Math Expressions

Teacher Edition • Volume 1

Developed by
The Children's Math Worlds Research Project

PROJECT DIRECTOR AND AUTHOR
Dr. Karen C. Fuson

This material is based upon work supported by the
National Science Foundation
under Grant Numbers
ESI-9816320, REC-9806020, and RED-935373.

Any opinions, findings, and conclusions, or recommendations expressed in this material
are those of the author and do not necessarily reflect the views of the National Science Foundation.

HOUGHTON MIFFLIN HARCOURT

Teacher Reviewers

Kindergarten
Patricia Stroh Sugiyama
Wilmette, Illinois

Barbara Wahle
Evanston, Illinois

Grade 1
Sandra Budson
Newton, Massachusetts

Janet Pecci
Chicago, Illinois

Megan Rees
Chicago, Illinois

Grade 2
Molly Dunn
Danvers, Massachusetts

Agnes Lesnick
Hillside, Illinois

Rita Soto
Chicago, Illinois

Grade 3
Jane Curran
Honesdale, Pennsylvania

Sandra Tucker
Chicago, Illinois

Grade 4
Sara Stoneberg Llibre
Chicago, Illinois

Sheri Roedel
Chicago, Illinois

Grade 5
Todd Atler
Chicago, Illinois

Leah Barry
Norfolk, Massachusetts

Special Thanks

Special thanks to the many teachers, students, parents, principals, writers, researchers, and work-study students who participated in the Children's Math Worlds Research Project over the years.

Credits

Photos: 122 The Sundae Scoop by Stuart J. Murphy, illustrated by Cynthia Jabor. © Harper Collins, 2003. 491G © C. Voigt/zefa/Corbis.

Introducing

Math Expressions

A Fresh Approach to

Math Expressions is a comprehensive Kindergarten–Grade 5 mathematics curriculum that offers new ways to teach and learn mathematics. Combining the most powerful

Standards-Based Instruction

elements of standards-based instruction with the best of traditional approaches, *Math Expressions* uses objects, drawings, conceptual language, and real-world situations to help students build mathematical ideas that make sense to them.

Math Expressions implements state standards as well as the recommendations and findings from recent reports on math learning:

Curriculum Focal Points (NCTM, 2007)

Principles and Standards for School Mathematics (NCTM, 2000)

Adding It Up
(National Research Council, 2001)

How Students Learn Mathematics in the Classroom
(National Research Council, 2005)

HOUGHTON MIFFLIN HARCOURT

Math Expressions

Focused on Understanding

In *Math Expressions,* teachers create an inquiry environment and encourage constructive discussion. Students invent, question, and explore, but also learn

and Fluency

and practice important math strategies. Through daily Math Talk students explain their methods and, in turn, become more fluent in them.

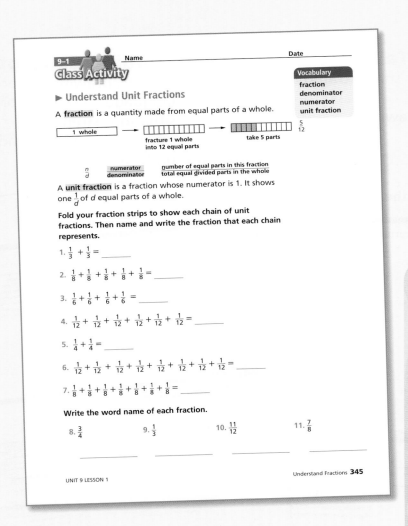

HOUGHTON MIFFLIN HARCOURT

Math Expressions

Organized for

Math Expressions is organized around five crucial classroom structures that allow children to develop deep conceptual

Quick Practice
Routines involve whole-class responses or individual partner practice.

Math Talk
Students share strategies and solutions orally and through proof drawings.

Building Concepts
Objects, drawings, conceptual language, and real-world situations strengthen mathematical ideas and understanding.

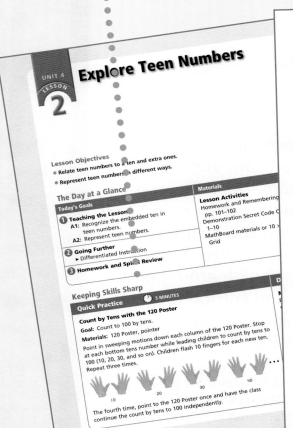

Classroom Success

understanding, and then practice, apply, and discuss
what they know with skill and confidence.

Helping Community
A classroom in which everyone is both
a teacher and a learner enhances
mathematical understanding,
competence, and confidence.

Student Leaders
Teachers facilitate students' growth by
helping them learn to lead practice and
discussion routines.

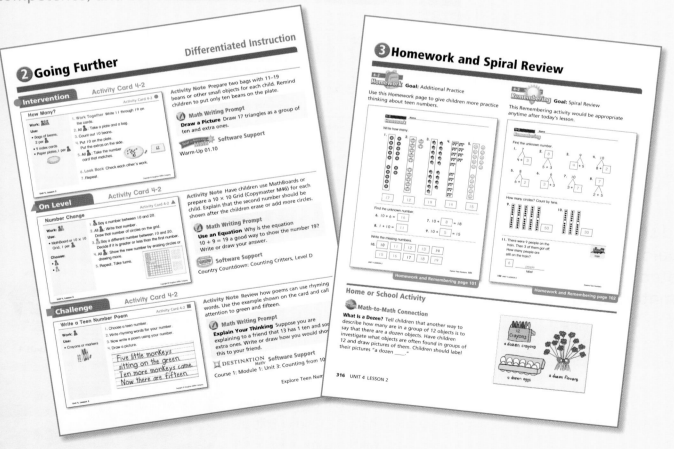

Differentiated for

Every **Math Expressions** lesson includes intervention, on level, and challenge differentiation to support classroom needs. Leveled Math Writing Prompts provide opportunities for in–depth thinking and analysis, and help prepare students for high-stakes tests.

"Activities and strategies should be developed and incorporated into instructional materials to assist teachers in helping all students become proficient in mathematics."

- *Adding It Up: Helping Children Learn Mathematics*, National Research Council (2001), p. 421

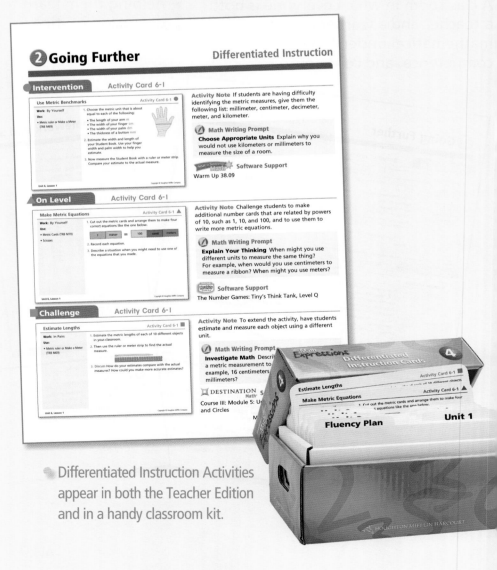

Differentiated Instruction Activities appear in both the Teacher Edition and in a handy classroom kit.

All Learners

Support for English Language Learners is included in each lesson. A special Math Center Challenge Easel with activities, projects, and puzzlers helps the highest math achievers reach their potential.

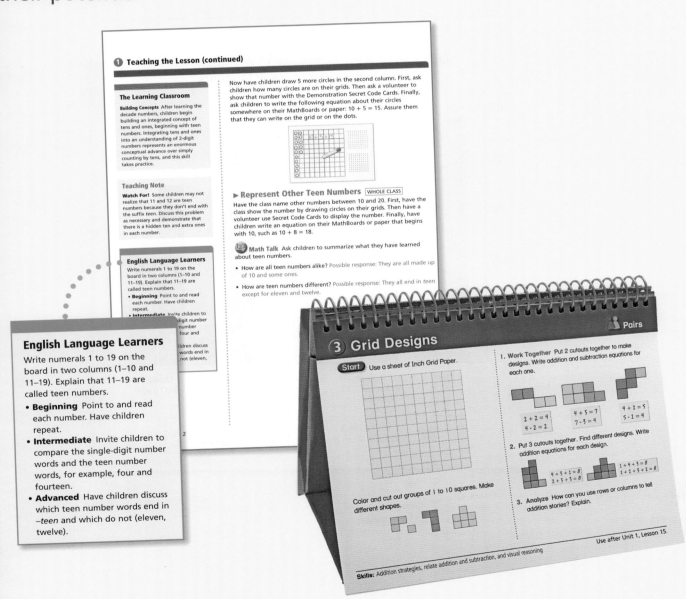

English Language Learners

Write numerals 1 to 19 on the board in two columns (1–10 and 11–19). Explain that 11–19 are called teen numbers.

- **Beginning** Point to and read each number. Have children repeat.
- **Intermediate** Invite children to compare the single-digit number words and the teen number words, for example, four and fourteen.
- **Advanced** Have children discuss which teen number words end in –*teen* and which do not (eleven, twelve).

Validated Through Ten

For twenty-five years, Dr. Karen Fuson, Professor Emeritus of Education and Psychology at Northwestern University, researched effective methods of teaching and learning mathematics.

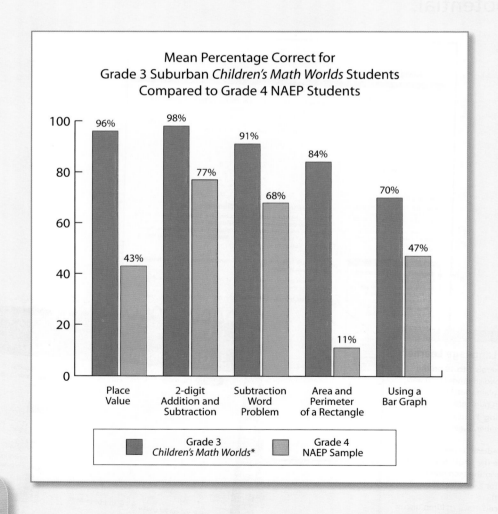

Mean Percentage Correct for
Grade 3 Suburban *Children's Math Worlds* Students
Compared to Grade 4 NAEP Students

Grade 3 *Children's Math Worlds**   Grade 4 NAEP Sample

"I have many children who cheer when it's math time."
- Grade 2 Teacher

Years of Research

During the last ten years, with the support of the National Science Foundation for the Children's Math Worlds research Project, Dr. Fuson began development of what is now the *Math Expressions* curriculum in real classrooms across the country.

Math Expressions
Grade 3
Percent At / Above Proficient
2006-2007

85%

71%

+14 points

Grade 3

■ 2006 (baseline)   ■ 2007

actual district results

Houghton Mifflin Harcourt
Math Expressions

Powered by

Math Expressions is highly accessible by all teachers. To ensure the program gets off to the right start, our educational consultants are available to support districts implementing **Math Expressions.** Unique Teacher Edition support and professional development options are also provided.

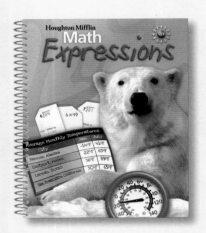

Teacher Edition

Written in a learn while teaching style, math background and learning in the classroom resources are embedded at point of use in the Teacher Edition.

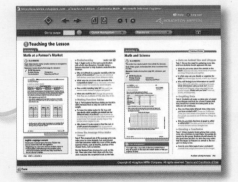

eTeacher Edition

Offers on-demand professional development
- Available 24/7
- Direct links in the eTE
- Math background, author talks, and classroom videos
- Relates to content being taught

Professional Development

Special in depth *Math Expressions* seminars are also available.

- **Administrator Institute**
  For administrators with school-based curriculum responsibilities

- **Level I Institute**
  For teachers who are new to *Math Expressions*

- **Level II Institute**
  For teachers who have at least 6 months' experience teaching *Math Expressions*

Components

New Hardcover Version Grades 3–5

	K	1	2	3	4	5
Core Components						
Teacher Edition	●	●	●	●	●	●
Student Activity Book*	●	●	●	●	●	●
Homework and Remembering	●	●	●	●	●	●
Assessment Guide	●	●	●	●	●	●
Teacher's Resource Book	●	●	●	●	●	●
MathBoards		●	●	●	●	●
Ready-Made Classroom Resources						
Individual Student Manipulatives Kit	●	●	●	●	●	●
Materials and Manipulatives Kit	●	●	●	●	●	●
Custom Manipulatives Kit	●	●	●	●	●	●
Math Center Challenge Easel	●	●	●	●	●	●
Differentiated Instruction Activities Kit	●	●	●	●	●	●
Literature Library	●	●	●	●	●	●
Anno's Counting Book Big Book	●					
Technology						
eTeacher Edition	●	●	●	●	●	●
eStudent Activity Book	●	●	●	●	●	●
Lesson Planner CD-ROM	●	●	●	●	●	●
ExamView Ways to Assess	●	●	●	●	●	●
Houghton Mifflin Harcourt Online Assessment System	●	●	●	●	●	●
MegaMath	●	●	●	●	●	●
Destination Math®	●	●	●	●	●	●
Soar to Success Math		●	●	●	●	●
Education Place	●	●	●	●	●	●

*Grades K–5 available as consumable workbook; Grades 3–5 available as Hardcover book with companion Activity Workbook.

Materials and Manipulatives for Grade 5

The essential materials needed for teaching *Math Expressions* are provided in the Student Activity Book and/or can be made from copymasters in the Teacher's Resource Book. However, many teachers prefer to use the more sturdy materials from the materials and manipulatives kits. This allows students to take home the paper materials (from the Student Activity Book) or the cardstock materials (made from the copymasters) to facilitate the connection between home and school.

Material or Manipulative in Grade 5	Pages in Student Activity Book	Copymasters in Teacher's Resource Book
Place Value Parade Poster*		
Class Multiplication Table Poster*		M47
Geometry and Measurement Poster*		
Division Cards*	20C–20L	M5–M14
Targets*		M3
Whole Number and Decimal Secret Code Cards*	86A–D, 88A–B	M75–M80
Demonstration Whole Number and Decimal Secret Code Cards*		
Base Ten Blocks		
Play Coins (pennies, nickels, dimes)		
Play Bills (1-dollar, 10-dollar, 100-dollar)		
Protractors		M24
2-Color Counters		
Blank Cubes and Stickers		
Pointer		
MathBoards		M113–M114

* These materials were developed specifically for this program under the leadership of Dr. Karen C. Fuson, director of the Children's Math Worlds Research Project and author of *Math Expressions.*

Using the Materials and Manipulatives for Each Unit

Material or Manipulative in Grade 5	Fluency Plan	Unit											
		1	2	3	4	5	6	7	8	9	10	11	12
Place Value Parade Poster				●				●					
Class Multiplication Table Poster	●	●						●				●	
Geometry and Measurement Poster			●										
Division Cards	●	●											
Targets	●												
Whole Number and Decimal Secret Code Cards				●									
Demonstration Whole Number and Decimal Secret Code Cards				●									
Base Ten Blocks				●			●	●		●			
Play Coins (pennies, nickels, dimes)				●		●		●		●		●	
Play Bills (1-dollar, 10-dollar, 100-dollar)				●				●	●			●	
Protractors					●					●		●	
2-Color Counters	●	●		●		●		●			●	●	
Blank Cubes and Stickers		●		●				●	●	●	●		●
Pointer		●		●		●							
MathBoards		●		●	●	●		●	●	●	●		

All materials for each unit (including those not in the kits) are listed in the planning chart for that unit.

Introduction

History and Development

Math Expressions is a K–5 mathematics program, developed from the Children's Math Worlds (CMW) Research Project conducted by Dr. Karen Fuson, Professor Emeritus at Northwestern University. This project was funded in part by the National Science Foundation.

The Research Project

The project studied the ways children around the world understand mathematical concepts, approach problem solving, and learn to do computation; it included ten years of classroom research and incorporated the ideas of participating students and teachers into the developing curriculum.

The research focused on building conceptual supports that include special language, drawings, manipulatives, and classroom communication methods that facilitate mathematical competence.

Curriculum Design

Within the curriculum, a series of learning progressions reflect recent research regarding children's natural stages when mastering concepts such as addition, subtraction, multiplication, and problem solving. These learning stages help determine the order of concepts, the sequence of units, and the positioning of topics.

The curriculum is designed to help teachers apply the most effective conceptual supports so that each child progresses as rapidly as possible.

During the research, students showed increases in standardized test scores as well as in broader measures of student understanding. These results were found for a wide range of both urban and suburban students from a variety of socio-economic groups.

Philosophy

Math Expressions incorporates the best practices of both traditional and reform mathematics curricula. The program strikes a balance between promoting children's natural solution methods and introducing effective procedures.

Building on Children's Knowledge

Because research has demonstrated that premature instruction in formalized procedures can lead to mechanical, unthinking behavior, established procedures for solving problems are not introduced until students have developed a solid conceptual foundation. Children begin by using their own knowledge to solve problems and then are introduced to research-based accessible methods.

In order to promote children's natural solution methods, as well as to encourage students to become reflective and resourceful problem solvers, teachers need to develop a helping and explaining culture in their classrooms.

Student Interactions

Collaboration and peer helping deepen children's commitment to values such as responsibility and respect for others. *Math Expressions* offers opportunities for students to interact in pairs, small groups, whole-class activities, and special scenarios.

As students collaboratively investigate math situations, they develop communication skills, sharpen their mathematical reasoning, and enhance their social awareness. Integrating students' social and cultural worlds into their emerging math worlds helps them to find their own voices and to connect real-world experiences to math concepts.

Main Concept Streams

Math Expressions focuses on crucially important core concepts. These core topics are placed at grade levels that enable students to do well on standardized tests. The main related concept streams at all grade levels are number concepts and an algebraic approach to word problems.

Breaking apart numbers, or finding the embedded numbers, is a key concept running through the number concept units.

- Kindergartners and first-graders find the numbers embedded within single-digit numbers and find the tens and ones in multi-digit numbers.

- Second- and third-graders continue breaking apart multi-digit numbers into ones and groups of tens, hundreds, and thousands. This activity facilitates their understanding of multi-digit addition and subtraction as well as solving word problems.

- Second-, third-, and fourth-graders work on seeing the repeated groups within numbers, and this awareness helps them to master multiplication and division.

- Fourth- and fifth-graders approach fractions as sums of unit fractions using length models. This permits them to see and comprehend operations on fractions.

Students work with story problems early in kindergarten and continue throughout the other grades. They not only solve but also construct word problems. As a result, they become comfortable and flexible with mathematical language and can connect concepts and terminology with meaningful referents from their own lives. As part of this process, students learn to make math drawings that enable teachers to see student thinking and facilitate communication.

Concepts and skills in algebra, geometry, measurement, and graphing are woven in between these two main streams throughout the grades. In grades two through five, geometry and measurement mini-units follow each regular unit.

Program Features

Many special features and approaches contribute to the effectiveness of *Math Expressions.*

Quick Practice

The opening 5 minutes of each math period are dedicated to activities (often student-led) that allow students to practice newly acquired knowledge. These *consolidating activities* help students to become faster and more accurate with the concepts. Occasionally, *leading activities* prepare the ground for new concepts before they are introduced. Quick Practice activities are repeated so that they become familiar routines that students can do quickly and confidently.

Drawn Models

Special manipulatives are used at key points. However, students move toward math drawings as rapidly as possible.

These drawn models help students relate to the math situation, facilitate students' explanations of the steps they took to solve the problem, and help listeners comprehend these explanations.

The drawings also give teachers insight into students' mathematical thinking, and leave a durable record of student work.

Language Development

Math Expressions offers a wealth of learning activities that directly support language development. In addition to verbalizing procedures and explanations, students are encouraged to write their own problems and describe their problem-solving strategies in writing as soon as they are able.

Homework Assignments

To help students achieve a high level of mathematical performance, students complete homework assignments every night. Families are expected to identify a homework helper to be responsible for monitoring the student's homework completion and to help if necessary.

Remembering Activities

Remembering Activities provide practice with the important concepts covered in all the units to date. They are ideal for spare classroom moments when students need a quick refresher of what they have learned so far. These pages are also valuable as extra homework pages that promote cumulative review as an ongoing synthesis of concepts.

Student Leaders

Student Leaders lead Quick Practice activities and can help as needed during the solving phase of Solve and Discuss. Such experiences build independence and confidence.

Math Talk

A significant part of the collaborative classroom culture is the frequent exchange of mathematical ideas and problem-solving strategies, or Math Talk. There are multiple benefits of Math Talk:

- Describing one's methods to another person can clarify one's own thinking as well as clarify the matter for others.

- Another person's approach can supply a new perspective, and frequent exposure to different approaches tends to engender flexible thinking.

- In the collaborative Math Talk classroom, students can ask for and receive help, and errors can be identified, discussed, and corrected.

- Student math drawings accompany early explanations in all domains, so that all students can understand and participate in the discussion.

- Math Talk permits teachers to assess students' understanding on an ongoing basis. It encourages students to develop their language skills, both in math and in everyday English.

- Math Talk enables students to become active helpers and questioners, creating student-to-student talk that stimulates engagement and community.

The key supports for Math Talk are the various participant structures, or ways of organizing class members as they interact. The teacher always guides the activity to help students to work both as a community and also independently. Descriptions of the most common participant structures follow.

Math Talk Participant Structures

Solve and Discuss (Solve, Explain, Question, and Justify) at the Board

The teacher selects 4 to 5 students (or as many as space allows) to go to the classroom board and solve a problem, using any method they choose. Their classmates work on the same problem at their desks. Then the teacher picks 2 or 3 students to explain their methods. Students at their desks are encouraged to ask questions and to assist their classmates in understanding.

> **Benefits:** Board work reveals multiple methods of solving a problem, making comparisons possible and communicating to students that different methods are acceptable. The teacher can select methods to highlight in subsequent discussions. Spontaneous helping occurs frequently by students working next to each other at the board. Time is used efficiently because everyone in the class is working. In addition, errors can be identified in a supportive way and corrected and understood by students.

Student Pairs

Two students work together to solve a problem, to explain a solution method to each other, to role play within a mathematical situation (for example, buying and selling), to play a math game, or to help a partner having difficulties. They are called helping pairs when more advanced students are matched with students who are struggling. Pairs may be organized formally, or they may occur spontaneously as help is needed. Initially, it is useful to model pair activities, contrasting effective and ineffective helping.

> **Benefits:** Pair work supports students in learning from each other, particularly in applying and practicing concepts introduced

Math Talk (continued)

Student Pairs (continued)

applying and practicing concepts introduced in whole-class discussion. Helping pairs often foster learning by both students as the helper strives to adopt the perspective of the novice. Helping almost always enables the helper to understand more deeply.

Whole-Class Practice and Student Leaders

This structure can be either teacher-led or student-led. When students lead it, it is usually at the consolidation stage, when children understand the concept and are beginning to achieve speed and automaticity. It is an excellent way for students to work together and learn from each other.

> **Benefits:** Whole-class practice lets the less advanced students benefit from the knowledge of the more advanced students without having to ask for help directly. It also provides the teacher with a quick and easy means of assessing the progress of the class as a whole.

Scenarios

The main purpose of scenarios is to demonstrate mathematical relationships in a visual and memorable way. In scenario-based activities, a group of students is called to the front of the classroom to act out a particular situation. Scenarios are useful when a new concept is being introduced for the first time. They are especially valuable for demonstrating the physical reality that underlies such math concepts as embedded numbers (break-aparts) and regrouping.

> **Benefits:** Because of its active and dramatic nature, the scenario structure often fosters a sense of intense involvement among children. In addition, scenarios create meaningful contexts in which students can reason about numbers and relate math to their everyday lives.

Step-by-Step at the Board

This is a variation of the Solve and Discuss structure. Again, several children go to the board to solve a problem. This time, however, a different student performs each step of the problem, describing the step before everyone does it. Everyone else at the board and at their desks carries out that step. This approach is particularly useful in learning multi-digit addition, subtraction, multiplication, and division. It assists the least-advanced students the most, providing them with accessible, systematic methods.

> **Benefits:** This structure is especially effective when students are having trouble solving certain kinds of problems. The step-by-step structure allows students to grasp a method more easily than doing the whole method at once. It also helps students learn to verbalize their methods more clearly, as they can focus on describing just their own step.

Small Groups

Unstructured groups can form spontaneously if physical arrangements allow (for example, desks arranged in groups of four or children working at tables). Spontaneous helping between and among students as they work on problems individually can be encouraged.

For more structured projects, assign students to specific groups. It is usually a good idea to include a range of students and to have a strong reader in each group. Explain the problem or project and guide the groups as necessary. When students have finished, call a pair from each group to present and explain the results of their work or have the entire group present the results, with each member explaining one part of the solution or project. Having lower-performing students present first allows them to contribute, while higher-performing students expand on their efforts and give the fuller presentation.

> **Benefits:** Students learn different strategies from each other for approaching a problem or task. They are invested in their classmates' learning because the presentation will be on behalf of the whole group.

Volume 1 Contents

Basic Facts Fluency Plan

Big Idea   Basic Multiplication and Division Situations

Big Idea   Patterns and Strategies

Unit 1   Multiplication and Division Word Problems

Unit 2 Perimeter and Area

Big Idea **Perimeter and Area of Rectangles**

Big Idea **Perimeter and Area of Triangles**

Big Idea **Perimeter and Area of Other Polygons**

Unit 3   Addition and Subtraction of Whole Numbers and Decimals

Big Idea   Decimal Concepts

Big Idea   Read and Write Whole Numbers and Decimals

REAL WORLD Problem Solving

REAL
WORLD
Problem
Solving

Big Idea Multi-Digit Word Problems

MINI
UNIT

Unit 4 Circles, Polygons, and Angles

Big Idea Angles and Polygons

Unit 5 Addition and Subtraction with Fractions

REAL WORLD Problem Solving

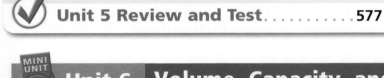

Unit 6   Volume, Capacity, and Weight

Big Idea   **Volume, Length, and Area**

Big Idea Measures of Capacity, Mass, and Weight

REAL WORLD Problem Solving

Big Idea Temperature and Time

REAL WORLD Problem Solving

Volume 2 Contents

Unit 7   Multiplication and Division with Whole Numbers and Decimals

Big Idea   Multiplication with Whole Numbers

Big Idea   Multiplication with Decimal Numbers

Unit 8   Algebra, Functions, and Graphs

Unit 9   Multiplication and Division with Fractions

Unit 10 Patterns and Transformations

Unit 11 Ratio, Proportion, and Percent

Unit 12   Three-Dimensional Figures

Pacing Guide

Basic Facts Fluency Plan This grade level begins with basic multiplication and division. Depending on the needs of your students, these fluency lessons may take approximately one week. Units 5 and 9 build strong conceptual development and skill fluency at a level often seen in the curricula of countries that rank high in math performance. In the first year, many classes may not cover all of the content of the later unit(s). As more students experience *Math Expressions* in the previous grade(s) and teachers become familiar with the program, earlier units move more rapidly, and later material can be covered in more depth. Some lessons in every unit, but especially the geometry and measurement mini-units, can be omitted if they do not focus on important state or district goals. Be sure **Student Leaders** lead the Quick Practice activities that begin each lesson, as they provide needed practice on core grade-level skills as well as support the growth of students as they lead these activities.

Unit	First Year — Pacing Suggestions	Days	Later Years — Pacing Suggestions	Days
1	This unit reviews problem solving models from the previous grades, but it also includes algebraic ideas and notations.	18	This unit will provide a strong foundation for multiplication and division skills and applying multiplication and division to word problems.	14
2	These are important Grade 5 geometry concepts.	10	These are important Grade 5 geometry concepts.	8
3	Generalize earlier student ideas about whole number place value and multi-digit addition and subtraction methods to decimal ideas and computation. Develop Math Talk and word problem-solving skills.	31	This unit will go more quickly for students who had *Math Expressions* in Grade 4, but there are still important ideas to develop about decimals. Develop Math Talk concepts and word problem-solving skills.	24
4	Teach only important district and state goals.	7	This will go more rapidly for students who had *Math Expressions* Unit 4 in Grade 4.	7
5	This unit is a core Grade 5 mastery unit. Students need to understand how all fractions are made from unit fractions and how addition, subtraction, and comparing require the same unit fraction.	30	For this core Grade 5 mastery unit, deepen Math Talk as students explain the use of unit fractions in building any fraction and in adding, subtracting, and comparing fractions.	23
6	Teach only important district and state goals.	5	Teach only important district and state goals.	7
7	For this core Grade 5 mastery unit, students need to master and explain one multiplication and one division method. Many will master and explain more methods.	32	You can move more quickly with students who had *Math Expressions* Grade 4 units on multi-digit multiplication and division.	27
8	This unit includes important algebraic concepts involving expressions, equations, and inequalities.	5	Extend knowledge of functions to coordinate graphs.	7
9	Generalize multiplication of fractions in the first five lessons. Omit division lessons 10 to 14 unless the subject matter is an important district and state goal.	10	With an advanced class, be sure to include division lessons 10 to 14.	15
10	Good for building students' understanding of patterns and spatial visualization.	4	Emphasize building students' understanding of patterns and spatial visualization.	3
11	Explore percent, decimal, and fraction relationships in lessons 10 and 11.	4	This unit takes students to an advanced understanding of ratio and proportion.	16
12	Teach only important district and state goals.	4	Teach only important district and state goals.	3
All Units	**Total Days**	**160**	**Total Days**	**154**

Correlation to NCTM Curriculum Focal Points and Connections for Grade 5

Grade 5 Curriculum Focal Points

1 *Number and Operations* and *Algebra*: Developing an understanding of and fluency with division of whole numbers

Students apply their understanding of models for division, place value, properties, and the relationship of division to multiplication as they develop, discuss, and use efficient, accurate, and generalizable procedures to find quotients involving multidigit dividends. They select appropriate methods and apply them accurately to estimate quotients or calculate them mentally, depending on the context and numbers involved. They develop fluency with efficient procedures, including the standard algorithm, for dividing whole numbers, understand why the procedures work (on the basis of place value and properties of operations), and use them to solve problems. They consider the context in which a problem is situated to select the most useful form of the quotient for the solution, and they interpret it appropriately.

1.1 find quotients involving multi-digit dividends	U7 L12, L15–17, L20
1.2 select and appropriate methods to estimate quotients or calculate them mentally	U7 L12, L15, L16
1.3 develop fluency with efficient procedures, including the standard algorithm, for dividing whole numbers and use them to solve problems	U7 L12, L15–17, L20
1.4 select the most useful form of the quotient and interpret it appropriately	U7 L17

2 *Number and Operations*: Developing an understanding of and fluency with addition and subtraction of fractions and decimals

Students apply their understandings of fractions and fraction models to represent the addition and subtraction of fractions with unlike denominators as equivalent calculations with like denominators. They apply their understandings of decimal models, place value, and properties to add and subtract decimals. They develop fluency with standard procedures for adding and subtracting fractions and decimals. They make reasonable estimates of fraction and decimal sums and differences. Students add and subtract fractions and decimals to solve problems, including problems involving measurement.

2.1 represent addition of fractions with unlike denominators as equivalent calculations with like denominators	U5 L14–16; U9 L9
2.2 represent subtraction of fractions with unlike denominators as equivalent calculations with like denominators	U5 L14–16; U9 L9
2.3 add decimals	U3 L4, L7, L8, L11; U5 L19
2.4 subtract decimals	U3 L4, L9; U5 L19
2.5 estimate fraction sums and differences	U5 L20
2.6 estimate decimal sums and differences	U3 L10, L15; U5 L20
2.7 add and subtract fractions to solve problems, including problems involving measurement	U5 L1, L3, L4, L7–10, L14–16; U9 L3, L9
2.8 add and subtract decimals to solve problems, including problems involving measurement	U3 L4, L7–10, L21

3 *Geometry* and *Measurement* and *Algebra:* **Describing three-dimensional shapes and analyzing their properties, including volume and surface area**
Students relate two-dimensional shapes to three-dimensional shapes and analyze properties of polyhedral solids, describing them by the number of edges, faces, or vertices as well as the types of faces. Students recognize volume as an attribute of three-dimensional space. They understand that they can quantify volume by finding the total number of same-sized units of volume that they need to fill the space without gaps or overlaps. They understand that a cube that is 1 unit on an edge is the standard unit for measuring volume. They select appropriate units, strategies, and tools for solving problems that involve estimating or measuring volume. They decompose three-dimensional shapes and find surface areas and volumes of prisms. As they work with surface area, they find and justify relationships among the formulas for the areas of different polygons. They measure necessary attributes of shapes to use area formulas to solve problems.

3.1 relate two-dimensional shapes to three-dimensional shapes	U12 L1–3
3.2 analyze properties of polyhedral solids, describing them by the number of edges, faces, or vertices as well as the types of faces	U6 L1, L2; U12 L1–3
3.3 recognize volume as an attribute of three-dimensional space	U6 L1, L2
3.4 find the total number of same-sized units of volume needed to fill the space without gaps or overlaps	U6 L1, L2
3.5 understand that a cube that is 1 unit on an edge is the standard unit for measuring volume	U6 L1, L2
3.6 select appropriate units, strategies, and tools for solving problems that involve estimating or measuring volume	U6 L1, L2
3.7 decompose three-dimensional shapes	U12 L1–3
3.8 find surface areas and volumes of prisms	U6 L1, L2; U12 L1
3.9 find and justify relationships among the formulas for the areas of different polygons	U2 L3–5
3.10 measure necessary attributes of shapes to use area formulas to solve problems	U2 L5, L6

Connections to the Focal Points

4 *Algebra:* Students use patterns, models, and relationships as contexts for writing and solving simple equations and inequalities. They create graphs of simple equations. They explore prime and composite numbers and discover concepts related to the addition and subtraction of fractions as they use factors and multiples, including applications of common factors and common multiples. They develop an understanding of the order of operations and use it for all operations.

4.1 use patterns, models, and relationships as contexts for writing and solving equations	Fluency Plan L1–5; U1 L1–7, L9–11; U3 L6, L18, L19, L20; U5 L4, L15; U7 L9; U8 L3, L5; U10 L2; U11 L1
4.2 use patterns, models, and relationships as contexts for writing and solving inequalities	U3 L2; U5 L2, L9; U8 L4
4.3 create graphs of simple equations	U8 L7; Extension L4

Connections to the Focal Points (cont.)	
4.4 explore prime and composite numbers	U8 L1
4.5 use factors and multiples, including applications of common factors and common multiples	Fluency Plan L3–6; U1 L4, L8; U5 L11–14; U8 L1; U11 L1–8, L12, L13
4.6 develop and use the order of operations	U1 L6, L9; U8 L2
5 *Measurement:* Students' experiences connect their work with solids and volume to their earlier work with capacity and weight or mass. They solve problems that require attention to both approximation and precision of measurement.	
5.1 relate solids and volume to capacity and weight or mass	U6 L1, L3, L4
5.2 solve problems that require attention to both approximation and precision of measurement	U2 L1, L2, L6; U4 L1, L2, L4, L6, L7; U6 L3–5
6 *Data Analysis:* Students apply their understanding of whole numbers, fractions, and decimals as they construct and analyze double-bar and line graphs and use ordered pairs on coordinate grids.	
6.1 construct and analyze double-bar graphs	U3 L14
6.2 construct and analyze line graphs	U3 L16, L17
6.3 use ordered pairs on coordinate grids	U8 L6, L7; U10 L4; Extension L4
7 *Number and Operations:* Building on their work in grade 4, students extend their understanding of place value to numbers through millions and millionths in various contexts. They apply what they know about multiplication of whole numbers to larger numbers. Students also explore contexts that they can describe with negative numbers (e.g., situations of owing money or measuring elevations above and below sea level.)	
7.1 understand place value to numbers through millions and millionths	U3 L1–6, L10, L12, L13; U7 L20
7.2 apply multiplication of whole numbers to larger numbers	U7 L1–6
7.3 describe contexts with negative numbers	U6 L6; Extension L1–3

NCTM Standards and Expectations Correlation for Grade 5

Number and Operations Standard	
Understand numbers, ways of representing numbers, relationships among numbers, and number systems	
• understand the place-value structure of the base-ten number system and be able to represent and compare whole numbers and decimals;	U3 L1–6, L13, L20; U7 L1, L7–11
• recognize equivalent representations for the same number and generate them by decomposing and composing numbers;	Fluency Plan L2, L4; U3 L2, L5, L10; U5 L6, L11–14, L17–20; U7 L2–4, L14; U9 L1, L5, L7, L9, L11, L14; U11 L10
• develop understanding of fractions as parts of unit wholes, as parts of a collection, as locations on number lines, and as divisions of whole numbers;	U5 L1–5, L17–20; U7 L14, L17; U9 L2–6, L8, L10; U11 L10–12
• use models, benchmarks, and equivalent forms to judge the size of fractions;	U5 L2, L5–6, L9, L11–13; U9 L1, L7; U11 L10–11
• recognize and generate equivalent forms of commonly used fractions, decimals, and percents;	U3 L2–3; U5 L5, L11–14, L17–20; U7 L7, L17; U9 L7, L9; U11 L10–12
• explore numbers less than 0 by extending the number line and through familiar applications;	U3 L1, L4; U10 L4; Extension L1–4
• describe classes of numbers according to characteristics such as the nature of their factors.	Fluency Plan L3–4; U1 L8; U8 L1
Understand meanings of operations and how they relate to one another	
• understand various meanings of multiplication and division;	Fluency Plan L1–4; U1 L2, L7, L9–10; U3 L1; U7 L2; U9 L1–2, L4, L8, L10–13
• understand the effects of multiplying and dividing whole numbers;	Fluency Plan L4–5; U1 L1, L2, L7, L9; U7 L1, L3–6, L7–10, L14–21; U9 L1, L3, L13
• identify and use relationships between operations, such as division as the inverse of multiplication, to solve problems;	Fluency Plan L4; U1 L3, L8, L10; U7 L12; U9 L5–6, L8, L10–13
• understand and use properties of operations, such as the distributivity of multiplication over addition.	Fluency Plan L4; U1 L10–11; U3 L11; U7 L2–4; U8 L3, L5; U9 L5–6
Compute fluently and make reasonable estimates	
• develop fluency with basic number combinations for multiplication and division and use these combinations to mentally compute related problems, such as 30 × 50;	Fluency Plan L4–5; U3 L11; U7 L1, L5–8, L10, L18, L20; U11 L7–9
• develop fluency in adding, subtracting, multiplying, and dividing whole numbers;	Fluency Plan L1–6; U1 L3–4, L8–9; U3 L7–8; U6 L3–4; U7 L6, L11, L13–16, L18; U8 L1–2; U11 L2, L7–9

NCTM Standards and Expectations Correlation for Grade 5 (cont.)

Number and Operations Standard (cont.)	
Compute fluently and make reasonable estimates (cont.)	
• develop and use strategies to estimate the results of whole-number computations and to judge the reasonableness of such results;	U3 L10–13; U6 L2–4; U7 L5–6, L10, L15–17
• develop and use strategies to estimate computations involving fractions and decimals in situations relevant to students' experience;	U3 L6, L9, L13–15; U6 L2–4; U7 L7, L10–11, L17, L20–21; U9 L6, L9–10
• use visual models, benchmarks, and equivalent forms to add and subtract commonly used fractions and decimals;	U3 L4; U5 L1, L3–4, L7–10, L14–16; U9 L14
• select appropriate methods and tools for computing with whole numbers from among mental computation, estimation, calculators, and paper and pencil according to the context and nature of the computation and use the selected method or tools.	Fluency Plan L1–4; U1 L4, L7–8; U3 L7–10, L18–21; U7 L1–4, L8, L10–11, L17, L20–21; U11 L5–6, L8

Algebra Standard	
Understand patterns, relations, and functions	
• describe, extend, and make generalizations about geometric and numeric patterns;	U3 L3, L5, L15–16; U6 L1–2; U7 L1, L5, L8–10, L18–19; U9 L4, L15; U10 L1–3; U11 L1–4
• represent and analyze patterns and functions, using words, tables, and graphs.	Fluency Plan L4; U1 L5; U3 L15–17; U7 L8–10; U8 L5–7; U9 L4; U10 L1–2; U11 L1–6, L8, L14–16; Extension L4
Represent and analyze mathematical situations and structures using algebraic symbols	
• identify such properties as commutativity, associativity, and distributivity and use them to compute with whole numbers;	Fluency Plan L2, L4; U1 L6–7, L10; U3 L11; U9 L6
• represent the idea of a variable as an unknown quantity using a letter or a symbol;	U1 L2–3, L5–7, L9; U3 L18–19; U5 L13; U8 L3–5; U9 L6, L10–11; U11 L7–8
• express mathematical relationships using equations.	U1 L1, L5–10; U3 L18–19; U6 L2, L5; U7 L2, L21; U8 L3–5
Use mathematical models to represent and understand quantitative relationships	
• model problem situations with objects and use representations such as graphs, tables, and equations to draw conclusions.	U1 L1, L4–7, L11; U2 L2; U3 L5–6; U7 L18–19; U8 L3, L5; U9 L4; U11 L1–6
Analyze change in various contexts	
• investigate how a change in one variable relates to a change in a second variable;	U6 L2; U8 L5; U11 L2–9
• identify and describe situations with constant or varying rates of change and compare them.	U11 L1–9

Geometry Standard	
Analyze characteristics and properties of two- and three-dimensional geometric shapes and develop mathematical arguments about geometric relationships	
• identify, compare, and analyze attributes of two- and three-dimensional shapes and develop vocabulary to describe the attributes;	U2 L3–5; U4 L1–7; U6 L1–2; U12 L1–3
• classify two- and three-dimensional shapes according to their properties and develop definitions of classes of shapes such as triangles and pyramids;	U2 L3–5; U4 L1–6: U12 L1–3
• investigate, describe, and reason about the results of subdividing, combining, and	U2 L3–4
• explore congruence and similarity;	U4 L3, L5; U10 L3; U11 L13; U12 L4
• make and test conjectures about geometric properties and relationships and develop logical arguments to justify conclusions.	U4 L2, L7; U6 L1–2; U9 L15; U12 L2, L4
Specify locations and describe spatial relationships using coordinate geometry and other representational systems	
• describe location and movement using common language and geometric vocabulary;	U10 L3–4
• make and use coordinate systems to specify locations and to describe paths;	U8 L6; U10 L3–4; Extension L4
• find the distance between points along horizontal and vertical lines of a coordinate system.	U8 L6; U10 L4
Apply transformations and use symmetry to analyze mathematical situations	
• predict and describe the results of sliding, flipping, and turning two-dimensional shapes;	U4, L4–5; U10 L3–4
• describe a motion or a series of motions that will show that two shapes are congruent;	U4 L5; U10 L3–4
• identify and describe line and rotational symmetry in two- and three-dimensional shapes and designs.	U4 L5; U12 L4

NCTM Standards and Expectations Correlation for Grade 5 (cont.)

Geometry Standard (cont.)	
Use visualization, spatial reasoning, and geometric modeling to solve problems	
• build and draw geometric objects;	U2 L2–5; U4 L1–6; U10 L3–4; U12 L1–3
• create and describe mental images of objects, patterns, and paths;	U2 L3, L5; U6 L1; U12 L3–4
• identify and build a three-dimensional object from two-dimensional representations of that object;	U12 L1–3
• identify and draw a two-dimensional representation of a three-dimensional object;	U6 L1; U12 L3
• use geometric models to solve problems in other areas of mathematics, such as number and measurement;	U2 L1–5; U4 L1, L4, L7; U6 L1–3, L5; U7 L2; U12 L2
• recognize geometric ideas and relationships and apply them to other disciplines and to problems that arise in the classroom or in everyday life.	U9 L15; U10 L3; U11 L16, U12 L1
Measurement Standard	
Understand measurable attributes of objects and the units, systems, and processes of measurement	
• understand such attributes as length, area, weight, volume, and size of angle and select the appropriate type of unit for measuring each attribute;	U2 L1–6; U4 L1–2; U5 L9; U6 L1–5
• understand the need for measuring with standard units and become familiar with standard units in the customary and metric systems;	U2 L1–6; U3 L9; U6 L1–6; U7 L23
• carry out simple unit conversions, such as from centimeters to meters, within a system of measurement;	U2 L1, L6; U6 L1, L5
• understand that measurements are approximations and how differences in units affect precision;	U2 L1, L6; U4 L7; U6 L2, L5
• explore what happens to measurements of a two-dimensional shape such as its perimeter and area when the shape is changed in some way.	U2 L2–3, L6; U6 L2
Apply appropriate techniques, tools, and formulas to determine measurements	
• develop strategies for estimating the perimeters, areas, and volumes of irregular shapes;	U2 L2, L5; U6 L1–2

Measurement Standard (cont.)	
Apply appropriate techniques, tools, and formulas to determine measurements (cont.)	
• select and apply appropriate standard units and tools to measure length, area, volume, weight, time, temperature, and the size of angles;	U2 L1–6; U4 L1–2, L4, L6–7; U6 L1–6; U11 L13–16
• select and use benchmarks to estimate measurements;	U2 L1–2, L6; U5 L8; U6 L5
• develop, understand, and use formulas to find the area of rectangles and related triangles and parallelograms;	U1 L5; U2 L1–6; U6 L2
• develop strategies to determine the surface areas and volumes of rectangular solids.	U6 L1–2, L5; U12 L1–2
Data Analysis and Probability Standard	
Formulate questions that can be addressed with data and collect, organize, and display relevant data to answer them	
• design investigations to address a question and consider how data-collection methods affect the nature of the data set;	U3 L17; U7 L22–23; U11 L17
• collect data using observations, surveys, and experiments;	U3 L17, L21–22; U5 L6, L17, L21; U7 L22–23; U11 L17
• represent data using tables and graphs such as line plots, bar graphs, and line graphs;	U1 L2, L7; U2 L2; U3 L12, L15–17, L21–22; U4 L6; U5 L17, L21
• recognize the differences in representing categorical and numerical data.	U3 L21–22
Select and use appropriate statistical methods to analyze data	
• describe the shape and important features of a set of data and compare related data sets, with an emphasis on how the data are distributed;	U3 L13, L16, L21; U4 L6; U7 L13, L22
• use measures of center, focusing on the median, and understand what each does and does not indicate about the data set;	U3 L9; U7 L13, L15–16, L21–22; U9 L14
• compare different representations of the same data and evaluate how well each representation shows important aspects of the data.	U3 L4; U4 L6; U7 L22
Develop and evaluate inferences and predictions that are based on data	
• propose and justify conclusions and predictions that are based on data and design studies to further investigate the conclusions or predictions.	U1 L11; U7 L22; U11 L12, L17

NCTM Standards and Expectations Correlation for Grade 5 (cont.)

Data Analysis and Probability Standard (cont.)	
Understand and apply basic concepts of probability	
• describe events as likely or unlikely and discuss the degree of likelihood using such words as certain, equally likely, and impossible;	U5 L17
• predict the probability of outcomes of simple experiments and test the predictions;	U5 L17, L21; U11 L12
• understand that the measure of the likelihood of an event can be represented by a number from 0 to 1.	U5 L17, L21; U11 L12

Problem Solving Standard	
• build new mathematical knowledge through problem solving;	U1 L1–4, L6, L9, L11; U2 L2–3, L5; U3 L5, L10, L16–22; U5 L3, L12, L14–17, L21; U6 L2; U7 L3–4, L6–7, L10–11, L14, L17, L19, L22; U9 L6–9, L12; U11 L3–5, L11; U12 L1
• solve problems that arise in mathematics and in other contexts;	U1 L1, L3, L7; U2 L2–3, L6; U3 L7, L20–21; U5 L4–5, L9, L13, L18–19; U6 L2; U7 L4–7, L9, L11, L16, L18, L20–21; U8 L5, L7; U9 L5–6, L9–10, L12–14; U11 L5–8, L11–12, L16; U12 L1
• apply and adapt a variety of appropriate strategies to solve problems;	U1 L1–5, L7, L11; U2 L3; U3 L10–11, L13, L18, L20–22; U5 L1, L3–5, L7, L10, L14, L16, L18–19; U6 L2; U7 L4–6, L10, L14, L17–21; U8 L7; U9 L5–6, L9–10, L12–15; U11 L5–9, L11, L16–17
• monitor and reflect on the process of mathematical problem solving.	U1 L1–2, L4, L10; U3 L10; U5 L15–17, L21; U7 L7, L9, L16–17, L21; U8 L4; U9 L6–7, L9, L12–13; U11 L2–7, L12

Reasoning and Proof Standard	
• recognize reasoning and proof as fundamental aspects of mathematics;	Fluency Plan L4; U1 L4, L11; U5 L12–13
• make and investigate mathematical conjectures;	Fluency Plan L4; U1 L11; U2 L2–3, L6; U3 L22; U4 L1–3, L7; U5 L1, L14, L17; U6 L1; U7 L23; U9 L12, L15
• develop and evaluate mathematical arguments and proofs;	U1 L11; U3 L22; U5 L6, L12, L14; U9 L15; U10 L3; U11 L3–4
• select and use various types of reasoning and methods of proof.	Fluency Plan L4; U1 L4; U3 L22; U5 L6, L12–13; U7 L12, L23; U9 L15

Communication Standard	
• organize and consolidate their mathematical thinking through communication;	Fluency Plan L2; U1 L3; U2 L2; U3 L15, L19, L22; U5 L7–8, L21; U6 L1, L3–4; U7 L1, L12–14, L16, L20; U8 L5; U9 L11, L14; U11 L2–3, L10
• communicate their mathematical thinking coherently and clearly to peers, teachers, and others;	Fluency Plan L2, L5; U1 L3; U2 L2; U3 L1–12, L18, L21–22; U5 L6, L9–10, L14; U6 L1, L3–4; U7 L1–6, L15, L18, L20–21, L23; U9 L11, L15; U11 L1, L3, L7, L10, L17

Communication Standard (cont.)	
• analyze and evaluate the mathematical thinking and strategies of others;	Fluency Plan L5; U1 L2; U3 L8, L15, L18, L20–22; U7 L6–10, L15–17, L21–22
• use the language of mathematics to express mathematical ideas precisely.	U1 L11; U2 L2; U3 L4, L7, L9–12, L15, L18–20; U5 L9–10, L14, L16, L21; U6 L1, L4–6; U7 L7, L11, L17–18, L21, L23; U8 L5; U11 L1–2, L9, L11, L17

Connections Standard	
• recognize and use connections among mathematical ideas;	Fluency Plan L4; U1 L11; U6 L2; U7 L3, L8–9, L13, L18, L22; U9 L15; U10 L4
• understand how mathematical ideas interconnect and build on one another to produce a coherent whole;	Fluency Plan L4; U1 L5; U5 L1; U6 L2; U7 L8–9, L13, L18, L22; U8 L1; U10 L4; U11 L10–11, L17; Extension L4
• recognize and apply mathematics in contexts outside of mathematics.	U1 L5, L11; U5 L1; U7 L3, L22–23; U8 L4–6; U9 L15; U11 L17

Representation Standard	
• create and use representations to organize, record, and communicate mathematical ideas;	Fluency Plan L2–3; U1 L1–3, L5; U3 L4, L12, L22; U4 L1; U5 L2, L8, L21; U7 L2, L7, L23; U8 L1, L3–7; U11 L1–2, L11, L17; U12 L1–3
• select, apply, and translate among mathematical representations to solve problems;	Fluency Plan L2–4; U1 L2–3, L5; U3 L2, L18; U5 L9, L14, L19; U7 L2; U9 L15; U11 L4, L11
• use representations to model and interpret physical, social, and mathematical phenomena.	U1 L1–3; U3 L22; U4 L3–4; U5 L6, L9, L11, L21; U6 L1–2; U7 L22–23; U8 L1, L3–7; U9 L15; U11 L1–2, L4, L17; U12 L1

Basic Facts Fluency Plan

THESE FLUENCY LESSONS develop students' concepts of multiplication and division as equal groups, arrays, and area represented in real-world situations. Students identify patterns in multiples for each number 1 to 12 and practice them to build fluency. Students examine the inverse relationship between multiplication and division. This Fluency Plan is designed to meet the needs of all students.

Skills Trace

Grade 4	Grade 5
• Identify patterns in basic multiplication and division facts.	• Use strategies for basic multiplication and division facts.
• Model equal groups, arrays, and area word problems for multiplication and division.	• Model equal groups, arrays, and area word problems for multiplication and division.
• Understand and apply properties of multiplication.	• Understand and apply properties of multiplication.
• Develop fluency with addition, subtraction, multiplication, and division facts.	• Develop fluency with multiplication and division facts.

Fluency Plan   Contents

Fluency Plan   Assessment

✓ Unit Objectives	Assessment	Lessons
FP.1 Diagnose fluency with multiplication and division.	Diagnostic Checkups	1
FP.2 Provide practice with multiplication and division.	Practice	1, 2, 3, 4, 5, 6
FP.3 Assess fluency with multiplication and division.	Final Quizzes	6

Assessment and Review Resources

Formal Assessment

Teacher's Resource Book
- Diagnostic Quiz for Basic Multiplication (TRB M58)
- Diagnostic Quiz for Basic Division (TRB M59)

Test Generator CD-ROM
- Test Bank Items

Informal Assessment

Teacher Edition
- Ongoing Assessment (in every lesson)
- Quick Practice (in every lesson)
- Math Talk (in every lesson)

Math Talk
▸ The Learning Classroom (pp. 8, 18, 21, 24, 30)
▸ Math Talk in Action (p. 19)
▸ In Activities (pp. 5, 12, 18, 22, 30, 37)
▸ Solve and Discuss (p. 8)
▸ Student Pairs (p. 38)
  Helping Partners (pp. 14, 23, 42)
▸ Scenarios (p. 31)

Review Opportunities

Homework and Remembering
- Review of recently taught topics
- Spiral Review

Teacher's Resource Book
- Basic Multiplication Practice (TRB M60)
- Basic Division Practice (TRB M61)
- Multiplication for 3s, 4s, 6s, 7s, 8s, 9s (TRB M62)
- Division for 3s, 4s, 6s, 7s, 8s, 9s (TRB M63)
- Multiplication for 6s, 7s, 8s (TRB M64)
- Division for 6s, 7s, 8s (TRB M65)

Test Generator CD-ROM
- Custom review sheets

Planning for Fluency

Lesson NCTM Focal Points NCTM Standards	Resources	Materials for Lesson Activities	Materials for Going Further
FP-1 **Multiplication as Equal Groups** NCTM Focal Point: 4.1 NCTM Standards: 1, 2, 6, 8, 10	TE pp. 1–10 SAB pp. 1–6 H&R pp. 1–2 AC FP-1	None	✓ Counters Centimeter-Grid Paper (TRB M18) Scissors Crayons Calculator Math Journals
FP-2 **Arrays and Area** NCTM Focal Point: 4.1 NCTM Standards: 2, 4, 6, 10	TE pp. 11–16 SAB pp. 7–10 H&R pp. 3–4 AC FP-2 MCC 1	None	Inch-Grid Paper (TRB M1) Scissors Centimeter-Grid Paper (TRB M18) Crayons Game Cards (TRB M2) Math Journals
FP-3 **Explore the Multiplication Table** NCTM Focal Points: 4.1, 4.5 NCTM Standards: 1, 2, 7, 10	TE pp. 17–26 SAB pp. 11–12 H&R pp. 5–6 AC FP-3 MCC 2	✓ Class Multiplication Table Poster ✓ Targets Blank Multiplication Tables (TRB M67)	Scissors Square sheets of paper ✓ Class Multiplication Table Poster Index cards Centimeter-Grid Paper (TRB M18) Calculators Math Journals
FP-4 **Discover Multiplication Patterns** NCTM Focal Points: 4.1, 4.5 NCTM Standards: 6, 7, 9	TE pp. 27–34 SAB pp. 13–16 H&R pp. 7–8 AC FP-4 MCC 3	None	✓ Counters or blocks Hundreds Grid (TRB M82) Crayons or markers Math Journals
FP-5 **Multiplication Strategies** NCTM Focal Points: 4.1, 4.5 NCTM Standards: 1, 2, 8	TE pp. 35–40 SAB pp. 17–20 H&R pp. 9–10 AC FP-5	None	Math Journals
FP-6 **Multiplication and Division Practice** NCTM Focal Point: 4.5 NCTM Standards: 1, 8	TE pp. 41–46 SAB pp. 20A–20L, 21–22 H&R pp. 11–12 AC FP-6 MCC 4	The Factor Field ✓ Division Cards	Crayons or markers The Factor Field ✓ Division Cards Math Journals

Resources/Materials Key: TE: Teacher Edition   SAB: Student Activity Book   H&R: Homework and Remembering
AC: Activity Cards   MCC: Math Center Challenge   AG: Assessment Guide   ✓: Grade 5 kits   TRB: Teacher's Resource Book

NCTM Standards and Expectations Key: 1. Number and Operations   2. Algebra   3. Geometry
4. Measurement   5. Data Analysis and Probability   6. Problem Solving   7. Reasoning and Proof   8. Communication
9. Connections   10. Representation

Hardcover Student Book	**Manipulatives and Materials**
• Together, the Hardcover Student Book and its companion Activity Workbook contain all of the pages in the consumable Student Activity Book.	• Essential materials for teaching *Math Expressions* are available in the Grade 5 kits. These materials are indicated by a ✓ in these lists. At the front of this Teacher Edition is more information about kit contents, alternatives for the materials, and use of the materials.

Fluency Plan Teaching Resources

Differentiated Instruction

Individualizing Instruction

Activities	Level	Frequency
	• Intervention • On Level • Challenge	All 3 in every lesson
Math Writing Prompts	Level	Frequency
	• Intervention • On Level • Challenge	All 3 in every lesson
Math Center Challenges	For advanced students	
	4 in every unit	

Reaching All Learners

	Lessons	Pages
English Language Learners	1, 2, 3, 4, 5, 6	7, 13, 20, 28, 30, 36, 43
Extra Help	Lessons	Pages
	1, 2, 3	4, 13, 14, 20
Special Needs	Lessons	Pages
	1, 6	6, 42
Advanced Learners	Lesson	Page
	3	22

Strategies for English Language Learners

Present this problem to all students. Offer the different levels of support to meet students' levels of language proficiency.

Objective Review multiplication vocabulary.

Problem Write $3 \times 2 = 6$ on the board. Have students read the equation aloud. Write *factor* and *product*.

Newcomer

- Point and say: **3 times 2 equals 6. This is a multiplication equation.** Have students repeat.
- Say: **We multiply 3 times 2. 3 and 2 are *factors*. 6 is the *product*.** Have students repeat.

Beginning

- Say: **In multiplication, the numbers we multiply are factors.** Ask: **Are 3 and 2 factors?** yes
- Say: **The answer is the product.** Ask: **Is 6 a factor or the product?** product

Intermediate

- Say: **In multiplication, the numbers we multiply are factors. 3 and 2 are __.** factors
- Say: **The answer is the product. 6 is the __.** product

Advanced

- Say: **We multiply the factors.** Ask: **Which numbers are the factors?** 3, 2
- Say: **The answer is the product.** Ask: **Which number is the product?** 6
- Continue with other simple problems.

Connections

Literature Connections
Lesson 3, page 26
Lesson 4, page 34

Math-to-Math Connection
Lesson 5, page 40

Science Connection
Lesson 6, page 46

Sports Connection
Lesson 2, page 16

Independent Learning Activities

Ready-Made Math Challenge Centers

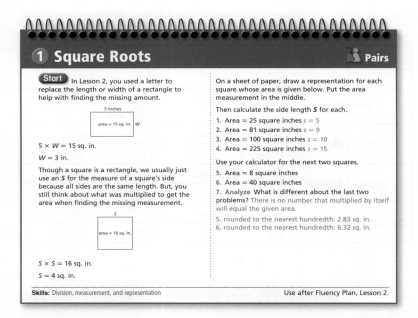

① Square Roots — Pairs

Start In Lesson 2, you used a letter to replace the length or width of a rectangle to help with finding the missing amount.

5 inches

area = 15 sq. in. | W

$5 \times W = 15$ sq. in.

$W = 3$ in.

Though a square is a rectangle, we usually just use an S for the measure of a square's side because all sides are the same length. But, you still think about what was multiplied to get the area when finding the missing measurement.

s

area = 16 sq. in.

$S \times S = 16$ sq. in.

$S = 4$ sq. in.

On a sheet of paper, draw a representation for each square whose area is given below. Put the area measurement in the middle.

Then calculate the side length S for each.
1. Area = 25 square inches $s = 5$
2. Area = 81 square inches $s = 9$
3. Area = 100 square inches $s = 10$
4. Area = 225 square inches $s = 15$

Use your calculator for the next two squares.
5. Area = 8 square inches
6. Area = 40 square inches
7. Analyze What is different about the last two problems? There is no number that multiplied by itself will equal the given area.

5. rounded to the nearest hundredth: 2.83 sq. in.
6. rounded to the nearest hundredth: 6.32 sq. in.

Skills: Division, measurement, and representation   Use after Fluency Plan, Lesson 2.

Grouping Pairs

Materials Calculator

Objective Given the square area, students find the square root.

Connections Measurement and Representation

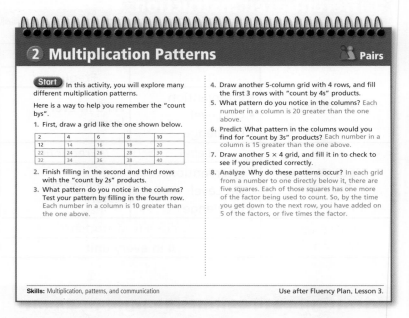

② Multiplication Patterns — Pairs

Start In this activity, you will explore many different multiplication patterns.

Here is a way to help you remember the "count bys".

1. First, draw a grid like the one shown below.

2	4	6	8	10
12	14	16	18	20
22	24	26	28	30
32	34	36	38	40

2. Finish filling in the second and third rows with the "count by 2s" products.
3. What pattern do you notice in the columns? Test your pattern by filling in the fourth row. Each number in a column is 10 greater than the one above.

4. Draw another 5-column grid with 4 rows, and fill the first 3 rows with "count by 4s" products.
5. What pattern do you notice in the columns? Each number in a column is 20 greater than the one above.
6. Predict What pattern in the columns would you find for "count by 3s" products? Each number in a column is 15 greater than the one above.
7. Draw another 5 × 4 grid, and fill it in to check to see if you predicted correctly.
8. Analyze Why do these patterns occur? In each grid from a number to one directly below it, there are five squares. Each of those squares has one more of the factor being used to count. So, by the time you get down to the next row, you have added on 5 of the factors, or five times the factor.

Skills: Multiplication, patterns, and communication   Use after Fluency Plan, Lesson 3.

Grouping Pairs

Materials None

Objective Students write the multiples of a given number in rows of five and identify a pattern.

Connections Computation and Communication

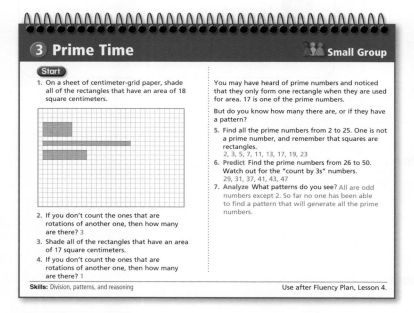

③ Prime Time — Small Group

Start
1. On a sheet of centimeter-grid paper, shade all of the rectangles that have an area of 18 square centimeters.

2. If you don't count the ones that are rotations of another one, then how many are there? 3
3. Shade all of the rectangles that have an area of 17 square centimeters.
4. If you don't count the ones that are rotations of another one, then how many are there? 1

You may have heard of prime numbers and noticed that they only form one rectangle when they are used for area. 17 is one of the prime numbers.

But do you know how many there are, or if they have a pattern?

5. Find all the prime numbers from 2 to 25. One is not a prime number, and remember that squares are rectangles.
2, 3, 5, 7, 11, 13, 17, 19, 23
6. Predict Find the prime numbers from 26 to 50. Watch out for the "count by 3s" numbers.
29, 31, 37, 41, 43, 47
7. Analyze What patterns do you see? All are odd numbers except 2. So far no one has been able to find a pattern that will generate all the prime numbers.

Skills: Division, patterns, and reasoning   Use after Fluency Plan, Lesson 4.

Grouping Small Group

Materials Centimeter-Grid Paper (TRB M18), calculator (optional)

Objective Students find the prime numbers 2–49.

Connections Algebra and Reasoning

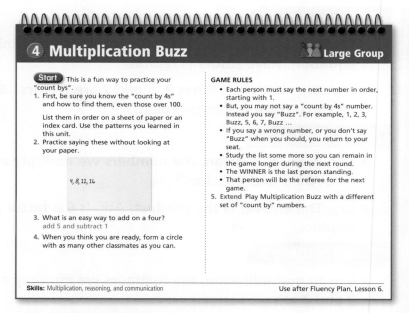

④ Multiplication Buzz — Large Group

Start This is a fun way to practice your "count bys".
1. First, be sure you know the "count by 4s" and how to find them, even those over 100.

List them in order on a sheet of paper or an index card. Use the patterns you learned in this unit.
2. Practice saying these without looking at your paper.

4, 8, 12, 16

3. What is an easy way to add on a four? add 5 and subtract 1
4. When you think you are ready, form a circle with as many other classmates as you can.

GAME RULES
- Each person must say the next number in order, starting with 1.
- But, you may not say a "count by 4s" number. Instead you say "Buzz". For example, 1, 2, 3, Buzz, 5, 6, 7, Buzz …
- If you say a wrong number, or you don't say "Buzz" when you should, you return to your seat.
- Study the list some more so you can remain in the game longer during the next round.
- The WINNER is the last person standing.
- That person will be the referee for the next game.
5. Extend Play Multiplication Buzz with a different set of "count by" numbers.

Skills: Multiplication, reasoning, and communication   Use after Fluency Plan, Lesson 6.

Grouping Large Group

Materials Index cards

Objective Students play a game in which they use the multiples of a given number.

Connections Computation and Communication

Ready-Made Math Resources

Technology — Tutorials, Practice, and Intervention

Use online, individualized intervention and support to bring students to proficiency.

Help students practice skills and apply concepts through exciting math adventures.

Extend and enrich students' understanding of skills and concepts through engaging interactive lessons and activities.

Visit **Education Place**
www.eduplace.com

Visit www.eduplace.com/mx2t/ and find family, teacher, and student materials, activities, games, and more.

Literature Links

Anno's Mysterious Multiplying Jar

Anno's Mysterious Multiplying Jar
In this beautifully illustrated book by Masaichiro and Mitsumasa Anno, students will see how the concept of factorials is demonstrated in an imaginative story context.

Literature Connections

- *Math Strategies That Multiply: The Best of Times,* by Greg Tang, illustrated by Harry Briggs (Scholastic Press, 2002)

- *One Grain of Rice: A Mathematical Folktale,* by Demi (Scholastic, 1997)

Math Background

Putting Research into Practice for Basic Facts Fluency

From Our Curriculum Research Project

We found that we needed to consider affective, social, motivational, self-regulatory, and self-image aspects of learning and not just focus on building mathematical conceptions. Thus, students need to be helped to see themselves as included in the world of mathematics. They need to be taken seriously as learners so that they can begin to see themselves as learners. Mathematization (starting with students' experiences), the co-construction of understandings in a collaborative classroom, and involvement in learning-goal setting and evaluation all contribute to students' growth.

Traditional and reform practices are usually posed as alternatives. We found many elements of value in both perspectives, especially in the context of urban schools. We wove these elements into a fabric of teaching-learning activities that would support teachers' and students' construction and use of mathematical meanings linked to the traditional mathematical symbols and words of the culture. In each mathematics domain the teacher connects students' experiences, words, meanings, object and drawn representations, and methods to the traditional mathematical symbols, words, and methods of that domain. These meaning connections define what we call the referential classroom: referents for mathematical symbols and words are used pervasively within the classroom.

—Karen Fuson, Author
Math Expressions

From Current Research:
Multiply with MI: Using Multiple Intelligences to Master Multiplication

Students can extend their understanding of multiplication and division as they consider the inverse relationship between the two operations. Another way their knowledge can grow is through new multiplicative situations, such as rates (3 candy bars for 59 cents each), comparisons (the book weighs 4 times as much as the tablet), and combinations (the number of outfits possible from 3 shirts and 2 pairs of shorts). Examining the effect of multiplying or dividing numbers can also lead to a deeper understanding of these operations. For example, dividing 28 by 14 and comparing the result to dividing 28 by 7 can lead to the conjecture that the smaller the divisor, the larger the quotient. With models or calculators, students can explore dividing by numbers between 0 and 1, such as $\frac{1}{2}$, and find that the quotient is larger than the original number. Explorations such as these help dispel common, but incorrect, generalizations such as "division always makes things smaller."

Further meaning for multiplication should develop as students build and describe area models, showing how a product is related to its factors. Using area models, properties of operations, such as the commutativity of multiplication, become more apparent. Other relationships can be seen by decomposing and composing area models. For example, a model for 20×6 can be split in half and the halves rearranged to form a 10×12 rectangle, showing the equivalence of 10×12 and 20×6. The distributive property is particularly powerful as the basis of many efficient multiplication algorithms.

National Council for School Mathematics. *Principles and Standards for School Mathematics* (Number and Operations Standard for Grades 3–5). Reston: NCTM, 2000. p. 151.

Other Useful References: Multiplication and Division

Sherin, B. & Fuson, K., "Multiplication strategies and the appropriation of computational resources." *Journal for Research in Mathematics Education*, 36 (4), (2005) pp. 347–395.

This paper outlines student strategies for learning single-digit multiplication and division. *Math Expressions* Grades 3, 4, and 5 use approaches based on this research.

Van de Walle, John A. Paper-and-Pencil Computation with Whole Numbers *Elementary and Middle School Mathematics: Teaching Developmentally* (Fourth Edition). New York: Longman, 2001. pp. 221–234.

As you teach these lessons, emphasize understanding of this term.

• count-bys

See the Teacher Glossary on pp. T6–T17.

Getting Ready to Teach Multiplication and Division Facts Fluency

Why Teach Basic Facts Fluency?

As a Grade 5 teacher, you are aware that some students are not fluent with multiplication and division facts. Unless you bring all students to a competent level, your teaching of multiplication and division algorithms as well as fraction concepts will be hampered by students who struggle to remember facts rather than concentrate on learning new mathematics.

Meeting the Needs of All Students

Before you begin Unit 1, use this Fluency Plan to help you bring all students to a competent level of fluency. The students will fall into three categories: those who need strategy teaching, those who need fluency practice, and those who have achieved fluency. This section provides support for all three.

Multiplication and Division Checkups
Fluency Plan Lesson 1

Begin Lesson 1 by giving the Diagnostic Checkups for basic multiplication facts and related division facts. Then use student performance on the checkups to group your students according to fluency:

• Developing Fluency (students who need to learn facts and concepts)

• Building Fluency (students who need to practice facts and understand concepts)

• Achieved Fluency (students who are ready to extend facts and concepts)

Multiplication and Division Facts Study Plan Students who are developing or building fluency should set up a Study Plan for homework. They should list any multiplication and division facts they missed in the Checkups. Have them study these facts and review them at home with a family member. Students should update their Study Plans often to include only those multiplication and division facts they still need to study.

Helping Students Who Need to Learn Strategies

The *Math Expressions* approach for helping students learn their basic multiplication and division facts is to teach learning strategies based on patterns and the inverse relationship between multiplication and division and to offer a variety of structured practice.

Learning Strategies

Strategies for learning the facts build on visual supports and patterns. Among the tools used in the Fluency Plan are the Class Multiplication Table, Targets, count-by patterns, and drawings that relate multiplication and division.

Equal Groups, Arrays, and Area
Fluency Plan Lessons 1 and 2

Students must recognize four common situations in which we use multiplication and division. Two of these situations (equal groups and arrays and areas) are listed below with examples. The other two situations (combinations and comparisons) are presented in Unit 1. Multiplication and division are taught together so that students can see that one operation is the reverse of the other.

Equal Groups

A sport shop sells tennis balls in boxes of 6.

Multiplication: Dana bought 3 boxes. How many balls did she buy?

Division: Adam needs 18 balls. How many boxes should he buy?

Arrays and Area

An **array** is made of objects arranged in a rectangular shape. We can find the product by multiplying the number of columns by the number of rows.

The **area** of a rectangle is an array of touching square units. The floor shown here is 5 yards long and 3 yards wide. To find the area, we multiply the length times the width.

In division situations, the product and a factor are known, and one solves to find the unknown factor.

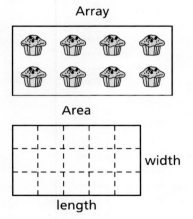

Array

Area

width

length

Targets
Fluency Plan Lesson 3

A special tool called a Target enables individuals to focus on just the multiplications and divisions that they need to practice. The Target is used either independently or with an in-class practice partner.
The shaded overlay with the transparent L-shape and the Target circle can be moved to any product. The ends of the L show the factors, and the Target shows the product. Covering the product provides multiplication practice, while covering one end of the L provides division practice. Students can use the target with the multiplication tables at the back of the Student Book.

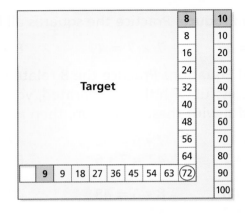

Count-by Patterns
Fluency Plan Lessons 2 and 4

Focusing on predictable patterns can facilitate learning multiplication and division. With some multiplication count-bys, the pattern is obvious, as with the 10s, 5s, and 2s.

With other count-bys, students may need help seeing the pattern as shown on the right. Students examine patterns for all of the multiplication count-bys.

1	11	21	31	41	51	61	71
2	12	22	(32)	42	52	62	(72)
3	13	23	33	43	53	63	73
4	14	(24)	34	44	54	(64)	74
5	15	25	35	45	55	65	75
6	(16)	26	36	46	(56)	66	76
7	17	27	37	47	57	67	77
(8)	18	28	38	(48)	58	68	78
9	19	29	39	49	59	69	79
10	20	30	(40)	50	60	70	(80)

Multiplication Strategies
Fluency Plan Lessons 2 and 5

Add or Subtract from a Known Product This strategy involves starting with a known product and then adding or subtracting a factor to arrive at an unknown product.

If you know $7 \times 7 = 49$

    Think: $6 \times 7 = 49 - 7 = 42$

       $7 \times 6 = 42$

If you know $7 \times 7 = 49$

    Think: $7 \times 8 = 49 + 7 = 56$

       $8 \times 7 = 56$

Multiplication Strategies (continued)

These strategies focus on the 6, 7s, and 8s.

Square Products Practice the squares all by themselves

$6 \times 6 = 36$ $7 \times 7 = 49$ $8 \times 8 = 64$

Related Equations Practice the 8 related equations separately. When students are successful with them separated, you can mix them up. When students are successful with these mixed up, then mix them with other products.

$6 \cdot 7 = 42$	$7 \cdot 6 = 42$	$42 \div 7 = 6$	$42 \div 6 = 7$
$42 = 6 \cdot 7$	$42 = 7 \cdot 6$	$6 = 42 \div 7$	$7 = 42 \div 6$
$6 \cdot 8 = 48$	$8 \cdot 6 = 48$	$48 \div 8 = 6$	$48 \div 6 = 8$
$48 = 6 \cdot 8$	$48 = 8 \cdot 6$	$6 = 48 \div 8$	$8 = 48 \div 6$
$7 \cdot 8 = 56$	$8 \cdot 7 = 56$	$56 \div 8 = 7$	$56 \div 7 = 8$
$56 = 7 \cdot 8$	$56 = 8 \cdot 7$	$7 = 56 \div 8$	$8 = 56 \div 7$

Ongoing Assessment and Practice for All Students

Students should continually work toward fluency for basic multiplication and division facts. Use structured practice sheets to assist students in monitoring their own learning. In the Teacher's Resource Book (TRB) you will find several pages for diagnosing and practicing basic multiplication and division.

TRB M58 Diagnostic Quiz for Basic Multiplication TRB M59 Diagnostic Quiz for Basic Division	TRB M66 Scrambled Multiplication Tables TRB M67 Blank Multiplication Tables
TRB M60 Basic Multiplication Practice TRB M61 Basic Division Practice	TRB M68 Multiplication for 10s, 11s, 12s TRB M69 Division for 10s, 11s, 12s
TRB M62 Multiplication for 3s, 4s, 6s, 7s, 8s, 9s TRB M63 Division for 3s, 4s, 6s, 7s, 8s, 9s	TRB M83 Factor Puzzles for 3s, 4s, 6s, 7s, 8s, 9s TRB M84 Factor Puzzles for 6s, 7s, 8s
TRB M64 Multiplication for 6s, 7s, 8s TRB M65 Division for 6s, 7s, 8s	TRB M85 Blank Factor Puzzles

Helping Students Who Need Practice

Fluency Days provide students with in-class opportunities to assess themselves on basic multiplication and division. Students can monitor their own learning through the use of hands-on materials and quick activities. If your students need more practice to build fluency, include a Fluency Day in your teaching plan. Use one or more of the activities suggested below.

Independent Practice

Have students who know the facts but are not completely fluent use the following materials for independent practice.

Division Practice
Fluency Plan Lesson 6

Division Cards Students may practice with these cards individually or with a partner. Students first stack their cards so the slanted corners line up on the right. Then one student reads the problem, solves the problem mentally, and turns the card over to check the answer. Students then sort their cards into *Fast, Slow,* and *Don't Know* piles to help them prioritize their practice.

Division Cards (Front)

$6\overline{)12}$	$6\overline{)18}$	$6\overline{)24}$	$6\overline{)30}$
$6 \times F = 12$	$6 \times F = 18$	$6 \times F = 24$	$6 \times F = 30$
$6\overline{)36}$	$6\overline{)42}$	$6\overline{)48}$	$6\overline{)54}$
$6 \times F = 36$	$6 \times F = 42$	$6 \times F = 48$	$6 \times F = 54$
$7\overline{)14}$	$7\overline{)21}$	$7\overline{)28}$	$7\overline{)35}$
$7 \times F = 14$	$7 \times F = 21$	$7 \times F = 28$	$7 \times F = 35$
$7\overline{)42}$	$7\overline{)49}$	$7\overline{)56}$	$7\overline{)63}$
$7 \times F = 42$	$7 \times F = 49$	$7 \times F = 56$	$7 \times F = 63$

FLUENCY PLAN LESSON 6 — Division Cards **20G**

Division Cards (Back)

$6\overline{)30}^{5}$	$6\overline{)24}^{4}$	$6\overline{)18}^{3}$	$6\overline{)12}^{2}$
$6 \times 5 = 30$	$6 \times 4 = 24$	$6 \times 3 = 18$	$6 \times 2 = 12$
$6\overline{)54}^{9}$	$6\overline{)48}^{8}$	$6\overline{)42}^{7}$	$6\overline{)36}^{6}$
$6 \times 9 = 54$	$6 \times 8 = 48$	$6 \times 7 = 42$	$6 \times 6 = 36$
$7\overline{)35}^{5}$	$7\overline{)28}^{4}$	$7\overline{)21}^{3}$	$7\overline{)14}^{2}$
$7 \times 5 = 35$	$7 \times 4 = 28$	$7 \times 3 = 21$	$7 \times 2 = 14$
$7\overline{)63}^{9}$	$7\overline{)56}^{8}$	$7\overline{)49}^{7}$	$7\overline{)42}^{6}$
$7 \times 9 = 63$	$7 \times 8 = 56$	$7 \times 7 = 49$	$7 \times 6 = 42$

20H FLUENCY PLAN LESSON 6 — Division Cards

Factor Field In this activity, students practice division by reading each division on the Division Cards and then placing the card on the Factor Field section that corresponds to the answer.

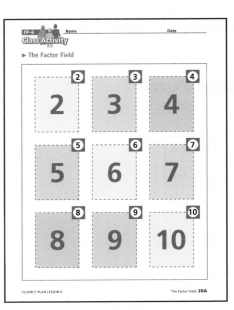

Factor Practice
Unit 1 Lessons 4 and 8

Factor the Footprints In this game, students practice finding factors with a partner by naming all the possible factor pairs that they can find for each number as they follow along the footprints on the game board.

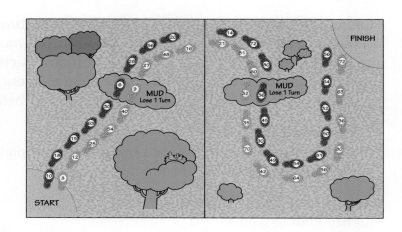

Scrambled Multiplication Tables These scrambled tables are multiplication tables with the rows and columns moved around. Students complete the missing factors (or products) in each table.

×	3	6	1	7	10	4	9	5	2	8
4	12	24	4	28	40	16	36	20	8	32
8	24	48	8	56	80	32	72	40	16	64
6	18	36	6	42	60	24	54	30	12	48
2	6	12	2	14	20	8	18	10	4	16
5	15	30	5	35	50	20	45	25	10	40
3	9	18	3	21	30	12	27	15	6	24
9	27	54	9	63	90	36	81	45	18	72
10	30	60	10	70	100	40	90	50	20	80
1	3	6	1	7	10	4	9	5	2	8
7	21	42	7	49	70	28	63	35	14	56

Factor Puzzles Students use their knowledge of factors and products to fill in the rows and columns of the multiplication table section that the Factor Puzzle numbers come from. They multiply to solve the puzzle.

Factor Puzzle

```
      5   7
   2 |10 |14 |  2
   6 | n |42 |  6
      5   7
```

$n = \underline{\ \ 30\ \ }$

Multiplication and Division Diagnostic Quizzes
Fluency Plan Lesson 6

Diagnostic multiplication and division quizzes are provided as tools to assess students' fluency after you have taught strategies or given opportunities for practice. These quizzes are structured for diagnosing needed practice.

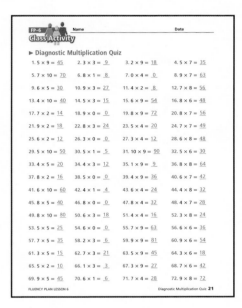

Activities for Students Who Have Achieved Fluency

Many students entering Grade 5 may be able to recall basic multiplication and division facts accurately and quickly. However, they should not move forward without the rest of the class but should instead use the activities described below until the whole class is ready to start Unit 1 together.

The activities described below are for those students who do not need extra teaching or practice for fluency.

Independent Activities

Math Center Challenges Four extended activities are provided for every unit. These activities are projects or investigations that will engage your more able students. You will find a description of the Math Center Challenges for the Fluency Plan on page 1F.

Challenge Activities Student Activity Cards describe independent activities related to the lesson content at three different ability levels. The Challenge Activity Card is pictured in the Differentiated Instruction section of each lesson.

Writing Word Problems Students can write word problems. Ask a Teacher Assistant or a volunteer parent to type the problems into a class booklet with an answer key at the end; or have a separate answer booklet with all the different solutions for the problems. The problems can be mixed single-step problems and multistep problems. Save the booklets to use with Unit 1.

Partner Activities

Helping Partners A student who has achieved fluency can function as a coach to help a less advanced students practice and plan effective practice methods. They can help students use different strategies. This individualized help and encouragement can be very helpful to a student in need of both.

Inventing Rhymes Students can work with a partner to write rhymes that will help everyone remember the hardest multiplication and division facts. They can lead the class to practice with them.

Inventing Songs Students can work with a partner to write songs that will help everyone remember the hardest multiplication and division facts. They can lead the class to practice with them.

Group Activities

Making Posters Students can make pictographs or function tables where each picture represents 3 or 4, or 6, 7, and 8 and then lead the class to practice with them.

Creating Board Games Some students may enjoy working in a group and creating a game board with question cards that require students to give the answers to the harder facts: 6s, 7, 8s. Students can play these games with each other or with less advanced students.

Multiplication as Equal Groups

Lesson Objectives

● Recognize multiplication as a method of finding the total of equal groups.

● Understand everyday applications of multiplication and division.

The Day at a Glance

Today's Goals	Materials
1 **Teaching the Lesson** **A1:** Assess recall of basic multiplication and division. **A2:** Visualize equal groups to review multiplication and division concepts. **A3:** Use strategies to find the total of equal groups. **A4:** Write and solve word problems that use equal groups. **2** **Going Further** ▶ Differentiated Instruction **3** **Homework and Spiral Review**	**Lesson Activities** Student Activity Book pp. 1–6 or Student Hardcover Book pp. 1–6 and Activity Workbook pp. 1–4 (includes Checkups and Family Letters) Homework and Remembering pp. 1–2 **Going Further** Activity Cards FP-1 Counters Centimeter-Grid Paper (TRB M18) Scissors Crayons Calculator Math Journals

123 Use Math Talk today!

Keeping Skills Sharp

Quick Practice	Daily Routines
This section provides repetitive, short activities that either help students become faster and more accurate at a skill or help to prepare ground for new concepts. These activities are very important for students to do every day because they provide valuable practice and give you an opportunity to interact with students who may need guidance during the time when **Student Leaders** or students are working individually. Many teachers have students complete the Quick Practice at some time other than during math class. Quick Practice for the Fluency Plan will start in Lesson 2.	**Find a Pattern** Write the following numbers on the board. 22, 31, 27, 36, 32, 41. Have students find and explain the pattern(s). Then have students give the next three terms. Possible pattern: Add 9 and then subtract 4; $22 + 9 = 31$, $31 - 4 = 27$, $27 + 9 = 36$, $36 - 4 = 32$, $32 + 9 = 41$; 37, 46, 42

1 Teaching the Lesson

Basic Multiplication and Division

 10 MINUTES

Goal: Assess recall of basic multiplication and division.

Materials: Student Activity Book pp. 1–2 or Hardcover Book pp. 1–2 and Activity Workbook pp. 1–2

 NCTM Standards:
Number and Operations
Communication

Teaching Note

Common Errors On Student Book page 1, the Identity Property of Multiplication is represented by exercises 14, 18, 38, 50, 66, and 71. Remind those students who write incorrect answers for one or more of these exercises that when you multiply a number and 1, the result or product is that number.

The Zero Property of Multiplication is represented by exercises 6, 22, 30, 46, 58, and 67. Remind those students who write incorrect answers for one or more of these exercises that when you multiply any number and 0, the result or product is 0.

FP–1   Name _____   Date _____
Class Activity

▶ **Diagnostic Checkup for Basic Multiplication**

1. 7 × 5 = 35	2. 2 × 3 = 6	3. 9 × 9 = 81	4. 9 × 6 = 54
5. 6 × 2 = 12	6. 3 × 0 = 0	7. 3 × 4 = 12	8. 6 × 8 = 48
9. 5 × 9 = 45	10. 3 × 3 = 9	11. 2 × 9 = 18	12. 5 × 7 = 35
13. 6 × 10 = 60	14. 4 × 1 = 4	15. 6 × 4 = 24	16. 4 × 8 = 32
17. 5 × 2 = 10	18. 1 × 3 = 3	19. 3 × 9 = 27	20. 7 × 6 = 42
21. 7 × 2 = 14	22. 9 × 0 = 0	23. 8 × 9 = 72	24. 8 × 7 = 56
25. 8 × 10 = 80	26. 6 × 3 = 18	27. 4 × 4 = 16	28. 3 × 8 = 24
29. 5 × 5 = 25	30. 6 × 0 = 0	31. 7 × 9 = 63	32. 6 × 6 = 36
33. 9 × 2 = 18	34. 8 × 3 = 24	35. 5 × 4 = 20	36. 7 × 7 = 49
37. 5 × 10 = 50	38. 5 × 1 = 5	39. 10 × 9 = 90	40. 5 × 6 = 30
41. 6 × 5 = 30	42. 9 × 3 = 27	43. 4 × 2 = 8	44. 7 × 8 = 56
45. 8 × 2 = 16	46. 5 × 0 = 0	47. 4 × 9 = 36	48. 6 × 7 = 42
49. 9 × 5 = 45	50. 6 × 1 = 6	51. 7 × 4 = 28	52. 9 × 8 = 72
53. 4 × 10 = 40	54. 5 × 3 = 15	55. 6 × 9 = 54	56. 8 × 6 = 48
57. 8 × 5 = 40	58. 8 × 0 = 0	59. 8 × 4 = 32	60. 4 × 7 = 28
61. 3 × 5 = 15	62. 7 × 3 = 21	63. 5 × 9 = 45	64. 3 × 6 = 18
65. 7 × 10 = 70	66. 8 × 1 = 8	67. 0 × 4 = 0	68. 9 × 7 = 63
69. 4 × 5 = 20	70. 4 × 3 = 12	71. 1 × 9 = 9	72. 8 × 8 = 64

FLUENCY PLAN LESSON 1   Diagnostic Multiplication Checkup **1**

Student Activity Book page 1

▶ Diagnostic Checkup for Basic Multiplication

INDIVIDUALS

A goal of fifth-grade students is to be fluent with basic multiplication and division. Use Student Book pages 1 and 2 to assess their ability to recall the more difficult multiplications and divisions. The Fluency Plan, described in the overview, provides appropriate support for students of all abilities.

The Checkup for Multiplication can be used to diagnose where students need additional practice.

Students Who Miss	Need to Practice Multiplications
Column 1	2s, 5s, and 10s
Column 2	0s, 1s, and 3s
Column 3	4s and 9s
Column 4	6s, 7s, and 8s

FP–1
Class Activity

Name _____   Date _____

▶ Diagnostic Checkup for Basic Division

1. $12 \div 2 =$ _6_   2. $8 \div 1 =$ _8_   3. $36 \div 9 =$ _4_   4. $35 \div 7 =$ _5_

5. $20 \div 5 =$ _4_   6. $24 \div 3 =$ _8_   7. $12 \div 4 =$ _3_   8. $6 \div 6 =$ _1_

9. $6 \div 2 =$ _3_   10. $3 \div 3 =$ _1_   11. $18 \div 9 =$ _2_   12. $63 \div 7 =$ _9_

13. $20 \div 10 =$ _2_   14. $0 \div 1 =$ _0_   15. $40 \div 4 =$ _10_   16. $48 \div 8 =$ _6_

17. $18 \div 2 =$ _9_   18. $6 \div 3 =$ _2_   19. $8 \div 4 =$ _2_   20. $36 \div 6 =$ _6_

21. $8 \div 2 =$ _4_   22. $9 \div 1 =$ _9_   23. $9 \div 9 =$ _1_   24. $56 \div 7 =$ _8_

25. $40 \div 5 =$ _8_   26. $9 \div 3 =$ _3_   27. $36 \div 4 =$ _9_   28. $56 \div 8 =$ _7_

29. $80 \div 10 =$ _8_   30. $7 \div 1 =$ _7_   31. $45 \div 9 =$ _5_   32. $48 \div 6 =$ _8_

33. $5 \div 5 =$ _1_   34. $30 \div 3 =$ _10_   35. $16 \div 4 =$ _4_   36. $72 \div 8 =$ _9_

37. $10 \div 2 =$ _5_   38. $1 \div 1 =$ _1_   39. $54 \div 9 =$ _6_   40. $21 \div 7 =$ _3_

41. $25 \div 5 =$ _5_   42. $15 \div 3 =$ _5_   43. $32 \div 4 =$ _8_   44. $24 \div 8 =$ _3_

45. $90 \div 10 =$ _9_   46. $18 \div 3 =$ _6_   47. $63 \div 9 =$ _7_   48. $54 \div 6 =$ _9_

49. $45 \div 5 =$ _9_   50. $6 \div 1 =$ _6_   51. $20 \div 4 =$ _5_   52. $49 \div 7 =$ _7_

53. $15 \div 5 =$ _3_   54. $0 \div 3 =$ _0_   55. $28 \div 4 =$ _7_   56. $30 \div 6 =$ _5_

57. $16 \div 2 =$ _8_   58. $21 \div 3 =$ _7_   59. $81 \div 9 =$ _9_   60. $64 \div 8 =$ _8_

61. $30 \div 5 =$ _6_   62. $12 \div 3 =$ _4_   63. $27 \div 9 =$ _3_   64. $42 \div 7 =$ _6_

65. $40 \div 10 =$ _4_   66. $10 \div 1 =$ _10_   67. $24 \div 4 =$ _6_   68. $18 \div 6 =$ _3_

69. $35 \div 5 =$ _7_   70. $27 \div 3 =$ _9_   71. $72 \div 9 =$ _8_   72. $42 \div 6 =$ _7_

2 FLUENCY PLAN LESSON 1   Diagnostic Division Checkup

Student Activity Book page 2

▶ Diagnostic Checkup for Basic Division INDIVIDUALS

The Checkup for Division can be used to diagnose where students need additional practice.

Students Who Miss	Need to Practice Divisions
Column 1	2s, 5s, and 10s
Column 2	1s, and 3s
Column 3	4s and 9s
Column 4	6s, 7s, and 8s

Teaching Note

Common Error When dividing whole numbers, make sure students recognize that 0 and 1 require special attention. On Student Book page 2, remind those students who incorrectly answer exercises 2, 14, 22, 30, 38, 50, and 66 that when you divide any number by 1, the result or quotient is that number.

Have students note that the divisions in exercises 14 and 54 involve 0, and remind them that it is not possible for the divisor to be 0 because division by 0 is not meaningful. Lead them to understand that, when one of the numbers is 0, they need to be very careful about the order.

These divisions are possible.

$$0 \div 9 = 0 \qquad 6\overline{)0}^{\,0}$$

These divisions are not possible.

$$9 \div 0 = ? \qquad 0\overline{)6}^{\,?}$$

Ask students to write these two concepts, using their own words, and then write three number sentences that illustrate each concept.

Teaching the Lesson

Visualize Equal Groups

 20 MINUTES

Goal: Visualize equal groups to review multiplication and division concepts.

✓ **NCTM Standards:**
Communication
Number and Operations
Algebra
Representation

The Learning Classroom

Helping Community By discussing multiple strategies for math problems students become aware of other students' thinking. As students better understand each other's thinking, they become better "helpers." Instead of showing how they would solve problems, they are able to look at another student's work and help them to find mistakes in their own method."

Differentiated Instruction

Extra Help If students have trouble finding a strategy, ask a few leading questions to get them started. For example, ask leading questions such as, "What if we knew 3 × 6 but didn't know 4 × 6?" This will help them see that in many multiplication problems they can build on what they already know.

▶ **Concepts of Multiplication**

Make this drawing on the board. Explain that each package holds 6 yo-yos. Ask the students if they can supply a multiplication equation that shows the total number of yo-yos. (Elicit or demonstrate that there are three ways to write the multiplication sign.)

| 6 | 6 | 6 | 6 |

Equal Groups drawing

$$4 \times 6 = 24$$
$$4 \bullet 6 = 24$$
$$4 * 6 = 24$$

Now ask students how they could find the total number of yo-yos if they didn't actually know the answer or if they wanted to find a different way. Below are a few common strategies. At this point, it is important to encourage students to articulate what they already know and to help them think about the meaning of equal groups.

● We could add six 4 times. We call this the sixes *count-by*.

6, 12, 18, 24   Count by six 4 times.

● If we knew 2 × 6, we could take it twice.

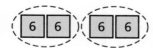   12 + 12 = 24

● If we knew 5 × 6, we could subtract 1 six.

| 6 | 6 | 6 | 6 | 6̶ | 30 − 6 = 24

● If we knew 3 × 6, we could add 1 six.

   18 + 6 = 24

Ask students to summarize how multiplication is different from addition. You have to add equal groups; the factors have different roles: one is the multiplier and the other is the multiplied.

Ask students whether they think of 4 × 6 as 4 groups of 6 (4 ×⑥) or groups of 4 taken 6 times (④ × 6). Explain that people in different countries think each of these ways and either is fine, though books in this country usually use the first way.

▶ Concepts of Division WHOLE CLASS

Explain that now we have 24 yo-yos and 4 packages. Draw this diagram on the board.

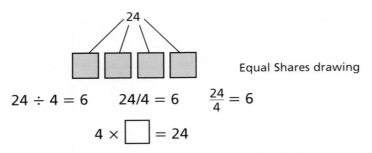

Equal Shares drawing

$$24 \div 4 = 6 \qquad 24/4 = 6 \qquad \frac{24}{4} = 6$$

$$4 \times \boxed{} = 24$$

Ask the class to supply an equation that shows how an equal number of yo-yos can be put in each package. (Elicit or demonstrate both division signs.)

Then ask for an equation that shows this situation with multiplication. Understanding that division is unknown multiplication (4 × what number = 24) is a crucial aspect of student thinking.

Now ask the class what would happen if we didn't know how many packages we needed. We know that we have 24 yo-yos, and we want to put 6 yo-yos in each package. How many packages would we need? Put the partial drawing shown below on the board and ask a volunteer to finish it. To help students, ask, "How many times do you need to add 6 to get 24?"

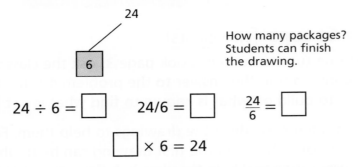

How many packages?
Students can finish
the drawing.

$$24 \div 6 = \boxed{} \qquad 24/6 = \boxed{} \qquad \frac{24}{6} = \boxed{}$$

$$\boxed{} \times 6 = 24$$

While the volunteer is working, have the class supply the various equations that show this problem.

Math Talk Ask students to summarize how these two division situations are alike and different. Be sure that students articulate these two different kinds of division in equal groups situations:

- dividing to find how many are in a group

- dividing to find how many groups

The unknown box in Equal Shares drawings shows this distinction.

Teaching Note

Math Symbols Review with students the different symbols that are used to indicate division. Explain that the symbol used does not affect the operation. For example, / and ÷ both represent division.

Activity 3

Strategies to Find Equal Groups

 15 MINUTES

Goal: Use strategies to find the total of equal groups.

Materials: Student Activity Book or Hardcover Book p. 3

 NCTM Standards:
Communication
Number and Operations
Algebra
Representation

Differentiated Instruction

Special Needs Some students may have trouble visualizing equal groups without seeing them. Have those students draw a picture of the total amount, using circles or tally marks. Guide the students to circle groups of equal amounts.

Try to move such students to using the numerical drawings as rapidly as possible because they facilitate numerical strategies and are much faster to draw.

The Learning Classroom

Helping Community Create a classroom where students are not competing but desire to collaborate and help one another. Communicate often that your goal as a class is that everyone understand the math you are studying. Tell students that this will require everyone working together to help each other.

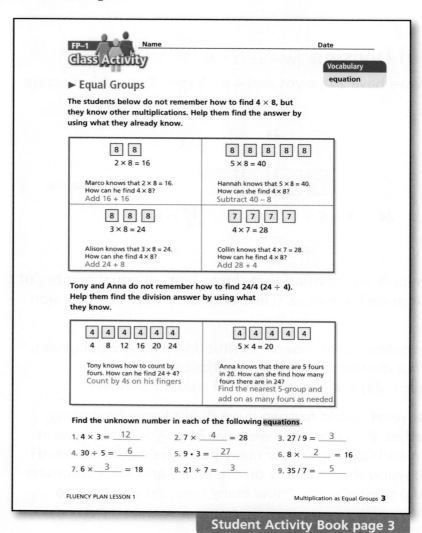

Student Activity Book page 3

▶ Equal Groups [INDIVIDUALS]

Have everyone turn to Student Book page 3. Ask the class to help each of the students to find the answer to the problem 4 × 8. They can discuss how to build on what is known to find what is not known.

Encourage students to adjust the drawings to help them. For example, the two boxes of 8 shown in the first drawing can be doubled. This visual representation will help the class link the concept to the equation.

$$\boxed{8}\ \boxed{8}\ \ \begin{array}{c}\fbox{8}\end{array}\ \begin{array}{c}\fbox{8}\end{array}$$
$$16\ \ +\ \ 16\ \ = 32$$

Be sure your students have some basic strategy for finding divisions. Adding on groups to find how many make the total is the most basic strategy. If students can count by 5, they can take a shortcut by using "fast fives."

Division Strategies

Adding-On Equal Groups
Example: 24 ÷ 4
Count by fours, using fingers to keep track of how many groups.

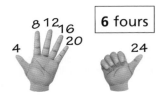

Fast Fives
Example: 24 ÷ 4
Start count-bys at 5 × 4, and add on as many fours as needed.

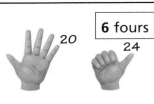

Equations Discuss the meaning of the word *equation*. Emphasize that an equation must include an equals sign. It is a statement that 2 or more quantities are equal. Point out that an equation can have an unknown number in any one of three positions.

$$\boxed{} \times 6 = 42 \qquad 7 \times \boxed{} = 42 \qquad 7 \times 6 = \boxed{}$$

Also point out to students that the product can be written on either side of the equals sign.

$$42 = \boxed{} \times 6 \qquad 42 = 7 \times \boxed{} \qquad \boxed{} = 7 \times 6$$

Ask students to quickly give the answers to exercises 1–9. Be sure that they understand all the forms of notation shown in this section. If they get stuck on any exercise, discuss possible solution strategies based on their understanding of equal groups.

Activity 4

Word Problems With Equal Groups

 25 MINUTES

Goal: Write and solve word problems that use equal groups.

Materials: Student Activity Book or Hardcover Book p. 4

 NCTM Standards:
Communication
Number and Operations
Algebra
Problem Solving

Ongoing Assessment

Ask students:

► What are two ways that you could show the number 12 by using equal groups?

► Explain how you can show 15 ÷ 3 by using equal groups.

The Learning Classroom

Math Talk Always start new topics by eliciting as much from students as possible. Students often know some things about new topics. This builds feelings of competence and confidence and helps create the classroom community where everyone is a teacher and a learner. So even where the directions for a lesson are directing you to do the talking, remember to always ask for students' own ideas first.

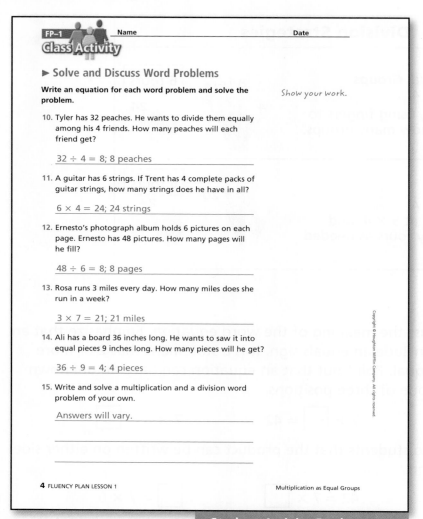

FP-1 Name _____ Date _____
Class Activity

► Solve and Discuss Word Problems

Write an equation for each word problem and solve the problem.   *Show your work.*

10. Tyler has 32 peaches. He wants to divide them equally among his 4 friends. How many peaches will each friend get?

     32 ÷ 4 = 8; 8 peaches

11. A guitar has 6 strings. If Trent has 4 complete packs of guitar strings, how many strings does he have in all?

     6 × 4 = 24; 24 strings

12. Ernesto's photograph album holds 6 pictures on each page. Ernesto has 48 pictures. How many pages will he fill?

     48 ÷ 6 = 8; 8 pages

13. Rosa runs 3 miles every day. How many miles does she run in a week?

     3 × 7 = 21; 21 miles

14. Ali has a board 36 inches long. He wants to saw it into equal pieces 9 inches long. How many pieces will he get?

     36 ÷ 9 = 4; 4 pieces

15. Write and solve a multiplication and a division word problem of your own.

     Answers will vary.
     _____
     _____

4 FLUENCY PLAN LESSON 1   Multiplication as Equal Groups

Student Activity Book page 4

► Solve and Discuss Word Problems

WHOLE CLASS   **Math Talk**

Begin using the **Solve and Discuss** classroom structure in which you send as many students to the board as possible. Students at the board solve by using a numerical drawing, or an equation, or finger methods while students at their seats also solve the problem. Then ask 2 or 3 students at the board to explain their method. These explanations are short, so you could ask more students to explain. With longer explanations, ask only 2 or 3 students because the class may lose attention for more. Explain that over time everyone will get a chance to explain their method.

For each problem on Student Book page 4, ask students to write both a multiplication and a division equation with an unknown box so that they can see the relationships between these operations. Also emphasize that it is important to label the answer with the kind of thing it is or with a measurement unit. This gives students a chance to look back at the problem to see if their answers make sense.

②Going Further

Intervention — Activity Card FP-1

Use Counters

Activity Card FP-1

Work: In Pairs

Use:
• Counters

Decide:
Who will be Student 1 and who will be Student 2 for the first round.

1. The counters show equal groups of 4 for the number 32. Notice how the equation describes the model of 8 groups with 4 in each group.

$8 \times 4 = 32$

2. Student 1: Use the counters to make another set of equal groups for the number 32.

3. Student 2: Write an equation that describes the equal groups.

4. Exchange roles and repeat the activity until you have found all the possible arrangements of equal groups for the number 32.
8×4; 4×8; 2×16; 16×2; 1×32; 32×1

Fluency Plan Lesson 1   Copyright © Houghton Mifflin Company

Activity Note Have students repeat the activity several times using different numbers, as time permits.

✎ Math Writing Prompt

Make a Drawing Make a drawing that shows $12 \div 3$. Write the multiplication equation that the drawing represents.

Soar to Success Math ★ Software Support

Warm-Up 12.21

On Level — Activity Card FP-1

Draw Models

Activity Card FP-1 ▲

Work: By Yourself

Use:
• Centimeter-Grid Paper (TRB M18)
• Scissors
• Crayons

1. Color squares on grid paper to make an array for each number listed below:

   6, 9, 10, 16

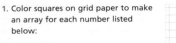

$3 \times 2 = 6$

2. Cut out each array. Then cut each array into equal groups and record the equation that matches the array.

3. Exchange with another student and compare your results.

4. Discuss Which number has the least number of possible arrangements of equal groups? 9: 1×9; 9×1; 3×3

Fluency Plan Lesson 1   Copyright © Houghton Mifflin Company

Activity Note Display the arrays that students make and then list all the possible arrays for each number. Discuss why only square numbers, such as 9, have an odd number of possible arrays.

✎ Math Writing Prompt

Explain Your Thinking Explain how equal groups are related to both $32 \div 8 = 4$ and $4 \times 8 = 32$. Use drawings if needed.

MegaMath Grades K-6 Software Support

The Number Games: Up, Up, and Array, Level D

Challenge — Activity Card FP-1

Look for Patterns

Activity Card FP-1 ■

Work: By Yourself

Use:
• Calculator

1. Use your calculator to answer each question.

   How many groups of 2 are in 32? 16

   How many groups of 2 are in 320? 160

   How many groups of 2 are in 3,200? 1,600

   How many groups of 2 are in 32,000? 16,000

2. Describe any patterns you discover. See below.

3. Predict Will the same patterns work for other sequences of numbers? Choose other numbers to test your prediction, and record your results.
   2. As the number all together increases by a factor of 10, the number of groups increases by a factor of 10.

Fluency Plan Lesson 1   Copyright © Houghton Mifflin Company

Activity Note Discuss the pattern of zeros in the quotients and dividends. Students can generate other patterns by dividing 32,000 by 2, 20, 200, and so on.

✎ Math Writing Prompt

Find a Strategy Create a new strategy for finding equal groups of two-digit numbers.

✦ DESTINATION Math· Software Support

Course III: Module 1: Unit 2: Finding Factors

③ Homework and Spiral Review

FP–1
Homework **Goal:** Additional Practice

✔ Include students' work for Homework page 1 as part of their portfolios.

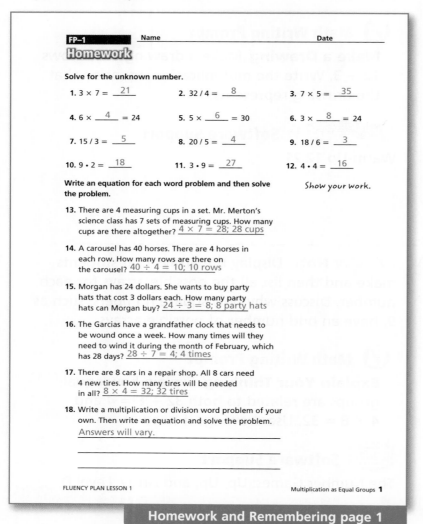

FP–1 Name _____ Date _____
Homework

Solve for the unknown number.

1. 3 × 7 = <u>21</u>   2. 32 / 4 = <u>8</u>   3. 7 × 5 = <u>35</u>

4. 6 × <u>4</u> = 24   5. 5 × <u>6</u> = 30   6. 3 × <u>8</u> = 24

7. 15 / 3 = <u>5</u>   8. 20 / 5 = <u>4</u>   9. 18 / 6 = <u>3</u>

10. 9 • 2 = <u>18</u>   11. 3 • 9 = <u>27</u>   12. 4 • 4 = <u>16</u>

Write an equation for each word problem and then solve the problem.   *Show your work.*

13. There are 4 measuring cups in a set. Mr. Merton's science class has 7 sets of measuring cups. How many cups are there altogether? <u>4 × 7 = 28; 28 cups</u>

14. A carousel has 40 horses. There are 4 horses in each row. How many rows are there on the carousel? <u>40 ÷ 4 = 10; 10 rows</u>

15. Morgan has 24 dollars. She wants to buy party hats that cost 3 dollars each. How many party hats can Morgan buy? <u>24 ÷ 3 = 8; 8 party hats</u>

16. The Garcias have a grandfather clock that needs to be wound once a week. How many times will they need to wind it during the month of February, which has 28 days? <u>28 ÷ 7 = 4; 4 times</u>

17. There are 8 cars in a repair shop. All 8 cars need 4 new tires. How many tires will be needed in all? <u>8 × 4 = 32; 32 tires</u>

18. Write a multiplication or division word problem of your own. Then write an equation and solve the problem. <u>Answers will vary.</u>

FLUENCY PLAN LESSON 1   Multiplication as Equal Groups **1**

Homework and Remembering page 1

FP–1
Remembering **Goal:** Spiral Review

This Remembering activity would be appropriate anytime after today's lesson.

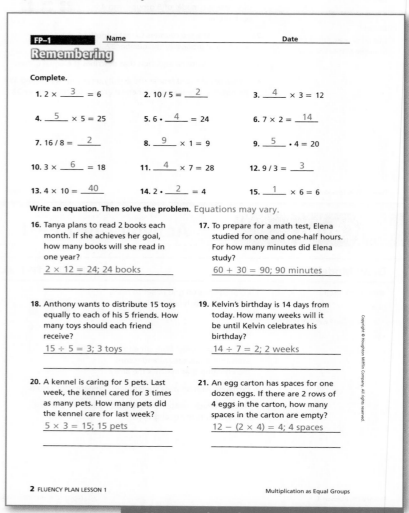

FP–1 Name _____ Date _____
Remembering

Complete.

1. 2 × <u>3</u> = 6   2. 10 / 5 = <u>2</u>   3. <u>4</u> × 3 = 12

4. <u>5</u> × 5 = 25   5. 6 • <u>4</u> = 24   6. 7 × 2 = <u>14</u>

7. 16 / 8 = <u>2</u>   8. <u>9</u> × 1 = 9   9. <u>5</u> • 4 = 20

10. 3 × <u>6</u> = 18   11. <u>4</u> × 7 = 28   12. 9 / 3 = <u>3</u>

13. 4 × 10 = <u>40</u>   14. 2 • <u>2</u> = 4   15. <u>1</u> × 6 = 6

Write an equation. Then solve the problem. Equations may vary.

16. Tanya plans to read 2 books each month. If she achieves her goal, how many books will she read in one year? <u>2 × 12 = 24; 24 books</u>

17. To prepare for a math test, Elena studied for one and one-half hours. For how many minutes did Elena study? <u>60 + 30 = 90; 90 minutes</u>

18. Anthony wants to distribute 15 toys equally to each of his 5 friends. How many toys should each friend receive? <u>15 ÷ 5 = 3; 3 toys</u>

19. Kelvin's birthday is 14 days from today. How many weeks will it be until Kelvin celebrates his birthday? <u>14 ÷ 7 = 2; 2 weeks</u>

20. A kennel is caring for 5 pets. Last week, the kennel cared for 3 times as many pets. How many pets did the kennel care for last week? <u>5 × 3 = 15; 15 pets</u>

21. An egg carton has spaces for one dozen eggs. If there are 2 rows of 4 eggs in the carton, how many spaces in the carton are empty? <u>12 − (2 × 4) = 4; 4 spaces</u>

2 FLUENCY PLAN LESSON 1   Multiplication as Equal Groups

Homework and Remembering page 2

Home and School Connection

Family Letter Have students take home the Family Letter on Student Book page 5 or Activity Workbook page 3. This letter explains how the concept of multiplication and division is developed in *Math Expressions*. It gives parents and guardians a better understanding of the learning that goes on in math class and creates a bridge between school and home. A Spanish translation of this letter is on Student Book page 6 and Activity Workbook page 4.

Student Activity Book Page 5

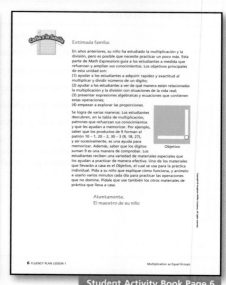

Student Activity Book Page 6

Arrays and Area

REAL WORLD Problem Solving

Vocabulary
array
row
column
area
length
width

Lesson Objectives

● **Understand and apply the terms *array* and *area*.**

● **Solve word problems that involve equal groups, areas, and arrays.**

● **Use simple algebraic notation to show the unknown in an area situation.**

The Day at a Glance

Today's Goals	Materials	

1 **Teaching the Lesson**
 A1: Review the difference between arrays and area, and apply knowledge to word problems.
 A2: Use simple algebraic notation, and apply it to area problems.
 	
 2 **Going Further**
 ▶ Differentiated Instruction
 	
 3 **Homework and Spiral Review**
	Lesson Activities
	 Student Activity Book pp. 7–10 or
	   Student Hardcover Book pp. 7–10
	 Homework and Remembering
	   pp. 3–4
		Going Further
		 Activity Cards FP-2
		 Inch-Grid Paper
		  (TRB M1)
		 Scissors
		 Centimeter-Grid
		  Paper (TRB M18)
		 Crayons
		 Game Cards (TRB M2)
		 Math Journals
		
		 123 *Use* **Math Talk** *today!*

Keeping Skills Sharp

Quick Practice ⏱ 5 MINUTES	**Daily Routines**
Goal: Practice basic multiplications, using Easy Finger Factors. **Easy Finger Factors** Ask for three volunteers to be **Student Leaders.** The first student leader gives a number from 0 to 5 by raising fingers on one hand and saying the number out loud. The second leader gives another number from 0 to 5 in the same way. The third leader gives a hand signal that the class will recognize as a go-signal. (This gives less advanced students time to think, ensuring that the class will answer in unison.) At that point, the seated students give the product of the two numbers. Repeat with other numbers.	**Homework Review** Let students work together to check their work. Initially, pair less able students with more able students. Remind students to use what they know about helping others. **Elapsed Time** Juan has to arrive at basketball practice at 12:15 P.M. It takes him 20 minutes to walk there. Along the way, he wants to stop for 10 minutes at his friend's house. At what time should Juan leave for practice? 11:45 A.M.

Teaching the Lesson

Compare Array and Area

 30 MINUTES

Goal: Review the difference between arrays and area, and apply knowledge to word problems.

Materials: Student Activity Book or Hardcover Book pp. 7–8

✓ **NCTM Standards:**
Problem Solving
Measurement
Representation

The Learning Classroom

Building Concepts To develop connections, remember to have students summarize. Have students take turns summarizing the previous day's lesson at the beginning of math class. They can just say one or two sentences. An alternative may be to have a student summarize at the end of the lesson. Either way, if you do this regularly, students will get used to making mental summaries of the math concepts discussed and making conceptual connections.

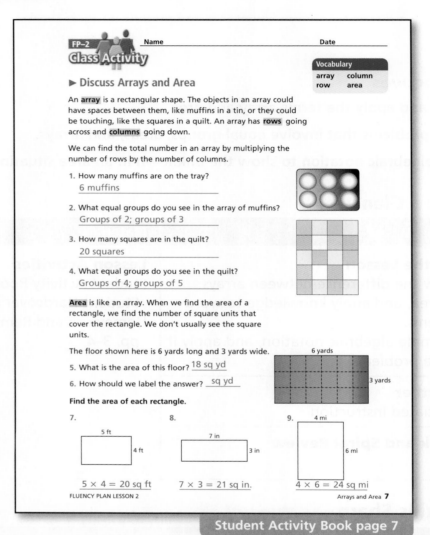

Student Activity Book page 7

▶ Discuss Arrays and Area

WHOLE CLASS

Math Talk

Ask questions to establish the meaning of *array* and *area*.

● **What is an array?** objects arranged in rows and columns **What is the meaning of area?** the total number of square units that cover a region, such as a rectangle.

● **How is a rectangle different from an array?** You can see the units of an array, but you can't see them on a rectangle.

Have students read and discuss the information on page 7 of the Student Book. Students should understand that the answer to an array problem is found by multiplying the number of rows by the number of columns and is the total number of objects, such as 12 cupcakes. The answer to an area problem is given in square units, 12 square feet. Be sure they can identify the abbreviation *sq*.

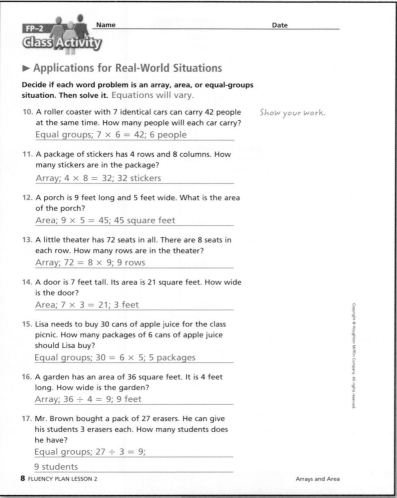

► Applications for Real-World Situations

Decide if each word problem is an array, area, or equal-groups situation. Then solve it. Equations will vary.

10. A roller coaster with 7 identical cars can carry 42 people at the same time. How many people will each car carry?
Equal groups; $7 \times 6 = 42$; 6 people

Show your work.

11. A package of stickers has 4 rows and 8 columns. How many stickers are in the package?
Array; $4 \times 8 = 32$; 32 stickers

12. A porch is 9 feet long and 5 feet wide. What is the area of the porch?
Area; $9 \times 5 = 45$; 45 square feet

13. A little theater has 72 seats in all. There are 8 seats in each row. How many rows are in the theater?
Array; $72 = 8 \times 9$; 9 rows

14. A door is 7 feet tall. Its area is 21 square feet. How wide is the door?
Area; $7 \times 3 = 21$; 3 feet

15. Lisa needs to buy 30 cans of apple juice for the class picnic. How many packages of 6 cans of apple juice should Lisa buy?
Equal groups; $30 = 6 \times 5$; 5 packages

16. A garden has an area of 36 square feet. It is 4 feet long. How wide is the garden?
Array; $36 \div 4 = 9$; 9 feet

17. Mr. Brown bought a pack of 27 erasers. He can give his students 3 erasers each. How many students does he have?
Equal groups; $27 \div 3 = 9$;
9 students

8 FLUENCY PLAN LESSON 2   Arrays and Area

Student Activity Book page 8

► Applications for Real-World Situations [INDIVIDUALS]

Ask students to solve problems 10–17 on page 8. Students need to identify the type of situation (equal groups, array, or area). If there is confusion, remind the class that equal groups are not connected to each other in rows and columns. They are separate groups. For example, 3 plates that each hold 4 cookies would be equal groups. A cookie sheet with 3 rows of 4 cookies would be an array. Make a drawing on the board, if necessary. Area does not involve objects at all, only measurements. It is the number of square units that cover a shape. For example, the area of the cookie sheet might be 4 square feet.

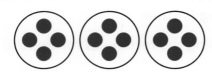

Equal Groups of Cookies   Array of Cookies

Extra Help If students are having trouble understanding the difference between equal groups, arrays, and area, have the students draw a picture. This can be very helpful when trying to solve word problems.

English Language Learners

Draw a 4×3 rectangle showing 4 unit squares across and 3 down. Write *array* and *area* on the board.

• **Beginning** Say: The array of unit squares is 4 across and 3 down. The area of the rectangle is 4×3. Ask: **What is 4×3?** 12
• **Intermediate** Ask: **What is the array of unit squares?** 4×3 **How do you find the area of the rectangle?** Multiply 4×3 **What is the area?** 12 square units
• **Advanced** Have students work in pairs. One partner names an array of unit squares in a rectangle and the other names the area.

Class Management

Looking Ahead In the next lesson, students will use Targets. These are on TRB page M3. Targets should be copied on transparencies (make sure your copy machine has the capability). You may want to set aside time before you begin the lesson for students to cut out their Targets.

If you have access to the *Math Expressions* materials kits, the Targets are included, so you will not have to prepare them.

Arrays and Area   **13**

Teaching the Lesson (continued)

Activity 2

Letter Notation for Area Problems

 25 MINUTES

Goal: Use simple algebraic notation, and apply it to area problems.

Materials: Student Activity Book or Hardcover Book pp. 9–10

 NCTM Standards:
Algebra
Measurement
Representation

Ongoing Assessment

Have students show 3 × 2 as equal groups, as an array, and as area.

Differentiated Instruction

Extra Help Some students may need a review of the formula for area of a rectangle.

Draw a rectangle on the board. Label the length and the width. Discuss the corresponding parts of the rectangle's dimensions and the formula.

Length 6 in.

Width 3 in.

Area = length × width
$A = l \times w$

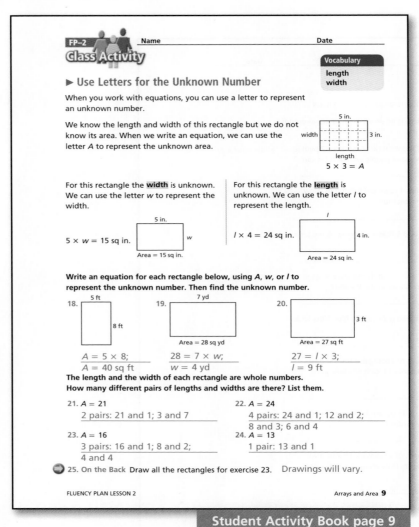

Student Activity Book page 9

► Use Letters for the Unknown Number INDIVIDUALS

Discuss exercises 18–20 on page 9 of the Student Book with the students. This is the introduction of simple algebraic expressions. Point out that every area problem has three parts: length, width, and area. If we know two of these parts, we can find the one that is unknown. The letters replace the answer box that students saw on the first day. They function in exactly the same way.

Exercises 21–24 give only the area. Students are asked to provide all the possible pairs of lengths and widths (assuming they are whole numbers). If students have trouble, for exercise 21 ask them "What number times what number equals 21?" Many students will produce the dimensions 7 × 3, but they may overlook the other possibility: 21 × 1. Some students may benefit from working with a **Helping Partner.**

Have students complete the page by drawing the rectangles for exercise 23.

②Going Further

Differentiated Instruction

● Intervention — Activity Card FP-2

Cover It — Activity Card FP-2 ●

Work: In Pairs

Use:
- Inch-Grid Paper (TRB M1)
- Scissors

1. **Work Together** Look for an object in your classroom that has a rectangular surface.
2. Cover the surface completely with inch squares.
3. Write three equations to represent the length, the width, and the area of your rectangle. Be sure to use the correct unit of measure for each.
4. **Explain** Why does area use a different unit of measure than length or width? Area is measured in square inches because it measures surface.

Fluency Plan Lesson 2   Copyright © Houghton Mifflin Company

Activity Note If the rectangle does not have whole unit dimensions in inches, have students estimate the length and width to the nearest inch.

 **Math Writing Prompt**

Make a Drawing Explain why 4 × 3 and 3 × 4 are equal to the same number. Draw equal groups, an array, or an area picture to support your answer.

Soar to Success Math **Software Support**

Warm-Up 45.24

▲ On Level — Activity Card FP-2

Draw and Compare — Activity Card FP-2 ▲

Work: In Small Groups

Use:
- Centimeter-Grid Paper (TRB M18)
- Crayons
- Game Cards (TRB M2)

1. Shuffle the cards. Then give two cards to each player.
2. Draw a rectangle on the grid paper, using the numbers on the cards for length and width.
3. Color the area of the rectangle, and write an equation for the area. Compare results. The player with the greatest area wins the round.
4. Repeat the activity until each player has won a round.

Fluency Plan Lesson 2   Copyright © Houghton Mifflin Company

Activity Note This activity demonstrates that sometimes there is a variety of dimensions for a given area. If there is a tie for greatest area, students should repeat the activity.

 Math Writing Prompt

Write a Problem Write a word problem about equal groups. Then write an equation to solve it.

MegaMath Grades K-6 **Software Support**

Ice Station Exploration: Polar Planes, Level Q

Challenge — Activity Card FP-2

Find Formulas — Activity Card FP-2 ■

Work: By Yourself

Use:
- Centimeter-Grid Paper (TRB M18)

1. 1, 4, 9, 16, 25, 36, 49, 64, 81, 100
2. Possible answer: A square number is a product of any number and itself. The area of a square is the product of the length of one side and itself.

1. The first three square numbers are 1, 4, and 9. Use grid paper to draw the first 10 square numbers. See left.
2. **Explain** Why does each drawing represent a square number? See left.
3. Use your drawings to help you write a formula to find the 100th square number. $n \times n =$ any square number where $n =$ the number of the term. $100 \times 100 = 10,000$

Fluency Plan Lesson 2   Copyright © Houghton Mifflin Company

Activity Note Review the definition of a square number before students begin the activity. Have students label each drawing to show its area in terms of length and width.

 Math Writing Prompt

Reasoning Skills Write a word problem about a 10 × 10 array. Explain how you decided what situation to use. Then write an equation to solve it.

DESTINATION Math **Software Support**
Course III: Module 1: Unit 2: Finding Factors

Arrays and Area   **15**

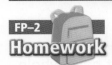 # ③ Homework and Spiral Review

FP-2
Homework **Goal:** Additional Practice

Use this Homework page to provide students with more practice using equal groups, arrays, and areas to solve problems.

FP-2
Remembering **Goal:** Spiral Review

This Remembering activity would be appropriate anytime after today's lesson.

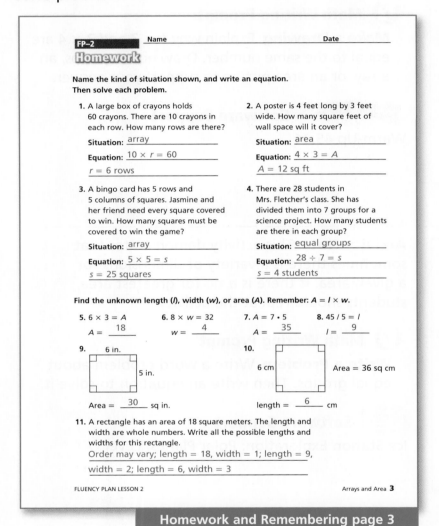

Homework and Remembering page 3

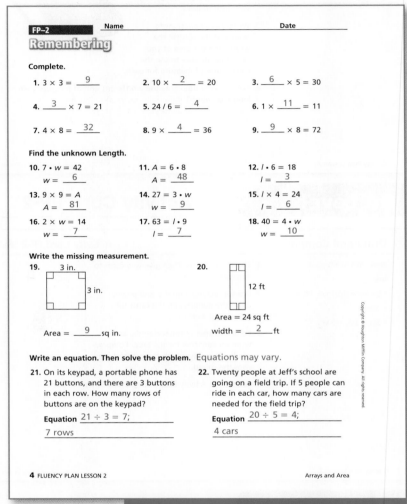

Homework and Remembering page 4

Home or School Activity

 ### Sports Connection

Olympics At the Olympics, athletes representing hundreds of countries from around the world compete in a wide variety of sporting events.

Have students research the official measurements for an Olympic pool. Then have them calculate the minimum area of a rectangular cover for an Olympic size pool.

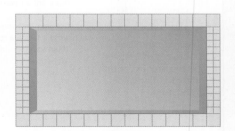

Explore the Multiplication Table

Vocabulary

column
row
Commutative Property
inverse operations
factor
product

Lesson Objectives

● Describe the patterns in the Multiplication Table.

● Understand that multiplication is commutative and that multiplication and division are inverse operations.

The Day at a Glance

Today's Goals	Materials
① Teaching the Lesson **A1:** Discuss the structure of the Multiplication Table and the patterns in it. **A2:** Learn to use the Target, and observe commutativity and inverse operations in the Multiplication Table. **A3:** Complete a blank Multiplication Table to assess basic multiplication. **② Going Further** ▶ Differentiated Instruction **③ Homework and Spiral Review**	**Lesson Activities** Student Activity Book pp. 11–12 or Student Hardcover Book pp. 11–12 and Blank Multiplication Tables (TRB M67) Homework and Remembering pp. 5–6 Class Multiplication Table Poster Targets **Going Further** Activity Cards FP-3 Centimeter-Grid Paper (TRB M18) Scissors Class Multiplication Table Poster Square sheets of paper Index cards Calculators Math Journals 123 Use Math Talk today!

Keeping Skills Sharp

Quick Practice ⏱ 5 MINUTES	Daily Routines
Goal: Practice basic multiplication, using Easy Finger Factors. **Easy Finger Factors** Ask for 3 volunteers to be **Student Leaders**. The two leaders each give a number from 0 to 5 by raising fingers on one hand and saying the number out loud. The third leader gives the hand signal, and the class gives the product of the two numbers. Repeat with other numbers. Watch to be sure the class does not say $5 \times 0 = 5$, for example. Some students get confused by the 0 and the 1 factors.	**Homework Review** Have student pairs resolve any homework issues. **Nonroutine Problem** Pat knit 4 rows and placed a bead every fifth stitch. Each row has the same number of beads and ends with a bead. She used a pack with 14 beads and had 2 beads left. How many stitches are on each row? 15 stitches; $14 - 2 = 12$ beads; $12 \div 4$ rows = 3 beads on each row; 3 beads $\times$ 5 stitches = 15 stitches

Teaching the Lesson

Patterns in the Multiplication Table

 20 MINUTES

Goal: Discuss the structure of the Multiplication Table and the patterns in it.

Materials: Student Activity Book or Hardcover Book p. 11, Class Multiplication Table Poster, Target (TRB M3)

✓ **NCTM Standards:**
Number and Operations
Representation

The Learning Classroom

Math Talk One of the goals of this discussion, in addition to finding patterns, is to begin the process of establishing a classroom community where students talk, listen, and question each other. Concentrate today on creating an accepting atmosphere so that students will feel comfortable making contributions.

Teaching Note

Class Multiplication Table Poster
This poster has 9 across and 12 down because some states require multiplications to 12. The table ends with 9 rather than 10 so that those 9 products can be seen every day by students to help learn the 9s.

For the lesson today, cover or fold the bottom 3 rows of the Class Multiplication Table Poster so that students can see a 9 by 9 table. They can see many patterns in this. Their page 11 also has the 10s in the table so that they can see those patterns also.

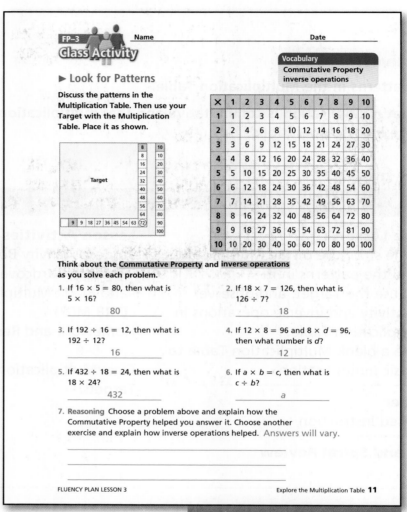

Student Activity Book page 11

► Look for Patterns WHOLE CLASS

Direct everyone's attention to the Multiplication Table on page 11 of the Student Book.

123 **Math Talk** Have students describe the arrangement of the table and any interesting patterns they see.

There are many patterns in the Multiplication Table, ranging from obvious (all the numbers in the bottom row end in zero) to extremely intricate (numbers on the various diagonals increase in predictable ways). Validate any pattern that students observe.

As with arrays, encourage the class to use the word *row* for the numbers going across and *column* for the numbers going down.

► The Structure of the Multiplication Table WHOLE CLASS

After a few minutes of open discussion, begin drawing attention to the overall structure of the table. Below are the important structural features to elicit from the students. Some of these may already have been mentioned during the previous discussion. (For a sample of classroom dialogue, see **Math Talk in Action** in the side column.)

1. Each row and each column show a particular count-by such as 5, 10, 15. The first number is the number to count by. If students have not already mentioned this feature, pick several rows and columns and ask students what they see.

2. Because the rows and columns are both made the same way, the Multiplication Table has ten row and column "twins." If students have not already noticed this feature, demonstrate matching row and column on the Class Multiplication Table Poster. Then ask students to find some "twins" on their own.

3. The answer to a multiplication problem (the product) is found by multiplying one number from the left column with another number from the top row. The product is in the square that forms the intersection of a column and a row.

Elicit or explain that the smaller numbers that are multiplied together are called *factors*. The answer is called the *product*. (When we multiply, we are finding the unknown product. When we divide, we are finding an unknown factor.)

 Math Talk in Action

What do you see when you look down the 3 column?

Tara: Each number going down is 3 more than the previous number.

Sam: It looks like skip counting by 3.

What do you see when you look across the 3 row?

Jai: This row is the same as the 3 column.

What about the 5 column and the 5 row?

Sam: Each number going across and down is 5 more than the previous number.

Are all columns and rows built this way?

Collin: Yes because mulitplication means repeatedly adding the same group.

Teaching Note

Language and Vocabulary As words relating to multiplication are used throughout the lesson, write the words on the board and review their meaning. Words emphasized in this activity include:

column
row
factor
product

Activity 2

The Target

 20 MINUTES

Goal: Learn to use the Target, and observe commutativity and inverse operations in the Multiplication Table.

Materials: Student Activity Book or Hardcover Book p. 11, Target (TRB M3)

 NCTM Standards:
Number and Operations
Algebra
Reasoning and Proof

Differentiated Instruction

Extra Help Some students may have difficulty manipulating the Target. Pair those students with other students who can help them until they become comfortable handling the square.

English Language Learners

Write *Commutative Property*, 6 × 5 = 30 and 5 × 6 = 30 on the board.

• **Beginning** Ask: **Are the products the same?** yes **Is this the Commutative Property?** yes

• **Intermediate** Say: **The order of the factors is ___.** different **The products are the ___.** same **This shows us the Commutative ___.** Property

• **Advanced** Have students tell how the equations are different and identify what property is shown.

▶ **Learn to Use the Target** WHOLE CLASS

Make sure each student has two Targets. (One will go home, and one will stay at school.) Have everyone experiment with the Target to see if they can explain how to practice multiplication with this device.

Multiplying: Position the Target on the Multiplication Table as shown, covering up the number in the circle with a finger. The transparent bars should be placed so that the factors are at each end. Students say the answer silently to themselves and then uncover the circle to see if they were right.

Now ask students if they can figure out how to practice division with the Target.

Dividing: Position the Target in the same way as before. Cover up the left end of the horizontal bar. Move the Target until the known factor appears at the top of the vertical bar and then move up or down until the product is in the circle. Solve the problem. Uncover the horizontal bar to see which number appears at the left end.

×	1	2	3	4	5	6	7	8	9	10
1	1	2	3	4	5	6	7	8	9	10
2	2	4	6	8	10	12	14	16	18	20
3	3	6	9	12	15	18	21	24	27	30
4	4	8	12	16	20	24	28	32	36	40
5	5	10	15	20	25	30	35	40	45	50
6	6	12	18	24	30	36	42	48	54	60
7	7	14	21	28	35	42	49	56	63	70
8	8	16	24	32	40	48	56	64	72	80
9	9	18	27	36	45	54	63	72	81	90
10	10	20	30	40	50	60	70	80	90	100

► Commutative and Inverse Relationships WHOLE CLASS

Ask everyone to multiply 8 × 7 and 7 × 8 using their Targets. Do they get the same answer? Yes If they know the answer to these two multiplication problems, what two division problems can they also solve? 56 ÷ 8 and 56 ÷ 7. Ask everyone to do these division problems with their Targets. Offer help as needed.

Now have the class contribute another multiplication problem. Students should do all four variations with the Targets. (Example: If they select 6 × 7, they should also do 7 × 6 and then 42 ÷ 7 and 42 ÷ 6.)

If students have trouble understanding the Commutative Property or inverse operations, encourage them to use area models to visualize the numbers. Drawing area models and then taking the models apart can help students to see how all of the numbers are related.

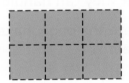 6 = 2 × 3

 6 ÷ 2 = 3

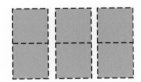 6 ÷ 3 = 2

The Commutative Property says that for any whole numbers *a* and *b*, *a* × *b* = *b* × *a*. Students can see a general argument by using an array:

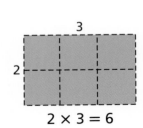
2 × 3 = 6

Rotate the area model.

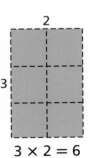
3 × 2 = 6

But the area did not change. This can be done for any area model, so *a* × *b* = *b* × *a*.

Activity continued ►

The Learning Classroom

Math Talk How did your students explain their math thinking today? Students are often unfamiliar with this process; they are accustomed to providing math answers only. Encouraging students to talk more fully about their thinking will take repeated efforts on your part. Expect this to be a building process that lasts for several weeks.

Classroom Management

Keeping Targets Safe Emphasize to students that they will be using these targets all year and that they need to keep them in safe places such as folders or fasten them to the inside cover of their book with a big paper clip. They also need to decide where to keep them safe at home and to make sure that their Homework Helper knows how important the Target is to keep safe so they can use it all year to get really fast.

Activity 2

Differentiated Instruction

Advanced Learners Some students may be ready to describe more details about their problem-solving strategies. You may want to encourage these students to do more explaining. Not only will they extend their own communication skills, they will model for other students how to talk about their thinking. The "child friendly language" may be more meaningful than your own way of talking about a concept.

▶ Use Critical Thinking INDIVIDUALS

Have everyone complete exercises 1–6 on page 11 of the Student Book. The questions in this section all involve higher-order thinking skills. As students consider the Commutative Property and inverse operations, they also receive some practice with easy algebraic expressions.

Some of these numbers may appear to be beyond the students' experience. That is done deliberately to ensure that they will apply the concepts of commutativity and inverse relationships and not just perform familiar computation.

If some students become intimidated when they encounter equations with large numbers, such as those in exercise 3, reassure them that they know how to solve these problems. They just need to think about the relationship between multiplication and division. Students will feel empowered when they realize that they can handle these exercises.

Math Talk When students complete the page, have a whole-class discussion of the answers to problem 7.

Create a Multiplication Table

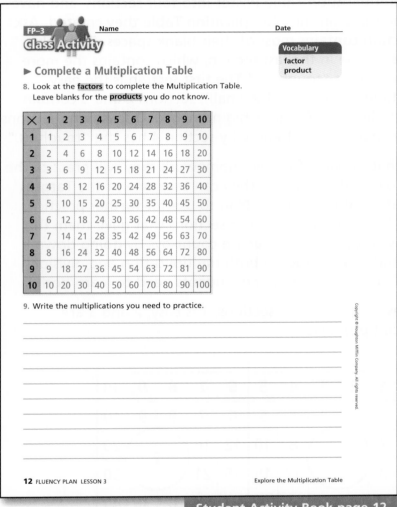

FP–3
Class Activity

Name _____ Date _____

Vocabulary
factor
product

▶ Complete a Multiplication Table

8. Look at the **factors** to complete the Multiplication Table.
   Leave blanks for the **products** you do not know.

✕	1	2	3	4	5	6	7	8	9	10
1	1	2	3	4	5	6	7	8	9	10
2	2	4	6	8	10	12	14	16	18	20
3	3	6	9	12	15	18	21	24	27	30
4	4	8	12	16	20	24	28	32	36	40
5	5	10	15	20	25	30	35	40	45	50
6	6	12	18	24	30	36	42	48	54	60
7	7	14	21	28	35	42	49	56	63	70
8	8	16	24	32	40	48	56	64	72	80
9	9	18	27	36	45	54	63	72	81	90
10	10	20	30	40	50	60	70	80	90	100

9. Write the multiplications you need to practice.

_____
_____
_____
_____
_____
_____
_____
_____

12 FLUENCY PLAN LESSON 3   Explore the Multiplication Table

Student Activity Book page 12

▶ Complete a Multiplication Table INDIVIDUALS

The goal today is to discover which multiplications students know quickly and which ones they should work on during practice sessions. Emphasize that this is not a test.

Give the class about 6 minutes to fill in the blank table on page 12 of the Student Book. Encourage students to leave a square blank when they do not immediately know the product. They should not take time to "figure it out." Tell students not to use count-bys because they are too slow. A faster strategy is needed for these problems.

When time is up, ask each student to write the multiplications that need practice. Ask volunteers to share the problems that are most difficult for them. Students may be surprised to learn that there is considerable agreement on which problems are difficult. You may wish to assign a **Helping Partner** for students who need help with strategies.

Activity continued ▶

 15 MINUTES

Goal: Complete a blank Multiplication Table to assess basic multiplication.

Materials: Student Activity Book p. 12 or Hardcover Book p. 12, Blank Multiplication Tables (TRB M67), Class Multiplication Table Poster

 NCTM Standards:
Number and Operations
Representation

The Learning Classroom

Helping Community Many students can learn to be productive helpers who support their classmates in various ways, from spontaneous helping with a small issue to sustained tutoring over time. Discuss what it means to be an effective helper (for example, be patient, help other students solve their way, don't do it for the other student, encourage and say nice things).

During work time, many *Math Expressions* teachers assign helpers to walk around and help those who need it and also assign **Helping Partners** for some students. Other helping occurs spontaneously among students sitting near each other. As students become better helpers, you can work at the board with students who are really struggling.

Activity 3

The Learning Classroom

Math Talk By discussing answers, students become aware of other students' thinking. They may discover that they share opinions and difficulties with others in their class.

 Ongoing Assessment

Have students discuss

► how they can show that multiplication is commutative.

► examples of the Commutative Property of Multiplication.

► Strategies for Effective Practice WHOLE CLASS

Divide the Class Multiplication Table Poster into four sections, and have the students do the same on the Multiplication Table they created. Ask the class which section contains most of their blank spaces. Probably most of the blanks will be in the last section, which contains the more difficult multiplications, or "toughies." The first section is the easy section (all 1 to 5 times 1 to 5; small × small); sections 2 and 3 contain more difficult multiplications (small × big numbers). Discuss why sections 2 and 3 are harder than section 1 and why section 4 has the "toughies."

Tell the students that as part of today's homework they will practice the multiplication problems they missed. They can take one of the Targets home for the duration of this Fluency Plan to use for further practice. Suggest that they focus on the section or sections that gave them the most trouble today. They can also practice count-bys by going down a column. Remind students to practice both multiplication and division because these will help each other, and students need to learn both.

The Quick Practices focus on these sections: 1 is easy, 2 and 3 are medium, 4 is difficult products.

×	1	2	3	4	5	6	7	8	9	10
1	1	2	3	4	5	6	7	8	9	10
2	2			8	10	12	14			20
3	3			12	15	18	21			30
4	4	8	12	16	20	24	28	32	36	40
5	5	10	15	20	25	30	35	40	45	50
6	6	12	18	24	30	36	42	48	54	60
7	7	14	21	28	35	42	49	56	63	70
8	8		3	32	40	48	56		4	80
9	9	18	27	36	45	54	63	72	81	90
10	10	20	30	40	50	60	70	80	90	100

② Going Further

Differentiated Instruction

● Intervention   Activity Card FP-3

Practice Triangles
Activity Card FP-3 ●

Work: In Pairs

Use:
• Scissors
• Square sheets of paper
• Class Multiplication Table Poster

1. **Work Together** List the multiplications that are most difficult for you to remember.

2. Make a triangle by folding a square sheet of paper along a diagonal. Then fold the triangle in half along the longest side. Unfold the paper to show 4 triangles. Cut out each triangle.

3. Write the product and factors of one multiplication on each corner of a triangle.

4. Make as many triangles as you need for your list. Take turns. One partner covers one corner. The other partner names the covered number. Continue until you can quickly name each covered number.

Fluency Plan Lesson 3   Copyright © Houghton Mifflin Company

Activity Note Extend the activity by having pairs of students exchange their triangles with other pairs and practice naming covered factors or products.

 **Math Writing Prompt**

Draw and Explain You know that $5 \times 4 = 20$. Explain why $20 \div 4$ must equal 5. Draw equal groups or arrays to support your answer.

Soar to Success Math **Software Support**
Warm-Up 12.27

▲ On Level   Activity Card FP-3

Find Facts
Activity Card FP-3 ▲

Work: In Pairs

Use:
• Index cards

1. **Work Together** Make two sets of index cards, one set numbered 0–10 and the other set numbered 0–9.

2. Shuffle the cards and place them face down in a pile.

3. Take turns. Pick two cards from the top of the pile and name the product of the two numbers. If the product is correct, you score the same number of points as the product. Then return the two cards to the bottom of the pile.

4. The player who earns 500 points first wins.

Fluency Plan Lesson 3   Copyright © Houghton Mifflin Company

Activity Note Partners should check each other's products as they are named before points are awarded at the end of each turn.

 Math Writing Prompt

Reasoning Skills Describe one of the patterns that appears in a multiplication table.

MegaMath **Software Support**
The Number Games: Up, Up, and Array, Level C

■ Challenge   Activity Card FP-3

Extending Tables
Activity Card FP-3 ■

Work: By Yourself

Use:
• Centimeter-Grid Paper (TRB M18)
• Calculator

1. Use grid paper to make a multiplication table. Write the numbers 1–12 across the top and the same numbers down the left side.

2. Complete the table, using a calculator if necessary.

3. **Write About It** Describe at least one horizontal pattern, one vertical pattern, and one diagonal pattern in the table. Possible patterns: Each number in the row or column beginning with 5 alternately ends in a 5 or a 0. Each number along the diagonal from the top left corner to the bottom right corner is a square number.

Fluency Plan Lesson 3   Copyright © Houghton Mifflin Company

Activity Note Have each student exchange tables with another student to check their work, and then have them compare patterns.

 **Math Writing Prompt**

9s Pattern Describe a pattern for all products of 9.

DESTINATION Math **Software Support**
Course III: Module 1: Unit 2: Finding Factors

③ Homework and Spiral Review

Homework **Goal:** Additional Practice

Use this Homework page to provide students with more practice with Multiplication Tables and Targets.

Remembering **Goal:** Spiral Review

This Remembering activity would be appropriate anytime after today's lesson.

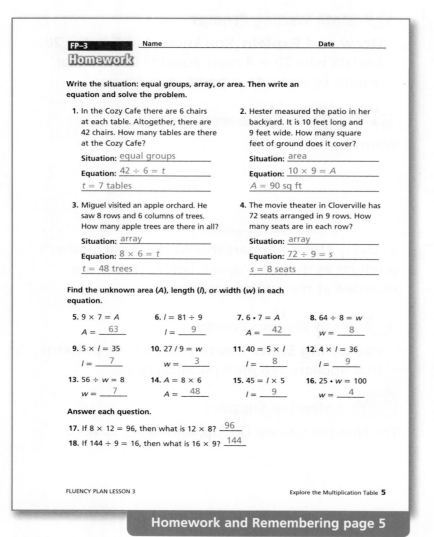

FP–3   Name _____ Date _____
Homework

Write the situation: equal groups, array, or area. Then write an equation and solve the problem.

1. In the Cozy Cafe there are 6 chairs at each table. Altogether, there are 42 chairs. How many tables are there at the Cozy Cafe?
   Situation: equal groups
   Equation: $42 \div 6 = t$
   t = 7 tables

2. Hester measured the patio in her backyard. It is 10 feet long and 9 feet wide. How many square feet of ground does it cover?
   Situation: area
   Equation: $10 \times 9 = A$
   A = 90 sq ft

3. Miguel visited an apple orchard. He saw 8 rows and 6 columns of trees. How many apple trees are there in all?
   Situation: array
   Equation: $8 \times 6 = t$
   t = 48 trees

4. The movie theater in Cloverville has 72 seats arranged in 9 rows. How many seats are in each row?
   Situation: array
   Equation: $72 \div 9 = s$
   s = 8 seats

Find the unknown area (A), length (l), or width (w) in each equation.

5. $9 \times 7 = A$ A = 63
6. $l = 81 \div 9$ l = 9
7. $6 \cdot 7 = A$ A = 42
8. $64 \div 8 = w$ w = 8
9. $5 \times l = 35$ l = 7
10. $27 \div 9 = w$ w = 3
11. $40 = 5 \times l$ l = 8
12. $4 \times l = 36$ l = 9
13. $56 \div w = 8$ w = 7
14. $A = 8 \times 6$ A = 48
15. $45 = l \times 5$ l = 9
16. $25 \cdot w = 100$ w = 4

Answer each question.

17. If $8 \times 12 = 96$, then what is 12×8? 96
18. If $144 \div 9 = 16$, then what is 16×9? 144

FLUENCY PLAN LESSON 3   Explore the Multiplication Table **5**

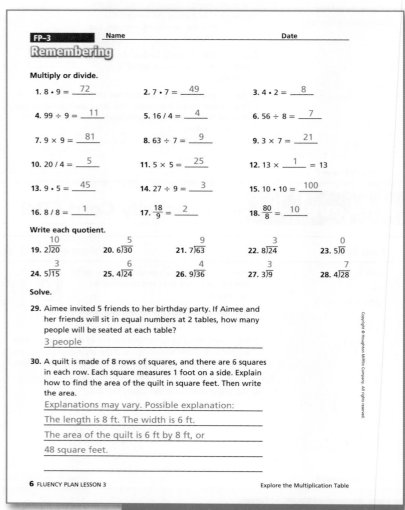

FP–3   Name _____ Date _____
Remembering

Multiply or divide.

1. $8 \cdot 9 =$ 72
2. $7 \cdot 7 =$ 49
3. $4 \cdot 2 =$ 8
4. $99 \div 9 =$ 11
5. $16 / 4 =$ 4
6. $56 \div 8 =$ 7
7. $9 \times 9 =$ 81
8. $63 \div 7 =$ 9
9. $3 \times 7 =$ 21
10. $20 / 4 =$ 5
11. $5 \times 5 =$ 25
12. $13 \times$ 1 $= 13$
13. $9 \cdot 5 =$ 45
14. $27 \div 9 =$ 3
15. $10 \cdot 10 =$ 100
16. $8 / 8 =$ 1
17. $\frac{18}{9} =$ 2
18. $\frac{80}{8} =$ 10

Write each quotient.

19. $2\overline{)20}$ → 10
20. $6\overline{)30}$ → 5
21. $7\overline{)63}$ → 9
22. $8\overline{)24}$ → 3
23. $5\overline{)0}$ → 0
24. $5\overline{)15}$ → 3
25. $4\overline{)24}$ → 6
26. $9\overline{)36}$ → 4
27. $3\overline{)9}$ → 3
28. $4\overline{)28}$ → 7

Solve.

29. Aimee invited 5 friends to her birthday party. If Aimee and her friends will sit in equal numbers at 2 tables, how many people will be seated at each table?
    3 people

30. A quilt is made of 8 rows of squares, and there are 6 squares in each row. Each square measures 1 foot on a side. Explain how to find the area of the quilt in square feet. Then write the area.
    Explanations may vary. Possible explanation:
    The length is 8 ft. The width is 6 ft.
    The area of the quilt is 6 ft by 8 ft, or
    48 square feet.

6 FLUENCY PLAN LESSON 3   Explore the Multiplication Table

Homework and Remembering page 5

Homework and Remembering page 6

Home or School Activity

 Literature Connection

Math Strategies That Multiply: The Best of Times Read *Math Strategies That Multiply: The Best of Times* by Greg Tang and illustrated by Harry Briggs (Scholastic Press, 2002).

This book uses poems and pictures to help students learn their multiplications. Challenge students to write their own poems. Some students may write songs, too. Have the students use **Scenarios** to act out their poems or songs with each other and the class.

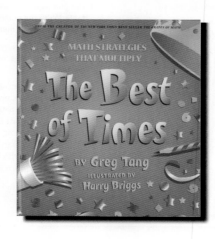

Discover Multiplication Patterns

REAL WORLD Problem Solving

Lesson Objectives

● Understand multiplicative relationships and patterns.

● Apply knowledge of patterns to problem-solving situations.

The Day at a Glance

Today's Goals	Materials	

1 **Teaching the Lesson**
 A1: Find and describe patterns in the count-bys.
 A2: Analyze and solve a problem.
 	
 2 **Going Further**
 ► Differentiated Instruction
 	
 3 **Homework and Spiral Review**
	Lesson Activities
	 Student Activity Book pp. 13–16 or
	   Student Hardcover Book pp. 13–16
	 Homework and Remembering
	   pp. 7–8
		Going Further
		 Activity Cards FP-4
		 Blocks or counters
		 Hundreds Grid
		  (TRB M82)
		 Crayons or markers
		 Math Journals
		
		 123 Use **Math Talk** today!

Keeping Skills Sharp

Quick Practice   🕐 5 MINUTES

Goal: Practice basic multiplications, using Medium Finger Factors.

Medium Finger Factors Explain to the class that they did the easy section of the Multiplication Table earlier and will do the medium sections today. Send 3 **Student Leaders** to the front. This time the first leader gives a factor from 6 to 10 by raising fingers on *both* hands and saying the number out loud. The second leader gives a factor from 0 to 5 by using one hand and says this number out loud. The third leader signals the class to respond with the product of the two factors. Repeat with other factors.

Daily Routines

Homework Review Have students explain how they found any incorrect answers. This will help find the error.

Strategy Problem Tanya painted a canvas with 4 colors. The canvas has a length of 18 in. and a width of 9 in. She painted red on a section that is the entire width but half the entire length. Blue, green, and purple equally share the remaining area. What is the difference in the area of the red and the green sections? 54 in.²; 81 in.² − 27 in.²

	18 in.		
3 in.	G		
3 in.	B		R	9 in.
3 in.	P		
	9 in.	9 in.	

Teaching the Lesson

Describe Patterns

 40 MINUTES

Goal: Find and describe patterns in the count-bys.

Materials: Student Activity Book or Hardcover Book pp. 13–15

✓ **NCTM Standards:**
Reasoning and Proof
Problem Solving

The Learning Classroom

Building Concepts The pattern found in 9s count-bys is useful for problem solving because each count-by is equal to a multiple of 10 minus the number of the count-by in the pattern: $10 - 1$, $20 - 2$, $30 - 3$, $40 - 4$, and so on. For example, finding 8×9 is the same as finding the 8th count-by. Find the 8th multiple of 10 and then subtract 8:
$8 \times 10 = 80$; $80 - 8 = 72$

Check the answer by seeing if the digits add up to 9:
$7 + 2 = 9$

English Language Learners

Write *horizontal, vertical,* and *diagonal* on the board. Draw an example of each line.

- **Beginning** Point to and identify each line. Have students repeat and hold out their arms in each direction.
- **Intermediate** Point and ask: **Is this line horizontal or vertical?** horizontal Continue with other lines.
- **Advanced** Have students identify each line.

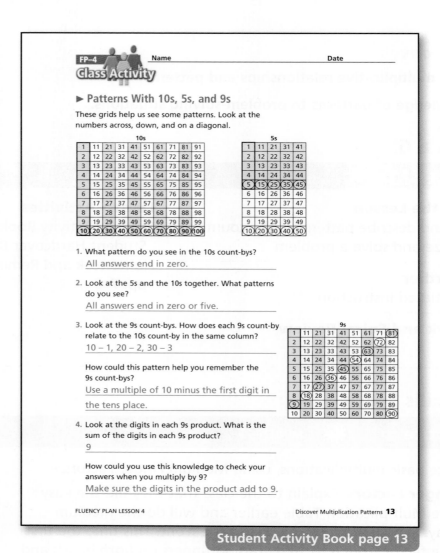

Student Activity Book page 13

▶ Patterns With 10s, 5s, 9s   WHOLE CLASS

Explain that the diagram for tens on page 13 is a hundred grid (numbers in order from 1 to 100) and not a multiplication table. The other diagrams each show part of a hundred grid. Discuss the exercises together.

5s and 10s Count-Bys Have students compare the patterns that they see in the 5s and 10s count-bys. They should notice that the gaps between the 10s count-bys are twice the size of the gaps between the 5s count-bys. There are twice as many 5s in that part of the diagram. They might also point out that the 10s always end in 0, while the 5s end in either 5 or 0.

9s Count-Bys The central 9s pattern is that 9 is 1 less than 10, 18 is 2 less than 20, 27 is 3 less than 30, and so on. This pattern can be expressed in a number of ways. Some students might say that the ones digits in the 9s pattern decrease by 1 (9, 8, 7, 6, and so on), while the tens digits increase by 1 (0, 1, 2, 3, 4, and so on).

A Visual Activity for Multiplying by 9 You might want to show your class or have a **Student Leader** show this hand activity in which students use their fingers to see the "tens-minus-ones" pattern for 9s.

Students put both hands up with the palms facing them, as shown.

They each bend down a single finger to show the multiplier. The position of this finger changes, but only one multiplier finger is ever bent down. Starting at the left, the first finger bent down means they are multiplying by 1, the second finger means 2, and so on.

The answer is decoded by seeing all fingers to the left of the bent finger as tens and all fingers to the right of the bent finger as ones.

1 × 9 = 9
(0 tens, 9 ones)

The first finger is bent down so no tens fingers are up, and 9 ones fingers are up.

2 × 9 = 18
(1 ten, 8 ones)

The second finger is bent down, so 1 tens finger is up, and 8 ones fingers are up.

3 × 9 = 27
(2 tens, 7 ones)

The third finger is bent down, so 2 tens fingers are up, and 7 ones fingers are up.

Activity continued ▶

Teaching Note

What to Expect From Students
In discussing the various count-bys, students may point out spatial relationships formed by some patterns as well as numeric relationships. For example, the first nine 9s count-bys form a "diagonal" across the grid (see Student Book page 13), and the 5s and 10s make horizontal rows.

The Learning Community

Student Leaders Select different student leaders for different tasks. Take time to help students get used to being leaders. Support them for the first few times, and encourage classmates to be supportive. Most students gain confidence themselves when they help others learn.

Teaching Note

Language and Vocabulary
Remind students that *products* and *count-bys* have the same meaning in this discussion. For example, in problem 4, *9s product* means *9s count-by*.

Teaching the Lesson (continued)

Activity 1

Class Management

Sometimes students take a while to formulate and verbalize their thinking. Be sure to have a role for the students who are in their seats waiting. For example, suggest that students in their seats get ready to be the next explainers. They should think of how they will explain their approach in two or three complete sentences. Or they can be thinking of good questions to ask the explainers to help everyone learn (one teacher calls these "good thinker questions"). **English Language Learners** may choose to explain their approaches or ask their "good thinker questions" in writing first. Then, when sharing with the class, they may read aloud their written materials or use them as notes.

The Learning Classroom

Math Talk Aspire to make your classroom a place where all students listen to understand one another. Explain to students that this is different from just being quiet when someone else is talking. This involves thinking about what a person is saying so that you could explain it yourself. Also, students need to listen so that they can ask a question or help the explainer. Remind students that listening can also help you learn that concept better.

FP-4
Class Activity

Name _____   Date _____

▶ **Patterns With Other Numbers**

On these grids, find patterns with 2s, 4s, and 8s.

5. Look at the ones digits in all the 2s, 4s, and 8s count-bys. What pattern do you see?
They are all even numbers.

6. Are the 2s, 4s, and 8s products even numbers or odd numbers?
even

On these grids, look for patterns with 3s and 6s.

7. Look at the 3s and 6s count-bys together. What pattern do you see?
Every other 3s count-by is a
6s count-by.

8. Look at the digits in each product. What is the sum of the digits in each of the products? Make a list. Write each different sum only once.
3, 6, 9, 12

Rewrite each pattern to make it correct.

9. 4, 8, 12, 18, 20, 24, 28   4, 8, 12, 16, 20, 24, 28

10. 18, 28, 36, 45, 54, 63, 70   18, 27, 36, 45, 54, 63, 72

14 FLUENCY PLAN LESSON 4   Discover Multiplication Patterns

Student Activity Book page 14

▶ Patterns With Other Numbers [WHOLE CLASS]

Math Talk Discuss exercises 5–8 as a class.

2s, 4s, and 8s Count-Bys On page 14, the class should notice that each pair of 2s make a 4, and that each pair of 4s make an 8. Ask the students if they can explain why this pattern exists. Because 4 is twice as large as 2, we "skip" every other 2s product to get the 4s products. And because 8 is twice as large as 4, we skip every other product again. Also note that the products are all even numbers. If necessary, review odd and even numbers.

3s and 6s Count-Bys Ask the students to find and compare as many patterns as they can in the 3s and 6s. Again, they should notice the "skip" pattern that was discussed with the 2s, 4s, and 8s. Ask them why this pattern exists. Because 6 is twice as large as 3, we skip every other 3s product to get the 6s products. Students should also discover that the digits in the products of the 3s and 6s always add up to 3, 6, or 9. (In the case of 48, the digits are added twice, 4 + 8 = 12, and 1 + 2 = 3.)

Ask students to use what they know about count-bys to find and correct the errors in the patterns in exercises 9 and 10.

▶ **Patterns in the Zeros and Ones** [WHOLE CLASS]

Ask for Ideas Ask the class what they know about multiplication and division with 1 and 0.

● The product of one and any number is that number, and any number divided by one is that number. $n \times 1 = n$ and $n \div 1 = n$.

● The product of zero and any number is zero, and zero divided by any other number is zero. $n \times 0 = 0$ and $0 \div n = 0$.

● It is not possible to divide by zero.

Have students complete exercises 11–21 on Student Book page 15.

▶ **Even-Odd Patterns** [WHOLE CLASS]

Students can find the answers to exercises 22–25 by trying a few sample problems. Even × Even = Even; Even × Odd = Even; Odd × Odd = Odd

● **Why is the product always an even number when one of the factors is even?** The even factor can be written as $2n$, so the product will contain $2n$, e.g., even • $5 = 2n • 5$, which is an even number because it is a multiple of 2.

Teaching Note

Math Background One way to understand that division by zero is impossible is to relate division and multiplication. For example, $12 \div 4 = 3$ because $3 \times 4 = 12$. To solve $12 \div 0 =$ what number, consider the related multiplication equation. Think: What number $\times 0 = 12$? There is no number multiplied by zero that equals 12.

The Learning Classroom

Scenario Structure To help students better understand that the product of an odd number multiplied by an even number is always even, have students act out the situation. Have 3 students stand at the front of the room, and ask them if they can divide themselves into two equal groups. no,; Point out that there is 1 person left over.

To model 2×3, have three more students come to the front of the room. Ask each group of 3 if they can divide themselves into two equal groups. no Now, have the 2 groups of 3 form 1 group of 6. Ask if they can divide themselves into two equal groups now. If so, why? yes, 2 groups of 3 because the two people left over can come together to form a pair.

Write on the board: odd number × even number = even product. Have students explain why this is true. Any odd number has a leftover 1 when you divide it by 2. If you multiply the odd number by an even number, you will have pairs of leftover 1s. The pairs of leftover 1s can be divided into two equal groups.

Teaching the Lesson (continued)

Applications

 10 MINUTES

Goal: Analyze and solve a problem.

Materials: Student Activity Book or Hardcover Book p. 16

 NCTM Standards:
Problem Solving
Reasoning and Proof
Connections

 Ongoing Assessment

Have students give a true statement about:

▶ 10s count-bys

▶ 5s count-bys

▶ 3s count-bys

▶ 6s count-bys

FP–4
Class Activity
Name _____ Date _____

▶ The Puzzled Penguin

Help the Puzzled Penguin understand how Lucy did the mental math.

Dear Math Students,

Today my friend Lucy and I sold lemonade for 5 cents a glass. When we were done, my friend said, "There are 24 nickels here, so we made $1.20."

"How did you figure that out so fast?" I asked.

Lucy answered, "I started by multiplying 24 by 10, and then I . . ."

At that moment Lucy heard her mother calling and had to leave. I can't figure out what Lucy did. Why would anyone start by multiplying by 10 when a nickel is worth only 5 cents? Can you explain Lucy's thinking?

Thanks for your help.
Puzzled Penguin

Answers will vary.

_____
_____
_____
_____
_____
_____
_____
_____
_____
_____

16 FLUENCY PLAN LESSON 4   Discover Multiplication Patterns

Student Activity Book page 16

▶ The Puzzled Penguin │ WHOLE CLASS │

Introduce the Puzzled Penguin to your class: "The Puzzled Penguin finds math in the real world. Sometimes, though, Puzzled Penguin gets confused. You can use what you have learned to help Puzzled Penguin understand the math. We'll get to help Puzzled Penguin on other days."

Direct students' attention to Student Book Page 16. Read the letter from the Puzzled Penguin together, and ask the class to try to explain the multiplication strategy probably used by Lucy.

Mental Math Your students already know that multiplying by 5 gives exactly half the result of multiplying by 10. This knowledge can be used as an aid in mental math. When dealing with multi-digit numbers, it is often simpler to multiply by 10 and then take half the answer than to try to multiply by 5 mentally.

For practice, ask your students to try multiplying the following numbers in their heads, using this strategy: 18×5, 28×5, 800×5.

Intervention — Activity Card FP-4

Make Models — Activity Card FP-4 ●

Work: By Yourself

Use:
• Blocks or counters

1. The models below show counting by 2s and by 4s.

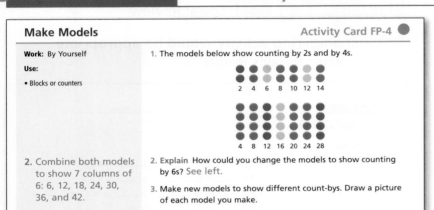

2. Combine both models to show 7 columns of 6: 6, 12, 18, 24, 30, 36, and 42.

2. Explain How could you change the models to show counting by 6s? See left.

3. Make new models to show different count-bys. Draw a picture of each model you make.

Fluency Plan Lesson 4   Copyright © Houghton Mifflin Company

Activity Note If students have difficulty with this activity, demonstrate how they can make a different model by simply adding another counter to each column of the model for counting by 2s.

 Math Writing Prompt

Explain Comparisons Explain how the 2s count-by pattern and the 4s count-by pattern are alike and different.

 **Software Support**

Warm-Up 12.15

On Level — Activity Card FP-4

Multiple Patterns — Activity Card FP-4 ▲

Work: In Pairs

Use:
• Hundred Grid (TRB M82)
• Crayons or markers

There are 100 people in line at the movie theater. Every sixth person gets a free drink. Every ninth person gets free popcorn. Use a hundred grid to find which people get both a free drink and free popcorn.

1. Working on your own, solve the problem. Then compare solutions with your partner. 18th, 36th, 54th, 72nd, and 90th people

2. Make up your own problem about multiplication patterns. Exchange with your partner and solve.

3. Discuss How would the solution to the problem above change if every 3rd person gets a free drink instead of every 6th person? Counting by 9s gives the solution: 9, 18, 27, 36, 45, 54, 63, 72, 81, 90, and 99.

Fluency Plan Lesson 4   Copyright © Houghton Mifflin Company

Activity Note Students can use the hundred grid to solve the problem by crossing off each number, counting first by 6s and then by 9s. Numbers crossed off twice are solution numbers.

 Math Writing Prompt

Make Comparisons Explain how the patterns for 2s count-bys and 3s count-bys are alike and different.

 Software Support

The Number Games: Up, Up, and Array, Level C

Challenge — Activity Card FP-4

Missing Factors — Activity Card FP-4 ■

Work: By Yourself

1. Look at the equations below. The value of the square is always the same. The value of the triangle is always the same.

$\square \times 6 = 48$

$\triangle \times \square = 72$

$\triangle \times \stackrel{\star}{} = 99$

2. Find the value of each symbol.
$\square = 8$ $\triangle = 9$ $\stackrel{\star}{} = 11$

3. Look Back How can you determine if your answers are correct? Substitute the values into the equations and solve.

4. Use symbols to write some equations of your own. Then write the equations that your symbols represent.

Fluency Plan Lesson 4   Copyright © Houghton Mifflin Company

Activity Note Students should recognize that any symbol, including letters, can be used to represent an unknown number.

 Math Writing Prompt

Relate Patterns Explain how 3s count-bys, 6s count-bys, and 9s count-bys are related.

 Software Support

Course III: Module 1: Unit 2: Finding Factors

③ Homework and Spiral Review

Homework **Goal:** Additional Practice

Use this Homework page to provide students with more practice with multiplication patterns.

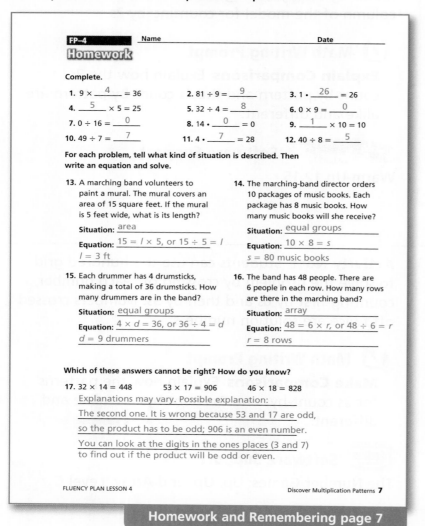

FP-4   Name _____ Date _____

Homework

Complete.

1. $9 \times \underline{4} = 36$ 2. $81 \div 9 = \underline{9}$ 3. $1 \cdot \underline{26} = 26$
4. $\underline{5} \times 5 = 25$ 5. $32 \div 4 = \underline{8}$ 6. $0 \times 9 = \underline{0}$
7. $0 \div 16 = \underline{0}$ 8. $14 \cdot \underline{0} = 0$ 9. $\underline{1} \times 10 = 10$
10. $49 \div 7 = \underline{7}$ 11. $4 \cdot \underline{7} = 28$ 12. $40 \div 8 = \underline{5}$

For each problem, tell what kind of situation is described. Then write an equation and solve.

13. A marching band volunteers to paint a mural. The mural covers an area of 15 square feet. If the mural is 5 feet wide, what is its length?

   Situation: area
   Equation: $15 = l \times 5$, or $15 \div 5 = l$
   $l = 3$ ft

14. The marching-band director orders 10 packages of music books. Each package has 8 music books. How many music books will she receive?

   Situation: equal groups
   Equation: $10 \times 8 = s$
   $s = 80$ music books

15. Each drummer has 4 drumsticks, making a total of 36 drumsticks. How many drummers are in the band?

   Situation: equal groups
   Equation: $4 \times d = 36$, or $36 \div 4 = d$
   $d = 9$ drummers

16. The band has 48 people. There are 6 people in each row. How many rows are there in the marching band?

   Situation: array
   Equation: $48 = 6 \times r$, or $48 \div 6 = r$
   $r = 8$ rows

Which of these answers cannot be right? How do you know?

17. $32 \times 14 = 448$ $53 \times 17 = 906$ $46 \times 18 = 828$

   Explanations may vary. Possible explanation:
   The second one. It is wrong because 53 and 17 are odd,
   so the product has to be odd; 906 is an even number.
   You can look at the digits in the ones places (3 and 7)
   to find out if the product will be odd or even.

FLUENCY PLAN LESSON 4   Discover Multiplication Patterns **7**

Homework and Remembering page 7

Remembering **Goal:** Spiral Review

This Remembering activity would be appropriate anytime after today's lesson.

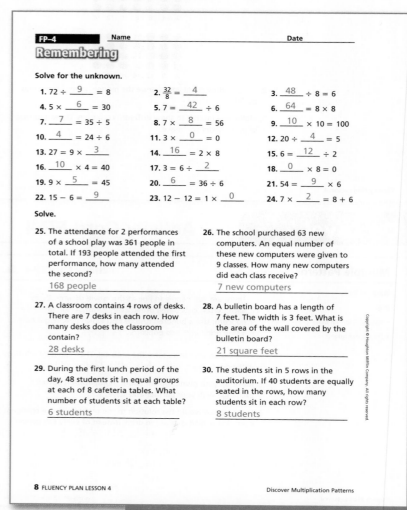

FP-4   Name _____ Date _____

Remembering

Solve for the unknown.

1. $72 \div \underline{9} = 8$ 2. $\frac{32}{8} = \underline{4}$ 3. $\underline{48} \div 8 = 6$
4. $5 \times \underline{6} = 30$ 5. $7 = \underline{42} \div 6$ 6. $\underline{64} = 8 \times 8$
7. $\underline{7} = 35 \div 5$ 8. $7 \times \underline{8} = 56$ 9. $\underline{10} \times 10 = 100$
10. $\underline{4} = 24 \div 6$ 11. $3 \times \underline{0} = 0$ 12. $20 \div \underline{4} = 5$
13. $27 = 9 \times \underline{3}$ 14. $\underline{16} = 2 \times 8$ 15. $6 = \underline{12} \div 2$
16. $\underline{10} \times 4 = 40$ 17. $3 = 6 \div \underline{2}$ 18. $\underline{0} \times 8 = 0$
19. $9 \times \underline{5} = 45$ 20. $\underline{6} = 36 \div 6$ 21. $54 = \underline{9} \times 6$
22. $15 - 6 = \underline{9}$ 23. $12 - 12 = 1 \times \underline{0}$ 24. $7 \times \underline{2} = 8 + 6$

Solve.

25. The attendance for 2 performances of a school play was 361 people in total. If 193 people attended the first performance, how many attended the second?

   168 people

26. The school purchased 63 new computers. An equal number of these new computers were given to 9 classes. How many new computers did each class receive?

   7 new computers

27. A classroom contains 4 rows of desks. There are 7 desks in each row. How many desks does the classroom contain?

   28 desks

28. A bulletin board has a length of 7 feet. The width is 3 feet. What is the area of the wall covered by the bulletin board?

   21 square feet

29. During the first lunch period of the day, 48 students sit in equal groups at each of 8 cafeteria tables. What number of students sit at each table?

   6 students

30. The students sit in 5 rows in the auditorium. If 40 students are equally seated in the rows, how many students sit in each row?

   8 students

8 FLUENCY PLAN LESSON 4   Discover Multiplication Patterns

Homework and Remembering page 8

Home or School Activity

 Literature Connection

One Grain of Rice: A Mathematical Folktale Read *One Grain of Rice: A Mathematical Folktale* by Demi (Scholastic Press, 1997) to the class. This is a folktale about a girl in India. The mathematics involves doubling each day for 30 days.

After reading this folktale to your class, ask students to act out the story, using counters. Then give students an opportunity to write some doubling stories of their own.

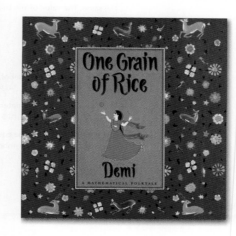

FLUENCY PLAN

LESSON

5

Multiplication Strategies

REAL WORLD Problem Solving

Lesson Objectives

- Understand how multiplication factors can be regrouped to solve problems.
- Apply knowledge of patterns, sequences, and multiplication properties to problem-solving situations.

The Day at a Glance

Today's Goals	Materials	
1 Teaching the Lesson **A1:** Discuss strategies that involve adding or subtracting from a known product to find an unknown product. **A2:** Discuss strategies that involve regrouping factors to find a product, and apply various strategies to specific multiplication situations.	**Lesson Activities** Student Activity Book pp. 17–18 or Student Hardcover Book pp. 17–18 Homework and Remembering pp. 9–10	**Going Further** Student Activity Book pp. 19–20 or Student Hardcover Book pp. 19–20 Activity Cards FP-5 Math Journals
2 Going Further ▶ Math Connection: Properties of Addition and Multiplication ▶ Differentiated Instruction		
3 Homework and Spiral Review		

123 *Use Math Talk today!*

Keeping Skills Sharp

Quick Practice ⏱ 5 MINUTES	Daily Routines
Goal: Practice basic multiplications with Difficult Finger Factors. **Difficult Finger Factors** The class will practice with factors from the difficult section of the Multiplication Table today. Send 3 **Student Leaders** to the front. For each turn, two leaders give factors from 6 to 10 by showing the number with fingers on both hands and saying the number aloud. The third leader signals the class to respond with the product of the two factors. Your class should be able to practice 15–20 multiplications during the Quick Practice.	**Homework Review** Ask students if they had difficulty with any part of the homework. Plan to set aside time to work with students needing extra help. **Strategy Problem** Gifts were given to the second, fifth, eleventh, and twenty-third persons visiting the museum. If this pattern continues and 6 gifts were given, how many people visited the museum? 95 people; Possible answer: the new term is equal to the previous term times 2 plus 1. Continue to find the sixth term, the total people visiting the museum; 47, 95

Multiplication Strategies **35**

Teaching the Lesson

Work With Known Products

 25 MINUTES

Goal: Discuss strategies that involve adding or subtracting from a known product to find an unknown product.

Materials: Student Activity Book or Hardcover Book p. 17

 NCTM Standards:
Number and Operations
Communication

Class Management

Looking Ahead In Lesson 6, students will use Division Cards and The Factor Field. For classroom activities, students can use the cards provided on Student Activity Book pp. 20A–L or Activity Workbook pp. 5–16, or they can take those cards home and you can make sturdy cards specifically for classroom use by copying TRB M4–M14 onto cardstock (make sure your copy machine has the capability). In either case, you may want to set aside time before you begin the lesson for students to cut out their cards.

The Division Cards are also included in the Materials kit.

English Language Learners

Make sure students understand "5 product." Write $5 \times 7 = 35$.

• **Beginning** Point and say: **35 is a 5 product. There are 5 groups of 7 in 35. There are 5 sevens.** Have students repeat.

• **Intermediate and Advanced** Ask: **Which number is the 5 product?** 35 **How many sevens are in 35?** 5

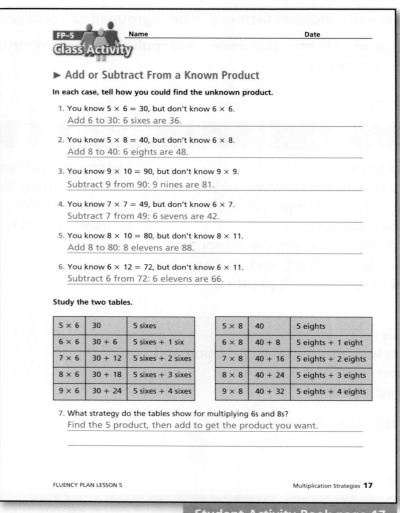

Student Activity Book page 17

▶ Add or Subtract From a Known Product [WHOLE CLASS]

Direct everyone's attention to problems 1–6. All of these questions focus on strategies that involve starting with a known product and then adding or subtracting a factor to arrive at an unknown product. Elicit the answers to these questions from the students rather than explaining the strategy yourself. Ask leading questions, such as "How many more than 5×6 is 6×6?" In some situations, such as those presented in problems 5 and 6, students can easily figure out products that are not part of the traditional multiplication table. This set of problems helps students realize that they often know more than they think they do.

Give students time to study the tables before beginning discussion of problem 7. These tables present an adding-on strategy based on 5-groups that works well for multiplying 6s and 8s. These two groups tend to be among the more difficult multiplications and divisions. Be sure that students see and understand the patterns in the tables.

More Work With Factors

FP-5
Class Activity

Name _____ Date _____

▶ **Make New Factors**

8. Look at the first array. Is 7 × 7 the same as
   5 sevens + 2 sevens? __yes__
   Mark the array to show that this is true.

9. How could you make new factors to solve 7 × 12?
   7 × 7 + 7 × 5 = 49 + 35 = 84

10. Look at the second array. Is 4 × 6 the same as
    3 × 8? __yes__
    Mark the array to show that this is true.

11. How could you make new factors to solve 18 × 3 quickly?
    Answers will vary. Possible answer: 10 × 3 + 8 × 3.

Show how you could make new factors to solve the problems. Possible answers given.

12. 5 × 18 $\underline{5 \times 10 + 5 \times 8}$ 13. 16 × 4 $\underline{10 \times 4 + 6 \times 4}$

14. 12 × 5 $\underline{6 \times 5 + 6 \times 5}$ 15. 14 × 4 $\underline{10 \times 4 + 4 \times 4}$

▶ **Apply Various Strategies**   Answers will vary.

Circle the name of the person who is right in each case. Explain why.

16. (David) says 9 × 6 is 54. Dana says it is 56. _____

17. David says 9 × 7 is 64. (Dana) says it is 63. _____

18. (David) says 8 × 7 is 56. Dana says it is 49. _____

19. David says 8 × 5 is 45. (Dana) says it is 40. _____

Rewrite each pattern to make it correct.

20. 3, 6, 10, 12, 15, 18, 21 $\underline{3, 6, 9, 12, 15, 18, 21}$

21. 8, 16, 24, 30, 32, 40, 45 $\underline{8, 16, 24, 32, 40, 48}$

18 FLUENCY PLAN LESSON 5   Multiplication Strategies

Student Activity Book page 18

▶ Make New Factors WHOLE CLASS

Once students realize that they can add or subtract one more factor to a known product, the door opens for making new factors in other ways. As the class discusses these problems, be aware that there are other ways of making new factors. For example, 7 × 7 can be seen as 6 × 7 + 1 × 7 or 3 × 7 + 4 × 7.

▶ Apply Various Strategies WHOLE CLASS

 Math Talk Students have a wide variety of strategies to use as they discuss problems 16–19. They can mention various ways of making new factors in order to build from the known to the unknown. Other special strategies are also shown in the answers on the student page. Let this be a relatively free discussion in which students share their own strategies.

Ask students to use what they know about count-bys to find and correct the errors in the patterns in exercises 20 and 21.

---

 25 MINUTES

Goal: Discuss strategies that involve regrouping factors to find a product, and apply various strategies to specific multiplication situations.

Materials: Student Activity Book or Hardcover Book p. 18

✓ **NCTM Standards:**
Number and Operations
Communication

Teaching Note

Properties of Multiplication The Distributive Property of Multiplication will be taught formally later in this book, along with the Commutative and Associative Properties. Students encounter all of these properties in various contexts before being introduced to them by name. Right now the essential thing is for students to see that making new factors (distributivity) is a potential solution strategy.

✓ Ongoing Assessment

During the discussion of problems 8–15, you can informally assess students' ability to ungroup and regroup factors as they work toward finding unknown products. Be sure that students understand that they should only break apart one factor and then multiply both parts by the other factor.

② Going Further

Math Connection: Properties of Addition and Multiplication

Goal: Identify and apply properties of addition and multiplication.

Materials: Student Activity Book or Hardcover Book pp. 19–20

✓ **NCTM Standards:**
Number and Operations
Algebra

▶ Discuss Properties | WHOLE CLASS |

In this activity, students will connect what they know about addition, multiplication, and their properties.

Commutative Property On the board, write the Commutative Property examples shown below. Compare and contrast the equations, and have students describe the property for addition and for multiplication, using their own words. Then invite volunteers to write their own examples.

Commutative Property
Addition	Multiplication
$10 + 15 = 15 + 10$	$9 \times 5 = 5 \times 9$

It is important for students to recognize that changing the *order* of the addends or factors does not change the sum or product.

Identity Property On the board, write the Identity Property examples shown below. Compare and contrast the equations, and have students describe the property for addition and for multiplication, using their own words. Then invite volunteers to write their own examples.

Identity Property
Addition	Multiplication
$8 + 0 = 8$	$7 \times 1 = 7$

The number 0 is called the *additive identity*. The number 1 is called the *multiplicative identity*.

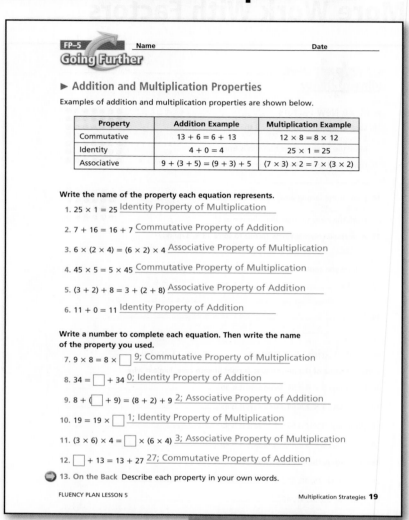

Associative Property Initiate a similar discussion as previously described for the Commutative Property. It is important for students to recognize that changing the *grouping* of the addends or factors does not change the sum or product.

Associative Property
Addition	Multiplication
$(6 + 4) + 5 = 6 + (4 + 5)$	$2 \times (3 \times 5) = (2 \times 3) \times 5$

▶ Addition and Multiplication Properties | PAIRS |

Have **Student Pairs** work cooperatively to complete exercises 1–12 on Student Book page 19. Then have students work individually to write descriptions for exercise 13.

Differentiated Instruction

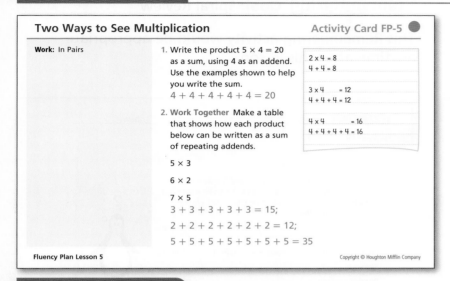

Two Ways to See Multiplication   Activity Card FP-5 ●

Work: In Pairs

1. Write the product $5 \times 4 = 20$ as a sum, using 4 as an addend. Use the examples shown to help you write the sum.
$4 + 4 + 4 + 4 + 4 = 20$

2. **Work Together** Make a table that shows how each product below can be written as a sum of repeating addends.

5 × 3

6 × 2

7 × 5

$3 + 3 + 3 + 3 + 3 = 15;$
$2 + 2 + 2 + 2 + 2 + 2 = 12;$
$5 + 5 + 5 + 5 + 5 + 5 + 5 = 35$

$2 \times 4 = 8$
$4 + 4 = 8$

$3 \times 4 = 12$
$4 + 4 + 4 = 12$

$4 \times 4 = 16$
$4 + 4 + 4 + 4 = 16$

Fluency Plan Lesson 5   Copyright © Houghton Mifflin Company

Activity Note Be sure students understand that the factor 4 in 4×5 represents the number of equal groups, and 5 represents the number in each group.

✏ Math Writing Prompt

Explain Your Thinking Tell why 3×5 is the same as $3 + 3 + 3 + 3 + 3$. Use words, numbers, or drawings.

 **Software Support**

Warm-Up 12.26

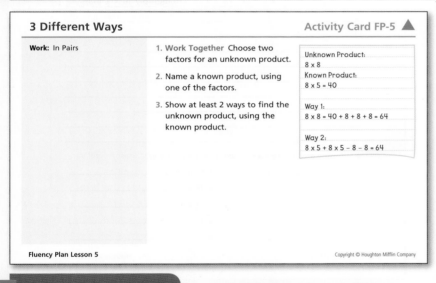

3 Different Ways   Activity Card FP-5 ▲

Work: In Pairs

1. **Work Together** Choose two factors for an unknown product.

2. Name a known product, using one of the factors.

3. Show at least 2 ways to find the unknown product, using the known product.

Unknown Product:
8 × 8
Known Product:
8 × 5 = 40

Way 1:
8 × 8 = 40 + 8 + 8 + 8 = 64

Way 2:
8 × 5 + 8 × 5 – 8 – 8 = 64

Fluency Plan Lesson 5   Copyright © Houghton Mifflin Company

Activity Note If students have difficulty, suggest that they first express the unknown product as the sum of two products. $8 \times 8 = 8 \times 5 + 8 \times 3$.

✏ Math Writing Prompt

Why Different Ways Are Important Tell why it is important to know different ways to use a product you know to find a product that you don't know. Give an example that shows your thinking.

  Software Support

The Number Games: Up, Up, and Array, Level C

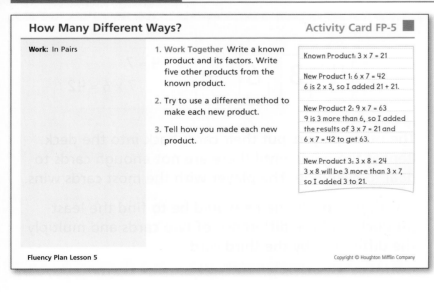

How Many Different Ways?   Activity Card FP-5 ■

Work: In Pairs

1. **Work Together** Write a known product and its factors. Write five other products from the known product.

2. Try to use a different method to make each new product.

3. Tell how you made each new product.

Known Product: 3 × 7 = 21

New Product 1: 6 × 7 = 42
6 is 2 × 3, so I added 21 + 21.

New Product 2: 9 × 7 = 63
9 is 3 more than 6, so I added the results of 3 × 7 = 21 and 6 × 7 = 42 to get 63.

New Product 3: 3 × 8 = 24
3 × 8 will be 3 more than 3 × 7, so I added 3 to 21.

Fluency Plan Lesson 5   Copyright © Houghton Mifflin Company

Activity Note Students must correctly interpret a known product such as 7×3 as the sum of 7 equal groups of 3. Then they can write new products by changing the size or the number of groups.

✏ Math Writing Prompt

Use a Known Product Show how you can use $3 \times 3 = 9$ to find $9 \times 9 = 81$. Explain your thinking for each step of your solution.

 **Software Support**

Course III: Module 1: Unit 2: Finding Factors

3 Homework and Spiral Review

FP–5 Homework · Goal: Additional Practice

Use this Homework page to provide students with more practice in using multiplication strategies.

FP–5 Remembering · Goal: Spiral Review

This Remembering activity would be appropriate anytime after this lesson.

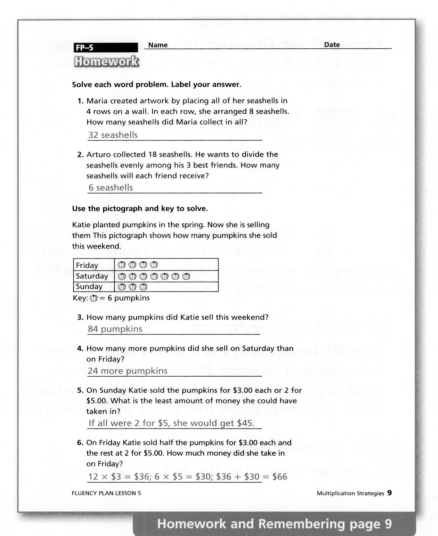

FP–5 Homework · Name · Date

Solve each word problem. Label your answer.

1. Maria created artwork by placing all of her seashells in 4 rows on a wall. In each row, she arranged 8 seashells. How many seashells did Maria collect in all?

   32 seashells

2. Arturo collected 18 seashells. He wants to divide the seashells evenly among his 3 best friends. How many seashells will each friend receive?

   6 seashells

Use the pictograph and key to solve.

Katie planted pumpkins in the spring. Now she is selling them This pictograph shows how many pumpkins she sold this weekend.

Friday	🎃 🎃 🎃
Saturday	🎃 🎃 🎃 🎃 🎃 🎃
Sunday	🎃 🎃 🎃

Key: 🎃 = 6 pumpkins

3. How many pumpkins did Katie sell this weekend?

   84 pumpkins

4. How many more pumpkins did she sell on Saturday than on Friday?

   24 more pumpkins

5. On Sunday Katie sold the pumpkins for $3.00 each or 2 for $5.00. What is the least amount of money she could have taken in?

   If all were 2 for $5, she would get $45.

6. On Friday Katie sold half the pumpkins for $3.00 each and the rest at 2 for $5.00. How much money did she take in on Friday?

   12 × $3 = $36; 6 × $5 = $30; $36 + $30 = $66

FLUENCY PLAN LESSON 5 · Multiplication Strategies 9

Homework and Remembering page 9

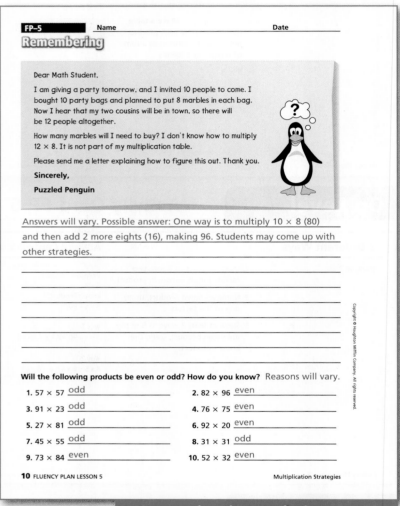

FP–5 Remembering · Name · Date

> Dear Math Student,
>
> I am giving a party tomorrow, and I invited 10 people to come. I bought 10 party bags and planned to put 8 marbles in each bag. Now I hear that my two cousins will be in town, so there will be 12 people altogether.
>
> How many marbles will I need to buy? I don't know how to multiply 12 × 8. It is not part of my multiplication table.
>
> Please send me a letter explaining how to figure this out. Thank you.
>
> Sincerely,
>
> Puzzled Penguin

Answers will vary. Possible answer: One way is to multiply 10 × 8 (80) and then add 2 more eights (16), making 96. Students may come up with other strategies.

Will the following products be even or odd? How do you know? Reasons will vary.

1. 57 × 57 odd
2. 82 × 96 even
3. 91 × 23 odd
4. 76 × 75 even
5. 27 × 81 odd
6. 92 × 20 even
7. 45 × 55 odd
8. 31 × 31 odd
9. 73 × 84 even
10. 52 × 32 even

10 FLUENCY PLAN LESSON 5 · Multiplication Strategies

Homework and Remembering page 10

Home or School Activity

Math-to-Math Connection

Greatest Product Game This game can be played with two or more players. Use index cards to make two sets of number cards, each with a digit from 0–9. The first player shuffles the cards and deals 3 cards to each person in the group. Players must try to find the greatest product that is the sum of two cards multiplied by the third card. The player with the highest product keeps his or her cards.

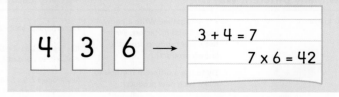

The other players put their cards back into the deck. Repeat the game until there are not enough cards to deal to everyone. The player with the most cards wins.

A variation of the game would be to find the least product: find the difference of two cards and multiply the difference by the third card.

Multiplication and Division Practice

Lesson Objectives

- Increase the speed and accuracy of division.
- Assess multiplication and division skills.

The Day at a Glance

Today's Goals	Materials
1 Teaching the Lesson **A1:** Use special materials to practice division. **A2:** Take multiplication and division quizzes, and correct mistakes. **2 Going Further** ▶ Differentiated Instruction **3 Homework and Spiral Review**	**Lesson Activities** Student Activity Book pp. 20A–20L and 21–22 or Student Hardcover Book pp. 21–22 and Activity Workbook pp. 5–18 (includes The Factor Field and Division Cards) Homework and Remembering pp. 11–12 **Going Further** Activity Cards FP-6 Crayons and markers The Factor Field Division Cards Math Journals 123 *Use* **Math Talk** *today!*

Keeping Skills Sharp

Quick Practice ⏱ 5 MINUTES	Daily Routines
Goal: Practice basic multiplication. **Difficult Finger Factors** Send three **Student Leaders** to the front. Two leaders will give factors from 6 to 10 by raising fingers on both hands and saying the number out loud. The third leader gives the hand signal, and the class responds with the product of the two factors. Repeat with other factors.	**Homework Review** For students who did not read the pictograph correctly, have them find the number each symbol stands for. Then have them skip count the symbols in each row and write the total at the end of each row. **Strategy Problem** There are four chapters in the book. Each chapter has 5 more pages in it than the previous chapter. If there are 150 pages in the four chapters, how many pages are in Chapter 3? 40 pages; Possible solutions: Estimate 160 ÷ 4 = 40 pages for each chapter, then use guess and check; $x + (x + 5) + (x + 5 + 5) + (x + 5 + 5 + 5) = 150$; x is Chapter 1, and it has 30 pages; Chapter 3 has 30 + 5 + 5 pages.

Teaching the Lesson

Division Practice

 30 MINUTES

Goal: Use special materials to practice division.

Materials: Student Activity Book pp. 20A–20L or Activity Workbook pp. 5–16 (See also: TRB M4–M14 and the *Math Expressions* materials kits.)

✔ **NCTM Standard:**
Number and Operations

Differentiated Instruction

Special Needs Some students may have a great number of division cards to practice. Have these students work with a **Helping Partner**. Have them focus on learning the easier problems first.

Have students share strategies for finding or remembering their more difficult divisions. Discuss how to use multiplication to do division.

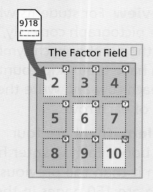

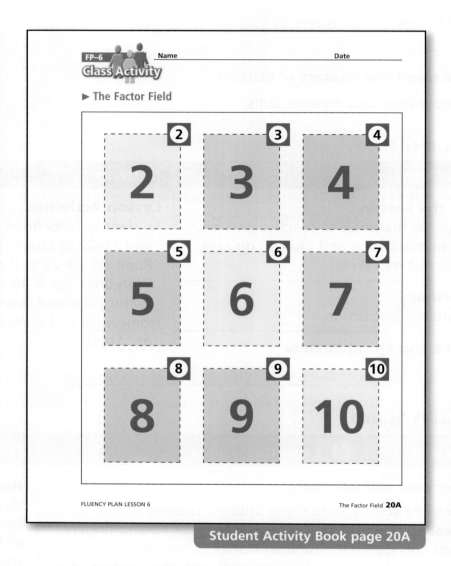

Student Activity Book page 20A

▶ The Factor Field [INDIVIDUALS]

Every student should have a set of Division Cards and a copy of *The Factor Field*. Have everyone mix up the cards and place them so the sides without the answers are face up. (The slanted corners of the cards will line up.)

Students read each problem and then place the card on The Factor Field in the section that corresponds to the answer. If students do not know an answer quickly, they should put the card aside.

When all the cards have been placed, students should confirm correct placement by picking up the cards in each section and turning them over to reveal that the answers are all the same.

If any cards were misplaced, they should be added to the pile to study later. Students should study these cards and then put the cards on the Factor Field again.

Diagnostic Quizzes

25 MINUTES

Goal: Complete multiplication and division quizzes, and correct mistakes.

Materials: Student Activity Book pp. 21–22 or Hardcover Book pp. 21–22 and Activity Workbook pp. 17–18

NCTM Standards:
Number and Operations
Communication

Student Activity Book page 21

FP–6
Class Activity

Name _____ Date _____

▶ Diagnostic Multiplication Quiz

1. 5 × 9 = _45_	2. 3 × 3 = _9_	3. 2 × 9 = _18_	4. 5 × 7 = _35_
5. 7 × 10 = _70_	6. 8 × 1 = _8_	7. 0 × 4 = _0_	8. 9 × 7 = _63_
9. 6 × 5 = _30_	10. 9 × 3 = _27_	11. 4 × 2 = _8_	12. 7 × 8 = _56_
13. 4 × 10 = _40_	14. 5 × 3 = _15_	15. 6 × 9 = _54_	16. 8 × 6 = _48_
17. 7 × 2 = _14_	18. 9 × 0 = _0_	19. 8 × 9 = _72_	20. 8 × 7 = _56_
21. 9 × 2 = _18_	22. 8 × 3 = _24_	23. 5 × 4 = _20_	24. 7 × 7 = _49_
25. 6 × 2 = _12_	26. 3 × 0 = _0_	27. 3 × 4 = _12_	28. 6 × 8 = _48_
29. 5 × 10 = _50_	30. 5 × 1 = _5_	31. 10 × 9 = _90_	32. 5 × 6 = _30_
33. 4 × 5 = _20_	34. 4 × 3 = _12_	35. 1 × 9 = _9_	36. 8 × 8 = _64_
37. 8 × 2 = _16_	38. 5 × 0 = _0_	39. 4 × 9 = _36_	40. 6 × 7 = _42_
41. 6 × 10 = _60_	42. 4 × 1 = _4_	43. 6 × 4 = _24_	44. 4 × 8 = _32_
45. 8 × 5 = _40_	46. 8 × 0 = _0_	47. 8 × 4 = _32_	48. 4 × 7 = _28_
49. 8 × 10 = _80_	50. 6 × 3 = _18_	51. 4 × 4 = _16_	52. 3 × 8 = _24_
53. 5 × 5 = _25_	54. 6 × 0 = _0_	55. 7 × 9 = _63_	56. 6 × 6 = _36_
57. 7 × 5 = _35_	58. 2 × 3 = _6_	59. 9 × 9 = _81_	60. 9 × 6 = _54_
61. 3 × 5 = _15_	62. 7 × 3 = _21_	63. 5 × 9 = _45_	64. 3 × 6 = _18_
65. 5 × 2 = _10_	66. 1 × 3 = _3_	67. 3 × 9 = _27_	68. 7 × 6 = _42_
69. 9 × 5 = _45_	70. 6 × 1 = _6_	71. 7 × 4 = _28_	72. 9 × 8 = _72_

FLUENCY PLAN LESSON 6

Diagnostic Multiplication Quiz **21**

English Language Learners

Review the word *factor*.

- **Beginning** Write the number 20. Say: **Let's list the factors that have a product of 20.** Write 2 and 10, 4 and 5, and 1 and 20. Say: **The factors of 20 are 2, 10, 4, 5, 1, and 20.** Have students repeat the factors.
- **Intermediate** Write the number 20. Say: **What factors have a product of 20?** Guide students to list the factors.
- **Advanced** Have students explain how to use multiplication and division to determine the factors of a number.

▶ Diagnostic Multiplication Quiz [INDIVIDUALS]

Explain that the quiz on Student Book page 21 will not be graded and that students should move on to the next exercise if they do not immediately know an answer. Allow 3 minutes for the quiz, and encourage students who finish early to check their work. Then read the answers and have students circle their mistakes.

Use the table below to identify where students need additional practice.

Students Who Miss	Need to Practice Multiplications
Column 1	2s, 5s, and 10s
Column 2	0s, 1s, and 3s
Column 3	4s and 9s
Column 4	6s, 7s, and 8s

Teaching the Lesson (continued)

Activity 2

✓ Ongoing Assessment

Have students compare the answers they missed on the multiplication quiz with those they missed on the division quiz and describe any relationships that can be observed. (For example, students who miss a fact such as 9 × 6 will also miss the related facts 54 ÷ 9 and 54 ÷ 6.)

FP–6

Class Activity

Name _____ Date _____

▶ **Diagnostic Division Quiz**

1. $30 \div 5 = \underline{6}$ 2. $12 \div 3 = \underline{4}$ 3. $27 \div 9 = \underline{3}$ 4. $42 \div 7 = \underline{6}$

5. $15 \div 5 = \underline{3}$ 6. $0 \div 3 = \underline{0}$ 7. $28 \div 4 = \underline{7}$ 8. $30 \div 6 = \underline{5}$

9. $8 \div 2 = \underline{4}$ 10. $9 \div 1 = \underline{9}$ 11. $9 \div 9 = \underline{1}$ 12. $56 \div 7 = \underline{8}$

13. $40 \div 10 = \underline{4}$ 14. $10 \div 1 = \underline{10}$ 15. $24 \div 4 = \underline{6}$ 16. $18 \div 6 = \underline{3}$

17. $40 \div 5 = \underline{8}$ 18. $9 \div 3 = \underline{3}$ 19. $36 \div 4 = \underline{9}$ 20. $56 \div 8 = \underline{7}$

21. $5 \div 5 = \underline{1}$ 22. $30 \div 3 = \underline{10}$ 23. $16 \div 4 = \underline{4}$ 24. $72 \div 8 = \underline{9}$

25. $16 \div 2 = \underline{8}$ 26. $21 \div 3 = \underline{7}$ 27. $81 \div 9 = \underline{9}$ 28. $64 \div 8 = \underline{8}$

29. $6 \div 2 = \underline{3}$ 30. $3 \div 3 = \underline{1}$ 31. $18 \div 9 = \underline{2}$ 32. $63 \div 7 = \underline{9}$

33. $90 \div 10 = \underline{9}$ 34. $18 \div 3 = \underline{6}$ 35. $63 \div 9 = \underline{7}$ 36. $54 \div 6 = \underline{9}$

37. $12 \div 2 = \underline{6}$ 38. $8 \div 1 = \underline{8}$ 39. $36 \div 9 = \underline{4}$ 40. $35 \div 7 = \underline{5}$

41. $18 \div 2 = \underline{9}$ 42. $6 \div 3 = \underline{2}$ 43. $8 \div 4 = \underline{2}$ 44. $36 \div 6 = \underline{6}$

45. $80 \div 10 = \underline{8}$ 46. $7 \div 1 = \underline{7}$ 47. $45 \div 9 = \underline{5}$ 48. $48 \div 6 = \underline{8}$

49. $25 \div 5 = \underline{5}$ 50. $15 \div 3 = \underline{5}$ 51. $32 \div 4 = \underline{8}$ 52. $24 \div 8 = \underline{3}$

53. $35 \div 5 = \underline{7}$ 54. $27 \div 3 = \underline{9}$ 55. $72 \div 9 = \underline{8}$ 56. $42 \div 6 = \underline{7}$

57. $20 \div 5 = \underline{4}$ 58. $24 \div 3 = \underline{8}$ 59. $12 \div 4 = \underline{3}$ 60. $6 \div 6 = \underline{1}$

61. $10 \div 2 = \underline{5}$ 62. $1 \div 1 = \underline{1}$ 63. $54 \div 9 = \underline{6}$ 64. $21 \div 7 = \underline{3}$

65. $20 \div 10 = \underline{2}$ 66. $0 \div 1 = \underline{0}$ 67. $40 \div 4 = \underline{10}$ 68. $48 \div 8 = \underline{6}$

69. $45 \div 5 = \underline{9}$ 70. $6 \div 1 = \underline{6}$ 71. $20 \div 4 = \underline{5}$ 72. $49 \div 7 = \underline{7}$

22 FLUENCY PLAN LESSON 6 Diagnostic Division Quiz

Student Activity Book page 22

▶ Diagnostic Division Quiz INDIVIDUALS

Explain that the quiz on Student Book page 22 will not be graded and that students should move on to the next exercise if they do not immediately know an answer. Allow 3 minutes for the quiz, and encourage students who finish early to check their work. Then read the answers and have students circle their mistakes.

Use the table below to identify where students need additional practice.

Students Who Miss	Need to Practice Divisions
Column 1	2s, 5s, and 10s
Column 2	1s, and 3s
Column 3	4s and 9s
Column 4	6s, 7s, and 8s

② Going Further

Intervention — Activity Card FP-6

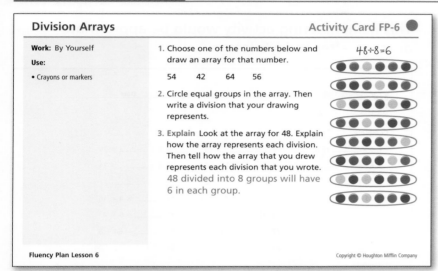

Division Arrays — Activity Card FP-6 ●

Work: By Yourself

Use:
• Crayons or markers

1. Choose one of the numbers below and draw an array for that number.

   54   42   64   56

2. Circle equal groups in the array. Then write a division that your drawing represents.

3. **Explain** Look at the array for 48. Explain how the array represents each division. Then tell how the array that you drew represents each division that you wrote. 48 divided into 8 groups will have 6 in each group.

$48 \div 8 = 6$

Fluency Plan Lesson 6   Copyright © Houghton Mifflin Company

Activity Note Have students compare their arrays with those of others and identify other possible arrays and division statements for each number.

✎ Math Writing Prompt

Explain Your Thinking Explain how you can use equal groups to solve basic division. Draw a picture if needed.

Soar to Success Math ★ **Software Support**

Warm-Up 13.22

On Level — Activity Card FP-6

Cover the Field — Activity Card FP-6 ▲

Work: In Pairs

Use:
• 1 set of Division Cards (TRB M5–M14)
• 2 The Factor Field (TRB M4)

1. Shuffle the cards and place them with the answers face down in a stack.

2. Take turns. Draw a card, read the problem aloud, and then give the answer. Check your answer.

3. If the answer matches the back of the card, place the card onto your Factor Field on the number that shows the answer.

4. If the answer you give is not correct, return the card to the bottom of the pile.

5. The first player to cover the Factor Field wins.

9)18

The Factor Field

2	3	4
5	6	7
8	9	10

Fluency Plan Lesson 6   Copyright © Houghton Mifflin Company

Activity Note After the cards are stacked, the slanted corners align if the correct side of each card is facing up. As the game progresses, multiple cards may be placed in each section of the Factor Field.

✎ Math Writing Prompt

Work Backward Explain how multiplication can be used to find division quotients. Give an example.

MegaMath Grades K–6 **Software Support**

The Number Games: Up, Up, and Array, Level G

Challenge — Activity Card FP-6

Write an Equation — Activity Card FP-6 ■

Work: By Yourself

1. Look at the function table below.

x	y
35	5
42	6
49	7
56	8
63	9

2. Write a division equation that shows the relationship between x and y. $y = x \div 7$

3. Use the equation to find the value of y when $x = 77$ and when $x = 84$. 11, 12

4. Make a function table of your own. Then write an equation that represents your table.

Fluency Plan Lesson 6   Copyright © Houghton Mifflin Company

Activity Note Most students will write the equation $x \div 7 = y$. You way want to point out that typically functions are written in the form of $y = x \div 7$.

✎ Math Writing Prompt

Explain Write a letter explaining how to find the product of 7×12 when you know the product of 7×6.

 DESTINATION Math **Software Support**

Course III: Module 1: Unit 2: Finding Factors

Multiplication and Division Practice   **45**

③ Homework and Spiral Review

FP–6

Homework **Goal:** Additional Practice

✔ Include students' work for Homework page 11 as part of their portfolios.

FP–6

Remembering **Goal:** Spiral Review

This Remembering activity would be appropriate anytime after today's lesson.

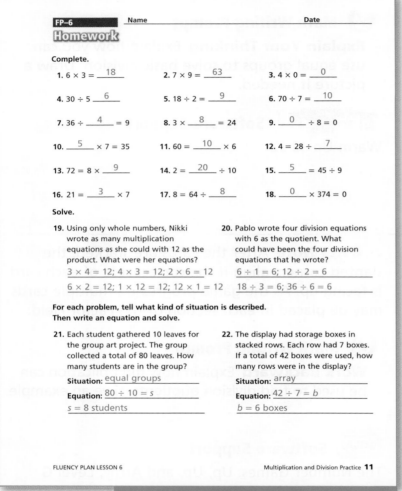

FP–6 Name ____ Date ____
Homework

Complete.

1. $6 \times 3 = \underline{18}$ 2. $7 \times 9 = \underline{63}$ 3. $4 \times 0 = \underline{0}$

4. $30 \div 5 = \underline{6}$ 5. $18 \div 2 = \underline{9}$ 6. $70 \div 7 = \underline{10}$

7. $36 \div \underline{4} = 9$ 8. $3 \times \underline{8} = 24$ 9. $\underline{0} \div 8 = 0$

10. $\underline{5} \times 7 = 35$ 11. $60 = \underline{10} \times 6$ 12. $4 = 28 \div \underline{7}$

13. $72 = 8 \times \underline{9}$ 14. $2 = \underline{20} \div 10$ 15. $\underline{5} = 45 \div 9$

16. $21 = \underline{3} \times 7$ 17. $8 = 64 \div \underline{8}$ 18. $\underline{0} \times 374 = 0$

Solve.

19. Using only whole numbers, Nikki wrote as many multiplication equations as she could with 12 as the product. What were her equations?
$3 \times 4 = 12; 4 \times 3 = 12; 2 \times 6 = 12$
$6 \times 2 = 12; 1 \times 12 = 12; 12 \times 1 = 12$

20. Pablo wrote four division equations with 6 as the quotient. What could have been the four division equations that he wrote?
$6 \div 1 = 6; 12 \div 2 = 6$
$18 \div 3 = 6; 36 \div 6 = 6$

For each problem, tell what kind of situation is described. Then write an equation and solve.

21. Each student gathered 10 leaves for the group art project. The group collected a total of 80 leaves. How many students are in the group?
Situation: equal groups
Equation: $80 \div 10 = s$
$s = 8$ students

22. The display had storage boxes in stacked rows. Each row had 7 boxes. If a total of 42 boxes were used, how many rows were in the display?
Situation: array
Equation: $42 \div 7 = b$
$b = 6$ boxes

FLUENCY PLAN LESSON 6   Multiplication and Division Practice **11**

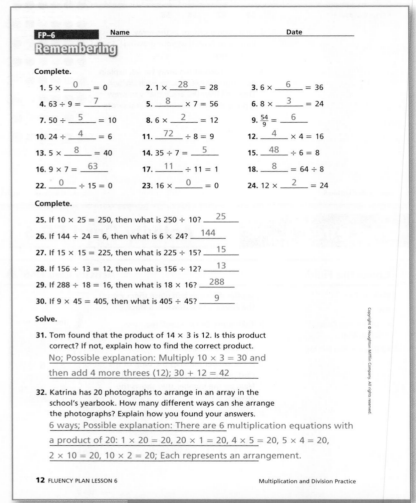

FP–6 Name ____ Date ____
Remembering

Complete.

1. $5 \times \underline{0} = 0$ 2. $1 \times \underline{28} = 28$ 3. $6 \times \underline{6} = 36$

4. $63 \div 9 = \underline{7}$ 5. $\underline{8} \times 7 = 56$ 6. $8 \times \underline{3} = 24$

7. $50 \div \underline{5} = 10$ 8. $6 \times \underline{2} = 12$ 9. $\frac{54}{9} = \underline{6}$

10. $24 \div \underline{4} = 6$ 11. $\underline{72} \div 8 = 9$ 12. $\underline{4} \times 4 = 16$

13. $5 \times \underline{8} = 40$ 14. $35 \div 7 = \underline{5}$ 15. $\underline{48} \div 6 = 8$

16. $9 \times 7 = \underline{63}$ 17. $\underline{11} \div 11 = 1$ 18. $\underline{8} = 64 \div 8$

22. $\underline{0} \div 15 = 0$ 23. $16 \times \underline{0} = 0$ 24. $12 \times \underline{2} = 24$

Complete.

25. If $10 \times 25 = 250$, then what is $250 \div 10$? $\underline{25}$

26. If $144 \div 24 = 6$, then what is 6×24? $\underline{144}$

27. If $15 \times 15 = 225$, then what is $225 \div 15$? $\underline{15}$

28. If $156 \div 13 = 12$, then what is $156 \div 12$? $\underline{13}$

29. If $288 \div 18 = 16$, then what is 18×16? $\underline{288}$

30. If $9 \times 45 = 405$, then what is $405 \div 45$? $\underline{9}$

Solve.

31. Tom found that the product of 14×3 is 12. Is this product correct? If not, explain how to find the correct product.
No; Possible explanation: Multiply $10 \times 3 = 30$ and then add 4 more threes (12); $30 + 12 = 42$

32. Katrina has 20 photographs to arrange in an array in the school's yearbook. How many different ways can she arrange the photographs? Explain how you found your answers.
6 ways; Possible explanation: There are 6 multiplication equations with a product of 20: $1 \times 20 = 20$, $20 \times 1 = 20$, $4 \times 5 = 20$, $5 \times 4 = 20$, $2 \times 10 = 20$, $10 \times 2 = 20$; Each represents an arrangement.

12 FLUENCY PLAN LESSON 6   Multiplication and Division Practice

Homework and Remembering page 11

Homework and Remembering page 12

Home or School Activity

Science Connection

Drinking Water Many health experts recommend that we drink a certain amount of water every day. One easy-to-remember recommendation is eight 8-ounce glasses a day.

Suppose a person drinks 64 ounces of water in one day. Have students find out how many cups, pints, and quarts are equivalent to 64 ounces. Suggest that students use the library or Internet to find other recommendations. How much would that be in a week? a year?

LIQUID MEASURE		
8 oz	=	1 cup
16 oz	=	1 pint
32 oz	=	1 qt

Multiplication and Division Word Problems

SOLVING WORD PROBLEMS is an essential part of the *Math Expressions* curriculum because these problems connect the outside world with the classroom. In their own lives, students encounter mathematical situations that require them to understand the relationships between known and unknown quantities. This unit encourages students to analyze the structure and language of different types of word problems and to discuss different models that can be used to solve word problems. They use algebraic notation to examine more complex problems including functions.

Skills Trace

Grade 4	Grade 5
• Solve combination problems.	• Solve combination problems.
• Solve comparison problems.	• Solve comparison problems.
• Write situation and solution equations.	• Write situation and solution equations.
• Solve multistep problems.	• Solve multistep problems.
• Use the properties of multiplication.	• Use the properties of multiplication.
• Write an equation to solve a problem.	• Write an equation to solve a problem.
• Write a rule and an equation for a function.	• Write a rule and an equation for a function.

Unit 1 Contents

Unit 1   Assessment

✓ Unit Objectives Tested	Unit Test Items	Lessons
1.1 Identify and write rules for a function table.	10–11	5
1.2 Solve algebraic equations involving multiplication and division.	12–15	1, 6
1.3 Identify and use properties of multiplication.	5–6, 16–17	10
1.4 Identify factor pairs.	1–4	8
1.5 Solve one-step multiplication and division problems, including combination and comparison problems.	7–9, 18	1, 2, 3, 4, 7, 11
1.6 Solve multistep problems involving multiplication and division.	19–20	1, 6, 9, 11

Assessment and Review Resources

Formal Assessment

Student Activity Book
- Unit Review and Test (pp. 53–54)

Assessment Guide
- Quick Quiz 1 (p. A2)
- Quick Quiz 2 (p. A3)
- Test A—Open Response (pp. A4–A5)
- Test B—Multiple Choice (pp. A6–A9)
- Performance Assessment (pp. A10–A12)

Test Generator CD-ROM
- Open Response Test
- Multiple Choice Test
- Test Bank Items

Informal Assessment

Teacher Edition
- Ongoing Assessment (in every lesson)
- Quick Practice (in every lesson)
- Math Talk (in every lesson)
- Portfolio Suggestions (p. 125)

123 Math Talk
- The Learning Classroom (pp. 76, 80, 86, 87, 89, 105, 110, 112)
- Math Talk in Action (pp. 63, 75)
- In Activities (pp. 51, 80, 94, 113, 118, 119, 120)
- Solve and Discuss (pp. 63, 68, 74, 76, 89, 104)
- Student Pairs (pp. 50, 76, 90, 97, 98) Helping Partners (pp. 70, 114)
- Small Groups (pp. 52, 58, 76, 90, 114)

Review Opportunities

Homework and Remembering
- Review of recently taught topics
- Spiral Review

Teacher Edition
- Unit Review and Test (pp. 123–126)

Test Generator CD-ROM
- Custom review sheets

Lesson NCTM Focal Points NCTM Standards	Resources	Materials for Lesson Activities	Materials for Going Further
1-1 **Make Combinations** NCTM Focal Point: 4.1 NCTM Standards: 1, 2, 6, 7, 9, 10	TE pp. 47–54 SAB pp. 23–26 H&R pp. 13–14 AC 1-1 MCC 5	None	Inch-Grid Paper (TRB M1) Colored blocks Colored pencils or markers ✓ Number cubes ✓ Letter cube Math Journals
1-2 **Understand Comparisons** NCTM Focal Point: 4.1 NCTM Standards: 1, 5, 6, 10	TE pp. 55–60 SAB pp. 27–32 H&R pp. 15–16 AC 1-2	Grid paper	✓ Number cubes Math Journals
1-3 **Practice With Multiplication Problems** NCTM Focal Point: 4.1 NCTM Standards: 1, 6, 8, 10	TE pp. 61–66 SAB pp. 33–34 H&R pp. 17–18 AC 1-3	None	✓ Counters or blocks Index cards Square sheet of paper Ruler Paper clip Math Journals
1-4 **Write Word Problems** NCTM Focal Points: 4.1, 4.5 NCTM Standards: 1, 6, 7	TE pp. 67–72 SAB pp. 35–36 H&R pp. 19–20 AC 1-4 AG Quick Quiz 1	Completed Homework p. 17 (optional) Multiplication and Division Practice (TRB M62–M65) (optional) Scrambled Multiplication Tables (TRB M66–M67) (optional)	Scissors ✓ Number cubes Timer or watch with second hand Grid Paper (TRB M17) Crayons or markers Math Journals
1-5 **Functions** NCTM Focal Point: 4.1 NCTM Standards: 2, 6, 9, 10	TE pp. 73–78 SAB pp. 37–38 H&R pp. 21–22 AC 1-5	None	Math Journals
1-6 **Equations With Parentheses** NCTM Focal Points: 4.1, 4.6 NCTM Standards: 2, 6, 8	TE pp. 79–84 SAB pp. 39–40 H&R pp. 23–24 AC 1-6	None	Large sheets of paper Markers Math Journals

Resources/Materials Key: TE: Teacher Edition   SAB: Student Activity Book   H&R: Homework and Remembering
AC: Activity Cards   MCC: Math Center Challenge   AG: Assessment Guide   ✓: Grade 5 kits   TRB: Teacher's Resource Book

NCTM Standards and Expectations Key: **1.** Number and Operations **2.** Algebra **3.** Geometry
4. Measurement **5.** Data Analysis and Probability **6.** Problem Solving **7.** Reasoning and Proof
8. Communication **9.** Connections **10.** Representation

Lesson NCTM Focal Points NCTM Standards	Resources	Materials for Lesson Activities	Materials for Going Further
1-7 **Combinations and Comparisons** NCTM Focal Point: 4.1 NCTM Standards: 1, 2, 5, 6	TE pp. 85–92 SAB pp. 41–42 H&R pp. 25–26 AC 1-7	Index cards (optional)	✓ Counters ✓ Number cubes Grid Paper (TRB M17) ✓ MathBoard materials Math Journals
1-8 **Practice With Factors** NCTM Focal Point: 4.5 NCTM Standard: 1	TE pp. 93–100 SAB pp. 43–44D H&R pp. 27–28 AC 1-8 MCC 6,7	Factor the Footprints (TRB M15–M16) ✓ Class Multiplication Table Poster Game token Tape	Index cards Grid Paper (TRB M17) ✓ MathBoard materials Math Journals
1-9 **Multistep Problems** NCTM Focal Points: 4.1, 4.6 NCTM Standards: 1, 2	TE pp. 101–108 SAB pp. 45–46 H&R pp. 29–30 AC 1-9	None	✓ Counters Math Journals
1-10 **Properties of Multiplication** NCTM Focal Point: 4.1 NCTM Standards: 1, 2, 7, 10	TE pp. 109–116 SAB pp. 47–50 H&R pp. 31–32 AC 1-10 MCC 8 AG Quick Quiz 2	None	Grid Paper (TRB M17) Math Journals
1-11 **Use Mathematical Processes** NCTM Focal Point: 4.1 NCTM Standards: 6, 7, 8, 9, 10	TE pp. 117–122 SAB pp. 51–52 H&R pp. 33–34 AC 1-11	None	✓ Number cubes Math Journals
Unit Review and Test	TE pp. 123–126 SAB pp. 53–54 AG Unit 1 Tests		

Hardcover Student Book

- Together, the Hardcover Student Book and its companion Activity Workbook contain all of the pages in the consumable Student Activity Book.

Manipulatives and Materials

- Essential materials for teaching *Math Expressions* are available in the Grade 5 kits. These materials are indicated by a ✓ in these lists. At the front of this Teacher Edition is more information about kit contents, alternatives for the materials, and use of the materials.

Independent Learning Activities

Ready-Made Math Challenge Centers

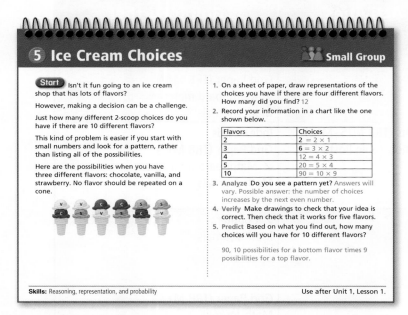

Grouping Small Group

Materials Chips or markers (optional)

Objective Students represent all the possible choices for arrangements of two scoops of ice cream and identify a number pattern.

Connections Probability and Reasoning

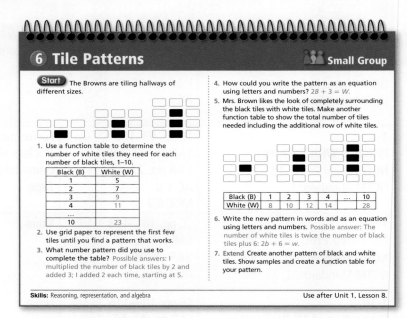

Grouping Small Group

Materials Centimeter-Grid Paper (TRB M18), colored tiles (optional)

Objective Students create a function table and identify function rules for arrangements of tiles.

Connections Algebra and Representation

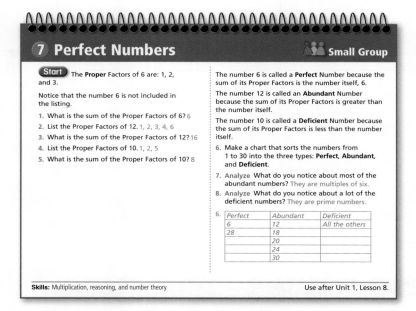

Grouping Small Group

Materials None

Objective Students identify perfect, abundant, deficient numbers.

Connections Algebra and Reasoning

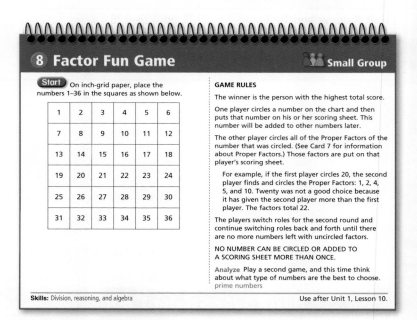

Grouping Small Group

Materials Two pencils of different colors, Inch-Grid Paper (TRB M1)

Objective Students find factors of numbers while playing a game.

Connections Computation and Reasoning

Ready-Made Math Resources

Technology — Tutorials, Practice, and Intervention

Use online, individualized intervention and support to bring students to proficiency.

Help students practice skills and apply concepts through exciting math adventures.

Extend and enrich students' understanding of skills and concepts through engaging, interactive lessons and activities.

Visit **Education Place**®
www.eduplace.com

Visit www.eduplace.com/mx2t/ and find family, teacher, and student materials, activities, games, and more.

Literature Links

O, Say Can You See?

O, Say Can You See?

This book by Sheila Keenan and Ann Boyajian tells the story behind well-known American symbols. It also provides facts about them that can be a springboard for problem-solving situations. Here's an example: How many more stairs did the workers at Mount Rushmore climb than visitors to the Statue of Liberty?

Literature Connections

Math-terpieces: The Art of Problem-Solving, by Greg Tang, illustrated by Greg Paprocki (Scholastic Press, 2003)

The Sundae Scoop, by Stuart J. Murphy, illustrated by Cynthia Jabar (Harper Collins, 2003)

Unit 1 Teaching Resources

Differentiated Instruction

Individualizing Instruction

Activities	Level	Frequency
	• Intervention • On Level • Challenge	All 3 in every lesson

Math Writing Prompts	Level	Frequency
	• Intervention • On Level • Challenge	All 3 in every lesson

Math Center Challenges	For advanced students
	4 in every unit

Reaching All Learners

English Language Learners	Lessons	Pages
	1, 2, 3, 4, 5, 6, 7, 8, 9, 10, 11	48, 56, 63, 68, 75, 80, 88, 94, 102, 113, 118
Extra Help	Lessons	Pages
	1, 4, 5, 8	49, 69, 74, 97
Special Needs	Lesson	Page
	4	70
Advanced Learners	Lessons	Pages
	1, 7, 8, 10	52, 90, 96, 98, 114

Strategies for English Language Learners

Present this problem to all students. Offer the different levels of support to meet students' levels of language proficiency.

Objective Make sure students understand the relationship between verbs and nouns in mathematical terms.

Problem Write *add, addition, subtract, subtraction, multiply, multiplication, divide,* and *division* on the board. Write $4 + 4 = 8$ and $4 - 2 = 2$.

Newcomer

• Say: **The plus sign means "add."** *Add* **is an action word. We add 4 plus 4.** *Addition* **is not an action word. 4 plus 4 shows addition.** Continue with other operations.

Beginning

• Ask: **Does the plus sign tell us to add?** yes **Is** *add* **an action word?** yes *Addition* **is not an action word. This problem uses addition.** Continue with other operations.

Intermediate

• Say: **The plus sign means __.** add Ask: **Is** *add* **a verb?** yes **Is** *addition* **a verb?** no **Is it a noun?** yes

• Say: **The minus sign means __.** subtract Ask: **Is** *subtract* **a verb?** yes *Subtraction* **is a __.** noun Continue with other operations.

Advanced

• Have students use short sentences and examples to tell the relationship between the verbs and nouns on the board.

Connections

 Art Connection
Lesson 3, page 66

 Language Arts Connections
Lesson 5, page 78
Lesson 6, page 84
Lesson 7, page 92
Lesson 10, page 116

 Literature Connections
Lesson 1, page 54
Lesson 11, page 122

 Math-to-Math Connection
Lesson 4, page 72

 Science Connection
Lesson 8, page 100

Social Studies Connection
Lesson 9, page 108

Math Background

Putting Research into Practice for Unit 1

From Our Curriculum Research Project: Analyzing the Structure and Language of Word Problems

In this unit, students analyze a variety of word-problem structures for real-world multiplication and division situations. Multiplication and division are taught together so students can see that one operation is the inverse of the other.

• Students relate these types of situations to each other and differentiate multiplication situations (unknown product) from division situations (unknown factor).

• Students use algebraic expressions and equations as well as drawings to represent and solve problems.

Different types of multiplication and division problems are presented:

Equal Groups problems involve objects that are separated into groups with the same number in each group.

Array problems involve objects organized in equal rows and columns that are not connected.

Area problems do not involve objects. They involve the number of square units that cover a shape.

Combination problems involve objects that can be organized in a table that has rows and columns of equal groups.

Comparison problems involve one quantity that is a number of times as many as or as much as another.

Throughout the unit, students discuss, draw, and/or model the relationships described in the problems.

—Karen Fuson, Author
Math Expressions

From Current Research: Strategic Competence

Strategic Competence refers to the ability to formulate mathematical problems, represent them, and solve them.

Not only do students need to be able to build representations of individual situations, but they also need to see that some representations share common mathematical structures. Novice problem solvers are inclined to notice similarities in surface features of problems, such as the characters or situations described in the problem. More expert problem solvers focus more on the structural relationships within problems, relationships that provide the clues for how problems might be solved.

For example, one problem might ask students to determine how many different sacks of five blocks can be made using red and green blocks, and another might ask how many different ways hamburgers can be ordered with or without each of the following: catsup, onions, pickles, lettuce, and tomato. Novices would see these problems as unrelated; experts would see both as involving five choices between two things: red and green, or with and without.

National Research Council. "Strategic Competence." *Adding It Up: Helping Children Learn Mathematics.* Washington, D.C.: National Academy Press, 2001. pp. 124–125.

Other Useful References: Solving Problems

Carpenter, Thomas P., Fennena, E., Franks, M.L., Empson, S.B., & Levi, L.W. *Children's Mathematics: Cognitively Guided Instruction.* Portsmouth, NH: Heinemann, 1999.

Mulligan, Joanne T. and Mitchelmore, Michael C. Young children's intuitive models of multiplication and division. *Journal for Research in Mathematics Education,* May 1997, Vol. 28, Issue 3, pp. 309–330.

Getting Ready to Teach Unit 1

In this unit students learn about different problem types for multiplication and division. This builds on the multiplication and division problem types studied in fourth grade.

As you teach this unit, emphasize understanding of these terms.
• situation equation
• solution equation
See the Teacher Glossary on pp. T6–T17.

Representing Word Problems

Writing Equations
Lesson 3

In this unit, students represent a word problem with a situation equation.

A *situation equation* shows the action or the relationships in a problem.

Then they may rewrite the situation equation as a solution equation.

A *solution equation* shows the operation that is performed to solve the problem.

Although these equations are the same for the simplest problems, they are different for the most difficult problems. When the numbers in a problem are small, students may be able to find the answer from a situation equation without having to write and solve a solution equation. When the numbers are greater (such as the multi-digit numbers in later units) or the situation is more complex, many students will find it helpful to use both equations. In Lesson 3, we discuss the distinction and, for this lesson only, students should write both equations so that they can experience the distinction.

Unknown Product
Lessons 1, 2, 3, 4, 6, 7, and 9

The easiest problems for students to solve are the Equal Groups, Array, and Combination problems that involve an *unknown product*. For these problems, the situation equation is also the solution equation (multiply the two known factors to find the unknown product).

Equal Groups Problems

Situation and Solution Equation → Multiplier × Group Size = $\boxed{\text{Product}}$

Array and Combination Problems

Situation and Solution Equation → Row × Column = $\boxed{\text{Product}}$

Unknown First Factor
Lessons 1, 3, and 7

Problems that are more difficult for students to solve are those with an *unknown first factor* in the situation equation. Although the solution equations for these problems involve division, students can find the unknown first factor from the situation equation if they count by the known second factor up to the product, or use a more advanced strategy. For multidigit numbers, students will need to write or at least think of the solution equation that shows the division inverse operation, and then perform the multi-digit division.

Equal Groups problems

Situation Equation → $\boxed{\text{Multiplier}}$ × Group Size = Product

Solution Equation → Product ÷ Group Size = $\boxed{\text{Multiplier}}$

Array, Area, and Combination problems

Situation Equation → $\boxed{\text{Row}}$ × Column = Product

Solution Equation → Product ÷ Column = $\boxed{\text{Row}}$

Unknown Second Factor
Lessons 1, 3, and 7

The most difficult problems for students to solve are those with an **unknown second factor** in the situation equation because these equations don't give the group size to use as a count-by number. But students can use the Commutative Property to write a multiplication solution equation with the unknown factor as the first number. Or as with the above problems, they can write a solution equation that is a division problem. For multidigit numbers, students will need to write or at least think of the solution equation that shows the division inverse operation, and then perform the multidigit division.

Equal Groups problems

Situation Equation → Multiplier × $\boxed{\text{Group Size}}$ = Product

Solution Equation → $\boxed{\text{Group Size}}$ × Multiplier = Product

Solution Equation → Product ÷ Multiplier = $\boxed{\text{Group Size}}$

Array, Area, and Combination problems

Situation Equation → Row × $\boxed{\text{Column}}$ = Product

Solution Equation → $\boxed{\text{Column}}$ × Row = Product

Solution Equation → Product ÷ Row = $\boxed{\text{Column}}$

What to Expect from Students The distinction between the unknown first factor and the unknown second factor may get blurred in actual use because in the real world there are two meanings for multiplication equations: 2 × 5 can mean 2 groups of 5 or 2 taken 5 times. Students may use either meaning, even though the more common meaning in this country is the former (2 × 5 means 2 groups of 5). Because some students in other countries have learned the latter meaning, *Math Expressions* allows students to be flexible. Therefore, for students who use the latter meaning, unknown first-factor problems will be the most difficult to solve because the group count-by number is not known. However, many students should be becoming facile in their use of the Commutative Property, so this distinction will become even less important as their facility increases.

Comparison Problems
Lessons 2 and 7

Some comparisons involve multiplication and division. Students are encouraged to draw simple comparison bars to help them visualize the comparison. Students begin to use unit-fraction language (one third as many).

Sarah picked 15 apples while her little brother Eli picked 3 apples. How many times as many apples did Sarah pick as her brother?

Each comparison can be said two ways:

Multiplication Sarah picked 5 times as many as Eli.

Division Eli picked $\frac{1}{5}$ as many as Sarah.

Students learn that division involves a unit fraction.

Multistep Problems
Lessons 6 and 9

Solutions for multistep problems can be found in a variety of ways. Most students will use separate steps to find the answer, and that is fine. Some students may be able to write a single equation, using parentheses. As long as students can explain their thinking, and that thinking fits the problem situation, any equation that leads students to the correct answer is acceptable.

Problem Solving Summary

In *Math Expressions* a research-based, algebraic problem-solving approach that focuses on problem types is used: interpret the problem, represent the situation with a math drawing or an equation, solve the problem, and check that the answer makes sense.

Representing Word Problems

Students using *Math Expressions* are taught a variety of ways to represent word problems. Some are conceptual in nature (making math drawings), while others are symbolic (writing equations). Students move from using math drawings to solving problems symbolically with equations. This table summarizes the representation methods taught in this unit.

Problem-Solving Approach
• Interpret the problem.
• Represent the situation.
• Solve the problem.
• Check that the answer makes sense.

Problem Type	Model	Equation
Equal Groups Seth had 5 bags with 2 apples in each bag.	10 5 × (2) (2) (2) (2) (2)	Unknown Product $2 \times 5 = n$ Unknown Factors $n \times 5 = 10;\ 10 \div 5 = n$ $2 \times n = 10;\ 10 \div 2 = n$
Array Jenna has 2 rows of stamps with 5 stamps in each row.	5 2 ○ ○ ○ ○ ○ ○ ○ ○ ○ ○	Unknown Product $2 \times 5 = n$ Unknown Factors $n \times 5 = 10;\ 10 \div 5 = n$ $2 \times n = 10;\ 10 \div 2 = n$
Area The floor of the kitchen is 2 meters by 5 meters.	5 2 ▭	Unknown Product $2 \times 5 = n$ Unknown Factors $n \times 5 = 10;\ 10 \div 5 = n$ $2 \times n = 10;\ 10 \div 2 = n$
Combination Katone packed 2 pairs of pants and 5 shirts.	c t h p e W | Wc | Wt | Wh | Wp | We R | Rc | Rt | Rh | Rp | Re	Unknown Product $2 \times 5 = n$ Unknown Factors $n \times 5 = 10;\ 10 \div 5 = n$ $2 \times n = 10;\ 10 \div 2 = n$
Comparison Katie picked 5 times as many flowers as Benardo. Benardo picked 2 flowers.	$B = \frac{1}{5} \times K$ B | 2 | K | 2 | 2 | 2 | 2 | 2 | $K = 5 \times B$	Unknown Product $2 \times 5 = n$ Unknown Factors $n \times 5 = 10;\ 10 \div 5 = n$ $2 \times n = 10;\ 10 \div 2 = n$

Use Mathematical Processes
Lesson 11

The NCTM process skills of problem solving, reasoning and proof, communication, connections, and representation are interwoven through all lessons throughout the year. The last lesson of this unit allows students to extend their use of mathematical processes to other situations.

NCTM Process Skill	Activity and Goal
Representation	1: Represent data in a table. 3: Make a drawing to represent and solve a problem.
Communication	2, 4: Share reasoning. 4: Discuss the patterns in a problem.
Connections	1: Math and Science: Number Sense and Data
Reasoning and Proof	5: Make and test generalizations using algebraic notation. 1: Use reasoning to predict from a table of data.
Problem Solving	2: Write an equation to solve a problem. 2: Solve problems involving estimation.

Basic Multiplication and Division Fluency

Students should continually work toward fluency for basic multiplication and division facts. Use checkups to assist students in monitoring their own learning. In the Teacher's Resource Book (TRB) you will find several pages for diagnosing and practicing basic multiplication and division.

TRB M58 Diagnostic Quiz for Basic Multiplication	TRB M66 Scrambled Multiplication Tables
TRB M59 Diagnostic Quiz for Basic Division	TRB M67 Blank Multiplication Tables
TRB M60 Basic Multiplication Practice	TRB M68 Multiplication for 10s, 11s, 12s
TRB M61 Basic Division Practice	TRB M69 Division for 10s, 11s, 12s
TRB M62 Multiplication for 3s, 4s, 6s, 7s, 8s, 9s	TRB M83 Factor Puzzles for 3s, 4s, 6s, 7s, 8s, 9s
TRB M63 Division for 3s, 4s, 6s, 7s, 8s, 9s	TRB M84 Factor Puzzles for 6s, 7s, 8s
TRB M64 Multiplication for 6s, 7s, 8s	TRB M85 Blank Factor Puzzles
TRB M65 Division for 6s, 7s, 8s	

See the Basic Facts Fluency Plan for information about practice materials.

Make Combinations

REAL WORLD Problem Solving

Lesson Objectives

- Connect combinations to multiplication of equal groups.
- Write equations to solve word problems that involve multiplication.

The Day at a Glance

Today's Goals	Materials

1 **Teaching the Lesson**
  A1: Use multiplication to solve combination problems.
  A2: Use a tree diagram to represent combinations.
  A3: Write an equation, using a letter to represent the unknown.
 	
2 **Going Further**
  ▶ Problem Solving Strategy: Guess and Check
  ▶ Differentiated Instruction
 	
3 **Homework and Spiral Review**
	Lesson Activities
	Student Activity Book pp. 23–25 or Student Hardcover Book pp. 23–25 and Activity Workbook p. 19
	Homework and Remembering pp. 13–14
		Going Further
		Student Activity Book p. 26 or Student Hardcover Book p. 26
		Activity Cards 1-1
		Inch-Grid Paper (TRB M1)
		Colored blocks
		Colored pencils or markers
		Number cubes
		Letter cube
		Math Journals

123 Use Math Talk today!

Keeping Skills Sharp

Quick Practice ⏱ 5 MINUTES	Daily Routines
Goal: Practice basic multiplications, using Medium Finger Factors. **Medium Finger Factors** Explain to the class that they did the easy section of the Multiplication Table earlier and will do the medium sections today. Again, send 3 **Student Leaders** to the front. This time the first leader gives a factor from 6 to 10 by raising fingers on *both* hands and saying the number out loud. The second leader gives a factor from 0 to 5 by using one hand. The third leader gives the hand signal, and the class responds with the product of the two factors. Repeat with other numbers.	**Logic** Felipe created a three-digit number. The hundreds digit is 3 greater than the ones digit. The product of the tens and the ones digits is 42. The sum of the hundreds and the ones digits is 15. What is the 3-digit number? 976; Use only one-digit numbers; Hundreds and Ones: 9 + 6 = 15 and 6 + 3 = 9; Tens: 6 × 7 = 42

1 Teaching the Lesson

Combinations as Multiplication

 25 MINUTES

Goal: Use multiplication to solve combination problems.

Materials: Student Activity Book or Hardcover Book p. 23

 NCTM Standards:
Number and Operations
Problem Solving
Representation

The Learning Classroom

Student Leaders Having Student Leaders lead Quick Practice activities is a key element of *Math Expressions*. Try to help Student Leaders take over leading Quick Practices as soon as possible. Choose socially confident students to begin. Before long, many students will want to be Student Leaders and, after a few weeks, all students will be ready to try their turn.

English Language Learners

Write *combine* and *combination* on the board. Say: *Combine* means "put together."

- **Beginning** Say: I combine milk and chocolate to make chocolate milk. Ask: **Is chocolate milk a combination?** yes
- **Intermediate** Ask: **What do I combine to make a cheese sandwich?** bread and cheese Say: **A sandwich is a __.** combination
- **Advanced** Have students tell about different combinations they can make.

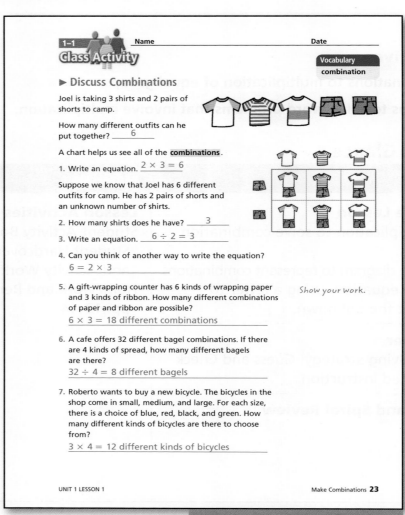

Student Activity Book page 23

▶ Discuss Combinations WHOLE CLASS

Have students look at the top of page 23 and list all the different outfits until they find all 6. Ask students to discuss how making a table can help them show their combinations. Elicit how to make a table without drawing pictures.

- There are 2 pairs of shorts on the side and 3 shirts at the top. What equation could we write that will show there are 6 outfits? $2 \times 3 = 6$

The combination table has rows and columns that are equal groups, and multiplication means adding equal groups.

Complete exercises 1–4 with the students. Have students solve problems 5–7. For problem 7, ask the students how they can solve a word problem that has no numbers. Count the number of bicycle sizes and the number of colors given.

Tree Diagrams (Optional)

▶ Make a Tree Diagram `WHOLE CLASS`

Write the five bicycle accessories and the incomplete tree diagram shown below on the board.

helmet
mirror
odometer
trail tires
handlebar padding

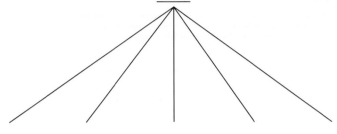

Explain that Conner is buying a bicycle and one accessory item from the list and that a tree diagram can be used to find the number of choices that he has. Then invite a volunteer to complete the tree diagram.

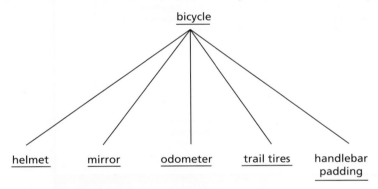

Discuss Have students suppose that the situation changes in this way: Conner has a choice of two bicycles—red or blue. Then invite volunteers to draw on the board a tree diagram that shows the number of combinations he has to choose from. There are 10 combinations altogether.

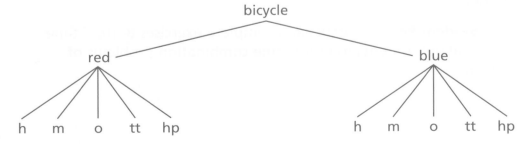

The abbreviations for the bicycle accessories are h: helmet, m: mirror, o: odometer, tt: trail tires, and hp: handlebar padding.

Generalize Students should generalize that the total number of branches represents the total number of different combinations.

Activity continued ▶

  30 MINUTES

Goal: Use a tree diagram to represent combinations.

Materials: Student Activity Book p. 24 or Student Hardcover Book p. 24 and Activity Workbook p. 19

 NCTM Standards:
Problem Solving
Representation
Connections

Differentiated Instruction

Extra Help Some students may find it helpful to think of the branches of a tree diagram as paths, and use a fingertip to trace the various paths that connect the top of the tree to the bottom.

Activity 2

Teaching Note

Math Background Finding combinations and finding probabilities are related concepts. In their study of probability, students will apply their understanding of combinations to write ratios that describe the likelihood of an event.

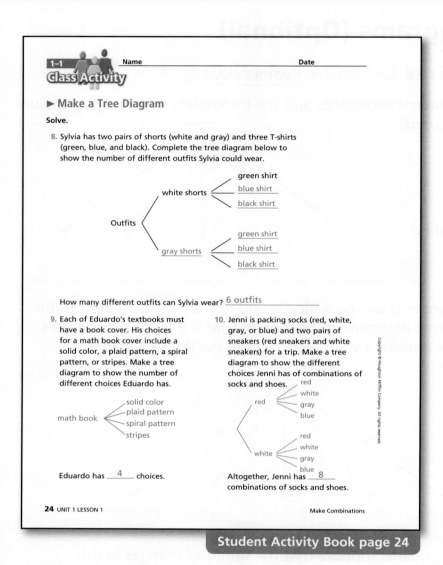

Student Activity Book page 24

► Make a Tree Diagram PAIRS

Point out that the tree diagram on Student Book page 24 is horizontal. Explain that at tree diagram can be drawn in a horizontal or vertical direction.

Allow **Student Pairs** to discuss and complete exercises 8–10. If time permits, allow students to write some combination problems of their own.

Equations With Letters

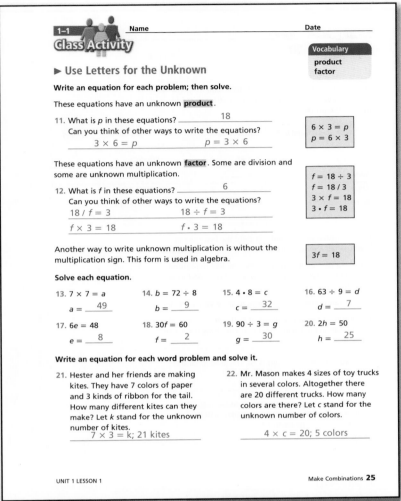

Student Activity Book page 25

1-1
Class Activity
Name _____ Date _____

Vocabulary
product
factor

▶ **Use Letters for the Unknown**

Write an equation for each problem; then solve.

These equations have an unknown **product**.

11. What is *p* in these equations? _____18_____
Can you think of other ways to write the equations?
$3 \times 6 = p$ $p = 3 \times 6$

$6 \times 3 = p$
$p = 6 \times 3$

These equations have an unknown **factor**. Some are division and some are unknown multiplication.

12. What is *f* in these equations? _____6_____
Can you think of other ways to write the equations?
$18 / f = 3$ $18 \div f = 3$
$f \times 3 = 18$ $f \cdot 3 = 18$

$f = 18 \div 3$
$f = 18 / 3$
$3 \times f = 18$
$3 \cdot f = 18$

Another way to write unknown multiplication is without the multiplication sign. This form is used in algebra.

$3f = 18$

Solve each equation.

13. $7 \times 7 = a$ 14. $b = 72 \div 8$ 15. $4 \cdot 8 = c$ 16. $63 \div 9 = d$
$a = \underline{49}$ $b = \underline{9}$ $c = \underline{32}$ $d = \underline{7}$

17. $6e = 48$ 18. $30f = 60$ 19. $90 \div 3 = g$ 20. $2h = 50$
$e = \underline{8}$ $f = \underline{2}$ $g = \underline{30}$ $h = \underline{25}$

Write an equation for each word problem and solve it.

21. Hester and her friends are making kites. They have 7 colors of paper and 3 kinds of ribbon for the tail. How many different kites can they make? Let *k* stand for the unknown number of kites.
$7 \times 3 = k$; 21 kites

22. Mr. Mason makes 4 sizes of toy trucks in several colors. Altogether there are 20 different trucks. How many colors are there? Let *c* stand for the unknown number of colors.

$4 \times c = 20$; 5 colors

UNIT 1 LESSON 1

Make Combinations **25**

---

 30 MINUTES

Goal: Write an equation, using a letter to represent the unknown.

Materials: Student Activity Book or Hardcover Book p. 25

 NCTM Standards:
Algebra
Problem Solving

Teaching Note

Math Symbols One reason we don't write the times sign (×) in Algebra is that in equations we often use the letter *x* to represent the unknown. $4 \times x = 12$ can be confusing.

Students should become familiar with all forms of multiplication and division.

3×4	$3 \cdot n$	$3 * 4$	$3n$
$10 \div 2$	$2\overline{)10}$	$\frac{10}{2}$	$10/2$

The asterisk and slash are used on computers.

Ongoing Assessment

Have students:

▶ show the different ways that 2 shapes and 3 different colors could be combined. Use a table.

▶ give an example of an equation with an unknown number.

▶ Use Letters for the Unknown [WHOLE CLASS]

Problems 11 and 12 on page 25 give students experience solving algebraic equations. Many students will be unfamiliar with expressions such as 3*f*. Give several additional examples until they feel comfortable with this notation.

$4s = 12$ $49 = 7b$ $5w = 35$ $60 = 10d$ $7t = 56$

Have the class use mental math to complete exercises 13–20. Point out that any letter may be used to represent an unknown number.

Math Talk Help students write and discuss equations for exercises 21–22. There will usually be two or more ways to write the equation. Students can either write division equations or equations with unknown multiplication to find the unknown factor. Have students share equations and then discuss why the equations can be different and each still correct for the situation.

② Going Further

Problem Solving Strategy: Guess and Check

Goal: Use the Guess and Check strategy to solve problems.

Materials: Student Activity Book or Hardcover Book p. 26

✓ **NCTM Standards:**
Problem Solving
Number and Operations
Reasoning and Proof

▶ Guess and Check [SMALL GROUPS]

Invite a volunteer to read aloud the paragraph at the top of Student Book page 26. Point out that the Guess and Check strategy involves making a reasonable first guess, and then making successive guesses if necessary. Make sure students understand that they should not make "random" successive guesses. Instead, they should use their previous guess and their reasoning skills to make the successive guesses.

Complete exercises 1 and 2 collectively as a class. Have **Small Groups** work together to complete exercises 3–5, and discuss the solutions as a group.

1-1
Going Further
Name _____ Date _____

▶ **Guess and Check**

The product of two numbers is 24. Their sum is 11. The table below shows how the Guess and Check strategy can be used to solve the problem.

First Guess: 6 and 4	Second Guess: ___ and ___	Third Guess: 8 and 3
Product: 24	Product: ___	Product: 24
Sum: 10	Sum: ___	Sum: 11
Check:	Check:	Check:
Is the product 24? yes	Is the product 24? ___	Is the product 24? yes
Is the sum 11? no	Is the sum 11? ___	Is the sum 11? yes

1. Work with a partner and complete the first column of the table for a guess of 6 and 4.

2. Make a new guess and use it to complete the second column. Complete the third column if you need to make another guess.

Use the Guess and Check strategy to solve each problem.

3. The sum of the ages in years of Karl and his sister Sabrina is 18. Sabrina is 4 years older that Karl. How old is Karl?
   Karl is 7 years old.

4. The sum of three numbers is 10. The product of the numbers is 30. What are the numbers?
   2, 3, and 5

5. In a pasture, there are goats and chickens. Eileen counted 10 heads and 28 legs. How many goats and how many chickens are in the pasture?
   4 goats and 6 chickens

26 UNIT 1 LESSON 1   Make Combinations

Student Activity Book page 26

Differentiated Instruction

Advanced Learners Have students write their own Guess and Check problems on index cards, with the answers on the back. Ask them to trade problems with classmates, solve the problems, and discuss the methods they used to solve them.

52 UNIT 1 LESSON 1

Differentiated Instruction

Draw Combinations
Activity Card 1-1 ●

Work: In Pairs

Use:
- Inch-Grid Paper (TRB M1)
- Colored blocks (6 different colors)
- Colored pencils or markers

1. Use blocks to model different combinations of colors. Choose two blocks. Then model as many combinations as you can for pairs of blocks, using the remaining four blocks.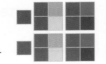

2. Record each model that you make by coloring squares on grid paper. How many possible combinations are there in all? 8

3. Predict How many combinations are possible, using one of three colors for the first block in a pair and one of three other colors for the second block? 9

4. Repeat the activity to check your prediction.

Unit 1, Lesson 1   Copyright © Houghton Mifflin Company

Activity Note If additional colored blocks are available, students may use more than 6 blocks. Making a table to record results will reinforce the connection between products and combinations.

✎ **Math Writing Prompt**

Make a Table Make a table that shows how many different combinations there are for 3 kinds of shapes and 3 different colors. Explain.

Soar to Success Math ★ **Software Support**

Warm-Up 52.06

Missing Numbers
Activity Card 1-1 ▲

Work: In Small Groups

Use:
- 2 Number cubes (labeled 1–6)
- 1 Letter cube (labeled a–f)

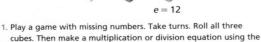
$c = 3$

$e = 12$

1. Play a game with missing numbers. Take turns. Roll all three cubes. Then make a multiplication or division equation using the two numbers and the letter that you roll.

2. Solve the equation. If your solution is correct, you earn 2 points. If your solution is not correct, other players can earn 1 point by solving the equation.

3. Continue taking turns writing and solving equations for 8 rounds. The player with the greatest number of points wins.

Unit 1, Lesson 1   Copyright © Houghton Mifflin Company

Activity Note Before students begin the activity, discuss how to choose the operations and the placement of the numbers in the equations to ensure solutions that are whole numbers.

✎ **Math Writing Prompt**

Write a Problem Write a multiplication word problem in which one of the factors is unknown.

MegaMath Grades K-6 **Software Support**

Ice Station Exploration: Arctic Algebra, Level C

Evaluate Expressions
Activity Card 1-1 ■

Work: In Pairs

Use:
- 2 Number cubes (labeled 1–6 and 7–12)

Decide:
Who will be Student 1 and who will be Student 2 for the first round.

1. Student 1: Roll the 7–12 cube and write an addition or multiplication expression using a letter and the number that was rolled.

Written: $12 + n$
Rolled: 5
Answer: $12 + 5 = 17$

2. Student 2: Roll the 1–6 cube and use that number to evaluate the expression.

3. Score the same number of points for each correct answer that you write.

4. Continue taking turns writing expressions and rolling the number cubes. The player with the greater score after 10 rounds wins.

Unit 1, Lesson 1   Copyright © Houghton Mifflin Company

Activity Note Suggest that students use opposite operations to check each evaluation. For the given example, solving the subtraction $17 - 5 = 12$ shows that the solution $n = 5$ is correct.

✎ **Math Writing Prompt**

Reasoning Skills Use the letters a, b, and c to write a related division equation for $a \times b = c$. Explain your thinking.

✳ **DESTINATION** Math® **Software Support**

Course III: Module 1: Unit 2: Finding Factors

③ Homework and Spiral Review

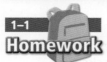

Homework **Goal:** Additional Practice

Use this Homework page to provide students with more practice with making combinations and solving word problems.

Remembering **Goal:** Spiral Review

This Remembering activity would be appropriate anytime after today's lesson.

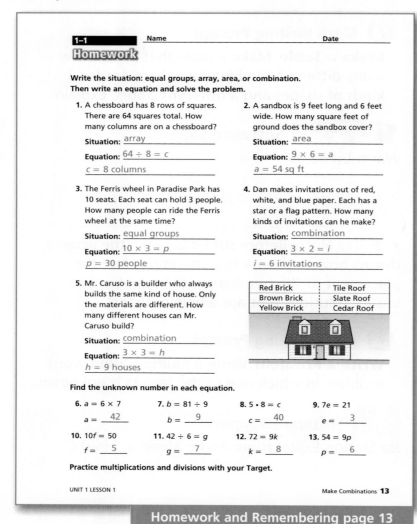

1–1 Name _____ Date _____
Homework

Write the situation: equal groups, array, area, or combination.
Then write an equation and solve the problem.

1. A chessboard has 8 rows of squares. There are 64 squares total. How many columns are on a chessboard?

   Situation: _array_

   Equation: _64 ÷ 8 = c_

   c = 8 columns

2. A sandbox is 9 feet long and 6 feet wide. How many square feet of ground does the sandbox cover?

   Situation: _area_

   Equation: _9 × 6 = a_

   _a = 54 sq ft_

3. The Ferris wheel in Paradise Park has 10 seats. Each seat can hold 3 people. How many people can ride the Ferris wheel at the same time?

   Situation: _equal groups_

   Equation: _10 × 3 = p_

   p = 30 people

4. Dan makes invitations out of red, white, and blue paper. Each has a star or a flag pattern. How many kinds of invitations can he make?

   Situation: _combination_

   Equation: _3 × 2 = i_

   i = 6 invitations

5. Mr. Caruso is a builder who always builds the same kind of house. Only the materials are different. How many different houses can Mr. Caruso build?

   Situation: _combination_

   Equation: _3 × 3 = h_

   h = 9 houses

Red Brick	Tile Roof
Brown Brick	Slate Roof
Yellow Brick	Cedar Roof

Find the unknown number in each equation.

6. $a = 6 × 7$
   $a = \underline{42}$

7. $b = 81 ÷ 9$
   $b = \underline{9}$

8. $5 · 8 = c$
   $c = \underline{40}$

9. $7e = 21$
   $e = \underline{3}$

10. $10f = 50$
    $f = \underline{5}$

11. $42 ÷ 6 = g$
    $g = \underline{7}$

12. $72 = 9k$
    $k = \underline{8}$

13. $54 = 9p$
    $p = \underline{6}$

Practice multiplications and divisions with your Target.

UNIT 1 LESSON 1   Make Combinations **13**

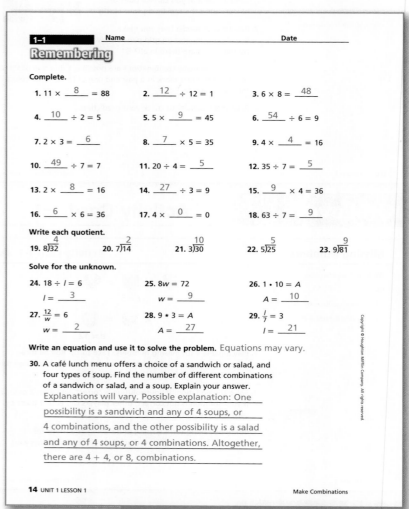

1–1 Name _____ Date _____
Remembering

Complete.

1. $11 × \underline{8} = 88$
2. $\underline{12} ÷ 12 = 1$
3. $6 × 8 = \underline{48}$
4. $\underline{10} ÷ 2 = 5$
5. $5 × \underline{9} = 45$
6. $\underline{54} ÷ 6 = 9$
7. $2 × 3 = \underline{6}$
8. $\underline{7} × 5 = 35$
9. $4 × \underline{4} = 16$
10. $\underline{49} ÷ 7 = 7$
11. $20 ÷ 4 = \underline{5}$
12. $35 ÷ 7 = \underline{5}$
13. $2 × \underline{8} = 16$
14. $\underline{27} ÷ 3 = 9$
15. $\underline{9} × 4 = 36$
16. $\underline{6} × 6 = 36$
17. $4 × \underline{0} = 0$
18. $63 ÷ 7 = \underline{9}$

Write each quotient.

19. $8\overline{)32}$ → 4
20. $7\overline{)14}$ → 2
21. $3\overline{)30}$ → 10
22. $5\overline{)25}$ → 5
23. $9\overline{)81}$ → 9

Solve for the unknown.

24. $18 ÷ l = 6$
    $l = \underline{3}$
25. $8w = 72$
    $w = \underline{9}$
26. $1 · 10 = A$
    $A = \underline{10}$
27. $\frac{12}{w} = 6$
    $w = \underline{2}$
28. $9 · 3 = A$
    $A = \underline{27}$
29. $\frac{l}{7} = 3$
    $l = \underline{21}$

Write an equation and use it to solve the problem. Equations may vary.

30. A café lunch menu offers a choice of a sandwich or salad, and four types of soup. Find the number of different combinations of a sandwich or salad, and a soup. Explain your answer.
    Explanations will vary. Possible explanation: One
    possibility is a sandwich and any of 4 soups, or
    4 combinations, and the other possibility is a salad
    and any of 4 soups, or 4 combinations. Altogether,
    there are 4 + 4, or 8, combinations.

14 UNIT 1 LESSON 1   Make Combinations

Homework and Remembering page 13

Homework and Remembering page 14

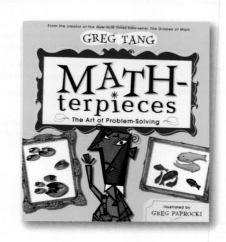

Home or School Activity

Literature Connection

Math-terpieces: The Art of Problem-Solving Read *Math-terpieces: The Art of Problem-Solving* by Greg Tang and illustrated by Greg Paprocki (Scholastic Press, 2003) to the class.

This is a book inspired by the artwork of twelve artists. The book focuses on improving problem-solving skills by using problems based on combinations and permutations.

Ask students to write and act out their own problem based on a piece of art.

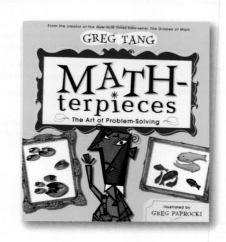

GREG TANG
MATH-terpieces
The Art of Problem-Solving

Illustrated by
GREG PAPROCKI

54 UNIT 1 LESSON 1

Understand Comparisons

REAL WORLD Problem Solving

Lesson Objectives

- Understand multiplicative comparisons expressed two ways.
- Solve word problems and complete tables that involve comparisons.

Vocabulary
comparison

The Day at a Glance

Today's Goals	Materials
1 Teaching the Lesson **A1:** Use multiplication to solve comparison problems. **A2:** Use tables and graphs to make comparisons. **2 Going Further** ▸ Differentiated Instruction **3 Homework and Spiral Review**	**Lesson Activities** Student Activity Book pp. 27–32 or Student Hardcover Book pp. 23–32 and Activity Workbook pp. 20–21 (includes Family Letters) Homework and Remembering pp. 15–16 Grid paper **Going Further** Activity Cards 1-2 Number cubes Math Journals 123 Use Math Talk today!

Keeping Skills Sharp

Quick Practice ⏱ 5 MINUTES	Daily Routines
Goal: Practice basic multiplications, using Medium Finger Factors. **Medium Finger Factors:** Send 3 **Student Leaders** to the front. The first leader gives a factor from 6 to 10 by raising fingers on *both* hands and saying the number aloud. The second leader gives a factor from 0 to 5 by using one hand. The third leader gives the hand signal, and the class responds with the product of the two factors. Repeat with other numbers.	**Homework Review** Ask students to place their homework at the corner of their desks. See whether any problem caused difficulty for many students. **What Went Wrong?** Doug is making shirt-and-pants outfits from 2 shirts and 3 pairs of pants. He says if he had one more shirt, there would still only be six outfits. Explain what Doug may have done incorrectly. What is the correct number of outfits? Doug added the number of shirts and pants instead of multiplying; $3 \times 3 = 9$; 9 outfits

❶ Teaching the Lesson

Comparisons as Multiplication

 35 MINUTES

Goal: Use multiplication to solve comparison problems.

Materials: Student Activity Book or Hardcover Book pp. 27–28

✔ **NCTM Standards:**
Number and Operations
Problem Solving
Representation

The Learning Classroom

Building Concepts When discussing how numbers compare, some students may give additive comparisons:

There are 4 more squares than circles; there are 4 fewer circles than squares. That is fine, but point out that we will be talking about comparisons that involve multiplication today. Discuss with students the meaning of the unit fraction $\frac{1}{3}$ as meaning dividing into 3 equal parts and taking one part (1 of 3 equal parts). So $\frac{1}{3} \times n$ means you divide n into 3 equal parts and take one part.

English Language Learners

Write *comparison* on the board. Draw these groups on the board.

Say: **Let's compare.** Ask: **How many groups of 2 circles are there?** 1 **Of 2 squares?** 3 **Are there 3 times as many squares as circles?** yes

▶ Express Comparisons Two Ways   WHOLE CLASS

Draw 2 circles and 6 squares on the board. Ask your class to compare the number of circles to the number of squares.

Try to elicit from students that there are two ways to state the comparison in a multiplicative way:

1. There are 3 times as many squares as circles.
   $$3 \times smaller\ number = larger\ number$$

2. There are $\frac{1}{3}$ as many circles as squares.
   $$\frac{1}{3} \times larger\ number = smaller\ number$$

When making comparisons that show multiplication, it is crucial that students practice saying both kinds of comparing sentences. It is easier for students to solve problems using the first sentence. They can always switch from $\frac{1}{n} \times large\ number$ to $n \times small\ number$ when solving a problem.

1–2
Class Activity

Name _____   Date _____

Vocabulary
comparison

▶ Comparisons With Unknown Numbers

You can use multiplication to solve **comparison** problems. All comparison problems involve a smaller amount and a larger amount.

1. There are 3 times as many deer as moose in the forest. If there are 5 moose, how many deer are there? *(The larger amount is unknown.)*

	$3 \times m$
Deer (3m)	
Moose (m)	5

   _____15 deer_____

2. There are $\frac{1}{3}$ as many moose as deer in the forest. If there are 15 deer, how many moose are there? *(The smaller amount is unknown.)*

Deer (d)	15
Moose ($\frac{1}{3}$ d)	
	$\frac{1}{3} \times d$

   _____5 moose_____

3. There are 5 moose in the forest. There are 15 deer. How many times as many deer as moose are there? *(The multiplier is unknown.)*

	___ $\times m$
Deer (3m)	15
Moose (m)	5

   _____3 times_____

4. Use the scoreboard to write 3 multiplication comparison word problems. Let each number be the unknown.
   Word problems will vary.

Red Team	Blue Team
6	24

   _____
   _____
   _____
   _____
   _____
   _____
   _____
   _____
   _____

Student Activity Book page 27

► Comparisons With Unknown Numbers [WHOLE CLASS]

Have everyone turn to page 27 in the Student Book. Point out the boxes that show comparison bars. These are useful tools for visualizing comparisons. Discuss problems 1–4. Notice that problem 2 reveals that if you know that there are $\frac{1}{3}$ as many moose as deer, you also can say that there are 3 times as many deer as moose.

1-2
Class Activity

Name _____ Date _____

► Solve Comparison Problems

Draw comparison bars, write an equation, and solve each problem. Equations may vary.

Show your work.

5. Farmer Ruiz has 6 times as many cows as goats. He has 7 goats. How many cows does he have?
Let c = the number of cows.
$c = 6 \times 7; c = 42$

Cows | 6 × | 7 | 7 | 7 | 7 | 7 | 7
Goats | 7

6. Nadia hiked 20 miles this weekend. Her sister Maria hiked only $\frac{1}{4}$ as many miles. How many miles did Maria hike?
Let m = the number of miles Maria hiked.
$\frac{1}{4} \times 20 = m; m = 5$

Nadia | 4 × | 20
Maria | 5 | $\frac{1}{4}$ ×

7. A baker made 35 apple pies today. He also made 7 peach pies. How many times as many apple pies as peach pies did he make?
Let t = how many times as many.
$7t = 35; t = 5$

Apple | — × | 35
Peach | 7

8. Nate practiced the trumpet for 10 hours last week. This week he practiced only $\frac{1}{5}$ as long. How long did Nate practice this week?
Let h = the number of hours Nate practiced this week.
$\frac{1}{5} \times 10 = h; h = 2$

Last week | 5 × | 10
This week | 2 | $\frac{1}{5}$ ×

9. How many times as many dark crayons are there as light crayons?
Let t = how many times as many.
$3t = 9; t = 3$

28 UNIT 1 LESSON 2   Understand Comparisons

Student Activity Book page 28

► Solve Comparison Problems [WHOLE CLASS]

In problems 5–9 on Student Book page 28, ask the class to draw comparison bars, write an equation using an appropriate letter to show the unknown number, and solve the word problems. Often several different equations will be possible.

Teaching Note

What to Expect from Students
Initially, students may find it helpful to draw comparison bars to show "who has more" and "how many times as many." Later, many students will not need to draw the comparison bars.

In problem 4, there are 3 kinds of word problems that are possible, depending on which amount is unknown:

The Red Team scored 6 points. The Blue Team scored 4 times as many points. How many points did the Blue Team score? (unknown larger amount) 24

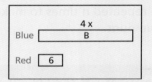

The Blue Team scored 24 points. The Red Team scored $\frac{1}{4}$ as many points. How many points did the Red Team score? (unknown smaller amount) 6

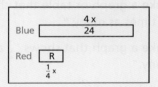

The Red Team scored 6 points. The Blue Team scored 24 points. How many times as many points did the Blue Team score as the Red Team? (unknown multiplier) 4

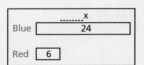

Understand Comparisons **57**

Teaching the Lesson (continued)

Activity 2

Data That Show Comparisons

 20 MINUTES

Goal: Use tables and graphs to make comparisons.

Materials: Student Activity Book pp. 29–30 or Hardcover Book p. 29 and grid paper

✓ **NCTM Standards:**
Data Analysis and Probability
Problem Solving
Representation

Teaching Note

Math Background Multiplication means adding equal groups. In multiplication comparison situations, the small amount is the equal group that is repeated n times to make the large amount.

 Ongoing Assessment

Ensure that students understand multiplication comparisons by having them:

► make a graph or table that shows "2 times as many."

► make a graph that shows "$\frac{1}{2}$ as many."

► explain the difference.

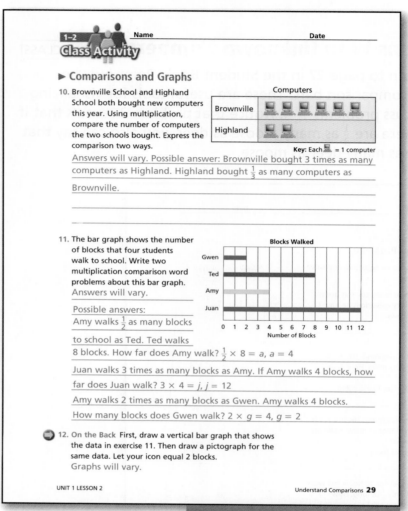

Student Activity Book page 29

► Comparisons and Graphs [WHOLE CLASS]

Have everyone discuss the table and graph problems 10 and 11 on Student Book page 29. For problem 11, students should say their multiplication comparing sentences using two forms. Practice with students how to say a comparing sentence using a whole number if they are given a comparing sentence in fraction form.

Math Talk If time permits, divide the students into **Small Groups** and ask each group to put a picture graph on the board for the other students to discuss in comparative terms. The graph should use simple-to-draw icons, such as squares, circles, dollar signs, or stick figures. The multiplication must come out even. (For example, one row must be exactly 2, 3, 4, or 5 times as much as the other row.) Also have students discuss how pictographs are the same and how they are different. You can display the same kind of data on each.

②Going Further

Differentiated Instruction

●Intervention — Activity Card 1-2

Make Predictions
Activity Card 1-2 ●

Work: In Pairs

Use:
• 2 Number cubes (labeled 1–6)

1. **Predict** When you roll two number cubes, which sums are more likely to be rolled?

2. Roll the cubes 50 times and record each sum.

3. **Look Back** Analyze your results and write comparisons to describe the outcome of the experiment.

4. **Math Talk** Which sum is most likely to occur? Which sum is least likely? Discuss why some sums happen more often than others. 7 is the most likely sum because there are more ways to make 7 than any other possible sum. The sums 2 and 12 are least likely because there is only one way to make each sum.

Unit 1, Lesson 2   Copyright © Houghton Mifflin Company

Activity Note To help students understand the outcome of their experiment, have them make a table of each possible sum and all possible combinations of two numbers that make each sum.

 Math Writing Prompt

Write a Problem Write a comparison problem using "times as many."

 **Software Support**

Warm-Up 52.04

▲On Level — Activity Card 1-2

Write Comparison Statements
Activity Card 1-2 ▲

Work: By Yourself

2. Possible statements: There are 2 more dogs than cats. (addition) There are $\frac{1}{2}$ as many cats as dogs. (multiplication)

1. The bar graph compares the number of dogs to the number of cats in a neighborhood.

2. Use the data in the graph to write as many comparison statements as you can to describe the graph.

3. Include both addition and multiplication statements in your comparisons, and classify each one.

4. **Math Talk** What clue words suggest a comparison based on multiplication? What clue words suggest an addition comparison? Possible answer: *More than* and *less than* suggest addition. *As many as* suggests multiplication.

Unit 1, Lesson 2   Copyright © Houghton Mifflin Company

Activity Note Be sure that students can distinguish between using *twice as many* and *2 more* in comparison statements. Use other sets of data, such as 6 dogs and 3 cats, to emphasize the distinction.

 Math Writing Prompt

Write a Problem Write a comparison problem using "$\frac{1}{2}$ as many."

 Software Support

The Number Games: ArachnaGraph, Level B

■Challenge — Activity Card 1-2

Venn Diagrams
Activity Card 1-2 ■

Work: In Small Groups

1. Copy the Venn diagram below.

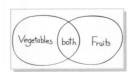

2 **Work Together** Ask members of your group to choose *vegetables, fruits,* or *both* to describe foods they like.

3. Write each student's name in the correct part of the Venn diagram.

4. Use the completed Venn diagram to write comparison statements about the data.

Unit 1, Lesson 2   Copyright © Houghton Mifflin Company

Activity Note To reinforce understanding, have groups combine their data into a single Venn diagram and write new comparison statements describing the results.

 Math Writing Prompt

Reasoning Skills Explain why the data in a Venn diagram can't be shown on a bar graph.

 Software Support

Course III: Module 1: Unit 2: Identifying Common Factors

Understand Comparisons   **59**

③ Homework and Spiral Review

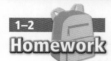

Homework **Goal:** Additional Practice

Use this Homework page to provide students with more practice with multiplicative comparisons.

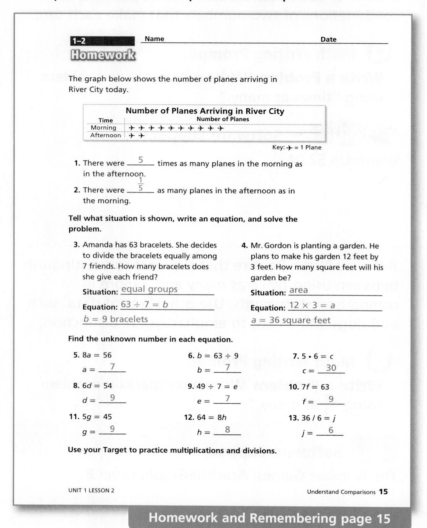

1-2
Name _____ Date _____
Homework

The graph below shows the number of planes arriving in River City today.

Number of Planes Arriving in River City

Time	Number of Planes
Morning	✈ ✈ ✈ ✈ ✈ ✈ ✈ ✈ ✈ ✈
Afternoon	✈ ✈

Key: ✈ = 1 Plane

1. There were __5__ times as many planes in the morning as in the afternoon.

2. There were __$\frac{1}{5}$__ as many planes in the afternoon as in the morning.

Tell what situation is shown, write an equation, and solve the problem.

3. Amanda has 63 bracelets. She decides to divide the bracelets equally among 7 friends. How many bracelets does she give each friend?

Situation: __equal groups__

Equation: __$63 \div 7 = b$__

__$b = 9$ bracelets__

4. Mr. Gordon is planting a garden. He plans to make his garden 12 feet by 3 feet. How many square feet will his garden be?

Situation: __area__

Equation: __$12 \times 3 = a$__

__$a = 36$ square feet__

Find the unknown number in each equation.

5. $8a = 56$
$a = $ __7__

6. $b = 63 \div 9$
$b = $ __7__

7. $5 \cdot 6 = c$
$c = $ __30__

8. $6d = 54$
$d = $ __9__

9. $49 \div 7 = e$
$e = $ __7__

10. $7f = 63$
$f = $ __9__

11. $5g = 45$
$g = $ __9__

12. $64 = 8h$
$h = $ __8__

13. $36 / 6 = j$
$j = $ __6__

Use your Target to practice multiplications and divisions.

UNIT 1 LESSON 2

Understand Comparisons **15**

Homework and Remembering page 15

Remembering **Goal:** Spiral Review

This Remembering activity would be appropriate anytime after today's lesson.

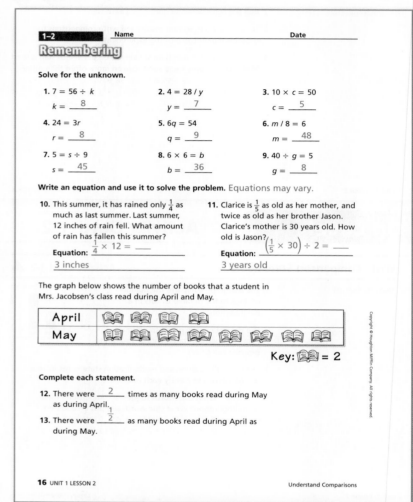

1-2
Name _____ Date _____
Remembering

Solve for the unknown.

1. $7 = 56 \div k$
$k = $ __8__

2. $4 = 28 / y$
$y = $ __7__

3. $10 \times c = 50$
$c = $ __5__

4. $24 = 3r$
$r = $ __8__

5. $6q = 54$
$q = $ __9__

6. $m / 8 = 6$
$m = $ __48__

7. $5 = s \div 9$
$s = $ __45__

8. $6 \times 6 = b$
$b = $ __36__

9. $40 \div g = 5$
$g = $ __8__

Write an equation and use it to solve the problem. Equations may vary.

10. This summer, it has rained only $\frac{1}{4}$ as much as last summer. Last summer, 12 inches of rain fell. What amount of rain has fallen this summer?

Equation: __$\frac{1}{4} \times 12 = $__

__3 inches__

11. Clarice is $\frac{1}{5}$ as old as her mother, and twice as old as her brother Jason. Clarice's mother is 30 years old. How old is Jason?

Equation: __$\left(\frac{1}{5} \times 30\right) \div 2 = $__

__3 years old__

The graph below shows the number of books that a student in Mrs. Jacobsen's class read during April and May.

| April | 📖 📖 📖 📖 |
| May | 📖 📖 📖 📖 📖 📖 📖 📖 |

Key: 📖 = 2

Complete each statement.

12. There were __2__ times as many books read during May as during April.

13. There were __$\frac{1}{2}$__ as many books read during April as during May.

16 UNIT 1 LESSON 2

Understand Comparisons

Homework and Remembering page 16

Home or School Activity

Home and School Connection

Family Letter Have students take home the Family Letter on Student Book page 31 or Activity Workbook page 20. This letter explains the type of real-world situations that students experience and how they write an equation to solve them. Factor puzzles and how to solve them are explained. A Spanish translation of this letter is on Student Book page 32 and Activity Workbook page 21.

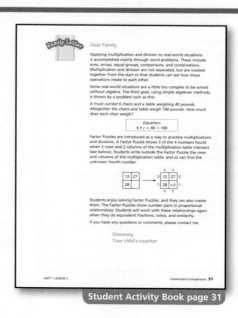

Student Activity Book page 31

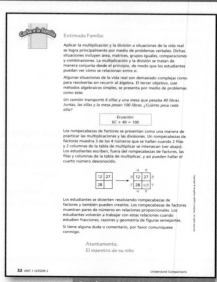

Student Activity Book page 32

Practice With Multiplication Problems

Lesson Objectives

- Understand the everyday applications of multiplication and division.
- Generate and solve simple algebraic equations to represent multiplicative situations.

Vocabulary

area	array
combination	comparison
equal groups	

The Day at a Glance

Today's Goals	Materials	

1 Teaching the Lesson
Recognize multiplication situations.
 	
2 Going Further
▶ Differentiated Instruction
 	
3 Homework and Spiral Review
	Lesson Activities
	Student Activity Book pp. 33–34 or
	  Student Hardcover Book pp. 33–34
	Homework and Remembering
	  pp. 17–18
		Going Further
		Activity Cards 1-3
		Counters or blocks
		Index cards, square
		  sheet of paper
		Ruler, paper clip
		Math Journals

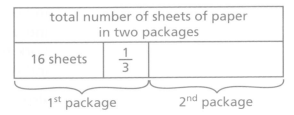
Use Math Talk today!

Keeping Skills Sharp

Quick Practice ⏱ 5 MINUTES	Daily Routines
Goal: Practice basic multiplication. **Medium Finger Factors** Once again, send three **Student Leaders** to the front. The first leader gives a factor from 6 to 10 by raising fingers on both hands and saying the number out loud. The second leader gives a factor from 0 to 5 by using one hand. The third leader gives the hand signal, and the class responds with the product of the two factors. Repeat with other numbers.	**Homework Review** Let students work together to check their work. **Nonroutine Problem** Hoon bought two packages of paper. Each package has the same number of sheets. He used 16 sheets of paper from one package, leaving $\frac{1}{3}$ of that package. How many sheets of paper did Hoon buy in all? 48 sheets; $16 \div 2 = 8$; $16 + 8 = 24$; $24 + 24 = 48$

total number of sheets of paper in two packages		
16 sheets	$\frac{1}{3}$	
1st package		2nd package

① Teaching the Lesson

Activity 1

Recognize Multiplication Situations

 30 MINUTES

Goal: Recognize multiplication situations.

Materials: Student Activity Book or Hardcover Book pp. 33–34

 NCTM Standards:
Number and Operations
Problem Solving
Representation
Communication

The Learning Classroom

Helping Community When students explaining at the board have difficulty, they usually welcome help from another student. Allowing other students to help instead of you will enable them to assume responsibility for one another's learning. Ask who they would like to help them. You can move on to another explainer while they redo their work. Of course, sometimes it is fine to go ahead and have the whole class help the student, while you lead with questions.

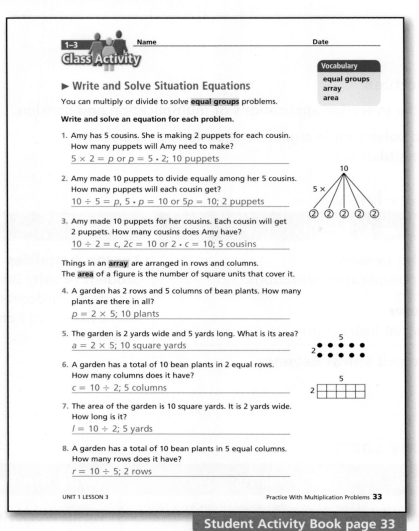

Student Activity Book page 33

► Introduce Situation and Solution Equations

WHOLE CLASS

Ask for Ideas Give students the opportunity to describe the different types of multiplication and division situations that have been discussed so far. Elicit these 4 situations (equal groups, array/area, comparisons, and combinations) with a brief description, an example word problem, and an example math drawing for each kind. Explain that the class will work together on student pages that show all of these types of problems and will discuss how each type is like and different from other types.

Also introduce students to the terms *situation equation* and *solution equation*. Explain that a situation equation shows the situation in the problem, and the solution equation shows how you are going to think about it to solve the problem. So, for a division problem, you might write $28 \div 7 = ?$ as a situation equation, but you would actually think $7 \times ? = 28$ to find the answer. That is your solution equation.

► Write and Solve Situation Equations   WHOLE CLASS

Equal Groups Direct students' attention to problems 1–3 on Student Book page 33. Invite several students to work at the board. Ask students to use **Solve and Discuss** to write and solve an equation for the first word problem, using the letter *p* for the unknown number of puppets. Discuss how the drawing shows 5 equal groups of 2, or 2 taken 5 times.

Have students do the same for the next word problem. Many students will write a division equation. If no one writes a multiplication equation, elicit one from the class.

Now have students write one division equation and one multiplication equation for the third problem, using *c* for the unknown number of cousins. You may point out that students can use any letter they want for an unknown, but that often the first letter of the unknown quantity is used, as *c* is used here to represent the unknown number of cousins.

Arrays and Area Review with the class how area is different from an array.

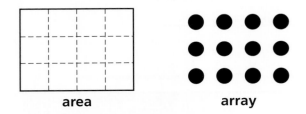

area   array

Have students generate equations and answers for problems 4–8 on page 33. The equations will be exactly the same in consecutive problems, but the label for the answer will be different. Students can use *a*, *b,* and *c* or any letter they choose for the unknowns.

 Math Talk in Action

Now, as a class, have students look at the problems in which a multiplication equation was used to solve. Discuss the similarities between these problems.

What is similar about the problems using a multiplication equation?

Ji Sun: You have to find a total.

Rafael: The amount of equal groups and the number of objects in each of those groups are given.

What is similar about the problems that use a division equation?

Benjamin: A total number of objects is given.

Aida: And, either the amount of equal groups or the number of objects in each of those groups is given.

Activity continued ▶

The Learning Classroom

Helping Community It will be important to take some class time to discuss *good helping*. You may have students create a list that can be posted in the classroom. It is important that they understand that good helping does not mean telling answers, but taking other students through steps so that they come up with the answers themselves.

English Language Learners

Draw a 2 × 3 dot array and an equivalent area rectangle. Write *area* and *array* below the drawings.

• **Beginning** Point to the array. Ask: **How many rows are there?** 2 **How many columns?** 3 Ask: **Do the dots touch each other?** no Ask similar questions about the area model.

• **Intermediate** Point to the area model. Say: **The total space in the rectangle is the ___.** area Ask: **Are area and array the same thing?** no

• **Advanced** Have students tell how area and array are different.

Teaching the Lesson (continued)

Activity 1

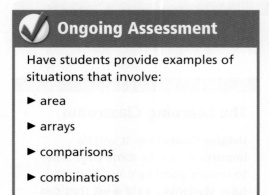

Ongoing Assessment

Have students provide examples of situations that involve:

► area

► arrays

► comparisons

► combinations

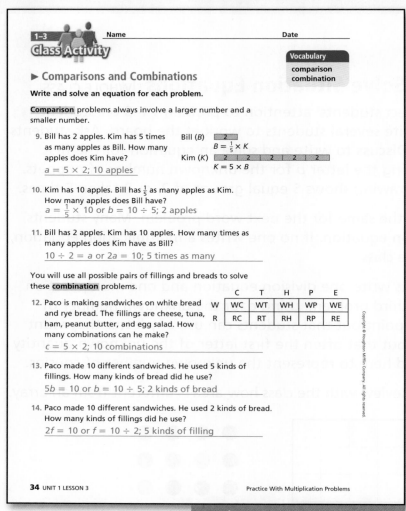

Student Activity Book page 34

The following text appears on Student Activity Book page 34:

1-3
Class Activity

Name _____ Date _____

► **Comparisons and Combinations**

Write and solve an equation for each problem.

Comparison problems always involve a larger number and a smaller number.

9. Bill has 2 apples. Kim has 5 times as many apples as Bill. How many apples does Kim have?
Bill (B) [2] $B = \frac{1}{5} \times K$
Kim (K) [2 | 2 | 2 | 2 | 2] $K = 5 \times B$
$a = 5 \times 2$; 10 apples

10. Kim has 10 apples. Bill has $\frac{1}{5}$ as many apples as Kim. How many apples does Bill have?
$a = \frac{1}{5} \times 10$ or $b = 10 \div 5$; 2 apples

11. Bill has 2 apples. Kim has 10 apples. How many times as many apples does Kim have as Bill?
$10 \div 2 = a$ or $2a = 10$; 5 times as many

You will use all possible pairs of fillings and breads to solve these **combination** problems.

12. Paco is making sandwiches on white bread and rye bread. The fillings are cheese, tuna, ham, peanut butter, and egg salad. How many combinations can he make?

	C	T	H	P	E
W	WC	WT	WH	WP	WE
R	RC	RT	RH	RP	RE

$c = 5 \times 2$; 10 combinations

13. Paco made 10 different sandwiches. He used 5 kinds of fillings. How many kinds of bread did he use?
$5b = 10$ or $b = 10 \div 5$; 2 kinds of bread

14. Paco made 10 different sandwiches. He used 2 kinds of bread. How many kinds of fillings did he use?
$2f = 10$ or $f = 10 \div 2$; 5 kinds of filling

34 UNIT 1 LESSON 3   Practice With Multiplication Problems

► Comparisons and Combinations WHOLE CLASS

Comparisons Work through problems 9–11 on Student Book page 34. The equation for problem 9 is the easiest to set up. The situation in problem 10 can be set up two ways. Students can either multiply by the fraction or divide by a whole number. The situation in problem 11 can also be set up with either a multiplication equation or a division equation.

Combinations Work through problems 12–14 on page 34. Students often are not given numbers for combination problems, but must count the items to find the numbers to be multiplied. In this case, there are 5 kinds of fillings and 2 kinds of bread. The chart shows that 10 combinations are possible if Paco makes sandwiches with just one filling. Ask your students to say all the combinations shown on the chart out loud (white bread with cheese, and so on). Then have everyone generate the various equations.

②Going Further

Differentiated Instruction

Intervention   Activity Card 1-3

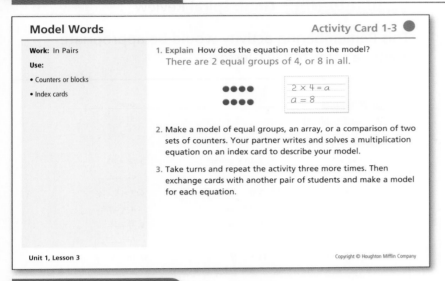

Model Words   Activity Card 1-3 ●

Work: In Pairs

Use:
• Counters or blocks
• Index cards

1. **Explain** How does the equation relate to the model? There are 2 equal groups of 4, or 8 in all.

  $2 \times 4 = a$ $a = 8$

2. Make a model of equal groups, an array, or a comparison of two sets of counters. Your partner writes and solves a multiplication equation on an index card to describe your model.

3. Take turns and repeat the activity three more times. Then exchange cards with another pair of students and make a model for each equation.

Unit 1, Lesson 3   Copyright © Houghton Mifflin Company

Activity Note Review how to model equal groups, arrays, and comparisons of two sets of counters if necessary, before students begin the activity. Discuss how the factors of the equation relate to the models.

 **Math Writing Prompt**

Make a Drawing Draw an array that shows 15 counters. Tell how to write an equation for the array.

Soar to Success Math ★ Software Support

Warm-Up 12.23

On Level   Activity Card 1-3

Multiplication Challenge   Activity Card 1-3 ▲

Work: In Small Groups

Use:
• Square sheet of paper
• Ruler
• Paper clip

1. Draw diagonals on the paper to make 4 equal sections. Label each section as shown.

2. Use a pencil point to hold the paper clip in the center of the square. Take turns spinning the clip.

3. Read the label where the clip stops. Then create a multiplication problem for your group to solve that matches the label.

4. **Work Together** Solve the problem. Repeat the activity until each player has taken a turn.

Unit 1, Lesson 3   Copyright © Houghton Mifflin Company

Activity Note Suggest that students write their problems on a sheet of paper. If time allows, have groups exchange problems and solve them for additional practice.

 Math Writing Prompt

Compare and Contrast Explain how arrays and area are alike. Explain how they are different.

MegaMath Software Support

The Number Games: Up, Up, and Array, Level C

Challenge   Activity Card 1-3

Combinations   Activity Card 1-3 ■

Work: In Pairs

Method 1: $2 \times 3 = 6$

Method 2:

Method 3:

1. **Work Together** Show three methods to find the total number of possible combinations for an ice cream dessert.

2. On your own, write a problem about combinations that you can solve by using the multiplication $3 \times 2 \times 4$. Exchange with your partner to solve.

3. **Compare** Tell which method of finding combinations you prefer and why. Students should discover that the table method does not work for more than 2 categories of choices.

Unit 1, Lesson 3   Copyright © Houghton Mifflin Company

Activity Note Students can use the ice cream problem as the basis for a three-factor combination problem by adding a choice of 4 toppings to the given choices of serving and flavors.

 Math Writing Prompt

Reasoning Skills Describe at least four different situations that 3×5 can represent.

✴ DESTINATION Math® Software Support

Course III: Module 6: Unit 1: Looking at Chance

Practice With Multiplication Problems   **65**

Homework and Spiral Review

---

1-3
Homework **Goal:** Additional Practice

Have students save this completed Homework page for use in the next lesson.

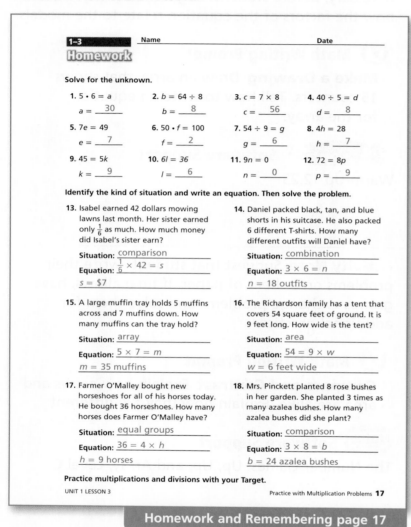

1-3 Name _____ Date _____
Homework

Solve for the unknown.

1. $5 \cdot 6 = a$
   $a =$ __30__
2. $b = 64 \div 8$
   $b =$ __8__
3. $c = 7 \times 8$
   $c =$ __56__
4. $40 \div 5 = d$
   $d =$ __8__

5. $7e = 49$
   $e =$ __7__
6. $50 \cdot f = 100$
   $f =$ __2__
7. $54 \div 9 = g$
   $g =$ __6__
8. $4h = 28$
   $h =$ __7__

9. $45 = 5k$
   $k =$ __9__
10. $6l = 36$
    $l =$ __6__
11. $9n = 0$
    $n =$ __0__
12. $72 = 8p$
    $p =$ __9__

Identify the kind of situation and write an equation. Then solve the problem.

13. Isabel earned 42 dollars mowing lawns last month. Her sister earned only $\frac{1}{6}$ as much. How much money did Isabel's sister earn?
    Situation: __comparison__
    Equation: $\frac{1}{6} \times 42 = s$
    $s = \$7$

14. Daniel packed black, tan, and blue shorts in his suitcase. He also packed 6 different T-shirts. How many different outfits will Daniel have?
    Situation: __combination__
    Equation: $3 \times 6 = n$
    $n = 18$ outfits

15. A large muffin tray holds 5 muffins across and 7 muffins down. How many muffins can the tray hold?
    Situation: __array__
    Equation: $5 \times 7 = m$
    $m = 35$ muffins

16. The Richardson family has a tent that covers 54 square feet of ground. It is 9 feet long. How wide is the tent?
    Situation: __area__
    Equation: $54 = 9 \times w$
    $w = 6$ feet wide

17. Farmer O'Malley bought new horseshoes for all of his horses today. He bought 36 horseshoes. How many horses does Farmer O'Malley have?
    Situation: __equal groups__
    Equation: $36 = 4 \times h$
    $h = 9$ horses

18. Mrs. Pinckett planted 8 rose bushes in her garden. She planted 3 times as many azalea bushes. How many azalea bushes did she plant?
    Situation: __comparison__
    Equation: $3 \times 8 = b$
    $b = 24$ azalea bushes

Practice multiplications and divisions with your Target.

UNIT 1 LESSON 3   Practice with Multiplication Problems **17**

Homework and Remembering page 17

1-3
Remembering **Goal:** Spiral Review

This Remembering activity would be appropriate anytime after today's lesson.

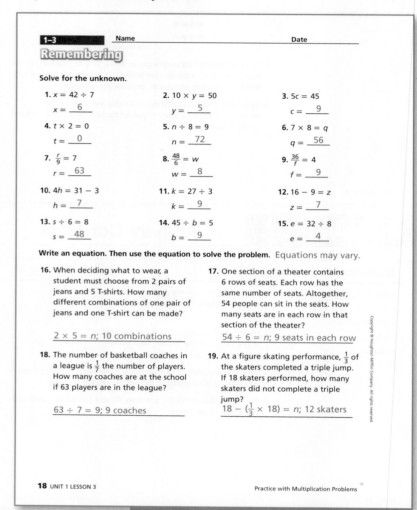

1-3 Name _____ Date _____
Remembering

Solve for the unknown.

1. $x = 42 \div 7$
   $x =$ __6__
2. $10 \times y = 50$
   $y =$ __5__
3. $5c = 45$
   $c =$ __9__

4. $t \times 2 = 0$
   $t =$ __0__
5. $n \div 8 = 9$
   $n =$ __72__
6. $7 \times 8 = q$
   $q =$ __56__

7. $\frac{r}{9} = 7$
   $r =$ __63__
8. $\frac{48}{6} = w$
   $w =$ __8__
9. $\frac{36}{f} = 4$
   $f =$ __9__

10. $4h = 31 - 3$
    $h =$ __7__
11. $k = 27 \div 3$
    $k =$ __9__
12. $16 - 9 = z$
    $z =$ __7__

13. $s \div 6 = 8$
    $s =$ __48__
14. $45 \div b = 5$
    $b =$ __9__
15. $e = 32 \div 8$
    $e =$ __4__

Write an equation. Then use the equation to solve the problem. Equations may vary.

16. When deciding what to wear, a student must choose from 2 pairs of jeans and 5 T-shirts. How many different combinations of one pair of jeans and one T-shirt can be made?
    $2 \times 5 = n$; 10 combinations

17. One section of a theater contains 6 rows of seats. Each row has the same number of seats. Altogether, 54 people can sit in the seats. How many seats are in each row in that section of the theater?
    $54 \div 6 = n$; 9 seats in each row

18. The number of basketball coaches in a league is $\frac{1}{7}$ the number of players. How many coaches are at the school if 63 players are in the league?
    $63 \div 7 = 9$; 9 coaches

19. At a figure skating performance, $\frac{1}{3}$ of the skaters completed a triple jump. If 18 skaters performed, how many skaters did not complete a triple jump?
    $18 - (\frac{1}{3} \times 18) = n$; 12 skaters

18 UNIT 1 LESSON 3   Practice with Multiplication Problems

Homework and Remembering page 18

Home or School Activity

**Art Connection**

Arrays and Patterns Many patterns for tiles, bricks, and paving stones are made by using different colors and shadings in arrays.

Have students find different designs that are made with arrays and use multiplication to find the number of tiles or bricks in those arrays. Then have students create their own designs on grid paper.

Write Word Problems

Lesson Objectives

- Write and share solutions to multiplication and division word problems.

- Consolidate single-digit multiplications and corresponding divisions in a variety of contexts.

Vocabulary

factor
product

The Day at a Glance

Today's Goals	Materials

1 Teaching the Lesson
A1: Share and solve word problems written for homework.
A2: Practice multiplication by using Scrambled Multiplication Tables.

2 Going Further
▸ Differentiated Instruction

3 Homework and Spiral Review

Lesson Activities
Student Activity Book pp. 35–36 or
  Student Hardcover Book pp. 35–36
  and Activity Workbook p. 22
Homework and Remembering
  pp. 19–20
Completed Homework p.17
  (optional)
Multiplication and Division Practice
  (TRB M62–M65) (optional)
Scrambled Multiplication Tables
  (TRB M66–M67) (optional)
Quick Quiz 1 (Assessment Guide)

Going Further
Activity Cards 1-4
Scissors
Number cubes
Timer or watch with
  second hand
Grid Paper (TRB M17)
Crayons or markers
Math Journals

123 Use Math Talk today!

Keeping Skills Sharp

Quick Practice ⏱ 5 MINUTES	Daily Routines

Goal: Practice basic multiplications with Difficult Finger Factors.

Difficult Finger Factors The class will practice with factors from the difficult section of the Multiplication Table today. Send 3 **Student Leaders** to the front. Two leaders will give factors from 6 to 10 by raising fingers on both hands and saying the number aloud. The third leader gives the hand signal, and the class responds with the product of the two factors. Repeat with other factors.

Homework Review Have students help each other resolve homework problems.

Strategy Problem Tyler, Kyra, and Emily finished the race in first, second, and third places. Tyler finished 1 second behind Emily. How many different ways could they have finished the race? 3 ways; Make an organized list and delete items based on the conditions; Tyler cannot be first and always has to be behind Emily. K, E, T; E, K, T; E, T, K

Teaching the Lesson

Word Problem Festival

 20 MINUTES

Goal: Share and solve word problems written for homework.

Materials: Student Activity Book or Hardcover Book p. 35, completed Homework p. 17 (optional)

✔ **NCTM Standards:**
Number and Operations
Problem Solving

 Class Management

Advance Preparation Try to discuss all four types of word problems in this activity. It will probably be necessary to prepare ahead of time by getting one problem of each type written on the board or an overhead transparency. Circulate around the room and try to enlist your volunteers ahead of time, looking at the word problems your students wrote, and identifying one of each type. When all four problems are written on the board or transparency, be sure to focus students' attention on one problem at a time.

English Language Learners

Provide support with writing word problems.

• **Beginning** Write an example of each kind of problem on the board. Have students change the numbers or items to write their own problems.

• **Intermediate and Advanced** Have students work in pairs. Circulate around the room providing support.

| 1-4 **Class Activity** | Name _____ | Date _____ |

▶ Share Solutions

Write 4 multiplication or division word problems for the class to solve. Write one problem for each of the 4 types shown below.

Equal Groups	Array or Area

Comparison	Combination

UNIT 1 LESSON 4   Write Word Problems **35**

Student Activity Book page 35

▶ Share Solutions WHOLE CLASS

Write Problems If you assigned the homework for Lesson 10, students should use those problems for this lesson. They can write their solutions in the corresponding spaces on page 35.

If you did not assign the homework for Lesson 10, give students time to write a problem of each type on page 35.

Math Talk Ask a student volunteer to share a word problem. Invite several students to use **solve and Discuss** to solve it at the board while the others work at their seats. Ask students to explain their solutions. All students should have written an appropriate equation and a labeled answer. After solving, have the students discuss what problem type they just solved (equal groups, array, area, comparison, or combinations).

Now ask someone to contribute a different kind of word problem, and repeat the same process. Eventually, examples of all four types should be included. (Include either an array or area; both types are not necessary.)

Ask for division problems so that there is a mix of multiplication and division. For some problems, either division or unknown multiplication equations (such as $7a = 35$) can be used. Try to elicit both methods.

Activity 2

Scrambled Tables

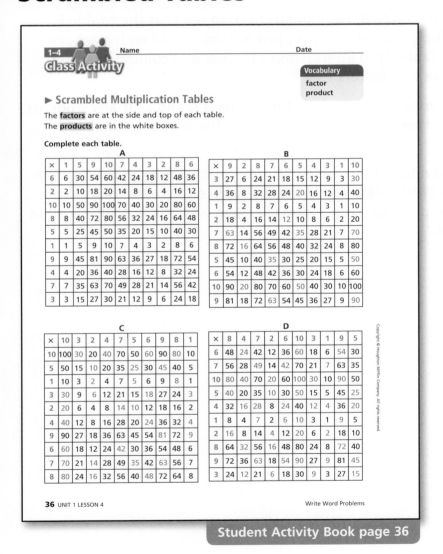

Student Activity Book page 36

 35 MINUTES

Goal: Practice multiplication by using Scrambled Multiplication Tables.

Materials: Student Activity Book p. 36 or Student Hardcover Book p. 36 and Activity Workbook p. 22, Multiplication and Division Practice (TRB M62–M65) (optional), Scrambled Multiplication Tables (TRB M66–M67) (optional)

 NCTM Standards:
Number and Operations
Reasoning and Proof

Differentiated Instruction

Extra Help If students have trouble getting started on Table A, suggest that students scan whole columns until they find a column they recognize. Students can search for easy columns if they want to, such as 2s, 5s, 9s, 10s. Once they have some column numbers written in, they can find rows by picking a product in one of those columns and putting the unknown factor in the row at the left. But let students discover all of these strategies and explain them to each other. Do not turn this into some kind of algorithm. Students enjoy the challenge of scrambled multiplication tables and solve them in different ways.

Activity continued ▶

① Teaching the Lesson (continued)

Activity 2

The Learning Classroom

Helping Community Continue to create a classroom where students are not competing, but desire to collaborate and help one another. Communicate often that your goal as a class is for everyone to understand the math you are studying. Tell students that this will require everyone to work together to help each other. Assign helping partners to students as needed.

 Quick Quiz

See Assessment Guide for Unit 1 Quick Quiz 1.

 Ongoing Assessment

Have students write a multiplication problem for:

► equal groups

► array

► area

► comparison

► combination

Differentiated Instruction

Special Needs If students need structured practice to achieve fluency in basic multiplication or division, you can use the practice sheets (TRB M62–65)

► Scrambled Multiplication Tables INDIVIDUALS

Have everyone look at Table A on page 36 of the Student Book. Review the terms *factor* and *product*. Explain that in a *scrambled* multiplication table, the rows and the columns have been moved around, but that each row and column still shows all the products for some factors. Ask the class to label each column and row with the correct factor. Allow the students to work alone for a minute. Then go over the missing factors.

Table B has a few missing products along with the missing factors. Allow students to work alone for a minute. Then ask the class to share some strategies for figuring out the factors. Many students will start by locating some of the easy multiplications, such as the 10s row and column and the 1s row and column. Make sure everyone has caught on to the basic process. Then allow the class to finish Table B.

As students finish Table B, have them check to see that their table is correct by multiplying some factors, just as they would with a regular Multiplication Table. (The intersection of a row and column gives the product of those two factors.)

Now have everyone work alone to finish Tables C and D. If any students are confused, either work with them or give them each a **Helping Partner**.

You can find additional Scrambled Multiplication Tables in the Teacher Resource Book (TRB M66). If students would like to create their own scrambled multiplication tables, provide them with Blank Multiplication Tables (TRB M67).

② Going Further

● Intervention   Activity Card 1-4

Mixed-Up Multiplication   Activity Card 1-4 ●

Work: In Pairs

Use:
• 2 Pairs of scissors

Decide:
Who will be Student 1 and who will be Student 2 for the first round.

1. Student 1: Choose a number from 2 to 10. Write the set of multiplications for your number.

2. Student 2: Choose a different number from 2 to 10. Write the set of multiplications for your number on the same sheet of paper as your partner.

3. **Work Together** Cut the paper into strips so that each multiplication is on a separate strip.

4. Student 1: Choose a strip and cover up either the product or one of the factors. Your partner names the missing number. Exchange roles and repeat the activity 10 times.

1	x	7	= 7
2	x	7	= 14
3	x	7	= 21
4	x	7	= 28
5	x	7	= 35
6	x	7	= 42

Unit 1, Lesson 4   Copyright © Houghton Mifflin Company

Activity Note Have students set aside those strips that are difficult for them to answer correctly. Have partners use those strips a second time to reinforce learning.

✎ Math Writing Prompt

Define Terms Write a sentence that includes the words *multiply*, *factor*, and *product*.

 **Software Support**

Warm-Up 14.22

▲ On Level   Activity Card 1-4

Fast Multiplication   Activity Card 1-4 ▲

Work: In Small Groups

Use:
• 2 Number cubes, labeled 1–6
• Timer or watch with a second hand

Decide:
Who will keep time and who will toss the number cubes.

1. Toss the number cubes and find the product of the digits. Then begin timing 20 seconds.

2. On your own, write as many multiplications with that product as possible in 20 seconds.

3. When the 20 seconds are over, exchange papers with another student to check your work.

4. Exchange roles and repeat the activity three more times.

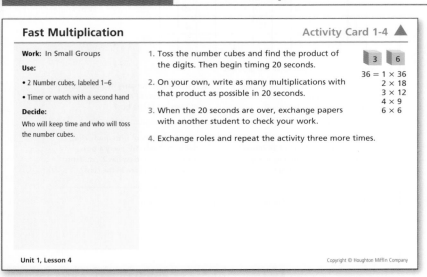

```
  [3]  [6]

36 = 1 × 36
     2 × 18
     3 × 12
     4 × 9
     6 × 6
```

Unit 1, Lesson 4   Copyright © Houghton Mifflin Company

Activity Note After the activity is completed, discuss strategies for finding as many products as possible for a given number. Use patterns such as doubling one factor and halving another.

✎ Math Writing Prompt

Word Problems Write an equal groups problem. Then solve the problem.

 Software Support

Ice Station Exploration: Arctic Algebra, Level C

■ Challenge   Activity Card 1-4

Multiplication Patterns   Activity Card 1-4 ■

Work: By Yourself

Use:
• Grid Paper (TRB M17)
• Crayons or markers

1. Make a pattern on grid paper. Color one square. Then use a different color for all of the surrounding squares.

2. Repeat the coloring process to fill the page, using a different color each time.

3. Write a multiplication to show the number of squares for each color.

4. Describe a pattern that represents your multiplications.

1 SQUARE ▩
8 SQUARES ▦
16 SQUARES ☐

The pattern after the first square is 8, 16, 24, 32, 40, 48...

1×8=8, 2×8=16, 3×8=24, 4×8=32...

Unit 1, Lesson 4   Copyright © Houghton Mifflin Company

Activity Note Students may repeat the activity using a row of two squares or some other configuration to start, if time permits.

✎ Math Writing Prompt

Use Patterns Describe how you could make your own scrambled multiplication table.

  Software Support

Course III: Module 1: Unit 2: Finding Factors

③ Homework and Spiral Review

 **Homework** **Goal:** Additional Practice

Use this Homework page to provide students with more practice with multiplication and division.

 **Remembering** **Goal:** Spiral Review

This Remembering activity would be appropriate anytime after today's lesson.

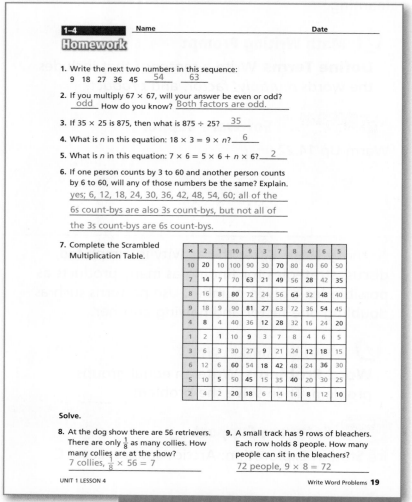

1-4 Name _____ Date _____

Homework

1. Write the next two numbers in this sequence:
   9 18 27 36 45 __54__ __63__

2. If you multiply 67 × 67, will your answer be even or odd?
   __odd__ How do you know? __Both factors are odd.__

3. If 35 × 25 is 875, then what is 875 ÷ 25? __35__

4. What is n in this equation: 18 × 3 = 9 × n? __6__

5. What is n in this equation: 7 × 6 = 5 × 6 + n × 6? __2__

6. If one person counts by 3 to 60 and another person counts by 6 to 60, will any of those numbers be the same? Explain.
   yes; 6, 12, 18, 24, 30, 36, 42, 48, 54, 60; all of the
   6s count-bys are also 3s count-bys, but not all of
   the 3s count-bys are 6s count-bys.

7. Complete the Scrambled Multiplication Table.

×	2	1	10	9	3	7	8	4	6	5
10	20	10	100	90	30	70	80	40	60	50
7	14	7	70	63	21	49	56	28	42	35
8	16	8	80	72	24	56	64	32	48	40
9	18	9	90	81	27	63	72	36	54	45
4	8	4	40	36	12	28	32	16	24	20
1	2	1	10	9	3	7	8	4	6	5
3	6	3	30	27	9	21	24	12	18	15
6	12	6	60	54	18	42	48	24	36	30
5	10	5	50	45	15	35	40	20	30	25
2	4	2	20	18	6	14	16	8	12	10

Solve.

8. At the dog show there are 56 retrievers. There are only $\frac{1}{8}$ as many collies. How many collies are at the show?
   7 collies, $\frac{1}{8}$ × 56 = 7

9. A small track has 9 rows of bleachers. Each row holds 8 people. How many people can sit in the bleachers?
   72 people, 9 × 8 = 72

UNIT 1 LESSON 4   Write Word Problems **19**

Homework and Remembering page 19

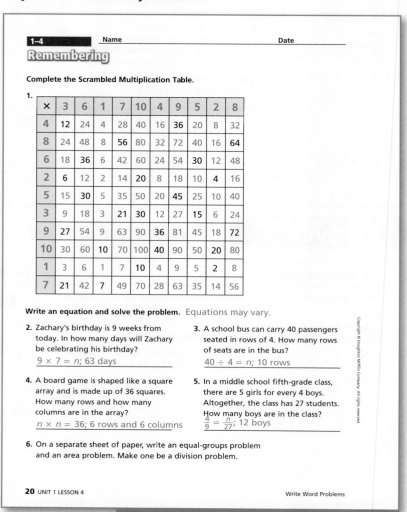

1-4 Name _____ Date _____

Remembering

Complete the Scrambled Multiplication Table.

1.

×	3	6	1	7	10	4	9	5	2	8
4	12	24	4	28	40	16	36	20	8	32
8	24	48	8	56	80	32	72	40	16	64
6	18	36	6	42	60	24	54	30	12	48
2	6	12	2	14	20	8	18	10	4	16
5	15	30	5	35	50	20	45	25	10	40
3	9	18	3	21	30	12	27	15	6	24
9	27	54	9	63	90	36	81	45	18	72
10	30	60	10	70	100	40	90	50	20	80
1	3	6	1	7	10	4	9	5	2	8
7	21	42	7	49	70	28	63	35	14	56

Write an equation and solve the problem. Equations may vary.

2. Zachary's birthday is 9 weeks from today. In how many days will Zachary be celebrating his birthday?
   9 × 7 = n; 63 days

3. A school bus can carry 40 passengers seated in rows of 4. How many rows of seats are in the bus?
   40 ÷ 4 = n; 10 rows

4. A board game is shaped like a square array and is made up of 36 squares. How many rows and how many columns are in the array?
   n × n = 36; 6 rows and 6 columns

5. In a middle school fifth-grade class, there are 5 girls for every 4 boys. Altogether, the class has 27 students. How many boys are in the class?
   $\frac{4}{9} = \frac{n}{27}$; 12 boys

6. On a separate sheet of paper, write an equal-groups problem and an area problem. Make one be a division problem.

20 UNIT 1 LESSON 4   Write Word Problems

Homework and Remembering page 20

Home or School Activity

 Math-to-Math Connection

Class Data Have students collect data about their class, such as who buys lunch or how students travel to school. Then have students choose a way to display the data. They might choose a table, graph, or other graphic representation. Next, tell students to write 2 conclusions about the data. Challenge them to use multiplication or division in their comparisons.

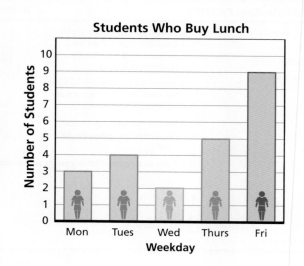

Functions

Lesson Objectives

● **Describe a function, and express it as an equation.**

● **Connect functions to real-world situations.**

Vocabulary

function
variable

The Day at a Glance

Today's Goals	Materials	
1 **Teaching the Lesson** **A1:** Identify and apply the rule of an input-output table. **A2:** Write an equation to express a function that models a real-world situation. **2** **Going Further** ▶ Differentiated Instruction **3** **Homework and Spiral Review**	**Lesson Activities** Student Activity Book pp. 37–38 or Student Hardcover Book pp. 37–38 and Activity Workbook pp. 23–24 Homework and Remembering pp. 21–22	**Going Further** Activity Cards 1-5 Math Journals

Use **Math Talk** *today!*

Keeping Skills Sharp

Quick Practice ⏱ 5 MINUTES	**Daily Routines**
Goal: Practice basic multiplication. **Materials:** pointer, Class Multiplication Table Poster **Multiplication in Motion** Tell students that they will need to remember their numbers. The students quickly count off from 2 to 10, repeating the sequence until every student in the class has a number. Then the **Student Leader** uses a pointer to point to a product on the Class Multiplication Table Poster. Ask Student Leaders to select difficult products. Every student who has a number that is a factor of this product stands. Then, going in order, the standing students announce the factors. At the end, the Student Leader names the factor pairs. (Many numbers, such as 24, will have more than 2 possible factors.) Repeat with other products.	**Homework Review** If students give incorrect answers, have them explain their work. This will determine whether the error is conceptual or procedural. **Strategy Problem** Charlie cut a whole piece of pipe into halves. Then he cut each half into thirds. He used four of the thirds for a project that needed 36 cm of pipe. What was the original length of the pipe? 54 cm; 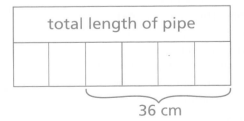 $36 \div 4 = 9; 9 \times 6 = 54$

Teaching the Lesson

Function Tables

 25 MINUTES

Goal: Identify and apply the rule of an input-output table.

Materials: Student Activity Book p. 37 or Student Hardcover Book p. 37 and Activity Workbook p. 23

✔ **NCTM Standards:**
Algebra
Connections
Representation

Teaching Note

Language and Vocabulary Review with the students the meaning of the word *function*. A *function* is a relationship between paired numbers. It can be described by a rule, an equation, or a table of values. Each input value can have only one output value. In this lesson, each function rule consists of an operation and a number.

Differentiated Instruction

Extra Help After working through the Student Book pages, you may offer extra help to students who are having difficulty. Have five students go to the board and ask each to draw one of the five input-output tables from page 37, leaving one column blank (have some be the input column and some be the output column). Then have students close their books and take turns telling the answer while you fill in the tables. Finally, repeat for the five horizontal function tables on page 38, alternating leaving the top or bottom row blank.

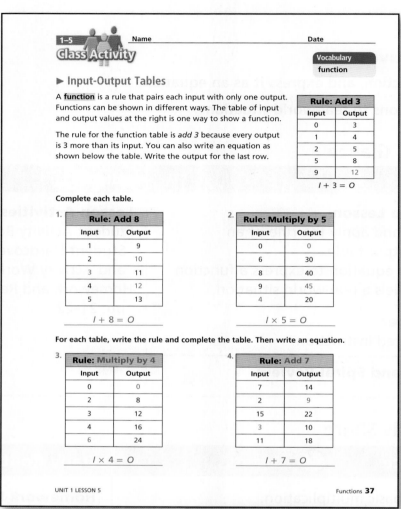

Student Activity Book page 37

▶ Input-Output Tables [WHOLE CLASS]

Identify the Rule Read aloud the introduction at the top of Student Book page 37 or read it together. Invite students to look at the first input-output table and consider the following:

● Which numbers are shown as inputs for this function? 0, 1, 2, 5, 9

● For the first input-output pair, the input is 0. Why is the output 3? The rule is to add 3.

● What output is missing in the last row of the table? 12 Write the output.

● Is $0 = I + 3$ also a rule for this function? Yes an equation can describe a rule for a function.

Have the students complete exercises 1–4. To complete exercises 3 and 4, the students must first identify the rule, then complete the table and write an equation. Use **Solve and Discuss** for exercises 3 and 4.

Activity 2

Real-World Applications

1–5 Class Activity

Name ______________________ Date ____________

Vocabulary
variable

▶ Functions and Equations

Functions can describe many situations in your everyday life. The table below shows late fees for an overdue library book.

A function table will often contain variables. A **variable** is a letter that is used to represent an unknown number.

We can represent the input (number of days late) by the variable *d* and the late fee by the variable *f*.

5. Write the rule in words and as an equation.

Rule in Words	Late fee equals days times ten cents.				
Equation	$f = 10d$				
Number of Days Late (d)	1	2	3	4	5
Late Fee (f)	10¢	20¢	30¢	40¢	50¢

For each function table, write the rule in words and as an equation. Then complete the table.

6.

Rule in Words	Number of wheels equals bicycles times two.				
Equation	$w = 2b$				
Bicycles (b)	1	2	3	4	5
Wheels (w)	2	4	6	8	10

7.

Rule in Words	Number of wheels equals tricycles times three.				
Equation	$w = 3t$				
Tricycles (t)	1	2	3	4	5
Wheels (w)	3	6	9	12	15

8.

Rule in Words	Cost in dollars equals 7 times number of tickets.				
Equation	$d = 7t$				
Tickets (t)	1	2	3	4	5
Cost in dollars (d)	7	14	21	28	35

9.

Rule in Words	One inch of rain equals 10 inches of snow.				
Equation	$s = 10r$				
Inches of rain (r)	0	1	2	3	4
Inches of snow (s)	0	10	20	30	40

38 UNIT 1 LESSON 5 Functions

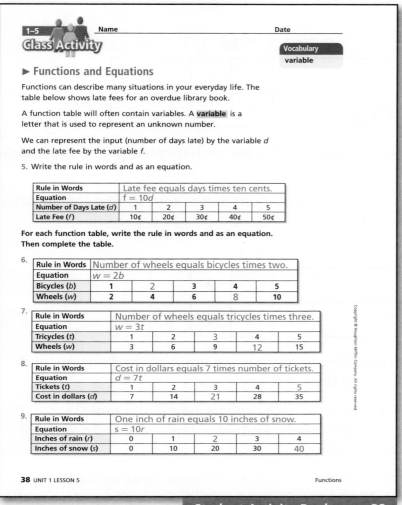

Student Activity Book page 38

▶ Functions and Equations INDIVIDUALS

On Student Book page 38, read exercise 5 aloud or read it together. Have students look at the table that shows number of days late and late fees. Invite students to compare each pair of numbers in the table and then decide the rule that describes their relationship. These function tables are a way for students to practice basic multiplication and division. Some students may realize that they can use count-bys to complete the tables.

After a rule has been agreed upon, ask the students to decide if the rule is true for *each* pair of numbers in the table. Then have students continue by writing the rule in words.

Ask volunteers to tell what equation can be written for this rule. $10d = f$ or $f = 10d$ Be sure to elicit both equations. Explain that often the output variable is written on the left side of the equation.

Activity continued ▶

25 MINUTES

Goal: Write an equation to express a function that models a real-world situation.

Materials: Student Activity Book p. 38 or Student Hardcover Book p. 38 and Activity Workbook p. 24

NCTM Standards:
Algebra
Problem Solving
Connections
Representation

Math Talk in Action

Give students the opportunity to share their descriptions of the rule. Possible descriptions might include:

James: The late fee is 10 cents each day.

Dani: You multiply the days by 10 to get the number of cents.

Tyler: The late fee is 10 times the day number.

English Language Learners

Make sure students understand *variable*. Model problem 5 on the board. Say: **We use letters to represent the input and output in a function because there are many different numbers. Each letter is a *variable*.**

Activity 2

The Learning Classroom

Math Talk The **Solve and Discuss** structure of conversation is used throughout the *Math Expressions* program. The teacher selects four or five students to go to the board and solve a problem, using any method they choose. The other students work on the same problem at their desks. Then the teacher asks the students at the board to explain their methods. Students at their desks are encouraged to ask questions and to assist each other in understanding the problem. Thus, students actually solve, explain, question, and justify. Usually ask only two or three students to explain because classes do not like to sit through more explanations, and time is better spent on the next issue.

Ongoing Assessment

Have students:

► create a table to represent the relationship between dogs and paws.

► write an equation for the function.

► Functions and Equations WHOLE CLASS

If students have difficulty writing equations, you may want to take some time for this exercise. Write the following equation and table on the board.

$$output = input + 1$$

input	1	2	3	4	5
output	2	3	4	5	6

● Is the rule *output = input + 1* true for each number pair in the table?
yes

Then erase letters from the words *input* and *output* so that the equation and table look like this:

$$o = i + 1$$

i	1	2	3	4	5
o	2	3	4	5	6

Point out that the variable i represents the input of the function, and the variable o represents the output.

● Is the rule $o = i + 1$ true for each number pair in the table? yes
Emphasize that both equations (output = input + 1 and $o = i + 1$) represent the same function.

Now have students study the bicycles-and-wheels function table on Student Book page 38 and then write a rule in words and as an equation in the space provided (exercise 6). They should then complete exercise 7, working cooperatively if necessary, to recognize that $w = 3 \times t$ can be written in a simpler way as $w = 3t$.

Math Talk Use **Solve and Discuss** for exercises 8 and 9. You might choose to have **Student Pairs** or **Small Groups** work together.

You may help students to see that function tables can be written horizontally or vertically by having them rewrite one or more of the tables in this lesson in the other form. Elicit that *input-output table* is another name for a function table.

②Going Further

Differentiated Instruction

Intervention — Activity Card 1-5

Functions
Activity Card 1-5

Work: In Pairs

Decide:
Who will be Student 1 and who will be Student 2 for the first round.

1. Student 1: Choose a number for the input. Choose a rule from the list below.

> Add 5
> Subtract 1
> Multiply by 2

2. Student 2: Solve for the output, using the number and the rule your partner has chosen.

3. Student 1: Check your partner's work.

4. Change roles and repeat the activity 5 more times.

Unit 1, Lesson 5
Copyright © Houghton Mifflin Company

Activity Note Reinforce understanding by having students write expressions such as Input + 5 = Output, Input − 1 = Output, and Input × 2 = Output.

 Math Writing Prompt

Define Terms Explain what *input* and *output* mean. Use an example.

 **Software Support**

Warm-Up 30.04

On Level — Activity Card 1-5

Generate a Pattern
Activity Card 1-5

Work: In Pairs

2.

$f = 3y$	
y	f
1	3
2	6
3	9
4	12
5	15

1. On your own, write a multiplication rule for the relationship below. Use y to represent the number of yards. Use f to represent the number of feet.

> 1 yard = 3 feet

2. **Work Together** Create and complete a function table for the relationship, using the rule that you wrote. Then describe the relationship using words. The values representing f are 3s count-bys. So as y increases by 1, f increases by 3.

3. **Look Back** How could you use the given relationship between yards and feet to check the rule that you wrote and the function table that you made? Substituting the number 3 for f in the rule should give 1 as the value for y.

Unit 1, Lesson 5
Copyright © Houghton Mifflin Company

Activity Note Ask students to write the rule without the operation symbols × or •. Some students may incorrectly write the rule as y = 3f. Have them substitute 3 for f in their rule to check their work before making the function table.

 Math Writing Prompt

Reasoning Explain how a multiplication rule can give count-bys as outputs.

 Software Support

Ice Station Exploration: Arctic Algebra, Level K

Challenge — Activity Card 1-5

Growth Over Time
Activity Card 1-5

Work: In Pairs

1.

Start Height = 60 in.		
Day Number	Daily Growth	Total Height
1	60 + 8	68
2	68 + 8	76
3	76 + 8	84
4	84 + 8	92
5	92 + 8	100
6	100 + 8	108
7	108 + 8	116
8	116 + 8	124

1. Bamboo plants can grow very fast under certain conditions. Use the information below to make a table and solve the problem. 8 days

> Growth rate: 8 inches per day
> Beginning height: 5 feet
> Target height: 10 feet
>
> How many days will it take the plant to reach its target height?

2. **Work Together** Write an equation that you can use to find the height of the bamboo plant in inches for any day.
8 in. × day number + 60 = height in inches on a given day

Unit 1, Lesson 5
Copyright © Houghton Mifflin Company

Activity Note If students are having difficulty writing the equation, ask them to first write an expression for the total amount of growth after any given day. 8 in. × day number

 Math Writing Prompt

Problem Solving Explain how to find how many days it will take a bamboo plant to reach a height of 45 feet, if it grows 8 inches each day.

 DESTINATION Math® **Software Support**

Course III: Module 6: Unit 1: Displaying and Analyzing Data

Functions **77**

③ Homework and Spiral Review

1–5
Homework   **Goal:** Additional Practice

Use this Homework page to provide students with more practice with functions.

1–5
Remembering   **Goal:** Spiral Review

This Remembering activity would be appropriate anytime after today's lesson.

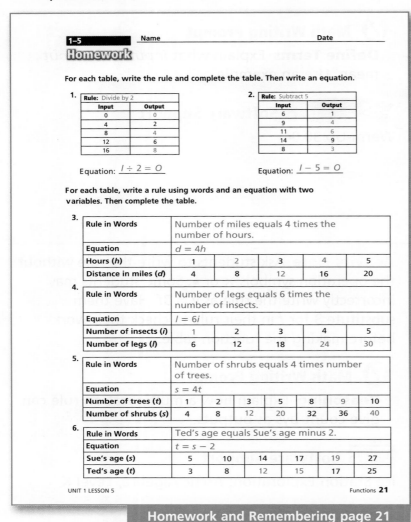

1–5   Name _____ Date _____
Homework

For each table, write the rule and complete the table. Then write an equation.

1. **Rule:** Divide by 2

Input	Output
0	0
4	2
8	4
12	6
16	8

Equation: $I \div 2 = O$

2. **Rule:** Subtract 5

Input	Output
6	1
9	4
11	6
14	9
8	3

Equation: $I - 5 = O$

For each table, write a rule using words and an equation with two variables. Then complete the table.

3.

Rule in Words	Number of miles equals 4 times the number of hours.				
Equation	$d = 4h$				
Hours (h)	1	2	3	4	5
Distance in miles (d)	4	8	12	16	20

4.

Rule in Words	Number of legs equals 6 times the number of insects.				
Equation	$l = 6i$				
Number of insects (i)	1	2	3	4	5
Number of legs (l)	6	12	18	24	30

5.

Rule in Words	Number of shrubs equals 4 times number of trees.						
Equation	$s = 4t$						
Number of trees (t)	1	2	3	5	8	9	10
Number of shrubs (s)	4	8	12	20	32	36	40

6.

Rule in Words	Ted's age equals Sue's age minus 2.					
Equation	$t = s - 2$					
Sue's age (s)	5	10	14	17	19	27
Ted's age (t)	3	8	12	15	17	25

UNIT 1 LESSON 5   Functions **21**

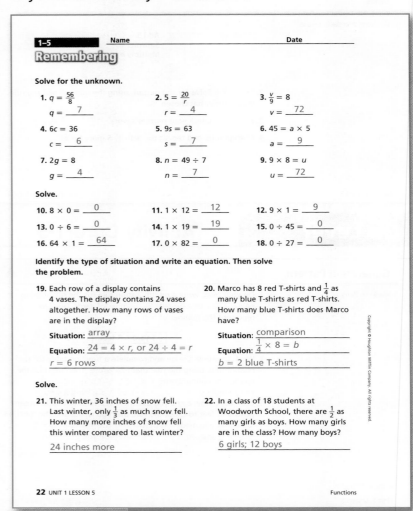

1–5   Name _____ Date _____
Remembering

Solve for the unknown.

1. $q = \frac{56}{8}$ $q = \underline{7}$
2. $5 = \frac{20}{r}$ $r = \underline{4}$
3. $\frac{v}{9} = 8$ $v = \underline{72}$
4. $6c = 36$ $c = \underline{6}$
5. $9s = 63$ $s = \underline{7}$
6. $45 = a \times 5$ $a = \underline{9}$
7. $2g = 8$ $g = \underline{4}$
8. $n = 49 \div 7$ $n = \underline{7}$
9. $9 \times 8 = u$ $u = \underline{72}$

Solve.

10. $8 \times 0 = \underline{0}$
11. $1 \times 12 = \underline{12}$
12. $9 \times 1 = \underline{9}$
13. $0 \div 6 = \underline{0}$
14. $1 \times 19 = \underline{19}$
15. $0 \div 45 = \underline{0}$
16. $64 \times 1 = \underline{64}$
17. $0 \times 82 = \underline{0}$
18. $0 \div 27 = \underline{0}$

Identify the type of situation and write an equation. Then solve the problem.

19. Each row of a display contains 4 vases. The display contains 24 vases altogether. How many rows of vases are in the display?

Situation: array

Equation: $24 = 4 \times r$, or $24 \div 4 = r$

$r = 6$ rows

20. Marco has 8 red T-shirts and $\frac{1}{4}$ as many blue T-shirts as red T-shirts. How many blue T-shirts does Marco have?

Situation: comparison

Equation: $\frac{1}{4} \times 8 = b$

$b = 2$ blue T-shirts

Solve.

21. This winter, 36 inches of snow fell. Last winter, only $\frac{1}{3}$ as much snow fell. How many more inches of snow fell this winter compared to last winter?

24 inches more

22. In a class of 18 students at Woodworth School, there are $\frac{1}{2}$ as many girls as boys. How many girls are in the class? How many boys?

6 girls; 12 boys

22 UNIT 1 LESSON 5   Functions

Homework and Remembering page 21   Homework and Remembering page 22

Home or School Activity

Language Arts Connection

The Math Machine Imagine a math machine that produces an output number for every number that is input.

If a machine uses the rule $4 + x$, then 4 is added to each input number to produce an output number. For example, if the input number is 5, then the output number is $4 + 5$, or 9.

Write a story about a math machine, including what it looks like and how it works.

UNIT 1 · LESSON 6

Equations With Parentheses

REAL WORLD Problem Solving

Lesson Objectives

- Understand everyday applications of multiplication and division.
- Generate and solve algebraic equations that involve grouping with parentheses.

Vocabulary

equation
parentheses

The Day at a Glance

Today's Goals	Materials

1 Teaching the Lesson
A1: Use parentheses to group numbers in an equation.
A2: Solve word problems with mixed operations by writing the corresponding equations.
2 Going Further
▶ Differentiated Instruction
3 Homework and Spiral Review
	Lesson Activities
	Student Activity Book pp. 39–40 or
	  Student Hardcover Book pp. 39–40
	Homework and Remembering
	  pp. 23–24
	
	Going Further
	Activity Cards 1-6
	Large sheets of paper
	Markers
	Math Journals

123 Use Math Talk today!

Keeping Skills Sharp

Quick Practice ⏱ 5 MINUTES	Daily Routines

Goal: Practice basic multiplication.
 	
Materials: pointer, Class Multiplication Table Poster
 	
Multiplication in Motion The students quickly count off from 2 to 10, repeating the sequence until every student in the class has a number. Then the **Student Leader** uses a pointer to point to a product on the Class Multiplication Table Poster in the medium or difficult sections of the table. Every student who has a number that is a factor of this product stands. Then, going in order, the standing students announce the factors. At the end, the Student Leader names the factor pairs. Repeat with the other products.
	Homework Review Ask students if they had difficulty with any part of the homework. Plan to set aside some time to work with students needing extra help.
	
	Mental Math Find the rule for each set of input and output pairs, (input, output).
	
	1. (49, 7), (21, 3), (35, 5), (56, 8)
	   divide by 7
	
	2. (6, 17), (4, 11), (9, 26), (2, 5)
	   multiply by 3 and subtract 1

Teaching the Lesson

Activity 1

Introduce Parentheses

 20 MINUTES

Goal: Use parentheses to group numbers in an equation.

Materials: Student Activity Book or Hardcover Book p. 39

✔ **NCTM Standards:**
Algebra
Communication

The Learning Classroom

Math Talk Aspire to make your classroom a place where all students listen to understand one another. Explain to students that this is different from just being quiet when someone else is talking. This involves thinking about what a person is saying so that you could explain it yourself or help them explain it more clearly. Also, students need to listen so that they can ask a question or help the explainer. Listening can also help them learn more about a concept.

English Language Learners

Write $(6 - 5) + (7 \times 2)$, *operation*, and *parentheses* on the board. Say: **Subtraction, addition, and multiplication are operations.**

- **Beginning** Point and say: **These are parentheses.** Have students repeat.
- **Intermediate** Point and ask: **How many operations are shown?** 3 **Is the subtraction inside or outside the parentheses?** inside
- **Advanced** Ask: **Which operation is not inside the parentheses?** addition

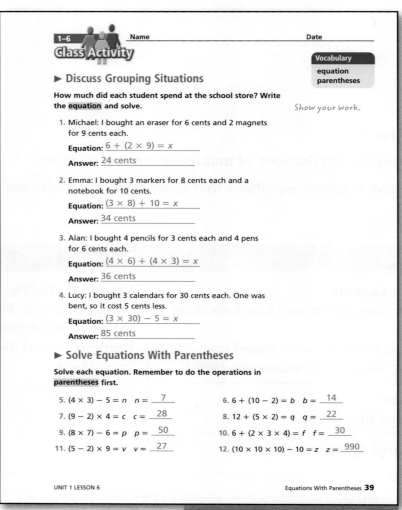

1–6
Class Activity

Name _____ Date _____

Vocabulary
equation
parentheses

► **Discuss Grouping Situations**

How much did each student spend at the school store? Write the **equation** and solve.   *Show your work.*

1. Michael: I bought an eraser for 6 cents and 2 magnets for 9 cents each.
   Equation: $6 + (2 \times 9) = x$
   Answer: 24 cents

2. Emma: I bought 3 markers for 8 cents each and a notebook for 10 cents.
   Equation: $(3 \times 8) + 10 = x$
   Answer: 34 cents

3. Alan: I bought 4 pencils for 3 cents each and 4 pens for 6 cents each.
   Equation: $(4 \times 6) + (4 \times 3) = x$
   Answer: 36 cents

4. Lucy: I bought 3 calendars for 30 cents each. One was bent, so it cost 5 cents less.
   Equation: $(3 \times 30) - 5 = x$
   Answer: 85 cents

► **Solve Equations With Parentheses**

Solve each equation. Remember to do the operations in **parentheses** first.

5. $(4 \times 3) - 5 = n$ n = 7
6. $6 + (10 - 2) = b$ b = 14
7. $(9 - 2) \times 4 = c$ c = 28
8. $12 + (5 \times 2) = q$ q = 22
9. $(8 \times 7) - 6 = p$ p = 50
10. $6 + (2 \times 3 \times 4) = f$ f = 30
11. $(5 - 2) \times 9 = v$ v = 27
12. $(10 \times 10 \times 10) - 10 = z$ z = 990

UNIT 1 LESSON 6   Equations With Parentheses **39**

Student Activity Book page 39

► Discuss Grouping Situations

WHOLE CLASS   Math Talk

For problem 1, students write an equation that corresponds with this situation. Invite one or two students to work at the board. They will likely write two equations because they have not seen complex long equations before (for example, $1 \times 6 = 6$, $2 \times 9 = 18$, $6 + 18 = 24$). A few might write $6 + 2 \times 9 = x$. Introduce writing the whole problem in one equation if no student solves it that way. Then raise the issue of how to solve the equation $6 + 2 \times 9 = x$: add first or multiply first.

Let students solve the equation and compare results. There are different answers, depending on which operation they do first. (If they add $6 + 2 = 8$ and then multiply by 9, they will get 72. If they multiply $2 \times 9 = 18$ and add that to 6, they will get 24.) Which one is right? If they read the problem again, they will see that the answer is 24 cents.

Use Parentheses Explain that parentheses can be used to group the numbers in an equation. The parentheses tell us which operations to do first. They are removed after the operation inside them is performed. The equation is written and solved this way:

$$6 + (2 \times 9) = c$$
$$6 + 18 = 24$$

Repeat this procedure for Emma's purchases. Ask students to write an equation that uses parentheses for grouping. Again, invite several students to work at the board. During the discussion be sure to explain that the second equation is the simplified version.

$$(3 \times 8) + 10 = c$$
$$24 + 10 = 34 \text{ cents}$$

Then have students write equations for Alan's and Lucy's purchases and solve them. Note that the equation for Alan's purchases requires two sets of parentheses and that Lucy's situation involves subtraction rather than addition.

Alan: $(4 \times 3) + (4 \times 6) = c$
$12 + 24 = 36$ cents

Lucy: $(3 \times 30) - 5 = c$
$90 - 5 = 85$ cents

▶ Solve Equations With Parentheses WHOLE CLASS

Most of the equations in exercises 5–12 can be solved quickly. Ask students to give the simplified version of the equation orally, and then you can write it on the board. After that, students may give the answer orally. For example, in the first problem, students would call out "12 minus 5 equals *n*." After you write that simplified equation on the board, students would call out "*n* = 7." This procedure reinforces the two-step process: simplifying and then solving.

▶ Using the = and ≠ Signs

Write these number sentences on the board.

$3 + 2 = 5$ $5 = 3 + 2$ $3 + 1 \neq 5$ $5 \neq 3 + 1$

Explain that an equals sign shows that two quantities have the same value. An "is not equal to" sign shows that two quantities do not have the same value. A statement using ≠ is called an *inequality*. While students work at their desks, have volunteers come to the board and write four equalities, using the equals sign. Then ask another student to write four inequalities, using the ≠ sign. Have students read the statements on the board.

Teaching Note

Math Background It may be helpful to understand the difference between an expression and an equation. An expression can be a number, a variable or an unknown represented by a letter, or any combination of numbers, variables, operation signs, and grouping symbols. An equation is a number sentence with an equals sign, showing that two expressions are equal. Knowing how to use parentheses as a grouping symbol is a key skill in algebra, so it is important that your students get a good start on this topic.

Teaching Note

Language and Vocabulary The symbols ≠, <, and > are used to write inequalities.

$3 \neq 2$

$3 > 2$

$2 < 3$

Activity 2

Multistep Word Problems

 25 MINUTES

Goal: Solve word problems with mixed operations by writing the corresponding equations.

Materials: Student Activity Book or Hardcover Book p. 40

 NCTM Standards:
Problem Solving
Algebra

 Ongoing Assessment

Check student understanding of the use of parentheses to set up problems by observing students at work on the problems on Student Book page 40. Be sure that they choose the right numbers to group as they analyze the problems.

Teaching Note

These problems were chosen to be relatively easy to show with equations so that students could practice and discuss using parentheses in equations. In later units students will encounter 2-step problems that are too difficult to represent in a single equation and do not need such a representation for students to solve them. So do not always require an equation because that may be more difficult than just solving the problem.

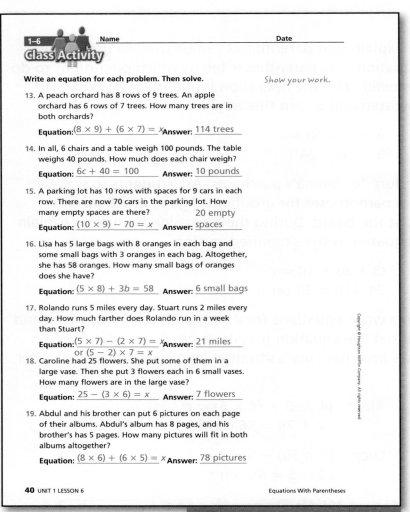

Student Activity Book page 40

Content of Student Activity Book page 40:

1–6 **Class Activity**

Name _____ Date _____

Write an equation for each problem. Then solve. *Show your work.*

13. A peach orchard has 8 rows of 9 trees. An apple orchard has 6 rows of 7 trees. How many trees are in both orchards?
    Equation: $(8 \times 9) + (6 \times 7) = x$ Answer: 114 trees

14. In all, 6 chairs and a table weigh 100 pounds. The table weighs 40 pounds. How much does each chair weigh?
    Equation: $6c + 40 = 100$ Answer: 10 pounds

15. A parking lot has 10 rows with spaces for 9 cars in each row. There are now 70 cars in the parking lot. How many empty spaces are there?
    Equation: $(10 \times 9) - 70 = x$ Answer: 20 empty spaces

16. Lisa has 5 large bags with 8 oranges in each bag and some small bags with 3 oranges in each bag. Altogether, she has 58 oranges. How many small bags of oranges does she have?
    Equation: $(5 \times 8) + 3b = 58$ Answer: 6 small bags

17. Rolando runs 5 miles every day. Stuart runs 2 miles every day. How much farther does Rolando run in a week than Stuart?
    Equation: $(5 \times 7) - (2 \times 7) = x$ or $(5 - 2) \times 7 = x$ Answer: 21 miles

18. Caroline had 25 flowers. She put some of them in a large vase. Then she put 3 flowers each in 6 small vases. How many flowers are in the large vase?
    Equation: $25 - (3 \times 6) = x$ Answer: 7 flowers

19. Abdul and his brother can put 6 pictures on each page of their albums. Abdul's album has 8 pages, and his brother's has 5 pages. How many pictures will fit in both albums altogether?
    Equation: $(8 \times 6) + (6 \times 5) = x$ Answer: 78 pictures

40 UNIT 1 LESSON 6   Equations With Parentheses

▶ Use Parentheses to Solve Complex Word Problems [INDIVIDUALS]

Ask students to write an equation for each word problem before solving it on Student Book page 40. In most cases the equation will need to be simplified before it can be solved. Learning how to write these equations is just as important as finding the answer.

Be sure students write an algebraic equation with a letter for the unknown quantity, not just an expression. Afterwards, discuss each problem. There may be more than one way to approach some problems. Ask volunteers to show and explain their work.

Intervention
Activity Card 1-6

Two Ways With Parentheses Activity Card 1-6

Work: In Pairs

1. $(4 + 3) \times 2 = 14$;
   $4 + (3 \times 2) = 10$;
   $(10 - 3) \times 2 = 14$;
   $10 - (3 \times 2) = 4$;
   $(6 \times 5) - 4 = 26$;
   $6 \times (5 - 4) = 6$;
   $(8 \times 4) - 3 = 29$;
   $8 \times (4 - 3) = 8$

1. **Work Together** Evaluate each pair of expressions.

$(4 + 3) \times 2$	$(10 - 3) \times 2$
$4 + (3 \times 2)$	$10 - (3 \times 2)$
$(6 \times 5) - 4$	$(8 \times 4) - 3$
$6 \times (5 - 4)$	$8 \times (4 - 3)$

2. **Compare** Which pairs have the same value for both expressions and which do not? All pairs have a different value for each of the two expressions.

3. **Math Talk** How does using parentheses affect the order in which you perform the operations of addition, subtraction, multiplication, and division? Operations inside parentheses are always done first.

Unit 1, Lesson 6 Copyright © Houghton Mifflin Company

Activity Note Reinforce the concept of working within parentheses first before students begin the activity. Encourage students to rewrite each expression to show the value within the parentheses.

✎ Math Writing Prompt

Explain Your Thinking Write an equation for this situation: Add 3 to the product of 4 and 5. Explain why you wrote it as you did.

Soar to Success Math ★ **Software Support**

Warm-Up 14.28

On Level
Activity Card 1-6

Shopping Spree Activity Card 1-6 ▲

Work: In Small Groups

Use:
• Large sheets of paper
• Markers

1. Each member of your group must spend exactly $35 at the Farmer's Market. Use the chart to choose what you will buy. Each shopping list must include at least 2 different items.

Farmers' Market	
Bunch of Carrots	$2
Bag of Spinach	$3
Basket of Apples	$4
Watermelon	$5
Basket of Pears	$6
Bunch of Radishes	$1
Pound of Potatoes	$2
Pound of Tomatoes	$4
Quart of Raspberries	$7

2. **On Your Own** Write an equation to show the total cost of your purchases.

3. **Compare** How did your group spend exactly $35 at the market by choosing 2 items? 3 items? More than 3 items?

Unit 1, Lesson 6 Copyright © Houghton Mifflin Company

Activity Note If time permits, have groups compare their equations and lists with other groups to see a variety of equations that are possible with 2, 3, or more than 3 items whose total cost is $35.

✎ Math Writing Prompt

Reasoning Skills Tell why it is important to use parentheses when you solve problems that have more than one step. Give an example to explain.

MegaMath Grades K-6 **Software Support**

Ice Station Exploration: Arctic Algebra, Level H

Challenge
Activity Card 1-6

Is the Answer the Same? Activity Card 1-6 ■

Work: By Yourself

Possible answer:

$a = 10 + 4 \times 5 - 3 \times 6$
$a = 12$

$a = (10 + 4) \times 5 - 3 \times 6$
$a = 52$

$a = 10 + (4 \times 5) - 3 \times 6$
$a = 12$

$a = 10 + 4 \times (5 - 3) \times 6$
$a = 58$

$a = 10 + 4 \times 5 - (3 \times 6)$
$a = 12$

1. Write an equation with five numbers and four operations without using parentheses. For example, $a = 10 + 4 \times 5 - 3 \times 6$.

2. Solve the equation to find the value of a, using the order of operation rules.

3. Rewrite the equation four times, using parentheses in a different place each time.

4. **Explain** Are any of your solutions the same? Why might some solutions be the same and others be different? Operations inside parentheses are done first. The number that an equation simplifies to depends on the order in which the operations are performed.

Unit 1, Lesson 6 Copyright © Houghton Mifflin Company

Activity Note Some students may use parentheses around more than one operation at a time. In that case, they will need to use order of operations within the parentheses as well as in the equation as a whole.

✎ Math Writing Prompt

The Same Answer Think of an equation with three numbers that would have the same answer no matter where you place parentheses. Explain.

✦ DESTINATION Math® **Software Support**

Course III: Module 2: Unit 3: Two-digit Multipliers

③ Homework and Spiral Review

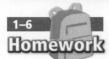

1–6
Homework **Goal:** Additional Practice

You can quickly review this homework to assess how well the class understands the use of parentheses.

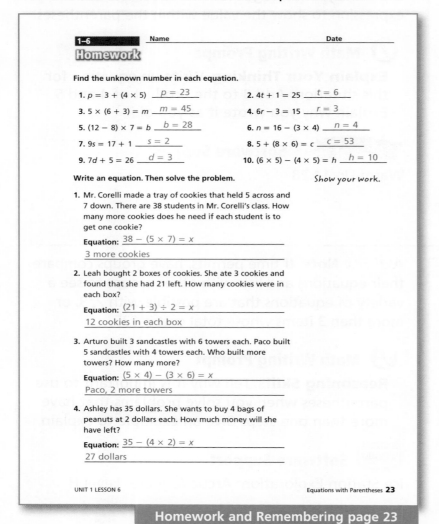

1–6 Name _____ Date _____
Homework

Find the unknown number in each equation.

1. $p = 3 + (4 \times 5)$ ___ $p = 23$
2. $4t + 1 = 25$ ___ $t = 6$
3. $5 \times (6 + 3) = m$ ___ $m = 45$
4. $6r - 3 = 15$ ___ $r = 3$
5. $(12 - 8) \times 7 = b$ ___ $b = 28$
6. $n = 16 - (3 \times 4)$ ___ $n = 4$
7. $9s = 17 + 1$ ___ $s = 2$
8. $5 + (8 \times 6) = c$ ___ $c = 53$
9. $7d + 5 = 26$ ___ $d = 3$
10. $(6 \times 5) - (4 \times 5) = h$ ___ $h = 10$

Write an equation. Then solve the problem. *Show your work.*

1. Mr. Corelli made a tray of cookies that held 5 across and 7 down. There are 38 students in Mr. Corelli's class. How many more cookies does he need if each student is to get one cookie?

   Equation: $38 - (5 \times 7) = x$
   3 more cookies

2. Leah bought 2 boxes of cookies. She ate 3 cookies and found that she had 21 left. How many cookies were in each box?

   Equation: $(21 + 3) \div 2 = x$
   12 cookies in each box

3. Arturo built 3 sandcastles with 6 towers each. Paco built 5 sandcastles with 4 towers each. Who built more towers? How many more?

   Equation: $(5 \times 4) - (3 \times 6) = x$
   Paco, 2 more towers

4. Ashley has 35 dollars. She wants to buy 4 bags of peanuts at 2 dollars each. How much money will she have left?

   Equation: $35 - (4 \times 2) = x$
   27 dollars

UNIT 1 LESSON 6   Equations with Parentheses **23**

Homework and Remembering page 23

1–6
Remembering **Goal:** Spiral Review

This Remembering activity would be appropriate anytime after this lesson.

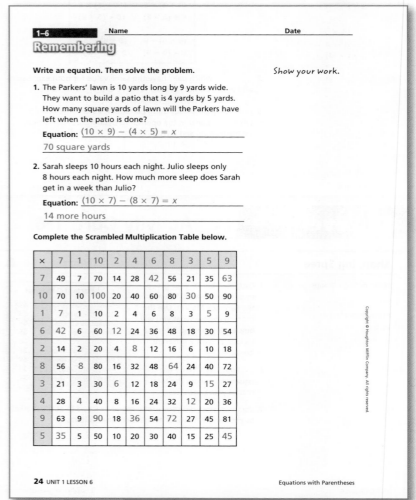

1–6 Name _____ Date _____
Remembering

Write an equation. Then solve the problem.   *Show your work.*

1. The Parkers' lawn is 10 yards long by 9 yards wide. They want to build a patio that is 4 yards by 5 yards. How many square yards of lawn will the Parkers have left when the patio is done?

   Equation: $(10 \times 9) - (4 \times 5) = x$
   70 square yards

2. Sarah sleeps 10 hours each night. Julio sleeps only 8 hours each night. How much more sleep does Sarah get in a week than Julio?

   Equation: $(10 \times 7) - (8 \times 7) = x$
   14 more hours

Complete the Scrambled Multiplication Table below.

×	7	1	10	2	4	6	8	3	5	9
7	49	7	70	14	28	42	56	21	35	63
10	70	10	100	20	40	60	80	30	50	90
1	7	1	10	2	4	6	8	3	5	9
6	42	6	60	12	24	36	48	18	30	54
2	14	2	20	4	8	12	16	6	10	18
8	56	8	80	16	32	48	64	24	40	72
3	21	3	30	6	12	18	24	9	15	27
4	28	4	40	8	16	24	32	12	20	36
9	63	9	90	18	36	54	72	27	45	81
5	35	5	50	10	20	30	40	15	25	45

24 UNIT 1 LESSON 6   Equations with Parentheses

Homework and Remembering page 24

Home or School Activity

Language Arts Connection

Parentheses and Punctuation Just as parentheses tell what order to do operations in an equation, punctuation helps to make the meaning of a sentence clear. Quotation marks and commas let the reader know who said or did something. Write the following sentence on the board.

   Jacob said Caleb likes to play soccer.

Ask students to decide whether Jacob or Caleb likes to play soccer and then add punctuation that makes the meaning clear. Ask students to write more sentences that can be punctuated in different ways to mean different things. Challenge students to write a sentence that needs parentheses to make its meaning clear.

84 UNIT 1 LESSON 6

Combinations and Comparisons

REAL
WORLD
**Problem
Solving**

Vocabulary

combination
comparison
misleading

Lesson Objective

● Solve multiple combination and comparison problems.

The Day at a Glance

Today's Goals	Materials

1 Teaching the Lesson
A1: Represent and solve combination problems that have more than two factors.
A2: Solve comparison word problems that have misleading language.
 	
2 Going Further
► Differentiated Instruction
 	
3 Homework and Spiral Review
	Lesson Activities
	Student Activity Book pp. 41–42 or
	  Student Hardcover Book pp. 41–42
	Homework and Remembering
	  pp. 25–26
	Index cards (optional)
	
	Going Further
	Activity Cards 1-7
	Counters
	Number cubes
	Grid Paper (TRB M17)
	MathBoard materials
	Math Journals
	
	123 Use **Math Talk** today!

Keeping Skills Sharp

Quick Practice ⏱ 5 MINUTES	Daily Routines
Goal: Practice basic multiplication. **Materials:** pointer, Class Multiplication Table Poster **Multiplication in Motion** The students count off from 2 to 10, repeating the sequence until every student has a number. Then the **Student Leader** uses a pointer to point to a product on the Class Multiplication Table Poster. Again, the leader points only to products that are in the difficult section. Every student who has a number that is a factor of this product stands. Then, going in order, the standing students announce the factors. At the end, the Student Leader names the factor pairs. Repeat with other products.	**Homework Review** Have students show their work at the board. Encourage the class to ask clarifying questions and make comments. **Who's Right?** Colby and Lily need to simplify the expression $3 + (2 \times 4)$. Colby said the value is 20. Lily said the value is 11. Which student is incorrect? Explain why. Colby is incorrect; First, he added and then multiplied 5 times 4, instead of first multiplying and then adding $3 + 8$.

Teaching the Lesson

Activity 1

Problems With Multiple Combinations

 25 MINUTES

Goal: Represent and solve combination problems that have more than two factors.

Materials: Student Activity Book or Hardcover Book p. 41

✔ **NCTM Standards:**
Number and Operations
Algebra
Problem Solving
Data Analysis and Probability

The Learning Classroom

Math Talk Always start by eliciting student ideas about a new topic. Students will increase their engagement in classes if they believe that their contributions will be heard. This may involve allowing for interruptions from students during teacher explanations of content. The teacher continues to decide what is important to continue exploring, but allows students to "own" new ideas or strategies. Often students come up with and explain strategies that the teacher was about to teach.

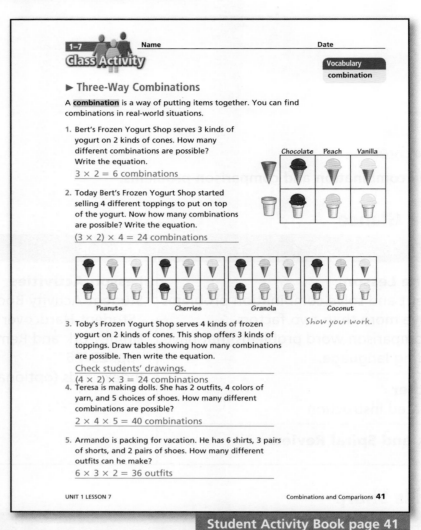

Student Activity Book page 41

► Three-Way Combinations WHOLE CLASS

Have students solve the problems on Student Book page 41. For the first problem, you can find the number of combinations by using two factors: 3 × 2 = 6. The second problem adds another element—different toppings. Because each of the 6 different cones can now have 4 different toppings, the expression from problem 1 gets multiplied by 4. Write the equation on the board: (3 × 2) × 4 = 24. Check to be sure that students understand.

Students can draw tables like the ones they just discussed to find the answer to problems. Have them draw *empty* tables (no pictures). They should discover that Toby's Frozen Yogurt Shop also offers 24 possible combinations.

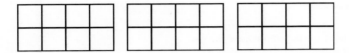

Write the equation that corresponds with this situation: $(4 \times 2) \times 3 = 24$.

Ask students if they notice anything interesting about the equations in problems 2 and 3. Help students see that the answer is the same even though the numbers are grouped differently: $(3 \times 2) \times 4$ has the same value as $(4 \times 2) \times 3$. Explain that they will learn about the mathematical reason for this in a later lesson.

▶ Practice With Combinations   WHOLE CLASS

For problems 4–5 on page 41 of the Student Book, students can multiply the numbers together to find the total number of combinations. Sometimes a strategic choice can make the multiplication easier. The numbers in problem 4, for example, are not given in the best order for multiplying. Discuss with students how these numbers could be reordered to make computation easier. Multiply 2×5 and then $\times 4$

The Learning Classroom

Math Talk You can create math conversations by eliciting multiple strategies for solving problems. When you ask, "Did anyone solve this problem differently?" your students will pay greater attention to the work on the board because they will be comparing and contrasting it with their own math strategies. The comparisons and contrasts that result can naturally prompt significant math talk.

Teaching the Lesson (continued)

Activity 2

Comparison Problems With Misleading Language

 25 MINUTES

Goal: Solve comparison word problems that have misleading language.

Materials: Student Activity Book or Hardcover Book p. 42, index cards (optional)

✔ **NCTM Standards:**
Number and Operations
Algebra

English Language Learners

Write *compare* and *combine* on the board. Ask: **Do these words mean the same thing?** no

- **Beginning** Say: *Compare* means "to tell how items are the same or different." Ask: **Does** *combine* **mean "to put items together"?** yes
- **Intermediate** Ask: **Which word means "to relate two items"?** compare Say: *Combine* means "put items ___." together
- **Advanced** Have students work in pairs to think of examples of when they compared or combined in math.

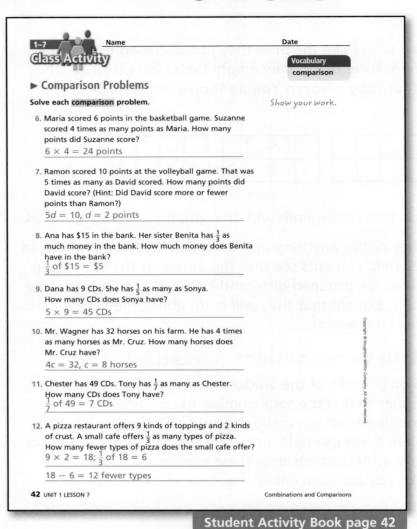

Student Activity Book page 42

► Comparison Problems WHOLE CLASS

Direct students' attention to problems 6 and 7 on page 42 of the Student Book. These two problems look similar, but they are different. Problem 6 is a multiplication comparison problem that students can probably solve easily because the comparing sentence directs the solution. Problem 7 is likely to confuse many students if they do not think about the situation carefully.

The comparing sentence is **misleading**: it says "5 times as many" so students may solve as 5 × 10. But the sentence says Ramon made 5 times as many points as David, so David made fewer points. If *d* represents David's points, then $5d = 10$ points and $d = 2$ points.

Use Comparison Bars The most difficult part of solving problems that have misleading comparison language is keeping track of who has more and who has less. Show students how to draw and label quick comparison bars to help them see Ramon's and David's points in Problem 7. They should not try to make the proportions accurate, but just make a quick sketch.

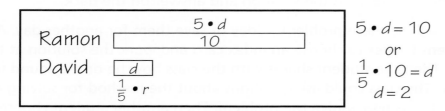

$5 \bullet d = 10$

or

$\frac{1}{5} \bullet 10 = d$

$d = 2$

Now ask students to draw comparison bars to help them solve Problems 9 and 11, which also have misleading language.

9.

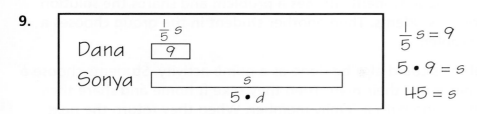

$\frac{1}{5} s = 9$

$5 \bullet 9 = s$

$45 = s$

Dana has $\frac{1}{5}$ as many as Sonya.

Sonya has 5 times as many as Dana.

11.

Chester
$7 \bullet t$
49

Tony
t
$\frac{1}{7} \bullet c$

$7 \bullet t = 49$

or

$\frac{1}{7} \bullet 49 = t$

$7 = t$

Tony has $\frac{1}{7}$ as many as Chester.

Chester has 7 times as many as Tony.

Math Talk Use **Solve and Discuss** for problems 8, 10, and 12. Decide for each problem whether the language was leading (it suggested the correct solution) or misleading (it suggested the incorrect solution). Lead students to say the comparing sentence or question both ways to see which is leading.

Activity continued ▶

① Teaching the Lesson (continued)

Activity 2

The Learning Classroom

Student Leaders When students explain their work, they need to stand beside their work and point to parts of it as they explain. Using a pointer that does not obscure any work enables all students to see the part of the drawing or math symbols that is being explained.

Some students may have difficulty with problem 12 because it is a combination *and* comparison problem. Tell students to find the number of combinations for the types of pizzas the restaurant offers and then use that information in solving the comparison problem.

Optional Writing Activity One way to know if students understand a problem type is to ask them to write a problem using a similar structure.

Have students write their own comparison and combination problems on large index cards with the solution and answer on the back.

You could use these problems today or save them for another day. Ask a **Student Leader** to choose an index card and work the solution at the board. Then the student shares with the class how he or she found the answer. The class could ask questions about the method for solving or offer other ways to solve the problem. Then another student chooses a different problem.

This activity could also be done by students working in **Small Groups** or **Student Pairs**. One student chooses a problem and shares the solution with the other students. Then another student in the group chooses a different problem.

These problems could also be done as a home activity. Students choose a problem that is not their own. Then they take it home and share their method of solving with a family member. When they return the next day, they could also share their method with the class.

Advanced Learners could write complex problems like problem 12 and work on each other's problems on the practice days, while other students are practicing basic multiplications and divisions.

② Going Further

Differentiated Instruction

● Intervention   Activity Card 1-7

Many Times   Activity Card 1-7 ●

Work: In Small Groups

Use:
• 60 Counters
• Number cubes

Decide:
Who will be the "caller" for your group.

1. **Caller:** Form a group of less than 10 counters. Then roll the number cube and use the number to call out, "_____ times as many!"

2. **Work Together** Make a model to match that number of counters.

3. Change callers and repeat the activity until each member of the group has taken a turn as caller.

4. **Math Talk** Is 5 times as many as 4 counters the same as 4 times as many as 5 counters? Why or why not? Yes, because $5 \times 4 = 20$ and $4 \times 5 = 20$.

Unit 1, Lesson 7   Copyright © Houghton Mifflin Company

Activity Note Have students count the total number of counters that they use to match the caller's instruction and then write a multiplication equation to represent each total.

 Math Writing Prompt

Explain Your Thinking Why are parentheses not necessary in this multiplication $4 \times (5 \times 2)$?

 **Software Support**

Warm-Up 12.20

▲ On Level   Activity Card 1-7

Grid Combination   Activity Card 1-7 ▲

Work: In Pairs

Use:
• Grid Paper (TRB M17)

1. You can use grid paper to model the product of 3 numbers. How does the example below show the product $3 \times 2 \times 4 = 24$? 24 grid squares are shaded.

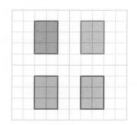

2. Use congruent rectangles on a grid to model the same product in two other ways. Possible answer: Three 2-by-4 rectangles and two 3-by-4 rectangles

Unit 1, Lesson 7   Copyright © Houghton Mifflin Company

Activity Note Extend the activity by having students show the product with a different set of three factors, such as $2 \times 6 \times 3$ or $2 \times 12 \times 1$. Display and compare the different models.

 Math Writing Prompt

Make a List Create a menu with 2 drinks, 4 dinners, and 3 desserts. Then list all possible combinations of 1 drink, 1 dinner, and 1 dessert.

 Software Support

The Number Games: Up, Up, and Array, Level D

■ Challenge   Activity Card 1-7

Tree Diagrams   Activity Card 1-7 ■

Work: By Yourself

Use:
• MathBoard materials

1. Use your MathBoard to show all the ways that one or more of the digits 1, 2, and 3 can be arranged to form a 3-digit number. 27 numbers can be made.

2. Copy and complete the diagram below to begin the activity. The diagram shows all the possible numbers with 1 in the hundreds place.

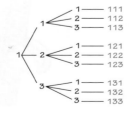

Unit 1, Lesson 7   Copyright © Houghton Mifflin Company

Activity Note Tell students that there are a total of 27 possible three-digit numbers using the digits 1, 2, and 3. Emphasize that each place value in the number can be any one of the three digits.

 Math Writing Prompt

Create a Problem Write a three-way combination problem.

 **Software Support**

Course III: Module 6: Unit 1: Looking at Chance

Combinations and Comparisons   **91**

③ Homework and Spiral Review

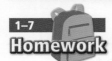

1-7
Homework Goal: Additional Practice

Use this Homework page to provide students with more practice with combinations and comparisons.

1-7
Remembering Goal: Spiral Review

This Remembering activity would be appropriate anytime after today's lesson.

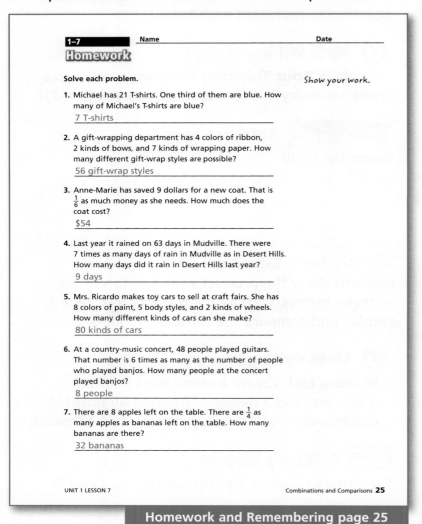

1-7 Name _____ Date _____
Homework

Solve each problem.   *Show your work.*

1. Michael has 21 T-shirts. One third of them are blue. How many of Michael's T-shirts are blue?
   7 T-shirts

2. A gift-wrapping department has 4 colors of ribbon, 2 kinds of bows, and 7 kinds of wrapping paper. How many different gift-wrap styles are possible?
   56 gift-wrap styles

3. Anne-Marie has saved 9 dollars for a new coat. That is $\frac{1}{6}$ as much money as she needs. How much does the coat cost?
   $54

4. Last year it rained on 63 days in Mudville. There were 7 times as many days of rain in Mudville as in Desert Hills. How many days did it rain in Desert Hills last year?
   9 days

5. Mrs. Ricardo makes toy cars to sell at craft fairs. She has 8 colors of paint, 5 body styles, and 2 kinds of wheels. How many different kinds of cars can she make?
   80 kinds of cars

6. At a country-music concert, 48 people played guitars. That number is 6 times as many as the number of people who played banjos. How many people at the concert played banjos?
   8 people

7. There are 8 apples left on the table. There are $\frac{1}{4}$ as many apples as bananas left on the table. How many bananas are there?
   32 bananas

UNIT 1 LESSON 7   Combinations and Comparisons **25**

Homework and Remembering page 25

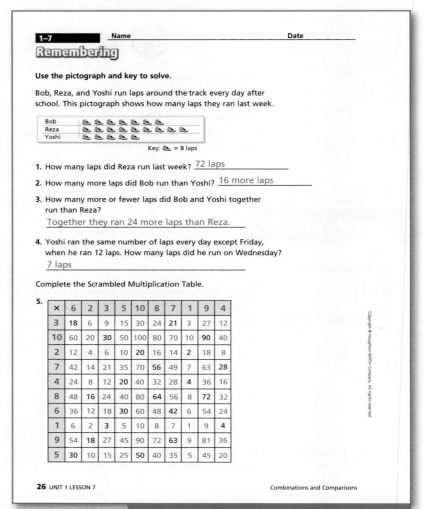

1-7 Name _____ Date _____
Remembering

Use the pictograph and key to solve.

Bob, Reza, and Yoshi run laps around the track every day after school. This pictograph shows how many laps they ran last week.

Bob	👟 👟 👟 👟 👟 👟 👟 👟 👟
Reza	👟 👟 👟 👟 👟 👟 👟 👟 👟
Yoshi	👟 👟 👟 👟 👟

Key: 👟 = 8 laps

1. How many laps did Reza run last week? 72 laps

2. How many more laps did Bob run than Yoshi? 16 more laps

3. How many more or fewer laps did Bob and Yoshi together run than Reza?
   Together they ran 24 more laps than Reza.

4. Yoshi ran the same number of laps every day except Friday, when he ran 12 laps. How many laps did he run on Wednesday?
   7 laps

Complete the Scrambled Multiplication Table.

5.

×	6	2	3	5	10	8	7	1	9	4
3	18	6	9	15	30	24	21	3	27	12
10	60	20	30	50	100	80	70	10	90	40
2	12	4	6	10	20	16	14	2	18	8
7	42	14	21	35	70	56	49	7	63	28
4	24	8	12	20	40	32	28	4	36	16
8	48	16	24	40	80	64	56	8	72	32
6	36	12	18	30	60	48	42	6	54	24
1	6	2	3	5	10	8	7	1	9	4
9	54	18	27	45	90	72	63	9	81	36
5	30	10	15	25	50	40	35	5	45	20

26 UNIT 1 LESSON 7   Combinations and Comparisons

Homework and Remembering page 26

Home or School Activity

Language Arts Connection

Letters and Words Have your students look at an English dictionary. Ask, "Did you ever think that combining just 26 letters could make so many words?" Point out that some letters are used in more words than others. According to experts, E, T, and A are the most frequently used letters in the English language.

Tell your students to list all of the ways that the letters E, T, and A can be combined, using each letter once. They should try to identify which combinations are actual words and then use a dictionary to check.

Can you guess what English word is used **THE** most?

Practice With Factors

Lesson Objective

- Find factors to solve puzzles that involve proportional relationships.

The Day at a Glance

Today's Goals	Materials

1 Teaching the Lesson
A1: Find factors to solve puzzles that involve proportional relationships.
A2: Practice finding factors.
 	
2 Going Further
▶ Differentiated Instruction
 	
3 Homework and Spiral Review
	Lesson Activities
	Student Activity Book pp. 43–44D or
	  Student Hardcover Book pp. 43–44
	  and Activity Workbook pp. 25–30
	  (includes Factor the Footprints
	  game board)
	Homework and Remembering
	  pp. 27–28
	Factor Footprints (TRB M15–M16)
	Class Multiplication Table Poster
	Game token (for each student)
	Tape
	
	Going Further
	Activity Cards 1-8
	Index cards
	Grid Paper (TRB M17)
	MathBoard materials
	Math Journals

123 *Use* **Math Talk** *today!*

Keeping Skills Sharp

Quick Practice ⏱ 5 MINUTES	Daily Routines
Goal: Practice division. **Materials:** Division Cards **Division in Motion** The students count off from 2 to 10, repeating the sequence until every student in the class has a number. Then two **Student Leaders** take turns reading a division problem from the Division Cards. Every student whose assigned number is the answer stands. One Student Leader gives a hand signal, and the standing students all say the answer in unison.	**Homework Review** Have students discuss the problems from their homework. Have students help each other resolve any misunderstandings. **Multiple Solution** The craft store is having a sale on red fabric: 2 yards cost $8, 3 yards cost $12, 4 yards cost $14, 5 yards cost $18, 6 yards cost $22. What is the least expensive way to buy 10 yards? Explain. 6 yd for $22 and 4 yd for $14 or two pieces 5 yd each for $18 each. Either way, she pays $36 for 10 yards.

Teaching the Lesson

Factor Puzzles

 30 MINUTES

Goal: Find factors to solve puzzles that involve proportional relationships.

Materials: Class Multiplication Table Poster, Student Activity Book pp. 43–44 or Student Hardcover Book pp. 43–44 and Activity Workbook pp. 25–26

✓ **NCTM Standards:**
Number and Operations

English Language Learners

Model a picture puzzle or draw a picture of a half-completed puzzle.

• **Beginning** Say: **This is a puzzle. I have to use the pieces I have to finish the picture.**
• **Intermediate** Ask: **Can I put pieces wherever I want to complete the puzzle?** no Say: **I have to put the pieces where they _____ together.** fit
• **Advanced** Have students tell how to finish a puzzle.

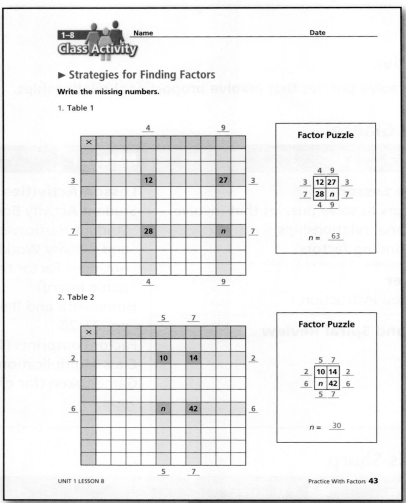

Student Activity Book page 43

▶ Strategies for Finding Factors

WHOLE CLASS

Math Talk

Ask the class to look at Table 1 on page 43 of the Student Book. This shows a part of the Multiplication Table. Work with the class to determine the row and column numbers, and then fill in the eight blanks provided around the table. You may want to use the discussion points that follow.

Students can use count-bys to find the factors.

1. **What count-by has 12 and 27?** The 3s.
   Tell the students to write 3 in the pair of blanks to the left and right of that row.

2. **What count-by has 12 and 28?** The 4s.
   Tell the students to write 4 above and below that column.

3. **What row are the 28 and _n_ in? How do you know?** We know that 28 is in the 4s column, so we can ask, "4 times what is 28?" The answer is 7. So 28 and _n_ must be in the 7s row.
   Tell the students to write 7 to the left and right of this row.

4. **What column are the 27 and _n_ in? How do you know?** We know that 27 is in the 3s row, so we can ask, "3 times what is 27?" The answer is 9. So 27 and _n_ must be in the 9s column.
   Tell the students to write 9 above and below this column.

5. **What number is _n_? How can we find out?** Look at the numbers written on the outside of the table. _n_ is in the 7s row and the 9s column. Multiply 7 × 9. So _n_ = 63.

6. On the Class Multiplication Table Poster, circle the four numbers that make up this puzzle: 12 and 27 from Row 3; 28 and 63 from Row 7. **Do they form a rectangle?** yes **What column are 12 and 28 in?** column 4 **What column are 27 and 63 in?** column 9 **So how does a Factor Puzzle relate to the multiplication table?** It comes from the intersections of 2 rows and 2 columns of the multiplication table.

7. Ask students to look at the Factor Puzzle next to Table 1. Have students solve this puzzle, using the same strategy they used when these numbers were in a larger table.

As students complete the puzzle, discuss alternate ways to solve it. Students should mention that it doesn't matter if they work with the rows or columns first. For this puzzle, step 2 could have come before step 1, and step 4 could have come before step 3. You solve the row and column in which you know 2 numbers first, then the row and column in which you know one number, and then you find the unknown number.

Give your students a few minutes to find the row and column numbers for Table 2. Then have them solve the Factor Puzzle next to it. Ask students to describe their strategies.

Activity continued ▶

① Teaching the Lesson (continued)

Activity 1

Differentiated Instruction

Advanced Learners Give students Blank Factor Puzzles (TRB M85). Students can make up their own factor puzzles, exchange them with a classmate, and then solve them. They may enjoy using 11s and 12s or numbers greater than 12 × 12.

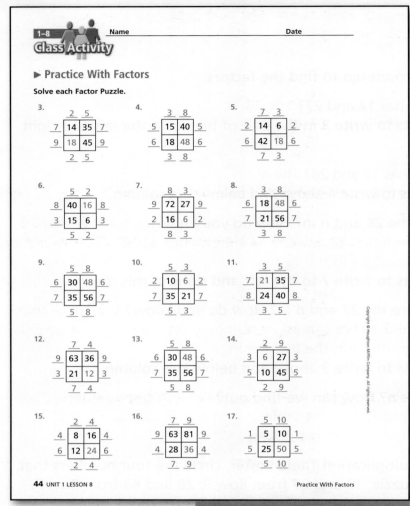

Student Activity Book page 44

▶ Practice With Factors WHOLE CLASS

Write this Factor Puzzle on the board.

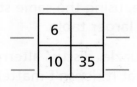

Include the following points in a discussion.

● Name a factor pair for 10 that are different from 1 and 10. 2 and 5. Write the factors outside one row and in one column.

```
        2
     ┌─────┬─────┐
     │  6  │     │
   5 ├─────┼─────┤ 5
     │ 10  │ 35  │
     └─────┴─────┘
        2
```

● Why do we write the 2 in the column and not in the row? Because 2 is a factor of 6 and 10 but not 35

● 2 times what number = 6? 3 Write 3s outside the remaining row.

```
        2
     ┌─────┬─────┐
   3 │  6  │     │ 3
     ├─────┼─────┤
   5 │ 10  │ 35  │ 5
     └─────┴─────┘
        2
```

● 5 times what number = 35? 7 Write 7s outside the remaining column.

```
        2     7
     ┌─────┬─────┐
   3 │  6  │     │ 3
     ├─────┼─────┤
   5 │ 10  │ 35  │ 5
     └─────┴─────┘
        2     7
```

● The missing number is the product of which two numbers? 3 and 7 What is the missing number? 21 Write 21 in the box.

```
        2     7
     ┌─────┬─────┐
   3 │  6  │ 21  │ 3
     ├─────┼─────┤
   5 │ 10  │ 35  │ 5
     └─────┴─────┘
        2     7
```

Have the class turn to page 44 in the Student Book. This page has more Factor Puzzles for the students to solve. **Student Pairs** can work together to verify their work by finding the four cells on a Multiplication Table. Their answer is correct if the cells form a rectangle.

The Learning Classroom

Building Concepts To support building coherence, have students take turns briefly summarizing the previous day's lesson at the beginning of each math class. Alternatively you may have a student summarize at the end of each class. Either way, if you do this regularly, students will get used to making mental summaries of math concepts and making conceptual connections.

Differentiated Instruction

Extra Help If students need extra practice with factor puzzles, you can provide them with Factor Puzzles for 3s, 4s, 6s, 7s, 8s, 9s (TRB M83) or Factor Puzzles for 6s, 7s, 8s (TRB M84).

Activity 2

Factor the Footprints

 25 MINUTES

Goal: Practice finding factors.

Materials: *Factor the Footprints* game board, Student Activity Book pp. 44A–44D or Activity Workbook pp. 27–30, small game token for each student, tape

 NCTM Standard:
Number and Operations

 Ongoing Assessment

Have students:

► determine pairs of factors for 12, 18, 24, 36.

► explain how they found the pairs of factors.

Differentiated Instruction

Advanced Learners Invite students to invent games of their own, using factors or other mathematical concepts. Have students determine strategies for winning the game and then write a set of directions for using those strategies to play.

► Factor the Footprints PAIRS

Setting Up Divide the class into pairs. Each pair will need the *Factor the Footprints* game board. Each person will need a token of some kind. The students tape the game board pages together as shown:

from Student Activity Book pages 44A and 44C

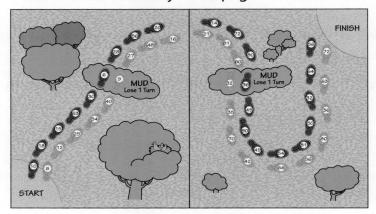

Activity Workbook pages 27 and 29

Game Rules One player will follow the trail of dark footprints, and the other will follow the trail of light footprints. Placing the marker on the first footprint, the first player names all the possible factor pairs for the number shown. The factor 1 is not permitted. The factors should be given in equation form, as in $3 \times 6 = 18$. The player moves forward one space for each correct equation named. The second player does the same, following a different trail. The first player to reach the Finish wins the game.

Playing the Game Player 1 has landed on a footprint marked 12. He says, "6 × 2 equals 12 and 4 × 3 equals 12." He has given 2 equations, so he moves ahead 2 spaces. (Reversing the order of the factors to produce another equation is not permitted.) It is now Player 2's turn. She has landed on a footprint marked 40. She says, "8 × 5 equals 40" and "2 × 20 equals 40." She also says, "4 × 10 equals 40." Generating factors that are not part of the regular Multiplication Table is allowed, so she moves ahead 3 spaces.

Disputed Equations and Lost Turns If one player gives an equation that the other player believes to be incorrect, they can consult the Multiplication Table or check by using other strategies. A player who gives an incorrect equation loses that turn. Players who land in one of the two mud puddles on the board also lose a turn.

Have **Student Pairs** switch trails and play a second game if time permits.

② Going Further

● Intervention — Activity Card 1-8

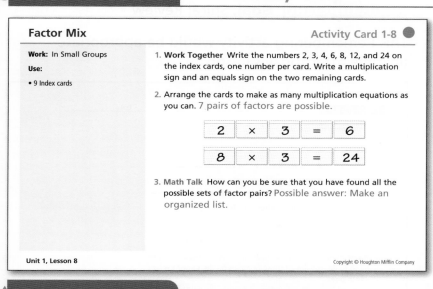

Factor Mix — Activity Card 1-8 ●

Work: In Small Groups

Use:
• 9 Index cards

1. **Work Together** Write the numbers 2, 3, 4, 6, 8, 12, and 24 on the index cards, one number per card. Write a multiplication sign and an equals sign on the two remaining cards.

2. Arrange the cards to make as many multiplication equations as you can. 7 pairs of factors are possible.

| 2 | × | 3 | = | 6 |

| 8 | × | 3 | = | 24 |

3. **Math Talk** How can you be sure that you have found all the possible sets of factor pairs? Possible answer: Make an organized list.

Unit 1, Lesson 8   Copyright © Houghton Mifflin Company

Activity Note Encourage students to the list the pairs of factors for each number to ensure that they find all possible equations.

✎ Math Writing Prompt

Write a Definition Use the words *multiply* and *product* to explain what factors are.

Soar to Success Math ★ **Software Support**

Warm-Up 14.28

▲ On Level — Activity Card 1-8

Factor Grids — Activity Card 1-8 ▲

Work: In Pairs

Use:
• Grid Paper (TRB M17)

1. **Work Together** Outline rectangles on grid paper to model the factors of 6, 12, 15, and 16.

2. Write a multiplication equation for each rectangle model that you make.

Unit 1, Lesson 8   Copyright © Houghton Mifflin Company

Activity Note Suggest that students make a list of factors for each number before they begin the activity. Students should use each factor pair as the length and width of a rectangle on the grid.

✎ Math Writing Prompt

Explain Your Thinking What number is a factor of every whole number? Why?

MegaMath Grades K-6 **Software Support**

Ice Station Exploration: Arctic Algebra, Level C

■ Challenge — Activity Card 1-8

Common Factors — Activity Card 1-8 ■

Work: By Yourself

Use:
• MathBoard materials

1. List all the factors of each pair of numbers below on your MathBoard.

| 24 and 32 | 12 and 20 |
| 30 and 18 | 36 and 42 |

2. Then circle the common factors for each pair. The first pair of factors is listed below.

24: ①②3④6⑧12 24
32: ①②④⑧16 32

3. **Look Back** Which two factors are common to all eight numbers? How could you have predicted this outcome? 1 and 2; 1 is a factor of every whole number and 2 is a factor of all even numbers.

Unit 1, Lesson 8   Copyright © Houghton Mifflin Company

Activity Note Check students' work to be sure that they have listed all factor pairs before finding common factors.

✎ Math Writing Prompt

Write Number Clues Choose any two-digit number. Then write 3 clues to describe it. Use the word *factor* in at least 1 clue. Challenge a partner to use the clues to name the number.

DESTINATION Math® **Software Support**

Course III: Module 1: Unit 2: Identifying Common Factors

 # Homework and Spiral Review

1-8 Homework Goal: Additional Practice

Use this Homework page to provide students with more practice with basic proportional relationships.

1-8 Remembering Goal: Spiral Review

This Remembering activity would be appropriate anytime after today's lesson.

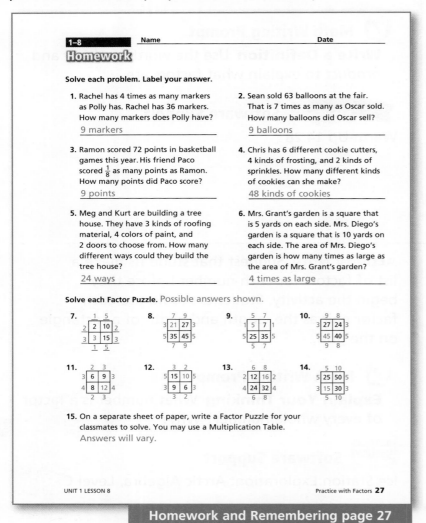

1-8 Homework   Name _____ Date _____

Solve each problem. Label your answer.

1. Rachel has 4 times as many markers as Polly has. Rachel has 36 markers. How many markers does Polly have?
   9 markers

2. Sean sold 63 balloons at the fair. That is 7 times as many as Oscar sold. How many balloons did Oscar sell?
   9 balloons

3. Ramon scored 72 points in basketball games this year. His friend Paco scored $\frac{1}{8}$ as many points as Ramon. How many points did Paco score?
   9 points

4. Chris has 6 different cookie cutters, 4 kinds of frosting, and 2 kinds of sprinkles. How many different kinds of cookies can she make?
   48 kinds of cookies

5. Meg and Kurt are building a tree house. They have 3 kinds of roofing material, 4 colors of paint, and 2 doors to choose from. How many different ways could they build the tree house?
   24 ways

6. Mrs. Grant's garden is a square that is 5 yards on each side. Mrs. Diego's garden is a square that is 10 yards on each side. The area of Mrs. Diego's garden is how many times as large as the area of Mrs. Grant's garden?
   4 times as large

Solve each Factor Puzzle. Possible answers shown.

7.
8.
9.
10.
11.
12.
13.
14.

15. On a separate sheet of paper, write a Factor Puzzle for your classmates to solve. You may use a Multiplication Table.
   Answers will vary.

UNIT 1 LESSON 8   Practice with Factors **27**

Homework and Remembering page 27

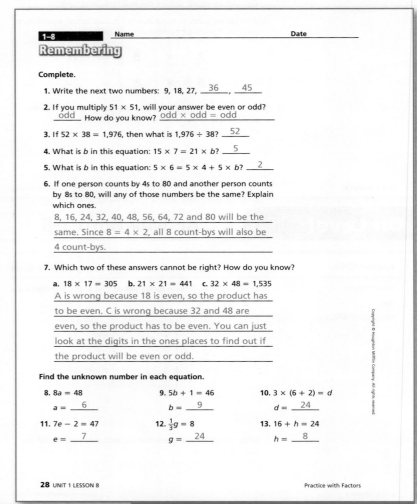

1-8 Remembering   Name _____ Date _____

Complete.

1. Write the next two numbers: 9, 18, 27, __36__, __45__

2. If you multiply 51 × 51, will your answer be even or odd? __odd__ How do you know? __odd × odd = odd__

3. If 52 × 38 = 1,976, then what is 1,976 ÷ 38? __52__

4. What is b in this equation: 15 × 7 = 21 × b? __5__

5. What is b in this equation: 5 × 6 = 5 × 4 + 5 × b? __2__

6. If one person counts by 4s to 80 and another person counts by 8s to 80, will any of those numbers be the same? Explain which ones.
   8, 16, 24, 32, 40, 48, 56, 64, 72 and 80 will be the same. Since 8 = 4 × 2, all 8 count-bys will also be 4 count-bys.

7. Which two of these answers cannot be right? How do you know?
   a. 18 × 17 = 305   b. 21 × 21 = 441   c. 32 × 48 = 1,535
   A is wrong because 18 is even, so the product has to be even. C is wrong because 32 and 48 are even, so the product has to be even. You can just look at the digits in the ones places to find out if the product will be even or odd.

Find the unknown number in each equation.

8. 8a = 48
   a = __6__

9. 5b + 1 = 46
   b = __9__

10. 3 × (6 + 2) = d
    d = __24__

11. 7e − 2 = 47
    e = __7__

12. $\frac{1}{3}g$ = 8
    g = __24__

13. 16 + h = 24
    h = __8__

28 UNIT 1 LESSON 8   Practice with Factors

Homework and Remembering page 28

Home or School Activity

 ### Science Connection

Herbivores and Carnivores In general, herbivores, animals that eat only plants, sleep less than carnivores, animals that eat only meat. Ask students to do research to find the names of some carnivores and herbivores and to see how long they sleep each day (on average).

Then ask students to calculate how many days it takes for each of their animals to sleep for a total of 24 hours.

DAILY SLEEPING HABITS	
Animal	**Number of Hours**
Cow	4 hours
Giraffe	2 hours
Horse	3 hours
Seal	6 hours
Tiger	16 hours

UNIT 1

LESSON

9

Multistep Problems

REAL WORLD Problem Solving

Lesson Objectives

● Solve multistep problems involving equations with multiplication chains.

● Solve equations with several unknowns.

The Day at a Glance

Today's Goals	Materials
① Teaching the Lesson **A1:** Solve and discuss word problems with multiplication chains. **A2:** Solve equations that include algebraic expressions. **② Going Further** ▶ Math Connection: Order of Operations ▶ Differentiated Instruction **③ Homework and Spiral Review**	**Lesson Activities** Student Activity Book pp. 45–46 or Student Hardcover Book pp. 45–46 Homework and Remembering pp. 29–30 **Going Further** Activity Cards 1-9 Counters Student Activity Book p. 45 or Student Hardcover Book p. 45 Math Journals

123 Use Math Talk today!

Keeping Skills Sharp

Quick Practice ⏱ 5 MINUTES	Daily Routines
Goal: Practice division skills. **Materials:** Division Cards **Division in Motion** The students count off from 2 to 10, repeating the sequence until everyone has a number. Then two **Student Leaders** take turns reading a division problem from the Division Cards. Every student whose number is the answer stands. One Student Leader gives a hand signal, and the standing students all say the answer in unison.	**Homework Review** Have a volunteer share a Factor Puzzle. Invite several students to solve it at the board, while the others work at their seats. **Nonroutine Problem** Of the 55 students surveyed, 30 had dogs, 20 had cats, and 10 have both a dog and a cat. The rest of the students have no pet. How many students have no pet? Use a Venn diagram to show your answer. 15 students

Neither: 15

Dogs 30 – 10 20 | Both 10 | Cats 20 – 10 10

Teaching the Lesson

Comparison Chains

 30 MINUTES

Goal: Solve and discuss word problems with multiplication chains.

Materials: Student Activity Book or Hardcover Book pp. 45–46

✔ **NCTM Standards:**
Number and Operations
Algebra

Teaching Note

What to Expect From Students
Most students will not use parentheses and will instead write and solve the second equation, $4 + 12 + 16 = 32$ days. That is fine. You may find that some students will write $4 + 12 = 16 + 16 = 32$. Let them know they have the right idea, but that the notation needs to be changed a little. $4 + 12$ does not equal $16 + 16$. These equations can be written separately [$4 + 12 = 16$ and $16 + 16 = 32$] or combined using parentheses: $(4 + 12) + 16 = 32$.

English Language Learners

Write *algebra*, *Algebraic Equation*, and $3f \times 7 = 21$ on the board. Say: **Algebra is math with variables.**

• **Beginning** Ask: **Does this equation have a variable?** yes **Is it an algebraic equation?** yes

• **Intermediate and Advanced** Say: **This equation has the variable __.** *f* Ask: **What kind of equation is it?** algebraic

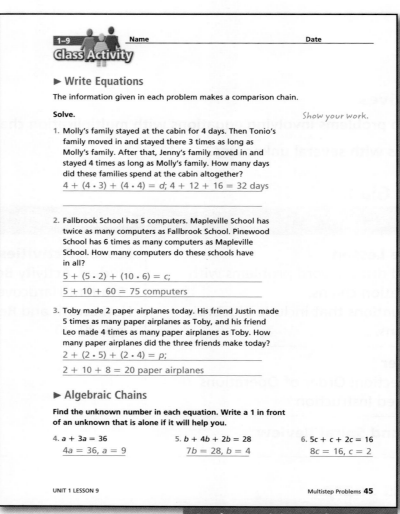

Student Activity Book page 45

▶ Write Equations WHOLE CLASS

Discuss with the class the first two problems on page 45 of the Student Book. In each of these problems, students need to read carefully to determine which numbers are multiplied.

Problem 1 The original number (4 days) is multiplied each time.

$4 + (4 \times 3) + (4 \times 4)$
$4 + 12 + 16 = 32$ days

Problem 2 The comparison chain develops differently. The original number is multiplied to make the second number, and then the second number (*not* the original number) is multiplied to make the third number. Again, most students will not bother with the parentheses and will simply multiply as they go.

$5 + (5 \times 2) + (10 \times 6)$
$5 + 10 + 60 = 75$ computers

Problem 3 This problem is similar to problem 1, with the original number being multiplied each time.

$2 + 10 + 8 = 20$ paper airplanes

▶ Algebraic Chains WHOLE CLASS

Combine Like Terms Ask students to look at the equation in exercise 4 on page 45 of the Student Book. How many times is the variable *a* being added altogether? 4 If your class has difficulty with this, give them another equation type that is familiar to them, such as $a + 4 = 12$. When *a* is by itself, it always means $1a$ (or $1 \times a$). Therefore, the first equation really means $1a + 3a$.

These equation chains can be solved in two steps. First, add all of the unknowns together. Then solve.

Problem 4 $a + 3a = 36$
or $1a + 3a = 36$
$4a = 36$, so $a = 9$

Problem 5 $b + 4b + 2b = 28$
or $1b + 4b + 2b = 28$
$7b = 28$, so $b = 4$

Problem 6 $5c + c + 2c = 16$
or $5c + 1c + 2c = 16$
$8c = 16$, so $c = 2$

Activity continued ▶

The Learning Classroom

Helping Community One reason that students are uncomfortable doing math work and thinking in public is that they may not be correct. You can help students change their perspective on errors. For example, you can respond to errors as opportunities for learning. You can model this for students as you make your own errors, by saying, "Oh, that's OK, I see what I did." Fixing your errors models a healthy approach for students.

① Teaching the Lesson (continued)

Activity 1

Teaching Note

Watch for! Students may be inexperienced in creating algebraic equations to solve word problems. You may need to remind students that a variable w in isolation really means $1w$. So $w + 3w = 4w$.

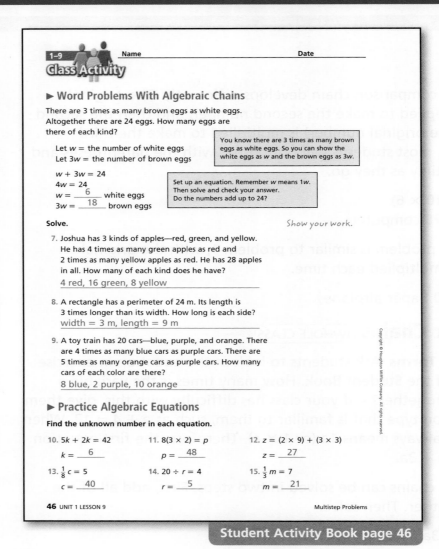

Student Activity Book page 46

▶ Word Problems With Algebraic Chains `WHOLE CLASS`

Have students look at the problem at the top of Student Book page 46. Work through the problem together. It will serve as a model for the other problems on this page.

These problems give the totals and the multipliers. To find each answer, students need to set up an algebraic equation with a variable for the first unknown quantity. Once they have found the first unknown quantity, they can find the others.

Math Talk Use **Solve and Discuss** for exercises 7, 8, and 9. Give students an opportunity to share their ideas for using variables to represent the problem.

Remind them that finding the first unknown is not enough. They also need to go back and find the other answers.

Problem 7 red + green + yellow = 28

$r + 4r + 2r = 28$

$7r = 28$

$r = 4$, so 4 red, 16 green, and 8 yellow apples

Remind students that $r = 1 \times r = 1r$.

Problem 8 $w + 3w + w + 3w = 24$

$8w = 24$

$w = 3$, so the rectangle is 3 meters by 9 meters.

This equation could also be set up with parentheses:

$2(w + 3w) = 24$

Problem 9 purple cars + blue cars + orange cars = 20

$p + 4p + 5p = 20$

$10p = 20$

$p = 2$, so 2 purple cars, 8 blue cars, and 10 orange cars

Check Answers Remind students to add the separate answers in each problem to decide if they get the correct total. In the last problem, for example, they should add 2 + 8 + 10 to see if they get 20, the total number of cars on the train. This is a good self-check.

Activity 2

Consolidation of Equations

▶ Practice Algebraic Equations [WHOLE CLASS]

Ask students to solve for the unknown quantity in each equation in Exercises 10–15 on page 46 of the Student Book.

Invite some students to work at the classroom board.

Some students may have trouble with exercise 11: $8(3 \times 2) = p$. If so, remind them that $8(3 \times 2)$ is just like $8n$. It means the quantity in parentheses is taken 8 times, so it can be simplified to 8×6, or 48.

 20 MINUTES

Goal: Solve equations that include algebraic expressions.

Materials: Student Activity Book or Hardcover Book p. 46

 NCTM Standards:
Number and Operations
Algebra

 Ongoing Assessment

Have students discuss:

▶ how to determine which number is multiplied to solve comparison chains.

▶ how to set up equations to solve word chains.

▶ how to self-check results from algebraic equations.

② Going Further

Math Connection: Order of Operations

Goal: Use Order of Operations

✔ **NCTM Standards:**
Number and Operations
Algebra

In this activity, students connect what they know about operations with rules governing the order of those operations.

Write the two sentences shown below on the board. Be sure to include the quotation marks in each sentence you write.

> Jill said, "Amy is first in line."
>
> "Jill," said Amy, "is first in line."

Ask the students to compare the sentences.

● In the first sentence, who is speaking? Jill Who is first in line? Amy

● In the second sentence, who is speaking? Amy Who is first in line? Jill

Have students note that although the words in each sentence are identical, punctuation changes the meaning of the sentences.

Write the expression shown below on the board.

$$8 + 4 \div 2$$

Have students note that the expression contains two different operations, then ask:

● If you add first, then divide, what number does the expression simplify to? 6

● If you divide first, then add, what number does the expression simplify to? 10

Point out that only one answer is correct, and ask students to describe what additional information they might need to help decide which answer is correct. Lead their discussion to suggest when more than one operation is present, a set of rules is needed to help decide which operation is completed first.

Write the following rules on the board. As you write, ask the students to write the rules in their Math Journals.

Order of Operations

● Work inside parentheses.

● Multiply and divide, from left to right.

● Add and subtract, from left to right.

Have students look again at the expression $8 + 4 \div 2$ on the board. Ask:

● We said the expression could be simplified to 6 or to 10. Which is correct? 10 Why? The Order of Operations states that multiplication and division must be completed before addition and subtraction.

Write the expression $13 - 3 \cdot 2 + 5$ on the board and have students apply the Order of Operations to simplify the expression.

$$13 - 3 \cdot 2 + 5$$
$$13 - 6 + 5$$
$$7 + 5$$
$$12$$

Encourage students to write a variety of numerical expressions such as those used in this activity, or lengthier expressions. Each expression should include at least one addition or subtraction and at least one multiplication or division. The students should simplify each expression they write, then exchange expressions and compare their answers with those of their classmates.

Differentiated Instruction

Counter Chains
Activity Card 1-9

Work: In Small Groups

Use:
- Counters
- Student Book p. 45

1. Use counters to model the first three word problems on Student Book page 45.

2. Follow the example for Problem 1. Count the total number of counters to find the total number of days. 32 days

3. Use the same method to model and solve the remaining two problems. 75 computers; 20 paper airplanes

4 counters for Molly's family

3 groups of 4 counters for Tonio's family

4 groups of 4 counters for Jenny's family

Unit 1, Lesson 9

Copyright © Houghton Mifflin Company

Activity Note Unlike Problems 1 and 3, Problem 2 requires students to use the number of computers they model for the second school as the basis for the number they model for the third school.

 **Math Writing Prompt**

Write Comparision Sentences Use the phrase "times as many" to write a sentence about your ears and toes.

Soar to Success Math **Software Support**

Warm-Up 12.20

Guess and Check
Activity Card 1-9

Work: In Pairs
Possible solution:

Equation:
$m = 8$
$t = 2m$
$b = 2m \div 2$

$t = 2 \cdot 8$
Since Tyler is twice as old as Megan and Megan is 8, Tyler is 16.

$b = 2 \cdot 8 \div 2$
Since Brandon is half as old as Tyler and Tyler is twice Megan's age, Brandon is 8.

1. **Work Together** Solve the problem below, using any method you choose.

> Tyler is twice as old as Megan. Brandon is half as old as Tyler. How old are Tyler and Brandon if Megan is 8 years old?

2. **Math Talk** What method did you use to solve the problem? Tell why you chose that method. What other methods could you have used?

Unit 1, Lesson 9

Copyright © Houghton Mifflin Company

Activity Note Students may write equations, make models, or use guess and check to solve the problem. Students must recognize that Megan's age must be the starting point for any method they choose.

 **Math Writing Prompt**

Write Your Own Write a word problem for this equation: $n + 4n = 25$.

MegaMath Grades K-6 **Software Support**

Ice Station Exploration: Arctic Algebra, Level I

Inverse Equations
Activity Card 1-9

Work: By Yourself

1. Copy the equation below.
   $5n + 7 = 22$

2. Use inverse operations to write two more equations that have the same solution. $5n = 22 - 7$; $7 = 22 - 5n$

3. Solve all three equations to be sure that the solutions are the same.

4. Repeat the activity for each equation below.
   $37 = 9f + 1$ $18 - 4p = 10$

5. **Explain** How does using inverse operations help you to write two more equations with the same solution?
   Possible answer: Addition and subtraction are inverse operations. So every sum of two different addends can also be expressed as the difference between the sum and one of the addends.

Unit 1, Lesson 9

Copyright © Houghton Mifflin Company

Activity Note Be sure that students understand how inverse operations relate to writing multiple equations that express the same relationship.

 **Math Writing Prompt**

Explain Your Thinking Is the following true? How do you know? $4n + 3n + n = 6n + 2n$

DESTINATION Math **Software Support**
Course III: Module 2: Unit 1: Whole Number Sums

③ Homework and Spiral Review

1–9
Homework **Goal:** Additional Practice

✓ Include students' work for page 29 as part of their portfolios.

1–9
Remembering **Goal:** Spiral Review

This Remembering activity would be appropriate anytime after today's lesson.

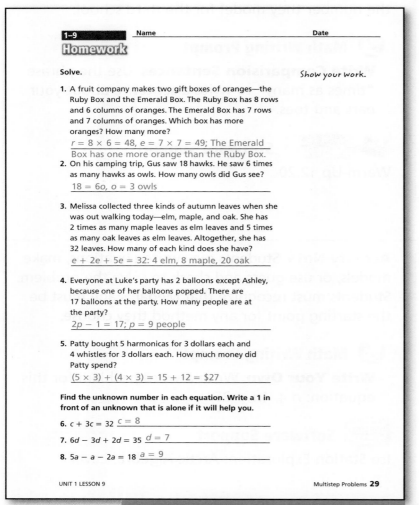

1–9 Name _____ Date _____
Homework

Solve.   *Show your work.*

1. A fruit company makes two gift boxes of oranges—the Ruby Box and the Emerald Box. The Ruby Box has 8 rows and 6 columns of oranges. The Emerald Box has 7 rows and 7 columns of oranges. Which box has more oranges? How many more?
   $r = 8 \times 6 = 48$, $e = 7 \times 7 = 49$; The Emerald Box has one more orange than the Ruby Box.

2. On his camping trip, Gus saw 18 hawks. He saw 6 times as many hawks as owls. How many owls did Gus see?
   $18 = 6o$, $o = 3$ owls

3. Melissa collected three kinds of autumn leaves when she was out walking today—elm, maple, and oak. She has 2 times as many maple leaves as elm leaves and 5 times as many oak leaves as elm leaves. Altogether, she has 32 leaves. How many of each kind does she have?
   $e + 2e + 5e = 32$: 4 elm, 8 maple, 20 oak

4. Everyone at Luke's party has 2 balloons except Ashley, because one of her balloons popped. There are 17 balloons at the party. How many people are at the party?
   $2p - 1 = 17$; $p = 9$ people

5. Patty bought 5 harmonicas for 3 dollars each and 4 whistles for 3 dollars each. How much money did Patty spend?
   $(5 \times 3) + (4 \times 3) = 15 + 12 = \$27$

Find the unknown number in each equation. Write a 1 in front of an unknown that is alone if it will help you.

6. $c + 3c = 32$ $c = 8$

7. $6d - 3d + 2d = 35$ $d = 7$

8. $5a - a - 2a = 18$ $a = 9$

UNIT 1 LESSON 9   Multistep Problems **29**

Homework and Remembering page 29

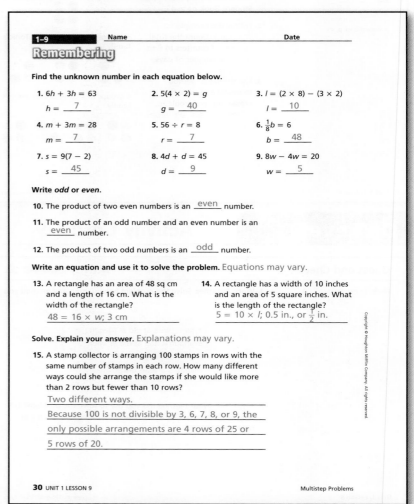

1–9 Name _____ Date _____
Remembering

Find the unknown number in each equation below.

1. $6h + 3h = 63$
   $h = \underline{7}$

2. $5(4 \times 2) = g$
   $g = \underline{40}$

3. $l = (2 \times 8) - (3 \times 2)$
   $l = \underline{10}$

4. $m + 3m = 28$
   $m = \underline{7}$

5. $56 \div r = 8$
   $r = \underline{7}$

6. $\frac{1}{8}b = 6$
   $b = \underline{48}$

7. $s = 9(7 - 2)$
   $s = \underline{45}$

8. $4d + d = 45$
   $d = \underline{9}$

9. $8w - 4w = 20$
   $w = \underline{5}$

Write odd or even.

10. The product of two even numbers is an __even__ number.

11. The product of an odd number and an even number is an __even__ number.

12. The product of two odd numbers is an __odd__ number.

Write an equation and use it to solve the problem. Equations may vary.

13. A rectangle has an area of 48 sq cm and a length of 16 cm. What is the width of the rectangle?
    $48 = 16 \times w$; 3 cm

14. A rectangle has a width of 10 inches and an area of 5 square inches. What is the length of the rectangle?
    $5 = 10 \times l$; 0.5 in., or $\frac{1}{2}$ in.

Solve. Explain your answer. Explanations may vary.

15. A stamp collector is arranging 100 stamps in rows with the same number of stamps in each row. How many different ways could she arrange the stamps if she would like more than 2 rows but fewer than 10 rows?
    Two different ways.
    Because 100 is not divisible by 3, 6, 7, 8, or 9, the only possible arrangements are 4 rows of 25 or 5 rows of 20.

30 UNIT 1 LESSON 9   Multistep Problems

Homework and Remembering page 30

Home or School Activity

Social Studies Connection

Number Systems As people worked with numbers and learned to count and do operations, they also invented math symbols.

Copy this table on the board.

Symbol	First Use
+, −	1498
=	1557
×	1637
÷	1659

Have your students copy it, make a time line, and write two equations that people in 1600 could write and two equations that they could not write.

History of Math Symbols

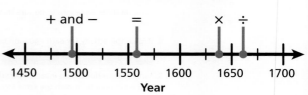

UNIT 1 LESSON 10

Properties of Multiplication

REAL WORLD Problem Solving

Lesson Objective

- Analyze and apply the Commutative, Associative, and Distributive Properties.

Vocabulary

Commutative Property
Associative Property
Distributive Property
expression
example
counterexample

The Day at a Glance

Today's Goals	Materials
1 **Teaching the Lesson** **A1:** Define and apply the Commutative, Associative, and Distributive Properties. **A2:** Prove or disprove whether the Commutative, Associative, and Distributive Properties apply to all operations. **2** **Going Further** ▶ Extension: Evaluate an Expression ▶ Differentiated Instruction **3** **Homework and Spiral Review**	**Lesson Activities** Student Activity Book pp. 47–49 or Student Hardcover Book pp. 47–49 Homework and Remembering pp. 31–32 Quick Quiz 2 (Assessment Guide) **Going Further** Student Activity Book p. 50 or Student Hardcover Book p. 50 Activity Cards 1-10 Grid Paper (TRB M17) Math Journals *Use* **Math Talk** *today!*

Keeping Skills Sharp

Quick Practice 5 MINUTES	Daily Routines
Goal: Practice division skills. **Materials:** Division Cards **Division in Motion** The students count off from 2 to 10, repeating the sequence until everyone has a number. Then two **Student Leaders** take turns reading a division problem from the Division Cards. Every student who has the number that is the answer stands. One Student Leader gives a hand signal, and the standing students all say the answer in unison.	**Homework Review** Send students to the board to show and explain their solutions. Have the class ask clarifying questions and make comments. **Logic** Use *always*, *sometimes*, or *never* to complete each sentence. 1. The product of 2 and any number is ____ an odd number. never 2. The product of 3 and any number is ____ an even number. sometimes 3. The product of 4 and any number is ____ an even number. always

Properties of Multiplication   **109**

Teaching the Lesson

Explore Multiplication Properties

 30 MINUTES

Goal: Define and apply the Commutative, Associative, and Distributive Properties.

Materials: Student Activity Book or Hardcover Book pp. 47–48

 NCTM Standards:
Number and Operations
Algebra

Class Management

Are your students still directing their explanations to you rather than the other students? Remember to move to the side or the back of the room and direct the class from there. Also, you should not do all the talking. Pause after posing a question and wait for students to answer. Ask, "Why do you think this is so?" rather than giving all the explanations. Soon the students will learn to start questioning themselves. Many teachers find that this is their most difficult challenge, but that it really pays off when they succeed.

The Learning Classroom

Math Talk To help students understand what you mean when you say, "explain your thinking," solve one of the problems at the board as if you were the student. Be sure to tell them about all the parts of your problem and the thinking you used to solve it.

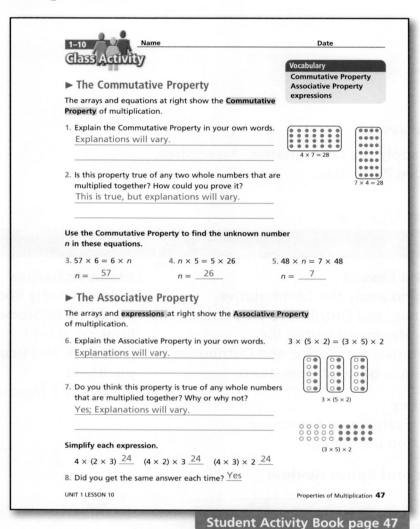

Student Activity Book page 47

► The Commutative Property WHOLE CLASS

The three properties discussed in this lesson have already been introduced in various problem-solving situations, but they have not been identified by name. Since your students have already encountered them before in other contexts, they will probably catch on rather quickly.

Direct students' attention to problems 1–2 on page 47 in the Student Book. Explain that multiplication has three properties that often make problems easier to solve. Have everyone read and answer the questions in this section. Elicit several explanations of the Commutative Property from various students so that everyone is clear about the term. The factors can be put in a different order. The factors can be flipped without changing the product.

If your students know the word *commuter* or *commute*, you might want to make that connection: a commuter moves from one place to another. Similarly, the factors of a multiplication problem can be moved from one place to another without changing the product. Have students complete exercises 3–5.

Ask students to give an algebraic equation for the Commutative Property, using *a* and *b* as variables for any numbers. $a \times b = b \times a$ or $ab = ba$.

▶ The Associative Property WHOLE CLASS

Students encountered this property when they did combination problems with three or more numbers. After looking over the arrays on page 47 of the Student Book, elicit several explanations of the Associative Property from the class.

● The factors can be grouped together in different ways without changing the product.

If your students know the word *associate*, you might want to make that connection: the factors can associate with each other in any way. It should be clear from the arrays that any grouping can take place without changing the product.

Explain that being able to multiply different factors first can sometimes make multiplication much easier. Give students the problem $(9 \times 4) \times 2$. It simplifies to 36×2. Now ask students if they can use the Associative Property to make the problem easier: $9 \times (4 \times 2)$ simplifies to 9×8. It is easier to multiply 9×8 than to multiply 36×2.

Ask students to give an algebraic equation for the Associative Property, using *a*, *b*, and *c* as variables for any numbers. $a \times (b \times c) = (a \times b) \times c$ or $a(bc) = (ab)c$.

Activity continued ▶

① Teaching the Lesson (continued)

Activity 1

 **Quick Quiz**

See Assessment Guide for Unit 1 Quick Quiz 2.

The Learning Classroom

Math Talk This may be a good day to talk with the class about what makes a good explanation. Students may want to produce a list on poster board that can be displayed in the classroom for later reference. Students may make suggestions such as these.

1) Write your work so that everyone can see it.

2) Talk loud enough for other students to hear.

3) Use a pointer to point at your work.

4) Say how you arrived at the answer, not just the answer.

5) Stand to the side of your work when you talk.

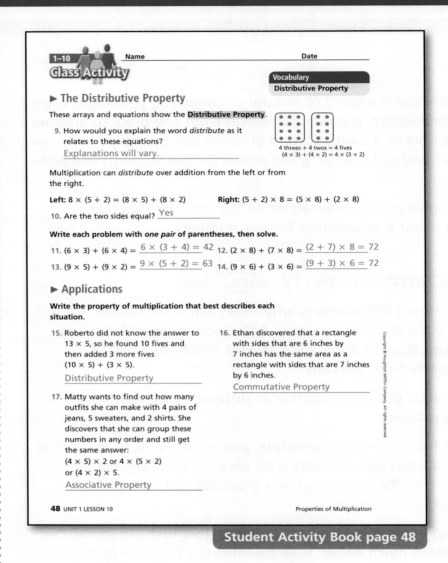

Student Activity Book page 48

▶ The Distributive Property [WHOLE CLASS]

Students encountered this property as one possible strategy for solving multiplication problems they did not know. ($7 \times 8 = 5$ eights $+ 2$ eights $= 40 + 16 = 56$.) After discussing the array in exercise 9 on page 48, elicit several explanations of the Distributive Property.

● If two numbers are added together and multiplied by the same factor, the multiplication can be done to the total $a \times (b + c)$ or to one number at a time $(a \times b) + (a \times c)$. In other words, the multiplication can be "spread out" or distributed. We say that multiplication is distributive over addition.

There is often an advantage in doing the multiplication to the total or, stated another way, first simplifying the problem so that it has only one pair of parentheses.

▶ Applications [WHOLE CLASS]

Direct students' attention to Problems 15–17 on page 48. Read the problems together, and have the students discuss which properties were applied in each situation described.

Reasoning and Properties

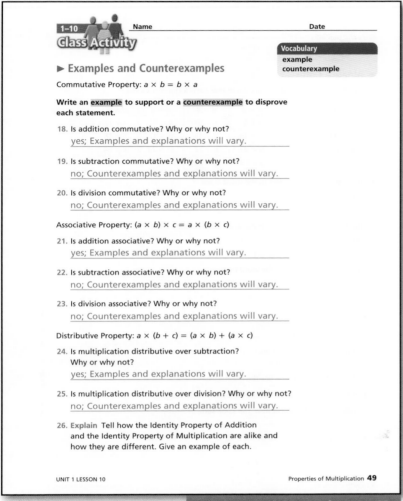

Class Activity

Name _____ Date _____

Vocabulary
example
counterexample

▶ **Examples and Counterexamples**

Commutative Property: $a \times b = b \times a$

Write an example to support or a counterexample to disprove each statement.

18. Is addition commutative? Why or why not?
    yes; Examples and explanations will vary.

19. Is subtraction commutative? Why or why not?
    no; Counterexamples and explanations will vary.

20. Is division commutative? Why or why not?
    no; Counterexamples and explanations will vary.

Associative Property: $(a \times b) \times c = a \times (b \times c)$

21. Is addition associative? Why or why not?
    yes; Examples and explanations will vary.

22. Is subtraction associative? Why or why not?
    no; Counterexamples and explanations will vary.

23. Is division associative? Why or why not?
    no; Counterexamples and explanations will vary.

Distributive Property: $a \times (b + c) = (a \times b) + (a \times c)$

24. Is multiplication distributive over subtraction? Why or why not?
    yes; Examples and explanations will vary.

25. Is multiplication distributive over division? Why or why not?
    no; Counterexamples and explanations will vary.

26. **Explain** Tell how the Identity Property of Addition and the Identity Property of Multiplication are alike and how they are different. Give an example of each.

UNIT 1 LESSON 10   Properties of Multiplication **49**

Student Activity Book page 49

▶ **Examples and Counterexamples** | WHOLE CLASS |

In problems 18–25 on page 49 of the Student Book, students are asked to try some experiments to decide which properties are unique to multiplication and which ones are true for other operations. Students should use examples and counterexamples to help them decide. The process of testing and discovery is the important part of reasoning and proof.

 Math Talk Before students discuss exercise 26, ask what they remember about the Identity Property. Include these ideas.

● The Identity Property of Addition states that adding 0 to any number gives the original number: $5 + 0 = 5$.

● The Identity Property of Multiplication states that multiplying any number by 1 gives the original number: $5 \cdot 1 = 5$.

● The word *identity* is used for this property because the sum or product is identical to the original addend or factor.

 20 MINUTES

Goal: Prove or disprove whether the Commutative, Associative, and Distributive Properties apply to all operations.

Materials: Student Activity Book or Hardcover Book p. 49

✔ **NCTM Standards:**
Reasoning and Proof
Algebra

Teaching Note

Language and Vocabulary
Students use examples to test a property or argument. Introduce the word *counterexample*. When students use examples to disprove a property or argument, the examples are called counterexamples.

English Language Learners
Write *prove* and *disprove* on the board.

● **Beginning** Ask: Does *prove* mean "to show something is true"? yes Say: *Disprove* means "to show something is false."

● **Intermediate and Advanced** Say: *Prove* means "to show something is __." true *Disprove* means "to show something is __." false

 Ongoing Assessment

Have students give an example of:

▶ the Commutative Property.

▶ the Associative Property.

▶ the Distributive Property.

Going Further

Extension: Evaluate an Expression

Goal: Use substitution to simplify algebraic expressions.

Materials: Student Activity Book or Hardcover Book p. 50

✔ **NCTM Standards:**
Number and Operations
Representation
Algebra

▶ Introduce Substitution | WHOLE CLASS |

An important algebraic skill is the ability to simplify an expression by using substitution. On the board, write several addition expressions that contain two variables, such as those shown below.

$a + b$ $n + s$ $c + c$

For each expression, say a number that each variable represents, and then ask students to use addition to simplify the expression. For example, have students simplify $a + b$ when $a = 3$ and $b = 5$.
$a + b = 3 + 5 = 8$

Invite volunteers to write other addition expressions and state a value for each variable. As a class, use substitution to simplify the expressions.

▶ Algebra Code | INDIVIDUALS |

Complete exercise 1 on Student Book page 50 as a class. Have students write the value of each letter on the line below the letter and then write the sum of the numbers.

Ask students to work individually or paired with a **Helping Partner** to complete exercises 2–4.

Exercise 5 is designed as a challenge; have students work in **Small Groups** to complete the challenge, then share their solutions. Some groups may enjoy the challenge of finding the greatest and least possible sums for a three letter word.

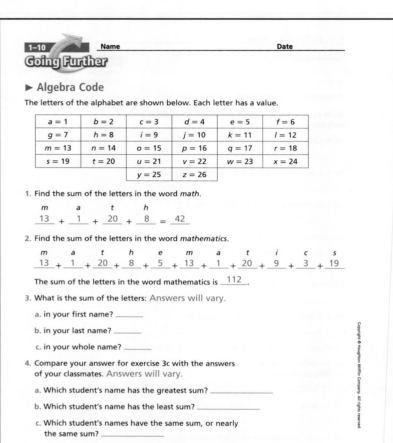

Student Activity Book page 50

Differentiated Instruction

Advanced Learners Have students choose a name that has duplicate or triplicate letters in it. Ask them to write an algebraic expression that combines like terms. Then have them use the chart on Student Book page 50 to substitute values for each letter and solve.

Lillian
$3l + 2i + a + n$
$(3 • 12) + (2 • 9) + 1 + 14$
$36 + 18 + 15$
69

Differentiated Instruction

Intervention   Activity Card 1-10

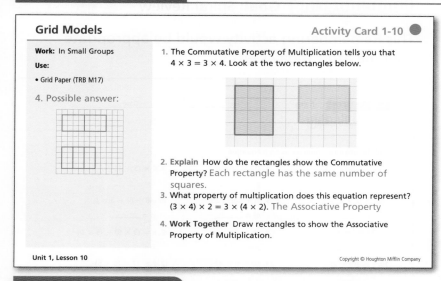

Grid Models   Activity Card 1-10 ●

Work: In Small Groups

Use:
• Grid Paper (TRB M17)

4. Possible answer:

1. The Commutative Property of Multiplication tells you that 4 × 3 = 3 × 4. Look at the two rectangles below.

2. **Explain** How do the rectangles show the Commutative Property? Each rectangle has the same number of squares.

3. What property of multiplication does this equation represent? (3 × 4) × 2 = 3 × (4 × 2). The Associative Property

4. **Work Together** Draw rectangles to show the Associative Property of Multiplication.

Unit 1, Lesson 10   Copyright © Houghton Mifflin Company

Activity Note Tell students to draw one rectangle for each product in parentheses to help them model the Associative Property. Then they can use the remaining factor on each side of the equation to complete both parts of the model.

 Math Writing Prompt

Explain a Property Explain the Commutative Property. Be sure to use the word *order.*

 **Software Support**

Warm-Up 12.36

On Level   Activity Card 1-10

Mental Math   Activity Card 1-10 ▲

Work: In Pairs

1. The example on the right shows how to find the product 5 × 26 using multiplication properties and mental math.

     5 × 26 =
     5 × (20 + 6) =
     (5 × 20) + (5 × 6) =
     100 + 30 =
     130

2. What property does the example use to find the product 5 × 26? Distributive Property

3. On your own, find each product, using either paper and pencil or mental math. Take turns choosing a method for each problem. Your partner uses the method you did not choose.

9 × 31	6 × 107	7 × 52	8 × 105
279	642	364	840

Unit 1, Lesson 10   Copyright © Houghton Mifflin Company

Activity Note Multiplication properties can make computations easier to do mentally. Partners can race to see who can find each product faster. Have them exchange solutions to check their work.

 Math Writing Prompt

Explain Your Thinking Explain the Associative Property. Try to use the word *associate* in your description.

 Software Support

The Number Games: Up, Up, and Array, Level J

Challenge   Activity Card 1-10

Use Substitution   Activity Card 1-10 ■

Work: By Yourself

1. Use substitution to show the properties of multiplication. Copy the equation and then choose a different value for each variable. $ab = ba$

2. Substitute the value you chose for each variable. Then simplify both sides of the equation to show that the Commutative Property is true for multiplication.

3. Repeat the activity for the Associative Property of Multiplication and the Distributive Property.

4. **Compare** The Identity Property of Multiplication can be expressed as $a \times 1 = a$. How does this compare to the Identity Property of Addition? Possible answer: The Identity Property of Addition can be expressed as $a + 0 = a$.

Unit 1, Lesson 10   Copyright © Houghton Mifflin Company

Activity Note Be sure that students can recall the commutative, associative, and distributive properties and can express each property in algebraic terms before beginning this activity.

 Math Writing Prompt

True or False For all whole numbers *a, b,* and *c,* if *a* is greater than *b,* then *a* − *c* is greater than *b* − *c.* Give an example or a counterexample.

 DESTINATION Math· **Software Support**

Course III: Module 1: Unit 2: Finding Factors

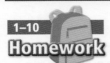

③ Homework and Spiral Review

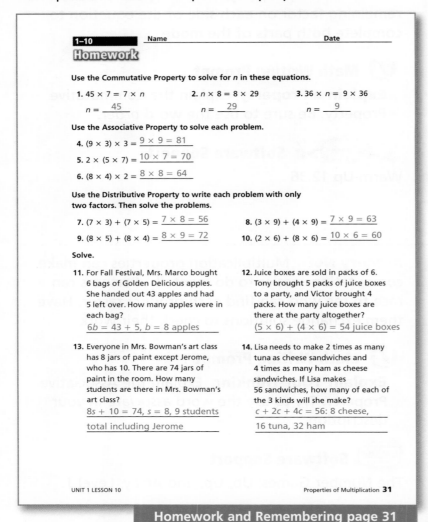

1–10 Homework **Goal:** Additional Practice

Use this Homework page to provide students with more practice with multiplication properties.

1–10 Homework

Name _____ Date _____

Use the Commutative Property to solve for *n* in these equations.

1. $45 \times 7 = 7 \times n$
n = __45__

2. $n \times 8 = 8 \times 29$
n = __29__

3. $36 \times n = 9 \times 36$
n = __9__

Use the Associative Property to solve each problem.

4. $(9 \times 3) \times 3 = $ __$9 \times 9 = 81$__

5. $2 \times (5 \times 7) = $ __$10 \times 7 = 70$__

6. $(8 \times 4) \times 2 = $ __$8 \times 8 = 64$__

Use the Distributive Property to write each problem with only two factors. Then solve the problems.

7. $(7 \times 3) + (7 \times 5) = $ __$7 \times 8 = 56$__

8. $(3 \times 9) + (4 \times 9) = $ __$7 \times 9 = 63$__

9. $(8 \times 5) + (8 \times 4) = $ __$8 \times 9 = 72$__

10. $(2 \times 6) + (8 \times 6) = $ __$10 \times 6 = 60$__

Solve.

11. For Fall Festival, Mrs. Marco bought 6 bags of Golden Delicious apples. She handed out 43 apples and had 5 left over. How many apples were in each bag?
__$6b = 43 + 5,\ b = 8$ apples__

12. Juice boxes are sold in packs of 6. Tony brought 5 packs of juice boxes to a party, and Victor brought 4 packs. How many juice boxes are there at the party altogether?
__$(5 \times 6) + (4 \times 6) = 54$ juice boxes__

13. Everyone in Mrs. Bowman's art class has 8 jars of paint except Jerome, who has 10. There are 74 jars of paint in the room. How many students are there in Mrs. Bowman's art class?
__$8s + 10 = 74,\ s = 8$, 9 students__
__total including Jerome__

14. Lisa needs to make 2 times as many tuna as cheese sandwiches and 4 times as many ham as cheese sandwiches. If Lisa makes 56 sandwiches, how many of each of the 3 kinds will she make?
__$c + 2c + 4c = 56$: 8 cheese,__
__16 tuna, 32 ham__

UNIT 1 LESSON 10   Properties of Multiplication **31**

Homework and Remembering page 31

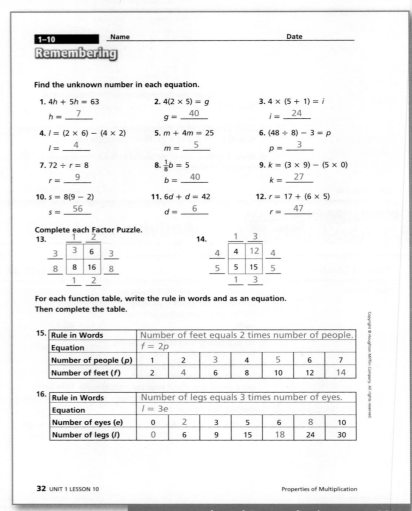

1–10 Remembering **Goal:** Spiral Review

This Remembering activity would be appropriate anytime after today's lesson.

1–10 Remembering

Name _____ Date _____

Find the unknown number in each equation.

1. $4h + 5h = 63$
h = __7__

2. $4(2 \times 5) = g$
g = __40__

3. $4 \times (5 + 1) = i$
i = __24__

4. $l = (2 \times 6) - (4 \times 2)$
l = __4__

5. $m + 4m = 25$
m = __5__

6. $(48 \div 8) - 3 = p$
p = __3__

7. $72 \div r = 8$
r = __9__

8. $\frac{1}{8}b = 5$
b = __40__

9. $k = (3 \times 9) - (5 \times 0)$
k = __27__

10. $s = 8(9 - 2)$
s = __56__

11. $6d + d = 42$
d = __6__

12. $r = 17 + (6 \times 5)$
r = __47__

Complete each Factor Puzzle.

13.

	1	2	
3	3	6	3
8	8	16	8
	1	2	

14.

	1	3	
4	4	12	4
5	5	15	5
	1	3	

For each function table, write the rule in words and as an equation. Then complete the table.

15.

Rule in Words	Number of feet equals 2 times number of people.						
Equation	$f = 2p$						
Number of people (*p*)	1	2	3	4	5	6	7
Number of feet (*f*)	2	4	6	8	10	12	14

16.

Rule in Words	Number of legs equals 3 times number of eyes.						
Equation	$l = 3e$						
Number of eyes (*e*)	0	2	3	5	6	8	10
Number of legs (*l*)	0	6	9	15	18	24	30

32 UNIT 1 LESSON 10   Properties of Multiplication

Homework and Remembering page 32

Home or School Activity

 Language Arts Connection

Suffixes in Math Explain that a suffix is something added to the end of a root word that changes its meaning. For example, the suffix *-itive* can change a verb to an adjective. The suffix *-itive* means "having the ability or quality of." Sometimes the spelling of the root word changes a little when the suffix is added.

Ask students to use a dictionary to find the definitions of the verbs *add*, and *multiply*. Then use the meanings of those verbs and the suffix *-itive* to write their own definitions for the adjectives *additive* and *multiplicative*.

Verb:	create
Definition:	to make something new
Adjective:	creative
Definition:	having the ability to make something new

Use Mathematical Processes

REAL WORLD Problem Solving

Lesson Objectives

● Apply mathematical concepts and skills in meaningful contexts.

● Reinforce the NCTM process skills embedded in this unit with a variety of problem-solving situations.

The Day at a Glance

Today's Goals	Materials
1 Teaching the Lesson **A1: Science Connection** Organize data in a table; analyze data and make predictions. **A2: Problem Solving** Write expressions and equations to show that a problem has multiple solutions. **A3: Representation** Use a drawing to prove the solution to a problem. **A4: Communication** Use drawings and expressions to see a pattern when adding and subtracting. **A5: Reasoning and Proof** Develop and test generalizations. **2 Going Further** ▶ Differentiated Instruction **3 Homework and Spiral Review**	**Lesson Activities** Student Activity Book pp. 51–52 or Student Hardcover Book pp. 51–52 Homework and Remembering pp. 33–34 **Going Further** Activity Cards 1-11 Number cubes Math Journals 123 *Use* **Math Talk** *today!*

Keeping Skills Sharp

Quick Practice/Daily Routines	Classroom Management
If you wish to include Quick Practice or a Daily Routine, choose content based on the needs of your class.	Select activities from this lesson that support important goals and objectives, or that help students prepare for state or district tests.

Activity 1

Math and Science

 30 MINUTES

Goal: Organize data in a table; analyze data and make predictions.

Materials: Student Activity Book or Hardcover Book p. 51

 NCTM Standards:
Connections
Representation
Problem Solving

Name _____ Date _____

▶ **Math and Science**

Strong winds can form during thunderstorms. If the conditions are right, these winds can develop into a swirling column of air called a funnel cloud. When a funnel cloud touches the ground, it is called a tornado.

The Fujita scale (F-scale) classifies tornados by their wind speeds. Tornados in classes F0 and F1 cause light to moderate damage. F2 and F3 tornados can cause severe damage. Less than 2 out of every 100 tornados, or 2%, are strong enough to totally flatten buildings. These tornados are in the F4 or F5 category.

Tornados often occur along a line of thunderstorms. During a strong storm system, a meteorologist recorded these tornado wind speeds.

	F-scale Classifications	
Category	Wind Speed (in miles per hour)	
F0	40–72	
F1	73–112	
F2	113–157	
F3	158–206	
F4	207–260	
F5	260–318	

119	70	88	110	98
109	111	94	87	89
106	125	79	144	55
108	100	161	105	113

1. Organize this data in a table using the F-scale classifications.
   Tables may vary. Check student's work.

2. How many tornados were recorded in all? _____20_____

3. How many tornados can be categorized as F0 or F1? Support your answer.
   15; Possible answer: F0 is 42–72 mph: 55, 70; F1 is 73–112 mph: 79, 87,
   88, 89, 94, 98, 100, 105, 106, 108, 109, 110, 111

Suppose a large storm system generates 140 tornados. Assume that the ratio of F-scale classifications in this storm system is approximately the same as in the storm system on your chart.
4. How many of the tornados in this system would likely be classified as F2–F5? Explain your reasoning.
   According to my storm chart there would be 0 F4 or F5 tornados, but if 2 out of every 100 are F4 or F5, there could be some because 140 > 100.

Possible answer: Since 140 ÷ 20 = 7, there would be about 7 times as many tornados in each classification, or 7 × 4 = 28 F2 tornados and 7 × 1 = 7 = 7 F3 tornados.

UNIT 1 LESSON 11   Use Mathematical Processes **51**

Student Activity Book page 51

▶ **Introduce the Activity** Math Talk

Task 1 During a class discussion on tornados, make sure students understand that destructive tornados are infrequent. Before students begin organizing the data, discuss questions 2 and 3.

▶ Without analyzing the data, how many tornados do you think will be classified as F4 or F5? Why? 0, because less than 2 out of every 100 tornados are classified as F4 or F5.

▶ **Organizing Data**

Task 2 Tell students that they need to organize the wind speed data so that they can easily see how many tornados fall into each category

▶ What kinds of tables have you used to organize data? Possible answers: Function tables, two-column tables, frequency or tally tables

▶ What do you think would be the most helpful way of organizing this data? Possible answer: Sort data into the 6 classifications of tornados.

▶ **Use Data to Make Predictions**

Task 3

▶ Which type of tornado occurred most often? F1

▶ How many tornados had wind speeds greater than 206 mph? 0

Discuss Talk about exercise 4 and have students share their reasoning. Have volunteers explain their estimates for the number of F5 tornados and the reason they feel their estimate is valid.

English Language Learners

Write *classify* and *category* on the board.

• **Beginning** Say: We put tornados in groups. Ask: Are the groups called categories? yes Is this classifying? yes

• **Intermediate and Advanced** Say: *Category* is another word for "__." group *Classify* means "put things in __." categories

Rock Climbing Safety

30 MINUTES

Goal: Write expressions and equations to show that a problem has multiple solutions.

Materials: Student Activity Book or Hardcover Book p. 52

 NCTM Standards:
Problem Solving
Communication

1–11
Name _____ Date _____

► Rock Climbing Safety

Rock climbing is an exciting and dangerous sport. To protect climbers from falls, rock climbers usually work in pairs. A combination of camming devices, carabiners, and rope reduce how far a climber can fall if he or she slips. These devices limit a fall to about twice the distance a climber is from the last spot where a camming device was inserted.

Miguel and Cameron are preparing to climb to the top of a 75-foot peak. They will insert camming devices approximately every 20 feet. Use this information and the information above to solve these problems.

5. Will 3 camming devices be enough? How do you know?
   Yes, the last camming device will be placed at about
   60 ft. They will have only 15 ft more to climb.

6. They will need at least twice as much rope as the distance they will climb. Write and solve an equation to find the amount of rope they need.
   Sample: $r = 2 \times 75 = 150$ ft

7. Cameron is the lead climber. She placed the second camming device and climbed about 10 more feet. Write and solve an equation to approximate the total distance Cameron has climbed so far.
   Sample: $d = (2 \times 20) + 10 = 40 + 10 = 50$ ft

8. Suppose Cameron placed the third camming device, climbed about 5 feet, and then slipped. Write and solve an equation to show approximately how far she fell.
   Sample: $d = 2 \times 5$ ft $= 10$ ft

9. When Cameron regains her footing after her fall, how much farther must she climb to reach the top of the peak? Use an expression to show how to solve the problem.
   20 ft; Sample: $75 - (3 \times 20 + 5 - 10)$

52 UNIT 1 LESSON 11   Use Mathematical Processes

Student Activity Book page 52

► Rock Climbing Safety Equipment

Task 1 Discuss rock climbing and its safety measures. Ask students if they have ever seen people rock climb or climb walls.

► Would the same protections described for rock climbing be needed for climbing a 10-ft wall? Answers may vary.

► Have students determine the greatest distance Cameron or Miguel could fall. About 40 feet; If the slip is just before placing a camming device, the fall would be 2 × 20 or 40 ft.

► Use Reasoning   Math Talk

Task 2 Discuss reasoning students used to solve the problems.

► How can you prove your answer to problem 5? Possible answer: I can draw a picture to show where the camming devices would be placed and to show that there would be only 15 ft after the last camming device.

► How can you be sure the equations you wrote for problems 6-8 are correct? Answers may vary.

► Is there more than one possible answer for problems 6-8? Answers may vary.

► Using Parentheses   Math Talk

Task 3 There are many possible expressions that could be used to solve problem 9. Have students check their expression to see if they need to use parentheses. Have volunteers write their expressions on the board and explain why the expression describes the situation.

Activity 3

Climbing Challenge

 15 MINUTES

Goal: Use a drawing to prove the solution to a problem.

 NCTM Standards:
Representation   Reasoning and Proof

Suppose you are climbing a rock. At 50 ft you cannot find a spot to grab to climb higher. So you climb down 10 ft, move to the right a distance and then climb back up 10 ft. At what height are you? 50 ft

Representation

Hold a whole-class discussion of the problem.

▶ Write an expression and make a drawing to prove your answer. $50 - 10 + 10$

▶ How would your drawing change if you climbed 78 feet before you decided to climb down 10 feet, move to the right, and climb back up 10 feet? I would change 50 to 78.

Activity 4

Going Up

 15 MINUTES

Goal: Use drawings and expressions to see a pattern when adding and subtracting.

 NCTM Standards:
Communication   Representation

Suppose you get on an elevator at the third floor. You ride up 4 floors, down 2 floors, up 7 floors, and down 9 floors. What floor are you on now? the third floor

Communication

Discuss how a picture or expression can communicate the situation in this problem.

▶ Write an expression to solve the problem that involves only 3 numbers? $3 + 11 - 11$

Have students write their own elevator problems that start and stop on the same floor.

▶ What pattern do you see in all of the elevator problems? Possible answer: The number of floors up and down is always the same.

Activity 5

Develop Generalizations

 15 MINUTES

Goal: Develop and test generalizations.

 NCTM Standards:
Reasoning and Proof   Communication

Explain why the statement below is true. Include a numerical example to support your reasoning.

$$a + b - b = a$$

Use the statement below to make a generalization. Use the generalization to complete the second equation.

$$a + b - a = b \qquad 43 + 38 - 43 = ?$$

If you add two values and then subtract the first value, the result is the second value; 38.

Reasoning and Proof

(123) Math Talk Discuss the term *generalization* and how to test a generalization. The discussion should include these points

▶ Is the value of both of the *a*s the same? yes

▶ Is the value of both of the *b*s the same? yes

▶ If the same quantity is added and then subtracted from another value, does the value change? no

▶ Ask students to use the generalization to complete this equation:
$27 + 66 - 66 = ?$ 27

▶ Give students an opportunity to develop and test generalizations of their own.

② Going Further

● Intervention   Activity Card 1-11

Equation-Problem Match   Activity Card 1-11 ●

Work: In Pairs

Use:
• 2 Number Cubes, labeled 1–6

1. Roll the number cubes. Each partner uses the two numbers to write an equation using any operation.

6 × 4 = 24

2. Partners exchange equations and on a separate piece of paper write a word problem that matches their partner's equation.

3. **Work Together** Partners review the equations and word problems to see if they are matches.

4. Switch equations and word problems with another pair. Match their equations with their word problems.

Unit 1, Lesson 11   Copyright © Houghton Mifflin Company

Activity Note Students write equations and problems to match the equations. You may want pairs of students to check each other's work.

 Math Writing Prompt

Choose any pair of numbers you rolled. Write 4 different problems—one for each operation (addition, subtraction, multiplication, and division).

Soar to Success Math ★ Software Support

Warm-Up 12.31

▲ On Level   Activity Card 1-11

Sum Prediction   Activity Card 1-11 ▲

Work: In Small Groups

Use:
• 2 Number cubes, labeled 1–6

1. Copy the table. Take turns rolling the number cubes and recording their sum in the table.

2. Roll the number cubes 20 times and record the sums.

3. **Predict** If you roll the number cubes 40 times, how many times do you think you will roll each sum? Roll the number cubes 20 more times to test your prediction.

4. **Predict** How many times would you need to roll the number cubes to get a sum of 12 two different times? Explain why you named that number of times.

Sum	Tally	Total
2		
3	I	
4	III	
5		
6	I	
7	II	
8	II	
9		
10	I	
11		
12		

Unit 1, Lesson 11   Copyright © Houghton Mifflin Company

Activity Note This activity can be done individually, in pairs, or in groups. Students make predictions based on the sums they roll.

 Math Writing Prompt

Write a prediction question based on 120 rolls. Predict the answer, and then give the question to a friend to predict.

 Software Support

Fraction Action: Last Chance Canyon, Level D

■ Challenge   Activity Card 1-11

Number Riddles   Activity Card 1-11 ■

Work: By Yourself

1. I am a number. Multiply me by any number and you will see the number you started with. What number am I? 1

2. I reduce numbers to nothing. Multiply me by any number and I will eliminate it. What number am I? 0

3. **Predict** Without multiplying, decide if these two expressions are equal. Explain your reasoning.

(3 × 4) × 2

(4 × 2) × 3

equal, Associative Property of Multiplication

4. Dena says that the product of 5(8 × 7) is the same as the product of 8(35). Is she correct? Explain.
yes, Associative Property of Multiplication

Unit 1, Lesson 11   Copyright © Houghton Mifflin Company

Activity Note This activity involves the understanding of the Identity, Zero, and Associative Properties of Multiplication.

 Math Writing Prompt

Write a multiplication expression using 3 numbers. Rearrange the numbers with different orders and groupings. Is the product always the same? What properties tell you that this will always be so?

 DESTINATION Math· Software Support

Course III: Module 1: Unit 2: Finding Factors

③ Homework and Spiral Review

✓ Include students' completed Homework page as part of their portfolios.

This Remembering page would be appropriate anytime after today's lesson.

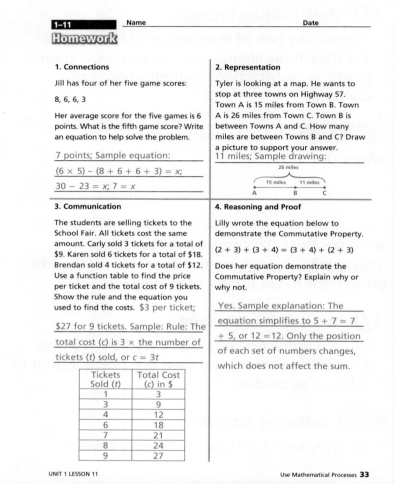

1-11 Name _____ Date _____
Homework

1. Connections

Jill has four of her five game scores:

8, 6, 6, 3

Her average score for the five games is 6 points. What is the fifth game score? Write an equation to help solve the problem.

7 points; Sample equation:

$(6 \times 5) - (8 + 6 + 6 + 3) = x;$

$30 - 23 = x; 7 = x$

2. Representation

Tyler is looking at a map. He wants to stop at three towns on Highway 57. Town A is 15 miles from Town B. Town A is 26 miles from Town C. Town B is between Towns A and C. How many miles are between Towns B and C? Draw a picture to support your answer.
11 miles; Sample drawing:

26 miles
15 miles   11 miles
A   B   C

3. Communication

The students are selling tickets to the School Fair. All tickets cost the same amount. Carly sold 3 tickets for a total of $9. Karen sold 6 tickets for a total of $18. Brendan sold 4 tickets for a total of $12. Use a function table to find the price per ticket and the total cost of 9 tickets. Show the rule and the equation you used to find the costs. $3 per ticket;

$27 for 9 tickets. Sample: Rule: The

total cost (c) is 3 × the number of

tickets (t) sold, or c = 3t

Tickets Sold (t)	Total Cost (c) in $
1	3
3	9
4	12
6	18
7	21
8	24
9	27

4. Reasoning and Proof

Lilly wrote the equation below to demonstrate the Commutative Property.

$(2 + 3) + (3 + 4) = (3 + 4) + (2 + 3)$

Does her equation demonstrate the Commutative Property? Explain why or why not.

Yes. Sample explanation: The

equation simplifies to 5 + 7 = 7

+ 5, or 12 = 12. Only the position

of each set of numbers changes,

which does not affect the sum.

UNIT 1 LESSON 11   Use Mathematical Processes **33**

Homework and Remembering page 33

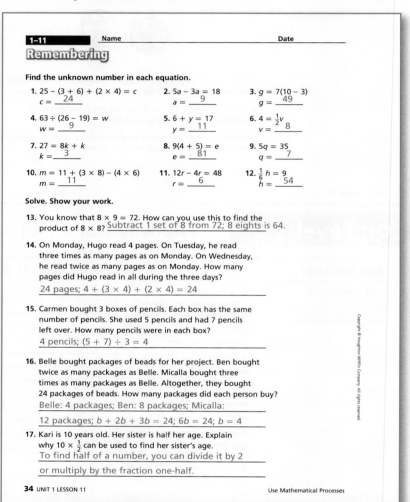

1-11 Name _____ Date _____
Remembering

Find the unknown number in each equation.

1. $25 - (3 + 6) + (2 \times 4) = c$
$c = $ 24

2. $5a - 3a = 18$
$a = $ 9

3. $g = 7(10 - 3)$
$g = $ 49

4. $63 \div (26 - 19) = w$
$w = $ 9

5. $6 + y = 17$
$y = $ 11

6. $4 = \frac{1}{2}v$
$v = $ 8

7. $27 = 8k + k$
$k = $ 3

8. $9(4 + 5) = e$
$e = $ 81

9. $5q = 35$
$q = $ 7

10. $m = 11 + (3 \times 8) - (4 \times 6)$
$m = $ 11

11. $12r - 4r = 48$
$r = $ 6

12. $\frac{1}{6}h = 9$
$h = $ 54

Solve. Show your work.

13. You know that $8 \times 9 = 72$. How can you use this to find the product of 8×8? Subtract 1 set of 8 from 72; 8 eights is 64.

14. On Monday, Hugo read 4 pages. On Tuesday, he read three times as many pages as on Monday. On Wednesday, he read twice as many pages as on Monday. How many pages did Hugo read in all during the three days?
24 pages; $4 + (3 \times 4) + (2 \times 4) = 24$

15. Carmen bought 3 boxes of pencils. Each box has the same number of pencils. She used 5 pencils and had 7 pencils left over. How many pencils were in each box?
4 pencils; $(5 + 7) \div 3 = 4$

16. Belle bought packages of beads for her project. Ben bought twice as many packages as Belle. Micalla bought three times as many packages as Belle. Altogether, they bought 24 packages of beads. How many packages did each person buy?
Belle: 4 packages; Ben: 8 packages; Micalla:
12 packages; $b + 2b + 3b = 24; 6b = 24; b = 4$

17. Kari is 10 years old. Her sister is half her age. Explain why $10 \times \frac{1}{2}$ can be used to find her sister's age.
To find half of a number, you can divide it by 2
or multiply by the fraction one-half.

34 UNIT 1 LESSON 11   Use Mathematical Processes

Homework and Remembering page 34

Home or School Activity

 Literature Connection

The Sundae Scoop Have students read *The Sundae Scoop,* by Stuart J. Murphy and illustrated by Cynthia Jabar (Harper Collins, 2003). As they read the book, have them record all of the options for sundaes. Then have students survey a group of 10 classmates and ask them to choose a preference for a sundae. Use the survey results to predict what options to offer at a class sundae party.

As a challenge, have students find the number of scoops in 1 gallon of ice cream. Then have them predict the number of gallons of each flavor of ice cream they would need for a party for the entire school.

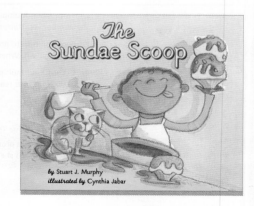

Unit Review and Test

Lesson Objective
- Assess student progress on unit objectives.

The Day at a Glance

Today's Goals	Materials
1 **Assessing the Unit** ▸ Assess student progress on unit objectives. ▸ Use activities from unit lessons to reteach content. **2** **Extending the Assessment** ▸ Use remediation for common errors. There is no homework assignment on a test day.	Unit 1 Test, Student Activity Book pp. 53–54 or Student Hardcover Book pp. 53–54 and Activity Workbook p. 31 Unit 1 Test, Form A or B, Assessment Guide (optional) Unit 1 Performance Assessment, Assessment Guide (optional)

Keeping Skills Sharp

Quick Practice 5 MINUTES	
Goal: Review any skills you choose to meet the needs of your class. If you are doing a unit review day, use any of the Quick Practice activities that provide support for your class. If this is a test day, omit Quick Practice.	**Review and Test Day** You may want to choose a quiet game or other activity (reading a book or working on homework for another subject) for students who finish early.

Assess Unit Objectives

 45 MINUTES (more if schedule permits)

Goal: Assess student progress on unit objectives.

Materials: Student Activity Book pp. 53–54 or Student Hardcover Book pp. 53–54 and Activity Workbook p. 31, Assessment Guide (optional)

▶ Review and Assessment

If your students are ready for assessment on the unit objectives, you may use either the test on the Student Book pages or one of the forms of the Unit 1 Test in the Assessment Guide to assess student progress.

If you feel that students need some review first, you may use the test on the Student Book pages as a review of unit content, and then use one of the forms of the Unit 1 Test in the Assessment Guide to assess student progress.

To assign a numerical score for all of these test forms, use 5 points for each question.

You may also choose to use the Unit 1 Performance Assessment. Scoring for that assessment can be found in its rubric in the Assessment Guide.

▶ Reteaching Resources

The chart at the right lists the test items, the unit objectives they cover, and the lesson activities in which the objective is covered in this unit. You may revisit these activities with students who do not show mastery of the objectives.

U1–Test
Unit Test

Name _____ Date _____

Name all the factor pairs for each number.

1. 10 <u>1 and 10, 2 and 5</u>
2. 15 <u>1 and 15,3 and 5</u>
3. 21 <u>1 and 21,3 and 7</u>
4. 16 <u>1 and 16,2 and 8, 4 and 4</u>

Complete each equation.

5. If $(5 \cdot 3) + (5 \cdot 4) = 35$, then $5(3 + 4) = $ <u>35</u>.
6. If $A \times B = 132$, then $B \times A$ must = <u>132</u>.

Solve.

7. A roller coaster holds 28 people. There are 7 identical cars. How many people can ride in each car?
   <u>4 people</u>

8. Dana made a rectangular quilt with 72 squares. There are 9 squares down. How many squares are there across?
   <u>8 squares</u>

9. A pancake shop serves 3 kinds of pancakes, 5 kinds of syrup, and 2 kinds of juice. How many different breakfast combinations are possible with one of each kind of item?
   <u>30 combinations</u>

For each function table, write the rule in words and as an equation. Then complete the table.

10.
Rule in Words	Output equals input plus 5.					
Equation	$O = I + 5$					
Input (I)	0	2	3	4	5	6
Output (O)	5	7	8	9	10	11

11.
Rule in Words	Number of tickets equals 4 times number of rides.				
Equation	$t = 4r$				
Rides (r)	1	2	3	4	5
Tickets (t)	4	8	12	16	20

UNIT 1 TEST   53

Student Activity Book page 53

Unit Test Items	Unit Objectives Tested	Activities to Use for Reteaching
10–11	**1.1** Identify and write rules for a function table.	Lesson 5, Activities 1–2
12–15	**1.2** Solve algebraic equations involving multiplication and division.	Lesson 1, Activity 2 Lesson 6, Activity 1
5–6, 16–17	**1.3** Identify and use properties of multiplication.	Lesson 10, Activities 1–2
1–4	**1.4** Identify factor pairs.	Lesson 8, Activities 1–2

Student Activity Book page 54

U1–Test
Unit Test ✓

Name _____ Date _____

Solve each equation.

12. $3j = 24$ 13. $90 = 10k$ 14. $80 \cdot 0 = s$ 15. $n = 24 - (7 \times 2)$

$j = \underline{\ 8\ }$ $k = \underline{\ 9\ }$ $s = \underline{\ 0\ }$ $n = \underline{\ 10\ }$

Use the Properties of Multiplication to solve for _n_.

16. $659 \times 1{,}357 = 1{,}357 \times n$ 17. $(201 \times 340) \times 980 = n \times (340 \times 980)$

$n = \underline{\ 659\ }$ $n = \underline{\ 201\ }$

Solve.

Show your work.

18. Katie swam 3 lengths of the pool. Kurt swam twice as many lengths as Katie. Rosa swam 4 times as many lengths as Kurt. How many lengths did Rosa swim?
    24 lengths

19. Laura bought 3 yo-yos for 8 cents each and 4 whistles for 10 cents each. How much money did Laura spend?
    64 cents

20. **Extended Response** Rolando wants to carpet the living room and dining room of his house. The living room is 10 yards by 6 yards. The dining room is 7 yards by 5 yards. How many square yards of carpet will Rolando need? Explain how you solved the problem. Write one equation that can be used to solve the problem.
    Possible explanation: The area of the living room is
    $10 \times 6 = 60$ square yards. The area of the dining
    room is $7 \times 5 = 35$ square yards. The total amount
    of carpeting needed is $60 + 35 = 95$ square yards.
    $(6 \cdot 10) + (7 \cdot 5) =$ total square yards

*Item 20 also assesses the Process Skills of Problem Solving, Communication, and Representation.

54 UNIT 1 TEST

Unit Test Items	Unit Objectives Tested	Activities to Use for Reteaching
7–9, 18	**1.5** Solve one-step multiplication and division problems, including combination and comparison problems.	Lesson 1, Activity 1 Lesson 2, Activities 1–2 Lesson 3, Activities 1–2 Lesson 4, Activity 1 Lesson 7, Activity 1 Lesson 11, Activity 1
19–20	**1.6** Solve multistep problems involving multiplication and division.	Lesson 1, Activity 2 Lesson 6, Activity 1 Lesson 9, Activities 1–2 Lesson 11, Activity 2

► Assessment Resources

Free Response Tests
Unit 1 Test, Student Activity Book pages 53–54 or Student Hardcover Book pp. 53–54 and Activity Workbook p. 31
Unit 1 Test, Form A, Assessment Guide

Extended Response Item
The last item in the Student Book test and in the Form A test will require an extended response as an answer.

Multiple Choice Test
Unit 1 Test, Form B, Assessment Guide

Performance Assessment
Unit 1 Performance Assessment, Assessment Guide
Unit 1 Performance Assessment Rubric, Assessment Guide

► Portfolio Assessment

Teacher-selected Items for Student Portfolios:
- Homework, Lessons 9 and 11
- Class Activity work, Lessons 3, 5, 7, and 11

Student-selected Items for Student Portfolios:
- Favorite Home or School Activity
- Best Writing Prompt

② Extending the Assessment

Unit Objective 1.1
Identify and write rules for a function table.

Common Error: Has Difficulty Identifying a Pattern Rule

Remediation Try creating a table with 3 rows. Then work with students to recognize the pattern by asking questions. For example:

Stars	1	2	3
Rule	× 5	× 5	× 5
Points	5	10	15

What must you do to the 1 to get 5? What must you do to the 2 to get 10? And so on.

Then ask, "What do you think you must do to get the 10th number in the pattern?" Extend the table to show that the answer will be 50.

Unit Objective 1.2
Solve algebraic equations involving multiplication and division.

Common Error: Confuses Sums and Products of Zero

Remediation Discuss with students why multiplying by zero gives zero but adding 0 gives that number. Some students call multiplying by 0 "zero zapping" to remind themselves that the number disappears and becomes 0.

Unit Objective 1.3
Identify and use the properties of multiplication.

Common Error: Uses Properties Incorrectly

- The Commutative Property lets you change the order of the factors.

- The Associative Property lets students operate with addends or factors in any order to make a computation easier.

Unit Objective 1.4
Identify factor pairs.

Common Error: Does Not Know Basic Multiplications and Divisions

Remediation The rhythmic recitation of count-bys can help students recognize factors for specific numbers.

Give students practice reciting count-bys orally. Then follow with oral practice using the corresponding multiplications.

Unit Objective 1.5
Solve one-step multiplication and division problems, including combination and comparison problems.

Common Error: Can't Distinguish Between a Multiplication and a Division Problem

Remediation Have students work in pairs to analyze a variety of multiplication and division problems. Have them list the similarities and differences of each problem. For example:

- Both problems involve equal groups.

- When you need to find a product, you use multiplication.

- When you are finding an unknown factor, you use division.

Unit Objective 1.6
Solve multistep problems involving multiplication and division.

Common Error: Doesn't Complete All the Steps

Remediation: Before solving, have students make a list of all the steps necessary to solve the problem. Then they can connect each step to a mathematical operation.

Perimeter and Area

THIS UNIT EXPLORES perimeter and area of rectangles, parallelograms, and triangles. Students derive the formulas for parallelograms and right triangles. A big idea for this unit is that perimeter and area are two different measurements of the same shape and that each has its own kind of unit of measurement: linear units for perimeter and square units for area. Students will use what they learn about area in this unit again in Unit 7, where area is used as a graphic model for multi-digit multiplication.

Skills Trace

Grade 4	Grade 5
• Find the perimeter and area of rectangles.	• Find the perimeter and area of rectangles.
• Distinguish between linear units for perimeter and square units for area.	• Distinguish between linear units for perimeter and square units for area.
• Derive the formula for the perimeter of a parallelogram from a rectangle.	• Find the perimeter and area of parallelograms.
• Find perimeter and area of complex figures.	• Derive the formula for the area of a triangle from the formula for the area of a parallelogram.
• Estimate measurements.	• Find perimeter and area of complex figures.
	• Estimate measurements.

Unit 2   Contents

 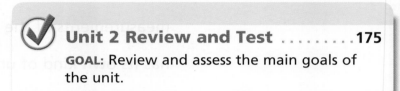

Unit 2   Assessment

✓ Unit Objectives Tested	Unit Test Items	Lessons
2.1 Find perimeter and area of polygons.	1–4	2, 3, 4
2.2 Use customary and metric measures to solve problems involving perimeter and area.	5, 6, 9, 10	1, 2, 6
2.3 Find perimeter and area of complex figures.	7, 8	5

Assessment and Review Resources

Formal Assessment	Informal Assessment	Review Opportunities
Student Activity Book • Unit Review and Test (pp. 81–82) **Assessment Guide** • Quick Quiz 1 (p. A13) • Quick Quiz 2 (p. A14) • Quick Quiz 3 (p. A15) • Test A—Open Response (pp. A16–A18) • Test B—Multiple Choice (pp. A19–A22) • Performance Assessment (pp. A23–A25) **Test Generator CD-ROM** • Open Response Test • Multiple Choice Test • Test Bank Items	**Teacher Edition** • Ongoing Assessment (in every lesson) • Math Talk (in every lesson) • Portfolio Suggestions (p. 177) **123 Math Talk** ▸ The Learning Classroom (pp. 129, 138) ▸ Math Talk in Action (pp. 131, 138, 161, 167) ▸ In Activities (pp. 129, 153, 158, 168, 171) ▸ Solve and Discuss (pp. 137, 140, 145) ▸ Student Pairs (pp. 128, 132, 148, 170, 171) Helping Partner (pp. 138, 139, 168) ▸ Small Groups (pp. 132, 172)	**Homework and Remembering** • Review of recently taught topics • Spiral Review **Teacher Edition** • Unit Review and Test (pp. 175–178) **Test Generator CD-ROM** • Custom review sheets

Planning Unit 2

Lesson NCTM Focal Points NCTM Standards	Resources	Materials for Lesson Activities	Materials for Going Further
2-1 **Square Units and Area** NCTM Focal Point: 5.2 NCTM Standard: 4	TE pp. 127–134 SAB pp. 55–58 H&R pp. 35–36 AC 2-1 MCC 9	Make a Meter Stick (TRB M21) Scissors Tape Centimeter-Grid Paper (TRB M18)	Centimeter-Grid Paper (TRB M18) Grid Paper (TRB M17) Push pins or tacks Board for push pins String, Ruler Math Journals
2-2 **Perimeter and Area of Rectangles** NCTM Focal Point: 5.2 NCTM Standards: 3, 4, 6, 7, 8	TE pp. 135–142 SAB pp. 59–64 H&R pp. 37–38 AC 2-2 MCC 10 AG Quick Quiz 1	Centimeter rulers Centimeter-Grid Paper (TRB M18) (optional)	Centimeter-Grid Paper (TRB M18) Math Journals

2-3
Area of Right Triangles and Parallelograms
NCTM Focal Point: 3.9
NCTM Standards: 3, 4, 6, 7
	TE pp. 143–150
	SAB pp. 65–68
	H&R pp. 39–40
	AC 2-3
	MCC 11
		Acute and Obtuse Triangles (TRB M19)
		Scissors
		Centimeter-Grid Paper (TRB M18)
		Centimeter rulers
		Geoboard/Dot Paper (TRB M20) and
		   markers (optional)
			Centimeter-Grid Paper (TRB M18) or
			   Geoboard/Dot Paper (TRB M20)
			Scissors
			Straws
			Math Journals

2-4 **The Area of Any Triangle** NCTM Focal Point: 3.9 NCTM Standards: 3, 4	TE pp. 151–156 SAB pp. 68A–72 H&R pp. 41–42 AC 2-4 AG Quick Quiz 2	Estimate Perimeter and Area (TRB M72) (optional) Scissors Rulers Grid paper (optional)	Centimeter rulers Centimeter-Grid Paper (TRB M18) Scissors Math Journals

Resources/Materials Key: TE: Teacher Edition   SAB: Student Activity Book   H&R: Homework and Remembering
AC: Activity Cards   MCC: Math Center Challenge   AG: Assessment Guide   ✓: Grade 5 kits   TRB: Teacher's Resource Book

NCTM Standards and Expectations Key: **1.** Number and Operations **2.** Algebra **3.** Geometry
4. Measurement **5.** Data Analysis and Probability **6.** Problem Solving **7.** Reasoning and Proof
8. Communication **9.** Connections **10.** Representation

Lesson NCTM Focal Points NCTM Standards	Resources	Materials for Lesson Activities	Materials for Going Further
2-5 **Consolidate Perimeter and Area** NCTM Focal Points: 3.9, 3.10 NCTM Standards: 3, 4, 6	TE pp. 157–164 SAB pp. 73–76 H&R pp. 43–44 AC 2-5 MCC 12	Centimeter rulers	Centimeter-Grid Paper (TRB M18) Markers Math Journals
2-6 **Customary Units of Length** NCTM Focal Points: 3.10, 5.2 NCTM Standards: 4, 7	TE pp. 165–174 SAB pp. 77–80 H&R pp. 45–46 AC 2-6 AG Quick Quiz 3	Inch and centimeter ruler Yardstick or meter stick Customary tape measure	Scissors Colored paper Inch-Grid Paper (TRB M1) Math Journals
Unit Review and Test	TE pp. 175–178 SAB pp. 81–82 AG Unit 2 Tests		

Hardcover Student Book

- Together, the Hardcover Student Book and its companion Activity Workbook contain all of the pages in the consumable Student Activity Book.

Manipulatives and Materials

- Essential materials for teaching *Math Expressions* are available in the Grade 5 kits. These materials are indicated by a ✓ in these lists. At the front of this Teacher Edition is more information about kit contents, alternatives for the materials, and use of the materials.

Independent Learning Activities

Ready-Made Math Challenge Centers

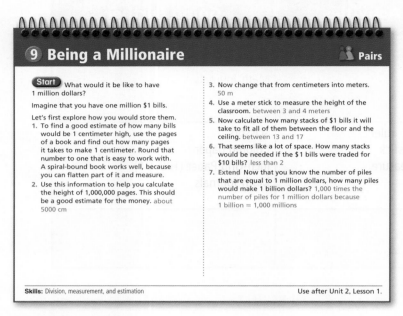

⑨ Being a Millionaire 👥 Pairs

Start What would it be like to have 1 million dollars?

Imagine that you have one million $1 bills.

Let's first explore how you would store them.
1. To find a good estimate of how many bills would be 1 centimeter high, use the pages of a book and find out how many pages it takes to make 1 centimeter. Round that number to one that is easy to work with. A spiral-bound book works well, because you can flatten part of it and measure.
2. Use this information to help you calculate the height of 1,000,000 pages. This should be a good estimate for the money. about 5000 cm

3. Now change that from centimeters into meters. 50 m
4. Use a meter stick to measure the height of the classroom. between 3 and 4 meters
5. Now calculate how many stacks of $1 bills it will take to fit all of them between the floor and the ceiling. between 13 and 17
6. That seems like a lot of space. How many stacks would be needed if the $1 bills were traded for $10 bills? less than 2
7. Extend Now that you know the number of piles that are equal to 1 million dollars, how many piles would make 1 billion dollars? 1,000 times the number of piles for 1 million dollars because 1 billion = 1,000 millions

Skills: Division, measurement, and estimation   Use after Unit 2, Lesson 1.

Grouping Pairs

Materials Metric ruler, Meter Stick (TRB M21), calculator (optional)

Objective Students estimate the height of stacks of bills.

Connections Computation and Estimation

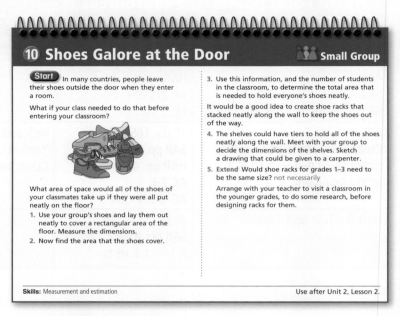

⑩ Shoes Galore at the Door 👥 Small Group

Start In many countries, people leave their shoes outside the door when they enter a room.

What if your class needed to do that before entering your classroom?

What area of space would all of the shoes of your classmates take up if they were all put neatly on the floor?
1. Use your group's shoes and lay them out neatly to cover a rectangular area of the floor. Measure the dimensions.
2. Now find the area that the shoes cover.

3. Use this information, and the number of students in the classroom, to determine the total area that is needed to hold everyone's shoes neatly.

It would be a good idea to create shoe racks that stacked neatly along the wall to keep the shoes out of the way.
4. The shelves could have tiers to hold all of the shoes neatly along the wall. Meet with your group to decide the dimensions of the shelves. Sketch a drawing that could be given to a carpenter.
5. Extend Would shoe racks for grades 1–3 need to be the same size? not necessarily

Arrange with your teacher to visit a classroom in the younger grades, to do some research, before designing racks for them.

Skills: Measurement and estimation   Use after Unit 2, Lesson 2.

Grouping Small Group

Materials Metric ruler or Meter Stick (TRB M21)

Objective Students determine the area needed for storing a class' shoes.

Connections Measurement and Real World

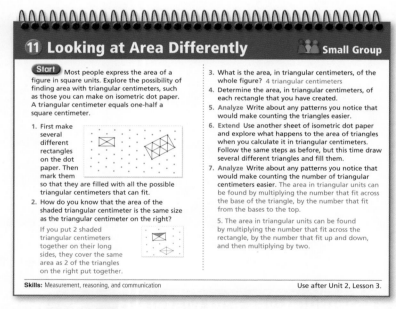

⑪ Looking at Area Differently 👥 Small Group

Start Most people express the area of a figure in square units. Explore the possibility of finding area with triangular centimeters, such as those you can make on isometric dot paper. A triangular centimeter equals one-half a square centimeter.

1. First make several different rectangles on the dot paper. Then mark them so that they are filled with all the possible triangular centimeters that can fit.
2. How do you know that the area of the shaded triangular centimeter is the same size as the triangular centimeter on the right?

If you put 2 shaded triangular centimeters together on their long sides, they cover the same area as 2 of the triangles on the right put together.

3. What is the area, in triangular centimeters, of the whole figure? 4 triangular centimeters
4. Determine the area, in triangular centimeters, of each rectangle that you have created.
5. Analyze Write about any patterns you notice that would make counting the triangles easier.
6. Extend Use another sheet of isometric dot paper and explore what happens to the area of triangles when you calculate it in triangular centimeters. Follow the same steps as before, but this time draw several different triangles and fill them.
7. Analyze Write about any patterns you notice that would make counting the number of triangular centimeters easier. The area in triangular units can be found by multiplying the number that fit across the base of the triangle, by the number that fit from the bases to the top.

5. The area in triangular units can be found by multiplying the number that fit across the rectangle, by the number that fit up and down, and then multiplying by two.

Skills: Measurement, reasoning, and communication   Use after Unit 2, Lesson 3.

Grouping Small Group

Materials Isometric Dot Paper (TRB M45)

Objective Students explore the possibility of using triangles as units for measuring area.

Connections Measurement and Communication

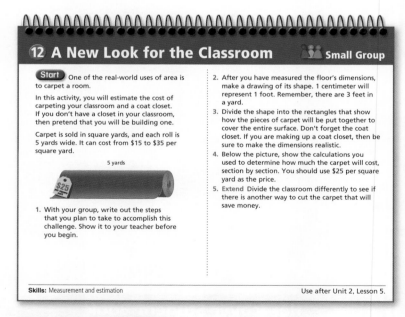

⑫ A New Look for the Classroom 👥 Small Group

Start One of the real-world uses of area is to carpet a room.

In this activity, you will estimate the cost of carpeting your classroom and a coat closet. If you don't have a closet in your classroom, then pretend that you will be building one.

Carpet is sold in square yards, and each roll is 5 yards wide. It can cost from $15 to $35 per square yard.

5 yards

1. With your group, write out the steps that you plan to take to accomplish this challenge. Show it to your teacher before you begin.

2. After you have measured the floor's dimensions, make a drawing of its shape. 1 centimeter will represent 1 foot. Remember, there are 3 feet in a yard.
3. Divide the shape into the rectangles that show how the pieces of carpet will be put together to cover the entire surface. Don't forget the coat closet. If you are making up a coat closet, then be sure to make the dimensions realistic.
4. Below the picture, show the calculations you used to determine how much the carpet will cost, section by section. You should use $25 per square yard as the price.
5. Extend Divide the classroom differently to see if there is another way to cut the carpet that will save money.

Skills: Measurement and estimation   Use after Unit 2, Lesson 5.

Grouping Small Group

Materials Meter Stick (TRB M21)

Objective Students determine the area of the classroom and use it to estimate the cost of carpeting.

Connections Measurement and Real World

Ready-Made Math Resources

Technology — Tutorials, Practice, and Intervention

Use online, individualized intervention and support to bring students to proficiency.

Help students practice skills and apply concepts through exciting math adventures.

Extend and enrich students' understanding of skills and concepts through engaging interactive lessons and activities.

Visit **Education Place**
www.eduplace.com

Visit Education Place www.eduplace.com
Visit **www.eduplace.com/mx2t/** and find family, teacher, and student materials, activities, games, and more.

Literature Link

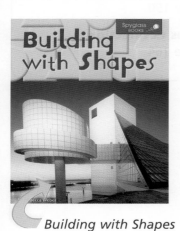

Building with Shapes

Building with Shapes
This book by Rebecca Weber explores three-dimensional shapes and the perimeter of each shape in the book. How could the area inside those shapes be determined? Which shapes would be the easiest in terms of area to measure? Which would be the most difficult?

Unit 2 Teaching Resources

Differentiated Instruction

Individualizing Instruction

Activities	Level	Frequency
	• Intervention • On Level • Challenge	All 3 in every lesson
Math Writing Prompts	Level	Frequency
	• Intervention • On Level • Challenge	All 3 in every lesson
Math Center Challenges	For advanced students	
	4 in every unit	

Reaching All Learners

	Lessons	Pages
English Language Learners	1, 2, 3, 4, 5, 6	127, 135, 143, 151, 157, 165
Extra Help	Lessons	Pages
	1, 2, 3, 5	130, 137, 147, 158
Special Needs	Lesson	Page
	5	160
Advanced Learners	Lessons	Pages
	2, 3, 5, 6	137, 148, 161, 171

Strategies for English Language Learners

Present this problem to all students. Offer the different levels of support to meet students' levels of language proficiency.

Objective Review vocabulary for *area* and *perimeter*.

Problem Draw and label a 6 × 7 rectangle on the board. Write *length, width, area,* and *perimeter*.

Newcomer

- Gesture and say: *Area is length × width. Perimeter is length + width + length + width.*
- Have students trace the rectangle in the air and repeat.

Beginning

- Gesture and say: *Area is the space inside. Area is length × width.* Have students repeat. Ask: **Is the *area* 6 × 7?** yes
- Continue with *perimeter*.

Intermediate

- Ask: **Is the *width* 6?** yes **Is the *length* 7?** yes **Is the space inside the *area* or *perimeter*?** area **Do we multiply *length × width* to find *area*?** yes **Is the *area* 42 units squared?** yes
- Continue with perimeter.

Advanced

- Have students identify the *length* and *width*. Say: **The space inside is the __.** area **The distance around is the __.** perimeter
- Say: **We add the sides to find __.** perimeter **We multiply *length × width* to find __.** area

Connections

Language Arts Connection
Lesson 2, page 142

Math-to-Math Connection
Lesson 4, page 156

Real-World Connection
Lesson 6, page 174

Science Connection
Lesson 3, page 150

Social Studies Connection
Lesson 5, page 164

Math Background

Putting Research into Practice for Unit 2

From Our Curriculum Research Project
Perimeter and Area

Initial classroom research showed that students made four kinds of errors in solving perimeter and area problems. The design of area and perimeter activities was refined to help students avoid these errors by deepening their understanding.

1. ***Visualizing and differentiating units*** Many students had difficulty visualizing the length units for perimeter and the square units for area and remembering which was which because area and perimeter problems are typically presented by showing a rectangle with a number on two sides. Students need to see the same rectangle with length units around all the sides to show the perimeter and the same rectangle filled with square units to show the area. It is important for students initially to see and to draw two versions of a rectangle: one with the perimeter length units and the other with the area square units.

2. ***Calculating only part of the perimeter*** Students need to become aware that opposite sides of a rectangle are congruent and to write the lengths of all sides on the figure initially to visualize and understand perimeter. Such experiences also help students avoid adding only the two numbers shown on the rectangle to find the perimeter.

3. ***Choosing the dimensions of a parallelogram*** Students confuse which sides of a parallelogram to use for perimeter and for area. Again, drawing length units all around the sides of a parallelogram helps students use both (slanting) sides and the top and bottom of a parallelogram for perimeter. For understanding why the height measure is used for area, it is helpful for students to decompose a parallelogram by cutting along any vertical height (not just the height at a vertex as is commonly done) and rearranging the parallelogram into a rectangle so that they see how the slanting sides disappear into the interior of the rectangle and are not involved at all in the area. Area requires only the measure of the base to tell the number of squares in a row along the bottom of the parallelogram and the measure of the height to tell the number of such rows of squares.

4. ***Finding twice the area of a triangle*** Students forget to take half of the product of the base and the height. Avoiding this error requires strong visualization of triangles as half of parallelograms, so students need to see how different kinds of triangles make parallelograms. Seeing a right triangle as half of a rectangle is particularly helpful. After this, students need practice in finding the areas of related parallelograms and triangles so that taking one-half becomes more automatic. Seeing the related parallelogram is a cue that the area of a triangle is half of its related parallelogram.

For all students, some discussion of language is helpful. The area of a rectangle is traditionally given as *length times width,* but the language used in formulas for parallelograms and triangles shifts to *base times height.* Students need to discuss that *length times width* is the same as *base times height* for rectangles. This gives them an integrated view of the areas of rectangles and parallelograms (and triangles) as working with *base times height.*

—Karen Fuson, Author
Math Expressions

Other Useful References: Perimeter and Area

National Council of Teachers of Mathematics. *Learning and Teaching Measurement* (NCTM 2003 Yearbook). Ed. Douglas H. Clements. Reston: NCTM, 2003.

National Council of Teachers of Mathematics. *Principles and Standards for School Mathematics.* Reston: NCTM, 2000.

Van de Walle, John A. *Elementary and Middle School Mathematics: Teaching Developmentally.* 4th ed. New York: Addison, 2001.

Getting Ready to Teach Unit 2

Measurement and Geometry

In this unit, students use the multiplication and division skills they previously learned to calculate and understand the areas of triangles and other shapes. In turn, they will use area models to visualize work with fractions and decimals later this year.

Measurement and Geometry are interconnected and support each other in many ways. For students to understand area and perimeter for triangles and parallelograms, students must be able to think spatially about these shapes.

Perimeter and Area of Rectangles (including squares)
Lessons 1 and 2

Students review the formulas for the perimeter and area of rectangles and derive the formula for the perimeter and area of a square. As students calculate the perimeter of rectangles, they add and subtract units of measure including compound units.

Perimeter and Area of Parallelograms and Triangles
Lessons 3 and 4

Students manipulate right triangles to see that two congruent right triangles can always form a rectangle. This allows them to generalize from the formula for finding the area of a rectangle, which they have already learned, to a strategy for finding the area of a right triangle.

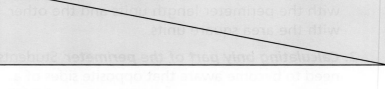

Then, students cut apart parallelograms to show that any parallelogram can be reconstructed into a rectangle. From this, students are able to develop a strategy to find area of any parallelogram.

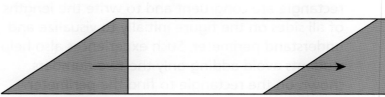

And, once students are comfortable with their strategy to find the area of parallelograms, they can show that any triangle is really half of a parallelogram, leading to the strategy for finding the area of any triangle.

Developing formulas to find the area of parallelograms and triangles ensures that students understand what the formulas mean, and helps students to apply and generalize the formulas later, when presented with complex figures in Lesson 5.

Estimating Measurements

Lesson 6

Students use customary units to calculate perimeter and area. They add and subtract measurements including compound units. As students measure real world objects, they estimate and then measure to the nearest half inch, quarter inch, and eighth inch.

Basic Multiplication and Division Fluency

Students should continually work toward fluency for basic multiplication and division facts. Use checkups to assist students in monitoring their own learning. In the Teacher's Resource Book (TRB) you will find several pages for diagnosing and practicing basic multiplication and division.

TRB M58 Diagnostic Quiz for Basic Multiplication	TRB M66 Scrambled Multiplication Tables
TRB M59 Diagnostic Quiz for Basic Division	TRB M67 Blank Multiplication Tables
TRB M60 Basic Multiplication Practice	TRB M68 Multiplication for 10s, 11s, 12s
TRB M61 Basic Division Practice	TRB M69 Division for 10s, 11s, 12s
TRB M62 Multiplication for 3s, 4s, 6s, 7s, 8s, 9s	TRB M83 Factor Puzzles for 3s, 4s, 6s, 7s, 8s, 9s
TRB M63 Division for 3s, 4s, 6s, 7s, 8s, 9s	TRB M84 Factor Puzzles for 6s, 7s, 8s
TRB M64 Multiplication for 6s, 7s, 8s	TRB M85 Blank Factor Puzzles
TRB M65 Division for 6s, 7s, 8s	

See the Basic Facts Fluency Plan for information about practice materials.

Square Units and Area

REAL WORLD Problem Solving

Lesson Objectives

● **Define and relate common metric units of area.**

● **Select the appropriate metric unit for measuring a particular object.**

Vocabulary

meter
decimeter
centimeter
millimeter

The Day at a Glance

Today's Goals	Materials	
1 Teaching the Lesson **A1:** Visualize square metric units and build a square meter from smaller units. **A2:** Measure classroom objects and calculate the area. **2 Going Further** ▶ Differentiated Instruction **3 Homework and Spiral Review**	**Lesson Activities** Student Activity Book pp. 55–58 or Student Hardcover Book pp. 55–58 and Activity Workbook pp. 32–33 (includes Family Letters) Homework and Remembering pp. 35–36 Make a Meter Stick (TRB M21) Scissors Tape Centimeter-Grid Paper (TRB M18)	**Going Further** Activity Cards 2-1 Centimeter-Grid Paper (TRB M18) Grid Paper (TRB M17) Push pins or tacks Board for push pins String Ruler Math Journals

123 *Use* **Math Talk** *today!*

Keeping Skills Sharp

Daily Routines	English Language Learners
Strategy Problem Gina sold 30 tickets to the play. She sold 4 times as many student tickets as adult tickets. Two-thirds of the student tickets sold were unreserved seats. How many of the student tickets sold were for reserved seats? 8 reserved-seat student tickets; $4t + t = 30$; $5t = 30$, $t = 6$, $4 \times 6 = 24$, one-third of $24 = 8$	Write: mm^2, cm^2, dm^2, and m^2 on the board. Model 1 m^2. Ask: **Are these *square units*?** yes **Is this 1 m^2?** yes ● **Beginning** Point to dm^2 and say: **This means *decimeter squared*.** Draw and label 1 dm^2. ● **Intermediate** Point to dm^2 and ask: **Is this decimeter or centimeter squared?** decimeter Draw and label 1 dm^2. ● **Advanced** Model each unit. Have students identify each abbreviation.

Teaching the Lesson

Activity 1

Relate Metric Area Measures

 25 MINUTES

Goal: Visualize square metric units and build a square meter from smaller units.

Materials: Scissors (1 per student), Make a Meter Stick (TRB M21), tape

✔ **NCTM Standard:**
Measurement

▶ Metric Unit Lengths WHOLE CLASS

Ask for Ideas Ask students to share anything they know about metric units of length. Then distribute Make a Meter Stick (TRB M21). Before students cut out the strips, have them look at the top of the first strip and find mm, cm, and dm. Ask students to approximate each length by holding their fingers apart. (mm: fingers almost touch; cm: a small finger width; dm: almost an index finger to thumb stretch).

Have **Student Pairs** work together to make their own meter. Each student cuts out the first 2 strips along the exterior solid lines and tapes them together on the back and front. Students then cut out the third strip and tape it to the first two. Repeat the process for the fourth strip. Have pairs confirm that their strips are taped together in the correct order and that no measures are covered up. Pairs can place one strip on top of the other to confirm that they are approximately the same length.

▶ Choose the Appropriate Unit

WHOLE CLASS

One of the fundamental skills of measuring involves choosing an appropriate unit. To practice this skill, have students suppose they were asked to measure the distance from school to their homes, and then ask them to give a variety of reasons why it is not practical to use millimeters, centimeters, decimeters, and (possibly) meters to measure the distance.

Offer the following questions for additional practice. For each question, have students give a reason to support their answer. Explanations will vary.

● Suppose you must make a variety of measurements in our classroom. What would you choose to measure if you were to measure using meters? Sample answer: The length, width, or height of our classroom.

● What would you choose to measure if you were to measure using decimeters? Sample answer: The width and height of the chalkboard.

● What would you choose to measure if you were to measure using centimeters? Sample answer: The length, width, and thickness of a large textbook.

● What would you choose to measure if you were to measure using millimeters? Sample answer: The length and width of a scrap of paper.

Generalize Give students an opportunity to share general strategies that can be used to help choose an appropriate measurement unit.

▶ Measure Classroom Objects

Act It Out Allow students time to use their meter strips or centimeter rulers to measure a variety of small objects (such as the length of a paper clip and the width of a pencil) to the nearest millimeter. Repeat the activity using larger objects and centimeters and decimeters. To measure to the nearest meter, have them measure a dimension inside the classroom (such as length or width), or outside the classroom (such as the length or width of a hallway).

Estimate If time permits, offer students an opportunity to estimate lengths using informal benchmarks. An example of an informal benchmark is the length of a shoe; students will find that the distance of their shoes—placed heel-to-toe 4 times—is about 1 meter. Other examples include the width of the widest part of one of their hands (about 1 decimeter) and the width of their narrowest fingernail (about 1 centimeter).

Encourage students to use these or other informal benchmarks of their own design to estimate various distances or measures in the classroom, and then compare estimates.

The Learning Classroom

Math Talk You must direct student math talk for it to be productive. Over time, as students become more skilled at discussing their thinking and talking directly with each other, you will fade into the background more. But you will always monitor, clarify, extend, and ultimately make the decisions about how to direct the math conversation so that it is productive for your students.

▶ Discuss Measurement Concepts

(123) **Math Talk** Have students look at their meter strips as you informally discuss these measurement concepts:

Iteration For measurement, any measuring tool has units that repeat.

● Describe the repeating units on your meter strip.

Partitioning Any measuring tool has large units divided into smaller units that are the same size.

● How are the units on your meter strip the same?

Compensatory Principle More smaller units than larger units are needed to measure any distance.

● If you measured the width of the classroom in meters and in centimeters, would the number of meters be greater or less than the number of centimeters? Explain how you know. less

Transitivity This concept involves the relationship of three elements. For example, if Object A is longer than Object B and Object B is longer than Object C, then Object A is longer than Object C. Demonstrate this concept by placing a new pencil and a pen on the overhead.

● Is the pencil longer or shorter than the pen? longer

Replace the pencil with a short crayon.

● Is the pen longer or shorter than the crayon? longer

● Without directly comparing them, is the pencil longer or shorter than the crayon? How do you know? longer

Activity continued ▶

① Teaching the Lesson (continued)

Activity 1

▶ Precision in Measurement WHOLE CLASS

Approximations Make sure students understand that all measurements are approximations. In other words, no measurements are exact.

To help them understand this concept, draw a short line segment on the board. Using a meterstick, invite a volunteer to measure the length of the segment to the nearest meter, invite a second volunteer to measure to the nearest centimeter, and invite a third volunteer to measure to the nearest millimeter. Discuss the measurements and lead students to conclude that although the measurement in millimeters is more precise than in centimeters or meters, we could measure the segment with more precision if the meterstick had divisions smaller than millimeters.

Therefore, all three measurements are not exact. Instead, they are simply approximations (with some more useful than others) of the length of the segment.

Precision Make sure students understand that the units they use to measure an object affect the precision of the measurement. For example, measuring the width of a sheet of paper in centimeters produces a more precise measurement than using decimeters. Lead students to generalize that the smaller the unit, the more precise the measurement, and vice versa.

Accuracy It is also important for students to understand that all tools must be used as accurately as possible. In other words, remind them that the greater the care that is used to make a measurement, the greater the precision, and vice versa.

Activity 2

Calculate Metric Area

 20 MINUTES

Goal: Measure classroom objects and calculate the area.

Materials: Student Activity Book or Hardcover Book pp. 55–56, Centimeter-Grid Paper (TRB M18), Scissors

 NCTM Standard:
Measurement

▶ Explore Metric Area WHOLE CLASS

Ask for Ideas Ask students to share what they know about the area of rectangles. Be sure to discuss that area is the number of square units that cover a figure and that the area of a rectangle is length times width ($l \times w$) because there are w rows of length l (this is just a basic multiplication situation). We can also think of the area of a rectangle as base times height ($b \times h$), or h rows of length b.

Direct students' attention to Student Book page 55. Ask them to identify the square millimeter (sq mm or mm²), square centimeter (sq cm or cm²), and square decimeter (sq dm or dm²). Work through questions 1 through 4 together. For 1 and 2 be sure that the explanations include seeing multiples of rows:

1. 10 rows of 10 knots each is 100 (look at the square centimeter to see the 100 square millimeters: a knot is in each of those squares).

2. There would be $10 \times 10 = 100$ millimeters (knots) across the top of the square decimeter and 100 rows of such knots, so 100×100 which is $10 \times 10 \times 100 = 10 \times 1,000 = 10,000$.

Differentiated Instruction

Extra Help If students have difficulty multiplying with multiples of 10, give them practice and discuss the pattern of the zeros.

$10 \times 10 = $ ____ 100
$10 \times 100 = $ ____ 1,000
$10 \times 1,000 = 10,000$
$100 \times 100 = $ ____ 10,000
$100 \times 1,000 = $ ____ 100,000

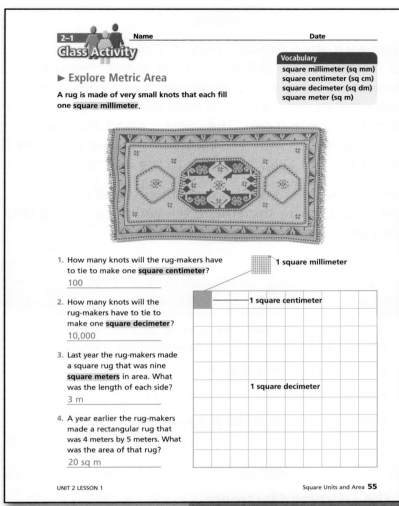

Student Activity Book page 55

Within the activity image:
- 2–1 **Class Activity** Name _____ Date _____
- ► Explore Metric Area
- A rug is made of very small knots that each fill one **square millimeter**.
- Vocabulary: square millimeter (sq mm), square centimeter (sq cm), square decimeter (sq dm), square meter (sq m)

1. How many knots will the rug-makers have to tie to make one **square centimeter**? 100
2. How many knots will the rug-makers have to tie to make one **square decimeter**? 10,000
3. Last year the rug-makers made a square rug that was nine **square meters** in area. What was the length of each side? 3 m
4. A year earlier the rug-makers made a rectangular rug that was 4 meters by 5 meters. What was the area of that rug? 20 sq m

 1 square millimeter
1 square centimeter
1 square decimeter

UNIT 2 LESSON 1 — Square Units and Area **55**

► Construct a Square Meter   WHOLE CLASS

Give each student a pair of scissors and 4 copies of the Centimeter-Grid Paper (TRB M18). Explain that students are going to create a rug with an area of one square meter, using the grids. Encourage them to brainstorm methods for making the square meter.

● How can we find a square decimeter in the grid? Count 10 cm by 10 cm.

Have students cut out a square decimeter on each of their copies of Centimeter-Grid Paper.

● How many decimeters are in one meter? 10

● Then how many square decimeters are in one square meter? 10 rows of 10 decimeters; 10 × 10 = 100

● If we need 100 square decimeters to make a square meter how should we place the square decimeters to make a square? 10 across and 10 down

Act It Out Have students carry out the plan by making a square meter on the floor. If you have fewer than 25 students, you will need to cut out a few extra masters. When students are finished, discuss the results. A sample dialogue appears in the side column.

Math Talk in Action

This is one square meter. Suppose that a family will sit around this rug and drink tea. How many people can comfortably sit around the rug?

Mara: Probably four. It is the size of a small kitchen table.

That's a good way to think of it. Now, how many centimeters are there along each side of a square meter?

Hamid: 100

So how many square centimeters do we have in this square meter?

Hamid: 100 × 100 or 10,000

Good. Now think about all the little square millimeters. Each represents a knot in the rug. How many knots did it take to make this rug? How can we figure it out?

Jamyce: We just found out that there are 10,000 square centimeters in this square meter. Each square centimeter contains 100 square millimeters, or 100 knots. So 10,000 × 100 = 1,000,000.

That's right. Now we can imagine what 1 million looks like.

The Learning Classroom

Scenario The main purpose of a scenario is to demonstrate mathematical relationships in a visual and memorable way. In this case, students will use square-decimeter cut-outs to act out a situation. Because of its active and dramatic nature, the scenario structure fosters a sense of intense involvement among children. Scenarios create meaningful contexts in which students relate math to their everyday lives.

Activity continued ▶

Activity 2

2–1

Class Activity

Name _____ Date _____

► **Identify the Appropriate Unit**

What metric unit is the most sensible unit for measuring each of the following? Possible answers are given.

5. the area of a postage stamp
   square millimeters

6. the length of a noodle
   centimeters

7. the area of a tabletop
   square decimeters

8. the length of a ladybug
   millimeters

9. the area of an envelope
   square centimeters

10. the length of a sidewalk
    meters

Name an object you can measure using each of these units. Possible answers are given.

11. millimeter
    length of a paper clip

12. centimeter
    length of a textbook

13. decimeter
    length of a car

14. square millimeter
    area of a baseball card

15. square meter
    area of a driveway

56 UNIT 2 LESSON 1   Square Units and Area

Student Activity Book page 56

► **Identify the Appropriate Unit**

WHOLE CLASS

Ask students to read Student Book page 56.

● What kind of measurement unit is appropriate for exercise 6? length units

● What kind of measurement unit is appropriate for exercise 7? square units, for area

Explain that sometimes the unit selected is a matter of how precise the measurements need to be. In exercise 7 for example, measuring the tabletop in centimeters will give a more accurate answer than decimeters, but it will be harder to calculate mentally (for example, 3×5 dm is easier to multiply than 31×52 cm).

Have students work together in **Student Pairs** or **Small Groups** to complete exercises 5–15.

► **Calculate the Area of Real-World Objects** SMALL GROUPS

Give each **Small Group** a copy of TRB M18 to use to measure sq cm and sq dm. Have teams measure something using sq cm, sq dm, and sq m. Give one team the square meter and have them measure something with it first. They pass it on to another team. All teams will need to use this square meter, so teams need to keep it moving to the next team.

When most teams are finished, discuss and compare the results. Invite students to tell which measuring unit they chose and the approximate area.

☑ **Ongoing Assessment**

Observe the students as they measure the objects and estimate area. Use questioning to assess understanding.

► Why did you choose that unit?

► What is the smallest unit that you know?

► What is the greatest unit that you know?

The Learning Classroom

Student Pairs Initially, it is useful to model pair activities for students by contrasting effective and ineffective ways of working together. For example, pairs may want to find the answers independently and then compare their answers, or they may want to work together on the solution. Stress that when working as pairs the effort is collaborative and one student in the pair should not be doing most of the work. When students effectively work in pairs, it often fosters learning in both students.

②Going Further

Differentiated Instruction

Intervention   Activity Card 2-1

String Rectangles   Activity Card 2-1 ●

Work: In Pairs

Use:
• Centimeter-Grid Paper (TRB M18)
• Pushpins or tacks
• Board for push pins (tacks)
• String

1. **Work Together** Attach the grid paper to the board. Use pushpins and string to make a rectangle on the grid.

2. On your own, calculate the area of the rectangle in square centimeters. Remember: Area = $l \times w$.

3. Compare results with your partner and check your work by counting squares.

4. **Math Talk** How can you be sure that the figure you made is a rectangle? Possible answer: It has 4 corners, each of which is a right angle on the grid.

Unit 2, Lesson 1   Copyright © Houghton Mifflin Company

Activity Note Review the properties of a rectangle before students begin the activity. Then have students place the push pins to mark 4 corners and wrap the string around the tacks to create the edges.

 **Math Writing Prompt**

Explain Your Thinking Explain how to multiply 20 × 10.

Soar to Success Math **Software Support**

Warm-Up 45.26

On Level   Activity Card 2-1

The Predict and Verify Game   Activity Card 2-1 ▲

Work: In Pairs

Use:
• Centimeter-Grid Paper (TRB M18) or centimeter ruler

1. One partner draws a rectangle.

2. The other partner predicts the area of the rectangle in square millimeters.

3. **Work Together** Use the grid paper or a ruler to measure the length and the width of the rectangle to the nearest millimeter. Then calculate its area.

4. If the difference between the prediction and the actual area is within 25 mm², the player who made the prediction scores a point.

5. Take turns drawing rectangles and predicting their area until one player has 10 points.

Unit 2, Lesson 1   Copyright © Houghton Mifflin Company

Activity Note Have students draw all the rectangles on a single sheet of paper. This will enable them to make visual comparisons to inform their predictions.

 Math Writing Prompt

Summarize In your own words, describe how millimeters, centimeters, decimeters, and meters are related. Then describe how square units of each measure are related.

MegaMath Grades K-6 **Software Support**

Ice Station Exploration: Polar Planes, Level Q

Challenge   Activity Card 2-1

Calculate Area   Activity Card 2-1 ■

Work: By Yourself

1. The dimensions of the rectangle and the square below are in different units.

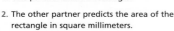

2. *Rectangle A:*
   450 mm = 45 cm;
   3 dm = 30 cm;
   area = 45 × 30 =
   1,350 sq cm =
   135,000 sq mm
   Square B: 4 m =
   400 cm; area = 400 ×
   400 = 160,000 sq cm =
   16,000,000 sq mm

2. Find the area of each figure in square centimeters and in square millimeters.

3. Explain How did you change square centimeters to square millimeters? Possible answer: I multiplied by 100, because 100 mm = 1 cm, and so 100 sq mm = 1 sq cm.

Unit 2, Lesson 1   Copyright © Houghton Mifflin Company

Activity Note Students will need to convert units before computing the area of the rectangle. They may choose to convert units before or after computing the area of the square.

 Math Writing Prompt

Problem Solving A garden is a 10-meter square. Each side of the garden has 6 fence posts. How many fence posts enclose the garden?

 DESTINATION Math· **Software Support**

Course III: Module 5: Unit 1: Rectangles and Squares

Square Units and Area   **133**

③ Homework and Spiral Review

2–1 Homework Goal: Additional Practice

This Homework page provides students with practice in metric measurements relating and calculating area and perimeter.

2–1 Remembering Goal: Spiral Review

This Remembering activity is appropriate anytime after today's lesson.

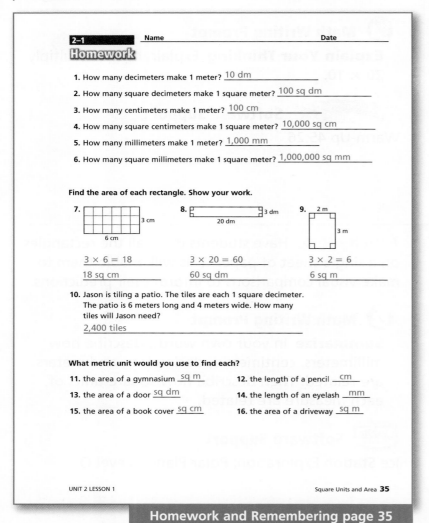

2–1	Name _____ Date _____
Homework	

1. How many decimeters make 1 meter? 10 dm
2. How many square decimeters make 1 square meter? 100 sq dm
3. How many centimeters make 1 meter? 100 cm
4. How many square centimeters make 1 square meter? 10,000 sq cm
5. How many millimeters make 1 meter? 1,000 mm
6. How many square millimeters make 1 square meter? 1,000,000 sq mm

Find the area of each rectangle. Show your work.

7. 3 cm, 6 cm
$3 \times 6 = 18$
18 sq cm

8. 3 dm, 20 dm
$3 \times 20 = 60$
60 sq dm

9. 2 m, 3 m
$3 \times 2 = 6$
6 sq m

10. Jason is tiling a patio. The tiles are each 1 square decimeter. The patio is 6 meters long and 4 meters wide. How many tiles will Jason need?
2,400 tiles

What metric unit would you use to find each?

11. the area of a gymnasium sq m
12. the length of a pencil cm
13. the area of a door sq dm
14. the length of an eyelash mm
15. the area of a book cover sq cm
16. the area of a driveway sq m

UNIT 2 LESSON 1   Square Units and Area **35**

Homework and Remembering page 35

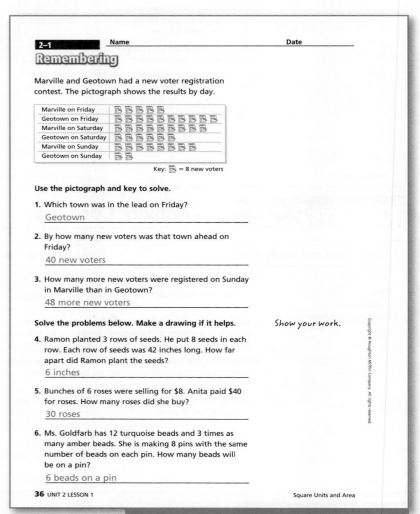

2–1	Name _____ Date _____
Remembering	

Marville and Geotown had a new voter registration contest. The pictograph shows the results by day.

Marville on Friday	
Geotown on Friday	
Marville on Saturday	
Geotown on Saturday	
Marville on Sunday	
Geotown on Sunday	

Key: = 8 new voters

Use the pictograph and key to solve.

1. Which town was in the lead on Friday?
Geotown

2. By how many new voters was that town ahead on Friday?
40 new voters

3. How many more new voters were registered on Sunday in Marville than in Geotown?
48 more new voters

Solve the problems below. Make a drawing if it helps.   *Show your work.*

4. Ramon planted 3 rows of seeds. He put 8 seeds in each row. Each row of seeds was 42 inches long. How far apart did Ramon plant the seeds?
6 inches

5. Bunches of 6 roses were selling for $8. Anita paid $40 for roses. How many roses did she buy?
30 roses

6. Ms. Goldfarb has 12 turquoise beads and 3 times as many amber beads. She is making 8 pins with the same number of beads on each pin. How many beads will be on a pin?
6 beads on a pin

36 UNIT 2 LESSON 1   Square Units and Area

Homework and Remembering page 36

Home and School Connection

Family Letter Have students take home the Family Letter on Student Book page 57 or Activity Workbook page 32. This letter explains how the concepts of measuring perimeter and area are developed in *Math Expressions*. It gives parents and guardians a better understanding of the learning that goes on in math class and creates a bridge between school and home. A Spanish translation of this letter is on Student Book page 58 and Activity Workbook page 33.

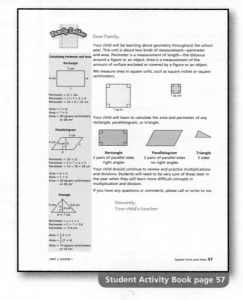

Student Activity Book page 57

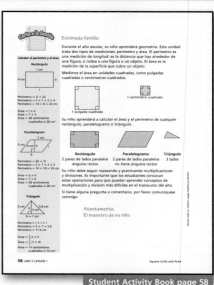

Student Activity Book page 58

134 UNIT 2 LESSON 1

Perimeter and Area of Rectangles

REAL WORLD **Problem Solving**

Lesson Objectives

● Construct rectangles of given widths and lengths.

● Distinguish between the area and the perimeter of a rectangle.

Vocabulary
perimeter
area
square centimeter
square unit
base
height

The Day at a Glance

Today's Goals	Materials	
1 Teaching the Lesson **A1:** Construct rectangles and visualize perimeter and area. Derive general formulas for calculating perimeter and area. **A2:** Measure to find perimeter and area. **2 Going Further** ▶ Math Connection: Make Estimates ▶ Differentiated Instruction **3 Homework and Spiral Review**	**Lesson Activities** Student Activity Book pp. 59–62 or Student Hardcover Book pp. 59–62 and Activity Workbook p. 34 Homework and Remembering pp. 37–38 Quick Quiz 1 (Assessment Guide) Centimeter rulers Centimeter-Grid Paper (TRB M18) (optional)	**Going Further** Student Activity Book pp. 63–64 or Student Hardcover Book pp. 63–64 and Activity Workbook p. 35 Activity Cards 2-2 Centimeter-Grid Paper (TRB M18) Math Journals

123 *Use* **Math Talk** *today!*

Keeping Skills Sharp

Daily Routines	English Language Learners
Homework Review Set aside time to work with students who had difficulty with the homework. **Estimate or Exact Answer?** Jamal is placing new baseboards in a closet. The length of the closet is 5 ft 8 in. Its width is 4 ft 10 in. Can Jamal estimate the number of feet of baseboard he needs or does he need an exact amount? Explain. Possible answer: Either; Jamal can round the measures up to the greater number of feet (length to 6 ft and the width to 5 ft), and he will have a little more baseboard than he needs. Or, he can calculate the exact amount, if the store will sell him non-whole-unit amounts of baseboard.	Draw and label a 4 × 5 dm rectangle on the board. Write *perimeter* = 4 + 5 + 4 + 5, *area* = 4 × 5. ● **Beginning** Point and ask: **Is *perimeter* the distance around a figure?** yes **Is *area* the space inside a figure?** yes ● **Intermediate** Ask: **Which is the distance around a figure, *perimeter* or *area*?** perimeter ● **Advanced** Have students identify *perimeter* and *area* on a figure.

1 Teaching the Lesson

Visualize Perimeter and Area

 20 MINUTES

Goal: Construct rectangles and visualize perimeter and area. Derive general formulas for calculating perimeter and area.

Materials: Student Activity Book pp. 59–60 or Hardcover Book pp. 59–60 and Activity Workbook p. 34, centimeter rulers (1 per student)

✓ **NCTM Standards:**
Measurement
Communication

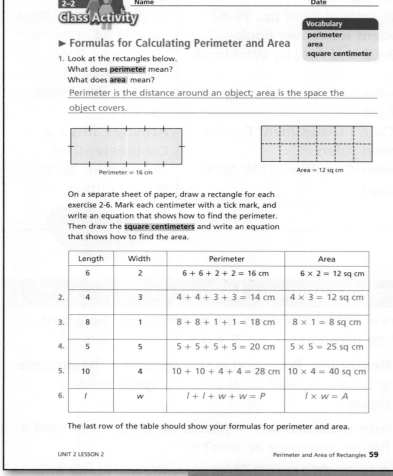

Student Activity Book page 59

▶ Formulas for Calculating Perimeter and Area [WHOLE CLASS]

Ask for Ideas Ask students to share what they know about the perimeter and area of rectangles. Have students make drawings as necessary to clarify their points.

Explain that students sometimes mix up perimeter and area, so they are going to do activities to help them visualize and remember these. They will also be finding a general formula for each. Have students look at the drawings on page 59 and discuss how they can visualize those to help find perimeter and area. Have students complete exercise 1 and discuss answers briefly. For exercises 2 through 6, explain that some students might want to make two rectangles as shown below to see perimeter and area more clearly. Have students label sides numerically as below.

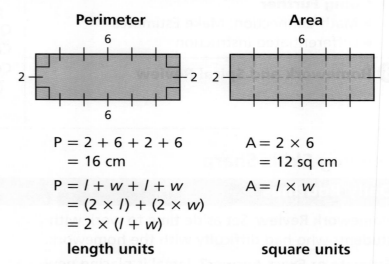

Perimeter	Area
$P = 2 + 6 + 2 + 6$ $\quad = 16$ cm	$A = 2 \times 6$ $\quad = 12$ sq cm
$P = l + w + l + w$ $\quad = (2 \times l) + (2 \times w)$ $\quad = 2 \times (l + w)$	$A = l \times w$
length units	**square units**

Discuss the general formulas students found for exercise 6. Have students summarize what they have learned about perimeter and area of rectangles. The rectangle formulas depend on knowing that opposite sides of rectangles are congruent (have the same lengths), so be sure that students noticed this when drawing and measuring their rectangles.

Student Activity Book page 60

▶ Perimeter and Area of a Square

WHOLE CLASS

Ask For Ideas Give students an opportunity to share what they know about perimeter and area. Make sure the discussion includes these ideas:

● Perimeter is a measure of the distance around a figure. Finding perimeter usually involves one or two operations (addition or multiplication and addition).

● Area is the amount of surface covered or enclosed by a figure. Finding area may involve one, two, or more than two operations, and is a measure of square units.

Have students work **Individually** to complete exercises 7–9 at the top of Student Book page 60.

Exercise 10 As a class, use **Solve and Discuss** to complete exercise 10. Make sure the discussion includes this concept: By definition, a rectangle is a quadrilateral with four right angles. Opposite sides are both congruent and parallel. Since a square also has these same characteristics, a square is a rectangle. The formulas that are used to find the perimeter and area of a rectangle can also be used to find the perimeter and area of a square.

Exercises 11–13 Have students individually complete exercise 11. Students should generalize that to find the area of a square they can multiply any side length times itself. Then have students complete exercises 12 and 13 as a class.

Differentiated Instruction

Advanced Learners Challenge your advanced learners to explain how mental math and a range of estimates can be used to check the answer for exercise 11. Possible explanation: 76 is about halfway between 70 and 80, so the product of 76^2 should be about halfway between the product of 70^2 or 4,900 and 80^2 or 6,400; that number is 5,650.

Differentiated Instruction

Extra Help Some students may find it helpful to draw the situations in exercises 12 and 13 on grid paper. The grid will enable them to count lines to find the perimeter and see that it doubles, and to count small squares to find the area and see that it is four times as great.

Teaching the Lesson (continued)

Real-World Applications

 20 MINUTES

Goal: Measure to find perimeter and area.

Materials: Student Activity Book or Hardcover Book pp. 61–62

 NCTM Standard:
Measurement

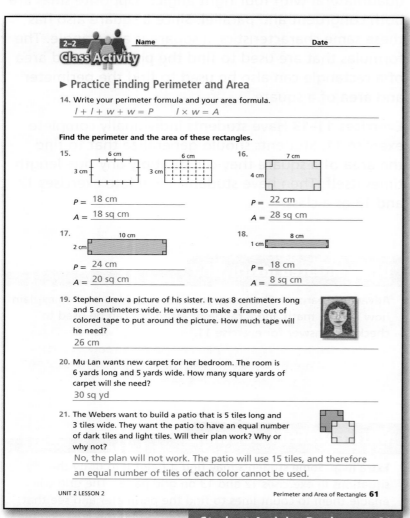

Student Activity Book page 61

▶ Practice Finding Perimeter and Area

WHOLE CLASS

As a class, discuss exercises 14–18 on Student Book page 61. Ask students to use the general formulas to find the perimeter and area for each exercise. Then have students complete exercises 19–21 individually or with a **Helping Partner**.

 Math Talk in Action

Let's consider problem 21. What answer did you get?

Marco: I said their plan won't work because 5 tiles by 3 tiles means they want 5 × 3 = 15 tiles. You can't have half of the tiles light and half of the tiles dark when it's an odd number.

Good. Did anyone use a different method to come up with an answer?

Linh: I drew the patio and shaded every other tile darker. There was one extra darker one when I was done.

That's a good method, too.

Design a Patio Challenge pairs of students to make a new design for a rectangular patio with an equal number of light and dark tiles. Ask them to draw the rectangular patio square tile by square tile. Then ask them to shade half the tiles to see if their design works. Possible answers: 4 tiles × 5 tiles; 4 tiles × 3 tiles

Students who are finished quickly can investigate other patio designs that will work.

 Ongoing Assessment

As students work on their patio designs, ask questions about how to find the area and perimeter of their designs. Make sure they understand that perimeter is measured in length units and area is measured in square units.

The Learning Classroom

Math Talk You can create math conversations by eliciting multiple strategies for solving problems. When you ask, "Did anyone do this problem differently?" your students will pay greater attention to the work on the board because they will be comparing and contrasting it with their own math strategies. The comparisons and contrasts that result can naturally springboard to significant math talk.

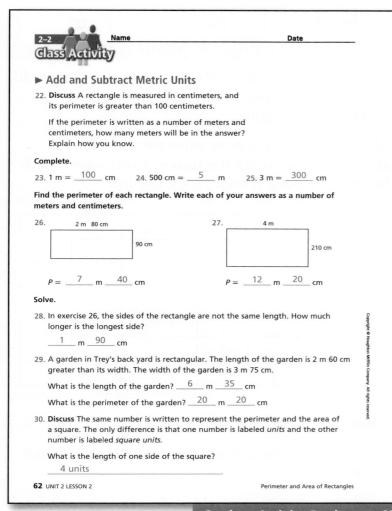

Student Activity Book page 62

► Add and Subtract Metric Units

WHOLE CLASS

Subtracting Metric Units Have students recall that whenever they subtract two numbers, they must rename or "borrow" whenever the number being subtracted is greater than the number they are subtracting from.

Point out that the same idea is true when subtracting two measures, and then review the relationships that linear metric units share.

1 m = 10 dm = 100 cm = 1,000 mm

Write 1 m 50 cm − 80 cm on the board and discuss how renaming 1 meter as 100 centimeters is used to complete the subtraction.

1 m 50 cm = 100 cm + 50 cm = 150 cm

−   80 cm   −   80 cm

                                 70 cm

Adding Metric Units Write 1 m 50 cm + 80 cm on the board and discuss how regrouping 100 centimeters as 1 meter is used to complete the addition.

1 m   50 cm

+   80 cm

1 m 130 cm = 2 m 30 cm

Generalize Discuss possible answers and explanations for open-ended exercise 22 at the top of Student Book page 62. Lead students to generalize that if the perimeter is greater than 100 cm and less than 200 cm, 100 cm will be regrouped as 1 meter because 100 cm = 1 meter. If the perimeter is greater than 200 and less than 300, 200 cm will be regrouped as 2 meters because 200 cm = 2 meters. And so on.

Exercises 23–30 Have students work **Individually** or paired with a **Helping Partner** to complete exercises 23–29. As a class, discuss exercise 30.

Teaching Note

Watch For! As they complete exercises 26–29, watch for opportunities to remind students that answers of 100 or more centimeters must be regrouped as meters and centimeters.

 **Quick Quiz**

See Assessment Guide for Unit 2 Quick Quiz 1.

② Going Further

Math Connection: Make Estimates

Goal: Estimate the area and perimeter of an irregular figure on a grid.

Materials: Student Activity Book pp. 63–64 or Hardcover Book p. 63 and Activity Workbook p. 35

✔ **NCTM Standards:**
Geometry
Measurement
Problem Solving
Reasoning and Proof

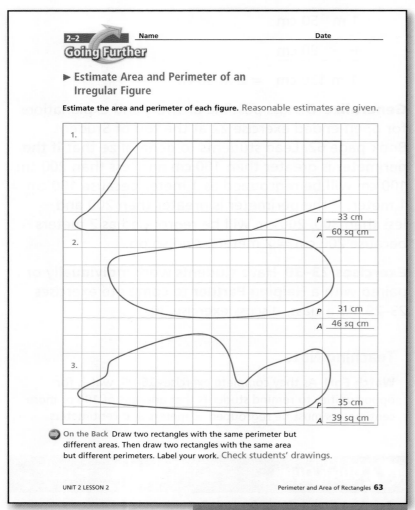

Student Activity Book page 63

In this activity, students will be connecting area and perimeter with estimation.

▶ Estimate Area and Perimeter of an Irregular Figure WHOLE CLASS

Ask students to describe different strategies that could be used to make a reasonable estimate of the perimeter of the figure.

To demonstrate one way to estimate the area, ask students to draw, inside the figure, a rectangle that is as large as possible. It might look like this:

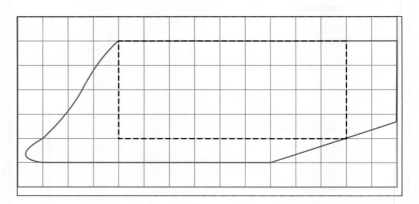

● What is the area of your rectangle? 36 sq cm

● How many whole unit squares are still outside your rectangle? 18

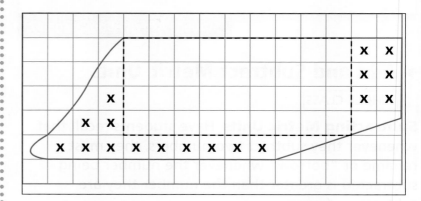

● What is the total area so far? 54 sq cm

● How many partial squares are along the edges? 11

● About how much area do they cover? 5 or 6 sq cm

● What do you estimate is the area of the irregular figure? 60 sq cm

Invite students to **Solve and Discuss** the other exercises in a similar manner.

Differentiated Instruction

Birthday Rectangles   Activity Card 2-2 ●

Work: In Pairs

Use:
• Centimeter-Grid Paper (TRB M18)

1. On your own, draw a rectangle on grid paper. Use your birth month for the width and your birth date for the length. Which birth month and date does the rectangle shown represent? April 10

2. **Work Together** Calculate the area and the perimeter of both rectangles. Remember:

$$A = l \times w \qquad P = (2 \times l) + (2 \times w)$$

3. **Predict** Of all possible birth dates, which one will have the greatest area? Which birth date will have the least area? How many birth dates are squares? 12/31; 1/1; 12

Unit 2, Lesson 2   Copyright © Houghton Mifflin Company

Activity Note Make sure students understand that January = 1, February = 2, and so on.

Math Writing Prompt

Explain Your Thinking Explain how to multiply 20 × 10.

Soar to Success Math ★ **Software Support**

Warm-Up 44.30, 45.26

Which One Is It?   Activity Card 2-2 ▲

Work: In Pairs

1. On your own, draw and label a rectangle.

2. Calculate the perimeter and area of your rectangle. Record one measurement correctly and the other incorrectly.

P = 50 cm (correct)
A = 141 sq cm (incorrect)

3. Exchange papers with your partner. Decide which measurement is correct. Then correct the measurement that is recorded incorrectly.

4. **Math Talk** Matt drew a square to exchange with his partner. How could his partner check each measurement by using division? Possible answer: Divide area by length to see if the quotient equals the width; divide the perimeter by 4 to see if the quotient equals the length of a side.

Unit 2, Lesson 2   Copyright © Houghton Mifflin Company

Activity Note Before students begin the activity, review how to find the perimeter and area of a rectangle.

Math Writing Prompt

Summarize In your own words, describe how millimeters, centimeters, decimeters, and meters are related. Then describe how square units of each measure are related.

MEGA MATH Grades K-6 **Software Support**

Ice Station Exploration: Polar Planes, Levels P and Q

Make Rectangles   Activity Card 2-2 ■

Work: By Yourself

1. Rectangles with different measures can have the same area. Draw and label as many rectangles as you can with an area of 24 square units. Use only whole numbers for the length and width of your rectangles.
1 × 24; 2 × 12; 3 × 8; 4 × 6

2. Draw all the possible rectangles with a perimeter of 24 units.
1 × 11; 2 × 10; 3 × 9; 4 × 8; 5 × 7; 6 × 6

3. **Explain** What strategy did you use to find all the possible rectangles? Possible answer: For area, I made an organized list of the factors of 24. For perimeter, I made an organized list of number pairs whose sum equals 12.

Unit 2, Lesson 2   Copyright © Houghton Mifflin Company

Activity Note Students should use only whole numbers.

Math Writing Prompt

Problem Solving A garden is a 10-meter square. Each side of the garden has 6 fence posts. How many fence posts enclose the garden?

DESTINATION Math **Software Support**

Course III: Module 5: Unit 1: Rectangles and Squares

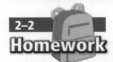

③ Homework and Spiral Review

Homework **Goal:** Additional Practice

✓ Include students' Homework for page 37 as part of their portfolios.

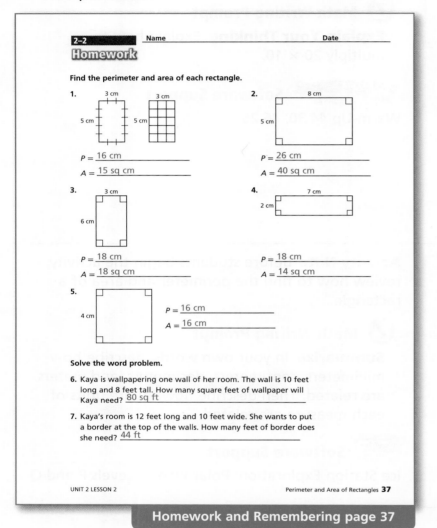

Remembering **Goal:** Spiral Review

This Remembering activity is appropriate anytime after today's lesson.

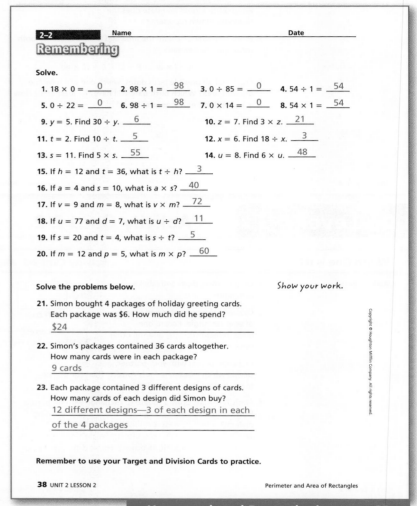

Home or School Activity

 Language Arts Connection

Measure a Room Have students write instructions for someone to follow to measure the perimeter of a rectangular room. Then they explain what it means to measure the area of a room. Explain how measuring perimeter is different from measuring area.

> Measure the lengths of two adjacent walls of the room.
> To find perimeter, add the lengths. Multiply by 2.
> To find area, just multiply one length by the other.

MINI UNIT 2

LESSON 3

Area of Right Triangles and Parallelograms

REAL WORLD Problem Solving

Vocabulary

acute angle
right angle
obtuse angle
triangle
rectangle
parallelogram
base
perpendicular
height

Lesson Objectives

● Classify angles by size, and classify triangles by the size of their angles.

● Derive formulas for areas of parallelograms and right triangles.

The Day at a Glance

Today's Goals	Materials
1 Teaching the Lesson **A1:** Recognize different kinds of angles and triangles. **A2:** Derive the formula for perimeter and area of a right triangle using a rectangle. **A3:** Identify the height of a parallelogram. Derive the formula for perimeter and area of a parallelogram using a rectangle. **2 Going Further** ▶ Problem Solving Strategy: Simpler Problems ▶ Differentiated Instruction **3 Homework and Spiral Review**	**Lesson Activities** Student Activity Book pp. 65–67 or Student Hardcover Book pp. 65–67 and Activity Workbook pp. 36–38 Homework and Remembering pp. 39–40 Acute and Obtuse Triangles (TRB M19) Scissors Centimeter-Grid Paper (TRB M18) Centimeter rulers Geoboard/Dot Paper (TRB M20) and markers (optional)	**Going Further** Student Activity Book p. 68 or Student Hardcover Book p. 68 Activity Cards 2-3 Centimeter-Dot Paper (TRB M25) or Centimeter-Grid Paper (TRB M18) Scissors Straws, 2 per student Math Journals

123 **Use Math Talk today!**

Keeping Skills Sharp

Daily Routines	English Language Learners
Homework Review Have students work together to check their work. **Algebra** Write the rule for each function table shown below.	Write *triangle*, *quadrilateral*, and *parallelogram* on the board. Below each term, draw a simple example.

Daily Routines (continued)

Input	2	5	7	9	10
Output	5	17	25	33	37

Output = Input × 4 − 3

Input	2	4	5	8	10
Output	9	15	18	27	33

Output = Input × 3 + 3

English Language Learners (continued)

● **Beginning** Identify each shape and its properties. Have students repeat.

● **Intermediate** Point to each shape. Ask questions such as: **How many sides are there? Is it a quadrilateral or triangle? Are the sides parallel? Is it a parallelogram?**

● **Advanced** Have students identify each shape and tell about its properties.

1 Teaching the Lesson

Angles and Triangles

 15 MINUTES

Goal: Recognize different kinds of angles and triangles.

Materials: Student Activity Book p. 65 or Hardcover Book p. 65, Acute and Obtuse Triangles (TRB M19), scissors

 NCTM Standards:
Geometry
Measurement
Reasoning and Proof

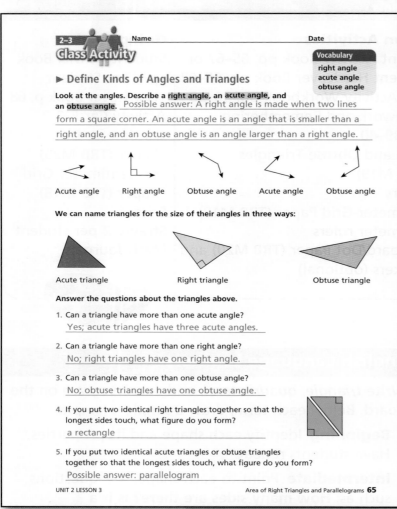

Student Activity Book page 65

▶ Define Kinds of Angles and Triangles

WHOLE CLASS

Direct students' attention to the angles at the top of Student Book page 65. Ask students to explain the

difference between an acute angle, a right angle, and an obtuse angle. If students need more practice, they can use two pencils to make angles.

Have students look at the three kinds of triangles shown in the illustrations. Use the following questions to help students define kinds of triangles.

● Can a triangle have more than one acute angle? Yes; a triangle can have as many as three acute angles.

Help students see that the other two triangles have two acute angles. Therefore, the definition of an acute triangle is one that has three acute angles or one in which all of the angles are acute.

● Can a triangle have more than one right angle? no

Students can try to draw such a triangle; they won't be able to close the figure. Therefore, the definition of a right triangle is a triangle that has one right angle.

● Can a triangle have more than one obtuse angle? no

Again, students will not be able to close the figure if they try to draw it. Therefore, the definition of an obtuse triangle is a triangle with one obtuse angle.

● If you put two identical right triangles together so that the longest sides touch, what figure is formed? a rectangle or a quadrilateral

Emphasize that a right triangle is half of a rectangle. Since a rectangle is a kind of parallelogram, a right triangle is also half of a parallelogram. If necessary, review the definition of a parallelogram (opposite sides are parallel).

For question 5, students can visualize the answer or experiment with the triangle cutouts on TRB M19.

Explore Right Triangles

 15 MINUTES

Goal: Derive the formula for perimeter and area of a right triangle using a rectangle.

Materials: Student Activity Book p. 66 or Hardcover Book p. 66 and Activity Workbook p. 36, Centimeter-Grid Paper (TRB M18)

 NCTM Standards:
Geometry
Measurement

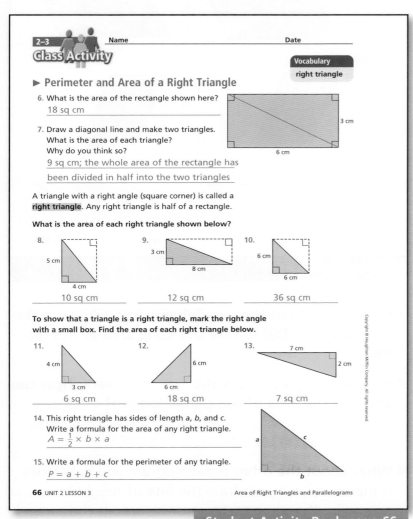

Student Activity Book page 66

► Perimeter and Area of a Right Triangle WHOLE CLASS

123 Math Talk Using **Solve and Discuss,** have students solve exercises 6 and 7. Help students see that each right triangle formed by a diagonal of a rectangle is exactly half the area of the rectangle. Assign exercises 8–13. Finally, ask students to complete exercises 14 and 15, generating a formula for calculating the area, and then the perimeter, of a right triangle:

$$Area = \frac{1}{2} \; base \times height \qquad Perimeter = a + b + c$$

Discuss the area formula and ask volunteers to explain why the formula works.

Teaching Note

What to Expect from Students When finding the area of a triangle, students may approach the multiplication in several ways. They may multiply the base by the height and then divide the result by 2. They may take $\frac{1}{2}$ of the base (or of the height) and then multiply that number by the height (or base). The answer will be the same.

Example: base = 6, height = 4

Option 1: $6 \times 4 = 24$, $24 \div 2 = 12$. The area is 12 square units.

Option 2: $\frac{1}{2}$ of $6 = 3$ and $3 \times 4 = 12$. The area is 12 square units.

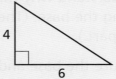

✓ Ongoing Assessment

Have students complete the following activity:

On Centimeter-Grid Paper draw a line 6 cm long. Draw a perpendicular line from one end, 8 cm long. Complete the triangle. What is the area of the triangle? Measure the longest side. What is the perimeter of the triangle?

Activity 3

Area of a Parallelogram

 30 MINUTES

Goal: Identify the height of a parallelogram. Derive the formula for perimeter and area of a parallelogram using a rectangle.

Materials: Student Activity Book pp. 66A–67 or Hardcover Book p. 67 and Activity Workbook pp. 37–38, scissors, centimeter rulers, geoboards and rubber bands or Geoboard/Dot Paper (TRB M20) and markers (optional)

 NCTM Standards:
Geometry
Measurement

▶ Experiment With Parallelograms
| WHOLE CLASS |

Have students look at the vertical dotted line inside each parallelogram. Explain that this line shows the height of the parallelogram. Elicit from students a definition of height, and discuss it.

● Each dotted line segment shows the height of the parallelogram. What is *height*? a line segment that is perpendicular to the base (or forms a right angle with the base)

● Can we draw a height in more than one place along the base? yes

Students should understand why the line can be drawn from anywhere along the base. (The parallel lines stay the same distance apart.)

Have students measure the base and height of each parallelogram while you write them on the board. Ask students to cut out each pair of parallelograms. Then have them cut along the heights of the identical parallelograms 16 and 17 and switch the pieces to align them along the slanted sides. Discuss that the slanted sides fit on the same slant because they are parallel (and they disappear inside the rectangle).

Help students find the area of the new parallelograms.

● What figure was formed when you switched the pieces around? a rectangle

● If the base is 6 cm and the height is 3 cm, what is the area of this rectangle? 18 sq cm

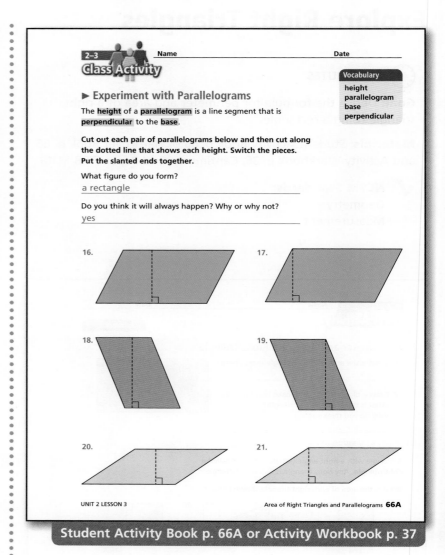

Student Activity Book p. 66A or Activity Workbook p. 37

● Now think about the parallelogram you cut to make the rectangle. Did it have the same area as this rectangle? Yes, it is made of the same two pieces.

● Put the two pieces back the way they were. How can you find the area of this parallelogram? Multiply the base times the height. That is the same as multiplying the length times the width of the rectangle.

● What about the other parallelogram you cut? Does it matter where you draw the line of height? No, we can make the same rectangle; the area is the same.

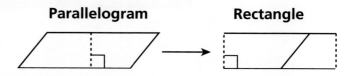

The parallelogram becomes a rectangle.

Ask the class to experiment with the other two pairs of parallelograms to see if the results are always the same. Can they always make a rectangle by switching the pieces? If so, then the formula for finding the area of a parallelogram must be generally true:

$$A = base \times height$$

Discuss with students the terminology difference commonly used for rectangles (length and width) and for parallelograms (base and height). The words *base* and *height* can also be used for the length and width of a rectangle, so the same formula can be used for a rectangle as for a parallelogram: area = base × height.

▶ Find the Area of a Parallelogram

INDIVIDUALS

Have students complete exercises 22–25 on Student Book page 67 and discuss why *h* is used in one formula and *s* in the other. Invite students to complete the exercises on the page.

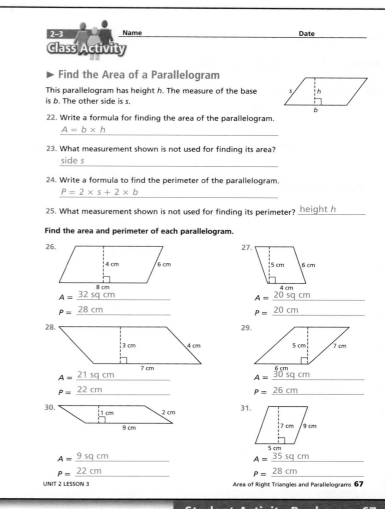
Student Activity Book page 67

🖐 Alternate Approach

Geoboards If geoboards are available, students can use different colors of rubber bands (or different color markers if you are using TRB M20), to make overlapping rectangles and parallelograms on geoboards. When the bases of the two figures are the same length (same number of dots) and the heights of the two figures are the same length, the triangles on each end are congruent. So, the sum of the common area and the area of one triangle must be the same as the area of the rectangle.

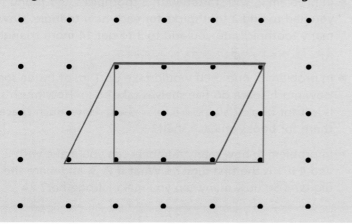

Teaching Note

Watch For! In writing the formulas, make sure students use *h*, and not *s* for the height. When measuring perimeter, students need to understand that they are measuring the distance around the whole parallelogram so they need to use *s* rather than *h*. Students can measure *s* and *h* to prove that the two measurements are different in parallelograms, and using the wrong measurement will result in errors.

Differentiated Instruction

Extra Help If students confuse which measures to use for perimeter and for area, suggest that they write the missing side lengths. For perimeter, use all the side lengths. For area, have them circle the measure of the base and the height of each figure.

Area of Right Triangles and Parallelograms **147**

Going Further

Problem Solving Strategy: Simpler Problems

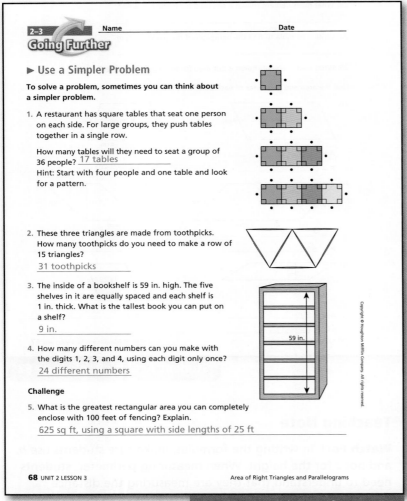

Student Activity Book page 68

Differentiated Instruction

Advanced Learners Students can use a string or a ribbon of known length to form a variety of shapes. Then using a ruler and various formulas, students will discover that for any length, a circle is the shape that encloses the greatest area.

► Use a Simpler Problem PAIRS

Discuss problem 1.

● How many people can sit around one table? 4

● When you put two tables together, how many people can sit around them? Draw a picture to help you decide. 6

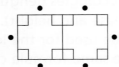

● When you put three tables together, how many people can sit around them? 8

● What number pattern is starting to happen? 4, 6, 8 even numbers

● How is the number pattern related to the number of tables? Subtract 2 from the number of people and divide by 2 to get the number of tables.

● How can you use the pattern to solve the problem? 36 − 2 = 34; 34 ÷ 2 = 17; they need 17 tables

Have **Student Pairs** continue with the other problems.

 ### Class Management

Walk around the room and observe the pairs as they solve the problems. Make sure students remember to solve the original problem after modeling it in a simpler way.

► In problem 2, you started with 3 toothpicks and found that you had to add 2 toothpicks for each new triangle. How many toothpicks do you add to 3 to get 14 more triangles? 2 × 14 = 28; 28 + 3 = 31 toothpicks

► In problem 3, one shelf would take up 1 in. of inside space. How much space do five shelves take? 5 in. How much space is left for books? 59 in. − 5 in. = 54 in. How much space is there for books on each shelf? 54 ÷ 6 = 9 in.

► In problem 4, how many numbers can you make with 2, 3, and 4 if 1 is the first digit? 6 What if 2, 3, and 4 are the first digits? 6 So how many can you make altogether? 24

Differentiated Instruction

Intervention   Activity Card 2-3

Make a Parallelogram   Activity Card 2-3 ●

Work: In Pairs

Use:
- Centimeter Grid (TRB M18) or Dot Paper (TRB M20)
- Scissors

1. **Work Together** Draw a rectangle with a diagonal on a grid or dot paper. Cut out the rectangle and then cut along the diagonal to make two right triangles.

2. Put the triangles together to make a parallelogram that is not a rectangle.

3. **Compare** How does the area of the rectangle compare to the area of the parallelogram? They are equal.

Unit 2, Lesson 3   Copyright © Houghton Mifflin Company

Activity Note If students have difficulty placing the two triangles to make a parallelogram, suggest that they align the shortest side of each triangle so that the right angles are not touching.

✎ **Math Writing Prompt**

Make a Drawing Show how to find the height of a parallelogram with a base measuring 8 cm and an area of 24 sq cm.

Soar to Success Math ⭐ **Software Support**

Warm-Up 45.26

On Level   Activity Card 2-3

Investigate Math   Activity Card 2-3 ▲

Work: By Yourself

Use:
- Centimeter-Grid Paper (TRB M18)

1. Draw a line 3 cm long on the grid paper. Beginning at one end of the line, draw a second line 4 cm long that is perpendicular to the first line.

2. Connect the two lines to make a right triangle. How long is the third side? 5 cm

3. Draw a square on each side of your triangle. Find the area of each square.

4. **Compare** Find the sum of the areas of the two smaller squares. How does the sum compare to the area of the third square? $3 \times 3 = 9$ cm²; $4 \times 4 = 16$ cm²; $5 \times 5 = 25$ cm². $9 + 16 = 25$; They are equal.

Unit 2, Lesson 3   Copyright © Houghton Mifflin Company

Activity Note After students complete the activity, ask them to use what they have observed to describe how to find a third side of a right triangle, given the lengths of the other two sides.

✎ **Math Writing Prompt**

Use Reasoning A right triangle has sides of 5 cm, 12 cm, and 13 cm. Which sides are perpendicular? How do you know? What is the area?

MegaMath Grades K-6 **Software Support**

Ice Station Exploration: Polar Planes, Level Q

Challenge   Activity Card 2-3

Straw Quadrilaterals   Activity Card 2-3 ■

Work: By Yourself

Use:
- Two straws

1. Cut two straws at the same place to make two pairs of congruent segments.

2. Use the straws to make a rectangle. Measure the length and width, and then estimate the area.

3. Push the straws to change the rectangle into a parallelogram.

4. Measure the base and height.

5. **Compare** How does the area of the figure change? What measure does not change? The area decreases but the perimeter does not change.

Unit 2, Lesson 3   Copyright © Houghton Mifflin Company

Activity Note As students manipulate the straws to make different parallelograms, remind them that opposite sides must be parallel. Be sure that students remember base and height are perpendicular.

✎ **Math Writing Prompt**

Investigate Math What is the least possible perimeter of a parallelogram with a base of 6 cm and a height of 3 cm? Explain your answer.

✳ **DESTINATION Math** **Software Support**

Course III: Module 5: Unit 1: Parallelograms and Trapezoids

Area of Right Triangles and Parallelograms   **149**

③ Homework and Spiral Review

2-3

Homework **Goal:** Additional Practice

✓ Include students' Homework for page 39 as part of their portfolios.

2-3

Remembering **Goal:** Spiral Review

This Remembering activity is appropriate anytime after today's lesson.

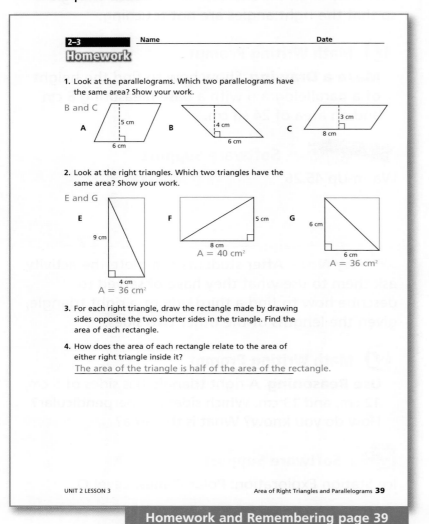

2-3 Name _____ Date _____

Homework

1. Look at the parallelograms. Which two parallelograms have the same area? Show your work.

B and C

A [5 cm, 6 cm] B [4 cm, 6 cm] C [3 cm, 8 cm]

2. Look at the right triangles. Which two triangles have the same area? Show your work.

E and G

E [9 cm, 4 cm, A = 36 cm²] F [5 cm, 8 cm, A = 40 cm²] G [6 cm, 6 cm, A = 36 cm²]

3. For each right triangle, draw the rectangle made by drawing sides opposite the two shorter sides in the triangle. Find the area of each rectangle.

4. How does the area of each rectangle relate to the area of either right triangle inside it?
   The area of the triangle is half of the area of the rectangle.

UNIT 2 LESSON 3   Area of Right Triangles and Parallelograms **39**

Homework and Remembering page 39

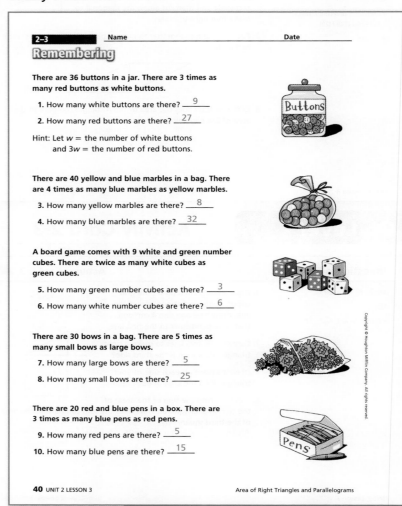

2-3 Name _____ Date _____

Remembering

There are 36 buttons in a jar. There are 3 times as many red buttons as white buttons.

1. How many white buttons are there? __9__

2. How many red buttons are there? __27__

Hint: Let w = the number of white buttons
     and $3w$ = the number of red buttons.

There are 40 yellow and blue marbles in a bag. There are 4 times as many blue marbles as yellow marbles.

3. How many yellow marbles are there? __8__

4. How many blue marbles are there? __32__

A board game comes with 9 white and green number cubes. There are twice as many white cubes as green cubes.

5. How many green number cubes are there? __3__

6. How many white number cubes are there? __6__

There are 30 bows in a bag. There are 5 times as many small bows as large bows.

7. How many large bows are there? __5__

8. How many small bows are there? __25__

There are 20 red and blue pens in a box. There are 3 times as many blue pens as red pens.

9. How many red pens are there? __5__

10. How many blue pens are there? __15__

40 UNIT 2 LESSON 3   Area of Right Triangles and Parallelograms

Homework and Remembering page 40

Home or School Activity

Science Connection

Traction Action The parallelogram is used in the design of tires to give better traction on the road. Look for and list other examples of products or designs that use the parallelogram.

The Area of Any Triangle

Lesson Objectives

- Find the area of any triangle.

- Identify the height of any triangle.

- Recognize that the area of a triangle is always one half the area of a parallelogram with the same height and base.

Vocabulary

triangle
parallelogram
area
base
height

The Day at a Glance

Today's Goals	Materials	
1 Teaching the Lesson **A1:** Cut out identical triangles to construct parallelograms, and discover the formula for the area of a triangle. **A2:** Draw and measure triangles and parallelograms.	**Lesson Activities** Student Activity Book pp. 68A–72 or Student Hardcover Book pp. 69–72 and Activity Workbook pp. 39–42 Homework and Remembering pp. 41–42	**Going Further** Activity Cards 2-4 Centimeter rulers Centimeter-Grid Paper (TRB M18) Scissors Math Journals
2 Going Further ▶ Differentiated Instruction	Quick Quiz 2 (Assessment Guide) Estimate Perimeter and Area (TRB M72) (optional)	
3 Homework and Spiral Review	Scissors Rulers Grid paper (optional)	

123 **Use Math Talk today!**

Keeping Skills Sharp

Daily Routines	English Language Learners
Homework Review Have students discuss and help each other resolve any problems from their homework. **Nonroutine Problem** There are four teams—Blue, Red, Green, and Yellow. Each team plays the other teams twice. The Blue team won 1 out of every 3 games played. If they did not tie in any games, how many games did the Blue team lose? 4; 3 other teams × 2 = 6 games played; 6 = 2 sets of 3. Since they won 1 out of 3 games, they won 2 games. 6 games − 2 won = 4 lost	Draw an acute triangle *ABC* with base *AC* on the board. Label the *base* and each *vertex*. Say: *Base* is the bottom. Each point is a *vertex*. • **Beginning** Ask: **Is *AC* the base?** yes **Is *B* a *vertex*?** yes • **Intermediate** Ask: **Is *AC* the *base* or a *vertex*?** base **How many *vertices* are there?** 3 **Name the vertices?** *A, B, C* • **Advanced** Say: *AC* is a ____. base The vertices are ____. A, B, C

Teaching the Lesson

Area of Triangles

 30 MINUTES

Goal: Cut out identical triangles to construct parallelograms, and discover the formula for the area of a triangle.

Materials: scissors, Student Activity Book pp. 68A–70 or Hardcover Book pp. 69–70 and Activity Workbook p. 39, Estimate Perimeter and Area (TRB M72) (optional)

✔ **NCTM Standards:**
Geometry
Measurement

► Experiment With Triangles   WHOLE CLASS

Have students cut out the two acute triangles and follow the directions. No matter which sides students place together (*a*, *b*, or *c*), students will discover that the result is a parallelogram. Students can repeat the exercise using the obtuse triangles. The results will be the same. Students have already discovered that two right triangles make a rectangle (which is a special kind of parallelogram). They can conclude that every triangle is half of a parallelogram.

► Calculate the Area of a Triangle

WHOLE CLASS

Invite students to answer questions 1 and 2 on page 69. Then have them use *A* to represent area, *b* to represent base, and *h* to represent height as they complete exercise 3. The following formula will allow them to find the area of any kind of triangle: $A = \frac{1}{2} b \times h$ or $A = b \times h \div 2$. Students can use the formula to answer questions 4 and 5.

Discuss questions 6 to 8. The height of an acute triangle is easy to find because it is inside the triangle. The height of a right triangle is the same as one of its sides. (*ZW* is not ⊥ *XY*; it is not the height.) The height of an obtuse triangle is outside the triangle.

Teaching Note

If your state standards require estimation of perimeter and area, have students complete the Estimate Perimeter and Area page (TRB M72).

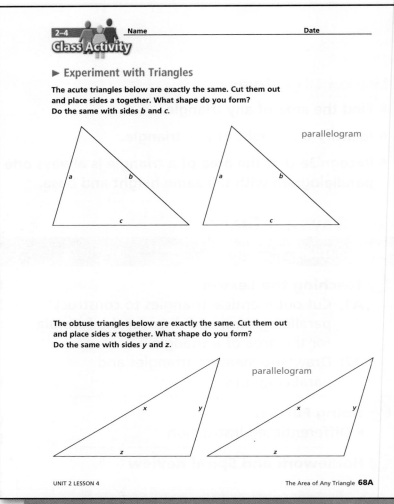

Student Activity Book p. 68A or Activity Workbook p. 39

In question 6, line segment *AE* shows the height of the obtuse triangle. A line segment must start at a vertex and be perpendicular to the base. Students can think of the base as being extended to meet the line.

You may want to draw this on the board. (Remind students that line segment *AE* can also be written as $\overline{AE}$.)

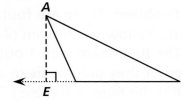

 Quick Quiz

See Assessment Guide for Unit 2 Quick Quiz 2.

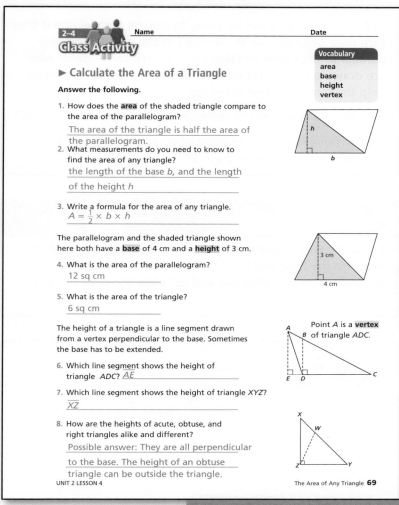

Student Activity Book page 69

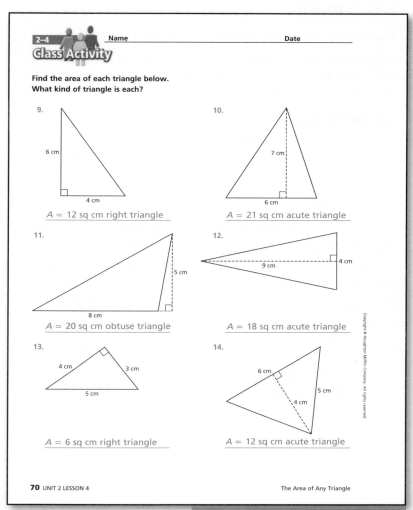

Student Activity Book page 70

In question 7, line segment *XZ* shows the height of the right triangle. The side is already perpendicular to the base, so no special lines need to be drawn.

The height of a right triangle is the same as one of the sides. $\overline{ZW}$ is not perpendicular to $\overline{XY}$, so it is not the height of the triangle.

Teaching Note

What to Expect from Students The order of operations does not matter here. If a triangle has a base of 8 and a height of 3, students can take $\frac{1}{2}$ of the base (4) and multiply it by the height ($4 \times 3 = 12$). Or they can multiply the base times the height (24) and take half of that entire quantity (12). The results will be the same.

● Does it matter if side *XZ* or side *ZY* is called the height? No; $\overline{XZ}$ is perpendicular to $\overline{ZY}$. If you turn the triangle so that $\overline{XZ}$ is the base, then $\overline{ZY}$ will be the height.

Math Talk For question 8, emphasize that the height of an obtuse triangle is a line segment outside the triangle. The base must be extended to see that it is perpendicular. Also, allow students to share and discuss all similarities and differences. Draw triangles on the board to demonstrate each point.

Have students calculate the area of the triangles in exercises 9–14 on Student Book page 70.

The Area of Any Triangle **153**

Activity 2

Triangles and Parallelograms

 15 MINUTES

Goal: Draw and measure triangles and parallelograms.

Materials: rulers, Student Activity Book pp. 71–72 or Hardcover Book pp. 71–72 and Activity Workbook pp. 41–42, grid paper (optional)

 NCTM Standards:
Geometry   Measurement

▶ Draw Parallelograms and Triangles

INDIVIDUALS

Students often forget to take half when finding the area of a triangle. These drawings will facilitate visual images of triangles as half of parallelograms. Have students complete exercises 15 to 30. Discuss the two different kinds of congruent triangles (acute and obtuse) that can be made from any parallelogram.

 Class Management

Tell students that it can be easier to draw a parallel line if they turn their page so that the bottom of the parallelogram is parallel to their desk or table edge. Watch for students who are drawing lines that do not look parallel. Ask questions to help them make better drawings.

▶ Does your line look the same distance everywhere from *AC*?

▶ How can you line up an edge of your ruler with *AC* and make a parallel line through *B*?

 Ongoing Assessment

Ask students to draw a parallelogram on grid paper and to measure the base and height. Have them divide their parallelogram into triangles and calculate the area of each triangle.

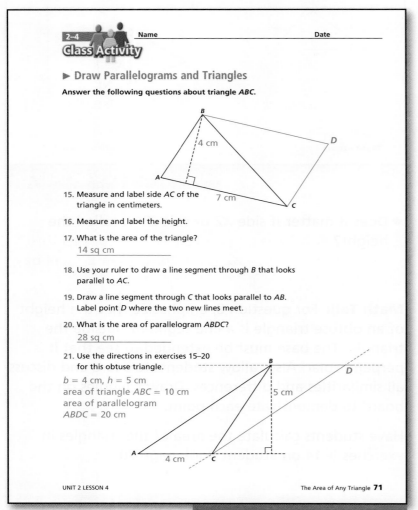

Student Activity Book page 71

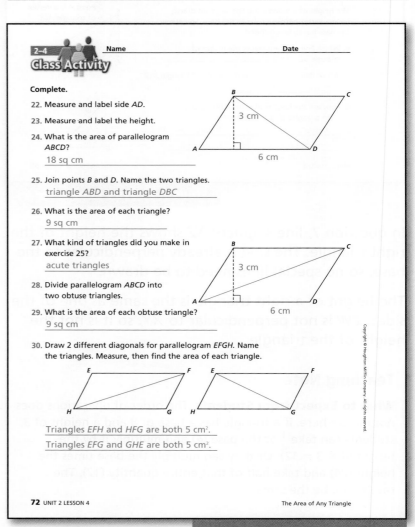

Student Activity Book page 72

Intervention   Activity Card 2-4

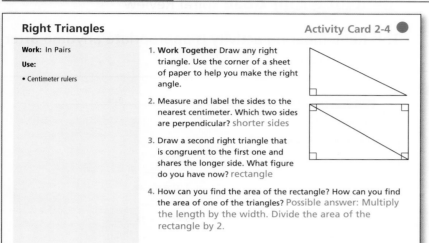

Right Triangles   Activity Card 2-4 ●

Work: In Pairs

Use:
• Centimeter rulers

1. **Work Together** Draw any right triangle. Use the corner of a sheet of paper to help you make the right angle.

2. Measure and label the sides to the nearest centimeter. Which two sides are perpendicular? shorter sides

3. Draw a second right triangle that is congruent to the first one and shares the longer side. What figure do you have now? rectangle

4. How can you find the area of the rectangle? How can you find the area of one of the triangles? Possible answer: Multiply the length by the width. Divide the area of the rectangle by 2.

Unit 2, Lesson 4   Copyright © Houghton Mifflin Company

Activity Note Encourage students to use the corner of a sheet of paper to make the right angles of the rectangle as they draw the second triangle.

 Math Writing Prompt

Make a Drawing What kind of triangle do you make when you cut a square in half along a diagonal? Draw an example and explain how to find the area of the triangle.

 **Software Support**

Warm-Up 45.26

On Level   Activity Card 2-4

Divide Rectangles   Activity Card 2-4 ▲

Work: In Pairs

Use:
• Centimeter-Grid Paper (TRB M18)
• Scissors

1. **Work Together** Draw a rectangle on grid paper. Measure the sides to the nearest centimeter. Then estimate the perimeter and area.

2. Cut the rectangle into two triangles and estimate the area of each triangle.

3. Use the triangles to make a parallelogram that is not a rectangle. Measure the sides and estimate the perimeter.

4. **Math Talk** Which quadrilateral has the greater perimeter? Is this always true? Explain. The parallelogram always has a greater perimeter because its slanted sides are longer than the vertical sides of the rectangle.

Unit 2, Lesson 4   Copyright © Houghton Mifflin Company

Activity Note To help students understand why the parallelogram will always have a greater perimeter, point out that the diagonal of the rectangle is always longer than either side.

 Math Writing Prompt

Explain Your Thinking Explain how you know the area of a triangle is one half the area of a parallelogram with the same base and height.

 Software Support

Ice Station Exploration: Polar Planes, Levels P and Q

Challenge   Activity Card 2-4

Draw Triangles   Activity Card 2-4 ■

Work: By Yourself

Use:
• Centimeter rulers

1. Draw any triangle with a base of 12 cm and a height of 4 cm. Many triangles are possible.

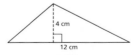

2. Find the area of the triangle. Then measure the sides to the nearest centimeter and label each side on your drawing.

3. Estimate the perimeter.

4. **Predict** Make a different triangle with the same base and height. Will the perimeter change? Measure and record your results. Yes, the perimeter will change unless the two triangles are mirror images of each other.

Unit 2, Lesson 4   Copyright © Houghton Mifflin Company

Activity Note The greatest perimeter will occur when the triangle is a right triangle.

 Math Writing Prompt

Investigate Math Can you put two copies of the same triangle together to make a quadrilateral that is not a parallelogram? Explain how.

 DESTINATION Math® **Software Support**

Course III: Module 5: Unit 1: Triangles

③ Homework and Spiral Review

Homework **Goal:** Additional Practice

For this Homework page, students find the perimeter and area of various regular polygons.

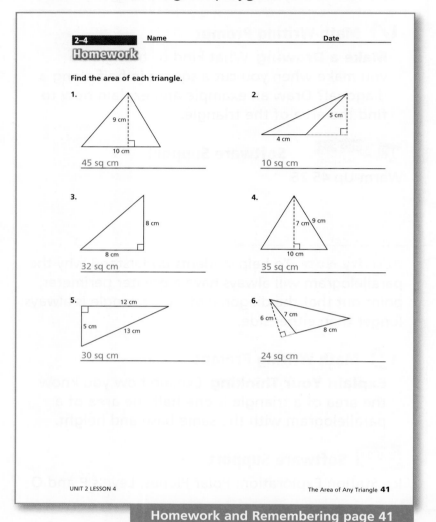

Remembering **Goal:** Spiral Review

This Remembering activity is appropriate anytime after today's lesson.

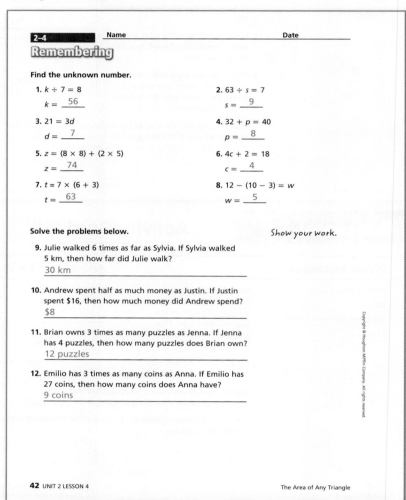

Homework and Remembering page 41

Homework and Remembering page 42

Home or School Activity

Math-to-Math Connection

Triangular Numbers Students build triangles by starting with one dot and adding new rows with one more dot each time. Invite them to investigate the number of dots. The total number of dots in each triangle is called a triangular number. Have students find the next three triangular numbers.

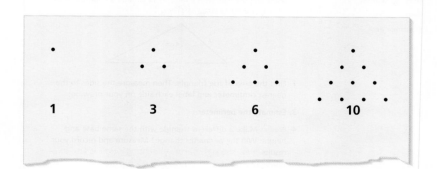

Consolidate Perimeter and Area

Lesson Objectives

● Select or infer the dimensions needed to find the area and perimeter of triangles and parallelograms.

● Find the perimeter and area of complex geometric figures composed of multiple smaller shapes.

The Day at a Glance

Today's Goals	Materials
1 **Teaching the Lesson** **A1:** Identify necessary dimensions for calculating area and perimeter. **A2:** Find the area and perimeter of various triangles and parallelograms. **A3:** Visualize and discuss strategies for finding the area and perimeter of complex geometric figures. **A4:** Estimate the area of regular polygons. **2** **Going Further** ▶ Differentiated Instruction **3** **Homework and Spiral Review**	**Lesson Activities** Student Activity Book pp. 73–76 or Student Hardcover Book pp. 73–76 Homework and Remembering pp. 43–44 Centimeter rulers **Going Further** Activity Cards 2-5 Centimeter-Grid Paper (TRB M18) Markers Math Journals

123 *Use Math Talk today!*

Keeping Skills Sharp

Daily Routines	English Language Learners
Homework Review Have students discuss and help each other resolve any problems from their homework. **Reasoning** Julieta said that when the lengths of a rectangle are doubled, the area also doubles. Is she correct? Explain. Draw and label rectangles with measurements to support your explanation. No; Possible explanation. Each side doubles and you multiply, not add, to find the area. $l = 4m$ $A = 8m^2$ $w = 2m$ $l = 8m$ $A = 32m^2$ $w = 4m$	Draw a complex figure made up of a rectangle and a triangle on the board. Write *complex figure*. Ask: **Is complex the opposite of simple?** yes ● **Beginning** Ask: **Does this figure have different shapes in it?** yes Say: **It is a complex figure.** Have students repeat. ● **Intermediate** Ask: **Is this a simple or a complex figure?** complex figure ● **Advanced** Have students tell why the figure on the board is a *complex figure*.

Teaching the Lesson

Appropriate Measurements

 20 MINUTES

Goal: Identify necessary dimensions for calculating area and perimeter.

Materials: Student Activity Book or Hardcover Book p. 73

✔ **NCTM Standards:**
Geometry
Measurement
Problem Solving

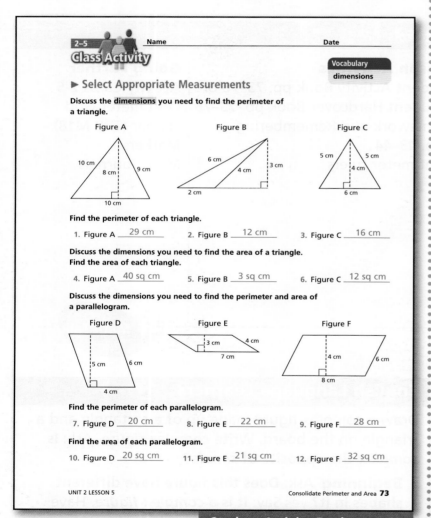

Student Activity Book page 73

▶ **Select Appropriate Measurements**

WHOLE CLASS

 Math Talk Have the class discuss exercises 1–6.

When calculating the perimeter or area of a geometric figure, students will often be presented with dimensions that they do not need. The exercises on this page will help them make the appropriate discriminations.

● Why don't you need the height of each triangle to find the perimeter? The height isn't a part of the distance around the triangle.

● For what kind of triangle might the height be part of the perimeter? Why? A right triangle, because one of the perpendicular sides can be the height.

Before beginning exercises 7–9, be sure your students understand that opposite sides of a parallelogram, like opposite sides of a rectangle, are equal in length.

● Why don't you need the height of each parallelogram to find the perimeter? The height isn't a part of the distance around the parallelogram.

● For what kind of parallelogram might the height be part of the perimeter? Why? A rectangle or a square, a perpendicular side can be the height.

● For exercises 10–12, why doesn't the formula we use include $\frac{1}{2}$, which is the same as dividing by 2? The figures are parallelograms. We divide by 2 when the figure is a triangle, because its area is $\frac{1}{2}$ the area of a parallelogram.

Differentiated Instruction

Extra Help For students who forget to divide by 2 when they find the area of a triangle, give them this extra practice. Name each figure on Student Book page 73 in the order below. Ask students to decide whether they should divide by 2 after they multiply the base times the height. D (*bh*), C (*bh* ÷ 2), A (*bh* ÷ 2), F (*bh*), E (*bh*) and B (*bh* ÷ 2).

Activity 2

Applications

 15 MINUTES

Goal: Find the area and perimeter of various triangles and parallelograms.

Materials: Student Activity Book or Hardcover Book p. 74

✔ **NCTM Standards:**
Geometry
Measurement

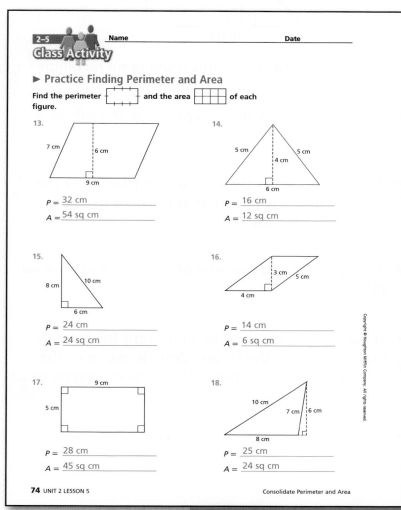

Student Activity Book page 74

► **Practice Finding Perimeter and Area**

WHOLE CLASS

Have students complete exercises 13–18, determining which dimensions they need to use each time. Students will need to supply the missing dimensions of parallelograms to find the perimeter, using their knowledge that opposite sides are equal. Alternatively, they can add the two sides that are given and then multiply by 2. They can use the same process for the rectangle in exercise 17 since rectangles are special kinds of parallelograms.

Students will need to ignore all sides except the base when finding the area of both triangles and parallelograms.

 Ongoing Assessment

Tell students that the formula $A = b \times h$ can be used to find the area of any parallelogram. Ask them to use a diagram to explain the formula. Then ask, "How can you change this formula and use it to find the area of any triangle?"

Teaching Note

What to Expect from Students The major error students make in finding the perimeter of rectangles and parallelograms is to forget to add the unlabeled sides. Suggest that students label all sides whenever they are asked for perimeter. They can drop this step when it is no longer needed.

The major error in finding the area of triangles is to forget to take half. Suggest that whenever students are asked to find the area of a triangle, they visualize the parallelogram made by 2 triangles and write $\frac{1}{2}$ by the triangle as a reminder to take half after they have found the product of the base and the height.

The major error in finding the area of a parallelogram is using the slanting side instead of the height. Have students visualize how the slanting side disappears when the parallelogram becomes a rectangle to show its square units and thus its area.

Teaching the Lesson (continued)

Activity 3

Area and Perimeter of Complex Figures

 25 MINUTES

Goal: Visualize and discuss strategies for finding the area and perimeter of complex geometric figures.

Materials: Student Activity Book or Hardcover Book p. 75

✔ **NCTM Standards:**
Geometry
Measurement

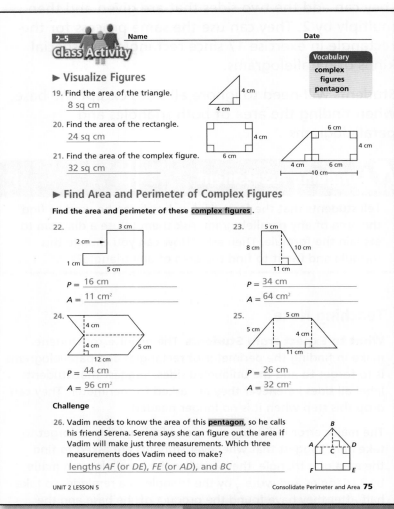

Student Activity Book page 75

▶ **Visualize Figures** [WHOLE CLASS]

Have students complete exercises 19 and 20. The figure in exercise 21 is a combination of the first two. Be sure that students do not assume that this shape is a combination of the triangle and the rectangle just because it looks that way. Ask probing questions to be sure that they can identify all the unknown dimensions.

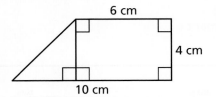

- **How do you know that this is the same rectangle?** It has the same length and width.

- **How do you know the height of the triangle in exercise 19?** The height is 4 cm because the height of this triangle is also one side of the rectangle.

- **How do you know the area of the triangle in the complex figure is the same as the area of the triangle in exercise 19?** The triangles have congruent bases and congruent heights.

- **How can you find the area of the figure in exercise 21?** Add the areas of the figures from exercises 19 and 20: 8 sq cm + 24 sq cm = 32 sq cm.

- **In exercise 21, we used two different formulas to find the area of the figure. Why does one of the formulas include $\frac{1}{2}$, which is the same as dividing by 2?** The product of a base and a height gives the area of a parallelogram. Two identical triangles form a parallelogram, so the formula for finding the area of a triangle is $\frac{1}{2}$ of the area of the formula for a parallelogram.

Differentiated Instruction

Special Needs For students who have difficulty seeing the figures that make up the complex figures in exercises 22–25, have them shade one of the figures. For #22, shade the large square; for #23, shade the rectangle; for #24, shade the top parallelogram; and for #25 shade the rectangle.

▶ Find Area and Perimeter of Complex Figures INDIVIDUALS

Help students find the area and perimeter of the complex figures in exercises 22–25. Remind students that they can find unknown lengths by using what they know about triangles and parallelograms.

Exercise 22: Students can find the length of the right side by adding the two lengths on the opposite side: 2 cm + 1 cm. They can find the length of the top of the small projecting rectangle by subtracting 3 cm from 5 cm. Students can now find the perimeter. They can find the area by adding the areas of the two combined rectangles together: 2 sq cm + 9 sq cm.

Exercise 23: The perimeter is the sum of the lengths. The dotted line that is the height of the embedded right triangle is 8 cm because it is directly opposite the other 8-cm side of the rectangle. To find the base of the triangle, students subtract 5 cm from 11 cm. Once they know these dimensions, students can find the area of the two figures separately and add them together.

Exercise 24: The figure is made up of two identical parallelograms. By applying their knowledge that opposite sides are equal, students can supply all the outside dimensions and find the perimeter. To find the area of the whole figure, students can find the area of one parallelogram and then multiply by 2.

Exercise 25: The right side of this figure is identical to the left side, so students can conclude that the right side is 5 cm long. They can now find the perimeter. They can find the length of the base of each right triangle by subtracting the top length (5 cm) from the bottom length (11 cm), which gives 6 cm. Because there are two triangles, the base of each is half of that measurement, or 3 cm. Students can now find the area of the rectangle (20 sq cm) and the two right triangles (6 sq cm + 6 sq cm) and add them together.

 Math Talk in Action

Look exercise 22 on Student Book page 75. Describe how to decompose the figure to find the area.

Carlos: We can divide the shape into two rectangles.

Yes, that's correct. How can we find the dimensions of the figures?

Madison: Two sides of the larger rectangle are 3 cm so it is a square. We multiply 3 × 3 = 9 sq cm.

That's correct Madison, but how do we know each side is 3 cm?

Madison: We can add 1 cm and 2 cm.

Yea, we can. How can we determine the dimensions of the smaller rectangle?

Teisha: We can subtract 3 cm from 5 cm to determine the length. Now we know the dimensions are 1 cm and 2 cm and the area is 1 × 2 or 2 sq cm.

Good. So what is the area of the whole figure?

Tyler: We add 9 + 2 for a total of 11 sq cm.

Differentiated Instruction

Advanced Learners Discuss strategies for solving exercise 26. To solve this problem, students need to see the embedded rectangle and triangle. The first measurement they need is the base of the triangle (*AD*), which is also one side of the rectangle. The other necessary measurements are the height of the triangle (*BC*) and the other side of the rectangle (either *AF* or *DE*, which are the same length).

Activity 4

Area of Regular Polygons

 15 MINUTES

Goal: Estimate the area of regular polygons.

Materials: centimeter rulers, Student Activity Book or Hardcover Book p. 76

 NCTM Standards:
Geometry
Measurement

▶ Area of a Regular Pentagon

WHOLE CLASS

Ask for Ideas Ask students to share what they remember about different types of triangles. As each triangle is named, ask that student to sketch one on the board. Discuss each triangle.

right triangle - one right angle

acute triangle - three acute angles

obtuse triangle - one obtuse angle

equilateral triangle - all sides equal

isosceles triangle - at least two equal sides. Students should make the connection that an equilateral triangle is also an isosceles triangle.

scalene triangle - no equal sides

Discuss Students should make the connection that an equilateral triangle has three equal sides and three equal angles. An isosceles triangle has two equal sides and two equal angles. A scalene triangle has no equal sides and no equal angles.

On the board, draw a rough sketch of a regular pentagon. Mark a point as close to the center of the pentagon as possible, and then join the point by line segments to each vertex of the pentagon.

● How many triangles are there? 5

● Are they all congruent? Yes; the pentagon is regular so their bases are all the same. The distances to the center are all the same.

● If the area of the whole pentagon is 10 sq cm, what is the area of each triangle? 2 sq cm

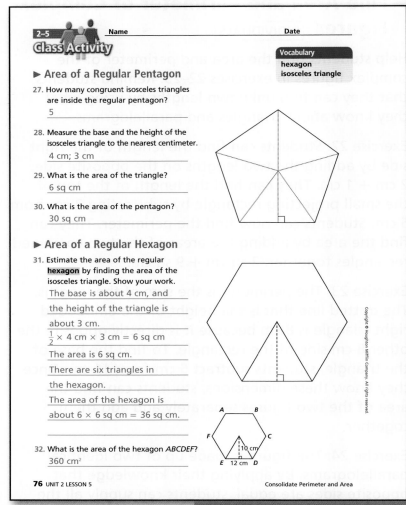

Student Activity Book page 76

● How can you find the area of the whole pentagon by measuring? Measure the base and height of one triangle and find its area. Then multiply by 5.

Have the students complete exercises 27 and 28 on Student Book page 76. Before completing exercises 29 and 30, ask the students to estimate the area of the regular pentagon, and after the remaining exercises have been completed, compare their estimates with their answers to exercise 30.

▶ Area of a Regular Hexagon   INDIVIDUALS

Students apply what they've learned to estimate the area of the hexagon in exercise 31, and then to find the actual area of the hexagon in exercise 32.

② Going Further

● Intervention   Activity Card 2-5

Make a Figure   Activity Card 2-5 ●

Work: By Yourself

Use:
• Centimeter-Grid Paper (TRB M18)

1. Draw two different parallelograms on grid paper. Use the same base and height for each figure.

2. Find the area for each figure. What do you notice? Both areas are equal.

3. Explain Can parallelograms with the same base and area ever have different areas? Why or why not?
No, the areas will always be the same. Possible explanation: You can cut both parallelograms and rearrange them to make the same rectangle.

Unit 2, Lesson 5   Copyright © Houghton Mifflin Company

Activity Note If students have difficulty explaining why the areas must be the same, have them cut each parallelogram along a vertical line from base to top and rearrange the pieces to make the same rectangle.

✏ Math Writing Prompt

Make a Drawing Draw two figures that have the same area and different perimeters. Explain why the perimeters are different.

Soar to Success Math ★ Software Support
Warm-Up 45.26

▲ On Level   Activity Card 2-5

Use Reasoning   Activity Card 2-5 ▲

Work: By Yourself

1. The base of each figure below has the same length. What do you notice about the height of each figure? same height

2. Which figure has the greater perimeter? How do you know?
The non-rectangular parallelogram has the greater perimeter because its slanted sides are longer than the sides of the rectangle.

Unit 2, Lesson 5   Copyright © Houghton Mifflin Company

Activity Note Reinforce the concept that the slanted sides of a parallelogram are longer by drawing a line connecting the base to the corner of the top of the figure. The longest side of the resulting right triangle is the always the side opposite the right angle.

✏ Math Writing Prompt

Explain Explain how to find the area of a right triangle with sides 5 cm, 12 cm, and 13 cm long.

MegaMath Software Support
Ice Station Exploration: Polar Planes, Level P

■ Challenge   Activity Card 2-5

Estimate Area   Activity Card 2-5 ■

Work: By Yourself

Use:
• Centimeter-Grid Paper (TRB M18)
• Markers

1. Draw the outline of a picture on centimeter grid paper.

2. Estimate the area of the picture by counting squares. First count all the whole squares inside the picture.

3. Then count the partial squares along the edges of the picture. Count each partial square as a whole square, a half square, or nothing, depending on how close each partial square appears to be to each benchmark.

4. Combine the values of all the squares you counted. Record the area of your picture. Then use color to decorate your figure if you like.

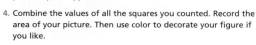

Unit 2, Lesson 5   Copyright © Houghton Mifflin Company

Activity Note Be sure that students understand the three benchmarks for evaluating partial squares. Display their finished pictures with area estimates.

✏ Math Writing Prompt

Area of a Trapezoid Sketch a trapezoid. Use what you know about triangles and parallelograms to explain what measurements you need to find the area of the trapezoid.

✦ DESTINATION Math® Software Support
Course III: Module 5: Unit 2: The Coordinate Plane

③ Homework and Spiral Review

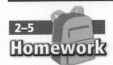

2–5
Homework **Goal:** Additional Practice

✓ Include students' Homework for page 43 as part of their portfolios.

2–5
Remembering **Goal:** Spiral Review

This Remembering activity is appropriate anytime after today's lesson.

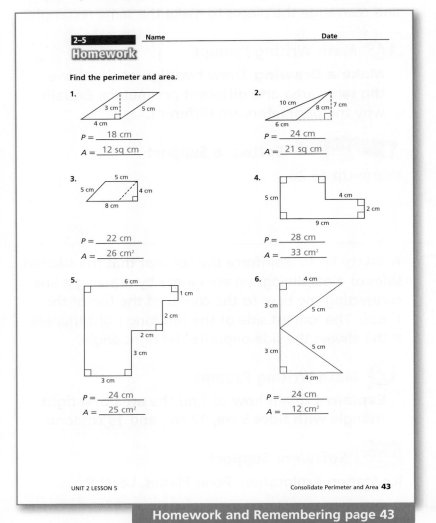

2–5
Homework

Name _____ Date _____

Find the perimeter and area.

1.
3 cm 5 cm
4 cm
P = 18 cm
A = 12 sq cm

2.
10 cm 8 cm 7 cm
6 cm
P = 24 cm
A = 21 sq cm

3.
5 cm 5 cm 4 cm
8 cm
P = 22 cm
A = 26 cm²

4.
5 cm 4 cm 2 cm
9 cm
P = 28 cm
A = 33 cm²

5.
6 cm 1 cm 2 cm 2 cm 3 cm 3 cm
P = 24 cm
A = 25 cm²

6.
4 cm 3 cm 5 cm 5 cm 3 cm 4 cm
P = 24 cm
A = 12 cm²

UNIT 2 LESSON 5   Consolidate Perimeter and Area **43**

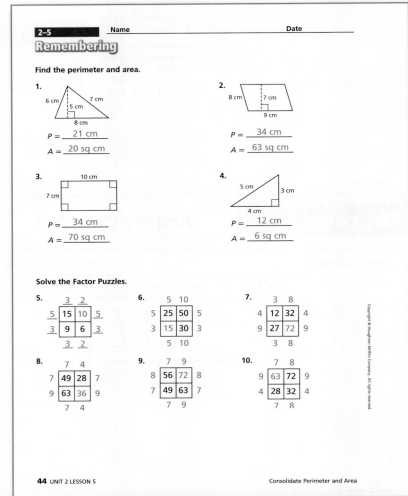

2–5
Remembering

Name _____ Date _____

Find the perimeter and area.

1.
6 cm 7 cm 5 cm
8 cm
P = 21 cm
A = 20 sq cm

2.
8 cm 7 cm
9 cm
P = 34 cm
A = 63 sq cm

3.
10 cm 7 cm
P = 34 cm
A = 70 sq cm

4.
5 cm 3 cm
4 cm
P = 12 cm
A = 6 sq cm

Solve the Factor Puzzles.

5.
	3	2	
5	15	10	5
3	9	6	3
	3	2	

6.
	5	10	
5	25	50	5
3	15	30	3
	5	10	

7.
	3	8	
4	12	32	4
9	27	72	9
	3	8	

8.
	7	4	
7	49	28	7
9	63	36	9
	7	4	

9.
	7	9	
8	56	72	8
7	49	63	7
	7	9	

10.
	7	8	
9	63	72	9
4	28	32	4
	7	8	

44 UNIT 2 LESSON 5   Consolidate Perimeter and Area

Homework and Remembering page 43

Homework and Remembering page 44

Home or School Activity

🌐 **Social Studies Connection**

Quilts Quilts are made up of complex figures sewn together to make a pattern. Have students research online or in books such as Mary Cobb's *The Quilt-Block History of Pioneer Days with Projects Kids Can Make* (The Millbrook Press, 1995, Illustrator Jan Davey Ellis). Have them find and draw at least three different examples of quilt patterns and describe each one using the language of geometry.

Customary Units of Length

Lesson Objectives

- Calculate perimeter and area in customary units.
- Estimate distances using benchmarks.
- Estimate and measure perimeter and area in customary units.

Vocabulary

inch	square inch
foot	square foot
yard	square yard

The Day at a Glance

Today's Goals	Materials	
① Teaching the Lesson **A1:** Calculate the perimeter and area of various figures. **A2:** Estimate distances using informal bench marks, measure lengths to the nearest half-, quarter, and eighth-inch. **② Going Further** ► Differentiated Instruction **③ Homework and Spiral Review**	**Lesson Activities** Student Activity Book pp. 77–80 or Student Hardcover Book pp. 77–80 and Activity Workbook p. 43 Homework and Remembering pp. 45–46 Quick Quiz 3 (Assessment Guide) Inch and centimeter ruler Yardstick or meter stick Customary tape measure	**Going Further** Activity Cards 2-6 Scissors Colored paper Inch-Grid Paper (TRB M1) Math Journals

123 *Use* **Math Talk** *today!*

Keeping Skills Sharp

Daily Routines	English Language Learners
Homework Review Send students to the board to show their work. **Strategy Problem** Hugo has 12 red and 12 white tiles. The area of each tile is 1 square inch. He uses the tiles to make a rectangle with a length that is 5 inches greater than the width. Each row in the rectangle has the same number of each red tile and white tiles. Describe the rectangle. Sketch one possible arrangement of the tiles. Possible answer: There are 24 tiles. The factor pairs of 24 are: 1, 24; 2, 12; 3, 8; 4, 6. 8 – 3 = 5, so there are 3 rows of 8 tiles with 4 red and 4 white tiles per row. There are several ways to arrange the tiles within the rows.	Write *in.*, *ft*, and *yd* on the board. Identify the meaning of each abbreviation. Draw three squares that show the following measures (areas): 1 sq in., 1 sq ft, and 1 sq yd. • **Beginning** Point to the figure that measures 1 sq ft and ask: **Is this a 1 sq in. or 1 sq ft?** 1 sq ft Continue with other units. • **Intermediate** Ask: **Are the areas of these figures measured in square units?** yes **Which figure has an area of 1 sq ft?** Have students point to the correct figure • **Advanced** Have students identify the square units.

1 Teaching the Lesson

Inches, Feet, and Yards

 20 MINUTES

Goal: Calculate the perimeter and area of various figures.

Materials: Student Activity Book or Hardcover Book pp. 77–79

 NCTM Standards:
Measurement
Reasoning and Proof

▶ Convert Units | WHOLE CLASS |

Review the customary units of length and ask questions about equivalent units.

● **What units do you usually use to measure the length of things at home?** Possible answers: inches, feet, and yards

● **Name some things that are about one inch long or wide.** Possible answers: width of a thumb, quarter, thickness of a textbook

● **Name some things that are about one foot long or wide.** Possible answers: a person's foot, a box of tissue (or cereal), length of a book

● **Name some things that are about one yard long or wide.** Possible answers: my desk, a window, a picture on the wall

● **How many inches are equal to one foot?** 12

● **How many feet are equal to one yard?** 3

● **So, how many inches are equal to one yard?** $3 \times 12 = 36$

Review the abbreviations for inch, yard, and foot. Write *in.*, *ft*, and *yd* on the board. Explain that we write *in.* with a period so we don't confuse it with the word *in*. The other abbreviations do not need periods.

Now lead a discussion on how to convert among units. On the board, write:

48 in. = _____ ft

_____ ft = 15 yards

● **If you know a stick is 48 in. long, how can you find its length in feet?** There are 12 in. in a foot, so divide by 12; $48 \div 12 = 4$ ft.

● **If you know a lawn is 15 yd long, how can you find its length in feet?** There are 3 ft in every one of the 15 yards, so multiply $3 \times 15 = 45$ ft.

● **When you convert from a small unit to a larger unit, what operation do you use? Why?** Division; the number of units will decrease.

● **When you convert from a large unit to a smaller unit, what operation do you use? Why?** Multiplication; you need more of the smaller units to measure the same length.

Compare a Meter and a Yard Discuss the relative sizes of meters and yards.

● **Which metric unit looks about the same length as a yard?** a meter

Have students measure a meter in inches.

● **About how long is a meter in inches?** 39 in.

● **Which is longer, a meter or a yard?** A meter; a yard is only 36 in.

Compare a Mile and a Kilometer Discuss the units you would use to measure long distances, such as the distance across a large city. Give students this rule for finding the approximate number of kilometers in one mile.

1 mile ≈ 1.6 km

As a class, make table that shows the approximate number of kilometers in 1 mile, 2 miles, 3 miles and so on. Ask if anyone knows how far he or she lives from school. Then calculate that distance in kilometers. For example, 1.5 mi × 1.6 km per mi = 2.4 km.

Invite students to complete exercises 1–9.

Vocabulary
inch (in.)
foot (ft)
yard (yd)
1 ft = 12 in.
1 yd = 3 ft
= 36 in.

▶ **Convert Units**

The **inch** (in.), **foot** (ft), and **yard** (yd) are commonly used units of measure in the Customary System of Measurement.

Complete.

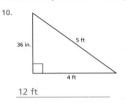
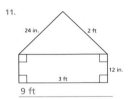

1. 24 in. = _2_ ft
2. 24 ft = _8_ yd
3. 12 ft = _144_ in.
4. _60_ in. = 5 ft
5. _18_ ft = 6 yd
6. 12 yd = _36_ ft
7. 72 in. = _2_ yd
8. _108_ in. = 3 yd
9. 10 yd = _360_ in.

▶ **Calculate Perimeter**

Calculate the perimeter of each figure in feet.

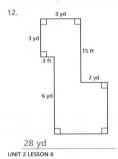

10.
36 in.
5 ft
4 ft
12 ft

11.
24 in.
2 ft
3 ft
12 in.
9 ft

Calculate the perimeter of each figure in yards.

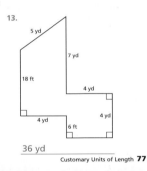

12.
3 yd
3 yd
15 ft
3 ft
2 yd
6 yd
28 yd

13.
5 yd
7 yd
18 ft
4 yd
4 yd
4 yd
6 ft
36 yd

UNIT 2 LESSON 6 | Customary Units of Length **77**

Student Activity Book page 77

▶ Calculate Perimeter INDIVIDUALS

Have students complete exercises 10–13. Remind students that they cannot add two numbers unless they are expressed in the same units. For example, when you add two nickels and three dimes, you need to convert the units to find the total amount in cents.

Math Talk in Action

Look exercise 13 on Student Book page 77. Describe how we can find the perimeter.

Hirva: We can add the measurements for all the sides.

Yes we can. How can we find the dimensions of the rectangle at the bottom?

Brooke: Since the top measurement is 4 yd, the bottom measurement must be 4 yd.

Good. Now, can we just add all the measurements?

Jackson: No, some of the measurements are in feet and the directions are to find the perimeter in yards. We need to change them to all yards.

That's right. How should we do that?

Manny: There are 3 feet in a yard and 3 is a factor of 18 and 6. So, we can divide 18 ft to become 6 yd and 6 ft to become 2 yd.

Correct. What do we do now?

Marcella: We add 5 + 7 + 4 + 4 + 4 + 2 + 4 + 6. The total is 36 yd, which is the perimeter.

Teaching Note

Watch For! Be aware of students who simply add the measurements shown. Remind them that there are some dimensions left unmarked that need to be included in the perimeter. Students can find these dimensions by looking at the total lengths of the opposite sides.

Activity continued ▶

① Teaching the Lesson (continued)

Activity 1

▶ Convert Compound Units WHOLE CLASS

 Math Talk Review units of length and ask questions about converting compound units.

● **What customary units do we use to measure length?** *Possible answers: inches, feet, and yards*

● **When we convert inches to feet, we use multiples of 12 inches to convert to an exact number of feet. For example, 12 inches is what number of feet?** *1 foot*

● **Twenty-four inches is what number of feet?** *2 feet*

● **Suppose we have a number of inches between 12 and 24, such as 20. How could we use subtraction to convert 20 inches to feet and inches?** *Subtract 12 inches from 20. The 12 inches we subtract represent 1 foot, and there are 8 inches left over. So 20 inches is the same as 1 foot 8 inches.*

● **How could we use division to convert 20 inches to feet and inches?** *Divide 20 inches by 12 and write the remainder. The whole number part of the quotient represents the number of feet, and the remainder represents the number of inches.*

On the board, ask volunteers to demonstrate each method and convert 42 inches to feet and inches. *3 ft 6 in.*

Generalize Suggest, or invite volunteers to suggest, conversions of larger units to smaller units. Complete each conversion as a class, then have students state a general method that can be used to convert any number of larger units to smaller units.

The Learning Classroom

Helping Partners Often it is useful to pair a struggling student with a student who is stronger in a particular area. The helping partner needs to help the other student understand how to solve a problem, rather than just showing the student what to do. Helping pairs often foster learning in both students as the helper strives to adopt the perspective of the novice.

2–6
Class Activity

▶ Convert Compound Units

A compound unit is a measurement that contains two different units. For example, if your height were measured in feet and inches, the measurement would be a compound unit.

Convert these units.

14. 1 yd = __3__ ft
15. 1 ft = __12__ in.
16. 1 yd = __36__ in.
17. 2 ft 6 in. = __30__ in.
18. 5 yd 2 ft = __17__ ft
19. 3 yd 3 in. = __111__ in.
20. 9 yd 1 ft = __28__ ft
21. 4 yd 10 in. = __154__ in.
22. 6 ft 5 in. = __77__ in.
23. 12 in. = __1__ ft
24. 3 ft = __1__ yd
25. 36 in. = __1__ yd
26. 19 ft = __6__ yd __1__ ft
27. 84 in. = __2__ yd __1__ ft
28. 54 in. = __4__ ft __6__ in.
29. 45 in. = __1__ yd __9__ in.
30. 99 in. = __8__ ft __3__ in.
31. 32 ft = __10__ yd __24__ in.

▶ Add and Subtract Units of Length

Add or subtract.

32.	33.	34.
7 feet 10 inches + 3 feet 5 inches 11 feet 3 inches	9 yards 2 inches − 5 yards 8 inches 3 yards 30 inches	2 yards 2 feet + 4 yards 6 feet 8 yards 2 feet

35.	36.	37.
8 feet 3 inches − 4 feet 9 inches 3 feet 6 inches	6 yards 10 inches + 2 yards 30 inches 9 yards 4 inches	10 yards 1 feet − 3 yards 2 feet 6 yards 2 feet

38. Beth is 5 feet 3 inches tall. Her best friend is 4 feet 11 inches tall. How many inches taller is Beth?
4 inches taller

39. In a long jump competition, Ty jumped 13 feet 2 inches. How many inches farther than 4 yards did he jump?
14 inches farther

78 UNIT 2 LESSON 6   Customary Units of Length

Student Activity Book page 78

▶ Add and Subtract Units of Length
 WHOLE CLASS

On the board, sketch a rectangle and label its length as 5 feet 7 inches and its width as 2 feet 10 inches. Invite volunteers to demonstrate how subtraction can be used to find how much greater the length is than the width, and how addition can be used to find the perimeter. *2 feet 9 inches; P = 16 ft 10 in.*

Make sure all students understand the regrouping relationships shared by inches, feet, and yards (1 foot is regrouped as 12 inches and 1 yard is regrouped as 3 feet). Then have students work individually or with a **Helping Partner** to complete exercises 14–39 on Student Book page 78.

▶ Calculate Area WHOLE CLASS

As a class, discuss the customary units used to measure area.

- Draw a square that is one inch on each side. What is the area of your square? 1 sq in.

- Draw a square that is one foot on each side. What is the area of your square? 1 sq ft

- What is the area of a square that is one yard on each side? 1 sq yd

Compare Square Meters and Square Yards Students constructed a square meter in Lesson 1 of this unit. Ask them to use 3 one-foot lengths to show an area of one square yard.

- What unit of area looks about the same size as one square yard? 1 sq m

Discuss the relative sizes of one square meter and one square yard.

- Which is greater, one square meter or one square yard? 1 sq m because each side of a meter square is greater than a yard

Assign exercises 40–45. Remind students that they need to convert dimensions into the same units before they can multiply them, and that some dimensions may be missing. Students can find missing dimensions by looking at the opposite sides.

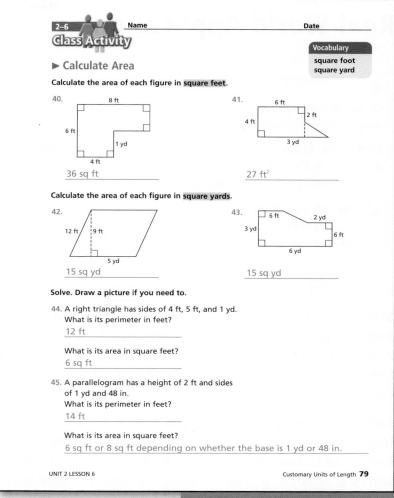

Activity 2

Real-World Applications

 40 MINUTES

Goal: Estimate distances using informal benchmarks; measure lengths to the nearest half-, quarter-, and eighth-inch.

Materials: Student Activity Book p. 80 or Hardcover Book p. 80 and Activity Workbook p. 43, inch and centimeter ruler, yardstick or meter stick, customary tape measure

 NCTM Standard:
Measurement
Reasoning and Proof

▶ Use Paces to Estimate PAIRS

Student Pairs will use the table at the top of Student Book page 80 to complete this activity. An alternative way to record the collected data is to copy the table on the board or overhead and extend it so all of the data can be recorded in one place.

Explain that informal benchmarks can be used to estimate length or distance. Point out, for example, that the heights of horses can be informally estimated in "hands" with the width of a "hand" being 4 inches. (A horse that is about 14 hands tall is about 14 × 4 or 56 inches tall.) A more familiar unit for most students is a pace—the length of one stride as measured from heel-to-heel or toe-to-toe.

Direct students to work with a partner and count the number of paces that are needed to walk the length and the width of the classroom, and record the data in the exercise 46 table. Then have them measure the length of their pace by walking a few steps and stopping in stride. A partner measures the length of the stride and records the data in the table. (Encourage

---

2–6
Class Activity

Name _____ Date _____

▶ Use Paces to Estimate

46. Work with a partner to complete the first two rows of the table. Use data collected by your classmates to complete the remaining rows.

Pair		Number of Paces	Length of a Pace	Estimate of Classroom
1	Width:			
	Length:			
2	Width:			
	Length:			
3	Width:			
	Length:			

▶ Measure Real-World Objects

47. Choose five different objects from your classroom. Complete the table below by estimating the length of each object to the nearest whole inch. Then measure to the nearest $\frac{1}{2}$, $\frac{1}{4}$, and $\frac{1}{8}$ inch.

Object	Estimate	Measure		
	to the nearest whole inch	to the nearest $\frac{1}{2}$ inch	to the nearest $\frac{1}{4}$ inch	to the nearest $\frac{1}{8}$ inch

80 UNIT 2 LESSON 6   Customary Units of Length

students to use other ratios, such as 2 paces is about 36 inches or 1 yard.) Partners then work together to complete the last column of the table.

Discuss Compare the collected data.

● What were the greatest and least estimates for the length and width of our classroom?

● Within what range are most of the estimates?

● If we choose only one estimate for the length and one estimate for the width of our classroom, which estimates should we choose? Why?

● What is a reasonable estimate for the perimeter of our classroom?

▶ Measure Real-World Objects [PAIRS]

Precision and Measurement Make sure students understand that measuring a length involves a specified degree of precision. For example, have students suppose their heights were measured to the nearest foot (their heights would be 5 feet) and measured to the nearest inch (their heights would be 4 feet and a number of inches or 5 feet and a number of inches). Then have them suggest reasons why stating their heights in feet and inches is more precise than simply stating the heights in feet.

Have **Student Pairs** choose a variety of classroom objects (such as a marker, a button, and a paper clip) and estimate the length and/or width of each to the nearest whole inch. Then have them measure to the nearest $\frac{1}{2}$, $\frac{1}{4}$, and $\frac{1}{8}$ inch. Students should record the measurements in the table for exercise 47.

Generalize After the activity has been completed, have students compare and discuss their findings. Lead them to generalize that the smaller the measurement unit, the greater the precision of the measurement, and vice versa.

Differentiated Instruction

Advanced Learners Challenge your advanced learners to describe real-world measurement situations and the degree of precision that is likely to be needed for each situation. For example, measuring the perimeter of a garden to the nearest inch is likely to represent too much precision when purchasing lengths of fencing to surround the garden. Instead, measuring to the nearest foot and purchasing at least that number of feet of fencing is sufficient.

✓ Ongoing Assessment

Encourage students to explain their thinking by asking questions such as the following:

▶ What customary units of measurement are best for measuring the area of a book cover, the school yard, or a classroom?

▶ Units of Measure and Benchmarks (Optional) [INDIVIDUALS]

(123) **Math Talk** Discuss informal benchmarks that students can use to gain a sense of how metric and customary linear units of measure compare. For example, have students suppose they are watching an Olympic race that is 1500 meters long. To give them a sense of how far 1500 meters is, point out that because it is about 0.93 miles, we can say in a general way that the race is about 1 mile long.

Give students an opportunity to suggest estimates for the following relationships (and others they might suggest). Reasonable answers are shown. Some students may find it helpful to compare inch rulers and centimeter rulers, or yardsticks and meter sticks, during the discussion.

1 in. = _____ cm about 2.5 or $2\frac{1}{2}$
1 dm = _____ in. about 4
1 yd = _____ cm about 90
1 yd = _____ m about 0.9 or $\frac{9}{10}$
1 mi = _____ m about 1,600
1 mi = _____ km about 1.6
1 km = _____ mi about 0.6 or $\frac{5}{8}$

Then have students use the relationships and their understanding of arithmetic to develop informal benchmarks. For example, they may conclude that since 1 yard is about 90 centimeters and 1 meter is 100 centimeters, a reasonable estimate of 1 yard is about 1 meter. Or, since 1 kilometer is about $\frac{5}{8}$ of a mile, 3 kilometers is about $\frac{5}{8} + \frac{5}{8} + \frac{5}{8}$ or $\frac{15}{8}$ miles, and $\frac{15}{8}$ is close to $\frac{16}{8}$, which is another name for 2; so 3 kilometers is about the same as 2 miles.

Encourage students to record the informal benchmarks in their Math Journals.

Activity continued ▶

Activity 2

▶ Carpet the Classroom SMALL GROUPS

Have students measure the length and width of the classroom in feet. Draw a rectangle on the board, about the same shape as the classroom. Label the dimensions.

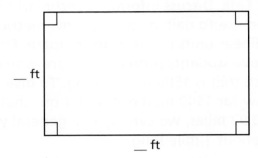

Explain to students that they are going to make a plan to use carpet tiles to cover the classroom floor. The carpet tiles come in two sizes: one-foot squares and two-foot squares. Students will estimate the number of tiles they need.

Divide the class into two **Small Groups**. The pairs in one group will estimate the number of one-foot squares; the pairs in the other group, two-foot squares. Students need to be sure they have enough tiles to cover the whole floor — they can't have too few.

When the students have made their estimates, bring them together and discuss the results.

● How many one-foot squares do you need?

● How do you know you'll have enough to cover the whole floor? We added an extra foot to each length estimate before we multiplied to find the area.

● How many two-foot squares do you need?

● How did you find the total? We divided each length by 2 to find the number of tiles that fit along each wall. Then we multiplied to find the number of tiles to cover the area.

● How do you know you'll have enough to cover the whole floor? We made sure to add an extra tile along each wall.

Discuss the relationship among the two results.

● What is the area of a two-foot tile? 4 sq ft

● How many one-foot tiles do you need to cover the same area as a two-foot tile covers? 4

● How can you use the number of one-foot tiles to find the number of two-foot tiles? divide by 4

● How can you use the number of two-foot tiles to find the number of one-foot tiles? multiply by 4

Invite students to check their results.

● Multiply the number of two-foot tiles by 4. Is it about the same as the estimate for one-foot tiles? Yes, it's close.

● Why might it be a bit different? The two-foot tiles are much bigger. With two-foot tiles you might have more leftover tiles after you cut them down along the edges.

Quick Quiz

See Assessment Guide for Unit 2 Quick Quiz 3.

② Going Further

Differentiated Instruction

Intervention   Activity Card 2-6

Make a Square Yard   Activity Card 2-6 ●

Work: In Small Groups

Use:
• Scissors
• Paper at least 12 inches on each side

1. Measure a one-foot square on paper and cut out nine copies of the square.

2. Arrange the squares to make one square yard. What is the perimeter of the square yard? 12 feet, or 4 yards

3. Now rearrange the squares to make other shapes. Write the area and perimeter of each new shape. Area = 1 sq yd, or 9 sq ft; Perimeters will vary: for figure shown, 20 ft

Unit 2, Lesson 6   Copyright © Houghton Mifflin Company

Activity Note Students should draw the first square in the corner of the paper. Have students use the square corner of a second sheet of paper to help them make three more right angles for the square.

 **Math Writing Prompt**

Change Units If a rectangle is 24 in. × 36 in., what is its perimeter in feet? What is its area in square feet?

Soar to Success Math ✦ **Software Support**

Warm-Up 45.26

On Level   Activity Card 2-6

Investigate Math   Activity Card 2-6 ▲

Work: In Pairs

Use:
• Inch-Grid Paper (TRB M1)

1. A complex figure combines several simple geometric figures, as shown below. On your grid paper, draw a different complex figure with an area of 60 inches. Label all the dimensions of your figure.

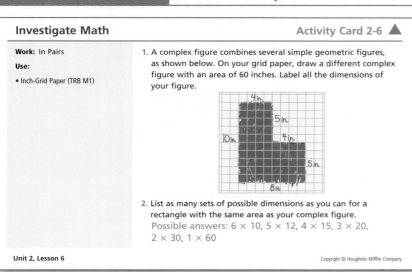

2. List as many sets of possible dimensions as you can for a rectangle with the same area as your complex figure. Possible answers: 6 × 10, 5 × 12, 4 × 15, 3 × 20, 2 × 30, 1 × 60

Unit 2, Lesson 6   Copyright © Houghton Mifflin Company

Activity Note Students can make multiple copies of their figure to cut out and rearrange to find possible dimensions for a rectangle with the same area. They can also make an organized list of factor pairs.

 Math Writing Prompt

Explain Your Thinking Will cutting up and rearranging a figure change its perimeter or area? Explain your answer.

MegaMath Grades K-6 **Software Support**

Ice Station Exploration: Polar Planes, Level R

Challenge   Activity Card 2-6

Use Reasoning   Activity Card 2-6 ■

Work: By Yourself

2. Possible answer: I made a large rectangle with an area of 90 sq yd. The area of the dotted rectangle is 30 sq yd. The area of the figure is 90 − 30 = 60 sq yd.

1. Copy the L-shaped figure. Include the labels.

2. Tell how to use subtraction to find the area of the figure. Use your drawing to help you explain your method.

3. Draw another complex figure whose area you can find by using subtraction.

4. Exchange papers with another student. Use subtraction to find the area of their figure.

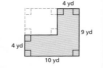

Unit 2, Lesson 6   Copyright © Houghton Mifflin Company

Activity Note Some students may recognize that they can find the area of a complex figure by decomposing it into smaller shapes such as rectangles and combining the areas to find the total.

 Math Writing Prompt

Investigate Math How many square inches are in a square foot? Use your answer to estimate how many square inches are in a square meter.

 DESTINATION Math **Software Support**

Course III: Module 5: Unit 1: Rectangles and Squares

Customary Units of Length   **173**

③ Homework and Spiral Review

2-6
Homework **Goal:** Additional Practice

This Homework page provides students with practice calculating the perimeter and area of various figures in customary units.

2-6
Remembering **Goal:** Spiral Review

This Remembering activity is appropriate anytime after today's lesson.

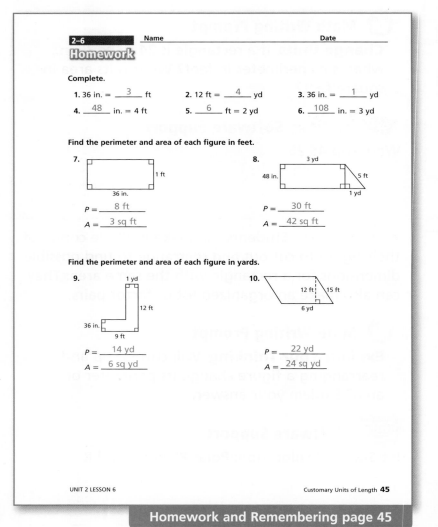

Homework and Remembering page 45

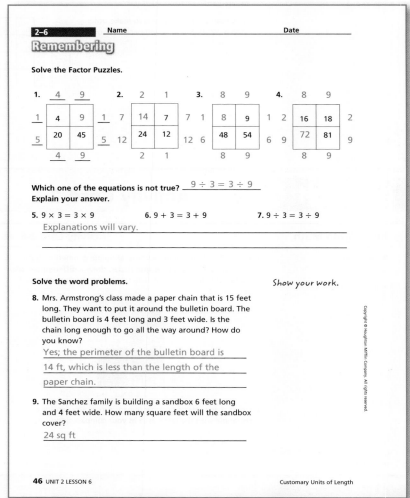

Homework and Remembering page 46

Home or School Activity

 Real-World Connection

Customary Measurement Ask students why it is important to measure in units that are a consistent size. What measurement system is used in most of the world? Ask students why they think units such as inches, feet, and yards are called *customary units*.

174 UNIT 2 LESSON 6

Unit Review and Test

Lesson Objective

● **Assess student progress on unit objectives.**

The Day at a Glance

Today's Goals	Materials
1 Assessing the Lesson ► Assess student progress on unit objectives. ► Use activities from unit lessons to reteach content. **2 Going Further** ► Use remediation for common errors. There is no homework assignment on a test day.	Unit 2 Test, Student Activity Book or Student Hardcover Book pp. 81–82 Unit 2 Test, Form A or B, Assessment Guide (optional) Unit 2 Performance Assessment, Assessment Guide (optional)

Keeping Skills Sharp

Daily Routines ⏱ 5 MINUTES	
If you are doing a unit review day, go over the homework. If this is a test day, omit the homework review.	**Review and Test Day** You may want to choose a quiet game or other activity (reading a book or working on homework for another subject) for students who finish early.

Assessing the Unit

Assess Unit Objectives

45 MINUTES (more if schedule permits)

Goal: Assess student progress on unit objectives.

Materials: Student Activity Book or Student Hardcover Book pp. 81–82, Assessment Guide (optional)

▶ Review and Assessment

If your students are ready for assessment on the unit objectives, you may use either the test on the Student Book pages or one of the forms of the Unit 2 Test in the Assessment Guide to assess student progress.

If you feel that students need some review first, you may use the test on the Student Book pages as a review of unit content, and then use one of the forms of the Unit 2 Test in the Assessment Guide to assess student progress.

To assign a numerical score for all of these test forms, use 10 points for each question.

You may also choose to use the Unit 2 Performance Assessment. Scoring for that assessment can be found in its rubric in the Assessment Guide.

▶ Reteaching Resources

The chart lists the test items, the unit objectives they cover, and the lesson activities in which the objective is covered in this unit. You may revisit these activities with students who do not show mastery of the objectives.

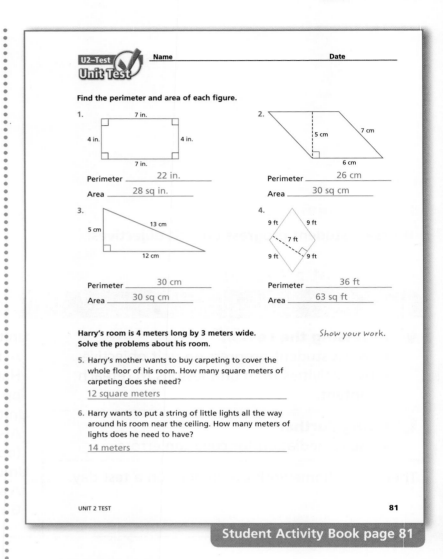

Student Activity Book page 81

Unit Test Items	Unit Objectives Tested	Activities to Use for Reteaching
1–4	**2.1** Find perimeter and area of polygons.	Lesson 2, Activities 1–2 Lesson 3, Activities 2–3 Lesson 4, Activity 1
5, 6, 9, 10	**2.2** Use customary and metric measurements to solve problems involving perimeter and area.	Lesson 1, Activities 1–2 Lesson 2, Activities 2–3 Lesson 6, Activity 1
7, 8	**2.3** Find perimeter and area of complex figures.	Lesson 5, Activity 3

176 UNIT 2

Name _____ **Date** _____

Find the perimeter and area of each figure.

7.

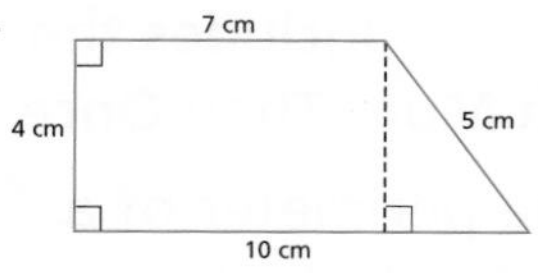

7 cm
4 cm
5 cm
10 cm

8.

3 ft
7 ft
2 ft
2 ft
2 ft
9 ft

Perimeter _____ 26 cm _____

Area _____ 34 sq cm _____

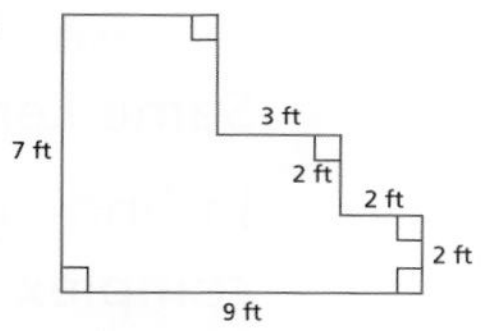

Perimeter _____ 32 ft _____

Area _____ 44 sq ft _____

Solve.

Show your work on your paper or in your journal.

9. A parallelogram has a height of 4 meters and sides of 5 meters and 7 meters. What is its area in square meters?

_____ 28 sq m _____

10. **Extended Response** Gina is framing a picture that is 9 in. wide and 10 in. high. She has 3 ft of framing material. Does she have enough material to frame the picture? Explain your answer.
(Remember: 1 ft = 12 in.)

No. The perimeter of the picture is 38 in.

She would need more than that to frame the

picture. She has 3 ft of frame. That is only

36 in.

_____

_____

82 UNIT 2 TEST

Student Activity Book page 82

► Assessment Resources

Free Response Tests
Unit 2 Test, Student Book pages 81–82
Unit 2 Test, Form A, Assessment Guide

Extended Response Item
The last item in the Student Book test and in the Form A test will require an extended response as an answer.

Multiple Choice Test
Unit 2 Test, Form B, Assessment Guide

Performance Assessment
Unit 2 Performance Assessment, Assessment Guide
Unit 2 Performance Assessment Rubric, Assessment Guide

► Portfolio Assessment

Teacher-selected Items for Student Portfolios:

- Homework, Lessons 2, 3, and 5
- Class Activity work, Lessons 4 and 6

Student-selected Items for Student Portfolios

- Favorite Home or School Activity
- Best Writing Prompt

Extending the Assessment

Unit Objective 2.1

Find perimeter and area of polygons.

Common Error: Doesn't Use All Measurements

In finding perimeter, students may fail to use the lengths of all sides of a polygon.

Remediation Remind students that the number of addends used to find the perimeter must equal the number of sides of the polygon. Suggest that it may help to count the sides and the addends as a check that all sides have been included.

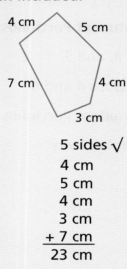

5 sides √
    4 cm
    5 cm
    4 cm
    3 cm
 + 7 cm
  23 cm

Unit Objective 2.2

Use customary and metric measurements to solve problems involving perimeter and area.

Common Error: Doesn't Label the Answer

In writing answers to problems, students may not include a unit of measure with their numerical answers.

Remediation Point out that a measurement problem usually requires a unit of measure with the answer. Emphasize that it is important to look back at the problem to see what unit of measure is needed for the label.

Common Error: Forgets to Convert Units

In setting up the computation needed to find an answer, students may not be using the same unit for all dimensions.

Remediation Remind students that they need to compute with the same unit of measure. Suggest that they check to see that all units of measure are the same and that they stop to convert any measurements that are not the same before doing any computation.

Unit Objective 2.3

Find perimeter and area of complex figures.

Common Error: Includes the Same Length More Than Once

In finding the perimeter of a complex figure, students may lose track of how the lengths of the sides relate to the whole figure and may include a length more than once.

Remediation Remind students that they need to use only the lengths of the line segments that are around the edges of the figure to find the perimeter. Suggest that they mark each side as they include it in the addends they are using to find the perimeter.

Common Error: Includes Part of the Area More Than Once

When decomposing a complex figure, students may include part of the area more than once.

Remediation Remind students that they first separate the figure into smaller parts for which they can find the area. Suggest that they shade each part of the complex figure as they find its area to prevent including it in another part. They might even write in the area for each part of the figure.

Addition and Subtraction of Whole Numbers and Decimals

UNIT 3 DEVELOPS the concept of place value for whole numbers and decimals. Students gain a deeper understanding of addition and subtraction of whole numbers and decimals and the relationship involved in these operations. Students read, interpret, and pose problems for pictographs, bar graphs, and line graphs. They discuss and solve change, collection, and comparison problems, and continue to use algebraic notation in situation and solution equations.

Skills Trace

Grade 4	Grade 5
• Understand place value from thousandths to thousands.	• Understand place value from billionths to billions.
• Compare and order whole numbers and decimals (hundredths).	• Compare and order whole numbers and decimals (thousandths).
• Round whole numbers and decimals to estimate sums and differences.	• Round whole numbers and decimals to estimate sums and differences.
• Use the Commutative, Associative, and Distributive Properties.	• Use the Commutative, Associative, and Distributive Properties.
• Use different models to write a decimal in standard form, word form, and as a fraction.	• Use different models to write a decimal in standard form, word form, expanded form, and as a fraction.
• Write an equation to solve problems involving whole numbers and decimals.	• Write an equation to solve problems involving whole numbers and decimals.
• Interpret and make a pictograph, bar graph, and line graph.	• Interpret and make a pictograph, bar graph (double), and line graph (double and triple).
• Distinguish between and match the appropriate graphs for numerical and categorical data.	• Distinguish between and match the appropriate graphs for numerical and categorical data, and discrete and continuous data.

Unit 3 Contents

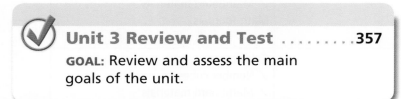

Planning Unit 3

Lesson NCTM Focal Points NCTM Standards	Resources	Materials for Lesson Activities	Materials for Going Further
3-1 **Decimals as Equal Divisions** NCTM Focal Point: 7.1 NCTM Standards: 1, 8, 9, 10	TE pp. 179–186 SAB pp. 83–84 H&R pp. 47–48 AC 3-1	✓ Pointer ✓ Play money (optional) Patterns from Billions to Billonths (TRB M22)	✓ MathBoard materials Centimeter-Grid Paper (TRB M18) Markers Math Journals
3-2 **Equate and Compare** NCTM Focal Points: 4.2, 7.1 NCTM Standards: 1, 10	TE pp. 187–198 SAB pp. 85–86D H&R pp. 49–50 AC 3-2 MCC 13	✓ MathBoard materials Whole Numbers and Number Lines (TRB M73) (optional) Small 10 × 10 Grids (TRB M74) ✓ Secret Code Cards (optional) Ruler Scissors	✓ MathBoard materials Grid Paper (TRB M17) Math Journals
3-3 **Thousands to Thousandths** NCTM Focal Point: 7.1 NCTM Standards: 1, 8, 10	TE pp. 199–208 SAB pp. 87–90 H&R pp. 51–52 AC 3-3	✓ Secret Code Cards Scissors ✓ Place Value Parade Poster ✓ MathBoard materials	✓ Number cubes ✓ Counters Ruler Math Journals
3-4 **Adding and Subtracting Decimals** NCTM Focal Points: 2.3, 2.4, 2.8, 7.1 NCTM Standards: 1, 4, 10	TE pp. 209–216 SAB pp. 90A–92 H&R pp. 53–54 AC 3-4 AG Quick Quiz 1	✓ MathBoard materials ✓ Secret Code Cards Scissors Tape ✓ Place Value Parade Poster (optional)	Grid paper ✓ MathBoard materials Math Journals
3-5 **Billions to Billionths** NCTM Focal Point: 7.1 NCTM Standards: 1, 6, 8, 10	TE pp. 217–228 SAB pp. 93–98 H&R pp. 55–56 AC 3-5	✓ Secret Code Cards Scissors Tape	Index cards Paper clips ✓ MathBoard materials Math Journals
3-6 **Use Place Value** NCTM Focal Points: 4.1, 7.1 NCTM Standards: 1, 7, 8, 10	TE pp. 229–236 SAB pp. 99–100 H&R pp. 57–58 AC 3-6 AG Quick Quiz 2	✓ Pointer	Calculators ✓ Number cubes ✓ MathBoard materials Math Journals
3-7 **Add Whole Numbers and Decimals** NCTM Focal Points: 2.3, 2.8 NCTM Standards: 1, 4, 8	TE pp. 237–242 SAB pp. 101–102 H&R pp. 59–60 AC 3-7 MCC 14	Calculators (optional)	Centimeter tape measures ✓ MathBoard materials ✓ Play money Math Journals
3-8 **Addition to Millions** NCTM Focal Points: 2.3, 2.8 NCTM Standards: 1, 8	TE pp. 243–248 SAB pp. 103–104 H&R pp. 61–62 AC 3-8	None	Place-value charts Calculators ✓ MathBoard materials Math Journals

Resources/Materials Key: TE: Teacher Edition SAB: Student Activity Book H&R: Homework and Remembering
AC: Activity Cards MCC: Math Center Challenge AG: Assessment Guide ✓: Grade 5 kits TRB: Teacher's Resource Book

NCTM Standards and Expectations Key: **1.** Number and Operations **2.** Algebra **3.** Geometry
4. Measurement **5.** Data Analysis and Probability **6.** Problem Solving **7.** Reasoning and Proof
8. Communication **9.** Connections **10.** Representation

Lesson NCTM Focal Points NCTM Standards	Resources	Materials for Lesson Activities	Materials for Going Further
3-9 **Subtract Whole and Decimal Numbers** NCTM Focal Points: 2.4, 2.8 NCTM Standards: 1, 4, 8	TE pp. 249–258 SAB pp. 105–106 H&R pp. 63–64 AC 3-9	Calculators (optional) ✓ Base ten blocks (optional)	✓ Play money Calculators ✓ MathBoard materials Math Journals
3-10 **Place Value Word Problems** NCTM Focal Points: 2.6, 2.8, 7.1 NCTM Standards: 1, 6, 8	TE pp. 259–264 SAB pp. 107–110 H&R pp. 65–66 AC 3-10	None	Index cards Math Journals
3-11 **Properties and Strategies** NCTM Focal Point: 2.4 NCTM Standards: 1, 2, 6, 8	TE pp. 265–270 SAB pp. 111–112 H&R pp. 67–68 AC 3-11 AG Quick Quiz 3	None	Index cards Grid Paper (TRB M17) Math Journals
3-12 **Pictographs With Large Numbers** NCTM Focal Point: 7.1 NCTM Standards: 1, 5, 8, 10	TE pp. 271–278 SAB pp. 113–114 H&R pp. 69–70 AC 3-12 MCC 15	None	✓ Counters Math Journals
3-13 **Round Numbers on Graphs** NCTM Focal Point: 7.1 NCTM Standards: 1, 8	TE pp. 279–286 SAB pp. 115–118 H&R pp. 71–72 AC 3-13	✓ Secret Code Cards (optional)	Math Journals
3-14 **Bar Graphs and Rounding** NCTM Focal Point: 6.1 NCTM Standards: 1, 2, 5, 8	TE pp. 287–292 SAB pp. 119–120 H&R pp. 73–74 AC 3-14 MCC 16	None	Connecting cubes Grid Paper (TRB M17) Math Journals
3-15 **Round and Estimate With Decimals** NCTM Focal Point: 2.6 NCTM Standards: 1, 6, 7, 9	TE pp. 293–300 SAB pp. 121–122 H&R pp. 75–76 AC 3-15	None	Calculator (optional) Math Journals
3-16 **Discrete and Continuous Data** NCTM Focal Point: 6.2 NCTM Standards: 5, 8, 9, 10	TE pp. 301–310 SAB pp. 123–128 H&R pp. 77–78 AC 3-16	Ruler	Grid Paper (TRB M17) Math Journals
3-17 **Graphs With Decimal Numbers** NCTM Focal Point: 6.2 NCTM Standards: 1, 2, 5, 6	TE pp. 311–316 SAB pp. 129–132 H&R pp. 79–80 AC 3-17 AG Quick Quiz 4	None	Grid Paper (TRB M17) Meter stick Math Journals

Lesson NCTM Focal Points NCTM Standards	Resources	Materials for Lesson Activities	Materials for Going Further
3-18 **Classify Word Problems** NCTM Focal Point: 4.1 NCTM Standards: 1, 2, 6, 8, 10	TE pp. 317–324 SAB pp. 133–136 H&R pp. 81–82 AC 3-18	None	✓ Counters Math Journals
3-19 **Situation and Solution Equations** NCTM Focal Point: 4.1 NCTM Standards: 1, 2, 6, 8	TE pp. 325–332 SAB pp. 137–140 H&R pp. 83–84 AC 3-19	None	✓ MathBoard materials Index cards Centimeter ruler Centimeter-Grid Paper (TRB M18) Math Journals
3-20 **Comparison Problems** NCTM Focal Point: 4.1 NCTM Standards: 1, 6, 8, 10	TE pp. 333–340 SAB pp. 141–142 H&R pp. 85–86 AC 3-20	Newspaper advertisements (optional)	✓ Counters Bag or sack Math Journals
3-21 **Two-Step Word Problems** NCTM Focal Point: 2.8 NCTM Standards: 1, 5, 6, 8, 10	TE pp. 341–350 SAB pp. 143–146 H&R pp. 87–88 AC 3-21 AG Quick Quiz 5	None	Ruler ✓ Play money Math Journals
3-22 **Use Mathematical Processes** NCTM Standards: 6, 7, 8, 9, 10	TE pp. 351–356 SAB pp. 147–148 H&R pp. 89–90 AC 3-22	None	Centimeter-Grid Paper (TRB M18) ✓ Play money Math Journals
Unit Review and Test	TE pp. 357–360 SAB pp. 149–150 AG Unit 3 Tests		

Resources/Materials Key: TE: Teacher Edition   SAB: Student Activity Book   H&R: Homework and Remembering
AC: Activity Cards   MCC: Math Center Challenge   AG: Assessment Guide   ✓: Grade 5 kits   TRB: Teacher's Resource Book

Hardcover Student Book

- Together, the Hardcover Student Book and its companion Activity Workbook contain all of the pages in the consumable Student Activity Book.

Manipulatives and Materials

- Essential materials for teaching *Math Expressions* are available in the Grade 5 kits. These materials are indicated by a ✓ in these lists. At the front of this Teacher Edition is more information about kit contents, alternatives for the materials, and use of the materials.

Unit 3   Assessment

✅ Unit Objectives Tested	Unit Test Items	Lessons
3.1 Read, write and identify the place value of decimals and whole numbers.	1–4	1–3, 5–6
3.2 Compare, order, and round numbers; estimate sums and differences.	5–8, 9–12	2, 5, 13–15
3.3 Add and subtract whole numbers and decimals.	9–12	4, 7–9, 11
3.4 Interpret and make pictographs, bar graphs, and line graphs.	13–18	12, 14, 16–17
3.5 Solve a variety of problems involving addition and subtraction of whole numbers and decimals.	19–20	10, 18–21

Assessment and Review Resources

Formal Assessment

Student Activity Book
- Unit Review and Test (pp. 149–150)

Assessment Guide
- Quick Quiz 1 (p. A26)
- Quick Quiz 2 (p. A27)
- Quick Quiz 3 (p. A28)
- Quick Quiz 4 (p. A29)
- Quick Quiz 5 (p. A30)
- Test A—Open Response (pp. A31–A32)
- Test B—Multiple Choice (pp. A33–A36)
- Performance Assessment (pp. A37–A39)

Test Generator CD-ROM
- Open Response Test
- Multiple Choice Test
- Test Bank Items

Informal Assessment

Teacher Edition
- Ongoing Assessment (in every lesson)
- Quick Practice (in every lesson)
- Math Talk (in every lesson)
- Portfolio Suggestions (p. 359)

🔢 Math Talk
- ▸ The Learning Classroom (pp. 195, 196, 261, 272, 282, 294, 303, 312, 322, 342)
- ▸ Math Talk in Action (pp. 190, 211, 234, 254, 336, 345, 347)
- ▸ In Activities (pp. 195, 204, 219, 221, 233, 239, 246, 268, 276, 283, 289, 294, 322, 327, 352)
- ▸ Solve and Discuss (pp. 181, 196, 212, 230, 240, 250, 252, 256, 262, 267, 303, 314, 345, 347)
- ▸ Student Pairs (pp. 189, 203, 204, 214, 222, 224, 256, 261, 298, 305, 306, 346, 348)
  Helping Partners (pp. 194, 196, 225, 308, 346)
- ▸ Small Groups (pp. 189, 194, 203, 246, 256, 296, 304, 306, 343, 348)

Review Opportunities

Homework and Remembering
- Review of recently taught topics
- Spiral Review

Teacher Edition
- Unit Review and Test (pp. 357–360)

Test Generator CD-ROM
- Custom review sheets

Independent Learning Activities

Ready-Made Math Challenge Centers

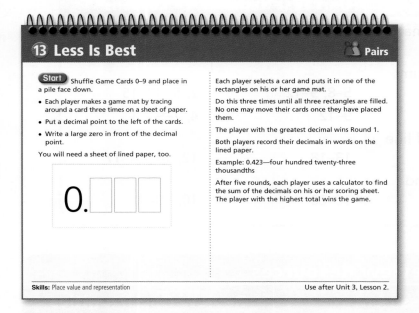

13 Less Is Best — Pairs

Start Shuffle Game Cards 0–9 and place in a pile face down.

- Each player makes a game mat by tracing around a card three times on a sheet of paper.
- Put a decimal point to the left of the cards.
- Write a large zero in front of the decimal point.

You will need a sheet of lined paper, too.

Each player selects a card and puts it in one of the rectangles on his or her game mat.

Do this three times until all three rectangles are filled. No one may move their cards once they have placed them.

The player with the greatest decimal wins Round 1.

Both players record their decimals in words on the lined paper.

Example: 0.423—four hundred twenty-three thousandths

After five rounds, each player uses a calculator to find the sum of the decimals on his or her scoring sheet. The player with the highest total wins the game.

Skills: Place value and representation
Use after Unit 3, Lesson 2.

Grouping Pairs
Materials Calculator, Game Cards (TRB M2)
Objective Students compare decimal numbers and write values in words.
Connections Computation and Representation

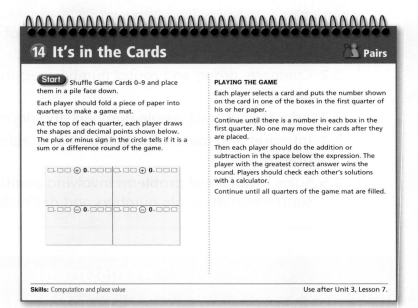

14 It's in the Cards — Pairs

Start Shuffle Game Cards 0–9 and place them in a pile face down.

Each player should fold a piece of paper into quarters to make a game mat.

At the top of each quarter, each player draws the shapes and decimal points shown below. The plus or minus sign in the circle tells if it is a sum or a difference round of the game.

PLAYING THE GAME

Each player selects a card and puts the number shown on the card in one of the boxes in the first quarter of his or her paper.

Continue until there is a number in each box in the first quarter. No one may move their cards after they are placed.

Then each player should do the addition or subtraction in the space below the expression. The player with the greatest correct answer wins the round. Players should check each other's solutions with a calculator.

Continue until all quarters of the game mat are filled.

Skills: Computation and place value
Use after Unit 3, Lesson 7.

Grouping Pairs
Materials Calculator (optional), Game Cards (TRB M2)
Objective Students add and subtract decimal numbers.
Connections Computation and Reasoning

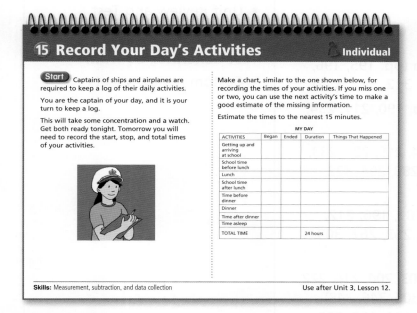

15 Record Your Day's Activities — Individual

Start Captains of ships and airplanes are required to keep a log of their daily activities.

You are the captain of your day, and it is your turn to keep a log.

This will take some concentration and a watch. Get both ready tonight. Tomorrow you will need to record the start, stop, and total times of your activities.

Make a chart, similar to the one shown below, for recording the times of your activities. If you miss one or two, you can use the next activity's time to make a good estimate of the missing information.

Estimate the times to the nearest 15 minutes.

MY DAY

ACTIVITIES	Began	Ended	Duration	Things That Happened
Getting up and arriving at school				
School time before lunch				
Lunch				
School time after lunch				
Time before dinner				
Dinner				
Time after dinner				
Time asleep				
TOTAL TIME			24 hours	

Skills: Measurement, subtraction, and data collection
Use after Unit 3, Lesson 12.

Grouping Individual
Materials Watch
Objective Students record time and calculate duration.
Connections Measurement and Representation

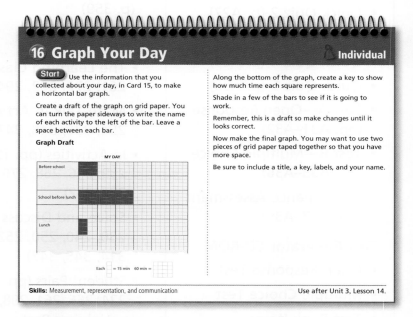

16 Graph Your Day — Individual

Start Use the information that you collected about your day, in Card 15, to make a horizontal bar graph.

Create a draft of the graph on grid paper. You can turn the paper sideways to write the name of each activity to the left of the bar. Leave a space between each bar.

Graph Draft

Along the bottom of the graph, create a key to show how much time each square represents.

Shade in a few of the bars to see if it is going to work.

Remember, this is a draft so make changes until it looks correct.

Now make the final graph. You may want to use two pieces of grid paper taped together so that you have more space.

Be sure to include a title, a key, labels, and your name.

Skills: Measurement, representation, and communication
Use after Unit 3, Lesson 14.

Grouping Individual
Materials Colored pencils or markers, Grid Paper (TRB M17)
Objective Students graph data from their daily log.
Connections Statistics and Communication

Ready-Made Math Resources

Technology — Tutorials, Practice, and Intervention

Use online, individualized intervention and support to bring students to proficiency.

Help students practice skills and apply concepts through exciting math adventures.

Extend and enrich students' understanding of skills and concepts through engaging interactive lessons and activities.

Visit **Education Place**
www.eduplace.com

Visit www.eduplace.com/mx2t/ and find family, teacher, and student materials, activities, games, and more.

Literature Link

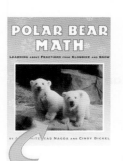

Polar Bear Math: Learning About Fractions from Klondike and Snow

Polar Bear Math: Learning About Fractions from Klondike and Snow

Authors Ann Whitehead Nagda and Cindy Bickel present a story about two orphaned polar bear cubs in the Denver zoo in this book that provides information about the bear pair and adding fractions. The layout in this book is unique, with the zoo story presented on the right side of each spread, and a lesson on fractions on the left side. The book includes great photographs.

Differentiated Instruction

Individualizing Instruction

Activities	Level	Frequency
Activities	• Intervention • On Level • Challenge	All 3 in every lesson
Math Writing Prompts	**Level**	**Frequency**
Math Writing Prompts	• Intervention • On Level • Challenge	All 3 in every lesson
Math Center Challenges	For advanced students	
Math Center Challenges	4 in every unit	

Reaching All Learners

	Lessons	Pages
English Language Learners	1, 2, 3, 4, 5, 6, 7, 8, 9, 10, 11, 12, 13, 14, 15, 16, 17, 18, 19, 20, 21, 22	180, 192, 204, 211, 219, 231, 238, 245, 251, 260, 266, 273, 280, 288, 297, 305, 314, 319, 328, 335, 343, 352
	Lessons	**Pages**
Extra Help	2, 3, 4, 6, 7, 9, 13, 17, 19, 21	190, 206, 213, 234, 239, 253, 254, 280, 313, 328, 345, 346
	Lessons	**Pages**
Special Needs	1, 2, 6, 8, 13	181, 192, 231, 246, 281
	Lessons	**Pages**
Advanced Learners	3, 4, 5, 6, 15, 20, 21	203, 206, 214, 218, 226, 234, 296, 298, 335, 346

Strategies for English Language Learners

Objective Identify and read *fraction* and *decimal notation*.

Problem Write 1, $\frac{8}{10}$, 0.8, 1 $\frac{8}{10}$, 1.8, *whole number, fraction, decimal,* and *mixed number* on the board.

Newcomer

- Point to each number, read it aloud and identify it. Have students repeat.

Beginning

- Ask: **Is 1 a *whole number*?** yes **Is $\frac{8}{10}$ a *decimal* or a *fraction*?** fraction **Is 0.8 a *decimal*?** yes

- Say: **1 $\frac{8}{10}$ and 1.8 are *mixed numbers*.** Have students repeat.

Intermediate

- Ask: **Which is a *whole number*?** 1 **A *fraction*?** $\frac{8}{10}$ **A *decimal*?** 0.8

- Say: **1 $\frac{8}{10}$ is a *whole number* and a _____.** fraction **It's a *mixed number*.**

- Ask: **Is 1.8 a *mixed number*?** yes

Advanced

- Students identify the *whole number, fraction, and decimal.*

- Say: **When we mix *whole numbers* and *fractions* or *decimals*, we get *mixed numbers*.** Ask: **Which numbers are *mixed numbers*?** 1 $\frac{8}{10}$, 1.8

Connections

Art Connection
Lesson 12, page 278

Language Arts Connections
Lesson 4, page 216
Lesson 18, page 324

Multicultural Connection
Lesson 14, page 292

Music Connection
Lesson 11, page 270

Real-World Connections
Lesson 1, page 186
Lesson 13, page 286
Lesson 21, page 350

Science Connections
Lesson 6, page 236
Lesson 9, page 258
Lesson 10, page 264
Lesson 17, page 316

Social Studies Connections
Lesson 5, page 228
Lesson 7, page 242
Lesson 8, page 248
Lesson 15, page 300
Lesson 19, page 332
Lesson 20, page 340

Sports Connection
Lesson 22, page 356

Technology Connections
Lesson 2, page 198
Lesson 16, page 310

Math Background

Putting Research into Practice for Unit 3

From Our Curriculum Research Project: Understanding Problem Situations

High-level goals are achieved by enabling all students to enter the mathematical activity at their own level. Teachers accomplish this by using rich and varied language about a given problem so that all students come to understand the problem situation, by mathematizing (focusing on the mathematical features of) a situation to which all students can relate (and that may be generated by a student), and by having students draw models of the problem situation. Cumulative experiencing and practicing of important knowledge skills helps students move through developmental trajectories to more advanced methods. Peer helping provides targeted assistance when necessary. The knowledge of the helper also increases. Assessment provides feedback to all and permits realistic adjustments of proximal learning goals by students and by the teacher.

—Karen Fuson, Author
  Math Expressions

From Current Research: Accessible Methods for Multi-Digit Addition

Method B [New Groups Below] is taught in China and has been invented by students in the United States. In this method the new 1 or regrouped 10 (or new hundred) is recorded on the line separating the problem from the answer . . . [it] requires that children understand what to do when they get 10 or more in a given column. . . . Method C [Show Subtotals], reflecting more closely many students' invented procedures, reduces the problem [of carrying] by writing the total for each kind of unit on a new line. The carrying-regrouping-trading is done as part of the adding of each kind of unit. Also, Method C can be done in either direction.

Method A: New Groups Above

```
The new →1 1← The new
hundred   186   ten
         +749
          935
```

Method B: New Groups Below

```
            186
           +749
The new →  1 1  ← The new
hundred     935   ten
```

Method C: Show Subtotals

```
              186
             +749
              800
The new  → 120
hundred
The new  →  15
ten        ___
            935
```

National Research Council. "Developing Proficiency with Whole Numbers." *Adding It Up: Helping Children Learn Mathematics*. Washington, D.C.: National Academy Press, 2001. 203.

Other Useful References: Addition and Subtraction

Number and Operations Standard for Grades 3–5. *Principles and Standards for School Mathematics*. Reston, VA: National Council of Teachers of Mathematics, 2000. 148–155.

Van de Walle, John A., *Elementary and Middle School Mathematics: Teaching Developmentally*. 3rd ed. New York: Longman, 1998. 213–221.

Carpenter, Thomas P., Fennena, E., Franks, M.L., Empson, S.B., & Levi, L.W. *Children's Mathematics: Cognitively Guided Instruction*. Portsmouth, NH: Heinemann, 1999

Getting Ready to Teach Unit 3

Place Value Concepts

This unit broadens and deepens students' experiences with very large and very small numbers which are explored from billions to billionths. Students write these numbers in word form, standard form, and expanded form. They are provided with a variety of models to visualize decimals.

Visualizing Tenths, Hundredths, and Thousandths
Lessons 1 and 2

MathBoards A special feature on the MathBoard allows students to visualize tenths and hundredths and to establish equivalent decimals.

This can be extended to thousandths.

This long 100-bar feature of the MathBoard is also available on TRB M113.

0	0.1	0.2	0.3	0.4	0.5	0.6	0.7	0.8	0.9	1.0
0	0.10	0.20	0.30	0.40	0.50	0.60	0.70	0.80	0.90	1.00
0	0.100	0.200	0.300	0.400	0.500	0.600	0.700	0.800	0.900	1.000

Money The tenths place is made by dividing 1 whole (such as a dollar) into 10 equal parts. The hundredths place is made by dividing each tenth into 10 equal parts. The thousandths place is represented by a tenth of a penny.

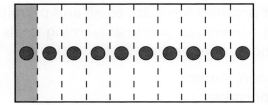

$\frac{1}{10}$ 1 of 10 equal parts

$ 0.10   one dime or one tenth

0.1   1 in the tenths place

Area Models Tenths and hundredths are represented by 10 × 10 grids. One thousandth is represented as one square divided into 10 parts.

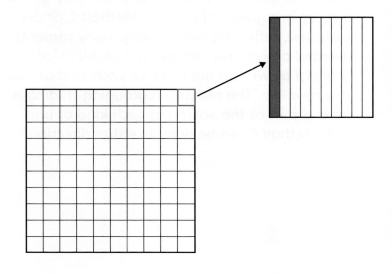

As you teach this lessons emphasize understanding of these terms.

- break-apart drawing
- change-plus problem
- change-minus problem
- collection situations
- leading language
- misleading language
- ungroup

See the Teacher Glossary on pp. T6–T17.

Number Lines A number line is a model of distance (from zero). It is closest to the model of a ruler.

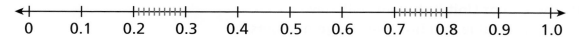

Secret Code Cards
Lessons 3 and 4

Students explore place value by assembling Secret Code Cards for both multi-digit whole numbers and decimals through thousandths.

These cards emphasize place value and help students visualize the expanded form of the numbers.

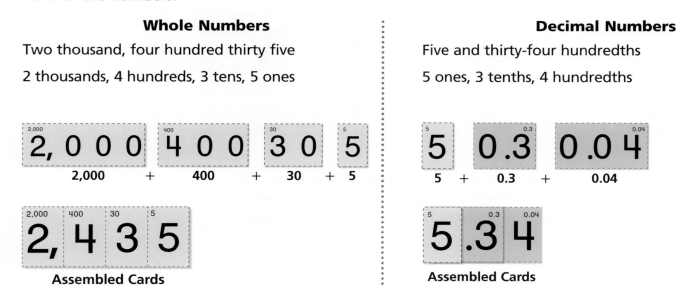

Large Numbers Students place their secret code cards on a large numbers frame. This gives them the ability to visualize and read very large numbers without writing them.

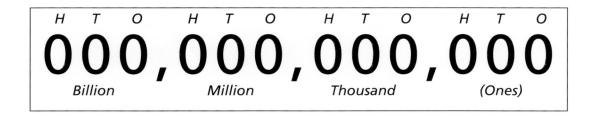

Place Value Extended from Billions to Billionths
Lesson 3

Thousands to Thousandths By the end of Unit 3 students will have a comprehensive understanding of place value and how very large numbers and decimal numbers relate to each other. The Place Value Parade helps everyone see the ten-for-one trades between places and the symmetry around the ones place. The Place Value Parade is also provided as a poster in the Materials Kit.

× 10 (Larger) →   **Place Value Parade**   ÷ 10 (Smaller) →

Thousands	Hundreds	Tens	ONES	Tenths	Hundredths	Thousandths
1,000.	100.	10.	1.	0.1	0.01	0.001
$\dfrac{1,000}{1}$	$\dfrac{100}{1}$	$\dfrac{10}{1}$	$\dfrac{1}{1}$	$\dfrac{1}{10}$	$\dfrac{1}{100}$	$\dfrac{1}{1,000}$
$1,000.00	$100.00	$10.00	$1	$0.10	$0.01	$0.001

Billions to Billionths Students create a place value chart that show from billions to billionths. They can see that regardless of the number of places, there is always symmetry around the ones place. They can also see the base ten relationships between places.

Patterns From Billions to Billionths

billions	hundred millions	ten millions	millions	hundred thousands	ten thousands	thousands	hundred	tens	ONES	tenths	hundredths	thousandths	ten thousandths	hundred thousandths	millionths	ten millionths	hundred millionths	billionths
1,000,000,000	100,000,000	10,000,000	1,000,000	100,000	10,000	1,000	100	10	1	0.1	0.01	0.001	0.0001	0.00001	0.000001	0.0000001	0.00000001	0.000000001
										$\frac{1}{10}$	$\frac{1}{100}$	$\frac{1}{1,000}$	$\frac{1}{10,000}$	$\frac{1}{100,000}$	$\frac{1}{1,000,000}$	$\frac{1}{10,000,000}$	$\frac{1}{100,000,000}$	$\frac{1}{1,000,000,000}$

Whole and Decimal Computation

Using place value concepts, students examine the major aspects of adding and subtracting large numbers and decimals numbers.

- We must add and subtract like places (line up the places).

- We may need to regroup in addition (10 or more in the place).

- We may need to ungroup in subtraction (get enough to subtract).

Add and Subtract Whole Numbers
Lessons 7, 8, and 9

Students analyze three addition methods shown below. They analyze two subtraction methods: Ungroup Place-by-Place and Ungroup All at Once (See pages 250–252).

New Groups Below

Step 1
```
  769
+ 584
 ₁
    3
```

Step 2
```
  769
+ 584
 ₁₁
   53
```

Step 3
```
  769
+ 584
 ₁₁₁
1,353
```

New Groups Above

Step 1
```
 ₁
 769
+ 584
   3
```

Step 2
```
 ₁₁
 769
+ 584
  53
```

Step 3
```
 ₁₁₁
 769
+ 584
1,353
```

Subtotal Method: The hundreds, tens, and ones are added separately.

Left to Right:
```
  769
+ 584
 1200
  140
   13
1,353
```

Right to Left:
```
  769
+ 584
   13
  140
 1200
1,353
```

Add and Subtract Decimals
Lessons 4, 7, 9, and 15

The MathBoard allows students to see why unlike places cannot be added.

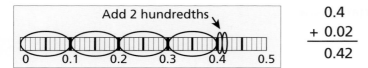

Add 2 hundredths

```
  0.4
+ 0.02
 0.42
```

Data and Graphs

In the practical world, pictographs, bar graphs, and lines graphs are often used to show both whole numbers and decimals. Students analyze different types of data and match them to appropriate graphs.

Types of Graphs
Lessons 12–14, 16, and 17

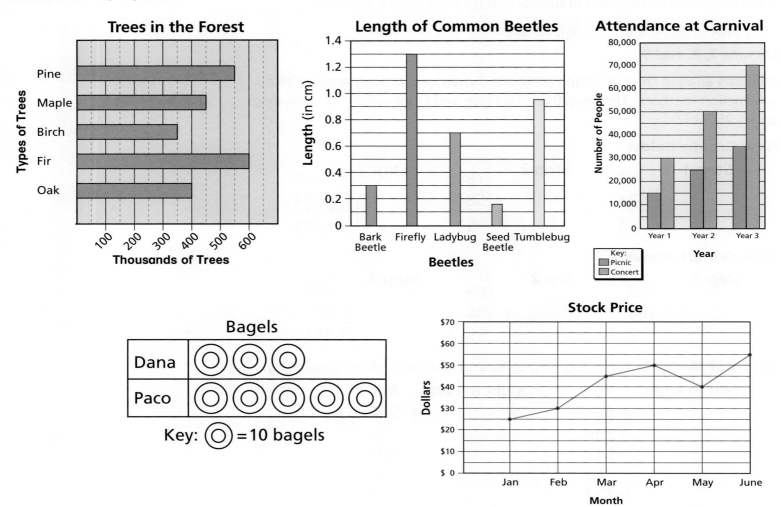

Types of Data
Lessons 16 and 22

Numerical and Categorical Data Students discuss the difference between categorical and numerical data. They collect data and decide if the data are categorical or numerical. They match graphs with appropriate data.

Discrete and Continuous Data Students discuss the difference between discrete and continuous data. They collect data and decide if the data are categorical or numerical. They match graphs with appropriate data.

Problem Solving

Students using *Math Expressions* are taught a variety of ways to represent word problems. Students move from using math drawings to solving problems symbolically with equations.

Representing Word Problems
Lessons 18 and 19

When students read and represent problems, they often translate the words in the order they appear in a problem. This literal translation may result in an equation that represents the problem but is not in a form that students can use to find the solution. This unit emphasizes using a break-apart model to represent addition and subtraction problems. Students use the model to write a situation equation and a solution equation to solve word problems.

Break-Apart Model

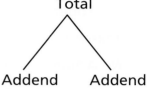

Change Problems
Lessons 18 and 19

Some addition and subtraction situations involve change (increasing or decreasing), where the starting number, the change, or the result will be unknown. Most students can solve problems in their heads when they involve basic addition and subtraction. When word problems involve larger numbers, it is important for students to understand how to set up situation and solution equations to represent them.

Change Plus (Increase)	Change Minus (Decrease)
Unknown Total (sum) Six children were playing tag in the yard. Three more children came to play. How many children are playing in the yard now? *Solution Equation*: $6 + 3 = n$	**Unknown Result (difference)** Jake has 10 trading cards. He gave 3 to his brother. How many trading cards does he have left? *Solution Equation*: $10 - 3 = n$
Unknown Start Some children were playing tag in the yard. Three more children came to play. Now there are 9 children in the yard. How many children were in the yard originally? *Situation Equation*: $n + 3 = 9$ *Solution Equation*: $9 - 3 = n$	**Unknown Start** Jake has some trading cards. He gave 3 to his brother. Now Jake has 7 trading cards left. How many cards did he start with? *Situation Equation*: $n - 3 = 7$ or $7 + n = 10$ *Solution Equation*: $7 + 3 = n$
Unknown Change Six children were playing tag in the yard. Some more children came to play. Now there are 9 children in the yard. How many children came to play? *Situation Equation*: $6 + n = 9$ *Solution Equation*: $9 - 6 = n$	**Unknown Change** Jake has 10 trading cards. He gave some to his brother. Now Jake has 7 trading cards left. How many cards did he give to his brother? *Situation Equation*: $10 - n = 7$ or $7 + n = 10$ *Solution Equation*: $10 - 7 = n$

Collection Problems
Lessons 18 and 19

Collection problems involve putting together (joining) or taking apart (separating) groups physically or conceptually. All of the objects in the groups are there from the beginning, and in many problems, there is no action at all.

Put Together: Two addends are put together to make the total.

Take Apart: The total is taken apart to make the two addends.

No Action: The problem describes the total and the addends.

Break-Apart Model

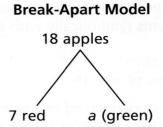

Put Together (Join)	Take Apart (Separate)	No Action
Unknown Total (sum)	**Unknown Total** (sum)	**Unknown Total** (sum)
Ana put 9 dimes and 4 nickels in her pocket. How many coins did she put in her pocket?	Jenna put 14 flowers in a red vase and 12 flowers in a blue vase. How many flowers did she start with?	There are 11 red and 7 green apples in a bowl. How many apples are in the bowl?
Solution Equation: $9 + 4 = c$	*Solution Equation*: $14 + 12 = f$	*Solution Equation*: $11 + 7 = a$
Unknown Addend (partner)	**Unknown Addend** (partner)	**Unknown Addend** (partner)
Ana put 13 coins in her pocket. Nine coins are dimes and the rest are nickels. How many are nickels?	Jenna has 26 flowers. She put 14 flowers in a red vase and the rest of the flowers in a blue vase. How many flowers are in the blue vase?	There are 18 red and green apples in a bowl. Seven apples are red. The rest of the apples are green. How many apples are green?
Situation Equation: $13 = 9 + c$	*Situation Equation*: $26 = 14 + f$	*Situation Equation*: $18 = 7 + a$
Solution Equation: $13 - 9 = c$	*Solution Equation*: $26 - 14 = f$	*Solution Equation*: $18 - 7 = a$
Unknown Addend (partner)	**Unknown Addend** (partner)	**Unknown Addend** (partner)
Ana put 13 coins in her pocket. Some coins are dimes and 4 coins are nickels. How many coins are dimes?	Jenna has 26 flowers. She put some flowers in a red vase and 12 flowers in a blue vase. How many flowers are in the red vase?	There are 18 red and green apples in a bowl. Some apples are red and 11 apples are green. How many apples are red?
Situation Equation: $13 = c + 4$	*Situation Equation*: $26 = f + 12$	*Situation Equation*: $18 = a + 11$
Solution Equation: $13 - 4 = c$	*Solution Equation*: $26 - 12 = f$	*Solution Equation*: $18 - 11 = a$

Comparison Problems
Lessons 18 and 20

Two amounts can be compared by multiplication and division as we did in Unit 1, or they can be compared by addition and subtraction, as we will do in this unit. When working with comparison problems, focus the instruction on helping students understand the language.

Questions Students always need to decide which amount is larger and which is smaller. For additive comparisons, the comparing question can be asked in two ways, with either amount as the subject of the sentence.

• Who has more? (or Who has fewer?)

• How many more? (or How many fewer?)

Models In both kinds of situations, comparison bars can help with the solution. With addition comparison bars, the difference is shown by an oval so that the two compared amounts in the rectangle can be clearly seen. The unknown may be the smaller quantity, the larger quantity, or the difference between the quantities.

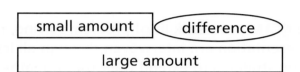

Language Emphasize that students must read word problems carefully—more than once, if necessary. Sometimes a word or phrase in a problem may suggest subtraction, but one must add to find the answer. Other times a word or phrase may suggest addition, but subtraction is used to find the answer. Students must understand the situation, not just look at the numbers and a key word.

Leading Language	Misleading Language
Fewer suggests subtraction; use subtraction	*Fewer suggests subtraction; use addition*
Problem The nursery has 83 rose bushes and 66 lilac bushes. How many fewer lilac bushes than rose bushes are in the garden?	**Problem** There are 10 dogs at the kennel. There are 6 fewer dogs than cats. How many cats are at the kennel?
Question Are there more rose bushes or lilac bushes?	**Question** Are there more dogs or cats?
Model There are more rose bushes, so the number of rose bushes is the larger number.	**Model** There are more cats, so the number of cats is the larger number.
Rose: \[83 rose bushes \] Lilac: \[66 lilac bushes \](d)	Cats: \[c (cats) \] Dogs: \[10 dogs \](6)
Solution Equation $83 - 66 = d$	**Solution Equation** $10 + 6 = c$
There are 17 fewer lilac bushes in the nursery.	There are 16 cats at the kennel.

Two-Step Problems
Lesson 21

The equations that students write for multistep problems may include more than one operation. Sometimes the order in which these operations are completed is not important. In other problems, students must find the answer to a *hidden question* and use that answer to answer the question of the problem. We use the term *hidden questions* just to make the conceptual point that students may need to answer these questions even if they do not appear in the problem.

Students also discuss problems

• problems with not enough or too much information

• problems with no solution or multiple solutions

Use Mathematical Processes
Lesson 22

The NCTM process skills of problem solving, reasoning and proof, communication, connections, and representation are interwoven through all lessons throughout the year. The last lesson of this unit allows students to extend their use of mathematical processes to other situations.

NCTM Process Skill	Activity and Goal
Representation	1: Represent data in a table. 2: Represent data in a graph.
Communication	2: Discuss the data in a graph. 5: Share reasoning.
Connections	1: Math and Social Studies: Number Sense and Data 2: Draw conclusions; make predictions.
Reasoning and Proof	3: Make a generalization. 3: Use reasoning to make a true equation.
Problem Solving	1: Design an investigation. 4: Use the process of elimination to solve a problem.

Basic Multiplication and Division Fluency

Students should continually work toward fluency for basic multiplication and division facts. Use checkups to assist students in monitoring their own learning. In the Teacher's Resource Book (TRB) you will find several pages for diagnosing and practicing basic multiplication and division.

TRB M58 Diagnostic Quiz for Basic Multiplication
TRB M59 Diagnostic Quiz for Basic Division

TRB M60 Basic Multiplication Practice
TRB M61 Basic Division Practice

TRB M62 Multiplication for 3s, 4s, 6s, 7s, 8s, 9s
TRB M63 Division for 3s, 4s, 6s, 7s, 8s, 9s

TRB M64 Multiplication for 6s, 7s, 8s
TRB M65 Division for 6s, 7s, 8s

TRB M66 Scrambled Multiplication Tables
TRB M67 Blank Multiplication Tables

TRB M68 Multiplication for 10s, 11s, 12s
TRB M69 Division for 10s, 11s, 12s

TRB M83 Factor Puzzles for 3s, 4s, 6s, 7s, 8s, 9s
TRB M84 Factor Puzzles for 6s, 7s, 8s
TRB M85 Blank Factor Puzzles

See the Basic Facts Fluency Plan for information about practice materials.

Decimals as Equal Divisions

REAL WORLD Problem Solving

Lesson Objectives

- Understand decimals as equal divisions of a whole.
- Relate fractions and decimals.

The Day at a Glance

Today's Goals	Materials	
1 Teaching the Lesson **A1:** Explore models for relating fractions and decimals. **A2:** Read and write decimals and fractions. **2 Going Further** ▶ Differentiated Instruction **3 Homework and Spiral Review**	**Lesson Activities** Student Activity Book pp. 83–84 or Student Hardcover Book pp. 83–84 Homework and Remembering pp. 47–48 Pointer Play money (optional) Patterns from Billions to Billionths (TRB M22)	**Going Further** Activity Cards 3-1 MathBoard materials Centimeter-Grid Paper (TRB M18) Markers Math Journals 123 Use Math Talk today!

Keeping Skills Sharp

Quick Practice	Daily Routines
This section provides repetitive, short activities that either help students become faster or more accurate at a skill or help to prepare ground for new concepts. Quick Practice for this unit will start with Lesson 2.	**Strategy Problem** Each photograph in a series has different dimensions that follow a pattern. The 1st photo has a length that is half its width and an area of 8 in.^{2} The 2nd is a square with an area of 16 in.^{2} The 3rd has a width that is 2 inches less than the length and an area of 24 in.^{2} What are the dimensions and area of the fifth frame? Explain your answer. 40 in.^{2}, l = 10 in., w = 4 in.; 1st photo $A = 2 \times 4 = 8$ in.^{2}; 2nd photo $A = 4 \times 4 = 16$ in.^{2}; 3rd photo $A = 6 \times 4 = 24$ in.^{2}; In each photo, w = 4 in., length equals the figure number times 2, and the area equals the photo number times 8. So, 5th photo $A = 5 \times 8 = 40$ in.^{2}, w = 4 in., $l = 5 \times 2 = 10$ in.

Teaching the Lesson

Relate Fractions and Decimals

 15 MINUTES

Goal: Explore models for relating fractions and decimals.

Materials: Student Activity Book or Hardcover Book pp. 83–84, pointer, Patterns from Billions to Billionths (TRB M22)

✔ **NCTM Standards:**
Number and Operations
Representation
Connections

English Language Learners

Write 0.5 and $\frac{1}{2}$ on the board.

- **Beginning** Point and say: $0.5 = \frac{1}{2}$. Ask: **Is 0.5 decimal or fraction notation?** decimal
- **Intermediate** Ask: **Does $0.5 = \frac{1}{2}$?** yes **Which is decimal notation?** 0.5 Say: $\frac{1}{2}$ is _____. fraction notation
- **Advanced** Have students tell the relationship between the numbers and identify the notation.

▶ Meanings and Notations | WHOLE CLASS |

Ask For Ideas Give students an opportunity to share what they know about fraction and decimal relationships, and about how fraction and decimal notation is alike and is different. To initiate the discussion, write the word name *one-tenth* on the board and ask them to explain what it means and describe how it is written. One-tenth means one of ten equal parts and is written as 0.1 and as $\frac{1}{10}$.

Zero Before the Decimal Point Explain that it is customary to write a zero before the decimal point whenever we write a decimal number that is less than 1.

Writing a zero helps alert us to the presence of the decimal point, and without the zero, it is more likely that the decimal point will be overlooked.

Writing a zero is also helpful conceptually because it reminds us that the number is less than 1 but greater than 0.

Some students may also find that the zero helps make decimal numbers look more like their equivalent fractions. For example, 0.1 and $\frac{1}{10}$, 0.01 and $\frac{1}{100}$, and 0.001 and $\frac{1}{1,000}$.

3–1 **Class Activity** Name Date

▶ Discuss Fractions and Decimals

Fractions and decimals are special kinds of numbers. They tell the number of equal parts a whole is divided into, and the number of those parts that are being taken or described.

Fraction notation shows a whole divided into any number of equal parts.

1. 1 Whole
4 equal parts
$\frac{1}{4} + \frac{1}{4} + \frac{1}{4} + \frac{1}{4}$
1 part $\frac{1}{4}$
1 of 4 equal parts

2. 1 Whole
5 equal parts
$\frac{1}{5} + \frac{1}{5} + \frac{1}{5} + \frac{1}{5} + \frac{1}{5}$
3 parts $\frac{3}{5}$
3 of 5 equal parts

Decimal notation shows places to the right of the ones place. The tenths place shows 1 whole (such as a dollar) divided into 10 equal parts. The hundredths place shows each tenth divided into 10 equal parts.

3. $\frac{1}{10}$ 1 of 10 equal parts
$ 0.10 one dime or one tenth of a dollar
0.1 1 in the tenths place

4. $\frac{1}{100}$ 1 of 100 equal parts
$0.01 one penny or one-hundredth of a dollar
0.01 1 in the hundredths place

The thousandths place shows each hundredth divided into 10 equal parts.

5. $\frac{1}{10}$ of a penny
$\frac{1}{1,000}$ 1 of 1,000 equal parts
$0.001 one-tenth of penny or one-thousandth of a dollar
0.001 1 in the thousandths place

UNIT 3 LESSON 1 Decimals as Equal Divisions **83**

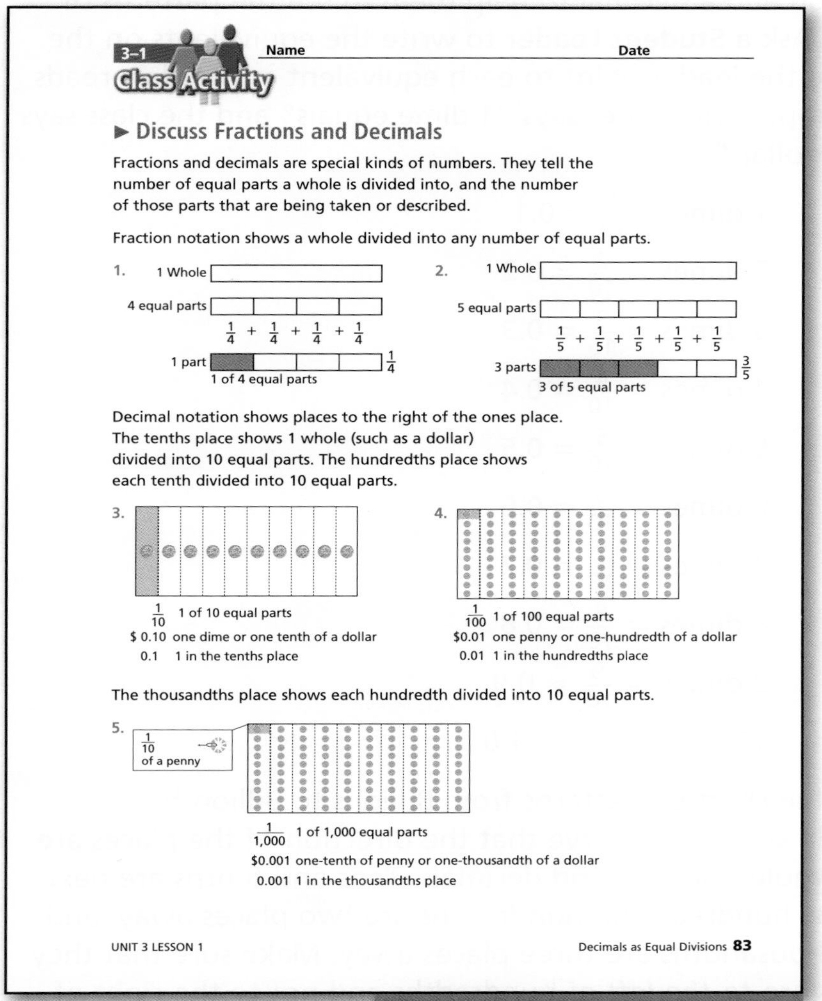

Student Activity Book page 83

▶ Discuss Fractions and Decimals WHOLE CLASS

Math Talk As a class, read the information at the top of page 83. Use **Solve and Discuss** to identify the patterns in exercises 1–5. For each exercise, ask:

- **How many equal parts are in the whole? Explain how you know.** The denominator of the fraction and/or the place value of the decimal identify the number of equal parts in the whole.
- **How many of those equal parts are being taken or described? Explain how you know.** The numerator of the fraction and/or the decimal number without regard to its place value (for example 0.08 describes eight parts) identify the number of equal parts that are being taken or described.

Activity continued ▶

Differentiated Instruction

Materials: pennies and dimes

Special Needs Some students may benefit from using dimes and pennies to model exercises 3 and 4.

Class Management

Looking Ahead In Lessons 2–5 and 13 in this unit, students will use Secret Code Cards. These can be found on Student Activity Book pages 86A–86D and 88A–88B, Activity Workbook pages 45–50, and TRB pages M75–M80. For classroom activities, students can use the cards provided in the Student Activity Book or the Activity Workbook. If you would like students to take those cards home, you can make sturdy cards specifically for classroom use by copying the copymaster onto cardstock (make sure your copy machine has the capability).

If you have access to the *Math Expressions* materials kits, the Secret Code Cards are included, so you will not have to prepare them.

Exercise 3 Students may find it helpful to list the amounts from 1 to 10 dimes as a fraction and a decimal to help them to see the patterns of dimes to dollars. Ask a **Student Leader** to write the equivalents on the board. Then have the leader point to each equivalent as the class reads it aloud. For example, the leader says "1 dime equals" and the class says "one-tenth of a dollar."

$$1 \text{ dime} = \frac{1}{10} = 0.1$$

$$2 \text{ dimes} = \frac{2}{10} = 0.2$$

$$3 \text{ dimes} = \frac{3}{10} = 0.3$$

$$4 \text{ dimes} = \frac{4}{10} = 0.4$$

$$5 \text{ dimes} = \frac{5}{10} = 0.5$$

$$6 \text{ dimes} = \frac{6}{10} = 0.6$$

$$7 \text{ dimes} = \frac{7}{10} = 0.7$$

$$8 \text{ dimes} = \frac{8}{10} = 0.8$$

$$9 \text{ dimes} = \frac{9}{10} = 0.9$$

$$10 \text{ dimes} = \frac{10}{10} = 1.0$$

Use the place value chart on Patterns from Billions to Billionths (TRB M22) to help students observe that the direction of the places are "opposite" for whole numbers and decimals. Tens and tenths are next to the ones place, hundreds and hundredths are two places away, and thousands and thousandths are three places away. Make sure that they recognize tenths are *to the left* of hundredths and not to the right of them as tens are to the right of hundreds.

Discuss money ($0.10 is one dime and one tenth of a dollar, and $0.01 is one penny and one hundredth of a dollar) with students to help them remember this pattern.

<u>tenths</u>	<u>hundredths</u>	<u>thousandths</u>
dime	penny	tenth of a penny

Read and Write Decimals and Fractions

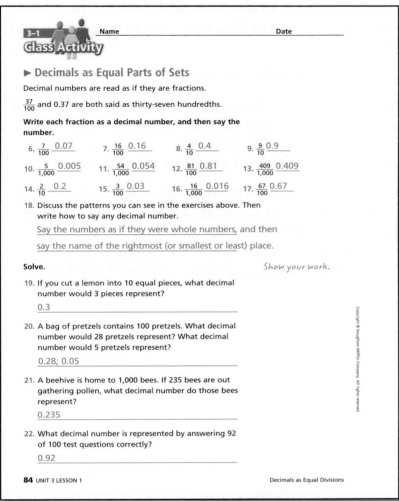

Student Activity Book page 84

 35 MINUTES

Goal: Read and write decimals and fractions.

Materials: Student Activity Book or Hardcover Book p. 84

 NCTM Standards:
Number and Operations
Communication

Teaching Note

Language and Vocabulary Most fractions are read and spoken by saying the numerator as a whole number and then saying the denominator with "*-th*" added to its end. Note, however, that several of the largest unit fractions ($\frac{1}{2}$, $\frac{1}{3}$, and $\frac{1}{5}$) do not follow this pattern. Instead, they have special names for their denominators: $\frac{1}{2}$ is one-*half*, $\frac{1}{3}$ is one-*third*, and $\frac{1}{5}$ is one-*fifth* (not one-*fiveth*).

Make sure students are aware of and understand this pattern, which can be used to complete exercises 6–17 Student Book page 84.

▶ Decimals as Equal Parts of Sets WHOLE CLASS

Before students start this activity, write the following on the board. You may want to ask students to copy it into their math journals.

Decimal Place Values

<u>thousands</u> <u>hundreds</u> <u>tens</u> ones • <u>tenths</u> <u>hundredths</u> <u>thousandths</u>

Invite a volunteer to read aloud the two sentences at the top of Student Book page 84. Then share the **Language and Vocabulary Note** in the adjacent column with students.

Activity continued ▶

Teaching the Lesson (continued)

 Ongoing Assessment

Ask students to describe relationships that equivalent fractions and decimals share.

 Class Management

Looking Ahead If your students need early mastery of simple fraction and decimal equivalencies (halves, thirds, fourths, fifths, sixths, and eighths) to prepare for state or district tests, you can complete Lesson 18 in Unit 5 at the appropriate time.

 Class Management

One part of making everyone responsible for listening to one another is to make sure that the explainers are talking loudly enough and that they are talking to the whole class, not just you. Move to the side or the back of the class so that students have to look at their classmates to see you (you can direct things from the side or the back and you have an interesting new view of your class).

One teacher has students use a pretend microphone initially to remind them to talk loudly. Another teacher has her students pretend that their parent is sitting in the back of the classroom listening to them. A third teacher uses the "finger wiggle" to hold her students accountable for really listening to one another. Rather than interrupting one another when they can't hear well, the student listeners subtly wiggle their finger in the air to indicate that they can't hear the speaker.

Exercises 6–17 After these exercises have been completed, give students an opportunity to discuss any patterns they observed when reading and speaking the names.

Exercise 18 As a class, discuss possible answers.

Exercises 19–22 These exercises ask students to write a decimal number for a part of a set of 10, 100, and 1,000. As with fractions, make sure students understand that a whole may represent 1 divided into a number of equal parts, or the number of things or objects in a set.

End the activity with a whole-class drill in which you say (or students say) a variety of whole numbers and students say those same numbers as decimal numbers. (Encourage students to have fun emphasizing the "-*th*" at the end of each decimal number.) For example, you say *eight hundred forty-two* and students say *eight hundred forty-two thousandths.*"

● Intervention   Activity Card 3-1

Write It Two Ways — Activity Card 3-1 ●

Work: In Pairs

Use:
• MathBoard materials

3. Possible explanation: The first number has a 0 in the hundredths place and an 8 in the thousandths place. The second number has an 8 in the hundredths place and a 0 in the thousandths place.

1. Each partner writes the following numbers as a fraction and as a decimal.

> twenty-three hundredths
> eight tenths
> three hundred eighteen thousandths
> sixty-three hundredths
> three tenths
> five hundred nine thousandths

2. Partners compare their fractions and decimals and make any corrections needed.

3. Math Talk Write these numbers in decimal form. Explain how they are different.

>   two hundred eight thousandths 0.208
>   two hundred eighty thousandths 0.280

Unit 3, Lesson 1   Copyright © Houghton Mifflin Company

Activity Note All of the numbers are greater than 0 and less than 1. Be sure students understand that they should start each number with 0 in ones place.

 Math Writing Prompt

Explain Your Thinking Write "twelve hundredths" and "twelve thousandths" as a fraction and as a decimal. Explain how they are different?

 **Software Support**

Warm-Up 4.18

▲ On Level   Activity Card 3-1

Express It — Activity Card 3-1 ▲

Work: By Yourself

1. Write a decimal and a fraction for the number shown on the grid. $0.53; \frac{53}{100}$

2. Explain How did you know how to write the decimal? 53 out of 100 squares = 0.53

3. Write the equivalent decimal for each fraction below.

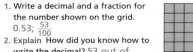

$\frac{3}{10}$ 0.3 $\frac{23}{100}$ 0.23 $\frac{308}{1,000}$ 0.308

4. Write the equivalent fraction for each decimal below.

0.7 $\frac{7}{10}$ 0.85 $\frac{85}{100}$ 0.044 $\frac{44}{1,000}$

Unit 3, Lesson 1   Copyright © Houghton Mifflin Company

Activity Note Have students who finish early work in pairs to show other decimal values on grid paper.

 Math Writing Prompt

Explain Your Thinking Why can we think of decimals as equal divisions of a whole number? Use money as an example.

 Software Support

Fraction Action: Number Line Mine, Level N

■ Challenge   Activity Card 3-1

What's That Decimal? — Activity Card 3-1 ■

Work: In Pairs

Use:
• Centimeter-Grid Paper (TRB M18)
• Markers

1. Write a fraction for the decimal number modeled on the grid. $0.72; \frac{72}{100}$

2. Each partner marks off two 10 × 10 squares on the grid paper and represents a fraction on each 10 × 10 grid. Write each fraction value below its grid.

> 0.72 = ?

3. Partners exchange grids, verify that the fraction value written is correct and writes it as a decimal.

4. Represent What does it mean when we say that decimals are equal divisions of a whole? Possible answer: It means that when we divide a whole into 10, 100, or 1000 equal pieces, we can use a decimal number to name the parts of the whole we are talking about.

Unit 3, Lesson 1   Copyright © Houghton Mifflin Company

Activity Note Students can use any type of grid paper as long as they can mark off a 10 × 10 grid on it. Students do not need to color in the shaded parts completely.

 Math Writing Prompt

Describe Relationships How are decimals related to fractions that have a denominator of 10, 100, or 1,000?

 DESTINATION Math® **Software Support**

Course III: Module 4: Unit 1: Tenths, Hundredths, and Thousandths

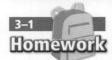

3 Homework and Spiral Review

Homework **Goal:** Additional Practice

Use this Homework page to provide students with more practice writing fractions with denominators of 10, 100 and 1,000 as decimals.

Remembering **Goal:** Spiral Review

This Remembering page would be appropriate anytime after today's lesson.

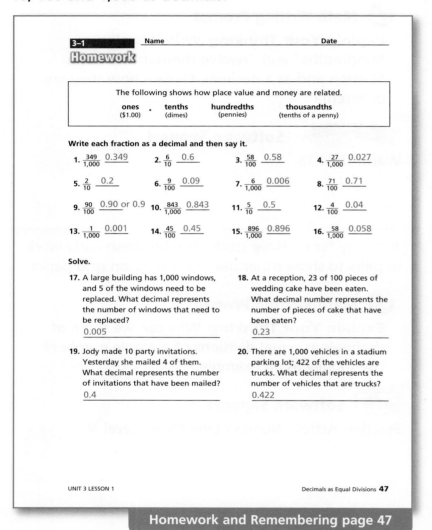

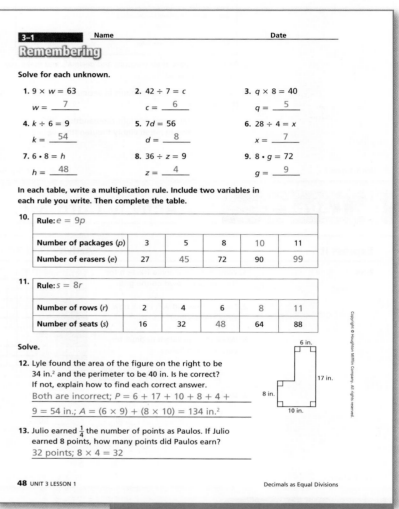

Homework and Remembering page 47

Homework and Remembering page 48

Home or School Activity

 Real-World Connection

Comparisons Have students use catalogues to find pictures of items that they can use to make comparison statements that use multiplication.

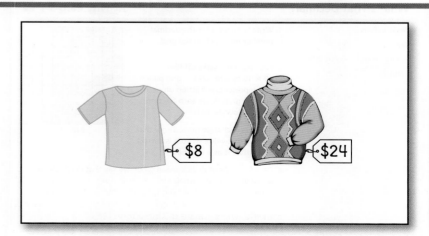

Equate and Compare

Lesson Objective
● Model and identify equivalent decimals.

The Day at a Glance

Today's Goals	Materials	
1 Teaching the Lesson **A1:** Recognize equivalent decimals using tenths, hundredths, and thousandths. **A2:** Represent decimals using a variety of models. **2 Going Further** ▶ Differentiated Instruction **3 Homework and Spiral Review**	**Lesson Activities** Student Activity Book pp. 85–86D or Student Hardcover Book pp. 85–86 and Activity Workbook pp. 44–48 (includes Secret Code Cards) Homework and Remembering pp. 49–50 MathBoard materials Whole Numbers and Number Lines (TRB M73) (optional) Small 10 × 10 Grids (TRB M74) Ruler Scissors	**Going Further** Activity Cards 3-2 MathBoard materials Grid Paper (TRB M17) Math Journals

123 Use Math Talk today!

Keeping Skills Sharp

Quick Practice ⏱ 5 MINUTES

Goal: Practice writing fractions as decimals.

Write Decimals Have students work in small groups. Send a **Student Leader** to the board to write three fractions that are less than one that have the same numerator and the denominators 10, 100, and 1,000. Then, the student leader signals to write the decimal form of each fraction, and then calls on a group to write their decimals on the board. The class reviews the decimals. Groups receive one point for each correct decimal. Repeat with different fractions until one group earns 10 points and wins the game.

Daily Routines

Homework Review Let students work together to check their work.

Nonroutine Problem Tyra and Kyle bought packages of paper plates. Each package had the same number of plates. Tyra bought a total of 32 plates and Kyle bought a total of 56 plates. How many paper plates could have been in each package? Explain how you found your answer. 1, 2, 4, or 8 paper plates; The 8s count-by has both 32 and 56. Also, 1, 2, and 4 are factors of 32 and 56.

① Teaching the Lesson

Decimal Equivalents

 25 MINUTES

Goal: Recognize equivalent decimals using tenths, hundredths, and thousandths.

Materials: MathBoard materials, Student Activity Book p. 85 or Hardcover Book p. 85 and Activity Workbook p. 44, Whole Numbers and Number Lines (TRB M73), Small 10 × 10 Grids (TRB M74)

 NCTM Standards:
Number and Operations
Representation

Teaching Note

Fraction Models The bar used in this activity is similar to the fraction bars used in Unit 5. If your students need practice with decimals on number lines, they can draw a number line below the long 100-bar and use the bar as a guide to divide and label the number line.

 Class Management

Preparing Materials There is a copymaster version of each MathBoard feature. The long 100-bar can be found on TRB M113. The fraction bars can be found on TRB M114. If your class does not have MathBoards, you can make photocopies of these copymasters for students to use. You may wish to place a photocopy of this copymaster in a sheet protector for each student, or you can laminate the copies, and have students write on them with dry-erase markers. By taping an enlarged sheet-protected or laminated photocopy of these TRB pages to the classroom board, you can also create a Demonstration MathBoard.

▶ Visualize Decimal Equivalents WHOLE CLASS

Visualize Tenths Have each student position the MathBoard so the long bar divided into 100 equal parts is at the top. Tell the class that the bar shows one whole. Then ask them to label one end 0 and the other end 1.0, and then label each heavy tick mark by tenths.

| 0 | 0.1 | 0.2 | 0.3 | 0.4 | 0.5 | 0.6 | 0.7 | 0.8 | 0.9 | 1.0 |

Visualize Hundredths Ask students to name the number of very small equal units that are shown on the bar between the heavy tick marks and explain what each unit represents 100; one hundredth Then have them write the number of hundredths under each number of tenths.

| 0 | 0.1 | 0.2 | 0.3 | 0.4 | 0.5 | 0.6 | 0.7 | 0.8 | 0.9 | 1.0 |
| 0 | 0.10 | 0.20 | 0.30 | 0.40 | 0.50 | 0.60 | 0.70 | 0.80 | 0.90 | 1.00 |

Visualize Equivalent Decimals Name a pair of equivalent decimals, such as 0.5 and 0.50, and draw an oval around the distance from 0 to those labels. Ask students to explain why 0.5 = 0.50. The distance from 0 is 5 of 10 equal parts and 50 of 100 equal parts. Since the distances are identical, the decimals representing those distances (0.5 and 0.50) are equivalent.

Extend to Thousandths Have students suppose the bar is divided into thousandths (which means that each hundredth would be divided into 10 very tiny equal parts.) Ask them to name the number of thousandths there would be from zero to the one-tenth mark. 10 in each hundredth, so 100 thousandths Then have them write the number of thousandths under each number of hundredths.

0	0.1	0.2	0.3	0.4	0.5	0.6	0.7	0.8	0.9	1.0
0	0.10	0.20	0.30	0.40	0.50	0.60	0.70	0.80	0.90	1.00
0	0.100	0.200	0.300	0.400	0.500	0.600	0.700	0.800	0.900	1.000

Select three equivalent decimals (such as 0.6, 0.60, and 0.600, and draw an oval around the distance from 0 to those labels. Ask students to explain why 0.6 = 0.60 = 0.600. The distance from 0 is 6 of 10 equal parts, 60 of 100 equal parts, and 600 of 1,000 equal parts. Since the distances are identical, the decimals representing those distances (0.6, 0.60, and 0.600) are equivalent.

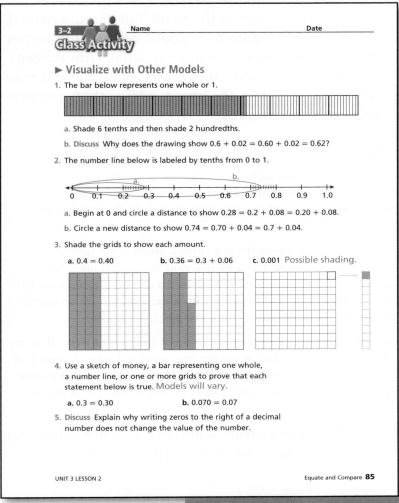

Student Activity Book page 85

▶ Visualize with Other Models [WHOLE CLASS]

Have students work through exercises 1–4 as a class, in **Student Pairs**, or in **Small Groups.** The exercises give students an opportunity to visualize decimals in a variety of ways, and reinforce the concept that tenths are ten times as big as hundredths, which are ten times as big as thousandths.

Activity continued ▶

Teaching Note

What to Expect From Students
Throughout this activity, emphasize the order of the decimal places to the right of the ones place, and the idea that tenths are greater than hundredths and hundredths are greater than thousandths.

ones . tenths hundredths thousandths

ones	>	tenths
tenths	>	hundredths
hundredths	>	thousandths

The visual representations shown on Student Book page 85 and the money shown on page 86 can be used to help students more thoroughly understand these relationships.

Teaching Note

Math Background The models in this lesson show three different meanings of fractions. The use of money represents fractions as parts of a set. Fraction bars represent fractions as parts of a whole. Number lines represent fractions as distance (from zero).

Activity 1

Differentiated Instruction

Extra Help Distribute Whole Numbers and Number Lines (TRB M73) if students need practice placing numbers on a number line.

Teaching Note

Why Discuss Zeros? Today's discussion is important because it is often easier for students to compare, add, and subtract decimal numbers when they write zeros so that the numbers have the same number of decimal places. It is important for them to understand, however, that we can only write zeros when the zeros do not change the value of the number.

Exercise 5 The goal for students in completing exercises 1–4 is to observe general patterns and use them to complete exercise 5. Discuss exercise 5 as a class (discussion examples are shown in the Math Talk feature below). Then ask students to make a general statement about why writing zeroes to the right of a decimal number does not change its value. (This concept may be difficult for some students to understand, and these students may need to copy a summary statement from the board, while others can write a general statement using their own words).

 Math Talk in Action

Chantel: 0.3 = 0.30 because 3 dimes is the same as 30 pennies, and 30 pennies is the same as 30 hundredths. And 30 hundredths is the same as 0.300 because a thousandth is one-tenth of a penny (one of those penny slivers). So for 30 pennies, there are 30 × 10 or 300 thousandths.

Jorge: I thought about the squares. Three-tenths is 3 vertical strips in a square, and each strip can be divided into 10 equal parts by drawing horizontal lines, so three-tenths is thirty hundredths. And each of the hundredths can be divided into 10 equal parts by drawing horizontal lines, and there will be a thousand in all, so each is one-thousandth. That means for 30 hundredths there are 300 thousandths.

Erica: I used the hundreds bar and thought about it like Jorge did except that all of my divisions were vertical. So I just had tinier but more decimal units as I moved from 3 of the tenths strips to 30 of the smaller hundredths strips to 300 of the tiny thousandths strips (so tiny that I can't actually draw them but I can see them when I think about them).

Extra Practice If you would like to provide additional practice using grids to model decimal numbers, distribute Small 10 × 10 Grids (TRB M74).

Patterns in Decimal Secret Code Cards

▶ Making Decimal Numbers [WHOLE CLASS]

Explain that students will be using the Decimal Secret Code Cards in this activity (and in the next three lessons) to help understand decimal numbers.

Have students cut along the dotted lines **on the front of** the Decimal Secret Code Cards to make tenths, hundredths, and thousandths cards. After the cards have been cut out, encourage suggestions from students about how the cards can be organized. (Any method that keeps the tenths together, the hundredths together, and the thousandths together is acceptable.)

Discuss Patterns Give students an opportunity to discuss patterns that can be seen on the backs of the cards. (The tenths show dimes, the hundredths show pennies, and the thousandths show tenths of pennies.)

⏱ **35 MINUTES**

Goal: Represent decimals using a variety of models.

Materials: Student Activity Book pp. 86 and 86A–86D or Hardcover Book p. 86 and Activity Workbook pp. 45–48, ruler, scissors

✓ **NCTM Standards:**
Number and Operations
Representation

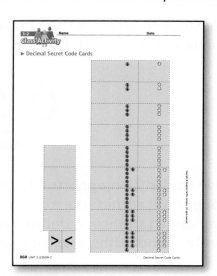

Tenths and Hundredths

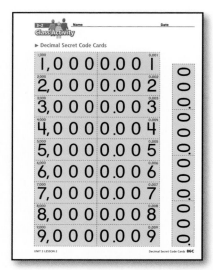

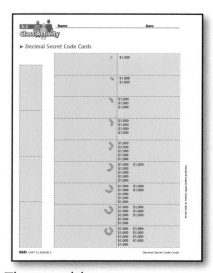

Thousands and Thousandths

Activity continued ▶

Activity 2

Differentiated Instruction

Special Needs If students are having difficulty manipulating the paper Secret Code Cards, laminate the page of cards before cutting them out.

English Language Learners

Write 0.564, *tenths, hundredths,* and *thousandths* on the board.

• **Beginning** Point and ask: **Is 5 in the *tenths* or *hundredths* place?** tenths Continue with other digits.

• **Intermediate** Ask: **Which number is in the *tenths* place?** 5 Continue with other digits.

• **Advanced** Have students identify the place value of each digit. Continue with 1,564.287.

Teaching Note

Place Value The Decimal Secret Code Cards were designed to emphasize place value. As students assemble the cards to make decimal numbers, they must identify each place and the card that represents it.

Modeling Decimal Numbers Ask students to move the fronts of the cards around to learn how they can be arranged to show decimal numbers. (Tenths are placed first, hundredths are placed to the right of tenths, and then thousandths are placed to the right of hundredths. Or thousandths are placed first, hundredths are placed to the left of thousandths, and then tenths are placed to the left of hundredths.)

Have students select the cards that can be used to show the decimal number 0.268. (Students select the cards representing 2 tenths, 6 hundredths, and 8 thousandths.)

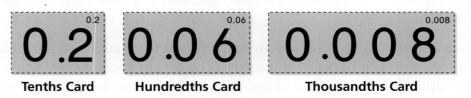

Tenths Card   Hundredths Card   Thousandths Card

Ask students to place the cards on top of each other to display the number in standard form.

Assembled Cards

Give students an opportunity to explain what the little numbers in the upper right corner of each card represent when the cards have been overlapped to show a decimal number. (The numbers represent the tenths, hundredths, and thousandths that make up the decimal number.)

▶ Use Inequality Signs to Compare | WHOLE CLASS |

Inequality Signs Ask students to describe the meanings of the inequality symbols > and < that are used for comparing numbers, and on the board write an example of how each symbol is used to compare the whole numbers 12 and 15. 15 > 12 (15 is greater than 12) and 12 < 15 (12 is less than 15.)

Write Equivalent Decimals Write 0.6 and 0.28 on the board and ask the class to decide which decimal number is greater.

Some students may think that 0.28 is greater than 0.6 because 28 is greater than 6. (This is a very common error.) Have the class brainstorm how to avoid making this kind of error. One such way is:

- How could we make 0.6 and 0.28 have the same number of decimal places? write a 0 to the right of 0.6

- Would writing a zero to the right of 0.6 change the value of 0.6? Explain why or why not. No; when a whole is divided into 10 and into 100 equal parts, 6 of 10 equal parts is the same amount as 60 of 100 equal parts, so 0.6 = 0.60.

Write the following pairs of numbers on the board and invite volunteers to complete each comparison.

0.6 > 0.28   0.28 < 0.6   0.60 > 0.28   0.28 < 0.60

Use Models To Compare Have students find the Decimal Secret Code Cards for 0.3, 0.03, and 0.003. Using the cards and the < and > inequality signs, ask them to arrange all possible comparisons of the three decimal numbers. Sample comparisons include 0.3 > 0.03, 0.3 > 0.003, 0.03 > 0.003, 0.03 < 0.3, 0.003 < 0.3, and 0.003 < 0.03.

To check their work, suggest that students use the backs of the cards and think about the values of the dimes, pennies, and tenths of pennies. dimes > pennies > tenths of pennies; tenths > hundredths > thousandths

Repeat the activity using the Decimal Secret Code Cards for 0.8, 0.08, and 0.008.

Activity continued ▶

Watch For! Some students have difficulty deciding which decimal number is greater because they extend their knowledge of whole number patterns incorrectly. For example, 420 is greater than 85, so these students assume that 0.420 must be greater than 0.85. Today's activities will help students recognize that a *longer* decimal number is not necessarily a *greater* decimal number.

Remind all of your students that decimal numbers are easier to compare when each has the same number of decimal places: 0.420 < 0.850.

Ongoing Assessment

Ask students to compare decimal numbers:

► Are all of these numbers equal? Give a reason to support your answer.

0.72 0.7200 0.720

► Compare each pair of numbers by writing > or <.

0.5 ◯ 0.36

0.4 ◯ 0.78

0.61 ◯ 0.2

0.32 ◯ 0.9

 Class Management

Decimal Secret Code Cards
Distribute an envelope to each student for storage of the Secret Code Cards, or have students fold a blank sheet of paper to form a type of envelope.

Address Student Misconceptions Some students may be misled by examples in which the whole number comparisons are opposite the decimal number comparisons. To address this error, write the problems shown below on the board and have students solve them as a class, as individuals with **Helping Partners**, or in **Small Groups**.

As they work, encourage them to use the dimes, pennies, and tenths of pennies on the backs of their Decimal Secret Code Cards to help complete the comparisons.

Suggest that students who prefer to use paper and pencil to write zeroes to the right of the numbers so that each has the same number of decimal places.

Discuss the different methods that were used to find the solutions and write the solutions on the board.

Write On Board	Solutions
17 ◯ 9 but 0.17 ◯ 0.9	17 > 9 but 0.17 < 0.9
73 ◯ 138 but 0.73 ◯ 0.138	73 < 138 but 0.73 > 0.138
456 ◯ 8 but 0.456 ◯ 0.8	456 > 8 but 0.456 < 0.8

Some students may also be misled by comparisons that involve the same non-zero digits arranged in different ways. To address this error, write the problems shown below on the board and have students again solve them as a class, as individuals with helping partners, or in small groups. Discuss the solutions and write them on the board.

Write On Board	Solutions
0.006 ◯ 0.6	0.006 < 0.6
0.60 ◯ 0.06	0.60 > 0.06
0.600 ◯ 0.060	0.600 > 0.060
0.6 ◯ 0.60 ◯ 0.600	0.6 = 0.60 = 0.600
0.06 ◯ 0.060	0.06 = 0.060

▶ Summarize Decimal Numbers [WHOLE CLASS]

(123) **Math Talk** Have students look at the two examples at the top of Student Activity Book page 86 and summarize everything they know about decimal numbers. Their summary should include these concepts:

- The decimal places are ordered from left to right in this way—tenths, hundredths, and thousandths.

- Tenths are greater than (>) hundredths and hundredths are greater than (>) thousandths because 1 divided into ten equal parts (tenths) makes a larger unit than that 1 divided into a hundred equal parts (hundredths), which makes a larger unit than 1 divided into a thousand equal parts (thousandths).

- The –*ths* ending for the decimal places reminds us that we are taking or describing small, equal parts of 1, and the larger the number of such parts, the smaller the unit parts will be.

- We do not read or say decimal numbers by reading or saying the value of each position. For example, 0.275 is not *two tenths seven hundredths five thousandths*. Although that is its value, we read and say the amount as a fraction: *two hundred seventy-five thousandths*.

- We can visualize tenths as dimes to remind ourselves that tenths are greater than hundredths because dimes are greater than pennies.

Activity continued ▶

The Learning Classroom

Math Talk Having students use their own words and examples to discuss what they have learned is an effective way to be sure they understand a concept. Invite a student to go to the board and summarize the class discussion. For this lesson, ask students to summarize what they know about decimal numbers.

Activity 2

The Learning Classroom

Math Talk The **Solve and Discuss** structure of conversation is used throughout the *Math Expressions* program. The teacher selects four or five students to go to the board and solve a problem, using any method they choose. The other students work on the same problem at their desks. Then the teacher asks the students at the board to explain their methods. Students at their desks are encouraged to ask questions and to assist each other in understanding the problem. Thus, students actually solve, explain, question, and justify. Usually ask only two or three students to explain because classes do not like to sit through more explanations, and time is better spent on the next issue.

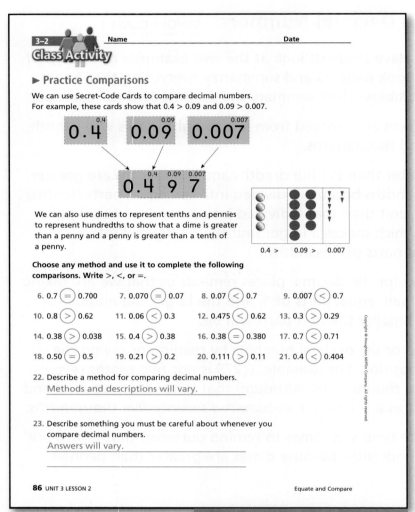

Student Activity Book page 86

► Practice Comparisons   WHOLE CLASS

On Student Book page 86, have students complete exercises 6–21 in the way that is best suited for the individuals in your class. You may wish to assign some of your advanced students to be **Helping Partners** for those students who may have difficulty completing the comparisons. Encourage students who finish early to write more difficult comparison problems on the board for other early finishers to complete.

Use **Solve and Discuss** to complete exercises 22 and 23 as a class.

Have students organize and store their Secret Code Cards (which will be used again in Lesson 3).

② Going Further

Differentiated Instruction

● Intervention   Activity Card 3-2

Equal or Not Equal?   Activity Card 3-2 ●

Work: In Pairs

Use:
• MathBoard materials

1. On your own, copy and complete the comparisons using either = (equal to) or ≠ (not equal to).

2. Model each decimal on the decimal bar of your MathBoard.

3. Exchange with your partner to check your work.

4. **Math Talk** How does understanding place value help you to compare 4.0 and 0.4?
Possible answer: The value of a digit increases as you move from right to left in the place value chart. So 4.0 and 0.4 cannot be equal.

0.2	0.02 ≠
0.5	0.50 =
60	0.60 ≠
0.17	0.71 ≠
3.9	3.09 ≠
4.0	0.4 ≠
0.720	0.72 =
8.08	8.8 ≠
0.045	0.0450 =
1.010	1.100 ≠

Unit 3, Lesson 2   Copyright © Houghton Mifflin Company

Activity Note After students have completed the activity, use their work as examples to show how to identify equal decimal numbers. Ask volunteers to explain their answers.

 Math Writing Prompt

Show and Tell Make a drawing of dimes and pennies to show why 0.5 is greater than 0.05.

 **Software Support**

Warm-Up 8.37

▲ On Level   Activity Card 3-2

Decimal Models   Activity Card 3-2 ▲

Work: By Yourself

Use:
• 2 sheets of Grid Paper (TRB M17) cut into six squares, each measuring 10 × 10

1. Each 10 × 10 grid sheet represents one whole. What does each column or row represent? What does each square represent? one tenth; one hundredth

2. Model the three given decimal pairs by shading parts of two grids, as shown in the sample below. Then write a comparison statement, using the symbol <, >, or =.

0.2 > 0.02   0.15 < 0.51   0.90 = 0.9
0.2 and 0.02   0.51 and 0.15   0.90 and 0.9

0.71 > 0.17

Unit 3, Lesson 2   Copyright © Houghton Mifflin Company

Activity Note Review decimal place value before students begin the activity. If students have difficulty, suggest that they use a decimal place value chart to identify the value of each digit.

 Math Writing Prompt

Equivalent Decimals Explain why 3 and 3.00 have the same value.

 Software Support

Fraction Action: Number Line Mine, Level P

■ Challenge   Activity Card 3-2

Inequalities   Activity Card 3-2 ■

Work: In Pairs

Use:
• MathBoard materials

1. The inequality symbols below can be used to describe real-life situations.

> ≥ means "is greater than or equal to"
> ≤ means "is less than or equal to"

2. Example. An elevator can carry a maximum of 1,200 lb. Let w = the weight that the elevator can carry.

$$w \leq 1{,}200$$

3. Write an inequality for the this situation: You must be 18 years old or older to vote. Possible answer: Age in years = a; $a \geq 18$.

4. Take turns describing real-life situations and writing an inequality to describe the situation.

Unit 3, Lesson 2   Copyright © Houghton Mifflin Company

Activity Note When students have completed the activity, ask volunteers to explain how each situation relates to a limit and why they chose the symbol they used to describe the situation.

 Math Writing Prompt

Explain Your Thinking Does writing zero in a decimal number change the value of the number? Give examples to explain your answer.

 **Software Support**

Course III: Module 1: Unit 1: Ordering and Rounding Whole Numbers

③ Homework and Spiral Review

Use this Homework page to provide students with more practice with decimal equivalents.

This Remembering activity would be appropriate anytime after today's lesson.

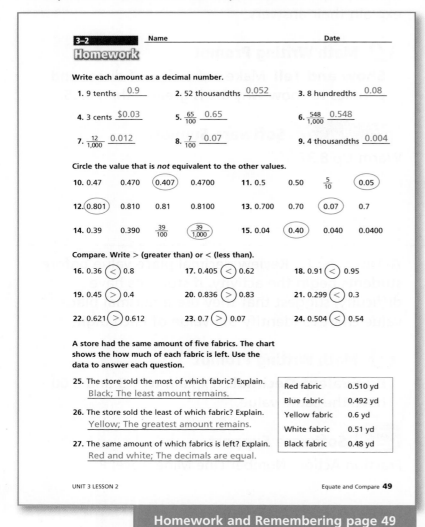

3-2 Homework   Name _____ Date _____

Write each amount as a decimal number.

1. 9 tenths __0.9__   2. 52 thousandths __0.052__   3. 8 hundredths __0.08__

4. 3 cents __$0.03__   5. $\frac{65}{100}$ __0.65__   6. $\frac{548}{1,000}$ __0.548__

7. $\frac{12}{1,000}$ __0.012__   8. $\frac{7}{100}$ __0.07__   9. 4 thousandths __0.004__

Circle the value that is *not* equivalent to the other values.

10. 0.47   0.470   (0.407)   0.4700   11. 0.5   0.50 $\frac{5}{10}$ (0.05)

12. (0.801)   0.810   0.81   0.8100   13. 0.700   0.70   (0.07)   0.7

14. 0.39   0.390 $\frac{39}{100}$ ($\frac{39}{1,000}$)   15. 0.04   (0.40)   0.040   0.0400

Compare. Write > (greater than) or < (less than).

16. 0.36 (<) 0.8   17. 0.405 (<) 0.62   18. 0.91 (<) 0.95

19. 0.45 (>) 0.4   20. 0.836 (>) 0.83   21. 0.299 (<) 0.3

22. 0.621 (>) 0.612   23. 0.7 (>) 0.07   24. 0.504 (<) 0.54

A store had the same amount of five fabrics. The chart shows the how much of each fabric is left. Use the data to answer each question.

Red fabric	0.510 yd
Blue fabric	0.492 yd
Yellow fabric	0.6 yd
White fabric	0.51 yd
Black fabric	0.48 yd

25. The store sold the most of which fabric? Explain.
    __Black; The least amount remains.__

26. The store sold the least of which fabric? Explain.
    __Yellow; The greatest amount remains.__

27. The same amount of which fabrics is left? Explain.
    __Red and white; The decimals are equal.__

UNIT 3 LESSON 2   Equate and Compare **49**

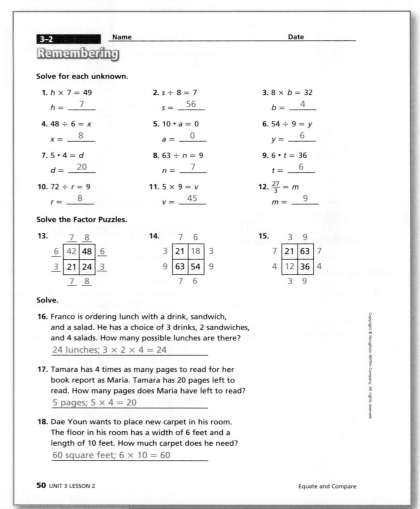

3-2 Remembering   Name _____ Date _____

Solve for each unknown.

1. $h \times 7 = 49$
   $h = $ __7__
2. $s \div 8 = 7$
   $s = $ __56__
3. $8 \times b = 32$
   $b = $ __4__

4. $48 \div 6 = x$
   $x = $ __8__
5. $10 \cdot a = 0$
   $a = $ __0__
6. $54 \div 9 = y$
   $y = $ __6__

7. $5 \cdot 4 = d$
   $d = $ __20__
8. $63 \div n = 9$
   $n = $ __7__
9. $6 \cdot t = 36$
   $t = $ __6__

10. $72 \div r = 9$
    $r = $ __8__
11. $5 \times 9 = v$
    $v = $ __45__
12. $\frac{27}{3} = m$
    $m = $ __9__

Solve the Factor Puzzles.

13.
	7	8
6	42	48	6
3	21	24	3
	7	8

14.
	7	6
3	21	18	3
9	63	54	9
	7	6

15.
	3	9
7	21	63	7
4	12	36	4
	3	9

Solve.

16. Franco is ordering lunch with a drink, sandwich, and a salad. He has a choice of 3 drinks, 2 sandwiches, and 4 salads. How many possible lunches are there?
    __24 lunches; 3 × 2 × 4 = 24__

17. Tamara has 4 times as many pages to read for her book report as Maria. Tamara has 20 pages left to read. How many pages does Maria have left to read?
    __5 pages; 5 × 4 = 20__

18. Dae Youn wants to place new carpet in his room. The floor in his room has a width of 6 feet and a length of 10 feet. How much carpet does he need?
    __60 square feet; 6 × 10 = 60__

50 UNIT 3 LESSON 2   Equate and Compare

Homework and Remembering page 49   **Homework and Remembering page 50**

Home or School Activity

 Technology Connection

Calculator Zeros Calculators show that writing zeros before or after a decimal does not change its value. Tell students to enter the decimal 3.10 into a calculator by pressing these keys:

Did the calculator show 3.1 after the equals sign was pressed? This is the calculator's way of showing that 3.10 = 3.1. Have students experiment by copying the chart and entering the decimals shown on the right.

Enter	Calculator Display
0.6 =	
00.7000 =	
010.010 =	
0.500 =	
0000000009. =	
0.20000000000 =	

Thousands to Thousandths

Lesson Objectives

- Read, write, and model whole and decimal numbers.
- Compare and order decimal numbers.

The Day at a Glance

Today's Goals	Materials
1 Teaching the Lesson **A1:** Read, write, and model numbers from thousands to thousandths. **A2:** Write, compare, and order decimal numbers. **2 Going Further** ▶ Differentiated Instruction **3 Homework and Spiral Review**	**Lesson Activities** Student Activity Book pp. 87–90 or Student Hardcover Book pp. 87–90 and Activity Workbook pp. 49–52 (includes Family Letters) Homework and Remembering pp. 51–52 Scissors Secret Code Cards (from Lesson 2) Place Value Parade Poster MathBoard materials **Going Further** Activity Cards 3-3 Number cubes Counters Ruler Math Journals

123 *Use* **Math Talk** *today!*

Keeping Skills Sharp

Quick Practice ⏱ 5 MINUTES	Daily Routines
Read Decimal Numbers Send two **Student Leaders** to the board and have them each write four different decimal numbers. (No number should be smaller than thousandths.) Leaders use the pointer to point to the numbers in order and says them out loud, omitting the place value name. The class responds with the place value name, emphasizing the *-ths* sound. **Example** Student Leader writes 0.23. Student Leader says "twenty-three." Class says "hundred*ths*."	**Homework Review** Have student solve and discuss any problems. **Multistep Problem** Ty needs $115 for a trip. He has $25 saved. To earn the rest, Ty works 3 hours per day 3 days per week. He received a $2 an hour raise and now earns $8 an hour. For taxes, $5 per day is subtracted from his earnings. If Ty works for one week, how many more days must he work to earn the money? 5 days; $115 – $25 = $90; $57 per week ($8 × 9 hr = $72 – $15 = $57); $90 – $57 = $33 more needed; $19 per day ($8 × 3 hr = 24 – $5 = $19); $33 – $19 = $14 to earn in 2nd day of second week

Teaching the Lesson

Symmetry Around the Ones

 45 MINUTES

Goal: Read, write, and model numbers from thousands to thousandths.

Materials: Student Activity Book pp. 87 and 88A–B or Hardcover Book p. 87 and Activity Workbook pp. 49–50, Decimal Secret Code Cards from Lesson 2, scissors, Place Value Parade Poster

✔ **NCTM Standards:**
Number and Operations
Representation

Teaching Note

Math Background On the Place Value Parade the row of place names or fractions is symmetrical, with the line of symmetry passing through the ones place. On either side of the ones, the other place values match up: tens with tenths, hundreds with hundredths, and thousands with thousandths.

The places become larger to the left and smaller to the right of 1. Each place to the left is 10 times as large, and each place to the right is $\frac{1}{10}$ as large. Stated another way, moving one place to the left multiplies the place value by 10, and moving one place to the right divides the place value by 10.

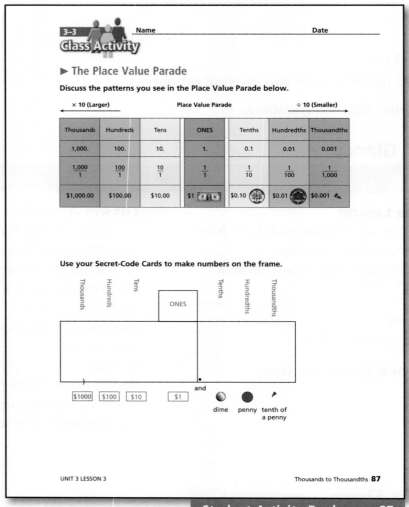

Student Activity Book page 87

▶ The Place Value Parade   WHOLE CLASS

Ask students to explain how the names and values of decimal number places (tenths, hundredths, and thousandths) relate to those for whole numbers. Then have students study the chart on Student Book page 87 and describe any patterns they see. (Two of the most important patterns are summarized in the column to the left. You may want to display the Place Value Parade poster to refer to during the discussion.)

A common misconception by students is to assume that the place value system is symmetric around the decimal point (instead of the ones place). To address this misconception, ask "Where is the *oneths* place?" Make sure students understand that the first place to the right of the decimal point is the tenths place because as we move to the right in our place value system, each place value is divided by 10 to make the next place value. So the place to the right of the ones place is 1 ÷ 10 or the fraction $\frac{1}{10}$ and the decimal 0.1 because it is 1 of 10 equal parts.

▶ Making Numbers with Secret Code Cards [WHOLE CLASS]

In this lesson, students will use the Secret Code Cards that they cut out previously (Lesson 2), and the hundreds, tens, and ones Secret Code Cards to model whole numbers and decimal numbers. Have students cut along the dotted lines **on the front** of the hundreds, tens, and ones cards. Once students have cut out all of the Secret Code Cards, they will use them to model whole numbers and decimal numbers.

Discuss Give students an opportunity to discuss patterns that can be seen on the backs of the cards. (The backs show the number of $1, $10, $100, or $1,000 bills that appear on the fronts of the cards.)

Modeling Whole Numbers Have students select the cards that can be used to form the whole number 2,435. (Students select the cards representing 2 thousands, 4 hundreds, 3 tens, and 5 ones.)

Ask students to place the cards on top of each other to display the number in standard form.

Assembled Cards

Ask students to explain what the little numbers in the upper right corner of each card represent when the cards have been overlapped to show a whole number. They represent the number of ones, tens, hundreds, and thousands that make up the whole number.

Activity continued ▶

 Class Management

Decimal Secret Code Cards In this activity, students will use the Decimal Secret Code Cards that were cut out in Lesson 2 and saved. If they did not cut out the thousands cards at that time, they will need to cut them out now.

Hundreds, Tens, and Ones

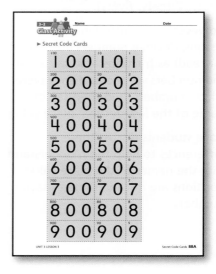

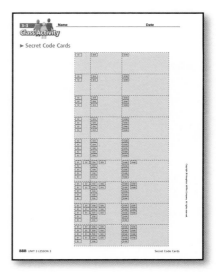

① Teaching the Lesson (continued)

Activity 1

Teaching Note

Math Background There is a distinction between knowing place value places and knowing how to say numbers. For example, to say whole numbers through thousands, we say (or read) the number in a place and then say the name of that place value, except that the tens place is spoken in an inconsistent way, and we do not say the name of the ones place. For tens, the place name *tens* shortened to the *–ty* ending, as in sixty, seventy, etc. (twenty, thirty, and fifty are irregular and are not said as twoty, threety, fivety).

However, as discussed in earlier lessons, decimal numbers are spoken (or read) as fractions—we say all of the numbers we see as if they were whole numbers, and then say the name of the last decimal place value.

Have students discuss these differences to help them understand that the names of the place value positions are not the same as saying numbers.

Modeling Decimal Numbers Now ask students to use the frame at the bottom of Student Book page 87 to make numbers that have whole and decimal parts (such as 5.34, for example).

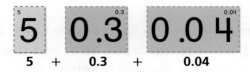

5   +   0.3   +   0.04

Assembled Cards

If students do not know the convention of saying *and* for the decimal point, write the decimal numbers below on the board and have students say each number aloud.

5.34 five and thirty-four hundredths

2.6 two and six tenths

972.8 nine hundred seventy-two and eight tenths

Challenge students to use their cards and form pairs of numbers that sound alike, and then read each pair of numbers aloud. (Encourage them to have fun emphasizing the "*-th*" sound at the end of each decimal number.) Adjust the difficulty of the examples according to the needs of your students, and be sure some examples include numbers with zeros, such as 40.07 and 2,009.80.

8,000.07 eight thousand, and seven hundredths

8,700 eight thousand, seven hundred

900 nine hundred

0.09 nine hundredths

Remind students that the backs of their Secret Code Cards show the values they are making with the fronts of the cards.

Word Names Have students look at the decimal numbers above. (Write them all on the board.) Ask volunteers to write the word name for each number while other students write the word name at their seats. For additional practice, have students make decimal numbers on the frame and then write their word names.

Reading Decimals Stress the importance of clearly speaking decimal numbers that end in *–ths* so that a listener can understand that it is a decimal number and not a whole number that is being named. For example, 400 or 0.04 (4 hundred or 4 hundredths).

Also stress the importance of not reading or saying "*and*" when reading or saying whole numbers. For example, if *four hundred and thirty seven* is spoken, a listener might think of the decimal number 400.37 (*four hundred and thirty-seven hundredths*) or the decimal number 400.037 (*four hundred and thirty-seven thousandths*) instead of 437.

Extra Practice Ask students who can benefit from reading or understanding more about decimal numbers to place Decimal Secret Code Cards on the frame. The students can then work together and take turns reading the place value names from the frame (e.g., 0.2 will be 2 tenths, 0.05 will be 5 hundredths, 0.308 with be 308 thousandths, etc.).

Ongoing Assessment

▶ Do whole numbers include the word "and" whenever they are read or spoken? Give an example to support your answer.

▶ Do fractions include the word "and" whenever they are read or spoken? Give an example to support your answer.

▶ Do mixed numbers include the word "and" whenever they are read or spoken? Give an example to support your answer.

▶ Do decimal numbers include the word "and" whenever they are read or spoken? Give an example to support your answer.

Teaching the Lesson (continued)

Places to the Left Are Larger

 45 MINUTES

Goal: Write, compare, and order decimal numbers.

Materials: Student Activity Book p. 88 or Hardcover Book p. 88, MathBoard materials, Secret Code Cards from Activity 1

 NCTM Standards:
Number and Operations
Communication
Representation

Class Management

Secret Code Cards The cards will be used through Lesson 13. After this activity has been completed, students should store their new whole number Secret Code Cards with their Decimal Secret Code Cards. Or you might choose to collect the cards and store them for your students.

English Language Learners

Write $2\frac{1}{3}$ on the board. Say: **A** *mixed number* is a *whole number* and a *fraction*.

- **Beginning** Ask: **Is 2 a** *whole number*? yes **Is $\frac{1}{3}$ a** *fraction*? yes Say: **$2\frac{1}{3}$ is a** *mixed number*. Have students repeat.
- **Intermediate and Advanced** Ask: **Which is a** *whole number*? 2 **A** *fraction*? $\frac{1}{3}$ Say: **$2\frac{1}{3}$ a __.** mixed number

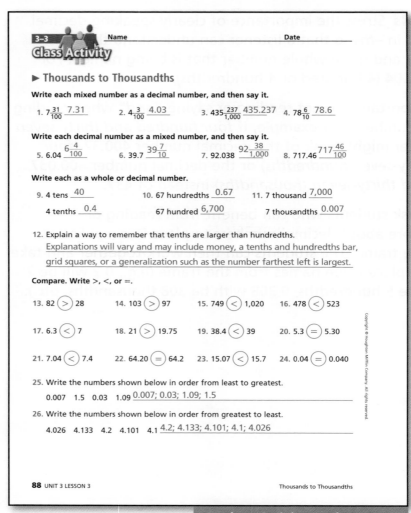

Student Activity Book page 88

▶ Thousands to Thousandths WHOLE CLASS

Work through exercises 1–11 on Student Book page 88 as a class or arrange students to work together in **Student Pairs**.

Math Talk Be sure that these points emerge in the work and discussion of the exercises:

- A *mixed number* is made up of a whole number and a fraction. We say "*and*" after the whole number just as we say "*and*" for the decimal point in a decimal number.

$$7\frac{31}{100} \text{ and } 7.31 \text{ means } 7 + \frac{31}{100}$$

- Some students may benefit from using Secret Code Cards on the frame for exercises 9–11.

- For exercise 12, be sure to use the Place Value Parade and the frame to emphasize how each place to the left is getting larger (ten times as large as the place to its right), and emphasize that this relationship is the same on both sides of the decimal point.

Compare Decimals to Thousandths Give students an opportunity to describe any general patterns that can be seen as they complete the comparisons in exercises 13–24. Along with their work on the Place Value Parade, students should now be able to recognize that the left-most place in a number is always the largest place, and conclude that if both numbers have the same left-most place values, the greater digit in that place represents the larger number. (The backs of the Secret Code Cards can help with this understanding.)

Suggest that students make the pairs of numbers and then check the backs of the cards. (Students will need to work in pairs for those times when they need two cards with the same number in the same place). As they work, students should begin to generalize that the larger number will have more places to the left of the decimal point (because the other number has a 0 in each of those places).

Generalize For the problems that involve the = sign (such as exercise 20: 5.3 and 5.30), students can use the frame at the bottom of page 87 to remind themselves that adding zeros to the right of a decimal number does not change the value of the number. In a related way, they can recognize that adding zeros to the left of a whole number does not change the value of the number. These facts enable them to articulate the overall pattern: *We only change the value if we move a number to a different place.*

Order Decimals to Thousandths Before students complete exercises 25 and 26, write these decimal numbers on the board.

     8.02   3.12   0.789 3.06 0.8

Give students an opportunity to discuss how to decide which number is smallest (or least), which number is largest (or greatest), and then decide how the other numbers compare.

Culminate the discussion by inviting one volunteer to write the numbers in order from greatest to least, and another to write the numbers in order from least to greatest.

> **Teaching Note**
>
> **Watch For!** A common error some students make when comparing numbers is to assume that the number with the greatest number of digits is the greatest number.
>
> These students may find it helpful to assume that the numbers being compared represent money. For example, if the numbers 42.63 and 42.549 are being compared, the students can decide that 42.63 is greater than 42.549 because $42.63 is greater than $42.54.
>
> By comparing numbers as money amounts whenever possible, students develop the habit of comparing from left to right because dollars and cents are read from left to right.

Activity continued ▶

① Teaching the Lesson (continued)

Activity 1

✔ Ongoing Assessment

Ask students to find:

▶ 0.03 + 0.6

▶ 0.4 − 0.75

▶ Subtract Decimals [WHOLE CLASS]

Have students use the MathBoard to subtract 0.4 − 0.02. Students should use the side of the MathBoard with the long bar, and keep the labeling of tenths, but wipe away the addition.

Using Models Have students circle 4 sections to show 4 tenths.

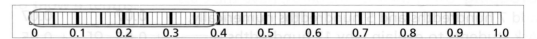

Now tell the class we want to subtract 2 hundredths from the 4 tenths, and ask them to explain how we can show the subtraction on the bar. *by circling 2 of the hundredths within the 4 tenths* Have them circle 2 hundredths and then use paper and pencil or their Secret Code Cards to subtract 0.02 from 0.4.

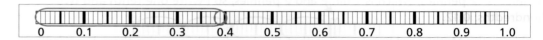

Ungrouping Discuss the methods that were used to subtract, including aligning like places, adding a zero, and ungrouping 1 tenth as 10 hundredths. Ask students to subtract 0.7 − 0.005 and discuss aligning, adding zeros, and ungrouping as they work.

Have students subtract 0.9 − 0.5 and 0.09 − 0.05. For all of these problems, students can use the MathBoard or think about dimes (tenths) or pennies (hundredths) as needed.

Extend to Thousandths Without using MathBoards, ask the class to subtract numbers that involve thousandths, such as 0.4 − 0.002, 0.04 − 0.002, 0.7 − 0.003, and 0.07 − 0.003.

Explain that thinking about dimes, pennies, and tenths of pennies can be helpful. Be sure that students use place value or money names when they explain ungrouping or subtracting (ten tenths minus two tenths, not ten minus two.)

▶ Mixed Practice [WHOLE CLASS]

Use **Solve and Discuss** at the board for these problems.

0.73 + 0.8	0.8 − 0.73	0.061 − 0.09
0.008 + 0.006	0.008 + 0.06	0.6 − 0.008

Relate Decimals and Metric Lengths

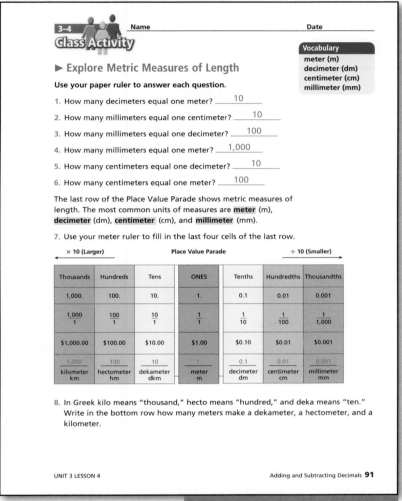

Student Activity Book page 91

The Student Activity Book page shows:

3-4 Class Activity — Name / Date

▶ Explore Metric Measures of Length

Vocabulary: meter (m), decimeter (dm), centimeter (cm), millimeter (mm)

Use your paper ruler to answer each question.

1. How many decimeters equal one meter? **10**
2. How many millimeters equal one centimeter? **10**
3. How many millimeters equal one decimeter? **100**
4. How many millimeters equal one meter? **1,000**
5. How many centimeters equal one decimeter? **10**
6. How many centimeters equal one meter? **100**

The last row of the Place Value Parade shows metric measures of length. The most common units of measures are **meter** (m), **decimeter** (dm), **centimeter** (cm), and **millimeter** (mm).

7. Use your meter ruler to fill in the last four cells of the last row.

× 10 (Larger) — Place Value Parade — ÷ 10 (Smaller)

Thousands	Hundreds	Tens	ONES	Tenths	Hundredths	Thousandths
1,000.	100.	10.	1.	0.1	0.01	0.001
$\frac{1,000}{1}$	$\frac{100}{1}$	$\frac{10}{1}$	$\frac{1}{1}$	$\frac{1}{10}$	$\frac{1}{100}$	$\frac{1}{1,000}$
$1,000.00	$100.00	$10.00	$1.00	$0.10	$0.01	$0.001
1,000 kilometer km	100 hectometer hm	10 dekameter dkm	1 meter m	0.1 decimeter dm	0.01 centimeter cm	0.001 millimeter mm

8. In Greek kilo means "thousand," hecto means "hundred," and deka means "ten." Write in the bottom row how many meters make a dekameter, a hectometer, and a kilometer.

▶ Explore Metric Measures of Length [WHOLE CLASS]

Have students cut on the dotted lines around the 4 parts of the meter stick. When they tape the parts together, they will need an overlap of 1 mm so there are only 10 mm in each taped section.

Ask for Ideas Invite students to find 1 dm, 1 cm, and 1 mm on their meter sticks, and then give them an opportunity to brainstorm about other words they know that are related to the prefixes: *deci* means "ten" decimal, decade; *centi* means "hundred" century; centipede; *milli* means "thousand" millennium, millipede.

As they work to complete exercises 1–7 on Student Book page 91, ask students to discuss the patterns they see in the Place Value Parade (especially those relating metric units to money and to place value relationships).

Activity continued ▶

20 MINUTES

Goal: Relate metric lengths and measure objects using metric units of length.

Materials: Student Activity Book pages 90A–92 or Hardcover Book pages 91–92 and Activity Workbook pp. 53–54, scissors, tape, Place Value Parade poster (optional)

✓ **NCTM Standards:**
Measurement
Representation

Differentiated Instruction

Extra Help Metric length can be a visual support for understanding tenths, hundredths, and thousandths. Using the metric names based on 1 meter (centimeter, decimeter, millimeter) can be challenging for some students. The Place Value Parade Poster will permit students to learn these lengths over time.

Meter Stick

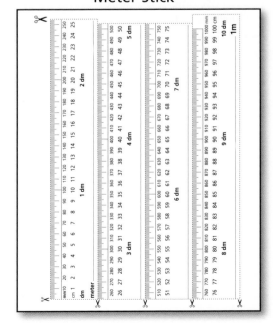

① Teaching the Lesson (continued)

Activity 2

Teaching Note

Language and Vocabulary Lead a discussion about ways to remember the meanings of the prefixes *deci, centi,* and *milli.*

There are 10 years in a *deca*de.

There are 10 *deci*meters in a meter.

There are 100 years in a *cent*ury.

There are 100 *centi*meters in a meter.

There are 1,000 years in a *mill*ennium.

There are 1,000 *milli*meters in a meter.

Differentiated Instruction

Advanced Learners Have students make a decameter by taping together 10 of their paper meters. The decameter strip can then be used to identify where to cut a string so that it is 1 decameter long, and also used to identify where to mark intervals of 1 meter on the string. The string can then be used to measure objects outside the classroom.

Quick Quiz

See Assessment Guide for Unit 3 Quick Quiz 1.

3–4
Class Activity

Name _____ Date _____

► **Measuring Real-World Objects**

Read each measurement below. Say the number of meters, decimeters, centimeters, and millimeters.

For example, 7.284 m is 7 meters, 2 decimeters, 8 centimeters, and 4 millimeters.

9. 7.284 m   10. 45.132 m   11. 29.16 m   12. 304 m   13. 16.02 m

14. Measure two objects in your classroom using a metric ruler.

_____

_____

15. Add the lengths of the two objects you measured.

_____

Write your own problems.

16. Write an addition word problem using the measurements in exercises 9 and 11.
Answers will vary.

_____

_____

_____

_____

17. Write a subtraction word problem using the measurements in exercises 10 and 12.
Answers will vary.

_____

_____

_____

_____

92 UNIT 3 LESSON 4   Adding and Subtracting Decimals

Student Activity Book page 92

► Explore Metric Measures of Length PAIRS

For exercises 9–13 on page 92, have students read the units aloud.

Choose Appropriate Units Ask **Student Pairs** to name the metric unit they would use to measure the length of the classroom (m), the length of a thumb (cm), the height of a desk (dm), and the width of a pen (mm). Then have them actually measure the objects.

Estimate Measurements Ask each student to choose an object, estimate its length, and record the estimate. Then ask them to measure the actual length and compare it to the estimate.

After students complete exercises 14–17, ask them to discuss how the metric system relates to our system of place value. In each system, the value of the units are × 10 as you move left and ÷ 10 as you move right.

②Going Further

Intervention   Activity Card 3-4

Subtract Decimals Using a Place-Value Chart   Activity Card 3-4 ●

Work: In Pairs

Use:
• Grid paper

tens	ones		tenths	hundredths	thousandths
	4	.	8	7	0
	3	.	4	6	2
	1	.	4	0	8

1. The example shows how to use a place-value chart to subtract decimals.

2. **Math Talk** Why are there more zeros in the answer than in the number that was subtracted from?

3. **Work Together** Make a place-value chart like the one shown. Use it to solve each subtraction problem below.

3.1 − 0.67 2.43   2.754 − 1.423 1.331   6 − 0.86 5.14

4.225 − 1.6 2.625 9.75 − 3.69 6.06   8.105 − 4.31 3.795

2. Possible answer: You need a placeholder in the thousandths place of 4.87 so you can subtract thousandths.

Unit 3, Lesson 4   Copyright © Houghton Mifflin Company

Activity Note Remind students to use zeros as placeholders as needed. Have them record each step in the subtraction to show ungrouping, as they have done with whole numbers.

 Math Writing Prompt

Explain Your Thinking What strategies have you found that help you to subtract decimal numbers? Explain why your strategies are helpful.

 **Software Support**

Warm-Up 22.35

On Level   Activity Card 3-4

Solve Problems with Decimals   Activity Card 3-4 ▲

Work: In Pairs

1. Make a drawing to represent each problem. Then work together to solve each problem.

> • Reggie measured two pieces of string. The blue piece was 8.35 centimeters long. The red piece was 9.2 centimeters long. How much longer was the red piece of string? Drawings will vary; 0.85 cm longer
>
> • One diamond weighs 1.856 karats and another weighs 0.98 karats. How much more does the first diamond weigh? Drawings will vary; 0.876 karats more

2. **On Your Own** Write and solve two problems that require subtracting decimals to thousandths. Exchange with your partner to check your answers.

Unit 3, Lesson 4   Copyright © Houghton Mifflin Company

Activity Note Check that students are correctly interpreting the problems and drawing appropriate diagrams to model subtraction. Also check that students are aligning digits correctly for subtraction.

 Math Writing Prompt

Real-World Experience Describe two situations in which you would subtract decimal numbers. Write about why you would need to subtract.

 Software Support

The Number Games: Tiny's Think Tank, Level L

Challenge   Activity Card 3-4

Find the Missing Decimal Number   Activity Card 3-4 ■

Work: In Pairs

Use:
• MathBoard materials

1. Copy the missing number problems below onto your MathBoard.

8.195	8.195
− 4.32	− 0.852

2. **Work Together** Find the missing numbers. 3.875; 7.343

3. By yourself, write three missing number problems on your MathBoard. Exchange boards with your partner to solve.

Unit 3, Lesson 4   Copyright © Houghton Mifflin Company

Activity Note Remind students of the number properties that allow them to subtract the difference to find each missing number. Check to see that students are aligning digits properly.

 Math Writing Prompt

Apply How can addition help you check the answer to a decimal subtraction problem? Explain. Include an example.

 **Software Support**

Course III: Module 4: Unit 2: Subtracting Decimals

③ Homework and Spiral Review

Homework **Goal:** Additional Practice

✓ Include student's Homework for page 53 as a part of their portfolios.

Remembering **Goal:** Spiral Review

This Remembering activity would be appropriate anytime after today's lesson.

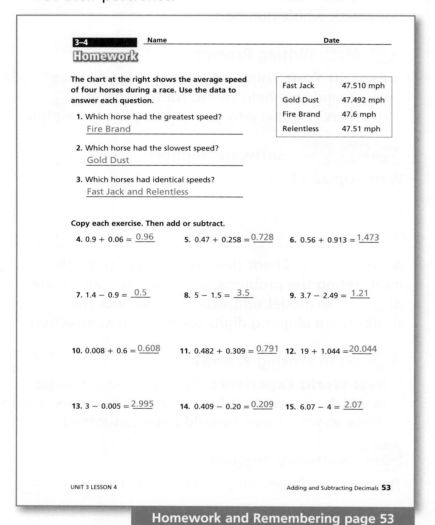

3-4 Name _____ Date _____
Homework

The chart at the right shows the average speed of four horses during a race. Use the data to answer each question.

Fast Jack	47.510 mph
Gold Dust	47.492 mph
Fire Brand	47.6 mph
Relentless	47.51 mph

1. Which horse had the greatest speed?
   Fire Brand

2. Which horse had the slowest speed?
   Gold Dust

3. Which horses had identical speeds?
   Fast Jack and Relentless

Copy each exercise. Then add or subtract.

4. $0.9 + 0.06 = \underline{0.96}$ 5. $0.47 + 0.258 = \underline{0.728}$ 6. $0.56 + 0.913 = \underline{1.473}$

7. $1.4 - 0.9 = \underline{0.5}$ 8. $5 - 1.5 = \underline{3.5}$ 9. $3.7 - 2.49 = \underline{1.21}$

10. $0.008 + 0.6 = \underline{0.608}$ 11. $0.482 + 0.309 = \underline{0.791}$ 12. $19 + 1.044 = \underline{20.044}$

13. $3 - 0.005 = \underline{2.995}$ 14. $0.409 - 0.20 = \underline{0.209}$ 15. $6.07 - 4 = \underline{2.07}$

UNIT 3 LESSON 4   Adding and Subtracting Decimals **53**

Homework and Remembering page 53

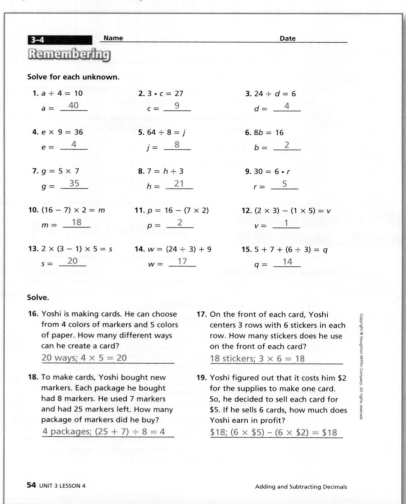

3-4 Name _____ Date _____
Remembering

Solve for each unknown.

1. $a \div 4 = 10$
   $a = \underline{40}$

2. $3 \cdot c = 27$
   $c = \underline{9}$

3. $24 \div d = 6$
   $d = \underline{4}$

4. $e \times 9 = 36$
   $e = \underline{4}$

5. $64 \div 8 = j$
   $j = \underline{8}$

6. $8b = 16$
   $b = \underline{2}$

7. $g = 5 \times 7$
   $g = \underline{35}$

8. $7 = h \div 3$
   $h = \underline{21}$

9. $30 = 6 \cdot r$
   $r = \underline{5}$

10. $(16 - 7) \times 2 = m$
    $m = \underline{18}$

11. $p = 16 - (7 \times 2)$
    $p = \underline{2}$

12. $(2 \times 3) - (1 \times 5) = v$
    $v = \underline{1}$

13. $2 \times (3 - 1) \times 5 = s$
    $s = \underline{20}$

14. $w = (24 \div 3) + 9$
    $w = \underline{17}$

15. $5 + 7 + (6 \div 3) = q$
    $q = \underline{14}$

Solve.

16. Yoshi is making cards. He can choose from 4 colors of markers and 5 colors of paper. How many different ways can he create a card?
    20 ways; $4 \times 5 = 20$

17. On the front of each card, Yoshi centers 3 rows with 6 stickers in each row. How many stickers does he use on the front of each card?
    18 stickers; $3 \times 6 = 18$

18. To make cards, Yoshi bought new markers. Each package he bought had 8 markers. He used 7 markers and had 25 markers left. How many package of markers did he buy?
    4 packages; $(25 + 7) \div 8 = 4$

19. Yoshi figured out that it costs him $2 for the supplies to make one card. So, he decided to sell each card for $5. If he sells 6 cards, how much does Yoshi earn in profit?
    $18; $(6 \times \$5) - (6 \times \$2) = \$18$

54 UNIT 3 LESSON 4   Adding and Subtracting Decimals

Homework and Remembering page 54

Home or School Activity

 Language Arts Connection

Metric Prefixes A *prefix* is added to the beginning of a root word that changes its meaning. In the metric system, all the units of length have a prefix added to the root word *meter*. So, if you know the meaning of the prefix, you also know the meaning of the unit. For example, *kilo–* means "one thousand," so *kilometer* means "one thousand meters."

Have students find words in a dictionary that use the metric prefixes shown in the table at right. Have them write the meanings of the words they find.

Prefix	Meaning
kilo-	one thousand
hecto-	one hundred
deka-	ten
deci-	one tenth
centi-	one hundredth
milli-	one thousandth

Billions to Billionths

Lesson Objectives

- Recognize place values from billions to billionths.
- Read, write, compare, and order very large numbers.
- Represent numbers in different ways.

Vocabulary

standard form
word form
short word form
expanded form

The Day at a Glance

Today's Goals	Materials

1 Teaching the Lesson
- **A1:** Model whole numbers in millions and billions.
- **A2:** Recognize place values from billions to billionths.
- **A3:** Compare and order large numbers; represent numbers in different ways.

2 Going Further
- ► Extension: Different Systems of Numeration
- ► Differentiated Instruction

3 Homework and Spiral Review

Lesson Activities
Student Activity Book pp. 93–97, or
Hardcover Book pp. 93, 95–97 and
Activity Workbook pp. 55–59
Homework and Remembering
pp. 55–56
Secret Code Cards from previous lessons
Scissors
Tape

Going Further
Student Activity Book
p. 98 or Hardcover
Book p. 98
Activity Cards 3-5
Index cards
Paper clips
MathBoard materials
Math Journals

123 Use **Math Talk** today!

Keeping Skills Sharp

Quick Practice 🕐 5 MINUTES	Daily Routines

Goal: Continue practice with decimals and metric lengths.

Read Decimal Numbers Have a **Student Leader** write four decimal numbers on the board. (No number should be smaller than thousandths.) The leader points to each and says it aloud, omitting the place value name. The class says the place value name, emphasizing the *–ths* at the end. For example, the leader writes 0.32 and says "thirty-two." The class says "hundredths."

Metric Lengths The student leader writes a metric length abbreviation on the board (m, dm, cm, or mm). The students say the name of the unit and show the approximate length with their hands. Repeat in random order.

Homework Review As you circulate during Quick Practice, see whether any problem caused difficulty for many students.

Algebra Write the rule for each given function table below.

Input	2	4	7	8	10
Output	3	7	13	15	19

Output = Input × 2 − 1

Input	3	5	6	8	10
Output	13	21	25	33	41

Output = Input × 4 + 1

Teaching the Lesson

Reading Large Numbers

 45 MINUTES

Goal: Model whole numbers in millions and billions.

Materials: Student Activity Book p. 93 or Hardcover Book p. 93 and Activity Workbook p. 55, Secret Code Cards

✓ **NCTM Standards:**
Number and Operations
Representation

Differentiated Instruction

Advanced Learners Students can make up riddles and use Secret Code Cards to solve the riddles. For example, "I'm thinking of a number that is greater than one billion, but less than one billion, two hundred fifty million." Other students build numbers to satisfy the criteria.

Teaching Note

Math Background Each group of 3 digits in a number is usually called a *period*. In this lesson, students learn about the thousands period, the millions period, and the billions period, although they will not be asked to use the term.

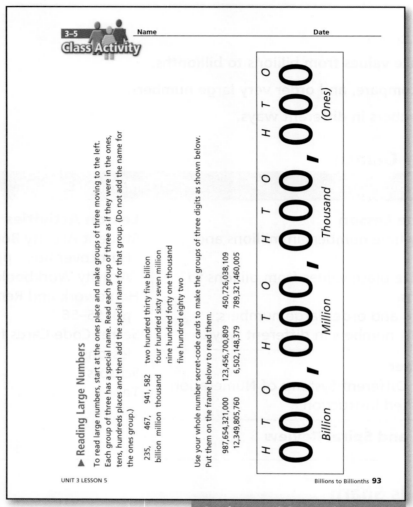

Student Activity Book page 93

▶ Build Numbers with Secret Code Cards WHOLE CLASS

Ask for Ideas Give students an opportunity to share what they know about saying or writing numbers that are larger than one thousand. If these numbers are not new to them, complete this lesson as a quick review and an opportunity for students to articulate patterns that can be seen in the numbers.

If students can benefit from more experience with larger numbers, emphasize the patterns that are present as you complete this lesson, and also provide plenty of practice so that the patterns can be applied. (Students will get more practice in Lesson 6 and in the Quick Practices in Lessons 7, 8, and 9), so complete mastery of these skills is not the goal of today's activities.)

Reading Numbers Use the top of Student Book page 93 to summarize or introduce reading large numbers. Make sure students can recognize the patterns for the example. (We are saying hundreds, tens, and ones for the billions, as well as for the millions, thousands, and ones; we do not say the grouping word for ones).

Have students use their Secret Code Cards to make numbers on the frame for at least three of the numbers on page 93. Encourage students to have fun reading the numbers by saying the group names (*billion, million,* and *thousand*) loudly (or softly) for emphasis. Have students describe issues with zeros as they arise in the examples.

Using Zeros Write the following examples on the board, and have 2 or 3 different **Student Leaders** lead the class in saying the numbers aloud.

105,000,006	520,000,000,000
6,000,000	19,070,000
20,020,020,020	38,038,038,038
5,005,005,005	900,800,700,600

Math Talk Have students summarize issues and patterns related to zeros. Be sure to discuss these ideas:

- Although there are three digits between commas (e.g., the hundreds, tens, and ones numbers), there may not be three numbers to say.

- Any of the hundreds, tens, or ones numbers can be zero.

- Remember not to say *and* when there is a zero. (For example, 809 is not said as *eight hundred and nine* because the word "*and*" represents a decimal point.)

- We do not have to write zeros to the left of the first non-zero digit in a number; we just begin with the first non-zero digit. (For example, 35,000,000 is not 035,000,000.) But we must write zeros in places between the first digit and the digit in the ones place so that every digit in a number is in its correct place.

Activity 2

Symmetry Around the Ones Place

 30 MINUTES

Goal: Recognize place values from billions to billionths.

Materials: Student Activity Book pp. 94A–95 or Student Hardcover Book page 95 and Activity Workbook pp. 57–59, scissors, tape

 NCTM Standards:
Number and Operations
Representation

▶ Patterns from Billions to Billionths [WHOLE CLASS]

Direct students to cut out and tape together the Patterns from Billions to Billionths chart. Students should cut (or fold and tear) the page in half horizontally, place the ONES columns on top of each other, and tape the two parts together. Then have them:

● circle the words *thousands, millions,* and *billions*.

● find and circle *thousandths* and describe the relationship between the *thousands* and *thousandths* positions. each is 3 places from the ONES place

● find and circle *millionths* and describe the relationship between the *millions* and *millionths* positions each is 6 places from the ONES place

● find and circle *billionths* and describe the relationship between the *billions* and *billionths* positions each is 9 places from the ONES place

● describe the relationships between the numbers of zeros in the whole number, in the fraction denominator, and in the decimal for a position. The number of zeros is the same for the whole number and for the fraction because the fraction denominator tells the number of equal parts; the number of zeros in the decimal number is one less because there is no *oneths* place. (However, if we include the 0 in the ones place when writing the decimal number, then the number of zeros is the same.

Patterns From Billions to Billionths

billions	hundred millions	ten millions	millions	hundred thousands	ten thousands	thousands	hundred	tens	ONES	tenths	hundredths	thousandths	ten thousandths	hundred thousandths	millionths	ten millionths	hundred millionths	billionths
1,000,000,000	100,000,000	10,000,000	1,000,000	100,000	10,000	1,000	100	10	1	0.1	0.01	0.001	0.0001	0.00001	0.000001	0.0000001	0.00000001	0.000000001
										$\frac{1}{10}$	$\frac{1}{100}$	$\frac{1}{1,000}$	$\frac{1}{10,000}$	$\frac{1}{100,000}$	$\frac{1}{1,000,000}$	$\frac{1}{10,000,000}$	$\frac{1}{100,000,000}$	$\frac{1}{1,000,000,000}$

(123) **Math Talk** Discuss direction by asking students to name the direction in which the places are getting larger and getting smaller. larger: going to the left; smaller: going to the right

Generalize Discuss how regrouping and ungrouping in a place is related to the adjacent place. For example, how many tens make a hundred? How many hundreds make a ten? Have students discuss and state a general rule that describes these regrouping and ungrouping relationships. 10 of any place make 1 in the place to the left (the next larger place), and 1 in any place makes 10 in the place to the right (the next smaller place). Make sure students recognize that these relationships are true both to the left and to the right of the decimal point. (These consistent relationships make our number system a base-ten system.)

Compare Write the numbers shown below on the board. Have students say the numbers and discuss how to decide which number is largest and which number is smallest, and then explain how the remaining numbers compare to those two numbers. (Make sure they understand that the zero written in the ones place of the decimal number 0.36 is not considered when comparing because its only value is as a placeholder to help ensure that the decimal point is not overlooked.)

45.089   2,000,650   5.689   0.36

This consistency makes the system a base-ten system. Explain this to students because we did not define the new places in Activity 1; we just explained how we read large numbers. These same relationships apply no matter how many places to the left or to the right we go.

Research If time permits during school hours, encourage interested students to do Internet-related research to find situations in the real world where very large and very small numbers are used. (They can use this information to write and solve word problems and share them with the class.)

Activity continued ▶

Teaching Note

Infinite Ask students to name the word that means that numbers go on and on getting bigger and bigger, or on and on getting smaller and smaller. Infinite; numbers can get infinitely larger or smaller. We do not have names for all of the places in such a number, but it is important for students to generalize that for any number, we can write a different number that is larger or smaller.

Activity 2

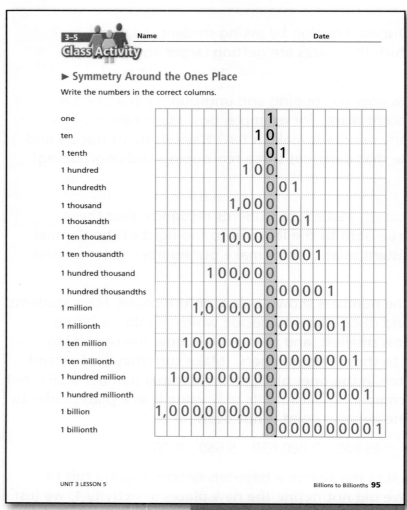

Student Activity Book page 95

▶ Symmetry Around the Ones Place   WHOLE CLASS

Have students discuss the patterns they see in the three numbers on Student Book page 95. Then ask **Student Pairs** to work together to complete the remainder of the chart, discussing the pattern for each related pair of numbers (such as 1 hundred and 1 hundredth, 1 thousand and 1 thousandth, and so on) as they work.

Make sure they write a zero in the ones place of each decimal number so that the number of zeros will be the same for each pair. Also make sure they write commas whenever appropriate to the left of a decimal point, and recognize that commas are not used to the right of a decimal point.

The Learning Classroom

Student Pairs Initially, it is useful to model pair activities for students by contrasting effective and ineffective helping. For example, students need to help partners solve a problem their way, rather than doing the work for the partner. Helping pairs often foster learning in both students as the helper strives to adopt the perspective of the novice.

Summary The numbers from billions to billionths in Activities 1 and 2 gave students an opportunity to see that our base-ten number system is symmetric around the ones place, and continues infinitely in both directions. Since decimal numbers to some of the lesser places such as millionths and billionths are not common, our work with decimal numbers in this text is through thousandths, which provides a sufficient understanding for common real-world situations.

These important concepts were also highlighted in Activities 1 and 2:

- Whole numbers and decimal numbers have related place value names that are alike except for the *–th* at the end of the decimal number places (which show that they are equal small parts of one whole).

- Related whole number and decimal places have the same number of zeroes if we include the 0 in the ones place of the decimal numbers. The decimal places are, however, one place closer to the decimal point than are the whole number places because the *ones* place is in the whole numbers and there is no matching *oneths* decimal place (because one divided into ten equal parts makes *tenths*, the name of the first decimal place).

- Whole number and decimal places get smaller and smaller as they go to the right and larger and larger as they go to the left.

- All places are related by the same regrouping and ungrouping rules: 10 of any place make 1 in the place to the left (the next larger place), and 1 in any place makes 10 in the place to the right (the next smaller place).

- Whole numbers and decimals are alike in that neither are read by naming all of the place values. But they are different in how they are read. Whole numbers have groups of three that are read and then named with their special name (*billion, million,* and/or *thousand*). Decimal numbers are read as if they are whole numbers and then the name of the last place value is read to tell the name of the unit fraction for the decimal number.

 Ongoing Assessment

What is the largest and smallest place value in each number?

► 2,395

► 87,461

► 0.976

► 1.28

► 329.5

► 604,302

► 7,550,809

The Learning Classroom

Building Concepts To support building coherence, remember to have students summarize. Have students take turns summarizing the previous day's lesson at the beginning of math class. They can just say one or two sentences. Students do this in Japanese elementary school classes. An alternative may be to have a student summarize at the end of the lesson. Either way, if you do this regularly, students will get used to making mental summaries of the math concepts discussed and making conceptual connections.

Teaching the Lesson (continued)

Activity 3

Compare and Order Large Numbers

 30 MINUTES

Goal: Compare and order large numbers; represent numbers in different ways.

Materials: Student Activity Book pp. 96–97 or Hardcover Book pp. 96–97

NCTM Standards:
Number and Operations
Representation
Problem Solving

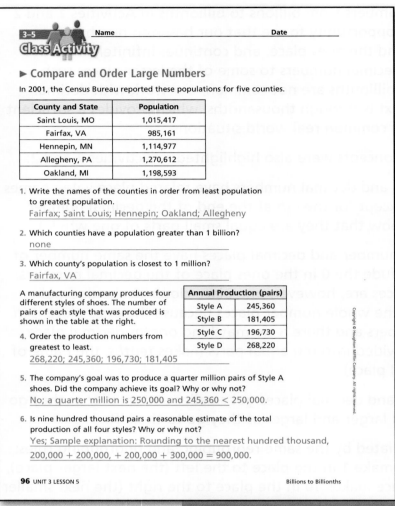

> 3–5
> **Class Activity**
>
> Name _____ Date _____
>
> ► **Compare and Order Large Numbers**
>
> In 2001, the Census Bureau reported these populations for five counties.
>
> | County and State | Population |
> |---|---|
> | Saint Louis, MO | 1,015,417 |
> | Fairfax, VA | 985,161 |
> | Hennepin, MN | 1,114,977 |
> | Allegheny, PA | 1,270,612 |
> | Oakland, MI | 1,198,593 |
>
> 1. Write the names of the counties in order from least population to greatest population.
>   Fairfax; Saint Louis; Hennepin; Oakland; Allegheny
>
> 2. Which counties have a population greater than 1 billion?
>   none
>
> 3. Which county's population is closest to 1 million?
>   Fairfax, VA
>
> A manufacturing company produces four different styles of shoes. The number of pairs of each style that was produced is shown in the table at the right.
>
> | Annual Production (pairs) | |
> |---|---|
> | Style A | 245,360 |
> | Style B | 181,405 |
> | Style C | 196,730 |
> | Style D | 268,220 |
>
> 4. Order the production numbers from greatest to least.
>   268,220; 245,360; 196,730; 181,405
>
> 5. The company's goal was to produce a quarter million pairs of Style A shoes. Did the company achieve its goal? Why or why not?
>   No; a quarter million is 250,000 and 245,360 < 250,000.
>
> 6. Is nine hundred thousand pairs a reasonable estimate of the total production of all four styles? Why or why not?
>   Yes; Sample explanation: Rounding to the nearest hundred thousand,
>   200,000 + 200,000, + 200,000 + 300,000 = 900,000.
>
> **96** UNIT 3 LESSON 5   Billions to Billionths

Student Activity Book page 96

► Act It Out | WHOLE CLASS

Introduce the activity by inviting five volunteers to each write a number in hundred thousands on a sheet of paper. The students then work together to determine the order of the numbers from least to greatest and stand at the front of the classroom and display the numbers in that order. Ask the seated students to confirm that the order is correct, and then ask a student to write the numbers on the board using the > and < comparison symbols. Repeat the activity twice—once for numbers in millions and once for numbers in billions. During one or both activities, change the order to greatest to least. (All students should have a turn at writing a number and standing at the front of the room.)

Have **Student Pairs** work together to complete exercises 1–6 on Student Book page 96.

The Learning Classroom

Scenario The main purpose of a scenario is to demonstrate mathematical relationships in a visual and memorable way. A group of students is called to the front of the room to act out a situation. Because of its active and dramatic nature, the scenario structure fosters a sense of intense involvement among children. Scenarios create meaningful contexts in which students relate math to their everyday lives.

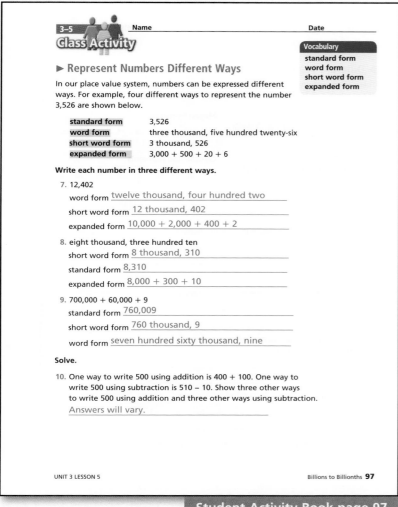

Name _____   Date _____

Vocabulary
standard form
word form
short word form
expanded form

▶ **Represent Numbers Different Ways**

In our place value system, numbers can be expressed different ways. For example, four different ways to represent the number 3,526 are shown below.

standard form	3,526
word form	three thousand, five hundred twenty-six
short word form	3 thousand, 526
expanded form	3,000 + 500 + 20 + 6

Write each number in three different ways.

7. 12,402
   word form _twelve thousand, four hundred two_
   short word form _12 thousand, 402_
   expanded form _10,000 + 2,000 + 400 + 2_

8. eight thousand, three hundred ten
   short word form _8 thousand, 310_
   standard form _8,310_
   expanded form _8,000 + 300 + 10_

9. 700,000 + 60,000 + 9
   standard form _760,009_
   short word form _760 thousand, 9_
   word form _seven hundred sixty thousand, nine_

Solve.

10. One way to write 500 using addition is 400 + 100. One way to write 500 using subtraction is 510 − 10. Show three other ways to write 500 using addition and three other ways using subtraction.
    Answers will vary.

Student Activity Book page 97

▶ Represent Numbers in Different Ways WHOLE CLASS

Ask for Ideas Give students an opportunity to discuss and describe different ways to write the same number. Make sure the discussion includes these forms for representing numbers:

2 million, 300 thousand (short word form)

2,300,000 (standard form)

2,000,000 + 300,000 (expanded from)

two million, three hundred thousand (word form)

2,100,000 + 200,000 = 2,300,000 (addition)

3,000,000 − 700,000 = 2,300,000 (subtraction)

Direct students to work individually or paired with a **Helping Partner** to complete exercises 7–10 on Student Book page 97.

Teaching Note

Math Background Expanded form can also be written as the sum of the product of each non-zero digit and a power of 10.

$1 \times 10^0 = 1$

$1 \times 10^1 = 10$

$1 \times 10^2 = 100$

$1 \times 10^3 = 1,000$

$1 \times 10^4 = 10,000$

$1 \times 10^5 = 100,000$

$1 \times 10^6 = 1,000,000$

$1 \times 10^7 = 10,000,000$

$1 \times 10^8 = 100,000,000$

$1 \times 10^9 = 1,000,000,000$

For example, the expanded form of 2,975 is $(2 \times 10^3) + (9 \times 10^2) + (7 \times 10^1) + (5 \times 10^0)$ which is the same as $(2 \times 1,000) + (9 \times 100) + (7 \times 10) + (5 \times 1)$.

At this grade level, we write the expanded form as 2,000 + 900 + 70 + 5.

Teaching Note

Ways to Write Numbers In this activity, students express a number in different ways. Discuss how there are an infinite number of ways to write a number when you include one or more operations in the expression. For example, here are six of the many ways to express 25.

20 + 5	19 + 6
30 − 5	5 × 5
100 ÷ 4	24.5 + 0.5

Going Further

Extension: Different Systems of Numeration

Goal: Write numbers using different systems of numeration.

Materials: Student Activity Book or Hardcover Book p. 98

✔ **NCTM Standards:**
Communication
Representation

▶ Different Systems of Numeration

WHOLE CLASS

Write this list on the board:

Basketball

Baseball

Hockey

Soccer

Other

Ask students to raise their hand to show their favorite sport to play. Have a volunteer record the numbers of hands raised for each sport on the list using tally marks.

Explain that many groups of people have developed ways of writing numbers, and that several of these systems were based on keeping score of something with tally marks. People would mark short line segments on wood or in the sand. These marks gradually became grouped in different ways, and became more complex symbols of numbers.

Lead a discussion about where we see Roman numerals today.

• on buildings, indicating when they were built

• on film credits, indicating when the film was made

• clock faces

• outlines for an article or book

• introductory pages of a book

• sporting events, such as the Olympics or Super Bowl

• successive generations, such as James Smith III

3–5
Going Further

▶ **Different Systems of Numeration**

There are many systems for writing numbers.
The numbers 1 to 10 are shown below using five different systems.

Tally System

Mayan Numerals

Grouped Tally System

Chinese Rod Numerals

Roman Numerals
I II III IV V VI VII VIII IX X

1. List some similarities you see in the number systems.
   Answers may vary. Possible answer: The numbers are grouped to make them easier to count. Some systems use lines and some use dots.

2. List some differences you see in the number systems.
   Answers may vary.

3. How might the symbol for 5 in the Roman system have come from a picture of a hand?
   Answers may vary. Possible answer: The 'V' is wide at the top and narrow at the bottom, like a hand.

4. What might the Roman symbol for 10 come from?
   Answers may vary. Possible answer: The X is made of two Vs, which are 5s, so 5 + 5 = 10.

5. **Math Journal** Write an addition or subtraction equation using one set of symbols.
   Answers may vary. Possible answer: V + III = VIII.

98 UNIT 3 LESSON 5   Billions to Billionths

Student Activity Book page 98

Have students look at the different number systems shown on Student Book page 98. Discuss where they see the influence of tally marks.

What other patterns do they see?

Have students work in pairs to answer questions 1–5. Discuss students' answers as a class.

Differentiated Instruction

Advanced Learners Some students may be interested in conducting research to find how these groups of people represented numbers greater than 10, or to find number systems developed by other groups of people. If possible, provide resources for them to use, and set aside some time for them to share what they learn with the class.

Differentiated Instruction

Intervention — Activity Card 3-5

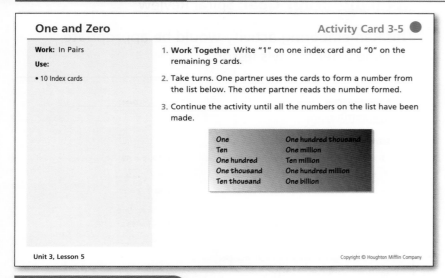

One and Zero   Activity Card 3-5

Work: In Pairs
Use:
• 10 Index cards

1. **Work Together** Write "1" on one index card and "0" on the remaining 9 cards.

2. Take turns. One partner uses the cards to form a number from the list below. The other partner reads the number formed.

3. Continue the activity until all the numbers on the list have been made.

One	One hundred thousand
Ten	One million
One hundred	Ten million
One thousand	One hundred million
Ten thousand	One billion

Unit 3, Lesson 5   Copyright © Houghton Mifflin Company

Activity Note After students have completed the activity, discuss with them any patterns that they used to help them form and name the numbers.

Math Writing Prompt

Explain Number Names When you add the sound *–ths* to the end of the word *million*, how does it change its meaning?

 **Software Support**

Warm-Up 2.19

On Level — Activity Card 3-5

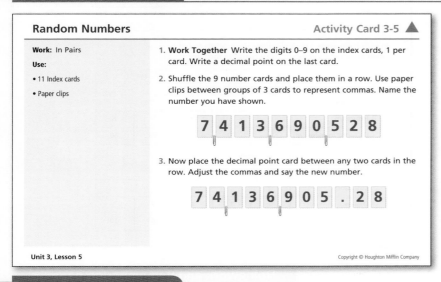

Random Numbers   Activity Card 3-5

Work: In Pairs
Use:
• 11 Index cards
• Paper clips

1. **Work Together** Write the digits 0–9 on the index cards, 1 per card. Write a decimal point on the last card.

2. Shuffle the 9 number cards and place them in a row. Use paper clips between groups of 3 cards to represent commas. Name the number you have shown.

7 4 1 3 6 9 0 5 2 8

3. Now place the decimal point card between any two cards in the row. Adjust the commas and say the new number.

7 4 1 3 6 9 0 5 . 2 8

Unit 3, Lesson 5   Copyright © Houghton Mifflin Company

Activity Note Remind students to count by 3s from right to left, beginning with the decimal point, when placing the commas within a number.

Math Writing Prompt

Explain Your Thinking When you write a number, how is inserting a comma different from inserting a decimal point?

 Software Support

The Number Games: Tiny's Think Tank, Level A

Challenge — Activity Card 3-5

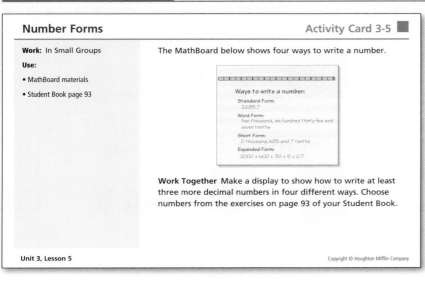

Number Forms   Activity Card 3-5

Work: In Small Groups
Use:
• MathBoard materials
• Student Book page 93

The MathBoard below shows four ways to write a number.

Ways to write a number:
Standard Form:
2,635.7
Word Form:
two thousand, six hundred thirty-five and seven tenths
Short Form:
2 thousand, 635 and 7 tenths
Expanded Form:
2000 + 600 + 30 + 5 + 0.7

Work Together Make a display to show how to write at least three more decimal numbers in four different ways. Choose numbers from the exercises on page 93 of your Student Book.

Unit 3, Lesson 5   Copyright © Houghton Mifflin Company

Activity Note Encourage students to include both decimal and whole numbers in their display. Discuss any patterns that students observe among the four number forms.

Math Writing Prompt

How Many Bills? How many $1-bills equal one million dollars? How many $10-bills? How many $100-bills? How many $1,000-bills?

 **Software Support**

Course III: Module 4: Unit 1: Tenths, Hundredths, and Thousandths

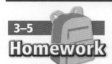 **Homework and Spiral Review**

3-5 Homework **Goal:** Additional Practice

Use this Homework page to provide more practice with numbers from billions to billionths.

3-5 Remembering **Goal:** Spiral Review

This Remembering activity would be appropriate anytime after today's lesson.

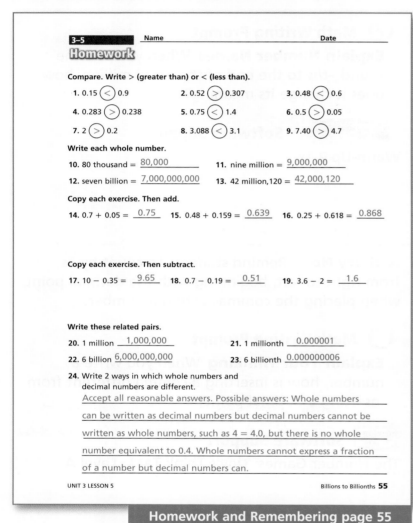

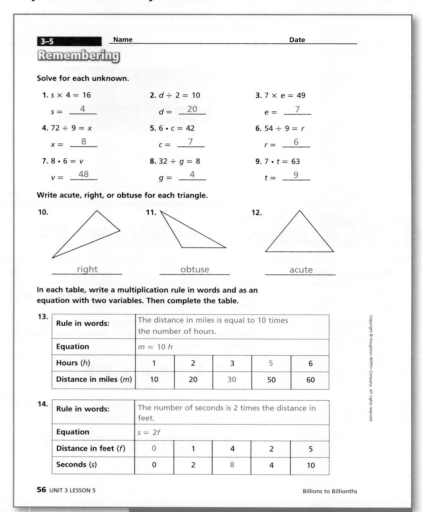

3-5 Name _____ Date _____
Homework

Compare. Write > (greater than) or < (less than).

1. 0.15 (<) 0.9   2. 0.52 (>) 0.307   3. 0.48 (<) 0.6

4. 0.283 (>) 0.238   5. 0.75 (<) 1.4   6. 0.5 (>) 0.05

7. 2 (>) 0.2   8. 3.088 (<) 3.1   9. 7.40 (>) 4.7

Write each whole number.

10. 80 thousand = 80,000   11. nine million = 9,000,000

12. seven billion = 7,000,000,000   13. 42 million,120 = 42,000,120

Copy each exercise. Then add.

14. 0.7 + 0.05 = 0.75   15. 0.48 + 0.159 = 0.639   16. 0.25 + 0.618 = 0.868

Copy each exercise. Then subtract.

17. 10 − 0.35 = 9.65   18. 0.7 − 0.19 = 0.51   19. 3.6 − 2 = 1.6

Write these related pairs.

20. 1 million 1,000,000   21. 1 millionth 0.000001

22. 6 billion 6,000,000,000   23. 6 billionth 0.000000006

24. Write 2 ways in which whole numbers and decimal numbers are different.
Accept all reasonable answers. Possible answers: Whole numbers
can be written as decimal numbers but decimal numbers cannot be
written as whole numbers, such as 4 = 4.0, but there is no whole
number equivalent to 0.4. Whole numbers cannot express a fraction
of a number but decimal numbers can.

UNIT 3 LESSON 5   Billions to Billionths **55**

3-5 Name _____ Date _____
Remembering

Solve for each unknown.

1. $s \times 4 = 16$ 2. $d \div 2 = 10$ 3. $7 \times e = 49$
$s = \underline{4}$ $d = \underline{20}$ $e = \underline{7}$

4. $72 \div 9 = x$ 5. $6 \cdot c = 42$ 6. $54 \div 9 = r$
$x = \underline{8}$ $c = \underline{7}$ $r = \underline{6}$

7. $8 \cdot 6 = v$ 8. $32 \div g = 8$ 9. $7 \cdot t = 63$
$v = \underline{48}$ $g = \underline{4}$ $t = \underline{9}$

Write acute, right, or obtuse for each triangle.

10.   11.   12.

___right___   ___obtuse___   ___acute___

In each table, write a multiplication rule in words and as an equation with two variables. Then complete the table.

13.
Rule in words:	The distance in miles is equal to 10 times the number of hours.				
Equation	$m = 10h$				
Hours (h)	1	2	3	5	6
Distance in miles (m)	10	20	30	50	60

14.
Rule in words:	The number of seconds is 2 times the distance in feet.				
Equation	$s = 2f$				
Distance in feet (f)	0	1	4	2	5
Seconds (s)	0	2	8	4	10

56 UNIT 3 LESSON 5   Billions to Billionths

Homework and Remembering page 55

Homework and Remembering page 56

Home or School Activity

 Social Studies Connection

Commas or Dots? Your students will find it interesting that in many other countries dots are used as we use commas—as separators in whole numbers, and commas are used as we use dots—as decimal points. Invite students to research this topic. Ask them to choose five countries and find out how people in those countries use commas and dots in numbers.

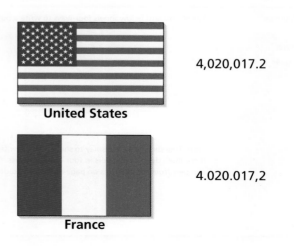

4,020,017.2

United States

4.020.017,2

France

Use Place Value

Lesson Objectives

- Make the greatest and the least possible numbers using a given set of numbers.

- Recognize relationships among place values to billions.

The Day at a Glance

Today's Goals	Materials

1 Teaching the Lesson
A1: Use place value concepts to increase or decrease numbers.
A2: Use a dot array to visualize large and small numbers.
 	
2 Going Further
▶ Math Connection: Reasoning and Proof
▶ Differentiated Instruction
 	
3 Homework and Spiral Review
	Lesson Activities
	Student Activity Book pp. 99–100
	  or Student Hardcover Book
	  pp. 99–100
	Homework and Remembering
	  pp. 57–58
	Pointer
	Quick Quiz 2 (Assessment Guide)
	
	Going Further
	Activity Cards 3-6
	Calculators
	Number cubes
	MathBoard materials
	Math Journals

123 Use Math Talk today!

Keeping Skills Sharp

Quick Practice ⏱ 5 MINUTES

Goal: Practice saying decimal and metric lengths.

Read Decimal Numbers Have a **Student Leader** write four decimal numbers on the board. The leader points to each and says it aloud, omitting the place value name. The class says the place value name. (No number should be smaller than thousandths.) For example, the leader writes 0.81 and says "eighty-one." The class says "hundredths."

Metric Lengths The **Student Leader** writes a metric length abbreviation on the board (m, dm, cm, or mm). The students say the name of the unit and show the approximate length with their hands. Repeat in random order.

Daily Routines

Homework Review Have students explain how they found their answers and look for any errors.

Elapsed Time Wilson attended a seminar that started at 8:30 A.M. The schedule of events is shown below.

Seminar Schedule	
Welcome	15 min
First Meeting	2 hr 25 min
Second Meeting	2 hr 35 min
Workshop	1 hr 20 min
Finale	25 min

At what time did the seminar end? 3:30 P.M.

Teaching the Lesson

Apply Place Value Concepts

 35 MINUTES

Goal: Use place value concepts to increase or decrease numbers.

Materials: Student Activity Book or Hardcover Book p. 99

✓ **NCTM Standards:**
Number and Operations
Communication

Teaching Note

Language and Vocabulary
The word *digit* is derived from a Latin word that means *finger*, and it is sometimes assumed that our base-ten number system is based on the fact we have 10 fingers.

Digit is also the name of the numerals we write in any place of a number. There are ten such digits (0, 1, 2, 3, 4, 5, 6, 7, 8, and 9), and numbers in our number system are formed by one or more of these digits.

The terms *increase* and *decrease* are derived from a Latin word that means *to grow*. *Increase* can be thought of as *growing up/becoming more*, and *decrease* can be thought of as *growing down/becoming less*. (The "d" in "decrease" and in "down" can be a helpful memory aid for some students.)

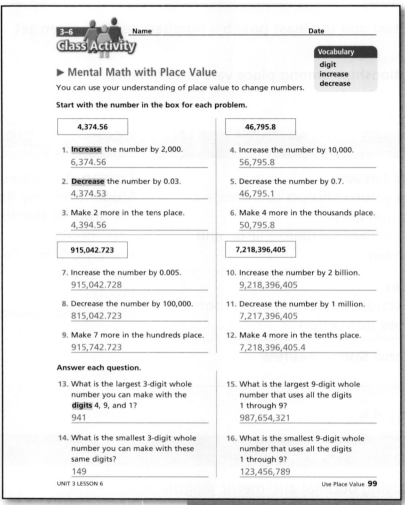

Student Activity Book page 99

▶ Mental Math with Place Value [WHOLE CLASS]

Ask for Ideas Elicit what students know about the vocabulary words *digit, increase,* and *decrease.* (See the Language note at the left.)

Use **Solve and Discuss** to work through exercises 1–12. Explain that these exercises are an interesting way for students to apply their knowledge of the names of the places in our base-ten number system.

Exercises 1–12 require students to decide the place value of the amount to be increased or decreased, and then find that same place value in the given number.

● Underlining or circling the place value in the given number can help students focus on that place, and then on the digit in that place, to help decide if the digit should be increased or decreased.

● Only exercise 6 requires grouping or ungrouping.

For exercises 13–16, encourage students to develop general rules that can be used to help solve the problems.

Exercises 13–16 require the following understandings of what was discussed in yesterday's lesson about the base-ten system:

- The places get larger to the left and smaller to the right. So to make the largest number with given digits, we write the *largest* of those digits in the largest place, write the next-largest digit in the next-largest place, and so on.

- To make the smallest number with given digits, we reverse this process and write the smallest of those digits in the largest place, the next-smallest in the next-largest place, and so on.

Exercises such as those in this activity frequently appear on tests. They incorporate an understanding of place value names, not knowledge about how to read numbers. Reading large numbers will be reviewed at the end of Activity 2.

Additional Practice To give yourself time to work with students who could benefit from additional help, ask your advanced students to pose and answer place-value questions of their own design.

Teaching the Lesson (continued)

Visualize Large and Small Numbers

 25 MINUTES

Goal: Use a dot array to visualize large and small numbers.

Materials: Student Activity Book or Hardcover Book p. 100, pointer

✓ **NCTM Standards:**
Number and Operations
Representation

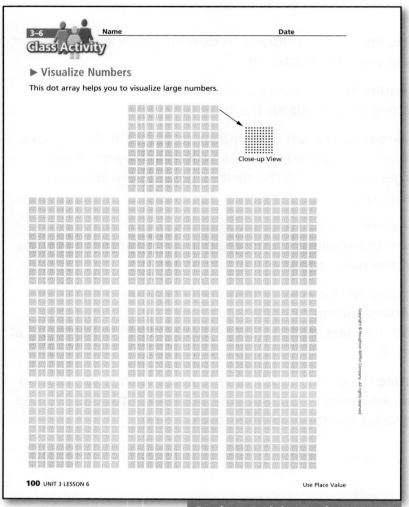

Student Activity Book page 100

Teaching Note

Student Helpers Take this opportunity to have one or more student helpers write each quantity on the board for you. Choose helpers who have grasped the concepts so they can write the quantities easily.

one tiny square = 100 dots

one row of tiny squares = 100 dots × 10 tiny squares = 1,000 dots

one large square = 1,000 dots × 10 rows = 10,000 dots

one page = 10,000 dots × 10 large squares = 100,000 dots

▶ Visualize Numbers [WHOLE CLASS]

Large Numbers Direct students' attention to the dot array on Student Book page 100, and use the questions below to guide them as they find the number of dots on the page, and then find the number of pages needed to make a million dots. Write each quantity on the board as you move through the activity, and have students label the quantities on the arrays.

● How many dots are in one of the tiny squares? 100

● How many dots are in one row of tiny squares? 1,000

● How many dots are in one large square? 10,000

● How many dots are on the whole page? 100,000

● How many pages are needed to make a million dots? 10

Math Talk **How Many Pages to Make a Billion Dots?**

You might choose to discuss with students the number of pages that would be needed to make a display of one billion dots. Use the following questions as springboards for discussion.

● Imagine a long row of one million dots that we can make by taping together the ten pages of 100,000 dots. A square of ten of these long rows would be how many dots? 10 × 1 million = 10 million

● A huge row of ten of these squares would be how many dots? 10 × 10 million = 100 million

● A gigantic square made of ten of these huge rows would be how many dots? 10 × 100 million = 1 billion

► Read Large Numbers WHOLE CLASS

Ask a **Student Leader** to go to the board and write a large number. Then have the student use the pointer to point to each group of three digits (such as those in the thousands) and read only the numbers. The class responds with the grouping name.

Example: 68,723,985,103

Leader: 68	**Leader:** 723	**Leader:** 985	**Leader:** 103
Class: billion	**Class:** million	**Class:** thousand	**Class:** ones

Repeat with a different student and number.

 Ongoing Assessment

Ask students to:

► Increase 5,681,004 by 10,000.

► Decrease 40,125.67 by 0.1.

► Make the largest possible three-digit number using the digits 5, 8, and 2.

► Make the smallest possible three-digit number using the digits 4, 9, and 1.

 Quick Quiz

See Assessment Guide for Unit 3 Quick Quiz 2.

Going Further

Math Connection: Reasoning and Proof

Goal: Justify ideas or solutions for mathematical statements or equations.

✓ **NCTM Standards:**
Number and Operations
Reasoning and Proof

Differentiated Instruction

Materials: MathBoard materials

Extra Help Provide MathBoard materials to students who have difficulty with the first example so they can make proof drawings showing that

3 tens + 5 ones = 35,

2 tens + 15 ones = 35, and

1 ten + 25 ones = 35.

Differentiated Instruction

Advanced Learners Give students an opportunity to write equations of their own design and exchange them with a classmate. Both students should discuss the solutions.

▶ Reasoning About a Problem

WHOLE CLASS

In this activity, students connect equations and reasoning.

Write $35 = \square$ tens $+ \square$ ones on the board.

- **What numbers can we write in the boxes?** Most students will say 3 (tens) and 5 (ones).

- **What other numbers can we write in the boxes?** Give students an opportunity to suggest a variety of numbers. If they insist that only 3 and 5 can be written in the boxes, write 2 in the tens box.

- **If we write 2 in the tens box, what number must we write in the ones box?** 15

Write 1 in the tens box and elicit from students that another way to write 35 is to write 25 in the ones box.

 ### Math Talk in Action

Write $35 + 2 = \square + 3$ on the board.

- **What number can we write in the box to make this number sentence true? Explain your answer.**

Marcus: 37, because $35 + 2 = 37$.

Jenny: You forgot the 3; $35 + 2 = 37 + 3 = 40$.

José: The sums on each side of the equals sign must have the same value.

Nick: We write 34 in the box because $35 + 2$ equals 37 and $34 + 3$ equals 37.

Tanisha: You don't need to add to find the answer. Since one more is being added to the number in the box, that number must be one less than 35, or 34.

Practice Write the equations shown below on the board. Have **Student Pairs** work together to find the value of *n* in each equation, and explain their answers.

$$60 + 46 = n + 56 \quad 50 \qquad n + n - 6 = 6 \quad 6$$

$$75 - 50 = 85 - n \quad 60 \qquad 2n - 10 = 10 \quad 10$$

$$50 + 6 - 3 = 25 + 25 + (2 \bullet 3) - n \quad 3$$

Differentiated Instruction

Intervention — Activity Card 3-6

Powers of Ten
Activity Card 3-6

Work: In Pairs

Use:
• Calculators

1. Take turns using a calculator to multiply. One partner uses the calculator first to find the product of 10 × 10.

2. The other partner writes the product and its word name in a table. 100; one hundred

Multiplication	Product	Word Name
10 × 10 =		

3. Trade roles. Find the next product: 10 × 10 × 10. Record the product as a number and its word name in the table.
1,000; one thousand

4. Continue taking turns, adding another factor of 10 each time until you reach a product of one million.

5. **Math Talk** Describe any patterns you see in the factors and the products you wrote. Possible answer: The number of zeros in the factors equals the number of zeros in the product.

Activity Note Remind students to include commas in the appropriate places when they write the products shown on their calculators.

Math Writing Prompt

Explain Number Names Which would you rather have: a million $1-bills or a thousand $100-bills? Explain your choice.

Soar to Success Math **Software Support**
Warm-Up 12.33

On Level — Activity Card 3-6

Roll With It
Activity Card 3-6 ▲

Work: In Pairs

Use:
• Number cube, labeled 1–6

1. One partner rolls the number cube. The result is the number of times the other partner will roll the number cube.

2. The second partner rolls the number cube the required number of times and records each roll.

Greatest: 65,311
Least: 11,356

3. **Work Together** Write the greatest possible number and the least possible number, using all the digits recorded.

4. Trade roles and repeat the activity.

Activity Note After students have completed the activity, discuss the strategies they used for finding the greatest and the least number.

Math Writing Prompt

Explain Your Thinking How can you arrange any four digits to make the greatest possible whole number? Explain your reasoning.

MegaMath **Software Support**
Fraction Action: Number Line Mine, Level A

Challenge — Activity Card 3-6

Place-Value Code
Activity Card 3-6 ■

Work: In Pairs

Use:
• MathBoard materials

1. Use the place-value code to solve problems.

Place-Value Code
$H = 10$
$n = 100$
$p = 1,000$
$s = 1,000,000$

2. Copy each equation below. Then use the code to find each missing variable.

$p = 10 \times \underline{} \; n$ $s = 1,000 \times \underline{} \; p$ $p = 100 \times \underline{} \; H$

3. Write your own code and problems. Exchange with other pairs to solve.

Activity Note An alternative approach to solving the equations can be writing a number for each missing factor, based on the code. Students can use either approach.

Math Writing Prompt

Write Steps How can you change 5,420,300 to 6,000,000 by using only four steps? Each step can involve only one place value.

DESTINATION Math **Software Support**
Course III: Module 1: Unit 1: Whole Numbers to One Million

③ Homework and Spiral Review

3-6 Homework **Goal:** Additional Practice

Use this Homework page to provide students with more practice with place value methods.

3-6 Remembering **Goal:** Spiral Review

This Remembering activity would be appropriate anytime after today's lesson.

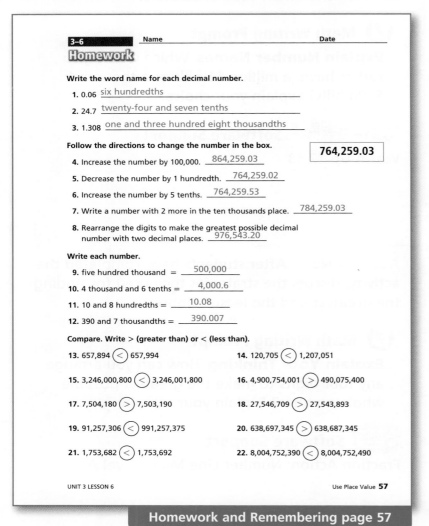

3-6 Homework Name _____ Date _____

Write the word name for each decimal number.

1. 0.06 <u>six hundredths</u>

2. 24.7 <u>twenty-four and seven tenths</u>

3. 1.308 <u>one and three hundred eight thousandths</u>

Follow the directions to change the number in the box.

Box: **764,259.03**

4. Increase the number by 100,000. <u>864,259.03</u>

5. Decrease the number by 1 hundredth. <u>764,259.02</u>

6. Increase the number by 5 tenths. <u>764,259.53</u>

7. Write a number with 2 more in the ten thousands place. <u>784,259.03</u>

8. Rearrange the digits to make the greatest possible decimal number with two decimal places. <u>976,543.20</u>

Write each number.

9. five hundred thousand = <u>500,000</u>

10. 4 thousand and 6 tenths = <u>4,000.6</u>

11. 10 and 8 hundredths = <u>10.08</u>

12. 390 and 7 thousandths = <u>390.007</u>

Compare. Write > (greater than) or < (less than).

13. 657,894 < 657,994

14. 120,705 < 1,207,051

15. 3,246,000,800 < 3,246,001,800

16. 4,900,754,001 > 490,075,400

17. 7,504,180 > 7,503,190

18. 27,546,709 > 27,543,893

19. 91,257,306 < 991,257,375

20. 638,697,345 > 638,687,345

21. 1,753,682 < 1,753,692

22. 8,004,752,390 < 8,004,752,490

UNIT 3 LESSON 6 — Use Place Value **57**

Homework and Remembering page 57

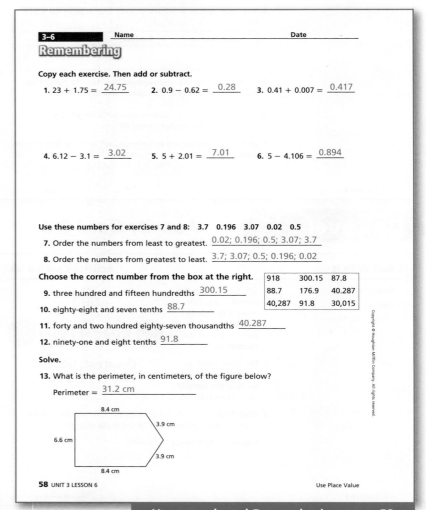

3-6 Remembering Name _____ Date _____

Copy each exercise. Then add or subtract.

1. 23 + 1.75 = <u>24.75</u>   2. 0.9 − 0.62 = <u>0.28</u>   3. 0.41 + 0.007 = <u>0.417</u>

4. 6.12 − 3.1 = <u>3.02</u>   5. 5 + 2.01 = <u>7.01</u>   6. 5 − 4.106 = <u>0.894</u>

Use these numbers for exercises 7 and 8: 3.7 0.196 3.07 0.02 0.5

7. Order the numbers from least to greatest. <u>0.02; 0.196; 0.5; 3.07; 3.7</u>

8. Order the numbers from greatest to least. <u>3.7; 3.07; 0.5; 0.196; 0.02</u>

Choose the correct number from the box at the right.

918	300.15	87.8
88.7	176.9	40.287
40,287	91.8	30,015

9. three hundred and fifteen hundredths <u>300.15</u>

10. eighty-eight and seven tenths <u>88.7</u>

11. forty and two hundred eighty-seven thousandths <u>40.287</u>

12. ninety-one and eight tenths <u>91.8</u>

Solve.

13. What is the perimeter, in centimeters, of the figure below?

Perimeter = <u>31.2 cm</u>

8.4 cm
3.9 cm
6.6 cm
3.9 cm
8.4 cm

58 UNIT 3 LESSON 6 — Use Place Value

Homework and Remembering page 58

Home or School Activity

Science Connection

Millions and Billions of Miles Explain to students that large numbers are used often in astronomy. Ask students to find the distances (in miles) of all the planets from the sun, and then write those distances in order from least to greatest.

Planet Distances	
Planet	**Average Distance from the Sun (in miles)**
Earth	93,000,000
Jupiter	483,600,000
Mars	141,600,000
Mercury	36,000,000
Neptune	2,794,400,000
Saturn	886,700,000
Uranus	1,784,000,000
Venus	67,200,000

Add Whole Numbers and Decimals

REAL WORLD Problem Solving

Lesson Objectives

- **Align numbers to prepare for addition.**
- **Explain different methods for addition.**

The Day at a Glance

Today's Goals	Materials	
1 Teaching the Lesson **A1:** Discuss various strategies for making a new ten when adding. **A2:** Analyze and add different types of numbers. **2 Going Further** ▶ Differentiated Instruction **3 Homework and Spiral Review**	**Lesson Activities** Student Activity Book pp. 101–102 or Student Hardcover Book pp. 101–102 Homework and Remembering pp. 59–60 Calculators (optional)	**Going Further** Activity Cards 3-7 Centimeter tape measures MathBoard materials Play money Math Journals

123 *Use* **Math Talk** *today!*

Keeping Skills Sharp

Quick Practice ⏱ 5 MINUTES

Goal: Identify place-value groups in large numbers and display approximate metric lengths.

Read Large Numbers Have a **Student Leader** write a number with 6 to 12 digits on the board. The leader points to each group of digits and reads the numbers. The class says the group name.

Example: 923,405,172

Student Leader: 923	Class: *million*
Student Leader: 405	Class: *thousand*
Student Leader: 172	Class: (no group name)

Metric Lengths The **Student Leader** writes a metric length abbreviation on the board (m, dm, cm, or mm). The students say the name of the unit and show the approximate length with their hands. Repeat in random order.

Daily Routines

Homework Review Let students work together to check their work.

Nonroutine Problem The teacher had two pieces of fabric with equal lengths. She cut one into 10 equal pieces and the other into 100 equal pieces. Carla used 7 out of the 10 pieces. Each piece is 10 in. long. Rodrigo used 74 out of the 100 pieces. Each piece is 1 in. long. Who had fewer inches of fabric remaining? Express this amount as a fraction and a decimal of the whole piece. Rodrigo; Rodrigo: 26 in., $100 - 74 = 26$; Carla: $(10 \times 10) - (7 \times 10) = 30$ in.; $\frac{26}{100}$ and 0.26

1 Teaching the Lesson

Discuss Ways to Regroup

 20–25 MINUTES

Goal: Discuss various strategies for making a new ten when adding.

 NCTM Standards:
Number and Operations
Communication

Teaching Note

Different Methods This lesson reviews basics before adding with large numbers. Go quickly in this lesson if your students are successful with these small numbers. All of the same issues will be addressed in the next lesson.

Activity 1 is checking on what methods students use to add. Advantages of each method are discussed on page 245. The Secret-Code Cards can help students see the values they are adding The *Subtotal Method* especially benefits from the Secret Code Cards.

English Language Learners

Model the *Subtotal Method* for 3-digit addition.

• **Beginning** Point to a *subtotal*. Ask: **Is this the answer?** no **Is this a *subtotal*?** yes **Is a *subtotal* part of the answer?** yes
• **Intermediate** Ask: **When we add each part, do we get 3 *totals*?** no **3 *subtotals*?** yes
• **Advanced** Have students tell about the difference between *subtotal* and *total*.

► **Student-Generated Addition Methods** [WHOLE CLASS]

Send several students to the board and ask them to solve this problem, while others work at their seats.

$$\begin{array}{r} 769 \\ + 584 \\ \hline \end{array}$$

Invite several students to explain their methods. Be sure that the explainers use place value words in their explanations. They should not just say, "I carried a one." (Ask them, "One *what?*")

Elicit any different methods your students use and discuss each of them. The most common methods appear below. The New Groups Below and New Groups Above methods involve making one new group of ten in the next larger place whenever there is a total of ten or more in one place.

New Groups Below

Step 1	Step 2	Step 3
$\begin{array}{r} 769 \\ +584 \\ \underline{1} \\ 3 \end{array}$	$\begin{array}{r} 769 \\ +584 \\ \underline{1\,1} \\ 53 \end{array}$	$\begin{array}{r} 769 \\ +584 \\ \underline{1\,1\,1} \\ 1{,}353 \end{array}$

New Groups Above

Step 1	Step 2	Step 3
$\begin{array}{r} {\scriptstyle 1} \\ 769 \\ +584 \\ \hline 3 \end{array}$	$\begin{array}{r} {\scriptstyle 1\,1} \\ 769 \\ +584 \\ \hline 53 \end{array}$	$\begin{array}{r} {\scriptstyle 1\,1\,1} \\ 769 \\ +584 \\ \hline 1{,}353 \end{array}$

Subtotal Method: Hundreds, tens, and ones are added separately.

Left to Right:	**Right to Left:**
$\begin{array}{r} 769 \\ +584 \\ \hline 1200 \\ 140 \\ 13 \\ \hline 1{,}353 \end{array}$	$\begin{array}{r} 769 \\ +584 \\ \hline 13 \\ 140 \\ 1200 \\ \hline 1{,}353 \end{array}$

You do not need to discuss all of the methods. Focus on the methods that your students *actually* use. In Lesson 8, the class will be exposed to all three of these methods in the context of adding very large numbers.

Activity 2

Add Unlike Amounts

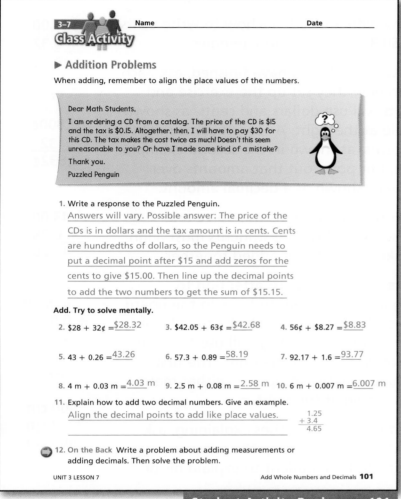

3-7
Class Activity

Name _____ Date _____

▶ **Addition Problems**

When adding, remember to align the place values of the numbers.

Dear Math Students,
I am ordering a CD from a catalog. The price of the CD is $15 and the tax is $0.15. Altogether, then, I will have to pay $30 for this CD. The tax makes the cost twice as much! Doesn't this seem unreasonable to you? Or have I made some kind of a mistake?
Thank you.
Puzzled Penguin

1. Write a response to the Puzzled Penguin.
   Answers will vary. Possible answer: The price of the
   CDs is in dollars and the tax amount is in cents. Cents
   are hundredths of dollars, so the Penguin needs to
   put a decimal point after $15 and add zeros for the
   cents to give $15.00. Then line up the decimal points
   to add the two numbers to get the sum of $15.15.

Add. Try to solve mentally.

2. $28 + 32¢ = $28.32   3. $42.05 + 63¢ = $42.68   4. 56¢ + $8.27 = $8.83

5. 43 + 0.26 = 43.26   6. 57.3 + 0.89 = 58.19   7. 92.17 + 1.6 = 93.77

8. 4 m + 0.03 m = 4.03 m   9. 2.5 m + 0.08 m = 2.58 m   10. 6 m + 0.007 m = 6.007 m

11. Explain how to add two decimal numbers. Give an example.
    Align the decimal points to add like place values.
    $$\begin{array}{r} 1.25 \\ + 3.4 \\ \hline 4.65 \end{array}$$

12. On the Back Write a problem about adding measurements or adding decimals. Then solve the problem.

UNIT 3 LESSON 7   Add Whole Numbers and Decimals **101**

Student Activity Book page 101

▶ Discuss Addition Problems WHOLE CLASS   Math Talk

The Puzzled Penguin Have the class turn to page 101 in the Student Book and discuss the Puzzled Penguin activity. Students should see that the penguin has added *unlike* amounts (dollars and cents) and has therefore arrived at the wrong total. Ask students how they would set up the problem for addition. Have a volunteer write the problem vertically on the board and solve it.

$$\begin{array}{r} \$15.00 \\ + 0.15 \\ \hline \$15.15 \end{array}$$

Discuss why the problem is set up this way. Encourage students to justify the alignment by talking about the size of the places rather than simply "lining up the decimal points." If students give a rule about lining up the decimals, ask them the reason for the rule. Elicit from them that only *like* amounts can be added (you can't add dollars to dimes or pennies).

Activity continued ▶

20–25 MINUTES

Goal: Analyze and add different types of numbers.

Materials: Student Activity Book or Hardcover Book pp. 101–102, calculators (optional)

 NCTM Standards:
Number and Operations
Measurement

Teaching Note

What to Expect From Students Students may readily see the answer without actually aligning and adding. If so, point out that it will not always be this easy to find the answer. For complex problems, they will need to align like place values.

Teaching Note

Math Drawings These drawings help less-advanced students. Single-digit methods for adding are shown on page 240. Make sure today that any students who are still *counting all* (making drawings for both numbers and counting all of them) move on to *counting on* (counting on from the larger number as many as are in the other number). See page 240.

Differentiated Instruction

Extra Help Use the Secret Code Cards and focus on the quantities on the back for students who do not understand about adding like quantities.

Activity 2

The Learning Classroom

Quick Practice This would be a good time to review the relationships among different lengths in the metric system.

- ? cm = 1 m   100
- 1 cm = ? m   0.01
- ? dm = 1 m   10
- 1 dm = ? m   0.1
- ? mm = 1 m   1000
- 1 mm = ? m   0.001

Ask students to talk about patterns that they observe.

Ongoing Assessment

Have students solve these exercises and discuss how to line up the decimal points.

- ► $208.11 + $0.89
- ► 67 dm + 48 cm
- ► 412 + 0.789

Add Money Amounts Invite three students to go to the board and solve exercises 2–4 on page 101 of the Student Book. Give each student a different exercise to solve. The students at their seats can work on all three exercises.

If necessary, review with all students how to write cents as dollars: 32¢ = $0.32 (3 dimes and 2 pennies).

When the students at the board have finished, ask each of them to explain how they set up the exercise and why. Most students will use dollars and cents, as shown in the first example at the right. A few students might decide to use all cents, as shown in the second example. That is acceptable, but point out that amounts over one dollar are usually shown as a decimal amount.

```
  $28.00
+  0.32
  $28.32

    or

  2,800¢
     32
  2,832¢
```

Add Numbers Now have students use **Solve and Discuss** for exercises 5–7. This time students must align the problems so like amounts are added together.

```
  43.00
+  0.26
  43.26
```

Add Metric Units Direct students' attention to exercises 8–10. Again, send three students to the board to solve and discuss these exercises. Students will need to decide which measuring unit they will use for their answer and then convert one of the units. The first exercise, for example, can be set up with either meters or centimeters, as shown at the right.

```
  4.00 m
+ 0.03 m
  4.03 m

    or

  400 cm
+   3 cm
  403 cm
```

As each student at the board finishes explaining, ask the seated students if anyone set up the exercise differently. If so, invite that student to explain his or her approach.

In this unit, students will be adding and subtracting like measuring units and like place values. It is important to align numbers so that like place values are added together.

Have students complete exercises 11–12. Allow students to share examples and use these examples to explain how to add decimals. Have the class ask clarifying questions and verify the answer. Then, have other students share their word problems. Allow students time to solve the problem and discuss the solution as a class. Students can use calculators to check their mental math.

② Going Further

Differentiated Instruction

● Intervention   Activity Card 3-7

Metric Sums	Activity Card 3-7 ●

Work: In Pairs

Use:
- Centimeter tape measure
- MathBoard materials

1. Use a tape measure to help you add metric sums. Take turns marking off each addend.

2. Find the sum of 2 dm + 8 cm. Begin by marking off 2 dm on the tape measure. How many centimeters does 1 decimeter equal? 2 decimeters? 10 cm; 20 cm

3. Next, your partner marks off 8 cm more on the tape measure. What sum does the tape show? 28 cm

4. Use the tape measure to help you find each sum.
   Possible answers are given. Units of measure may vary.
   11 cm + 5 mm 11.5 cm   1 dm + 2 cm 12 cm
   2 dm + 10 mm 21 cm   10 mm + 10 cm 11 cm

Unit 3, Lesson 7   Copyright © Houghton Mifflin Company

Activity Note Review linear metric conversions before students begin the activity. Be sure that students are comfortable reading different intervals on the metric tape measure.

✏️ **Math Writing Prompt**

Explain Relationships When adding money, when should you regroup pennies for dimes? When should you regroup dimes for dollars?

Soar to Success Math ⭐ **Software Support**

Warm-Up 41.29

▲ On Level   Activity Card 3-7

Money Sums	Activity Card 3-7 ▲

Work: In Pairs

Use:
- Play money (dollars, dimes, and pennies)

1. Find the sum of 56¢ + $2.75. Model each addend using dollars and coins.

2. Combine like money to find the sum. How many dollars are there? How many dimes? How many pennies?
   2 dollars, 12 dimes, 11 pennies

3. Trade pennies for dimes and then trade dimes for dollars. What is the sum? $3.31

4. Write 3 other sums to find and exchange them with your partner to model each solution.

Unit 3, Lesson 7   Copyright © Houghton Mifflin Company

Activity Note Before students begin the activity, review money equivalencies for regrouping pennies as dimes and dimes as dollars. Remind students that the decimal point separates dollars from cents.

✏️ **Math Writing Prompt**

Write a Correction Explain why Tyler has the wrong sum for this addition and explain how to find the correct sum. 35.2 + 1.46 = 4.98.

MegaMath Grades K-6 **Software Support**

The Number Games: Buggy Bargains, Level E

■ Challenge   Activity Card 3-7

Inequalities	Activity Card 3-7 ■

Work: By Yourself

Use:
- MathBoard materials

1. Copy and complete the exercise set on your MathBoard.

   170 + 25 = 19.5   17.0 + 2.5 = 19.5
   361 + 145 = 18.11   3.61 + 14.5 = 18.11
   91 + 109 = 10.19   9.1 + 1.09 = 10.19
   50 + 505 = 55.05   50 + 5.05 = 55.05
   864 + 329 = 119.3   86.4 + 32.9 = 119.3
   210 + 19 = 22.9   21.0 + 1.9 = 22.9
   101 + 101 = 11.11   10.1 + 1.01 = 11.11

2. Place the decimal points in each addend to match the given sum.

3. **Look Back** Explain the strategies you used to decide where to place each decimal point.

Unit 3, Lesson 7   Copyright © Houghton Mifflin Company

Activity Note Students can use number sense to decide where to place each decimal point. By looking at the sum, students can eliminate one or more options for placement in each addend.

✏️ **Math Writing Prompt**

Explain Multi-Step Problems Write the steps you would follow to solve 9 m + 5 mm = ____.

✴️ **DESTINATION Math·** **Software Support**

Course III: Module 4: Unit 2: Adding Decimals

Add Whole Numbers and Decimals   **241**

3 Homework and Spiral Review

3–7
Homework **Goal:** Additional Practice

Use this Homework page to provide more practice with adding whole and decimal numbers.

3–7
Remembering **Goal:** Spiral Review

This Remembering activity would be appropriate anytime after today's lesson.

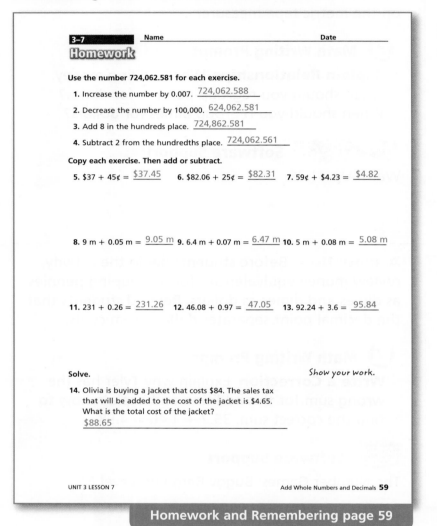

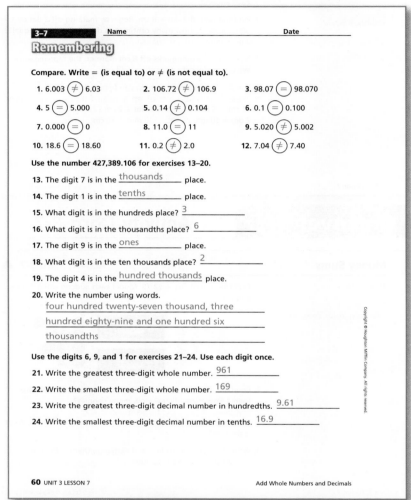

Homework and Remembering page 59

Homework and Remembering page 60

Home or School Activity

Social Studies Connection

Lots of Time Have students research the length of time for the following.

decade = 10 years
century = 100 years
millennium = 1,000 years

Have students look up several events in history and make a chart estimating how long ago each event happened.

Historical Event	When?
Christopher Columbus sailed to the Americas.	about 5 centuries ago
Paper was invented in China.	about 2 millennia ago
The first known writing system was developed.	about 5 millennia ago
"The Star-Spangled Banner" was written.	about 2 centuries ago

Addition to Millions

Lesson Objectives

- Align numbers according to their place values to prepare for adding.
- Use and explain different methods for addition.

The Day at a Glance

Today's Goals	Materials

1 Teaching the Lesson
A1: Discuss the advantages and disadvantages of different addition methods.
A2: Solve addition problems using different methods.
2 Going Further
▶Differentiated Instruction
3 Homework and Spiral Review
	Lesson Activities
	Student Activity Book
	  pp. 103–104 or Student
	  Hardcover Book
	  pp. 103–104
	Homework and
	  Remembering pp. 61–62 **Going Further**
	Activity Cards 3-8
	Place-value charts
	Calculators
	MathBoard materials
	Math Journals

123 Use Math Talk today!

Keeping Skills Sharp

Quick Practice   ⏱ 5 MINUTES

Goal: Identify place-value groups in large numbers and display approximate metric lengths.

Read Large Numbers Have a **Student Leader** write a number with 6 to 12 digits on the board. The leader points to each group of digits and reads the numbers. The class says the group name.

Example: 42,103,685,093

Leader: 42   Class: *billion*

Leader: 103   Class: *million*

Leader: 685   Class: *thousand*

Leader: 093   Class: *ones*

Metric Lengths The **Student Leader** writes a metric length abbreviation on the board (m, dm, cm, or mm). The students say the name of the unit and show the approximate length with their hands. Repeat in random order.

Daily Routines

Homework Review Send students to the board to show their work and explain each step.

What Went Wrong? Adam wanted to place a fence around his garden that measures 7.3 yd long and 2.5 yd wide. He found the perimeter to be 1.96 yd. He knows this amount is incorrect. Why? What happened? Give the correct perimeter.

The perimeter must be greater than the length of any side and this perimeter is less than the length of each side. He used 0.73 yd for the length and 0.25 yd for the width. The perimeter is 19.6 yd.

Teaching the Lesson

Addition Methods

 20–25 MINUTES

Goal: Discuss the advantages and disadvantages of different addition methods.

Materials: Student Activity Book or Hardcover Book p.103

✓ **NCTM Standards:**
Number and Operations
Communication

Teaching Note

Math Background Remind students when adding decimal numbers that they should align the numbers by their place values. Ask them to explain why. *cannot add unlike values, such as dollars and dimes*

Tell students we are going to refer to the horizontal line drawn under the problem as the *problem line.* In the New Groups Below method, the ten groups are written on the problem line.

3-8
Class Activity

Name _____ Date _____

▶ **Compare Different Methods**

There are many ways to add numbers. These methods each show the new groups in a different way. Each method has its own advantages and disadvantages.

New Groups Below

	Step 1	Step 2	Step 3	Step 4	Step 5	Step 6
	787.608	787.608	787.608	787.608	787.608	787.608
	+561.739	+561.739	+561.739	+561.739	+561.739	+561.739
	7	47	347	9.347	49.347	1,349.347

New Groups Above

	Step 1	Step 2	Step 3	Step 4	Step 5	Step 6
	1	1	1 1	1 1	1 1 1	1 1 1
	787.608	787.608	787.608	787.608	787.608	787.608
	+561.739	+561.739	+561.739	+561.739	+561.739	+561.739
	7	47	347	9.347	49.347	1,349.347

Subtotal Method

	Step 1	Step 2	Step 3	Step 4	Steps 5 & 6	Step 7
	787.608	787.608	787.608	787.608	787.608	787.608
	+561.739	+561.739	+561.739	+561.739	+561.739	+561.739
	1,200.000	1,200.000	1,200.000	1,200.000	1,200.000	1,200.000
		140.000	140.000	140.000	140.000	140.000
			8.000	8.000	8.000	8.000
				1.300	1.300	1.300
					0.030	0.030
					0.017	+0.017
						1,349.347

UNIT 3 LESSON 8   Addition to Millions **103**

Student Activity Book page 103

▶ Compare Different Methods   WHOLE CLASS

Real-World Situations Write the numbers 786.608 and 561.739 on the board. Suggest that it is unlikely that students will encounter a real-world situation in which the place-values in a number range from hundreds to thousandths. Discuss why this is true and give this example. One motorcycle weighs 787 pounds. Ask students if they think there is any advantage to knowing a more precise weight for the motorcycle.

Lead students to see that the smaller an object is, the more value there may be to knowing a more precise weight. For example, precious materials such as gold might be weighed to thousandths.

Tell students that the addition in this lesson is practice. They will see three different addition methods but do not have to master all of them. However, using and discussing the methods is useful in understanding the place-value concepts used in addition.

Share Methods There are three different methods of addition on page 103 in the Student Book. Have students look at the student page and discuss how

- the first method shows the new groups below on the problem line waiting to be added last.
- the second method shows the new groups above the top number where they will be added first.
- the third method shows place value groups as subtotals.

After you discuss each method, ask students to think about the advantages and disadvantages of each method. You may want to have students discuss this page in pairs or in groups of three and then ask volunteers to share their ideas with the class.

New Groups Below

Advantages:

- Addition is easier because the extra 1 is added last: you add the numbers you see and increase that by 1.
- The new teen subtotal can be seen clearly. (For example, you can see the 17 in Step 1.)

Disadvantages:

- More parents know New Groups Above.

New Groups Above

Advantages:

- The method is known to many people.

Disadvantages:

- Adding is more difficult if you add the columns from top to bottom, because you have to remember your first total. (For example, $7 + 1 = 8$ and then do $8 + 5 = 13$.)
- Teen subtotals are separated.

Subtotal Method

Advantages:

- You can add in either direction. (We show left to right.)
- You do not need to insert numbers for new groups.

Disadvantages:

- The problem takes up more space. With big numbers like this, it is easy to get a number in the wrong column.

The Learning Classroom

Building Concepts This is the perfect place to emphasize that there is more than one way to solve a problem.

Teaching Note

What to Expect From Students *Math Expressions* emphasizes New Groups Below over the more traditional New Groups Above because the New Groups Below method is less prone to error. However, by fifth grade, most students have become accustomed to their own methods. Students may use any method they understand, can explain, and is fast enough. (For example, making drawings for very large numbers is not feasible. Students should record their method numerically for such problems.)

What to Expect From Parents Parents have been very accepting of New Groups Below because it is similar to New Groups Above and they can see the advantages of this method.

English Language Learners

Write *advantage* and *disadvantage* on the board. Say: **An *advantage* is positive or good. A *disadvantage* is negative or not good.** Ask simple questions to help students tell about the *advantages* and *disadvantages* for each method. For example, ask: **Does the *subtotal method* take more time?** yes **Is that an *advantage* or *disadvantage?*** disadvantage

Teaching the Lesson (continued)

Activity 2

Practice and Explain

 20–25 MINUTES

Goal: Solve addition problems using different methods.

Materials: Student Activity Book p. 104 or Hardcover Book p. 104

 NCTM Standards:
Number and Operations
Communication

Differentiated Instruction

Special Needs Some students have trouble aligning columns of numbers. With longer computation problems such as these, you might want to have these students use lined notebook paper. Before writing the problem, have them turn the paper sideways so that the lines are vertical. The vertical lines will help them align the columns more precisely.

 Ongoing Assessment

Tell students to solve each problem and then write the name of the method they chose to use.

► 203.6 + 78,493

► 2,700,508 + 2.009

► 978,859.97 + 4,341.05

► 0.975 + 369.235

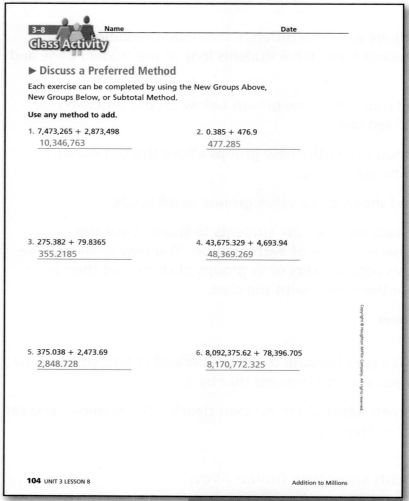

Student Activity Book page 104

The worksheet shown reads:

3–8
Class Activity

Name _____ Date _____

► **Discuss a Preferred Method**

Each exercise can be completed by using the New Groups Above, New Groups Below, or Subtotal Method.

Use any method to add.

1. 7,473,265 + 2,873,498
   10,346,763

2. 0.385 + 476.9
   477.285

3. 275.382 + 79.8365
   355.2185

4. 43,675.329 + 4,693.94
   48,369.269

5. 375.038 + 2,473.69
   2,848.728

6. 8,092,375.62 + 78,396.705
   8,170,772.325

104 UNIT 3 LESSON 8   Addition to Millions

► Discuss a Preferred Method

WHOLE CLASS   **Math Talk** 123

Have everyone solve exercises 1–6 on page 104 of the Student Book, using any method. Invite as many students as possible to solve at the board while the rest of the students solve at their seats. You may want to have the seated students work in **Small Groups**. When explanations are given, emphasize place value language to describe how new groups of tens are made.

Invite the class to comment or ask questions when explanations are given. As a class, discuss why students do not choose to use certain methods and if they always use the same method, or if they use specific methods for different types of addition.

② Going Further

Differentiated Instruction

Intervention — Activity Card 3-8

Line Up!

Activity Card 3-8

Work: In Pairs

Use:
• Place-value charts

1. You can use a place-value chart to help you add large numbers. The chart below shows how to add 4,763,052 + 829,476. What is the sum? 5,592,528

	M,	HTh	TTh	Th,	H	T	O
Regroup	1		1		1		
	4,	7	6	3,	0	5	2
+		8	2	9,	4	7	6
Sum	5,	5	9	2,	5	2	8

2. Possible answer: There were 12 thousands in the sum, so one group of 10 thousands was regrouped into 1 group of ten thousands.

2. Notice that one row of the chart is labeled "Regroup." What does the digit 1 mean in the ten thousands (TTh) column of that row?

3. Copy the place-value chart. Take turns with your partner. Write addition problems of whole numbers to millions. Then use the chart to find the sum.

Unit 3, Lesson 8

Copyright © Houghton Mifflin Company

Activity Note Be certain students understand the abbreviation for the place values on the chart. If students have difficulty placing the digits, suggest that they begin with the ones digit and work up.

✎ Math Writing Prompt

Write Number Names Use the digits 0 to 9 to write a number in standard form. Use each digit once. Now write the same number in word form.

 **Software Support**

Warm-Up 10.33

On Level — Activity Card 3-8

Choose Your Method

Activity Card 3-8

Work: In Pairs

Use:
• Calculator
• MathBoard materials

1. There are different ways to solve problems: mental math, paper and pencil, and a calculator. Work with your partner to decide which method works best for each problem below.

Problem	Solution	Method
1,200 + 700	1,900	MM
97.984 + 3.5107	101.4947	C
651 + 326	977	PP
13,500 + 6,100	19,600	MM
15.42 + 6.8	22.22	PP
99,999,999 + 999,999	100,999,998	C

2. **Work Together** Copy the chart. Solve each problem and then explain why you chose the method you used.
Methods may vary.

Unit 3, Lesson 8

Copyright © Houghton Mifflin Company

Activity Note Before students begin the activity, discuss the different methods and when each method might be most reasonable to choose.

✎ Math Writing Prompt

Explain Your Thinking When is mental math a good method to choose when you need to add? Give examples to explain your thinking.

 Software Support

The Number Games: Tiny's Think Tank, Level L

Challenge — Activity Card 3-8

Grade a Quiz

Activity Card 3-8

Work: By Yourself

Use:
• MathBoard materials

1. 17.3; regrouping omitted in tenths place
2. correct
3. 126.45; did not align by place value
4. correct
5. 1,207,180.8; wrote a decimal point instead of a comma in the second addend and left off the last two digits

1. Puzzled Penguin found five sums on his math quiz. Copy the quiz onto your MathBoard and check each answer.

> Name: Puzzled Penguin
> 1. 9.8 + 7.5 = 16.3
> 2. 261,792 + 17,975 = 282,767
> 3. 107.15 + 19.3 = 109.08
> 4. 0.6419 + 64.19 = 64.8319
> 5. 312,546.8 + 894,634 = 313,441.4

2. If an answer is wrong, find the correct sum. Then explain the mistake that the Puzzled Penguin made.

Unit 3, Lesson 8

Copyright © Houghton Mifflin Company

Activity Note Students can identify the error in exercise 5 by using number sense. The difference between the sum and the first addend is less than 1,000. So 894.6 was used as the second addend.

✎ Math Writing Prompt

Explain a Process Give an example to explain why it is important to align digits by place value when you add.

 **Software Support**

Course III: Module 4: Unit 2: Adding Decimals

Addition to Millions   **247**

3 Homework and Spiral Review

Homework 3-8   Goal: Additional Practice

Use this Homework page to provide students with more practice with addition to millions.

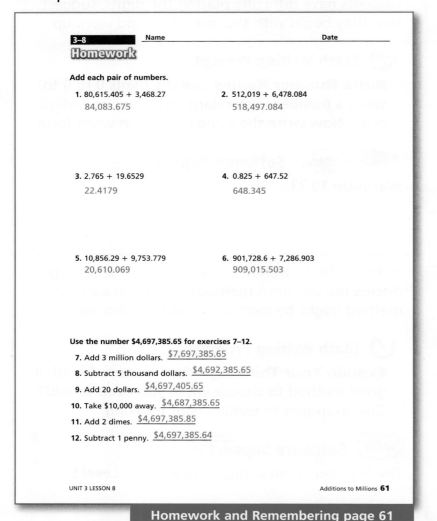

3-8   Name _____ Date _____

Homework

Add each pair of numbers.

1. 80,615.405 + 3,468.27
84,083.675

2. 512,019 + 6,478.084
518,497.084

3. 2.765 + 19.6529
22.4179

4. 0.825 + 647.52
648.345

5. 10,856.29 + 9,753.779
20,610.069

6. 901,728.6 + 7,286.903
909,015.503

Use the number $4,697,385.65 for exercises 7–12.

7. Add 3 million dollars. $7,697,385.65

8. Subtract 5 thousand dollars. $4,692,385.65

9. Add 20 dollars. $4,697,405.65

10. Take $10,000 away. $4,687,385.65

11. Add 2 dimes. $4,697,385.85

12. Subtract 1 penny. $4,697,385.64

UNIT 3 LESSON 8   Additions to Millions **61**

Homework and Remembering page 61

Remembering 3-8   Goal: Spiral Review

This Remembering activity would be appropriate anytime after today's lesson.

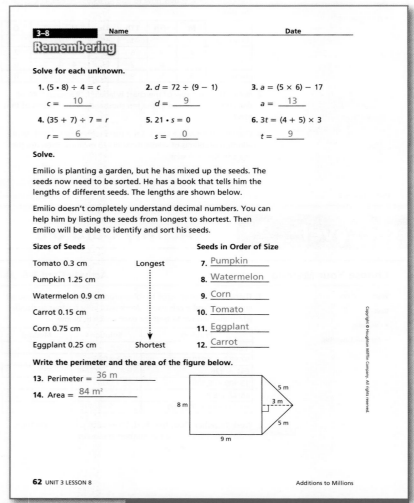

3-8   Name _____ Date _____

Remembering

Solve for each unknown.

1. $(5 \cdot 8) \div 4 = c$
$c = 10$

2. $d = 72 \div (9 - 1)$
$d = 9$

3. $a = (5 \times 6) - 17$
$a = 13$

4. $(35 + 7) \div 7 = r$
$r = 6$

5. $21 \cdot s = 0$
$s = 0$

6. $3t = (4 + 5) \times 3$
$t = 9$

Solve.

Emilio is planting a garden, but he has mixed up the seeds. The seeds now need to be sorted. He has a book that tells him the lengths of different seeds. The lengths are shown below.

Emilio doesn't completely understand decimal numbers. You can help him by listing the seeds from longest to shortest. Then Emilio will be able to identify and sort his seeds.

Sizes of Seeds

Tomato 0.3 cm   Longest

Pumpkin 1.25 cm

Watermelon 0.9 cm

Carrot 0.15 cm

Corn 0.75 cm

Eggplant 0.25 cm   Shortest

Seeds in Order of Size

7. Pumpkin

8. Watermelon

9. Corn

10. Tomato

11. Eggplant

12. Carrot

Write the perimeter and the area of the figure below.

13. Perimeter = 36 m

14. Area = 84 m²

62 UNIT 3 LESSON 8   Additions to Millions

Homework and Remembering page 62

Home or School Activity

 Social Studies Connection

Millions of People Every 10 years, the U.S. Census Bureau counts all the people in each state. The Bureau also groups the 50 states into four regions, as shown in the map at right. Have students research to find the population data that the Census Bureau collected for each region in 1990 and 2000 (shown in table). Then have your students calculate the total U.S. population in 1990 and in 2000.

State Region	Population 1990	Population 2000
Northeast	50,809,229	53,594,378
Midwest	59,668,632	64,392,776
South	85,445,930	100,236,820
West	52,786,082	63,197,932

U.S. State Regions

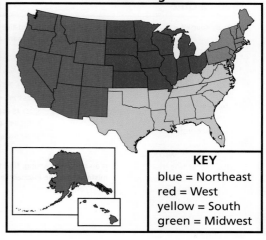

KEY
blue = Northeast
red = West
yellow = South
green = Midwest

248 UNIT 3 LESSON 8

UNIT 3

LESSON 9

Subtract Whole and Decimal Numbers

REAL WORLD Problem Solving

Lesson Objectives

- **Explore the relationship between addition and subtraction.**
- **Explain solution methods for multi-digit subtraction.**

The Day at a Glance

Today's Goals	Materials
1 Teaching the Lesson **A1:** Discuss regrouping to subtract and relate regrouping in subtraction to addition. **A2:** Explain subtraction methods and apply them to real-world problems. **2 Going Further** ▶ Differentiated Instruction **3 Homework and Spiral Review**	**Lesson Activities** Student Activity Book pp. 105–106 or Student Hardcover Book pp. 105–106 Homework and Remembering pp. 63–64 Base ten blocks (optional) Calculators (optional) **Going Further** Activity Cards 3-9 Play money Calculators MathBoard materials Math Journals

123 **Use Math Talk today!**

Keeping Skills Sharp

Quick Practice ⏱ 5 MINUTES	Daily Routines
Goal: Identify place-value groups in large numbers and display approximate metric lengths. **Read Large Numbers** Have a **Student Leader** write a number with 6 to 12 digits on the board. The leader points to each group of digits and reads the numbers. The class says the group name. **Example:** 42,103,685,093 Leader: 42 Class: *billion* Leader: 103 Class: *million* Leader: 685 Class: *thousand* Leader: 093 Class: *ones* **Metric Lengths** The **Student Leader** writes a metric length abbreviation on the board (m, dm, cm, or mm). The students say the name of the unit and show the approximate length with their hands. Repeat in random order.	**Homework Review** Send students to the board to show their work and explain each step. **What Went Wrong?** Adam wanted to place a fence around his garden that measures 7.3 yd long and 2.5 yd wide. He found the perimeter to be 1.96 yd. He knows this amount must be incorrect. What happened? Give the correct perimeter. Possible answer: The perimeter must be greater than the length of any side. He used 0.73 yd for the length and 0.25 yd for the width. The perimeter is 19.6 yd.

1 Teaching the Lesson

Ungroup With Zeros

 20–25 MINUTES

Goal: Discuss regrouping to subtract and relate regrouping in subtraction to addition.

Materials: Base ten blocks (optional)

 NCTM Standards:
Number and Operations
Communication

Teaching Note

Watch For! Remind students to show how they ungroup on their paper, drawing lines through the numbers as they ungroup.

Teaching Note

Math Background Students are given subtraction across zeros first to show that numbers can be ungrouped from the left. Ungrouping all at once from the left is natural because we read from left to right, and this method leads to fewer errors. For these reasons, this method is emphasized in the earlier grades in *Math Expressions*. However, by fifth grade, most students have become adept at one particular method. There is no need to suggest a change unless the student is clearly struggling.

 Alternate Approach

Base Ten Blocks Have students use hundreds, tens, and ones blocks as they work through the sample problem in Activity 1. If students have trouble conceptualizing ungrouping, provide additional problems for students to practice with the base ten blocks.

► **Discuss Student Methods** WHOLE CLASS

Using **Solve and Discuss**, have students share methods for subtracting these numbers.

$$\begin{array}{r} 400 \\ -\ 164 \\ \hline \end{array}$$

Ask the students to explain how they would ungroup to get enough tens and ones to subtract 6 tens and 4 ones. Explain that there are two basic methods:

Ungroup Place by Place Ungroup 1 hundred to make 10 tens, leaving 3 hundreds. Then ungroup 1 ten to make 10 ones, leaving 9 tens.

$$\begin{array}{r} \overset{9}{\overset{3\ \cancel{10}\,10}{\cancel{400}}} \\ -164 \\ \hline \end{array}$$

Ungroup All at Once Ungroup 400 to make 3 hundreds (300), 9 tens (90), and 10 ones.

$$400 = 300 + 90 + 10$$

$$\begin{array}{r} \overset{3\ 9\ 10}{\cancel{400}} \\ -164 \\ \hline \end{array}$$

Some students may use drawings to show the ungrouping. Each box in the drawing represents a hundred, each line segment represents a ten, and each circle represents a one. The crossed out hundred-box has been ungrouped as 10 tens, and the crossed out ten-segment has been ungrouped as 10 ones.

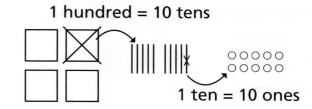

1 hundred = 10 tens

1 ten = 10 ones

Students can also show on the math drawing taking away the known addends to find the unknown addend.

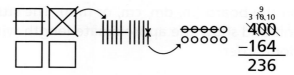

Notice that you can subtract from the left or from the right once all necessary ungrouping has been done.

▶ Relate Addition and Subtraction WHOLE CLASS

Begin by drawing this break-apart drawing on the board.

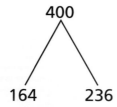

Ask the class to discuss how the drawing shows the relationship between addition and subtraction.

- Which number is the total? the top number

- What do we get if we subtract one of the bottom numbers from the total? We get the other bottom number.

Struggling students may benefit from break-apart drawings as they relate addition and subtraction or solve word problems with unknown addends.

Check Subtraction Using the same set of numbers, ask the class to add the two smaller numbers *without* grouping. Have one student work at the board and ungroup the larger number to subtract. What do we notice about the ungrouped numbers in both problems? They are the same. In subtracting you ungroup to get the numbers you would get if you added without grouping.

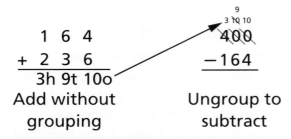

Add without grouping

Ungroup to subtract

This is a good time to reinforce that addition and subtraction are inverse operations. This example shows why we can use addition to check subtraction work.

Check to be sure that students understand that when adding, they still must make 1 new group in the next-left place for each ten in a given place. What was just being discussed is how the ungrouped top number ready for subtraction (the ungrouped total) is the same as the total in addition before it is grouped in those places that have ten or more (too many to write in that place).

Teaching Note

Language and Vocabulary
Students may use a variety of terms for *ungrouping*. Other common terms are *trading* and *borrowing*. Any of these terms are acceptable, as long as students understand what they are used for: ungrouping one unit from a place value to make ten of the units in the next place to the right. You may want to review the definition of ungrouping for **English learners**. Remind them that to ungroup is to break apart into a new group in order to subtract. Hundreds can be ungrouped into tens, and tens can be ungrouped into ones.

English Language Learners
Write *opposite* and *inverse operations* on the board. Model a subtraction and addition problem using the same numbers.
- **Beginning** Ask: **Is addition the opposite of subtraction?** yes Say: **They are *inverse operations*.** Have students repeat.
- **Intermediate** Ask: **What is the *opposite* of addition?** subtraction **Are they *inverse operations*?** yes
- **Advanced** Say: **Addition *undoes* _____.** subtraction **They are *inverse _____*. operations**

Teaching the Lesson (continued)

Activity 2

Solve Any Subtraction Problem

 20-25 MINUTES

Goal: Explain subtraction methods and apply them to real-world problems.

Materials: Student Activity Book or Hardcover Book pp. 105–106, calculators (optional)

✔ **NCTM Standards:**
Number and Operations
Measurement
Communication

Teaching Note

What to Expect From Students
With these problems, some students will ungroup from the left, and some from the right. Try to elicit an explanation of both methods, if possible. In addition, some students will ungroup everything before they subtract, while others will subtract as they ungroup. Again, both of these methods are acceptable.

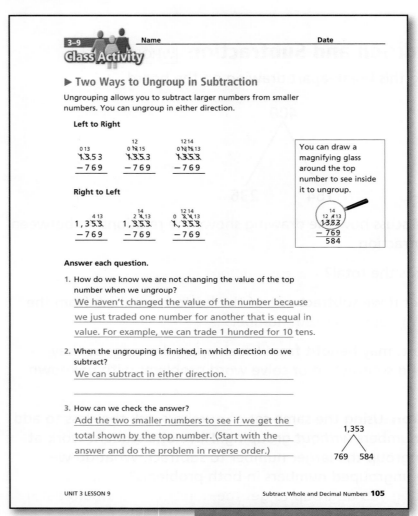

Student Activity Book page 105

▶ Two Ways to Ungroup in Subtraction WHOLE CLASS

Use **Solve and Discuss** to elicit student solution methods for the problem shown below. Ask students to explain the ungrouping process using place value language. (They should not say "borrowed a one," but "ungrouped [or borrowed or traded] one hundred or one ten.")

$$\begin{array}{r} 1353 \\ -\ 769 \end{array}$$

Ask students to look at page 105 in the Student Book. There they can see the same example ungrouped two ways. Tell students they can draw a magnifying glass around the top number to "see inside" it to help them ungroup. If all of your students used the same method, be sure to discuss the other way. Then have students answer the three questions shown.

Practice Subtraction This bank of exercises can be used for mastery of subtraction if students need extra practice. Subsequent days will include more practice on addition and subtraction of decimal numbers, so you don't need to wait for mastery of subtracting decimals.

You may want to suggest that students add to check their subtraction answers, thereby getting addition practice also. They could also use a calculator to check their answers.

1. $45,384 - 28,946 = 16,438$

2. $137,355 - 18,967 = 118,388$

3. $15,044 - 498 = 14,546$

4. $34,568,999 - 8,479,345 = 26,089,654$

5. $4,508 - 3,305 = 1,203$

6. $7,000 - 4,813 = 2,187$

7. $51,006 - 897 = 50,109$

8. $100,000,000 - 510,000 = 99,490,000$

9. $9,612 - 5,000 = 4,612$

10. $43,080 - 8,948 = 34,132$

11. $17,856 - 96 = 17,760$

12. $73,000 - 37,000 = 36,000$

13. $5,000,000,000 - 493,000,000 = 4,507,000,000$

14. $826,005 - 18,785 = 807,220$

15. $93,000 - 6,130 = 86,870$

16. $5,132 - 4,987 = 145$

17. $7,400,000,034 - 7,300,000,921 = 99,999,113$

18. $651,300 - 85,076 = 566,224$

19. $9,005 - 3,999 = 5,006$

20. $5,000,000 - 3,500,000 = 1,500,000$

Activity continued ▶

① Teaching the Lesson (continued)

Activity 2

Differentiated Instruction

Extra Help When a subtraction requires ungrouping, a common error is to ignore the ungrouping and simply subtract the smaller digit in each place from the larger digit, as shown below.

Common Error
$$\begin{array}{r} 1,353 \\ -\ 769 \\ \hline 1,416 \end{array}$$

If you observe this error, encourage those students to perform all of the ungroupings before subtracting any numbers.

The magnifying glass on Student Book page 105 is used to highlight the three ungroupings that are needed to complete the subtraction.

A way for students to begin the subtraction is to draw a loop (large enough for all of the ungroupings) around the top number as a way of reminding themselves to check if all of the top numbers are big enough to subtract the bottom numbers.

The magnifying glass also shows the concept that ungrouping does not change the value of the number. Ungrouping simply shifts equal quantities across columns.

 Math Talk in Action

On the board, model the subtraction shown below, and have students explain each of the ungroupings that are needed to find the answer.

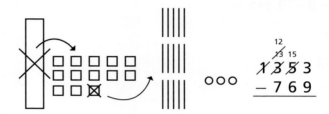

Alyssa: We need to subtract 7 hundreds from 3 hundreds, so we need more hundreds, because 7 is greater than 3. We ungroup 1 thousand to be ten hundreds that we write in the hundreds place.

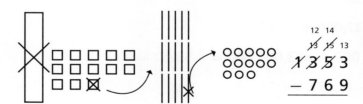

Riley: We need to subtract 6 tens from 5 tens. We need more tens because 6 is more than 5. So we ungroup 1 of the 13 hundreds and get 10 tens for it. That leaves 12 hundreds, and makes 15 tens in the tens column.

Marie: We need to subtract 9 ones from 3 ones, but 9 is more than 3. So we get 10 more ones by ungrouping a ten. That leaves 14 tens and gives us 13 ones.

Complete the subtraction by having some students subtract from the left and others from the right. Check how all of your students are subtracting to learn which of them may need help to move to the "forward unknown addend methods" described on the next page. Some students will benefit from such a move.

Larger Numbers Present a variety of subtractions that include larger numbers and one or more ungroupings. Point out that students may use any method to complete the subtractions, and be sure they know that all of the ungroupings can be performed at one time, or as needed.

Invite pairs of volunteers to work at the board and perform all of the ungroupings for the subtractions shown below. Ask one student in each pair to ungroup from the left, and ask the other student to ungroup from the right.

45,384 – 28,946   137,355 – 18,967

651,300 – 85,076   15,034 – 6,572

▶ Single-Digit Subtraction Methods WHOLE CLASS

Some fifth grade students may still perform single-digit subtractions slowly or inaccurately. Many students count down to solve these problems. However, if the starting number is counted when counting down, the result will be a wrong answer. These students may benefit from shifting to a forward unknown addend method, which changes the subtraction to an addition, and enables them to count up to find the answer.

For example, the subtraction 13 – 9 = ? is the same as 9 + ? = 13.

Think: 13 – 9 = ?	9 + ? = 13
Count Down	Count Up
Start with 13.	Start with 9.
Count to 9: 12, 11, 10, 9 is 4.	Count to 13: 10, 11, 12, 13 is 4.

An alternative way involves making a ten.

Think: 9 + ? = 13
Make a Ten
9 + 1 makes 10 + 3 more in 13 is 4: 9 + 4 = 13

Activity continued ▶

The Learning Classroom

Helping Community Students may fear doing their math work in public because they are afraid to be incorrect. Emphasize that errors help us learn. A safe culture develops in this type of classroom because students do not fear criticism when they make mistakes. You can model this for students as you make your own errors. Fixing your errors models a healthy approach for students.

Activity 2

Tell students to solve each problem and then write the name of the method they chose to use.

► 6,300 − 427

► 3,001 − 135

► 5,020 − 123

► 1,001,001 − 96,452

3–9
Class Activity

Name _____ Date _____

► **Real-World Problems**

Solve each problem.

Show your work.

4. One year the Sahara Desert received 0.791 inches of rain. That same year the rain forest in Brazil received 324 inches. How much more rain fell in the rain forest that year than in the desert?

   323.209 inches

5. A newborn kangaroo measures about 0.02 meters in height. An adult kangaroo can measure up to 2.7 meters in height. How much shorter is the baby kangaroo than the tallest adult?

   2.68 meters

6. Jack and Lelia have each been saving money. Jack has $136.83, and Lelia has nineteen dollars. How much less money does Lelia have than Jack?

   $117.83

7. Colleen owns a tree nursery. Her tallest maple tree measures 2.32 meters, and her shortest measures 0.4 meters. What is the difference in their heights?

   1.92 meters

106 UNIT 3 LESSON 9   Subtract Whole and Decimal Numbers

Student Activity Book page 106

The Learning Classroom

Helping Community When stronger math students finish their work early, let them help others who might be struggling. Many students enjoy the role of helping other students. In their "helper" role, students who might become bored challenge themselves as they explain math content to others.

► **Real-World Problems** WHOLE CLASS

Next, have the class use **Solve** and **Discuss** with the word problems on page 106 of the Student Book. Invite several students to work at the board while the others work at their seats alone or in **Student Pairs** or **Small Groups**. Students can explain at their seats before discussing as a class. The major issue with these problems is subtracting like units, which is done most easily by aligning like places in a vertical subtraction. Use the Decimal Secret-Code Cards or the metric rulers as needed to help students see the like places they need to align for these problems.

② Going Further

Intervention — Activity Card 3-9

Across Zeros — Activity Card 3-9 ●

Work: In Pairs

Use:
• Play money

1. **Work Together** Use play money to model the following subtraction: $300 – $279

2. Model 3 hundreds with $100-bills and take away 2.

3. Ungroup the remaining hundred into 10 tens and take away 7 tens.

4. How can you ungroup the remaining bills so you can take away 9 ones? What is $300 – $279? Ungroup the three tens into 30 ones; $21

Unit 3, Lesson 9   Copyright © Houghton Mifflin Company

Activity Note After students have completed the activity, have them model and solve the following problems: $200 – $148 $52; $400 – $327 $73; $500 – $216 $84

📝 **Math Writing Prompt**

Real-World Situation Write about a real-world situation in which you would need to add or subtract decimals.

Soar to Success Math ★ **Software Support**

Warm-Up 11.25

On Level — Activity Card 3-9

Choose Your Method — Activity Card 3-9 ▲

Work: In Pairs

Use:
• Calculators
• MathBoard materials

1. There are different ways to solve problems: mental math, paper and pencil, and a calculator. Decide which method works best for each problem below.

Problem	Solution	Method
950 – 250	700	MM
13.402 – 8.979	4.423	C
639 – 564	75	PP
5,000 – 2,000	3,000	MM
9.85 – 2.27	7.58	PP
10,213 – 9,999.85	213.15	C

2. **Work Together** Solve each problem. Did the method you choose work well? If not, what method might work better? Answers will vary.

Unit 3, Lesson 9   Copyright © Houghton Mifflin Company

Activity Note Before students begin the activity, discuss the different methods and when each method might be most reasonable to choose.

📝 **Math Writing Prompt**

Make Connections Explain how addition and subtraction are related. Give an example.

MegaMath Grades K-6 **Software Support**

The Number Games: Tiny's Think Tank, Level L

Challenge — Activity Card 3-9

Check It! — Activity Card 3-9 ■

Work: In Pairs

Use:
• MathBoard materials

1. What is the inverse operation for subtraction? addition

You can use addition to check subtraction.

Solve:
507.8 – 269.5 = 238.3

Check:
238.3 + 269.5 = 507.8 ✓

2. Make up five subtraction exercises on your own. Then exchange with your partner and solve.

3. Exchange again and use addition to check the answers.

Unit 3, Lesson 9   Copyright © Houghton Mifflin Company

Activity Note Review the concept of inverse operations before students begin the activity. Encourage students to write subtraction exercises using whole and decimal numbers.

📝 **Math Writing Prompt**

Explain a Process Write a subtraction example that involves regrouping. Then explain how you would regroup to solve it.

✦ **DESTINATION** Math® **Software Support**

Course III: Module 4: Unit 2: Subtracting Decimals

③ Homework and Spiral Review

3-9
Homework **Goal:** Additional Practice

Use this Homework page to provide more practice subtracting whole numbers and decimal numbers.

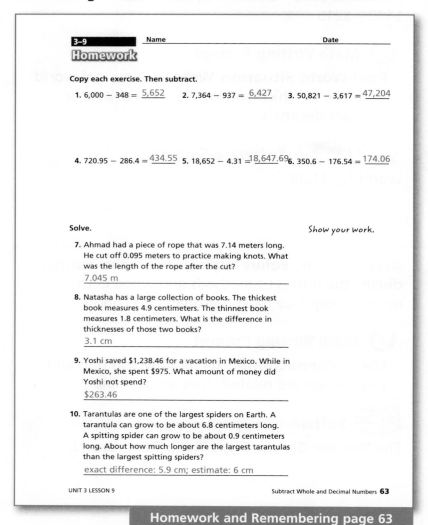

3-9 Name _____ Date _____
Homework

Copy each exercise. Then subtract.

1. 6,000 − 348 = _5,652_ 2. 7,364 − 937 = _6,427_ 3. 50,821 − 3,617 = _47,204_

4. 720.95 − 286.4 = _434.55_ 5. 18,652 − 4.31 = _18,647.69_ 6. 350.6 − 176.54 = _174.06_

Solve. *Show your work.*

7. Ahmad had a piece of rope that was 7.14 meters long. He cut off 0.095 meters to practice making knots. What was the length of the rope after the cut?
   _7.045 m_

8. Natasha has a large collection of books. The thickest book measures 4.9 centimeters. The thinnest book measures 1.8 centimeters. What is the difference in thicknesses of those two books?
   _3.1 cm_

9. Yoshi saved $1,238.46 for a vacation in Mexico. While in Mexico, she spent $975. What amount of money did Yoshi not spend?
   _$263.46_

10. Tarantulas are one of the largest spiders on Earth. A tarantula can grow to be about 6.8 centimeters long. A spitting spider can grow to be about 0.9 centimeters long. About how much longer are the largest tarantulas than the largest spitting spiders?
    exact difference: 5.9 cm; estimate: 6 cm

UNIT 3 LESSON 9   Subtract Whole and Decimal Numbers **63**

Homework and Remembering page 63

3-9
Remembering **Goal:** Spiral Review

This Remembering activity would be appropriate anytime after today's lesson.

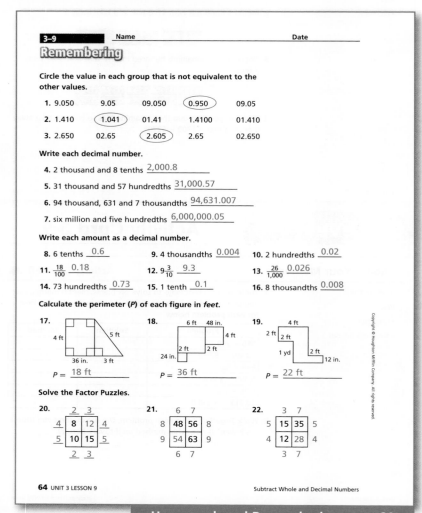

3-9 Name _____ Date _____
Remembering

Circle the value in each group that is not equivalent to the other values.

1. 9.050   9.05   09.050   (0.950)   09.05
2. 1.410   (1.041)   01.41   1.4100   01.410
3. 2.650   02.65   (2.605)   2.65   02.650

Write each decimal number.

4. 2 thousand and 8 tenths _2,000.8_
5. 31 thousand and 57 hundredths _31,000.57_
6. 94 thousand, 631 and 7 thousandths _94,631.007_
7. six million and five hundredths _6,000,000.05_

Write each amount as a decimal number.

8. 6 tenths _0.6_   9. 4 thousandths _0.004_   10. 2 hundredths _0.02_
11. $\frac{18}{100}$ _0.18_   12. $9\frac{3}{10}$ _9.3_   13. $\frac{26}{1,000}$ _0.026_
14. 73 hundredths _0.73_   15. 1 tenth _0.1_   16. 8 thousandths _0.008_

Calculate the perimeter (P) of each figure in feet.

17.   18.   19.
P = _18 ft_   P = _36 ft_   P = _22 ft_

Solve the Factor Puzzles.

20.   21.   22.

64 UNIT 3 LESSON 9   Subtract Whole and Decimal Numbers

Homework and Remembering page 64

Home or School Activity

Science Connection

Seeing Colors Ask, "Did you know that all the colors we see are just different waves of light?" Then tell students that every color light wave has a different length. Have students research to find the ranges of wave lengths for some common colors. Then ask, Which of these colors has the greatest range of wavelengths? Which color has the smallest range?

Color	Wavelength of Light	
	Shortest	Longest
Blue	0.045 cm	0.05 cm
Green	0.052 cm	0.0565 cm
Yellow	0.0565 cm	0.059 cm
Orange	0.059 cm	0.0625 cm
Red	0.0625 cm	0.074 cm

258 UNIT 3 LESSON 9

Place Value Word Problems

Lesson Objectives

● Solve problems with large numbers and decimal numbers.

● Write word problems.

The Day at a Glance

Today's Goals	Materials
1 **Teaching the Lesson** **A1:** Solve and explain problems with large numbers and decimals. **A2:** Work in pairs or small groups to generate word problems. **2** **Going Further** ► Problem Solving Strategy: Is an Exact or Estimated Answer Needed? ► Differentiated Instruction **3** **Homework and Spiral Review**	**Lesson Activities** Student Activity Book pp. 107–109 or Student Hardcover Book pp.107–109 Homework and Remembering pp. 65–66 **Going Further** Student Activity Book p. 110 or Student Hardcover Book p. 110 Activity Cards 3-10 Index cards Math Journals

123 Use Math Talk today!

Keeping Skills Sharp

Quick Practice ⏱ 5 MINUTES	Daily Routines
Goal: Practice counting and saying place-value groups by counting by 10s, 100s, and 1,000s aloud. **Large Count-Bys** Have the class count in unison by 10s to 100, by 100s to 1,000, by 1,000s to 10,000, by 10,000s to 100,000, by 100,000s to 1,000,000, and by 1,000,000s to 10,000,000. Write the first several numbers in each series as the students are counting. **Examples:** Count by 10s to 100: 10, 20, 30, 40, 50… Count by 100s to 1,000: 100, 200, 300, 400… Count by 1,000s to 10,000: 1,000, 2,000, 3,000…	**Homework Review** Have students discuss and help each other resolve any problems from the homework. **Logic** Franco, Tom, Gail, and Jaqui want to run for club president, vice-president, treasurer, and secretary. Gail does not want to be treasurer or secretary. Tom does not want to be vice-president or treasurer. How many ways can they run? 6 ways

P	F	J	G	G	T	T
VP	G	G	J	F	G	G
T	J	F	F	J	F	J
S	T	T	T	T	J	F

Teaching the Lesson

Solve and Explain Word Problems

 15–20 MINUTES

Goal: Solve and explain problems with large numbers and decimals.

Materials: Student Activity Book or Hardcover Book p. 107

✔ **NCTM Standards:**
Problem Solving
Number and Operations
Communication

Teaching Note

What to Expect From Students
Students will use a variety of methods to solve these problems. For example, problem 3 can be solved mentally by some students who have a clear sense of place value. Other students will need to carry out the subtraction on paper. Have students discuss their different solution methods.

English Language Learners

On the board, write: *How long ago did sharks appear on earth?* Underline *How long*.

• **Beginning** Say: In this question *how long* means how many years. Ask: **Is the answer about 395 million years?** yes
• **Intermediate** Ask: In this question, does *how long* mean *how many years*? yes
• **Advanced** Say: In this question, *how long* means *how many* _____. years

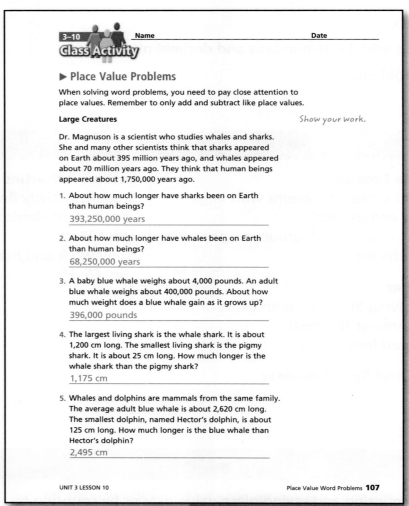

3–10
Class Activity
Name _____ Date _____

▶ **Place Value Problems**

When solving word problems, you need to pay close attention to place values. Remember to only add and subtract like place values.

Large Creatures   *Show your work.*

Dr. Magnuson is a scientist who studies whales and sharks. She and many other scientists think that sharks appeared on Earth about 395 million years ago, and whales appeared about 70 million years ago. They think that human beings appeared about 1,750,000 years ago.

1. About how much longer have sharks been on Earth than human beings?
   393,250,000 years

2. About how much longer have whales been on Earth than human beings?
   68,250,000 years

3. A baby blue whale weighs about 4,000 pounds. An adult blue whale weighs about 400,000 pounds. About how much weight does a blue whale gain as it grows up?
   396,000 pounds

4. The largest living shark is the whale shark. It is about 1,200 cm long. The smallest living shark is the pigmy shark. It is about 25 cm long. How much longer is the whale shark than the pigmy shark?
   1,175 cm

5. Whales and dolphins are mammals from the same family. The average adult blue whale is about 2,620 cm long. The smallest dolphin, named Hector's dolphin, is about 125 cm long. How much longer is the blue whale than Hector's dolphin?
   2,495 cm

UNIT 3 LESSON 10   Place Value Word Problems **107**

Student Activity Book page 107

▶ Place Value Problems ⬚WHOLE CLASS⬚

Explain that problems 1–5 on page 107 of the Student Book are like other problems students have seen except that they have large numbers. Invite several students to work at the board while the other students work at their seats. Then ask one or two students at the board to explain how they solved the problem. Some students will need to convert 395 million and 70 million into numerals before they can work with the numbers.

Follow the same basic procedures for problems 6–9. In problems 7, 8, and 9, the alignment of the decimal numbers is crucial to solving the problem. If necessary, have students explain how to correctly set up the problems.

Activity 2

Student-Generated Word Problems

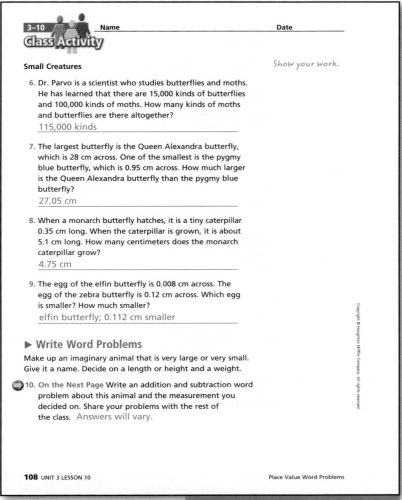

3-10
Class Activity

Name _____ Date _____

Small Creatures

Show your work.

6. Dr. Parvo is a scientist who studies butterflies and moths. He has learned that there are 15,000 kinds of butterflies and 100,000 kinds of moths. How many kinds of moths and butterflies are there altogether?
   115,000 kinds

7. The largest butterfly is the Queen Alexandra butterfly, which is 28 cm across. One of the smallest is the pygmy blue butterfly, which is 0.95 cm across. How much larger is the Queen Alexandra butterfly than the pygmy blue butterfly?
   27.05 cm

8. When a monarch butterfly hatches, it is a tiny caterpillar 0.35 cm long. When the caterpillar is grown, it is about 5.1 cm long. How many centimeters does the monarch caterpillar grow?
   4.75 cm

9. The egg of the elfin butterfly is 0.008 cm across. The egg of the zebra butterfly is 0.12 cm across. Which egg is smaller? How much smaller?
   elfin butterfly; 0.112 cm smaller

▶ **Write Word Problems**
Make up an imaginary animal that is very large or very small. Give it a name. Decide on a length or height and a weight.

10. On the Next Page Write an addition and subtraction word problem about this animal and the measurement you decided on. Share your problems with the rest of the class. Answers will vary.

108 UNIT 3 LESSON 10

Place Value Word Problems

Student Activity Book page 108

▶ Write Word Problems PAIRS

Using the prompt on page 108, students should work in **Student Pairs** to create some problems of their own. Give them about 10 minutes to come up with two problems about an imaginary animal.

If some groups have trouble getting started, try asking:

● How long is your animal? How much does it weigh?

● Does it have a tail? How long is the tail?

● About how many of these animals are there on Earth? Or does it live on another planet? How far away is that planet?

Then have various pairs volunteer to describe their animal and to present some problems for the rest of the class to solve.

 20–25 MINUTES

Goal: Work in pairs or small groups to generate word problems.

Materials: Student Activity Book or Hardcover Book pp. 108–109

 NCTM Standards:
Problem Solving
Number and Operations
Communication

The Learning Classroom

Math Talk Emphasize to students that this is a good time to exchange problem solving strategies and to help each other clarify their thinking about problems. Ask students to check each other's work so they can correct their own errors. **English learners** having difficulty generating word problems may choose to draw or diagram their problems first and then work with a partner to find the best words to communicate the problems and their solution strategies.

 Ongoing Assessment

Tell students to write and solve one original problem and note the method they used to solve it.

---

② Going Further

Problem Solving Strategy: Is an Exact or Estimated Answer Needed?

Goal: Determine whether a problem requires an exact answer or an estimated answer.

Materials: Student Activity Book or Hardcover Book p. 110

 NCTM Standards:
Number and Operations
Problem Solving

▶ Is an Exact or Estimated Answer Needed? [WHOLE CLASS]

In this activity, students connect exact or estimated answers and problem solving.

You may choose to wait for this activity until after working with rounding in Lessons 11 and 12. Only very simple rounding is needed in this activity, so if you use the activity now, simply review what students learned about rounding in earlier grades.

Have students read the introduction at the top of the page. Discuss the difference between an exact answer and an estimated answer.

Then read the example problem scenario and the first row of questions in the box. Ask:

● **How are the questions alike?** They both ask about the total number of apples.

● **What word is different in the second question?** about

● **What does that word tell you?** I can estimate the answer.

Solve both problems together as a class.

```
  29          29  ⟶  30
 +13         +13  ⟶ +10
 ---         ----------
  42               40
```

Point out that the word *about* is used in the estimated answer sentence.

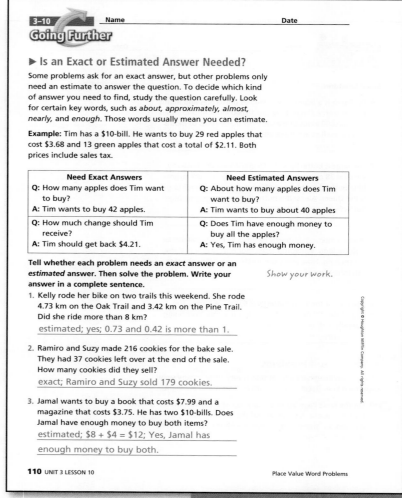

Student Activity Book page 110

Then discuss the next example. Have students identify the estimation words. Point out in the last estimation question that since we know the apples cost about $6.00, we know that $10 is enough to buy them.

Have students solve problems 1–3 independently. Suggest that they underline the question in each problem and circle any key estimation words. Remind students to use estimation words, such as *about*, when they write their estimated answers.

Math Talk After students solve all the problems, review the answers together as a class. Use **Solve and Discuss** to encourage students to talk about how they decided whether an exact or estimated answer was needed for each problem.

Differentiated Instruction

Intervention

Activity Card 3-10

Add or Subtract?   Activity Card 3-10

Work: By Yourself
Use:

• 12 Index cards

3. Possible answer: *Earn*
is an addition word
because earning money
adds to my income.
Spend is a subtraction
word because
spending money
reduces the amount of
money that I have.

1. Write each word in the list below on an index card, 1 word per card.

> plus, minus, more, less, sum, difference
> earn, spend, increase, decrease, up, down

2. Shuffle all the cards. Then sort the cards into two groups: Addition Words and Subtraction Words.

3. **Math Talk** Explain how you decided which category to choose for the words *earn* and *spend*.

4. Pick a card. Then write a word problem using that word and solve it.

Unit 3, Lesson 10   Copyright © Houghton Mifflin Company

Activity Note If time permits, have students choose additional cards and use the words in sentences to reinforce the distinction between addition and subtraction scenarios.

 Math Writing Prompt

Estimate Write a word problem that requires an estimated answer. Then solve the problem.

 **Software Support**

Warm-Up 10.07, 11.06

On Level

Activity Card 3-10

Two Mix   Activity Card 3-10 ▲

Work: In Pairs
Problem sets will vary.

Possible problem set:

22 + 22 = 44
22 + 2.2 = 24.2
22 + 0.22 = 22.22
2.2 + 2.2 = 4.4
2.2 + 0.22 = 2.42
0.22 + 0.22 = 0.44

1. **Work Together** Write six addition problems. Follow the rules below.

• Each addend uses only the digit 2.
• Each addend must have exactly two digits.
• Each problem must have a different sum.
• The addends can be whole numbers or decimals.

2. **Math Talk** How many different pairs of addends are possible? 9; Each addend can be 22, 2.2, or 0.22, so there are three possible choices for the second addend with each choice for the first addend.

Unit 3, Lesson 10   Copyright © Houghton Mifflin Company

Activity Note Be sure students understand that the zero they would ordinarily use to precede the decimal point in a number such as 0.22 does not count as one of the two digits in the two addends.

 Math Writing Prompt

Explain Use examples to show that addition and subtraction are inverse operations.

 Software Support

The Number Games: Tiny's Think Tank, Level L

Challenge

Activity Card 3-10

Elapsed Time   Activity Card 3-10 ■

Work: By Yourself

1. You can regroup hours to find elapsed time. Look at the example. If you regroup 3 hours, you have 2 hours and how many minutes? 60

2	85
3̸ hr 25 min	
−1 hr 53 min	
1 hr 32 min	

2. **Explain** How is regrouping to find elapsed time different from regrouping to subtract 578 − 486? Regrouping is done with groups of 60, not 100.

3. Find the elapsed time for each problem below.

1 hr 15 min − 45 min 30 min

2 hr 7 min − 1 hr 20 min 47 min

5 hr 30 min −3 hr 57 min 1 hr 33 min

8 hr − 4 hr 20 min 3 hr 40 min

10 hr − 35 min 9 hr 25 min

Unit 3, Lesson 10   Copyright © Houghton Mifflin Company

Activity Note If necessary, remind students that 1 h = 60 min, so they use groups of 60, not 100, when they regroup.

 Math Writing Prompt

Write a Problem Use your state population and the total population of another state to write a story problem.

 Software Support

Course III: Module 2: Unit 1: Differences Between Large Numbers

③ Homework and Spiral Review

3-10
Homework **Goal:** Additional Practice

Use this Homework page to provide students with more practice with place value problems.

3-10
Remembering **Goal:** Spiral Review

This Remembering activity would be appropriate anytime after today's lesson.

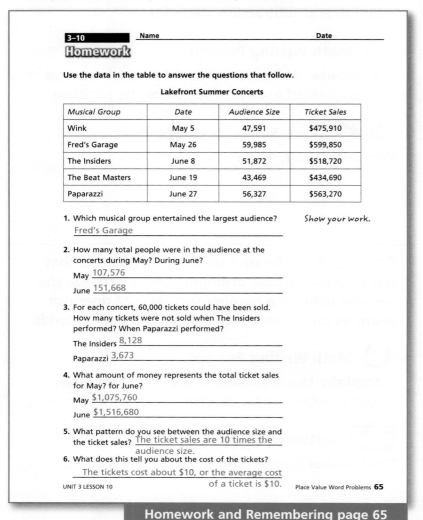

3-10 Name _____ Date _____
Homework

Use the data in the table to answer the questions that follow.

Lakefront Summer Concerts

Musical Group	Date	Audience Size	Ticket Sales
Wink	May 5	47,591	$475,910
Fred's Garage	May 26	59,985	$599,850
The Insiders	June 8	51,872	$518,720
The Beat Masters	June 19	43,469	$434,690
Paparazzi	June 27	56,327	$563,270

1. Which musical group entertained the largest audience? *Show your work.*
   Fred's Garage

2. How many total people were in the audience at the concerts during May? During June?
   May 107,576
   June 151,668

3. For each concert, 60,000 tickets could have been sold. How many tickets were not sold when The Insiders performed? When Paparazzi performed?
   The Insiders 8,128
   Paparazzi 3,673

4. What amount of money represents the total ticket sales for May? for June?
   May $1,075,760
   June $1,516,680

5. What pattern do you see between the audience size and the ticket sales? The ticket sales are 10 times the audience size.
6. What does this tell you about the cost of the tickets?
   The tickets cost about $10, or the average cost of a ticket is $10.

UNIT 3 LESSON 10   Place Value Word Problems **65**

Homework and Remembering page 65

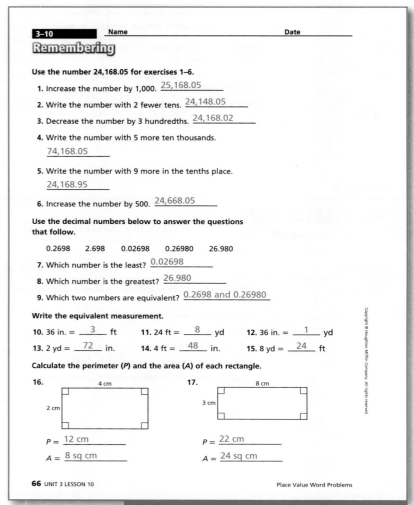

3-10 Name _____ Date _____
Remembering

Use the number 24,168.05 for exercises 1–6.
1. Increase the number by 1,000. 25,168.05
2. Write the number with 2 fewer tens. 24,148.05
3. Decrease the number by 3 hundredths. 24,168.02
4. Write the number with 5 more ten thousands.
   74,168.05
5. Write the number with 9 more in the tenths place.
   24,168.95
6. Increase the number by 500. 24,668.05

Use the decimal numbers below to answer the questions that follow.

   0.2698   2.698   0.02698   0.26980   26.980
7. Which number is the least? 0.02698
8. Which number is the greatest? 26.980
9. Which two numbers are equivalent? 0.2698 and 0.26980

Write the equivalent measurement.
10. 36 in. = ___3___ ft   11. 24 ft = ___8___ yd   12. 36 in. = ___1___ yd
13. 2 yd = ___72___ in.   14. 4 ft = ___48___ in.   15. 8 yd = ___24___ ft

Calculate the perimeter (*P*) and the area (*A*) of each rectangle.
16.   4 cm
   2 cm

17.   8 cm
   3 cm

   P = 12 cm   P = 22 cm
   A = 8 sq cm   A = 24 sq cm

66 UNIT 3 LESSON 10   Place Value Word Problems

Homework and Remembering page 66

Home or School Activity

 Science Connection

Animal Facts Scientists divide all animals into groups called *classes*, such as mammals, birds, insects, and fish.

The animal fact cards at right give information about the largest and smallest animals in three different classes.

Have students use the facts to write three addition or subtraction word problems about the animals. Tell students to exchange problems with a friend and solve.

UNIT 3
LESSON
11

Properties and Strategies

REAL WORLD Problem Solving

Lesson Objectives

- Use the Commutative, Associative, and Distributive properties to compute mentally.
- Apply properties to real-world situations.

Vocabulary

Commutative Property of Addition
Associative Property of Addition
Distributive Property

The Day at a Glance

Today's Goals	Materials
1 Teaching the Lesson **A1:** Use properties to compute mentally with large numbers and decimal numbers. **A2:** Identify Communicative, Associative, and Distributive Properties in real-world contexts. **2 Going Further** ▶ Differentiated Instruction **3 Homework and Spiral Review**	**Lesson Activities** Student Activity Book pp. 111–112 or Student Hardcover Book pp. 111–112 Homework and Remembering pp. 67–68 Quick Quiz 3 (Assessment Guide) **Going Further** Activity Cards 3-11 Index cards Grid Paper (TRB M17) Math Journals 123 *Use Math Talk today!*

Keeping Skills Sharp

Quick Practice ⏱ 5 MINUTES	Daily Routines
Goal: Practice counting and saying place-value groups by counting by 10s, 100s, and 1,000s aloud. **Large Count-Bys** Have the class count in unsion by 10s to 100, by 100s to 1,000, by 1,000s to 10,000, by 10,000s to 100,000, by 100,000s to 1,000,000, and by 1,000,000s to 10,000,000. Write the first several numbers in each series as the students are counting. **Examples:** By 10s to 100: 10, 20, 30, 40, 50… By 100s to 1,000: 100, 200, 300, 400… By 1,000s to 10,000: 1,000, 2,000, 3,000…	**Homework Review** Have students discuss problems from the homework. **Strategy Problem** Each student needs 5 inches. Paul and Mari did not have any. The teacher gave Paul $\frac{1}{4}$ of the string from the school supply closet. Then Paul gave $\frac{1}{2}$ of this to Mari. Mari had just enough string. How much string is left in the school supply closet? 30 in.; Mari had 5 in. that is half of 10 in. 10 in. is one fourth of 40 in. 40 − 10 = 30

Teaching the Lesson

Use Properties

 20-25 MINUTES

Goal: Use properties to compute mentally with large numbers and decimal numbers.

Materials: Student Activity Book or Hardcover Book pp. 111–112

✓ **NCTM Standards:**
Number and Operations
Algebra
Communication

Teaching Note

Language and Vocabulary Remind students about the definitions of the Commutative and Associative Properties of Addition.

Commutative Property:
$a + b = b + a$

Associative Property:
$a + (b + c) = (a + b) + c$

English Language Learners

For problems 5 and 6, write out the numbers on the board.

- **Beginning** Point to and identify each number. Have students repeat.
- **Intermediate and Advanced** Point to each number. Have students identify it. Write 10,000,000. Ask: **In problem 5, which 2 numbers can we add to get 10 million?** 8 million, 2 million

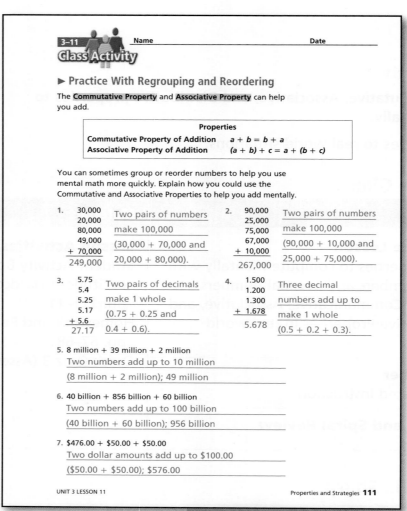

Student Activity Book page 111

▶ Numbers With Multiple Addends WHOLE CLASS

Write this addition problem on the board.

$$50,000 + 25,000 + 38,000 + 75,000 + 50,000 =$$

Ask the class if there is a quick way to solve it using mental math.

Show students that, by pairing the numbers as shown, we can make two groups of 100,000. Then it is easier to find the total.

$$100,000 + 100,000 + 38,000 = 238,000$$

Ask the students how we know that it is all right to reorder the numbers and to group them together in this way. Students may remember the Commutative Property of Addition and the Associative Property of Addition, which state that numbers can be added in reverse order or regrouped.

▶ Practice With Regrouping and Reordering

WHOLE CLASS

Have students **Solve and Discuss** the exercises on pages 111–112 of the Student Book. For exercises 1–7, students need to find meaningful ways to group and reorder numbers so that they can add them mentally.

Next, have students turn to Student Book page 112. To best solve exercises 8–10, students need to recognize that the sum of two pairs of factors that share a factor can be simplified into just one pair of factors.

$$(7 \times 25) + (7 \times 75) = 7 \times (25 + 75) = 7 \times 100 = 700$$

This is much easier than completing the multiplication first, and then adding the results.

Teaching Note

Watch For! Some students may confuse applications of the Associative and Distributive Properties because both use parentheses. Make sure students understand that

▶ the Associative Property uses parentheses to show which numbers should be added or multiplied first. Only one operation is involved.

▶ the Distributive Property uses parentheses to show whether you multiply/divide or add/subtract first. Two operations are involved.

 Class Management

Looking Ahead Have students bring in pictographs from newspapers and magazines for the next lessons. Students can share their graphs and discuss the information presented.

Teaching the Lesson (continued)

Real-World Applications

 20-25 MINUTES

Goal: Identify Commutative, Associative, and Distributive Properties in real-world contexts.

Materials: Student Activity Book p. 112 or Hardcover Book p. 112

✔ **NCTM Standards:**
Number and Operations
Algebra
Problem Solving

Teaching Note

Language and Vocabulary Help students remember the meanings of Commutative, Associative, and Distributive Properties by associating them with real-world situations. For example, a *commuter* covers the same distance going to and coming from work each day, we *associate* with different groups of people, and we *distribute* grades to everyone in the class, leaving no one out. For quick reference, remind **English learners** to record in their notebook the definitions of Commutative and Associative Properties along with the above examples.

 **Quick Quiz**

See Assessment Guide for Unit 3 Quick Quiz 3.

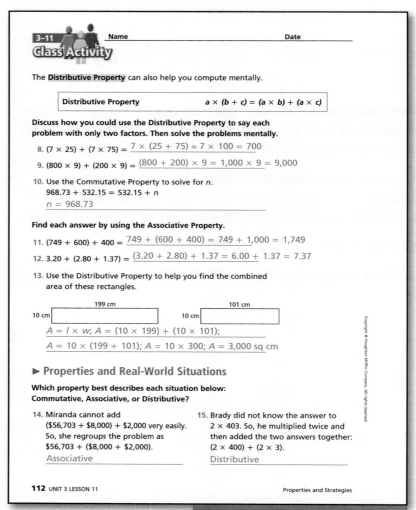

Student Activity Book page 112

The page 112 activity shows:

The **Distributive Property** can also help you compute mentally.

| Distributive Property | $a \times (b + c) = (a \times b) + (a \times c)$ |

Discuss how you could use the Distributive Property to say each problem with only two factors. Then solve the problems mentally.

8. $(7 \times 25) + (7 \times 75) = \underline{7 \times (25 + 75) = 7 \times 100 = 700}$

9. $(800 \times 9) + (200 \times 9) = \underline{(800 + 200) \times 9 = 1{,}000 \times 9 = 9{,}000}$

10. Use the Commutative Property to solve for n.
$968.73 + 532.15 = 532.15 + n$
$\underline{n = 968.73}$

Find each answer by using the Associative Property.

11. $(749 + 600) + 400 = \underline{749 + (600 + 400) = 749 + 1{,}000 = 1{,}749}$

12. $3.20 + (2.80 + 1.37) = \underline{(3.20 + 2.80) + 1.37 = 6.00 + 1.37 = 7.37}$

13. Use the Distributive Property to help you find the combined area of these rectangles.

$A = l \times w; A = (10 \times 199) + (10 \times 101);$
$A = 10 \times (199 + 101); A = 10 \times 300; A = 3{,}000$ sq cm

▶ **Properties and Real-World Situations**

Which property best describes each situation below: Commutative, Associative, or Distributive?

14. Miranda cannot add ($56,703 + $8,000) + $2,000 very easily. So, she regroups the problem as $56,703 + ($8,000 + $2,000).
Associative

15. Brady did not know the answer to 2×403. So, he multiplied twice and then added the two answers together: $(2 \times 400) + (2 \times 3)$.
Distributive

112 UNIT 3 LESSON 11 — Properties and Strategies

▶ Properties and Real-World Situations | WHOLE CLASS

Math Talk Have students answer questions 14–15 on page 112 of the Student Book. Tell students to try solving these problems without referring to the definitions on the previous page. Discuss why these word problems exemplify these properties.

Then tell students to describe a situation that illustrates the Commutative Property. For example,

A school carnival earned $45.00 on Friday morning and $35.00 on Friday afternoon. On Saturday, the carnival earned $35.00 in the morning and $45.00 in the afternoon. The carnival earned exactly the same amount on both days.

Allow students to share their word problems with the class. Discuss why each is or is not a good example.

② Going Further

Differentiated Instruction

Hundred Pairs   Activity Card 3-11 ●

Work: By Yourself

Use:
• 9 Index cards

1. Write the hundred numbers 100–900 on the nine index cards, 1 number per card.

2. Pair the cards to make it easy to find the sum of all nine numbers using mental math. Look for four pairs that have the same sum. 100 + 900; 200 + 800; 300 + 700; 400 + 600

3. Which sum did you choose? Which card will be left over? 1,000; 500

4. What is the sum of the nine numbers? 4,500

5. Repeat the activity adding tens. Erase (or mark out) the last zero in each number on the cards to use the cards again.

6. **Predict** What is the sum of the first nine counting numbers? 45

Unit 3, Lesson 11   Copyright © Houghton Mifflin Company

Activity Note If students have difficulty pairing the numbers, suggest that pairing the greater numbers with the lesser numbers will make it easier to find pairs with the same sum.

 Math Writing Prompt

Draw and Describe Draw a picture that illustrates the Associative Property of Addition. Explain how the picture shows the property.

 **Software Support**

Warm-Up 10.30

Area Models   Activity Card 3-11 ▲

Work: In Pairs

Use:
• Grid Paper (TRB M17)

1. Copy the three rectangles onto grid paper. Write the area of each rectangle on the model. A = 35 sq units; B = 20 sq units; C = 55 sq units

2. Use the equation below to explain how the model shows the Distributive Property.

$$(5 \times 7) + (5 \times 4) = 5 \times 11$$

A + B = C; The rectangles A and B combined have the same length and width as rectangle C. Therefore the sum of their areas equals the area of rectangle C.

Unit 3, Lesson 11   Copyright © Houghton Mifflin Company

Activity Note Students may find it easier to interpret the model if they draw rectangles A and B sharing a common width. This will demonstrate that their total areas equal the area of Rectangle C.

 Math Writing Prompt

Explain Properties How can you use the Commutative and Associative Properties to make it easier to find the sum of the digits 1–9?

 Software Support

Ice Station Exploration: Polar Planes, Level Q

Backward Distribution   Activity Card 3-11 ■

Work: By Yourself

Use:
• Grid Paper (TRB M17)

2. Yes; Any model with two addends whose sum equals 8 units as the length and a width of 5 units will show the Distributive Property. For example: 6 × 5 and 2 × 5

1. A rectangle has a length of 8 units and a width of 5 units. You can use the Distributive Property to separate the rectangle into two new rectangles. The combined area of the two new rectangles is equal to the area of the first rectangle.

2. **Explain** Is there another way to use the dimensions 8 units by 5 units to show the Distributive Property?

3. Draw a rectangle for each of the dimensions on the table. Use the Distributive Property to separate them into two new rectangles. Draw the two new rectangles and find their areas.

length	width
7 units	10 units
12 units	3 units
15 units	9 units

Unit 3, Lesson 11   Copyright © Houghton Mifflin Company

Activity Note To reinforce the concept of the Distributive Property, have students label each length and width of the rectangles they draw and write an equation such as: $(3 \times 5) + (5 \times 5) = 40$.

 Math Writing Prompt

Write Your Own Some word problems can be solved by using the Distributive Property. Write a word problem that you can solve in this way.

 DESTINATION Math® **Software Support**

Course III: Module 5: Unit 1: Rectangles and Squares

③ Homework and Spiral Review

3–11
Homework **Goal:** Additional Practice

Use this Homework page to provide students with more practice with properties and strategies.

3–11
Remembering **Goal:** Spiral Review

This Remembering activity would be appropriate anytime after today's lesson.

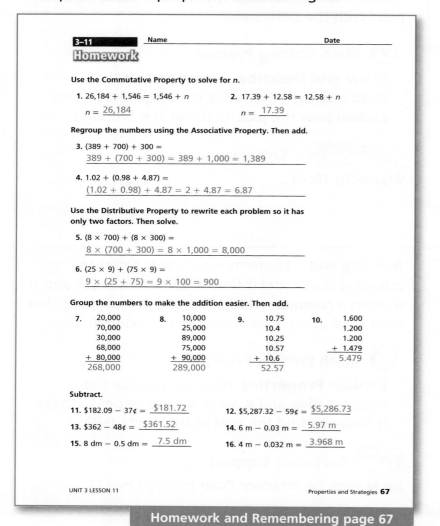

3–11 Name _____ Date _____
Homework

Use the Commutative Property to solve for n.

1. $26{,}184 + 1{,}546 = 1{,}546 + n$ 2. $17.39 + 12.58 = 12.58 + n$
   $n = \underline{26{,}184}$ $n = \underline{17.39}$

Regroup the numbers using the Associative Property. Then add.

3. $(389 + 700) + 300 =$
   $389 + (700 + 300) = 389 + 1{,}000 = 1{,}389$

4. $1.02 + (0.98 + 4.87) =$
   $(1.02 + 0.98) + 4.87 = 2 + 4.87 = 6.87$

Use the Distributive Property to rewrite each problem so it has only two factors. Then solve.

5. $(8 \times 700) + (8 \times 300) =$
   $8 \times (700 + 300) = 8 \times 1{,}000 = 8{,}000$

6. $(25 \times 9) + (75 \times 9) =$
   $9 \times (25 + 75) = 9 \times 100 = 900$

Group the numbers to make the addition easier. Then add.

7.	8.	9.	10.
20,000	10,000	10.75	1.600
70,000	25,000	10.4	1.200
30,000	89,000	10.25	1.200
68,000	75,000	10.57	+ 1.479
+ 80,000	+ 90,000	+ 10.6	5.479
268,000	289,000	52.57	

Subtract.

11. $\$182.09 - 37¢ = \underline{\$181.72}$ 12. $\$5{,}287.32 - 59¢ = \underline{\$5{,}286.73}$

13. $\$362 - 48¢ = \underline{\$361.52}$ 14. $6\text{ m} - 0.03\text{ m} = \underline{5.97\text{ m}}$

15. $8\text{ dm} - 0.5\text{ dm} = \underline{7.5\text{ dm}}$ 16. $4\text{ m} - 0.032\text{ m} = \underline{3.968\text{ m}}$

UNIT 3 LESSON 11   Properties and Strategies **67**

Homework and Remembering page 67

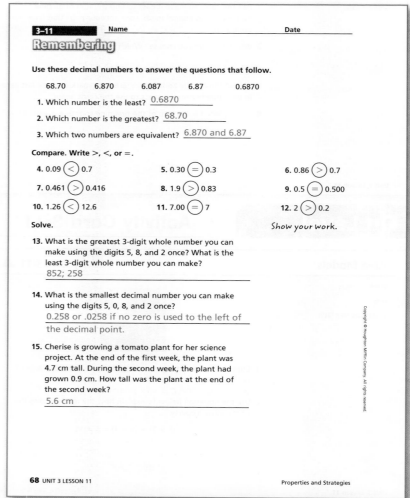

3–11 Name _____ Date _____
Remembering

Use these decimal numbers to answer the questions that follow.

68.70   6.870   6.087   6.87   0.6870

1. Which number is the least? $\underline{0.6870}$
2. Which number is the greatest? $\underline{68.70}$
3. Which two numbers are equivalent? $\underline{6.870 \text{ and } 6.87}$

Compare. Write $>$, $<$, or $=$.

4. $0.09 \boxed{<} 0.7$ 5. $0.30 \boxed{=} 0.3$ 6. $0.86 \boxed{>} 0.7$
7. $0.461 \boxed{>} 0.416$ 8. $1.9 \boxed{>} 0.83$ 9. $0.5 \boxed{=} 0.500$
10. $1.26 \boxed{<} 12.6$ 11. $7.00 \boxed{=} 7$ 12. $2 \boxed{>} 0.2$

Solve.   *Show your work.*

13. What is the greatest 3-digit whole number you can make using the digits 5, 8, and 2 once? What is the least 3-digit whole number you can make?
    852; 258

14. What is the smallest decimal number you can make using the digits 5, 0, 8, and 2 once?
    0.258 or .0258 if no zero is used to the left of the decimal point.

15. Cherise is growing a tomato plant for her science project. At the end of the first week, the plant was 4.7 cm tall. During the second week, the plant had grown 0.9 cm. How tall was the plant at the end of the second week?
    5.6 cm

68 UNIT 3 LESSON 11   Properties and Strategies

Homework and Remembering page 68

Home or School Activity

Music Connection

Orchestra Arrangements Have students research seating arrangements for a symphony orchestra. The instruments are arranged into four "families"—strings, woodwinds, brass, and percussion. A typical number of musicians in the strings family is:

First Violins = 10 musicians   Cellos = 5 musicians
Second Violins = 13 musicians   Double Basses = 2 musicians
Violas = 7 musicians   Harp = 1 musician

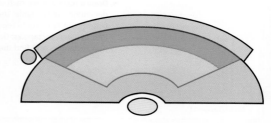

Have students discuss how they can use the properties of addition to find the total number of musicians in the strings section.

Pictographs With Large Numbers

UNIT 3
LESSON
12

REAL
WORLD
**Problem
Solving**

Lesson Objectives

● **Understand progressively larger increments to one million.**

● **Read and construct pictographs with large numbers.**

The Day at a Glance

Today's Goals	Materials	

1 Teaching the Lesson
A1: Discuss pictographs with increasingly large numbers.
A2: Read pictographs with large numbers.
A3: Construct pictographs with large numbers.
 	
2 Going Further
▸ Differentiated Instruction
 	
3 Homework and Spiral Review
	Lesson Activities
	Student Activity Book pp. 113–114
	  or Student Hardcover Book
	  pp. 113–114
	Homework and Remembering
	  pp. 69–70
		Going Further
		Activity Cards 3-12
		Counters
		Math Journals

123 Use **Math Talk** today!

Keeping Skills Sharp

Quick Practice ⏱ 5 MINUTES	Daily Routines
Goal: Practice counting aloud by 10s, 100s, and 1,000s. **Large Count-Bys** Have the class count in unison by 10s to 100, by 100s to 1,000, by 1,000s to 10,000, by 10,000s to 100,000, by 100,000s to 1,000,000, and by 1,000,000s to 10,000,000. Write the first several numbers in each series as the students are counting. **Examples:** By 10s to 100: 10, 20, 30, 40, 50… By 100s to 1,000: 100, 200, 300, 400… By 1,000s to 10,000: 1,000, 2,000, 3,000…	**Homework Review** As you circulate, see whether any problem caused difficulty for many students. **Mental Math** Find the number that is 0.1 greater and the number that is 0.1 less than each of the given numbers. **1.** 6,789 6,789.1; 6,788.9 **2.** 874.025 874.125; 873.925 **3.** 89,105.13 89,105.23; 89,105.03 **4.** 971,355.4 971,355.5; 971,355.3

Pictographs With Large Numbers **271**

Teaching the Lesson

Activity 1

Discuss Pictographs With Large Numbers

 15-20 MINUTES

Goal: Discuss pictographs with increasingly large numbers.

✔ **NCTM Standards:**
Number and Operations
Data Analysis and Probability
Communication

Teaching Note

Math Background Tell students that a pictograph uses the same symbol for each category. A key (value) for that picture is always provided.

The Learning Classroom

Math Talk Always start new topics by eliciting as much from students as possible. Students often know some things about new topics. This builds feelings of competence and confidence and helps create the classroom community where everyone is a teacher and a learner. So even where the directions for a lesson are directing you to do the talking, remember to always ask for students' own ideas first.

▶ **Pictographs With Weighted Symbols** WHOLE CLASS

Make a simple pictograph on the board such as the one shown here. Explain that it shows the number of bagels that two people have.

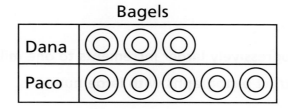

Establish a Key Discuss with students what they might do if Dana had 30 bagels and Paco had 50. Help students come to the conclusion that it would take a lot of space and time to draw 30 bagels. Explain that each picture represents 10 bagels. Introduce the concept of a key showing that each bagel on the pictograph represents 10 bagels. Then draw the key on the board below the pictograph.

Tell students to count Dana's bagels using the new key: 10, 20, 30. Then have them count Paco's bagels: 10, 20, 30, 40, 50.

Change the Condition Ask the class what could be done if Dana had 300 bagels and Paco had 500. Change the key so that each bagel represents 100. Invite a student to go to the board and fix the key.

Key: ⊙ =100 bagels

Then ask the student to lead the class in counting Dana's bagels and Paco's bagels using the new key: 100, 200, 300, and so on.

Continue to increase the quantity of bagels by a factor of 10 until you reach a million. Have a student adjust the key each time and then lead the class in counting the number of bagels. Point out to the students that the graph itself never changes.

Graphs With Rounded Units Give students some 2- and 3-digit numbers that have not been rounded to the nearest ten, hundred, or thousand, and discuss the implications for making pictographs.

Help students see that pictographs don't always show the exact number of items. Sometimes the numbers have been rounded. Ask students:

● What if Dana had 31 bagels and Paco had 59? What would you do?

Here, 10 is our rounding unit. We would make the key show that 1 bagel picture = 10 bagels. Then, we would round each number to the nearest 10. We would still show 3 bagels on the graph for Dana because 31 is closer to 30 than to 40. But we would show 6 bagels for Paco instead of 5 because 59 is closer to 60 than it is to 50.

● What if Dana had 395 bagels and Paco had 612? What would you do?

We could make the key show that 1 bagel picture = 100 bagels. Then, we would round to the nearest 100. Dana has 395 bagels, which rounds to 400. Paco has 612 bagels, which rounds to 600.

When numbers in any table or graph are very large, they are usually estimates. Very large quantities cannot be counted, so estimates are used. You can include the word estimate or estimated in the title or the key of the graph.

Activity continued ▶

Teaching Note

What to Expect From Students
This discussion should move rapidly if your students have had previous exposure to rounding. At this point, students only need to see that graphs are sometimes based on estimates and that we choose the *nearest rounding* unit when we represent a number in a pictograph.

Teaching Note

Vocabulary When creating a pictograph, it is important to decide what number each symbol will stand for. We call this the *rounding unit*. Every number in the data will need to be rounded to this place value. For example, if the rounding unit is 100, every number will need to be rounded to the nearest 100.

English Language Learners
Write *estimate* on the board. Point to the pictograph. Say: **When the numbers in a pictograph are very big we can *estimate*.**

- **Beginning** Ask: **Is an *estimate* exact?** no **Is it *near* the exact number?** yes
- **Intermediate** Ask: **Does *estimate* mean use the exact number or a number *near* the exact number?** near
- **Advanced** Say: **An *estimate* is not _____.** exact **It is *near* the _____.** exact number

Activity 1

Teaching Note

What to Expect from Students
Some students might have used quarter units in the past. Encourage students to round to the nearest rounding unit or halfway point. For instance, they would round 37 to 35 and 38 to 40.

Find the Halfway Point Restore the key on the bagel graph so that 1 bagel picture = 10 bagels. Now ask how many bagel pictures we would draw if Dana had 35 bagels. Some students may say that they would use the larger rounding unit, 40, because this number is exactly halfway between 30 and 40. Point out that there is another possibility—a half bagel. Explain that half pictures are sometimes used on pictographs to show a number that is right between two rounding units. Demonstrate by drawing a half bagel on the graph.

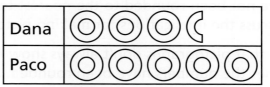

Key: ◯ = 10 bagels

Ask students to identify the halfway point between:

- 200 and 300   250
- 6,000 and 7,000   6500
- 10,000 and 20,000   15,000

Activity 2

Read Pictographs With Large Numbers

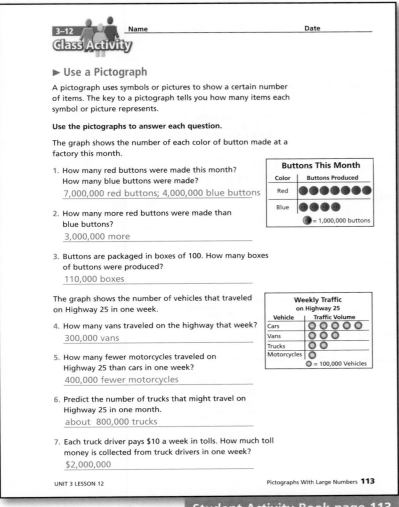

Student Activity Book page 113

Content of Student Activity Book page 113:

3–12 Class Activity

Name _____ Date _____

▶ **Use a Pictograph**

A pictograph uses symbols or pictures to show a certain number of items. The key to a pictograph tells you how many items each symbol or picture represents.

Use the pictographs to answer each question.

The graph shows the number of each color of button made at a factory this month.

1. How many red buttons were made this month? How many blue buttons were made?
   7,000,000 red buttons; 4,000,000 blue buttons

2. How many more red buttons were made than blue buttons?
   3,000,000 more

3. Buttons are packaged in boxes of 100. How many boxes of buttons were produced?
   110,000 boxes

Buttons This Month

Color	Buttons Produced
Red	
Blue	

= 1,000,000 buttons

The graph shows the number of vehicles that traveled on Highway 25 in one week.

4. How many vans traveled on the highway that week?
   300,000 vans

5. How many fewer motorcycles traveled on Highway 25 than cars in one week?
   400,000 fewer motorcycles

6. Predict the number of trucks that might travel on Highway 25 in one month.
   about 800,000 trucks

7. Each truck driver pays $10 a week in tolls. How much toll money is collected from truck drivers in one week?
   $2,000,000

Weekly Traffic on Highway 25

Vehicle	Traffic Volume
Cars	
Vans	
Trucks	
Motorcycles	

= 100,000 Vehicles

UNIT 3 LESSON 12   Pictographs With Large Numbers **113**

⏱ **10–15 MINUTES**

Goal: Read pictographs with large numbers.

Materials: Student Activity Book or Hardcover Book p. 113

✔ **NCTM Standards:**
Number and Operations
Data Analysis and Probability

The Learning Classroom

Building Concepts To support building coherence, have students take turns briefly summarizing the previous day's lesson at the beginning of each math class. Alternatively, you may have a student summarize at the end of each lesson. Either way, if you do this regularly, students will get used to making mental summaries of math concepts and making conceptual connections.

▶ Use a Pictograph WHOLE CLASS

Have students turn to page 113 and answer the questions about the pictographs. Direct their attention to the key for each graph. Have students identify the rounding unit and then use count-bys to answer exercises 1–7. The rounding unit in the first graph, for example, is a million, so the first question can by answered by counting: 1 million, 2 million, 3 million, and so on.

As each question is answered, ask a volunteer to write the number on the board. Check the position of the commas.

Next, have students turn to page 114 and complete exercises 8–10.

Teaching the Lesson (continued)

Construct Pictographs With Large Numbers

 15-20 MINUTES

Goal: Construct pictographs with large numbers.

Materials: Student Activity Book or Hardcover Book p. 114

✓ **NCTM Standards:**
Number and Operations
Data Analysis and Probability
Representation

Teaching Note

What to Expect From Students
Students should keep their drawings simple and neat while they work on making their graphs mathematically accurate. Tell students that one of the important advantages of using pictographs is that the reader can quickly read and interpret the data. It is imperative that the presentation be neat and accurate, and that it include details such as the title and key.

Teaching Note

Math Symbols When you reach problem 9, review the halfway point. Elicit from students that the half-figure on the graph shows the halfway point between 60,000,000 and 70,000,000.

 Ongoing Assessment

► Observe the students as they construct their pictographs. Ensure that all students round correctly and include appropriate keys.

► Ask students to explain what the key is used for in a pictograph.

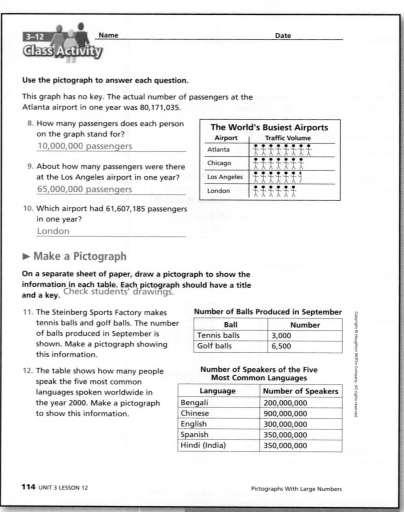

Student Activity Book page 114

► Make a Pictograph WHOLE CLASS

Math Talk Have students complete exercises 11 and 12 on page 114 in the Student Book. Ask students to draw pictographs to show the information in each table. Have them use simple grids with crossed lines as shown on the student book page.

Discuss what rounding unit should be shown in the key. Ask students if there will be any halfway points. Have students discuss the results when they are finished. Allow students to share their pictographs with the class. Then, compare and contrast the pictographs and discuss how different rounding units affect the final pictograph.

② Going Further

Differentiated Instruction

● Intervention Activity Card 3-12

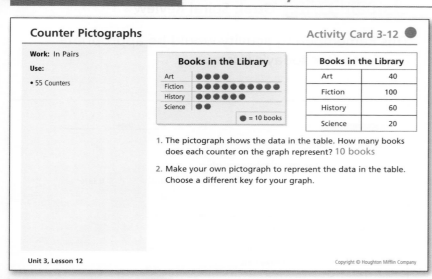

Counter Pictographs Activity Card 3-12 ●

Work: In Pairs
Use:
• 55 Counters

Books in the Library

Art	● ● ● ●
Fiction	● ● ● ● ● ● ● ● ● ●
History	● ● ● ● ● ●
Science	● ●

 ● = 10 books

Books in the Library

Art	40
Fiction	100
History	60
Science	20

1. The pictograph shows the data in the table. How many books does each counter on the graph represent? 10 books

2. Make your own pictograph to represent the data in the table. Choose a different key for your graph.

Unit 3, Lesson 12   Copyright © Houghton Mifflin Company

Activity Note Give students the following numbers to choose for the key to their graph: 1 counter = 20, 5, or 4 books.

📝 **Math Writing Prompt**

Make Connections Why do you think a pictograph key is called a key? Explain.

Soar to Success Math ★ **Software Support**

Warm-Up 50.11

▲ On Level Activity Card 3-12

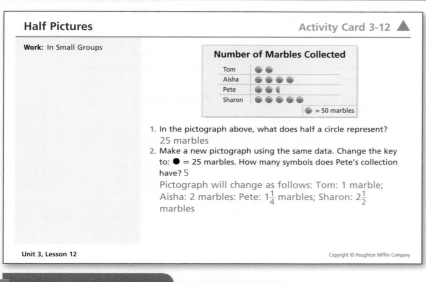

Half Pictures Activity Card 3-12 ▲

Work: In Small Groups

Number of Marbles Collected

Tom	● ●
Aisha	● ● ● ●
Pete	● ● ◖
Sharon	● ● ● ● ●

 ● = 50 marbles

1. In the pictograph above, what does half a circle represent? 25 marbles

2. Make a new pictograph using the same data. Change the key to: ● = 25 marbles. How many symbols does Pete's collection have? 5
Pictograph will change as follows: Tom: 1 marble; Aisha: 2 marbles: Pete: $1\frac{1}{4}$ marbles; Sharon: $2\frac{1}{2}$ marbles

Unit 3, Lesson 12   Copyright © Houghton Mifflin Company

Activity Note Suggest that students make a table showing the data that the original graph represents before making a graph with a different key.

📝 **Math Writing Prompt**

Same and Different Explain the similarities and differences between a bar graph and a pictograph.

MegaMath Grades K-6 **Software Support**

The Number Games: ArachnaGraph, Level A

■ Challenge Activity Card 3-12

Compare Graphs Activity Card 3-12 ■

Work: In Pairs

1. Use the data to make two graphs — a bar graph and a pictograph. Decide who makes each graph.

Sports Balls Sold

Baseballs: 90
Footballs: 45
Basketballs: 60

2. **Work Together** List at least three similarities and three differences between the two graphs.

3. **Math Talk** Which graph makes it easier to compare the numbers sold in each category? Which graph makes it easier to quickly name the exact number sold in each category?

Unit 3, Lesson 12   Copyright © Houghton Mifflin Company

Activity Note In comparing the two graphs, students may find that it is easier to identify specific values on the bar graph if the number of symbols on the pictograph is very large.

📝 **Math Writing Prompt**

Explain Your Thinking Why is it sometimes necessary to show fractional symbols on a pictograph?

✦ **DESTINATION** Math® **Software Support**

Course III: Module 6: Unit 1: Displaying and Analyzing Data

Pictographs With Large Numbers **277**

③ Homework and Spiral Review

3-12 Homework **Goal:** Additional Practice

✓ Include student's Homework for page 69 as a part of their portfolios.

3-12 Remembering **Goal:** Spiral Review

This Remembering activity would be appropriate anytime after today's lesson.

3-12
Homework

Name _____ Date _____

Use the information in each problem to make a pictograph.

1. The Horizon Book Company needs a pictograph showing the number of books sold this year. Using the information shown, make a pictograph. Give your graph a title and a key. Answers will vary. Possible answer:

| Children | 500,000 |
| Adults | 700,000 |

Books Sold this Year	
Books for Children	● ● ● ● ●
Books for Adults	● ● ● ● ● ● ●

Key: ● = 100,000 Books

2. The Melodic Music Company needs a pictograph showing the number of CDs sold this year. Using the information shown, make a pictograph. Remember to include the title and the key. Answers will vary. Possible answer:

Rock	40,000
Country	30,000
Jazz	15,000
Classical	5,000

Number of CDs Sold	
Rock	● ● ● ●
Country	● ● ●
Jazz	● ◖
Classical	◖

Key: ● = 10,000 CDs

3. Ask 2 questions about your pictograph for problem 2 and then answer them. Check students' work.

_____

_____

_____

_____

UNIT 3 LESSON 12   Pictographs with Large Numbers **69**

3-12
Remembering

Name _____ Date _____

Answer each question about the decimal numbers.

58.76   5.876   0.05876   5.8760   0.5876

1. Which number is the smallest?
   0.05876

2. Which number is the greatest?
   58.76

3. Which two numbers are equivalent?
   5.876 and 5.8760

Write each number.

4. seven tenths
   0.7

5. thirty million
   30,000,000

6. eight hundredths
   0.08

7. four million one
   4,000,001

8. forty-five thousand six
   45,006

9. seven hundred fifty thousand ten
   750,010

10. eighty thousand twenty-nine
    80,029

11. two thousandths
    0.002

For each measurement, write an equivalent length in decimeters (dm), centimeters (cm), and millimeters (mm).

12. 13.74 m   137.4 dm   1,374 cm   13,740 mm
13. 0.85 m   8.5 dm   85 cm   850 mm

70 UNIT 3 LESSON 12   Pictographs with Large Numbers

Homework and Remembering page 69

Homework and Remembering page 70

Home or School Activity

Art Connection

Stone Age Art Ancient people made art on rocks. Today, people call these images petroglyphs. Petroglyphs are found all over the world. Some are more than 20,000 years old! Common images include people, animals, and handprints. Experts believe these images may have been used to record history.

Have students find a picture of an ancient petroglyph and use it as a symbol to make a pictograph about their family.

UNIT 3
LESSON
13

Round Numbers on Graphs

REAL
WORLD
Problem
Solving

Lesson Objectives

● Read scales that show large rounded numbers to 100 million.

● Identify the halfway point between two numbers that are multiples of ten.

● Estimate by rounding large numbers.

Vocabulary

scale
estimate
front-end estimation

The Day at a Glance

Today's Goals	Materials	
1 Teaching the Lesson **A1:** Round large numbers with the aid of a scale or number line, then round without visual aids. **A2:** Round large numbers for the purpose of estimation in real-world contexts. **2 Going Further** ► Math Connection: Estimation Methods ► Differentiated Instruction **3 Homework and Spiral Review**	**Lesson Activities** Student Activity Book pp. 115–117 or Student Hardcover Book pp. 115–117 Homework and Remembering pp. 71–72 Secret Code Cards (optional)	**Going Further** Student Activity Book p. 118 or Student Hardcover Book p. 118 Activity Cards 3-13 Math Journals 123 *Use* **Math Talk** *today!*

Keeping Skills Sharp

Quick Practice 🕐 5 MINUTES	Daily Routines
Goal: Use the halfway point of a group of numbers to facilitate rounding. **The Halfway Point** Send 3 **Student Leaders** to the board. The first writes the numbers vertically as the class counts by 100s to 1,000. The next writes the numbers as the class counts by 1,000s to 10,000. The third writes the numbers as the class counts by 10,000s to 100,000. **Student Leaders** take turns circling a pair of consecutive numbers in the list. As they do so, they should ask, "What is the halfway point?" The class responds with the number. For example, 400 and 300 are circled. The class responds "350."	**Homework Review** Ask several students to share their pictographs. Have the class ask clarifying questions about each. If necessary, model asking questions. **Nonroutine Problem** Alexis said she subtracted a 5-digit number from a 6-digit number to find a 4-digit difference. Is this possible? Create an example to support your answer. Yes; Possible example: 101,000 − 96,000 = 5,000

Teaching the Lesson

Use Scales to Round Large Numbers

 25 MINUTES

Goal: Round large numbers with the aid of a scale or number line, then round without visual aids.

Materials: Student Activity Book or Hardcover Book pp. 115–116, Secret Code Cards (optional)

✔ **NCTM Standards:**
Number and Operations
Communication

Differentiated Instruction

Extra Help When working through the first example, the answer may not be apparent to everyone. If students hesitate, ask them to identify the halfway point. 75 Then ask if 76 is larger or smaller than 75. larger Because 76 is larger than 75, it is closer to 80 than to 70.

English Language Learners

Draw a weight scale and a rounding scale on the board. Write *scale*. Say: **These are different scales**.

• **Beginning** Point to each scale and say: **We use the *weight scale* to measure weight. The *rounding scale* helps us round numbers.**

• **Intermediate** Point to the weight scale and ask: **Is this scale for measuring weight or rounding?** measuring weight Point to the rounding scale and say: **This is a rounding _____.** scale

• **Advanced** Have students tell what each *scale* is used for.

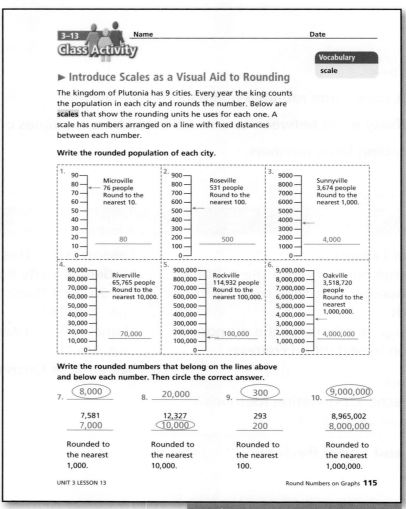

▶ Introduce Scales as a Visual Aid to Rounding

WHOLE CLASS

Have the class turn to page 115. Introduce the word *scale* (numbers arranged in equal "increments"). Have students discuss how the scales on this page are similar to the count-bys that they have been practicing in the Quick Practice.

Ask students to round the population of each city in Plutonia, using the scale to help them position the number. Then ask:

● What is the rounding unit of the scale in exercise 1? 10

● What are we counting by? 10s

● Between which 2 numbers on the scale does the population of Microville fall? between 70 and 80 Put an arrow between these numbers.

3-13

Class Activity

Name _____ Date _____

Vocabulary
estimate

► **Practice With Rounding**

Round to the nearest ten.

11. 23 _20_

12. 75 _80_

13. 156 _160_

Round to the nearest hundred.

14. 291 _300_

15. 1,610 _1,600_

16. 834 _800_

Round to the nearest thousand.

17. 2,315 _2,000_

18. 10,987 _11,000_

19. 15,204 _15,000_

Round to the nearest 10 thousand.

20. 30,986 _30,000_

21. 65,713 _70,000_

22. 9,506 _10,000_

► **Round to Estimate**

When you **estimate** you find a number that is close to the exact number.

Solve each problem by rounding.

Show your work.

23. Herminio has a stamp collection. He has 689 American stamps and 226 foreign stamps. About how many stamps does Herminio have in all?
   Possible answer: 900 stamps

24. Karinne bought a glass of lemonade for 59 cents and a pretzel for 39 cents. Is $1 enough to pay for both items?
   yes

25. The Brown Owl Bookstore has 1,897 novels and 1,405 comic books. About how many more novels does the store have than comic books?
   Possible answer: 500 novels

26. Mebrahtom drove 47 miles before noon. He drove 52 miles after noon. He said he drove nearly 100 miles altogether. Is he right?
   yes

116 UNIT 3 LESSON 13

Round Numbers on Graphs

Differentiated Instruction

Special Needs Fifth-grade students vary widely in their previous exposure to rounding. If your students are having difficulty and this is an important topic for your state or district, you may want to spend an extra day on it. You might try using the Secret Code Cards to help students see the rounded number with zeros that is hiding behind the string of digits. For example, 14,856 is really 14,000 with an extra 856. Is that 856 closer to zero or closer to 1,000? Then the nearest 1,000 is really 15,000.

Teaching Note

Before students do page 116, have them summarize the usual rounding rules.

If the digit to the right of the place to which you want to round is:

• less than 5, round down.

• more than 5, round up.

• 5, round up.

● Is 76 closer to 70 or closer to 80? closer to 80

● So, what would we round the population of Microville to? 80

Tell students that as the numbers get larger, the process still remains the same. Before they begin each exercise, have them identify the rounding unit.

When students reach exercise 7, they will generate the round numbers that go directly above and below the given number. These are called **rounding frames.**

► **Practice With Rounding** [WHOLE CLASS]

Direct students' attention to Student Book page 116. Ask them to round each number as indicated in the directions.

Teaching the Lesson (continued)

Activity 2

Round to Estimate

 25 MINUTES

Goal: Round large numbers for the purpose of estimation in real-world contexts.

Materials: Student Activity Book or Hardcover Book pp. 116–117

✔ **NCTM Standard:**
Number and Operations

The Learning Classroom

Math Talk You must direct student math talk for it to be productive. Over time, as students become more skilled at discussing their thinking and talking directly with each other, you will fade into the background more. But you will always monitor, clarify, extend, and ultimately make the decisions about how to direct the math conversation so that it is productive for your student.

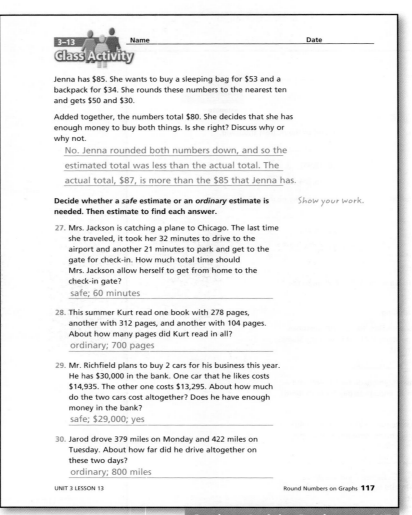

3-13 Name _____ Date _____
Class Activity

Jenna has $85. She wants to buy a sleeping bag for $53 and a backpack for $34. She rounds these numbers to the nearest ten and gets $50 and $30.

Added together, the numbers total $80. She decides that she has enough money to buy both things. Is she right? Discuss why or why not.

No. Jenna rounded both numbers down, and so the
estimated total was less than the actual total. The
actual total, $87, is more than the $85 that Jenna has.

Decide whether a *safe* estimate or an *ordinary* estimate is needed. Then estimate to find each answer.   *Show your work.*

27. Mrs. Jackson is catching a plane to Chicago. The last time she traveled, it took her 32 minutes to drive to the airport and another 21 minutes to park and get to the gate for check-in. How much total time should Mrs. Jackson allow herself to get from home to the check-in gate?
    safe; 60 minutes

28. This summer Kurt read one book with 278 pages, another with 312 pages, and another with 104 pages. About how many pages did Kurt read in all?
    ordinary; 700 pages

29. Mr. Richfield plans to buy 2 cars for his business this year. He has $30,000 in the bank. One car that he likes costs $14,935. The other one costs $13,295. About how much do the two cars cost altogether? Does he have enough money in the bank?
    safe; $29,000; yes

30. Jarod drove 379 miles on Monday and 422 miles on Tuesday. About how far did he drive altogether on these two days?
    ordinary; 800 miles

UNIT 3 LESSON 13   Round Numbers on Graphs **117**

Student Activity Book page 117

▶ Round to Estimate [WHOLE CLASS]

Explain that we often round numbers because it allows us to solve problems faster. The answer won't be an exact answer, but an estimate. Sometimes an estimate, something close to the real answer, is good enough. Discuss each problem on pages 116–117 of the Student Book with your students.

● Look at problem 23. Are these numbers easy to work with? no

● If we rounded each number to the nearest hundred, would these numbers be easier to work with? yes

● What are the rounded numbers? 700 and 200

● Look at problem 24. Can you estimate to answer the question? yes

● What would be a good rounding unit for these numbers? ten

● What are the rounded numbers? 60 and 40

Safe Estimates Have students read and discuss the problem at the top of on page 117 of the Student Book. Ask questions to help the class discover Jenna's mistake:

- Did Jenna round correctly? yes

- Did she add correctly? yes

- Then what went wrong? An estimate is always slightly off. In this case, Jenna rounded both numbers down, and so the estimated total was less than the actual total. The actual total, $87, is more than the $85 that Jenna has.

Elicit from students the idea that in some cases, such as when time or money are involved, we need to make sure that our estimates make sense—we round up to make sure that we will have enough time or money.

 Math Talk **Make an Appropriate Estimate** Discuss problems 27–30 on Student Book page 117. Before making an estimate, students should first decide whether a *safe estimation* or an *ordinary estimation* should be used. Have students decide whether they need to round up to be safe.

- **Problem 27** Safe Estimation

Getting to the airport on time is crucial, and traffic conditions can vary widely. Therefore, Mrs. Jackson should leave plenty of time and make a safe estimation. If she just followed the normal rules of rounding, she would add 20 + 30 = 50 minutes. This is not going to be enough time. It took longer than that to reach the airport last time she made the trip, and it could take even longer this time.

- **Problem 28** Ordinary Estimation

Rounding to the nearest hundred, we can figure out that Kurt read 300 + 300 + 100 = 700 pages this summer.

- **Problem 29** Safe Estimation

A safe estimation is needed because Mr. Richfield cannot spend more money than he has. Some students will be able to see immediately that he has enough money to buy the 2 cars because both amounts are less than half ($15,000) of the whole ($30,000). Other students will estimate the long way, rounding both amounts up to play it safe. To the nearest thousand, $15,000 + $14,000 = $29,000.

- **Problem 30** Ordinary Estimation

Rounding to the nearest hundred, we can figure out that Jarod drove 400 + 400 = 800 miles.

Going Further

Math Connection: Estimation Methods

Goal: Explore estimation strategies.

Materials: Student Activity Book or Hardcover Book p. 118

✔ **NCTM Standards:**
Number and Operations

▶ Find a Range of Estimates WHOLE CLASS

In this activity students connect rounding to other ways of estimating.

Round Up to Overestimate Write the phrase shown below on the board and ask students to discuss possible methods to produce the overestimate.

An overestimate of 4,629 + 1,405 is ___.

Explain that overestimating a sum involves rounding each addend up so that the sum of the rounded addends is greater than the exact sum. This is the maximum estimate. Invite a volunteer to the board to demonstrate how to complete the overestimate by first rounding each addend to the next thousand.

$$\begin{array}{rll} 4,629 & \text{rounds up to} & 5,000 \\ + 1,405 & \text{rounds up to} & + 2,000 \\ \hline & & 7,000 \end{array}$$

Round Down to Underestimate We round down to produce an underestimate, or minimum estimate. Write the phrase shown below on the board and invite a volunteer to complete the arithmetic.

An underestimate of 4,629 + 1,405 is ___.

$$\begin{array}{rll} 4,629 & \text{rounds down to} & 4,000 \\ + 1,405 & \text{rounds down to} & + 1,000 \\ \hline & & 5,000 \end{array}$$

A Range of Estimates Lead students to generalize that the estimates produced by rounding down and up (5,000 and 7,000) represent a *range* of possible answers for the exact sum of 4,629 + 1,405. The range of estimates falls between the minimum and maximum estimates.

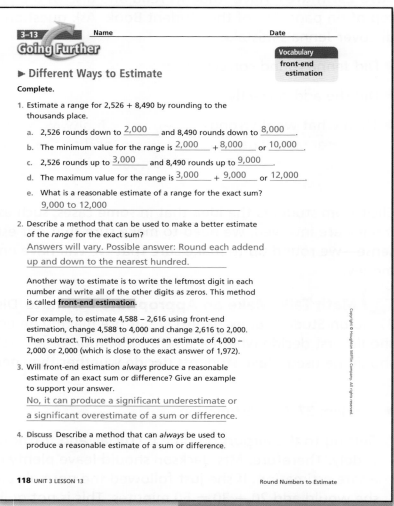

Student Activity Book page 118

▶ Different Ways to Estimate WHOLE CLASS

As a class, complete all of the exercises on Student Book page 118.

Exercise 2 At the board, invite volunteers to demonstrate the arithmetic that proves the reasonableness of each method that is suggested.

Exercise 3 Challenge students to provide a variety of examples for which front-end estimation produces significant underestimates and significant overestimates.

Exercise 4 Have students record the method in their Math Journals.

Differentiated Instruction

Intervention
Activity Card 3-13

About Time   Activity Card 3-13

Work: In Pairs

1. Answers may vary. Possible answers:
17 min is about 15 min; 3 hr, 42 min is about 4 hr; 41 hr is about 2 days; 23 days is about 3 weeks

1. On your own, copy and complete the chart.

> Round to estimate each amount of time.
>
> 17 minutes
>
> about _____ minutes
>
> 3 hours, 42 minutes
>
> about _____ hours
>
> 41 hours
>
> about _____ days
>
> 23 days
>
> about _____ weeks

2. **Work Together** Take turns giving your partner an amount of time to round.

Unit 3, Lesson 13   Copyright © Houghton Mifflin Company

Activity Note Before students begin the activity, have them make or review a chart showing equivalent measures of time for hours, days, and weeks.

Math Writing Prompt

Make Connections Describe a situation when you might want to round numbers.

 **Software Support**

Warm-Up 48.14

On Level
Activity Card 3-13

More Is Better   Activity Card 3-13 ▲

Work: In Pairs

1. Possible answers: Overestimating helps you to avoid being late for an event, having too little money for purchases, or not having enough food at a party.

1. Partners discuss why each situation described at the right might require overestimating.

2. **Math Talk** Describe three situations in which underestimating may be needed. Explain your thinking. Possible answers: Estimating the weight that elevators can carry, the time remaining before a bill is due, or the number of calories in dessert.

> • Your bus to school leaves at 8:30 A.M.
> • A movie you want to see starts at 7:00 P.M.
> • You have exactly $10 to buy school supplies.
> • 12 people are coming to your birthday party.

Unit 3, Lesson 13   Copyright © Houghton Mifflin Company

Activity Note As part of the discussion, encourage students to include the consequences of estimating incorrectly in the given situations and the new situations that they describe.

Math Writing Prompt

Write Rules What are the possibilities for rounding whole numbers to the nearest ten? Use examples to illustrate your answer.

 Software Support

Fraction Action: Number Line Mine, Level C

Challenge
Activity Card 3-13

Schedules   Activity Card 3-13 ■

Work: By Yourself

1. Think about the things that you need to do tomorrow. Then make a schedule for the day similar to the sample one below.

> **Thursday**
> | Get Dressed | 7:00 A.M. |
> | Eat Breakfast | 7:15 A.M. |
> | Walk to School | 7:45 A.M. |

2. Include the time you will begin each activity. Be sure to include time for sleeping and meals.

3. Use your schedule to calculate the time you have to complete each activity.

Unit 3, Lesson 13   Copyright © Houghton Mifflin Company

Activity Note After students have completed the activity, have them compare schedules with others in the class and discuss strategies for calculating the time allotted for each activity.

Math Writing Prompt

Reasoning When you round 199 to the nearest ten and to the nearest hundred, why do you get the same result?

  Software Support

Course III: Module 1: Unit 1: Ordering and Rounding Whole Numbers

③ Homework and Spiral Review

3–13
Homework **Goal:** Additional Practice

Use this Homework page to provide students with more practice with rounding methods.

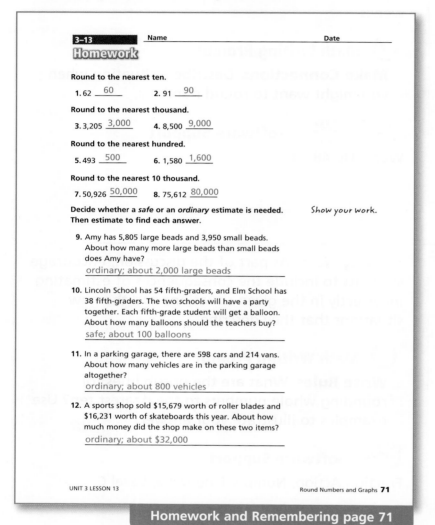

3–13   Name _____   Date _____
Homework

Round to the nearest ten.

1. 62 __60__   2. 91 __90__

Round to the nearest thousand.

3. 3,205 __3,000__   4. 8,500 __9,000__

Round to the nearest hundred.

5. 493 __500__   6. 1,580 __1,600__

Round to the nearest 10 thousand.

7. 50,926 __50,000__   8. 75,612 __80,000__

Decide whether a *safe* or an *ordinary* estimate is needed. Then estimate to find each answer.   *Show your work.*

9. Amy has 5,805 large beads and 3,950 small beads. About how many more large beads than small beads does Amy have?
   ordinary; about 2,000 large beads

10. Lincoln School has 54 fifth-graders, and Elm School has 38 fifth-graders. The two schools will have a party together. Each fifth-grade student will get a balloon. About how many balloons should the teachers buy?
    safe; about 100 balloons

11. In a parking garage, there are 598 cars and 214 vans. About how many vehicles are in the parking garage altogether?
    ordinary; about 800 vehicles

12. A sports shop sold $15,679 worth of roller blades and $16,231 worth of skateboards this year. About how much money did the shop make on these two items?
    ordinary; about $32,000

UNIT 3 LESSON 13   Round Numbers and Graphs **71**

Homework and Remembering page 71

3–13
Remembering **Goal:** Spiral Review

This Remembering activity would be appropriate anytime after today's lesson.

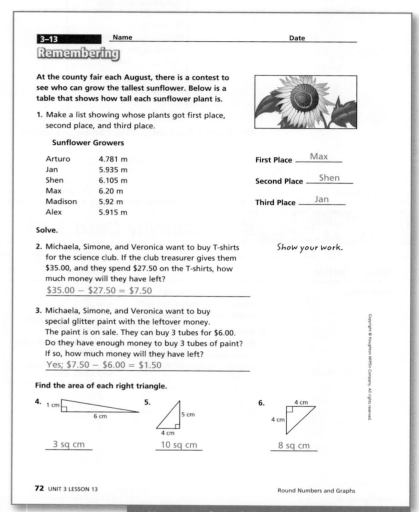

3–13   Name _____   Date _____
Remembering

At the county fair each August, there is a contest to see who can grow the tallest sunflower. Below is a table that shows how tall each sunflower plant is.

1. Make a list showing whose plants got first place, second place, and third place.

   Sunflower Growers

Arturo	4.781 m
Jan	5.935 m
Shen	6.105 m
Max	6.20 m
Madison	5.92 m
Alex	5.915 m

   First Place __Max__

   Second Place __Shen__

   Third Place __Jan__

Solve.

2. Michaela, Simone, and Veronica want to buy T-shirts for the science club. If the club treasurer gives them $35.00, and they spend $27.50 on the T-shirts, how much money will they have left?   *Show your work.*
   $35.00 − $27.50 = $7.50

3. Michaela, Simone, and Veronica want to buy special glitter paint with the leftover money. The paint is on sale. They can buy 3 tubes for $6.00. Do they have enough money to buy 3 tubes of paint? If so, how much money will they have left?
   Yes; $7.50 − $6.00 = $1.50

Find the area of each right triangle.

4. 1 cm / 6 cm
   3 sq cm

5. 5 cm / 4 cm
   10 sq cm

6. 4 cm / 4 cm
   8 sq cm

72 UNIT 3 LESSON 13   Round Numbers and Graphs

Homework and Remembering page 72

Home or School Activity

 Real-World Connection

Shopping Trip Tell students that nearly everyone uses rounding and estimation when they shop. Explain that when shopping, you need to make sure you have enough money to pay for all the items, including the tax, which adds to the total. For this reason, it's usually best to round up each item's price so that you don't go over your limit.

Have students use grocery store advertisements to practice estimating. Tell them to pick five or more items and estimate the total cost. Then find the exact cost to compare.

Students can also try the skill in the real world. Tell them to try to estimate the total cost as they shop the next time they go to the grocery store with their family.

286 UNIT 3 LESSON 13

Bar Graphs and Rounding

REAL
WORLD
**Problem
Solving**

Lesson Objectives

● Read and construct bar graphs with large numbers.

● Round numbers to the hundred millions.

● Identify the halfway point with numbers to the hundred millions.

Vocabulary

bar graph
double-bar graph

The Day at a Glance

Today's Goals	Materials

1 Teaching the Lesson
A1: Discuss bar graphs with large numbers.
A2: Make bar graphs.
 	
2 Going Further
▶ Differentiated Instruction
 	
3 Homework and Spiral Review
	Lesson Activities
	Student Activity Book pp. 119–120
	  or Student Hardcover Book
	  pp. 119–120 and Activity
	  Workbook p. 60
	Homework and Remembering
	  pp. 73–74
		Going Further
		Activity Cards 3-14
		Connecting cubes
		Homework p. 73
		Grid Paper (TRB M17)
		Math Journals
		
		123 Use
		Math Talk
		today!

Keeping Skills Sharp

Quick Practice ⏱ 5 MINUTES	Daily Routines
Goal: Use the halfway point of a group of numbers to facilitate rounding. **The Halfway Point** Send three **Student Leaders** to the board. The first writes the numbers vertically as the class counts by 100s to 1,000. Then next writes the numbers as the class counts by 1,000s to 10,000. The third student writes the numbers as the class counts by 10,000s to 100,000. **Student Leaders** take turns circling pairs of consecutive numbers in the list. They ask, "What is the halfway point?" The class responds with the number. For example, 6,000 and 7,000 are circled. The class responds "6,500."	**Homework Review** Ask students if they had difficulty with any part of the homework. Set aside time to work with students needing extra help. **Who's Right?** Dagmar factored 8, Gregg factored 9, and Francesca factored 10. They said that the numbers all have the same amount of factors. Is this correct? Explain your answer. No; 8 and 10 have four factors. 8: 1, 2, 4, 8; 10: 1, 2, 5, 10; 9 has only 3 factors, 1, 3, and 9.

Teaching the Lesson

Interpret Bar Graphs

 20 MINUTES

Goal: Discuss bar graphs with large numbers.

Materials: Student Activity Book or Hardcover Book p. 119

 NCTM Standards:
Number and Operations
Algebra
Communication

Class Management

Student Helpers Continue to invest time in discussing effective ways to help others (for example, ask questions to help them see the next step, ask them to say what they know about the problem, be encouraging). Fifth graders can learn to be very effective helpers, even leading review sessions with groups while you work with the strugglers.

English Language Learners

Write *data* on the board. Point to the graphs on Student Activity Book page 119.

- **Beginning** Say: The information we show in graphs is *data*. Have students repeat.
- **Intermediate** Ask: Is the amount of ticket sales an example of *data*? yes
- **Advanced** Say: The information we show with a graph is _____. data

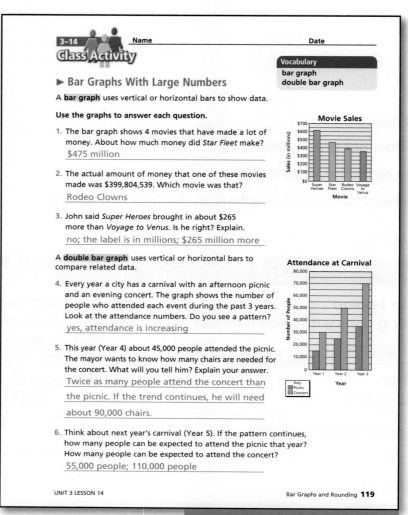

Student Activity Book page 119

▶ Bar Graphs With Large Numbers WHOLE CLASS

Begin by having your students look at the scale on the "Movie Sales" graph on Student Book page 119. Ask:

● What is the rounding unit on this scale? Hundred millions

● What are we counting by on this scale? 100 millions

Be sure everyone notices the word millions in the label on the left. Explain that on a bar graph, large numbers are often represented this way. Explain that writing all the zeros would take up too much space.

Math Talk Discuss the problems that go with each bar graph.

● **Problem 1** Have a student read problem 1 aloud. Explain that reading a bar graph where the bar does not touch any line exactly is always a matter of estimation. This bar is about halfway between the dotted lines for $450 million and $500 million. A good estimate would be $475 million. Ask a volunteer to write $475 million on the board.

● **Problem 2** Have a student read problem 2 aloud. $399,804,539 is just under $400 million. The movie *Rodeo Clowns* is the answer because the bar for *Rodeo Clowns* is just under the $400 million line.

● **Problem 3** Ask a student to read problem 3 aloud. John is wrong because the label on the left indicates the dollars are in millions. So the answer is $265 million, not $265.

Double-Bar Graph Direct students' attention to the key on the "Attendance at Carnival" graph. Be sure they understand that the darker bar represents the number of people who attended the picnic and the lighter bar represents the number people who attended the band concert. Then ask them what the rounding unit is. 10,000

● **Problem 4** Have a student read problem 4 aloud. Ask students to look at the bars on the graph and describe any patterns they see. Students might notice that about twice as many people attend the concert as the picnic each year, that attendance at the picnic increases by about 10,000 each year, and that attendance at the concert increases by about 20,000 each year.

● **Problem 5** Ask a student to read problem 5 aloud. Remind students that they can use any of the patterns they recognized in problem 4 to make an estimate for the number of chairs for the concert. Students might notice that the number will probably be twice as much as 45,000 or 20,000 more than the year before, which was 70,000. So, the best estimate is 90,000 chairs.

● **Problem 6** Have a student read problem 6 aloud. Remind students that we already concluded that the Year 4 figures would be 45,000 people at the picnic and 90,000 people at the band concert. We can find the Year 5 figures by calculating that 10,000 more than 45,000 is 55,000 and 20,000 more than 90,000 is 110,000. We also know that the second bar must be twice as long as the first. $55,000 \times 2 = 110,000$. So, we know that if the pattern continues, the Year 5 figures will be 55,000 and 110,000.

Teaching Note

What to Expect from Students
How did your students explain their math thinking today? Students are often unfamiliar with this process; they are accustomed to providing math answers only. Encouraging students to talk more fully about their thinking will take repeated efforts on your part. Expect this to be a building process that lasts for several weeks.

Teaching the Lesson (continued)

Activity 2

Make Bar Graphs

 30 MINUTES

Goal: Make bar graphs.

Materials: Student Activity Book or Hardcover Book p. 120 and Activity Workbook p. 60

✔ **NCTM Standard:**
Data Analysis and Probability

 Ongoing Assessment

Ask students to:

▶ explain the difference between a bar graph and a double-bar graph.

▶ define scale.

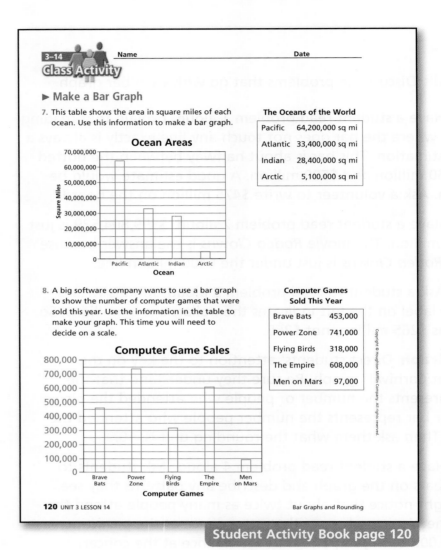

Student Activity Book page 120

▶ Make a Bar Graph [WHOLE CLASS]

Oceans Areas Have everyone turn to Student Book page 120. The first bar graph has a scale and labels for the students. Their task is to draw the bars. Discuss the rounding units on the scale (10 million) and have students identify the halfway points. Then, discuss how the numbers in the table might be rounded to make them easier to graph.

Computer Game Sales The second bar graph does not have a scale indicated—only the calibration lines and labels. Students will need to determine their own scale.

Discuss what rounding units would make a good scale. Increments of 100,000 would work best. If students propose something else, let them give it a try. They will discover if it is not workable.

Have students work independently on their graphs. Offer help as needed. Then discuss the results as a class.

290 UNIT 3 LESSON 14

② Going Further

● Intervention   Activity Card 3-14

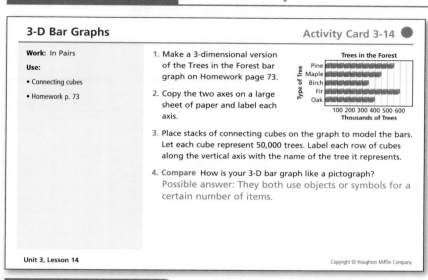

3-D Bar Graphs   Activity Card 3-14 ●

Work: In Pairs

Use:
- Connecting cubes
- Homework p. 73

1. Make a 3-dimensional version of the Trees in the Forest bar graph on Homework page 73.

2. Copy the two axes on a large sheet of paper and label each axis.

3. Place stacks of connecting cubes on the graph to model the bars. Let each cube represent 50,000 trees. Label each row of cubes along the vertical axis with the name of the tree it represents.

4. **Compare** How is your 3-D bar graph like a pictograph? Possible answer: They both use objects or symbols for a certain number of items.

Unit 3, Lesson 14   Copyright © Houghton Mifflin Company

Activity Note Ask students if it is possible to make the graph if each cube represents 100,000 trees. Students should realize that whole cubes cannot represent the number of pine, birch, or maple trees in the data.

 Math Writing Prompt

Make Connections Explain how a bar graph is like a pictograph and how it is different.

 **Software Support**

Warm-Up 50.12

▲ On Level   Activity Card 3-14

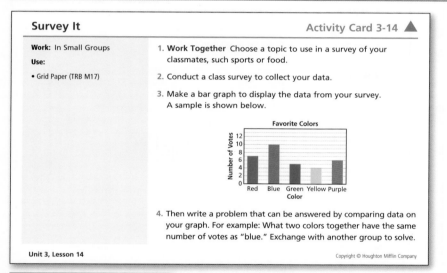

Survey It   Activity Card 3-14 ▲

Work: In Small Groups

Use:
- Grid Paper (TRB M17)

1. **Work Together** Choose a topic to use in a survey of your classmates, such sports or food.

2. Conduct a class survey to collect your data.

3. Make a bar graph to display the data from your survey. A sample is shown below.

4. Then write a problem that can be answered by comparing data on your graph. For example: What two colors together have the same number of votes as "blue." Exchange with another group to solve.

Unit 3, Lesson 14   Copyright © Houghton Mifflin Company

Activity Note Discuss the intervals that students chose for the vertical axes on their graphs. Ask if another interval would have been possible, and why they chose the one they did.

 Math Writing Prompt

Explain Your Thinking Some bar graphs need keys, and others do not. Explain why this is so. Give examples to support your thinking.

 Software Support

The Number Games: ArachnaGraph, Level C

■ Challenge   Activity Card 3-14

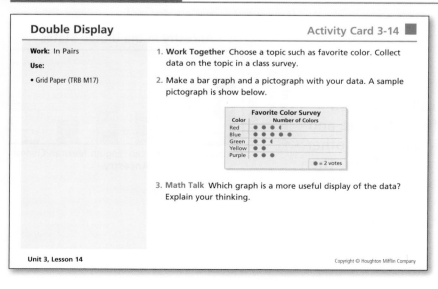

Double Display   Activity Card 3-14 ■

Work: In Pairs

Use:
- Grid Paper (TRB M17)

1. **Work Together** Choose a topic such as favorite color. Collect data on the topic in a class survey.

2. Make a bar graph and a pictograph with your data. A sample pictograph is show below.

3. **Math Talk** Which graph is a more useful display of the data? Explain your thinking.

Unit 3, Lesson 14   Copyright © Houghton Mifflin Company

Activity Note You may want to have students make a bar graph of the given data first.

 Math Writing Prompt

In Your Own Words Explain how you choose the scale when making a bar graph.

 **Software Support**

Course III: Module 6: Unit 1: Displaying and Analyzing Data

③ Homework and Spiral Review

3–14
Homework **Goal:** Additional Practice

✔ Include students' Homework for page 73 as part of their portfolios.

3–14
Remembering **Goal:** Spiral Review

This Remembering activity would be appropriate anytime after today's lesson.

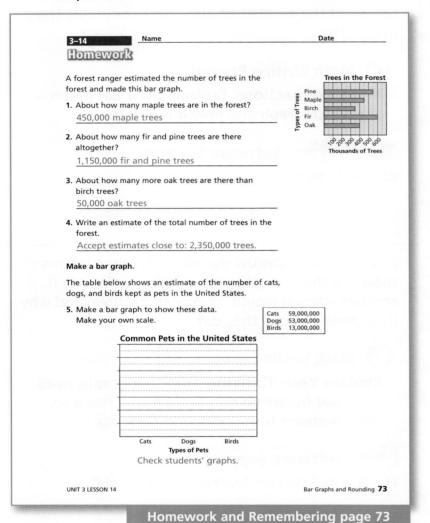

3–14 Name _____ Date _____	
Homework	

A forest ranger estimated the number of trees in the forest and made this bar graph.

Trees in the Forest
(bar graph with Types of Trees: Pine, Maple, Birch, Fir, Oak; x-axis Thousands of Trees 100 200 300 400 500 600)

1. About how many maple trees are in the forest?
   450,000 maple trees

2. About how many fir and pine trees are there altogether?
   1,150,000 fir and pine trees

3. About how many more oak trees are there than birch trees?
   50,000 oak trees

4. Write an estimate of the total number of trees in the forest.
   Accept estimates close to: 2,350,000 trees.

Make a bar graph.

The table below shows an estimate of the number of cats, dogs, and birds kept as pets in the United States.

5. Make a bar graph to show these data.
   Make your own scale.

   Cats 59,000,000
   Dogs 53,000,000
   Birds 13,000,000

Common Pets in the United States

Cats   Dogs   Birds
Types of Pets
Check students' graphs.

UNIT 3 LESSON 14   Bar Graphs and Rounding **73**

Homework and Remembering page 73

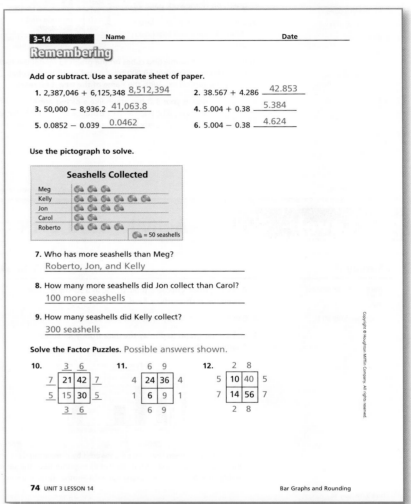

3–14 Name _____ Date _____	
Remembering	

Add or subtract. Use a separate sheet of paper.

1. 2,387,046 + 6,125,348 8,512,394   2. 38.567 + 4.286 42.853
3. 50,000 − 8,936.2 41,063.8   4. 5.004 + 0.38 5.384
5. 0.0852 − 0.039 0.0462   6. 5.004 − 0.38 4.624

Use the pictograph to solve.

Seashells Collected

Meg	🐚 🐚 🐚
Kelly	🐚 🐚 🐚 🐚 🐚 🐚
Jon	🐚 🐚 🐚 🐚 🐚 🐚
Carol	🐚 🐚
Roberto	🐚 🐚 🐚 🐚

🐚 = 50 seashells

7. Who has more seashells than Meg?
   Roberto, Jon, and Kelly

8. How many more seashells did Jon collect than Carol?
   100 more seashells

9. How many seashells did Kelly collect?
   300 seashells

Solve the Factor Puzzles. Possible answers shown.

10.
	3	6	
7	21	42	7
5	15	30	5
	3	6	

11.
	6	9	
4	24	36	4
1	6	9	1
	6	9	

12.
	2	8	
5	10	40	5
7	14	56	7
	2	8	

74 UNIT 3 LESSON 14   Bar Graphs and Rounding

Homework and Remembering page 74

Home or School Activity

 Multicultural Connection

Melting Pot Explain to students that people sometimes call the United States a "melting pot" because people from so many different places and cultures live here. Suggest to students that they ask their parents or other family members to tell them about where their ancestors came from. Then invite students to discuss some traditions their family practices that reflect their ancestry. Have students work in small groups to make a class graph about their ancestry. Students can write word problems that can be solved using the graph.

Ancestry in the United States
(bar graph; Number of People (in millions) 0–60; Ancestry: German, Irish, African, English, Mexican, Chinese)

Round and Estimate With Decimals

Lesson Objectives

● Use a number line and place value to round decimals

● Estimate decimal sums and differences.

The Day at a Glance

Today's Goals	Materials	
① Teaching the Lesson **A1:** Use a number line to round decimal numbers. **A2:** Use rounding to estimate decimal sums and differences. **② Going Further** ▶ Differentiated Instruction **③ Homework and Spiral Review**	**For Lesson Activities** Student Activity Book pp. 121–122 or Student Hardcover Book pp. 121–122 Homework and Remembering pp. 75–76	**Going Further** Activity Cards 3-15 Calculator (optional) Math Journals 123 Use Math Talk today!

Keeping Skills Sharp

Quick Practice   ⏱ 5 MINUTES

Goal: Use the halfway point of a group of numbers to facilitate rounding.

The Halfway Point Send 3 **Student Leaders** to the board. The first writes the numbers vertically as the class counts by 100,000s to a million. The next writes the numbers as the class counts by millions to 10 million. The third writes the numbers as the class counts by 10 millions to 100 million.

Now have each **Student Leader** take turns circling pairs of consecutive numbers in the list. As they do so, they ask, "What is the halfway point?" The class responds with the number. For example, 200,000 and 300,000 are circled. The class responds "250,000."

Daily Routines

Homework Review Have students explain their work. Look for errors.

Combinations Linh has red, white, and black shirts. She has khaki, black, and white pants. She does not wear the same color shirt and pants together, and does not wear white with black. Can she make 8 outfits? If not, what could she do so she can? Possible answer: No, she can only make 5 outfits. If she bought a blue shirt, she could make 8 outfits, because it does not match any pants.

Teaching the Lesson

Round With Decimals

30 MINUTES

Goal: Use a number line to round decimal numbers.

Materials: Student Activity Book or Hardcover Book p. 121

✔ **NCTM Standards:**
Numbers and Operations
Connections
Problem Solving

The Learning Classroom

Math Talk This may be a good day to talk with the class for a few minutes about what makes a good explanation. They may want to produce a list that can be posted on the wall of the classroom on a poster board for later reference. They may make suggestions such as: 1) write your work so everyone can see it, 2) talk loudly, 3) point to the numbers as you talk, 4) say how you arrived at the answer, not just the answer, 5) stand to the side of your work when you talk, etc.

▶ Round To the Nearest Whole Number WHOLE CLASS

On the board or overhead, draw a number line by tenths from 4.0 to 5.0 as shown below.

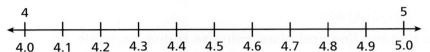

 Math Talk Plot a point at 4.7 and discuss how the number line can be used to round 4.7 to the nearest whole number.

● On this number line, 4.7 is between which two whole numbers? 4 and 5

● What number is exactly halfway between 4 and 5? 4.5

● Is 4.7 to the right or to the left of 4.5? to the right

● Is 4.7 closer to 4 or closer to 5? closer to 5

● What is 4.7 rounded to the nearest whole number? 5

Generalize Ask students to explain why 4 is not the correct answer. Make sure their explanations include the generalization that because 4.5 is exactly halfway between 4 and 5, and 4.7 is to the right of 4.5, 4.7 is closer to 5 than to 4; therefore 4.7 rounds to 5.

Plot a point at 4.4 and invite volunteers to explain how the number line can be used to round 4.4 to the nearest whole number. 4.4 rounds to 4 Plot a point at 4.5 and lead students to conclude that a number that is exactly halfway between two numbers always rounds up.

▶ Round To the Nearest Tenth WHOLE CLASS

On the board or overhead, draw a number line by hundredths from 1.6 to 1.7 as shown below.

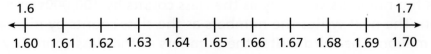

Plot a point at 1.62 and invite volunteers to use what they know about rounding to the nearest whole number to explain why 1.62 rounds to 1.6 when rounded to the nearest tenth. Then plot a point at 1.68 and at 1.65 and repeat the activity. 1.68 and 1.65 round to 1.7

▶ Round To the Nearest Hundredth   WHOLE CLASS

Have students recall decimal place value by asking:

- A decimal number in tenths has how many digits to the right of the decimal point? one

- How many digits to the right of the decimal point does a decimal number in hundredths have? two

- A decimal number in thousandths has how many digits to the right of the decimal point? three

Invite volunteers to name several examples of decimal numbers in tenths, in hundredths, and in thousandths.

Write 8.057 on the board. Have students name the digit in each place of the number. ones: 8; tenths: 0; hundredths: 5; thousandths: 7

- Suppose we round 8.057 to the nearest whole number. Why is the digit in the tenths place of our number important?

Connection To help answer the question, encourage students think about how a number line in tenths would be used to round 8.057 to the nearest whole number, and then relate that concept to a method that does not involve a number line. Using a number line involves deciding if a number is less than halfway, halfway, or more than halfway. In the same way, a method for rounding numbers without a number line involves deciding if the digit to the right of the rounding place is less than 5, equal to 5, or greater than 5.

- Explain why the digit in the tenths place of 8.057 tells us that the number rounds to 8 instead of to 9. The 0 in the tenths place is less than 5.

- What digits would have to be in the tenths place of our number for it to round to 9 instead of to 8? 5, 6, 7, 8, or 9

Generalize Have students state a general method that can be used to round any number to a given place value. If the digit to the right of the rounding place is 5 or more, the digit in the rounding place increases by 1; if the digit to the right of the rounding place is less than 5, the digit in the rounding place does not change.

Activity continued ▶

✓ Ongoing Assessment

Make sure students understand the concept of rounding by asking them to complete each of the following sentences.

- ▶ If we round a number to the nearest whole number, the answer will be a count-by _____ number. ones

- ▶ If we round a number to the nearest tenth, the answer will be a count-by _____ number. tenths

- ▶ If we round a number to the nearest hundredth, the answer will be a count-by _____ number. hundredths

Ask students to give an example of each situation.

Activity 1

Differentiated Instruction

Advanced Learners Ask your advanced students to make number lines that show ten thousandths. The tick marks between the numbers will show thousandths—0.001, 0.002, and so on. After students have made their number lines, have them write a number to thousandths, such as 0.1643, and place a point at its estimated position. (a little to the right of the halfway point between 0.001 and 0.002)

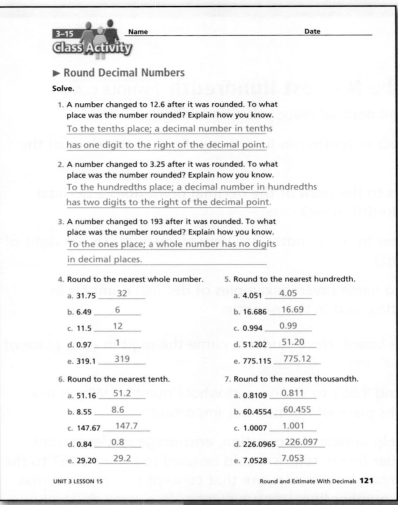

3-15
Class Activity

Name _____ Date _____

► **Round Decimal Numbers**

Solve.

1. A number changed to 12.6 after it was rounded. To what place was the number rounded? Explain how you know.
   To the tenths place; a decimal number in tenths
   has one digit to the right of the decimal point.

2. A number changed to 3.25 after it was rounded. To what place was the number rounded? Explain how you know.
   To the hundredths place; a decimal number in hundredths
   has two digits to the right of the decimal point.

3. A number changed to 193 after it was rounded. To what place was the number rounded? Explain how you know.
   To the ones place; a whole number has no digits
   in decimal places.

4. Round to the nearest whole number.
   a. 31.75 ___32___
   b. 6.49 ___6___
   c. 11.5 ___12___
   d. 0.97 ___1___
   e. 319.1 ___319___

5. Round to the nearest hundredth.
   a. 4.051 ___4.05___
   b. 16.686 ___16.69___
   c. 0.994 ___0.99___
   d. 51.202 ___51.20___
   e. 775.115 ___775.12___

6. Round to the nearest tenth.
   a. 51.16 ___51.2___
   b. 8.55 ___8.6___
   c. 147.67 ___147.7___
   d. 0.84 ___0.8___
   e. 29.20 ___29.2___

7. Round to the nearest thousandth.
   a. 0.8109 ___0.811___
   b. 60.4554 ___60.455___
   c. 1.0007 ___1.001___
   d. 226.0965 ___226.097___
   e. 7.0528 ___7.053___

UNIT 3 LESSON 15   Round and Estimate With Decimals **121**

Student Activity Book page 121

► Round To the Nearest Thousandth (Optional)

| WHOLE CLASS |

Write 3.6405 on the board and ask students to name the digit in the thousandths place and ten-thousandths place of the number. thousandths: 0; ten-thousandths: 5

Have students extend what they know about rounding to the nearest hundredth to explain how to round 3.6405 to the nearest thousandth. 3.6405 rounds to 3.641 because the digit to the right of the rounding place is 5 or more.

► Round Decimal Numbers | WHOLE CLASS |

As a class, complete exercises 1–3 on Student Book page 121. Have students work in **Small Groups** to complete exercises 4–6. Exercise 7 is optional; you may choose to use it as a challenge.

Determine Reasonable Answers

▶ Estimate Sums ⬚ WHOLE CLASS

Ask For Ideas Remind students of the importance of checking their work, and then ask them to describe different methods they have used in the past to check answers.

On the board, write the addition 7.934 + 5.825 and discuss how rounding to the nearest whole number can be used to make a reasonable estimate of the exact sum. A reasonable estimate is 14 because 7.934 rounds to 8, 5.825 rounds to 6, and 8 + 6 = 14.

Invite a volunteer to find the exact sum of the numbers and write it on the board. Ask students to explain how the estimate can be used to help decide if the volunteer's answer is reasonable. Using a estimate to decide if a sum is reasonable involves comparing—compare the exact sum and the estimate. If the exact sum is close to the estimate, the sum is reasonable; if the exact sum is not close to the estimate, the sum is not reasonable.

Then ask students to debate the value of estimating the sum by rounding to the nearest tenth or rounding to the nearest hundredth. Lead them to conclude that although estimates can be made by rounding to either decimal place, the goal of using estimates to check answers simply involves general approximations. For addends such as 7.934 + 5.825, the precision of rounding to the nearest whole number is enough to help decide if an exact answer is reasonable.

Generalize Make sure students understand that the goal of estimating is to provide only a general approximation of an exact answer, and although some estimates are better than others, more than one estimate can likely be made for many exact answers.

▶ Estimate Differences ⬚ WHOLE CLASS

On the board, write the subtraction 4.107 − 3.288 and as described above, estimate the difference by rounding to the nearest whole number, find the exact difference and use the estimate to decide if the difference is reasonable, and then debate the value of making an estimate by rounding to a lesser place value.

 30 MINUTES

Goal: Use rounding to estimate decimal sums and differences.

Materials: Student Activity Book or Hardcover Book p. 122

 NCTM Standards:
Number and Operations
Problem Solving
Reasoning and Proof

English Language Learners

Write 71 + 27 = 98, *reasonable estimate*, 100, and 90 on the board. Say: **A *reasonable estimate* is a good or close estimate.**

- **Beginning** Say: **The *reasonable estimate* is 100.**
- **Intermediate** Ask: **Which estimate is closer?** 100 Say: **100 was the _____.** reasonable estimate
- **Advanced** Have students identify the *reasonable estimate*.

Activity continued ▶

❶ Teaching the Lesson (continued)

Activity 2

Advanced Learners Remind your advanced learners that the goal of estimating is to provide only a general approximation of an exact answer, and then point out that mental math can often be used to make the general approximations or estimates.

As they complete today's activity, encourage them to use mental math to make estimates whenever possible.

The Learning Classroom

Helping Community When stronger math students finish their work early, give them an opportunity to help other who might be struggling. Many students enjoy the role of helping other students. In their "helper" role, students who might become bored challenge themselves as they explain math content to others.

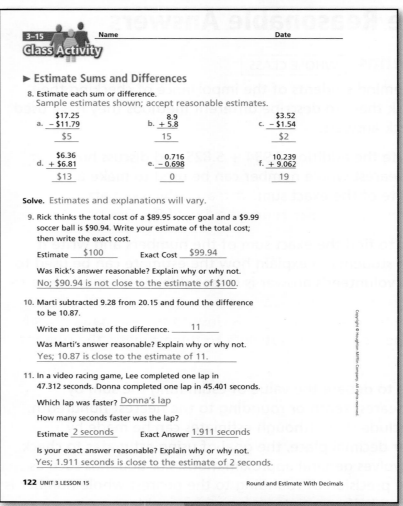

3–15
Class Activity

Name _____ Date _____

▶ **Estimate Sums and Differences**

8. Estimate each sum or difference.
   Sample estimates shown; accept reasonable estimates.

   a. $17.25
      − $11.79
      _____$5_____

   b. 8.9
      + 5.8
      _____15_____

   c. $3.52
      − $1.54
      _____$2_____

   d. $6.36
      + $6.81
      _____$13_____

   e. 0.716
      − 0.698
      _____0_____

   f. 10.239
      + 9.062
      _____19_____

Solve. Estimates and explanations will vary.

9. Rick thinks the total cost of a $89.95 soccer goal and a $9.99 soccer ball is $90.94. Write your estimate of the total cost; then write the exact cost.

   Estimate ___$100___   Exact Cost ___$99.94___

   Was Rick's answer reasonable? Explain why or why not.
   No; $90.94 is not close to the estimate of $100.

10. Marti subtracted 9.28 from 20.15 and found the difference to be 10.87.

    Write an estimate of the difference. ___11___

    Was Marti's answer reasonable? Explain why or why not.
    Yes; 10.87 is close to the estimate of 11.

11. In a video racing game, Lee completed one lap in 47.312 seconds. Donna completed one lap in 45.401 seconds.

    Which lap was faster? Donna's lap

    How many seconds faster was the lap?

    Estimate 2 seconds   Exact Answer 1.911 seconds

    Is your exact answer reasonable? Explain why or why not.
    Yes; 1.911 seconds is close to the estimate of 2 seconds.

122 UNIT 3 LESSON 15   Round and Estimate With Decimals

Student Activity Book page 122

▶ Estimate Sums and Differences PAIRS

Have **Student Pairs** work together to complete exercises 8–11 on Student Book page 122. Each exercise involves an estimate, and have the partners discuss different ways each estimate could be made (such as rounding to the nearest whole number or to the nearest tenth), then choose one of the ways and use it to complete the estimate.

For exercise 11, make sure students understand that in a race measured by elapsed time, the lesser time is the faster time.

Intervention — Activity Card 3-15

Estimates and Exact Costs   Activity Card 3-15

Work: By Yourself

1. Write 6 different prices that round to $0.70, some greater than and some less than $0.70. Pick two of the prices and use them to complete the problem.

> Josh wants to buy a pen for _____ and a stamp for _____.
> He has $1.40. Does he have enough money to buy the pen and stamp?

2. Estimate the total cost of the two items, and predict whether Josh has enough money. Then find the actual total and solve the problem. Repeat the activity using other prices.

3. **Look Back** Review your estimates and your predictions. Does your estimation strategy work? If not, is there another strategy that does?

Unit 3, Lesson 15   Copyright © Houghton Mifflin Company

Activity Note Discuss why using prices that round up to 70¢ ensures that Josh has enough money each time.

✎ Math Writing Prompt

Explain Your Thinking Write two decimal numbers that have an estimated sum of 1.0. Explain how to round each number and how to estimate the sum.

 **Software Support**

Warm-Up 23.22

On Level — Activity Card 3-15

Can I Afford This?   Activity Card 3-15 ▲

Work: In Small Groups
Use: Calculator (optional)

1. Choose one person to be the shopkeeper. Other group members decide on an amount under $3.00 to spend.

> The Hobby Shop
> Items and Prices
> Chalk – $0.28   Paper – $0.47
> Glitter – $0.75   Paste – $0.36
> Marker – $0.63   Yarn – $0.11
> Paint Brush – $0.54
> Ribbon – $0.32

2. Each group member chose as many items as he/she thinks they can afford, lists the actual prices and estimates the total price.

3. The shopkeeper calculates the cost of the items on each list.

4. As a group, members compare their estimates with the calculated total cost and decide if their estimation strategy was useful.

5. Repeat the activity, taking turns as shopkeeper.

Unit 3, Lesson 15   Copyright © Houghton Mifflin Company

Activity Note Students may want to round all the prices before selecting items to simplify that process.

✎ Math Writing Prompt

You Decide Use two ways to estimate the answer to 6.47 − 0.682. Decide which estimate is closer to the actual answer and explain why.

 Software Support

The Number Games: Buggy Bargains, Level I

Challenge — Activity Card 3-15

Same Estimated and Exact Answer   Activity Card 3-15 ■

Work: In Pairs

1. The example below shows an estimated sum and the exact sum of 0.59 + 0.21. Notice that the two sums are the same.

> 0.59 + 0.21
> 0.59 rounds to 0.6
> 0.21 rounds to 0.2
> 0.6 + 0.2 = 0.8 Estimate
> 0.59 + 0.21 = 0.8 Exact Answer

2. Work together to write two addition problems and two subtraction problems in which an estimated and an exact answer are the same.

3. **Math Talk** What similarities do you see in the problems? How did you choose the numbers for each problem? The last digit of each number cannot be equal to 5 but must add to 10 for the addition problems; for the subtraction problems, they can be any digits but must be equal.

Unit 3, Lesson 15   Copyright © Houghton Mifflin Company

Activity Note If students have difficulty, point out the last digits in the example, 9 and 1. Ask how those digits affect the rounded values and the sum.

✎ Math Writing Prompt

Explain Your Thinking Can you round a decimal money amount to the nearest dollar and to the nearest ten dollars and have the answers be the same? Explain why or why not.

 DESTINATION Math® **Software Support**

Course III: Module 4: Unit 1: Ordering and Rounding

③ Homework and Spiral Review

3-15
Homework **Goal:** Additional Practice

✓ Include students' Homework for page 75 as a part of their portfolios.

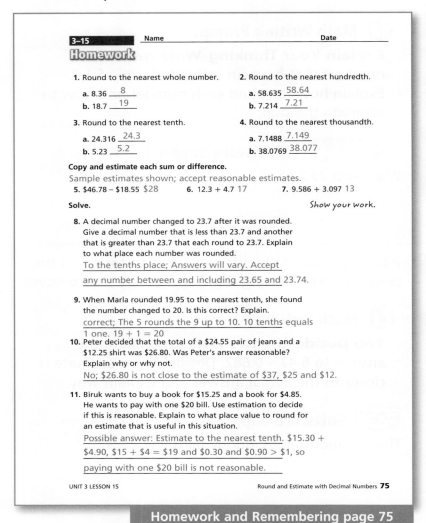

3-15 Name _____ Date _____
Homework

1. Round to the nearest whole number.
   a. 8.36 ___8___
   b. 18.7 ___19___

2. Round to the nearest hundredth.
   a. 58.635 ___58.64___
   b. 7.214 ___7.21___

3. Round to the nearest tenth.
   a. 24.316 ___24.3___
   b. 5.23 ___5.2___

4. Round to the nearest thousandth.
   a. 7.1488 ___7.149___
   b. 38.0769 ___38.077___

Copy and estimate each sum or difference.
Sample estimates shown; accept reasonable estimates.
5. $46.78 – $18.55 $28   6. 12.3 + 4.7 17   7. 9.586 + 3.097 13

Solve. *Show your work.*

8. A decimal number changed to 23.7 after it was rounded. Give a decimal number that is less than 23.7 and another that is greater than 23.7 that each round to 23.7. Explain to what place each number was rounded.
   To the tenths place; Answers will vary. Accept any number between and including 23.65 and 23.74.

9. When Marla rounded 19.95 to the nearest tenth, she found the number changed to 20. Is this correct? Explain.
   correct; The 5 rounds the 9 up to 10. 10 tenths equals 1 one. 19 + 1 = 20

10. Peter decided that the total of a $24.55 pair of jeans and a $12.25 shirt was $26.80. Was Peter's answer reasonable? Explain why or why not.
   No; $26.80 is not close to the estimate of $37, $25 and $12.

11. Biruk wants to buy a book for $15.25 and a book for $4.85. He wants to pay with one $20 bill. Use estimation to decide if this is reasonable. Explain to what place value to round for an estimate that is useful in this situation.
   Possible answer: Estimate to the nearest tenth. $15.30 + $4.90, $15 + $4 = $19 and $0.30 and $0.90 > $1, so paying with one $20 bill is not reasonable.

UNIT 3 LESSON 15   Round and Estimate with Decimal Numbers **75**

Homework and Remembering page 75

3-15
Remembering **Goal:** Spiral Review

This Remembering page would be appropriate anytime after today's lesson.

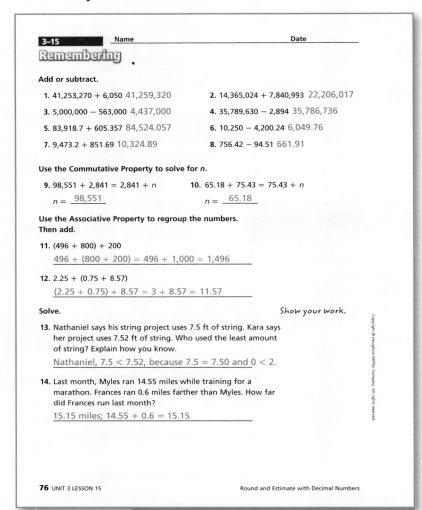

3-15 Name _____ Date _____
Remembering

Add or subtract.

1. 41,253,270 + 6,050 41,259,320   2. 14,365,024 + 7,840,993 22,206,017
3. 5,000,000 – 563,000 4,437,000   4. 35,789,630 – 2,894 35,786,736
5. 83,918.7 + 605.357 84,524.057   6. 10,250 – 4,200.24 6,049.76
7. 9,473.2 + 851.69 10,324.89   8. 756.42 – 94.51 661.91

Use the Commutative Property to solve for n.

9. 98,551 + 2,841 = 2,841 + n   10. 65.18 + 75.43 = 75.43 + n
   n = ___98,551___   n = ___65.18___

Use the Associative Property to regroup the numbers. Then add.

11. (496 + 800) + 200
   496 + (800 + 200) = 496 + 1,000 = 1,496

12. 2.25 + (0.75 + 8.57)
   (2.25 + 0.75) + 8.57 = 3 + 8.57 = 11.57

Solve. *Show your work.*

13. Nathaniel says his string project uses 7.5 ft of string. Kara says her project uses 7.52 ft of string. Who used the least amount of string? Explain how you know.
   Nathaniel, 7.5 < 7.52, because 7.5 = 7.50 and 0 < 2.

14. Last month, Myles ran 14.55 miles while training for a marathon. Frances ran 0.6 miles farther than Myles. How far did Frances run last month?
   15.15 miles; 14.55 + 0.6 = 15.15

76 UNIT 3 LESSON 15   Round and Estimate with Decimal Numbers

Homework and Remembering page 76

Home or School Activity

Social Studies Connection

Decimal Distances Discuss how maps sometimes show distances as decimal numbers. Have students do research on the Internet to find some distances between towns. Then have them draw a simple map to show the distance. Have them write one addition and one subtraction word problem for their map.

Discrete and Continuous Data

REAL
WORLD
**Problem
Solving**

Lesson Objectives

- Compare and contrast discrete and continuous data represented in tables and graphs.
- Interpret double and triple line graphs.
- Make single line graphs.

Vocabulary

discrete data
continuous data

The Day at a Glance

Today's Goals	Materials
1 Teaching the Lesson **A1:** Identify data as discrete or continuous. **A2:** Classify graphs as displays of discrete or continuous data. **A3:** Analyze double and triple line graphs. **A4:** Construct single line graphs. **2 Going Further** ▶ Differentiated Instruction **3 Homework and Spiral Review**	**Lesson Activities** Student Activity Book pages 123–128 or Student Hardcover Book pages 123–128 and Activity Workbook page 61 Homework and Remembering pages 77–78 **Going Further** Activity Cards 3-16 Grid Paper (TRB M17) Math Journals

123 *Use* **Math Talk** *today!*

Keeping Skills Sharp

Quick Practice ⏱ 5 MINUTES	Daily Routines
Goal: Round decimals to the nearest tenth, hundredth, or thousandth. **Round Decimals** Ask the class: ● If we round to the nearest tenth, how many numbers will be after the decimal point? 1 ● If we round to the nearest hundredth, how many numbers will be after the decimal point? 2 ● If we round to the nearest thousandth, how many numbers will be after the decimal point? 3 Have several students write 4-digit decimal numbers on the board. Round each number to the nearest thousandth, hundredth, and tenth.	**Homework Review** Have students share their solutions as the class asks clarifying questions and makes comments. **Geometry** A given right triangle has a perimeter of 12 m and an area of 6 m². Is it possible to make a rectangle with whole number dimensions that has the same perimeter and area? Give examples to support your answer. No; Possible answer: You can match perimeter or area but not both. Examples will vary.

① Teaching the Lesson

Analyze Data

 15 MINUTES

Goal: Identify data as discrete or continuous.

Materials: Student Activity Book or Hardcover Book p. 123

 NCTM Standards:
Data Analysis and Probability
Representation

Teaching Note

Language and Vocabulary Explain to students that data is a plural noun. Datum is the singular noun. There we say, for example, "the data are about trees." We don't say, "the data is about trees."

▶ Discuss Discrete Data [WHOLE CLASS]

Invite a volunteer to read aloud the paragraph about discrete data that is shown at the top of Student Book page 123. Encourage students to suggest other examples of discrete data. To initiate the discussion, share these additional examples:

● The number of people in a family.

● The number of books on a shelf.

● The number of heads or tails outcomes when a coin is tossed.

▶ Discuss Continuous Data [WHOLE CLASS]

Invite a volunteer to read aloud the paragraph about continuous data that is shown at the top of Student Book page 123. Encourage students to suggest other examples of continuous data. To initiate the discussion, ask:

● Suppose you were asked to find the total number of times your heart beats in three minutes, and you record the total number of times after one minute, after two minutes, and after three minutes. What kind of data would those three numbers represent—discrete or continuous? Give a reason to support your answer.

Lead students to conclude that the three numbers represent continuous data because each represents an *accumulation* of heart beats. For example, although the number recorded at 1 minute is a single number, it represents the total number of heartbeats from 0 to 60 seconds; the number recorded at 2 minutes represents the total number of heartbeats from 60 seconds to 120 seconds, and so on. In other words, the number of heartbeats are accumulating over time.

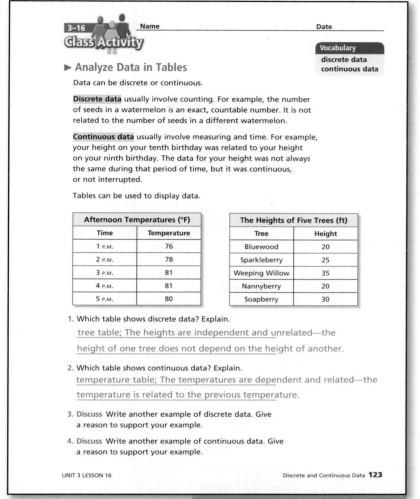

The following is the content shown on Student Activity Book page 123:

3–16 Class Activity

Name _____ Date _____

► **Analyze Data in Tables**

Data can be discrete or continuous.

Discrete data usually involve counting. For example, the number of seeds in a watermelon is an exact, countable number. It is not related to the number of seeds in a different watermelon.

Continuous data usually involve measuring and time. For example, your height on your tenth birthday was related to your height on your ninth birthday. The data for your height was not always the same during that period of time, but it was continuous, or not interrupted.

Tables can be used to display data.

Afternoon Temperatures (°F)	
Time	Temperature
1 P.M.	76
2 P.M.	78
3 P.M.	81
4 P.M.	81
5 P.M.	80

The Heights of Five Trees (ft)	
Tree	Height
Bluewood	20
Sparkleberry	25
Weeping Willow	35
Nannyberry	20
Soapberry	30

1. Which table shows discrete data? Explain.
   tree table; The heights are independent and unrelated—the height of one tree does not depend on the height of another.

2. Which table shows continuous data? Explain.
   temperature table; The temperatures are dependent and related—the temperature is related to the previous temperature.

3. Discuss Write another example of discrete data. Give a reason to support your example.

4. Discuss Write another example of continuous data. Give a reason to support your example.

UNIT 3 LESSON 16   Discrete and Continuous Data **123**

► **Analyze Data in Tables** ｜WHOLE CLASS｜

123 **Math Talk** Discuss the tables on Student Book page 123. Make sure students have a general understanding of how discrete and continuous data differ.

Use **Solve and Discuss** for exercises 1–4. For exercises 3 and 4, discuss the different examples students provide, and then have the class decide by consensus what type of data each example represents.

Activity 2

Compare Graphs

 15 MINUTES

Goal: Classify graphs as displays of discrete or continuous data.

Materials: Student Activity Book or Hardcover Book pp. 124–125

 NCTM Standards:
Data Analysis and Probability
Representation
Connections

Teaching Note

What to Expect From Students
Some students may need help relating discrete and continuous data to graphs. Describe what "accumulate" means. Then point out that on a bar graph, there is no "accumulation" of data between any of the bars. In other words, the values are independent of each other, and do not influence or affect each other in any way.

Contrast that idea with the data "accumulating" between any two points on a line graph. In other words, the value of every point on the graph depends in some way on the value of the point or points that precede it.

Encourage students to think of the concept of accumulating whenever they are asked to classify data as discrete or continuous.

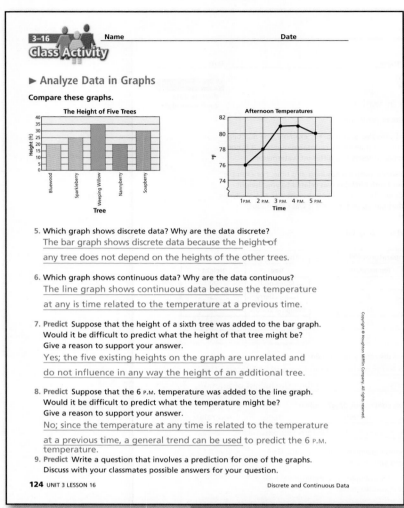

Student Activity Book page 124

▶ Analyze Data in Graphs SMALL GROUPS

Have students work in **Small Groups** to complete exercises 5–9 on Student Book page 124. Upon completion of each exercise, encourage the groups to share their answers, and discuss and explain any discrepancies.

3–16
Class Activity

Name _____ Date _____

▶ **Choose the Appropriate Graph**

Write *bar graph* or *line graph* for each situation.

10. A graph showing the height of each student in a class.
    bar graph

11. A graph showing the height of a seedling each day for a month.
    line graph

12. A graph showing your heart rate during from the beginning of a recess until the end of the recess.
    line graph

13. A graph showing the number of people who attended each performance of a school play.
    bar graph

14. A graph showing temperature of water that is being brought to a boil in a kettle.
    line graph

15. A graph showing the quiz scores for each student in a class.
    bar graph

16. Describe a situation or a group of data for which a bar graph would be an appropriate display.
    Situations and data will vary.
    _____
    _____

17. Describe a situation or a group of data for which a line graph would be an appropriate display.
    Situations and data will vary.
    _____
    _____

UNIT 3 LESSON 16   Discrete and Continuous Data **125**

Student Activity Book page 125

▶ **Choose an Appropriate Graph** [PAIRS]

Have **Student Pairs** discuss and complete exercises 10–15 on Student Book page 125. Use exercises 16 and 17 as springboards for discussion by completing them as a whole-class activity. An alternative is to have students complete the two exercises individually, with volunteers sharing their answers with the class.

Teaching the Lesson (continued)

Graphs with More Than One Line

 15 MINUTES

Goal: Analyze double and triple line graphs.

Materials: Student Activity Book or Hardcover Book pp. 126–127

✓ **NCTM Standards:**
Data Analysis and Probability
Connections
Communication

The Learning Classroom

Small Groups By discussing the problem situation and listening to other students' ideas, students become aware of other students' thinking. Instead of always following their own line of thinking, students working in small groups are able to come up with solutions they might not think of on their own.

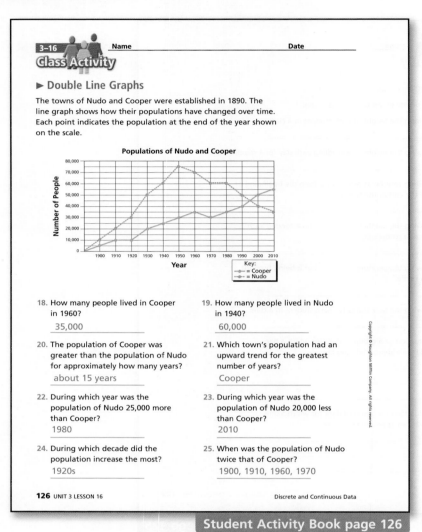

Student Activity Book page 126

▶ **Double Line Graphs** PAIRS — Math Talk

Begin the activity by having students note what each line of the graph represents. Then ask **Student Pairs** to complete exercises 18–25.

Support an Argument Graphically Ask **Small Groups** to suppose their group works for the town of Cooper. They need to estimate the number of students there will be in school in 2030. Currently, about one tenth of the total population is in school.

Allow time for discussion. Then ask each group to name the number of students they estimate will be in school in 2030, explain why they named that number, and use the graph to support their answers. A reasonable argument can be made for a wide range of students in school in 2030.

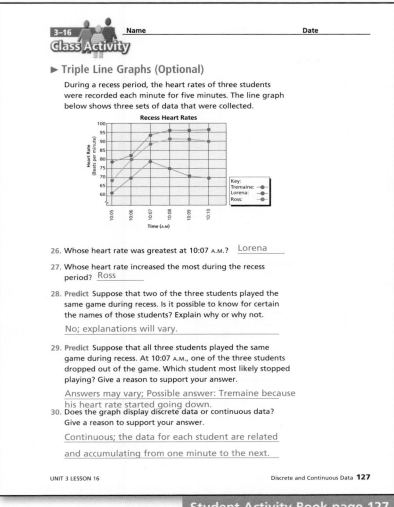

▶ Triple Line Graphs (Optional) [WHOLE CLASS]

Make sure students understand that a triple bar graph simply displays an additional set of data when compared to a double bar graph. Introduce the activity by asking students to describe the concept of a trend, and make sure they understand that with respect to numerical data, a trend is a general tendency or general direction (such as up or down) of the data.

Have students work cooperatively as a class to complete exercises 26–30 on Student Book page 127.

Teaching Note

Watch For! As students complete the activity, watch for opportunities to remind them of the importance of a legend or key when working with line graphs that display more than one line.

Activity 4

Construct a Line Graph

 15 MINUTES

Goal: Construct line graphs.

Materials: Student Activity Book p. 128 or Student Hardcover Book p.128 and Activity Workbook p. 61; ruler

 NCTM Standards:
Data Analysis and Probability
Representation

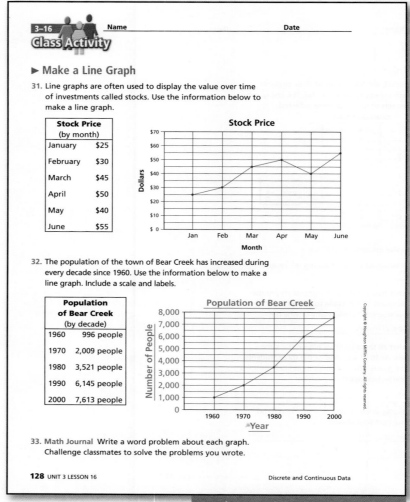

Student Activity Book page 128

▶ Make a Line Graph INDIVIDUALS

Begin by having students look again at the line graphs in the previous activities. Then ask them to name all of the different parts of a line graph, and have a volunteer record those parts in a list on the board or overhead.

Ask students to work individually or paired with a **Helping Partner** to complete the activity on Student Book page 128. For exercise 32, students will need to choose a scale for the graph. You might choose to have them perform this portion of the activity as a class by naming possible scales and discussing the advantages and/or disadvantages of each scale. (A good choice is increments of 1,000.)

The Learning Classroom

Helping Partners Often it is useful to pair a struggling student with a student who is stronger in a particular area. The helping partner needs to help the other student understand how to solve a problem, rather than just showing the student what to do. Helping pairs often foster learning in both students as the helper strives to adopt the perspective of the novice.

②Going Further

● Intervention   Activity Card 3-16

Count and Graph   Activity Card 3-16 ●

Work: By Yourself

Use:
• Grid Paper (TRB M17)

1. Count the number of boys and girls in your class.

2. Make a bar graph similar to the one below to graph your data.

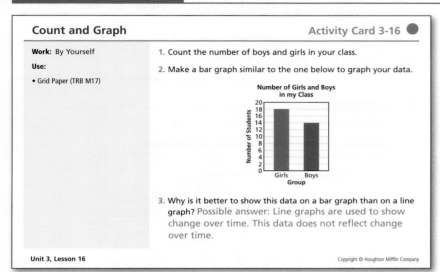

Number of Girls and Boys in my Class

3. Why is it better to show this data on a bar graph than on a line graph? Possible answer: Line graphs are used to show change over time. This data does not reflect change over time.

Unit 3, Lesson 16   Copyright © Houghton Mifflin Company

Activity Note Review the rationale for choosing either a line graph or a bar graph before students begin the activity.

✎ Math Writing Prompt

Make Connections Give an example of data that would best be shown on a line graph.

Soar to Success Math ★ Software Support

Warm-Up 50.07

▲ On Level   Activity Card 3-16

Change the Scale   Activity Card 3-16 ▲

Work: By Yourself

Use:
• Grid Paper (TRB M17)

1. Review the graph below.

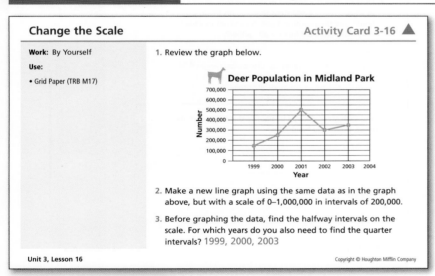

Deer Population in Midland Park

2. Make a new line graph using the same data as in the graph above, but with a scale of 0–1,000,000 in intervals of 200,000.

3. Before graphing the data, find the halfway intervals on the scale. For which years do you also need to find the quarter intervals? 1999, 2000, 2003

Unit 3, Lesson 16   Copyright © Houghton Mifflin Company

Activity Note Suggest that students make a table of the data shown in the first graph before beginning the new graph. Be sure that students correctly calculate half and quarter intervals.

✎ Math Writing Prompt

Explain Your Thinking How do you choose the scale for a line graph? Give an example.

MegaMath Grades K-6 Software Support

The Number Games: ArachnaGraph, Level J

■ Challenge   Activity Card 3-16

Misleading Graphs   Activity Card 3-16 ■

Work: In Pairs

1. Students should notice that (1) there are inconsistent intervals on the graph, (2) the scale does not start at 0, and (3) no data is shown for Dazzle for 2000 and 2001.

1. **Work Together** Identify three things about the graph on the right that make it misleading.

2. Make a new graph of the data that is not misleading. You may need to add some data.

3. **Look Back** Describe at least one conclusion about sales that your graph will support.

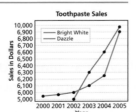

Toothpaste Sales

Unit 3, Lesson 16   Copyright © Houghton Mifflin Company

Activity Note After students have revised the graph, discuss how the conclusions that can be drawn from each graph differ.

✎ Math Writing Prompt

Collect Data Collect some data about your town or school. Choose a graph to display your data.

✦ DESTINATION Math® Software Support

Course III: Module 6: Unit 1: Displaying and Analyzing Data

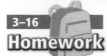 **Homework and Spiral Review**

③ Homework and Spiral Review

3-16
Homework **Goal:** Additional Practice

✓ Include student's Homework for page 77 as part of their portfolios.

3-16
Remembering **Goal:** Spiral Review

This Remembering activity would be appropriate anytime after today's lesson.

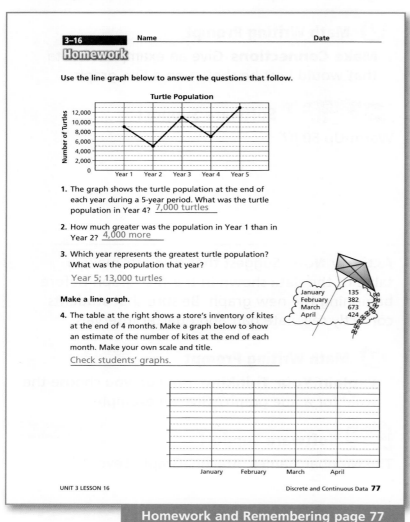

3-16 Name _____ Date _____
Homework

Use the line graph below to answer the questions that follow.

Turtle Population

(line graph: Number of Turtles on vertical axis 0 to 12,000; Year 1 through Year 5 on horizontal axis)

1. The graph shows the turtle population at the end of each year during a 5-year period. What was the turtle population in Year 4? __7,000 turtles__

2. How much greater was the population in Year 1 than in Year 2? __4,000 more__

3. Which year represents the greatest turtle population? What was the population that year?
   __Year 5; 13,000 turtles__

Make a line graph.

4. The table at the right shows a store's inventory of kites at the end of 4 months. Make a graph below to show an estimate of the number of kites at the end of each month. Make your own scale and title.
   __Check students' graphs.__

January	135
February	382
March	673
April	424

(blank grid with months January, February, March, April)

UNIT 3 LESSON 16

Discrete and Continuous Data **77**

Homework and Remembering page 77

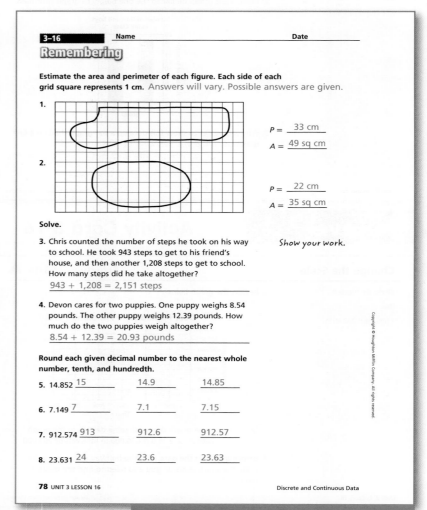

3-16 Name _____ Date _____
Remembering

Estimate the area and perimeter of each figure. Each side of each grid square represents 1 cm. *Answers will vary. Possible answers are given.*

1. *(figure on grid)*

   P = __33 cm__

   A = __49 sq cm__

2. *(figure on grid)*

   P = __22 cm__

   A = __35 sq cm__

Solve.

Show your work.

3. Chris counted the number of steps he took on his way to school. He took 943 steps to get to his friend's house, and then another 1,208 steps to get to school. How many steps did he take altogether?
   __943 + 1,208 = 2,151 steps__

4. Devon cares for two puppies. One puppy weighs 8.54 pounds. The other puppy weighs 12.39 pounds. How much do the two puppies weigh altogether?
   __8.54 + 12.39 = 20.93 pounds__

Round each given decimal number to the nearest whole number, tenth, and hundredth.

5. 14.852 __15__   __14.9__   __14.85__

6. 7.149 __7__   __7.1__   __7.15__

7. 912.574 __913__   __912.6__   __912.57__

8. 23.631 __24__   __23.6__   __23.63__

78 UNIT 3 LESSON 16

Discrete and Continuous Data

Homework and Remembering page 78

Home or School Activity

 Technology Connection

Computer Graphing There are many kinds of computer software available for making graphs. You may have such software in your school. Graphing software is a good tool for enhancing your students' projects.

Have students do research at the library or on the Internet to find the population of your state for the five past years. Then have them use a computer to make a graph of that data.

Have students explain:

- the kind of graph they made.
- why they chose that graph for their data.

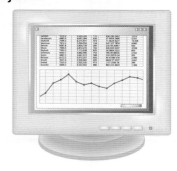

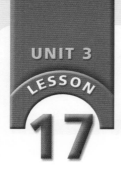

Graph With Decimal Numbers

REAL WORLD **Problem Solving**

Lesson Objectives

● **Round decimal numbers to the nearest tenth, hundredth, and thousandth.**

● **Read and construct graphs with decimal scales and decimal numbers.**

The Day at a Glance

Today's Goals	Materials	
1 **Teaching the Lesson** **A1:** Read and discuss line graphs and bar graphs with decimal numbers. **A2:** Round decimal numbers and construct a bar graph with the results. **2** **Going Further** ▶ Math Connection: Histograms ▶ Differentiated Instruction **3** **Homework and Spiral Review**	**Lesson Activities** Student Activity Book pp. 129–131 or Student Hardcover Book pp. 129–131 and Activity Workbook p. 62 Homework and Remembering pp. 79–80 Quick Quiz 4 (Assessment Guide)	**Going Further** Student Activity Book or Hardcover Book p. 132 Activity Cards 3-17 Grid Paper (TRB M17) Meter stick Math Journals 123 *Use* **Math Talk** *today!*

Keeping Skills Sharp

Quick Practice ⏱ 5 MINUTES	Daily Routines
Goal: Round decimals to the nearest tenth, hundredth, or thousandth. **Round Decimals** Ask the class: ● If we round to the nearest tenth, how many numbers will be after the decimal point? 1 ● If we round to the nearest hundredth, how many numbers will be after the decimal point? 2 ● If we round to the nearest thousandth, how many numbers will be after the decimal point? 3 Have several students write 4-digit numbers on the board. Round each number to the nearest thousandth, hundredth, and tenth.	**Homework Review** For students, who did not read the line graph correctly, review the population for each year. **Homework Review** Tara earned twice as many point as Jerome. Jerome's points are exactly three times more than Wylie's points. Altogether they have 40 points. How many points does each person have? Wylie: 4 pts; Jerome: 12 pts; Tara: 24 pts; Guess Wylie has 3 pts. Jerome: 3(4) = 12 pts; Tara: 2(12) = 24 pts; 3 + 12 + 24 ≠ 40. Too low, so give Wylie more points to raise the overall team score.

Teaching the Lesson

Activity 1

Discuss Decimal Graphs

 20 MINUTES

Goal: Read and discuss line graphs and bar graphs with decimal numbers.

Materials: Student Activity or Hardcover Book p. 129

✓ **NCTM Standards:**
Algebra
Data Analysis and Probability

Teaching Note

Language and Vocabulary
Students may be familiar with the terms "*x*-axis" and "*y*-axis" used when describing data on a graph. The *x*-axis is the horizontal axis. Remind students that a horizontal line is like the horizon line when they look at a sunset. The *y*-axis is the vertical axis. Remind students that a vertical line is straight up and down. Students should get used to this terminology since it will be used in later grades.

The Learning Classroom

Math Talk Encourage students to discuss some of the places they would commonly see bar graphs used. Many of them will say newspapers or magazines. Ask them to brainstorm several situations when a graph would be helpful.

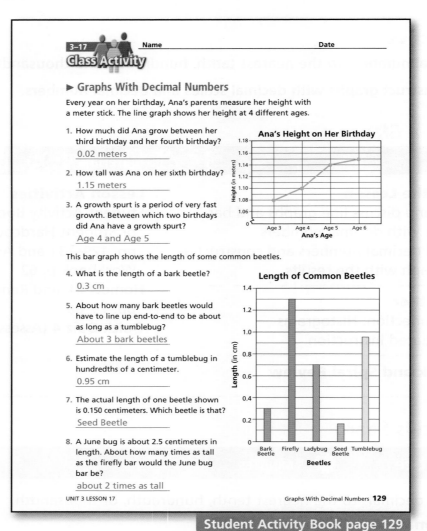

Student Activity Book page 129

▶ Graphs With Decimal Numbers | WHOLE CLASS |

Line Graphs With Decimal Numbers Discuss the scale of the line graph on page 129 in the Student Book.

- What decimal numbers does it have? hundredths

- How far apart are the numbers on the scale? 0.02 apart

Have students discuss and answer exercises 1–3.

Bar Graphs With Decimal Numbers Discuss the scale of the bar graph on page 129 in the Student Book.

- What decimal numbers does it have? tenths

- How far apart are the numbers on the scale? 0.2 apart

Have students discuss and answer exercises 4–8.

Construct a Decimal Graph

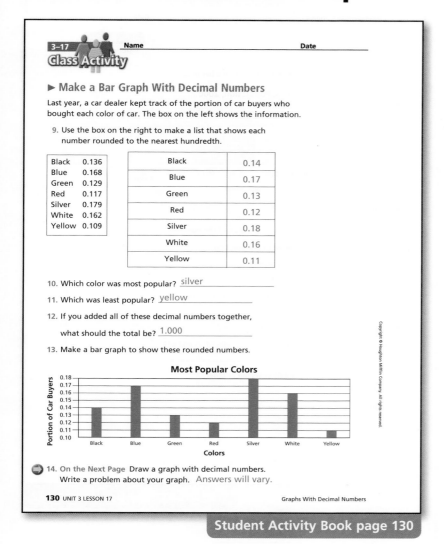

Student Activity Book page 130

▶ Make a Bar Graph With Decimal Numbers

WHOLE CLASS

Ask students to explain the data:

● **What does the entry 0.136 mean?** one hundred thirty-six thousandths, which is the fraction of all the car-buyers who bought black cars

● **What number would represent all the data?** one

Now work together to round the decimals in the table to the nearest hundredth. Ask the class how many digits there will be after the decimal point. 2 digits

Make a Bar Graph Let each student work independently to construct the bar graph of car colors. Remind everyone that the colors should be presented in order of popularity. If necessary, work together to list the cars in order from most popular to least popular.

---

 30 MINUTES

Goal: Round decimal numbers and construct a bar graph with the results.

Materials: Student Activity Book pp. 130–131 or Hardcover Book pp. 130–131 and Activity Workbook p. 62

 NCTM Standards:
Number and Operations
Algebra
Data Analysis and Probability

Ongoing Assessment

Give students the following data: 0.59, 0.0304, 1.98, 0.78 Ask students to:

▶ choose the number that is closest to one whole.

▶ draw a vertical axis starting at 0 with a scale of 0.04 and make a bar graph of the data.

Quick Quiz

See Assessment Guide for Unit 3 Quick Quiz 4.

Differentiated Instruction

Extra Help When rounding, sometimes it helps to write both choices above and below the number to be rounded, and to fill in with the extra zero.

0.180

0.179

0.170

Remind the class that a number ending in 5 (the halfway point) will be rounded up to the next larger hundredth.

Going Further

Math Connection: Histograms

Goal: Understand the difference between bar graphs and histograms and read histograms to solve problems.

Materials: Student Activity Book or Hardcover Book p. 132

✔ **NCTM Standards:**
Data Analysis and Probability
Problem Solving

▶ Read a Histogram

In this activity, students will connect bar graphs to histograms.

Have students look at the population graph on page 132. Use the information on the page to discuss with students how this graph is like and different from a bar graph. Then read the text below the graph.

Point out that the first and last age intervals on this histogram have larger ranges than the rest. The first interval is limited (by 0 and 14), but the last interval is only limited by the lowest age, 75. The rest of the intervals cover ranges of 10 years.

123 Math Talk As a class, use **Solve and Discuss** to answer questions 1–7. Lead students to use the space between two marks on the vertical scale to estimate the data shown by each bar's height. For example, the bar for ages 65–74 ends about halfway between 10 and 20 on the scale. So, 15 million would be a good estimate for halfway between 10 and 20 on the scale. Point out that some of the questions involve adding data for two intervals. Identify which questions this occurs in and why.

English Language Learners

Write *range* on the board. Say: **A *range* is a group of numbers.** Have student tell their ages. Write the range.

• **Beginning** Say: The age of students in this class *ranges* from (state range).

• **Intermediate and Advanced** Ask: Is this the *range* of ages in our class? yes

---

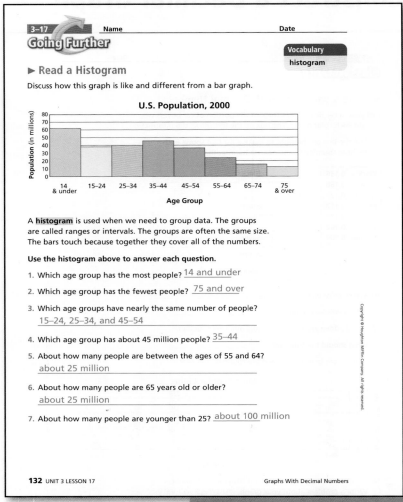

Student Activity Book page 132

▶ Extend WHOLE CLASS

You can extend this activity by showing students how to make a histogram. Write the following data table on the board. Then graph the data on a histogram on an overhead transparency.

Football Game Points Scored	
Point Range	**Number of Games**
0–9	3
10–19	7
20–29	9
30–39	5

Differentiated Instruction

Coin Scale   Activity Card 3-17 ●

Work: In Pairs

Use:

• Grid Paper (TRB M17)

1. Make a bar graph to show the decimal value of a U.S. penny, nickel, dime, quarter, and half-dollar.

2. Use the model below. Choose a title for your graph and label each axis.

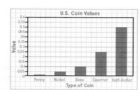

3. What scale and interval did you choose for your graph? Explain your choice. Possible answer: 0–0.6, because the value of the penny is 0.01 and the half-dollar is 0.5. The interval is 0.05 to make it possible to show the value of both the penny and the half-dollar in a reasonable vertical space.

Unit 3, Lesson 17   Copyright © Houghton Mifflin Company

Activity Note Be sure that students understand that the decimal value of each coin is expressed as a decimal part of $1. Remind students to choose a scale that allows them to show each value clearly.

 Math Writing Prompt

Number Sense If a graph has a scale of 0 to 1, do you think most of the data graphed will be decimals? Explain your thinking.

 **Software Support**

Warm-Up 50.07

Metric Lengths   Activity Card 3-17 ▲

Work: In Small Groups

Use:

• Grid Paper (TRB M17)
• Meter stick

1. **Work Together** Measure the length of the stride of each person in your group. Record the measurement in meters to the nearest 5 cm.

2. Record the data in a bar graph similar to the one shown below.

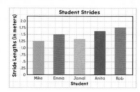

3. **Compare** Write a statement that compares some of the data in your graph.

Unit 3, Lesson 17   Copyright © Houghton Mifflin Company

Activity Note Be sure that students make the connection between decimal parts of a whole and the metric system. For example, 0.25 meter is 25 cm.

 Math Writing Prompt

Make Connections Describe a set of data that you would use a scale in decimal numbers to graph.

 Software Support

The Number Games: ArachnaGraph, Level C

Decimal Billions   Activity Card 3-17 ■

Work: In Pairs

Use:

• Grid Paper (TRB M17)

1. Research the world population for these years.

Year	1950	1960	1970	1980	1990	2000
Population						

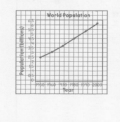

2. Display the data you find to make a line graph. Explain how you chose the scale and interval for your graph.

3. **Math Talk** Would it make sense to show the same data on a bar graph? Why or why not? Possible answer: No, the graph shows change over time. A bar graph is used to compare data.

   2. Possible explanations will focus on the size and range of the data and its precision. See sample.

Unit 3, Lesson 17   Copyright © Houghton Mifflin Company

Activity Note Discuss the accuracy with which world population data is given and how this relates to the appropriate scale for graphing such data.

 Math Writing Prompt

Draw Conclusions Write a conclusion based on a graph that you have drawn in this unit.

 Software Support

Course III: Module 6: Unit 1: Displaying and Analyzing Data

 Homework and Spiral Review

③ Homework and Spiral Review

3–17 Homework **Goal:** Additional Practice

3–17 Homework **Goal:** Additional Practice

Use this Homework page to provide students with more practice with graphing methods.

3–17 Remembering **Goal:** Spiral Review

This Remembering activity would be appropriate anytime after today's lesson.

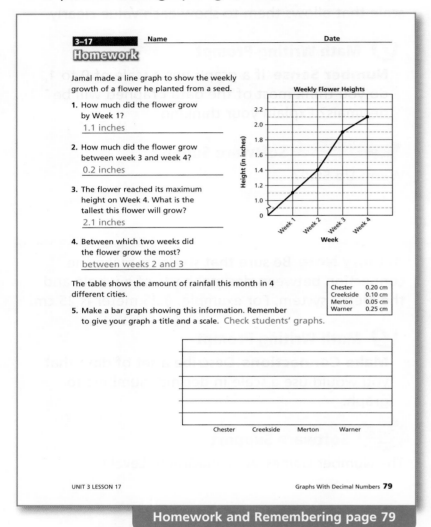

Homework and Remembering page 79

3-17 Homework   Name   Date

Jamal made a line graph to show the weekly growth of a flower he planted from a seed.

1. How much did the flower grow by Week 1?
1.1 inches

2. How much did the flower grow between week 3 and week 4?
0.2 inches

3. The flower reached its maximum height on Week 4. What is the tallest this flower will grow?
2.1 inches

4. Between which two weeks did the flower grow the most?
between weeks 2 and 3

The table shows the amount of rainfall this month in 4 different cities.

Chester	0.20 cm
Creekside	0.10 cm
Merton	0.05 cm
Warner	0.25 cm

5. Make a bar graph showing this information. Remember to give your graph a title and a scale. Check students' graphs.

UNIT 3 LESSON 17   Graphs With Decimal Numbers **79**

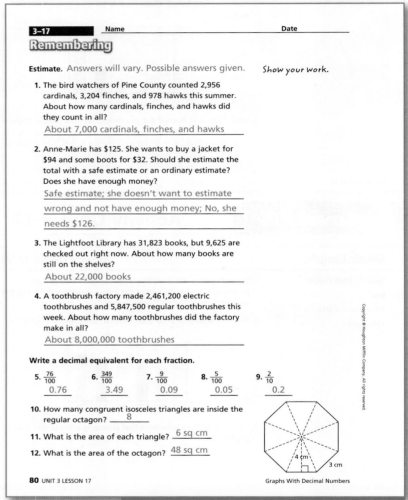

Homework and Remembering page 80

3-17 Remembering   Name   Date

Estimate. Answers will vary. Possible answers given.   *Show your work.*

1. The bird watchers of Pine County counted 2,956 cardinals, 3,204 finches, and 978 hawks this summer. About how many cardinals, finches, and hawks did they count in all?
About 7,000 cardinals, finches, and hawks

2. Anne-Marie has $125. She wants to buy a jacket for $94 and some boots for $32. Should she estimate the total with a safe estimate or an ordinary estimate? Does she have enough money?
Safe estimate; she doesn't want to estimate wrong and not have enough money; No, she needs $126.

3. The Lightfoot Library has 31,823 books, but 9,625 are checked out right now. About how many books are still on the shelves?
About 22,000 books

4. A toothbrush factory made 2,461,200 electric toothbrushes and 5,847,500 regular toothbrushes this week. About how many toothbrushes did the factory make in all?
About 8,000,000 toothbrushes

Write a decimal equivalent for each fraction.

5. $\frac{76}{100}$ 0.76

6. $\frac{349}{100}$ 3.49

7. $\frac{9}{100}$ 0.09

8. $\frac{5}{100}$ 0.05

9. $\frac{2}{10}$ 0.2

10. How many congruent isosceles triangles are inside the regular octagon?   8

11. What is the area of each triangle?   6 sq cm

12. What is the area of the octagon?   48 sq cm

80 UNIT 3 LESSON 17   Graphs With Decimal Numbers

Home or School Activity

 ## Science Connection

Your Weather Explain to students that scientists called meteorologists collect and study data about weather. Since weather changes over time, they often display the data they collect on line graphs and histograms.

Have students collect weather data for your community for one week. Each day, they should record the amount of precipitation (rain or snow) and the high temperature. At the end of the week, have them make one line graph (and possibly one histogram) to show each set of data that they collected. Then tell them to use their completed graphs to describe the weather in their community that week.

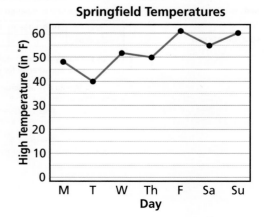

316 UNIT 3 LESSON 17

Classify Word Problems

Lesson Objectives

- Understand and apply a classification system for common addition and subtraction situations.

- Solve word problems with both additive and multiplicative comparisons.

Vocabulary
change-plus problem
change-minus problem
collection situations

The Day at a Glance

Today's Goals	Materials
1 Teaching the Lesson **A1:** Classify addition and subtraction word problems. **A2:** Represent, solve, and discuss various kinds of comparison word problems. **2 Going Further** ▶ Differentiated Instruction **3 Homework and Spiral Review**	**Lesson Activities** Student Activity Book pp. 133–136 or Student Hardcover Book pp. 133–136 Homework and Remembering pp. 81–82 **Going Further** Activity Cards 3-18 Counters Math Journals 123 *Use* **Math Talk** *today!*

Keeping Skills Sharp

Quick Practice ⏱ 5 MINUTES	**Daily Routines**
Round Decimals Send several **Student Leaders** to the board. Each should write a decimal number with 4 digits after the decimal point (for example, 0.1752). They ask the class to round each number to the nearest thousandth, hundredth, and tenth. After each response, the leader writes the rounded decimal to the right of the original decimal number.	**Homework Review** Have students discuss the problems from their homework. Encourage students to help each other resolve any misunderstandings. **Reasoning** Write the following problem on the board. $2.6581 + 14.7 = 17.3581$ Have students write another addition problem involving decimals that has the same sum. Possible answer: $9.86 + 7.4981 = 17.3581$

Teaching the Lesson

Addition and Subtraction Situations

 30 MINUTES

Goal: Classify addition and subtraction word problems.

Materials: Student Activity Book or Hardcover Book pp. 133–135

NCTM Standards:
Number and Operations
Algebra
Representation
Communication

Teaching Note

Math Background Some addition and subtraction situations involve a change. The change can be an increase or a decrease. In a change problem, the starting number, the change, or the result will be unknown. An equation with a letter can be used to show a change situation.

Change Plus Situations

Unknown Start	Unknown Change	Unknown Result
$n + 2 = 5$	$3 + n = 5$	$3 + 2 = n$

Change Minus Situations

Unknown Start	Unknown Change	Unknown Result
$n - 2 = 3$	$5 - n = 3$	$5 - 2 = n$

Situation and Solution Equations

• A *situation equation* shows the action or the relationships in a problem.

• A *solution equation* shows the operation you perform to solve the problem.

For simple numbers, students may find the answer from a situation equation. They do not always need to write a solution equation.

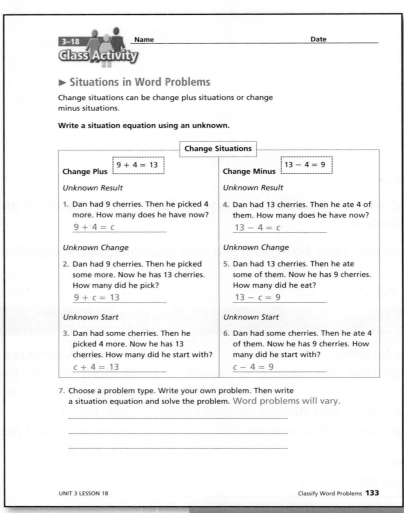

Student Activity Book page 133

► Situations in Word Problems WHOLE CLASS

Change Situations Direct students' attention to page 133 of the Student Book. Explain that situation equations are a good way to represent these change problems. Situation equations use an unknown to show the situation. Students can use the letter c for the unknown number of cherries. Invite a few students to work at the class board. It can be helpful for students to label some or all parts of their equations. Then discuss the solution equations, especially for problems 3 and 6.

Change Plus	Change Minus
1. $9 + 4 = c$	4. $13 - 4 = c$
2. $9 + c = 13$	5. $13 - c = 9$
3. $c + 4 = 13$	6. $c - 4 = 9$

Student Activity Book page 134

Class Activity

Name _____ Date _____

Collection situations can have an unknown total or an unknown partner.

**Make a Break-Apart drawing and write a situation equation.
Use a variable for the unknown.**

Collection Situations

```
        13
       /  \
      9    4
```

Unknown Total

Put Together

8. Ana put 9 dimes and 4 nickels in her pocket. How many coins did she put in her pocket?

$9 + 4 = c$

Take Apart

9. Ana put 9 coins in her purse and 4 coins in her bank. How many coins did she have in the beginning?

$9 + 4 = c$

No Action

10. Ana has 9 dimes and 4 nickels. How many coins does she have in all?

$9 + 4 = c$

Unknown Partner

Put Together

11. Ana put 13 coins in her pocket. Nine are dimes and the rest are nickels. How many nickels are in her pocket?

$9 + n = 13$

Take Apart

12. Ana had 13 coins. She had 9 dimes and the rest were nickels. She put all 9 dimes in her purse and all the nickels in her bank. How many nickels did she put in her bank?

$9 + n = 13$

No Action

13. Ana has 13 coins. She has 9 dimes and the rest are nickels. How many are nickels?

$9 + n = 13$

14. Choose a problem type. Write your own problem. Then write an equation and solve the problem.

Answers will vary.

_____

_____

134 UNIT 3 LESSON 18   Classify Word Problems

English Language Learners

Write $7 + n = 15$, *unknown*, and *variable* on the board.

- **Beginning** Point and say: **The *n* is a *variable*. It represents the partner we don't know.** Ask: **Is it an *unknown partner*?** yes
- **Intermediate** Ask: **Does *n* represent an *unknown partner* or *total*?** partner **Is it a *variable*?** yes
- **Advanced** Say: **We don't know the partner, it is _____.** unknown **We represent it with the *variable* _____.** *n*

Collection Situations Ask the class to look at student page 134. Have students quickly read the word problems to themselves. Then discuss how collection situations differ from change situations. Ask:

● What is the difference between a collection situation and a change situation? In a collection situation, all of the objects are there from the beginning. We don't add or subtract anything. We just move them around or classify them.

Activity continued ▶

Teaching Note

Math Background Students are exposed to these different addition and subtraction problem types so that they will be aware of the many variations. They are definitely not expected to internalize all the subcategories or to label each word problem they encounter. This classification system will help them to understand the unknown quantity in a word problem and how it can be related to the known quantities. Equations, break-apart drawings, and comparison bars are all representations that help students to see these relationships.

Teaching Note

Math Background Different equations are possible for any word problem. For problem 13, the equation $13 - 9 = n$ is also correct. Equations such as $13 - 9 = n$ and $9 + n = 13$ are called *equivalent equations* because they have the same solution.

Explain that break-apart drawings are a good way to represent collection problems because they show the total and the parts without showing any change (plus or minus). Ask the students to draw a break-apart drawing for each of these collection situations. They can use the letter *c* for coins, *n* for nickels, and *d* for dimes. (There are only two kinds of break-apart drawings for these six problems—one for an unknown total and one for an unknown addend.)

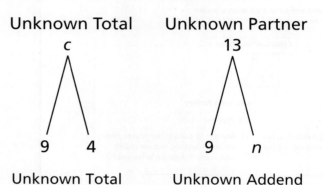

In problems 11–13, the unknown addend is always 4. Ask the class to invent a word problem about Ana and her coins in which the unknown addend is 9. Ana has 13 coins. 4 are nickels and the rest are dimes. How many are dimes? Then have everyone make a break-apart drawing and write an equation for that situation.

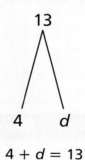

$$4 + d = 13$$

Student Activity Book page 135 content

Additive comparison situations ask how many more or how many fewer. They can have an unknown quantity or an unknown difference.

Make a Break-Apart drawing and write an equation for each situation.

Comparison Situations

13

9 4

Unknown Difference

How Many More?

15. Ali has 9 balloons. Lisa has 13 balloons. How many more balloons does Lisa have than Ali?

$13 - 9 = c$

How Many Fewer?

16. Ali has 9 balloons. Lisa has 13 balloons. How many fewer balloons does Ali have than Lisa?

$13 - 9 = c$

Unknown Quantity

Leading Language

17. Ali has 9 balloons. Lisa has 4 more than Ali. How many balloons does Lisa have?

$9 + 4 = c$

Misleading Language

18. Ali has 9 balloons. He has 4 fewer than Lisa. How many balloons does Lisa have?

$9 + 4 = c$

19. Write a comparison problem with an unknown difference. Draw comparison bars, write an equation, and solve.

Answers will vary.

20. Write a comparison problem with an unknown quantity. Draw comparison bars, write an equation, and solve.

Answers will vary.

Comparison Situations Direct everyone's attention to exercises 15–20 on page 135. Ask students how these comparison bars are different from the comparison bars they drew for multiplication comparisons and why they are this way. Ask the class to read each problem and then draw comparison bars showing which quantity is unknown.

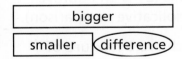

Additive comparisons compare a smaller to a bigger quantity. Many students think of these situations as smaller + difference = bigger.

Have students write and solve word problems for exercises 19 and 20 with a partner. Have them draw comparison bars in the space to the right.

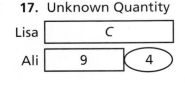

15. Unknown Difference

Lisa | 13
Ali | 9 | C

17. Unknown Quantity

Lisa | C
Ali | 9 | 4

Teaching Note

Math Background Two amounts can be compared by multiplication and division as we did in Unit 1, or they can be compared by addition and subtraction, as we are doing here. In both kinds of situations, comparison bars can help with the solution. You always need to decide which amount is bigger and which is smaller. But for multiplicative comparisons the comparing question asks, "How many times *a* is *b*?" and for additive comparisons the comparing question asks, "How much more is *a* than *b*?" Both kinds of comparing situations can ask the comparing sentence in two ways, with either amount the subject of the sentence. With additive comparison bars, the difference is shown by an oval so that the two compared amounts in the rectangle can be clearly seen.

Teaching the Lesson (continued)

Activity 2

Mixed Practice With Comparisons

 25 MINUTES

Goal: Represent, solve, and discuss various kinds of comparison word problems.

Materials: Student Activity Book or Hardcover Book p. 136

✔ **NCTM Standards:**
Number and Operations
Algebra
Communication
Problem Solving
Representation

The Learning Classroom

Math Talk

24. Troy spent $\frac{1}{8}$ as much as Jamie spent.
Jamie spent 8 times as much as Troy spent.

25. The length is 17.2 meters more than the width. The width is 17.2 meters less than the length.

26. How many fewer points did Martin score? How many more points did Alex score?

3–18
Class Activity

Name _____ Date _____

▶ **Additive and Multiplicative Comparison**

You can use comparison bars to represent quantities in additive and multiplicative comparison situations.

Show your work.

Solve.

21. Two speedboats entered the harbor. One was 9 feet long, and the other was 3 feet longer. What was the length of the longer boat?
    12 feet

    | 9 | |
    | 9 | 3 |

22. Later, two sailboats entered the harbor. One was 9 feet long. The other was 3 times as long. What was the length of the longer boat?
    27 feet

    | 9 | | |
    | 9 | 9 | 9 |

23. Ramona spent $72 at the theme park last week. Alicia spent $8 less than Ramona. How much money did Alicia spend?
    $64

24. Jamie spent $72 during the soccer trip. Troy spent $\frac{1}{8}$ as much as Jamie spent. How much money did Troy spend?
    $9

25. The length of a field is 123 meters. That is 17.2 meters more than the width. What is the width of the field?
    105.8 meters

26. Alex and Martin played video games last night. Alex scored 8,000 points and Martin scored 2,845 points. How many fewer points did Martin score?
    5,155 points

136 UNIT 3 LESSON 18   Classify Word Problems

Student Activity Book page 136

▶ **Solve Comparison Problems** [WHOLE CLASS]

123 Math Talk Have students turn to the word problems on page 136 and solve problems 21 and 22. Then ask the class to discuss the difference between these two comparison problems (21 is an additive comparison where the difference is 3; 22 is a multiplicative comparison).

Discuss the rest of the problems on the page, which are a mixture of additive and multiplicative comparisons. Invite some students to solve and explain at the board while the others work at their seats. For each problem be sure one explainer draws comparison bars and have students say the comparison both ways. (See also **Math Talk.**)

23. Alicia spent $8 less than Ramona.
    Ramona spent $8 more than Alicia.

②Going Further

Intervention   Activity Card 3-18

Counter Model	Activity Card 3-18 ●

Work: In Pairs

Use:
• Counters

1. Write an equation for each problem and use counters to model it. Then write the solution. The first one is modeled for you.

• Dan had 9 stars. Then he made 4 more. How many does he have now? 13

    $9 + 4 = c$

• Dan had 9 stars. Then he made some more. Now he has 13 stars. How many did he make? 4

• Dan had some stars. Then he made 4 more. Now he has 13 stars. How many did he have at the start? 9

2. **Explain** Why are these called Change Plus problems?

Possible answer: Each problem describes a number of items that are increased to make a new total.

Unit 3, Lesson 18   Copyright © Houghton Mifflin Company

Activity Note After students have completed the activity, have them write their own change plus equations and model them with counters.

✎ Math Writing Prompt

Compare and Contrast How are addition and subtraction alike? How are they different?

 **Software Support**

Warm-Up 10.13

On Level   Activity Card 3-18

All Possible Equations	Activity Card 3-18 ▲

Work: By Yourself

1. $a + 4 = 9$, $a = 5$;
$4 + a = 9$, $a = 5$;
$a - 4 = 9$, $a = 13$;
$9 + 4 = a$, $a = 13$;
$4 + 9 = a$, $a = 13$;
$9 - 4 = a$, $a = 5$;
$9 - a = 4$; $a = 5$

1. Write and solve all possible addition and subtraction equations using the whole numbers 4 and 9 and the letter a.

2. Choose one of the equations that you wrote. Write a change, a collection, or a comparison word problem that you could solve with that equation.

3. **Compare** How is a change word problem different from a comparison word problem? Give an example of each. Possible answer: A change word problem is about a number of items that is increased or decreased. A comparison word problem is about how the quantities of two different items compare. Examples will vary.

Unit 3, Lesson 18   Copyright © Houghton Mifflin Company

Activity Note Before students begin the activity, remind them that addition is commutative but subtraction is not.

✎ Math Writing Prompt

Write Your Own Use the numbers 7, 5, and 12 to write a change, a collection, and a comparison word problem.

 Software Support

Ice Station Exploration: Arctic Algebra, Level F

Challenge   Activity Card 3-18

Comparison Sentences	Activity Card 3-18 ■

Work: By Yourself

5 more than 3 is 8.

3 more than 5 is 8.

3 more than 2 is 5.

5 times 3 is 15.

3 times 5 is 15.

1. Copy the sentence form below.

____ _____ ____ is ____.

2. Write as many sentences as possible, using
• the digits 3 and 5 for two of the short blanks
• the phrase "more than" or "times" for the long blank
• any digit(s) you might need for the third short blank

3. **Write a Comparison** Choose one of the sentences that you wrote. Write a comparison word problem that your sentence can be used to solve.

Unit 3, Lesson 18   Copyright © Houghton Mifflin Company

Activity Note To vary this activity, have students work in pairs and challenge each other to complete the sentence using numbers other than 3 and 5.

✎ Math Writing Prompt

Explain Your Thinking List words or phrases that might be in multiplication comparison word problems. Make another list for addition comparison word problems. Explain your choices.

 DESTINATION Math Software Support

Course III: Module 1: Unit 1: Whole Numbers to One Million

Classify Word Problems   **323**

③ Homework and Spiral Review

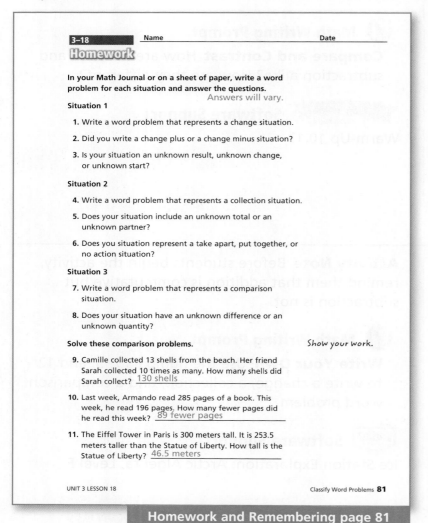

3-18
Homework **Goal:** Additional Practice

✓ Include students' work for page 81 as part of their portfolios.

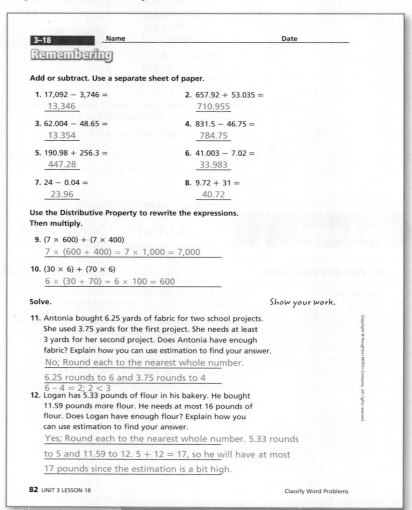

3-18
Remembering **Goal:** Spiral Review

This Remembering activity would be appropriate anytime after today's lesson.

3-18 Name _____ Date _____
Homework

In your Math Journal or on a sheet of paper, write a word problem for each situation and answer the questions.
Answers will vary.

Situation 1

1. Write a word problem that represents a change situation.

2. Did you write a change plus or a change minus situation?

3. Is your situation an unknown result, unknown change, or unknown start?

Situation 2

4. Write a word problem that represents a collection situation.

5. Does your situation include an unknown total or an unknown partner?

6. Does you situation represent a take apart, put together, or no action situation?

Situation 3

7. Write a word problem that represents a comparison situation.

8. Does your situation have an unknown difference or an unknown quantity?

Solve these comparison problems. *Show your work.*

9. Camille collected 13 shells from the beach. Her friend Sarah collected 10 times as many. How many shells did Sarah collect? _130 shells_

10. Last week, Armando read 285 pages of a book. This week, he read 196 pages. How many fewer pages did he read this week? _89 fewer pages_

11. The Eiffel Tower in Paris is 300 meters tall. It is 253.5 meters taller than the Statue of Liberty. How tall is the Statue of Liberty? _46.5 meters_

UNIT 3 LESSON 18 | Classify Word Problems **81**

Homework and Remembering page 81

3-18 Name _____ Date _____
Remembering

Add or subtract. Use a separate sheet of paper.

1. $17,092 - 3,746 =$ _13,346_

2. $657.92 + 53.035 =$ _710.955_

3. $62.004 - 48.65 =$ _13.354_

4. $831.5 - 46.75 =$ _784.75_

5. $190.98 + 256.3 =$ _447.28_

6. $41.003 - 7.02 =$ _33.983_

7. $24 - 0.04 =$ _23.96_

8. $9.72 + 31 =$ _40.72_

Use the Distributive Property to rewrite the expressions. Then multiply.

9. $(7 \times 600) + (7 \times 400)$
   $7 \times (600 + 400) = 7 \times 1,000 = 7,000$

10. $(30 \times 6) + (70 \times 6)$
    $6 \times (30 + 70) = 6 \times 100 = 600$

Solve. *Show your work.*

11. Antonia bought 6.25 yards of fabric for two school projects. She used 3.75 yards for the first project. She needs at least 3 yards for her second project. Does Antonia have enough fabric? Explain how you can use estimation to find your answer.
    No; Round each to the nearest whole number.
    6.25 rounds to 6 and 3.75 rounds to 4
    _$6 - 4 = 2; 2 < 3$_

12. Logan has 5.33 pounds of flour in his bakery. He bought 11.59 pounds more flour. He needs at most 16 pounds of flour. Does Logan have enough flour? Explain how you can use estimation to find your answer.
    Yes; Round each to the nearest whole number. 5.33 rounds
    to 5 and 11.59 to 12. $5 + 12 = 17$, so he will have at most
    17 pounds since the estimation is a bit high.

82 UNIT 3 LESSON 18 | Classify Word Problems

Homework and Remembering page 82

Home or School Activity

Language Arts Connection

Comparison Suffixes Tell students that a suffix is a word ending. Two suffixes that indicate comparison are *-er* and *–est*.

Have students make a list of words that describe measurement, such as *tall, short, heavy, cold, small,* etc. Then they should attach suffixes and use the new comparison words to write word problems.

> The low temperature on Wednesday was 15°. That was 12° colder than the low temperature on Tuesday. What was the low temperature on Tuesday?

UNIT 3
LESSON 19

Situation and Solution Equations

REAL WORLD **Problem Solving**

Lesson Objectives

- Solve word problems with unknown addends.
- Write a situation equation and convert it to a solution equation.

Vocabulary

situation equation
solution equation

The Day at a Glance

Today's Goals	Materials
1 **Teaching the Lesson** **A1:** Solve problems that require converting situation equations to solution equations. **A2:** Practice solving for a variety of unknowns in charts and word problems. **2** **Going Further** ▶ Differentiated Instruction **3** **Homework and Spiral Review**	**Lesson Activities** Student Activity Book pp. 137–140 or Student Hardcover Book pp. 137–140 and Activity Workbook pp. 63–64 Homework and Remembering pp. 83–84 **Going Further** Activity Cards 3-19 MathBoard materials Index cards Centimeter ruler Centimeter-Grid Paper (TRB M18) Math Journals 123 Use **Math Talk** today!

Keeping Skills Sharp

Quick Practice ⏱ 5 MINUTES	Daily Routines
Round Decimals Send several **Student Leaders** to the board. Each should write a decimal number with 4 digits after the decimal point (for example, 0.6752). They ask the class to round each number to the nearest thousandth, hundredth, and tenth. After each response, the leader writes the rounded decimal to the right of the original decimal number.	**Homework Review** Ask students to share their word problems while the class asks clarifying questions about each. **Nonroutine Problem** In a toothpaste survey, 5 of the first 15 people surveyed liked a toothpaste. If 30 people will be surveyed altogether, predict the number of people who will not like the toothpaste. Give a reason to support your answer. 20; Sample explanation: 10 of 15 is $\frac{2}{3}$, and $\frac{2}{3}$ of 30 is 20.

Situation and Solution Equations **325**

① Teaching the Lesson

Convert to Solution Equations

 25 MINUTES

Goal: Solve problems that require converting situation equations to solution equations.

Materials: Student Activity Book pp. 137–138 or Hardcover Book pp. 137–138 and Activity Workbook pp. 63–64

 NCTM Standards:
Number and Operations
Algebra
Communication
Problem Solving

The Learning Classroom

Helping Community Students at the board may get stuck. They usually welcome help from another student at that point. Allowing other students to help (instead of you) will lead them to assume responsibility for one another's learning. Ask who they would like to come help them. You can move on to another explainer while the students redo their work at the board. Of course, sometimes it is fine to have the whole class help the student as you guide the process.

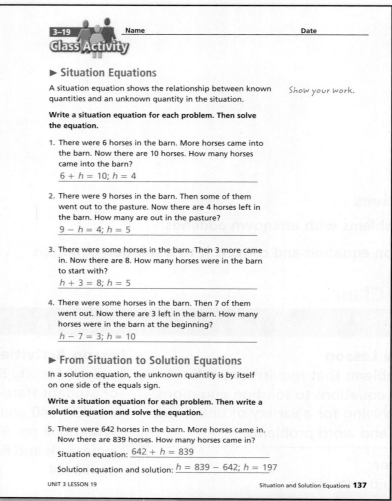

Student Activity Book page 137

> ▶ Situation Equations [WHOLE CLASS]

Problems 1–4 have been made deliberately easy so that students can see the relationship between the unknown and the known quantities.

Using the letter h as the unknown number of horses, ask students to write the equation that shows each situation. Ask a few student volunteers to work at the classroom board. Tell students not to solve the equations yet.

123 **Math Talk** Discuss the term *situation equation*. Explain that an equation that shows the real-world situation, as these equations do, can be called a situation equation. They can help show the problem to yourself or to a classmate.

Now discuss how these equations can be solved. Many students will automatically know the answers. Others will count on to find the unknown number, because all but 4 involve an unknown addend. *Example:* 6 + *what number* = 10? It takes 4 to get from 6 to 10, so $h = 4$.

Discuss student reasoning about problem 4. Some students think backwards (3 + 7 makes the 10 at the beginning), and others see the 3 and 7 as addends (partners) of the total, so add them to make 10.

Have students write one word problem that relates to the situation equation $a + 5 = 20$ and share their problems with the class. The class verifies that the equation relates to the word problem and then solves. Discuss how one equation has the same numeric answer, but represents something different each time.

▶ From Situation to Solution Equations WHOLE CLASS

Direct students' attention to problems 5–8 on Student Book pages 137–138.

Again, work together as a class to write situation equations, using the letter *h* for the unknown number of horses.

When the equations have all been written, discuss how they can be solved. For these equations, students will *not* be able to perform mental math or count on to find the answers. Students should realize at this point that solving situation equations with large numbers requires a method other than mental math or counting on.

For these larger numbers, students need to write solution equations that tell them what operation to do, or they should write a vertical computation. Labeling the equation to find the total can be helpful, as can making a break-apart drawing.

5. $642 + h = 839$
<small>now total</small>

$$\begin{array}{r} {\scriptstyle 713} \\ 8\cancel{3}9 \\ -642 \\ \hline 197 \end{array}$$

Activity continued ▶

Activity 1

Differentiated Instruction

Extra Help Some students may need more structure when identifying the total and the parts. It may be helpful to start by circling or underlining the total in the equation.

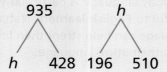

$$(935) - h = 428$$

Making a break-apart drawing that shows the total on top and the two parts on the bottom could also be helpful.

```
      935           h
      / \          / \
     h  428     196  510
```

English Language Learners

Write $10 - s = 7$, $10 - 7 = s$, *situation equation*, and *solution equation* on the board.

- **Beginning** Point and say: $10 - s = 7$ is the *situation equation*. We move the variable s and get $10 - 7 = s$. This is the *solution equation*. Have students repeat.
- **Intermediate** Ask: Does $10 - s$ tell us the problem or how to solve? problem Is it a *situation equation*? yes
- **Advanced** Have students tell the difference between the equations and identify them.

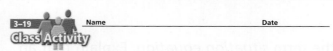

3–19 **Class Activity** — Name _____ Date _____

6. There were 935 horses in the barn. Then some of them went out to the pasture. Now there are 428 horses left in the barn. How many are out in the pasture?

   Show your work.

   Situation equation: $935 - h = 428$

   Solution equation and solution: $h = 935 - 428$; $h = 507$

7. There were some horses in the barn. Then 347 more came in. Now there are 736. How many horses were in the barn to start with?

   Situation equation: $h + 347 = 736$

   Solution equation and solution: $h = 736 - 347$; $h = 389$

8. There were some horses in the barn. Then 196 of them went out. Now there are 510 left in the barn. How many horses were in the barn at the beginning?

   Situation equation: $h - 196 = 510$

   Solution equation and solution: $h = 510 + 196$; $h = 706$

▶ **Word Problem Applications**

Workers at the Burlington Balloon Factory make a chart each day to keep track of the number of balloons. Today someone spilled juice on the chart. Some of the numbers cannot be read.

9. Write an equation you can solve to find each unknown number. Then solve the equation.

The Burlington Balloon Factory

Color of Balloon	Number at Beginning	Number made today	Number at end of day	Equation	Solution
Yellow	2,498	3,261		$2,498 + 3,261 = x$	$x = 5,759$
Red	1,945		4,147	$1,945 + r = 4,147$	$r = 2,202$
Blue		5,172	8,365	$b + 5,172 = 8,365$	$b = 3,193$
Pink	498		1,498	$498 + p = 1,498$	$p = 1,000$
White	3,456	500		$3,456 + 500 = w$	$w = 3,956$

138 UNIT 3 LESSON 19 — Situation and Solution Equations

Student Activity Book page 138

---

6. $935 - h = 428$
   total pasture barn

```
      935
      / \
     h   428
```

$$\begin{array}{r} \overset{2\,15}{9\cancel{3}\cancel{5}} \\ -428 \\ \hline 507 \end{array}$$

7. $h + 347 = 736$
   some more now

```
      736
      / \
     h   347
```

$$\begin{array}{r} \overset{12}{\overset{6\,13\,16}{7\cancel{3}\cancel{6}}} \\ -347 \\ \hline 389 \end{array}$$

8. $h - 196 = 510$
   some out left

```
       h
      / \
    196  510
```

$$\begin{array}{r} \overset{1}{196} \\ +510 \\ \hline 706 \end{array}$$

Solve With Various Unknowns

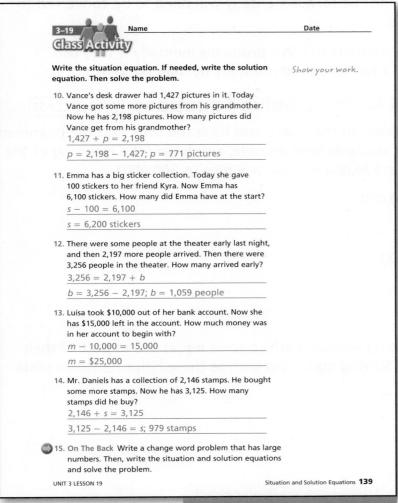

Student Activity Book page 139

The activity book page shows:

3–19
Class Activity
Name _____ Date _____

Write the situation equation. If needed, write the solution equation. Then solve the problem.

Show your work.

10. Vance's desk drawer had 1,427 pictures in it. Today Vance got some more pictures from his grandmother. Now he has 2,198 pictures. How many pictures did Vance get from his grandmother?
$1,427 + p = 2,198$
$p = 2,198 - 1,427; p = 771$ pictures

11. Emma has a big sticker collection. Today she gave 100 stickers to her friend Kyra. Now Emma has 6,100 stickers. How many did Emma have at the start?
$s - 100 = 6,100$
$s = 6,200$ stickers

12. There were some people at the theater early last night, and then 2,197 more people arrived. Then there were 3,256 people in the theater. How many arrived early?
$3,256 = 2,197 + b$
$b = 3,256 - 2,197; b = 1,059$ people

13. Luisa took $10,000 out of her bank account. Now she has $15,000 left in the account. How much money was in her account to begin with?
$m - 10,000 = 15,000$
$m = \$25,000$

14. Mr. Daniels has a collection of 2,146 stamps. He bought some more stamps. Now he has 3,125. How many stamps did he buy?
$2,146 + s = 3,125$
$3,125 - 2,146 = s; 979$ stamps

15. **On The Back** Write a change word problem that has large numbers. Then, write the situation and solution equations and solve the problem.

UNIT 3 LESSON 19 — Situation and Solution Equations **139**

 30 MINUTES

Goal: Practice solving for a variety of unknowns in charts and word problems.

Materials: Student Activity Book or Hardcover Book pp. 139–140

✔ **NCTM Standards:**
Number and Operations
Algebra
Communication
Problem Solving

▶ Word Problem Applications WHOLE CLASS

Have your students read exercise 9 from Student Book page 139, and look at the balloon factory chart. Every row has a missing number. Have students first write the situation equation, using any letter for the unknown that is meaningful to them. If necessary, they can convert it to a solution equation and solve for the missing number. Encourage your students to use mental math for the last two rows.

Yellow: situation: $2,498 + 3,261 = x$ $x = 5,759$

Red: situation: $1,945 + r = 4,147$ $r = 2,202$

Blue: situation: $b + 5,172 = 8,365$ $b = 3,193$

Pink: situation: $498 + p = 1,498$ $p = 1,000$

White: situation: $3,456 + 500 = w$ $w = 3,956$

Activity continued ▶

Teaching the Lesson (continued)

Activity 2

The Learning Classroom

Helping Community Students at the board may get stuck at some point. Allowing other students to help instead of you will help them to assume responsibility for one another's learning. Ask whom they would like to come up to help them. You can move on to another explainer while they redo their work. Of course, sometimes it is fine just to go ahead and have the whole class help the student with you leading with questions.

Working together as a class, solve problems 10–15 on page 139 of the Student Book. Invite some students to work at the board. Situation equations that cannot be solved mentally will need to be converted to solution equations.

Again, encourage students to solve problems mentally if they can. Problems 11 and 13 can be solved mentally by many students.

▶ Use Mental Math to Solve Equations WHOLE CLASS

Write these equations on the board and have the class find the unknown number quickly. If students have trouble, emphasize the meaning of the equation. *Example:* 500,000 + *what* will give us 600,000?

$500{,}000 + g = 600{,}000$ $g = 100{,}000$

$d + 788 = 6{,}788$ $d = 6{,}000$

$c - 20{,}000 = 30{,}000$ $c = 50{,}000$

$0.45 + l = 38.45$ $l = 38$

$k - 0.40 = 0.50$ $k = 0.90$

Students will be using mental math to solve equations as part of their homework today. Solving equations such as these helps reinforce place value concepts.

② Going Further

Intervention — Activity Card 3-19

Card Equations   Activity Card 3-19 ●

Work: In Pairs

Use:
- MathBoard materials
- 14 Index cards

1. Write the numbers 1–10 on ten of the cards. Write +, −, =, and *n* on the other four cards.

2. Shuffle the ten numbered cards and place them face down.

3. One person chooses two numbered cards and the other person chooses three of the other cards.

4. One person uses the cards to form an equation on the MathBoard. The other person solves the equation. See the example below.

$$n + 6 = 9$$
$$n = 9 - 6$$
$$n = 3$$

Unit 3, Lesson 19   Copyright © Houghton Mifflin Company

Activity Note Remind students to say "what number" when they read a variable in an equation.

 **Math Writing Prompt**

Explain Your Thinking If two numbers in a situation equation are 18 and 3, what is a possible solution? Explain your thinking.

Soar to Success Math ★ Software Support

Warm-Up 14.32

On Level — Activity Card 3-19

Inverse Operations   Activity Card 3-19 ▲

Work: In Pairs

1. One person writes a situation equation with two decimal numbers and a letter using one of the following forms.

_____ + _____ = _____

_____ − _____ = _____

2. The other person converts it to a solution equation and solves it, as shown below.

$$a + 1.2 = 5.75$$
$$a = 5.75 - 1.2$$
$$a = 4.55$$

3. Repeat the activity three times.

4. Possible answer: To isolate the variable, you must use the inverse operation. So the addition form will have a subtraction solution and vice versa.

4. Math Talk How are the situation equation and the solution equation related?

Unit 3, Lesson 19   Copyright © Houghton Mifflin Company

Activity Note Remind students to align decimal points when adding or subtracting. The solution should be stated as an equation using the variable.

 Math Writing Prompt

Support Your Answer If a situation equation has a subtraction sign, will the solution equation always have an addition sign? Give an example to support your answer.

MegaMath Grades K-6 Software Support

Ice Station Exploration: Arctic Algebra, Level Y

Challenge — Activity Card 3-19

Equations for Geometry   Activity Card 3-19 ■

Work: In Pairs

Use:
- Centimeter Ruler
- Centimeter-Grid Paper (TRB M18)

The drawing below shows a polygon with all right angles. All the sides are labeled to the nearest tenth of a centimeter except for side *x*. The equation shows how to find the value of *x*.

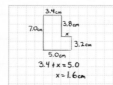

$$3.4 + x = 5.0$$
$$x = 1.6 \text{ cm}$$

1. On your own, use a centimeter ruler to draw a different polygon with all right angles. Label all side lengths except one to the nearest tenth. Use a letter to label the remaining side.

2. Exchange drawings with your partner. Write an equation and solve it to find the unknown side length on your partner's drawing.

Unit 3, Lesson 19   Copyright © Houghton Mifflin Company

Activity Note Tell students to put away their rulers after they complete their drawings.

 Math Writing Prompt

Explain Your Reasoning Describe how to find the area of the figure you drew for this activity. If necessary, include a sketch of how you divided the figure.

 DESTINATION Math· Software Support

Course III: Module 4: Unit 2: Subtracting Decimals

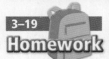

3 Homework and Spiral Review

Use this Homework page to provide students with more practice with situation and solution equations.

This Remembering activity would be appropriate anytime after today's lesson.

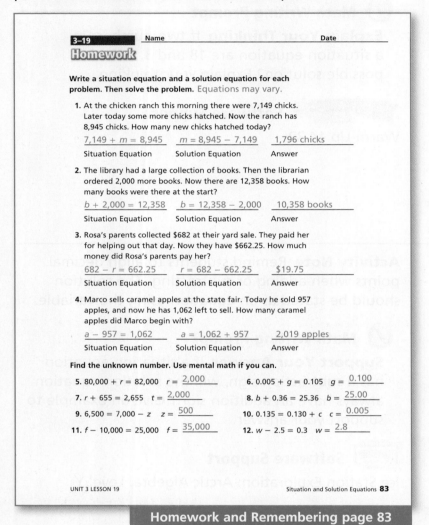

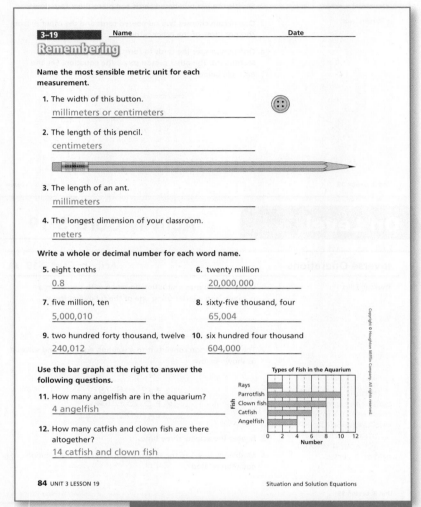

Homework and Remembering page 83

Homework and Remembering page 84

Home or School Activity

Social Studies Connection

Morse Code In 1840, Samuel Morse invented a code that was used to send telegraph messages. There is a Morse code for every letter and digit.

Give several of the digit codes to your students. Have them research to find the remaining digit codes, and then write equations "in Morse code." Students can exchange equations and solve them. For example:

$$\cdot \cdot \cdot \text{—} \text{—} + n = \text{—} \cdot \cdot \cdot \cdot$$

$$n = \cdot \cdot \cdot \text{—} \text{—}$$

MORSE CODE DIGITS	
Digit	Code
0	— — — — —
1	· — — — —
2	· · — — —
3	· · · — —
4	· · · · —
5	· · · · ·
6	— · · · ·

Comparison Problems

REAL WORLD Problem Solving

Lesson Objectives

- Solve addition and subtraction problems mentally using place value concepts.

- Represent and solve comparison word problems.

- Understand and apply comparison language.

Vocabulary

leading language
misleading language

The Day at a Glance

Today's Goals	Materials	
1 Teaching the Lesson **A1:** Solve a variety of comparison problems, including those with misleading language. **A2:** Solve and discuss mixed word problems with comparisons. **2 Going Further** ▸ Differentiated Instruction **3 Homework and Spiral Review**	**For Lesson Activities** Student Activity Book pp. 141–142 or Student Hardcover Book pp. 141–142 Homework and Remembering pp. 85–86 Newspaper advertisements (optional)	**Going Further** Activity Cards 3-20 Counters Bag or sack Math Journals 123 *Use* **Math Talk** *today!*

Keeping Skills Sharp

Quick Practice ⏱ 5 MINUTES	**Daily Routines**
Round Decimals Send several **Student Leaders** to the board. Each should write a decimal number with 4 digits after the decimal point (for example, 0.9743). They ask the class to round each number to the nearest thousandth, hundredth, and tenth. After each response, the leader writes the rounded decimal to the right of the original decimal number.	**Homework Review** Encourage students to help each other resolve any problems. **Estimation** Victoria will serve 58 guests one mini hamburger. Each hamburger uses $\frac{1}{8}$ lb of meat and a roll. Meat costs \$4.39 a pound and rolls cost \$3.82 for a package of 6. About how much will it cost to buy supplies for the guests? about \$80; 58 ≈ 60, 10 packs of rolls at \$4 each = \$40; 58 ≈ 64; 1 lb = 8 burgers; 8 lbs at about \$5 per lb = \$40; 40 + 40 = 80

Teaching the Lesson

Explore Comparison Situations

 25 MINUTES

Goal: Solve a variety of comparison problems, including those with misleading language.

Materials: Student Activity Book or Hardcover Book p. 141, newspaper advertisements (optional)

✓ **NCTM Standards:**
Number and Operations
Problem Solving
Communication
Representation

Teaching Note

Language and Vocabulary Try to use *less* or *fewer* in appropriate contexts. For a continuous quantity, such as water, we use *less*. For a quantity that can be counted, such as a number of cookies, we use *fewer*. (So, we say "less water," but "fewer cookies.") We also use less for whole numbers and for dollar amounts—5 is less than 7; 3 dollars is less than 4 dollars.

Try to use these terms correctly when you speak. However, it is not necessary to correct students when they use the wrong word. The distinction between *less* and *fewer* is difficult even for some adults.

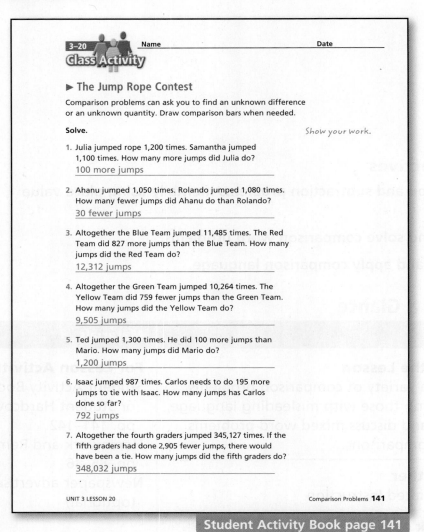

Student Activity Book page 141

▶ The Jump Rope Contest WHOLE CLASS

Unknown Difference Problems Have the class solve problems 1 and 2 on page 141 of the Student Book. This will be familiar territory to most students. They have already solved this type of problem in connection with graphs. Encourage students to solve the problems in their heads.

Discuss how comparisons can be stated two ways. Have students practice describing each situation using two comparisons:

1. If Julia did 100 *more* jumps than Samantha, then Samantha did 100 *fewer* jumps than Julia.

2. If Ahanu did 30 *fewer* jumps than Rolando, then Rolando did 30 *more* jumps than Ahanu.

Unknown Quantity Problems with Leading Language From a conceptual point of view, problems 3 and 4 will likely be easy for students. The word *more* will signal addition, and the word *fewer* will signal subtraction. However, the computation might be a challenge. Invite several students to work at the class board while the others work at their seats. Be sure all students check their answers.

3. 12,312 jumps

4. 9,505 jumps

Comparison Problems with Misleading Language Ask students to solve problem 5 on their own. This problem may be tricky for your class. The word *more* might lead students to believe that they should add, but they actually need to subtract. They know the larger quantity and the difference, so subtraction will give them the smaller quantity. Discuss the results. Be sure that these points are raised and that comparison bars are drawn.

- Who jumped more times?
- How many more times?
- How can we show this?
- How do comparison bars help?

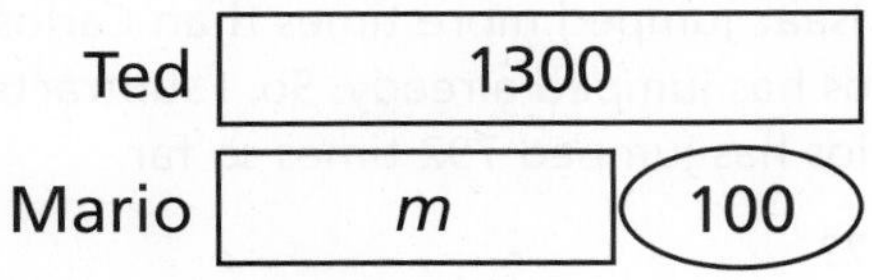

Ted | 1300
Mario | m | 100

Students will write different equations for comparison situations. Students may write $m + 100 = 1300$ or $1300 - 100 = m$

Activity continued ▶

Activity 1

The Learning Classroom

Building Concepts Constructing thoughtful questions and probing statements is often challenging while teaching a lesson. Here are some questions and statements that teachers have found useful. It is fine to use a few questions or statements repeatedly with your students. Students will begin to predict your probes and grow more comfortable responding to them.

▶ What is this problem about?

▶ Tell us what you see.

▶ Tell us your thinking.

▶ What would happen if...?

▶ Is that true for all cases?

▶ How can we check to be sure that this is a correct answer?

▶ What did you mean when you said...?

▶ What were you thinking when you decided to...?

Have all students draw comparison bars to help them solve problem 6 with some students working at the board so that everyone can compare and discuss.

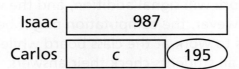

Emphasize to your class that the two most important questions to ask in a comparison problem are:

● Who has more (or less)?

● How much more (or less)?

If they focus on these questions, instead of just on the words *more* or *less*, they will be more likely to solve the problem correctly.

Tell students to draw comparison bars to help them solve the rest of the problems with misleading language. See Math Talk in Action below for a sample of classroom dialogue.

 Math Talk in Action

How did you solve problem 6?

Jenna: For problem 6, I asked myself, "Who jumped more?" Since Carlos needs to jump more to tie Isaac, then Isaac jumped more times than Carlos. Then I needed to find how many times Carlos has jumped already. So, I subtracted 195 from 987 and the difference is 792. So, Carlos has jumped 792 times so far.

How did you solve problem 7?

Thomas: Problem 7 said that if the fifth-graders had jumped 2,905 fewer it would have been a tie. That means that the fifth-graders jumped 2,905 more than the fourth-graders. So I added 345,127 and 2,905 and the sum is 348,032. So, the fifth-graders jumped 348,032 times.

Mixed Practice With Comparisons

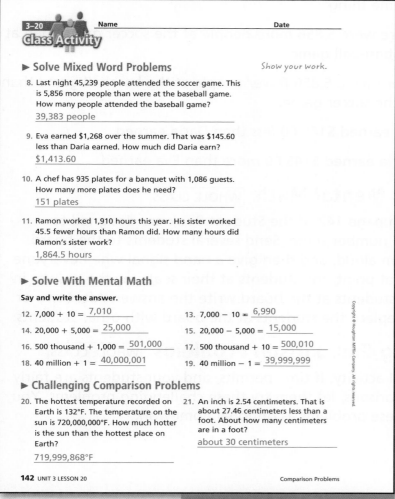

3-20
Class Activity

Name _____ Date _____

▶ Solve Mixed Word Problems   *Show your work.*

8. Last night 45,239 people attended the soccer game. This is 5,856 more people than were at the baseball game. How many people attended the baseball game?
   39,383 people

9. Eva earned $1,268 over the summer. That was $145.60 less than Daria earned. How much did Daria earn?
   $1,413.60

10. A chef has 935 plates for a banquet with 1,086 guests. How many more plates does he need?
    151 plates

11. Ramon worked 1,910 hours this year. His sister worked 45.5 fewer hours than Ramon did. How many hours did Ramon's sister work?
    1,864.5 hours

▶ Solve With Mental Math

Say and write the answer.

12. 7,000 + 10 = 7,010   13. 7,000 − 10 = 6,990

14. 20,000 + 5,000 = 25,000   15. 20,000 − 5,000 = 15,000

16. 500 thousand + 1,000 = 501,000   17. 500 thousand + 10 = 500,010

18. 40 million + 1 = 40,000,001 19. 40 million − 1 = 39,999,999

▶ Challenging Comparison Problems

20. The hottest temperature recorded on Earth is 132°F. The temperature on the sun is 720,000,000°F. How much hotter is the sun than the hottest place on Earth?
    719,999,868°F

21. An inch is 2.54 centimeters. That is about 27.46 centimeters less than a foot. About how many centimeters are in a foot?
    about 30 centimeters

142 UNIT 3 LESSON 20   Comparison Problems

Student Activity Book page 142

▶ Solve Mixed Word Problems   WHOLE CLASS

The different types of comparison problems are mixed together in problems 8–11. For each problem, send several students to work at the board while the other students work at their seats. Encourage students to use the comparison bars any time they are unsure of themselves.

🕐 **30 MINUTES**

Goal: Solve and discuss mixed word problems with comparisons.

Materials: Student Activity Book or Hardcover Book p. 142

✔ **NCTM Standards:**
Number and Operations
Problem Solving
Communication

Teaching Note

What to Expect From Students
Students may draw comparison bars different ways. Allow students to draw the bars in a way that makes sense to them. It does help if students consistently draw the larger amount first, but if a different method is working for students, let them use it.

This variation with the difference inside the larger amount is also acceptable. Students may draw this for particular problems or for all problems.

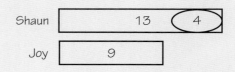

Teaching Note

Watch For! Some students might believe that comparison bars must always be drawn proportionally. Make sure these students understand that this is not the case. For example, a bar representing 10 does not have to be twice as long as a bar representing 5. These are only rough sketches in which it is important only that the bar representing the greater amount is longer than the bar representing the lesser amount.

Activity continued ▶

Activity 2

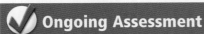 **Ongoing Assessment**

Watch your students closely as they are working through the mental math exercises. Are there some students who do not join in to answer? These students might require extra assistance with their mental math skills.

Problems 8 and 9 have misleading language. Say the comparing sentence out loud. Ask students to respond with the other comparing sentence that means the same thing:

8. Teacher: There were 5,856 *more* people at the soccer game than at the baseball game.

Students: There were 5,856 *fewer* people at the baseball game than at the soccer game.

9. Teacher: Eva earned $145.60 *less* than Daria earned.

Students: Daria earned $145.60 *more* than Eva earned.

▶ Solve With Mental Math WHOLE CLASS

Exercises 12–19 on page 142 of the Student Book are designed to improve students' number sense. Send several students to the board. Read each problem aloud, and then give a hand signal when everyone can answer. At that point, the students at their seats say the answer in unison while the students at the board write the answer. After two or three problems, replace the students at the board with other students.

▶ Challenging Comparison Problems WHOLE CLASS

This is an optional activity. If time permits, and your students are fairly secure with comparisons, let them try these challenging problems. You can also assign these problems as optional homework.

Intervention — Activity Card 3-20

Counter Comparisons — Activity Card 3-20

Work: In Pairs

Use:
• Counters
• Bag or sack

1. Place three handfuls of counters in the bag. Each partner takes one handful of counters from the bag and counts them.

2. **Work Together** Write a comparison problem about the counters, using your names. Here is a sample problem.

Annie's Counters   Devon's Counters

Annie has 12 counters. That is 5 more counters than Devon has. How many counters does Devon have?

3. Repeat the activity two more times. If you take the same number of counters, return them and take a different number.

Unit 3, Lesson 20   Copyright © Houghton Mifflin Company

Activity Note There are two possible comparison problems for each set of counters chosen. You can extend the activity by asking students to write both problems each time.

✎ Math Writing Prompt

Less Is More Write a word problem that includes the word *less*, but requires addition to solve.

Soar to Success Math ★ Software Support

Warm-Up 10.08

On Level — Activity Card 3-20

Combine Problems — Activity Card 3-20 ▲

Work: In Pairs

1. One partner writes an equation with a variable.

2. The other partner writes a word problem for the equation. An example is shown below.

$$987 + c = 1,910$$

Meg earned $987 during her first month at a new job. After two months, she had earned $1,910 altogether. How much did she earn during the second month?

3. **Work Together** Use the equation to solve the problem.

4. **Math Talk** How can you check your work? Possible answer: Substitute the solution into the equation in place of the variable and check if the equation is true.

Unit 3, Lesson 20   Copyright © Houghton Mifflin Company

Activity Note If students finish early, have them write another problem for the sample equation, such as: Meg earned $1,910 in two months. Her second month's earnings were $987 less than the total.

✎ Math Writing Prompt

Write an Equation Write a word problem about the sum 356. Then write an equation to solve it.

HARCOURT Mega Math Grades K-6 Software Support

Ice Station Exploration: Arctic Algebra, Level Y

Challenge — Activity Card 3-20

Number Patterns — Activity Card 3-20 ■

Work: In Pairs

1. **Work Together** Predict the next number in the pattern. Add 3, then 4, then 5, and so on. The next number is 21.

3, 6, 10, 15, ____

2. How does the pattern below differ from the first pattern?

3, 6, 9, 12, ____

3. **Write Your Own** Write a number pattern that does NOT add the same number each time. Challenge your partner to identify the pattern.

2. Possible answer: In this pattern, you add the same number, 3, each time. In the first pattern you add a different number each time.

Unit 3, Lesson 20   Copyright © Houghton Mifflin Company

Activity Note If students have difficulty identifying the first pattern, suggest that they write the difference between consecutive terms. Be sure that students write 4 or more numbers to specify a pattern.

✎ Math Writing Prompt

Make a Table Create a function table to show the price of 15 tickets when one ticket costs $2.25.

✴ DESTINATION Math®  Software Support

Course III: Module 2: Unit 1: Whole Number Sums

Comparison Problems   **339**

3 Homework and Spiral Review

3–20 **Homework** **Goal:** Additional Practice

Use this Homework page to provide students with more practice with comparison problems.

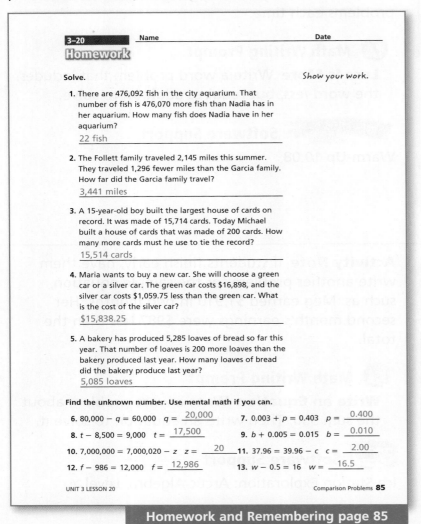

3–20 **Homework** Name ______ Date ______

Solve. *Show your work.*

1. There are 476,092 fish in the city aquarium. That number of fish is 476,070 more fish than Nadia has in her aquarium. How many fish does Nadia have in her aquarium?
   22 fish
2. The Follett family traveled 2,145 miles this summer. They traveled 1,296 fewer miles than the Garcia family. How far did the Garcia family travel?
   3,441 miles
3. A 15-year-old boy built the largest house of cards on record. It was made of 15,714 cards. Today Michael built a house of cards that was made of 200 cards. How many more cards must he use to tie the record?
   15,514 cards
4. Maria wants to buy a new car. She will choose a green car or a silver car. The green car costs $16,898, and the silver car costs $1,059.75 less than the green car. What is the cost of the silver car?
   $15,838.25
5. A bakery has produced 5,285 loaves of bread so far this year. That number of loaves is 200 more loaves than the bakery produced last year. How many loaves of bread did the bakery produce last year?
   5,085 loaves

Find the unknown number. Use mental math if you can.

6. $80{,}000 - q = 60{,}000$ $q =$ 20,000
7. $0.003 + p = 0.403$ $p =$ 0.400
8. $t - 8{,}500 = 9{,}000$ $t =$ 17,500
9. $b + 0.005 = 0.015$ $b =$ 0.010
10. $7{,}000{,}000 = 7{,}000{,}020 - z$ $z =$ 20
11. $37.96 = 39.96 - c$ $c =$ 2.00
12. $f - 986 = 12{,}000$ $f =$ 12,986
13. $w - 0.5 = 16$ $w =$ 16.5

UNIT 3 LESSON 20 Comparison Problems 85

Homework and Remembering page 85

3–20 **Remembering** **Goal:** Spiral eview

This emembering activity wou ld be appropriate anytime after today s lesson

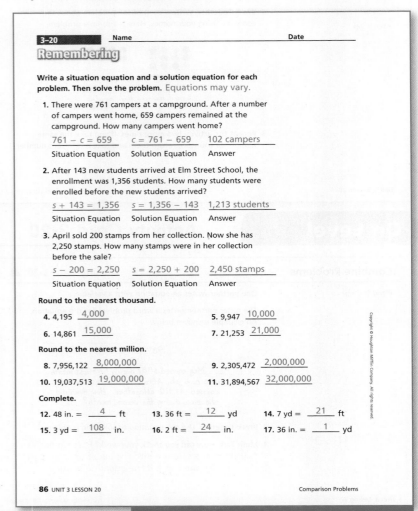

3–20 **Remembering** Name ______ Date ______

Write a situation equation and a solution equation for each problem. Then solve the problem. Equations may vary.

1. There were 761 campers at a campground. After a number of campers went home, 659 campers remained at the campground. How many campers went home?
   $761 - c = 659$ (Situation Equation) $c = 761 - 659$ (Solution Equation) 102 campers (Answer)
2. After 143 new students arrived at Elm Street School, the enrollment was 1,356 students. How many students were enrolled before the new students arrived?
   $s + 143 = 1{,}356$ (Situation Equation) $s = 1{,}356 - 143$ (Solution Equation) 1,213 students (Answer)
3. April sold 200 stamps from her collection. Now she has 2,250 stamps. How many stamps were in her collection before the sale?
   $s - 200 = 2{,}250$ (Situation Equation) $s = 2{,}250 + 200$ (Solution Equation) 2,450 stamps (Answer)

Round to the nearest thousand.

4. 4,195 4,000
5. 9,947 10,000
6. 14,861 15,000
7. 21,253 21,000

Round to the nearest million.

8. 7,956,122 8,000,000
9. 2,305,472 2,000,000
10. 19,037,513 19,000,000
11. 31,894,567 32,000,000

Complete.

12. 48 in. = 4 ft
13. 36 ft = 12 yd
14. 7 yd = 21 ft
15. 3 yd = 108 in.
16. 2 ft = 24 in.
17. 36 in. = 1 yd

86 UNIT 3 LESSON 20 Comparison Problems

Homework and Remembering page 86

Home or School Activity

Social Studies Connection

Great Lakes The Great Lakes are located in the northeastern part of the United States and along the Canadian border. Have students research the areas and depths of the different lakes that make up the Great Lakes.

Then have students make a bar graph to display their data.

GREAT LAKES FACTS

Lake	Total Area (in square miles)	Greatest Depth (in feet)
Erie	9,940	210
Huron	23,010	750
Michigan	22,178	923
Ontario	7,540	778
Superior	31,820	1,302

Two-Step Word Problems

Lesson Objectives

- Write and solve word problems that involve two steps.
- Identify relevant information in problems.

The Day at a Glance

Today's Goals	Materials

Today's Goals

1 Teaching the Lesson

A1: Solve and explain word problems with two or more steps.

A2: Work in pairs or small groups to write word problems from a map.

A3: Identify word problems with extra or missing information and ones with multiple or no solutions.

2 Going Further

▶ Math Connection: Double Bar Graphs
▶ Differentiated Instruction

3 Homework and Spiral Review

Materials

For Lesson Activities
Student Activity Book pp. 143–145
  or Student Hardcover Book
  pp. 143–145
Homework and Remembering
  pp. 87–88
Quick Quiz 5 (Assessment Guide)

Going Further
Student Activity Book
  or Hardcover Book
  p. 146
Ruler
Activity Cards 3-21
Play money
Math Journals

123 Use Math Talk today!

Keeping Skills Sharp

Quick Practice ⏱ 5 MINUTES	Daily Routines

Round Decimals Send several **Student Leaders** to the board. Each should write a decimal number with 4 digits after the decimal point (for example, 0.5384). They ask the class to round each number to the nearest thousandth, hundredth, and tenth. After each response, the leader writes the rounded decimal to the right of the original decimal number.

Homework Review Send students to the board to show and explain their solutions. Have the class ask clarifying questions and make comments.

Reasoning Have students describe two situations for which a line graph is the best display for the related data and two situations for which a bar graph is the best display. Line graph situations should be about continuous data. Bar graph situations should be about discrete data. Example: line graph: your height over the last 5 years; bar graph: the height of 5 people.

1 Teaching the Lesson

Solve and Explain Two-Step Problems

 25 MINUTES

Goal: Solve and explain word problems with two or more steps.

Materials: Student Activity Book or Hardcover Book p. 143

✓ **NCTM Standards:**
Number and Operations
Problem Solving
Communication

The Learning Classroom

Math Talk Have students practice explaining one another's work in their own words from their seats, or have them go to the board and point to the parts of a student's work as you or another student explains those parts.

Teaching Note

Math Background The two methods described for problem 4 illustrate the distributive property:

$10 \times (6,125 - 5,450) =$
$10 \times 6,125 - 10 \times 5,450$

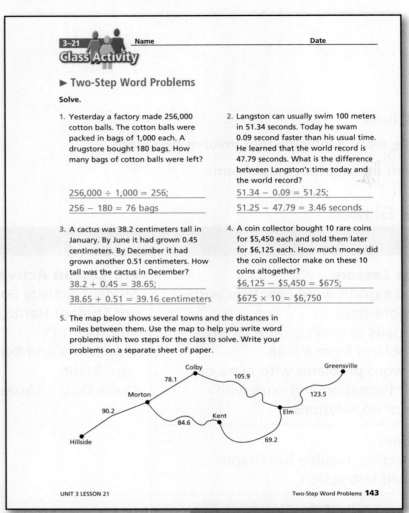

Student Activity Book page 143

▶ Two-Step Word Problems WHOLE CLASS

Have students work individually to solve problems 1–4. Explain that for these problems, most solution methods will take two steps. Invite several students to work at the board while the other students work at their seats. Then ask two students at the board to explain how they solved the problem. Choose students who had somewhat different approaches, if possible.

Note that there are sometimes different ways to solve a problem. Problem 4, for example, can be solved by writing:

$(\$6,125 - \$5,450) \times 10 = \$6,750$

or

$10(\$6,125 - \$5,450) = (10 \times 6,125) - (10 \times 5,450).$

Write Word Problems

▶ Student Generated Problems SMALL GROUPS

Have students work in **Small Groups** for problem 5. Using the map, students should work together to create some problems of their own. Give them about 10 minutes to write three problems that are based on the map. [If you are running short on time, have the whole class brainstorm to make up problems instead of dividing students into small groups.]

Remind the class to write both addition and subtraction problems. Below are a few examples:

● We drove from Elm to Greensville and back again. How far did we drive?

● I am driving from Hillside to Morton. I have gone 9.6 miles. How far do I still have to go before I reach Morton?

● Ella wants to drive from Morton to Elm. There are two routes. Which route will be shorter? How much shorter will it be?

After the allotted time, have various groups volunteer to present some of their map problems for the rest of the class to solve.

 30 MINUTES

Goal: Work in pairs or small groups to write word problems from a map.

 NCTM Standards:
Number and Operations
Problem Solving
Communication

 Ongoing Assessment

Write the following problem on the board. Have students solve it two different ways.

▶ Jose earned $4.75 each day for 10 days. Paul earned $3.95 each day for 10 days. How much more did Jose earn than Paul?

English Language Learners

Provide support with writing word problems. Have students work in pairs.

● **Beginning** Write a few different problems on the board. Have students copy them, then change some of the information and/or numbers.

● **Intermediate** Ask simple questions to give students ideas and help them organize their problem.

● **Advanced** Have students tell each other their story aloud first, then write it.

1 **Teaching the Lesson (continued)**

Activity 3

Determining Relevant Information

 30 MINUTES

Goal: Identify word problems with extra or missing information and differentiate between word problems that can and cannot be solved.

Materials: Student Activity Book or Hardcover Book pp. 144–145

✔ **NCTM Standards:**
Problem Solving
Number and Operations

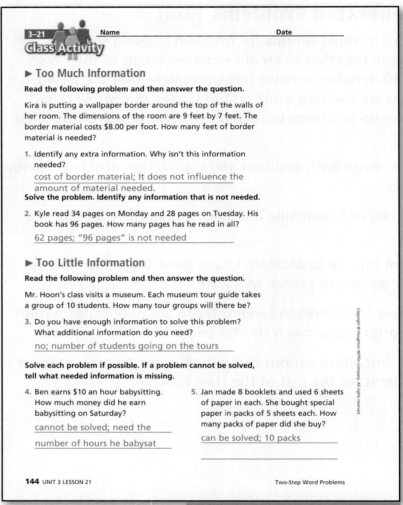

Student Activity Book page 144

▶ Too Much Information WHOLE CLASS

Write the following word problem on the board:

> Ryan sold 9 tickets to the school play for $6.00 each. There are 24 other students selling tickets. How much money did Ryan collect selling tickets?

Read the problem. Give students a minute or two to solve it, and then discuss the solution.

- How can we figure out how much money Ryan collected? Multiply the number of tickets he sold (9) by the price per ticket ($6).

- What numerical information is not needed to solve the problem? 24

- Why is it not needed? Doesn't affect the tickets Ryan sold.

Have students read the word problem at the top of Student Book page 144. As a class, discuss how to solve the problem. See the **Math Talk in Action** in the side column for a sample classroom discussion.

Students will approach the problem in different ways. Some may find it easier to identify information that is missing, while others may find it easier to identify unnecessary information. Encourage students to use both strategies by circling information they think is necessary and crossing out information they believe is not needed.

After students have solved exercise 1, use **Solve and Discuss** for exercise 2.

▶ Too Little Information [WHOLE CLASS]

Write the following word problem on the board:

> Ryan's class watched the school play in the auditorium. The teacher sat 10 students in each row. How many rows were filled?

Ask students to read it and give them a minute or two to try to solve it.

- Can this problem be solved? If not, why? no; doesn't say how many students are in Ryan's class

Ask the students to suggest how the problem can be revised so it can be solved. Revise the problem as a class and find the answer as a class.

Have students look at the word problem with exercise 3 on Student Book page 144. Discuss the answer and have students tell how they know what information is missing. Next, have students revise the problem and solve it. Allow students to share their revised problems with the class.

Use **Solve and Discuss** to complete exercises 4–5.

Have students revise the problem in exercise 4 and solve. Then, have students share their revised problems and discuss how to solve each one.

 Math Talk in Action

How did you know that the cost of material was not needed?

Evan: The cost of the material does not have anything to do with the length of the border. You would need the same amount of material no matter how much it cost.

Karen: To find the amount, you only need to know the length and width of the room, so I know I don't need to know the cost of the material.

Differentiated Instruction

Extra Help Before students start their work in the Student Book, suggest that they make and label a drawing to help them understand the problem.

Activity continued ▶

① Teaching the Lesson (continued)

Activity 3

Differentiated Instruction

Extra Help Students who are struggling with problems with more than one solution may benefit from working with a **Helping Partner**. Pair such students with a partner who can help them see other ways of looking at the problem.

Differentiated Instruction

Advanced Learners For students who complete the exercise easily suggest that they work as **Student Pairs** to write and solve problems with multiple solutions and with no solution. Pairs can then exchange their problems with another student pair and solve the problems they wrote.

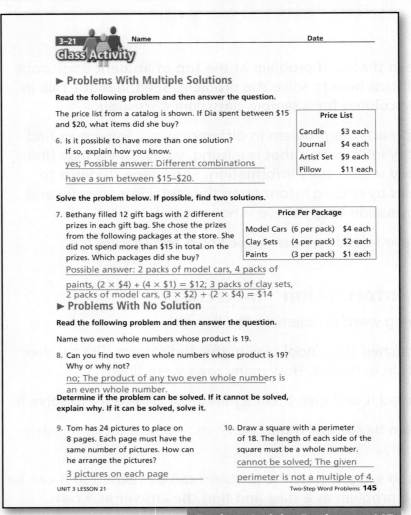

Student Activity Book page 145

▶ Problems With Multiple Solutions [WHOLE CLASS]

Ask students to draw a rectangle that has an area of 18 m², and then discuss the solution.

● Is it possible to draw a rectangle that has an area of 18 m²? If so, explain why. yes; any two factors of 18 can be used for the length and the width

● Is it possible that this problem has more than one solution? Explain. Yes, the factor pairs for 18 are: 1, 18; 2, 9; 3, 6. Each pair can form 2 different rectangles.

Invite volunteers to draw the six rectangles on the board. Then, discuss how this problem can be revised to have only solution. The discussion should include inserting a condition. For example, a rectangle with an area of 18 m² with a length that is half the width. Then, the only dimensions that meet the conditions are a length of 3 m and a width of 6 m.

Have students read the word problem at the top of Student Book page 145. As a class, discuss the answer to exercise 6. Then, have students find one solution each and share their solution with the class. Have the class confirm that the sum for each solution is between $15 and $20.

Use **Solve and Discuss** for exercise 7. See the **Math Talk in Action** below for a sample classroom dialogue.

 Math Talk in Action

Which prizes and how many packages of each prize did you have Bethany buy?

Juan: I had her put 1 clay set and 1 paint in each gift bag. She buys 3 packages of clay sets, $3 \times 4 = 12$, for, $3 \times \$2 = \$6$. She buys 4 packages of paints, $4 \times 3 = 12$, for $4 \times \$1 = \$4$. $\$6 + \$4 = \$10$, which is less than $15.

Youn Sue: I had her put clay sets in all 12 bags, too. But, as the second prize, I had her put model cars in 6 bags and paints in the other 6 bags. She buys 3 packages of clay sets for $6, 2 packages of paints for $2, and 1 package of model cars for $4. In all, she spends $12, which is less than $15.

▶ Problems With No Solution [WHOLE CLASS]

Ask students to draw a line with endpoints *A* and *B*. Give students a minute or two to draw the line, and then discuss it.

- Can this line be drawn? Explain why or why not. no, Lines do not have endpoints.

Ask the class to suggest how this description can be revised so a figure can be drawn. Then, have students draw the figure on the board.

Use **Solve and Discuss** to complete exercises 8–10.

Have students revise the problem in exercise 9 so that it cannot be solved. Allow students to share their revised problems with the class and explain how their revisions affected the problem.

Have students revise the problem in exercise 10 so that it can be solved. Then, allow several students to share their revised problems and discuss as a class how to solve each one.

Going Further

Math Connection: Double Bar Graphs

Goal: Interpret and make a double bar graph.

Materials: Student Activity Book or Hardcover Book p. 146, ruler

 NCTM Standard:
Data Analysis and Probability
Representation

▶ What To Expect from Students

WHOLE CLASS

In this activity, students connect single bar graphs to double bar graphs.

Choosing a Scale One of the most difficult aspects of drawing a bar (or line) graph involves choosing a sensible multiple for the numerical axis. If the multiple is too small, the axis may be too long to be practical. If the multiple is too large, the heights of the bars are more likely to fall between the lines of the graph and become difficult to interpret.

To help students refine this skill, write the data set {3, 17, 4, 31, 8} on the board and have them assume a bar will be drawn on a graph for each number. Then ask them to name possible multiples (such as by twos, by threes, and so on) that could be chosen for the numerical axis of the graph, and describe an advantage or disadvantage of each choice.

 Ongoing Assessment

Reinforce understanding of bar graphs by asking:

▶ Every bar graph is made up of what individual parts?

▶ Explain how to choose a sensible scale for the number axis of a bar graph.

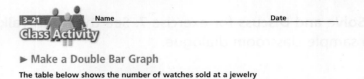

Student Activity Book page 146

▶ Make a Double Bar Graph   PAIRS

Have students complete exercises 1–3 on Student Book page 146 by working in **Student Pairs** or in **Small Groups**. Students will need a ruler to draw the graph.

Write a Problem If time permits, give students an opportunity to share their problems and their solutions.

Collect Data An alternative to exercises 2–3 is to have students make a double bar graph of data they collect, such as favorite subjects of their classmates. (A favorite subject graph would have numbers along one axis and favorite subjects along the other; the double bars would be the number of boys and the number of girls with that characteristic.)

Differentiated Instruction

Shopping Spree — Activity Card 3-21

Work: In Pairs

Use:
• Play money

1. Make a list of items and prices for a store similar to the one shown.

SCHOOL STORE	
Item	Price
Folder	$3.79
Box of Pencils	$2.39
Pen	$4.50
3-Ring Binder	$8.99
Spiral Notebook	$4.29
Ruler	$2.15

2. Take turns being shopper and cashier.

3. The shopper buys two or three items with a $20 bill. The cashier computes and gives the correct change.

4. The shopper checks the amount of change.

5. **Math Talk** How did you compute the correct change? Possible answers: Find the total cost of the items and subtract the sum from $20, or count on to reach $20.

Unit 3, Lesson 21 — Copyright © Houghton Mifflin Company

Activity Note Encourage students to try two different ways to compute the correct change. They can either accumulate the change while counting on from the total to $20 or subtract the total from $20.

 Math Writing Prompt

How Many Steps If you buy two items and receive change in return, how many steps are needed to find the correct change? Explain.

 **Software Support**

Warm-Up 21.35, 22.34

Write Problems for Equations — Activity Card 3-21

Work: In Pairs

1. **Work Together** Write a word problem for each equation:

$$s + 1.25 = 20.4$$
$$m = 129 + 26 - 33$$

2. Each partner writes two more equations using addition and subtraction with decimal numbers.

3. Partners exchange equations and write a word problem that can be solved with each equation.
   Possible answers: Tyra ran a race in 20.4 sec. That was 1.25 sec slower than Sonya. What was Sonya's time in seconds (s)? Alan had $129. He earned $26 more and spent $33. How much money (m) does he have now?

Unit 3, Lesson 21 — Copyright © Houghton Mifflin Company

Activity Note If students have difficulty writing word problems that involve decimal numbers, suggest that they consider situations involving sports or metric measures.

 Math Writing Prompt

Write a Problem Write a two-step word problem that can be solved in more than one way.

 Software Support

The Number Games: Tiny's Think Tank, Level L

Making Change — Activity Card 3-21

Work: In Pairs

1. Each partner writes a problem about buying two or more items and receiving change. Problems should include the following.

   • Each item costs less than $1.00.
   • The items are paid for with a $5-bill.

2. Partners exchange problems. Calculate the cost of the items and the amount of change owed. Show how to use the least possible number of coins and/or bills for change.

3. **Math Talk** Describe a real-world situation in which you might pay for a purchase with bills and coins and still receive change.

3. Possible answer: The cost of the purchase is $5.21. You give the cashier a $5 bill and a quarter and receive 4¢ in change.

Unit 3, Lesson 21 — Copyright © Houghton Mifflin Company

Activity Note Discuss strategies for making change using the least number of coins and bills.

 Math Writing Prompt

Too Much Information Write a two-step word problem. Include more information than is needed to solve the problem.

 DESTINATION Math Software Support

Course III: Module 4: Unit 2: Subtracting Decimals

Two-Step Word Problems **349**

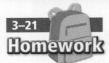

③ Homework and Spiral Review

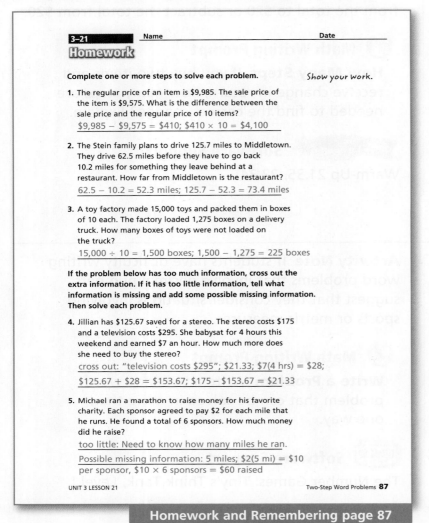

3–21
Homework **Goal:** Additional Practice

Use this Homework page to provide students with more practice with two-step word problems.

3–21 Name _____ Date _____
Homework

Complete one or more steps to solve each problem.   *Show your work.*

1. The regular price of an item is $9,985. The sale price of the item is $9,575. What is the difference between the sale price and the regular price of 10 items?
$9,985 − $9,575 = $410; $410 × 10 = $4,100

2. The Stein family plans to drive 125.7 miles to Middletown. They drive 62.5 miles before they have to go back 10.2 miles for something they leave behind at a restaurant. How far from Middletown is the restaurant?
62.5 − 10.2 = 52.3 miles; 125.7 − 52.3 = 73.4 miles

3. A toy factory made 15,000 toys and packed them in boxes of 10 each. The factory loaded 1,275 boxes on a delivery truck. How many boxes of toys were not loaded on the truck?
15,000 ÷ 10 = 1,500 boxes; 1,500 − 1,275 = 225 boxes

If the problem below has too much information, cross out the extra information. If it has too little information, tell what information is missing and add some possible missing information. Then solve each problem.

4. Jillian has $125.67 saved for a stereo. The stereo costs $175 and a television costs $295. She babysat for 4 hours this weekend and earned $7 an hour. How much more does she need to buy the stereo?
cross out: "television costs $295"; $21.33; $7(4 hrs) = $28;
$125.67 + $28 = $153.67; $175 − $153.67 = $21.33

5. Michael ran a marathon to raise money for his favorite charity. Each sponsor agreed to pay $2 for each mile that he runs. He found a total of 6 sponsors. How much money did he raise?
too little: Need to know how many miles he ran.
Possible missing information: 5 miles; $2(5 mi) = $10 per sponsor, $10 × 6 sponsors = $60 raised

UNIT 3 LESSON 21   Two-Step Word Problems **87**

Homework and Remembering page 87

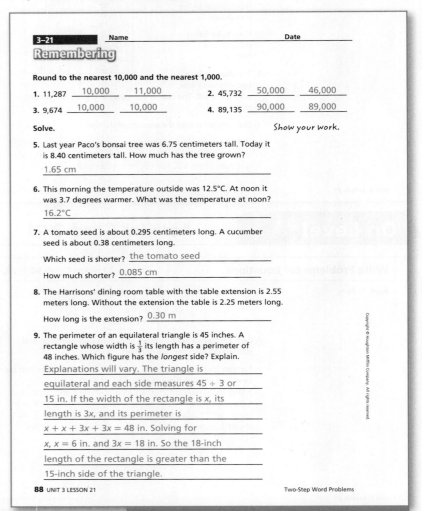

3–21
Remembering **Goal:** Spiral Review

This Remembering activity would be appropriate anytime after today's lesson.

3–21 Name _____ Date _____
Remembering

Round to the nearest 10,000 and the nearest 1,000.

1. 11,287 __10,000__ __11,000__   2. 45,732 __50,000__ __46,000__
3. 9,674 __10,000__ __10,000__   4. 89,135 __90,000__ __89,000__

Solve.   *Show your work.*

5. Last year Paco's bonsai tree was 6.75 centimeters tall. Today it is 8.40 centimeters tall. How much has the tree grown?
1.65 cm

6. This morning the temperature outside was 12.5°C. At noon it was 3.7 degrees warmer. What was the temperature at noon?
16.2°C

7. A tomato seed is about 0.295 centimeters long. A cucumber seed is about 0.38 centimeters long.
Which seed is shorter? the tomato seed
How much shorter? 0.085 cm

8. The Harrisons' dining room table with the table extension is 2.55 meters long. Without the extension the table is 2.25 meters long.
How long is the extension? 0.30 m

9. The perimeter of an equilateral triangle is 45 inches. A rectangle whose width is $\frac{1}{3}$ its length has a perimeter of 48 inches. Which figure has the *longest* side? Explain.
Explanations will vary. The triangle is equilateral and each side measures 45 ÷ 3 or 15 in. If the width of the rectangle is x, its length is $3x$, and its perimeter is $x + x + 3x + 3x = 48$ in. Solving for x, $x = 6$ in. and $3x = 18$ in. So the 18-inch length of the rectangle is greater than the 15-inch side of the triangle.

88 UNIT 3 LESSON 21   Two-Step Word Problems

Homework and Remembering page 88

Home or School Activity

 Real-World Connection

Perimeter and Area Ask your students to make up and solve a word problem about the perimeter and area of some part of their home. For example: a carpet, yard, garden, or driveway. Remind students to make sure they select the appropriate units to measure the part of their home they choose to work with.

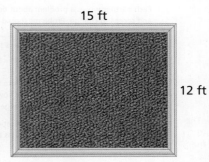

15 ft

12 ft

Carpet: Area = 12 × 15 = 180 square feet

UNIT 3
LESSON 22
Use Mathematical Processes

Lesson Objectives

- Apply mathematical concepts and skills in meaningful contexts.
- Reinforce the NCTM process skills embedded in this unit, and in previous units, with a variety of problem-solving situations.

Vocabulary
hypothesis

The Day at a Glance

Today's Goals	Materials

1 Teaching the Lesson
A1: Social Studies Connection Design an investigation; make a hypothesis, write a survey question, conduct a survey, organize and analyze the data to make predictions.
A2: Representation Classify and display survey data; compare graphs, collected data, and hypotheses.
A3: Reasoning and Proof Make and test a generalization from given data.
A4: Problem Solving Use the process of elimination to solve a problem.
A5: Communication Discuss using appropriate data displays.
 	
2 Going Further
▶ Differentiated Instruction
 	
3 Homework and Spiral Review
	Lesson Activities
	Student Activity Book pp. 147–148
	  or Hardcover Book pp. 147–148
	Homework and Remembering
	  p. 89–90
	
	Going Further
	Activity Cards 3-22
	Centimeter-Grid
	  Paper (TRB M18)
	Play money
	
	123 Use Math Talk today!

Keeping Skills Sharp

Quick Practice/Daily Routines	Classroom Management
If you wish to include Quick Practice or a Daily Routine, choose content based on the needs of your class.	Select activities from this lesson that support important goals and objectives, or that help students prepare for state or district tests.

Teaching the Lesson

Connections

Math and Social Studies

 30 MINUTES

Goal: Design an investigation; make a hypothesis, write a survey question, conduct a survey, organize and analyze the data to make predictions.

Materials: Student Activity Book or Hardcover Book p. 147

✔ **NCTM Standards:**
Connections   Representation
Communication Reasoning and Proof

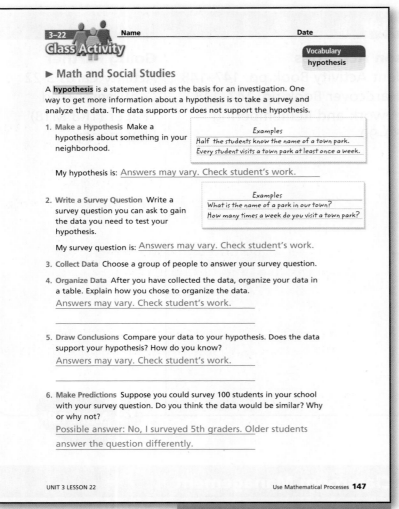

Student Activity Book page 147

▶ **Making Hypotheses**   Math Talk

Task 1 Hold a whole-class discussion on hypotheses. Introduce the term *hypothesis* and its plural form *hypotheses*.

▶ Have you seen or used a hypothesis before? If so, where? Possible answer: For a science experiment, I write what I think will happen during the experiment.

Review the hypotheses that students wrote in Exercise 1. As a class discuss if each hypothesis can be tested.

▶ **Testing Hypotheses**   Math Talk

Task 2 Before students answer Exercise 2, discuss the qualities of a good survey question.

▶ How can a survey become biased? Possible answer: The question influences the answer.

After students complete exercises 3 and 4, have volunteers share their tables. Discuss the differences in the tables.

▶ **Analyzing Data and Hypotheses**

Task 3 For exercise 5, allow students to share examples of supported and unsupported hypotheses. For exercise 6, ask students to share any predictions they think they can make based on the data they collected.

English Language Learners
Write *hypothesis* on the board.
• **Beginning** Ask: Is a *hypothesis* an educated guess? yes
• **Intermediate and Advanced** Say: An educated guess is a __. hypothesis

Displaying Survey Data

 30 MINUTES

Goal: Classify and display survey data; compare graphs, collected data, and hypotheses.

Materials: Student Activity Book or Hardcover Book p. 148

✓ **NCTM Standards:**
Representation   Communication
Reasoning and Proof

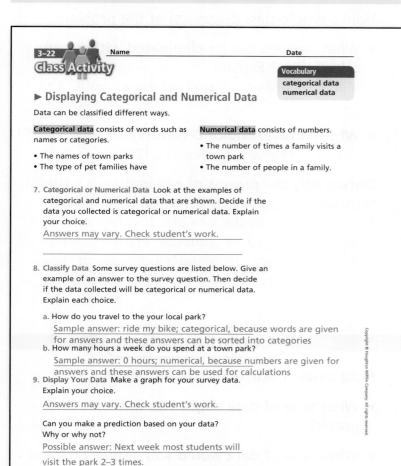

Student Activity Book page 148

▶ Classifying Survey Data

Task 1 Have a whole-class discussion on data types. Tell students that *numerical data* is as it sounds— data that is consists of numbers. The number of pets you own and the temperature recorded each hour are examples of numerical data. *Categorical data* is data that are words. Favorite color and types of pets are categorical data.

Have students share their survey questions and their answers to exercise 7. Then, have students change the wording of their survey questions so that it collects the other type of data. Allow students to share answers. As a class, review the answers to exercise 8.

▶ Choosing a Data Display

Task 2 Before students complete exercise 9, have them brainstorm a list of data displays such as bar graphs, picture graphs, line plots, and so on. Discuss what type of data—*numerical* or *categorical*—is appropriate for each type of data display.

Have several volunteers share their survey question and their display choice.

▶ Comparing Data Displays

Task 3 Once students have made their data displays, have them share the displays with the class. Discuss the merits of each display.

If time permits, allow students to share their predictions.

Activity 3

Does It Add Up?

 15 MINUTES

Goal: Make and test a generalization from given data.

✓ **NCTM Standards:**
Reasoning and Proof
Communication

Write this expression on the board.

$$58 + 43 = 56 + d$$

Reasoning and Proof

Hold a class discussion. Give students an opportunity to form a generalization.

▶ **How can we find the value of d without adding 56 + 43?** Ask students to explain their reasoning. 56 is 2 less than 58, so d must be 2 more than 43, or 45.

Ask students to write another problem that supports their generalization.

Activity 4

Process of Elimination

 15 MINUTES

Goal: Use the process of elimination to solve a problem.

✓ **NCTM Standards:**
Problem Solving
Reasoning and Proof

During the school year (Sept.–June), Yara reads about 1 book per month. Over the summer she read 7 books. About how many books does Yara read in one year? D

A 7   **B** 10   **C** 12   **D** 17

Problem Solving

Hold a whole-class discussion of the problem.

▶ **What answers can be eliminated without any calculations? Explain.** A: 7 books - summer alone; B: 10 books - school year alone; C: this is 1 a month all year.

▶ **Why is answer choice D correct?** 10 school year + 7 over the summer = 17

Discuss why the process of elimination is a useful technique. In some problems the numbers are large and the calculations are difficult. Knowing when you can simply eliminate answers can be helpful, even if you eliminate only one or two answer choices.

Activity 5

Daily Data

 15 MINUTES

Goal: Discuss using appropriate data displays.

✓ **NCTM Standards:**
Representation
Communication

Suppose I graph the temperature for the next 5 hours. Which type of graph would be most appropriate? Why? Discuss the merits of line graph versus bar graph for this data.

Communication

Hold a class discussion of the problem.

▶ **What type of data might you find on a line graph?** numerical

▶ **What type of data would you display on a bar graph?** categorical or numerical

▶ **Would you display categorical and/or numerical data on a bar graph?** can display both on a bar graph

▶ **Would you display categorical and/or numerical data on a line graph?** numerical only

---

Intervention — Activity Card 3-22

Decimal Sums and Differences — Activity Card 3-22

Work: In Pairs

Use:
• Centimeter-Grid Paper (TRB M17)

1. Write the greatest and least decimal numbers you can using the digits 4, 7, 0, and 1 once. Both decimal numbers must be less than 1. 0.741; 0.147

2. One partner finds the sum of the two decimal numbers and the other finds the difference. Use grid paper to align the digits, if necessary. 0.888; 0.594

3. **Work Together** Decide if the sum should be greater or less than the decimal numbers you created. Repeat for the difference. Then, use this information to check your answers.

4. Switch work and check using the opposite operation.

3. The sum should be greater and the difference should be less than the greater decimal number.

Unit 3, Lesson 22   Copyright © Houghton Mifflin Company

Activity Note Students use their knowledge of place value to add and subtract decimals. You may wish to review the decimals prior to students adding and subtracting them.

 **Math Writing Prompt**

Write a Problem Have students write a word problem for the addition and the subtraction and share their problems with the class.

Soar to Success Math ★ Software Support

Warm-Up 21.36, 22.35

On Level — Activity Card 3-22

Before and After Amounts — Activity Card 3-22 ▲

Work: In Pairs

Use:
• Play money

1. Find the value of each group of money shown and write this amount in decimal form. $2.77; $4.29

Before   After

2. Find the value of the missing amount of money. $1.52

3. **Write About It** Write a situation equation related to the groups. Then, write a solution equation to find the amount of money that is missing. $m + \$2.77 = \$4.29$; $\$4.29 - \$2.77 = m$

4. **Look Back** How can you check your answer?

Unit 3, Lesson 22   Copyright © Houghton Mifflin Company

Activity Note Review the relationship between money and place values.

 Math Writing Prompt

Write a Word Problem Have students write a word problem based on the given amounts. The person must buy more than one item and prices must be given.

MegaMath Grades K-6 Software Support

The Number Games: Tiny's Think Tank, Level L

Challenge — Activity Card 3-22

Soccer Game Data — Activity Card 3-22 ■

Work: In Small Groups

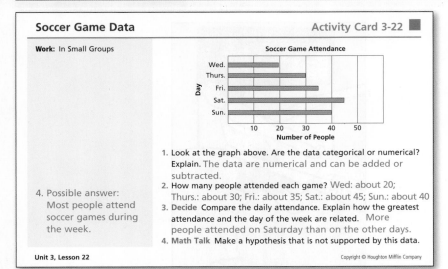

Soccer Game Attendance

1. Look at the graph above. Are the data categorical or numerical? Explain. The data are numerical and can be added or subtracted.

2. How many people attended each game? Wed: about 20; Thurs.: about 30; Fri.: about 35; Sat.: about 45; Sun.: about 40

3. **Decide** Compare the daily attendance. Explain how the greatest attendance and the day of the week are related. More people attended on Saturday than on the other days.

4. **Math Talk** Make a hypothesis that is not supported by this data.

4. Possible answer: Most people attend soccer games during the week.

Unit 3, Lesson 22   Copyright © Houghton Mifflin Company

Activity Note Review the definition of hypothesis. An example of a hypothesis that is not supported is that Friday is the favorite night to attend a game.

 Math Writing Prompt

Draw a Conclusion Have students write a conclusion based on the data given in the bar graph, such as Wednesday had about one-half the attendance of Sunday.

 DESTINATION Math· Software Support

Course III: Module 6: Unit 1: Displaying and Analyzing Data

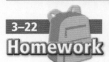

✔ Include students' completed Homework page as part of their portfolios.

This Remembering page would be appropriate anytime after today's lesson.

3–22   Name _____ Date _____
Homework

1. Connections Lorenzo is a realtor and wants to become a member of the Million Dollar Club. To do this he must have at least $1 million in sales. So far, he has sold three homes for $256,900, $373,100, and $284,400. How can you quickly tell if these sales will allow him to be a member? If they can't, how much more does he need in sales? Possible answer: Round to the nearest hundred thousand and add; $1,000,000. Round to the nearest ten thousand and add; $910,000. Lorenzo doesn't have enough sales. He needs $1,000,000 − ($256,900 + $373,100 + $284,400), or $85,600 more.

2. Representation Susan owns a card shop. She kept a record of the number of cards sold each month for one year. Then, she used a line graph to graph the data she collected. Explain what the line graph showed and how she might use the data. Possible answer: The line graph shows the total, cumulative card sales by month, for example, the number for February represents the total number of cards sold in January and February. The line segments will show the months when the most and the least cards were sold, or help her see when sales are strong or weak.

3. Communication Hanna bought 4 pencils for 9¢ each, two notebooks for $1.58 each, and one pack of paper for $3.17 each. She paid with $10 and received $3.58 in change. Is the change correct? If not, identify the correct amount of change and why the error was made. No; Possible answer: it is too much.; The change received should have been: (4 × $0.09) + (2 × $1.58) + $3.17 = $6.69; $10 − $6.69 = $3.31; The difference is $0.27, the price of three pencils. So, she was probably charged for only one pencil.

4. Reasoning and Proof Can you draw a square that has an area and a perimeter that are not the same, such as, an area of 16 m² and a perimeter of 20 m? Explain your answer. Yes; a 5-meter square has a perimeter of 5 m × 4, or 20 m, and an area of 5 m × 5 m, or 25 m². The only square that has the same number of units when you find the area and perimeter is a square that measures 4 units. Perimeter = 4 units × 4 = 16 units Area = 4 units × 4 units = 16 square units

UNIT 3 LESSON 22   Use Mathematical Processes **89**

Homework and Remembering page 89

3–22   Name _____ Date _____
Remembering

Use the number 149,578.324 for exercises 1–6.

1. Increase the number by 5 more hundredths.
149,578.374

2. Decrease the number by 1 hundred thousand.
49,578.324

3. Decrease the number by 4 tens.
149,538.324

4. Increase the number by one hundred thirteen thousandths.
149,578.437

Solve.

5. Last week, Jillian drove 113.4 miles and 49.67 miles. So far this week, she has driven 152.89 miles. How many more miles will she have to drive this week to equal the miles driven last week?
10.18 miles; (113.4 + 49.67) − 152.89 = 10.18

Write a situation equation and a solution equation. Then solve.

6. The charity held a banquet as a fundraiser. After paying $1,796 in expenses from the money collected, the charity has $4,853 left. How much did the charity collect in all at the party?

$m − \$1,796 = \$4,853$ $\$4,853 + \$1,796 = m$ $6,649

Situation Equation   Solution Equation   Answer

7. Skyler bought 214 more baseball cards at a flea market. He now has 567 baseball cards in his collection. How many baseball cards did he have before the purchase?

$b + 214 = 567$ $567 − 214 = b$ 353 baseball cards

Situation Equation   Solution Equation   Answer

90 UNIT 3 LESSON 22   Use Mathematical Processes

Homework and Remembering page 90

Home or School Activity

 **Sports Connection**

Decimal Results Have students locate the times for the first and second place finishers in both a long and a short running event, such as a marathon and a 40-meter dash. In which race(s) are decimal numbers used to report the result? Are they to different decimal places? If so, explain why.

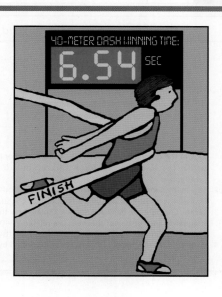

Unit Review and Test

UNIT 3

Lesson Objective

● **Assess student progress on unit objectives.**

The Day at a Glance

Today's Goals	Materials
1 Assessing the Unit ► Assess student progress on unit objectives. ► Use activities from unit lessons to reteach content. **2 Extending the Assessment** ► Use remediation for common errors. There is no homework assignment on a test day.	Unit 3 Test, Student Activity Book or Student Hardcover Book pp. 149–150 Unit 3 Test, Form A or B, Assessment Guide (optional) Unit 3 Performance Assessment, Assessment Guide (optional)

Keeping Skills Sharp

Quick Practice 🕐 5 MINUTES	
Goal: Review any skills you choose to meet the needs of your class. If you are doing a unit review day, use any of the Quick Practice activities that provide support for your class. If this is a test day, omit Quick Practice.	**Review and Test Day** You may want to choose a quiet game or other activity (reading a book or working on homework for another subject) for students who finish early.

Assess Unit Objectives

🕐 **45 MINUTES** (more if schedule permits)

Goal: Assess student progress on unit objectives.

Materials: Student Activity Book or Hardcover Book pp.149–150, Assessment Guide (optional)

▶ Review and Assessment

If your students are ready for assessment on the unit objectives, you may use either the test on the Student Book pages or one of the forms of the Unit 3 Test in the Assessment Guide to assess student progress.

If you feel that students need some review first, you may use the test on the Student Book pages as a review of unit content, and then use one of the forms of the Unit 3 Test in the Assessment Guide to assess student progress.

To assign a numerical score for all of these test forms, use 5 points for each question.

You may also choose to use the Unit 3 Performance Assessment. Scoring for that assessment can be found in its rubric in the Assessment Guide.

▶ Reteaching Resources

The chart at the right lists the test items, the unit objectives they cover, and the lesson activities in which the objective is covered in this unit. You may revisit these activities with students who do not show mastery of the objectives.

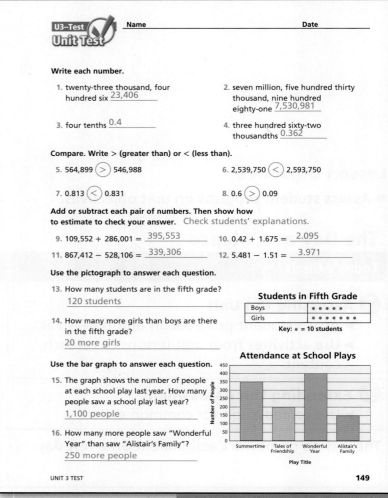

Student Activity Book page 149

Unit Test Items	Unit Objectives Tested	Activities to Use for Reteaching
1–4	**3.1** Read, write, and identify the place value of decimals and whole numbers.	Lessons 1–3, Activities 1–2 Lesson 5–6, Activities 1–2
5–8, 9–12	**3.2** Compare, order, and round numbers; estimate sums and differences.	Lesson 2, Activities 1–2 Lesson 5, Activities 1–2 Lessons 13–15, Activities 1–2
9–12	**3.3** Add and subtract whole numbers and decimals.	Lesson 4, Activities 1–2 Lessons 7–9, Activities 1–2 Lesson 11, Activities 1–2

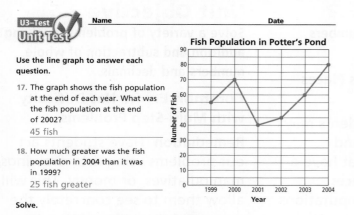

U3–Test
Unit Test

Name _____ Date _____

Use the line graph to answer each question.

Fish Population in Potter's Pond

17. The graph shows the fish population at the end of each year. What was the fish population at the end of 2002?

    45 fish

18. How much greater was the fish population in 2004 than it was in 1999?

    25 fish greater

Solve.

19. This week Roberto ran 5.83 miles on Monday and 6.6 miles on Tuesday. Last week he ran a total of 12.09 miles on Monday and Tuesday. Did he run more or less last week? How much more or less?

    less, 0.34 mi less

Show your work.

* 20. **Extended Response** The distance between Chicago and Los Angeles is 1,742 miles. The distance between Chicago and Philadelphia is 665 miles. The distance between Chicago and Detroit is 427 miles less than the distance between Chicago and Philadelphia. Explain how to find how much greater the distance between Chicago and Los Angeles is than the distance between Chicago and Detroit.

    First find the distance between Chicago and
    Detroit, 665 − 427 = 238. Then subtract the
    distance from 1,742, 1,742 − 238 = 1,504. The
    distance between Chicago and Los Angeles is
    1,504 miles more than the distance between
    Chicago and Detroit.

    *Item 20 also assesses the Process Skills of Problem Solving and Communication.

150 UNIT 3 TEST

Student Activity Book page 150

Unit Test Items	Unit Objectives Tested	Activities to Use for Reteaching
13–18	**3.4** Interpret and make pictographs, bar graphs, and line graphs.	Lesson 12, Activities 1–3 Lesson 14, Activities 1–2 Lesson 16, Activities 1–3 Lesson 17, Activities 1–2
19–20	**3.5** Solve a variety of problems involving addition and subtraction of whole numbers and decimals.	Lesson 10, Activities 1–2 Lessons 18–20, Activities 1–2 Lesson 21, Activities 1–3

▶ Assessment Resources

Free Response Tests
Unit 3 Test, Student Activity Book or Hardcover Book pp. 149–150
Unit 3 Test, Form A, Assessment Guide

Extended Response Item
The last item in the Student Book test and in the Form A test will require an extended response as an answer.

Multiple Choice Test
Unit 3 Test, Form B, Assessment Guide

Performance Assessment
Unit 3 Performance Assessment, Assessment Guide
Unit 3 Performance Assessment Rubric, Assessment Guide

▶ Portfolio Assessment

Teacher-selected Items for Student Portfolios:

- Homework, Lessons 4, 12, 14, 15, 16, 18, and 22
- Class Activity work, Lessons 9, 14, 18, 20, and 22

Student-selected Items for Student Portfolios:

- Favorite Home or School Activity
- Best Writing Prompt

② Extending the Assessment

Unit Objective 3.1

Read, write, and identify the place value of decimals and whole numbers.

Common Error: Omits Zeros

Remediation Students may sometimes omit one or more zeros when writing the standard form of a number given in word form. Have these students use Secret Code Cards, a place value chart, or a grid to record the standard form of the number. This will help them recognize and understand that zeros are sometimes used as placeholders in a number.

Unit Objective 3.2

Compare, order, and round numbers; estimate sums and differences.

Common Error: Compares Digits in Different Places

Remediation Have these students use Secret Code Cards or grid paper as they make their comparisons. For each comparison, have students place or write the numbers, one above the other, and align the numbers by place value. Remind students to compare digits beginning at the greatest, or leftmost, place of the numbers.

Unit Objective 3.3

Add and subtract whole numbers and decimals.

Common Error: Aligns Places Incorrectly

Remediation Some students may have difficulty adding and subtracting decimals that have a different number of places, especially when the computations are presented horizontally. Have students carefully rewrite the computations vertically on grid paper or lined paper turned sideways. This will enable them to use a column or a line for vertical alignment of the decimal points as well as the various places in the numbers.

Unit Objective 3.4

Interpret and make pictographs, bar graphs, and line graphs.

Common Error: Misreads Pictographs

Remediation Some students do not use the information in the key when reading the data presented in pictographs. For students to learn to read the key, they need to see a number of pictographs and practice including the information in the key when interpreting the data.

Unit Objective 3.5

Solve a variety of problems involving addition and subtraction of whole numbers and decimals.

Common Error: Has Difficulty with Multi-Step Problems

Remediation Have students act out problems using lists, drawings, manipulatives, or money. This will allow them to see concretely the steps, and the order of the steps, that must be performed.

Common Error: Doesn't Know How to Begin

Remediation Have students work in pairs to work through a problem. Then have students solve similar problems in which they can apply a similar strategy.

Circles, Polygons, and Angles

IN THIS UNIT, students are involved in hands-on activities to investigate how angles and lines combine in polygons and circles. They apply their discoveries about angles in a circle to describe rotational symmetry and to interpret and create circle graphs. Students then use what they have learned about circumference to investigate the relationship between diameter and circumference of a circle.

Skills Trace

Grade 4	Grade 5
• Use a protractor to determine the measure of an angle that is a multiple of 10°. • Classify triangles by their angles and sides. • Identify two-dimensional figures with line and rotational symmetry. • Interpret circle graphs. • Identify congruent figures.	• Use a protractor to determine the measure of any angle; measure internal angles in triangles, quadrilaterals, and circles. • Classify polygons by their angles and sides. • Identify two-dimensional figures with line and rotational symmetry. • Model turns of a circle. • Interpret and create circle graphs. • Explore circumference. • Identify congruent figures.

Unit 4   Contents

Unit 4   Assessment

✓ Unit Objectives Tested	Unit Test Items	Lessons
4.1 Identify and measure angles.	1, 2	1
4.2 Find the measure of an unknown angle in a polygon.	3, 4	1, 2
4.3 Identify congruent figures.	5	3
4.4 Identify the position of an object after it has been turned.	6	4
4.5 Identify lines of symmetry.	7	5
4.6 Solve problems using a circle graph.	8–10	6

Assessment and Review Resources

Formal Assessment

Student Activity Book
- Unit Review and Test (pp. 177–178)

Assessment Guide
- Quick Quiz 1 (p. A40)
- Quick Quiz 2 (p. A41)
- Test A—Open Response (pp. A42–A43)
- Test B—Multiple Choice (pp. A44–A45)
- Performance Assessment (pp. A46–A48)

Test Generator CD-ROM
- Open Response Test
- Multiple Choice Test
- Test Bank Items

Informal Assessment

Teacher Edition
- Ongoing Assessment (in every lesson)
- Math Talk (in every lesson)
- Portfolio Suggestions (p. 409)

123 **Math Talk**
- ▸ Math Talk in Action (pp. 378, 379, 380, 403)
- ▸ In Activities (pp. 363, 372, 385, 391, 398)
- ▸ Solve and Discuss (pp. 371, 379, 380, 386, 392)
- ▸ Student Pairs (p. 380)
- ▸ Small Groups (pp. 402, 403, 404)

Review Opportunities

Homework and Remembering
- Review of recently taught topics
- Spiral Review

Teacher Edition
- Unit Review and Test (pp. 407–410)

Test Generator CD-ROM
- Custom review sheets

Planning Unit 4

Lesson NCTM Focal Points NCTM Standards	Resources	Materials for Lesson Activities	Materials for Going Further
4-1 **Lines and Angles** NCTM Focal Point: 5.2 NCTM Standards: 3, 4, 7, 10	TE pp. 361–368 SAB pp. 151–156 H&R pp. 91–92 AC 4-1	Rulers ✓ Protractors	Regular paper Marker ✓ Protractors Math Journals
4-2 **Polygons and Angles** NCTM Focal Point: 5.2 NCTM Standards: 3, 4, 7	TE pp. 369–374 SAB pp. 157–160 H&R pp. 93–94 AC 4-2	Rulers Scissors ✓ Protractors	Rulers ✓ Protractors Math Journals
4-3 **Compare and Contrast Polygons** NCTM Standards: 1, 3, 7	TE pp. 375–382 SAB pp. 161–164 H&R pp. 95–96 AC 4-3 MCC 17 AG Quick Quiz 1	✓ MathBoard materials or Dot Paper (TRB M20) (optional) Scissors Straightedge Centimeter-Grid Paper (TRB M18)	Centimeter-Dot Paper (TRB M25) Tracing paper Scissors Math Journals
4-4 **Circles and Angles** NCTM Focal Point: 5.2 NCTM Standards: 3, 4	TE pp. 383–388 SAB pp. 165–168 H&R pp. 97–98 AC 4-4 MCC 18	Rulers Circles (TRB M86) (optional) ✓ Protractors Grid paper or Dot Paper (TRB M20) (optional)	Rulers Analog clock Tracing paper ✓ Protractors Math Journals
4-5 **Symmetry** NCTM Standard: 3	TE pp. 389–394 SAB pp. 169–172 H&R pp. 99–100 AC 4-5 MCC 19	Rectangular paper, unlined Scissors	Centimeter-Dot Paper (TRB M25) Math Journals
4-6 **Circle Graphs** NCTM Focal Point: 5.2 NCTM Standards: 3, 4, 5	TE pp. 395–400 SAB pp. 173–174 H&R pp. 101–102 AC 4-6	Rulers ✓ Protractors	Math Journals

Resources/Materials Key: TE: Teacher Edition   SAB: Student Activity Book   H&R: Homework and Remembering
AC: Activity Cards   MCC: Math Center Challenge   AG: Assessment Guide   ✓: Grade 5 kits   TRB: Teacher's Resource Book

NCTM Standards and Expectations Key: **1.** Number and Operations **2.** Algebra **3.** Geometry
4. Measurement **5.** Data Analysis and Probability **6.** Problem Solving **7.** Reasoning and Proof
8. Communication **9.** Connections **10.** Representation

Lesson NCTM Focal Points NCTM Standards	Resources	Materials for Lesson Activities	Materials for Going Further
4-7 **Circumference** NCTM Focal Point: 5.2 NCTM Standards: 3, 4, 7	TE pp. 401–406 SAB pp. 175–176 H&R pp. 103–104 AC 4-7 MCC 20 AG Quick Quiz 2	Rulers Cans of various sizes String	Strip of paper Scissors Cans String Rulers Circular object Math Journals
Unit Review and Test	TE pp. 407–410 SAB pp. 177–178 AG Unit 4 Tests		

Hardcover Student Book

- Together, the Hardcover Student Book and its companion Activity Workbook contain all of the pages in the consumable Student Activity Book.

Manipulatives and Materials

- Essential materials for teaching *Math Expressions* are available in the Grade 5 kits. These materials are indicated by a ✓ in these lists. At the front of this Teacher Edition is more information about kit contents, alternatives for the materials, and use of the materials.

Independent Learning Activities

Ready-Made Math Challenge Centers

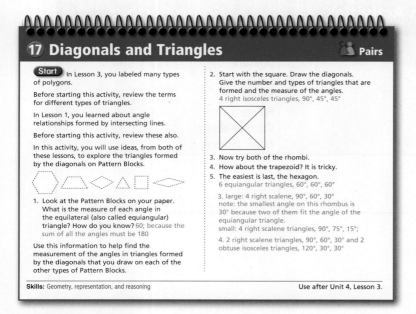

Grouping Pairs

Materials Ruler, Pattern Blocks (TRB M28)

Objective Students name different types of triangles and give the angle measures.

Connections Geometry and Representation

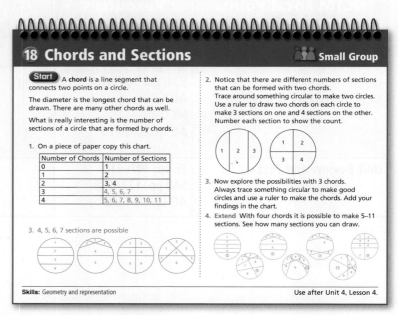

Grouping Small Group

Materials Ruler, something circular to trace

Objective Students explore the different number of sections of a circle that can be made with chords.

Connections Geometry and Reasoning

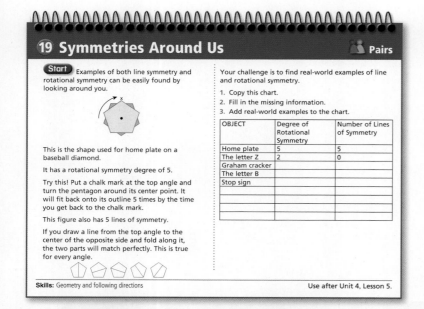

Grouping Pairs

Materials None

Objective Students identify the symmetries in real-world objects.

Connections Geometry and Real World

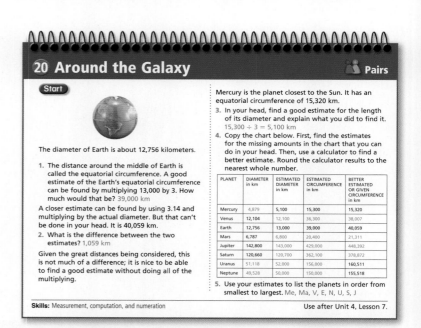

Grouping Pairs

Materials Calculator

Objective Students use estimates to find circumference and to order the planets.

Connections Measurement and Computation

Ready-Made Math Resources

Technology — Tutorials, Practice, and Intervention

Use online, individualized intervention and support to bring students to proficiency.

Help students practice skills and apply concepts through exciting math adventures.

Visit **Education Place®**
www.eduplace.com

Extend and enrich students' understanding of skills and concepts through engaging, interactive lessons and activities.

Visit www.eduplace.com/mx2t/ and find family, teacher, and student materials, activities, games, and more.

Literature Links

Sir Cumference and the Great Knight of Angleland: A Math Adventure

Sir Cumference and the Great Knight of Angleland: A Math Adventure

Introducing geometry has never been more fun. This tale, set in a medieval timeframe, follows an aspiring knight, Radius (son of Sir Cumference) on his quest through a maze of angles. Students will learn to use a protractor, which is included in the book, in this mathematics adventure by Cindy Neuschwander.

Literature Connection

Sir Cumference and the Dragon of Pi, by Cindy Neuschwander, illustrated by Wayne Geehan (Charlesbridge Publishing, 1999)

Unit 4   Teaching Resources

Differentiated Instruction

Individualizing Instruction

Activities	Level	Frequency
	• Intervention • On Level • Challenge	All 3 in every lesson
Math Writing Prompts	Level	Frequency
	• Intervention • On Level • Challenge	All 3 in every lesson
Math Center Challenges	For advanced students	
	4 in every unit	

Reaching All Learners

English Language Learners	Lessons	Pages
	1, 2, 3, 4, 5, 6, 7	361, 369, 375, 383, 389, 395, 401
Extra Help	Lesson	Pages
	1	365, 366
Special Needs	Lesson	Page
	5	391
Advanced Learners	Lessons	Pages
	1, 3, 6	363, 380, 398

Strategies for English Language Learners

Present this problem to all students. Offer the different levels of support to meet students' levels of language proficiency.

Objective Review *angle, degree, right, acute,* and *obtuse.*

Problem Draw a square and mark the angles on the board. Draw an *acute,* and an *obtuse angle.* Say: **Squares have *right angles.* Right angles are 90 degrees**. Write 90°, *degrees, right, acute,* and *obtuse angle.*

Newcomer

- Have students trace a *right angle* in the air with a finger and repeat.
- Say: **This *angle* is smaller than 90°. It is *acute*.** Have students trace and repeat. Continue with *obtuse.*

Beginning

- Point and ask: **Is this *angle* smaller than 90°?** yes Say: **It is *acute*.** Have students repeat. Continue with other angles.

Intermediate

- Point and ask: **Is this *angle* greater or less than 90°?** less Say: **It is *acute*.** Have students repeat. Continue with *obtuse.*

Advanced

- Have students identify compare the other angles. Define *acute* and *obtuse.* Have students identify each angle.

Connections

Art Connection
Lesson 2, page 374

Language Arts Connection
Lesson 3, page 382

Literature Connection
Lesson 7, page 406

Science Connections
Lesson 4, page 388
Lesson 5, page 394

Social Studies Connection
Lesson 6, page 400

Math Background

Putting Research into Practice for Unit 4

From Current Research: Developing Angle Concepts

An important and difficult geometric figure for students to understand and be able to use is the angle. In the course of schooling, students need to encounter multiple mathematical conceptions of angle, including: (a) angle as movement, as in rotation or sweep; (b) angle as a geometric shape, a delineation of space by two intersecting lines; and (c) angle as a measure, a perspective that encompasses the other two. Although as preschoolers, they encounter and use angles intuitively in their play, children have many misconceptions about angles. They typically believe that angle measures are influenced by the lengths of the intersecting lines or by the angle's orientation in space. The latter conception decreases with age, but the former is robust at every age. Some researchers have suggested that students in the elementary grades should develop separate mental models of angle as movement and angle as shape.

There is some research on instructional approaches that attempt to develop the two models of angles. With appropriate instruction, Logo's Turtle Geometry can support the development of measures of rotations. The students, however, rarely connected these rotations to models of the space in the interior of figures traced by the turtle. Simple modifications to Logo helped students perceive the relationship between turns and traces (the path made by Logo's turtle), and the students could then use turns to measure static intersections of lines. Another approach used multiple concrete analogies such as turns, slopes, meetings, bends, directions, corners, and openings to help children develop general angle concepts by recognizing common features of these situations. Other research took as the starting point children's experience with physical rotations, especially rotations of their own bodies. In time, students were able to assign numbers to certain turns and integrate turn-as-body-motion with turn-as-number.

An understanding of angle requires novel forms of mental structuring, the coordination of several potential models, and an integration of those models. The long developmental process is best begun in the early grades. Common admonitions to teach angles as turns run the risk of students developing only one concept of angle since they rarely spontaneously relate situations involving rotations to those involving shape and form.

Kilpatrick, Jeremy, Jane Swafford, Bradford Findell, eds. *Adding It Up: Helping Children Learn Mathematics.* Mathematics Learning Study Committee, National Research Council. Washington: NAP, 2001. p. 286.

Other Useful References: Circles, Polygons, and Angles

Learning Math: Geometry. Annenberg/CPB Learner.org. 1997–2004. <www.learner.org/resources/series167.html>.

Learning Math: Measurement. Annenberg/CPB Learner.org. 1997–2004. <www.learner.org/resources/series184.html>.

National Council of Teachers of Mathematics. *Learning and Teaching Measurement* (NCTM 2003 Yearbook). Ed. Douglas H. Clements. Reston: NCTM, 2003.

National Council of Teachers of Mathematics. *Mathematics Teaching in the Middle School* (Focus Issue: Measurement) 9.8 (Apr. 2004).

National Council of Teachers of Mathematics. *Mathematics Teaching in the Middle School* (Focus Issue: Geometry) 3.6 (Mar. 1998).

National Council of Teachers of Mathematics. *Principles and Standards for School Mathematics.* Reston: NCTM, 2000.

Getting Ready to Teach Unit 4

Analyzing Geometric Figures

Characteristics of Lines and Angles
Lesson 1

In order to classify polygons, students need to be familiar with certain characteristics of lines and angles. Parallel line segments run in the same direction, and will never meet, even if extended.

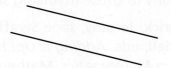

Perpendicular line segments that intersect form a 90° angle.

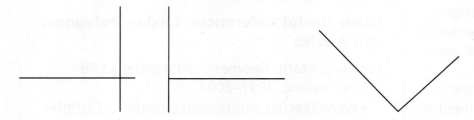

Measuring Angles with a Protractor
Lesson 1

In this unit, students will measure angles with a protractor. In order to use a protractor accurately, students need to align the vertex of the angle carefully with the center mark on the protractor and align one ray with the zero line. Some protractors are labeled clockwise *and* counterclockwise. Students should use what they already know about angles to choose which scale to read. Some practice as a class may be useful.

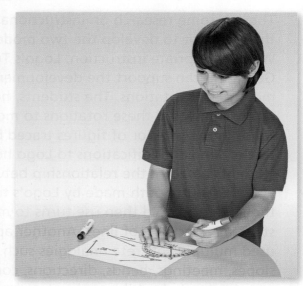

This protractor is not positioned correctly.

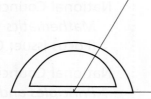

Does this angle measure 60° or 120°?

Building Concepts of Angles
Lessons 4, 5, and 6

In Lesson 4, students are asked to make a connection between angles as shapes—two line segments and the space between them—and angles as turns—the movement between one position and another. Seeing angles as turns will help students to describe rotational symmetry in Lesson 5.

Circle graphs are commonly used to show data. To read a circle graph, we need to have a fundamental understanding of angles in a circle. To create a circle graph, we also need a sense of proportion. If I survey 72 people, and 360° represents all of them, what angle in the circle represents each person? (360° ÷ 72 = 5°. Each response is represented by 5° on a circle graph.)

Rotations and Rotational Symmetry
Lesson 5

An exploration of rotational symmetry enables students to consolidate their understanding of angles, turns, and symmetry. If we can rotate (or turn) a figure around a center point in fewer than 360° and the figure appears unchanged, then the figure has rotational symmetry. The point around which you rotate is called the center of rotation, and the smallest angle you need to turn is called the angle of rotation.

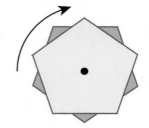

We can describe a figure with rotational symmetry in two ways: either by its rotation angle or by its degree of rotational symmetry. A regular pentagon fits on itself 5 times in one full turn. Its degree of rotational symmetry is 5.

We can divide 360° by 5 to determine the rotation angle, 72°. This regular pentagon has 72° rotational symmetry.

Basic Multiplication and Division Fluency

Students should continually work toward fluency for basic multiplication and division facts. Use checkups to assist students in monitoring their own learning. In the Teacher's Resource Book (TRB) you will find several pages for diagnosing and practicing basic multiplication and division.

TRB M58 Diagnostic Quiz for Basic Multiplication	TRB M66 Scrambled Multiplication Tables
TRB M59 Diagnostic Quiz for Basic Division	TRB M67 Blank Multiplication Tables
TRB M60 Basic Multiplication Practice	TRB M68 Multiplication for 10s, 11s, 12s
TRB M61 Basic Division Practice	TRB M69 Division for 10s, 11s, 12s
TRB M62 Multiplication for 3s, 4s, 6s, 7s, 8s, 9s	TRB M83 Factor Puzzles for 3s, 4s, 6s, 7s, 8s, 9s
TRB M63 Division for 3s, 4s, 6s, 7s, 8s, 9s	TRB M84 Factor Puzzles for 6s, 7s, 8s
TRB M64 Multiplication for 6s, 7s, 8s	TRB M85 Blank Factor Puzzles
TRB M65 Division for 6s, 7s, 8s	

See the Basic Facts Fluency Plan for information about practice materials.

Lines and Angles

Lesson Objectives

- Identify and draw lines, rays, and line segments.
- Measure angles.
- Classify angles according to their measures.

The Day at a Glance

Today's Goals	Materials
1 Teaching the Lesson A1: Draw and name the characteristics of various lines, rays, and angles. A2: Use a protractor to measure angles. A3: Identify vertical, complementary, and supplementary angles. **2 Going Further** ▶ Differentiated Instruction **3 Homework and Spiral Review**	**Lesson Activities** Student Activity Book pp. 151–156 or Student Hardcover Book pp. 151–156 and Activity Workbook pp. 65–67 (includes Family Letters) Homework and Remembering pp. 91–92 Rulers Protractors
	Going Further Activity Cards 4-1 Rectangular paper Marker Protractors Math Journals

123 *Use* **Math Talk** *today!*

Keeping Skills Sharp

Daily Routines	English Language Learners
Mental Math Find the number that is 0.1 greater than and the number that is 0.1 less than each of the given numbers. **1.** 5.768 5.868; 5.668 **2.** 6.14 6.24; 6.04 **3.** 3.2 3.3; 3.1 **4.** 10 10.1; 9.9	Draw a *line segment* on the board. Write *endpoint*. Point and say: **A *line segment* has 2 *endpoints*.** Have students repeat and trace the line segment in the air with a finger. Draw a *line* and a *ray*. • **Beginning** Point and say: **This is a *line*.** Ask: **Does it have any *endpoints*?** no Continue with ray. • **Intermediate and Advanced** Identify the *line* and *ray*. Have students tell about the endpoints.

Teaching the Lesson

Draw Lines, Rays, and Angles

 15 MINUTES

Goal: Draw and name the characteristics of various lines, rays, and angles.

Materials: Student Activity Book p. 151 or Hardcover Book p. 151 and Activity Workbook p. 65, rulers (1 per student)

✓ **NCTM Standards:**
Geometry
Representation

▶ **Identify Lines** WHOLE CLASS

Divide the board into six columns. Label the columns 1–6. Have students look at the instructions on Student Book page 151. Invite volunteers to come to the board and to record two characteristics of each figure from exercises 1–6. Some characteristics may be named more than once.

With a completed list of characteristics on the board, invite the students to discuss the characteristics and, by consensus, erase those that are not correct.

Have volunteers write the name of each geometric figure at the top of each column, and draw several different examples of that kind of figure, while the rest of the students complete exercises 1–6.

Ask students to complete exercises 7–12. As a class, discuss where we can see these figures in the world around us.

Teaching Note

Watch For! Some students may believe that a *point of intersection* can be formed only when two lines cross. Explain that a point of intersection is formed whenever two lines, rays, or line segments cross or meet. The line and the ray below share a common point: they intersect but do not cross.

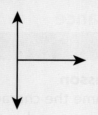

Definition	Sample of Characteristics
A **line** is set of points that form a straight path that extends infinitely in opposite directions.	a set of points; straight path; infinite length in opposite directions; length goes on and on
A **line segment** is a part of a line marked by two endpoints, and it includes the endpoints and all the points on the line between them.	a specific set of points, often with named endpoints; sides of a polygon; edge of a solid figure; a radius or a diameter of a circle; an arc (curve) on a circle
A **ray** is part of a line that begins at an endpoint and extends infinitely in one direction.	a set of points; part of a line; one endpoint; infinite length in one direction
An **angle** is formed by two rays sharing a common endpoint.	two rays; common endpoint
Parallel lines are lines that are equidistant from each other and in the same plane.	lines that do not intersect; always the same distance from each other
Perpendicular lines are lines that intersect or meet to form right (90°) angles.	lines that intersect; form right (90°) angles; square corners
Oblique lines are lines in the same plane that intersect to form nonright (acute or obtuse) angles.	lines that intersect; form nonright (acute or obtuse) angles

(123) **Math Talk** As a class, discuss how each figure was drawn using information given in the names. Students should mention the following in their discussion.

● The first letter in the name of the ray is the endpoint of the ray. The ray points in the direction of the second letter.

● The letter that is in the middle of the angle name is the vertex of the angle.

● Perpendicular lines form a square corner on the grid.

● Oblique lines intersect but do not form a square corner.

● To draw parallel lines, you had to choose a pair of either vertical or horizontal grid lines.

Then, as a class, discuss where these figures can be seen in the world around us, for example, the walls of the classroom.

► Interior and Exterior Angles

WHOLE CLASS

You may wish to introduce the concept of the interior and exterior of the angle. When a point is in the *interior* of an angle it is between the points that lie on each side of the angle. When a point is in the *exterior* of an angle it is not on the angle or in its interior.

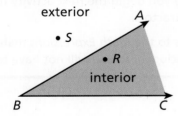

Sketch angle *ABC* above on the board. Ask if point *R* lies between the point on rays *AB* and *CB* or outside of them. inside Ask if point *R* is on the interior or exterior of the angle. interior Repeat the same process for point *S*, which is on the exterior of the angle.

Volunteers can to add additional points that are either interior or exterior to the angle. The class says "interior" or "exterior."

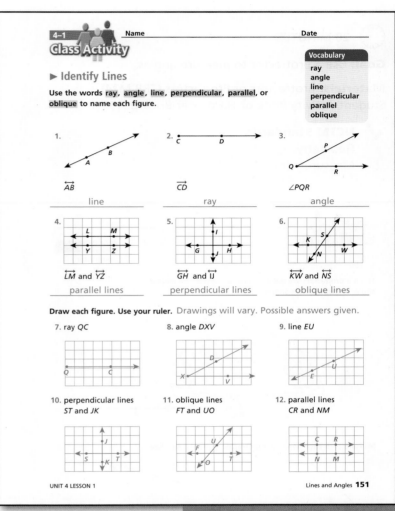

Differentiated Instruction

Advanced Learners *Skew lines* are two (or more) lines that are not parallel but never intersect because they lie in different planes. Lines *m* and *p* below are skew lines.

Students can use straws or craft sticks and clay (or other materials) to model skew lines.

Activity 2

Measure Angles With a Protractor

 20 MINUTES

Goal: Use a protractor to measure angles.

Materials: protractors or Protractors (TRB M24), Student Activity Book or Hardcover Book p. 152

 NCTM Standards:
Geometry
Measurement

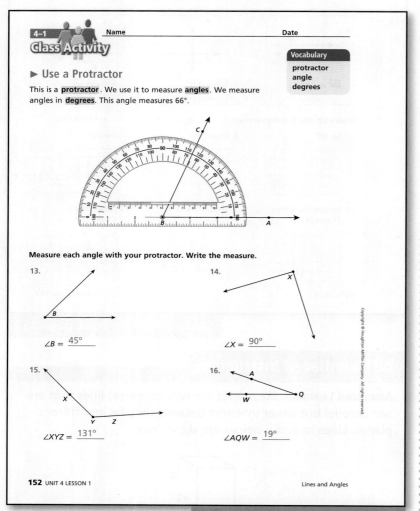

► **Use a Protractor**   WHOLE CLASS

Measure Angles in Degrees Draw a circle with a dot in its center on the board. Explain that one full turn around the circle is 360 degrees. An angle is a partial turn around a circle, and we measure an angle in *degrees* (rather than by the length of its rays).

Mark right angle *S* in the circle and ask how many degrees are in a quarter turn around the circle. 90 Then write ∠*S* = 90° on the board and point out that the symbol ° represents the word *degrees*. (You may wish to introduce the statement: M∠*S* = 90°, which is read "The measure of angle *S* is 90° degrees.")

Discuss the protractor on Student Book page 364. Allow time for students to find the 0 and 180 marks on the scales. Then ask why both scales end with 180 rather than 360. The ensuing discussion should lead students to understand that the protractor has two scales and that it shows the number of degrees in a half circle, 180°.

Help students align the base ray of the angle with the 0° mark on one of of the scales. Then demonstrate how to read the scale where the second ray of the angle intersects the scale.

Have students use their protractors to measure the angles in exercises 13–16.

Class Management

Looking Ahead In this activity and Lessons 2, 4, and 6, students will use protractors. TRB M24 shows a protractor with a clockwise scale and a counter-clockwise scale. For classroom activities, you can copy TRB M24 on transparencies (make sure your copy machine has the capability). You may want to set aside time before you begin the next activity for students to cut out their protractors.

If you have access to the *Math Expressions* materials kits, protractors are included, so you will not have to prepare them.

Find Unknown Angles

 25 MINUTES

Goal: Identify vertical, complementary, and supplementary angles.

Materials: Student Activity Book or Hardcover Book pp. 153–154, protractors or Protractors (TRB M24)

 NCTM Standards:
Geometry
Reasoning and Proof

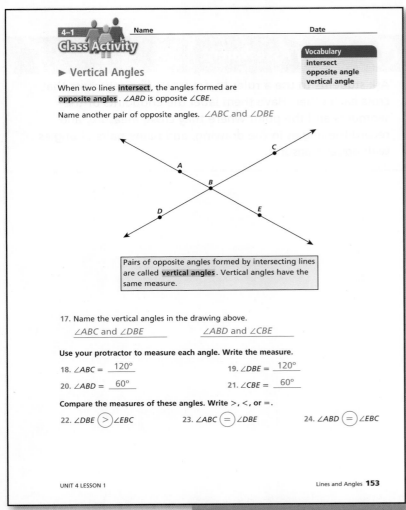

Student Activity Book page 153

▶ Vertical Angles [WHOLE CLASS]

Discuss the intersecting lines at the top of Student Book page 153.

● Name the angles formed by the intersecting lines.
∠ABD, ∠DBE , ∠CBE, ∠ABC

● Which pairs of angles are opposite each other?
∠ABD is opposite ∠CBE; ∠DBE is opposite ∠ABC

Read the definition of vertical angles given on the page. Ask students to apply the definition and to name the vertical angles in the figure. Have them complete exercises 17–24.

Discuss how the concept of vertical angles was helpful when answering exercise 18–21.

Differentiated Instruction

Extra Help Suggest that before students place their protractors they should decide if the angle to be measured is greater than or less than a right angle (90°). This will help them determine if the measure they find is reasonable.

Give this tip to students who are uncertain of which scale to use on the protractor: If the angle opens to the left, count up from the 0° mark on the left. If the angle opens to the right, count up from the 0° mark on the right.

Teaching Note

Math Symbols Discuss how the mathematical notation for these geometric figures shows the aspects of the figure.

line *AB*	$\overleftrightarrow{AB}$
parallel lines *ST* and *JK*	$\overleftrightarrow{ST} \parallel \overleftrightarrow{JK}$
ray *RT*	$\overrightarrow{RT}$
perpendicular lines *GH* and *UV*	$\overleftrightarrow{GH} \perp \overleftrightarrow{UV}$
line segment *LM*	$\overline{LM}$
angle *PQR*	∠*PQR*

Activity continued ▶

Activity 3

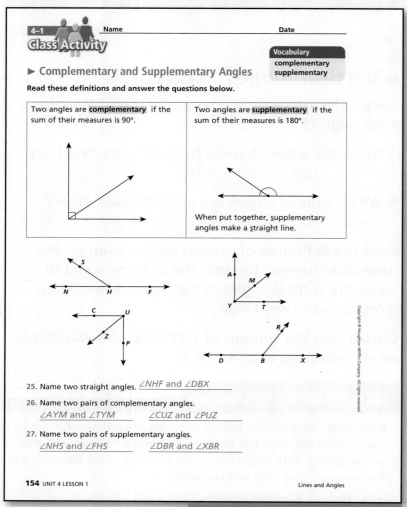

Student Activity Book page 154

▶ Complementary and Supplementary Angles WHOLE CLASS

Explain that a right angle has a measure of 90° and a straight angle has a measure of 180°. Draw an example of each angle on the board.

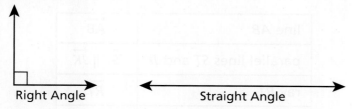

Right Angle   Straight Angle

Point out the symbol located at the vertex of the right angle. Explain that this symbol represents a right, or 90°, angle, and indicates perpendicular lines, rays, and line segments.

Read the definitions of complementary and supplementary angles given on the page. Ask students to use the definitions when completing the exercises.

366 UNIT 4 LESSON 1

Teaching Note

Language and Vocabulary Discuss the difference between *compliment* and *complement*. When you admire someone you are being *complimentary*. When angles are *complementary*, their measures total 90°. *Complementary* comes from the same root as *complete*. Together, the two angles complete a right angle.

Differentiated Instruction

Extra Help Some students confuse the definitions for supplementary and complementary. One way to remember is to think: <u>S</u>upplementary angles form a <u>s</u>traight angle and both words begin with the letter *s*.

✓ Ongoing Assessment

Ask students to use a ruler to draw two line segments that cross each other. Have them label the endpoints of the segments and the point where they cross, measure, and record the angles in the drawing, and name pairs of angles with equal measures.

Activity Card 4-1

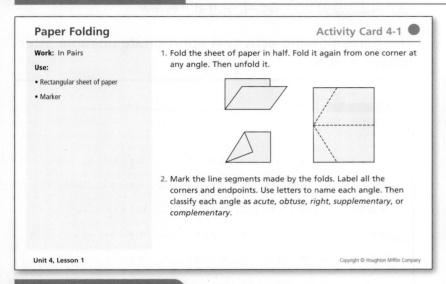

Paper Folding   Activity Card 4-1 ●

Work: In Pairs
Use:
• Rectangular sheet of paper
• Marker

1. Fold the sheet of paper in half. Fold it again from one corner at any angle. Then unfold it.

2. Mark the line segments made by the folds. Label all the corners and endpoints. Use letters to name each angle. Then classify each angle as *acute, obtuse, right, supplementary,* or *complementary.*

Unit 4, Lesson 1   Copyright © Houghton Mifflin Company

Activity Note Suggest that students first classify the angles as *acute*, *obtuse*, or *right*, and then identify angle pairs as *supplementary* or *complementary*.

 Math Writing Prompt

Make a Drawing Draw two right angles that share one side. Use your drawing to explain why the two right angles are supplementary.

 **Software Support**

Warm-Up 35.24

Activity Card 4-1

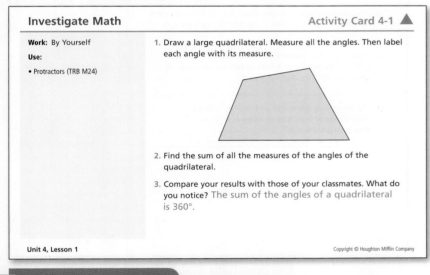

Investigate Math   Activity Card 4-1 ▲

Work: By Yourself
Use:
• Protractors (TRB M24)

1. Draw a large quadrilateral. Measure all the angles. Then label each angle with its measure.

2. Find the sum of all the measures of the angles of the quadrilateral.

3. Compare your results with those of your classmates. What do you notice? The sum of the angles of a quadrilateral is 360°.

Unit 4, Lesson 1   Copyright © Houghton Mifflin Company

Activity Note Angle measures may not total 360°, depending on the accuracy of the measurements. Demonstrate this fact by having students cut out each angle and connect the vertices to form a circle.

 Math Writing Prompt

Summarize Use symbols to describe all the straight geometric figures that contain two points, *A* and *B*.

 Software Support

Ice Station Exploration: Polar Planes, Level B

Activity Card 4-1

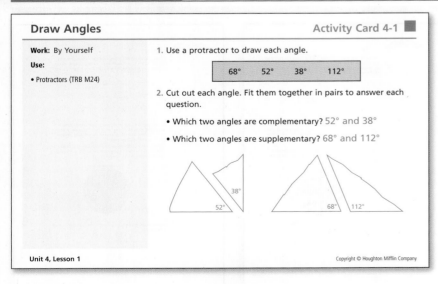

Draw Angles   Activity Card 4-1 ■

Work: By Yourself
Use:
• Protractors (TRB M24)

1. Use a protractor to draw each angle.

| 68° | 52° | 38° | 112° |

2. Cut out each angle. Fit them together in pairs to answer each question.
   • Which two angles are complementary? 52° and 38°
   • Which two angles are supplementary? 68° and 112°

Unit 4, Lesson 1   Copyright © Houghton Mifflin Company

Activity Note Review how to use a protractor. Students must draw the rays of each angle far enough to be able to align sides and identify the resulting pairs of angles.

 Math Writing Prompt

Use Logic Explain why an obtuse angle and an acute angle cannot be complementary. Explain why two acute angles cannot be supplementary.

 DESTINATION Math® **Software Support**

Course III: Module 5: Unit 1: Lines, Angles, and Circles

③ Homework and Spiral Review

<table>
</table>

4-1

Homework **Goal:** Additional Practice

For Homework, students draw and identify lines, rays, and angles.

4-1

Remembering **Goal:** Spiral Review

This Remembering activity is appropriate anytime after today's lesson.

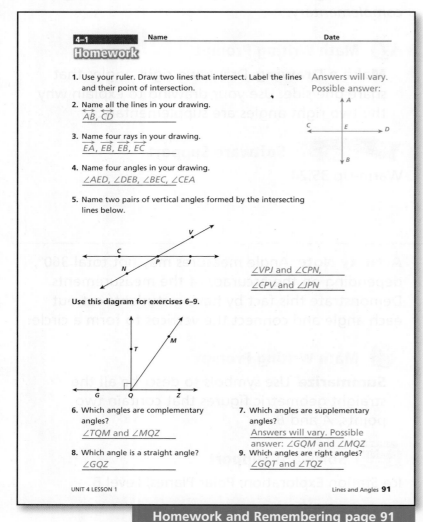

4-1 Name _____ Date _____

Homework

1. Use your ruler. Draw two lines that intersect. Label the lines and their point of intersection.

Answers will vary. Possible answer:

2. Name all the lines in your drawing.
$\overleftrightarrow{AB}$, $\overleftrightarrow{CD}$

3. Name four rays in your drawing.
$\overrightarrow{EA}$, $\overrightarrow{EB}$, $\overrightarrow{EB}$, $\overrightarrow{EC}$

4. Name four angles in your drawing.
∠AED, ∠DEB, ∠BEC, ∠CEA

5. Name two pairs of vertical angles formed by the intersecting lines below.

∠VPJ and ∠CPN,
∠CPV and ∠JPN

Use this diagram for exercises 6–9.

6. Which angles are complementary angles?
∠TQM and ∠MQZ

7. Which angles are supplementary angles?
Answers will vary. Possible answer: ∠GQM and ∠MQZ

8. Which angle is a straight angle?
∠GQZ

9. Which angles are right angles?
∠GQT and ∠TQZ

UNIT 4 LESSON 1   Lines and Angles **91**

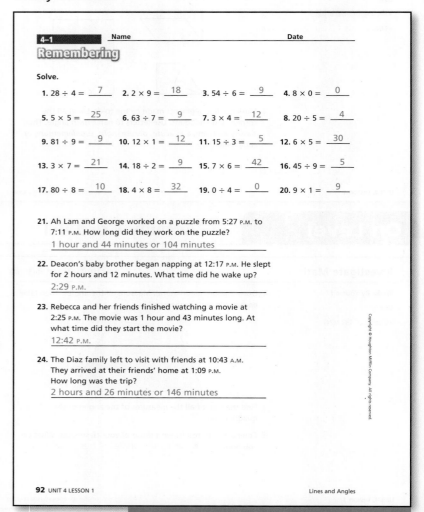

4-1 Name _____ Date _____

Remembering

Solve.

1. 28 ÷ 4 = **7**   2. 2 × 9 = **18**   3. 54 ÷ 6 = **9**   4. 8 × 0 = **0**

5. 5 × 5 = **25**   6. 63 ÷ 7 = **9**   7. 3 × 4 = **12**   8. 20 ÷ 5 = **4**

9. 81 ÷ 9 = **9**   10. 12 × 1 = **12**   11. 15 ÷ 3 = **5**   12. 6 × 5 = **30**

13. 3 × 7 = **21**   14. 18 ÷ 2 = **9**   15. 7 × 6 = **42**   16. 45 ÷ 9 = **5**

17. 80 ÷ 8 = **10**   18. 4 × 8 = **32**   19. 0 ÷ 4 = **0**   20. 9 × 1 = **9**

21. Ah Lam and George worked on a puzzle from 5:27 P.M. to 7:11 P.M. How long did they work on the puzzle?
1 hour and 44 minutes or 104 minutes

22. Deacon's baby brother began napping at 12:17 P.M. He slept for 2 hours and 12 minutes. What time did he wake up?
2:29 P.M.

23. Rebecca and her friends finished watching a movie at 2:25 P.M. The movie was 1 hour and 43 minutes long. At what time did they start the movie?
12:42 P.M.

24. The Diaz family left to visit with friends at 10:43 A.M. They arrived at their friends' home at 1:09 P.M. How long was the trip?
2 hours and 26 minutes or 146 minutes

92 UNIT 4 LESSON 1   Lines and Angles

Homework and Remembering page 91   **Homework and Remembering page 92**

Home and School Connection

Family Letter Have students take home the Family Letter on Student Activity Book page 155 or Activity Workbook page 66. This letter explains how the concepts of angles and measuring angles are developed in *Math Expressions*. It gives parents and guardians a better understanding of the learning that goes on in math class and creates a bridge between school and home. A Spanish translation of this letter is on Student Activity Book page 156 and Activity Workbook page 67.

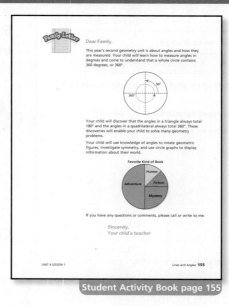

Student Activity Book page 155

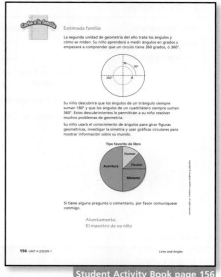

Student Activity Book page 156

368 UNIT 4 LESSON 1

Polygons and Angles

Lesson Objectives

- Discover the total measure of the interior angles of triangles and of quadrilaterals.
- Determine missing angle measures.

The Day at a Glance

Today's Goals	Materials	

1 **Teaching the Lesson**
A1: Cut and arrange angles to discover the total measure of the interior angles of a triangle.
A2: Use a protractor to find the total measure of the interior angles of a quadrilateral.
2 **Going Further**
▶ Differentiated Instruction
3 **Homework and Spiral Review**
	Lesson Activities
	Student Activity Book
	  pp. 157–160 or Student
	  Hardcover Book pp. 157–160
	  and Activity Workbook p. 68
	Homework and Remembering
	  pp. 93–94
	Rulers
	Scissors
	Protractors
		Going Further
		Activity Cards 4-2
		Rulers
		Protractors
		Math Journals

123 Use Math Talk today!

Keeping Skills Sharp

Daily Routines	English Language Learners
Homework Review If students give incorrect answers, have them share their work with the class. Have the class help locate and correct the error. **Nonroutine problem** There are 36 students participating in the math challenge teams this year. There is an even number of teams. The teachers want the greatest number of teams possible with at least 5 students per team. How many teams are there? 6 teams; The factors of 36 are: 1, 36; 2, 18; 3, 12; 4, 9; 6, 6. Only 6 and 6 fulfill the conditions.	Write *quadrilateral* on the board. Draw a rhombus, a regular trapezoid, and an irregular quadrilateral on the board. • **Beginning** Ask: Do all these figures have 4 sides? yes **Are they** *quadrilaterals*? yes **Does the sum of their** *angles* **equal 360°?** yes • **Intermediate** Say: These shapes all have 4 __ and __. sides, angles **They are** __. quadrilaterals **The sum of their** *angles* **equals** __. 360° • **Advanced** Have students identify the figures as *quadrilaterals* and tell about their properties.

① Teaching the Lesson

Activity 1

Interior Angles of a Triangle

 30 MINUTES

Goal: Cut and arrange angles to discover the total measure of the interior angles of a triangle.

Materials: Student Activity Book pp. 157–158 or Hardcover Book pp. 157–158 and Activity Workbook p. 68, rulers (1 per student), scissors

 NCTM Standards:
Measurement
Geometry
Reasoning and Proof

Class Management

Be sure students draw their own triangle on a separate sheet of paper, and do *not* cut out the triangle on Student Book page 157.

▶ **Measure Interior Angles of a Triangle**

⎡ WHOLE CLASS ⎤

Have students follow the directions for exercise 1.

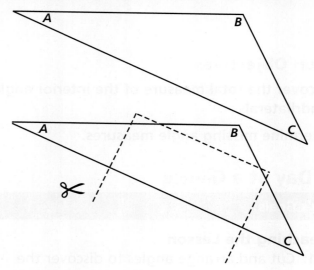

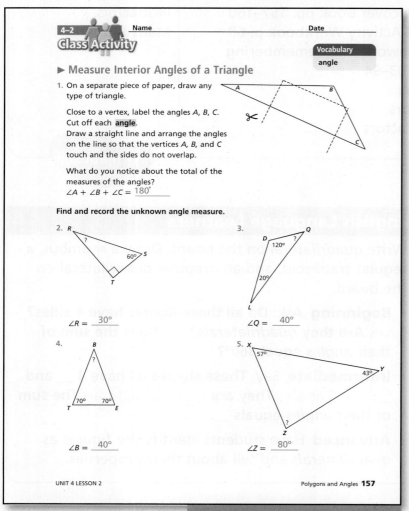

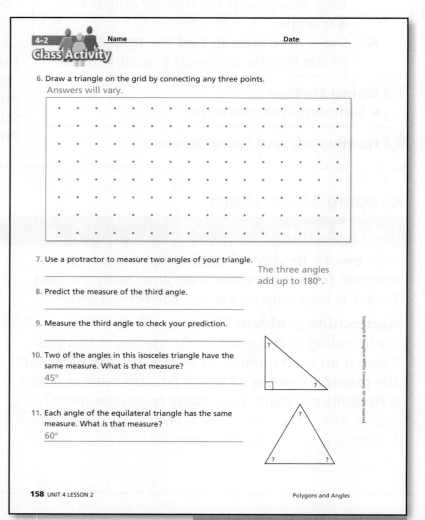

370 UNIT 4 LESSON 2   **Student Activity Book page 157**   **Student Activity Book page 158**

Now have students put the three angles together along a straight line (as shown).

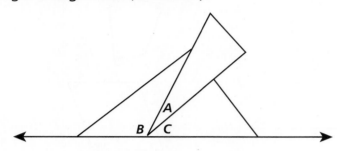

- The line represents a straight angle. What is the degree measure of a straight angle? 180°

- What is the total of the three angle measures of your triangle? 180°

Have students share their triangle proofs with other students and work together to create the generalization that the total of the angle measures of any triangle is 180°.

Find Unknown Angles Without Measuring To complete exercises 2–5, students must subtract the known angle measures, or the total of the known angle measures, from 180°.

Use **Solve and Discuss** for exercises 6–9. Ask students to suggest reasons why their predictions might be off by a degree or two, depending on the accuracy of their measurements.

Discuss the isosceles and equilateral triangles in exercises 10 and 11.

- What is the total measure of the two unknown angles in exercise 10? 180° − 90° = 90°

- If the two angles are the same size, what do you do to find the measure of each angle? Divide 90° by 2 to get 45°.

- What is the total measure of the three unknown angles in exercise 11? 180°

- If the three angles are the same size, what do you do to find the measure of each angle? Divide 180° by 3 to get 60°.

Interior Angles of a Quadrilateral

 30 MINUTES

Goal: Use a protractor to find the total measure of the interior angles of a quadrilateral.

Materials: Student Activity Book or Hardcover Book pp. 159–160, protractors or Protractors (TRB M24)

 NCTM Standards:
Measurement
Geometry
Reasoning and Proof

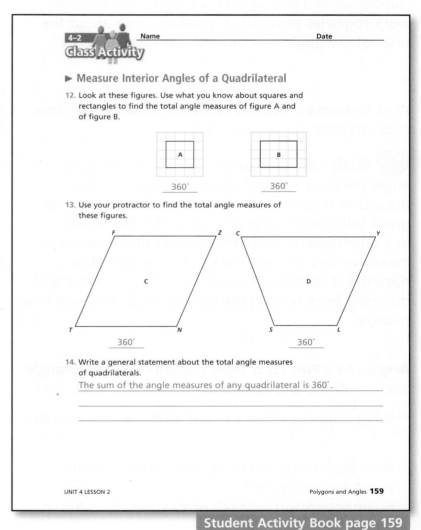

Student Activity Book page 159

Activity continued ▶

Activity 2

▶ Measure Interior Angles of a Quadrilateral WHOLE CLASS

Ask students to look at figures A and B in exercise 12 on Student Book page 159.

● **Without using a protractor, how can you determine the measure of each angle?** The grid shows that each figure is made up of four right angles.

● **What is the total of the measures of the angles of these rectangles?** $4 \times 90° = 360°$

Have students use their protractors to determine the angle measures, and the total of the angle measures, of figures C and D in exercise 13. After they have completed and compared their measures, students work together to create a generalization about the total of the angle measures of any quadrilateral: The total of the angle measures of any quadrilateral is 360°.

Find Unknown Angles Without Measuring Have students look at exercises 15–20.

Math Talk Discuss how to find the missing angle measure without using a protractor. The discussion should lead to the conclusion that when given information about three of the four angles in a quadrilateral, students can add the given angle measures and subtract the total from 360°. Then, have the class discuss how this method is similar and different from finding the missing angle measure in a triangle. Add the given angle measures but subtract for 180° rather than for 360°.

Angles in a Full Turn Have students make a rectangle and cut off the angles as described in exercise 21.

● **What happens when you put all the angles together?** They fit together around a point and leave no gaps.

● **How does this compare to the full angle around a circular protractor?** There are 360° in the quadrilateral, around the protractor, and around the point.

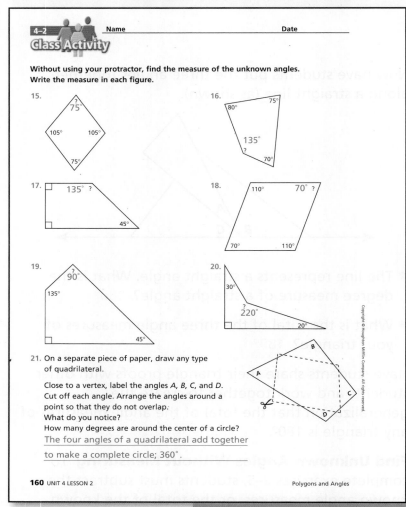

Student Activity Book page 160

✓ Ongoing Assessment

Ask students to draw any quadrilateral and to cut it into two pieces from one corner to the opposite corner.

▶ What two figures did you make?

▶ How does knowing that the total of the angle measures in a triangle is 180° tell you the total angle measures in a quadrilateral?

② Going Further
Differentiated Instruction

Draw Triangles   Activity Card 4-2 ●

Work: In Pairs

Use:
• 2 Rulers
• Protractors (TRB M24)

1. On your own, use a ruler to draw three triangles.

2. Measure and label two angles in each triangle.

3. Exchange triangles with your partner. Calculate the measure of the third angle in each triangle. Then check your calculation by measuring the angle.

4. What do you notice about the sum of the angles of each triangle? The sum equals 180°.

Unit 4, Lesson 2   Copyright © Houghton Mifflin Company

Activity Note Angle measures may not total 180°, depending on the accuracy of the measurements. Reinforce the concept by having students cut out each angle and align them to form a straight angle.

✓ **Math Writing Prompt**

Straight Angles In a right triangle, what is the sum of the measures of the non-right angles? What is another name for this pair of angles?

 **Software Support**

Warm-Up 35.32

Make a Drawing   Activity Card 4-2 ▲

Work: In Pairs

Use:
• Ruler

1. A quadrilateral is described below. Sketch what the figure might look like. Label the angle measures. See possible figure on left.

   • A quadrilateral has exactly one right angle.
   • Two of the other angles are congruent.
   • The fourth angle measures 60°.

2. **Math Talk** How did you decide what measure to use for the congruent angles? Possible answer: Add 90° + 60° and subtract the sum from 360°. Then divide the result by 2.

Unit 4, Lesson 2   Copyright © Houghton Mifflin Company

Activity Note Be sure students understand that congruent angles have equal measures. The 60° angle in the quadrilateral may be opposite or adjacent to the right angle.

✓ **Math Writing Prompt**

Use Logic Explain why a triangle can never have more than one right angle.

 Software Support

Ice Station Exploration: Polar Planes, Level B

Estimate Angles   Activity Card 4-2 ■

Work: In Pairs

Use:
• Protractors (TRB M24)

1. Play a game of estimating angles.

2. On your own, draw a large quadrilateral on a sheet of paper.

3. Exchange papers with your partner. Estimate the measure of each angle in the figure. Record the estimates on the drawing.

4. Exchange papers again and measure each angle. Find the difference between each estimate and the actual measure. Add the four differences. The player with the smaller difference wins.

5. **Math Talk** Discuss the strategies you used to make your estimates.

Unit 4, Lesson 2   Copyright © Houghton Mifflin Company

Activity Note After students explain their strategies for estimating the angles, discuss how benchmarks such as a 45° or 90° angle might be used to make a closer estimate, if no one has suggested this strategy.

✓ **Math Writing Prompt**

Investigate Math Explain how you can calculate the measure of any two angles in a parallelogram if you know the measure of the other two angles.

 DESTINATION Math® **Software Support**

Course III: Module 5: Unit 1: Lines, Angles, and Circles

Polygons and Angles   **373**

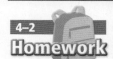

③ Homework and Spiral Review

4–2 **Homework** **Goal:** Additional Practice

✓ Include students' Homework for page 93 as part of their portfolios.

4–2 **Remembering** **Goal:** Spiral Review

This Remembering activity is appropriate anytime after today's lesson.

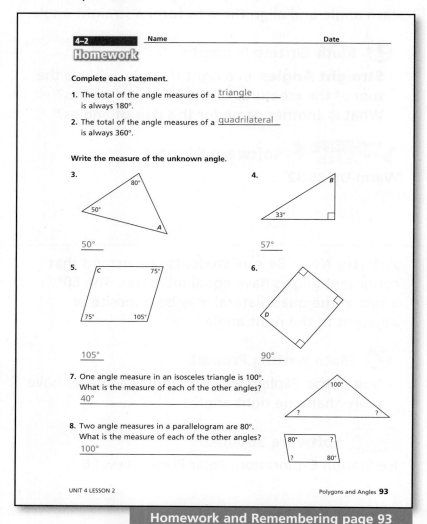

4–2 Name _____ Date _____
Homework

Complete each statement.

1. The total of the angle measures of a <u>triangle</u> is always 180°.

2. The total of the angle measures of a <u>quadrilateral</u> is always 360°.

Write the measure of the unknown angle.

3. [triangle with angles 80°, 50°, A]

   <u>50°</u>

4. [right triangle with angle 33°, B]

   <u>57°</u>

5. [parallelogram C, 75°, 75°, 105°]

   <u>105°</u>

6. [quadrilateral D with right angles]

   <u>90°</u>

7. One angle measure in an isosceles triangle is 100°. What is the measure of each of the other angles?
   <u>40°</u>
   [triangle with 100°, ?, ?]

8. Two angle measures in a parallelogram are 80°. What is the measure of each of the other angles?
   <u>100°</u>
   [parallelogram with 80°, ?, ?, 80°]

UNIT 4 LESSON 2   Polygons and Angles **93**

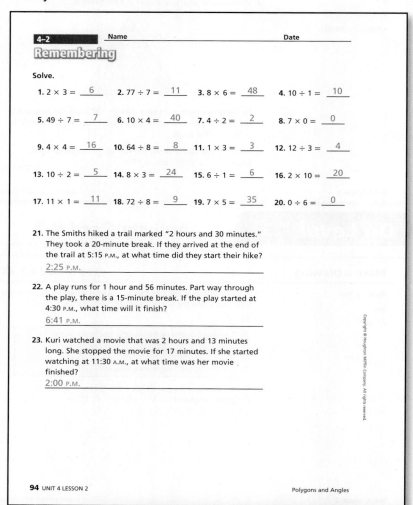

4–2 Name _____ Date _____
Remembering

Solve.

1. 2 × 3 = <u>6</u>   2. 77 ÷ 7 = <u>11</u>   3. 8 × 6 = <u>48</u>   4. 10 ÷ 1 = <u>10</u>

5. 49 ÷ 7 = <u>7</u>   6. 10 × 4 = <u>40</u>   7. 4 ÷ 2 = <u>2</u>   8. 7 × 0 = <u>0</u>

9. 4 × 4 = <u>16</u>   10. 64 ÷ 8 = <u>8</u>   11. 1 × 3 = <u>3</u>   12. 12 ÷ 3 = <u>4</u>

13. 10 ÷ 2 = <u>5</u>   14. 8 × 3 = <u>24</u>   15. 6 ÷ 1 = <u>6</u>   16. 2 × 10 = <u>20</u>

17. 11 × 1 = <u>11</u>   18. 72 ÷ 8 = <u>9</u>   19. 7 × 5 = <u>35</u>   20. 0 ÷ 6 = <u>0</u>

21. The Smiths hiked a trail marked "2 hours and 30 minutes." They took a 20-minute break. If they arrived at the end of the trail at 5:15 P.M., at what time did they start their hike?
   <u>2:25 P.M.</u>

22. A play runs for 1 hour and 56 minutes. Part way through the play, there is a 15-minute break. If the play started at 4:30 P.M., what time will it finish?
   <u>6:41 P.M.</u>

23. Kuri watched a movie that was 2 hours and 13 minutes long. She stopped the movie for 17 minutes. If she started watching at 11:30 A.M., at what time was her movie finished?
   <u>2:00 P.M.</u>

94 UNIT 4 LESSON 2   Polygons and Angles

Homework and Remembering page 93

Homework and Remembering page 94

Home or School Activity

 Art Connection

Mathematics and Art Have students make a design using quadrilaterals and triangles. Encourage students to use figures that fit together to create a visually pleasing design.

Compare and Contrast Polygons

Vocabulary

polygon
congruent
isosceles triangle
equilateral triangle
scalene triangle
acute triangle
obtuse triangle
right triangle
right trapezoid

Lesson Objectives

- Identify congruent polygons.
- Sort and classify polygons.

The Day at a Glance

Today's Goals	Materials

1 **Teaching the Lesson**
  A1: Identify congruent polygons.
  A2: Define, describe, sort, and classify polygons.
 	
2 **Going Further**
  ▶ Differentiated Instruction
 	
3 **Homework and Spiral Review**
	Lesson Activities
	Student Activity Book pp. 161–164
	  or Student Hardcover Book
	  pp. 161–164 and Activity
	  Workbook pp. 69–74
	Homework and Remembering
	  pp. 95–96
	Quick Quiz 1 (Assessment Guide)
	Dot Paper (TRB M20) or MathBoard
	  materials (optional)
	Scissors
	Straightedge
	Centimeter-Grid Paper (TRB M18)
		Going Further
		Activity Cards 4-3
		Centimeter-Dot Paper
		  (TRB M25)
		Tracing paper
		Scissors
		Math Journals

123 Use Math Talk today!

Keeping Skills Sharp

Daily Routines

Homework Review Encourage students to discuss and resolve the problems from their homework.

Who's Right? Lisa says it is possible to draw a triangle that has more than one right angle. Miguel says this is impossible. Who is correct? Explain your answer. Miguel is correct; Possible explanation: 2 right angles have a sum of 180°. A triangle must have three angles and a total sum of 180°. Also, it is impossible to connect two right angles to create a triangle.

English Language Learners

Write *polygon* on the board. Say: **A *polygon* has 3 or more straight sides.** Draw these figures on the board:

- **Beginning** Point and say: **Figure A has 3 straight sides.** Ask: **Is it a *polygon*?** yes Continue with other figures.

- **Intermediate** Point and say: **Figure A has __ straight sides.** 3 **It has __ sides.** straight **It is a __.** polygon Continue with other figures.

- **Advanced** Have students tell about each figure and identify the *polygons*.

Teaching the Lesson

Congruent Polygons

🕐 **20 MINUTES**

Goal: Identify congruent polygons.

Materials: Student Activity Book p. 161 or Hardcover Book p. 161 and Activity Workbook p. 69, Dot Paper (TRB M20) or MathBoard materials

✓ **NCTM Standard:**
Geometry

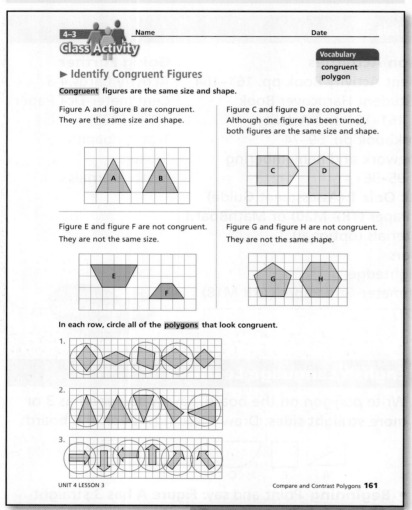

Student Activity Book page 161

▶ Identify Congruent Figures WHOLE CLASS

Introduce the word *polygon*, a figure with many sides. Discuss the examples of congruence and noncongruence at the top of Student Book page 161 (figures A–H). Ask students to give reasons why the pairs of figures do or do not appear to be congruent.

● **How can tracing one of the figures help you?** If the tracing fits exactly over the other figure, then the figures must be the same size and shape, or congruent.

● **How might the grid help you?** If some squares or parts of squares inside each figure don't match up, then the figures can't be congruent.

● **How did you know figures E and F weren't congruent?** Figure F looks smaller. It is smaller because there are fewer squares inside it.

● **How did you know figures G and H weren't congruent?** Figure H has more sides, so a tracing of it won't fit over figure G.

Have students complete exercises 1–3. If they have difficulty, they can count squares or use a tracing.

Teaching Note

Mathematical Notation You may wish to introduce the symbols that are used to represent congruency. Using these symbols (tick marks) helps students keep track of equal measures and determine congruency.

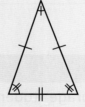 

✓ Ongoing Assessment

Have students draw two congruent triangles on dot paper or their MathBoard. Then ask them to draw a third triangle that is not congruent to the other triangles.

Classify Polygons

 40 MINUTES

Goal: Define, describe, sort, and classify polygons.

Materials: Student Activity Book pp. 162–162B or Hardcover Book p. 162 and Activity Workbook pp. 70–72, scissors

 NCTM Standard:
Geometry

▶ Identify Polygons WHOLE CLASS

Have students cut along the vertical and horizontal dotted lines. Students should not cut out the actual figures within each square.

Explain to students that they should compare and contrast the characteristics of the polygons as you discuss each one as a class. If students need help, the student glossary includes all of the polygons.

Remind students of the names of different figures and have them pick out the correct examples of each.

- Isosceles triangles have at least two congruent sides. Which figures are isosceles triangles? figures A, N, Q, W

- Equilateral triangles have all sides congruent. Which triangle is equilateral? figure W

- Scalene triangles have no congruent sides. Which figures are scalene triangles? figures F, S, V, L

- Which quadrilaterals are parallelograms? figures B, C, D, E, G, I, R

- Which parallelograms are also rhombuses? figures B, E, R

- Which quadrilaterals are rectangles? figures B, D, I, R

- Which rectangles are also squares? figures B, R

- Regular polygons have all sides and all angles congruent. Which polygons are regular? figures B, J, O, R, T, W

- Which polygons are pentagons? figures J, M

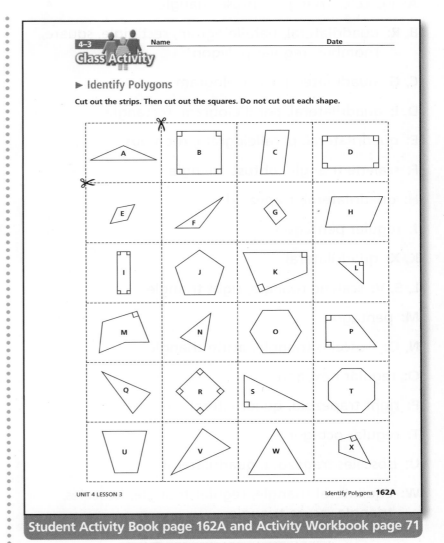

▶ Identify Polygons

Cut out the strips. Then cut out the squares. Do not cut out each shape.

UNIT 4 LESSON 3   Identify Polygons **162A**

Student Activity Book page 162A and Activity Workbook page 71

- Which is a hexagon? figure O an octagon? figure T

- Which figures are trapezoids? figures H, P, U

- Isosceles figures have at least two equal sides. Which figure is an isosceles trapezoid? figure U

- Acute triangles have all angles less than 90°. Which triangles are acute? figures N, Q, W

- Obtuse triangles have one angle greater than 90°. Which triangles are obtuse? figures F, A

- Right triangles have one angle equal to 90°. Which triangles are right triangles? figure L, S, V

- Right trapezoids have one angle equal to 90°. Which figure is a right trapezoid? figure P

Activity continued ▶

Compare and Contrast Polygons   **377**

Activity 2

Have students use what they've learned to label the backs of the figures.

A: isosceles triangle, obtuse triangle

B, R: quadrilateral, parallelogram, rectangle, square, rhombus, regular polygon

C, G: quadrilateral, parallelogram

D, I: quadrilateral, parallelogram, rectangle

E: quadrilateral, parallelogram, rhombus

F: scalene triangle, obtuse triangle

H: quadrilateral, trapezoid

J: regular pentagon

K, X: quadrilateral

L, S, V: scalene triangle, right triangle

M: pentagon

N, Q: isosceles triangle, acute triangle

O: regular hexagon

P: right trapezoid, quadrilateral

T: regular octagon

U: isosceles trapezoid, quadrilateral

W: equilateral triangle, regular triangle, isosceles triangle, acute triangle

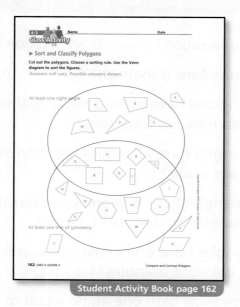

Student Activity Book page 162

▶ Sort and Classify Polygons WHOLE CLASS

Invite students to classify the polygons they have named by sorting them into different groups. As they work, encourage the students to use math vocabulary to describe the characteristics of the different groups. They may use all or only some of the polygons.

 **Math Talk in Action**

How did you sort the polygons?

Robbie: I sorted "quadrilaterals" and "not quadrilaterals." Figures B, C, D, E, G, H, I, K, P, R, U, and X are quadrilaterals. Figures A, F, J, L, M, N, O, Q, S, T, V, and W are not quadrilaterals.

Teresa: I sorted "right triangles" and "nonright triangles." Figures L, S, and V are right triangles. Figures A, F, N, Q, and W are nonright triangles.

How can you use the Venn Diagram to sort the polygons by their sides?

Taci: I sorted "perpendicular sides" and "parallel sides." Figures B, D, I, L, P, R, S, and V have perpendicular sides. Figures B, C, D, E, G, H, I, O, P, R, T, and U have parallel sides.

Darnell: Some polygons have both types of sides. Figures B, D, I, P, and R have both perpendicular and parallel sides.

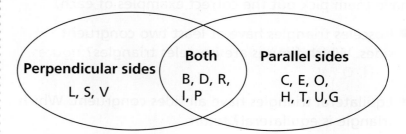

Make and Test Conjectures As a class brainstorm some rules that can be used to verify the classification of a polygon. The rules would include characteristics such as number of sides, types of angles, 1 or 2 pairs of opposite sides parallel, all sides equal in length.

Example: Rhombus — 4 equal sides, 2 sets of opposite sides parallel, opposite angles equal, no right angles. If a student states that a figure is a rhombus, he/she can test the conjecture using the rule. If the figure does not meet all of the requirements, it is not a rhombus.

Draw Angles and Polygons

 20 MINUTES

Goal: Sketch angles and polygons from given clues about side lengths and angle measures.

Materials: Student Activity Book pp. 163–164 or Hardcover Book pp. 163–164 and Activity Workbook pp. 73–74, straightedge (1 per student), Centimeter-Grid Paper (TRB M18), Dot Paper (TRB M20)

 NCTM Standards:
Geometry
Reasoning and Proof
Number and Operations

▶ Draw a Figure Using Clues WHOLE CLASS

On centimeter-grid paper, demonstrate how to create 45°, 90°, and 135° angles without using a protractor. Repeat using dot paper.

Tell students that you will write a description of a polygon on the board. Then write:

This polygon has at least one right angle and 180° as the total of its angle measures.

Discuss Have a class discussion on how to use the clues in the description to find the polygon that matches it. Be sure the discussion includes the following.

● The sum of the angles of a triangle 180°.

● A right triangle has one right angle.

Have a volunteer draw a right triangle on the board. Ask if there is any other figure that will fulfill the requirements of this description. no

Have students work individually to complete exercise 1. Then ask volunteers to share their figure.

Use **Solve and Discuss** to complete exercises 2–6.

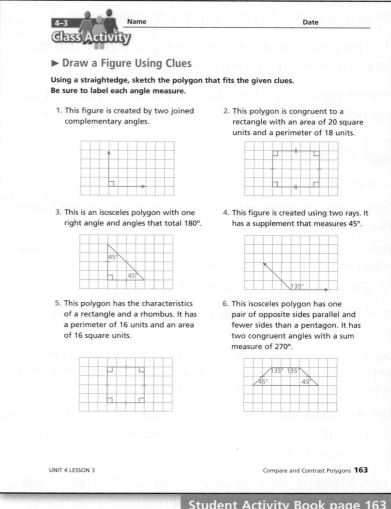

 Math Talk in Action

How did the clues in exercise 6 help you find the polygon and the measures of its angles?

Roberto: An isosceles triangle has fewer sides than a pentagon, but it does not have one pair of opposite sides parallel.

Karol: An isosceles trapezoid has 4 sides and 4 < 5.

Frank: An isosceles trapezoid has only one pair of opposite sides parallel.

Paula: The two obtuse angles have the total sum of 270° or a measure of 135° each.

Ronald: The total of the angle measures in a quadrilateral is 360°. So, this leaves 90° for the two congruent acute angles making each 45°.

Activity continued ▶

① Teaching the Lesson (continued)

Activity 3

▶ Draw Multiple Figures Using Clues

WHOLE CLASS

Write the following description on the board:

This polygon has at least three right angles and the total measure of its angles is 360°.

Discuss how to use the clues in the description to find the polygon or polygons that match it.

 Math Talk in Action

How did you find the polygons that best fit the clues?

Dora: A quadrilateral has a total measure of 360°, so the figure must be a quadrilateral.

Norman: Three right angles total 270°. 360° – 270° = 90°, so the fourth angle must be a right angle also.

Dora: Rectangles and squares have 4 right angles.

Norman: These are parallelograms. So is parallelogram an answer, too?

Dora: No, not all parallelograms had 4 right angles. Rectangles and squares are special parallelograms with 4 right angles, so the polygon could be a rectangle or a square.

Tell students that there will be more than one polygon that fits the clues in each of the exercises on Student Book page 164.

Have **Student Pairs** complete exercise 7. Then, allow pairs to share their figures and reasoning with the class.

Differentiated Instruction

Advanced Learners Have **Student Pairs** work individually to write on paper a set of clues that describe a figure. On the back of the paper, they draw a figure that meets *all* of the requirements of the clues. Students exchange papers and draw figures using the given clues. Then students verify that both figures meet all the requirements. Students then decide if the clues describe one figure only or if multiple figures satisfy the requirements of the clues. If multiple figures are possible, have students refine or add additional clues so that only one figure is possible.

4–3 | Name _____ Date _____
Class Activity

▶ Draw Multiple Figures Using Clues

Using a straightedge, sketch the polygons that fit the given clues.
Possible answers are given.

7. A polygon with no pairs of opposite sides parallel, at most 2 acute angles, and a total angle measure of < 200°. obtuse or right triangle

8. A polygon with less than 5 sides and all sides with equal lengths. equilateral triangle, square, or rhombus

9. A polygon with at most 5 sides, at least one pair of opposite sides parallel, and at least 2 right angles. square, rectangle, pentagon

10. A polygon with at most 2 pairs of opposite sides parallel and at most 2 acute angles. parallelogram, rhombus, trapezoid

11. This quadrilateral has 2 pairs of opposite sides parallel and at least one pair of congruent opposite angles that have a total angle measure of 180°. square or rectangle

12. A polygon with at most 5 sides, at least 1 acute and 1 obtuse angle, at least one pair of opposite sides congruent and one pair of opposite sides parallel. isosceles trapezoid, rhombus, parallelogram, pentagon

164 UNIT 4 LESSON 3   Compare and Contrast Polygons

Student Activity Book page 164

Use **Solve and Discuss** for exercises 8–12.

 Math Talk in Action

How did you use the clues in exercise 9 to find the polygons?

Lian: Triangles, quadrilaterals and pentagons are all polygons with at most 5 sides.

Enrico: Triangles do not have any pairs of opposite sides parallel.

Derek: Parallelograms, rhombi, squares, and rectangles are quadrilaterals with at least one pair of opposite sides parallel.

Charlie: Some pentagons have one pair of opposite sides parallel.

Carla: Parallelograms and rhombi do not have right angles. So, the answer must be squares, rectangles, and pentagons.

Antonio: To draw the pentagon, the base must form a right angle with each side, but the two remaining line segments at the top can connect and point in or out.

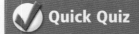 **Quick Quiz**

See Assessment Guide for Unit 4 Quick Quiz 1.

②Going Further

● Intervention — Activity Card 4-3

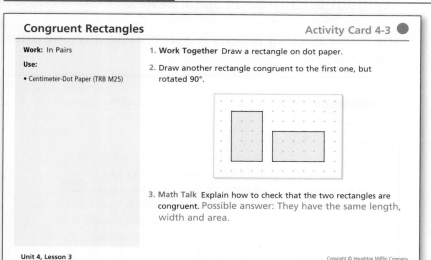

Congruent Rectangles — Activity Card 4-3 ●

Work: In Pairs

Use:
• Centimeter-Dot Paper (TRB M25)

1. **Work Together** Draw a rectangle on dot paper.

2. Draw another rectangle congruent to the first one, but rotated 90°.

3. **Math Talk** Explain how to check that the two rectangles are congruent. Possible answer: They have the same length, width and area.

Unit 4, Lesson 3 — Copyright © Houghton Mifflin Company

Activity Note Another way to demonstrate congruence is to trace the first figure and then place the tracing over the second figure, covering it completely and exactly.

 Math Writing Prompt

Squares Are all squares congruent to each other? Explain your answer.

 **Software Support**

Warm-Up 37.16

▲ On Level — Activity Card 4-3

Draw a 3-4-5 Right Triangle — Activity Card 4-3 ▲

Work: In Pairs

Use:
• Centimeter-Dot Paper (TRB M25)

1. Draw the triangle described below. Use dot paper to help you make your drawing accurate.

   • The triangle has two sides that measure 3 cm and 4 cm.
   • The two sides form a right angle.

2. Measure the third side. The third side is 5 cm.

3. **Math Talk** Multiply the length of the two shorter sides of your triangle by 2. Draw the new triangle. What do you notice about the measure of the third side of the new triangle? Possible answer: It equals 10, which is 5 × 2.

Unit 4, Lesson 3 — Copyright © Houghton Mifflin Company

Activity Note Using dot paper helps students make more accurate measurements. This activity presents one of the most common Pythagorean triples that students will study in more advanced mathematics.

 Math Writing Prompt

Impossible Triangles Can one angle of a right triangle be obtuse? Can an obtuse triangle have two congruent angles? Explain your answers.

 Software Support

Ice Station Exploration: Polar Planes, Level E

■ Challenge — Activity Card 4-3

Tiling — Activity Card 4-3 ■

Work: By Yourself

Use:
• Tracing paper
• Scissors

1. Any parallelogram can be used to tile a floor without overlapping or leaving any gaps.

2. Can you do the same with either one of the figures below? Predict which figure can be used to tile a floor.

   Regular pentagon   **Regular hexagon**

3. **Test your prediction.** Only the hexagon can be used to tile a floor with no overlaps or gaps.

Unit 4, Lesson 3 — Copyright © Houghton Mifflin Company

Activity Note Any regular polygon with an interior angle measure that divides evenly into 360° can be used. The hexagon interior angle measures 120°. The pentagon interior angle measures 108°. A square or equilateral triangle can also be used.

 Math Writing Prompt

Investigate Math What is another name for a regular triangle? For a regular quadrilateral?

 DESTINATION Math· **Software Support**

Course III: Module 5: Unit 2: Symmetry and Transformations

③ Homework and Spiral Review

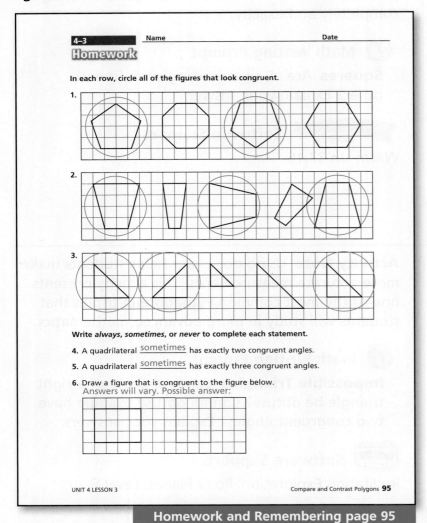

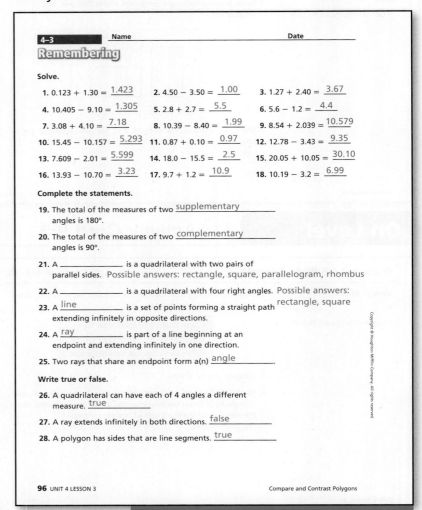

4-3 Homework — Goal: Additional Practice

For Homework, students identify and draw congruent figures.

Homework and Remembering page 95

4-3 Remembering — Goal: Spiral Review

This Remembering activity is appropriate anytime after today's lesson.

Homework and Remembering page 96

Homework page 95 (reproduced)

4-3 Homework Name _____ Date _____

In each row, circle all of the figures that look congruent.

1.

2.

3.

Write always, sometimes, or never to complete each statement.

4. A quadrilateral _sometimes_ has exactly two congruent angles.

5. A quadrilateral _sometimes_ has exactly three congruent angles.

6. Draw a figure that is congruent to the figure below.
   Answers will vary. Possible answer:

UNIT 4 LESSON 3   Compare and Contrast Polygons **95**

Remembering page 96 (reproduced)

4-3 Remembering Name _____ Date _____

Solve.

1. 0.123 + 1.30 = _1.423_
2. 4.50 − 3.50 = _1.00_
3. 1.27 + 2.40 = _3.67_
4. 10.405 − 9.10 = _1.305_
5. 2.8 + 2.7 = _5.5_
6. 5.6 − 1.2 = _4.4_
7. 3.08 + 4.10 = _7.18_
8. 10.39 − 8.40 = _1.99_
9. 8.54 + 2.039 = _10.579_
10. 15.45 − 10.157 = _5.293_
11. 0.87 + 0.10 = _0.97_
12. 12.78 − 3.43 = _9.35_
13. 7.609 − 2.01 = _5.599_
14. 18.0 − 15.5 = _2.5_
15. 20.05 + 10.05 = _30.10_
16. 13.93 − 10.70 = _3.23_
17. 9.7 + 1.2 = _10.9_
18. 10.19 − 3.2 = _6.99_

Complete the statements.

19. The total of the measures of two _supplementary_ angles is 180°.

20. The total of the measures of two _complementary_ angles is 90°.

21. A _____ is a quadrilateral with two pairs of parallel sides. Possible answers: rectangle, square, parallelogram, rhombus

22. A _____ is a quadrilateral with four right angles. Possible answers: rectangle, square

23. A _line_ is a set of points forming a straight path extending infinitely in opposite directions.

24. A _ray_ is part of a line beginning at an endpoint and extending infinitely in one direction.

25. Two rays that share an endpoint form a(n) _angle_.

Write true or false.

26. A quadrilateral can have each of 4 angles a different measure. _true_

27. A ray extends infinitely in both directions. _false_

28. A polygon has sides that are line segments. _true_

96 UNIT 4 LESSON 3   Compare and Contrast Polygons

Home or School Activity

Language Arts Connection

Names for Polygons

Polygons are named with prefixes that tell the number of sides they have. *Tri* means "three," *quad* means "four," *penta* means "five," *hexa* means "six," and *octa* means "eight."

A decameter is ten meters. What name would you give a ten-sided polygon? If *dodeca* means "twelve," what is the name of a twelve-sided polygon? How many sides do you think a heptagon or a nonagon have?

Circles and Angles

Lesson Objectives

- Identify angles of a circle.
- Identify turns about the center of a circle.
- Determine the position of an object after a turn or a series of turns.

Vocabulary

straight angle
reflex angle
circle
turn

The Day at a Glance

Today's Goals	Materials
1 **Teaching the Lesson** A1: Discuss and draw various angles of a circle. A2: Model turns of a circle. **2** **Going Further** ▶ Differentiated Instruction **3** **Homework and Spiral Review**	**Lesson Activities** Student Activity Book pp. 165–168 or Student Hardcover Book pp. 165–168 and Activity Workbook pp. 75–76 Homework and Remembering pp. 97–98 Rulers Circles (TRB M86) (optional) Protractors Grid paper or Dot Paper (TRB M20) (optional) **Going Further** Activity Cards 4-4 Ruler Analog clock Tracing paper Protractor Math Journals

123 *Use* **Math Talk** *today!*

Keeping Skills Sharp

Daily Routines	English Language Learners
Homework Review Ask students to place their homework at the corner of their desks. As you circulate, check whether any problem caused difficulty for many students. **Logic** Marita wrote a 3-digit number. The digit in the tenths place is 5 less than the digit in the ones place. The digit in the hundredths place is the sum of the digits in the tenths and the ones places. What are the possible numbers? 7.29, 6.17, or 5.05; If the digit in the ones place is > 7 or < 5, the conditions cannot be met.	Draw a circle on the board. Draw, identify, and label the center, *radius*, and *diameter*. • **Beginning** Point and say: **A *radius* connects the center to a point on the circle.** Have students trace the circle and radius in the air with a finger and repeat. Continue with *diameter*. • **Intermediate** Ask: **How may points on the circle does the *radius* touch?** 1 **The *diameter*?** 2 • **Advanced** Have students tell about the radius and the diameter.

Teaching the Lesson

Interior Angles of a Circle

 30 MINUTES

Goal: Discuss and draw various angles of a circle.

Materials: Student Activity Book pp. 165–166 or Hardcover Book pp. 165–166 and Activity Workbook p. 75, rulers (1 per student), Circles (TRB M86) (optional), protractors or Protractors (TRB M24) (1 per student), grid paper or Dot Paper (TRB M20) (optional)

✓ **NCTM Standards:**
Geometry
Measurement

▶ Review Parts of a Circle WHOLE CLASS

Ask for Ideas Invite a student to come to the board and draw a circle while other students draw a circle at their desk. Then write the words *diameter* and *radius* close to the circle.

As a class, define the term *diameter*: A line segment from one side of the circle to the other through the center. Invite a volunteer to draw and label a diameter on the circle while other students draw and label a diameter on their circles. As a class, define *radius*: A line segment that connects the center of the circle to any point on the circle. Invite a different volunteer to draw and label a radius on the circle while others draw and label a radius on their circles.

Discuss the relationship between a diameter and a radius of any circle. The discussion should lead students to understand the following relationships.

$$\text{diameter} = \text{radius} \times 2$$

$$\text{radius} = \text{diameter} \div 2 \text{ or } \frac{\text{diameter}}{2}$$

Give students this definition of a circle: All points equidistant from a given point form a circle. Point this out on a circle on the board and ask what it tells us about all the diameters and all the radii in the same circle. all diameters are equal; all radii are equal Students should also understand that every circle has an infinite number of diameters and radii.

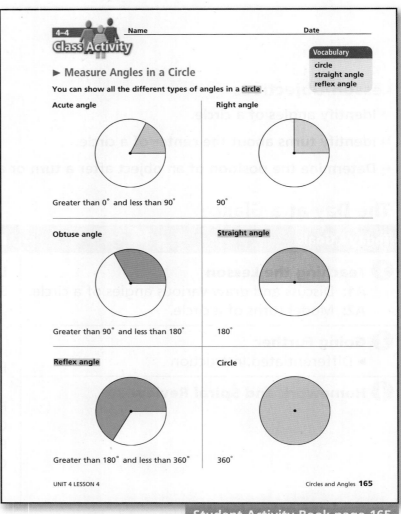

Student Activity Book page 165

▶ Measure Angles in a Circle WHOLE CLASS

Students should be familiar with acute, right, obtuse, and straight angles. Invite students to share ideas about how to remember the names of various angles.

- An acute angle has a measure that is greater than 0° and less than 90°.

- A right angle has a measure of exactly 90°.

- An obtuse angle has a measure that is greater than 90° and less than 180°.

- A straight angle has a measure of exactly 180°.

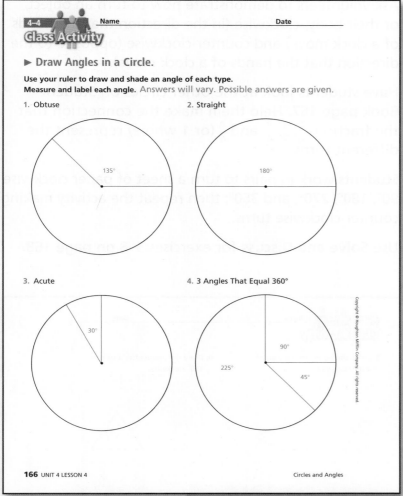

Student Activity Book page 166

Math Talk Students do not need to have mastery of a reflex angle, but a discussion of this angle helps students recognize that the total angle measure of a circle is 360°. Be sure the following points are discussed.

● A reflex angle has a measure that is greater than 180° and less than 360°.

● A circle has a measure of 360°.

As a class, discuss the number of right angles that can be included in a circle and why. 4; 4 × 90 = 360 Then, discuss the number of straight angles that can be included in a circle and how this relates to the number of right angles. 2; 2 × 180 = 360

▶ Draw Angles in a Circle   INDIVIDUALS

To practice drawing angles, have students use a protractor to draw angles with measures of 25°, 75°, 155°, and 180°. Students can draw on a separate piece of paper or in their Math Journals. Ask students to complete exercises 1–3, using a ruler and a protractor.

● Why will your new straight angles have the same measure as the example? all straight angles = 180°

● Label a diameter and a radius on the straight angle.

For exercise 4, be certain that students understand that they will draw three angles whose sum is 360°. Students can add the measures to confirm the sum. Extend the concept by having students use Circles (TRB M86) to draw and measure 4 or 5 angles whose sum is 360°.

▶ Find Missing Angles   INDIVIDUALS

Ask the students to measure (using a protractor) and label their acute and obtuse angles. They may have to extend the arms of the angles to measure them.

● The unshaded angle in your obtuse and acute angle figures is a reflex angle. How can you find the size of the reflex angle in each exercise without measuring? The whole circle is 360°, so subtract the measure of the shaded angle from 360.

Explementary Angles Since students have learned about complementary and supplementary angles, you may choose to introduce the idea that two angles are explementary (or conjugate) angles if their sum is 360°; either angle is the explement of the other.

Challenge students to make a list of different ways that conjugate angles can be combined to make a circle. For example: two straight angles, one acute angle and one reflex angle, one right angle and one reflex angle, or one obtuse angle and one reflex angle.

✓ Ongoing Assessment

Have students draw an acute angle on grid paper or dot paper. Ask them to measure their acute angle and label the measure of the reflex angle without actually measuring it. Have them repeat the procedure beginning with an obtuse angle.

Activity 2

Turns of a Circle

 30 MINUTES

Goal: Model turns of a circle.

Materials: Student Activity Book pp. 167–168 or Hardcover Book pp. 167–168 and Activity Workbook p. 76

 NCTM Standard:
Geometry

▶ **Turns and Degrees** WHOLE CLASS

Have students look at the circle at the top of Student Book page 167 and name the direction of movement that is represented by the arrows. counter-clockwise.

Ask volunteers to demonstrate how to turn an object, or their body, clockwise (in the direction that the hands of a clock move) and counter-clockwise (opposite to the direction that the hands of a clock move).

Have students look at the other circles on Student Book page 167. Help them make the connection that the fractions $\frac{1}{4}$, $\frac{1}{2}$, $\frac{3}{4}$, and $\frac{4}{4}$ (or 1 whole) represent the different turns.

Students work in pairs to turn a sheet of paper clockwise 90°, 180°, 270°, and 360°; then repeat the activity making counter-clockwise turns.

Use **Solve and Discuss** for exercises 5–8 on page 168.

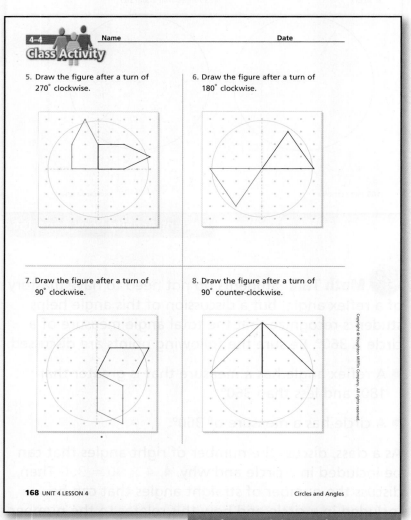

Student Activity Book page 167

Student Activity Book page 168

② Going Further

● Intervention   Activity Card 4-4

Use a Right Angle   Activity Card 4-4 ●

Work: In Pairs

Use:

• Ruler

1. **Work Together** Draw any triangle or quadrilateral.

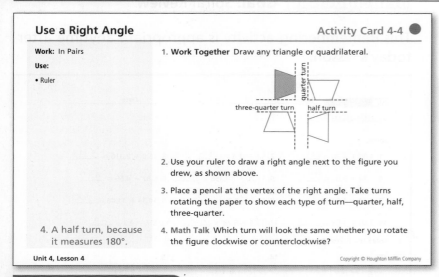

2. Use your ruler to draw a right angle next to the figure you drew, as shown above.

3. Place a pencil at the vertex of the right angle. Take turns rotating the paper to show each type of turn—quarter, half, three-quarter.

4. A half turn, because it measures 180°.

4. **Math Talk** Which turn will look the same whether you rotate the figure clockwise or counterclockwise?

Unit 4, Lesson 4   Copyright © Houghton Mifflin Company

Activity Note Suggest that students use the square corner of a piece of paper to help them draw the right angle accurately.

✐ Math Writing Prompt

Circle Angles If one angle drawn from the center of a circle measures 130°, what is the measure of the other angle that is formed? Explain.

Soar to Success Math ★ Software Support

Warm-Up 37.20

▲ On Level   Activity Card 4-4

Angles on a Clock   Activity Card 4-4 ▲

Work: In Pairs

Use:

• Analog clock

1. Possible answers:
Right angle: 3 o'clock
Obtuse angle:
4 o'clock Acute angle:
2 o'clock Straight
angle: 6 o'clock Reflex
angle: 7 o'clock

1. Use a clock to help you identify angles. Name a time when the hands form each of the following angles:

- a right angle
- an obtuse angle
- an acute angle
- a straight angle
- a reflex angle

2. **Math Talk** Does the clock above show more than one type of angle? Explain. Yes, the hands of the clock form both an obtuse and a reflex angle.

Unit 4, Lesson 4   Copyright © Houghton Mifflin Company

Activity Note Some students may name times such as 3:45 or 9:15 to show a straight angle. Review how the hour hand moves from one hour to the next.

✐ Math Writing Prompt

Explain Your Thinking Why does a 90° turn counterclockwise have the same effect as a 270° turn clockwise? Name another pair of turns that have the same effect.

HARCOURT MegaMath Grades K-6 Software Support

Ice Station Exploration: Polar Planes, Level B

■ Challenge   Activity Card 4-4

Measure the Time   Activity Card 4-4 ■

Work: By Yourself

Use:

• Tracing paper

• Protractor (TRB M24)

1. Predict the angle measure in degrees of clock hands that show the following times:

- 1:00
- 5:00
- 7:00
- 11:00

3. The clock shows two angles for each time, the sum of which is always 360°. Estimation strategies should include using benchmarks such as 45°, 90°, and 180°.

2. Make four tracings of the clock and show each time. Measure each angle formed by the hands of the clock. Record your results. 30° or 330°, 150° or 210°, 210° or 150°, 330° or 30°

3. **Explain** How many angles does the clock show for each time? What strategies did you use to make your estimates?

Unit 4, Lesson 4   Copyright © Houghton Mifflin Company

Activity Note Angle measures may vary depending on where students place tick marks for each number on the face of the clock. More importantly, the sum of both measures must always equal 360°.

✐ Math Writing Prompt

Turn Letters Which upper-case letters look the same after a reflection?

✦ DESTINATION Math® Software Support

Course III: Module 5: Unit 1: Lines, Angles, and Circles

③ Homework and Spiral Review

4–4
Homework **Goal:** Additional Practice

✓ Include students' Homework for page 97 as part of their portfolios.

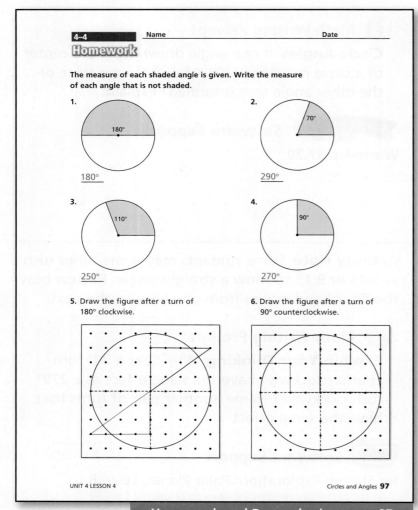

4–4
Remembering **Goal:** Spiral Review

This Remembering activity is appropriate anytime after today's lesson.

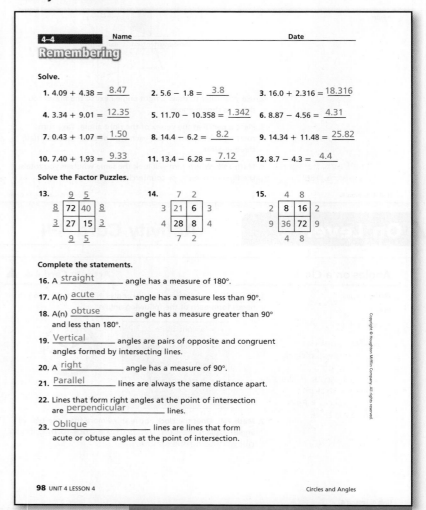

Home or School Activity

Science Connection

Rotations in Our World Earth rotates a full 360° every 24 hours. Ask students to describe other examples of rotations in astronomy or other examples of rotations in general science.

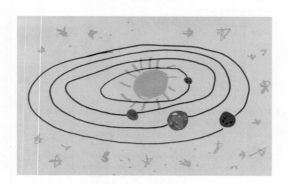

Symmetry

Vocabulary

line symmetry
line of symmetry
rotational symmetry
quarter turn
half turn

Lesson Objectives

● Recognize line symmetry and rotational symmetry.

● Determine the position of an object after a turn or a series of turns.

The Day at a Glance

Today's Goals	Materials	
① Teaching the Lesson **A1:** Review line symmetry and draw lines of symmetry on various figures. **A2:** Discover rotational symmetry in a variety of figures.	**Lesson Activities** Student Activity Book pp. 169–172 or Hardcover Book pp. 169–172 and Activity Workbook pp. 77–78 Homework and Remembering pp. 99–100 Rectangular paper, unlined Scissors	**Going Further** Activity Cards 4-5 Centimeter-Dot Paper (TRB M25) Math Journals
② Going Further ▶ Differentiated Instruction		
③ Homework and Spiral Review		

123 Use **Math Talk** today!

Keeping Skills Sharp

Daily Routines	English Language Learners
Homework Review Work with students needing extra help with specific homework problems. **Making Change** Deirdre bought one pencil for 54¢, one book for $4.35, and one book on sale for 65¢ off of $4. She paid with one $10 bill and six coins and received two $1 bills and one coin as change. If she did not receive a half-dollar coin, what coins did she use to pay? Explain. 1 quarter, 1 nickel, and 4 pennies; She spent $8.24. To receive $2 and 1 dime, she paid using $10.34. You can make 34¢ using 6 coins.	On the board, write: A *line of symmetry* divides a figure into 2 parts that match exactly. Draw a simple figure with a dotted line of symmetry on it. • **Beginning** Ask: **Do the two parts of the figure match exactly?** yes **Is the line a *line of symmetry*?** yes • **Intermediate** Say: **The two parts of the figure match exactly. The dotted line is __.** a line of symmetry • **Advanced** Draw other simple shapes and have students take turns drawing a line of symmetry on them. For each correct line students should say: This is a *line of symmetry*.

Teaching the Lesson

Line Symmetry

 20 MINUTES

Goal: Review line symmetry and draw lines of symmetry on various figures.

Materials: Student Activity Book p. 169 or Hardcover Book p. 169 and Activity Workbook p. 77, rectangular sheet of unlined paper (1 per student)

✓ **NCTM Standard:**
Geometry

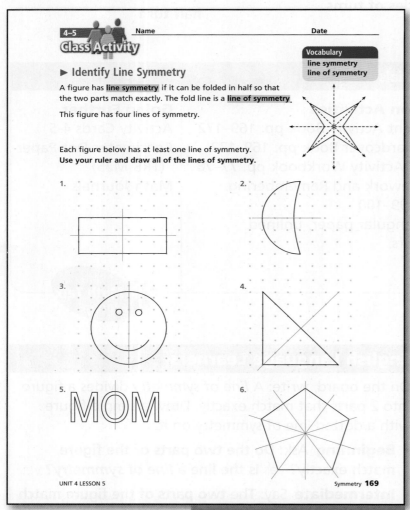

Student Activity Book page 169

▶ Identify Line Symmetry [WHOLE CLASS]

Some students may already know about line symmetry and lines of symmetry. Invite them to be student leaders as the class reviews these concepts.

Write on the board the terms *line symmetry* and *line of symmetry*.

Have students discuss what they already know about symmetry. Lines of symmetry have exact mirror images on each side.

Discuss the figure at the top of Student Book page 169. Give each student a rectangular sheet of unlined paper. Invite students to fold the paper in different ways.

● How many lines of symmetry does the paper rectangle have? two

Ask students to draw the lines of symmetry on the rectangle in exercise 1. Next, focus on the figures in exercises 2 and 3. Discuss the idea that figures may have many, few, or no lines of symmetry.

● How can the dot grid help you discover a line of symmetry? The dots match up on either side of the line.

Talk about exercise 4.

● How is the figure in exercise 4 different from the others? There is no line of symmetry either straight up and down the figure, or straight across it.

● Does it have any lines of symmetry? There is a line of symmetry that goes from the bottom left corner to the middle of the opposite side.

Define Line Symmetry Students should draw at least two different figures with line symmetry. They should draw the line(s) of symmetry for each figure. Invite them to define the terms *line symmetry* and *line of symmetry* in their own words.

Rotational Symmetry

 40 MINUTES

Goal: Discover rotational symmetry in two-dimensional figures.

Materials: unlined sheet of paper, scissors, Student Activity Book pp. 170–172 or Hardcover Book pp. 170–172 and Activity Workbook p. 78

 NCTM Standard:
Geometry

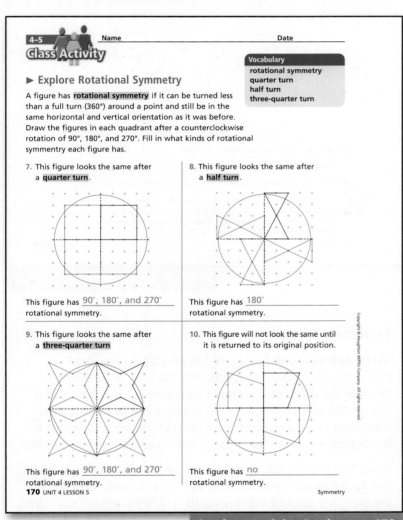

Student Activity Book page 170

Differentiated Instruction

Special Needs Students who have difficulty visualizing a rotation can trace and cut out each figure, and then rotate the figures about a fixed point at the center.

► Explore Rotational Symmetry

WHOLE CLASS

An exploration of rotational symmetry enables students to consolidate their understanding of angles, turns, and symmetry. Discuss the four turns shown on Student Book page 170 and help students make the connection that a fraction having a denominator of four ($\frac{1}{4}$, $\frac{2}{4}$ or $\frac{1}{2}$, $\frac{3}{4}$, and $\frac{4}{4}$ or 1) can be used to represent the turns.

A figure has rotational symmetry if it can be turned less than a full turn (360°) around a point and still look the same as it did before the turn.

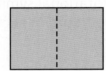

Invite students to fold a sheet of paper in half and cut it along the fold line.

On one sheet of paper, have students draw a figure that they think has 90° (quarter turn) rotational symmetry. Students can turn their drawings to verify their predictions. Next, on the other sheet of paper, invite them to draw a figure that they think has 180° (half turn) rotational symmetry. Again, have them verify their predictions. Encourage volunteers to share their drawings and predictions with their classmates.

Math Talk After discussing all of the examples of turns on Student Book page 170, have students look again at the first figure.

● What generalization can you make about a figure that has 90° rotational symmetry? Any figure having 90° rotational symmetry also has 180° and 270° rotational symmetry.

Teaching Note

Three-Dimensional Figures Rotational symmetry for 3-dimensional figures is covered in Unit 12 Lesson 4.

Activity continued ▶

Activity 2 OPTIONAL

Use **Solve and Discuss** for exercises 11–16.

● Does the triangle in exercise 11 have 90°, 180°, or 270° symmetry? No. It doesn't look exactly the same after those turns.

● Does it have another kind of rotational symmetry? Yes. It looks the same after a one-third turn.

Some students may discover what that means in terms of the rotation angle. (120°)

Have students complete exercises 17–19. Discuss exercise 17.

● Can a figure have line symmetry but not rotational symmetry? Yes. The figure in exercise 14 has only line symmetry.

● Can a figure have rotational symmetry but not line symmetry? Yes. The figure in exercise 15 has only rotational symmetry.

 Ongoing Assessment

Have students explain how to tell whether a figure has rotational symmetry. Then ask them to describe a design or logo that has rotational symmetry.

 Alternate Approach

Turn About the Center You can describe a figure with rotational symmetry in two ways: either by its rotation angle or by its degree of rotational symmetry. The regular pentagon fits on itself five times in one full turn. Its degree of rotational symmetry is 5. The number of times a figure fits on itself after one full turn is its degree of rotational symmetry.

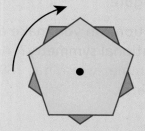

Ask students: What is the degree of rotational symmetry of each figure in exercises 7–12?

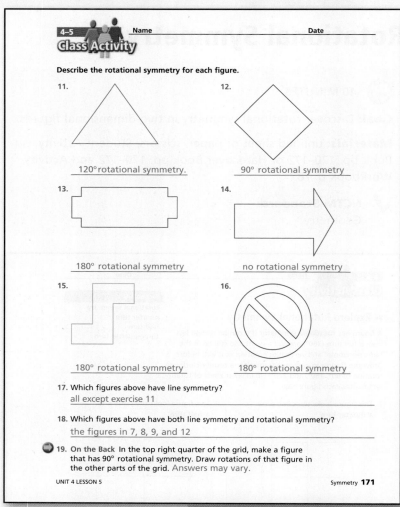

Student Activity Book page 171

Teaching Note

Math Background No figure has only 270° rotational symmetry. To help students understand why, invite them to think about the first occurrence of symmetry in a figure that has rotational symmetry. For example, a figure that has 180° rotational symmetry needs another 180° degrees to return to its original position. The total of the turns (180° + 180°) is 360°.

If the first occurrence of rotational symmetry in a figure is 270°, the figure would need another 270° to return to its original position. The total of the turns (270° + 270°) is greater than 360°.

You can generalize this fact as follows: The first time a figure has rotational symmetry can never be greater than 180° because no number greater than 180 can be a factor of 360, the degree measure of a circle. The greatest factor of any number is always less than or equal to that number divided by 2.

Intervention — Activity Card 4-5

Symmetry–The Other Half
Activity Card 4-5 ●

Work: In Pairs
Use:
• Centimeter-Dot Paper (TRB M25)

1. On your own, draw half a shape on dot paper. Then exchange papers with your partner.

2. Complete the missing half of the shape that your partner drew.

3. Exchange papers again. Draw a line of symmetry on the completed figure to check each other's work.

4. **Explain** How does the line of symmetry help you check the completed drawing? Possible answer: The line of symmetry divides a figure in half. Folding the drawing along the line of symmetry should match each part of one half exactly onto the other half.

Unit 4, Lesson 5   Copyright © Houghton Mifflin Company

Activity Note Some figures may have more than one line of symmetry. Have students draw the line of symmetry along the open side of the incomplete drawing before finishing the figure.

 Math Writing Prompt

Explain Your Thinking Draw half of a figure in your Math Journal. Explain how to draw the other half so that the whole figure has line symmetry.

 **Software Support**

Warm-Up 37.18

On Level — Activity Card 4-5

Symmetry Drawing
Activity Card 4-5 ▲

Work: In Pairs
1. Answer and possible explanation: Line symmetry, because folding the figure along the dotted line makes two congruent halves.

1. What type of symmetry can you find in the figure at the right? Explain your response.

2. **Work Together** Draw a figure that has line symmetry but not rotational symmetry.

3. Draw a second figure that has only rotational symmetry.

4. **Math Talk** Which figure was easier to draw? Explain your answer.

Unit 4, Lesson 5   Copyright © Houghton Mifflin Company

Activity Note If students have difficulty drawing a figure with only rotational symmetry, suggest that they analyze the figure in exercise 15 of Activity 2.

 Math Writing Prompt

Sort and Classify Describe the following quadrilaterals by line symmetry and rotational symmetry: trapezoid, isosceles trapezoid, parallelogram, rhombus, rectangle, square.

Software Support

Ice Station Exploration: Polar Planes, Levels K and L

Challenge — Activity Card 4-5

Regular Polygons
Activity Card 4-5 ■

Work: By Yourself
1. *triangle*: 3 lines of symmetry, 120° rotational angle, degree of rotational symmetry is 3; *square*: 4 lines of symmetry, 90° rotational angle, degree of rotational symmetry is 4; *pentagon*: 5 lines of symmetry, 72° rotational angle, degree of rotational symmetry is 5; *hexagon*: 6 lines of symmetry, 60° rotational angle, degree of rotational symmetry is 6.

1. Answer these questions about each polygon shown.

• How many lines of symmetry does it have?

• What is the degree of rotational symmetry?

• What is the angle of rotational symmetry?

2. **Predict** How are the number of sides of a regular polygon related to its line symmetry and its rotational symmetry?

Unit 4, Lesson 5   Copyright © Houghton Mifflin Company

Activity Note An *n*-sided regular polygon has *n* lines of symmetry. Its degree of rotational symmetry is *n*. Its angle of rotational symmetry is $360° \div n$.

 **Math Writing Prompt**

Investigate Math How many lines of symmetry can a figure have? How many times can a figure turn and still look exactly the same? Explain.

DESTINATION Math® Software Support
Course III: Module 5: Unit 2: Symmetry and Transformations

① Teaching the Lesson

Activity 1

Solve Problems Using a Circle Graph

 15 MINUTES

Goal: Read a circle graph.

Materials: Student Activity Book or Hardcover Book p. 173

✔ **NCTM Standards:**
Geometry
Data Analysis and Probability

4-6
Class Activity

Name _____ Date _____

▶ **Interpret Parts of a Circle Graph**

This circle graph represents a survey of students. The students were asked to name their favorite kind of book.

Favorite Books

Use the graph to answer the questions.

1. What kind of book was named twice as often as a humor book?
   mystery book

2. What kind of book was named half as often as an adventure book?
   mystery book

3. Is the number of students who chose either mystery or humor books more or less than the number of students who chose adventure books? Explain how you know.
   Answers will vary. Possible explanation: Since
   humor, fiction, or mystery choices equal adventure,
   mystery and humor, the number of students who
   chose mystery or humor is less than the number
   who chose adventure.

4. For this survey, 125 students named fiction books as their favorite kind of book. How many students named mystery books as their favorite kind of book?
   250 students

5. How many students were surveyed? Explain how you know.
   1,000; explanations may vary. Possible answer:
   Since 125 students named fiction as their favorite
   and they are $\frac{1}{8}$ of the sample, then
   8 × 125 students were surveyed.

UNIT 4 LESSON 6   Circle Graphs **173**

Student Activity Book page 173

▶ **Interpret Parts of a Circle Graph**

WHOLE CLASS

Direct the students' attention to the "Favorite Books" circle graph on Student Book page 173.

Ask what the graph represents. The results of a survey where students named their favorite kind of book. Point out that a circle graph shows data that emphasizes the relationships of the parts to the whole.

Discuss the relationship of each section to the whole circle. Encourage students to use the vocabulary and concepts from the previous days. If necessary, reinforce the idea that the entire graph represents one whole, or 1. Help students understand how the sections relate to each other.

● Use what you know about angles, degrees, and fractions to explain how adventure books relate to the whole circle. Line segment BE is a straight angle. It is 180°. Since the circle has 360°, Adventure represents 180° or one half of the circle.

● How do mystery books relate to the whole? Line segment AD and line segment AE form a right angle. A right angle is 90°. A circle has four 90° angles, so the section for mystery books is one fourth of the circle.

● How do the humor and fiction sections relate to each other? They appear to be the same size.

● How can we tell for sure? We can measure them. We can trace one and place it over the other.

 Class Management

Looking Ahead In the next lesson you will need cans of various sizes. Ask students to bring cans from home.

Use Questions on the Student Page As students answer the questions, they should begin to relate each section of the circle to a number of students that are represented by that section. Students should generalize that the greater the area of a section, the greater the amount of data the section represents, and vice versa.

Be sure that students compare the areas of the humor and mystery sections, and recognize that the area of the mystery section is approximately twice the area of the fiction section and that the area of the humor section is approximately one-half the area of the mystery section.

You may want to invite those who answered exercise 5 correctly to demonstrate different ways of finding the answer.

Have students pose and solve a few more questions about the graph.

Activity 2

Make a Circle Graph

 20 MINUTES

Goal: Use data to make a circle graph.

Materials: rulers, protractors or Protractors (TRB M24), Student Activity Book p. 174 or Hardcover Book p. 174 and Activity Workbook p. 79

 NCTM Standards:
Geometry
Measurement

▶ Plan and Make a Graph INDIVIDUALS

Discuss the data table and the marked circle on Student Book page 174. One way to determine the degree measure of a section of the circle is to use a protractor. Another way is to use arithmetic: since there are 360° in a circle and there are 12 sections on the given circle, each section represents 360 ÷ 12 or 30°.

To determine the number of sections to use for each number of pets, students first need to recognize that there is a total of 240 pets in our school. Therefore, each pet represents 360 ÷ 240 or 1.5° of the circle.

Students may want to use a variety of colors or cross-hatchings, or design their own method of differentiating the various sections from each other. Remind students that their graph is not complete without a name and labels.

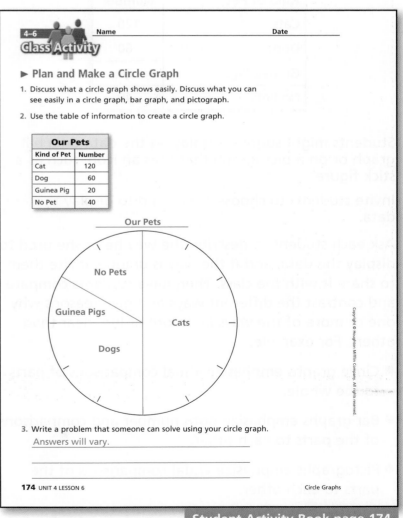

Student Activity Book page 174

Activity 3

Display the Same Data in Different Ways

 25 MINUTES

Goal: Display data different ways.

Materials: Student Activity Book or Hardcover Book p. 174

 NCTM Standards:
Data Analysis and Probability
Measurement

▶ Discuss Data Displays

WHOLE CLASS   **Math Talk**

Discuss different ways to display the data from the table on Student Book page 174.

Our Pets

Kind of Pet	Number
Cats	120
Dogs	60
Guinea Pigs	20
No Pets	40

Students might suggest displaying the data on a bar graph or on a pictograph that uses an icon, such as a stick figure.

Invite students to choose a way and to display the data.

Ask each student to describe the way he or she used to display the data, and if the way is unique, invite them to share it with the class. Then have students compare and contrast the different ways and give reasons why one or more of the ways are more or less clear than others. For example:

● Circle graphs emphasize visual comparisons of parts to the whole.

● Bar graphs emphasize both number and comparisons of the parts to each other.

● Pictographs emphasize visual comparisons of the parts to each other.

Write Problems Have students write problems that can be solved using their graphs. Discuss as many problems as time allows.

Differentiated Instruction

Advanced Learners Have students use encyclopedias, other reference books, or the computer to find data that can be displayed in more than one way. Then have them display the data in at least two ways and write two or three questions that can be answered using the data displays.

Ongoing Assessment

▶ Ask questions like the following:

If a circle graph is divided into 3 equal sections, what do you know about the data? The 3 sets of data represent the same amount.

If you have data from 72 students, how will you start to make a circle graph? Divide 360° by 72 to find the number of degrees for each student's data.

Why are a name and labels important? They tell what the graph is about.

The Learning Classroom

Helping Community Create a classroom where students are not competing, but desire to collaborate and help one another. Communicate often that your goal as a class is that everyone understands the math you are studying. Tell students that this will require everyone working together to help each other.

② Going Further

● Intervention   Activity Card 4-6

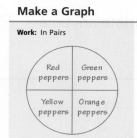

Make a Graph   Activity Card 4-6 ●

Work: In Pairs

1. **Work Together** Use the data to make a graph. Sample shown on left.

> **Bell Peppers for Sale**
>
> 90 red peppers
> 90 yellow peppers
> 90 green peppers
> 90 orange peppers

2. **Math Talk** How did you choose the type of graph you made? How did you decide how to organize the data in the graph? Possible response: The data show parts of a whole, so a circle graph is appropriate. Each of the four parts is an equal amount, so the graph is divided into four equal sections.

Unit 4, Lesson 6   Copyright © Houghton Mifflin Company

Activity Note Before students begin, remind them that the graph should make it easy to see what part of the total amount each type of pepper represents.

 Math Writing Prompt

Write a Question Find a graph in your math book or a magazine. Write a question that someone can answer using the graph.

 **Software Support**

Warm-Up 51.17

▲ On Level   Activity Card 4-6

Graph Data   Activity Card 4-6 ▲

Work: In Pairs
Possible answer:

Apples for Sale

Granny Smith   90
MᶜIntosh   180
Jonathan   90

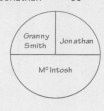

1. **Work Together** Decide how many apples are in each category. Choose 90, 90, and 180, or choose 45, 45, and 270.

> • A farmer has 360 apples for sale.
> • There are three kinds of apples: Jonathan, McIntosh, and Granny Smith.

2. Organize this data about the apples in a table. Then graph the data. Sample for data above shown on left.

3. **Math Talk** How did you decide what part of the graph represents each category of the data? Possible answer: The fractional part of 360 that each category represents equals the fractional part of the circle graph for that category.

Unit 4, Lesson 6   Copyright © Houghton Mifflin Company

Activity Note To vary the activity, have each partner choose a different set of numbers to use in the data table. Have each student write a sentence describing what the graph shows.

 Math Writing Prompt

How to Make a Circle Graph Write the steps for making a circle graph to help someone who missed this lesson.

 Software Support

The Number Games: ArachnaGraph, Level C

■ Challenge   Activity Card 4-6

Use Data to Make a Graph   Activity Card 4-6 ■

Work: By Yourself

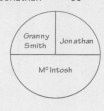

1. Use the numbers 60, 120, and 180 to make a data set. Choose a topic and use it to write a title for your data. Here is an example.

> **Favorite Colors**
>
> Red   60
> Green   120
> Blue   180

2. Make a circle graph to display your data. Sample for data above shown on left.

3. **Explain** How did you decide how large to make each section of your graph? Possible answer: The total number of votes is 360. So blue represents half of 360. Red and green together represent the other half. Green is $\frac{1}{3}$ of 360, which is twice as many as red.

Unit 4, Lesson 6   Copyright © Houghton Mifflin Company

Activity Note Students should begin by finding the total number of votes. Ask students to write a sentence about what their graph shows.

 Math Writing Prompt

Ask a Question Think of a good survey question. Ask 12 people the question and make a data table of your results. Then write the directions for making a circle graph from the data table.

 **DESTINATION** Math· **Software Support**

Course III: Module 5: Unit 1: Lines, Angles, and Circles

③ Homework and Spiral Review

Homework **Goal:** Additional Practice

You can quickly review this Homework to assess how well students understand how to make and use circle graphs.

Remembering **Goal:** Spiral Review

This Remembering activity is appropriate anytime after today's lesson.

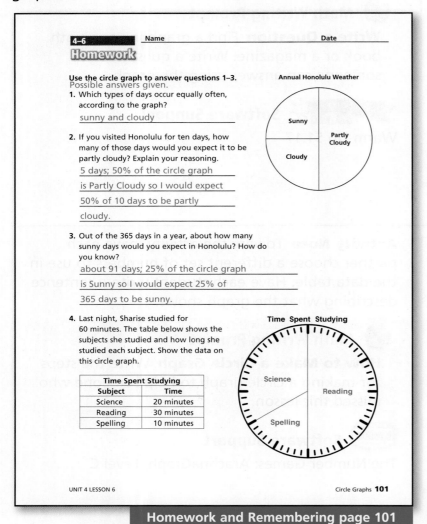

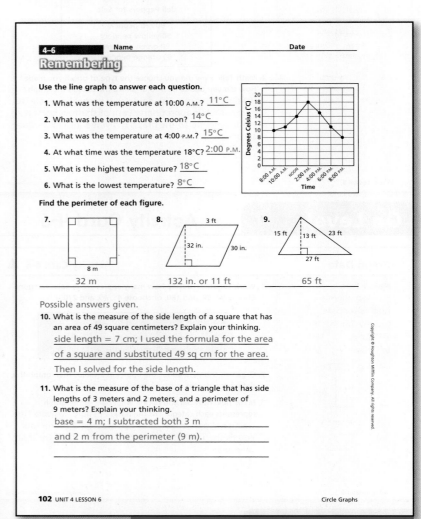

Homework and Remembering page 101

Homework and Remembering page 102

Home or School Activity

 Social Studies Connection

Graphs in the Media Have students collect graphs from newspapers, magazines, and the Internet. Students should tell whether they think each graph clearly shows the data and helps the reader to understand the message or story that goes with the graph. Have students explain what the different types of graphs (line graphs, bar graphs, and circle graphs) seem to be used for.

Circumference

Lesson Objectives

- Define and estimate circumference.

- Round lengths in millimeters to the nearest whole centimeter.

- Collect, record, and look for patterns in data.

Vocabulary

circumference
radius
diameter
pi

The Day at a Glance

Today's Goals	Materials	

1 Teaching the Lesson
A1: Discover the relationship shared by the diameter and the circumference of a circle.
A2: Estimate the circumference of a circle by using 3 as an approximation for π.
 	
2 Going Further
▶ Differentiated Instruction
 	
3 Homework and Spiral Review
	Lesson Activities
	Student Activity Book pp. 175–176
	  or Student Hardcover Book
	  pp. 175–176 and Activity Workbook
	  p. 80
	Homework and Remembering
	  pp. 103–104
	Quick Quiz 2 (Assessment Guide)
	Rulers
	Cans of various sizes
	String
		Going Further
		Activity Cards 4-7
		Strip of paper
		Scissors
		Cans
		String
		Rulers
		Circular object
		Math Journals
		
		123 Use **Math Talk** today!

Keeping Skills Sharp

Daily Routines	English Language Learners
Homework Review Let students work together to check their work. Initially, pair less able students with more able students. **Mental Math** Write one addition and one subtraction problem that each use 4.61 as the answer. Answers will vary. Possible answer: 2.35 + 2.26 = 4.61; 8.31 − 3.7 = 4.61	Draw a square and a circle on the board. Write *perimeter* and *circumference*. • **Beginning** Point and ask: **Is *perimeter* the distance around a square?** yes Say: ***Circumference* is the distance around a circle.** Have students repeat. • **Intermediate** Say: ***Perimeter* is the distance around a __.** square ***Circumference* is the distance around a __.** circle • **Advanced** Point to the two words and say: **The distance around a square is its __.** perimeter Say: **The distance around a circle is its __.** circumference

Teaching the Lesson

Explore Circumference

 30 MINUTES

Goal: Discover the relationship shared by the diameter and the circumference of a circle.

Materials: rulers (1 per small group of students), cans of various sizes (1 per small group of students), string, Student Activity Book p. 175 or Hardcover Book p. 175 and Activity Workbook p. 80

✔ **NCTM Standards:**
Measurement
Geometry
Reasoning and Proof

▶ Experiment With Circumference

SMALL GROUPS

Draw this picture on the board and discuss the terms *radius*, *diameter*, and *circumference* of a circle.

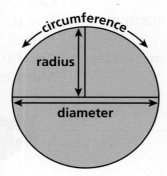

Make sure students understand that the terms *perimeter* and *circumference* represent the idea of "distance around."

● How can you remember which word is used for circles and which is used for polygons? You can use the starting sounds: perimeter for polygons, circumference for circles.

Give each **Small Group** of students one can and one sheet of paper. Have students record the type of can they have and draw a diagonal from one corner of the paper to the other. Students mark one end of the diagonal *Start.*

Have students place their can at the *Start* position and mark the diameter, the length across the can, on the diagonal.

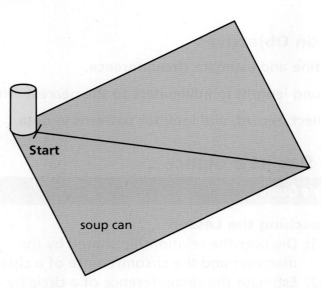

Next, have them make a mark on the top of the can. They place the can at *Start* and roll it one complete revolution, marking on the diagonal where it stops. This mark shows the circumference of the can.

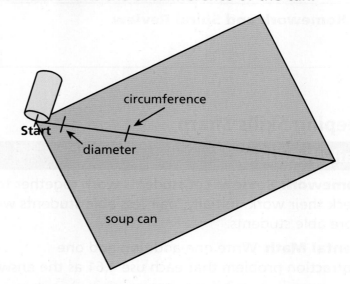

 Alternate Approach

Use String Students can mark the diameter and circumference of the can on a piece of string. They then measure each distance with a ruler.

Have students use a ruler to measure, in millimeters, the marks on their sheet of paper. Create a table on the board and invite students to compile and display their data. As a class, discuss the patterns in the table. For a sample of student dialogue, see Math Talk in Action. If necessary, direct students' attention to the "nearest cm" columns.

Student Activity Book page 175

Draw students' attention to Student Book page 175. Have them work in **Small Groups** to complete the first exercise using the class data from the board.

Invite students to discuss and generalize the relationship between the diameter and the circumference of the can. Students should discover that there is a pattern for all the can measurements.

● About how many times as long as the diameter is the circumference? about three times

If they are having difficulty, students can fold the paper to discover that the distance around is about three times as long as the diameter.

 Math Talk in Action

What patterns do you see in your measurements?

Olivia: The circumference of my can is three times the diameter.

Is there another way to say that?

Olivia: You could say the diameter is one third of the circumference.

Correct. Do you all have the same pattern for your can measurements?

Anil: Almost. The circumference of my can is about 17 cm and the diameter is about 6 cm. 3 × 6 is 18. 17 isn't exactly three times 6, but it's close.

That's good. The circumference of a circle is close to three times the diameter. Where is it easiest to see this in the table?

Félix: In the "nearest cm" columns. The numbers are smaller so they're easier to multiply or divide in your head.

That's true. The rounded circumference can also be exactly three times the rounded diameter.

 Ongoing Assessment

As students complete exercises 1–4, check that they are measuring accurately and converting millimeters to centimeters correctly.

Teaching Note

Watch For! In the next activity, some students might confuse diameter and radius in their calculations. For example, they might estimate the circumference by multiplying the radius, instead of the diameter, by 3.

 Quick Quiz

See Assessment Guide for Unit 4 Quick Quiz 2.

Activity 2

Estimate Circumference

 30 MINUTES

Goal: Estimate the circumference of a circle by using 3 as an approximation for π.

Materials: Student Activity Book or Hardcover Book p. 176

 NCTM Standards:
Measurement
Geometry
Reasoning and Proof

▶ Estimate Circumference Using Diameter WHOLE CLASS

Sketch a circle on the board. Invite volunteers, one at a time, to go to the board, draw a diameter on the circle, and assign it an estimated length. Each time, challenge the rest of the class to estimate the circumference of the circle. Repeat, beginning with a circumference and challenging students to estimate the diameter.

▶ Estimate Circumference Using Radius
WHOLE CLASS

Draw several circles and mark the radius and diameter on each. Discuss how the measures relate to circumference:

● How do the lengths of a diameter and a radius of a circle compare? The length of a diameter is twice the length of a radius and the length of a radius is one half the length of a diameter.

● What do you have to do to a radius before you can use it to find the circumference of a circle? multiply it by 2

● How can you find the diameter if you know the circumference? divide by 3

● After you find the diameter, what do you need to do to get the radius? divide your answer by 2

Use the circles on the board. Have volunteers assign a radius and challenge the students to find the circumference; then have volunteers assign a circumference and challenge the students to find the radius.

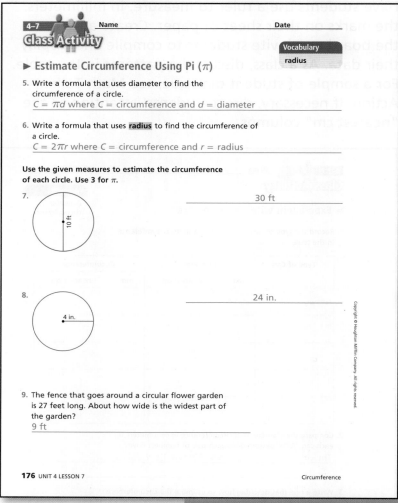

▶ Estimate Circumference Using Pi (π)
SMALL GROUPS

Explain that the relationship shared by circumference and diameter is called *pi* (π). Write the symbol on the board. Tell students that they will use 3 to represent π.

Have **Small Groups** complete the exercises using *C* for circumference, 3 for π, *d* for diameter, and *r* for radius.

Teaching Note

Language and Vocabulary Pi (π) is a constant ratio of the diameter of a circle to its circumference. Pi is an irrational number. It cannot be written as a fraction or as a repeating or terminating decimal. Pi is approximately 3.14 or $\frac{22}{7}$. A less precise estimate is obtained when 3 is used for π.

② Going Further

Intervention · Activity Card 4-7

Circumference · Activity Card 4-7

Work: In Pairs

Use:
• Ruler
• Scissors
• Strip of paper
• Large can

1. Draw a large circle on a sheet of paper by tracing the bottom of the can. Then mark a diameter on the circle.

2. **Work Together** Cut a strip of paper that is 3 times as long as the diameter.

3. Wrap the paper around the circle like a fence. Notice that it almost fits the circle exactly.

4. Measure the length of the paper strip that you wrapped around the circle. Divide the length by 3.

5. **Compare** How does the length of the paper strip compare to the diameter of the circle? Measure the diameter to check your response. Possible answer: The diameter of the circle is about $\frac{1}{3}$ as long as the paper that fits around the circumference.

Unit 4, Lesson 7   Copyright © Houghton Mifflin Company

Activity Note Have students locate the widest distance across the circle to mark the diameter accurately. Repeat the activity with different size circles to reinforce the concept.

✐ Math Writing Prompt

Understand Circumference Explain how to use the diameter of a circle to estimate the circumference of that circle.

Soar to Success Math ★ **Software Support**

Warm-Up 35.33

On Level · Activity Card 4-7

Calculate and Compare · Activity Card 4-7 ▲

Work: In Pairs

Use:
• Two cans of different sizes
• String
• Ruler

1. One partner traces the bottom of one can onto paper.

2. Then the partner measures the diameter of the circle and uses the diameter to estimate the circumference.

3. The other partner measures the circumference of the can using a string and a ruler, and then uses the circumference to estimate the diameter.

4. Compare results. Then switch roles and repeat the activity with the second can. Possible answer: The circumference is about 3 times the diameter.

5. **Math Talk** What do you notice about how the circumference relates to the diameter?

Unit 4, Lesson 7   Copyright © Houghton Mifflin Company

Activity Note Have students mark the diameter as accurately as possible by locating the widest distance across the circle. Pulling the string taut each time also increases the accuracy of measurements.

✐ Math Writing Prompt

You Decide You are checking your work and you find two measurements for a circle: $r = 4$ cm and $C = 12$ cm. Is this reasonable? Explain.

Harcourt MegaMath Grades K-6 **Software Support**

Ice Station Exploration: Polar Planes, Level P

Challenge · Activity Card 4-7

Polygons and Circles · Activity Card 4-7 ■

Work: By Yourself

Use:
• Large can (or other circular object)
• Ruler

1. Trace a circle three times onto a piece of paper.

2. Place three equally spaced dots around one of the circles and connect them with lines.

3. Repeat using four dots on the second circle and five dots on the third circle.

4. Identify the polygon inside each circle. equilateral triangle, square, regular pentagon.

5. **Math Talk** Measure the perimeter of each polygon and estimate the circumference of each circle. How does the perimeter of the polygon compare to the circumference of the circle as the number of dots increases? Possible answer: The difference between the two measures decreases.

Unit 4, Lesson 7   Copyright © Houghton Mifflin Company

Activity Note Placing the dots an equal distance apart around the circle creates regular polygons and makes it easier to estimate perimeter, but otherwise is not critical to the success of the activity.

✐ Math Writing Prompt

Explore Formulas Is $C \div 6$ a formula that you can use to estimate the radius of a circle? Explain why or why not.

✸ DESTINATION Math **Software Support**

Course III: Module 5: Unit 1: Lines, Angles, and Circles

③ Homework and Spiral Review

Homework **Goal:** Additional Practice

✓ Include students' Homework for page 103 as part of their portfolios.

Remembering **Goal:** Spiral Review

This Remembering activity is appropriate anytime after today's lesson.

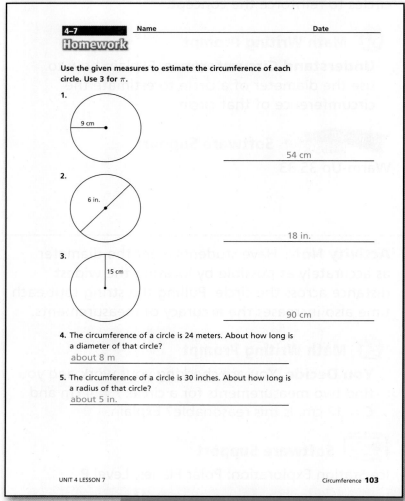

4-7 Name _____ Date _____
Homework

Use the given measures to estimate the circumference of each circle. Use 3 for π.

1.

9 cm

54 cm

2.

6 in.

18 in.

3.

15 cm

90 cm

4. The circumference of a circle is 24 meters. About how long is a diameter of that circle?
about 8 m

5. The circumference of a circle is 30 inches. About how long is a radius of that circle?
about 5 in.

UNIT 4 LESSON 7   Circumference **103**

Homework and Remembering page 103

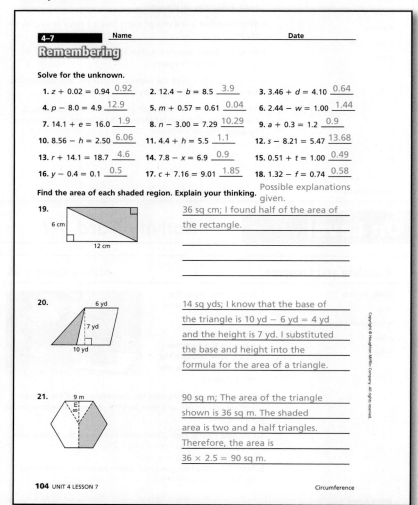

4-7 Name _____ Date _____
Remembering

Solve for the unknown.

1. $z + 0.02 = 0.94$ _0.92_   2. $12.4 - b = 8.5$ _3.9_   3. $3.46 + d = 4.10$ _0.64_
4. $p - 8.0 = 4.9$ _12.9_   5. $m + 0.57 = 0.61$ _0.04_   6. $2.44 - w = 1.00$ _1.44_
7. $14.1 + e = 16.0$ _1.9_   8. $n - 3.00 = 7.29$ _10.29_   9. $a + 0.3 = 1.2$ _0.9_
10. $8.56 - h = 2.50$ _6.06_   11. $4.4 + h = 5.5$ _1.1_   12. $s - 8.21 = 5.47$ _13.68_
13. $r + 14.1 = 18.7$ _4.6_   14. $7.8 - x = 6.9$ _0.9_   15. $0.51 + t = 1.00$ _0.49_
16. $y - 0.4 = 0.1$ _0.5_   17. $c + 7.16 = 9.01$ _1.85_   18. $1.32 - f = 0.74$ _0.58_

Find the area of each shaded region. Explain your thinking. Possible explanations given.

19.

6 cm

12 cm

36 sq cm; I found half of the area of the rectangle.

20.

6 yd
7 yd
10 yd

14 sq yds; I know that the base of the triangle is 10 yd − 6 yd = 4 yd and the height is 7 yd. I substituted the base and height into the formula for the area of a triangle.

21.

9 m
8 m

90 sq m; The area of the triangle shown is 36 sq m. The shaded area is two and a half triangles. Therefore, the area is 36 × 2.5 = 90 sq m.

104 UNIT 4 LESSON 7   Circumference

Homework and Remembering page 104

Home or School Activity

Literature Connection

Sir Cumference and the Dragon of Pi Read the book *Sir Cumference and the Dragon of Pi,* by Cindy Neuschwander, illustrated by Wayne Geehan (Charlesbridge Publishing, 1999). Encourage discussion of how the story relates to what students have learned about pi during math class.

Unit Review and Test

Lesson Objective

● Assess student progress on unit objectives.

The Day at a Glance

Today's Goals	Materials
1 Assessing the Unit ▸ Assess student progress on unit objectives. ▸ Use activities from unit lessons to reteach content. **2 Extending the Assessment** ▸ Use remediation for common errors. There is no homework assignment on a test day.	Unit 4 Test, Student Activity Book pp. 177–178 or Student Hardcover Book pp. 177–178 and Activity Workbook p. 81 Unit 4 Test, Form A or B, Assessment Guide (optional) Unit 4 Performance Assessment, Assessment Guide (optional)

Keeping Skills Sharp

Daily Routines 🕐 5 MINUTES	
If you are doing a unit review day, go over the homework. If this is a test day, omit the homework review.	**Review and Test Day** You may want to choose a quiet game or other activity (reading a book or working on homework for another subject) for students who finish early.

Assess Unit Objectives

🕐 **45 MINUTES** (more if schedule permits)

Goal: Assess student progress on unit objectives.

Materials: Student Activity Book pp. 177–178 or Hardcover Book pp. 177–178 and Activity Workbook p. 81, Assessment Guide (optional)

▶ Review and Assessment

If your students are ready for assessment on the unit objectives, you may use either the test on the Student Book pages or one of the forms of the Unit 4 Test in the Assessment Guide to assess student progress.

If you feel that students need some review first, you may use the test on the Student Book pages as a review of unit content, and then use one of the forms of the Unit 4 Test in the Assessment Guide to assess student progress.

To assign a numerical score for all of these test forms, use 10 points for each question.

You may also choose to use the Unit 4 Performance Assessment. Scoring for that assessment can be found in its rubric in the Assessment Guide.

▶ Reteaching Resources

The chart lists the test items, the unit objectives they cover, and the lesson activities in which the objective is covered in this unit. You may revisit these activities with students who do not show mastery of the objectives.

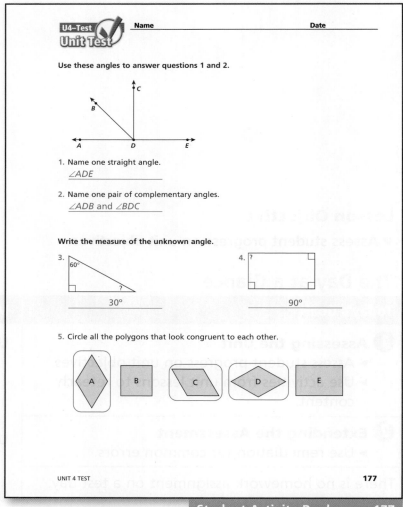

Student Activity Book page 177

Unit Test Items	Unit Objectives Tested	Activities to Use for Reteaching
1–2	**4.1** Identify and measure angles.	Lesson 1, Activity 1
3–4	**4.2** Find the measure of an unknown angle in a polygon.	Lesson 1, Activity 2 Lesson 2, Activity 2
5	**4.3** Identify congruent figures.	Lesson 3, Activity 1

Student Activity Book page 178

Unit Test Items	Unit Objectives Tested	Activities to Use for Reteaching
6	**4.4** Identify the position of an object after it has been turned.	Lesson 4, Activity 2
7	**4.5** Identify lines of symmetry.	Lesson 5, Activity 1
8–10	**4.6** Solve problems using a circle graph.	Lesson 6, Activity 1

▶ Assessment Resources

Free Response Tests
Unit 4 Test, Student Book pages 177–178
Unit 4 Test, Form A, Assessment Guide

Extended Response Item
The last item in the Student Book test and in the Form A test will require an extended response as an answer.

Multiple Choice Test
Unit 4 Test, Form B, Assessment Guide

Performance Assessment
Unit 4 Performance Assessment, Assessment Guide
Unit 4 Performance Assessment Rubric, Assessment Guide

▶ Portfolio Assessment

Teacher-selected Items for Student Portfolios:

- Homework, Lessons 2, 4, and 7
- Class Activity work, Lessons 3 and 6

Student-selected Items for Student Portfolios:

- Favorite Home or School Activity
- Best Writing Prompt

② Extending the Assessment

Unit Objective 4.1
Identify and measure angles.

Common Error: Misidentifies Complementary and Supplementary Angles

Some students may confuse complementary angles and supplementary angles.

Remediation Point out to these students that "s" is the first letter of *straight* and *supplementary,* and that supplementary angles form straight lines, or angles of 180°. The word *complementary* does not begin with "s" and complementary angles do not form straight lines.

Unit Objective 4.2
Find the measure of an unknown angle in a polygon.

Common Error: Confuses Sums of Angles of Polygons

Students may have difficulty remembering that the sum of the angles in a triangle is 180° and the sum of the angles in a rectangle is 360°.

Remediation Encourage these students to remember that a triangle has fewer angles than a rectangle, so the sum of its angles is less.

Unit Objective 4.3
Identify congruent figures.

Common Error: Determines Congruence Incorrectly

Some students may have difficulty determining the congruence, or lack of congruence, of two figures.

Remediation Encourage these students to use tracing paper or a ruler to help make their decisions.

Unit Objective 4.4
Identify the position of an object after it has been turned.

Common Error: Doesn't Connect Degree Measures to Fractional Turns

Some students may have difficulty recognizing that 90°, 180°, 270°, and 360° turns represent a one-quarter turn, a one-half turn, a three-quarter turn, and a full turn, respectively.

Remediation To help students make these connections, provide them with circles divided into fourths. Have them use their protractors to determine the angle measure of each quarter. Then ask students to label those measures and parts using appropriate fractions.

Unit Objective 4.5
Identify lines of symmetry.

Common Error: Identifies Too Few Lines of Symmetry

Students may identify some, but not all, of the lines of symmetry of a figure. For example, in a square, they may recognize the vertical and horizontal lines of symmetry, but not the lines of symmetry along the diagonals.

Remediation Encourage these students to orient the figure in different ways (upside-down, sideways, and so on) to help them identify all of the lines of symmetry.

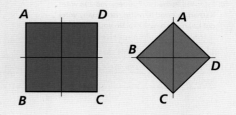

Unit Objective 4.6
Solve problems using a circle graph.

Common Error: Misreads the Graph

Students may misinterpret the graph.

Remediation Have students reread and check their answers before submitting their tests. Remind them that the size of each section is related to the number it represents, so the largest section indicates the greatest number and the smallest section indicates the least number.

Addition and Subtraction with Fractions

UNIT 5 BUILDS on the conceptual understanding of fractions that students have developed in previous grades. Activities help students develop strategies to add and subtract like and unlike fractions, and to use equivalent fractions. Students use a variety of representations in this unit to help them gain fluency with manipulating proper and improper fractions and mixed numbers. Students are expected to apply their understanding and skills with adding and subtracting fractions to numeric calculations and to real-world problem-solving situations.

Skills Trace

Grade 4	Grade 5
• Compare and order fractions. • Write fractions and decimals in equivalent forms. • Convert and use improper fractions and mixed numbers. • Add and subtract fractions and mixed numbers with like and unlike denominators. • Solve word problems involving addition and subtraction of fractions. • Express probabilities as fractions.	• Compare and order fractions, mixed numbers, and decimals. • Write fractions and decimals in equivalent forms. • Convert and use improper fractions and mixed numbers. • Add and subtract fractions and mixed numbers with like and unlike denominators. • Solve word problems involving addition and subtraction of fractions and mixed numbers. • Describe probability situations by finding fractional equivalents.

Unit 5   Contents

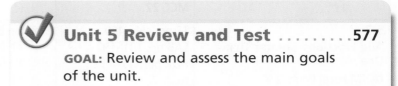

Planning Unit 5

Lesson NCTM Focal Points NCTM Standards	Resources	Materials for Lesson Activities	Materials for Going Further
5-1 **Build Unit Fractions** NCTM Focal Point: 2.7 NCTM Standards: 1, 6, 9	TE pp. 411–420 SAB pp. 179–182 H&R pp. 105–106 AC 5-1	✓ MathBoard materials	✓ Counters or plastic bread tags Grid Paper (TRB M17) Math Journals
5-2 **Compare Fractions** NCTM Focal Point: 4.2 NCTM Standards: 1, 10	TE pp. 421–428 SAB pp. 183–184 H&R pp. 107–108 AC 5-2 MCC 21	✓ MathBoard materials Colored pencils	Grid Paper (TRB M17) Fraction Bars for Adding and Subtracting (TRB M26) Math Journals
5-3 **Subtract Fractions** NCTM Focal Point: 2.7 NCTM Standards: 1, 2, 6	TE pp. 429–434 SAB pp. 185–186 H&R pp. 109–110 AC 5-3	None	Index cards Math Journals
5-4 **Fractional Addends of One** NCTM Focal Points: 2.7, 4.1 NCTM Standards: 1, 6	TE pp. 435–440 SAB pp. 187–188 H&R pp. 111–112 AC 5-4	✓ MathBoard materials	✓ Counters or plastic bread tags Unknown Addend Cards (TRB M27) Math Journals
5-5 **Relate Fractions and Wholes** NCTM Standards: 1, 6	TE pp. 441–448 SAB pp. 189–190 H&R pp. 113–114 AC 5-5 AG Quick Quiz 1	Pattern blocks or Pattern Blocks (TRB M28) (optional) Masking tape (optional) ✓ MathBoard materials	Pattern Blocks (TRB M28) Masking tape Chapter book Math Journals
5-6 **Fractions Greater Than One** NCTM Standards: 1, 7, 8, 10	TE pp. 449–454 H&R pp. 115–116 AC 5-6 MCC 22	Greeting cards or photos (optional) ✓ Pointer	Index cards Math Journals
5-7 **Add Fractions Greater Than One** NCTM Focal Point: 2.7 NCTM Standards: 1, 6, 7, 8	TE pp. 455–460 SAB pp. 191–192 H&R pp. 117–118 AC 5-7	Fraction Bars for Adding and Subtracting (TRB M26) (optional) Scissors (optional)	Fraction Circles (TRB M30) Math Journals
5-8 **Subtract Mixed Numbers** NCTM Focal Point: 2.7 NCTM Standards: 1, 8, 10	TE pp. 461–466 SAB pp. 193–194 H&R pp. 119–120 AC 5-8	✓ MathBoard materials Fraction Bars for Adding and Subtracting (TRB M26) (optional) Scissors (optional) Fraction Cards (TRB M29) (optional) Envelopes (optional)	Any cookbook Math Journals
5-9 **Comparison Situations** NCTM Focal Points: 2.7, 4.2 NCTM Standards: 1, 4, 6, 8, 10	TE pp. 467–474 SAB pp. 195–196 H&R pp. 121–122 AC 5-9	Inch rulers	✓ Play money Math Journals
5-10 **Mixed Practice With Like Fractions** NCTM Focal Point: 2.7 NCTM Standards: 1, 6, 8	TE pp. 475–480 SAB pp. 197–198 H&R pp. 123–124 AC 5-10 AG Quick Quiz 2	None	Math Journals

Resources/Materials Key: TE: Teacher Edition   SAB: Student Activity Book   H&R: Homework and Remembering
AC: Activity Cards   MCC: Math Center Challenge   AG: Assessment Guide   ✓: Grade 5 kits   TRB: Teacher's Resource Book

NCTM Standards and Expectations Key: **1.** Number and Operations **2.** Algebra **3.** Geometry
4. Measurement **5.** Data Analysis and Probability **6.** Problem Solving **7.** Reasoning and Proof
8. Communication **9.** Connections **10.** Representation

Lesson NCTM Focal Points NCTM Standards	Resources	Materials for Lesson Activities	Materials for Going Further
5-11 **Discover Equivalent Fractions** NCTM Focal Point: 4.5 NCTM Standards: 1, 7, 10	TE pp. 481–490 SAB pp. 199–202 H&R pp. 125–126 AC 5-11	✓ MathBoard materials	Equivalent Fractions (TRB M31) Ruler Fraction Match-Up Cards (TRB M32) Scissors Math Journals
5-12 **Equivalent Fractions and Multipliers** NCTM Focal Point: 4.5 NCTM Standards: 1, 6, 7	TE pp. 491–498 SAB pp. 203–204 H&R pp. 127–128 AC 5-12	✓ Class MathBoard Math Journals	Tens and Hundreds Grids (TRB M33) Timer or clock with a second hand Math Journals
5-13 **Solve Equivalence Problems** NCTM Focal Point: 4.5 NCTM Standards: 1, 6, 7	TE pp. 499–506 SAB pp. 205–206 H&R pp. 129–130 AC 5-13	Completed Homework p. 127 Math Journals	✓ MathBoard materials Ruler Index cards Math Journals
5-14 **Add and Subtract Unlike Fractions** NCTM Focal Points: 2.1, 2.2, 2.7, 4.5 NCTM Standards: 1, 6, 7, 8, 10	TE pp. 507–516 SAB pp. 207–208 H&R pp. 131–132 AC 5-14	✓ MathBoard materials	Fraction Circles (TRB M30) Scissors Math Journals
5-15 **Solve With Unlike Mixed Numbers** NCTM Focal Points: 2.1, 2.2, 2.7, 4.1 NCTM Standards: 1, 6	TE pp. 517–524 SAB pp. 209–210 H&R pp. 133–134 AC 5-15 MCC 23	None	✓ Play money Math Journals
5-16 **Practice With Unlike Mixed Numbers** NCTM Focal Points: 2.1, 2.2, 2.7 NCTM Standards: 1, 6, 8	TE pp. 525–530 SAB pp. 211–212 H&R pp. 135–136 AC 5-16 MCC 24	None	Ruler Index cards Grid Paper (TRB M17) Colored markers Math Journals
5-17 **Probability and Equivalent Fractions** NCTM Standards: 1, 5, 6, 7	TE pp. 531–540 SAB pp. 213–216 H&R pp. 137–138 AC 5-17 AG Quick Quiz 3	None	Spinner (TRB M34) Pencil and paper clip ✓ Coins Math Journals
5-18 **Fraction and Decimal Equivalencies** NCTM Standards: 1, 8	TE pp. 541–550 SAB pp. 217–219 H&R pp. 139–140 AC 5-18	✓ MathBoard materials Calculators (optional)	Equivalent Fractions (TRB M31) Index cards Ruler Math Journals
5-19 **Compare and Order Fractions and Decimals** NCTM Focal Points: 2.3, 2.4 NCTM Standards: 1, 8, 10	TE pp. 551–562 SAB pp. 217–218, 221–224 H&R pp. 141–142 AC 5-19	✓ MathBoard materials	✓ Play money Game Cards 1–9 (TRB M2) Ruler Math Journals

Lesson NCTM Focal Points NCTM Standards	Resources	Materials for Lesson Activities	Materials for Going Further
5-20 **Different Ways to Estimate** **(Optional)** NCTM Focal Points: 2.5, 2.6 NCTM Standards: 1, 6, 7	TE pp. 563–570 SAB pp. 225–226 H&R pp. 143–144 AC 5-20 AG Quick Quiz 4	None	Grid Paper (TRB M17) Index cards Math Journals
5-21 **Use Mathematical Processes** NCTM Standards: 6, 7, 8, 9, 10	TE pp. 571–576 SAB pp. 227–228 H&R pp. 145–146 AC 5-21	None	Sheets of paper Scissors Index cards Math Journals
Unit Review and Test	TE pp. 577–580 SAB pp. 229–230 AG Unit 5 Tests		

Resources/Materials Key: TE: Teacher Edition   SAB: Student Activity Book   H&R: Homework and Remembering
AC: Activity Cards   MCC: Math Center Challenge   AG: Assessment Guide   ✓: Grade 5 kits   TRB: Teacher's Resource Book

Hardcover Student Book

- Together, the Hardcover Student Book and its companion Activity Workbook contain all of the pages in the consumable Student Activity Book.

Manipulatives and Materials

- Essential materials for teaching *Math Expressions* are available in the Grade 5 kits. These materials are indicated by a ✓ in these lists. At the front of this Teacher Edition is more information about kit contents, alternatives for the materials, and use of the materials.

Unit 5   Assessment

✓ Unit Objectives Tested	Unit Test Items	Lessons
5.1 Add and subtract fractions and mixed numbers with like and unlike denominators.	1–2	1, 3, 7, 8, 14–16
5.2 Compare and order fractions, decimals, and mixed numbers.	4, 6–7	2, 9, 18–19
5.3 Relate fractions and wholes.	3	4–6
5.4 Find equivalent fractions.	5, 8	6, 11–13, 18–19
5.5 Express the probability of an event as a fraction.	9	17, 21
5.6 Solve problems involving fractions.	10	9–10, 14, 20

Assessment and Review Resources

Formal Assessment

Student Activity Book
- Unit Review and Test (pp. 229–230)

Assessment Guide
- Quick Quiz 1 (p. A49)
- Quick Quiz 2 (p. A50)
- Quick Quiz 3 (p. A51)
- Quick Quiz 4 (p. A52)
- Test A—Open Response (pp. A53–A54)
- Test B—Multiple Choice (pp. A55–A56)
- Performance Assessment (pp. A57–A59)

Test Generator CD-ROM
- Open Response Test
- Multiple Choice Test
- Test Bank Items

Informal Assessment

Teacher Edition
- Ongoing Assessment (in every lesson)
- Quick Practice (in every lesson)
- Math Talk (in every lesson)
- Portfolio Suggestions (p. 579)

�123 Math Talk
- ▸ The Learning Classroom (pp. 413, 430, 432, 477, 494, 543, 564)
- ▸ Math Talk in Action (pp. 519, 558, 564)
- ▸ In Activities (pp. 416, 425, 436, 450, 463, 464, 478, 483, 508, 526, 543, 546, 552, 553, 554, 567, 572)
- ▸ Solve and Discuss (pp. 430, 432, 444, 488, 502, 504, 518, 521, 535, 559)
- ▸ Student Pairs (pp. 415, 418, 437, 443, 446, 477, 485, 494, 522, 537, 538, 547, 557, 566, 573, 574)
  - Helping Partners (pp. 559, 560)
- ▸ Small Groups (pp. 415, 418, 437, 438, 472, 521, 548, 568, 573)
- ▸ Scenarios (pp. 442, 559)
- ▸ Step-by-Step at the Board (p. 519)

Review Opportunities

Homework and Remembering
- Review of recently taught topics
- Spiral Review

Teacher Edition
- Unit Review and Test (pp. 577–580)

Test Generator CD-ROM
- Custom review sheets

Independent Learning Activities

Ready-Made Math Challenge Centers

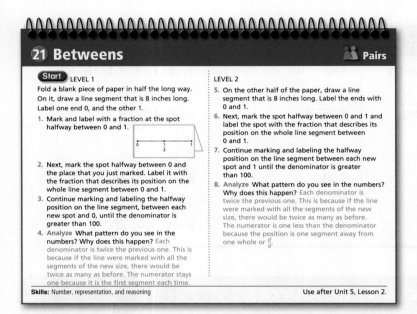

21 Betweens · Pairs

Start LEVEL 1

Fold a blank piece of paper in half the long way. On it, draw a line segment that is 8 inches long. Label one end 0, and the other 1.

1. Mark and label with a fraction at the spot halfway between 0 and 1.

2. Next, mark the spot halfway between 0 and the place that you just marked. Label it with the fraction that describes its position on the whole line segment between 0 and 1.

3. Continue marking and labeling the halfway position on the line segment, between each new spot and 0, until the denominator is greater than 100.

4. **Analyze** What pattern do you see in the numbers? Why does this happen? Each denominator is twice the previous one. This is because if the line were marked with all the segments of the new size, there would be twice as many as before. The numerator stays one because it is the first segment each time.

LEVEL 2

5. On the other half of the paper, draw a line segment that is 8 inches long. Label the ends with 0 and 1.

6. Next, mark the spot halfway between 0 and 1 and label the spot with the fraction that describes its position on the whole line segment between 0 and 1.

7. Continue marking and labeling the halfway position on the line segment between each new spot and 1 until the denominator is greater than 100.

8. **Analyze** What pattern do you see in the numbers? Why does this happen? Each denominator is twice the previous one. This is because if the line were marked with all the segments of the new size, there would be twice as many as before. The numerator is one less than the denominator because the position is one segment away from one whole or $\frac{d}{d}$.

Skills: Number, representation, and reasoning

Use after Unit 5, Lesson 2.

Grouping Pairs

Materials None

Objective Students locate and name halfway positions on a number line.

Connections Number and Reasoning

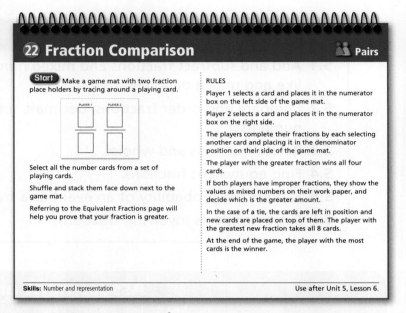

22 Fraction Comparison · Pairs

Start Make a game mat with two fraction place holders by tracing around a playing card.

PLAYER 1 PLAYER 2

Select all the number cards from a set of playing cards.

Shuffle and stack them face down next to the game mat.

Referring to the Equivalent Fractions page will help you prove that your fraction is greater.

RULES

Player 1 selects a card and places it in the numerator box on the left side of the game mat.

Player 2 selects a card and places it in the numerator box on the right side.

The players complete their fractions by each selecting another card and placing it in the denominator position on their side of the game mat.

The player with the greater fraction wins all four cards.

If both players have improper fractions, they show the values as mixed numbers on their work paper, and decide which is the greater amount.

In the case of a tie, the cards are left in position and new cards are placed on top of them. The player with the greatest new fraction takes all 8 cards.

At the end of the game, the player with the most cards is the winner.

Skills: Number and representation

Use after Unit 5, Lesson 6.

Grouping Pairs

Materials Playing cards, Equivalent Fractions (TRB M31)

Objective Students convert and compare improper fractions.

Connections Representation and Number

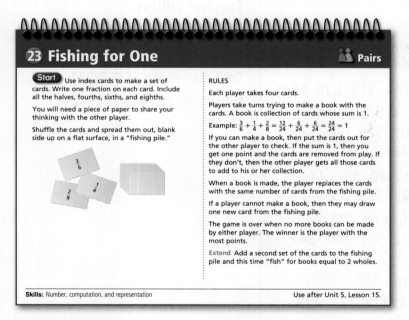

23 Fishing for One · Pairs

Start Use index cards to make a set of cards. Write one fraction on each card. Include all the halves, fourths, sixths, and eighths.

You will need a piece of paper to share your thinking with the other player.

Shuffle the cards and spread them out, blank side up on a flat surface, in a "fishing pile."

RULES

Each player takes four cards.

Players take turns trying to make a book with the cards. A book is collection of cards whose sum is 1.

Example: $\frac{3}{6} + \frac{1}{4} + \frac{2}{8} = \frac{12}{24} + \frac{6}{24} + \frac{6}{24} = \frac{24}{24} = 1$

If you can make a book, then put the cards out for the other player to check. If the sum is 1, then you get one point and the cards are removed from play. If they don't, then the other player gets all those cards to add to his or her collection.

When a book is made, the player replaces the cards with the same number of cards from the fishing pile.

If a player cannot make a book, then they may draw one new card from the fishing pile.

The game is over when no more books can be made by either player. The winner is the player with the most points.

Extend Add a second set of the cards to the fishing pile and this time "fish" for books equal to 2 wholes.

Skills: Number, computation, and representation

Use after Unit 5, Lesson 15.

Grouping Pairs

Materials Index cards

Objective Students collect fractions that have a sum of one.

Connections Number and Computation

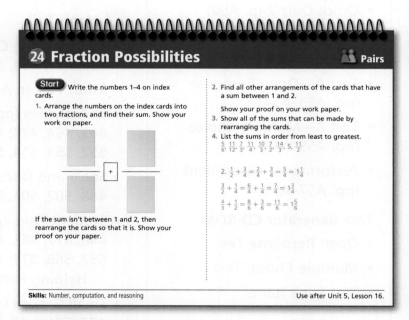

24 Fraction Possibilities · Pairs

Start Write the numbers 1–4 on index cards.

1. Arrange the numbers on the index cards into two fractions, and find their sum. Show your work on paper.

+

If the sum isn't between 1 and 2, then rearrange the cards so that it is. Show your proof on your paper.

2. Find all other arrangements of the cards that have a sum between 1 and 2.

Show your proof on your work paper.

3. Show all of the sums that can be made by rearranging the cards.

4. List the sums in order from least to greatest.

$\frac{5}{6}, \frac{11}{12}, \frac{7}{3}, \frac{7}{4}, \frac{10}{3}, \frac{7}{4}, \frac{14}{3}, 5, \frac{11}{2}$

2. $\frac{1}{2} + \frac{3}{4} = \frac{2}{4} + \frac{3}{4} = \frac{5}{4} = 1\frac{1}{4}$

$\frac{3}{2} + \frac{1}{4} = \frac{6}{4} + \frac{1}{4} = \frac{7}{4} = 1\frac{3}{4}$

$\frac{4}{3} + \frac{1}{2} = \frac{8}{6} + \frac{3}{6} = \frac{11}{6} = 1\frac{5}{6}$

Skills: Number, computation, and reasoning

Use after Unit 5, Lesson 16.

Grouping Pairs

Materials 4 index cards

Objective Students rearrange a set of numbers into fractions in order to find all the possible sums.

Connections Number and Computation

Ready-Made Math Resources

Technology — Tutorial, Practice, and Intervention

Use online, individualized intervention and support to bring students to proficiency.

Help students practice skills and apply concepts through exciting math adventures.

Extend and enrich students' understanding of skills and concepts through engaging interactive lessons and activities.

Visit **Education Place**
www.eduplace.com

Visit Education Place www.eduplace.com
Visit **www.eduplace.com/mx2t/** and find family, teacher, and student materials, activities, games, and more.

Literature Link

Fraction Action

Fraction Action
Loreen Leedy's lively cast of animal characters will introduce fractions in a word-problem context that is unique, colorful and animated.

Differentiated Instruction

Individualizing Instruction

Activities	Level	Frequency
	• Intervention • On Level • Challenge	All 3 in every lesson

Math Writing Prompts	Level	Frequency
	• Intervention • On Level • Challenge	All 3 in every lesson

Math Center Challenges	For advanced students	
	4 in every unit	

Reaching All Learners

	Lessons	Pages
English Language Learners	1, 2, 3, 4, 5, 6, 7, 8, 9, 10, 11, 12, 13, 14, 15, 16, 17, 18, 19, 20, 21	412, 422, 432, 436, 444, 450, 458, 463, 469, 476, 482, 487, 493, 500, 510, 519, 526, 532, 542, 547, 552, 567, 573
	Lessons	**Pages**
Extra Help	1, 2, 7, 8, 9, 11, 14, 18, 19	415, 418, 423, 426, 457, 462, 464, 468, 488, 513, 547, 558
	Lessons	**Pages**
Special Needs	1, 6, 10, 18	413, 451, 476, 547
Advanced Learners	**Lessons**	**Pages**
	5, 19, 20	445, 557, 565

Strategies for English Language Learners

Present this problem to all students. Offer the different levels of support to meet students' levels of language proficiency.

Objective Review language and vocabulary used with fractions.

Problem Draw a circle divided into 4 equal parts. Shade 1 part. Write *whole, part, fraction, numerator,* and *denominator*. Have students tell how many parts of the whole are shaded. Write $\frac{1}{4}$.

Newcomer

- Say: **1 of 4 parts is $\frac{1}{4}$. $\frac{1}{4}$ is a fraction.** Have students repeat.
- Point and say: **1 is the numerator. 4 is the denominator.** Have students repeat.

Beginning

- Ask: **Is this the fraction $\frac{1}{4}$? Does $\frac{1}{4}$ equal 1 of 4 equal parts?** yes
- Point and say: **4 is the total number of parts. 4 is the denominator.** Have students repeat. Continue with *numerator*.

Intermediate

- Say: **$\frac{1}{4}$ is a __.** fraction **It equals 1 of 4 equal __.** parts **Is $\frac{1}{4}$ of the circle shaded?** yes
- Say: **The denominator is 4. The total number of parts is the __.** denominator Continue with *numerator*.

Advanced

- Ask: **How much of the circle is shaded?** $\frac{1}{4}$
- Have students identify the numerator and denominator.

Connections

Art Connection
Lesson 5, page 448

Language Arts Connection
Lesson 10, page 480

Math-to-Math Connections
Lesson 2, page 428
Lesson 7, page 460
Lesson 11, page 490
Lesson 18, page 550

Multicultural Connection
Lesson 14, page 516

Real-World Connections
Lesson 3, page 434
Lesson 8, page 466
Lesson 13, page 506
Lesson 15, page 524
Lesson 17, page 540
Lesson 19, page 562
Lesson 20, page 570
Lesson 21, page 576

Science Connections
Lesson 4, page 440
Lesson 9, page 474

Social Studies Connection
Lesson 6, page 454

Sports Connections
Lesson 12, page 498
Lesson 16, page 530

Math Background

Putting Research into Practice for Unit 5

From Our Curriculum Research Project: Math Talk Is Important

A significant part of the collaborative classroom culture in *Math Expressions* is the frequent exchange of problem-solving strategies, or math talk. The benefits of math talk are multiple. Describing one's methods to another person can clarify one's own thinking as well as clarify the matter for others. Another person's approach can supply a new perspective, and frequent exposure to different approaches tends to engender flexible thinking. Math talk creates opportunities to understand errors and permits teachers to assess students' understanding on an ongoing basis. It encourages students to develop their language skills, both in math and in everyday English. Finally, math talk enables students to become active helpers and questioners, creating student-to-student talk that stimulates engagement and community.

—Karen Fuson, Author
  Math Expressions

From Current Research: Models of Fractions

During grades 3–5, students should build their understanding of fractions as parts of a whole and as division. They will need to see and explore a variety of models of fractions, focusing primarily on familiar fractions such as halves, thirds, fourths, fifths, sixths, eighths, and tenths. By using an area model in which part of a region is shaded, students can see how fractions are related to a unit whole, compare fractional parts of a whole, and find equivalent fractions. They should develop strategies for ordering and comparing fractions, often using benchmarks such as $\frac{1}{2}$ and 1. For example, fifth-graders can compare fractions such as $\frac{2}{5}$ and $\frac{5}{8}$ by comparing each with $\frac{1}{2}$; one is a little less than $\frac{1}{2}$, and the other is a little more. By using parallel number lines, each showing a unit fraction and its multiples (see fig. 5.1), students can see fractions as numbers, note their relationship to 1, and see relationships among fractions, including equivalence. They should also begin to understand that between any two fractions, there is always another fraction.

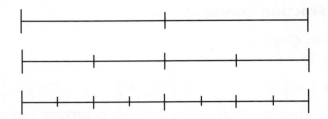

Fig. 5.1. Parallel number lines with unit fractions and their multiples

National Council of Teachers of Mathematics. *Principles and Standards for School Mathematics* (Number and Operations Standard for Grades 3–5). Reston: NCTM, 2000. p. 149

Other Useful References: Fractions

Kilpatrick, Jeremy, Jane Swafford, Bradford Findell, eds. *Adding It Up: Helping Children Learn Mathematics.* Mathematics Learning Study Committee, National Research Council. Washington: NAP, 2001 (especially Chapter 7: Developing Proficiency with Other Numbers).

Mack, Nancy K. "Connecting to Develop Computational Fluency with Fractions." *Teaching Children Mathematics* 11.4 (Nov. 2004): pp. 226–232.

National Council of Teachers of Mathematics. *Making Sense of Fractions, Ratios, and Proportions* (2002 Yearbook). Ed. Bonnie Litwiller. Reston: NCTM, 2002.

Reys, Barbara J., Rita Barger, Maxim Bruckheimer, Barbara Dougherty, Jack Hope, Linda Lembke, Zvia Markovits, Andy Parnas, Sue Reehm, Ruthi Sturdevant, and Marianne Weber. *Developing Number Sense in the Middle Grades: Addenda Series, Grades 5–8.* Curriculum and Evaluation Standards Addenda Series. Reston: NCTM, 1991. pp. 28–33.

Getting Ready to Teach Unit 5

Basic Fraction Concepts

Fraction Chains
Lesson 1

$$\frac{1}{3} + \frac{1}{3} + \frac{1}{3} = \frac{3}{3} = 1 \qquad \frac{1}{5} + \frac{1}{5} + \frac{1}{5} = \frac{3}{5} \qquad \frac{5}{8} = \frac{1}{8} + \frac{1}{8} + \frac{1}{8} + \frac{1}{8} + \frac{1}{8}$$

The unit fraction chains help students overcome typical errors in adding and subtracting fractions (adding and subtracting the tops and the bottoms, not just the tops.)

Visualizing Unit Fractions as Equal Parts of 1 Whole
Lesson 2

Students fold fraction strips to see each unit fraction $\frac{1}{d}$ as one of d equal parts of the whole. They see fraction bars on student pages throughout the unit. Fraction bars show the crucial inverse relationship between the number and the size of unit fractions: a larger d in $\frac{1}{d}$ means more but smaller equal parts. Fraction bars also show equivalent fractions ($\frac{2}{4} = \frac{3}{6} = \frac{4}{8}$).

$\frac{1}{3}$		$\frac{1}{3}$		$\frac{1}{3}$	
$\frac{1}{4}$	$\frac{1}{4}$		$\frac{1}{4}$		$\frac{1}{4}$

$\frac{1}{6}$	$\frac{1}{6}$	$\frac{1}{6}$	$\frac{1}{6}$	$\frac{1}{6}$	$\frac{1}{6}$

$\frac{1}{8}$	$\frac{1}{8}$	$\frac{1}{8}$	$\frac{1}{8}$	$\frac{1}{8}$	$\frac{1}{8}$	$\frac{1}{8}$	$\frac{1}{8}$

Fraction Partners of 1 Whole
Lesson 4

Students find "fraction partners" of 1 whole—two fractions with the same denominator that together form 1 whole. The model below shows 1 whole as the sum of $\frac{1}{4}$ and $\frac{3}{4}$. So $\frac{1}{4}$ and $\frac{3}{4}$ are partners of 1 whole.

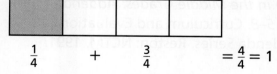

$$\frac{1}{4} \qquad + \qquad \frac{3}{4} \qquad = \frac{4}{4} = 1$$

Seeing 1 whole as $\frac{d}{d}$ ($\frac{4}{4}$, $\frac{7}{7}$, and so on) is crucial in understanding mixed numbers and ungrouping in subtracting mixed numbers.

As you teach these lessons emphasize understanding of these terms.

• non-unit fraction

• unit fraction

• unsimplify

See the Teacher Glossary on pp. T6–T17.

Equivalent Fractions
Lessons 11, 12, and 13

Students discuss fractions equivalent to $\frac{1}{2}$.

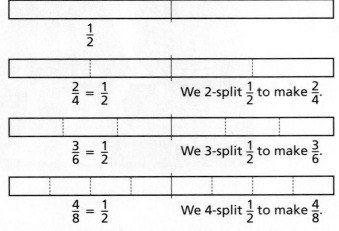

$\frac{1}{2}$

$\frac{2}{4} = \frac{1}{2}$ We 2-split $\frac{1}{2}$ to make $\frac{2}{4}$. $\frac{1 \times 2}{2 \times 2} = \frac{2}{4}$

$\frac{3}{6} = \frac{1}{2}$ We 3-split $\frac{1}{2}$ to make $\frac{3}{6}$. $\frac{1 \times 3}{2 \times 3} = \frac{3}{6}$

$\frac{4}{8} = \frac{1}{2}$ We 4-split $\frac{1}{2}$ to make $\frac{4}{8}$. $\frac{1 \times 4}{2 \times 4} = \frac{4}{8}$

$\frac{5}{10} = \frac{1}{2}$ We 5-split $\frac{1}{2}$ to make $\frac{5}{10}$. $\frac{1 \times 5}{2 \times 5} = \frac{5}{10}$

Mixed Numbers and Improper Fractions
Lesson 6

Students share a variety of ways to show represent $\frac{5}{4}$.

 $\frac{5}{4}$ 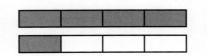 $\frac{5}{4}$

They also connect what they know about unit fractions to show that there is one whole, $\frac{4}{4}$, and $\frac{2}{4}$ more.

$$\boxed{\frac{1}{4} + \frac{1}{4} + \frac{1}{4} + \frac{1}{4}} + \frac{1}{4} = 1\frac{1}{4}$$

Modeling Fraction Operations

Like Denominators
Lessons 1 and 3

We focus on using fraction bars on the MathBoard to model addition and subtraction with like denominators. This fraction bar feature of the MathBoard is also available on TRB M114.

Addition Model for Fractions With Like Denominators:

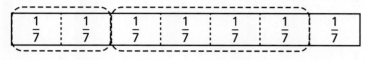

$$\frac{2}{7} + \frac{4}{7} = \frac{2+4}{7} = \frac{6}{7}$$

Subtraction Model for Fractions With Like Denominators:

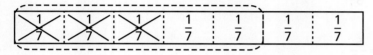

$$\frac{5}{7} - \frac{3}{7} = \frac{5-3}{7} = \frac{2}{7}$$

For both addition and subtraction, the critical step of adding or subtracting only the numerators is circled as a transition for understanding. That step can be omitted later.

Unlike Denominators
Lessons 14 and 15

Again students use their MathBoards to model addition and subtraction with unlike denominators.

Make $\frac{5}{6}$. How can you subtract $\frac{2}{3}$?

Sixths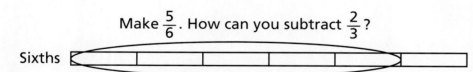

Change thirds into sixths and subtract.

Sixths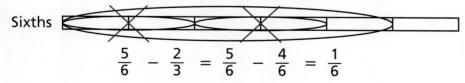

$$\frac{5}{6} - \frac{2}{3} = \frac{5}{6} - \frac{4}{6} = \frac{1}{6}$$

Relate Fractions and Decimals

Looking for Patterns
Lessons 18 and 19

Students discuss patterns they see in fraction and decimal equivalencies.

Fifths and Tenths

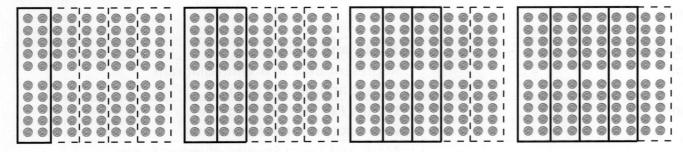

$$\frac{1}{5} = 0.20 = 0.2 = \frac{2}{10} \qquad \frac{2}{5} = 0.40 = 0.4 = \frac{4}{10} \qquad \frac{3}{5} = 0.60 = 0.6 = \frac{6}{10} \qquad \frac{4}{5} = 0.80 = 0.8 = \frac{8}{10}$$

Using Number Lines
Lesson 19

Equivalence Students write fraction and decimal equivalencies on number lines.

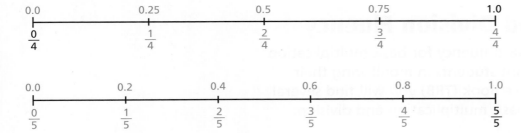

Compare Fractions and Decimals Students compare fractions and decimals as they estimate their placement on a number line

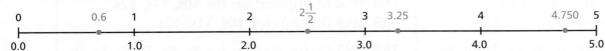

Ordering Fractions and Decimals Students use any method they choose including benchmarks to write fractions, mixed numbers and decimals in order.

$$\frac{5}{6}, \; 1\frac{2}{3}, \; \frac{7}{12}, \; 1\frac{1}{2}, \; \frac{1}{3} \qquad 1\frac{2}{3}, \; 1\frac{1}{2}, \; \frac{5}{6}, \; \frac{7}{12}, \; \frac{1}{3}$$

Use Mathematical Processes
Lesson 21

The NCTM process skills of problem solving, reasoning and proof, communication, connections, and representation are interwoven through all lessons throughout the year. The last lesson of this unit allows students to extend their use of mathematical processes to other situations.

NCTM Process Skill	Activity and Goal
Representation	1: Represent data in a Venn diagram. 2: Collect and display data.
Communication	3: Discuss fair and unfair games. 1, 2: Predict and share reasoning.
Connections	1: Math and Social Studies: Number Sense and Data
Reasoning and Proof	3: Use reasoning to determine whether a game is fair or unfair. 1: Use reasoning to place data in a Venn diagram.
Problem Solving	4, 5: Solve a problem with multiple solutions.

Basic Multiplication and Division Fluency

Students should continually work toward fluency for basic multiplication and division facts. Use checkups to assist students in monitoring their own learning. In the Teacher's Resource Book (TRB) you will find several pages for diagnosing and practicing basic multiplication and division.

TRB M58 Diagnostic Quiz for Basic Multiplication TRB M59 Diagnostic Quiz for Basic Division	TRB M66 Scrambled Multiplication Tables TRB M67 Blank Multiplication Tables
TRB M60 Basic Multiplication Practice TRB M61 Basic Division Practice	TRB M68 Multiplication for 10s, 11s, 12s TRB M69 Division for 10s, 11s, 12s
TRB M62 Multiplication for 3s, 4s, 6s, 7s, 8s, 9s TRB M63 Division for 3s, 4s, 6s, 7s, 8s, 9s	TRB M83 Factor Puzzles for 3s, 4s, 6s, 7s, 8s, 9s TRB M84 Factor Puzzles for 6s, 7s, 8s
TRB M64 Multiplication for 6s, 7s, 8s TRB M65 Division for 6s, 7s, 8s	TRB M85 Blank Factor Puzzles

See the Basic Facts Fluency Plan for information about practice materials.

Build Unit Fractions

REAL WORLD Problem Solving

Lesson Objectives

- Build other fractions from unit fractions.
- Add like fractions.
- Express information from pictures, stories, and data formats as fractions.

Vocabulary

unit fraction
non-unit fraction

The Day at a Glance

Today's Goals	Materials
1 Teaching the Lesson **A1:** Add unit fractions and non-unit fractions with like denominators. **A2:** Apply knowledge of fractions to real-life situations. **2 Going Further** ▶ Differentiated Instruction **3 Homework and Spiral Review**	**Lesson Activities** Student Activity Book pp. 179–182 or Student Hardcover Book pp. 179–182 and Activity Workbook pp. 82–84 (includes Family Letter) Homework and Remembering pp. 105–106 MathBoard materials	**Going Further** Activity Cards 5-1 Plastic bread tags or counters (2 colors) Grid Paper (TRB M17) Math Journals

123 **Use Math Talk today!**

Keeping Skills Sharp

Quick Practice ⏱ 5 MINUTES	Daily Routines
This section provides repetitive, short activities that either help students become faster and more accurate at a skill or help to prepare ground for new concepts. Quick Practice for this unit will start with Lesson 2.	**Reasoning** Is the following statement true or false? If false, explain why. Then reword the statement to make it true. **The circumference of a circle is a similar measure to the area of a square.** False; Possible answer: Circumference is the distance around a circle. Perimeter is the distance around a square. True: The circumference of a circle is a similar measure to the perimeter of a square.

① Teaching the Lesson

Add Like Fractions

 25 MINUTES

Goal: Add unit fractions and non-unit fractions with like denominators.

Materials: MathBoard materials

 NCTM Standards:
Number and Operations
Problem Solving

English Language Learners

Write $\frac{1}{4}$, $\frac{1}{5}$, and *unit fraction* on the board. Ask: **Is a unit fraction one part of a whole?** yes

- **Beginning** Ask: **Is $\frac{1}{4}$ one of 4 equal parts?** yes **Is $\frac{1}{4}$ a unit fraction.** yes Continue with $\frac{1}{5}$.
- **Intermediate** Say: $\frac{1}{4}$ and $\frac{1}{5}$ are __. unit fractions
- **Advanced** Have students tell about what each fraction represents and identify them as unit fractions.

Teaching Note

Math Background

Throughout the work on fractions, we may sometimes use the word *pieces* to refer to the unit fractions that make up a fraction. This helps make them be quantities (things) to students. But continue to emphasize that these pieces are unit fractions and are equal parts of a specific whole. Fractions are composed of unit fractions, and these unit fractions are added, subtracted, compared, simplified, and unsimplified. Operating with fractions requires operations with unit fractions, the equal parts of one specific whole.

▶ MathBoards and Unit Fractions WHOLE CLASS

Ask for Ideas Ask students to share what they know about fractions. This will give you some sense of where your class is. Don't worry about teaching the issues they raise. Just say you'll return to all of these points as you move through the fraction lessons.

Distribute the MathBoard materials. Ask students to discuss the patterns they see on the MathBoards, including the words on the left. They should identify and discuss these points:

- Each fraction bar has as many equal parts as the first part of the word on the left (four equal parts in fourths, six equal parts in sixths, etc.)
- The first part gets smaller as the number of parts gets bigger.
- All of these fractions are equal parts of the same 1 whole shown at the top. You can only compare fractions when they are parts of the same whole.
- Fractions are division situations where you know how many equal parts there are. The denominator (bottom number) tells how many parts/shares.

Tell students that they are going to label the first part of each bar as a unit fraction and write out at the right what this unit fraction means.

$\frac{1}{2}$	1 of 2 equal parts
$\frac{1}{3}$	1 of 3 equal parts
$\frac{1}{4}$	

Continue through to $\frac{1}{10}$.   1 of 10 equal parts

Have students discuss the pattern they see in the unit fractions:

As the number of equal parts increases, the size _____. decreases

Tell students that this is the most important and trickiest part of fractions: that a *bigger* number on the *bottom* of a unit fraction means that the unit fraction is *smaller*.

Have them look at the unit fractions they've written to see the pattern and then "Close your eyes. Visualize." to see the pattern in their mind to help them remember it.

Discuss the names for the unit fractions $\frac{1}{2}$, $\frac{1}{3}$, $\frac{1}{4}$, $\frac{1}{5}$, ... , $\frac{1}{10}$

$\frac{one}{half}$, $\frac{one}{third}$, $\frac{one}{fourth}$, $\frac{one}{fifth}$, $\frac{one}{sixth}$, ... , $\frac{one}{tenth}$

and the *-th* pattern in names for unit fractions.

▶ Add Unit Fractions on the MathBoard WHOLE CLASS

Now tell students that they will find patterns in the number of unit fractions in 1 whole. Have them label the rest of the unit fractions in each whole, one at a time as shown below. This activity is the set-up for adding fractions (on the next page) and is the visual basis for understanding fractions.

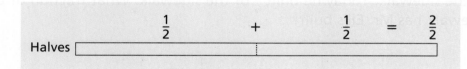

Ask students to discuss the patterns they see emerging for thirds, fourths, and fifths.

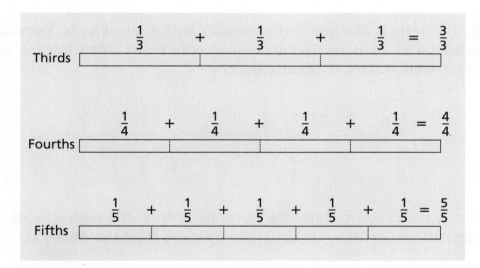

Discuss the meaning of $\frac{2}{2}$, $\frac{3}{3}$, $\frac{4}{4}$, and $\frac{5}{5}$.

● **What do you have when the numerator and denominator are the same?** one whole

● **How do you know?** There are a certain number of equal parts and we are using all of them.

Do at least the sixths, eighths, and tenths and discuss the patterns they see (e.g., $1 = \frac{6}{6}$ because it takes six of the $\frac{1}{6}$ to make the whole again).

Activity continued ▶

Teaching Note

Math Background

Fraction bars are length models. Length models have an advantage over the traditional circular models for fractions, such as pizzas or pies, because they can be constructed to be easily divided into equal parts. For example, a circle may be very difficult to divide into 7 equal parts, but a length model can be made 7 centimeters long and the centimeters can be marked easily.

Differentiated Instruction

Special Needs Work on the larger unit fractions of $\frac{1}{6}$ and above to be sure that students understand the general -*th* pattern. Then discuss and practice the irregular fractions: one-half, one-third, one-fifth.

The Learning Classroom

Math Talk Always start new topics by eliciting as much from students as possible. Students often know some things about new topics. This builds feelings of competence and confidence and helps create the classroom community where everyone is a teacher and a learner. So even where the directions for a lesson are directing you to do the talking, remember to always ask for students' own ideas first.

Activity 1

Teaching Note

Watch For! A typical student error when finding the sum of fractions is to add not only the numerators, but also the denominators. For example, students might write $\frac{2}{5} + \frac{1}{5} = \frac{3}{10}$. Writing unit fraction chains helps students see that the bottom number stays the same:

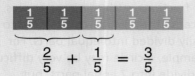

 Ongoing Assessment

Ask students:

▶ How can you tell what the unit fraction is?

▶ How can you build a non-unit fraction from unit fractions?

▶ How can you use unit fractions to add fractions with like denominators?

▶ Add Non-Unit Fractions on the MathBoard

WHOLE CLASS

Direct the students' attention to the fraction bar that shows sixths and have them erase the $= \frac{6}{6}$ at the end.

Give students the word problems below and ask everyone to solve them by circling fractions on the MathBoards. Ask them to write a fraction addition equation below the bar for each problem.

● Mr. Ellis is building a sidewalk with 6 equal parts. Yesterday he built $\frac{2}{6}$ of the sidewalk. Today he built $\frac{3}{6}$ of the sidewalk. What fraction of the sidewalk has Mr. Ellis built? $\frac{5}{6}$

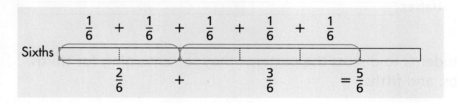

● Ms. Glennette is also building a sidewalk with 6 equal parts. Yesterday she built 4 of the parts. Today she built only 1 part. What fraction of the sidewalk has Ms. Glennette built? $\frac{5}{6}$

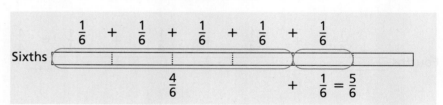

The first word problem states the fractions directly. The second word problem asks students to construct the fractions from the situation.

Discuss the fractions in the equations:

● Which fraction in the equations is a unit fraction? $\frac{1}{6}$

● Which fractions in the equations are not unit fractions? $\frac{2}{6}, \frac{3}{6}, \frac{4}{6}, \frac{5}{6}$

● How can you build these other fractions from the unit fraction $\frac{1}{6}$? by adding; $\frac{2}{6} = \frac{1}{6} + \frac{1}{6}, \frac{3}{6} = \frac{1}{6} + \frac{1}{6} + \frac{1}{6}$, and so on

Introduce the term *non-unit fraction* for fractions such as $\frac{2}{6}, \frac{3}{6}, \frac{4}{6}$, or $\frac{5}{6}$. Non-unit fractions are built by adding unit fractions. Ask students to name some other non-unit fractions. Answers will vary. Possible answers: $\frac{3}{16}, \frac{2}{7}, \frac{4}{5}$

Invite students to invent more sidewalk problems using sevenths, then eighths, ninths, and tenths. Ask a student volunteer to work at the Class MathBoard while the rest of the students solve the problems at their seats. Be sure students write an equation for each problem that is presented and discuss how each non-unit fraction is made by adding unit fractions.

▶ Add Fractions Without Fraction Bars WHOLE CLASS

Ask students to turn their MathBoards over to the blank side. Present the following addition equations and ask everyone to complete them without using the fraction bars, but writing unit fractions:

$$\frac{3}{8} + \frac{2}{8} = \left(\frac{1}{8} + \frac{1}{8} + \frac{1}{8}\right) + \left(\frac{1}{8} + \frac{1}{8}\right) = \frac{5}{8}$$

$$\frac{2}{5} + \frac{3}{5} = \left(\frac{1}{5} + \frac{1}{5}\right) + \left(\frac{1}{5} + \frac{1}{5} + \frac{1}{5}\right) = \frac{5}{5} = 1$$

$$\frac{4}{9} + \frac{2}{9} + \frac{1}{9} = \left(\frac{1}{9} + \frac{1}{9} + \frac{1}{9} + \frac{1}{9}\right) + \left(\frac{1}{9} + \frac{1}{9}\right) + \frac{1}{9} = \frac{7}{9}$$

Discuss the results.

- Which part of each fraction did not change when you added the fractions? the bottom numeral, or denominator

- How do you find the top numeral, or numerator, for the total? Add the numerators of the given fractions to get the numerator for the sum. This is because you are just counting all of the unit fractions that make those non-unit fractions.

- Did any of these fractions add to one whole? yes; the second pair

Ask students to discuss whether this general method will work for any fractions. Yes, you can write any fractions as the top number of unit fractions so you can always just add the top numbers to tell you how many of the bottom number unit fractions you have.

You can introduce the vocabulary *numerator* and *denominator* anytime. The words will appear on the student page in Lesson 3.

$$\frac{7\ \underline{\text{numerator}}}{9\ \text{denominator}} \quad \frac{\text{number of unit fractions}}{\text{divided equal parts}} = \frac{7\ \text{of the}}{\text{ninths}}$$

Teaching Note

What to Expect from Students
Some students may be confused about equivalent fractions when talking about unit and non-unit fractions. For example, the non-unit fraction $\frac{2}{4}$ is equivalent to the unit fraction $\frac{1}{2}$. A fraction is a unit fraction if it describes one of the equal parts only (as $\frac{1}{2}$ does). It is not necessary to discuss this if students do not bring it up on their own.

Differentiated Instruction

Extra Help If students need more practice adding fractions with like denominators without using fraction bars, have them work in **Student Pairs** or **Small Groups** to create and solve more addition questions by writing out the unit fractions. Encourage them to share and discuss their answers.

Activity 2

Fractions in Context

 25 MINUTES

Goal: Apply knowledge of fractions to real-world situations.

Materials: MathBoard materials; Student Book, pp. 179–180 or Hardcover Book pp. 179–180 and Activity Workbook p. 82

✔ **NCTM Standards:**
Number and Operations
Connections

Teaching Note

Watch For! Some students might confuse the "other" part with the whole. For example, they might say that E makes up $\frac{1}{4}$ of "Emily" because there is one E and there are four other letters. If so, ask them to find the total number of letters first and emphasize that this number is the whole.

Teaching Note

Math Background There are two basic kinds of fraction situations in the world. The whole may be a length (a piece of ribbon) or a shape (a pizza). The whole may be a set of things, and the fraction is made of some number of these things.

We use length models (fraction bars and number lines) to provide consistency across these two situations. The visual single whole length helps students stay in the fraction world, which operates differently from the whole-number world. For example, this visual whole helps students see that, although $3 < 4$, $\frac{1}{3} > \frac{1}{4}$ because $\frac{1}{3}$ has fewer unit fractions (3 rather than 4) and, therefore, each unit fraction $\frac{1}{3}$ is larger than $\frac{1}{4}$.

▶ Observe Fractions in the Classroom | WHOLE CLASS |

 Math Talk Have the students discuss some fractional amounts that relate to the classroom. It is important to emphasize that students need to find the total, or whole, first. These examples include 1 whole divided into *d* parts and things in a group in which the group is taken to be the 1 whole. Some examples include:

● Our window is divided into how many unit fractions? This will vary with the window.

● How many people are in the classroom? possible answer: 26

● How many people in the classroom are teachers? possible answer: 1

● What fraction of all the people in the room are teachers? $\frac{1}{26}$

● What fraction of all the people in the room are students? How do you know? $\frac{25}{26}$, because the whole has 26 equal parts and 25 of them are students

Write one or two students' names on the board. (For example, Emily and Waneta.)

● What fraction of the letters in Emily's name is the letter *E*? How do you know? $\frac{1}{5}$, because there are 5 letters altogether and one of them is an *E*.

● What fraction of the letters in Waneta's name is the letter *A*? How do you know? $\frac{2}{6}$, because there are 6 letters altogether and 2 of them are the letter *A*.

● What fraction of my fingers have a ring? possible answer: $\frac{1}{10}$.

● What fraction of the class is wearing blue today? Answers will vary.

If time permits, invite students to think of other fractions they can observe in the room.

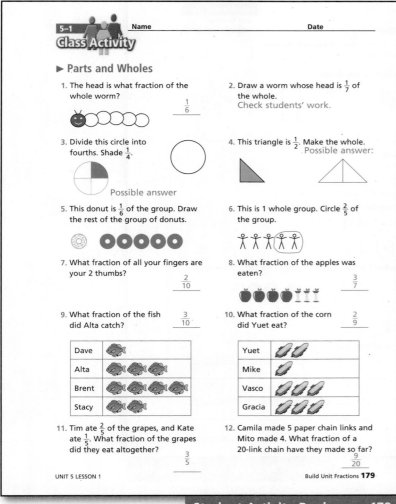

Student Activity Book page 179

▶ Parts and Wholes WHOLE CLASS

To emphasize that a unit fraction is one *equal* part of a whole, draw this figure on the board. Discuss the fraction of the circle that is shaded.

- **Does the shaded section show $\frac{1}{3}$? Why or why not?**
  No. Three of the shaded sections won't completely fill the circle.

- **Why might someone think that it shows $\frac{1}{3}$?** There are 3 sections and 1 section is shaded, but the sections aren't the same size.

- **What fraction does the shaded section show? Why?** The shaded section shows $\frac{1}{4}$ because the circle can be divided into 4 parts that are the exact size of the shaded section.

Have students look at Student Book page 179. Read and discuss the exercises as a class. When a drawing is required, send several volunteers to the board while the others draw on the back of their MathBoard or on a sheet of paper.

Activity continued ▶

① Teaching the Lesson (continued)

Activity 2

Teaching Note

Math Background During this unit, it is important that students maintain and improve their knowledge of basic multiplication and division. You will find suggestions for games and practice at the end of the Unit 5 Overview.

Differentiated Instruction

Extra Help If students continue to add both the denominators and the numerators of fractions, suggest that they rewrite the fractions in words and then read what they wrote. For example, "three fifths plus one fifth equals four fifths."

The Learning Classroom

Student Pairs Initially, it is useful to model pair activities for students by contrasting effective and ineffective helping. For example, students need to help partners solve a problem their way, rather than doing the work for the partner. Helping pairs often foster learning in both students as the helper strives to adopt the perspective of the novice.

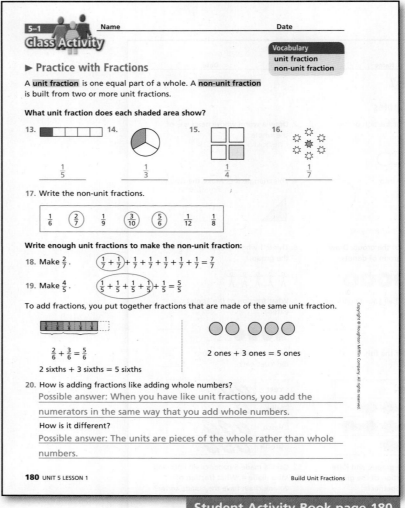

Student Activity Book page 180

▶ Practice With Fractions [WHOLE CLASS]

Discuss the definitions and exercises on Student Book page 180.

Discuss the last question in more detail. Emphasize that in math we always add like to like—tens to tens, ones to ones, sixths to sixths. If we added 2 tens and 3 ones, we would not get 5 of *anything* because the units are not the same. This rule applies to fractions, too. We add only *like* unit fractions. Adding fractions is different from adding whole numbers only because the units are pieces of the whole rather than whole numbers.

If the students understand the material well, they can complete the activity in **Student Pairs** or **Small Groups**. Exercise 20 may still require a class discussion.

2 Going Further

Intervention   Activity Card 5-1

Create a Whole   Activity Card 5-1 ●

Work: In Pairs

Use:
- 2 colors of identical plastic bread tags or counters, a little more than a large handful

1. Each partner picks up a small handful of items from different color groups.

2. Combine the items to form a whole. Name the unit fraction. Then name the fraction of the whole that each color represents.

The unit fraction is ⅟₇. ⅗ of the tags are blue and ⅘ of the tags are pink.

3. Write a sum to represent the two fractional parts of the whole that you made. Express the sum as a fraction. The sum of both fractions equals the whole expressed as a fraction equal to 1.

Unit 5, Lesson 1   Copyright © Houghton Mifflin Company

Activity Note Discuss what a unit fraction represents. Ask students to explain how to add fractions with the same denominator.

☑ Math Writing Prompt

Make a Drawing Use a drawing to show that $\frac{5}{5}$ is the same as one whole. Write an addition equation with unit fractions to go with your drawing.

Soar to Success Math   **Software Support**

Warm-Up 6.09

On Level   Activity Card 5-1

Divide the Whole   Activity Card 5-1 ▲

Work: In Pairs

Use:
- Grid Paper (TRB M17)

1. Take turns drawing a rectangle on grid paper.

2. **Work Together** Investigate different ways to divide the rectangle into equal parts. Use the grid to help you.

3. Write the unit fraction for each drawing. Then write an equation to show that the fractional parts equal the whole.

4. **Math Talk** How did you choose the unit fraction for each drawing? Possible answer: The denominator of the unit fraction equals the number of equal parts. The numerator is always 1.

Unit 5, Lesson 1   Copyright © Houghton Mifflin Company

Activity Note After the activity is complete, use students' work to create a display of sums of unit fractions that equal one whole.

☑ Math Writing Prompt

Analyze You are checking homework for your friend and find this: $\frac{5}{8} + \frac{1}{8} = \frac{6}{16}$. Write a note to your friend. Explain the error and how to fix it.

MEGA MATH Grades K-6   **Software Support**

Fraction Action: Fraction Flare Up, Level B

Challenge   Activity Card 5-1

Describe With Fractions   Activity Card 5-1 ■

Work: By Yourself

1. Choose a topic to investigate, such as the favorite colors of your classmates.

Favorite Color

2. Survey at least 10 of your classmates.

3. Make a pictograph to represent the data you collect in your survey.

⁵⁄₁₀ of the people prefer red, ²⁄₁₀ prefer yellow, ⁴⁄₁₀ prefer blue, and ¹⁄₁₀ prefer green.

4. **Summarize** Write a fractional statement to summarize the results of your survey.

Unit 5, Lesson 1   Copyright © Houghton Mifflin Company

Activity Note Remind students to identify the total number of people in the survey before writing the fractions to identify the part of the whole.

☑ Math Writing Prompt

Write a Problem What is your favorite activity? Write and solve a word problem about it, using fractions. Exchange with a classmate.

DESTINATION Math   **Software Support**

Course III: Module 3: Unit 1: Proper Fractions

③ Homework and Spiral Review

Homework **Goal:** Additional Practice

For Homework, students practice adding unit fractions.

Remembering **Goal:** Spiral Review

This Remembering activity is appropriate anytime after today's lesson.

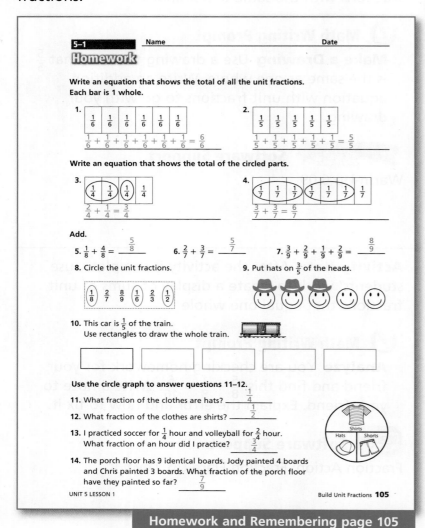

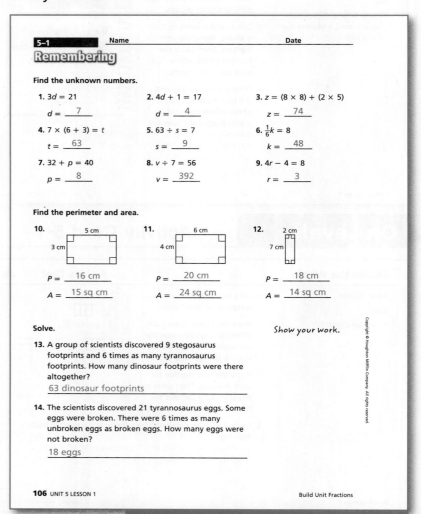

Home and School Connection

Family Letter Have students take home the Family Letter on Student Book page 181 or Activity Workbook page 83. This letter explains how the concept of fractions is developed in *Math Expressions*. It gives parents and guardians a better understanding of the learning that goes on in math class and creates a bridge between school and home. A Spanish translation of this letter is on Student Book page 182 and Activity Workbook page 84.

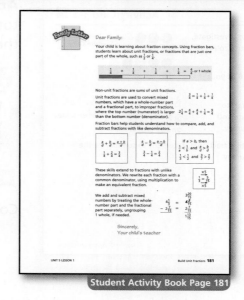

Student Activity Book Page 181

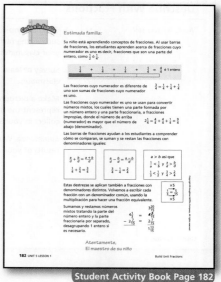

Student Activity Book Page 182

Compare Fractions

Lesson Objectives

- Compare unit fractions and fractions with like denominators.
- Express and refine comparative concepts.
- Apply greater than (>) and less than (<) notation.

Vocabulary

numerator
denominator

The Day at a Glance

Today's Goals	Materials	
1 **Teaching the Lesson** **A1:** Compare common fractions, using fraction bars, and apply findings to other fractions. **A2:** Compare fractions on the number line, and express ideas about comparative fraction size. **A3:** Write inequality signs to compare fractions.	**Lesson Activities** Student Activity Book pp. 183–184 or Student Hardcover Book pp. 183–184 and Activity Workbook page 85 Homework and Remembering pp. 107–108 MathBoard materials Colored pencils	**Going Further** Activity Cards 5-2 Grid Paper (TRB M17) Fraction Bars (TRB M26) Math Journals
2 **Going Further** ▸ Differentiated Instruction		
3 **Homework and Spiral Review**		

123 Use Math Talk today!

Keeping Skills Sharp

Quick Practice ⏱ 5 MINUTES	Daily Routines
Unit Fraction Parade Send six students to the board, and have them each write a unit fraction. In turn, each student gives an arm signal, and the class says each fraction out loud. Everyone checks to make sure all answers are unit fractions.	**Homework Review** Check if any problem caused difficulty for many students, and review as a class. **Mental Math** Find the number that is 0.1 greater and the number that is 0.01 less than each of the given numbers. 1. 470.26 2. 3,189.5 3. 25,317 4. 153.906 1. 470.36, 470.25; 2. 3,189.6, 3,189.49; 3. 25,317.1, 25,316.99; 4. 154.006, 153.896

Teaching the Lesson

Visualize With Fraction Bars

 25 MINUTES

Goal: Compare common fractions, using fraction bars, and apply findings to other fractions.

Materials: Student Activity Book or Hardcover Book p. 183

✔ **NCTM Standard:**
Number and Operations

Teaching Note

Watch For! Some students might be confused by the use of the greater than (>) and less than (<) signs. Tell them that the names of these signs come from how they are read. Emphasize that either sign can be correct for a given pair of numbers; the order the numbers are in determines which sign should be used. For example, both of the following are correct:

- $\frac{1}{6} > \frac{1}{8}$ "$\frac{1}{6}$ is greater than $\frac{1}{8}$"
- $\frac{1}{8} < \frac{1}{6}$ "$\frac{1}{8}$ is less than $\frac{1}{6}$"

To help students remember the proper usage, tell them that the wide end of the symbol is nearer to the greater number.

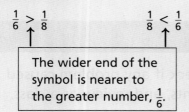

The wider end of the symbol is nearer to the greater number, $\frac{1}{6}$.

English Language Learners

Write $\frac{1}{2}$, $\frac{1}{4}$, $\frac{3}{4}$, *numerator*, and *denominator* on the board. Ask: **Which fractions have the same numerator?** $\frac{1}{2}$, $\frac{1}{4}$ **Denominator?** $\frac{1}{4}$, $\frac{3}{4}$

▶ **Review Comparison Signs (< and >)** WHOLE CLASS

Begin by asking students which number is greater, $\frac{1}{2}$ or $\frac{1}{3}$. Then ask a volunteer to draw fraction bars to show that the answer $\frac{1}{2}$ is correct.

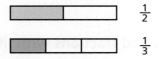

Discuss the drawing.

- How can you tell from the drawing that $\frac{1}{2}$ is greater than $\frac{1}{3}$? The shaded half is larger than the shaded third. You can see it easily because the bars are aligned.

- What has to be true about the fraction bars in order to compare the fractions? They have to be the same size to show the same whole.

- Why might the idea that $\frac{1}{2}$ is greater than $\frac{1}{3}$ be confusing? Because 3 is greater than 2, some people might expect the fraction with a denominator of 3 to be greater than the fraction with a denominator of 2.

On the board, write the mathematical notation that shows which fraction is greater.

$$\frac{1}{2} > \frac{1}{3} \qquad\qquad \frac{1}{3} < \frac{1}{2}$$

Review this notation with the class.

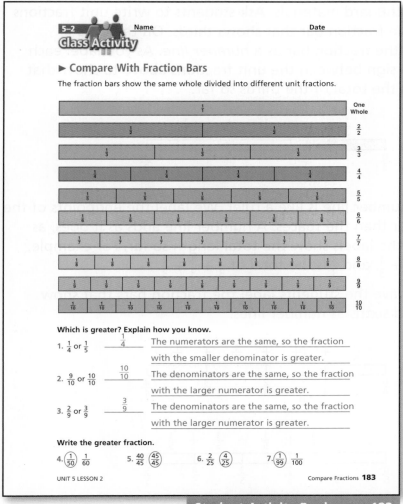

Student Activity Book page 183

▶ Compare With Fraction Bars WHOLE CLASS

Have the students turn to Student Book page 183. Discuss the fractions to the right of the fraction bars. Also review the pattern for unit fractions (as there are more equal parts, the unit fraction becomes smaller).

Ask the students to complete the exercises. In exercises 4–7, students will find that the fraction bars are not directly helpful. Instead, they must recognize and state these general principles:

● The larger the number of parts in a whole, the smaller each equal part must be. When the numerators are the same, the fraction with the smaller denominator is the greater fraction.

● When comparing fractions with like denominators, the parts are all the same size. So a fraction with a greater top number (numerator) will be greater because it has more parts.

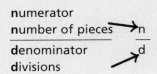

Activity 2

Visualize With Number Lines

 25 MINUTES

Goal: Compare fractions on the number line, and express ideas about comparative fraction size.

Materials: MathBoard materials

 NCTM Standard:
Number and Operations

Teaching Note

Changing the Total These number lines do not have arrows on the ends to make it easier to understand the points in this note. Ordinarily number lines will be drawn with arrows to show that they extend in either direction. But some students may need to draw them without arrows initially while they sort out the tick marks and lengths issues.

It is sometimes difficult to partition a given length into equal parts (even roughly equal parts). Students therefore may change the original total by erasing a leftover part they did not use or by adding a bit to make the last part equal. This is changing the total. It may not matter in some situations, but students need to be aware that this is what they are doing because it may matter a lot in other situations. One alternative is to build up a fraction from a given unit fraction. Draw a small unit fraction and then keep adding on equal lengths to make your 1 whole (draw three such lengths if the unit fraction is $\frac{1}{3}$). You can then circle your target fraction (e.g., $\frac{2}{3}$ of that whole). This does not work of course when you are finding equivalent fractions; these must have the same whole.

▶ **Construct Number Lines** WHOLE CLASS

Distribute the MathBoard materials. Ask students to write unit fractions centered above the fraction bar that shows thirds. On the class MathBoard, label the fraction bar as a *number line*. As you label each third, write a plus sign between the unit fractions above to show that you are recording the total of the thirds so far.

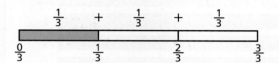

Point out that a number line is like a ruler. We label the endpoints of the number line rather than the spaces. A number line adds as it goes, as does a ruler, and the labels show the total length so far. For example, $\frac{2}{3}$ is the total of $\frac{1}{3} + \frac{1}{3}$, and $\frac{3}{3}$ is the total of $\frac{1}{3} + \frac{1}{3} + \frac{1}{3}$.

In a similar way, have the students label the fraction bars that show fourths, fifths, and sixths as number lines.

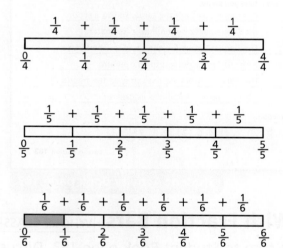

Ask everyone to shade $\frac{1}{6}$ of the appropriate number line. Then ask them to shade $\frac{2}{6}$, followed by $\frac{3}{6}$.

▶ Compare Fractions on the Number Line WHOLE CLASS

Allow the class ample opportunity to practice comparing fractions, using the number lines they created. Ask a volunteer to go to the board as the class recorder. Students take turns selecting two fractions from the same number line or from two different number lines. The class discusses which fraction is greater and why. The class recorder writes the inequality on the board. Be sure to include:

- unit fractions.

- same top numbers and different bottom numbers.

- different top numbers and same bottom numbers.

▶ Summarize the Big Ideas WHOLE CLASS

123 **Math Talk** Have the class discuss the main ideas about comparing fractions. Let students initiate the discussion, and encourage them to use the terms *numerator* and *denominator* whenever possible (but also use *top number* and *bottom number* to be sure everyone is following). Ask questions and elicit examples to ensure all topics are covered:

- If two fractions are unit fractions, which one is greater? The one with the smaller denominator is greater, for example, $\frac{1}{3}$ is greater than $\frac{1}{7}$.

- Why is this true? Because a smaller denominator means the whole has been divided into fewer equal parts, and so each part is larger.

- If two fractions have the same numerator—2, for example—but different denominators, which fraction is greater? The one with the smaller denominator. These fractions are built from unit fractions; for example, $\frac{2}{5}$ is greater than $\frac{2}{9}$, because each $\frac{1}{5}$ is greater than each $\frac{1}{9}$.

- If two fractions have the same denominator, which one is greater? The one with the greater numerator is the greater fraction. We are taking more equal parts of the same size; for example, $\frac{7}{8}$ is greater than $\frac{3}{8}$.

$$\frac{7}{8} = \frac{1}{8} + \frac{1}{8} + \frac{1}{8} + \frac{1}{8} + \frac{1}{8} + \frac{1}{8} + \frac{1}{8} \qquad \frac{3}{8} = \frac{1}{8} + \frac{1}{8} + \frac{1}{8}$$

- What if two fractions have a numerator and denominator that are the same, such as $\frac{4}{4}$ or $\frac{8}{8}$? Which fraction is greater? They are the same size. They are both equal to one whole.

- Emphasize again that you can only compare fractions made from the same whole. Ask students how they know that the fractions on the MathBoard are all equal parts (equal shares) of the same whole. Because you can see the 1 whole total that is divided into equal parts to make each kind of fraction.

Teaching Note

Drawing Number Line Errors
When students begin sketching number lines later in the unit, the fact that there is one more vertical tick mark than lengths is the source of many student errors.

In the number line below, there are 3 lengths that show thirds but 4 tick marks.

Students sometimes draw 3 tick marks with 2 lengths and label each tick mark $\frac{1}{3}$, $\frac{2}{3}$, $\frac{3}{3}$. They have created halves not thirds.

Student Error

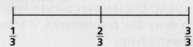

Or they may draw one whole number line and then make 3 marks between the end-points, creating fourths, not thirds.

Student Error

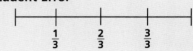

The Learning Classroom

Building Concepts To support building coherence, remember to have students summarize. They can just say one or two sentences. Students do this in Japanese elementary school classes. If you do this regularly, students will get used to making mental summaries of the math concepts discussed and making conceptual connections.

Activity 3

Use Inequality Symbols

 25 MINUTES

Goal: Write inequality signs to compare fractions.

Materials: colored pencils, Student Activity Book p. 184 or Hardcover Book p. 184 and Activity Workbook p. 85

 NCTM Standards:
Number and Operations
Representation

Differentiated Instruction

Extra Help You can make copies of Student Book page 184 so students can cut up the fraction bars to help them make the comparisons, if they need extra help.

Examples

This shading lets you compare $\frac{1}{2}$ to $\frac{2}{3}$:

$\frac{1}{2}$		$\frac{1}{2}$	
$\frac{1}{3}$	$\frac{1}{3}$		$\frac{1}{3}$

This shading does not:

$\frac{1}{2}$		$\frac{1}{2}$	
$\frac{1}{3}$		$\frac{1}{3}$	$\frac{1}{3}$

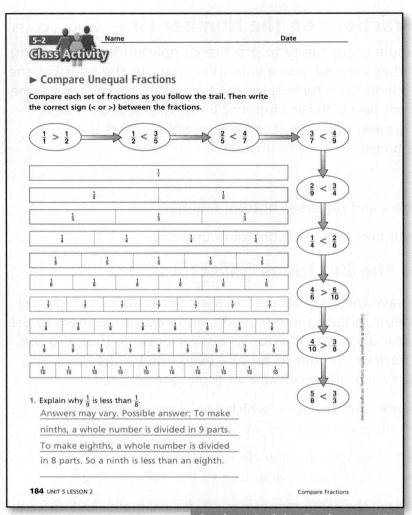

Student Activity Book page 184

► Compare Unequal Fractions INDIVIDUALS

Read and discuss the instructions with the class. Elicit methods from the students for comparing each pair of fractions. Some may use a ruler placed vertically to help them make the comparisons. Some may choose to shade sections of the bars.

They will encounter choices of sections to shade. Any option is acceptable, providing the sections can be compared vertically.

② Going Further

Differentiated Instruction

● Intervention   Activity Card 5-2

Compare Unit Fractions   Activity Card 5-2 ●

Work: In Pairs

Use:
• Grid Paper (TRB M17)

1. On your own, choose a denominator from 2 to 10. Your partner chooses a different denominator.

2. Draw two rectangles on grid paper. Use the two different numbers you chose as the length and width of each rectangle.

3. On your own, shade one row or column on one rectangle to show a unit fraction with the denominator you chose.

4. **Compare** Which unit fraction is greater? How can you use the shaded squares to verify your answer? *The unit fraction with the greater denominator is the lesser fraction. Count the shaded squares to verify.*

Unit 5, Lesson 2   Copyright © Houghton Mifflin Company

Activity Note This activity reinforces the concept that the denominator of a unit fraction indicates how many equal parts are in the whole. The fewer the parts, the greater the unit fraction is.

 Math Writing Prompt

In Your Own Words Explain how to tell which fraction is greater when two denominators are the same. Use the fractions $\frac{6}{10}$ and $\frac{4}{10}$ as an example.

 **Software Support**

Warm-Up 9.12

▲ On Level   Activity Card 5-2

Comparing Game   Activity Card 5-2 ▲

Work: In Pairs

Use:
• Fraction Bars (TRB M26)

1. Each partner writes a fraction that can be compared by using fraction bars.

2. Partners use these rules to compare their fractions.

> • Identical fractions: 0 points
>
> • Fractions with like numerators or denominators: I point for the greater fraction
>
> • Fractions with unlike numerators or denominators: I point for the lesser fraction
>
> • I0 points wins the game.

Unit 5, Lesson 2   Copyright © Houghton Mifflin Company

Activity Note Students should use Fraction Bars or MathBoard materials to help them compare fractions with unlike denominators.

 Math Writing Prompt

Compare and Contrast How are fraction bars and number lines alike? How are they different? How do you compare fractions using each of them?

 Software Support

Fraction Action: Fraction Flare Up, Level F

■ Challenge   Activity Card 5-2

Inequalities in Real Life   Activity Card 5-2 ■

Work: In Pairs

Parking
$0.50 per $\frac{1}{4}$ hour or less

1. Write inequalities. Use the symbols <, >, ≤, or ≥.

2. One partner names an amount spent on parking. The other partner writes an inequality to show how many hours they might have parked for that amount of money.

> t = time parked
> For $2.50, 1 < t ≤ 1¼
> For $5.00, 2¼ < t ≤ 2½
> For $6.00, 2¾ < t ≤ 3

3. Exchange roles and repeat the activity 5 times.

4. **Math Talk** Discuss how you chose the upper and lower limits for each inequality.

4. Possible answer: Since the charges are for each $\frac{1}{4}$ hour or less, I found the maximum number of hours for the charge and used that as the upper limit. Then I used $\frac{1}{4}$ hour less for the lower limit.

Unit 5, Lesson 2   Copyright © Houghton Mifflin Company

Activity Note Suggest that students calculate the cost of parking for one hour as a first step.

 Math Writing Prompt

Guess and Test To show that $\frac{2}{9} < \frac{3}{6}$, compare both to a fraction that shares a numerator with one and a denominator with the other: $\frac{2}{9} < \frac{3}{9} < \frac{3}{6}$; $\frac{2}{9} < \frac{2}{6} < \frac{3}{6}$. Will this method work for any two fractions? Give examples.

DESTINATION Math® Software Support

Course III: Module 3: Unit 1: Ordering and Rounding Fractions

Compare Fractions   **427**

 # ③ Homework and Spiral Review

5–2 Homework — **Goal:** Additional Practice

For Homework, students compare fractions.

5–2 Remembering — **Goal:** Spiral Review

This Remembering activity is appropriate anytime after today's lesson.

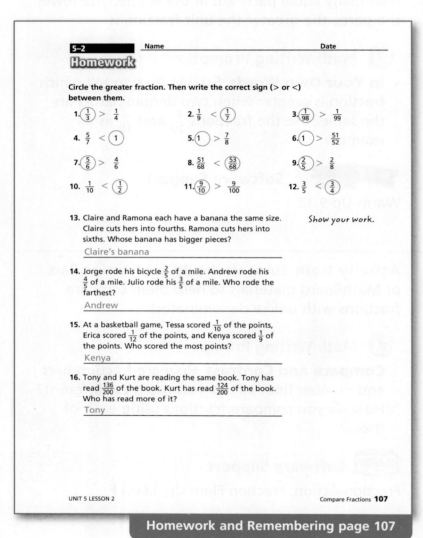

5–2 Homework — Name ___ Date ___

Circle the greater fraction. Then write the correct sign (> or <) between them.

1. $\left(\frac{1}{3}\right) > \frac{1}{4}$ 2. $\frac{1}{9} < \left(\frac{1}{7}\right)$ 3. $\left(\frac{1}{98}\right) > \frac{1}{99}$

4. $\frac{5}{7} < \left(1\right)$ 5. $\left(1\right) > \frac{7}{8}$ 6. $\left(1\right) > \frac{51}{52}$

7. $\left(\frac{5}{6}\right) > \frac{4}{6}$ 8. $\frac{51}{68} < \left(\frac{53}{68}\right)$ 9. $\left(\frac{2}{5}\right) > \frac{2}{8}$

10. $\frac{1}{10} < \left(\frac{1}{2}\right)$ 11. $\left(\frac{9}{10}\right) > \frac{9}{100}$ 12. $\frac{3}{5} < \left(\frac{3}{4}\right)$

13. Claire and Ramona each have a banana the same size. Claire cuts hers into fourths. Ramona cuts hers into sixths. Whose banana has bigger pieces?

Claire's banana

Show your work.

14. Jorge rode his bicycle $\frac{2}{5}$ of a mile. Andrew rode his $\frac{4}{5}$ of a mile. Julio rode his $\frac{3}{5}$ of a mile. Who rode the farthest?

Andrew

15. At a basketball game, Tessa scored $\frac{1}{10}$ of the points, Erica scored $\frac{1}{12}$ of the points, and Kenya scored $\frac{1}{9}$ of the points. Who scored the most points?

Kenya

16. Tony and Kurt are reading the same book. Tony has read $\frac{136}{200}$ of the book. Kurt has read $\frac{124}{200}$ of the book. Who has read more of it?

Tony

UNIT 5 LESSON 2   Compare Fractions **107**

Homework and Remembering page 107

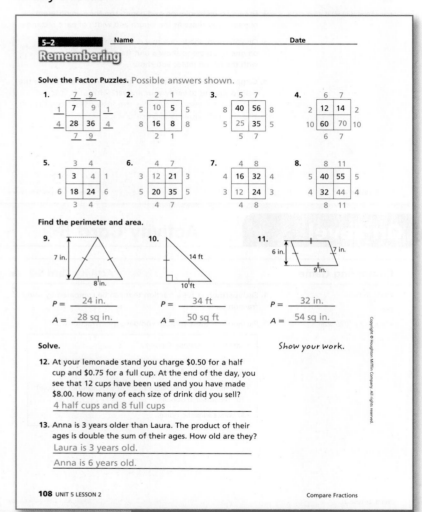

5–2 Remembering — Name ___ Date ___

Solve the Factor Puzzles. Possible answers shown.

1.
	7	9	
1	7	9	1
4	28	36	4
	7	9	

2.
	2	1	
5	10	5	5
8	16	8	8
	2	1	

3.
	5	7	
8	40	56	8
5	25	35	5
	5	7	

4.
	6	7	
2	12	14	2
10	60	70	10
	6	7	

5.
	3	4	
1	3	4	1
6	18	24	6
	3	4	

6.
	4	7	
3	12	21	3
5	20	35	5
	4	7	

7.
	4	8	
4	16	32	4
3	12	24	3
	4	8	

8.
	8	11	
5	40	55	5
4	32	44	4
	8	11	

Find the perimeter and area.

9. 7 in. / 8 in.

10. 14 ft / 10 ft

11. 6 in. / 7 in. / 9 in.

9. $P = $ _24 in._ $A = $ _28 sq in._

10. $P = $ _34 ft_ $A = $ _50 sq ft_

11. $P = $ _32 in._ $A = $ _54 sq in._

Solve.

Show your work.

12. At your lemonade stand you charge $0.50 for a half cup and $0.75 for a full cup. At the end of the day, you see that 12 cups have been used and you have made $8.00. How many of each size of drink did you sell?

4 half cups and 8 full cups

13. Anna is 3 years older than Laura. The product of their ages is double the sum of their ages. How old are they?

Laura is 3 years old.

Anna is 6 years old.

108 UNIT 5 LESSON 2   Compare Fractions

Homework and Remembering page 108

Home or School Activity

 ## Math-to-Math Connection

Measuring Carpenters, tailors, and others often measure small items by using fractions of an inch. Have students assemble a collection of items less than one inch long and measure them as accurately as possible, using a ruler. They can order the items by length and list the measurements from smallest to greatest.

Object	Length in inches
Letter A	$\frac{5}{16}$
Thumbtack	$\frac{3}{8}$
Macaroni	$\frac{7}{8}$

428 UNIT 5 LESSON 2

Subtract Fractions

UNIT 5 · LESSON 3

REAL WORLD **Problem Solving**

Lesson Objectives

- Subtract like fractions and mixed numbers.
- Understand simple algebraic notation for fractions.
- Solve problems with algebraic notation.

Vocabulary

numerator
denominator

The Day at a Glance

Today's Goals	Materials	
1 Teaching the Lesson **A1:** Solve word problems that involve simple subtraction of like fractions. **A2:** Use simple algebraic notation to express an unknown numerator (n) or denominator (d). **2 Going Further** ▶ Differentiated Instruction **3 Homework and Spiral Review**	**Lesson Activities** Student Activity Book pp. 185–186 or Student Hardcover Book pp. 185–186 Homework and Remembering pp. 109–110	**Going Further** Activity Cards 5–3 Index cards Math Journals

123 Use **Math Talk** today!

Keeping Skills Sharp

Quick Practice 🕐 5 MINUTES

Goal: Practice writing and comparing fractions.

Small Fraction Parade: Begin by writing the fraction $\frac{1}{2}$ on the board. Send six students to the board. The first student writes a unit fraction smaller than $\frac{1}{2}$. The next student writes a unit fraction smaller than the one just written. Continue in this way until each student has had a turn.

Have the class say each fraction aloud after it is written. Have the class check to be sure each fraction is smaller than the previous one.

Example:

$$\frac{1}{2} > \frac{1}{6} > \frac{1}{10} > \frac{1}{12} > \frac{1}{20} > \frac{1}{40} > \frac{1}{96}$$

Daily Routines

Homework Review Let students work together to check their work.

Nonroutine Problem A bar graph shows 9 red paints, 12 green paints, some blue paints, for a total of 30 paints. Brad displayed the same data on a circle graph. Explain how he made the circle graph and how to check if it is correct. $30 - (9 + 12) = 9$ blue; $360° ÷ 30 = 12°$ per paint; red and blue: $9 × 12° = 108°$; green: $12 × 12° = 144°$; $108° + 108° + 144° = 360°$, the total degrees in a circle.

Teaching the Lesson

Subtract Like Fractions

🕐 **20 MINUTES**

Goal: Solve word problems that involve simple subtraction of like fractions.

✓ **NCTM Standards:**
Number and Operations
Problem Solving

The Learning Classroom

Math Talk The **Solve and Discuss** structure of conversation is used throughout the *Math Expressions* program. The teacher selects four or five students to go to the board and solve a problem, using any method they choose. The other students work on the same problem at their desks. Then the teacher asks the students at the board to explain their methods. Students at their desks are encouraged to ask questions and to assist each other in understanding the problem. Thus, students actually solve, explain, question, and justify. Usually ask only two or three students to explain because classes do not like to sit through more explanations, and time is better spent on the next issue.

► Explore Methods of Subtraction WHOLE CLASS

 Math Talk Use **Solve and Discuss** with the student MathBoards to solve by using the eighths fraction bar.

● We had $\frac{5}{8}$ of a pizza. Then we ate $\frac{3}{8}$ of it. How much pizza is left? $\frac{2}{8}$

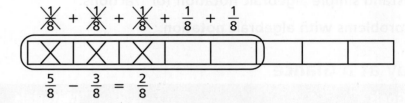

Have students share and discuss their methods with the class. Then ask students to solve this problem by using numerical methods without the sevenths fraction bar if they can.

● If $\frac{6}{7}$ of the class was in school and $\frac{2}{7}$ of the class went to the library, what fraction of the class is left? $\frac{4}{7}$

$$\frac{6}{7} - \frac{2}{7} = \frac{4}{7} \quad or \quad \cancel{\frac{1}{7}} + \cancel{\frac{1}{7}} + \frac{1}{7} + \frac{1}{7} + \frac{1}{7} + \frac{1}{7}$$

Encourage students to write chains of unit fractions (without the corresponding fraction bar).

Invite several students to contribute subtraction word problems of their own for everyone to solve. Those who need to solve on the fraction bars can do so while others can just write unit fractions. Discuss general patterns in subtraction.

The second top number is subtracted from the first and the bottom number stays the same because it tells what kind of unit fractions are being subtracted.

Activity 2

Algebraic Notation

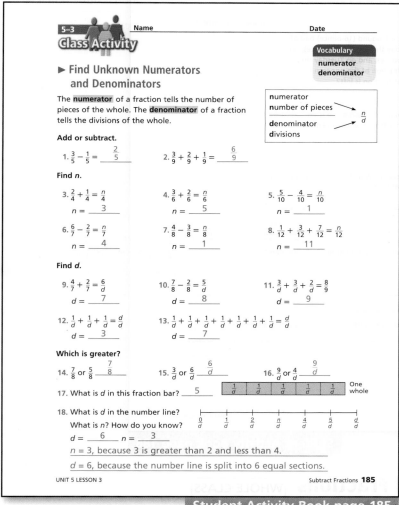

Student Activity Book page 185

► Find Unknown Numerators and Denominators

| WHOLE CLASS |

Review the terms *numerator* and *denominator*.

● What part is the numerator? the denominator? the top number; the bottom number

● What do the numbers mean? The numerator is the number of pieces and the denominator tells the divisions of the whole.

Explain that we can use the letters *n* and *d* to show an unknown numerator or denominator: $\frac{n}{d}$. When we know that the numerator and denominator are the same number, we can write $\frac{d}{d}$. Have students complete exercises 1–18 on Student Book page 185.

Activity continued ►

 30 MINUTES

Goal: Use simple algebraic notation to express an unknown numerator (*n*) or denominator (*d*).

Materials: Student Activity Book or Hardcover Book pp. 185–186

 NCTM Standards:
Number and Operations
Algebra

 Ongoing Assessment

Help students verbalize their understanding by asking them such questions as:

► How did you find *n*?

► What part of the fraction doesn't change when you add or subtract? How did that help you find *d*?

► If the denominators were given to you and the numerators were both *n*, would you be able to compare the fractions?

③ Homework and Spiral Review

5–3 Homework Goal: Additional Practice

✓ Include students' Homework for page 109 as part of their portfolios.

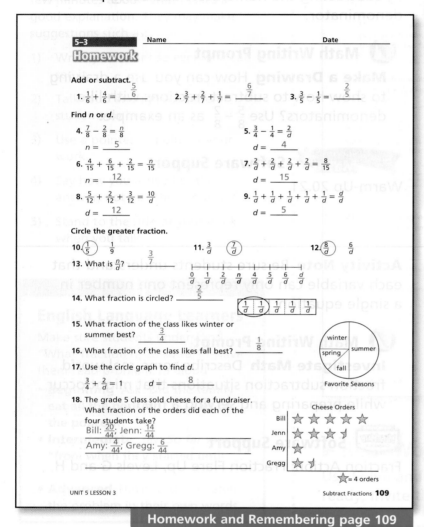

Homework and Remembering page 109

5–3 Remembering Goal: Spiral Review

This Remembering activity is appropriate anytime after today's lesson.

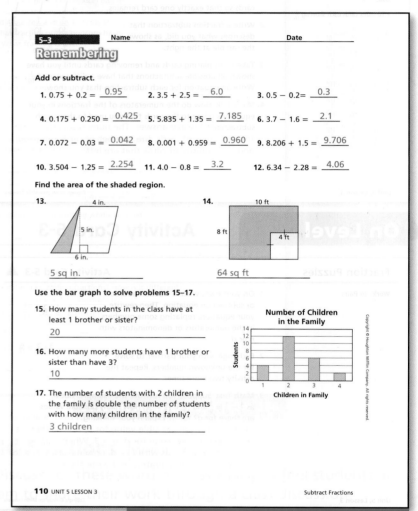

Homework and Remembering page 110

Home or School Activity

Real-World Connection

Printable Area The pages of books have margins around the edges where there is no print. Have students measure the dimensions of a full page from a book and also the dimensions of the rectangular portion containing print. Then have them calculate the fraction of the page that the margins take up.

Fractional Addends of One

REAL WORLD Problem Solving

Lesson Objectives

● Practice adding and subtracting fractions, with like denominators.

● Build fractions from unit fractions, and identify how many more it will take to make one whole.

Vocabulary

addend
sum

The Day at a Glance

Today's Goals	Materials
① Teaching the Lesson **A1:** Review like fractions, and generate fraction partners. **A2:** Solve problems that involve like fractions and fraction partners. **② Going Further** ► Differentiated Instruction **③ Homework and Spiral Review**	**Lesson Activities** Student Activity Book pp. 187–188 or Student Hardcover Book pp. 187–188 Homework and Remembering pp. 111–112 MathBoard materials **Going Further** Activity Cards 5-4 Plastic bread tags or counters Unknown Addend Cards (TRB M27) Math Journals

123 *Use* **Math Talk** *today!*

Keeping Skills Sharp

Quick Practice ⏱ 5 MINUTES	**Daily Routines**
Goal: Practice writing and comparing fractions. **Material:** pointer **Small Fraction Parade:** Begin by writing the fraction $\frac{1}{2}$ on the board. Send six students to the board. The first student writes a unit fraction smaller than $\frac{1}{2}$. The next student writes a unit fraction smaller than the one just written. Continue in this way. Have the class say the fractions as one student uses a pointer to point to them in order. At the end, ask someone to explain why the last fraction is smaller than $\frac{1}{2}$.	**Homework Review** Encourage students to help each other resolve any misunderstandings from the homework. **Multistep Problem** Apples cost \$0.25 for one-fifth pound. Bananas cost \$0.45 for a half pound. Kim bought three-fifths pound of apples and 1 pound of bananas. State an amount of money used to pay, and find the amount of change Kim received. Apples: \$0.25 + \$0.25 + \$0.25 = \$0.75; Bananas: \$0.45 + \$0.45 = \$0.90; Cost: \$0.75 + \$0.90 = \$1.65; Possible answer: Paid with \$5, received (\$5 − \$1.65) = \$3.35 in change.

Teaching the Lesson

Fractional Addends

 25 MINUTES

Goal: Review like fractions, and generate fraction partners.

Materials: MathBoard materials, Student Activity Book or Hardcover Book p. 187

✓ **NCTM Standard:**
Number and Operations

The Learning Classroom

Building Concepts Once students have demonstrated a solid understanding of the idea behind fraction partners, or addends that total 1, allow them to write the equations without shading the fraction bar. Students who are struggling should continue with the shading until they are comfortable with the concept.

English Language Learners

Write $\frac{5}{8} + \frac{2}{8} = \frac{7}{8}$, *addend*, and *sum* on the board.

• **Beginning** Say: $\frac{5}{8}$ and $\frac{2}{8}$ are addends. Ask: **Do we add the addends?** yes **Is the sum the total?** yes **Is $\frac{7}{8}$ the sum?** yes
• **Intermediate** Ask: **Are $\frac{5}{8}$ and $\frac{2}{8}$ addends or the sum?** addends Say: **$\frac{7}{8}$ is the __.** sum
• **Advanced** Have students identify the addends and sum.

▶ Find Embedded Fourths and Sixths WHOLE CLASS

Distribute the MathBoards, and direct students' attention to the fraction bar that shows fourths.

123 Math Talk As a class, discuss any patterns students found while completing the activity for both fourths and sixths. Be sure students mention that the sum of both numerators is equal to the denominator. The denominator represents the number of equal pieces that make the whole, and the numerator tells how many of the equal pieces were combined into the two separate pieces.

Ask the students how many fourths there are in one whole. Have everyone write, above the fraction bar, the equation that shows how the unit fractions add up to $\frac{4}{4}$, or one whole. Demonstrate on the class MathBoard.

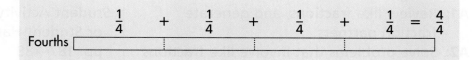

Tell the students that you want to find all the pairs of fractions, or fraction partners, that add to $\frac{4}{4}$. Have students shade the first section of the fraction bar and write the corresponding equation to the right.

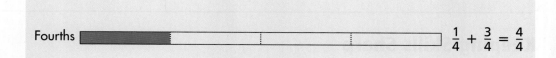

Elicit the other equations from the students. They should shade one more section of the fraction bar each time and then generate the other fraction partners.

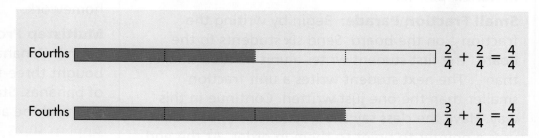

Have students independently repeat the activity by using the fraction bar that shows sixths. Invite a **Student Leader** to work on the class MathBoard.

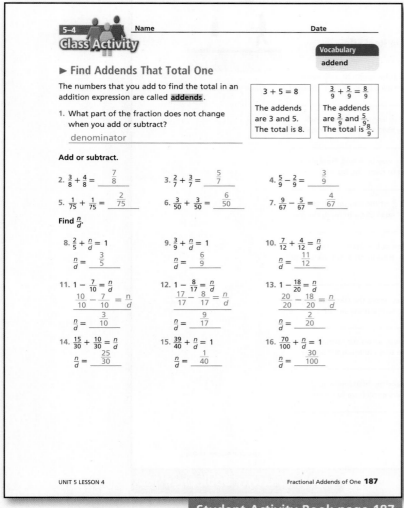

5–4
Class Activity

Name _____ Date _____

▶ **Find Addends That Total One**

Vocabulary
addend

The numbers that you add to find the total in an addition expression are called **addends**.

$3 + 5 = 8$	$\frac{3}{9} + \frac{5}{9} = \frac{8}{9}$
The addends are 3 and 5. The total is 8.	The addends are $\frac{3}{9}$ and $\frac{5}{9}$. The total is $\frac{8}{9}$.

1. What part of the fraction does not change when you add or subtract?

   denominator

Add or subtract.

2. $\frac{3}{8} + \frac{4}{8} = \frac{7}{8}$ 3. $\frac{2}{7} + \frac{3}{7} = \frac{5}{7}$ 4. $\frac{5}{9} - \frac{2}{9} = \frac{3}{9}$

5. $\frac{1}{75} + \frac{1}{75} = \frac{2}{75}$ 6. $\frac{3}{50} + \frac{3}{50} = \frac{6}{50}$ 7. $\frac{9}{67} - \frac{5}{67} = \frac{4}{67}$

Find $\frac{n}{d}$.

8. $\frac{2}{5} + \frac{n}{d} = 1$ 9. $\frac{3}{9} + \frac{n}{d} = 1$ 10. $\frac{7}{12} + \frac{4}{12} = \frac{n}{d}$

   $\frac{n}{d} = \frac{3}{5}$ $\frac{n}{d} = \frac{6}{9}$ $\frac{n}{d} = \frac{11}{12}$

11. $1 - \frac{7}{10} = \frac{n}{d}$ 12. $1 - \frac{8}{17} = \frac{n}{d}$ 13. $1 - \frac{18}{20} = \frac{n}{d}$

   $\frac{10}{10} - \frac{7}{10} = \frac{n}{d}$ $\frac{17}{17} - \frac{8}{17} = \frac{n}{d}$ $\frac{20}{20} - \frac{18}{20} = \frac{n}{d}$

   $\frac{n}{d} = \frac{3}{10}$ $\frac{n}{d} = \frac{9}{17}$ $\frac{n}{d} = \frac{2}{20}$

14. $\frac{15}{30} + \frac{10}{30} = \frac{n}{d}$ 15. $\frac{39}{40} + \frac{n}{d} = 1$ 16. $\frac{70}{100} + \frac{n}{d} = 1$

   $\frac{n}{d} = \frac{25}{30}$ $\frac{n}{d} = \frac{1}{40}$ $\frac{n}{d} = \frac{30}{100}$

UNIT 5 LESSON 4   Fractional Addends of One **187**

Student Activity Book page 187

▶ **Find Addends That Total One** SMALL GROUPS

Discuss the terms *addend* and *sum* with the class. Explain that when an entire fraction is unknown, not just the numerator or denominator, we can show the unknown fraction as $\frac{n}{d}$. Write these equations on the board, and ask students to identify whether an addend or the sum (total) is missing:

- $\frac{4}{6} + \frac{n}{d} = 1$ addend
- $\frac{n}{d} + \frac{1}{8} = 1$ addend
- $\frac{1}{16} + \frac{3}{16} = \frac{n}{d}$ sum

Ask the class to find $\frac{n}{d}$ in these equations:

- $\frac{n}{d} + \frac{1}{6} = 1$ $\frac{n}{d} = \frac{5}{6}$
- $1 - \frac{1}{6} = \frac{n}{d}$ $\frac{n}{d} = \frac{5}{6}$

Point out that the answers are the same and that students can think of unknown addend questions as subtraction questions. Students work in **Small Groups** or in **Student Pairs** to complete the exercises.

Alternate Approach

MathBoards To help students, **English Language Learners** in particular, understand visually that unknown addend questions are equivalent to subtraction questions, have students shade $\frac{1}{6}$ of the appropriate fraction bar and write the sum of unit fractions that give one whole above the bar.

$$1 - \frac{1}{6} = \frac{5}{6}$$

$$\cancel{\frac{1}{6}} + \frac{1}{6} + \frac{1}{6} + \frac{1}{6} + \frac{1}{6} + \frac{1}{6} = 1$$

$$\frac{1}{6} + \frac{5}{6} = 1$$

Subtracting involves crossing out the shaded sixth and seeing what is left. Finding the unknown addend involves looking at the unshaded sixths, which amounts to the same thing.

Teaching Note

Language and Vocabulary An addend is also known as a *summand*. In a subtraction expression, the corresponding terms are *minuend* (which derives from the Latin word for "diminish") and *subtrahend* (which derives from the Latin word for "subtract"). More commonly known is the term *difference*, which is the result of a subtraction.

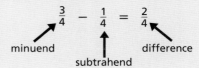

$$\frac{3}{4} - \frac{1}{4} = \frac{2}{4}$$

minuend   subtrahend   difference

Fractional Addends of One   **437**

Activity 2

Unknown Addends and Real-Life Applications

 25 MINUTES

Goal: Solve problems that involve like fractions and fraction partners.

Materials: Student Activity Book or Hardcover Book p. 188

 NCTM Standards:
Number and Operations
Problem Solving

 Ongoing Assessment

Visit the groups and ensure that students understand the idea of addends in the context of the problems on Student Book page 188. Ask questions such as:

► How many seventeenths are in one whole?

► How many more seventeenths are needed to make one whole?

► How can you write that as an equation?

Teaching Note

Mental Math Students should be able to determine these answers without using paper and pencil. Ask students to use mental math to solve exercises 19–24 and share their methods with the class.

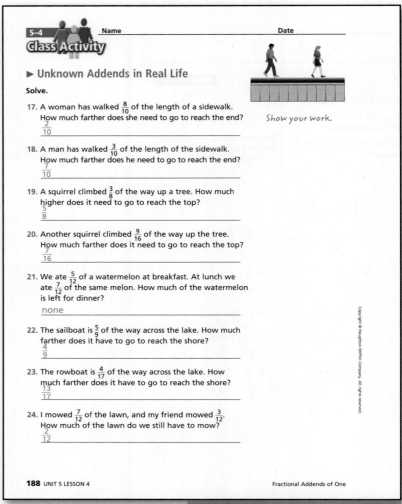

Student Activity Book page 188

The student activity page shows:

5-4 **Class Activity** Name _____ Date _____

► Unknown Addends in Real Life

Solve. *Show your work.*

17. A woman has walked $\frac{8}{10}$ of the length of a sidewalk. How much farther does she need to go to reach the end?
$\frac{2}{10}$

18. A man has walked $\frac{3}{10}$ of the length of the sidewalk. How much farther does he need to go to reach the end?
$\frac{7}{10}$

19. A squirrel climbed $\frac{3}{8}$ of the way up a tree. How much higher does it need to go to reach the top?
$\frac{5}{8}$

20. Another squirrel climbed $\frac{9}{16}$ of the way up the tree. How much farther does it need to go to reach the top?
$\frac{7}{16}$

21. We ate $\frac{5}{12}$ of a watermelon at breakfast. At lunch we ate $\frac{7}{12}$ of the same melon. How much of the watermelon is left for dinner?
none

22. The sailboat is $\frac{5}{9}$ of the way across the lake. How much farther does it have to go to reach the shore?
$\frac{4}{9}$

23. The rowboat is $\frac{4}{17}$ of the way across the lake. How much farther does it have to go to reach the shore?
$\frac{13}{17}$

24. I mowed $\frac{7}{12}$ of the lawn, and my friend mowed $\frac{3}{12}$. How much of the lawn do we still have to mow?
$\frac{2}{12}$

188 UNIT 5 LESSON 4   Fractional Addends of One

► Unknown Addends in Real Life SMALL GROUPS

Have students read question 17 on Student Book page 188 and point to the woman's location on the sidewalk. Discuss the problem.

● **How did you figure out where to point?** By counting 8 parts of the sidewalk.

● **Should you point to the beginning, the middle, or the end of the eighth part? Why?** the end; if it isn't at the end, she hasn't walked the full 8 parts yet.

● **How far does she have to go to reach the end?** 2 more parts

● **How can you say that as a fraction?** $\frac{2}{10}$

● **How can you find the answer without the picture?** You can figure out what you have to add to $\frac{8}{10}$ to get $\frac{10}{10}$, or one whole.

Read exercise 18. Ask students to point to the man's location on the sidewalk. Have students work in **Small Groups** to complete the page.

② Going Further

Intervention   Activity Card 5-4

Fraction Partner Practice   Activity Card 5-4 ●

Work: In Pairs
Use:
• Identical plastic bread tags in two
  colors or counters in two colors

1. Take turns thinking of a fraction. Then work together to find its fraction partner.

2. Write the equation that shows why the two fractions are partners.

3. Which two fractions does the picture show? What equation shows why the two fractions are partners? $\frac{4}{7}$ and $\frac{3}{7}$; $\frac{4}{7} + \frac{3}{7} = 1$

4. **Math Talk** Can a fraction have more than one partner? Can a fraction be its own partner? Explain your thinking. A fraction partner is the fraction that, when added to a fraction, equals 1. So each fraction has only one partner. Any fraction that equals $\frac{1}{2}$ is its own partner, since that fraction doubled equals 1.

Unit 5, Lesson 4   Copyright © Houghton Mifflin Company

Activity Note Review the meaning of a fraction partner before students begin. Be sure students understand that the denominator of the fraction determines the total number of items in the group.

✎ Math Writing Prompt

In Your Own Words Explain the terms *addend* and *fraction partner*. Use examples to illustrate.

Soar to Success Math ⭐ **Software Support**

Warm-Up 20.20

On Level   Activity Card 5-4

Matching Game   Activity Card 5-4 ▲

Work: In Pairs
Use:
• Unknown Addend Cards (TRB M27)

1. Place the cards face down. Take turns flipping over a pair of cards.

$$\frac{1}{5} + \frac{n}{d} = 1 \qquad \frac{4}{5}$$

2. If one card shows an equation and the other card shows the missing addend for the equation, keep the pair. Otherwise, turn the two cards face down again.

3. Continue taking turns and flipping over pairs of cards until no cards are left on the table. The player with more cards wins.

Unit 5, Lesson 4   Copyright © Houghton Mifflin Company

Activity Note Suggest that students think of the sum as a fraction with the same denominator as the addends. This will make it easier to recognize the missing addend.

✎ Math Writing Prompt

Summarize How is an unknown addend problem the same as a subtraction question?

MegaMath Grades K-6 **Software Support**

Fraction Action: Fraction Flare Up, Level G

Challenge   Activity Card 5-4

Write a Word Problem   Activity Card 5-4 ■

Work: By Yourself

1. Write a word problem that can be described by the equation below.

$$\frac{10}{60} + \frac{n}{d} = \frac{45}{60}$$

2. Then exchange with a classmate to solve the problem. Exchange once more to check your work.

3. **Summarize** Write a description of how the equation and your problem are related. Explain how you know that the solution is reasonable.

Unit 5, Lesson 4   Copyright © Houghton Mifflin Company

Activity Note If students have difficulty thinking of an appropriate scenario, remind them that an hour has 60 minutes and a minute has 60 seconds. So problems involving time can fit the equation.

✎ Math Writing Prompt

Explain Your Thinking Describe two different ways to find the unknown addend in the equation: $\frac{4}{7} + \frac{n}{d} = \frac{6}{7}$.

✴ DESTINATION Math **Software Support**

Course III: Module 3: Unit 2: Sums Involving Like Denominators

Fractional Addends of One   **439**

③ Homework and Spiral Review

Homework **Goal:** Additional Practice

For Homework, students continue doing operations with fractions.

Remembering **Goal:** Spiral Review

This Remembering activity is appropriate anytime after today's lesson.

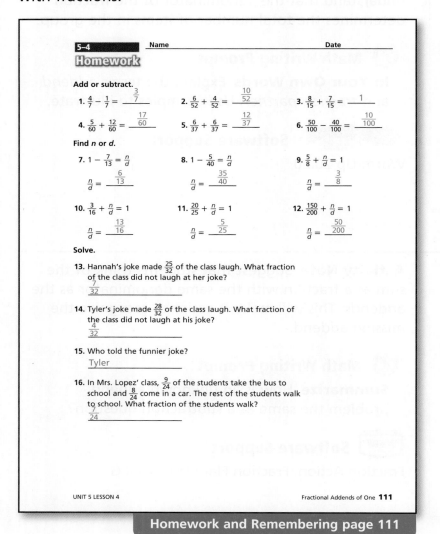

5–4 Name _____ Date _____
Homework

Add or subtract.

1. $\frac{4}{7} - \frac{1}{7} = \frac{3}{7}$ 2. $\frac{6}{52} + \frac{4}{52} = \frac{10}{52}$ 3. $\frac{8}{15} + \frac{7}{15} = \frac{1}{1}$

4. $\frac{5}{60} + \frac{12}{60} = \frac{17}{60}$ 5. $\frac{6}{37} + \frac{6}{37} = \frac{12}{37}$ 6. $\frac{50}{100} - \frac{40}{100} = \frac{10}{100}$

Find n or d.

7. $1 - \frac{7}{13} = \frac{n}{d}$ 8. $1 - \frac{5}{40} = \frac{n}{d}$ 9. $\frac{5}{8} + \frac{n}{d} = 1$

$\frac{n}{d} = \frac{6}{13}$ $\frac{n}{d} = \frac{35}{40}$ $\frac{n}{d} = \frac{3}{8}$

10. $\frac{3}{16} + \frac{n}{d} = 1$ 11. $\frac{20}{25} + \frac{n}{d} = 1$ 12. $\frac{150}{200} + \frac{n}{d} = 1$

$\frac{n}{d} = \frac{13}{16}$ $\frac{n}{d} = \frac{5}{25}$ $\frac{n}{d} = \frac{50}{200}$

Solve.

13. Hannah's joke made $\frac{25}{32}$ of the class laugh. What fraction of the class did not laugh at her joke?
$\frac{7}{32}$

14. Tyler's joke made $\frac{28}{32}$ of the class laugh. What fraction of the class did not laugh at his joke?
$\frac{4}{32}$

15. Who told the funnier joke?
Tyler

16. In Mrs. Lopez' class, $\frac{9}{24}$ of the students take the bus to school and $\frac{8}{24}$ come in a car. The rest of the students walk to school. What fraction of the students walk?
$\frac{7}{24}$

UNIT 5 LESSON 4   Fractional Addends of One **111**

Homework and Remembering page 111

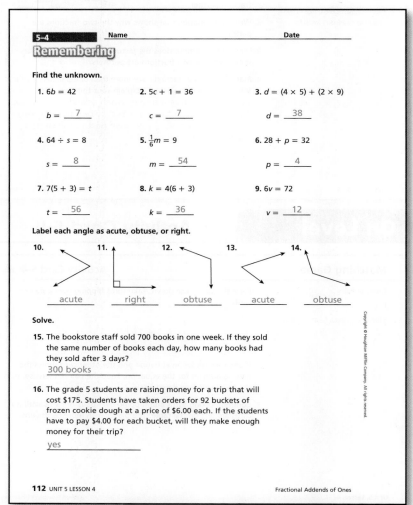

5–4 Name _____ Date _____
Remembering

Find the unknown.

1. $6b = 42$ 2. $5c + 1 = 36$ 3. $d = (4 \times 5) + (2 \times 9)$

 $b = 7$ $c = 7$ $d = 38$

4. $64 \div s = 8$ 5. $\frac{1}{6}m = 9$ 6. $28 + p = 32$

 $s = 8$ $m = 54$ $p = 4$

7. $7(5 + 3) = t$ 8. $k = 4(6 + 3)$ 9. $6v = 72$

 $t = 56$ $k = 36$ $v = 12$

Label each angle as acute, obtuse, or right.

10.   11.   12.   13.   14.

acute   right   obtuse   acute   obtuse

Solve.

15. The bookstore staff sold 700 books in one week. If they sold the same number of books each day, how many books had they sold after 3 days?
300 books

16. The grade 5 students are raising money for a trip that will cost $175. Students have taken orders for 92 buckets of frozen cookie dough at a price of $6.00 each. If the students have to pay $4.00 for each bucket, will they make enough money for their trip?
yes

112 UNIT 5 LESSON 4   Fractional Addends of Ones

Homework and Remembering page 112

Home or School Activity

Science Connection

Our Solar System The table shows the distances of the planets from the Sun in millions of kilometers. Have students read from the chart how far light from the Sun travels to get to Neptune. Using that distance as the denominator, have them write a fraction to show what part of the distance to Neptune the Sun's light travels to each planet.

For example: Distance to Earth = $\frac{150}{4,498}$

Have students pose and solve a problem like this one: Once sunlight reaches Earth, how much farther does it have to travel to get to Neptune?

Planet	Distance from Sun
Mercury	58
Venus	108
Earth	150
Mars	228
Jupiter	778
Saturn	1,427
Uranus	2,869
Neptune	4,498

Relate Fractions and Wholes

REAL
WORLD
**Problem
Solving**

Lesson Objectives

● **Understand that the size of a fraction depends on the size of the whole.**

● **Solve and explain open-ended word problems that relate fractions and wholes.**

The Day at a Glance

Today's Goals	Materials	

1 Teaching the Lesson
A1: Explore how fractional parts change as the whole changes.
A2: Represent the changing whole, and observe what happens to the fraction.
 	
2 Going Further
▶ Differentiated Instruction
 	
3 Homework and Spiral Review
	Lesson Activities
	Student Activity Book pp. 189–190
	  or Student Hardcover Book
	  pp. 189–190
	Homework and Remembering
	  pp. 113–114
	Pattern blocks or Pattern Blocks
	  (TRB M28) (optional)
	Masking tape (optional)
	MathBoard materials
	Quick Quiz 1 (Assessment Guide)
		Going Further
		Activity Cards 5-5
		Pattern Blocks
		  (TRB M28)
		Masking tape
		Chapter book
		Math Journals

123 Use
Math Talk
today!

Keeping Skills Sharp

Quick Practice ⏱ 5 MINUTES

Goal: Practice finding fraction partners.

How Many More to One? Invite six students to the board, and ask them to stand in pairs. The first person in each pair writes a fraction that is not a unit fraction and also writes a plus sign. The other member of the pair writes the addend that will make a total of 1, followed by "= 1." When everyone is done, ask the class to check each pair to see if it adds up to one whole.

Do these fractions add to one whole? $\frac{2}{8} + \frac{6}{8} = 1$

Together, the whole class reads the equation: "Two eighths plus six eighths equals one whole."

Daily Routines

Homework Review Have students share their work for incorrect answers. As a class, look for errors.

Reasoning Write the following on the board: 6.2 − 3.37 = 2.83. Have students write another subtraction problem that has a decimal difference that is less than the given difference and one with a decimal difference that is greater. Have students label each difference. Possible less than: 6.2 − 3.4 = 2.8; Possible greater than: 6.2 − 3.3 = 2.9

Activity 1

Change the Whole

 25 MINUTES

Goal: Explore how fractional parts change as the whole changes.

Materials: Student Activity Book or Hardcover Book pp. 189–190; pattern blocks or Pattern Blocks (TRB M28) (optional); masking tape (optional); MathBoard materials

✔ **NCTM Standard:**
Number and Operations

The Learning Classroom

Scenario The main purpose of a scenario is to demonstrate mathematical relationships in a visual and memorable way. A group of students is called to the front of the room to act out a situation. Because of its active and dramatic nature, the scenario structure fosters a sense of intense involvement among children. Scenarios create meaningful contexts in which students relate math to their everyday lives.

☑ **Ongoing Assessment**

Make sure students understand the general concept of the size of a fraction being relative to the size of the whole. Ask questions such as:

▶ What fraction of the name Elizabeth is vowels?

▶ If we shorten that to Beth, what is the fraction?

▶ What if we shorten it to Liza?

If possible, use variations of a student's name when asking the questions.

▶ **Discover That Fractions Are Relative to the Whole**

WHOLE CLASS   Math Talk 🄸🄸🄸

Use the **Scenario** structure and invite one student to step to the front of the room to represent a fraction.

What fraction of the group of students at the front of the class is the student? $\frac{1}{1}$, or one whole

Ask three more students to come to the front and form a group of four.

● What fraction of the group is the first student now? $\frac{1}{4}$

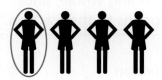

Have one more student come to the front, forming a group of five.

● What fraction of the group is the student now? $\frac{1}{5}$

● The person did not change. Why does the person represent a different fraction? The size of the group changed.

● If the first student were in a group of 25 people, what fraction would he or she represent? $\frac{1}{25}$

Explain that the same part, in this case the student, is a different fraction of different wholes.

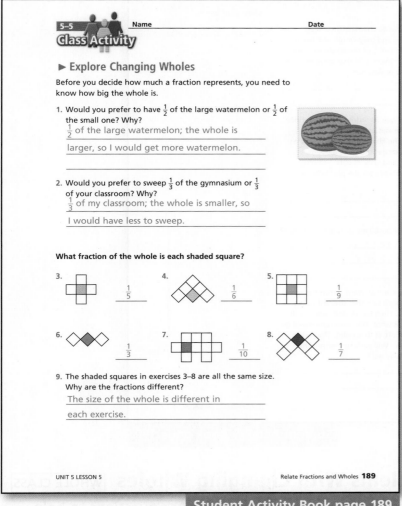

▶ Explore Changing Wholes [PAIRS]

Discuss questions 1 and 2 on Student Book page 189 with the class. Emphasize that the amount that a fraction represents depends on the size of the whole. Ask students to think of other real objects or situations that show this. Possible examples include:

- eating $\frac{1}{2}$ of a cherry or $\frac{1}{2}$ of an apple
- walking $\frac{1}{3}$ of a block or $\frac{1}{3}$ of a mile
- having $\frac{1}{4}$ of a dollar or $\frac{1}{4}$ of a million dollars in the bank

Have students work in **Student Pairs** to complete the exercises.

Teaching Note

Watch For! When doing exercises like 3–8 on Student Book page 189, some students forget to include the shaded square when they are counting the squares that make a whole. Suggest that students count the shaded square first and then continue counting the unshaded squares.

The Learning Classroom

Helping Community Create a classroom where students are not competing, but desire to collaborate and help one another. Communicate often that your goal as a class is that everyone understands the math you are studying. Tell students that this will require everyone working together to help each other.

Activity continued ▶

① Teaching the Lesson (continued)

Activity 1

Teaching Note

Math Background It may seem obvious to your students that the size of the fraction depends on the size of the whole. They know that half a cherry is not the same size as half a watermelon and that a fourth of an inch is not the same as a fourth of a yard. But many real-world fraction errors stem from students' failure to take this property of fractions into account. The problems in the Student Book should help students understand this concept.

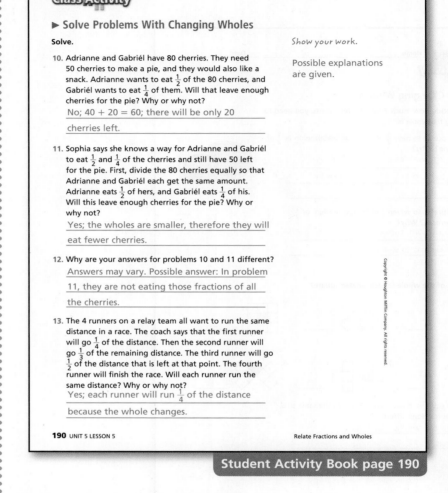

Student Activity Book page 190

English Language Learners

Draw a cake and a cupcake on the board. Draw $\frac{1}{4}$ of each. Write *size* and *whole*.

- **Beginning** Ask: Are the wholes all the same size? no Does $\frac{1}{4}$ of a cake equal $\frac{1}{4}$ of an cupcake? no
- **Intermediate** Say: The wholes are different __. sizes The size of $\frac{1}{4}$ of each whole is __. different
- **Advanced** Have students use short sentences to tell about the size of $\frac{1}{4}$ of each whole.

► Solve Problems With Changing Wholes WHOLE CLASS

Use **Solve and Discuss** for problems 10 and 11. Ask questions to help students see the big picture:

- Why does Sophia's plan work? It involves making the whole smaller.

- What happens to the amount a fraction represents when the whole gets smaller? It gets smaller, too.

- How can you see this in the number of cherries that Adrianne and Gabriél have for a snack? Originally, Adrianne wanted 40 cherries. With Sophia's plan, she gets 20. Gabriél wanted 20 at first, and now he gets 10.

Approaching Problem 13 This problem is more challenging. Choose an approach that suits your students.

- Divide the class into groups. Give students time to think about the problem and to discuss strategies. Then ask volunteers to go to the board and to explain how they solved the problem.

- **Act It Out:** Invite four students to the front of the room to be the relay team. Have another pair of students measure a 4-yard length to represent the length of the race and mark the beginning and end with masking tape. Involve the rest of the class by asking questions, such as how far a runner should move to represent his or her fraction of the race.

- Lead the class through the solution, using the MathBoard materials. Begin with the fraction bar for fourths and shade $\frac{1}{4}$. Ask what the whole is for the remaining part of the race at each step.

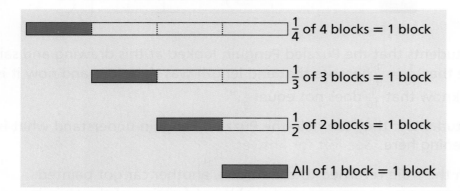

$\frac{1}{4}$ of 4 blocks = 1 block

$\frac{1}{3}$ of 3 blocks = 1 block

$\frac{1}{2}$ of 2 blocks = 1 block

All of 1 block = 1 block

The important thing for students to recognize is that the whole keeps changing. The different fractions are the same-size piece because they are each part of a different-size whole.

Emphasize with students that when fractions are parts of the same whole, the denominator does make different sized pieces, as they can see on the MathBoards: larger denominators make smaller but more unit fractions.

Remind students that they need to keep in mind what the whole is in their problem whenever they are working with fractions. Make this point again at the end of Activity 2. They cannot cut off pieces from a whole and have the fractions be part of the same whole. We cut off pieces here and in Activity 2 to emphasize that cutting off a piece *changes the whole* and, therefore, *changes the unit fraction*.

Students sometimes change the whole when they sketch fractions or fold fraction strips. They mark or fold equal parts, but if this is less than the whole, they may erase or tear off that extra piece. Emphasize that they are changing the whole and, therefore, the unit fraction when they do this.

Advanced Learners Pose this version of a famous problem that illustrates the concept of the size of a fraction being relative to the size of the whole:

A flea is on the carpet and spies a dog across the room. It manages to jump halfway to the dog, but it starts to feel tired. The next jump takes it halfway to the dog again, as does each jump after that. Will the flea ever reach the dog?

In theory, the answer is "No" because no jump ever takes the flea all the way to the dog. Each half is smaller than the one before. (In practice, the flea will be so close at some point that it can bite the dog anyway.)

Activity 2

Parts and Wholes Using MathBoards

25 MINUTES

Goal: Represent the changing whole, and observe what happens to the fraction.

Materials: MathBoard materials

 NCTM Standards:
Number and Operations
Problem Solving

Answer

On the MathBoards, the $\frac{1}{10}$ and $\frac{1}{9}$ are parts of the same whole shown at the top. With this whole, $\frac{1}{10} < \frac{1}{9}$. When you change the whole by cutting off that end piece, you have a different $\frac{1}{9}$. This $\frac{1}{9}$ is 1 of 9 equal parts of a smaller whole, so this $\frac{1}{9}$ is smaller than the $\frac{1}{9}$ shown on the MathBoard. They are different $\frac{1}{9}$ because they are parts of different wholes.

The Learning Classroom

Helping Community This activity is well suited to **Student Pairs,** particularly in a class with diverse abilities. Everyone benefits when you match students who are having difficulty with students who are having success.

 Quick Quiz

See Assessment Guide for Unit 5 Quick Quiz 1.

▶ **Construct Parts and Wholes** [WHOLE CLASS]

Distribute the MathBoard materials. Direct students' attention to the tenths fraction bar. Ask students to represent the following problems on their MathBoards.

A train has 10 cars. The first car is painted, and the rest are not. (Have everyone shade the first car.) What fraction of the train is painted? $\frac{1}{10}$

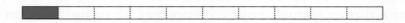

The last car dropped off the end of the train. (Have everyone draw a separating line and cross out the last car.) What fraction of the train is painted now? $\frac{1}{9}$; the whole has changed.

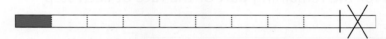

Tell students that the Puzzled Penguin looked at this drawing and said, "I see that $\frac{1}{10} = \frac{1}{9}$ because that end length was $\frac{1}{10}$ before and now it is $\frac{1}{9}$. But I know that $\frac{1}{10}$ does not equal $\frac{1}{9}$."

Ask students if they can help the Puzzled Penguin understand what is happening here. See left for answer.

When the train returned to the station, another car got painted. (Have everyone shade a second car.) What fraction of the train is painted now? $\frac{2}{9}$

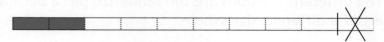

Then the last 2 cars were taken off the train. (Have everyone draw a new separating line and cross out the last 2 cars.) What fraction of the train is painted now? $\frac{2}{7}$

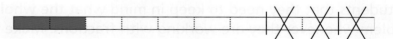

Today, the fifth car was painted. (Have everyone color the fifth car.) What fraction of the train is painted now? $\frac{3}{7}$

It is crucial that this activity does not encourage students to modify their wholes. If they do, you or other students can say, "Oh, what would Puzzled Penguin say here?" That you have a different fraction because you have changed the whole.

② Going Further

Differentiated Instruction

Name That Fraction
Activity Card 5-5 ●

Work: In Pairs

Use:
- Pattern Blocks (TRB M28), copies of 1 shape
- Masking tape

1. Mark one pattern block with a small piece of masking tape.

The pattern block is ⅛ of the tessellation.

2. A tessellation is a design with no gaps or overlapping shapes. Take turns. Make a small tessellation using the block you marked and several other identically shaped blocks. Record the total number of blocks in your design.

3. What fraction of your whole tessellation does the marked block represent?

Unit 5, Lesson 5   Copyright © Houghton Mifflin Company

Activity Note Before students name the fractional part, have them explain how they chose the number that they will use for the denominator of the fraction.

 Math Writing Prompt

Explain Your Thinking How can two different fractions describe the same amount? Use pictures and words in your explanation.

 **Software Support**

Warm-Up 6.08

Compare Halves
Activity Card 5-5 ▲

Work: In Pairs

Use:
- Any book divided into chapters

1. **Work Together** Use the Table of Contents to calculate the number of pages in each chapter of your book. Then calculate the number in half of each chapter.

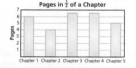

Pages in ½ of a Chapter

2. Use a bar graph or a pictograph to graph the results of your page count.

3. **Math Talk** How could you use the graph to find the number of pages in ¼ of each chapter? Find the halfway mark on each bar of the graph.

Unit 5, Lesson 5   Copyright © Houghton Mifflin Company

Activity Note For books with many chapters, students may select a few chapters to graph.

 Math Writing Prompt

Solve the Puzzle Half of Matt's coins are silver. Half of the silver coins are dimes. Half of the dimes are older than 1920, and half of those older dimes are in good condition. If 6 dimes are in good condition, how many coins are there?

 Software Support

Fraction Action: Fraction Flare Up, Level C

Create the Whole
Activity Card 5-5 ■

Work: In Pairs

1. On your own, draw a figure and tell whether it is ½ or ⅓ of a whole.

 ⅓

2. Exchange drawings with your partner and complete the drawing.

3. Repeat the activity, this time making a drawing that shows ⅖ of a whole.

4. **Explain** Is there more than one way to complete each drawing? Why or why not? Possible answer: Yes; changing the position of the parts of the drawing does not change the fractional part that was missing and is now restored.

Unit 5, Lesson 5   Copyright © Houghton Mifflin Company

Activity Note Have students use regular shapes or work on grid paper to make their drawings to make it easier to complete the whole.

 Math Writing Prompt

Make Your Own Work backwards to make a word problem that uses different fractions to represent the same amount. Check that your problem works by solving it.

 DESTINATION Math® **Software Support**

Course III: Module 3: Unit 1: Proper Fractions

③ Homework and Spiral Review

Homework **Goal:** Additional Practice

For Homework, students relate fractions and wholes.

Remembering **Goal:** Spiral Review

This Remembering activity is appropriate anytime after today's lesson.

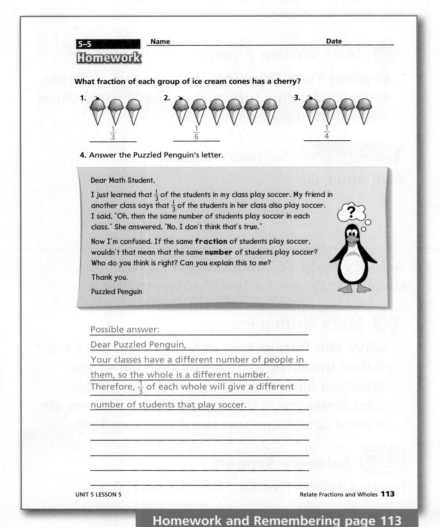

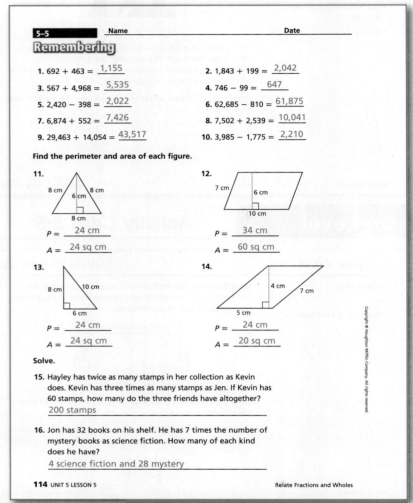

Homework and Remembering page 113

Homework and Remembering page 114

Home or School Activity

Art Connection

Sierpinski Carpet Fractal patterns occur in nature, but many artists create fractal patterns simply for their beauty. If you enlarge one section of a fractal pattern, it looks the same as the whole. The Sierpinski carpet is an example of a fractal pattern made of decreasing ninths.

Students can make their own Sierpinski carpet. On grid paper, have them draw a square that measures 27 squares by 27 squares. Have them divide the whole square into ninths and then color the center square, as shown. Students can then divide each uncolored ninth into ninths and color the center square of each one, and so on. If you use larger grid paper or a computer, you can continue this pattern several more times. Students can also experiment with different colors.

Fractions Greater Than One

Lesson Objectives

- Represent improper fractions and mixed numbers.
- Convert between improper fractions and mixed numbers.
- Apply the terms *improper fraction* and *mixed number*.

Vocabulary

improper fraction
mixed number

The Day at a Glance

Today's Goals	Materials
① Teaching the Lesson **A1:** Represent improper fractions and mixed numbers numerically and with drawings. **A2:** Explore ways to convert between mixed numbers and improper fractions.	**Lesson Activities** Homework and Remembering pp. 115–116 Greeting cards or photos (optional) Pointer	**Going Further** Activity Cards 5-6 Index cards Math Journals
② Going Further ▶ Differentiated Instruction	
③ Homework and Spiral Review	

123 Use **Math Talk** today!

Keeping Skills Sharp

Quick Practice ⏱ 5 MINUTES	Daily Routines
Goal: Recognize fractions that add to one. **How Many More to One?** Invite six students to the board, and ask them to stand in pairs. The first person in each pair writes a fraction that is not a unit fraction. The other member of the pair writes the addend that will make the fraction equal one. When they are done, ask the class to check that each pair of fractions equals one. $\frac{2}{8}$ $\frac{6}{8}$ Do these fractions add up to 1?	**Homework Review** Set aside time to work with students needing extra help. **Strategy Problem** Valerie made 1 lb of pizza dough. She cut the whole into 12 pieces and then placed it into packages. She sold one package and had $\frac{5}{6}$ of the whole left. She sold another package and had $\frac{2}{3}$ of the whole left. How much does the dough in each package weigh? How many packages were made? **Explain.** The whole was cut into twelfths. There are 2 pieces in each package weighing $\frac{2}{12}$ lb, or $\frac{1}{6}$ lb. There are 6 packages in all.

① Teaching the Lesson

Improper Fractions and Mixed Numbers

 20 MINUTES

Goal: Represent improper fractions and mixed numbers numerically and with drawings.

Materials: greeting cards or photos (optional)

 NCTM Standards:
Number and Operations
Representation

Teaching Note

Math Background In later lessons, students will add and subtract mixed numbers by separating the whole number part and the fractional part. Taking the time now to demonstrate that a mixed number represents the total of a whole number and a fraction will help students to separate the parts later.

English Language Learners

On the board, draw 2 pizzas divided into 8 slices. Write and say: **An improper fraction is greater than or equal to 1 whole.** Shade and write $\frac{9}{8}$.

• **Beginning** Ask: Does $\frac{8}{8} = 1$ whole? yes Say: $\frac{9}{8}$ is greater than 1 whole. $\frac{8}{8}$ and $\frac{9}{8}$ are improper fractions. Have students repeat.

• **Intermediate** Say: $\frac{8}{8}$ and $\frac{9}{8}$ are greater than or equal to 1 __. whole **They are** __. improper fractions

• **Advanced** Write $\frac{7}{8}, \frac{8}{8}$, and $\frac{9}{8}$. Have students identify the fraction, the whole, and the improper fractions.

► Introduce Fractions Greater Than One | WHOLE CLASS |

Write this chain of fractions on the board:

$$\frac{1}{4} + \frac{1}{4} + \frac{1}{4} + \frac{1}{4} + \frac{1}{4}$$

Math Talk Ask students for the total and add "$= \frac{5}{4}$" to the chain. Introduce the term *improper fraction*. Discuss its meaning with the class and explain that it is acceptable to write a fraction in this way.

● An improper fraction has a numerator that is greater than or equal to the denominator.

Invite several students to represent and explain this fraction on the board. There are a variety of ways they can show this. Be sure they demonstrate that the fraction is more than one whole.

  $\frac{5}{4}$ 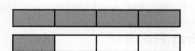 $\frac{5}{4}$

Go back to the original chain of unit fractions. Group the fractions to show that there is one whole ($\frac{4}{4}$) and $\frac{1}{4}$ more. Write the mixed number and elicit its meaning from the students.

$$\boxed{\frac{1}{4} + \frac{1}{4} + \frac{1}{4} + \frac{1}{4}} + \frac{1}{4} = 1\frac{1}{4}$$

Then present, on the board, another chain of unit fractions that totals more than one whole, for example, $\frac{1}{3} + \frac{1}{3} + \frac{1}{3} + \frac{1}{3} + \frac{1}{3}$.

Ask students to express the fraction chain as a mixed number.

● Can we make one whole? yes

● How many more thirds do we have? 2

Why do you think $1\frac{2}{3}$ is called a mixed number? It is a mixture of a whole number and a fractional part.

Be sure the class understands that $1\frac{2}{3}$ is pronounced "one **and** two thirds" and that it means the same thing as $1 + \frac{2}{3}$. To reinforce this point, ask students to write mixed numbers for the following:

$1 + \frac{1}{6}$ $\qquad\qquad$ $2 + \frac{7}{8}$ $\qquad\qquad$ $9 + \frac{2}{3}$

$5 + \frac{7}{10}$ $\qquad\qquad$ $4 + \frac{11}{12}$ $\qquad\qquad$ $20 + \frac{1}{5}$

▶ See Fractions With Several Wholes WHOLE CLASS

Draw this configuration on the board.

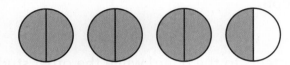

Ask the students to express the shaded parts as a mixed number and as an improper fraction. $3\frac{1}{2}$; $\frac{7}{2}$

▶ Build Mixed Numbers From Unit Fractions

WHOLE CLASS

Ask students to draw a chain of unit fractions that contains several wholes. They can choose any unit fraction they want. Send several students to the board to work while the others work in their Math Journals.

Ask students to write the improper fraction next to the chain and then to circle the individual wholes and write the mixed number. Students at their seats can trade papers to see and check each other's examples.

Example

$$\boxed{\frac{1}{3} + \frac{1}{3} + \frac{1}{3}} + \boxed{\frac{1}{3} + \frac{1}{3} + \frac{1}{3}} + \frac{1}{3} + \frac{1}{3} = \frac{8}{3} = 2\frac{2}{3}$$

Send another group of students to the board, and repeat the activity. Encourage students to build larger mixed numbers with 3, 4, or 5 as the whole number. Repeat the activity if you think your students would benefit from the practice.

Fractions as Word Names It may help students if they write the unit fraction as word name.

one third + one third + one third = three thirds, or 1
one third + one third + one third = three thirds, or 1
         one third + one third = two thirds

Eight thirds = Two and two-thirds

Differentiated Instruction

Special Needs Kinesthetic learners may benefit from arranging fractions of an object into wholes. Bring in several greeting cards or photos cut into quarters. Give each student 7 quarters (including 4 from one card and 3 from another), and ask each student to arrange the pieces into wholes.

• How many cards do you have?

• How many whole cards?

• How many part cards?

Students fit the pieces together to make one entire picture and see the three parts that are left over. They can now build $1\frac{3}{4}$.

Ongoing Assessment

Ask students to tell you what they are thinking as they get ready to change a chain of fractions into a mixed number.

Activity 2

Conversions

 30 MINUTES

Goal: Explore ways to convert between mixed numbers and improper fractions.

Material: pointer

 NCTM Standards:
Number and Operations
Reasoning and Proof
Communication

Teaching Note

What to Expect from Students

One approach to changing mixed numbers to improper fractions is to write all of the unit fractions and count the total number of parts. Try to move students into numeric methods.

- There are 4 fourths in 1 whole, so there must be 8 fourths in 2 wholes. Take these 8 fourths and add 3 extra fourths. The improper fraction is $\frac{11}{4}$.

Be sure students understand this line of reasoning before you proceed. Many students may need to "unbuild" the fraction: $2\frac{3}{4} = \frac{4}{4} + \frac{4}{4} + \frac{3}{4} = \frac{11}{4}$

A few students may want to use long division to change $\frac{9}{4}$ to a mixed number. Help them to see that the main answer will be the whole number (2 groups of 4 fourths) and that the remainder will be the numerator of the fractional part (1 group of 3 fourths left).

$$\begin{array}{r} 2\frac{3}{4} \\ 4\overline{)11} \\ \underline{8} \\ 3 \end{array}$$

Changing an improper fraction to a mixed number requires finding the $\frac{d}{d} = 1$ within the improper fraction:

$$\frac{9}{4} = \frac{4}{4} + \frac{4}{4} + \frac{1}{4} = 1 + 1 + \frac{1}{4} = 2\frac{1}{4}$$

$$\frac{10}{7} = \frac{7}{7} + \frac{3}{7} = 1 + \frac{3}{7} = 1\frac{3}{7}$$

▶ Change Mixed Numbers to Improper Fractions

WHOLE CLASS

Write this mixed number on the board, and ask students to change it to an improper fraction.

$$2\frac{3}{4}$$

Send several volunteers to the board while the other students work at their seats. Invite students at the board to explain their results. Other students can ask questions or help to clarify.

Students may use some or all of the following method, and some students may need to see unit fractions.

$$2\frac{3}{4} = 2 + \frac{3}{4} = 1 + 1 + \frac{3}{4} = \frac{4}{4} + \frac{4}{4} + \frac{3}{4} = \frac{11}{4}$$

Eventually some students will see the short cut of multiplying $2 \times 4 = 8$ instead of the third and fourth steps. Students can just write the above equation steps from right to left to change an improper fraction to a mixed number.

Give students several more mixed numbers to change to improper fractions. This time, ask them all to use numeric methods and to write out any steps they need. Again, invite several volunteers to work at the board while the others work at their seats.

$$3\frac{2}{5} \qquad \frac{17}{5} \qquad\qquad 2\frac{3}{8} \qquad \frac{19}{8}$$

▶ Change Improper Fractions to Mixed Numbers

WHOLE CLASS

Write the improper fraction $\frac{9}{4}$ on the board, and ask students to change it to a mixed number. Send several volunteers to the board while the others work at their seats. Invite the students at the board to use a pointer as they explain their results. Encourage other students to contribute to the explanations or to ask questions.

$$\frac{9}{4} \qquad 2\frac{1}{4}$$

Give the class a few more improper fractions to change to mixed numbers. Send several volunteers to the board to work. Ask students to use numeric methods and to write out any steps they need. Students who are struggling should be encouraged to use the "unbuilding" method described in the teaching note, which will help them to see the relationship between the parts and the whole.

$$\frac{10}{7} \qquad\qquad \frac{12}{5} \qquad\qquad \frac{8}{3} \qquad 1\frac{3}{7}, 2\frac{2}{5}, 2\frac{2}{3}$$

②Going Further

Differentiated Instruction

Intervention   Activity Card 5-6

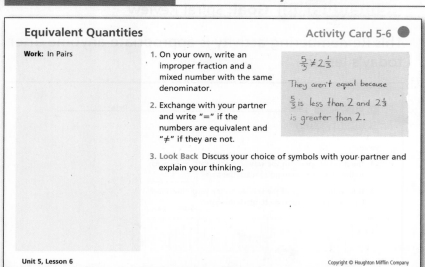

Equivalent Quantities   Activity Card 5-6 ●

Work: In Pairs

1. On your own, write an improper fraction and a mixed number with the same denominator.

2. Exchange with your partner and write "=" if the numbers are equivalent and "≠" if they are not.

3. **Look Back** Discuss your choice of symbols with your partner and explain your thinking.

$\frac{5}{3} \neq 2\frac{1}{3}$

They aren't equal because $\frac{5}{3}$ is less than 2 and $2\frac{1}{3}$ is greater than 2.

Unit 5, Lesson 6   Copyright © Houghton Mifflin Company

Activity Note Students can calculate how many unit fractions with the given denominator are equal to each quantity to decide if the two numbers are equivalent.

✐ **Math Writing Prompt**

Explain Your Thinking What does the fraction $\frac{9}{2}$ mean? Is $\frac{9}{2}$ greater than or less than 2? Explain how you decided.

Soar to Success Math ★ **Software Support**

Warm-Up 9.29

On Level   Activity Card 5-6

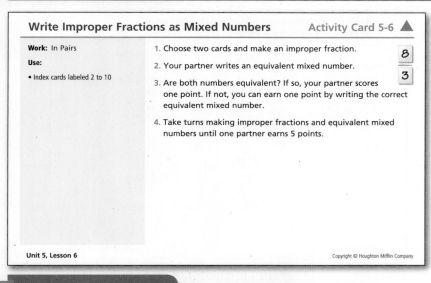

Write Improper Fractions as Mixed Numbers   Activity Card 5-6 ▲

Work: In Pairs
Use:
• Index cards labeled 2 to 10

1. Choose two cards and make an improper fraction.

2. Your partner writes an equivalent mixed number.

3. Are both numbers equivalent? If so, your partner scores one point. If not, you can earn one point by writing the correct equivalent mixed number.

4. Take turns making improper fractions and equivalent mixed numbers until one partner earns 5 points.

8
3

Unit 5, Lesson 6   Copyright © Houghton Mifflin Company

Activity Note Students should decide how many wholes are in the improper fraction and then how many fractional parts are left over to write the mixed number.

✐ **Math Writing Prompt**

In Your Own Words Is $\frac{13}{5}$ greater than or less than $2\frac{4}{5}$? Explain how you decided.

MEGAMATH Grades K-6 **Software Support**

Fraction Action: Number Line Mine, Level F

Challenge   Activity Card 5-6

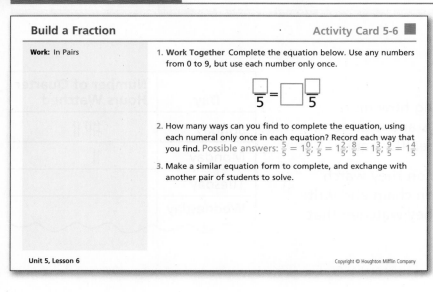

Build a Fraction   Activity Card 5-6 ■

Work: In Pairs

1. **Work Together** Complete the equation below. Use any numbers from 0 to 9, but use each number only once.

$$\frac{\square}{5} = \square\frac{\square}{5}$$

2. How many ways can you find to complete the equation, using each numeral only once in each equation? Record each way that you find. Possible answers: $\frac{5}{5} = 1\frac{0}{5}, \frac{7}{5} = 1\frac{2}{5}, \frac{8}{5} = 1\frac{3}{5}, \frac{9}{5} = 1\frac{4}{5}$

3. Make a similar equation form to complete, and exchange with another pair of students to solve.

Unit 5, Lesson 6   Copyright © Houghton Mifflin Company

Activity Note Students should realize that the format requires that the fraction be an improper fraction, so the numerator must be 5 or greater. $\frac{6}{5}$ cannot be chosen because $\frac{6}{5} = 1\frac{1}{5}$ uses 1 twice.

✐ **Math Writing Prompt**

Write Your Own Write a problem that can be answered by writing a mixed number as an improper fraction. Give the answer as well.

✦ **DESTINATION** Math· **Software Support**

Course III: Module 3: Unit 1: Improper Fractions

Fractions Greater Than One   **453**

③ Homework and Spiral Review

Homework **Goal:** Additional Practice

☑ Include students' Homework for page 115 as part of their portfolios.

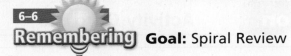

6–6

Remembering **Goal:** Spiral Review

This Remembering activity is appropriate anytime after today's lesson.

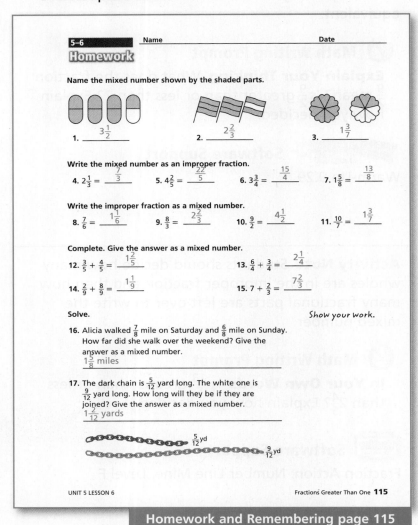

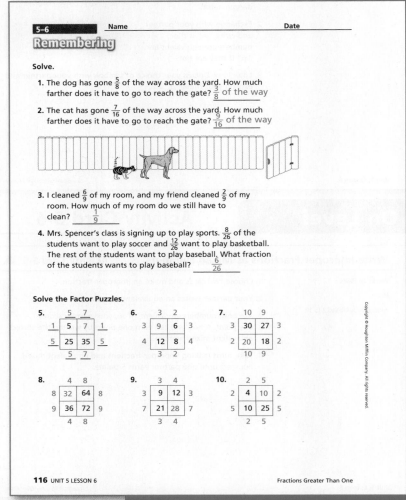

Homework and Remembering page 115

Homework and Remembering page 116

Home or School Activity

Social Studies Connection

Television Viewing Many groups are interested in knowing how much television we watch. Results are often gathered by surveys and used to develop programs, sell advertising time, and encourage healthy habits.

Have students keep track of every quarter hour of television they watch each day. At the end of the week they can make a fraction chain and write a mixed number to show how many hours of television they watched that week. Students can also graph their results.

Day	Number of Quarter Hours Watched
Sunday	⦀⦀ ‖
Monday	‖
Tuesday	
Wednesday	

Add Fractions Greater Than One

REAL
WORLD
**Problem
Solving**

Lesson Objectives

● Add mixed numbers, applying quick methods when appropriate.

● Read and represent mixed numbers on calibrated lines and rulers.

The Day at a Glance

Today's Goals	Materials	
1 **Teaching the Lesson** **A1:** Explore ways to add mixed numbers, and learn to represent mixed numbers on a number line. **A2:** Develop useful solution strategies for adding mixed numbers. **2** **Going Further** ▶ Differentiated Instruction **3** **Homework and Spiral Review**	**Lesson Activities** Student Activity Book pp. 191–192 or Student Hardcover Book pp. 191–192 Homework and Remembering pp. 117–118 Fraction Bars for Adding and Subtracting (TRB M26) (optional) Scissors (optional)	**Going Further** Activity Cards 5-7 Fraction Circles (TRB M30) Math Journals

123 *Use*
Math Talk
today!

Keeping Skills Sharp

Quick Practice	5 MINUTES	Daily Routines

Goal: Change fractions to mixed numbers.

Improper Fraction Parade: Invite six students to the board, and ask them to stand in pairs. The first person in each pair writes an improper fraction that only contains numbers less than 10. The other member of the pair writes the corresponding mixed number or whole number. When pairs are finished, ask the class to check each mixed number to see if it is correct.

For example, write $\frac{9}{4}$ and $2\frac{1}{4}$ on the board. Invite the class to read aloud each number together. Ask if the numbers show the same amount. Nine fourths equals two and one fourth.

Homework Review Have students discuss and check their solutions.

Reasoning Draw this graph on the board.

This circle graph shows how Gary planted geraniums, impatiens, and roses in his garden. He planted a total of 30 flowers. Find the amount of each type of flower. Use proportions. $\frac{1}{2} = \frac{3}{6} = \frac{n}{30}$; n = 15; 15 geraniums, 5 impatiens, 10 roses.

Teaching the Lesson

Explore Solution Methods

 25 MINUTES

Goal: Explore ways to add mixed numbers, and learn to represent mixed numbers on a number line.

Materials: Student Activity Book or Hardcover Book p. 191, Fraction Bars for Adding and Subtracting (TRB M26) (optional), scissors (optional)

✔ **NCTM Standards:**
Number and Operations
Problem Solving
Communication

Teaching Note

What to Expect from Students A few students may use drawings or number lines to solve the problem. These approaches are fine for now.

Generally, a good method is to add whole numbers and fractions separately and then add the totals together.

Some students may convert the numbers to improper fractions before adding.

(The final step of the swimming problem can be expanded as shown here.)

$$\frac{5}{3} + \frac{5}{3} = \frac{10}{3} = 3\frac{1}{3}$$

$$\frac{10}{3} = \frac{3}{3} + \frac{3}{3} + \frac{3}{3} + \frac{1}{3} = 3\frac{1}{3}$$

Other students may set up the problem in a vertical format, and add whole numbers and fractions separately.

▶ **Student-Generated Solutions** WHOLE CLASS

Write this word problem on the board and ask students to solve it by using a method of their choice. Invite volunteers to work at the board. For now, allow students to work through the problem without your direction.

> Celso swam $1\frac{2}{3}$ lengths of the swimming pool this morning and $1\frac{2}{3}$ lengths of the pool this afternoon. How many lengths did he swim today?

Have students discuss their solution strategies. Before moving on, be sure students see several methods.

Discuss how adding mixed numbers is like adding money: you add together the dollars and you add together the quarters (the fourths).

$$1\frac{3}{4}$$
$$+ 2\frac{2}{4}$$
$$= 3\frac{5}{4} = 4\frac{1}{4}$$

▶ **Represent and Add Mixed Numbers** WHOLE CLASS

Number Lines and Rulers Refer students to Student Book page 191 and have them look at the number line shown at the top of the page. The number line shows units divided into thirds. Many students are used to seeing fraction number lines with a total of only one whole, so this is a slight variation.

● The first finger points to $4\frac{2}{3}$. How much more to 5? $\frac{1}{3}$

● The second finger points to $9\frac{1}{3}$. How much more to 12? $2\frac{2}{3}$

Ask students to complete exercises 1–11 on their own; provide assistance as necessary. In exercises 3 and 4, students need to recognize that the two improper fractions convert to exact whole numbers (4 and 10). In exercise 5, $\frac{31}{3}$ is just $\frac{1}{3}$ more than 10, or $10\frac{1}{3}$.

In exercise 6, the best way to add the two mixed numbers on the number line is to add the two whole numbers first (4 + 1) and then to add the two fractional parts ($\frac{1}{3} + \frac{1}{3}$).

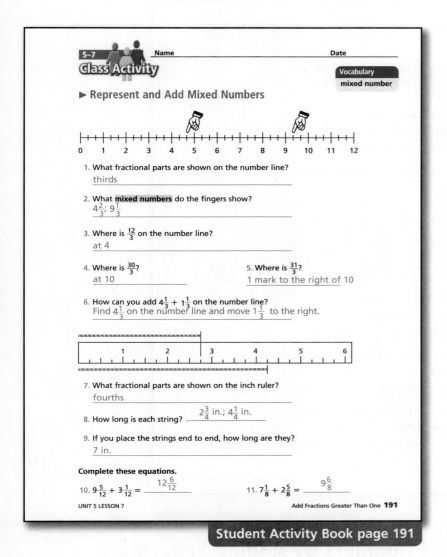

Student Activity Book page 191

Content of the activity page:

5–7
Class Activity

Name _____ Date _____

▶ **Represent and Add Mixed Numbers**

0 1 2 3 4 5 6 7 8 9 10 11 12

1. What fractional parts are shown on the number line?
   thirds

2. What **mixed numbers** do the fingers show?
   $4\frac{2}{3}$; $9\frac{1}{3}$

3. Where is $\frac{12}{3}$ on the number line?
   at 4

4. Where is $\frac{30}{3}$?
   at 10

5. Where is $\frac{31}{3}$?
   1 mark to the right of 10

6. How can you add $4\frac{1}{3} + 1\frac{1}{3}$ on the number line?
   Find $4\frac{1}{3}$ on the number line and move $1\frac{1}{3}$ to the right.

   1   2   3   4   5   6

7. What fractional parts are shown on the inch ruler?
   fourths

8. How long is each string? $2\frac{3}{4}$ in.; $4\frac{1}{4}$ in.

9. If you place the strings end to end, how long are they?
   7 in.

Complete these equations.

10. $9\frac{5}{12} + 3\frac{1}{12} = $ $12\frac{6}{12}$

11. $7\frac{1}{8} + 2\frac{5}{8} = $ $9\frac{6}{8}$

UNIT 5 LESSON 7   Add Fractions Greater Than One **191**

Differentiated Instruction

Extra Help Some students may find the Fraction Bars for Adding and Subtracting (TRB M26) useful when adding or subtracting mixed numbers. Have these students cut out the bars and use them to represent each mixed number to add, to trade parts for a whole as needed, and to represent the total of the mixed numbers.

✓ Ongoing Assessment

Observe students as they complete exercises 10 and 11. Do they write equations that show the whole numbers separate from the fractional parts? Do they first draw diagrams and then write equations to match the diagrams?

For exercise 8, the string on top of the ruler is $2\frac{3}{4}$ inches long and the string below the ruler is $4\frac{1}{4}$ inches long. Remind students to include units in their answers.

In exercise 9, some students may see that $\frac{3}{4}$ and $\frac{1}{4}$ add to 1 whole.

If not, point this out. A drawing may be helpful. Recognizing the addends of 1 is a useful strategy when adding mixed numbers.

Solve Without Number Lines Ask students to complete exercises 10 and 11. Invite several volunteers to work at the board. These exercises deal with larger whole numbers, so students may find it difficult to make drawings or to convert to improper fractions. At this point, students should see the value of adding whole numbers and fractions separately. Writing the equation vertically will help some students keep the wholes and the fractional parts separate.

Teaching the Lesson (continued)

Activity 2

Applications and Practice

 25 MINUTES

Goal: Develop useful solution strategies for adding mixed numbers.

Materials: Student Activity Book or Hardcover Book p. 192

☑ **NCTM Standards:**
Number and Operations
Reasoning and Proof

Teaching Note

Some students may need to write out the step where they change an improper fraction to a mixed number.

$1\frac{3}{5} + 2\frac{4}{5} = 3\frac{7}{5}$

$\frac{7}{5} = \frac{5}{5} + \frac{2}{5} = 1\frac{2}{5}$

$3 + 1\frac{2}{5} = 4\frac{2}{5}$

English Language Learners

Refer to Student Book page 192. Say: **We use a proof to show that something is true.** Write *proof* on the board.

• **Beginning** Say: This equation is a proof. It shows us we can add separately to add mixed numbers.

• **Intermediate** Ask: Does this proof tell us it is true that we can add separately to add mixed numbers? yes

• **Advanced** Have students tell what the *proof* shows is true.

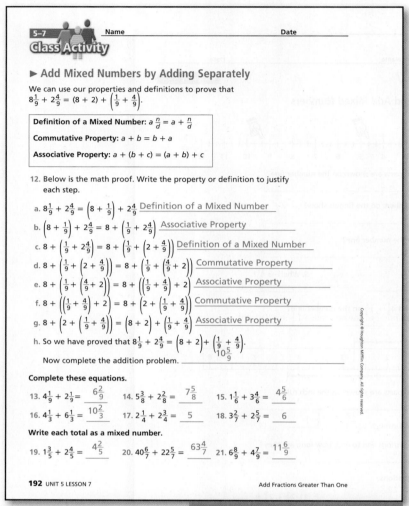

5–7

Class Activity

Name _____ Date _____

▶ **Add Mixed Numbers by Adding Separately**

We can use our properties and definitions to prove that
$8\frac{1}{9} + 2\frac{4}{9} = (8 + 2) + \left(\frac{1}{9} + \frac{4}{9}\right)$.

Definition of a Mixed Number: $a\frac{n}{d} = a + \frac{n}{d}$

Commutative Property: $a + b = b + a$

Associative Property: $a + (b + c) = (a + b) + c$

12. Below is the math proof. Write the property or definition to justify each step.

a. $8\frac{1}{9} + 2\frac{4}{9} = \left(8 + \frac{1}{9}\right) + 2\frac{4}{9}$ __Definition of a Mixed Number__

b. $\left(8 + \frac{1}{9}\right) + 2\frac{4}{9} = 8 + \left(\frac{1}{9} + 2\frac{4}{9}\right)$ __Associative Property__

c. $8 + \left(\frac{1}{9} + 2\frac{4}{9}\right) = 8 + \left(\frac{1}{9} + \left(2 + \frac{4}{9}\right)\right)$ __Definition of a Mixed Number__

d. $8 + \left(\frac{1}{9} + \left(2 + \frac{4}{9}\right)\right) = 8 + \left(\frac{1}{9} + \left(\frac{4}{9} + 2\right)\right)$ __Commutative Property__

e. $8 + \left(\frac{1}{9} + \left(\frac{4}{9} + 2\right)\right) = 8 + \left(\left(\frac{1}{9} + \frac{4}{9}\right) + 2\right)$ __Associative Property__

f. $8 + \left(\left(\frac{1}{9} + \frac{4}{9}\right) + 2\right) = 8 + \left(2 + \left(\frac{1}{9} + \frac{4}{9}\right)\right)$ __Commutative Property__

g. $8 + \left(2 + \left(\frac{1}{9} + \frac{4}{9}\right)\right) = (8 + 2) + \left(\frac{1}{9} + \frac{4}{9}\right)$ __Associative Property__

h. So we have proved that $8\frac{1}{9} + 2\frac{4}{9} = (8 + 2) + \left(\frac{1}{9} + \frac{4}{9}\right)$.

Now complete the addition problem. ___ $10\frac{5}{9}$

Complete these equations.

13. $4\frac{1}{9} + 2\frac{1}{9} =$ __$6\frac{2}{9}$__   14. $5\frac{3}{8} + 2\frac{2}{8} =$ __$7\frac{5}{8}$__   15. $1\frac{1}{6} + 3\frac{4}{6} =$ __$4\frac{5}{6}$__

16. $4\frac{1}{3} + 6\frac{1}{3} =$ __$10\frac{2}{3}$__   17. $2\frac{1}{4} + 2\frac{3}{4} =$ __5__   18. $3\frac{2}{7} + 2\frac{5}{7} =$ __6__

Write each total as a mixed number.

19. $1\frac{3}{5} + 2\frac{4}{5} =$ __$4\frac{2}{5}$__   20. $40\frac{6}{7} + 22\frac{5}{7} =$ __$63\frac{4}{7}$__   21. $6\frac{8}{9} + 4\frac{7}{9} =$ __$11\frac{6}{9}$__

192 UNIT 5 LESSON 7   Add Fractions Greater Than One

Student Activity Book page 192

▶ Add Mixed Numbers by Adding Separately

WHOLE CLASS

Refer students to Student Book page 192. The proof demonstrates why you can add fractions and whole numbers separately when adding mixed numbers together. Help students track the changes at each step and find the definition or property that explains why you can make each of these changes. Together, work through exercise 12.

Note that students will not be expected to use formal proofs at any point in Grade 5. This example of a proof is only an initial exposure.

Discuss exercises 13–21 as a class. Students can complete exercises 13–16 by using mental math. The total of the two fractions is less than 1. In exercises 17–18, each pair of fractions adds to 1.

In exercises 19–21, the two fractional parts add up to a number greater than 1. Here, students will see the importance of adding whole numbers and fractions separately.

② Going Further

Differentiated Instruction

Intervention   Activity Card 5-7

Add Fractions of Circles   Activity Card 5-7 ●

Work: In Pairs
Use:
• Fraction Circles (TRB M30)

1. Take turns. Name two mixed numbers with the same denominator. Your partner uses fraction circles to build the mixed numbers.

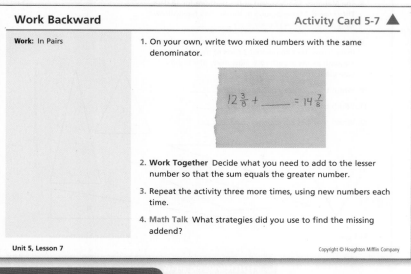

2. **Work Together** Add the mixed numbers and record the total.

3. Switch roles and repeat the activity.

Unit 5, Lesson 7   Copyright © Houghton Mifflin Company

Activity Note As students build each mixed number with fraction circles, they should trade parts of circles for whole circles whenever possible. Then they combine again, if possible, to find the sum.

 Math Writing Prompt

Make a Drawing Make an illustration that you might use to show a younger student how to add two mixed numbers. Write your explanation, too.

 **Software Support**

Warm-Up 5.13

On Level   Activity Card 5-7

Work Backward   Activity Card 5-7 ▲

Work: In Pairs

1. On your own, write two mixed numbers with the same denominator.

$$12\frac{3}{8} + \underline{\hspace{1cm}} = 14\frac{7}{8}$$

2. **Work Together** Decide what you need to add to the lesser number so that the sum equals the greater number.

3. Repeat the activity three more times, using new numbers each time.

4. **Math Talk** What strategies did you use to find the missing addend?

Unit 5, Lesson 7   Copyright © Houghton Mifflin Company

Activity Note Suggest that students count on from the first addend by fractional amounts until they reach the sum. Combining the fractions they name will give the missing addend.

 Math Writing Prompt

You Decide Jonathan adds $4\frac{3}{10}$ and $3\frac{8}{10}$ to get the sum $7\frac{1}{10}$. Dalia gets $7\frac{11}{10}$ as her answer. Who is correct? Explain your thinking.

 Software Support

Fraction Action: Number Line Mine, Level F

Challenge   Activity Card 5-7

Add It Your Way   Activity Card 5-7 ■

Work: In Pairs

1. Play a fraction addition game with eighths.

• Begin with "1" as the total. Add any number of eighths from $\frac{1}{8}$ to $\frac{8}{8}$ to the total, and say the equation.

$9\frac{2}{8}$

$9\frac{2}{8} + \frac{6}{8} = 10!$
I win again!

• Take turns. Continue adding eighths and saying the equation that gives the new total.

• The player who is able to make a final equation that adds to 10 is the winner.

2. **Math Talk** Discuss your strategies for choosing fractions to add.

Unit 5, Lesson 7   Copyright © Houghton Mifflin Company

Activity Note As students approach the sum of 9, choosing the last few addends will determine who wins the game. Whoever makes an equation that adds to 9 or more but less than 10 will not win.

 Math Writing Prompt

Write a Description Describe a situation when you might need to add mixed numbers. Name the numbers, and tell how you would add them.

 **Software Support**

Course III: Module 3: Unit 2: Sums Involving Like Denominators

Add Fractions Greater Than One   **459**

③ Homework and Spiral Review

5–7
Homework **Goal:** Additional Practice

On this Homework page, students solve equations and work with mixed numbers.

5–7
Remembering **Goal:** Spiral Review

This Remembering activity is appropriate anytime after today's lesson.

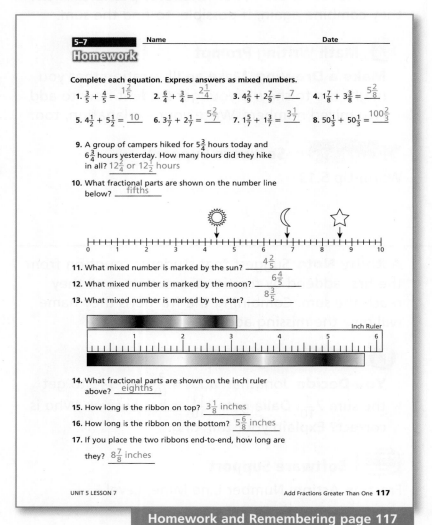

Homework and Remembering page 117

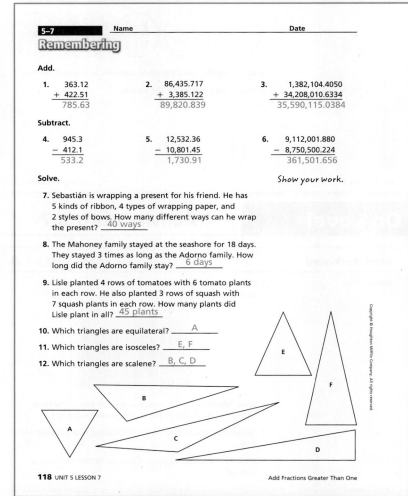

Homework and Remembering page 118

Home or School Activity

 Math-to-Math Connection

Add Fractions to Find Perimeter Measuring in the customary system often requires adding fractions. Have students draw a polygon, measure each side to the nearest $\frac{1}{8}$ inch, and calculate the perimeter of their polygon. Ask them to create a polygon with a perimeter as close as possible to 5 inches, 10 inches, or a measurement of their choice. Challenge them to create two different polygons with the same perimeter.

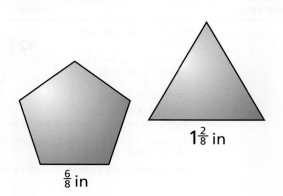

460 UNIT 5 LESSON 7

Subtract Mixed Numbers

Lesson Objectives

- Subtract mixed numbers with like denominators.

- Ungroup the first mixed number in a subtraction problem when necessary.

- Explain student-generated methods of subtraction to the class.

Vocabulary

mixed number
ungroup
add on

The Day at a Glance

Today's Goals	Materials	
1 **Teaching the Lesson** **A1:** Solve problems that involve subtraction of mixed numbers. **A2:** Practice ungrouping problems in real-world contexts. **2** **Going Further** ▶ Differentiated Instruction **3** **Homework and Spiral Review**	**Lesson Activities** Student Activity Book pp.193–194 or Student Hardcover Book pp. 193–194 Homework and Remembering pp. 119–120 Fraction Bars for Adding and Subtracting (TRB M26) (optional) Scissors (optional) Fraction Cards (TRB M29) (optional) Envelopes (optional) MathBoard materials	**Going Further** Activity Cards 5-8 Any cookbook Math Journals

123 Use
Math Talk
today!

Keeping Skills Sharp

Quick Practice ⏱ 5 MINUTES	**Daily Routines**
Goal: Change mixed numbers to improper fractions. **Mixed Number Parade:** Invite six students to the board, and ask them to stand in pairs. The first student in each pair writes a mixed number that only contains numbers less than 10. The other student writes the corresponding improper fraction. When they are finished, ask the class to check each improper fraction to see if it is correct. For example, write $1\frac{3}{8}$ and $\frac{8}{5}$ on the board, and invite the class to read aloud each number together.	**Homework Review** Review any problem that was difficult for many. **What Went Wrong?** Carmen had $19.50 to buy cheese. The cheese costs $3.25 per pound. He picked out two packages of cheese that weighed $2\frac{5}{8}$ lb and $3\frac{7}{8}$ lb. He did not have enough money to pay! Explain the error Carmen made. Find the correct total weight. He had enough money for at most 6 lb. He thought the total weight, $5\frac{12}{8}$ lb, was less than 6 lb, but it is greater.

1 Teaching the Lesson

Activity 1

Subtraction With Mixed Numbers

 30 MINUTES

Goal: Solve problems that involve subtraction of mixed numbers.

Materials: MathBoard materials, Fraction Bars for Adding and Subtracting (TRB M26) (optional), scissors (optional)

 NCTM Standards:
Number and Operations
Communication
Representation

Differentiated Instruction

Extra Help Some students may find the Fraction Bars for Adding and Subtracting (TRB M26) useful when adding and subtracting. Have students cut out the bars and use them to represent the fractions with which they are working. For example, to represent $\frac{3}{8}$ they can fold back some of the eighths bars so they do not show. When students need to ungroup a fraction in order to subtract from it, they can trade a whole for the equivalent set of parts.

► **Perform Simple Subtraction** WHOLE CLASS

Read aloud this word problem and ask students to solve it.

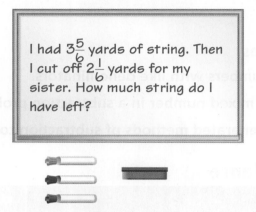

I had $3\frac{5}{6}$ yards of string. Then I cut off $2\frac{1}{6}$ yards for my sister. How much string do I have left?

Invite several students to work at the board. Many students will be able to solve this problem mentally; others may choose to use their MathBoards. You might remind those students who are struggling that they can subtract the whole numbers and the fractions separately.

When students are finished, invite them to show how they solved the problem. If students had difficulty, provide them with another problem of this type, such as $4\frac{7}{8} - 2\frac{3}{8}$.

► **Subtraction With Ungrouping** WHOLE CLASS

Write this equation on the board, and have students complete it. Again, invite several volunteers to work at the board.

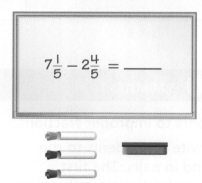

$7\frac{1}{5} - 2\frac{4}{5} = $ _____

There are many effective methods for solving problems like this one.

Ungroup Students may find it helpful to ungroup the first mixed number in some way. There are many ways to do this; eventually, the choice becomes a matter of personal preference. The ungrouping methods shown at the left are recommended for struggling students who are looking for guidance.

                                                    Ungroup

Expanded Notation $6\frac{6}{5}$

$7\frac{1}{5} = 6 + \frac{5}{5} + \frac{1}{5} = 6\frac{6}{5}$ $\cancel{7}\frac{\cancel{1}}{5}$

$\qquad\qquad\qquad - 2\frac{4}{5}$ $- 2\frac{4}{5}$

$\rule{3cm}{0.4pt}$

$\qquad\qquad\qquad\quad 4\frac{2}{5}$ $4\frac{2}{5}$

Add On Some students may add on from the smaller mixed number to the larger.

$$2\frac{4}{5} \quad \text{to 3} \quad \text{to 7} \quad \text{to } 7\frac{1}{5}$$

$$\vee \qquad \vee \qquad \vee$$

$$\frac{1}{5} \qquad 4 \qquad \frac{1}{5} = 4\frac{2}{5}$$

Use Improper Fractions Students may try to convert both numbers to improper fractions before subtracting: $\frac{36}{5} - \frac{14}{5} = \frac{22}{5}$, or $4\frac{2}{5}$. As it does with addition, this method can become cumbersome.

Math Talk Ask several students to demonstrate the method they used. Encourage students to share a variety of methods to provide exposure to different approaches. As students share their ideas, try to validate any method that reflects understanding. Invite students to ask questions and to help each other explain their approaches.

When a volunteer shows one of the ungrouping methods, ask the class how the subtraction of mixed numbers is like the subtraction of whole numbers (for example, $243 - 158$). As students respond, they should demonstrate an understanding that in order to subtract mixed numbers, you can ungroup a whole. So, to subtract $243 - 158$, you can ungroup a ten to subtract 8 from 13 ones.

Present students with several other problems of this type to solve; invite volunteers to share their methods. Two examples are at the right.

▶ Decide What to Do [WHOLE CLASS]

Invite several students to the board. Have each of them quickly write down two or three subtraction problems with mixed numbers. The problems can be easy or difficult.

Point to each problem and have the class respond by saying "ungroup" or "do not ungroup," depending on whether the first number needs to be changed to solve the problem. Have a volunteer explain how to decide. If necessary, repeat this activity until students respond quickly and confidently.

$$2\frac{2}{7} - 1\frac{4}{7} \underbrace{\quad \text{Ungroup!} \quad} \qquad 28\frac{7}{9} - 13\frac{5}{9} \underbrace{\quad \text{Do not ungroup!} \quad}$$

If no students write problems with large mixed numbers, like the second problem above, provide one or two of these problems yourself.

Teaching Note

Watch For! Some students may try to subtract the smaller fractional part from the larger fractional part even when this involves "going the wrong way." Encourage these students to use the vertical format. It resembles the ungrouping they already know in multi-digit subtraction.

Incorrect	Correct
$8\frac{3}{5}$	$8\frac{3}{5}$
$-1\frac{4}{5}$	$-1\frac{4}{5}$
$7\frac{1}{5}$	$6\frac{4}{5}$

$$5\frac{3}{5} - 1\frac{4}{5} \qquad 6\frac{2}{9} - 2\frac{7}{9}$$

English Language Learners

On the board, write $4\frac{2}{5} - 2\frac{3}{5}$ and $3\frac{5}{8} - 1\frac{3}{8}$. Also write *regroup* and *do not regroup*.

• **Beginning** Point and ask: **To subtract $2\frac{3}{5}$, do I regroup $4\frac{2}{5}$?** yes Point and say: **To subtract $1\frac{3}{8}$, I ___ $3\frac{5}{8}$.** do not regroup

• **Intermediate and Advanced** Have students identify which fraction they regroup and which fraction they do not regroup to subtract.

Teaching the Lesson (continued)

Activity 2

Subtraction Practice

 25 MINUTES

Goal: Practice ungrouping problems in real-world contexts.

Materials: Student Activity Book or Hardcover Book pp. 193–194; Fraction Cards (TRB M29), scissors, envelopes (optional)

✔ **NCTM Standards:**
Number and Operations
Representation

Differentiated Instruction

Extra Help Distribute one copy of Fraction Cards (TRB M29) to each pair of students. Have pairs cut out the fraction cards and place both sets of one type of fraction in an envelope. One partner selects a fraction from the envelope and subtracts the number from 42. Pairs continue to take turns choosing a fraction and subtracting it from the most recent answer. Students will need to ungroup in order to perform some subtractions.

 Ongoing Assessment

Throughout this lesson, as students subtract mixed numbers, observe whether they are ungrouping the first number only when necessary. Also check that they are not simply subtracting the smaller fractional part from the larger fractional part.

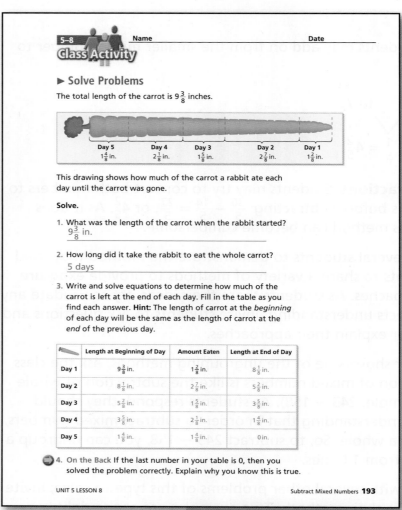

Student Activity Book page 193

► Solve Problems [INDIVIDUALS]

Refer students to Student Book page 193. Ensure that they understand the problem situation before having them work independently to complete the page.

Math Talk Have students share their equations used in exercise 3. Review as a class. Then allow students to share their explanation for exercise 4, and discuss as a class why the final answer should be zero. Students should mention that zero represents no remaining carrot. If time permits, have students decide the day the rabbit ate the most carrot and the least carrot and share their thinking with the class.

②Going Further

Differentiated Instruction

● Intervention   Activity Card 5-8

Write Fractions in Different Ways   Activity Card 5-8 ●

Work: In Pairs

1. Possible answer: Each whole equals $\frac{4}{4}$. So $3\frac{3}{4}$ = $1 + 2\frac{3}{4}$, which can be written as $\frac{4}{4} + 2\frac{3}{4}$ or $2\frac{7}{4}$.

1. Look at the example at the right. It shows three different ways to write the mixed number $3\frac{3}{4}$. How do you know that $3\frac{3}{4}$ equals $2\frac{7}{4}$?

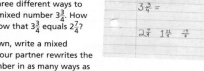

2. On your own, write a mixed number. Your partner rewrites the mixed number in as many ways as possible.

3. Switch roles and repeat the activity.

4. **Math Talk** What strategies did you use to find the different ways to write each fraction?

Unit 5, Lesson 8   Copyright © Houghton Mifflin Company

Activity Note This activity reinforces the concept that the whole number 1 can be written as a fraction with the same terms. So $2\frac{7}{4}$ can be written as $1 + 1\frac{7}{4}$ or $\frac{4}{4} + 1\frac{7}{4}$ or $1\frac{11}{4}$.

 Math Writing Prompt

Explain Your Thinking Describe how to change $3\frac{1}{8}$ to an improper fraction. Explain each step.

 **Software Support**

Warm-Up 5.13

▲ On Level   Activity Card 5-8

Representations for Subtraction   Activity Card 5-8 ▲

Work: In Pairs

1. **Work Together** Show as many ways as possible to complete the following subtraction: $2\frac{3}{10} - 1\frac{7}{10}$.

2. The fraction bars show the mixed number $2\frac{3}{10}$. How can you use the bars to complete the subtraction?

3. Another way might be to regroup before subtracting, using paper and pencil. Show how to use this method.

4. **Compare** Which do you prefer, regrouping with paper and pencil or using the fraction bars? Explain your choice.

Unit 5, Lesson 8   Copyright © Houghton Mifflin Company

Activity Note Other methods that students might use include converting to improper fractions or decimals.

 Math Writing Prompt

Solve a Problem Alejandro is making muffins. He needs $3\frac{3}{4}$ cups of flour, but has only $1\frac{1}{4}$ cups. How much flour must he borrow from his neighbor? Explain two ways to find the answer.

MEGAMATH Grades K-6 **Software Support**

Fraction Action: Number Line Mine, Level F

■ Challenge   Activity Card 5-8

Double the Recipe   Activity Card 5-8 ■

Work: By Yourself

Use:
• Cookbooks

1. Find a recipe that includes fractions and mixed numbers as part of the ingredient measures.

2. Rewrite the ingredients to double the recipe.

Unit 5, Lesson 8   Copyright © Houghton Mifflin Company

Activity Note If necessary, point out that to double a recipe, you can add the amount in the first recipe to itself.

 Math Writing Prompt

Summarize Explain why $6\frac{7}{8} - 2\frac{5}{8}$ is the same as $(6 - 2) + (\frac{7}{8} - \frac{5}{8})$.

 **Software Support**

Course III: Module 3: Unit 2: Sums Involving Like Denominators

Subtract Mixed Numbers   **465**

③ Homework and Spiral Review

Homework **Goal:** Additional Practice

On this Homework page, students solve problems involving subtraction with mixed numbers.

Remembering **Goal:** Spiral Review

This Remembering activity is appropriate anytime after today's lesson.

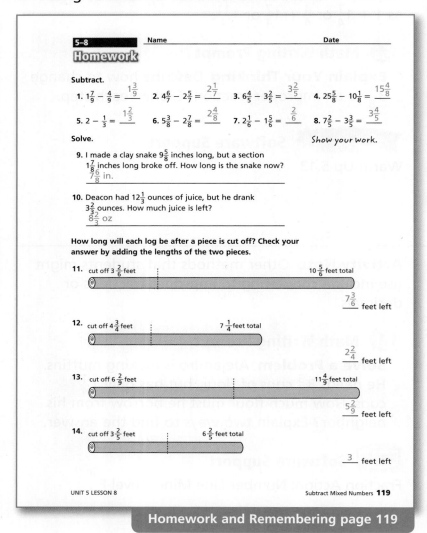

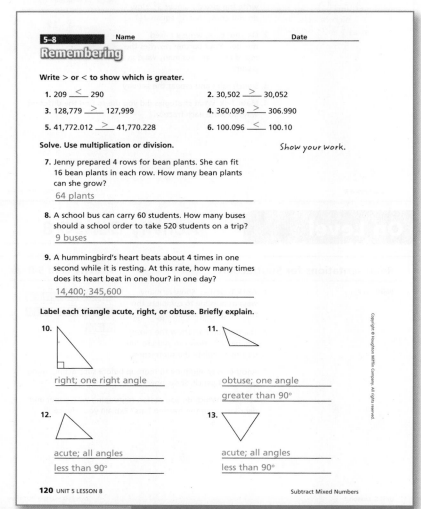

Home or School Activity

 ### Real-World Connection

Fractions and Mixed Numbers in Use Ask students to interview parents, guardians, and other adults they know to learn how they use fractions and mixed numbers in their everyday lives. They will likely find that the most common use is found in measuring: a cook preparing a recipe, a pharmacist preparing a prescription, a carpenter measuring lumber, or a machinist determining the depth of a hole.

Invite students to share their findings with the class or to prepare a bulletin board with the most interesting discoveries.

UNIT 5 LESSON 9

Comparison Situations

REAL WORLD Problem Solving

Lesson Objectives

- Compare the sizes of two like fractions or mixed numbers, and use subtraction to determine the exact difference.
- Construct a chart of comparative measurements.

Vocabulary

mixed number
subtract
add on

The Day at a Glance

Today's Goals	Materials
1 Teaching the Lesson **A1:** Compare fractions, and find the difference. **A2:** Solve problems that involve subtraction of mixed numbers. **A3:** Take real measurements of hands or feet, and make comparisons. **2 Going Further** ▸ Problem Solving Strategy: Applications With Mixed Numbers ▸ Differentiated Instruction **3 Homework and Spiral Review**	**Lesson Activities** Student Activity Book p. 195 or Student Hardcover Book p. 195 Homework and Remembering pp. 121–122 Inch rulers **Going Further** Student Activity Book p. 196 or Student Hardcover Book p. 196 Activity Cards 5-9 Play money Math Journals *Use Math Talk today!*

Keeping Skills Sharp

Quick Practice ⏱ 5 MINUTES

Goal: Compare fractions by using > and <.

Material: pointer

Which Fraction Is Less? Invite six pairs of students to the board. The first student in each pair writes a fraction. The other student then writes a different fraction with the same denominator.

Next, invite one student from each pair to remain at the board and to use a pointer to point to each set of fractions, asking "Which is less?" The class responds by pointing, and the student at the board writes > or < between the fractions. Have the whole class read aloud the inequality. For fractions such as $\frac{5}{12} < \frac{9}{12}$ the class would say, "Five twelfths is less than nine twelfths."

Daily Routines

Homework Review Have students discuss the problems from their homework. Encourage students to help each other resolve any misunderstandings.

Nonroutine Problem Sung Hoon made two decimal numbers using the digits 5, 6, and 7. He found 7.425 to be their sum. What is the difference of the two decimal numbers? 6.075; The decimal numbers are 6.75 and 0.675.

Teaching the Lesson

Compare Fractions

 15 MINUTES

Goal: Compare fractions, and find the difference.

✔ **NCTM Standards:**
Number and Operations
Communication
Representation

Differentiated Instruction

Extra Help If students are struggling to see why they can use subtraction to solve comparison problems, give them an analogous situation with whole numbers. This will help make relationships more apparent.

For example, Katie has 7 melons. Otto has 5 melons.

► Who has more? Katie

► How many more? 2 more

► How did you find this answer? I subtracted 5 from 7.

Students can also solve comparisons like this by adding on to the smaller number to make the larger number. They can use this strategy with fractions, too. It is especially effective with fractions that are less than 1.

► ### Solve Simple Comparisons With Like Fractions

WHOLE CLASS

Write the following word problem on the board and invite students to solve it and share their strategies.

> Katie has $\frac{2}{8}$ of a melon. Otto has $\frac{5}{8}$ of the same melon. Who has more? How much more?

Students must first see that Otto has more melon. They then need to determine that they can find out how much more by subtracting or by adding on. Some students may find this obvious; others may need to work with chains of unit fractions to see that Otto has $\frac{3}{8}$ more melon.

Katie $\frac{1}{8}$ + $\frac{1}{8}$

Otto $\frac{1}{8}$ + $\frac{1}{8}$ + $\left(\frac{1}{8} + \frac{1}{8} + \frac{1}{8}\right)$

Next, ask

● Who has less melon? How much less? Katie; $\frac{3}{8}$ less

Help students realize that the answer to a "how much less?" question is always the same as the answer to a "how much more?" question. Use fraction chains to illustrate this concept.

Give students this word problem to solve by using a method of their choice. Invite volunteers to share and explain their strategies.

> My black shoelace is $\frac{7}{12}$ yard long. My white shoelace is $\frac{9}{12}$ yard long. Which shoelace is shorter? How much shorter?

The two main numerical models will be variations of the following:
$\frac{7}{12} + \frac{n}{d} = \frac{9}{12}$ and $\frac{9}{12} - \frac{7}{2} = \frac{n}{d}$.

Compare With Mixed Numbers

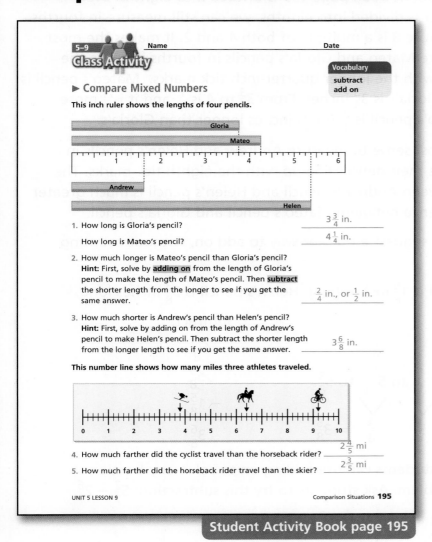

5–9
Class Activity

Name _____ Date _____

Vocabulary
subtract
add on

▶ **Compare Mixed Numbers**

This inch ruler shows the lengths of four pencils.

Gloria
Mateo

Andrew
Helen

1. How long is Gloria's pencil?

   How long is Mateo's pencil?

   $3\frac{3}{4}$ in.

   $4\frac{1}{4}$ in.

2. How much longer is Mateo's pencil than Gloria's pencil?
   Hint: First, solve by adding on from the length of Gloria's pencil to make the length of Mateo's pencil. Then **subtract** the shorter length from the longer to see if you get the same answer.

   $\frac{2}{4}$ in., or $\frac{1}{2}$ in.

3. How much shorter is Andrew's pencil than Helen's pencil?
   Hint: First, solve by adding on from the length of Andrew's pencil to make Helen's pencil. Then subtract the shorter length from the longer length to see if you get the same answer.

   $3\frac{6}{8}$ in.

This number line shows how many miles three athletes traveled.

0 1 2 3 4 5 6 7 8 9 10

4. How much farther did the cyclist travel than the horseback rider?

   $2\frac{4}{5}$ mi

5. How much farther did the horseback rider travel than the skier?

   $2\frac{3}{5}$ mi

UNIT 5 LESSON 9   Comparison Situations **195**

Student Activity Book page 195

🕐 **20 MINUTES**

Goal: Solve problems that involve subtraction of mixed numbers.

Materials: Student Activity Book or Hardcover Book p. 195

✔ **NCTM Standards:**
   Number and Operations
   Problem Solving
   Representation

▶ **Compare Mixed Numbers** WHOLE CLASS

Refer students to Student Book page 195, and work together to complete exercises 1–5. For all of these exercises, emphasize that a mixed number is a whole number plus a fractional part. For example, $3\frac{4}{5}$ is three wholes plus four fifths.

Compare Mixed Numbers by Using a Number Line As students complete exercises 1–5, remind them to find the difference first by adding on and then to check their answer by using subtraction. This process will help students realize why they can solve comparisons by subtracting or by adding on.

English Language Learners

Write *longer, shorter, longest,* and *shortest* on the board. Have students look at Student Book page 195.

• **Beginning** Ask: **Is Andrew's pencil *longer* or *shorter* than Gloria's?** shorter Continue with other comparisons.

• **Intermediate** Say: **Matteo's pencil is *shorter than* __.** Helen's **Helen's pencil is the __.** longest Continue with other comparisons.

• **Advanced** Have students use short sentences to compare the pencil lengths.

Activity continued ▶

Activity 2

Teaching Note

What to Expect from Students
Students may use one or more of these strategies to find the differences in exercises 4 and 5.

Count the Lengths Students can count the individual lengths between two athletes on the number line and then convert the improper fraction to a mixed number. For example, the cyclist traveled $\frac{14}{5}$ miles, or $2\frac{4}{5}$ miles, farther than the horseback rider.

Add On Students can start with the smaller number, add on to the next whole, add on the number of complete wholes, and then add on the remaining fraction.

Subtract Students can subtract the two mixed numbers by ungrouping the larger number as they did in Lesson 8.

The Learning Classroom

Helping Community When stronger math students finish their work early, let them help others who might be struggling. Many students enjoy the role of helping other students. In their "helper" role, students who might become bored challenge themselves as they explain math content to others.

The ruler on Student Book page 195 is divided into eighths. Even though the ruler is divided into eighths, we can still measure in fourths and halves because 8 is a multiple of both 4 and 2. It makes the most sense to measure Mateo and Gloria's pencils in fourths because the pencils line up with the longer quarter-inch tick marks. Mateo's pencil is $4\frac{1}{4}$ inches and Gloria's is $3\frac{3}{4}$ inches. From $3\frac{3}{4}$ to 4 is $\frac{1}{4}$, and it is $\frac{1}{4}$ more to $4\frac{1}{4}$, so Mateo's pencil is $\frac{2}{4}$ (or $\frac{1}{2}$) inches longer than Gloria's.

It makes the most sense to measure Andrew and Helen's pencils in eighths because their pencils line up with the eighth tick marks. The difference between Andrew's pencil and Helen's pencil is much greater than the difference between Mateo's pencil and Gloria's pencil.

Ask students to suggest a quicker way to add on, without counting every mark.

Andrew's pencil is $1\frac{5}{8}$ inches long. Helen's pencil is $5\frac{3}{8}$ inches long.

Add on:

From $1\frac{5}{8}$ to 2 to 5 to $5\frac{3}{8}$

$\frac{3}{8}$ 3 $\frac{3}{8}$ $= 3\frac{6}{8}$

Subtract:

$4\frac{11}{8}$

$\cancel{5}\frac{3}{8}$

$- 1\frac{5}{8}$

$3\frac{6}{8}$

Reinforce that students can use adding on to solve any fraction subtraction problem. Ask students to try this subtraction: $5\frac{2}{7} - 2\frac{6}{7}$.

From $2\frac{6}{7}$ to 3 to 5 to $5\frac{2}{7}$

$\frac{1}{7}$ 2 $\frac{2}{7}$ $= 2\frac{3}{7}$

Compare Mixed Numbers by Using Other Methods Have students look at the number line at the bottom of Student Book page 195, and ask them what fractional parts are shown. fifths

Encourage students to use any method of their choice to complete exercises 4 and 5. Invite students to share and explain the different methods they used.

Discuss Ungrouping Patterns Have students ungroup these mixed numbers to get them ready to subtract a larger fraction. Discuss why the new ungrouped fraction is $1 + \frac{n}{d} = \frac{d}{d} + \frac{n}{d} = \frac{d+n}{d}$.

$5\frac{3}{8} = 4 + 1 + \frac{3}{8} = 4 + \frac{8}{8} + \frac{3}{8} = 4\frac{11}{8}$ $\cancel{47}\frac{1}{6} = 46\frac{6}{6} + \frac{1}{6} = 46\frac{7}{6}$

Real-World Comparisons

▶ Make a Measurement Table WHOLE CLASS

Invite three students of different heights to the front of the classroom. Measure the hand or foot of each student to the nearest eighth of an inch and complete a table on the board.

Length of Hand

Samantha	$6\frac{7}{8}$ inches
Pedro	$7\frac{5}{8}$ inches
Robby	$6\frac{1}{8}$ inches

Next, ask students to make several comparisons, using the information in the table.

● Who has the longest hand? Pedro Who has the shortest hand? Robby

● How much shorter is Samantha's hand than Pedro's? $\frac{6}{8} = \frac{3}{4}$ inches

● How much longer is Pedro's hand than Robby's? $1\frac{4}{8} = 1\frac{1}{2}$ inches

If time permits, repeat the activity with a new group of students. Alternatively, you might have students work in groups of three to measure their own hands or feet and subtract to compare measurements.

 20 MINUTES

Goal: Take real measurements of hands or feet, and make comparisons.

Materials: inch rulers (1 per student)

 NCTM Standards:
Number and Operations
Measurement

 Ongoing Assessment

Watch students as they subtract to compare mixed numbers. Do they subtract accurately, even when the numbers begin with different whole numbers (for example, $7\frac{3}{8}$ and $6\frac{5}{8}$)?

② Going Further

Problem Solving Strategy: Applications With Mixed Numbers

Goal: Add and subtract mixed numbers to solve problems.

Materials: Student Activity Book or Hardcover Book p.196

✓ **NCTM Standards:**
Number and Operations
Problem Solving

▶ Solve and Discuss Problems

SMALL GROUPS   Math Talk

Refer students to the word problems on Student Book page 196. Working in **Small Groups**, have students select one of the four word problems and do the following:

● restate the problem in their own words to ensure that everyone understands it.

● agree on a strategy to solve the problem; students may suggest strategies such as adding, subtracting, drawing a diagram, or working backward.

Invite each group to explain to the rest of students class how they would solve their problem. Encourage other students to ask questions to be sure that they understand the strategies.

Next, ask groups to solve all four problems by using the suggested strategies or others of their choice.

When students have solved all four problems, discuss solutions as a class.

● What was your solution to problem 3?

● How can you check that the answer is correct?

● What might you do differently next time?

● Did anyone solve this problem in a different way?

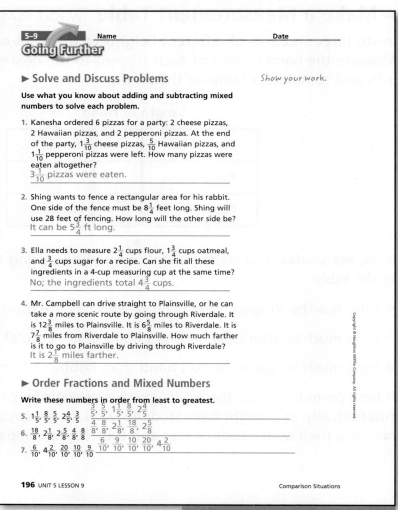

▶ Order Fractions and Mixed Numbers

INDIVIDUALS

For exercises 5–7 on Student Book page 196, students consolidate their understanding of fractions, fractions greater than one, improper fractions, and fractions that are equal to 1 as they compare and write these numbers in order.

Differentiated Instruction

Intervention   Activity Card 5-9

Benchmark Numbers   Activity Card 5-9 ●

Work: In Pairs

Use:

• Play money (dimes, quarters, nickels)

1. **Work Together** Select a coin or a small group of coins. Then copy and complete the table.

2. Use what you know about fractions to write decimal and fraction equivalents.

3. Repeat the activity several times. Include the following money amounts in your table: $0.10, $0.25, $0.50, and $0.75.

Unit 5, Lesson 9   Copyright © Houghton Mifflin Company

Activity Note Any group of coins can be described as a fractional part of $1 by using the denominator 100, for example, $0.37 = \frac{37}{100}$. Some money amounts can be described as part of $1 by using more than one fraction. $0.25 = \frac{25}{100} = \frac{1}{4}$.

✓ **Math Writing Prompt**

A Good Trade Or Not? Should you trade $0.60 for $\frac{1}{2}$ dollar? Explain why or why not.

Soar to Success Math ★ **Software Support**

Warm-Up 24.36

On Level   Activity Card 5-9

Fractions on a Number Line   Activity Card 5-9 ▲

Work: In Pairs

1. On your own, write five fractions or mixed numbers between 0 and 3 on a sheet of paper. Be sure that each fraction has 8 as the denominator.

2. Exchange papers. Draw a number line from 0 to 3, and place the fractions on the number line.

3. Exchange papers again to check your partner's work.

4. **Math Talk** How did you decide where to place the numbers on the line? Possible answer: For fractions less than 1, the numerator tells how many intervals between 0 and 1 to count to place the fraction. For mixed numbers, locate the whole number on the number line and then count on the number of intervals equal to the numerator of the fraction part of the mixed number.

Unit 5, Lesson 9   Copyright © Houghton Mifflin Company

Activity Note Students should make a number line with intervals between whole numbers divided into eighths to make it easier to locate the fractions.

✓ **Math Writing Prompt**

In Your Own Words A friend doesn't think that $1\frac{1}{8}$ is closer to $\frac{7}{8}$ than it is to $1\frac{7}{8}$. What might you say, write, or draw to convince him?

MegaMath Grades K-6 **Software Support**

Fraction Action: Number Line Mine, Level F

Challenge   Activity Card 5-9

Fractions and Decimals on a Number Line   Activity Card 5-9 ■

Work: In Pairs

1. On your own, write three fractions and three decimals between 0 and 3 on a sheet of paper.

2. Exchange papers and draw a number line from 0 to 3. Then place each fraction and decimal on the line.

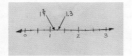

3. Exchange papers again to check your partner's work.

4. **Compare** Which is easier to locate on your number line, $1\frac{3}{8}$ or 1.8? Explain your thinking.

Unit 5, Lesson 9   Copyright © Houghton Mifflin Company

Activity Note Students should consider the denominators of the fractions they must locate on the number line as they choose the intervals between whole numbers on the number line they draw.

✓ **Math Writing Prompt**

Investigate Math How can you determine if $1\frac{7}{8}$ is closer to $2\frac{1}{8}$ or to 1.6?

✵ **DESTINATION** Math **Software Support**

Course III: Module 4: Unit 1: Tenths, Hundredths, and Thousandths

Comparison Situations   **473**

③ Homework and Spiral Review

5–9
Homework   **Goal:** Additional Practice

✔ Include students' Homework for page 121 as part of their portfolios.

5–9
Remembering   **Goal:** Spiral Review

This Remembering activity is appropriate anytime after today's lesson.

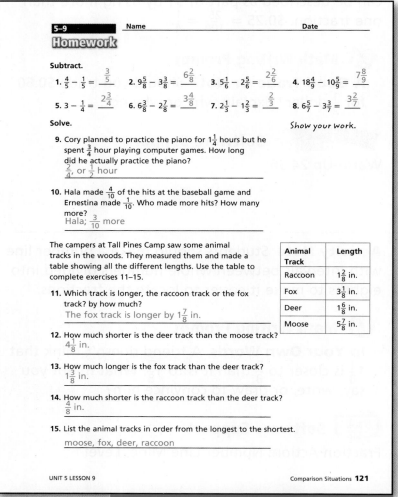

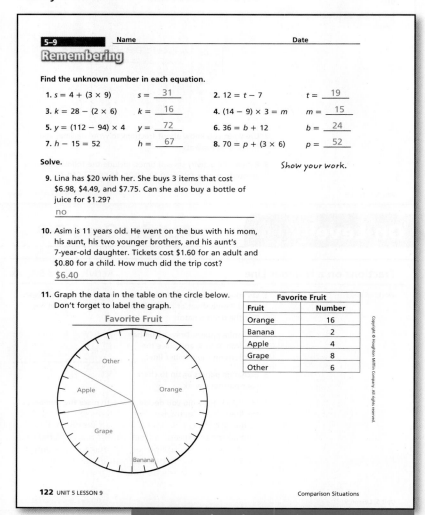

Home or School Activity

 Science Connection

Compare Animal Size Guidebooks to insects, birds, and other animals often include the length of the animal in inches as a mixed number.

Have students find a guidebook at home, at school, at a library, or on the Internet. Ask them to record the length of several interesting animals, using mixed numbers, and to create a word problem that involves comparing animals' sizes.

Monarch Butterfly
$3\frac{3}{8}$ to $4\frac{7}{8}$ inches

474   UNIT 5 LESSON 9

UNIT 5
LESSON
10

Mixed Practice With Like Fractions

REAL WORLD Problem Solving

Lesson Objectives

● Consolidate understanding of addition and subtraction with like fractions.

● Express the main concept of adding and subtracting like fractions.

Vocabulary
numerator
denominator

The Day at a Glance

Today's Goals	Materials
① Teaching the Lesson **A1:** Discuss a word problem presented by the Puzzled Penguin. **A2:** Present and solve fraction word problems. **② Going Further** ► Differentiated Instruction **③ Homework and Spiral Review**	**Lesson Activities** Student Activity Book pp. 197–198 or Student Hardcover Book pp. 197–198 Homework and Remembering pp. 123–124 Quick Quiz 2 (Assessment Guide) **Going Further** Activity Cards 5-10 Math Journals 123 *Use* **Math Talk** *today!*

Keeping Skills Sharp

Quick Practice ⏱ 5 MINUTES	Daily Routines
Goal: Compare fractions by using > and <. **Material:** pointer **Which Fraction Is Less?** Invite six pairs of students to the board. The first student in each pair writes a fraction. The other student then writes a different fraction with the same denominator. Next, invite one student from each pair to remain at the board and to use a pointer to point to each set of fractions, asking "Which is less?" The class responds by pointing, and the student at the board writes > or < between the fractions. Then have the whole class read aloud the inequality. For fractions such as $\frac{7}{10}$ and $\frac{3}{10}$, the class would say, "Seven tenths is greater than three tenths."	**Homework Review** If students give incorrect answers, have them explain how they found the answers. This can help you determine whether the error is conceptual or procedural. **Geometry** The dimensions of Ms. Fu's living room are 9 ft 5 in. by 10 ft 8 in. Ms. Fu received a price quote for installing new carpet that said the area of her living room is 102 square feet. Is the quoted area reasonable? How can she use estimation to check? Yes. Possible answer: 6 in. is half of a foot. 9 ft 5 in. ≈ 9 ft, because 5 < 6; 10 ft 8 in. ≈ 11 ft, because 8 > 6; $A = 9$ ft • 11 ft = 99 sq ft, which is ≈ 102 sq ft

1 Teaching the Lesson

The Puzzled Penguin

 20 MINUTES

Goal: Discuss a word problem presented by the Puzzled Penguin.

Materials: Student Activity Book or Hardcover Book p. 197

 NCTM Standards:
Number and Operations
Problem Solving
Communication

Differentiated Instruction

Special Needs For students who have difficulty writing, pair them with good writers who can write the students' ideas. Or allow the students to give their answers orally.

English Language Learners

Provide support with writing word problems. Have students work in **Student Pairs**.

• **Beginning** Write a word problem on the board. Have students change some of the words or numbers to write their own.
• **Intermediate** Ask simple questions to help students decide what to write.
• **Advanced** Have students tell each other a problem before writing it.

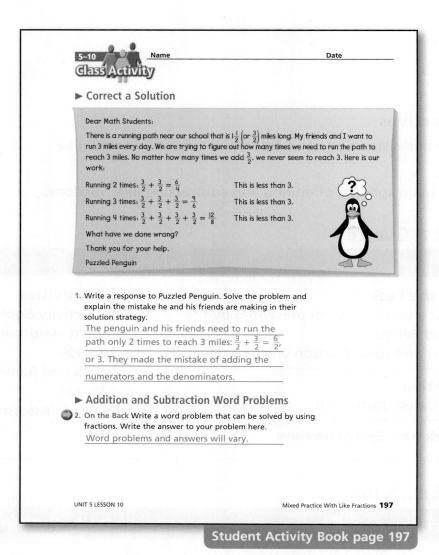

Student Activity Book page 197

▶ Correct a Solution ⎡WHOLE CLASS⎤

Explain that the class received a letter from the Puzzled Penguin. Refer students to Student Book page 197.

Give students several minutes to think about how they might respond to the letter. Then discuss their ideas as a class.

It is most important that students recognize that the Puzzled Penguin and his friends added both the numerators and the denominators of the fractions; they should have added only the numerators. To emphasize this point, you can pose this problem to the class:

● Suppose the Puzzled Penguin ran 3 miles (or $\frac{24}{8}$ miles) one day but his friend ran $\frac{1}{8}$ mile more. How can the Puzzled Penguin calculate how far his friend ran? Add $\frac{1}{8}$ to $\frac{24}{8}$.

- Should the Puzzled Penguin add the numerator and the denominator? No; $\frac{24}{8} + \frac{1}{8}$ is not equal to $\frac{25}{16}$. $\frac{25}{16} = 1\frac{9}{16}$, which is less than 3.

- How can the Puzzled Penguin use addition to find out how far his friend ran? He can add the numerators, but not the denominators: $\frac{24}{8} + \frac{1}{8} = \frac{25}{8}$, or $3\frac{1}{8}$.

- Does the answer $3\frac{1}{8}$ seem reasonable? Yes; $\frac{1}{8}$ is a small amount, so the answer should be a little more than 3. $3\frac{1}{8}$ is a little more than 3.

Invite students to complete exercise 1 and to compare their responses to the Puzzled Penguin with a partner.

► Choose the Correct Answer WHOLE CLASS

Write these three equations on the board. Tell students that one of them is correct and the other two are incorrect.

$$1.\ 7\tfrac{1}{8} - 5\tfrac{3}{8} \overset{?}{=} 2\tfrac{2}{8}$$
$$2.\ 7\tfrac{1}{8} - 5\tfrac{3}{8} \overset{?}{=} 1\tfrac{6}{8}$$
$$3.\ 7\tfrac{1}{8} - 5\tfrac{3}{8} \overset{?}{=} 2\tfrac{6}{8}$$

Working in **Student Pairs**, allow students several minutes to determine which equation is correct and to identify the errors that caused the incorrect answers in the other two equations. Invite pairs to share their ideas, and encourage questions from classmates. Students should realize that:

- equation 1 is incorrect. The person who completed the equation subtracted 5 from 7, but also subtracted $\frac{1}{8}$ from $\frac{3}{8}$; he or she should have subtracted $\frac{3}{8}$ from $\frac{1}{8}$.

- equation 2 is correct.

- equation 3 is incorrect. The person who completed it took apart 7 to create more eighths from which to subtract $\frac{3}{8}$, but he or she forgot to subtract 5 from 6 instead of from 7.

The Learning Classroom

Math Talk Ensure that all students agree that the Puzzled Penguin and his friends made the mistake of adding the denominators as well as the numerators.

► What did the Puzzled Penguin do wrong?

► Why was that a problem?

► How did that change their answer?

✓ Ongoing Assessment

During the class discussion, listen carefully to students' explanations. Are they able to clearly explain how errors occurred? Can they confidently identify correct equations?

Activity 2

Student-Generated Problems

 30 MINUTES

Goal: Present and solve fraction word problems.

Materials: Student Activity Book or Hardcover Book pp. 197–198

 NCTM Standards:
Number and Operations
Problem Solving
Communication

 Quick Quiz

See Assessment Guide for Unit 5 Quick Quiz 2.

▶ Addition and Subtraction Word Problems

WHOLE CLASS

Math Talk Refer students to exercise 2 on Student Book page 197, and have them write a word problem that can be solved by using fractions. To ensure balanced practice, you might ask certain students to write subtraction problems and others to write addition problems.

Invite one student at a time to read aloud his or her problem and to ask the rest of the class to solve it. Encourage students to discuss their solutions; have several students work at the board.

If any students present problems that include fractions with unlike denominators, ask them to make an adjustment.

● You are asking us to add fourths and fifths. Which shall we use?

② Going Further

● Intervention — Activity Card 5-10

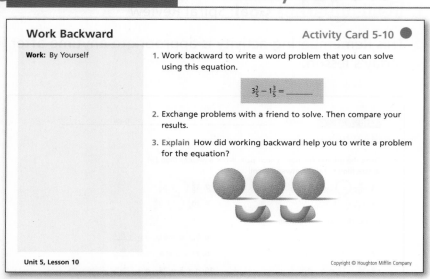

Work Backward   Activity Card 5-10 ●

Work: By Yourself

1. Work backward to write a word problem that you can solve using this equation.

$$3\tfrac{2}{5} - 1\tfrac{3}{5} = \underline{\qquad}$$

2. Exchange problems with a friend to solve. Then compare your results.

3. **Explain** How did working backward help you to write a problem for the equation?

Unit 5, Lesson 10   Copyright © Houghton Mifflin Company

Activity Note If students need help focusing on a topic, suggest that they consider situations involving objects that can be divided into 5 equal parts to match the fraction denominators.

Math Writing Prompt

In Your Own Words Look at a word problem you solved in this lesson. How did you determine that your solution was correct?

Soar to Success Math   **Software Support**

Warm-Up 20.21

▲ On Level — Activity Card 5-10

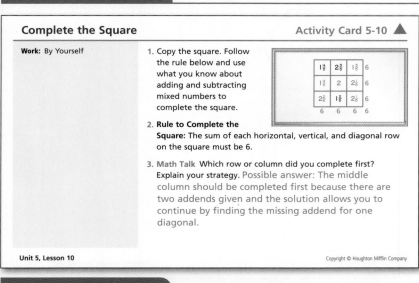

Complete the Square   Activity Card 5-10 ▲

Work: By Yourself

1. Copy the square. Follow the rule below and use what you know about adding and subtracting mixed numbers to complete the square.

$1\tfrac{4}{6}$	$2\tfrac{3}{6}$	$1\tfrac{5}{6}$	6
$1\tfrac{4}{6}$	2	$2\tfrac{2}{6}$	6
$2\tfrac{4}{6}$	$1\tfrac{3}{6}$	$2\tfrac{5}{6}$	6
6	6	6	6

2. **Rule to Complete the Square:** The sum of each horizontal, vertical, and diagonal row on the square must be 6.

3. **Math Talk** Which row or column did you complete first? Explain your strategy. Possible answer: The middle column should be completed first because there are two addends given and the solution allows you to continue by finding the missing addend for one diagonal.

Unit 5, Lesson 10   Copyright © Houghton Mifflin Company

Activity Note When students add the two mixed numbers in the top row, be sure that they regroup before counting on to 6. Have students exchange papers with other students to check their work.

Math Writing Prompt

Explain Your Thinking How did you find each missing number in the Complete the Square activity?

 MegaMath Grades K-6   **Software Support**

Fraction Action: Fraction Flare Up, Level G

■ Challenge — Activity Card 5-10

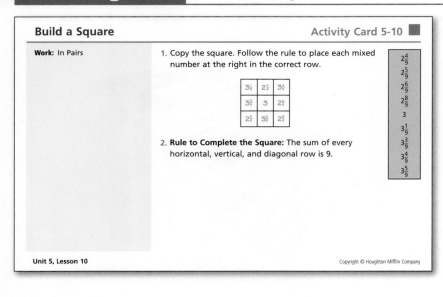

Build a Square   Activity Card 5-10 ■

Work: In Pairs

1. Copy the square. Follow the rule to place each mixed number at the right in the correct row.

$3\tfrac{1}{9}$	$2\tfrac{5}{9}$	$3\tfrac{3}{9}$
$3\tfrac{3}{9}$	3	$2\tfrac{7}{9}$
$2\tfrac{5}{9}$	$3\tfrac{4}{9}$	$2\tfrac{6}{9}$

$2\tfrac{4}{9}$
$2\tfrac{5}{9}$
$2\tfrac{6}{9}$
$2\tfrac{8}{9}$
3
$3\tfrac{1}{9}$
$3\tfrac{3}{9}$
$3\tfrac{4}{9}$
$3\tfrac{5}{9}$

2. **Rule to Complete the Square:** The sum of every horizontal, vertical, and diagonal row is 9.

Unit 5, Lesson 10   Copyright © Houghton Mifflin Company

Activity Note If students have difficulty, point out that the numerators of the fractions in each row, column, and diagonal must add to 9 or 18 for the sum of all three numbers to be a whole number.

Math Writing Prompt

Solve a Problem One day, a mouse ate $\tfrac{1}{5}$ of its food. On every day after that, it ate $\tfrac{1}{5}$ of the remaining food. When will it finish the food?

 DESTINATION Math· **Software Support**

Course III: Module 3: Unit 2: Sums Involving Like Denominators

Mixed Practice With Like Fractions   **479**

3 Homework and Spiral Review

Homework **Goal:** Additional Practice

On this Homework page, students solve problems involving the addition and subtraction of like fractions.

Remembering **Goal:** Spiral Review

This Remembering activity is appropriate anytime after today's lesson.

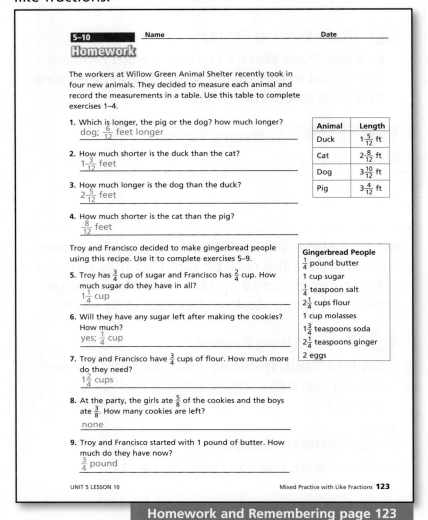

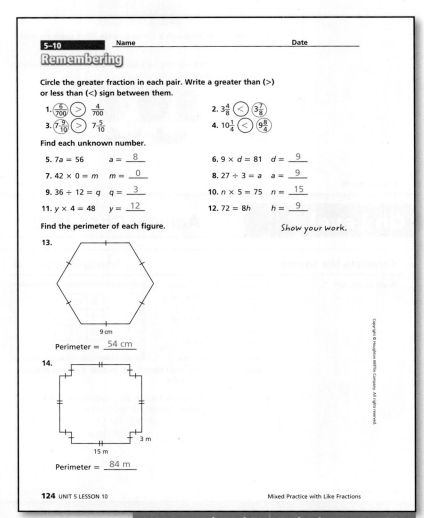

Homework and Remembering page 123

Homework and Remembering page 124

Home or School Activity

 Language Arts Connection

Media Advertisements Ask students to look for advertisements in newspapers or magazines. Have them estimate how many pages of advertising there are in one section of a newspaper or a group of pages in a magazine, to the nearest eighth of a page. They can add and subtract to compare the amount of advertising in different sections of the newspaper or in different publications.

Discover Equivalent Fractions

REAL WORLD Problem Solving

Vocabulary

equivalent fractions
multiplier
simplify
unsimplify

Lesson Objectives

● Generate and explain simple equivalent fractions.

● Understand and apply the terms *equivalent fraction* and *simplify*.

The Day at a Glance

Today's Goals	Materials	
1 **Teaching the Lesson** 　A1: Generate equivalent fractions, and discuss the multipliers. 　A2: Use a number line to create and visualize equivalent fractions. **2** **Going Further** 　► Differentiated Instruction **3** **Homework and Spiral Review**	**Lesson Activities** Student Activity Book pp. 199–202 or Student Hardcover Book pp. 199–202 and Activity Workbook pp. 86–88 Homework and Remembering pp. 125–126 MathBoard materials	**Going Further** Activity Cards 5-11 Equivalent Fractions (TRB M31) Ruler Fraction Match-Up Cards (TRB M32) Scissors Math Journals

123 **Use Math Talk today!**

Keeping Skills Sharp

Quick Practice ⏱ 5 MINUTES	**Daily Routines**
Goal: Recognize when to ungroup mixed numbers to solve a subtraction problem. **Material:** pointer **Ungroup** Invite six students to the board to write a subtraction problem involving mixed numbers; they should leave the problem unsolved. Ask one student to remain at the board and to use a pointer to point to each problem while the class responds, "ungroup" or "do not ungroup," depending on whether the first number needs to be changed to solve the problem.	**Homework Review** Have students discuss their work for each problem. Clarify any misunderstandings. **Mental Math** Find the number that is 0.01 greater and the number that is 0.1 less than each of the given numbers. **1.** 65.997　　**2.** 13,850.09 **3.** 4,201　　**4.** 738.1 1. 66.007, 65.897; 2. 13,850.1, 13,849.99; 3. 4,201.01, 4,200.9; 4. 738.11, 738

Teaching the Lesson

Explore Equivalence

 25 MINUTES

Goal: Generate equivalent fractions, and discuss the multipliers.

Materials: MathBoard materials

✔ **NCTM Standards:**
Number and Operations
Reasoning and Proof
Representation

English Language Learners

Draw 2 sandwiches on the board, one cut into halves and the other cut into fourths. Write *equivalent*.

• **Beginning** Ask: Is $\frac{1}{2}$ sandwich the same size as $\frac{2}{4}$ sandwich? yes Say: $\frac{1}{2}$ and $\frac{2}{4}$ are equivalent.

• **Intermediate** Say: One-half sandwich is the same size as ___. $\frac{2}{4}$ sandwich Ask: **Are $\frac{1}{2}$ and $\frac{2}{4}$ equivalent?** yes

• **Advanced** Say: *Equivalent* means "having an equal value." Ask: **What fraction of the sandwich is equivalent to $\frac{1}{2}$?** $\frac{2}{4}$

► **Generate Equivalent Halves** WHOLE CLASS

Write the fraction $\frac{1}{2}$ on the board. Ask students to suggest as many fractions as they can that are equivalent to one half. Create a long fraction equation on the board and write fractions in the order in which students generate them. Leave the fraction chain on the board.

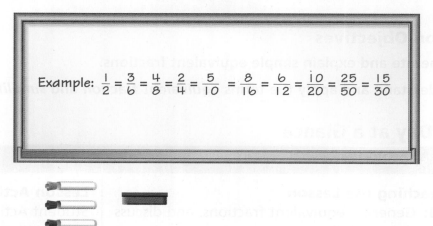

Example: $\frac{1}{2} = \frac{3}{6} = \frac{4}{8} = \frac{2}{4} = \frac{5}{10} = \frac{8}{16} = \frac{6}{12} = \frac{10}{20} = \frac{25}{50} = \frac{15}{30}$

Have students find all of the fractions on the MathBoard that equal $\frac{1}{2}$ and discuss relationships they see. Draw a vertical line segment at the end of each $\frac{1}{2}$ and write each fraction $= \frac{1}{2}$ as shown below to help with the search for patterns.

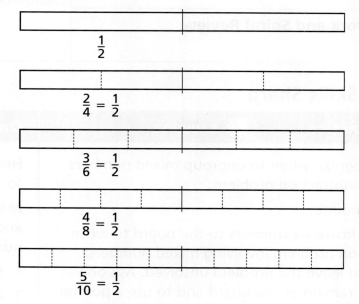

Have students focus on what is happening numerically to each fraction and what is happening to the fraction bar unit $\frac{1}{2}$ as it is written with a new unit fraction. We have found that the language *n*-split or *n*-fracture is helpful in describing what is happening.

After discussing, record as shown below the dividing of the $\frac{1}{2}$ length into smaller unit fractions ($\frac{1}{4}, \frac{1}{6}, \frac{1}{8}, \frac{1}{10}$) and the multiplying of the number of unit fractions to make an equivalent fraction (the same-sized part of the whole).

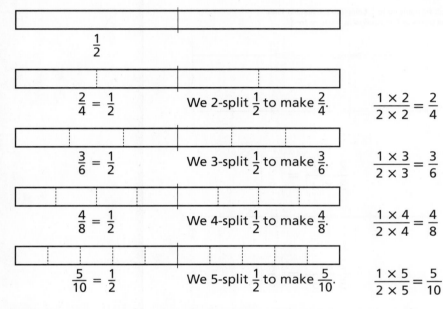

$\frac{2}{4} = \frac{1}{2}$ We 2-split $\frac{1}{2}$ to make $\frac{2}{4}$. $\frac{1 \times 2}{2 \times 2} = \frac{2}{4}$

$\frac{3}{6} = \frac{1}{2}$ We 3-split $\frac{1}{2}$ to make $\frac{3}{6}$. $\frac{1 \times 3}{2 \times 3} = \frac{3}{6}$

$\frac{4}{8} = \frac{1}{2}$ We 4-split $\frac{1}{2}$ to make $\frac{4}{8}$. $\frac{1 \times 4}{2 \times 4} = \frac{4}{8}$

$\frac{5}{10} = \frac{1}{2}$ We 5-split $\frac{1}{2}$ to make $\frac{5}{10}$. $\frac{1 \times 5}{2 \times 5} = \frac{5}{10}$

Discuss how multiplying the top and the bottom numbers in $\frac{1}{2}$ have different meanings. Multiplying the bottom unit fraction 2 gives the number of equal parts in the whole new fraction (it gives the new unit fraction number). Multiplying the top number 1 gives the number of the new unit fraction parts that are actually in the new equivalent fraction.

(123) Math Talk Now look at other equivalent fractions in your long equation and discuss what kind of *n*-split (or *n*-fracture) would create that unit fraction and what you would have to multiply the top and bottom by to get that fraction.

$\frac{1}{2} = \frac{8}{16}$ 8-split $\frac{1}{2}$ to make $\frac{8}{16}$ $\frac{1 \times 8}{2 \times 8} = \frac{8}{16}$

$\frac{1}{2} = \frac{100}{200}$ 100-split $\frac{1}{2}$ to make $\frac{100}{200}$ $\frac{1 \times 100}{2 \times 100} = \frac{100}{200}$

Discuss whether this would work for any multiplier. Yes, you could make equivalent fractions for $\frac{1}{2}$ by using any multiplier.

Teaching the Lesson (continued)

Equivalent Fractions on the Number Line

 30 MINUTES

Goal: Use a number line to create and visualize equivalent fractions.

Materials: Student Activity Book pp. 199–202 or Hardcover Book pp. 199–202 and Activity Workbook pp. 86–88; MathBoard materials (optional)

✔ **NCTM Standards:**
Number and Operations
Reasoning and Proof
Representation

Teaching Note

Same Whole Throughout all lessons on equivalent fractions, emphasize that the equivalent fractions must have the same whole. The MathBoards fractions all have the same whole, as do the number lines on the Student Book pages. But when you or students sketch equivalent fractions, be sure that the whole used for the original fraction stays the same whole for the new equivalent fraction. Sometimes students do not make equal partitions of a whole and add on a new piece or cross out part of the original whole, thus changing the whole without even knowing they are doing so.

This is also important when finding equivalent fractions to add, subtract, or compare. These fractions must have the same unit fraction (have same sized parts) **of the same whole**. Drawing them both on the same unit length ensures that they are parts of the same whole, and simplifying or unsimplifying one or both as needed ensures that they have the same unit fraction (the same denominator, called the common denominator).

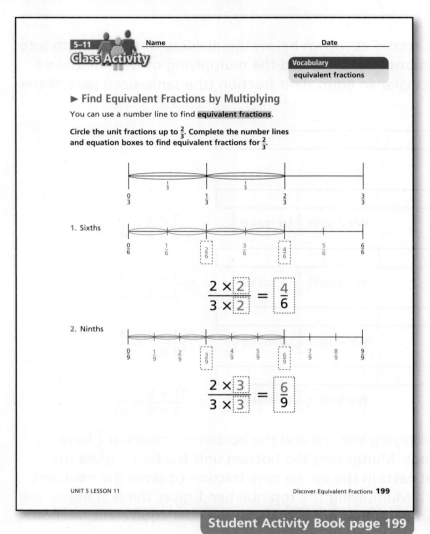

Student Activity Book page 199

▶ Find Equivalent Fractions by Multiplying [WHOLE CLASS]

Direct students' attention to the first number line on Student Book page 199. Explain that they will be finding equivalent fractions for $\frac{2}{3}$.

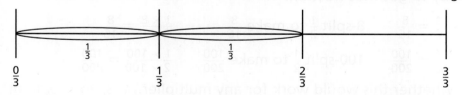

Explain that this number line shows the simplest way to write the fractions $\frac{1}{3}$ and $\frac{2}{3}$. Elicit from students the total of the circled thirds: $\frac{1}{3} + \frac{1}{3} = \frac{2}{3}$.

Direct students' attention to the number line in exercise 1, which shows sixths. Ask students to label all fractions shown on the line. The fractions that belong in the empty boxes are equivalent to $\frac{1}{3}$ and $\frac{2}{3}$.

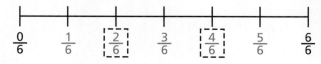

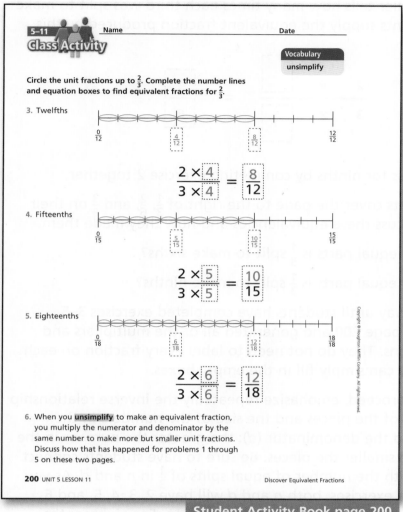

Alternate Approach

MathBoards If students would benefit from more practice seeing representations of equivalent fractions, have them work with the MathBoards. In **Student Pairs**, students can find equivalent fractions on the fraction bars and write equations to describe them.

$$\frac{1}{4} = \frac{2}{8}$$

Next, have students circle enough sixths to make $\frac{1}{3}$ and $\frac{2}{3}$. Then ask them to write the total above each part: $\frac{2}{6} + \frac{2}{6} = \frac{4}{6}$.

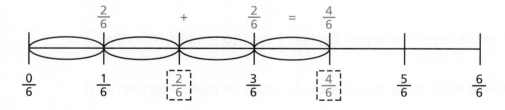

Use questions to encourage students to share their observations about the numbers on the line.

● How many sixths does it take to make $\frac{1}{3}$? 2 sixths

● How many sixths does it take to make $\frac{2}{3}$? 4 sixths

● How can $\frac{4}{6}$ be equal to $\frac{2}{3}$ when $\frac{4}{6}$ has bigger numbers than $\frac{2}{3}$? $\frac{4}{6}$ has twice as many pieces as $\frac{2}{3}$, but each piece is only half as big.

Activity continued ▶

Activity 2

Have students look at the equation box below the number line for sixths. Ask them to identify the multiplier and to write it in both stacked boxes. The multiplier tells how many times each third was split to make sixths. Have students supply the equivalent fraction produced by this multiplier.

$$\frac{2 \times \boxed{2}}{3 \times \boxed{2}} = \frac{\boxed{4}}{\boxed{6}}$$

Repeat the process for ninths by completing exercise 2 together.

Then have students cover the page to the right of $\frac{1}{3}$, $\frac{2}{6}$, and $\frac{3}{9}$ on their number lines. Discuss these equivalencies and how they made them.

● Into how many equal parts is $\frac{1}{3}$ split to make sixths? 2 equal parts

● Into how many equal parts is $\frac{1}{3}$ split to make ninths? 3 equal parts

Continue in this way until students have completed exercises 3–5 on Student Book page 200 and generated all of the multipliers and equivalent fractions. They do not need to label every fraction on each number line; they can simply fill in the empty boxes.

Key Idea As you proceed, emphasize repeatedly the inverse relationship between the size of the pieces and the size of the numbers in the numerator (n) and the denominator (d): the greater the number in the denominator, the smaller the pieces. Be sure to have students connect the multipliers with the number of equal splits of $\frac{1}{3}$ in n and d. As you work through the exercises, both n and d will have 2, 3, 4, 5, and 6 times as many parts as the original simple fraction. For eighteenths, there are 6 times as many parts, but each part is only $\frac{1}{6}$ the original size.

Ask students to cover page 200 to the right of $\frac{4}{12}$, $\frac{5}{15}$, and $\frac{6}{18}$.

● Into how many equal parts is $\frac{1}{3}$ split to make twelfths?
4 equal parts

● Into how many equal parts is $\frac{1}{3}$ split to make fifteenths?
5 equal parts

● Into how many equal parts is $\frac{1}{3}$ split to make eighteenths?
6 equal parts

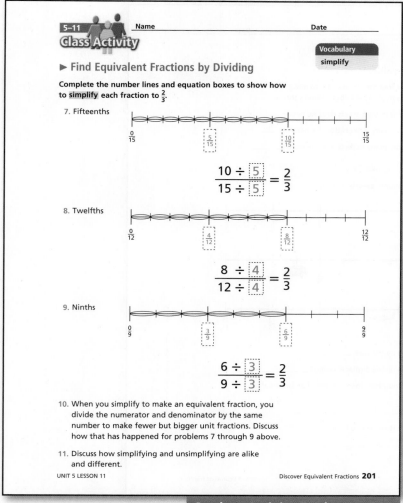

Student Activity Book page 201

► Find Equivalent Fractions by Dividing WHOLE CLASS

Ask students to look back at the equation in exercise 5 on Student Book page 200.

● How can you change $\frac{12}{18}$ back to $\frac{2}{3}$? Divide the numerator and denominator by 6.

Introduce the term *simplify:* to produce an equivalent fraction with lesser numerator and denominator. Have students complete exercises 7–11 on Student Book page 201. Then have them cover the whole page to the right of $\frac{1}{3}$.

● How many fifteenths are grouped together to make $\frac{1}{3}$? 5

● How can you find the number of thirds in $\frac{10}{15}$? Divide 10 and 15 by 5.

● How many twelfths are grouped together to make $\frac{1}{3}$? 4

● How can you find the number of thirds in $\frac{8}{12}$? Divide 8 and 12 by 4.

● How many ninths are grouped together to make $\frac{1}{3}$? 3

● How can you find the number of thirds in $\frac{6}{9}$? Divide 6 and 9 by 3.

Activity continued ▶

Teaching Note

Math Background Some math programs use the term *reduce* rather than *simplify*. The word *reduce*, however, can imply to students that the amount is actually getting smaller. Your students, **English Language Learners** in particular, should be aware of this alternate term because they may see it in other contexts, including some standardized math tests.

✓ Ongoing Assessment

Remind students that there are two ways to make equivalent fractions: simplify and unsimplify. Ask students how to simplify and unsimplify a given fraction.

▶ $\frac{4}{8}$ can be simplified to $\frac{1}{2}$. Explain what you need to do to simplify a fraction.

▶ $\frac{1}{2}$ can be unsimplified to $\frac{3}{6}$. Explain what you need to do to unsimplify a fraction.

① Teaching the Lesson (continued)

Activity 2

Differentiated Instruction

Extra Help If students are having difficulty, they can circle each fractional part of the number line and count the parts up to the equivalent fractions they are trying to find.

The Learning Classroom

Building Concepts Ask students to summarize what they have learned about how to make a new fraction that is equivalent to a given fraction. They should recognize that you can always multiply the numerator and denominator by the same whole number to make an equivalent fraction. They may also recognize that it is possible to divide the numerator and denominator by the same whole number to simplify a fraction if that number is a factor of both the numerator and the denominator.

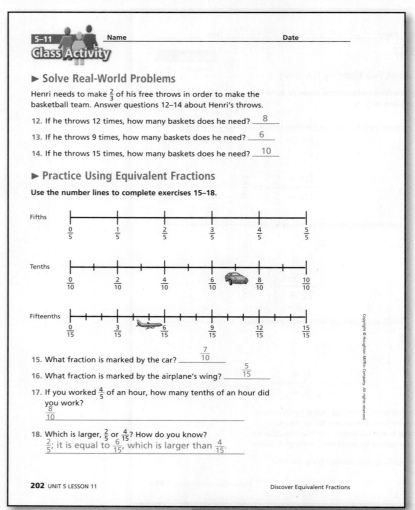

Student Activity Book page 202

The student activity page shows:

5–11 Class Activity — Name / Date

▶ Solve Real-World Problems

Henri needs to make $\frac{2}{3}$ of his free throws in order to make the basketball team. Answer questions 12–14 about Henri's throws.

12. If he throws 12 times, how many baskets does he need? __8__

13. If he throws 9 times, how many baskets does he need? __6__

14. If he throws 15 times, how many baskets does he need? __10__

▶ Practice Using Equivalent Fractions

Use the number lines to complete exercises 15–18.

15. What fraction is marked by the car? $\frac{7}{10}$

16. What fraction is marked by the airplane's wing? $\frac{5}{15}$

17. If you worked $\frac{4}{5}$ of an hour, how many tenths of an hour did you work? $\frac{8}{10}$

18. Which is larger, $\frac{2}{5}$ or $\frac{4}{15}$? How do you know? $\frac{2}{5}$; it is equal to $\frac{6}{15}$, which is larger than $\frac{4}{15}$.

202 UNIT 5 LESSON 11 — Discover Equivalent Fractions

▶ Solve Real-World Problems [WHOLE CLASS]

Use **Solve and Discuss** for problems 12–14 on Student Book page 202. Remind students to refer to the number lines on the previous pages and discuss how to use them to solve the problem.

▶ Practice Using Equivalent Fractions [INDIVIDUALS]

Refer students to Student Book page 202, and ask them to complete exercises 15–18.

② Going Further

Differentiated Instruction

Intervention   Activity Card 5-11

Find Equivalent Fractions   Activity Card 5-11 ●

Work: By Yourself

Use:
• Equivalent Fractions (TRB M31)
• Ruler

1. Use your ruler and the Equivalent Fractions page to find and write equivalent fractions.

2. Place the ruler vertically beside any fraction you choose. List all the fractions that align with the ruler.

$\frac{4}{7}$ and $\frac{2}{8}$ are equivalent.

3. **Math Talk** Why does using the ruler in this way help you to identify equivalent fractions? Possible answer: The ruler divides each line into the same fractional part because all the lines are the same length and are arranged in parallel to each other, aligned on the left.

Unit 5, Lesson 11   Copyright © Houghton Mifflin Company

Activity Note Be sure that students position the ruler vertically so that equivalent fractions appear in alignment along one side of the ruler. Students can align the bottom of the ruler with the bottom line.

> 🖉 **Math Writing Prompt**
>
> **Show Your Thinking** Use a diagram to explain why the fractions $\frac{2}{5}$ and $\frac{4}{10}$ are equivalent.

Soar to Success Math ★ **Software Support**

Warm-Up 9.22

On Level   Activity Card 5-11

Fraction Match-Up   Activity Card 5-11 ▲

Work: In Pairs

Use:
• Fraction Match-Up Cards (TRB M32)
• Scissors

1. Cut out the cards to play a match-up game.

2. Take turns turning over two cards. If the cards show equivalent fractions, keep the cards and take another turn.

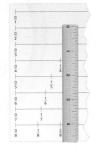

3. If the cards do not match, return them face down and end your turn.

4. The first player to collect five pairs of matching cards wins.

Unit 5, Lesson 11   Copyright © Houghton Mifflin Company

Activity Note Have students justify their fraction pairs as they accumulate them. After students complete the activity, discuss the strategies they used to identify equivalent fractions.

> 🖉 **Math Writing Prompt**
>
> **Use Reasoning** Write three equivalent fractions. Identify the simplest fraction, and explain why it is the simplest.

MEGA MATH Grades K–6 **Software Support**

Fraction Action: Fraction Flare Up, Level D

Challenge   Activity Card 5-11

Compare Fractions   Activity Card 5-11 ■

Work: In Pairs

Use:
• Equivalent Fractions (TRB M31)
• Ruler

1. Take turns predicting how two fractions compare. Write any two fractions with a denominator from 2 to 12. Your partner predicts which fraction is greater, or predicts that they are equivalent.

2. **Work Together** Check the prediction by lining up the left side of a ruler with the chosen or greater fraction on the Equivalent Fractions page. If the second fraction is less, it appears to the left of the ruler.

3. **Compare** The example shows that $\frac{1}{4}$ is greater than $\frac{1}{5}$. What fraction is equivalent to $\frac{1}{4}$? $\frac{2}{8}$

Unit 5, Lesson 11   Copyright © Houghton Mifflin Company

Activity Note It is important that students align the ruler with the fraction they have chosen as being greater before looking for the second fraction. If they do not see the second fraction on the left, it cannot be the lesser fraction.

> 🖉 **Math Writing Prompt**
>
> **Explain Your Thinking** Use equivalent fractions to explain why 25 cm is the same length as $\frac{1}{4}$ m.

✖ **DESTINATION Math** **Software Support**

Course III: Module 3: Unit 1: Equivalent Fractions

Discover Equivalent Fractions   **489**

③ Homework and Spiral Review

Homework **Goal:** Additional Practice

✔ Include students' Homework for page 125 as part of their portfolios.

Remembering **Goal:** Spiral Review

This Remembering activity is appropriate anytime after today's lesson.

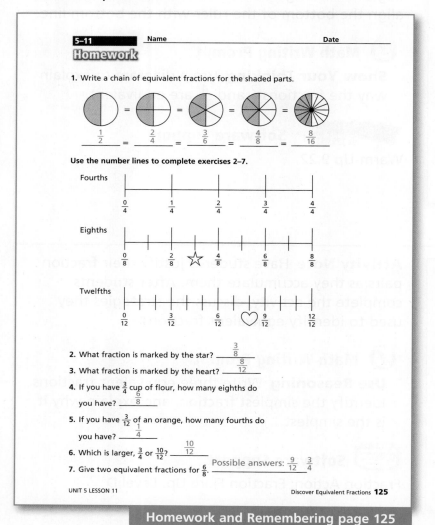

Homework and Remembering page 125

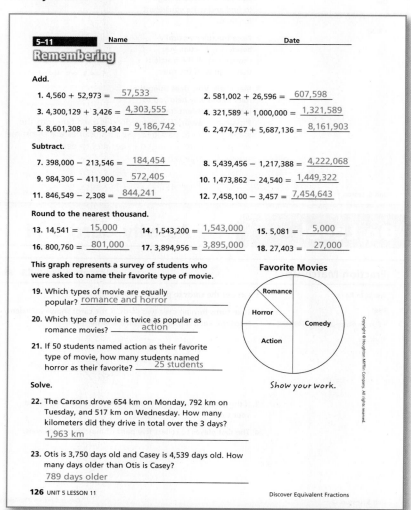

Homework and Remembering page 126

Home or School Activity

 Math-to-Math Connection

Fractions and Time Have students divide up their day by the number of hours spent at school, playing, sleeping, eating, and so on. Ask them to write fractions for each activity with a denominator of 24. Then they write equivalent fractions for each of their fractions by dividing. Ask them how many different denominators are possible for the equivalent fractions.

UNIT 5
LESSON
12

Equivalent Fractions and Multipliers

Vocabulary

multiplication
table
multiplier
simplify
unsimplify

Lesson Objectives

● **Understand the role of the multiplier in equivalent fractions.**

● **Simplify and unsimplify common fractions.**

The Day at a Glance

Today's Goals	Materials	

1 **Teaching the Lesson**
  A1: Discuss how equivalent fractions relate to the multiplication table.
  A2: Find equivalent fractions.
 	
2 **Going Further**
  ▶ Differentiated Instruction
 	
3 **Homework and Spiral Review**
	Lesson Activities
	Student Activity Book pp. 203–204 or Student Hardcover Book pp. 203–204 and Activity Workbook pp. 89–90
	Homework and Remembering pp. 127–128
	Class MathBoard
	Math Journals
		Going Further
		Activity Cards 5-12
		Tens and Hundreds Grids (TRB M33)
		Clock with second hand or a timer
		Math Journals

123 *Use* **Math Talk** *today!*

Keeping Skills Sharp

Quick Practice 🕐 5 MINUTES	**Daily Routines**
Goal: Recognize when to ungroup mixed numbers to solve a subtraction problem. **Material:** pointer **Ungroup** Invite six students to the board to write a subtraction problem involving mixed numbers; they should leave the problem unsolved. Ask one student to remain at the board and use a pointer to point to each problem while the class responds, "ungroup" or "do not ungroup," depending on whether the first number needs to be changed to solve the problem.	**Strategy Problem** Walter saw a display of towers made from boxes. The first tower used 1 box; the second tower used 8 boxes, the third used 27 boxes; the fourth used 64 boxes, and so on. If this pattern continued, how many boxes were in the one hundredth tower? Find the pattern. Rule: Multiply the figure number 3 times; example: $4 \times 4 \times 4 = 64$. Apply the pattern to the one hundredth term: $100 \times 100 \times 100 = 1,000,000$ boxes.

Equivalent Fractions and Multipliers **491**

Teaching the Lesson

Explore Equivalence

35 MINUTES

Goal: Discuss how equivalent fractions relate to the multiplication table.

Materials: Student Activity Book pp. 203–204 or Hardcover Book pp. 203–204 and Activity Workbook pp. 89–90; Class MathBoard

✔ **NCTM Standards:**
Number and Operations
Reasoning and Proof
Problem Solving

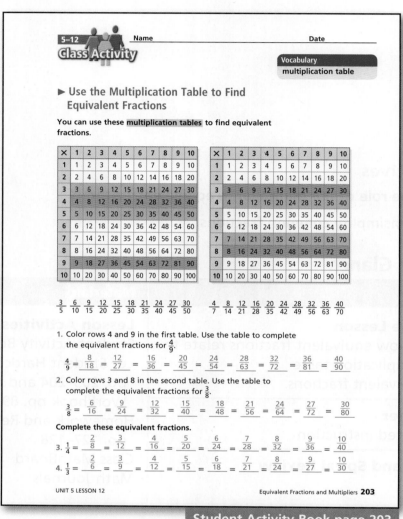

Student Activity Book page 203

▶ Use the Multiplication Table to Find Equivalent Fractions [WHOLE CLASS]

Write the fraction $\frac{3}{5}$ on the board. Ask students to suggest as many equivalent fractions as they can. It is fine if they are able to come up with only a few suggestions.

Refer students to Student Book page 203.

- What do you see at the top of the page? multiplication tables

- What does row 3 in each table show? multiples of 3

- What does row 5 in each table show? multiples of 5

Tell students to think of the numbers in row 3 as numerators and the numbers in row 5 as denominators.

- Why is $\frac{3}{5}$ equivalent to $\frac{6}{10}$? Both the numerator and denominator of $\frac{3}{5}$ have been multiplied by 2.

Draw students' attention to the row of fractions at the bottom of the first table.

- The first fraction, $\frac{3}{5}$, is the simplest fraction. Why can't we write it with smaller numbers for the numerator and denominator? You can't divide both numbers by the same whole number to make them smaller.

- What are the multipliers for the fractions, as you look across the row? 2, 3, 4, 5, 6, 7, 8, 9, 10

- Write the multiplier below each fraction. Where do you see the multipliers in the table? in the top row

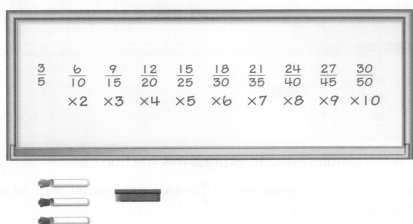

▶ Simplify and Unsimplify WHOLE CLASS

Encourage students to consult this chain of fractions as you discuss simplifying and unsimplifying. Relate the fractions to the columns in the first multiplication table on Student Book page 203.

- How can you change $\frac{3}{5}$ to $\frac{18}{30}$? Multiply the numerator and denominator by 6.

- How can you simplify $\frac{18}{30}$? Divide the numerator and denominator by 6.

- How can you change $\frac{3}{5}$ to $\frac{27}{45}$? Multiply the numerator and denominator by 9.

- How can you simplify $\frac{27}{45}$? Divide the numerator and denominator by 9.

Remind students that when they divide the numerator and denominator to make them smaller, they are simplifying the fraction to make larger unit fractions. Multiplying the numerator and denominator *un*simplifies the fraction by making smaller unit fractions. The two fractions still represent the same number; they are still the same part of the whole. This is why we call them *equivalent fractions*.

Activity continued ▶

Activity 1

▶ **Find Numerators and Denominators** [WHOLE CLASS]

Have students look at the second multiplication table on Student Book page 203. Ask them to write the multiplier below each fraction and to relate this multiplier to the column in the multiplication table.

(123) **Math Talk** Ask questions related to simplifying and unsimplifying the fractions. Also have students find fractions with specific numerators and denominators, such as the examples shown here.

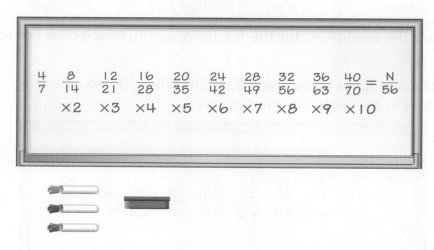

- What is the simplest way to express this fraction? $\frac{4}{7}$

- If I need a fraction equivalent to $\frac{4}{7}$ with a denominator of 56, what will the numerator be? 32

- How did you get 32? Since you multiplied the denominator by 8, you have to multiply the numerator by 8.

- If I need a fraction equivalent to $\frac{4}{7}$ with a numerator of 24, what will the denominator be? 42

$$\frac{4}{7} = \frac{24}{d}$$

- How did you get 42? Since you multiplied the numerator by 6, you have to multiply the denominator by 6.

Invite students to make up similar questions for their classmates to answer. For each question, encourage students to explain how they found the unknown number.

Have students complete exercises 1–4 on their own or in **Student Pairs**.

► Split Fraction Bars [INDIVIDUALS]

Refer students to Student Book page 204, and draw their attention to the fraction bar for $\frac{5}{6}$. Ask students how they can modify the bar to show twelfths. You can split each sixth in 2 parts.

Next, ask them how they can modify the bar to show eighteenths and twenty-fourths. You can split each sixth in 3 parts for eighteenths and 4 parts for twenty-fourths.

Ask students to split the bars as described and complete exercises 4–6. Invite a volunteer to demonstrate the first series of splits on the Class MathBoard.

When students are finished, have them split the fraction bars and find the equivalent fractions in exercises 7 and 8.

Teaching the Lesson (continued)

Activity 2

Equivalence Chains

 20 MINUTES

Goal: Find equivalent fractions.

Materials: Math Journals

 NCTM Standards:
Number and Operations
Reasoning and Proof

✔ Ongoing Assessment

Choose an unsimplified fraction, such as $\frac{10}{12}$, and ask students to make equivalent fractions with given multipliers or divisors.

► Write a simpler fraction, using 2 as a divisor.

► Write an equivalent fraction, using 3 as a multiplier.

► Generate Equivalent Fractions [WHOLE CLASS]

Write the fraction $\frac{3}{8}$ on the board, and leave room to the right for a row of equivalent fractions. Invite nine volunteers to line up at the board. Each student writes the next equivalent fraction in the series and places the multiplier below. Ask the rest of the class to write the same fraction chain in their Math Journals or on a sheet of paper, working ahead if possible. When the chain is complete, have students check it to make sure it is correct. Leave the fraction chain on the board for the next activity.

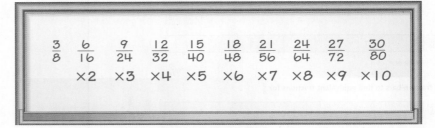

► Share a Giant Pizza [WHOLE CLASS]

Ask a girl and a boy to go to the board and to circle a fraction in the chain, except the first or the last. Above their fractions, have them label the letter *B* for boy and *G* for girl.

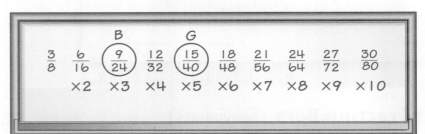

Have students pretend that these fractions represent slices of the same-sized giant pizza. Ask these questions.

● **What does each denominator represent?** the total number of slices

● **What does each numerator represent?** the number of slices that the boy or girl gets

● **Who gets more slices?** girl **larger slices?** boy

● **Who gets a larger amount, the girl or the boy? Why?** They get the same amount because both fractions are equivalent to $\frac{3}{8}$.

● **What does the boy's multiplier mean?** He has 3 times as many slices as the $\frac{3}{8}$ of a pizza. Each slice is only $\frac{1}{3}$ as large.

● **What does the girl's multiplier mean?** She has 5 times as many slices as the $\frac{3}{8}$ of a pizza. Each slice is only $\frac{1}{5}$ as large.

If time permits, have students generate another chain of equivalent fractions and repeat the activity.

Intervention   Activity Card 5-12

Decimals and Fractions   Activity Card 5-12 ●

Work: By Yourself

Use:
- Tens and Hundreds Grids (TRB M33)

1. Shade a different part of each grid.

2. Write a fraction and a decimal to represent the shaded part of each grid.

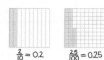

$\frac{2}{10} = 0.2$ $\frac{25}{100} = 0.25$

3. **Explain** How does the decimal you wrote show the shaded part of the grid? How does the fraction relate to the shaded part? Possible answers: The decimal shows how many columns out of 10 columns or how many squares out of 100 squares are shaded. The numerator of the fraction shows how many parts are shaded and the denominator shows how many parts are in the entire grid.

Unit 5, Lesson 12   Copyright © Houghton Mifflin Company

Activity Note Before students begin the activity, review what part of the whole grid each column of 10 unit squares represents, and what part of the whole grid each unit square represents.

 Math Writing Prompt

Explain Your Thinking Write a fraction with a denominator of 100. Use an example to explain what the numerator and denominator could represent.

 **Software Support**

Warm-Up 24.36

On Level   Activity Card 5-12

Equivalent Fractions   Activity Card 5-12 ▲

Work: In Pairs

1. On your own, write an improper fraction. Then write an equivalent fraction using a multiplier.

$\frac{13}{5} = \frac{26}{10}$

$2\frac{3}{5} = 2\frac{6}{10}$

2. Trade papers and rewrite both fractions as mixed numbers.

3. **Math Talk** Discuss the method you used to rewrite each improper fraction as a mixed number.

Unit 5, Lesson 12   Copyright © Houghton Mifflin Company

Activity Note After students trade papers, suggest that they check each other's equivalent fractions by identifying the multiplier used to write it.

 Math Writing Prompt

Correct or Not? Floyd used 2 as a multiplier to change $1\frac{2}{3}$ to $2\frac{4}{6}$. Are his mixed numbers equivalent? Explain why or why not.

 Software Support

Fraction Action: Number Line Mine, Level F

Challenge   Activity Card 5-12

Describe with Fractions   Activity Card 5-12 ■

Work: In Pairs

Use:
- Clock with a second hand or minute timer

1. On your own, write a whole number, a fraction with a denominator of 10, and a fraction with a denominator of 100.

$3 = 3.0 = \frac{3}{1}$

$\frac{5}{10} = 0.5 = \frac{1}{2} = \frac{50}{100}$

$\frac{75}{100} = 0.75 = \frac{15}{20} = \frac{150}{200}$

11 points ✓

2. Trade papers with your partner. Look at the time or set the timer, and write each number in as many equivalent ways as possible in one minute.

3. Each player scores 2 points for the first new form of each number and 1 point for each additional form.

Unit 5, Lesson 12   Copyright © Houghton Mifflin Company

Activity Note Use the examples to review equivalent ways to write fractions before students begin the activity.

 Math Writing Prompt

Investigate Math Explain how to use the whole numbers 2, 3, 4, 5, and so on as divisors to test if you can simplify a fraction. Can you simplify the fraction $\frac{35}{91}$?

DESTINATION Math **Software Support**

Course III: Module 3: Unit 1: Equivalent Fractions

③ Homework and Spiral Review

5–12
Homework **Goal:** Additional Practice

On this Homework page, students practice writing equivalent fractions.

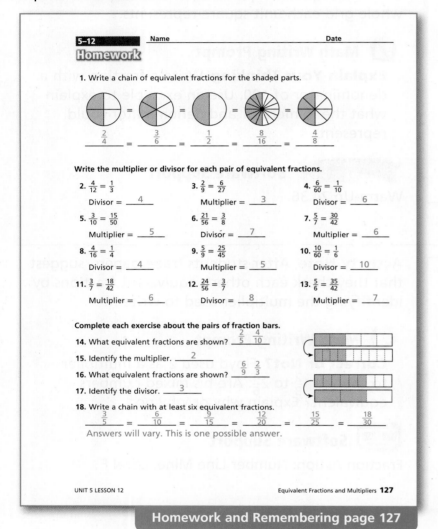

5–12 Name _____ Date _____
Homework

1. Write a chain of equivalent fractions for the shaded parts.

$$\frac{2}{4} = \frac{3}{6} = \frac{1}{2} = \frac{8}{16} = \frac{4}{8}$$

Write the multiplier or divisor for each pair of equivalent fractions.

2. $\frac{4}{12} = \frac{1}{3}$ **3.** $\frac{2}{9} = \frac{6}{27}$ **4.** $\frac{6}{60} = \frac{1}{10}$

Divisor = 4   Multiplier = 3   Divisor = 6

5. $\frac{3}{10} = \frac{15}{50}$ **6.** $\frac{21}{56} = \frac{3}{8}$ **7.** $\frac{5}{7} = \frac{30}{42}$

Multiplier = 5   Divisor = 7   Multiplier = 6

8. $\frac{4}{16} = \frac{1}{4}$ **9.** $\frac{5}{9} = \frac{25}{45}$ **10.** $\frac{10}{60} = \frac{1}{6}$

Divisor = 4   Multiplier = 5   Divisor = 10

11. $\frac{3}{7} = \frac{18}{42}$ **12.** $\frac{24}{56} = \frac{3}{7}$ **13.** $\frac{5}{6} = \frac{35}{42}$

Multiplier = 6   Divisor = 8   Multiplier = 7

Complete each exercise about the pairs of fraction bars.

14. What equivalent fractions are shown? $\frac{2}{5}$ $\frac{4}{10}$

15. Identify the multiplier. 2

16. What equivalent fractions are shown? $\frac{6}{9}$ $\frac{2}{3}$

17. Identify the divisor. 3

18. Write a chain with at least six equivalent fractions.

$$\frac{3}{5} = \frac{6}{10} = \frac{9}{15} = \frac{12}{20} = \frac{15}{25} = \frac{18}{30}$$

Answers will vary. This is one possible answer.

UNIT 5 LESSON 12   Equivalent Fractions and Multipliers **127**

Homework and Remembering page 127

5–12
Remembering **Goal:** Spiral Review

This Remembering activity is appropriate anytime after today's lesson.

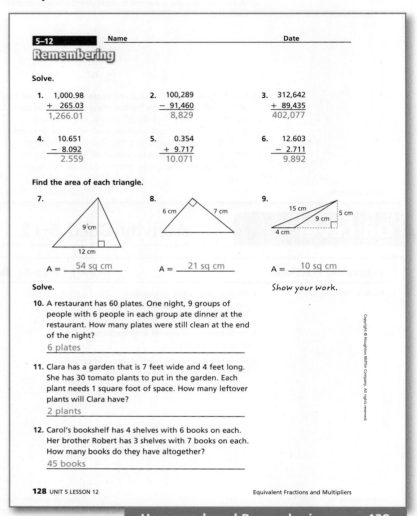

5–12 Name _____ Date _____
Remembering

Solve.

1. 1,000.98
     + 265.03
     1,266.01

2. 100,289
     − 91,460
     8,829

3. 312,642
     + 89,435
     402,077

4. 10.651
     − 8.092
     2.559

5. 0.354
     + 9.717
     10.071

6. 12.603
     − 2.711
     9.892

Find the area of each triangle.

7. (9 cm height, 12 cm base)   **8.** (6 cm, 7 cm)   **9.** (15 cm, 9 cm, 5 cm, 4 cm)

A = 54 sq cm   A = 21 sq cm   A = 10 sq cm

Solve.   Show your work.

10. A restaurant has 60 plates. One night, 9 groups of people with 6 people in each group ate dinner at the restaurant. How many plates were still clean at the end of the night?

6 plates

11. Clara has a garden that is 7 feet wide and 4 feet long. She has 30 tomato plants to put in the garden. Each plant needs 1 square foot of space. How many leftover plants will Clara have?

2 plants

12. Carol's bookshelf has 4 shelves with 6 books on each. Her brother Robert has 3 shelves with 7 books on each. How many books do they have altogether?

45 books

128 UNIT 5 LESSON 12   Equivalent Fractions and Multipliers

Homework and Remembering page 128

Home or School Activity

Sports Connection

Fractions in Baseball Have students write an improper fraction for $5\frac{2}{3}$, and have them consider this question: In baseball, how many outs has one pitcher made after $5\frac{2}{3}$ innings?

Have students describe what each part of the fraction means in their response. Then challenge them to think of other fractions used in baseball or a sport of their choice.

"Strike 3! You're out!"

UNIT 5
LESSON
13

Solve Equivalence Problems

REAL WORLD **Problem Solving**

Lesson Objective

● Generate and simplify fractions in real-world contexts.

Vocabulary
equivalent
simplify
unsimplify

The Day at a Glance

Today's Goals	Materials

1 **Teaching the Lesson**
A1: Generate an out-of-order equivalent-fraction chain, and compare equivalent fractions.
A2: Find unknown numerators and denominators of equivalent fractions.
A3: Generate and simplify fractions in real-world contexts.
 	
2 **Going Further**
▶ Math Connection: Factors and Multiples
▶ Differentiated Instruction
 	
3 **Homework and Spiral Review**
	Lesson Activities
	Student Activity Book pp. 205–206
	  or Student Hardcover Book
	  pp. 205–206
	Homework and Remembering
	  pp. 129–130
	Completed Homework p. 127
	Math Journals
	
	Going Further
	Activity Cards 5-13
	MathBoard materials
	Ruler
	Index cards
	Math Journals

123 Use **Math Talk** today!

Keeping Skills Sharp

Quick Practice ⏱ 5 MINUTES	**Daily Routines**
Goal: Generate equivalent fractions. **Equivalent Fraction Parade:** Write the fraction $\frac{1}{4}$ on the board. Invite six students to the board. Taking turns, each student writes a different fraction equivalent to $\frac{1}{4}$. The class says the fraction out loud and tells the multiplier that made that fraction from $\frac{1}{4}$. Fractions do not have to be in order; for example, $$\frac{1}{4} \quad \frac{3}{12} \quad \frac{2}{8} \quad \frac{5}{20}$$ At the end, the class reads the list together. "One fourth equals three twelfths," and so on.	**Homework Review** Before students do Activity 2, check their understanding of exercises 2–13. **Geometry** A rectangle has a perimeter of 36 cm and an area of 80 cm². A right, scalene triangle has the same perimeter. Its base is 3 cm longer than its height. The diagonal side is 3 cm longer than the base. The base is 12 cm long. What is the area of this triangle? height: 9 cm, base: 12 cm, diagonal: 15 cm; $A = (12 \div 2)\ 9 = 54$ cm².

Solve Equivalence Problems **499**

① Teaching the Lesson

Practice With Equivalence

 15 MINUTES

Goal: Generate an out-of-order equivalent-fraction chain, and compare equivalent fractions.

 NCTM Standards:
Number and Operations
Reasoning and Proof

English Language Learners

Write *unit fraction* on the board. Draw 2 pizzas. Divide one into fourths and one into eighths. Write $\frac{1}{4}$ and $\frac{1}{8}$.

- **Beginning** Ask: Are these unit fractions? yes Does $\frac{1}{4}$ have a bigger or smaller denominator? smaller Is $\frac{1}{4}$ of a pizza bigger or smaller than $\frac{1}{8}$? bigger
- **Intermediate** Ask: Which unit fraction has a larger denominator? $\frac{1}{8}$ Which is a larger slice? $\frac{1}{4}$
- **Advanced** Say: $\frac{1}{4}$ and $\frac{1}{8}$ are both unit __. fractions Have students compare the denominators and slices.

▶ The Pizza Activity `WHOLE CLASS`

Ask a boy and a girl to go to the board and to write a chain of equivalent fractions, as in Share a Giant Pizza in Lesson 12 Activity 2. This time the fractions should be written out of order. Ask each student to circle one fraction and to write *B* for *boy* and *G* for *girl* above the one he or she chose.

$$\frac{3}{8} \quad \overset{B}{\textcircled{\frac{9}{24}}} \quad \frac{18}{48} \quad \overset{G}{\textcircled{\frac{15}{40}}} \quad \frac{6}{16} \quad \frac{12}{32}$$

For each pair of fractions, ask the class these questions. Answers will vary; these answers are based on the example above.

- Who gets more slices of the giant pizza, the girl or the boy? the girl

- Who gets larger slices of the giant pizza, the girl or the boy? the boy

- Who gets a larger amount, the girl or the boy? Why? They get the same amount; there are more of the smaller slices and fewer of the larger slices; both fractions are equivalent to $\frac{3}{8}$.

- How do you know their two fractions are equivalent? because both fractions are also equivalent to $\frac{3}{8}$

Erase the circles and have another boy and girl circle and label two different fractions. Repeat the activity, emphasizing that the person with more slices has smaller slices. The total amount continues to be equal. If needed, have students generate another chain of equivalent fractions and repeat the activity.

Return to this activity occasionally to help students remember that a larger denominator means smaller shares (smaller unit fractions).

Equivalence With Unknown Parts

5–13
Class Activity

Name _____ Date _____

Vocabulary
equivalent
simplify
unsimplify

▶ Find Unknown Numerators and Denominators

Find n or d.

1. $\frac{1}{4} = \frac{n}{12}$ $n = \underline{\ 3\ }$ 2. $\frac{2}{5} = \frac{12}{d}$ $d = \underline{\ 30\ }$

3. $\frac{6}{36} = \frac{n}{6}$ $n = \underline{\ 1\ }$ 4. $\frac{4}{20} = \frac{2}{d}$ $d = \underline{\ 10\ }$

5. $\frac{2}{9} = \frac{n}{45}$ $n = \underline{\ 10\ }$ 6. $\frac{3}{8} = \frac{30}{d}$ $d = \underline{\ 80\ }$

7. $\frac{12}{16} = \frac{n}{4}$ $n = \underline{\ 3\ }$ 8. $\frac{14}{35} = \frac{2}{d}$ $d = \underline{\ 5\ }$

9. $\frac{15}{25} = \frac{n}{5}$ $n = \underline{\ 3\ }$ 10. $\frac{9}{36} = \frac{3}{d}$ $d = \underline{\ 12\ }$

11. $\frac{21}{28} = \frac{n}{4}$ $n = \underline{\ 3\ }$ 12. $\frac{12}{20} = \frac{6}{d}$ $d = \underline{\ 10\ }$

Two fractions are **equivalent** if either can be changed into the other by multiplying or dividing the numerator and denominator by the same number.

To **simplify** a fraction, divide the numerator and denominator by the same number to make a *smaller* number of *larger* unit fractions.

To **unsimplify** a fraction, multiply the numerator and denominator by the same number to make a *larger* number of *smaller* unit fractions.

Use the words *multiply*, *divide*, *simplify*, and *unsimplify* to complete the statements.

13. To change $\frac{3}{5}$ to $\frac{18}{30}$, __multiply__ the numerator and denominator by 6 in order to __unsimplify__ the fraction.

14. To change $\frac{18}{30}$ to $\frac{3}{5}$, __divide__ the numerator and denominator by 6 in order to __simplify__ the fraction.

UNIT 5 LESSON 13   Solve Equivalence Problems **205**

Student Activity Book page 205

---

25 MINUTES

Goal: Find unknown numerators and denominators of equivalent fractions.

Materials: Completed Homework p. 127, Math Journals, Student Activity Book or Hardcover Book p. 205

 NCTM Standards:
Number and Operations
Reasoning and Proof

The Learning Classroom

Helping Community Invite a few volunteers to work at the board and to discuss how they found the answer.

▶ Find Unknown Numerators and Denominators

WHOLE CLASS

Before beginning this activity, check students' understanding of exercises 2–7 on Homework page 127. They need to understand that the new equivalent fraction comes from multiplying or dividing both the numerator and denominator of the first fraction by the same number.

Write these two fractions on the board. Explain that n is an unknown numerator.

$$\frac{5}{8} = \frac{n}{24}$$

Have everyone write a value for n in their Math Journals. Discuss the answer as a class.

● What if we wanted to change $\frac{5}{8}$ to a fraction with 24 as the denominator? What would the multiplier be? Why? 3; because you have to multiply 8 by 3 to get 24

Activity continued ▶

Activity 2

Teaching Note

What to Expect from Students
Students will need to apply their knowledge of multipliers and divisors in order to solve these problems. Some extra notations may be helpful. Students may simply write the multiplier or divisor above the problem, or use arrows to help them track what they are doing. Encourage students to share their different approaches. Some students may be able to solve the problems without any special notation.

Unsimplify

$\times 3$

$\dfrac{5}{8} = \dfrac{n}{24}$ $\dfrac{5}{8} = \dfrac{n}{24}$ $\dfrac{5 \times 3}{8 \times 3} = \dfrac{15}{24}$
$\times 3$

Simplify

$\div 4$

$\dfrac{20}{32} = \dfrac{n}{8}$ $\dfrac{20}{32} = \dfrac{n}{8}$ $\dfrac{20 \div 4}{32 \div 4} = \dfrac{5}{8}$
$\div 4$

The Learning Classroom

Helping Community Students at the board may get stuck at some point. They usually welcome help from another student. Allowing other students to help instead of you will help them to assume responsibility for one another's learning. Ask who they would like to come up to help them. You can move on to another explainer while they redo their work. Of course, sometimes it is fine just to go ahead and have the whole class help the student with you leading with questions.

- What would you multiply the numerator, 5, by to get an equivalent fraction? Why? 3; the multiplier of the denominator was 3, so the multiplier of the numerator also has to be 3.

$$\dfrac{5}{8} = \dfrac{5 \times 3}{8 \times 3} = \dfrac{15}{24}$$

Repeat the activity, using an example with an unknown denominator.

$$\dfrac{9}{12} = \dfrac{3}{d} \qquad \dfrac{9 \div 3}{12 \div 3} = \dfrac{3}{4}$$

- We want to change $\dfrac{9}{12}$ to a fraction with 3 as the numerator. What will the divisor be? Why? 3; because you divide 9 by 3 to get 3

- What will you divide the denominator, 12, by to get an equivalent fraction? Why? 3; the divisor of the numerator was 3, so the divisor of the denominator also has to be 3.

Give the class some more equivalence problems to solve. Send several students to work on each problem at the board and to explain their methods. They should say whether they are simplifying or unsimplifying.

$$\dfrac{3}{5} = \dfrac{n}{40}\,24 \qquad \dfrac{7}{8} = \dfrac{28}{d}\,32 \qquad \dfrac{20}{32} = \dfrac{n}{8}\,5 \qquad \dfrac{3}{4} = \dfrac{21}{d}\,28$$

$$\dfrac{10}{15} = \dfrac{2}{d}\,3 \qquad \dfrac{42}{49} = \dfrac{n}{7}\,6 \qquad \dfrac{18}{81} = \dfrac{n}{9}\,2 \qquad \dfrac{63}{90} = \dfrac{7}{d}\,10$$

Have students complete exercises 1–12 on Student Book page 205.

▶ Simplifying Fractions WHOLE CLASS

(123) **Math Talk** Discuss with students why you might want to simplify a fraction. Possible answer: If the numbers are big, like $\dfrac{28}{56}$ or $\dfrac{19}{57}$, we have a better feel for what our answer is if we simplify them: $\dfrac{28}{56} = \dfrac{1}{2}$ and $\dfrac{19}{57} = \dfrac{1}{3}$.

To find the simplest form of a fraction, you just keep dividing top and bottom by a common factor. Sometimes this might take 2 or 3 steps:

$$\dfrac{90}{126} \overset{\div 3}{=} \dfrac{30}{42} \overset{\div 3}{=} \dfrac{10}{14} \overset{\div 2}{=} \dfrac{5}{7}$$

Use **Solve and Discuss** to simplify these fractions to the simplest form:

$$\dfrac{42}{48} \qquad \dfrac{40}{72} \qquad \dfrac{36}{45} \qquad \dfrac{36}{54} \qquad \dfrac{30}{42} \qquad \dfrac{48}{54} \qquad \dfrac{56}{63}$$

$$\dfrac{7}{8} \qquad \dfrac{5}{9} \qquad \dfrac{4}{5} \qquad \dfrac{6}{9} \qquad \dfrac{5}{7} \qquad \dfrac{8}{9} \qquad \dfrac{8}{9}$$

Activity 3

Applications

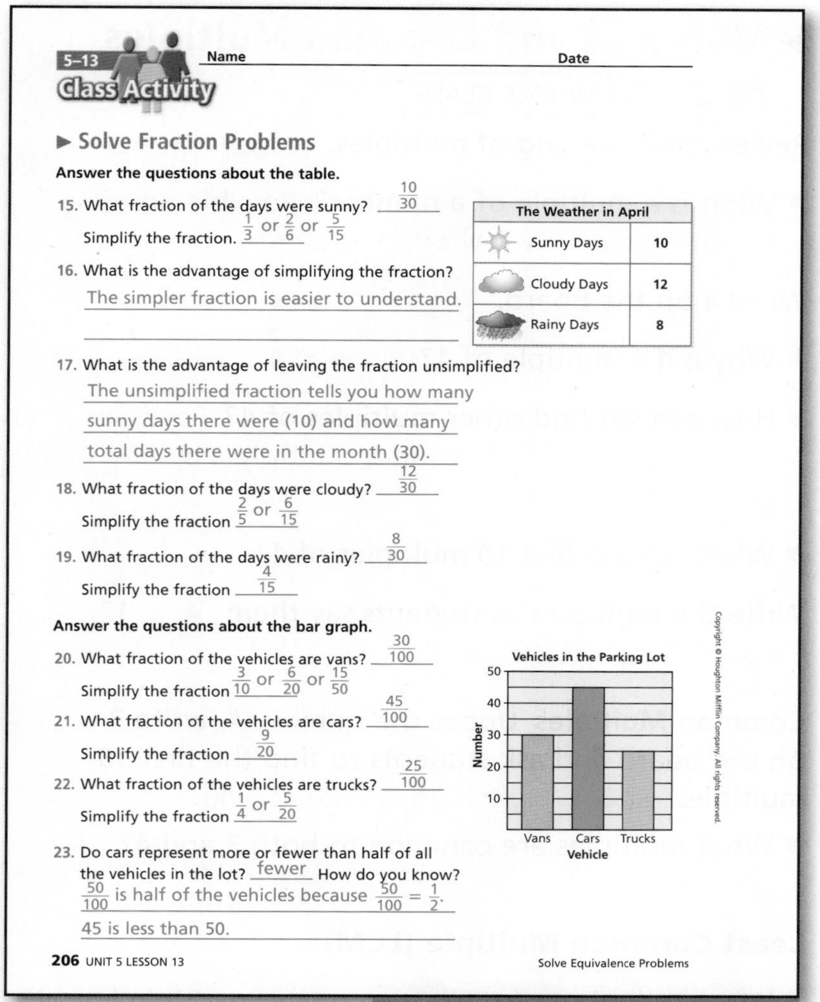
5–13 Class Activity

Name ______ Date ______

▶ Solve Fraction Problems

Answer the questions about the table.

15. What fraction of the days were sunny? $\frac{10}{30}$

Simplify the fraction. $\frac{1}{3}$ or $\frac{2}{6}$ or $\frac{5}{15}$

The Weather in April	
Sunny Days	10
Cloudy Days	12
Rainy Days	8

16. What is the advantage of simplifying the fraction?

The simpler fraction is easier to understand.

17. What is the advantage of leaving the fraction unsimplified?

The unsimplified fraction tells you how many sunny days there were (10) and how many total days there were in the month (30).

18. What fraction of the days were cloudy? $\frac{12}{30}$

Simplify the fraction $\frac{2}{5}$ or $\frac{6}{15}$

19. What fraction of the days were rainy? $\frac{8}{30}$

Simplify the fraction $\frac{4}{15}$

Answer the questions about the bar graph.

20. What fraction of the vehicles are vans? $\frac{30}{100}$

Simplify the fraction $\frac{3}{10}$ or $\frac{6}{20}$ or $\frac{15}{50}$

21. What fraction of the vehicles are cars? $\frac{45}{100}$

Simplify the fraction $\frac{9}{20}$

22. What fraction of the vehicles are trucks? $\frac{25}{100}$

Simplify the fraction $\frac{1}{4}$ or $\frac{5}{20}$

23. Do cars represent more or fewer than half of all the vehicles in the lot? fewer How do you know?

$\frac{50}{100}$ is half of the vehicles because $\frac{50}{100} = \frac{1}{2}$.

45 is less than 50.

206 UNIT 5 LESSON 13 Solve Equivalence Problems

Student Activity Book page 206

▶ Solve Fraction Problems INDIVIDUALS

Together, discuss the definitions and exercises 13 and 14 on Student Book page 205. Then have students apply these concepts by answering the questions about the chart and graph on Student Book page 206.

In exercises 15–19, students will need to find the total number of days in the month (30) before they can generate any fractions. This total (30 days) is the 1 whole, the denominator, for these problems.

For exercises 20–23, students will need to find the total number, the denominator, of vehicles (100) first. In problem 23, forty-five vehicles is less than half. Students may recognize quickly that 50 is half of 100, or they may have to compare $\frac{45}{100}$ to $\frac{50}{100}$.

15 MINUTES

Goal: Generate and simplify fractions in real-world contexts.

Materials: Student Activity Book or Hardcover Book pp. 205–206

NCTM Standards:
Number and Operations
Problem Solving

Ongoing Assessment

Ask students to explain different ways to change the same fraction.

- ▶ Explain how you can simplify the fraction $\frac{6}{9}$.
- ▶ Show how to unsimplify the fraction $\frac{6}{9}$.
- ▶ What do you know about the two new fractions?

②Going Further

Math Connection: Factors and Multiples

Goal: Determine common factors, as well as the GCF and LCM, of two numbers.

✓ **NCTM Standard:**
Number and Operations

▶ Factors and Common Factors

WHOLE CLASS

In this activity, students connect what they know about equivalent fractions with factors and multiples.

Review the meaning of *factors*.

● **What is a factor of a number?** Possible answer: A whole number that divides evenly into another whole number.

Write 28 on the board.

● **What are the factors of 28?**

Write the factors as students say them. 4 and 7, 1 and 28, 2 and 14

● **What number is a factor of every whole number?** 1

● **What property helps us know this?** Identity Property of Multiplication

Common Factors Write the number 42 on the board, under the number 28.

● **What are the factors of 42?**

Write the factors as students say them. 1 and 42, 2 and 21, 3 and 14, 6 and 7

● **What factors are common to both lists of factors?** 1, 2, 7, and 14

Greatest Common Factor (GCF)

● **What is the greatest common factor in both lists of factors?** 14

On the board, list other pairs of numbers: 12 and 15; 20 and 24; and 33 and 66. Use **Solve and Discuss** as students find the common factors and GCF of each pair of numbers.

12: 1, 2, 3, 4, 6, 12; 15: 1, 3, 5, 15; GCF: 3
20: 1, 2, 4, 5, 10, 20; 24: 1, 2, 3, 4, 6, 8, 12, 24; GCF: 4
33: 1, 3, 11, 33; 66: 1, 2, 3, 6, 11, 22, 33, 66; GCF: 33

▶ Multiples and Common Multiples Factors

WHOLE CLASS

Review the meaning of multiples.

● **What is a multiple of a number?** Possible answer: the product of two whole numbers

Write 4 on the board.

● **Why is 4 a multiple of 4?** $4 \times 1 = 4$

● **How can we find other multiples of 4?** Possible answers: use count-bys for 4; multiply 4 by any counting number

● **What are the first 10 multiples of 4?**

Write the multiples as students say them. 4, 8, 12, 16, 20, 24, 28, 32, 36, 40

Common Multiples Under the number 4, write 3 on the board and ask students to find the first 10 multiples. 3, 6, 9, 12, 15, 18, 21, 24, 27, 30

● **What multiples are common to both 3 and 4?** 12 and 24

Least Common Multiple (LCM)

● **What is the least (smallest) common multiple in both list of multiples?** 12

On the board, list other pairs of numbers: 5 and 10; 6 and 8; and 2 and 3. Use **Solve and Discuss** as students find the common multiples and LCM of each pair of numbers. 5 and 10 LCM: 10; 6 and 8 LCM: 24; 2 and 3 LCM: 6

Teaching Note

Math Background The GCF of the numerator and denominator can be used as a greatest common divisor (GCD) to simplify a fraction. The LCM of unlike denominators can be used as a least common denominator (LCD) to add or subtract fractions. However, it may be easier for students to simplify fractions and find common denominators using other methods.

Differentiated Instruction

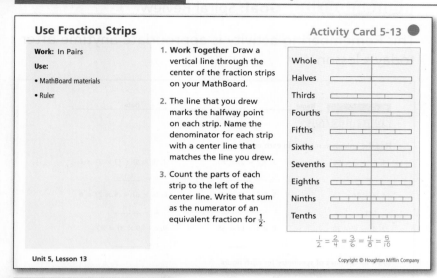

Use Fraction Strips   Activity Card 5-13 ●

Work: In Pairs

Use:
• MathBoard materials
• Ruler

1. **Work Together** Draw a vertical line through the center of the fraction strips on your MathBoard.

2. The line that you drew marks the halfway point on each strip. Name the denominator for each strip with a center line that matches the line you drew.

3. Count the parts of each strip to the left of the center line. Write that sum as the numerator of an equivalent fraction for $\frac{1}{2}$.

| Whole |
| Halves |
| Thirds |
| Fourths |
| Fifths |
| Sixths |
| Sevenths |
| Eighths |
| Ninths |
| Tenths |

$\frac{1}{2} = \frac{2}{4} = \frac{3}{6} = \frac{4}{8} = \frac{5}{10}$

Unit 5, Lesson 13   Copyright © Houghton Mifflin Company

Activity Note Students can locate the center of all the fraction strips by positioning the ruler to align with the center mark for halves and fourths.

✐ Math Writing Prompt
Make a Drawing Use a drawing to explain why $\frac{3}{4}$ is equivalent to $\frac{6}{8}$.

Soar to Success Math ★ **Software Support**
Warm-Up 24.36

Simpler Fractions   Activity Card 5-13 ▲

Work: In Pairs

Use:
• Index cards numbered 2 through 10

1. Place the cards face down. Each player turns over two cards and makes a proper fraction with the cards.

2. Write an equivalent fraction if possible by simplifying the first fraction. Otherwise, use a multiplier for the numerator and the denominator to write an equivalent fraction.

3. Your partner should challenge any fraction that he or she thinks is incorrect.

4. Score 2 points for a simplified fraction, 1 point for using a multiplier, and 0 points for an incorrect answer. Lose 2 points for making an incorrect challenge and earn 1 point for making a correct challenge. The first player to score 10 points wins.

 $\frac{2}{8} = \frac{1}{4}$

 $\frac{3}{7} = \frac{6}{14}$

Unit 5, Lesson 13   Copyright © Houghton Mifflin Company

Activity Note Have students justify their equivalent fractions by naming the multiplier that relates one fraction to the other. Students continue the activity until one player earns 10 points.

✐ Math Writing Prompt
Look for a Pattern Give an example of an ordered chain of equivalent fractions. Explain the number pattern shown by the denominators.

MEGA MATH Grades K-6 **Software Support**
Fraction Action: Number Line Mine, Level E

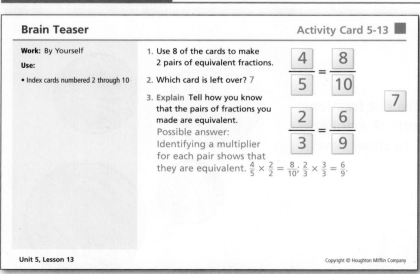

Brain Teaser   Activity Card 5-13 ■

Work: By Yourself

Use:
• Index cards numbered 2 through 10

1. Use 8 of the cards to make 2 pairs of equivalent fractions.

2. Which card is left over? 7

3. **Explain** Tell how you know that the pairs of fractions you made are equivalent.
Possible answer: Identifying a multiplier for each pair shows that they are equivalent. $\frac{4}{5} \times \frac{2}{2} = \frac{8}{10}, \frac{2}{3} \times \frac{3}{3} = \frac{6}{9}$.

$\frac{4}{5} = \frac{8}{10}$

$\frac{2}{3} = \frac{6}{9}$

7

Unit 5, Lesson 13   Copyright © Houghton Mifflin Company

Activity Note Possible pairs are shown. Other pairs can also be made by transposing the numerator of one fraction in a pair with the denominator of the other fraction in the same pair.

✐ Math Writing Prompt
Explain Your Thinking Why is it always possible to unsimplify a fraction, but often impossible to simplify it?

✸ DESTINATION Math **Software Support**
Course III: Module 3: Unit 1: Equivalent Fractions

③ Homework and Spiral Review

5–13
Homework **Goal:** Additional Practice

✓ Include students' Homework for page 129 as part of their portfolios.

5–13
Remembering **Goal:** Spiral Review

This Remembering activity is appropriate anytime after today's lesson.

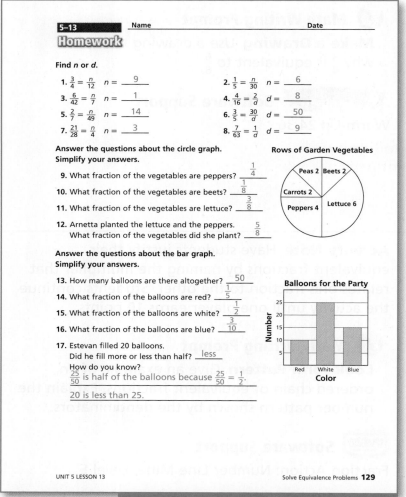

5–13
Homework   Name _____ Date _____

Find *n* or *d*.

1. $\frac{3}{4} = \frac{n}{12}$ $n = 9$ 2. $\frac{1}{5} = \frac{n}{30}$ $n = 6$
3. $\frac{6}{42} = \frac{n}{7}$ $n = 1$ 4. $\frac{4}{16} = \frac{2}{d}$ $d = 8$
5. $\frac{2}{7} = \frac{n}{49}$ $n = 14$ 6. $\frac{3}{5} = \frac{30}{d}$ $d = 50$
7. $\frac{21}{28} = \frac{n}{4}$ $n = 3$ 8. $\frac{7}{63} = \frac{1}{d}$ $d = 9$

Answer the questions about the circle graph. Simplify your answers.

Rows of Garden Vegetables

9. What fraction of the vegetables are peppers? $\frac{1}{4}$

10. What fraction of the vegetables are beets? $\frac{1}{8}$

11. What fraction of the vegetables are lettuce? $\frac{3}{8}$

12. Arnetta planted the lettuce and the peppers. What fraction of the vegetables did she plant? $\frac{5}{8}$

Answer the questions about the bar graph. Simplify your answers.

13. How many balloons are there altogether? 50

14. What fraction of the balloons are red? $\frac{1}{5}$

15. What fraction of the balloons are white? $\frac{1}{2}$

16. What fraction of the balloons are blue? $\frac{3}{10}$

17. Estevan filled 20 balloons. Did he fill more or less than half? $less$
How do you know?
$\frac{25}{50}$ is half of the balloons because $\frac{25}{50} = \frac{1}{2}$.
20 is less than 25.

Balloons for the Party

UNIT 5 LESSON 13   Solve Equivalence Problems **129**

Homework and Remembering page 129

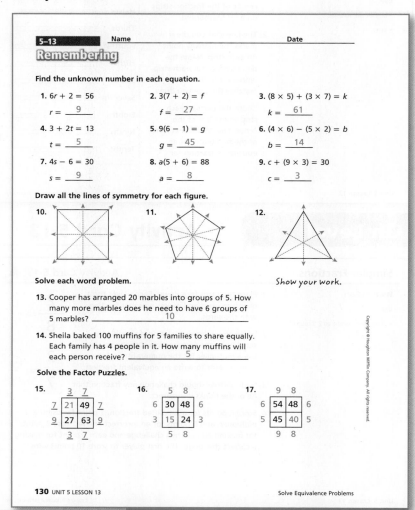

5–13
Remembering   Name _____ Date _____

Find the unknown number in each equation.

1. $6r + 2 = 56$ 2. $3(7 + 2) = f$ 3. $(8 \times 5) + (3 \times 7) = k$
   $r = 9$ $f = 27$ $k = 61$

4. $3 + 2t = 13$ 5. $9(6 - 1) = g$ 6. $(4 \times 6) - (5 \times 2) = b$
   $t = 5$ $g = 45$ $b = 14$

7. $4s - 6 = 30$ 8. $a(5 + 6) = 88$ 9. $c + (9 \times 3) = 30$
   $s = 9$ $a = 8$ $c = 3$

Draw all the lines of symmetry for each figure.

10.   11.   12.

Solve each word problem.   Show your work.

13. Cooper has arranged 20 marbles into groups of 5. How many more marbles does he need to have 6 groups of 5 marbles? 10

14. Sheila baked 100 muffins for 5 families to share equally. Each family has 4 people in it. How many muffins will each person receive? 5

Solve the Factor Puzzles.

15.
	3	7	
7	21	49	7
9	27	63	9
	3	7	

16.
	5	8	
6	30	48	6
3	15	24	3
	5	8	

17.
	9	8	
6	54	48	6
5	45	40	5
	9	8	

130 UNIT 5 LESSON 13   Solve Equivalence Problems

Homework and Remembering page 130

Home or School Activity

 Real-World Connection

Money Using 100 as the denominator, students write equivalent fractions for common coins: a half-dollar, a quarter, and a dime (tenth of a dollar). Students use an equivalent fraction with a numerator of 1 to show what fraction of a dollar is represented by a nickel.

$$\frac{1}{2} = \frac{n}{100} \qquad \frac{1}{4} = \frac{n}{100} \qquad \frac{1}{10} = \frac{n}{100} \qquad \frac{5}{100} = \frac{1}{d}$$

UNIT 5 LESSON 14

Add and Subtract Unlike Fractions

REAL WORLD Problem Solving

Lesson Objectives

● Add and subtract fractions with unlike denominators.

● Apply the terms *common denominator* and *least common denominator*.

Vocabulary

common denominator
least common denominator

The Day at a Glance

Today's Goals	Materials
1 Teaching the Lesson **A1:** Using MathBoards, visualize how to find a common denominator when adding or subtracting unlike fractions. **A2:** Rename fractions, and solve problems that involve adding and subtracting unlike fractions. **2 Going Further** ▶ Math Connection: Change Fractions to Simplest Form ▶ Differentiated Instruction **3 Homework and Spiral Review**	**Lesson Activities** Student Activity Book pp. 207–208 or Student Hardcover Book pp. 207–208 and Activity Workbook p. 91 Homework and Remembering pp. 131–132 MathBoard materials **Going Further** Activity Cards 5-14 Fraction Circles (TRB M30) Scissors Math Journals 123 Use Math Talk today!

Keeping Skills Sharp

Quick Practice ⏱ 5 MINUTES	**Daily Routines**
Goal: Write equivalent fractions. **Equivalent Fraction Parade** Write $\frac{2}{5}$ on the board. Have six students come to the board and take turns writing a new fraction equivalent to $\frac{2}{5}$. As each fraction appears, the writer turns and gives a signal. The class says the fraction and tells the multiplier that made that fraction from $\frac{2}{5}$. Fractions do not have to be in any special order; for example, $$\frac{2}{5} \qquad \frac{20}{50} \qquad \frac{12}{30} \qquad \frac{4}{10}$$ At the end, the class reads the list together. "Two fifths equals twenty fiftieths equals twelve thirtieths," and so on.	**Homework Review** Have students review the amount each bar of the bar graph represents. **Who's Right?** Shayne read 15 out of 50 pages in her book and Kenton read 27 out of 90 pages. Shayne said she had read more of her book than Kenton. Kenton said they actually read the same fraction of their books. Who is correct? **Explain.** Kenton; $\frac{15}{50} = \frac{3}{10} = \frac{27}{90}$ Both fractions simplify to the same fraction, so they are equivalent fractions.

① Teaching the Lesson

Rename Fractions

 25 MINUTES

Goal: Using MathBoards, visualize how to find a common denominator when adding or subtracting unlike fractions.

Materials: MathBoard materials

 NCTM Standards:
Number and Operations
Problem Solving
Representation
Communication

Teaching Note

Watch For! Some students may add numerators and denominators and write $\frac{1}{3} + \frac{1}{4} = \frac{2}{7}$. Look at $\frac{2}{7}$ on the MathBoard. $\frac{2}{7} < \frac{1}{3}$, so it can't be the total of $\frac{1}{3} + \frac{1}{4}$.

▶ **Student-Generated Solutions** WHOLE CLASS

Present the addition problem shown here. Invite several students to work at the board while the others work at their seats.

$$\frac{1}{2} + \frac{1}{3}$$

Math Talk This is an opportunity to see what your students already know about renaming and adding fractions. If no one is able to solve the problem, go directly to activity **Rename Fractions to Add or Subtract.** If some students know about renaming, let them explain their solutions to the class. Ask a few probing questions to help clarify the process. Throughout the lesson, use the term *common denominator* frequently to mean "have the same unit fraction."

● I see you changed $\frac{1}{2}$ to $\frac{3}{6}$ and $\frac{1}{3}$ to $\frac{2}{6}$. Why did you do that? Fractions need to have the same denominator before you can add them. They have to be made from the same unit fraction of the same whole.

● Yes, we need to give them a common denominator. What made you choose 6 as the common denominator? Why not 4 or 5? 6 is a product of both 2 and 3, so I can find equivalent fractions by using 6.

▶ **Rename Fractions to Add or Subtract** WHOLE CLASS

Students use the fraction bars on their MathBoards to solve the two problems shown below. This activity helps students visualize how to split two wholes into same sized unit fractions before adding or subtracting.

Addition Problem: $\frac{1}{3} + \frac{1}{4}$

Have students circle $\frac{1}{3}$ on the thirds fraction bar and try to add $\frac{1}{4}$.

● Why can't you add $\frac{1}{4}$ easily?

You can't tell where $\frac{1}{4}$ is on the $\frac{1}{3}$ bar.

Have students circle $\frac{1}{4}$ on the fourths bar.

Make $\frac{1}{3}$ and $\frac{1}{4}$ on different bars.

Thirds

Fourths

Make twelfths on both bars.

Thirds

Fourths

- How can you divide both fourths and thirds into same sized unit fractions? Split each third into 4 parts and split each fourth into 3 parts. That gives us twelfths on both bars.

Have students split the thirds and fourths on their MathBoards into twelfths. Explain that twelfths then become a common denominator (a common unit fraction) so that students can add the two fractions.

Ask,

- How many twelfths is $\frac{1}{4}$? 3 twelfths

Have students add $\frac{3}{12}$ to the $\frac{4}{12}$ already circled on the thirds fraction bar.

- What is the total of $\frac{1}{3} + \frac{1}{4}$? $\frac{7}{12}$

$$\text{Add } \frac{4}{12} + \frac{3}{12}.$$

Thirds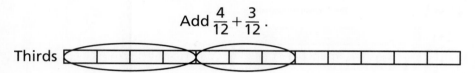

Subtraction Problem: $\frac{5}{6} - \frac{2}{3}$

Have students circle $\frac{5}{6}$ on the sixths fraction bar. Then challenge them:

- Try to subtract $\frac{2}{3}$. How can you do it without using the thirds fraction bar? We can write the thirds as sixths: $\frac{1}{3} = \frac{2}{6}$ and $\frac{2}{3} = \frac{4}{6}$. Then we can draw the four sixths on the sixths bar. The difference between $\frac{5}{6}$ and $\frac{2}{3}$ is $\frac{1}{6}$.

$$\text{Make } \frac{5}{6}. \text{ How can you subtract } \frac{2}{3}?$$

Sixths

Change thirds into sixths and subtract.

Sixths

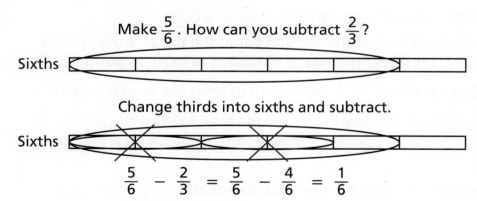

$$\frac{5}{6} - \frac{2}{3} = \frac{5}{6} - \frac{4}{6} = \frac{1}{6}$$

Teaching Note

Watch For! Some students may subtract numerators and denominators and write $\frac{5}{6} - \frac{2}{3} = \frac{3}{3}$. But $\frac{3}{3} = 1$ and $1 > \frac{5}{6}$, so this can't be correct.

Activity 2

Problems and Stories

 25 MINUTES

Goal: Rename fractions, and solve problems that involve adding and subtracting unlike fractions.

Materials: Student Activity Book pp. 207–208 or Hardcover Book pp. 207–208 and Activity Workbook p. 91, MathBoard materials

 NCTM Standards:
Number and Operations
Problem Solving
Representation
Communication

Teaching Note

Watch For! Some students may add both numerators and denominators to get: $\frac{1}{2} + \frac{1}{3} = \frac{2}{5}$. Ask those students,

▶ Where is $\frac{2}{5}$ on the fraction bar? before $\frac{1}{2}$ (It is less than $\frac{1}{2}$.)

▶ Why can $\frac{2}{5}$ not be the correct answer? $\frac{1}{2} + \frac{1}{3}$ must be greater than $\frac{1}{2}$.

English Language Learners

Write *common*, 3, and 5 on the board. Ask: **Is 15 a multiple of 3 and 5?** yes Say: **This is something 3 and 5 have in common.** Write $\frac{1}{3} + \frac{1}{5}$.

• **Beginning** Say: **The denominator has to be the same.** Ask: **Can 15 be the common denominator?** yes

• **Intermediate** Ask: **What has to be common to add $\frac{1}{3}$ and $\frac{1}{5}$?** denominator **Is 15 a good common denominator?** yes

• **Advanced** Say: **To add $\frac{1}{3}$ and $\frac{1}{5}$ we need to find a common __.** denominator Ask: **What number can we use?** 15

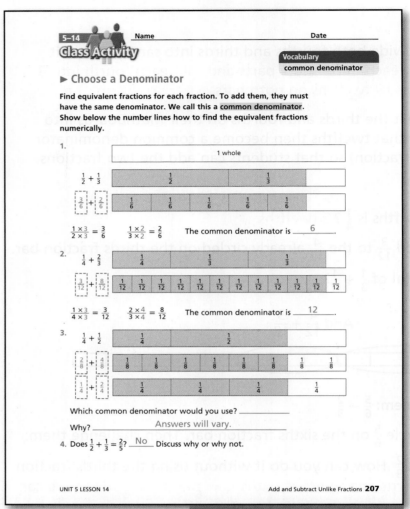

Student Activity Book page 207

▶ Choose a Denominator WHOLE CLASS

Have students look at the fraction bar at the top of Student Book page 207. Let students lead the discussion as much as possible.

The first bar shows $\frac{1}{2} + \frac{1}{3}$. Does it tell us what the total is called? No.

● How can we decide what to call the total? Divide the bar, using a fraction that can rename halves and thirds, a unit fraction that can make $\frac{1}{2}$ and also $\frac{1}{3}$.

● How can we find a fraction that does that? Multiply the two denominators: 2×3.

Have students complete exercise 1.

The second problem, $\frac{1}{4} + \frac{2}{3}$, is solved in a similar way. Ask students to explain how.

- What three fractions are added on the bar? $\frac{1}{4} + \frac{1}{3} + \frac{1}{3}$

- How can we find a common denominator? Multiply 4 by 3.

- What common denominator can we use? 12; This is the unit fraction that makes $\frac{1}{4}$ and $\frac{2}{3}$.

Have students complete exercise 2. Invite one student to show and explain a solution on the board. Encourage other students to ask questions.

- What is the total of $\frac{1}{4} + \frac{1}{3} + \frac{1}{3}$? $\frac{3}{12} + \frac{4}{12} + \frac{4}{12} = \frac{11}{12}$

The third bar raises an important issue: Do we always have to rename both fractions? Have students work on exercises 3–4 individually, and then discuss their answers as a class.

- What common denominator did you use? Some will have used 4; some may have used 8.

Ask those students who used 4 as the common denominator,

- Why didn't you use $2 \times 4 = 8$? because there is less multiplying to do if you use 4; 2 is a factor of 4, so 4 can be the unit fraction for $\frac{1}{4}$ and $\frac{1}{2}$

Discuss how sometimes one denominator is a factor of the other denominator. In this case, 2 is a factor of 4. So we can just use 4 as our new common denominator:

$$\frac{1}{4} + \frac{2}{4} = \frac{3}{4}$$

- Which common denominator would you choose if you were adding $\frac{1}{25}$ and $\frac{1}{50}$? 50; 25 is one of its factors.

Point out that it is helpful to look for a small denominator that works, especially with big numbers.

Exercise 4 will help students understand why a common denominator is used to add fractions with unlike denominators and why the denominators are not added. Have students look at $\frac{1}{2}$, $\frac{1}{3}$, and $\frac{2}{5}$ on their MathBoards during this discussion.

Activity continued ▶

Teaching Note

What to Expect from Students

▶ It is not always necessary for students to find the least common denominator before solving a problem. Sometimes it is better to use the obvious multiple than to spend extra time trying to find the smallest multiple.

▶ At this point it is also acceptable for students to give an answer that has not been simplified. Although the Answer Key for today's homework gives the answer in simplest form, your students may give unsimplified answers. Right now simplifying answers gets in the way of seeing the big idea of adding fractions with unlike denominators: that you need to change one or both fractions to have the same unit fraction, which is the common denominator.

Teaching the Lesson (continued)

Activity 2

Teaching Note

Least Common Denominator

As long as the numbers do not get too large, it is easier and faster for less-advanced students to use a common denominator found by multiplying the 2 denominators together because they only have to think of 1 method. Many can also use the larger denominator when the other denominator is a factor of it. The methods for systematically finding the Least Common Denominator (listing many multiples of each denominator and finding the smallest common multiple or using prime factorization) are much more complex and error-prone than using the product or thinking of a smaller common multiple. Sometimes, as in exercise 11, students can simplify one fraction so that its denominator becomes a factor of the other fraction.

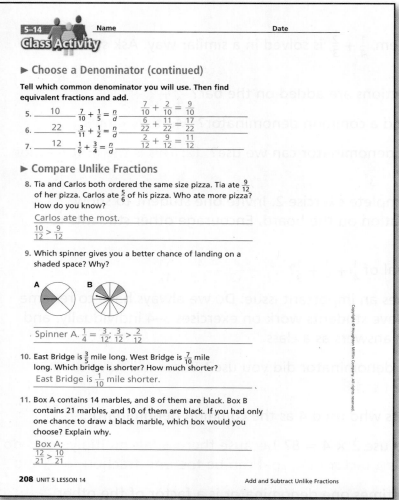

Student Activity Book page 208

Invite students to complete exercises 5–7 on Student Book page 208. Discuss their responses as a class.

For many equations, there are many denominators that students can use. However, there is usually one that will provide them with the simplest route to completing the equation. After students share their responses and explain them to others as needed, highlight these principles.

● From exercise 5: students should first look to see if one denominator is a factor of the other when finding a common denominator.

● From exercise 6: students should realize that they can always find a common denominator by multiplying the two given denominators together. However, this may produce a large denominator that is hard to work with, but is necessary when the denominators do not have a common factor.

● From exercise 7: students may multiply the two denominators together, but there may be a smaller denominator that is easier to work with, in this case 12.

At this point, send one student to the board to complete exercise 7, using 12 as a common denominator, and another to complete it, using 24. Compare the answers.

- Are they the same? Yes; $\frac{11}{12}$ is equal to $\frac{22}{24}$ because we could multiply the numerator and the denominator by 2 to get $\frac{22}{24}$.

Introduce the term *least common denominator* (the smallest possible common denominator).

Write these equations on the board, and ask students to tell what denominator they would choose in order to complete each equation. Invite input from other students.

$\frac{7}{16} + \frac{1}{4} = ?$ 16; 4 is a factor of 16.

$\frac{2}{9} + \frac{1}{6} = ?$ 18; Students may multiply the denominators together to get 54 or recognize that 9 and 6 both go into 36. Using 54 as a common denominator is easier for many students because they can see the numbers they need to multiply by (9 and 6).

$\frac{2}{3} - \frac{7}{12} = ?$ 12; 3 is a factor of 12.

▶ Compare Unlike Fractions   WHOLE CLASS

To compare unlike fractions, ask:

- Which is greater 3 or 6? 6

- Which is greater $\frac{1}{3}$ or $\frac{1}{6}$? $\frac{1}{3}$; fewer unit fractions (3, not 6) make each unit fraction larger

- Which is greater $\frac{2}{3}$ or $\frac{5}{6}$? What do we need to do before we decide? $\frac{5}{6}$; first we have to see them in the same units of the same whole, sixths. One fraction, $\frac{2}{3}$, has 4 sixths, and the other has 5 sixths.

Have students solve exercises 8–11 on Student Book page 208. Then discuss their strategies as a class.

- How did you compare the two fractions in each question? changed to like unit fractions

- What common denominator did you use? sixths

Have a student write an equation to compare the fractions on the board. Invite others to ask questions to clarify the solution.

In exercise 11, students must first use the total number of marbles in each box to build fractions; then they must find a common denominator and compare the fractions, $\frac{8}{14}$ and $\frac{10}{21}$. This is a case where it is easiest to simplify $\frac{8}{14}$ so that its new denominator 7 becomes a factor of 21.

$\frac{8}{14} \div \frac{2}{2} = \frac{4}{7} \times \frac{3}{3} = \frac{12}{21}$ $\frac{12}{21} > \frac{10}{21}$, so Box A has a higher probability that you will choose a blank marble.

Building Concepts Numbers must be in the same unit fraction before we can show that one number is larger than the other. With whole numbers, we count ones. With fractions, we count unit fractions.

Differentiated Instruction

Extra Help Pair students who are struggling with students who can solve these problems. Together, they may activate the strategies they need.

Going Further

Math Connection: Change Fractions to Simplest Form

▶ Review Greatest Common Factor

WHOLE CLASS

In this activity, students connect what they know about equivalent fractions with their knowledge of factors to simplify fractions.

Remind students of the meaning of greatest common factor (from Going Further, Lesson 13). The greatest common factor (GCF) of two numbers is the greatest number that divides evenly into both numbers.

- **What are the factors of 12?** 1, 2, 3, 4, 6, and 12

- **What are the factors of 16?** 1, 2, 4, 8, and 16

- **What is the GCF of 12 and 16?** 4

▶ Change Fractions to Simplest Form

WHOLE CLASS

Work together to simplify a fraction.

- **Simplify the fraction $\frac{12}{16}$.** $\frac{3}{4}$

- **What divisor did you use to simplify $\frac{12}{16}$?** 4

- **Can you simplify your answer, $\frac{3}{4}$?** No.

- **What is the GCF of 12 and 16?** 4

Tell students that $\frac{3}{4}$ is called the *simplest form* of the fraction.

The simplest form of a fraction is obtained when you use the GCF as the divisor. However, you can simplify in several steps until there is no common factor. This is often easier for students than finding the greatest common factor, which is a complex process.

📁 Class Management

Walk around the room and observe as students check their fractions for simplest form. Watch for students who do not divide by the greatest common factor.

- ▶ Is your new fraction in simplest form?

- ▶ By what number can you divide the numerator and the denominator?

- ▶ Did you divide by the greatest common factor?

Differentiated Instruction

Intervention   Activity Card 5-14

Activity Card 5-14

Add and Subtract With Fraction Circles   Activity Card 5-14

Work: In Pairs

Use:
- Fraction Circles (TRB M30)
- Scissors

1. Use fraction circles to solve $1\frac{1}{6} + \frac{2}{3}$. Use three circles, one showing one whole, one showing sixths, and one showing thirds.

2. Shade part or all of each circle to represent the two addends of the sum. How many sixths equal one third? How many sixths equal two thirds? 2; 4

3. Cut out the shaded parts of the circles showing thirds and sixths. Trade parts to combine thirds and sixths into one circle. What is $\frac{1}{6} + \frac{2}{3}$? $\frac{5}{6}$

4. What is $1\frac{1}{6} + \frac{2}{3}$? $1\frac{5}{6}$

Unit 5, Lesson 14   Copyright © Houghton Mifflin Company

Activity Note Fraction circles provide yet another visual representation of fractions as part of a whole. By cutting out fraction pieces for thirds and sixths, students can see that $\frac{1}{3} = \frac{2}{6}$ and then find the sum.

Math Writing Prompt

Explain Your Thinking Why can you only add fractions with the same denominator? Give an example to help you explain.

Soar to Success Math   Software Support

Warm-Up 20.22

On Level   Activity Card 5-14

Estimate Sums and Differences   Activity Card 5-14

Work: In Pairs

1. On your own, draw a number line from 0 to 5, showing whole numbers and halves.

2. Look at the first equation and then point to the mark on your number line nearest to the difference of the two numbers.

3. Compare estimates with your partner. If both agree, repeat the activity with the next equation in the list. If you disagree, discuss your strategies for estimating.

4. Continue the activity until you have estimated all the sums and differences in the list.

$4\frac{11}{12} - 3\frac{1}{8} = ?$

$3\frac{2}{7} + 1\frac{5}{8} = ?$

$\frac{4}{7} - \frac{1}{6} = ?$

$3\frac{11}{13} - 1\frac{5}{8} = ?$

Unit 5, Lesson 14   Copyright © Houghton Mifflin Company

Activity Note A useful strategy for estimating these sums and differences is to round each number to the nearest whole or half, and then add or subtract.

Math Writing Prompt

Create a Problem Write a real-world problem that can be solved by adding or subtracting fractions that have different denominators.

MegaMath Grades K-6   Software Support

Fraction Action: Fraction Flare Up, Level K

Challenge   Activity Card 5-14

Simplify   Activity Card 5-14

Work: In Pairs

1. On your own, write an addition or subtraction equation with fractions.

2. Use only denominators less than or equal to 10.

3. Exchange papers with your partner and find the sum or difference. Then simplify the answer.

4. Exchange papers again to check each other's work.

$3\frac{2}{9} + 2\frac{1}{6} = ?$

$\frac{7}{8} - \frac{2}{3} = ?$

Unit 5, Lesson 14   Copyright © Houghton Mifflin Company

Activity Note As they solve each other's equations, students should show the steps they used to find a common denominator. Students can use opposite operations to check each other's work.

Math Writing Prompt

In Your Own Words Describe the steps you follow to find a useful common denominator. Use an example to help you explain.

DESTINATION Math Software Support

Course III: Module 3: Unit 2: Working with Unlike Denominators

Add and Subtract Unlike Fractions   **515**

 **Homework and Spiral Review**

5–14

Homework **Goal:** Additional Practice

✔ Include students' Homework for page 131 as part of their portfolios.

5–14

Remembering **Goal:** Spiral Review

This Remembering activity is appropriate anytime after today's lesson.

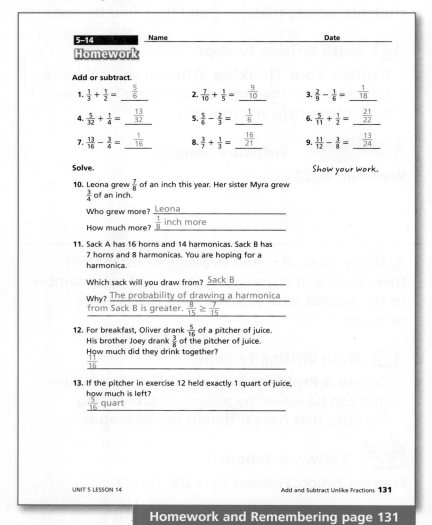

5–14 Name _____ Date _____

Homework

Add or subtract.

1. $\frac{1}{3} + \frac{1}{2} = \frac{5}{6}$ 2. $\frac{7}{10} + \frac{1}{5} = \frac{9}{10}$ 3. $\frac{2}{9} - \frac{1}{6} = \frac{1}{18}$

4. $\frac{5}{32} + \frac{1}{4} = \frac{13}{32}$ 5. $\frac{5}{6} - \frac{2}{3} = \frac{1}{6}$ 6. $\frac{5}{11} + \frac{1}{2} = \frac{21}{22}$

7. $\frac{13}{16} - \frac{3}{4} = \frac{1}{16}$ 8. $\frac{3}{7} + \frac{1}{3} = \frac{16}{21}$ 9. $\frac{11}{12} - \frac{3}{8} = \frac{13}{24}$

Solve.   *Show your work.*

10. Leona grew $\frac{7}{8}$ of an inch this year. Her sister Myra grew $\frac{3}{4}$ of an inch.

   Who grew more? Leona
   How much more? $\frac{1}{8}$ inch more

11. Sack A has 16 horns and 14 harmonicas. Sack B has 7 horns and 8 harmonicas. You are hoping for a harmonica.

   Which sack will you draw from? Sack B
   Why? The probability of drawing a harmonica from Sack B is greater. $\frac{8}{15} \geq \frac{7}{15}$

12. For breakfast, Oliver drank $\frac{5}{16}$ of a pitcher of juice. His brother Joey drank $\frac{3}{8}$ of the pitcher of juice. How much did they drink together?
   $\frac{11}{16}$

13. If the pitcher in exercise 12 held exactly 1 quart of juice, how much is left?
   $\frac{5}{16}$ quart

UNIT 5 LESSON 14   Add and Subtract Unlike Fractions **131**

Homework and Remembering page 131

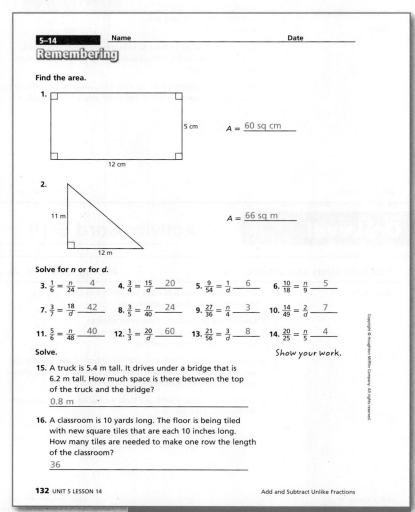

5–14 Name _____ Date _____

Remembering

Find the area.

1.

5 cm
12 cm
$A = $ 60 sq cm

2.

11 m
12 m
$A = $ 66 sq m

Solve for n or for d.

3. $\frac{1}{6} = \frac{n}{24}$ 4   4. $\frac{3}{4} = \frac{15}{d}$ 20   5. $\frac{9}{54} = \frac{1}{d}$ 6   6. $\frac{10}{18} = \frac{n}{9}$ 5

7. $\frac{3}{7} = \frac{18}{d}$ 42   8. $\frac{3}{5} = \frac{n}{40}$ 24   9. $\frac{27}{36} = \frac{n}{4}$ 3   10. $\frac{14}{49} = \frac{2}{d}$ 7

11. $\frac{5}{6} = \frac{n}{48}$ 40   12. $\frac{1}{3} = \frac{20}{d}$ 60   13. $\frac{21}{56} = \frac{3}{d}$ 8   14. $\frac{20}{25} = \frac{n}{5}$ 4

Solve.   *Show your work.*

15. A truck is 5.4 m tall. It drives under a bridge that is 6.2 m tall. How much space is there between the top of the truck and the bridge?
   0.8 m

16. A classroom is 10 yards long. The floor is being tiled with new square tiles that are each 10 inches long. How many tiles are needed to make one row the length of the classroom?
   36

132 UNIT 5 LESSON 14   Add and Subtract Unlike Fractions

Homework and Remembering page 132

Home or School Activity

 Multicultural Connection

Ancient Egyptian Fractions In ancient Egypt, people used the fractions $\frac{2}{3}$ and $\frac{3}{4}$ but, other than that, only fractions with a numerator of 1 were used. To show $\frac{5}{6}$, ancient Egyptians would write $\frac{1}{2} + \frac{1}{3}$. Challenge students to write other fractions as the ancient Egyptians would have written them. If they wish, they can use the number symbols that appear in ancient Egyptian writing.

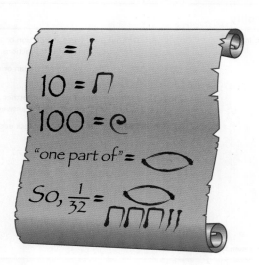

UNIT 5
LESSON
15

Solve With Unlike Mixed Numbers

REAL WORLD Problem Solving

Lesson Objectives

● Consolidate understanding of equivalent fractions and operations with unlike fractions.

● Express the main concept of equivalent fractions in writing, and refine it through class discussion.

The Day at a Glance

Today's Goals	Materials
1 Teaching the Lesson **A1:** Rename and ungroup to add and subtract mixed numbers. **A2:** Recognize common errors, and solve word problems with mixed fractions. **2 Going Further** ▶ Math Connection: Equations Involving Fractions ▶ Differentiated Instruction **3 Homework and Spiral Review**	**Lesson Activities** Student Activity Book p. 209 or Student Hardcover Book p. 209 Homework and Remembering pp. 133–134 **Going Further** Student Activity Book p. 210 or Student Hardcover Book p. 210 and Activity Workbook p. 92 Activity Cards 5-15 Play money Math Journals

123 Use Math Talk today!

Keeping Skills Sharp

Quick Practice ⏱ 5 MINUTES	Daily Routines
Goal: Practice finding common denominators. **Material:** pointer **Common Denominator Parade** Invite six students to the board. Each student writes an addition problem with two fractions in which one denominator is a factor of the other. No fraction can contain a number greater than 10. In turn, each person at the board uses a pointer to point to his or her problem and says, "Name a common denominator." At a signal, the class responds with the answer, which is the larger denominator. $\frac{1}{4} + \frac{1}{2}$ 4 is the common denominator.	**Homework Review** Send students to the board to show their work. Have each student at the board explain his or her solution. Encourage the rest of the class to ask clarifying questions and to make comments. **Nonroutine Problem** Is it possible to subtract two fractions and have a difference greater than 1? Give an example and counterexample to support your answer. Sometimes, when the minuend is an improper fraction; Example: $\frac{17}{4} - \frac{3}{4} = \frac{17}{4} = 4\frac{1}{4} > 1$; Counterexample: $\frac{5}{4} - \frac{3}{4} = \frac{2}{4} = \frac{1}{2} < 1$

Teaching the Lesson

Rename and Ungroup

 25 MINUTES

Goal: Rename and ungroup to add and subtract mixed numbers.

✔ **NCTM Standard:**
Number and Operations

Teaching Note

What to Expect from Students
Most students will need to write out extra steps for some processes, as for example:

Ungrouping using $\frac{d+n}{d}$:

F. $9\frac{3}{18} = 8 + \frac{18}{18} + \frac{3}{18} = 8\frac{21}{18}$

Simplifying using $\frac{d+n}{d} = 1 + \frac{n}{d}$:

E. $10\frac{17}{12} = 10 + \frac{12}{12} + \frac{5}{12} =$
$10 + 1 + \frac{5}{12} = 11\frac{5}{12}$

Finding equivalent fractions:

D. $4\frac{1}{3} = 4 + \frac{1 \times 5}{3 \times 5} = 4\frac{5}{15}$

 Ongoing Assessment

As students add and subtract, make sure they understand how to rename or ungroup, and why it is done. Ask questions such as:

▶ Why do we have to rename the fractions at this step?

▶ Why do we have to ungroup before we can subtract?

▶ How can we tell that the answer is in its simplest form?

▶ Rename and Ungroup to Solve WHOLE CLASS

Adding and subtracting mixed numbers with unlike fractions is quite complex. It requires finding equivalent fractions, adding or subtracting the whole numbers and fractions separately, and ungrouping if necessary for subtraction. Then two kinds of simplifying may be required if simplifying is necessary: simplifying a proper fraction to the simplest form and changing an improper fraction to a mixed number, which must be added to the whole number.

Use **Solve and Discuss** for these mixed-number addition and subtraction problems with unlike fractions.

A.
$$2\frac{3}{8} = 2\frac{3}{8}$$
$$-1\frac{1}{4} = 1\frac{2}{8}$$
$$\overline{1\frac{1}{8}}$$

B.
$$4\frac{1}{5} = 4\frac{3}{15}$$
$$+2\frac{1}{3} = 2\frac{5}{15}$$
$$\overline{6\frac{8}{15}}$$

C.
$$7\frac{5}{6} = 7\frac{10}{12}$$
$$-3\frac{1}{4} = 3\frac{3}{12}$$
$$\overline{4\frac{7}{12}}$$

D.
$$\phantom{4\frac{1}{3} =} 3\frac{20}{15}$$
$$4\frac{1}{3} = 4\frac{5}{15}$$
$$-2\frac{7}{15} = 2\frac{7}{15}$$
$$\overline{1\frac{13}{15}}$$

E.
$$6\frac{2}{3} = 6\frac{8}{12}$$
$$+4\frac{3}{4} = 4\frac{9}{12}$$
$$\overline{10\frac{17}{12} = 11\frac{5}{12}}$$

F.
$$\phantom{9\frac{1}{6} =} 8\frac{21}{18}$$
$$9\frac{1}{6} = 9\frac{3}{18}$$
$$-5\frac{7}{9} = 5\frac{14}{18}$$
$$\overline{3\frac{7}{18}}$$

If your students need more practice, give them these problems.

G.
$$\phantom{5\frac{2}{5} =} 4\frac{14}{10}$$
$$5\frac{2}{5} = 5\frac{4}{10}$$
$$-3\frac{7}{10} = 3\frac{7}{10}$$
$$\overline{1\frac{7}{10}}$$

H.
$$8\frac{1}{4} = 8\frac{5}{20}$$
$$+2\frac{4}{5} = 2\frac{16}{20}$$
$$\overline{10\frac{21}{20} = 11\frac{1}{20}}$$

I.
$$\phantom{7\frac{1}{8} =} 6\frac{27}{24}$$
$$7\frac{1}{8} = 7\frac{3}{24}$$
$$-4\frac{5}{12} = 4\frac{10}{24}$$
$$\overline{2\frac{17}{24}}$$

💬 Math Talk in Action

Let's solve exercise D by using Step-by-Step at the board.

Eric: The first step is to rename the fractions so that they both have the same denominator. The denominators are 3 and 15. 3 is a factor of 15, so 15 is a common denominator. We can rename $\frac{1}{3}$ as $\frac{5}{15}$.

$$4\tfrac{1}{3} = 4\tfrac{5}{15}$$
$$-2\tfrac{7}{15} = 3\tfrac{7}{15}$$

Max: You can't subtract $\frac{7}{15}$ from $\frac{5}{15}$ because $\frac{5}{15}$ is smaller. I'll ungroup. The 4 becomes a 3 because I'm giving a 1 to the fifteenths. One is the same as $\frac{15}{15}$. Adding $\frac{15}{15}$ to $\frac{5}{15}$, I get $\frac{20}{15}$.

$$4\tfrac{1}{3} = 4\overset{3\tfrac{20}{15}}{\tfrac{5}{15}}$$
$$-2\tfrac{7}{15} = 2\tfrac{7}{15}$$

Sara: Now we can subtract. First, I'll subtract the whole numbers: $3 - 2 = 1$. Then I'll subtract the fractions:

$$\frac{20}{15} - \frac{7}{15} = \frac{13}{15}.$$

$$4\tfrac{1}{3} = 4\overset{3\tfrac{20}{15}}{\tfrac{5}{15}}$$
$$-2\tfrac{7}{15} = 2\tfrac{7}{15}$$
$$\overline{\phantom{-2\tfrac{7}{15} = }1\tfrac{13}{15}}$$

Can anyone think of one more step?

Vanya: The last step is to see if the answer can be simplified. $\frac{13}{15}$ can't be regrouped and 13 and 15 have no common factors. The answer in simplest form is $1\frac{13}{15}$.

Good.

Teaching the Lesson (continued)

Activity 2

Practice With Mixed Numbers

 20 MINUTES

Goal: Recognize common errors, and solve word problems with mixed fractions.

Materials: Student Activity Book or Hardcover Book p. 209

✔ **NCTM Standards:**
Number and Operations
Problem Solving

Teaching Note

Watch For! Exercise 3 shows the difficulty that may result from selecting a large common denominator. The problem solver could have used 18 for the new denominator, but instead used 54. The chance of error may be greater with larger numbers. Also, a smaller common denominator can sometimes make it unnecessary to simplify.

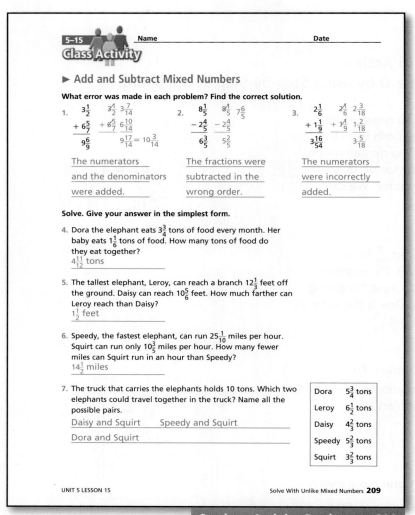

Student Activity Book page 209

▶ Add and Subtract Mixed Numbers WHOLE CLASS

Direct students' attention to exercises 1–3 on Student Book page 209. These show common errors that students need to be able to recognize. Give the class a minute to look over each problem before discussing it.

● In exercise 1, the denominators have been added as well as the numerators.

● Exercise 2 shows the "wrong-way" error that sometimes occurs with subtraction. Since $\frac{4}{5}$ annot be subtracted from $\frac{1}{5}$, the problem solver reversed the order and subtracted $\frac{1}{5}$ from $\frac{4}{5}$. Remind the class that regrouping is needed instead.

● The error in exercise 3 is less obvious. The numerators have been added incorrectly after renaming.

If students cannot spot some of the errors, revisit the discussion after they have found the correct solutions.

Word Problems With Mixed Numbers

Use **Solve and Discuss** for word problems 4–6.

Approach word problem 7 strategically so that students don't add together every possible pair of numbers to see if the sum is 10 tons or less. Break the class into **Small Groups** and ask them to brainstorm for strategies to make solving the problem easier. Have each group share its ideas with the class.

One good approach is to start with the heaviest elephant and work to the lightest, or vice versa.

- To see that the heaviest elephant, Leroy, cannot travel with any of the other elephants, students can check that even the lightest elephant, Squirt, is too heavy to go with Leroy. They can then deduce that the others are too heavy as well.

- Other students might instead find the unknown addend in $6\frac{1}{2} + x = 10$ to see that no elephant over $3\frac{1}{2}$ tons can travel with Leroy.

Some groups may also think of rounding. For example, to see that Dora and Speedy cannot ride together, students can round down to see that their total is more than 10 tons. To see that Daisy and Squirt can ride together, students can round up.

Extra Practice If time permits, use these exercises for extra practice. Give students the opportunity to share their solution methods.

1. $2\frac{1}{2} + 3\frac{2}{4}$

6

2. $6\frac{1}{4} + 3\frac{1}{8}$

$9\frac{3}{8}$

3. $7\frac{2}{8} + 5\frac{1}{16}$

$12\frac{5}{16}$

4. $4\frac{1}{2} + 3\frac{5}{16}$

$7\frac{13}{16}$

5. $5\frac{400}{1000} + 4\frac{60}{100}$

10

6. $2\frac{4}{5} + 5\frac{10}{100}$

$7\frac{90}{100}$ or $7\frac{9}{10}$

7. $6\frac{8}{12} - 3\frac{1}{6}$

$3\frac{1}{2}$

8. $5\frac{2}{3} - 4\frac{1}{6}$

$1\frac{3}{6}$ or $1\frac{1}{2}$

9. $8\frac{6}{12} - 2\frac{1}{3}$

$6\frac{2}{12}$ or $6\frac{1}{6}$

10. $7\frac{3}{5} - 2\frac{1}{10}$

$5\frac{5}{10}$ or $5\frac{1}{2}$

11. $9\frac{8}{10} - 3\frac{40}{100}$

$6\frac{40}{100}$ or $6\frac{2}{5}$

12. $10\frac{3}{4} - 1\frac{9}{16}$

$9\frac{3}{16}$

Teaching Note

What to Expect from Students
As your students present their solutions for problems 4, 5, and 6, be sure they explain both the renaming process and the ungrouping process. Being able to communicate and demonstrate is just as important as solving the problem.

Going Further

Math Connection: Equations Involving Fractions

Goal: Solve for an unknown in an equation.

Materials: Student Activity Book p. 210 or Hardcover Book p. 210 and Activity Workbook p. 92

✔ **NCTM Standard:**
Number and Operations

▶ Solve Equations Involving Fractions

PAIRS

Draw a fraction bar on the board, and shade a little more than half of it. Tell the class that the whole for this fraction bar is $1\frac{7}{10}$ and the shaded part is $\frac{9}{10}$.

Write $\frac{9}{10} + x = 1\frac{7}{10}$ above the fraction bar.

$$\frac{9}{10} \qquad + \qquad x \qquad = \qquad 1\frac{7}{10}$$

Discuss methods to find the unknown addend.

● How can we find out what fraction x represents?

Use mental math; $\frac{9}{10} + \frac{1}{10}$ equals 1, then add another $\frac{7}{10}$ to get $1\frac{7}{10}$. So x is $\frac{1}{10} + \frac{7}{10} = \frac{8}{10}$, or $\frac{4}{5}$.

● Can we subtract to find x? Yes. $1\frac{7}{10} - \frac{9}{10}$ is the same as $\frac{17}{10} - \frac{9}{10} = \frac{8}{10}$, or $\frac{4}{5}$.

Cross out the $\frac{9}{10}$ on the board to illustrate that subtracting $\frac{9}{10}$ from $1\frac{7}{10}$ gives x.

Have the class work in **Student Pairs** to complete the activity. To avoid frustration, make sure their answers to exercises 1–6 are correct before they proceed.

▶ Write an Equation   INDIVIDUALS

For exercise 8, discuss whether the students wrote a situation equation, a solution equation, or both.

Situation Equation: $n + \frac{3}{4} = 2\frac{7}{8}$

Solution Equation: $2\frac{7}{8} - \frac{3}{4} = n$

Ask students to choose an equation on the page and write a word problem that corresponds to it.

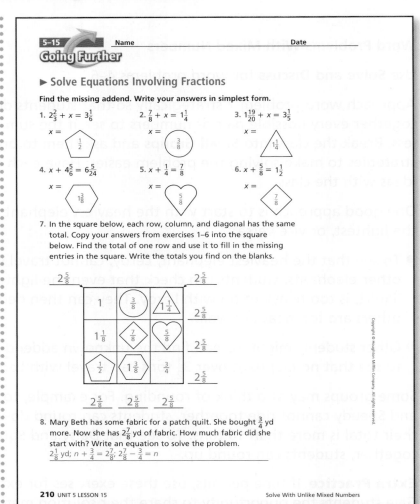

Student Activity Book page 210

Teaching Note

Magic Square Students will not need to find the sum of every row, column, and diagonal to complete the entries in exercise 7, but they should be encouraged to do so to check that each sum is the same. It will also give them extra practice adding fractions.

Teaching Note

Math Background Magic squares date back to around 2800 B.C. in Chinese literature with the magic square, *Loh-Shu*. Each number is represented by a symbol, and the magic number is 15.

Differentiated Instruction

Practice Regrouping   Activity Card 5-15 ●

Work: In Pairs

Use:

• Play money (dimes and pennies)

2. Replace the dime with 10 pennies to have 12 pennies altogether.

1. If a dime represents one whole, what does a penny represent? $\frac{1}{10}$

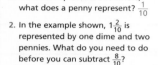

$1\frac{2}{10}$
$-\frac{8}{10}$

2. In the example shown, $1\frac{2}{10}$ is represented by one dime and two pennies. What do you need to do before you can subtract $\frac{8}{10}$?

3. Use money to model each sum or difference.

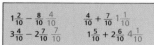

$1\frac{2}{10} - \frac{8}{10}$ $\frac{4}{10}$ $\frac{4}{10} + \frac{7}{10}$ $1\frac{1}{10}$

$3\frac{4}{10} - 2\frac{7}{10}$ $\frac{7}{10}$ $1\frac{5}{10} + 2\frac{6}{10}$ $4\frac{1}{10}$

Unit 5, Lesson 15   Copyright © Houghton Mifflin Company

Activity Note This activity reinforces the concept of renaming before adding or subtracting fractions. Familiarity with the relationship between dimes and pennies will help students to model the questions.

 **Math Writing Prompt**

Explain Your Thinking Use the example $\frac{3}{10} - \frac{1}{5}$ to explain why you may need to rename fractions before adding or subtracting.

Soar to Success Math ★ Software Support

Warm-Up 20.22

Estimate Sums and Differences   Activity Card 5-15 ▲

Work: In Pairs

1. On your own, write a mixed fraction.

2. **Work Together** Compare fractions with your partner. Who wrote the greater number?

$3\frac{4}{15}$ and $3\frac{5}{21}$

3. Estimate the sum and difference of the two fractions. Record both estimates.

4. Math Talk Calculate the sum and difference. How close was each estimate? What estimation strategy did you use? Could you have made a closer estimate?

Unit 5, Lesson 15   Copyright © Houghton Mifflin Company

Activity Note Students should use benchmarks of 0, $\frac{1}{2}$, and 1 to estimate sums and differences with fractions. Suggest that they use common denominators if necessary to compare fractions.

 Math Writing Prompt

Investigate Math Tell why you need to regroup in some addition or subtraction questions, and explain how to do it. Use an example.

MEGA MATH Grades K-6 Software Support

Fraction Action: Number Line Mine, Level J

Solve This!   Activity Card 5-15 ■

Work: By Yourself

1. The diagram below represents $2\frac{1}{2}$ acres that a farmer plants. The shaded squares represent land that is not yet plowed.

2. Calculate the fraction of the land that has already been plowed. $1\frac{11}{12}$ acres

3. **Summarize** Explain how you decided what fractional amounts to subtract from the $2\frac{1}{2}$ acres the farmer plants. Possible answer: Each large square represents 1 acre. So the first square is divided into ninths and the second into fourths. So I subtracted $\frac{3}{9}$ and $\frac{1}{4}$.

Unit 5, Lesson 15   Copyright © Houghton Mifflin Company

Activity Note Students may not interpret the model of the farm correctly because of the combination of two squares and one rectangle. Point out that the rectangle equals $\frac{1}{2}$ acre because it is half as large as one of the squares.

 Math Writing Prompt

Create and Solve Write a word problem that represents $3\frac{1}{5} + 2\frac{3}{7} - \frac{3}{10}$. Then solve it.

 DESTINATION Math® Software Support

Course III: Module 3: Unit 2: Working with Unlike Denominators

③ Homework and Spiral Review

Homework **Goal:** Additional Practice

✔ Include students' Homework for page 133 as part of their portfolios.

Remembering **Goal:** Spiral Review

This Remembering activity is appropriate anytime after today's lesson.

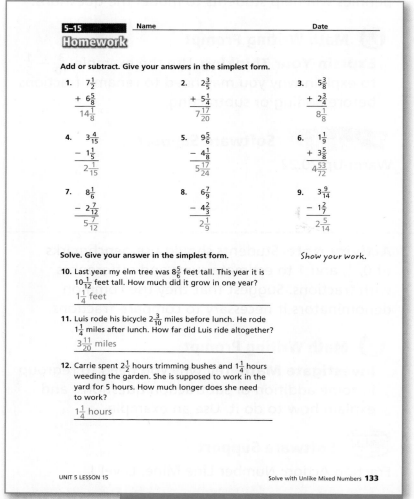

5–15   Name _____ Date _____

Homework

Add or subtract. Give your answers in the simplest form.

1. $7\frac{1}{2}$
    $+ 6\frac{5}{8}$
    $14\frac{1}{8}$

2. $2\frac{3}{5}$
    $+ 5\frac{1}{4}$
    $7\frac{17}{20}$

3. $5\frac{3}{8}$
    $+ 2\frac{3}{4}$
    $8\frac{1}{8}$

4. $3\frac{4}{15}$
    $- 1\frac{1}{5}$
    $2\frac{1}{15}$

5. $9\frac{5}{6}$
    $- 4\frac{1}{8}$
    $5\frac{17}{24}$

6. $1\frac{1}{9}$
    $+ 3\frac{5}{8}$
    $4\frac{53}{72}$

7. $8\frac{1}{6}$
    $- 2\frac{7}{12}$
    $5\frac{7}{12}$

8. $6\frac{7}{9}$
    $- 4\frac{2}{3}$
    $2\frac{1}{9}$

9. $3\frac{9}{14}$
    $- 1\frac{2}{7}$
    $2\frac{5}{14}$

Solve. Give your answer in the simplest form.

Show your work.

10. Last year my elm tree was $8\frac{5}{6}$ feet tall. This year it is $10\frac{1}{12}$ feet tall. How much did it grow in one year?
    $1\frac{1}{4}$ feet

11. Luis rode his bicycle $2\frac{3}{10}$ miles before lunch. He rode $1\frac{1}{4}$ miles after lunch. How far did Luis ride altogether?
    $3\frac{11}{20}$ miles

12. Carrie spent $2\frac{1}{2}$ hours trimming bushes and $1\frac{1}{4}$ hours weeding the garden. She is supposed to work in the yard for 5 hours. How much longer does she need to work?
    $1\frac{1}{4}$ hours

UNIT 5 LESSON 15   Solve with Unlike Mixed Numbers **133**

Homework and Remembering page 133

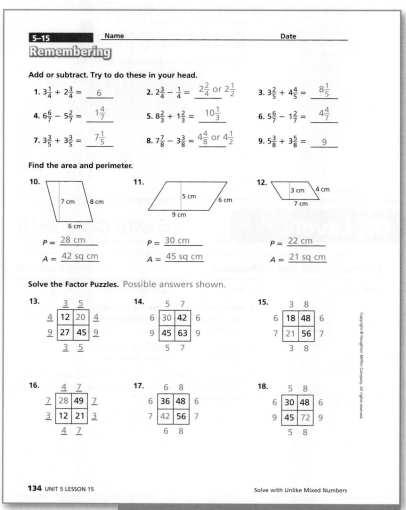

5–15   Name _____ Date _____

Remembering

Add or subtract. Try to do these in your head.

1. $3\frac{1}{4} + 2\frac{3}{4} =$ ___6___
2. $2\frac{3}{4} - \frac{1}{4} =$ ___$2\frac{2}{4}$ or $2\frac{1}{2}$___
3. $3\frac{2}{5} + 4\frac{4}{5} =$ ___$8\frac{1}{5}$___
4. $6\frac{6}{7} - 5\frac{2}{7} =$ ___$1\frac{4}{7}$___
5. $8\frac{2}{3} + 1\frac{2}{3} =$ ___$10\frac{1}{3}$___
6. $5\frac{6}{7} - 1\frac{2}{7} =$ ___$4\frac{4}{7}$___
7. $3\frac{3}{5} + 3\frac{3}{5} =$ ___$7\frac{1}{5}$___
8. $7\frac{7}{8} - 3\frac{3}{8} =$ ___$4\frac{4}{8}$ or $4\frac{1}{2}$___
9. $5\frac{3}{8} + 3\frac{5}{8} =$ ___9___

Find the area and perimeter.

10.
    7 cm   8 cm
    6 cm

    P = ___28 cm___
    A = ___42 sq cm___

11.
    5 cm   6 cm
    9 cm

    P = ___30 cm___
    A = ___45 sq cm___

12.
    3 cm   4 cm
    7 cm

    P = ___22 cm___
    A = ___21 sq cm___

Solve the Factor Puzzles. Possible answers shown.

13.
	3	5	
4	12	20	4
9	27	45	9
	3	5	

14.
	5	7	
6	30	42	6
9	45	63	9
	5	7	

15.
	3	8	
6	18	48	6
7	21	56	7
	3	8	

16.
	4	7	
7	28	49	7
3	12	21	3
	4	7	

17.
	6	8	
6	36	48	6
7	42	56	7
	6	8	

18.
	5	8	
6	30	48	6
9	45	72	9
	5	8	

134 UNIT 5 LESSON 15   Solve with Unlike Mixed Numbers

Homework and Remembering page 134

Home or School Activity

 Real-World Connection

Plan a Feast Have each student find a recipe for a dish to contribute to the feast. Make sure the recipe uses customary units of measurement. Have each student total the amount of dry ingredients and the amount of wet ingredients in their recipe, using cups. Keep track of the students' totals on a class chart. Then have everyone find the grand total, in cups, for each type of ingredient for the whole feast.

1 tablespoon = 3 teaspoons
$\frac{1}{4}$ cup = 4 tablespoons

UNIT 5

LESSON

16

Practice With Unlike Mixed Numbers

REAL WORLD Problem Solving

Lesson Objectives

● Consolidate understanding of equivalent fractions and operations with unlike fractions.

● Express the main concept of renaming and ungrouping fractions.

The Day at a Glance

Today's Goals	Materials

1 Teaching the Lesson
A1: Explain how to rename and ungroup fractions.
A2: Review and classify the various ways to find a common denominator.
 	
2 Going Further
▶ Differentiated Instruction
 	
3 Homework and Spiral Review
	Lesson Activities
	Student Activity Book pp. 211–212
	  or Student Hardcover Book
	  pp. 211–212
	Homework and Remembering
	  pp. 135–136
	
	Going Further
	Activity Cards 5-16
	Ruler
	Index cards
	Grid Paper (TRB M17)
	Colored markers
	Math Journals

Use Math Talk today!

Keeping Skills Sharp

Quick Practice ⏱ 5 MINUTES	Daily Routines
Goal: Practice finding common denominators. **Material:** pointer **Common Denominator Parade** Invite six students to the board. Each student writes an addition problem with two fractions in which one denominator is a factor of the other. No fraction can contain a number greater than 10. In turn, each person at the board uses a pointer to point to his or her problem and says, "Name a common denominator." At a signal, the class responds with the answer, which is the larger denominator. $\frac{5}{8} + \frac{3}{4}$ 8 is the common denominator.	**Homework Review** Let students work together to check their homework. Remind students to use what they know about helping others. **Strategy Problem** Rodney cut a long piece of wood into fourths. Then he cut each fourth in half. He gave away 6 of the pieces. The length of the two remaining pieces is 8 inches in all. How long was the original board? Answer is a form of 32 in.;

total length

8 in.

Practice With Unlike Mixed Numbers **525**

1 Teaching the Lesson

Activity 1

The Puzzled Penguin

25 MINUTES

Goal: Explain how to rename and ungroup fractions.

Materials: Student Activity Book or Hardcover Book p. 211

NCTM Standards:
Number and Operations
Problem Solving
Communication

Teaching Note

What to Expect from Students
This problem requires both renaming and ungrouping. First, students must change $9\frac{2}{5}$ to $9\frac{4}{10}$. Then they must change $9\frac{4}{10}$ to $8\frac{14}{10}$ so that they can subtract $\frac{7}{10}$.
The correct answer is $2\frac{7}{10}$ miles.

5–16 Class Activity

Name Date

► Rename and Ungroup Fractions

Dear Math Students,

I live in the town of Clear Springs. I am going on a hike with several of my friends next week. We would like to walk to Eagle Crest.

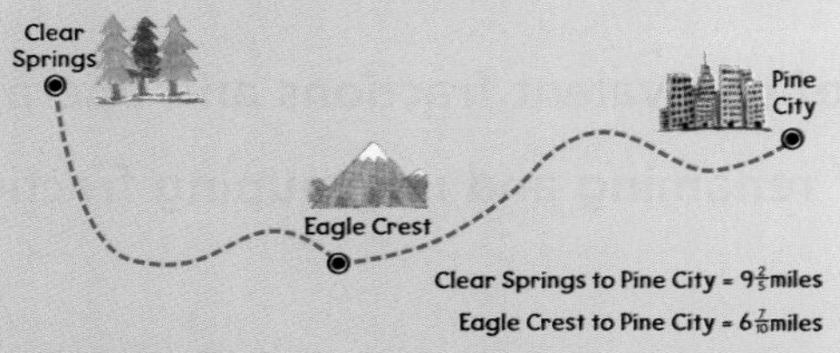

The map tells us the whole distance to Pine City and it tells us the distance from Eagle Crest to Pine City. But it does not tell us the distance from Clear Springs to Eagle Crest. We know we can subtract the smaller distance from the larger to get our answer. But we don't know how to subtract these numbers.

Can you help?

Your friend,

Puzzled Penguin

1. Write an answer to the Puzzled Penguin.
Possible answer: First, change $9\frac{2}{5}$ to $9\frac{4}{10}$. You cannot subtract the fractions because $\frac{4}{10}$ is less than $\frac{7}{10}$. So you change $9\frac{4}{10}$ to $8\frac{14}{10}$. Subtract. $8\frac{14}{10} - 6\frac{7}{10} = 2\frac{7}{10}$. Therefore, Clear Springs is $2\frac{7}{10}$ miles from Eagle Crest.

UNIT 5 LESSON 16 Practice With Unlike Mixed Numbers **211**

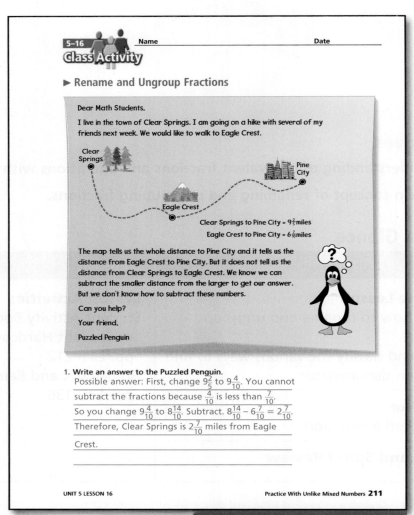

Student Activity Book page 211

► Rename and Ungroup Fractions WHOLE CLASS

Direct students' attention to the Puzzled Penguin letter on Student Book page 211 and read it together. Be sure everyone understands the basic problem before they reply to the Puzzled Penguin.

Math Talk Ask a few volunteers to read their letters to the class. The rest of the class should listen carefully for:

- steps that are explained clearly.
- steps that are left out.
- ideas that are still unclear.

Invite the students to ask questions or make suggestions for clarifying the explanation. You may want to collect the letters for students' portfolios or for parent conferences.

English Language Learners

Write *rename* and *ungroup* on the board. Model a subtraction problem requiring both.

- **Beginning** Say: **First, we find a common denominator.** Ask: **Is this renaming?** yes **Then do we ungroup?** yes
- **Intermediate** Ask: **What did I do first, rename or ungroup?** rename Say: **Then I __.** ungrouped
- **Advanced** Have students identify each step.

Review the Common Denominator

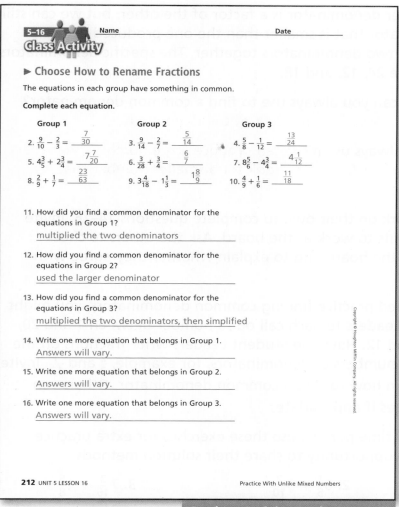

5–16
Class Activity

Name _____ Date _____

▶ **Choose How to Rename Fractions**

The equations in each group have something in common.

Complete each equation.

Group 1	Group 2	Group 3
2. $\frac{9}{10} - \frac{2}{3} = \underline{\frac{7}{30}}$	3. $\frac{9}{14} - \frac{2}{7} = \underline{\frac{5}{14}}$	4. $\frac{5}{8} - \frac{1}{12} = \underline{\frac{13}{24}}$
5. $4\frac{3}{5} + 2\frac{3}{4} = \underline{7\frac{7}{20}}$	6. $\frac{3}{28} + \frac{3}{4} = \underline{\frac{6}{7}}$	7. $8\frac{5}{6} - 4\frac{3}{4} = \underline{4\frac{1}{12}}$
8. $\frac{2}{9} + \frac{1}{7} = \underline{\frac{23}{63}}$	9. $3\frac{4}{18} - 1\frac{1}{3} = \underline{1\frac{8}{9}}$	10. $\frac{4}{9} + \frac{1}{6} = \underline{\frac{11}{18}}$

11. How did you find a common denominator for the equations in Group 1?
    multiplied the two denominators

12. How did you find a common denominator for the equations in Group 2?
    used the larger denominator

13. How did you find a common denominator for the equations in Group 3?
    multiplied the two denominators, then simplified

14. Write one more equation that belongs in Group 1.
    Answers will vary.

15. Write one more equation that belongs in Group 2.
    Answers will vary.

16. Write one more equation that belongs in Group 3.
    Answers will vary.

212 UNIT 5 LESSON 16   Practice With Unlike Mixed Numbers

Student Activity Book page 212

⏱ **25 MINUTES**

Goal: Review and classify the various ways to find a common denominator.

Materials: Student Activity Book or Hardcover Book p. 212

✓ **NCTM Standards:**
Number and Operations
Communication

▶ Choose How to Rename Fractions WHOLE CLASS

Have students work alone to complete exercises 2–10 on Student Book page 212. Then discuss their answers to questions 11, 12, and 13 as a class. Allow students to explain in their own words how they found a common denominator for the fractions in each group. Encourage other students to ask questions if an explanation is unclear to them.

Three basic situations are represented here:

Group 1: The two denominators have no common factor. They must be multiplied together to produce a new denominator for both fractions. The specific denominators in this group are 30, 20, and 63.

Activity continued ▶

Activity 2

 Ongoing Assessment

Students who can confidently rename, add, and subtract fractions have grasped the main points of this unit. As students work, watch for those who:

► choose difficult or incorrect common denominators

► neglect to ungroup wholes into parts in order to subtract

► make false starts

They may need a little more practice.

The Learning Classroom

Student Leaders Select different student leaders for different tasks. Take time to help students get used to being leaders. Support them for the first few times, and encourage classmates to be supportive. Most students gain confidence themselves when they help others learn.

Group 2: One denominator is a factor of the other, so we can use the larger denominator as the common denominator. The specific denominators in this group are 14, 28, and 18.

Group 3: Neither denominator is a factor of the other, but we can still find a denominator that is smaller than the one produced by multiplying the two denominators together. The specific denominators in this group are 24, 12, and 18.

● **Which method can you always use to find a common denominator?** the first method: using the product of the denominators

● **Why don't we always use it?** It can produce large numbers that are hard to work with. We need to look for a smaller number that is a multiple of both.

Have students work on their own to complete questions 14–16. Invite a couple of students to work at the board. Ask the others to check the equations on the board and to explain whether they agree with the responses.

If students still need practice finding common denominators, you might ask two **Student Leaders** to each call out a number between 1 and 20, for example, 3 and 12. Have the Student Leaders write fractions on the board with these numbers as denominators, for example, $\frac{2}{3}$ and $\frac{1}{12}$. Invite students to explain how to find a common denominator. Others can suggest alternatives if appropriate.

Extra Practice If time permits use these exercises for extra practice. Give students the opportunity to share their solution methods.

1. $3\frac{1}{2} + 2\frac{7}{8}$
$6\frac{3}{8}$

2. $6\frac{1}{5} + 5\frac{7}{10}$
$11\frac{9}{10}$

3. $7\frac{3}{16} + 1\frac{5}{8}$
$8\frac{13}{16}$

4. $5\frac{2}{4} + 6\frac{3}{8}$
$11\frac{7}{8}$

5. $7\frac{3}{12} + 2\frac{5}{6}$
$10\frac{1}{12}$

6. $2\frac{2}{3} + 5\frac{11}{12}$
$8\frac{7}{12}$

7. $6\frac{8}{10} - 5\frac{60}{100}$
$1\frac{20}{100}$ or $1\frac{1}{5}$

8. $11\frac{9}{12} - 3\frac{1}{3}$
$8\frac{5}{12}$

9. $9\frac{5}{6} - 2\frac{1}{12}$
$7\frac{9}{12}$ or $7\frac{3}{4}$

10. $10\frac{15}{16} - 4\frac{1}{2}$
$6\frac{7}{16}$

11. $11\frac{200}{1000} - 2\frac{10}{100}$
$9\frac{100}{1000}$ or $9\frac{1}{10}$

12. $6\frac{7}{10} - 1\frac{3}{5}$
$5\frac{1}{10}$

② Going Further

Intervention — Activity Card 5-16

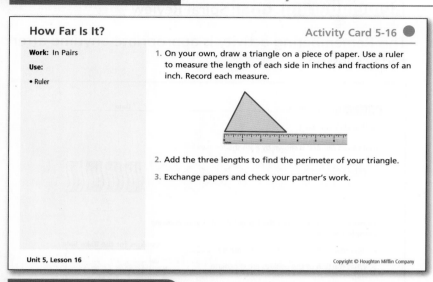

How Far Is It? — Activity Card 5-16 ●

Work: In Pairs

Use:
• Ruler

1. On your own, draw a triangle on a piece of paper. Use a ruler to measure the length of each side in inches and fractions of an inch. Record each measure.

2. Add the three lengths to find the perimeter of your triangle.

3. Exchange papers and check your partner's work.

Unit 5, Lesson 16   Copyright © Houghton Mifflin Company

Activity Note Before students begin the activity, review the fractional parts of an inch shown on the ruler. Students can also check their work by adding on, using the ruler.

 Math Writing Prompt

Make a Drawing How can you use a drawing to find a common denominator for $\frac{1}{2}$ and $\frac{1}{9}$? Explain what your drawing shows.

 **Software Support**

Warm-Up 20.22

On Level — Activity Card 5-16

Divide the Whole — Activity Card 5-16 ▲

Work: In Pairs

Use:
• Numbered index cards 1–20

1. **Work Together** Arrange four number cards to make two fractions.

2. On your own, find a common denominator and add the fractions.

3. **Compare** Does your sum equal the sum that your partner found? If not, work together to find the correct answer.

4. Award 1 point for each correct addition. Repeat the activity until one person wins 5 points.

$$\frac{7}{4} \qquad \frac{9}{11}$$

Unit 5, Lesson 16   Copyright © Houghton Mifflin Company

Activity Note Students can always find a common denominator by multiplying both denominators. Have students simplify each sum before comparing answers.

 Math Writing Prompt

Investigate Mathematics Show two ways to find a common denominator for $\frac{1}{2}$ and $\frac{1}{9}$.

 Software Support

Fraction Action: Fraction Flare Up, Level I

Challenge — Activity Card 5-16

Fraction Designs — Activity Card 5-16 ■

Work: By Yourself

Use:
• Grid Paper (TRB M17)
• Red, blue, yellow, green, and purple markers

2. Possible answer: Using the common denominator 60 for the total number of squares makes it easy to find the number of squares for each fractional part.

1. Draw a design on grid paper that matches the description below.

| $\frac{1}{3}$ red | $\frac{1}{4}$ blue | $\frac{1}{5}$ yellow |
| $\frac{1}{6}$ green | the rest purple | |

2. **Explain** How did you decide how many squares on the grid paper to use for the total design?

3. Share your design with your classmates and discuss how you chose the size of each fractional part.

red	blue	green	yellow
			purple

Unit 5, Lesson 16   Copyright © Houghton Mifflin Company

Activity Note If students have difficulty choosing the size of the overall design, suggest that they calculate and use the common denominator. One twentieth of the finished design should be purple.

 Math Writing Prompt

Agree or Disagree No two unlike fractions can have a common denominator of 31. Do you agree or disagree? Explain your reasoning.

✳ DESTINATION Math® **Software Support**

Course III: Module 3: Unit 1: Equivalent Fractions

③ Homework and Spiral Review

Homework **Goal:** Additional Practice

✓ Include students' Homework for page 135 as part of their portfolios.

Remembering **Goal:** Spiral Review

This Remembering activity is appropriate anytime after today's lesson.

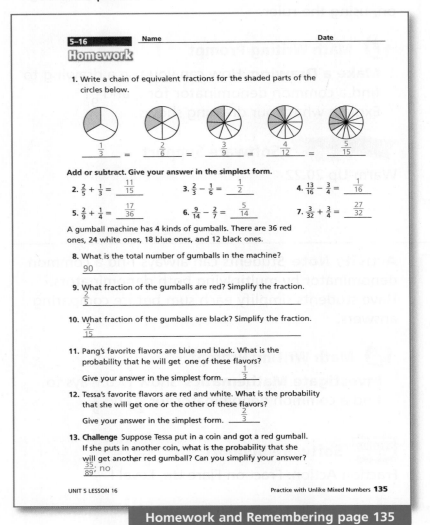

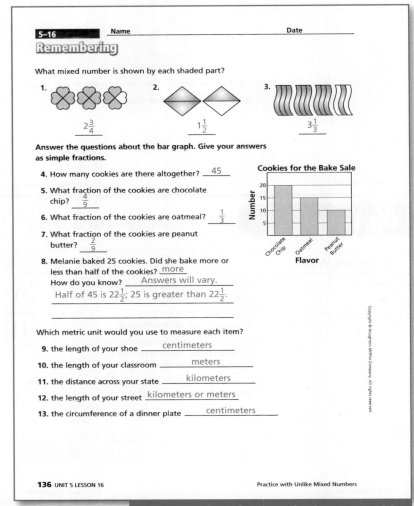

Homework and Remembering page 135

Homework and Remembering page 136

Home or School Activity

 Sports Connection

Shots Made Fractions can be used to track statistics in sports. You can track how many free throws a player makes in basketball, how many pitches a player hits in baseball, how many shots a player scores in hockey. Have students try an activity, such as shooting baskets or throwing beanbags at a target, and have them record their success rate as a fraction. Students can write a short report, using fractions to compare their results in a meaningful way.

Probability and Equivalent Fractions

Lesson Objectives

- Apply the language of probability.
- Solve probability situations by finding fractional equivalents.

Vocabulary

probability	impossible
likely	frequency table
unlikely	line plot
certain	

The Day at a Glance

Today's Goals	Materials
1 Teaching the Lesson **A1:** Use probability terminology to describe a simple probability situation. **A2:** Discuss situations involving probability. **2 Going Further** ▶ Math Connection: Line Plots and Probability ▶ Differentiated Instruction **3 Homework and Spiral Review**	**Lesson Activities** Student Activity Book pp. 213–215 or Student Hardcover Book pp. 213–215 Homework and Remembering pp. 137–138 Quick Quiz 3 (Assessment Guide) **Going Further** Student Activity Book p. 216 or Hardcover Book p. 216 and Activity Workbook p. 93 Activity Cards 5-17 Spinner (TRB M34) Pencil and paper clip Coins Math Journals

123 *Use* **Math Talk** *today!*

Keeping Skills Sharp

Quick Practice ⏱ 5 MINUTES	Daily Routines
Goal: Generate equivalent fractions. **Equivalent Fraction Parade** Write the fraction $\frac{1}{6}$ on the board. Invite six students to the board. Taking turns, each student writes a fraction equivalent to $\frac{1}{6}$, being careful not to write one that is already on the board. As each fraction appears, the writer turns and gives a signal. The class says the fraction out loud and tells the multiplier that made that fraction from $\frac{1}{6}$. Fractions do not have to be in any particular order; for example, $\quad\frac{1}{6}\qquad\frac{3}{18}\qquad\frac{4}{24}\qquad\frac{2}{12}$ At the end, the class reads the list together. "One sixth equals three eighteenths equals four twenty-fourths," and so on.	**Homework Review** Have students discuss the problems from their homework. Encourage students to help each other resolve any misunderstandings. **Strategy Problem** For her party, Tia bought 20 sets of prizes. Each set had the same number of prizes. She put $\frac{1}{4}$ of all the prizes in the piñata, $\frac{1}{2}$ of all the prizes in the gift bags, and the remaining 10 prizes became door prizes. How many prizes were in each set? $\frac{1}{4}+\frac{1}{2}=\frac{1}{4}+\frac{2}{4}=\frac{3}{4}$; $1-\frac{3}{4}=\frac{1}{4}$; The 10 door prizes are $\frac{1}{4}$ of the prizes, $10\times4=40$, $20\times2=40$. So, there are 2 prizes in each set.

① Teaching the Lesson

The Language of Probability

 20 MINUTES

Goal: Use probability terminology to describe a simple probability situation.

Materials: Student Activity Book or Hardcover Book p. 213

 NCTM Standards:
Data Analysis and Probability
Number and Operations
Reasoning and Proof

Teaching Note

Language and Vocabulary
Probability is sometimes called *chance*. Chance is a term often used to refer to something that happens unpredictably, such as a chance event. Probability is the mathematical science of measuring and estimating predictability. The mathematical probability of an event may also be referred to informally as the chance or chances of the event happening.

English Language Learners

Draw two scenes on the board, a sunny day and a very cloudy day. Write *more likely* and *less likely*.

• **Beginning** Point and say: **It is cloudy. It is more likely to rain.** Point and ask: **When it is sunny, is it less likely to rain?** yes
• **Intermediate** Ask: **When it is cloudy, is it more or less likely to rain?** more Say: **When it is sunny, it is __.** less likely
• **Advanced** Have students tell how *likely* it is to rain in each situation.

▶ **Use the Language of Probability** WHOLE CLASS

Begin by drawing on the board the two figures that follow. The figures represent marbles in a box. Use the first figure to demonstrate the meanings of *more likely* and *less likely*.

Use the second figure to demonstrate the meaning of *equally likely*. If these terms are used in a clear context, students will catch on quickly. No formal definitions should be needed.

● Look at the first box of marbles. If I reach in and take out a marble without looking, am I more likely to get a white one or a black one? Why? a white one; there are more white ones in the box

● Which color am I less likely to choose? Why? black; only 1 black marble and 3 white ones

● Suppose I had 99 white marbles and 1 black marble in the box. What is likely to happen when I draw a marble from the box? What is unlikely to happen? drawing a white one; drawing a black one

● Look at the second box of marbles. If I reach in and take out a marble without looking, am I more likely to draw a white one or a black one? Each is just as likely.

● How could you describe the likelihood of drawing white or black? equally likely

Draw another box that has all white marbles.

Tell the students that sometimes the likelihood of an event can be described by the words *certain* or *impossible*.

● Suppose I had no black marbles in the box. What is certain to happen when I draw a marble from the box? drawing a white one

● What is impossible when I draw a marble from the box? drawing a black one

Have students complete exercises 1–5 on Student Book page 213. Discuss any questions that arise.

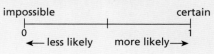

5–17

Class Activity

Name _____ Date _____

▶ **Use the Language of Probability**

Vocabulary
likely
unlikely
certain
impossible
probability

Use the words **likely**, **unlikely**, **certain**, or **impossible** to describe each event for the spinner.

1. Spinning a 2 _____ unlikely _____

2. Spinning a 3 _____ likely _____

3. Spinning a 5 _____ impossible _____

4. Spinning a number less than 5 _____ certain _____

5. Which numbers are you equally likely to spin? _____ 2 and 4 _____

▶ **Relate Probability to Fractions**

6. What is the total number of sections for the spinner? _____ 6 _____

7. How many sections have a 2 on them? _____ 1 _____

8. What is the **probability** of spinning a 2? _____ $\frac{1}{6}$ _____

9. How many sections have a 3 on them? _____ 4 _____

10. What is the probability of spinning a 3? _____ $\frac{4}{6}$, or $\frac{2}{3}$ _____

11. What is the probability of spinning a 4? _____ $\frac{1}{6}$ _____

12. What is the total of the three probabilities in exercises 8, 10, and 11? _____ 1 _____

13. What is the probability of spinning a number less than 5? _____ 1 _____

14. What is the probability of spinning a 5? _____ 0 _____

▶ **Solve Probability Problems**

15. What is the total number of sections for the spinner? _____ 6 _____
How many shaded sections are there? _____ 2 _____
What is the probability that the spinner will stop on a shaded section? _____ $\frac{2}{6}$, or $\frac{1}{3}$ _____
What is the probability that the spinner will stop on a white section? _____ $\frac{4}{6}$, or $\frac{2}{3}$ _____

UNIT 5 LESSON 17   Probability and Equivalent Fractions **213**

Student Activity Book page 213

▶ Relate Probability to Fractions | WHOLE CLASS |

Explain to the class what is meant by probability, a mathematical way of stating the likelihood that an event will happen. Explain that it is often expressed as a fraction, usually as simply as possible. When people talk about the likelihood of something happening, they are talking about probability. Discuss why.

There are four marbles altogether, and two of them are white. The probability that I will get a white marble is 2 out of 4. This can be expressed as a fraction, $\frac{2}{4}$.

● Can you make this fraction any simpler? yes; $\frac{1}{2}$

Activity continued ▶

Probability and Equivalent Fractions   **533**

Understand the Total Discuss the probabilities involved in the first box of marbles that you drew on the board and find the total. Do the same for the second box that you drew on the board. Elicit from students that the total of all fractions in a probability situation will always be one whole.

- Look at the first box of marbles again. What is the probability that I will get a black marble? 1 out of 4, or $\frac{1}{4}$

- What is the probability of drawing a white marble? 3 out of 4, or $\frac{3}{4}$

- What is the total of $\frac{1}{4}$ and $\frac{3}{4}$? $\frac{4}{4}$, or one whole

Ask the same questions about the second box.

- What is the probability of drawing a white marble? $\frac{1}{2}$

- What is the probability of drawing a black marble? $\frac{1}{2}$

- What is the total of $\frac{1}{2}$ and $\frac{1}{2}$? $\frac{2}{2}$, or one whole

- What do you think is the total of all the probabilities in any situation? 1

- Why will this always be true? Because each probability is expressed as the number of its occurrence out of the total number possible. So, these occurrences add up to the total.

Ask about the third box that you drew.

How many marbles are there altogether? 4

- How many white marbles are there? 4

- What is the probability of drawing a white marble? $\frac{4}{4}$, or 1

- What is the probability of something that is certain? 1

- How many black marbles are in the box? 0

- What is the probability of drawing a black marble? $\frac{0}{4}$, or 0

- What is the probability of something that is impossible? 0

Have students complete exercises 6–14. Discuss any questions that arise.

Activity 2

Probability Situations

5-17
Class Activity

Name _____ Date _____

16. Suppose you put the marbles in the box and take one out without looking.

What is the probability that you will get a white marble?
$\frac{4}{13}$

What is the probability that you will get a black marble?
$\frac{3}{13}$

What is the probability that you will get a gray marble?
$\frac{6}{13}$

MARBLES

17. Ellen made this spinner with 4 white sections and 2 shaded sections. She says that the spinner is more likely to stop on a white section than a shaded section. Do you agree? Why or why not?

No; even though there are more white sections,

the white sections only cover half the circle.

▶ **Make Predictions**

Solve. Explain your reasoning.

18. Suppose you have a can that contains 100 nuts. The label says that there are about 20 pecans, 30 walnuts, and 50 almonds. If you take out 10 nuts, how many of each kind would you expect to get?

You can expect to get 2 pecans, 3 walnuts, and

5 almonds.

100 Nuts

19. Mark found a box in the attic labeled "72 clown noses, 2 sizes." He took out 8 noses. Five of them were large and 3 of them were small. Out of the 72 total noses, how many are likely to be large? ___45___

How many are likely to be small? ___27___

214 UNIT 5 LESSON 17   Probability and Equivalent Fractions

Student Activity Book page 214

▶ **Solve Probability Problems**   Math Talk

WHOLE CLASS

Use **Solve and Discuss** as students complete problems 15–17 on Student Book pages 213–214.

Emphasize to students that they should begin every probability problem by finding the total number of possibilities. It will not always be as obvious as it is in problem 15. In this case, there are six total possibilities, so 6 will be the denominator of the fractions. The probability of landing on a dark section is 2 out of 6, or $\frac{2}{6}$, or $\frac{1}{3}$. The probability of landing on a white section is 4 out of 6, or $\frac{4}{6}$, or $\frac{2}{3}$.

Have students add the fractions to see if they get one whole.

$$\frac{1}{3} + \frac{2}{3} = \frac{3}{3}$$

Activity continued ▶

---

35 MINUTES

Goal: Discuss situations involving probability.

Materials: Student Activity Book or Hardcover Book pp. 213–215

✓ **NCTM Standards:**
Data Analysis and Probability
Number and Operations
Problem Solving

Teaching Note

Math Background Predicting results by using probabilities is almost never exact. Polls and surveys always state a margin of error with the results. For example, a poll may state that it is accurate within five percentage points, 19 times out of 20, or 95% of the time. This means that $\frac{1}{20}$ of the time, it may be even less accurate. In problem 18, 2 pecans, 3 walnuts, and 5 almonds are likely to be chosen, but often the distribution will be slightly different. For situations like problem 19, the prediction will rarely be exact, but should be close most of the time.

Problem 16 has three variables, but the procedure is the same. There are 13 possibilities. The probability of getting a white marble is 4 out of 13. The probability of getting a black marble is 3 out of 13. The probability of getting a gray marble is $\frac{6}{13}$. Ask students to add the three fractions to see if they get one whole. You might want to have several students try it at the board. They will need to use fractions with like denominators.

$$\frac{4}{13} + \frac{3}{13} + \frac{6}{13} = \frac{13}{13}$$

If students look closely at the spinner in problem 17, they will see that the sections are not all the same size. The four white sections are equal to the two shaded sections. If the lines were removed from the white sections, it would be easy to see that the spinner is divided into fourths. The probability of landing on a shaded section or a white section would be exactly equal.

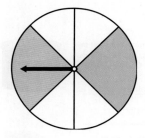

► **Make Predictions** [WHOLE CLASS]

Tell students that probabilities are used in real life to make predictions, such as in weather forecasting and taking polls for elections and other kinds of surveys. Discuss how to use probabilities for problem 18.

● What is the probability of choosing a pecan? $\frac{20}{100}$, or $\frac{1}{5}$

● What is the probability of choosing a walnut? $\frac{30}{100}$, or $\frac{3}{10}$

● What is the probability of choosing an almond? $\frac{50}{100}$, or $\frac{1}{2}$

● What do you expect to happen if you choose 10 nuts? How are they likely to be distributed? in the same fractions (proportions) as the whole can

Have students write equivalent fractions, using a denominator of 10 to make their predictions.

Problem 19 is similar except that it starts with the sample and then generalizes to the whole. Tell students that this situation is like polls that take samples of people to make predictions about the whole population. In the sample, $\frac{5}{8}$ of the noses are large and $\frac{3}{8}$ are small. Equivalent fractions with a denominator of 72 are $\frac{45}{72}$ and $\frac{27}{72}$. Therefore, out of a total of 72 noses, 45 are likely to be large and 27 are likely to be small.

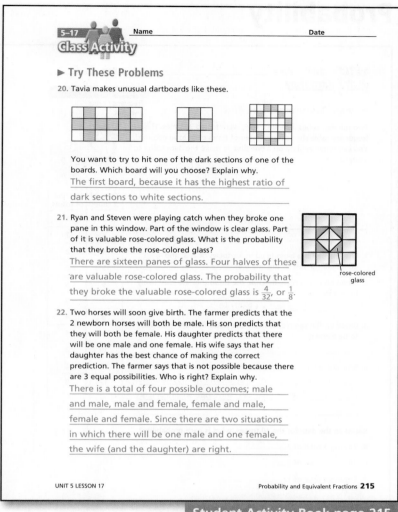

Student Activity Book page 215

▶ Try These Problems PAIRS

Your students can consolidate their understanding of probabilities as fractions as they work in **Student Pairs** to solve the problems on Student Book page 215.

The probability of hitting the dark sections of the dartboards in problem 20 is $\frac{5}{9}$ for the first, $\frac{4}{9}$ for the second, and $\frac{1}{3}$ for the third, after the fractions are simplified. You are most likely to hit a dark section on the first dartboard.

The key to solving problem 21 is to realize that each triangular section of rose-colored glass is exactly one half of a square. Since there are four triangular sections, they are the equivalent of two squares out of a total of 16 squares. The probability of hitting the rose-colored glass, then, is $\frac{2}{16}$, or $\frac{1}{8}$.

In problem 22, the wife and her daughter are right. There are four equally likely possibilities. Students will see this if you make a chart of all the combinations. The probability that there will be one male and one female is actually 2 out of 4.

Problem 22

Horse 1	Horse 2
Male	Male
Male	Female
Female	Male
Female	Female

② Going Further

Math Connection: Line Plots and Probability

Goal: Create a line plot from a frequency table.

Materials: Student Activity Book p. 216 or Hardcover Book p. 216 and Activity Workbook p. 93

✓ **NCTM Standards:**
Data Analysis and Probability
Number and Operations

▶ Read Data from a Line Plot INDIVIDUALS

In this activity, students connect what they know about probability with displays of data in a line plot.

Draw a number line on the board, and label it from 1 to 31. Ask a student to come to the board and put an X over the day of the month of his or her birthday.

```
                        x
1 2 3 4 5 6 7 8 9 10 11 12 13 14 15 16 17 18 19 20 21 22 23 24 25 26 27 28 29 30 31
```

The rest of the students call out their birthdays and the student at the board records each one on the number line, "stacking" the ones that occur more than once.

Tell the students that the completed number line is called a *line plot*. Ask questions about the final results.

● Which number is most frequent?

● Which number is least frequent?

● Why do you think 31 usually occurs less often on a line plot like this? Some months don't have 31 days.

● Should 30 occur less often than other numbers? maybe a little less because February has only 28 or 29 days

Have students complete the exercises on Student Book page 216.

Discuss the students' answer to exercise 7.

● Is the probability of tossing a 12 based on this sample the real probability? Why or why not? No, because it is possible to toss a 12; it just has not happened in these 30 trials.

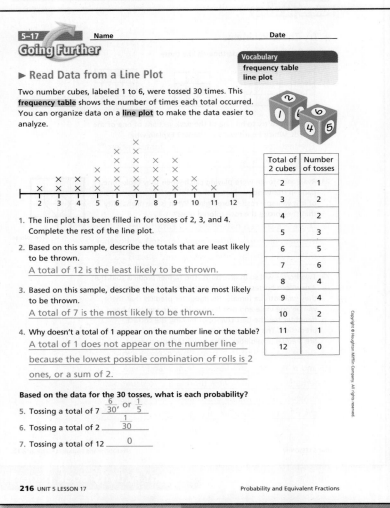

Student Activity Book page 216

▶ Take a Survey PAIRS

If time remains, **Student Pairs** can survey their classmates. Possible topics include number of pets or siblings or number of hours per day doing homework, reading, sleeping, or watching television.

Have students write conclusions about the data.

Make a Line Plot Students can make a frequency table and a line plot of their survey results.

Differentiated Instruction

Intervention Activity Card 5-17

Make a Spinner
Activity Card 5-17 ●

Work: In Small Groups

Use:
- Spinner (TRB M34)
- Pencil and paper clip

1. Make a spinner, using the pencil and paper clip to form a pointer as shown.

2. Find the probability of spinning each number from 1 to 8. Then find the probability of spinning an even or an odd number. $\frac{1}{8}$, $\frac{1}{2}$

3. **Predict** What results do you expect for 24 spins? Test your predictions and record your results. Possible prediction: The spinner will point to each number 3 times out of 24 spins.

Unit 5, Lesson 17

Copyright © Houghton Mifflin Company

Activity Note After students complete the activity, discuss why the results of their experiment may not match their predictions. Discuss the many ways that experiments may bias results, such as using a spinner that does not spin freely on a level surface.

 Math Writing Prompt

Make Predictions Describe what should happen if you toss a coin 100 times. Explain your thinking.

 **Software Support**

Warm-Up 52.03

On Level Activity Card 5-17

Find the Probability
Activity Card 5-17 ▲

Work: In Small Groups

1. There are 100 letter tiles in a board game. The frequency of the tiles that are vowels is listed in the table.

A – 9
E – 12
I – 9
O – 8
U – 4

2. **Work Together** Find the probability of picking any vowel from the 100 letters. $\frac{21}{50}$

3. **Compare** Find the probability of picking each vowel and then list the vowels in order from most likely to least likely to be picked. Which two vowels are equally likely? A and I
A – $\frac{9}{100}$
I – $\frac{9}{100}$
E – $\frac{3}{25}$
O – $\frac{2}{25}$
U – $\frac{1}{25}$

Unit 5, Lesson 17

Copyright © Houghton Mifflin Company

Activity Note Be sure that students understand the distinction between picking any vowel and picking a specific vowel. Discuss why there are more of some letters than others in the set of tiles (letters in English appear with different frequencies).

 Math Writing Prompt

Explain Your Thinking How does knowing about probability help you to make predictions?

 Software Support

Fraction Action: Last Chance Canyon, Level F

Challenge Activity Card 5-17

Tossing a Coin
Activity Card 5-17 ■

Work: By Yourself

Use:
- 2 different coins

1. List every possible outcome when you toss two different coins at once. HH, TT, HT, TH

2. **Predict** What is the likelihood of each outcome?

3. Conduct an experiment of tossing the coins 20 times, and record the results.

4. **Look Back** How did your predictions and your actual results compare? Possible answer: Results might differ if the coin is not perfectly balanced or the tossing technique biases the result.

penny	nickel
T	H
H	T
H	H
T	T

Unit 5, Lesson 17

Copyright © Houghton Mifflin Company

Activity Note Make sure students can recognize the four different outcomes that are possible when a penny and a nickel are tossed.

 Math Writing Prompt

In Your Own Words Explain why the results of an experiment are usually different from what you might predict using probability.

DESTINATION Math **Software Support**

Course III: Module 6: Unit 1: Looking at Chance

Probability and Equivalent Fractions **539**

Teaching the Lesson

Relating Easy Fractions and Decimals

 25 MINUTES

Goal: Identify patterns of equivalent fractions and decimals, using money models.

Materials: Student Activity Book or Hardcover Book p. 217, calculators (optional)

✔ **NCTM Standards:**
Numbers and Operations
Communication

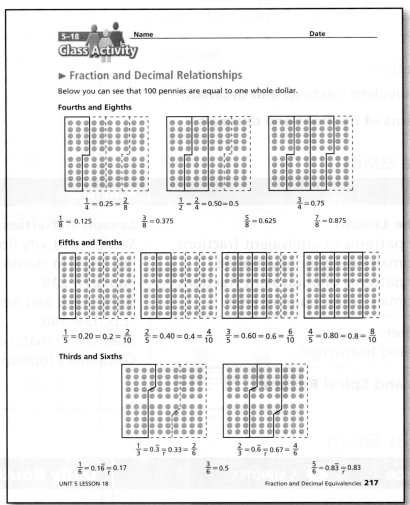

Student Activity Book page 217

English Language Learners

Draw four quarters on the board. Write $0.25, 25¢, $\frac{1}{4}$, and *equivalent*.

- **Beginning** Point and ask: **Is $0.25 a decimal?** yes **Does one quarter equal 25¢?** yes **Is one quarter equal to $\frac{1}{4}$ dollar?** yes **Is $\frac{1}{4}$ equivalent to 0.25?** yes
- **Intermediate and Advanced** Ask: **How many cents are in one quarter?** 25 **What fraction of $1 is a quarter?** $\frac{1}{4}$ Say: **The decimal 0.25 and the fraction $\frac{1}{4}$ are __.** equivalent

---

▶ **Fraction and Decimal Relationships** | WHOLE CLASS |

Ask for Ideas Ask students to share what they know about how fractions and decimals relate to each other and about how fraction and decimal notation are alike and different. (This discussion is a review of Unit 3 Lesson 1 and of other sources of student knowledge.) Ask them to include how thinking about dollars and cents can help with understanding these relationships.

(123) Math Talk Discuss patterns students see in the fraction and decimal equivalencies on Student Book page 217. Prompt the discussion by asking the questions below for several related fractions and decimals.

- **What is the whole?** The whole is one dollar, or 100 cents/pennies.

- **Without counting, how do we know the number of equal parts the whole is divided into?** The number of equal parts in the whole is shown on the bottom of a fraction (the denominator) and by the position (the place value) of the decimal (tenths or hundredths or thousandths).

- **How many of such parts are being taken (or described)?** The number of parts that are taken is shown on the top of a fraction (the numerator) and by the number written in a given position of the decimal. For example, 5 written in the tenths place for 0.5.

Students may discuss patterns they see between fractions and decimals, or within fractions or within decimals. They may also identify patterns for fractions with the same denominator or those with easily-related denominators.

Be sure that the talking points on the next two pages are a part of the discussion. (Although some of the points were covered in Unit 3 Lesson 1, all of your students will benefit from discussing them again). These concepts will become clearer for students when they work through Student Book page 218, and can be discussed again there (for example, the even and odd eighths).

Activity continued ▶

The Learning Classroom

Math Talk Having students use their own words and examples to discuss what they have learned is an effective way to be sure they understand a concept. Invite a student to go to the board and summarize the class discussion.

Discussion Points for Patterns in Fourths

- Fourths are multiples of $\frac{25}{100}$ (a dollar divided into 4 equal parts makes 4 quarters, and each equal part equals 25 cents); 0.25, 0.50, 0.75 are $\frac{1}{4}, \frac{2}{4}, \frac{3}{4}$.

- Eighths are half of fourths, so they are multiples of 0.125. The 0.005 is half of a penny (half of 0.01).

- The even-numerator eighths equal fourths $\left(\frac{2}{8} = \frac{1}{4}, \frac{4}{8} = \frac{2}{4}, \frac{6}{8} = \frac{3}{4}\right)$; the decimal equivalents have a zero in the thousandths place, so they can be expressed simply in hundredths: 0.25, 0.50, 0.75 are $\frac{2}{8}, \frac{4}{8}, \frac{6}{8}$.

- The odd-numerator eighths can be thought of as the previous even numerator eighth plus one more eighth, so they always have an extra half of a fourth (0.125) added on.

$$\frac{1}{8} = 0.125$$

$$\frac{3}{8} = \frac{2}{8} + \frac{1}{8} = 0.25 + 0.125 = 0.375$$

$$\frac{5}{8} = \frac{4}{8} + \frac{1}{8} = 0.50 + 0.125 = 0.625$$

$$\frac{7}{8} = \frac{6}{8} + \frac{1}{8} = 0.75 + 0.125 = 0.875$$

Discussion Points for Patterns in Fifths and Tenths

- Fifths are multiples of $\frac{20}{100}$ (a dollar divided into 5 equal parts makes 5 groups of 2 dimes, and each equal part equals 20 cents): 0.20, 0.40, 0.60, 0.80 are $\frac{1}{5}, \frac{2}{5}, \frac{3}{5}, \frac{4}{5}$.

- The groups of 2 dimes = 20 cents can be thought of as hundredths (as cents: 0.20, 0.40, 0.60, 0.80) or as dimes (as tenths: 0.2, 0.4, 0.6, 0.8 and as $\frac{2}{10}, \frac{4}{10}, \frac{6}{10}, \frac{8}{10}$).

Discussion Points for Patterns in Thirds and Sixths

- Thirds as decimals are multiples of $33\frac{1}{3}$: a dollar (1.00 = 100 cents) divided into 3 equal parts makes equal groups of $33\frac{1}{3}$.

- We can't ever make dividing by 3 come out even. For any place, we'll get 3 equal groups of $3\frac{1}{3}$. So we need to use rounded values for thirds. The little r's under the equals signs on Student Book page 217 shows that a decimal value has been rounded.

  $\frac{1}{3} = 0.33\frac{1}{3}$, which we round to 0.33

  $\frac{2}{3} = 0.66\frac{2}{3}$, which we round to 0.67

- We use the special notation of a bar over a numeral to show that the number goes on and on.

  $\frac{1}{3} = 0.\overline{3}$ $\frac{2}{3} = 0.\overline{6}$

  $\frac{1}{6} = 0.1\overline{6}$ $\frac{2}{6} = 0.\overline{3}$ $\frac{3}{6} = 0.5$

  $\frac{4}{6} = 0.\overline{6}$ $\frac{5}{6} = 0.8\overline{3}$

Calculators (optional) You may wish to have students use calculators to see that $\frac{1}{3}, \frac{2}{3}, \frac{1}{6}, \frac{2}{6}, \frac{4}{6}$, and $\frac{5}{6}$ result in nonterminating decimals. Ask students to enter the fractions as divisions, such as $1 \div 3$, $4 \div 6$, and so on.

Discussion Points for Patterns Across the Fractions

- Fifths can be written as tenths and fourths as hundredths, but eighths need thousandths to write all of the eighths (the even numerators can drop the 0 thousandths and be expressed as fourths in hundredths).

- Thirds and sixths actually have decimal equivalents that go on and on, but we usually round them off to hundredths;

  $\frac{1}{3}$ rounds to 0.33 and $\frac{2}{3}$ rounds to 0.67

  $\frac{1}{6}$ rounds to 0.17, $\frac{2}{6}$ rounds to 0.33, and $\frac{3}{6} = \frac{1}{2} = 0.5$

  $\frac{4}{6}$ rounds to 0.67 and $\frac{5}{6}$ rounds to 0.83

Tell students that the next two pages will help them see and remember these fraction and decimal equivalencies.

Teaching Note

Thirds and Sixths You do not have to emphasize the decimal equivalents for thirds and sixths if that is not a district or state goal. This lesson and the related practice materials are designed so that students can omit these fractions. However, it is helpful to discuss the values on Student Book page 217 as pennies because it will help students in future years understand these decimal values. Your advanced students will also find it interesting and are likely to have the ability to learn the values now.

Teaching Note

Visualizing Encourage your students to look again at the equal divisions on Student Book page 217, and try to make a mental picture of the values of fourths, eighths, and fifths (and thirds and sixths, for those who wish to do so). Tell your students to "*Close your eyes. Visualize!!!*" Can they see $\frac{1}{4}$? $\frac{3}{4}$? $\frac{1}{5}$? $\frac{3}{5}$?

Activity 2

Patterns and Number Lines

 35 MINUTES

Goal: Identify patterns of equivalent fractions and decimals, using number lines.

Materials: Student Activity Book or Hardcover Book pp. 218–219, MathBoard materials

 NCTM Standards:
Number and Operations

Teaching Note

Student Misunderstandings
Students often misunderstand number lines and think that the point represents the number. A number line is a length model in which the number represents the distance from 0 to the point where the number is located.

Teaching Note

Number Lines We are using vertical number lines because students can look across the numerators and the denominators to see relationships. Vertical number lines also make it easier for students to see how the decimal values are multiples of the unit decimals. In upcoming lessons, students will work with horizontal number lines. Both kinds of number lines help prepare them for work in the coordinate plane.

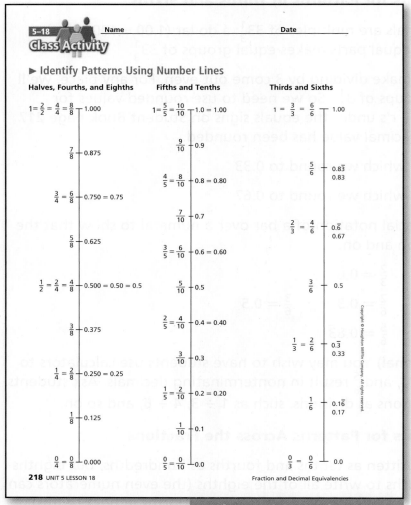

Student Activity Book page 218

▶ Identify Patterns Using Number Lines [WHOLE CLASS]

Have students turn to Student Book page 218. Ask them to imagine that each vertical number line is actually a tower of 100 pennies. (They can imagine pennies stacked on top of each other if that imagery is easier for them to visualize.)

Math Talk Discuss the patterns that can be seen. (This discussion reviews the patterns that were discussed in Activity 1, and students can now see those patterns on the number lines.) Emphasize especially the decimal values for the unit fractions $\frac{1}{4}$, $\frac{1}{8}$, $\frac{1}{5}$, $\frac{1}{3}$, and $\frac{1}{6}$, and emphasize how the other fractions are built from those unit fractions. For example, now students can see the pattern in the decimal values for eighths clearly: how it builds by adding 0.125 each time, making a new quarter ($0.25 = \frac{1}{4}$ of a dollar) every other time.

5–18
Class Activity

Name

Date

▶ Practice Fraction and Decimal Equivalencies

Study Chart

Eighths	Fourths	Fifths and Tenths	Thirds and Sixths
$\frac{1}{8} = 0.125$			$\frac{1}{6} = 0.1\overline{6}$ 0.17
		$\frac{1}{5} = \frac{2}{10} = 0.2$	
$\frac{2}{8} = 0.250$	$\frac{1}{4} = 0.25$		
			$\frac{2}{6} = \frac{1}{3} = 0.\overline{3}$ 0.33
$\frac{3}{8} = 0.375$		$\frac{2}{5} = \frac{4}{10} = 0.4$	
$\frac{4}{8} = 0.500$	$\frac{2}{4} = 0.50$		$\frac{3}{6} = 0.5$
		$\frac{3}{5} = \frac{6}{10} = 0.6$	
$\frac{5}{8} = 0.625$			$\frac{4}{6} = \frac{2}{3} = 0.\overline{6}$ 0.67
$\frac{6}{8} = 0.750$	$\frac{3}{4} = 0.75$		
		$\frac{4}{5} = \frac{8}{10} = 0.8$	$\frac{5}{6} = 0.8\overline{3}$ 0.83
$\frac{7}{8} = 0.875$			
$\frac{8}{8} = 1.000$	$\frac{4}{4} = 1.00$	$\frac{5}{5} = \frac{10}{10} = 1.0$	$\frac{6}{6} = \frac{3}{3} = 1$

UNIT 5 LESSON 18

Fraction and Decimal Equivalencies **219**

▶ Practice Fraction and Decimal Equivalencies [PAIRS]

Have students turn to the Study Chart on Student Book page 219. Ask them again to discuss briefly patterns they see. Then have **Student Pairs** work together to give the decimal equivalent for a fraction, and vice versa. For example, one student says a fraction, and the other student says and writes the fraction and then writes the decimal equivalent after an equals sign.

Ask students what would belong in the Fifths and Tenths column for $\frac{1}{2}$. Be sure students understand that the equivalent fraction $\frac{5}{10}$ needs to be used to represent $\frac{1}{2}$.

Study Strategies Elicit strategies from students that can be used in their studies. For example, they may choose to practice all of the eighths and then ask their partner to give them only eighths. Or they may choose to first practice the unit fractions or the more difficult fractions. Partner practice allows them to tailor their practice to their needs.

Activity continued ▶

Differentiated Instruction

Extra Help It is helpful for all students to use both auditory and visual modes when they practice fraction and decimal equivalencies. Using both modes also provides extra practice for **English Language Learners.** Walk around your classroom, and listen to be sure students say the fractions and decimals correctly.

Differentiated Instruction

Special Needs For students who have difficulty tracking fractions across the page, suggest that they fold a sheet of paper in half and place it straight across the number lines.

Fraction and Decimal Equivalencies **547**

① Teaching the Lesson (continued)

Activity 2

 Ongoing Assessment

State a variety of fractions and have students name an equivalent decimal number for each fraction.

State a variety of decimal numbers and have students name an equivalent fraction for each number.

Students can work on paper or on their MathBoards. Allow 2 to 4 minutes for one partner to ask questions and then students switch roles.

Complete two or three (or more if needed) cycles of such practice. Stress that students will be taking these three pages home, and their Home Helper can help them study in the same way.

An alternative is to have students keep Student Book pages 218 or 219 in their books and complete this practice briefly during Lessons 19 and 20. Students can practice the other two pages at home to prepare them for in-class practice.

You may want to have **Small Groups** practice with a **Student Leader.**

②Going Further

Differentiated Instruction

Intervention   Activity Card 5-18

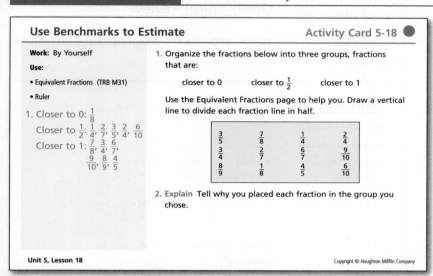

Activity Note Point out that the fraction $\frac{1}{4}$ is halfway between 0 and $\frac{1}{2}$, so it rounds to $\frac{1}{2}$. The fraction $\frac{3}{4}$ is halfway between $\frac{1}{2}$ and 1, so it rounds to 1.

Math Writing Prompt

Explain Your Reasoning The Puzzled Penguin wrote $\frac{1}{2} + \frac{1}{3} = \frac{2}{5}$. Explain why this is incorrect.

Soar to Success Math **Software Support**

Warm-Up 9.17

On Level   Activity Card 5-18

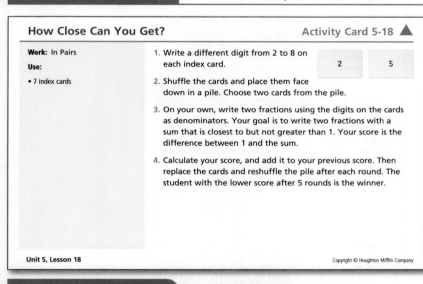

Activity Note For the cards in the example, the greatest possible sum would be $\frac{1}{2} + \frac{2}{5} = \frac{9}{10}$, and the student's score would be $\frac{1}{10}$.

Math Writing Prompt

Write the Steps Write the steps you would follow to estimate the sum of two fractions with unlike denominators.

MegaMath **Software Support**

Fraction Action: Fraction Flare Up, Level K

Challenge   Activity Card 5-18

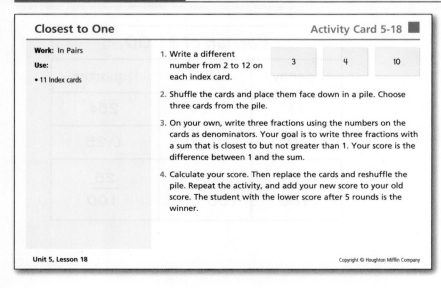

Activity Note Using the cards in the example, the greatest possible sum would be $\frac{1}{3} + \frac{1}{4} + \frac{4}{10} = \frac{59}{60}$, and the score would be $\frac{1}{60}$.

Math Writing Prompt

Write Your Own Write an addition word problem and a subtraction word problem that each include the fractions $\frac{2}{5}$ and $\frac{7}{8}$. Estimate each solution.

DESTINATION Math® **Software Support**

Course III: Module 3: Unit 2: Working with Unlike Denominators

Fraction and Decimal Equivalencies   **549**

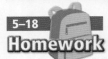 Homework and Spiral Review

Homework **Goal:** Additional Practice

Use this Homework page to provide students with more practice with fraction and decimal equivalencies.

Remembering **Goal:** Spiral Review

This Remembering page would be appropriate anytime after today's lesson.

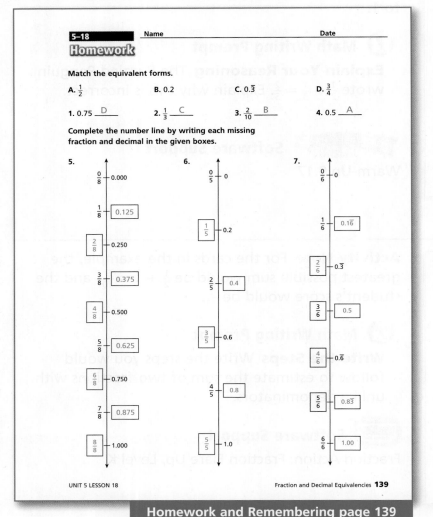

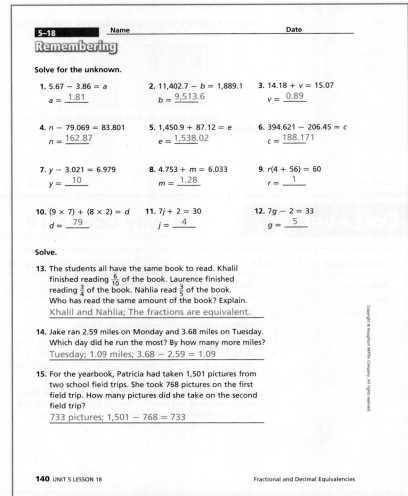

Homework and Remembering page 139

Homework and Remembering page 140

Home or School Activity

 Math-to-Math Connection

Relate Money to Fractions and Decimals Describe how coins in our money system are related to a whole dollar. Use both fractions and decimals in your answer. Include a table in your explanation to show these relationships.

Portion of $1.00		
1 penny	1 dime	1 quarter
1¢	10¢	25¢
0.01	0.10	0.25
$\frac{1}{100}$	$\frac{10}{100} = \frac{1}{10}$	$\frac{25}{100}$

UNIT 5
LESSON 19

Compare and Order Fractions and Decimals

REAL WORLD **Problem Solving**

Lesson Objectives

● **Use patterns and strategies to compare and order fractions and decimals.**

The Day at a Glance

Today's Goals	Materials

① Teaching the Lesson
  A1: Identify patterns to compare fractions with like denominators.
  A2: Identify strategies to compare fractions with unlike denominators.
  A3: Use number lines to represent, compare, and order fractions and decimals.

② Going Further
  ▶ Math Connection: Making Change
  ▶ Differentiated Instruction

③ Homework and Spiral Review

Lesson Activities
Student Activity Book pp. 217–218, 221–222 or Student Hardcover Book pp. 217–218, 221–222 and Activity Workbook pp. 94–95
Homework and Remembering pp. 141–142
MathBoard materials

Going Further
Student Activity Book pp. 223–224 or Student Hardcover Book pp. 223–224
Play money
Activity Cards 5-19
Game Cards 1–9 (TRB M2)
Ruler
Math Journals

123 *Use* **Math Talk** *today!*

Keeping Skills Sharp

Quick Practice ⏱ 5 MINUTES	Daily Routines

Goal: Practice finding common denominators.

Material: pointer

Common Denominator Parade Invite two students to the board. One student writes an addition problem with two fractions in which the denominators are greater than 1 and less than 10. The other writes an addition problem with two fractions in which the denominators are two different even numbers, either 4, 6, 8, or 10. In turn, each person uses a pointer to point to his or her problem and says, "Name a common denominator." The class responds with the answer, which is a common product of the two denominators.

$$\frac{7}{8} + \frac{5}{7} \qquad \frac{7}{8} + \frac{3}{4}$$

Discuss how to find the denominator in each.

Homework Review Have students share and discuss their work. Help them clarify any misunderstandings.

Estimate or Exact Answer? Alma put wallpaper on a wall with dimensions 6 ft 9 in. by 8 ft 4 in. She needed only one roll of pre-cut wallpaper to cover it. How many square feet does the roll of wallpaper need to cover? Explain if you found an estimate or an exact answer and why. Possible answer: Estimate; Using normal rounding rules finds the least amount on the roll; 6 ft 9 in. ≈ 7 ft; 8 ft 4 in. ≈ 8 ft; $7 \times 8 = 56$ sq ft; The roll had at least 56 square feet.

Compare and Order Fractions and Decimals **551**

Teaching the Lesson

Compare Easier Fractions

 20 MINUTES

Goal: Identify patterns to compare fractions with like denominators.

Materials: MathBoard materials, Student Activity Book or Hardcover Book p. 217

✔ **NCTM Standards:**
Number and Operations
Communication

English Language Learners

Write 0.2 > 0.05, 0.05 < 0.2, *compare, digit, tenths,* and *hundredths* on the board. Have students read the expressions aloud.

- **Beginning** Ask: Do these symbols mean "compare"? yes **Is the number 2 in the tenths or the hundredths place?** tenths
- **Intermediate** Say: These symbols mean __. compare Ask: **What digit is in the hundredths place?** 5
- **Advanced** Have students tell about the > and < signs and then identify the places of the digits.

▶ **Elicit Comparison Knowledge**

WHOLE CLASS

Math Talk

Ask for Ideas Ask students what they remember about comparing decimals. Be sure that they discuss the following points:

- The meanings of the < and > signs and how to remember what each sign means.

- The digits in the largest place are the only digits that matter (unless the digits are equal). The largest place is always the place that is farthest to the left. The number with the larger digit in the largest (left-most) place is the larger number.

- If the digits in the left-most (largest) place are the same, move to the next-largest place, and find the larger digit. If the digits are the same, continue moving one place at a time to the right until you find a place in which the digits differ. The larger digit in that place will identify the larger number.

- Why is this pattern true? Because the values of the smaller place values to the right are less than the largest place value that is being compared, so smaller place values are irrelevant.

Now ask students what they know about comparing fractions. Remember their responses, and try to incorporate them into the following sequence of activities that build fraction comparing knowledge. (For example, *See, this is the point that David made in our first discussion about fractions.*).

▶ Discuss Fraction Comparisons

| WHOLE CLASS |

Math Talk

Fractions with the Same Denominator Write the fraction comparisons shown below on the board, and have students copy them on their MathBoards. Encourage students to look at Student Book page 217 and complete the comparisons by writing < or > in each circle.

$$\frac{1}{4} \le \frac{2}{4} \qquad \frac{3}{8} \le \frac{5}{8} \qquad \frac{4}{5} \ge \frac{2}{5}$$

$$\frac{2}{3} \ge \frac{1}{3} \qquad \frac{7}{10} \ge \frac{6}{10}$$

Now have students look at their answers and describe the pattern they see for fractions that are made from the same unit fraction (e.g., whose denominators are the same number). More of the same unit fraction make a larger fraction. If the denominators are the same, the larger numerator is the larger fraction because it represents more unit fractions.

Fractions with the Same Numerator but Different Denominators Write the pairs of fractions shown below on the board and have students copy them on their MathBoards. Suggest that students look at Student Book page 217 as needed to decide which symbol (< or >) to write.

$$\frac{2}{4} \ge \frac{2}{5} \qquad \frac{3}{8} \le \frac{3}{5} \qquad \frac{2}{4} \le \frac{2}{3}$$

$$\frac{5}{8} \le \frac{5}{6} \qquad \frac{7}{8} \ge \frac{7}{10}$$

Now have students look at their answers and describe the pattern they see for fractions with the same numerator but with different denominators. (This relationship is opposite that of whole numbers: A larger denominator means more but smaller unit fractions, so the larger fraction here is always the fraction with the smaller denominator because it has fewer unit fractions. So, each unit fraction is larger.)

Activity 2

Compare Harder Fractions

 20 MINUTES

Goal: Identify strategies to compare fractions with unlike denominators.

Materials: MathBoard materials, Student Activity Book or Hardcover Book p. 218

✔ **NCTM Standards:**
Number and Operations
Communication

Teaching Note

Unit Fractions Some students may notice that some pairs are just one unit fraction away from 1

$(\frac{4}{5}$ ___ $\frac{5}{6}, \frac{7}{8}$ ___ $\frac{9}{10})$

When comparing two such fractions with numerators one less than the denominator, the fraction with the larger unit fraction (the smaller denominator) will be smaller because its missing unit fraction will make it be farther from 1. So $\frac{1}{5} > \frac{1}{6}$, and $\frac{4}{5} < \frac{5}{6}$ because $\frac{5}{6}$ will be closer to 1 than $\frac{4}{5}$.

▶ **Discuss Strategies for Comparing**

WHOLE CLASS

Math Talk

Fractions with Different Numerators and Different Denominators
Write the fraction comparisons shown below on the board, and have students copy them on their MathBoards. Suggest that students look at Student Book page 218 as needed to decide which symbol (< or >) to write.

$$\frac{2}{4} \leq \frac{3}{5} \qquad \frac{5}{8} \geq \frac{3}{5} \qquad \frac{2}{3} \geq \frac{5}{8}$$

$$\frac{4}{5} \leq \frac{5}{6} \qquad \frac{7}{8} \leq \frac{9}{10}$$

As they work, have students discuss the strategies they are using to find the largest fraction. These comparisons are more difficult than the earlier cases in which the top or bottom number was the same. Student Book page 218 can be used now because the scales are helpful for these comparisons. Many students may be using the decimal equivalents to find the larger number.

Common Denominator An alternative way to compare when the denominators are nearly the same is to find equivalent fractions that have the same denominator. You may wish to have students use this method as a quick review for finding equivalent fractions. Finding equivalent fractions with the same denominator is the general method for deciding which fraction is larger, but knowing the decimal equivalents for these easy fractions is an even easier method.

$$\frac{2}{4} < \frac{3}{5} \qquad \frac{5}{8} > \frac{3}{5} \qquad \frac{2}{3} > \frac{5}{8}$$

$$\frac{4}{5} < \frac{5}{6} \qquad \frac{7}{8} < \frac{9}{10}$$

$$\frac{10}{20} < \frac{12}{20} \qquad \frac{5}{40} < \frac{24}{40} \qquad \frac{16}{24} > \frac{15}{24}$$

$$\frac{24}{30} < \frac{25}{30} \qquad \frac{35}{40} < \frac{36}{40}$$

Fractions with Different Numerators and Different Denominators That Can Use "Benchmarks" Write the easier fraction comparisons shown below on the board, and have students copy them on their MathBoards. Students may have knowledge that enables them to identify the correct symbol simply by using their knowledge of being close to 1, close to 0, or greater than or less than one-half. This method is often called *using benchmarks* (the 0, 1, and $\frac{1}{2}$ are benchmarks). Since this method may be difficult for some students, stress that three patterns above are sufficient for making any fraction comparisons. Encourage your students to try and use these patterns without consulting Student Book pages 217 and 218, but they may use the pages if they so choose. Discuss each pair as students solve them.

$\frac{1}{4} \underline{<} \frac{9}{10}$ $\frac{4}{8} \underline{>} \frac{1}{8}$ $\frac{5}{6} \underline{>} \frac{1}{2}$

$\frac{2}{5} \underline{<} \frac{5}{8}$ $\frac{3}{5} \underline{>} \frac{1}{3}$ $\frac{2}{3} \underline{>} \frac{3}{8}$

The first two comparisons each include one fraction close to 0 and another fraction close to 1, so the fraction close to 1 will be larger.

The last four comparisons involve knowing whether a fraction is larger or smaller than $\frac{1}{2}$. In all cases, the fractions larger than $\frac{1}{2}$ are larger than the fractions that are less than or equal to $\frac{1}{2}$.

Give students an opportunity to discuss how they know if a fraction is more than or less than $\frac{1}{2}$. (To be more than half, the numerator must be more than half the denominator.) For fractions that have a denominator that is an odd number, half of the denominator will be a mixed number, such as $2\frac{1}{2}$ for a denominator of 5, so $\frac{3}{5}$ is more than half because $3 > 2\frac{1}{2}$.

Teaching Note

Watch For! Some students can find the larger of two fractions or decimals but may write an incorrect < or > sign. These students will find it helpful to circle the larger number, and then think about which sign will have its larger part pointed toward the circled larger number.

Activity 3

Fractions and Decimals

 30 MINUTES

Goal: Use number lines to represent, compare, and order fractions and decimals.

Materials: Student Activity Book pp. 221–222 or Student Hardcover Book pp. 221–222 and Activity Workbook pp. 94–95

✔ **NCTM Standards:**
Number and Operations
Representation

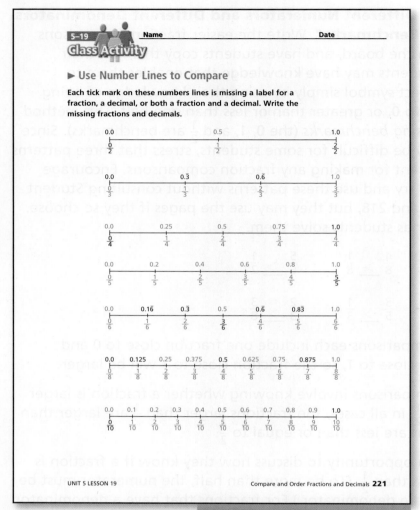

Student Activity Book page 221

▶ Use Number Lines to Compare WHOLE CLASS

On Student Book page 221, have students write the missing fractions and decimals on the number lines. The number lines show the equivalent fractions and decimals.

Then using the completed number lines, have students write several fraction and decimal comparisons (for example, $\frac{4}{5} < \frac{5}{6}$) to practice their understanding that the larger values are to the right on a positive horizontal number line.

Write Comparison Statements Have students choose 3 numbers from each number line and write comparison statements. Encourage students to use the inequality symbols.

Example: $\frac{1}{4} < \frac{2}{4} < \frac{3}{4}$ or $\frac{1}{4} < 0.5 < 1$

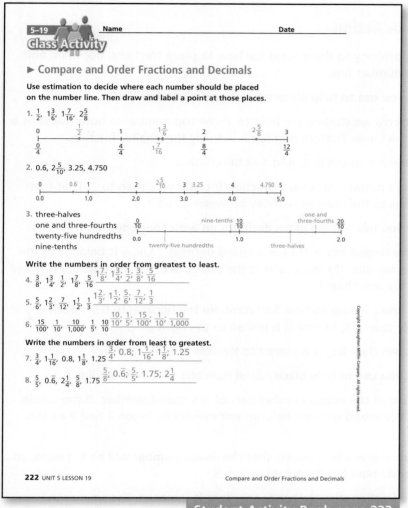

Student Activity Book page 222

▶ Compare and Order Fractions and Decimals [PAIRS]

Have **Student Pairs** work together to complete exercises 1–8 on Student Book page 222. The first three exercises involve using estimation to place numbers on a number line. The goal of these exercises is not for students to place the numbers exactly, but rather for them to demonstrate a general understanding of where the numbers should be.

Before starting exercises 4–8, alert students to the common error to watch for the words *greatest to least* and *least to greatest* in direction lines.

Write Comparison Statements Have students choose 3 numbers from each number line and write comparison statements. Encourage students to use the inequality symbols.

Examples: $\frac{8}{4} > 1\frac{7}{16} > \frac{1}{2}$ or $3.25 > 2\frac{5}{10} > 0.6$

Activity continued ▶

Teaching Note

Number Lines As students work with number lines, continue to emphasize the concept that the fractions and the decimals represent lengths (or distances) from 0. Have students circle several lengths or hold one finger at 0 and another finger at a fraction or decimal to help visualize this concept.

Differentiated Instruction

Advanced Learners Suggest that students make their own number lines and a list of fractions and decimals. They can exchange with a partner to place the fractions and decimals on the number line.

① Teaching the Lesson (continued)

Activity 3

Differentiated Instruction

Extra Help Pair students having difficulty with a **Helping Partner** to discuss and demonstrate different ways to compare fractions.

✓ Ongoing Assessment

Explain what it means for a fraction and a decimal number to be equivalent. Give an example to support your answer.

Describe two different ways to compare two fractions.

Describe two different ways to compare two decimal numbers.

Explain how to compare a fraction, a decimal, a mixed number, and a mixed decimal.

 Math Talk in Action

Give students an opportunity to share ideas for how to place fractions, decimals, and mixed numbers on a number line.

What strategies can you use to help place fractions on a number line?

Kai: The fraction patterns we studied are helpful. If the top number in both fractions is 1, the fraction with the larger bottom number is actually the smaller fraction.

Angela: Another pattern is to use 0, $\frac{1}{2}$, and 1 as benchmarks.

Garrett: Using Angela's pattern, let's say a fraction is closer to 1 than to $\frac{1}{2}$. That tells you that the fraction is to the right of halfway between $\frac{1}{2}$ and 1.

What strategies can you use to help place decimals on a number line?

Seth: I look first at the largest place. If I see a mixed decimal, I know it belongs to the right of 1 on the number line. If I see a zero in the ones place, I know that the number is greater than zero but less than 1.

Misty: On a number line $\frac{1}{2}$ is easy to find. So I compare the decimal to 0.5, which is $\frac{1}{2}$. If the decimal is greater than 0.5, I know it is placed to the right of $\frac{1}{2}$.

Bill: If the decimal is less than 0.5, it is placed to the left of $\frac{1}{2}$.

What strategies can you use to help place mixed numbers on a number line?

Christopher: I look first at the whole number part of the mixed number. If the whole number is 1, I know the mixed number belongs somewhere between 1 and 2 on the number line.

Emily: Once you know the whole numbers that the mixed number will be between, all you have to do is decide how big the fraction part is.

Matt: The bigger the fraction, the farther to the right it is placed. The smaller the fraction, the farther to the left it goes.

Math Connection: Making Change

Goal: Make change and compare and order money amounts.

Materials: coins and bills, Student Activity Book or Hardcover Book pp. 223–224

 NCTM Standards:
Number and Operations
Representation

► Count Coins   WHOLE CLASS

In this activity, students connect what they know about decimals and money with making change.

Act It Out Write the phrase "a music CD costs $11.59" on the board. Use the **Scenario** structure, and invite two volunteers to come to the front of the classroom. Ask them to use the bills and coins from the Manipulative Kit to model the amount of change that would be received if two 10-dollar bills were used to pay for the purchase.

Repeat the activity by inviting other volunteers to act out the amount of change for a $187.50 purchase paid for with two 100-dollar bills, and act out the amount of change for a $2.88 purchase paid for with one 10-dollar bill.

Encourage the seated students to ask clarifying questions and summarize the methods.

► Use Subtraction   WHOLE CLASS

Write $114.75 − $69.89 on the board and demonstrate how to find the difference ($44.86). Make sure students recognize that the subtraction begins in the pennies column. They will ungroup 1 dime for 10 pennies, 1 dollar for 10 dimes, 10 dollars for 10 ones, and 100 dollars for 10 tens.

► Make Change   INDIVIDUALS

Have students work individually or paired with a **Helping Partner** to complete exercises 1–6 on Student Book page 223. Use **Solve and Discuss** to complete exercises 7–8 as a whole-class activity.

5-19
Going Further
Name _____ Date _____

► Make Change

A $5 bill was used to purchase each item below. List the coins and bills that should be received as change.

1. paperback book
   $3.79 <u>1 penny, 2 dimes, one $1 bill</u>

2. pencil eraser
   35¢ <u>1 nickel, 1 dime, 2 quarters (or 1 half-dollar), four $1 bills</u>

A $20 bill was used to purchase each item below. List the coins and bills that should be received as change.

3. outdoor basketball
   $12.61 <u>4 pennies, 1 dime, 1 quarter, two $1 bills, one $5 bill</u>

4. canvas book bag
   $6.95 <u>1 nickel, three $1 bills, one $10 bill</u>

Use subtraction to make change for each situation.

5. Bought: jeans for $23.75
   Gave the clerk: one $50 bill

   Change: <u>$26.25</u>

6. Bought: groceries for $46.07
   Gave the clerk: three $20 bills

   Change: <u>$13.93</u>

Solve.

7. Hal has $70. After buying a hat for $9.50, mittens for $14.95, and a jacket for $36.50, does he have enough money to buy a pair of mittens for $15? Can Hal use an estimate to answer the question? Explain why or why not.
   <u>No; Sample explanation: Hal can round each amount to the nearest $5, then compare the sum of the amounts to $70 to learn he does not have enough money.</u>

8. A customer purchased an item and received $8.00 in change after giving the clerk a $20 bill and a nickel. What was the cost of the item?
   <u>$12.05</u>

UNIT 5 LESSON 19   Compare and Order Fractions and Decimals **223**

Student Activity Book page 223

The Learning Classroom

Scenario The main purpose of a scenario is to demonstrate mathematical relationships in a visual and memorable way. A group of students is called to the front of the room to act out a situation. Because of its active and dramatic nature, the scenario structure fosters a sense of intense involvement among children. Scenarios create meaningful contexts in which students relate math.

► ## Fractions of a Dollar [WHOLE CLASS]

Explain that in our system of currency, the benchmark unit is the dollar. We can divide this benchmark unit into equal parts, and represent the equal parts with coins. For example, if we divide 1 dollar into 4 equal parts, we can represent each equal part with a quarter.

One quarter is $\frac{1}{4}$ dollar, two quarters is $\frac{2}{4}$ dollar, three quarters is $\frac{3}{4}$ dollar, and so on. Have students examine the pattern $\frac{1}{4}, \frac{2}{4}, \frac{3}{4}, \frac{4}{4}, \frac{5}{4}, \frac{6}{4}, \ldots$. They can model the pattern using 1 quarter for the first term, 2 quarters for the second term, and so on. Students should notice that the numerator in each fraction represents the number of quarters in the model. Students should also notice that the denominator is always 4, since there are 4 quarters in a whole dollar.

Now have students write the pattern using mixed numbers: $\frac{1}{4}, \frac{2}{4}, \frac{3}{4}, 1, 1\frac{1}{4}, 1\frac{2}{4}, \ldots$. Have them use their model with quarters to show that $\frac{4}{4} = 1$ dollar, $\frac{5}{4} = 1$ dollar 1 quarter, $\frac{6}{4} = 1$ dollar 2 quarters, and so on.

Give students an opportunity to make similar connections for other coins.

► ## Compare and Order Money Amounts

[WHOLE CLASS]

Point out that comparing money amounts is the same as comparing decimals.

To compare money amounts, have students recall that we begin by comparing the digits in the greatest place. If the digits in that place are the same, we move one place to the right and compare the digits in that place. This pattern continues until the digits in a place are different.

Discuss the importance of finding equivalence when comparing amounts whose forms are different, such as $\frac{1}{4}$ dollar and $0.60. For comparisons such as these, it is important for students to recognize that they must convert $\frac{1}{4}$ dollar to dollars and cents, or convert $0.60 to some fraction of a dollar, before the amounts can be compared.

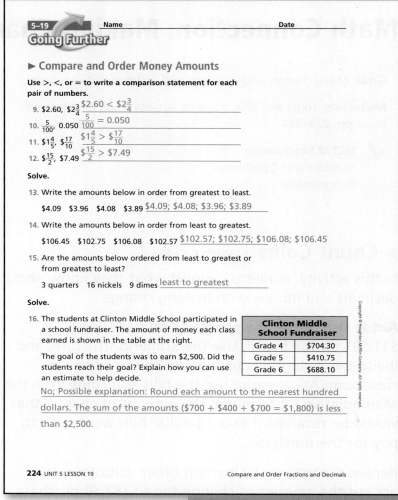

Student Activity Book page 224

On Student Book page 224, have students work individually or paired with a **Helping Partner** to complete exercises 9–15. Invite volunteers to share their answers for exercise 16 with the class.

Differentiated Instruction

Decimal and Fraction Patterns Activity Card 5-19

Work: In Pairs

Use:
• Game Cards 1–9 (TRB M2)

1. **Work Together** Copy and complete the table. Make 27 rows.

2. Shuffle the Game Cards.

3. One partner chooses a card and writes a decimal number from 0.1 to 0.009 with the digit on the card in the tenths place, and then writes two more decimal numbers, one with the digit on the card in the hundredths place, and one with the digit on the card in the thousandths place.

4. The partner writes the three numbers in the first column of the table, and then completes each of those rows.

5. Take turns until the table is complete.

Decimal	Number of equal parts	Number of parts in a whole	Fraction
0.1	1	10	$\frac{1}{10}$
			$\frac{1}{1,000}$
	2		
		100	
0.002			

Unit 5, Lesson 19   Copyright © Houghton Mifflin Company

Activity Note Help students identify patterns in the rows and columns. In the fourth column, for example, denominators of 10, 100, and 1,000 repeat.

✎ Math Writing Prompt

Summarize Explain how thousandths are different from hundredths and tenths. Explain how to write six thousandths as a decimal and as a fraction.

 **Software Support**

Warm-Up 24.36

On the Line Activity Card 5-19 ▲

Work: In Pairs

Use:
• Ruler

1. **Work Together** Make a number line from 0 to 1. Divide the number line into 10 equal intervals.

2. Label each interval with a decimal number. Which decimal number marks the halfway point on the line? 0.5

3. Take turns choosing a fraction from the list and locating it on the number line. Which fractions have a decimal equivalent on the line? $\frac{1}{2}, \frac{1}{5}, \frac{3}{5}, \frac{4}{5}$

4. **Math Talk** How did you locate the points for $\frac{1}{3}$ and $\frac{2}{3}$ on the number line? Which decimal number is close to each fraction? Possible answer: I used the ruler to divide the line into 3 equal parts and labeled the first interval $\frac{1}{3}$ and the second $\frac{2}{3}$; 0.3 and 0.6 are close to the fractions.

$\frac{1}{2}$
$\frac{1}{3}$
$\frac{1}{4}$
$\frac{1}{5}$
$\frac{3}{4}$
$\frac{2}{3}$
$\frac{4}{5}$
$\frac{3}{5}$

Unit 5, Lesson 19   Copyright © Houghton Mifflin Company

Activity Note To help students locate fractions on the number line, suggest that they rewrite each decimal tenth on the number line as a fraction in simplest form.

✎ Math Writing Prompt

Explain Why is it more likely that a metric measure will be expressed as a decimal than as a fraction? Is this true of a customary measure?

 Software Support

Fraction Action: Number Line Mine, Level N

Number Sense Activity Card 5-19 ■

Work: In Pairs

1. Match each given situation with one of the numbers below.

0.63 $17\frac{1}{2}$ $108\frac{3}{4}$ 9.95   1.25

Situations

• A 100-meter dash runner can run that distance at an amazing speed. The elapsed time was only _____ seconds! 9.95

• Joanie bought a snack. She paid with a 1-dollar bill. She received change back in the amount of _____ dollar. 0.63

• Milton used an inch ruler to measure the length of his computer keyboard. The keyboard measured _____ inches. $17\frac{1}{2}$

2. Write your own matching problems to share.

Unit 5, Lesson 19   Copyright © Houghton Mifflin Company

Activity Note Suggest that students begin by eliminating unreasonable answers for each situation. For example, because Joanie received change from $1, her lunch must cost less than $1.

✎ Math Writing Prompt

Number Sense Why do we express money amounts with decimal numbers? How could you express $1.50 as a mixed number?

 Software Support

Course III: Module 4: Unit 1: Ratios, Decimals, and Percents

Compare and Order Fractions and Decimals **561**

 # Homework and Spiral Review

5-19 Homework Goal: Additional Practice

Use this Homework page to provide students with more practice comparing and ordering fractions and decimals.

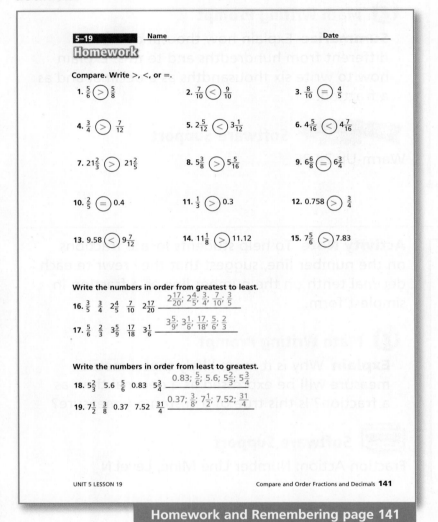

5-19 Homework   Name _____ Date _____

Compare. Write >, <, or =.

1. $\frac{5}{6}$ > $\frac{5}{8}$ 2. $\frac{7}{10}$ < $\frac{9}{10}$ 3. $\frac{8}{10}$ = $\frac{4}{5}$

4. $\frac{3}{4}$ > $\frac{7}{12}$ 5. $2\frac{5}{12}$ < $3\frac{1}{12}$ 6. $4\frac{5}{16}$ < $4\frac{7}{16}$

7. $21\frac{2}{3}$ > $21\frac{2}{5}$ 8. $5\frac{3}{8}$ > $5\frac{5}{16}$ 9. $6\frac{6}{8}$ = $6\frac{3}{4}$

10. $\frac{2}{5}$ = 0.4   11. $\frac{1}{3}$ > 0.3   12. 0.758 > $\frac{3}{4}$

13. 9.58 < $9\frac{7}{12}$ 14. $11\frac{1}{8}$ > 11.12   15. $7\frac{5}{6}$ > 7.83

Write the numbers in order from greatest to least.

16. $\frac{3}{5}$ $\frac{3}{4}$ $2\frac{4}{5}$ $\frac{7}{10}$ $2\frac{17}{20}$ $2\frac{17}{20}; 2\frac{4}{5}; \frac{3}{4}; \frac{7}{10}; \frac{3}{5}$

17. $\frac{5}{6}$ $\frac{2}{3}$ $3\frac{5}{9}$ $\frac{17}{18}$ $3\frac{1}{6}$ $3\frac{5}{9}; 3\frac{1}{6}; \frac{17}{18}; \frac{5}{6}; \frac{2}{3}$

Write the numbers in order from least to greatest.

18. $5\frac{2}{3}$ 5.6 $\frac{5}{6}$ 0.83 $5\frac{3}{4}$ $0.83; \frac{5}{6}; 5.6; 5\frac{2}{3}; 5\frac{3}{4}$

19. $7\frac{1}{2}$ $\frac{3}{8}$ 0.37   7.52 $\frac{31}{4}$ $0.37; \frac{3}{8}; 7\frac{1}{2}; 7.52; \frac{31}{4}$

UNIT 5 LESSON 19   Compare and Order Fractions and Decimals **141**

Homework and Remembering page 141

5-19 Remembering Goal: Spiral Review

This Remembering page would be appropriate anytime after today's lesson.

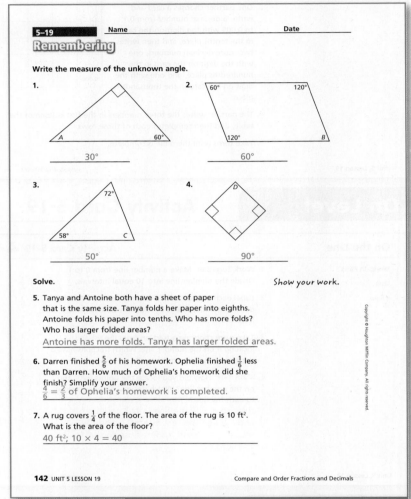

5-19 Remembering   Name _____ Date _____

Write the measure of the unknown angle.

1.   _____ 30°

2.   _____ 60°

3.   _____ 50°

4.   _____ 90°

Solve.   *Show your work.*

5. Tanya and Antoine both have a sheet of paper that is the same size. Tanya folds her paper into eighths. Antoine folds his paper into tenths. Who has more folds? Who has larger folded areas?
Antoine has more folds. Tanya has larger folded areas.

6. Darren finished $\frac{5}{6}$ of his homework. Ophelia finished $\frac{1}{6}$ less than Darren. How much of Ophelia's homework did she finish? Simplify your answer.
$\frac{4}{6} = \frac{2}{3}$ of Ophelia's homework is completed.

7. A rug covers $\frac{1}{4}$ of the floor. The area of the rug is 10 ft². What is the area of the floor?
40 ft²; 10 × 4 = 40

142 UNIT 5 LESSON 19   Compare and Order Fractions and Decimals

Homework and Remembering page 142

Home or School Activity

 ### Real-World Connection

Ordering Delia noticed that the bloom stalks on the irises in her garden grow to different heights. She measured the height of 8 bloom stalks and displayed them in a list. Order the heights of these blooms from least to greatest.

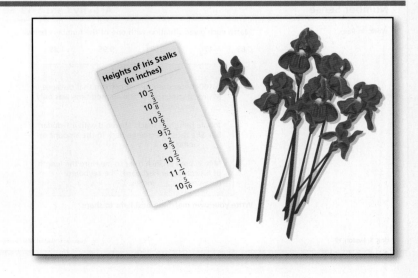

Heights of Iris Stalks (in inches)

$10\frac{1}{2}$
$10\frac{3}{8}$
$10\frac{5}{6}$
$9\frac{5}{12}$
$9\frac{2}{3}$
$10\frac{2}{5}$
$11\frac{1}{4}$
$10\frac{5}{16}$

Different Ways to Estimate (Optional)

REAL WORLD
Problem Solving

Lesson Objectives

● **Use a variety of methods to estimate sums and differences of fractions, mixed numbers, and decimals.**

Vocabulary
benchmark

The Day at a Glance

Today's Goals	Materials

1 Teaching the Lesson
A1: Use benchmarks and rounding to estimate with fractions and mixed numbers.
A2: Estimate sums and differences to check for reasonableness.
 	
2 Going Further
▶ Differentiated Instruction
 	
3 Homework and Spiral Review
	Lesson Activities
	Student Activity Book pp. 225–226
	  or Student Hardcover Book
	  pp. 225–226
	Homework and Remembering
	  pp. 143–144
	Quick Quiz 4 (Assessment Guide)
	
	Going Further
	Activity Cards 5-20
	Grid Paper (TRB M17)
	Index cards
	Math Journals

123 **Use Math Talk today!**

Keeping Skills Sharp

Quick Practice ⏱ 5 MINUTES	Daily Routines
Goal: Practice finding common denominators. **Material:** pointer **Common Denominator Parade** Invite two students to the board. One student writes an addition problem with two fractions in which the denominators are greater than 1 and less than 10. The other writes an addition problem with two fractions in which the denominators are two different even numbers, either 4, 6, 8, or 10. In turn, each person uses a pointer to point to his or her problem and says, "Name a common denominator." The class responds with the answer, which is a common product of the two denominators. $\frac{2}{3} + \frac{1}{4}$ $\frac{5}{6} + \frac{3}{4}$ Discuss the two types of addition problems and ask "Which is easier? Why?" Allow students to share their thinking.	**Homework Review** If students give incorrect answers, have them explain how they found the answers. This can help you determine whether the error is conceptual or procedural. **Nonroutine Problem** Write two fractions, using each of the numbers 2, 3, 4, and 7 only once. The sum of these fractions should simplify to $1\frac{1}{28}$. $\frac{3}{4}, \frac{2}{7}; \frac{3}{4} + \frac{2}{7} = \frac{21}{28} + \frac{8}{28} = \frac{29}{28} = 1\frac{1}{28}$

① Teaching the Lesson

Estimate with Fractions

 30 MINUTES

Goal: Use benchmarks and rounding to estimate with fractions and mixed numbers.

Materials: Student Activity Book or Hardcover Book p. 225

 NCTM Standards:
Number and Operations
Reasoning and Proof

The Learning Classroom

Math Talk Aspire to make your classroom a place where all students listen to understand one another. Point out that listening to understand is different than simply being quiet when someone else is talking. Listening to understand involves thinking about what a person is saying so that the listener could explain it in the same way. Listening to understand also creates opportunities to ask questions, or to help a person who is having difficulty with an explanation. Most of all, listening to understand can help each student to more thoroughly grasp the concepts that are being talked about.

▶ **Review Fraction Benchmarks**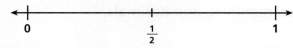

Ask for Ideas Ask students to recall benchmarks and give an example of how they are used. Benchmarks are reference numbers that are used to compare.

On the board or overhead, draw the number line shown below, and write the fraction $\frac{5}{8}$ nearby.

$$\begin{array}{ccc} 0 & \frac{1}{2} & 1 \end{array}$$

Math Talk in Action

Ask students to work at the board.

How can we use the number line to decide if $\frac{5}{8}$ is closer to 0, closer to $\frac{1}{2}$, or closer to 1?

Reggie: One way is to divide the number line into eighths. Eighths means eight equal parts. So we draw a tick mark halfway between 0 and $\frac{1}{2}$ and halfway between $\frac{1}{2}$ and 1. This will divide the number line into 4 equal parts, or fourths. Then we divide each of those equal parts in half to make eighths, and we label each tick mark in eighths.

Can anyone describe a different way?

Hannah: Change each benchmark to eighths. We can do this by multiplying the numerator and the denominator of each benchmark by the same number. Multiply both parts of $\frac{1}{2}$ by 4 to find that $\frac{1}{2} = \frac{4}{8}$.

Sean: Zero is the same as zero eighths, and 1 is the same as eight eighths. So in eighths, the benchmarks become $\frac{0}{8}$, $\frac{4}{8}$ and $\frac{8}{8}$.

Now we have two ways to compare. Is $\frac{5}{8}$ closer to 0, closer to $\frac{1}{2}$, or closer to 1?

Enrique: $\frac{5}{8}$ is closer to $\frac{1}{2}$.

▶ **Use Benchmarks to Add and Subtract** WHOLE CLASS

Fractions Write $\frac{3}{8} + \frac{5}{6}$ on the board. Ask a volunteer to explain how to use the 0, $\frac{1}{2}$, and 1 benchmarks to estimate the sum. $\frac{3}{8}$ is closer to $\frac{1}{2}$ than to 0 and $\frac{5}{6}$ is closer to 1 than to $\frac{1}{2}$; the estimate is $\frac{1}{2} + 1 = 1\frac{1}{2}$

Repeat the activity for $\frac{15}{16} - \frac{1}{3}$. $\frac{15}{16}$ is closer to 1 than to $\frac{1}{2}$ and $\frac{1}{3}$ is closer to $\frac{1}{2}$ than to 0; the estimate is $1 - \frac{1}{2} = \frac{1}{2}$

Mixed Numbers Remind students of the importance of checking their work as you write $2\frac{5}{6} + 7\frac{1}{8}$ on the board.

- **One way to check a sum of mixed numbers is to use an estimate, and one way to estimate is to round. How can rounding be used to estimate this sum?** (Lead students to conclude that rounding each addend to the nearest whole number is a good way to estimate the sum of mixed numbers.)

  Explain how to round $2\frac{5}{6}$ to the nearest whole number. Compare $\frac{5}{6}$ to $\frac{1}{2}$ and to 1; $\frac{5}{6}$ is closer to 1 than to $\frac{1}{2}$.

- **What whole number does $2\frac{5}{6}$ round to? Tell why.** $2\frac{5}{6}$ rounds up to 3 because $\frac{5}{6}$ rounds up.

  Explain how to round $7\frac{1}{8}$ to the nearest whole number. Compare $\frac{1}{8}$ to 0 and to $\frac{1}{2}$; $\frac{1}{8}$ is closer to 0 than to $\frac{1}{2}$.

- **What whole number does $7\frac{1}{8}$ round to? Tell why.** $7\frac{1}{8}$ rounds down to 7 because $\frac{1}{8}$ rounds down.

  Is $9\frac{23}{24}$ a reasonable answer for the sum of these mixed numbers? Explain why or why not. Yes; using rounding, an estimate of the sum is $3 + 7 = 10$, and 10 is close to $9\frac{23}{24}$. (The exact answer is $9\frac{23}{24}$.)

Invite volunteers to suggest other methods that can be used to estimate the sum, and write on the board to support their answers. Then write $5\frac{3}{10} - 1\frac{5}{8}$ on the board and ask questions similar to those shown above to lead students to estimate the difference.

Discuss Ask students to decide if this method will also work for 3 or more mixed numbers, and give reasons to support their answer.

Activity continued ▶

Differentiated Instruction

Advanced Learners Write the subtraction shown below on the board.

$$\begin{array}{r} 12\frac{2}{5} \\ -\ 3\frac{3}{4} \\ \hline \end{array}$$

Have students recall the concept of a *range* (the difference between the greatest and the least numbers in a set of data). Then challenge them to develop one or more ways to estimate a range for the exact difference of the numbers.

One such method involves comparing the fraction parts of the mixed numbers to identify the greater fraction. The mixed number associated with the greater fraction is rounded up and down to the nearest whole numbers. The rounded whole numbers and the whole number portion of the other mixed number are then used to establish the range.

For the example above, because $\frac{3}{4} > \frac{2}{5}$, we round $3\frac{3}{4}$ down to 3 and up to 4, and then subtract those numbers from 12.

Because we include only the greater fraction in our rounding, we ensure that the exact difference will fall within the range.

Activity 1

The Learning Classroom

Student Pairs Initially, it is useful to model activities in which students work in pairs by contrasting effective and ineffective helping. For example, students need to lead partners toward a solution, rather than doing the work for them. Helping pairs often foster learning in both students as the helper strives to adopt the perspective of the novice.

Ongoing Assessment

Make sure students understand the concept of benchmarks. Ask:

► What is a benchmark?

► What kinds of numbers can be used as benchmarks?

► Give an example of how a benchmark is used to estimate the sum or difference of two fractions or mixed numbers.

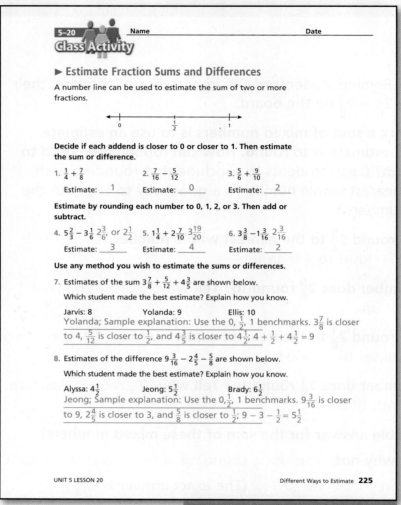

Student Activity Book page 225

► Estimate Fraction Sums and Differences PAIRS

Assign **Students Pairs** to work together and complete exercises 1–8 on Student Book page 225.

For exercises 7 and 8, point out that students may use any strategy they choose to estimate the sums and differences. Upon completion of the activity, invite a volunteer from each pair to share their answers for exercises 7 and 8 with the class.

In this lesson, students estimate sums and differences of fractions with unlike denominators. Elicit that students may use the same estimation strategies for fractions with like denominators as well.

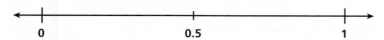

Estimate to Check for Reasonableness

▶ Decimals and Benchmarks WHOLE CLASS

Ask for Ideas Have students recall what they have learned about whole number and fraction benchmarks.

Draw the number line shown below on the board and point out that another kind of benchmark involves decimal numbers.

```
◄————————|————————————|————————————|————————►
         0           0.5           1
```

 Math Talk Write the decimal numbers 0.4 and 0.8 on the board. Invite a volunteer to work at the board and explain how the benchmarks 0, 0.5, and 1 can be used to decide if 0.4 is closer to 0 or closer to 1. Sample explanation: Draw four tick marks to the right and to the left of 0.5 to divide the distances into five equal parts, and then label the marks by tenths beginning with 0.1. We plot 0.4 and conclude that it is closer to 0 than to 1.

Then invite a second volunteer to work at the board and describe a different way to use the benchmarks 0, 0.5, and 1 to decide if 0.8 is closer to 0.5 or closer to 1. Sample explanation: Use mental math to compare. Since 8 is greater than 5, eight-tenths is greater than five-tenths, eight-tenths will be to the right of five-tenths on the number line. We plot 0.8 to see that it is closer to 1 than to 0.5.

 20 MINUTES

Goal: Estimate sums and differences to check for reasonableness.

Materials: Student Activity Book or Hardcover Book p. 226

✔ **NCTM Standards:**
Number and Operations
Problem Solving

English Language Learners
Write *estimate* and *reasonable* on the board. Ask: **Is an estimate exact?** no
• **Beginning** Say: An estimate is reasonable when it's close to the exact answer. Have students repeat.
• **Intermediate** Say: When an estimate is close to the exact answer it is __. reasonable
• **Advanced** Have students tell what makes a reasonable estimate.

Activity continued ▶

Activity 2

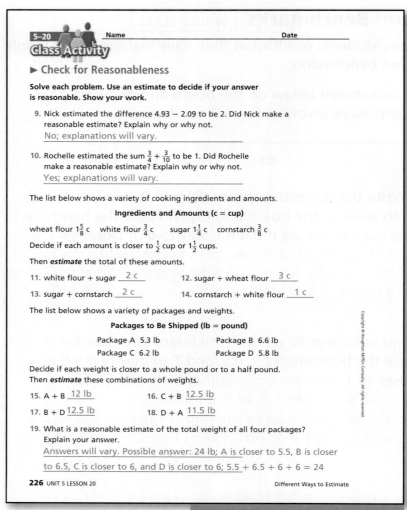

5–20

Class Activity

Name _____ Date _____

▶ **Check for Reasonableness**

Solve each problem. Use an estimate to decide if your answer is reasonable. Show your work.

9. Nick estimated the difference 4.93 − 2.09 to be 2. Did Nick make a reasonable estimate? Explain why or why not.
   No; explanations will vary.

10. Rochelle estimated the sum $\frac{3}{4} + \frac{3}{10}$ to be 1. Did Rochelle make a reasonable estimate? Explain why or why not.
    Yes; explanations will vary.

The list below shows a variety of cooking ingredients and amounts.

Ingredients and Amounts (c = cup)

wheat flour $1\frac{5}{8}$ c   white flour $\frac{3}{4}$ c   sugar $1\frac{1}{4}$ c   cornstarch $\frac{3}{8}$ c

Decide if each amount is closer to $\frac{1}{2}$ cup or $1\frac{1}{2}$ cups.

Then *estimate* the total of these amounts.

11. white flour + sugar __2 c__   12. sugar + wheat flour __3 c__

13. sugar + cornstarch __2 c__   14. cornstarch + white flour __1 c__

The list below shows a variety of packages and weights.

Packages to Be Shipped (lb = pound)

Package A 5.3 lb   Package B 6.6 lb
Package C 6.2 lb   Package D 5.8 lb

Decide if each weight is closer to a whole pound or to a half pound.
Then *estimate* these combinations of weights.

15. A + B __12 lb__   16. C + B __12.5 lb__

17. B + D __12.5 lb__   18. D + A __11.5 lb__

19. What is a reasonable estimate of the total weight of all four packages? Explain your answer.
    Answers will vary. Possible answer: 24 lb; A is closer to 5.5, B is closer to 6.5, C is closer to 6, and D is closer to 6; 5.5 + 6.5 + 6 + 6 = 24

226 UNIT 5 LESSON 20   Different Ways to Estimate

Student Activity Book page 226

Quick Quiz

See Assessment Guide for Unit 5 Quick Quiz 4.

▶ **Check for Reasonableness** SMALL GROUPS

Have students work in **Small Groups** to complete exercises 9–19 on Student Book page 226. Remind students that all of the answers in this activity involve estimates, not exact answers.

For all of the exercises on this page, some students may find it helpful to sketch and use number lines to make the estimates or to check their work.

Intervention   Activity Card 5-20

Compare Decimal Numbers   Activity Card 5-20 ●

Work: In Pairs

Use:
• Grid Paper (TRB M17)

1. To compare numbers, you can use a decimal point to align the numbers by place value.

0	.	5	3
1	.	7	

2. Copy the example at the right on grid paper. Name the place value of each column. ones, tenths, hundredths
3. Use < or > to write a comparison statement.
   0.53 < 1.7 or 1.7 > 0.53
4. **Compare** Use the alignment method shown above to help write comparison statements for each pair of numbers below.

0.27 and 1.9 0.27 < 1.9 or   4.4 and 0.99 4.4 > 0.99 or
              1.9 > 0.27   0.99 < 4.4
2.59 and 2.95 2.59 < 2.95 1.26 and 1.2 1.26 > 1.2
               or 2.95 > 2.59   or 1.2 < 1.26

Unit 5, Lesson 20   Copyright © Houghton Mifflin Company

Activity Note Remind students to compare place values from left to right. Point out that for 1.26 and 1.2, it is helpful to write a 0 in the hundredths place of 1.2 so that they are comparing 1.26 to 1.20.

 Math Writing Prompt

Make a List How many decimals in tenths are greater than 0.1 and less than 1? Explain how you know.

 **Software Support**

Warm-Up 8.37

On Level   Activity Card 5-20

Compare Decimals   Activity Card 5-20 ▲

Work: In Groups of 3

Use:
• 12 Index cards labeled 0.1, 0.2, 0.3, 0.4, 0.5, 0.6, 0.7, 0.8, 0.9, 1, 2, 3

1. **Student 1:** Shuffle the cards and select two to show the group. Then secretly write a number in tenths, hundredths, or thousandths that is between the two numbers.

0.3
2

2. **Student 2** and **Student 3:** Write a number in tenths, hundredths, or thousandths that is between the two numbers on the cards. Then write a comparison of your two numbers.

3. **Student 1:** Show your secret number. If your number is less than both other numbers, you earn 1 point. Otherwise, the player with the number less than and closer to your number earns 1 point. Exchange roles to play 10 rounds.

Unit 5, Lesson 20   Copyright © Houghton Mifflin Company

Activity Note Student 1 has an advantage if the least value possible is chosen. For example, if the cards show 0.2 and 3, choosing 0.201 ensures that no number can be less than 0.201.

 Math Writing Prompt

Summarize Explain to a younger student how to decide which decimal number is greater, 0.36 or 0.82. You may use a drawing to help you.

 Software Support

Fraction Action: Number Line Mine, Level Q

Challenge   Activity Card 5-20

Order Decimal Numbers   Activity Card 5-20 ■

Work: In Small Groups

1. On your own, write a number in tenths, hundredths, or thousandths that is between 0 and 20.

0.003 < 0.123 < 0.25
0.25 > 0.123 > 0.003

2. **Work Together** Write two comparison statements, each using all three numbers and the symbol < or >.

3. Repeat the activity for 10 rounds.

Unit 5, Lesson 20   Copyright © Houghton Mifflin Company

Activity Note Have students work in groups of 3. Each student writes one decimal. To make the second comparison, reverse the order of the numbers and the direction of the inequality symbol.

 Math Writing Prompt

Compare Measures Find the measurement in liters of two or more containers. Write an inequality that compares the capacities.

DESTINATION Math® **Software Support**

Course III: Module 4: Unit 1: Ordering and Rounding

③ Homework and Spiral Review

5–20

Homework **Goal:** Additional Practice

Use this Homework page to provide students with more practice with estimation.

5–20

Remembering **Goal:** Spiral Review

This Remembering page would be appropriate anytime after today's lesson.

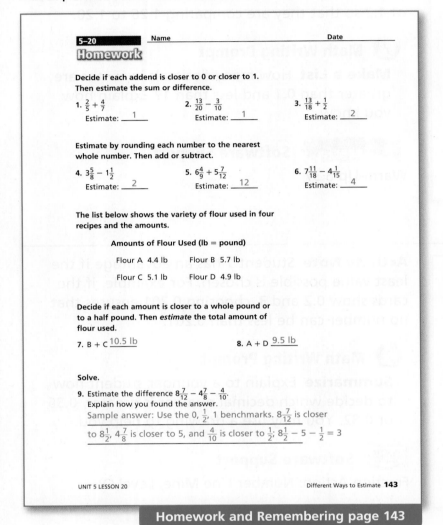

5–20 Name _____ Date _____
Homework

Decide if each addend is closer to 0 or closer to 1. Then estimate the sum or difference.

1. $\frac{2}{5} + \frac{4}{7}$
   Estimate: __1__

2. $\frac{13}{20} - \frac{3}{10}$
   Estimate: __1__

3. $\frac{13}{18} + \frac{1}{2}$
   Estimate: __2__

Estimate by rounding each number to the nearest whole number. Then add or subtract.

4. $3\frac{5}{8} - 1\frac{1}{2}$
   Estimate: __2__

5. $6\frac{4}{9} + 5\frac{7}{12}$
   Estimate: __12__

6. $7\frac{11}{18} - 4\frac{1}{15}$
   Estimate: __4__

The list below shows the variety of flour used in four recipes and the amounts.

Amounts of Flour Used (lb = pound)

Flour A 4.4 lb   Flour B 5.7 lb

Flour C 5.1 lb   Flour D 4.9 lb

Decide if each amount is closer to a whole pound or to a half pound. Then *estimate* the total amount of flour used.

7. B + C __10.5 lb__

8. A + D __9.5 lb__

Solve.

9. Estimate the difference $8\frac{7}{12} - 4\frac{7}{8} - \frac{4}{10}$.
   Explain how you found the answer.
   Sample answer: Use the 0, $\frac{1}{2}$, 1 benchmarks. $8\frac{7}{12}$ is closer
   to $8\frac{1}{2}$, $4\frac{7}{8}$ is closer to 5, and $\frac{4}{10}$ is closer to $\frac{1}{2}$; $8\frac{1}{2} - 5 - \frac{1}{2} = 3$

UNIT 5 LESSON 20   Different Ways to Estimate **143**

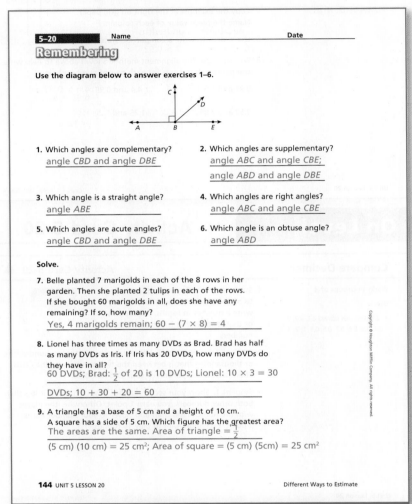

5–20 Name _____ Date _____
Remembering

Use the diagram below to answer exercises 1–6.

1. Which angles are complementary?
   angle *CBD* and angle *DBE*

2. Which angles are supplementary?
   angle *ABC* and angle *CBE*;
   angle *ABD* and angle *DBE*

3. Which angle is a straight angle?
   angle *ABE*

4. Which angles are right angles?
   angle *ABC* and angle *CBE*

5. Which angles are acute angles?
   angle *CBD* and angle *DBE*

6. Which angle is an obtuse angle?
   angle *ABD*

Solve.

7. Belle planted 7 marigolds in each of the 8 rows in her garden. Then she planted 2 tulips in each of the rows. If she bought 60 marigolds in all, does she have any remaining? If so, how many?
   Yes, 4 marigolds remain; $60 - (7 \times 8) = 4$

8. Lionel has three times as many DVDs as Brad. Brad has half as many DVDs as Iris. If Iris has 20 DVDs, how many DVDs do they have in all?
   60 DVDs; Brad: $\frac{1}{2}$ of 20 is 10 DVDs; Lionel: $10 \times 3 = 30$
   DVDs; $10 + 30 + 20 = 60$

9. A triangle has a base of 5 cm and a height of 10 cm. A square has a side of 5 cm. Which figure has the greatest area?
   The areas are the same. Area of triangle $= \frac{1}{2}$
   (5 cm) (10 cm) = 25 cm²; Area of square = (5 cm) (5cm) = 25 cm²

144 UNIT 5 LESSON 20   Different Ways to Estimate

Homework and Remembering page 143

Homework and Remembering page 144

Home or School Activity

 Real-World Connection

Estimations Have students use catalogues, the Internet, or newspaper ads to estimate the total cost of two or more items. Students should choose items with prices that are decimal numbers.

$8.35 $25.98

570 UNIT 5 LESSON 20

Use Mathematical Processes

REAL WORLD **Problem Solving**

Lesson Objectives

- Apply mathematical concepts and skills in meaningful contexts.
- Reinforce the NCTM process skills embedded in this unit, and in previous units, with a variety of problem-solving situations.

The Day at a Glance

Today's Goals	Materials	
1 Teaching the Lesson **A1: Social Studies Connection** Make a Venn diagram to represent real-world data, and use it to solve problems and to predict. **A2: Representation** Conduct a probability experiment, record results, and display results in a line plot; predict outcomes when an experiment changes. **A3: Reasoning and Proof** Differentiate between fair and unfair games involving spinners. **A4: Communication** Solve an open-ended problem involving equivalent fractions. **A5: Problem Solving** Identify and solve a problem with multiple solutions.	**Lesson Activities** Student Activity Book pp. 227–228 or Hardcover Book pp. 227–228 Homework and Remembering pp. 145–146	**Going Further** Activity Cards 5-21 Two sheets of paper Scissors Index cards Math Journals
2 Going Further ▶ Differentiated Instruction		
3 Homework and Spiral Review		

123 Use Math Talk today!

Keeping Skills Sharp

Quick Practice/Daily Routines	Classroom Management
If you wish to include Quick Practice or a Daily Routine, choose content based on the needs of your class.	Select activities from this lesson that support important goals and objectives, or that help students prepare for state or district tests.

Teaching the Lesson

Math and Social Studies

 30 MINUTES

Goals: Make a Venn diagram to represent real-world data, and use it to solve problems and to predict.

Materials: Student Activity Book or Hardcover Book p. 227

✔ **NCTM Standards:**
Connections   Representation
Communication Reasoning and Proof

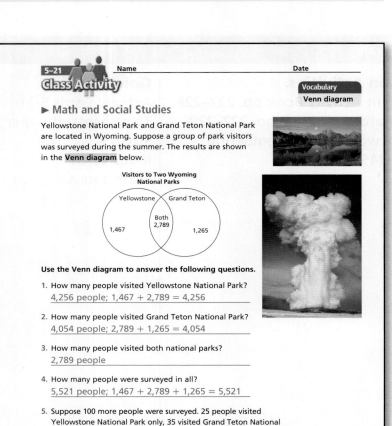

Student Activity Book page 227

▶ Creating a Venn Diagram

Task 1 Survey the class to find the students that like either blue or orange or both colors. Allow students to raise their hands only once.

Make a Venn diagram from the collected data. Discuss each section and the data it represents.

▶ What is one way to check the data in the Venn diagram? Possible answer: The 3 numbers must equal the total number of students who participated.

Then have students complete exercises 1–4 on Student Book page 227.

▶ Including More Data in a Display

Task 2 Have students work in pairs to create an empty Venn diagram with the same labels and title as shown on the Student Book page. Have students read and discuss exercise 5.

▶ How will the data in each section change? They will increase.

Find the new number of people who visited both parks. Then discuss which original numbers will increase by 25, 35, and 40.

▶ Predict Using Given Data

Math Talk

Task 3 Have students answer exercise 6 independently. Then discuss the answers as a class and compare.

Discuss Have students create other questions that require predictions based on the data given in the Venn diagram.

Have students read their questions to the class. Allow time for students to answer and then review each and how the given data are used.

Collect and Display Data

 30 MINUTES

Goals: Conduct a probability experiment, record results, and display results in a line plot; predict outcomes when an experiment changes.

Materials: Student Activity Book or Hardcover Book p. 228

 NCTM Standards:
Representation   Communication
Reasoning and Proof

Name _____   Date _____

▶ Collect and Display Data

You are going to roll two number cubes. One number cube has the numbers 1 through 6. Another number cube has the numbers 7 through 12.

7. On a separate sheet of paper, make a table like the one shown on the right. The table should include all 11 possible sums from rolling the two number cubes. Checks students' tables.

Total of 2 Cubes	Tally Marks	Number of Tosses
8		
9		

8. Roll the two number cubes together 20 times and record the results in your table. Checks students' results.

9. On a separate sheet of paper draw a line plot like the one shown below.

```
|---|---|---|---|---|---|---|---|---|---|---|
    8   9   10  11  12  13  14  15  16  17  18
```

Use your data to complete your line plot. Checks students' line plots.

10. Based on your collected data, describe the totals that are least and most likely to be thrown.
Answers will vary. Accept all reasonable answers.

11. **Predict** If you rolled the numbers cubes a total of 40 times, predict the number of tosses for each total.
Answers will vary. Accept all reasonable answers.

228 UNIT 5 LESSON 21   Use Mathematical Processes

Student Activity Book page 228

Teaching Note

In Lesson 17, students were given data and asked to analyze it. In this lesson, students collect their own data and analyze it.

▶ Organizing Possible Outcomes

Task 1 Explain that the set of all possible outcomes is called the *sample space*. Have students work in **Small Groups** to make an organized list of those outcomes.

▶ How can each outcome be found? Add a number from the first cube to all of the numbers on the second cube. Continue for each number on the first number cube.

Review each sum as a class. Then have students make the table.

▶ Creating a Data Display

Task 2 Have **Students Pairs** work together to compare the collected data. Review what each number on the base of the line plot represents and how to use the collected data to complete the line plot.

Then have students complete and share their line plots. Compare and contrast the results.

▶ Using Collected Data

Task 3 Have students share their line plots and answers to exercise 10. Allow the class time to verify that the answers are correct based on the line plot. Discuss how the answers are found.

Then discuss as a class possible ways to answer exercise 11. Allow students to share their line plots and answers with the class. Be sure the answers are reasonable.

English Language Learners

Write *probability* and *outcome*. Say: **In a probability problem, there are different possible results.**

• **Beginning** Ask: **Is a possible result an outcome?** yes
• **Intermediate and Advanced** Say: **A possible result in a probability problem is an __.** outcome

Activity 3

Fair and Unfair Games

 30 MINUTES

Goal: Differentiate between fair and unfair games involving spinners.

 NCTM Standards:
Reasoning and Proof   Communication

Develop a game that uses a spinner with 4 sections. Draw the spinner and describe how the game is played and scored. Then decide if the game is fair or unfair. Explain. Answers will vary.

Reasoning and Proof

Hold a whole-class discussion of fair and unfair games.

▶ What does it mean for a game to be fair? Each player has the same chance to win.

▶ What can make a game unfair? Possible answers: spinner has unequal sections; the scoring is skewed to one player.

Have students share their games and reasons for classifying the games as fair or unfair.

Activity 4

Equivalent Pieces

 10 MINUTES

Goal: Solve an open-ended problem involving equivalent fractions.

 NCTM Standards:
Communication   Reasoning and Proof

Tulah has $\frac{3}{4}$ yd of fabric. She cuts this into *at most* 15 and *at least* 8 smaller, equal pieces. How can she cut the fabric? What is the length of each new piece? Possible answer: She cut 9 pieces each $\frac{1}{12}$ yd long.

Communication

Remind students that $\frac{3}{4}$ is the whole in this situation, but the measurements are based on 1 yard. Discuss the meaning of *at most* and *at least*. Have **Student Pairs** discuss how to solve this problem. Here are sample questions.

▶ How can the amount of fabric she begins with be cut into 3 equal pieces? 3 pieces each $\frac{1}{4}$ yd long

▶ Now, cut one of the pieces in half. What do you get? 2 pieces each $\frac{1}{8}$ yd long

▶ Now, cut one piece that measures $\frac{1}{4}$ yard into 3 equal pieces. What do you get? 3 pieces each $\frac{1}{12}$ yd long

Activity 5

Multiple Amounts

 15 MINUTES

Goal: Identify and solve a problem with multiple solutions.

 NCTM Standards:
Problem Solving   Reasoning and Proof
Communication

Sam bought red and green apples. He wanted at least 1 more pound of red apples than green apples. The total purchase weighed $3\frac{1}{4}$ pounds. How much of each kind of apple did he buy? Possible answer: $2\frac{1}{8}$ lb red, $1\frac{1}{8}$ lb green

Problem Solving

Have students discuss clue words in the text that help them know there is more than one solution.

▶ Is there only one correct answer for this problem? Explain. No; any combination that meets the two conditions is correct.

Discuss ways to solve the problem. Then allow students to share their solutions. Have the class add each pair of amounts to check that the sum is $3\frac{1}{4}$ pounds and subtract to see that the difference is 1 pound or more.

Intervention — Activity Card 5-21

Fraction Sums and Differences — Activity Card 5-21 ●

Work In Pairs

Use:
• Two sheets of the same paper
• Scissors

1. Fold a sheet of paper into 4 equal sections and another sheet into 8 equal sections. Cut out the sections keeping sets separate.

2. Separate each set into two groups. Write an addition problem and a subtraction problem involving fractions that represents this action.

3. **Look Back** Should each sum have been the same? Why or why not? Yes; the whole for each set is 1.

4. **Analyze** Why was the minuend the same in each subtraction problem? Each subtraction begins with the whole, which is 1.

Unit 5, Lesson 21   Copyright © Houghton Mifflin Company

Activity Note Pair students so that at least one can easily cut equal sections.

 Math Writing Prompt

Explain Your Thinking Explain how $\frac{1}{4} + \frac{3}{8}$ can be modeled using the sets. Add two eighths and three eighths for a sum of five eighths.

 **Software Support**

Warm-Up 20.22

On Level — Activity Card 5-21

Pick a Card — Activity Card 5-21 ▲

Work: In Pairs

Use:
• 10 index cards

1. Write the numbers 1–10 each on a different index card. Place the cards face down.

2. Select a card, record the number, and replace the card in the deck. Repeat this for a total of 10 times.

3. **Look Back** What fraction of the recorded numbers were even? Simplify the fraction if needed. Answers will vary.

4. **Decide** If you continued this for a total of 20 times, how many times do you think an even number would be selected? Possible answer: Twice the recorded amount.

Unit 5, Lesson 21   Copyright © Houghton Mifflin Company

Activity Note Have students repeat the activity to see if the results change.

 Math Writing Prompt

Compare Write the probability of choosing an even number as a fraction. $\frac{5}{10}$ or $\frac{1}{2}$ Compare this probability to the actual results of the experiment.

 Software Support

Fraction Action: Last Chance Canyon, Level I

Challenge — Activity Card 5-21

Make a Number — Activity Card 5-21 ■

Work: In Small Groups

1. $3\frac{4}{5}, 3\frac{5}{4}, 4\frac{3}{5}, 4\frac{5}{3}, 5\frac{3}{4}, 5\frac{4}{3},$ 3.45, 3.54, 4.35, 4.53, 5.34, 5.43

1. Write as many different mixed and decimal numbers as you can using the digits 3, 4, and 5 once per number.

2. Be sure everyone in the group has written the same numbers.

3. **Work Together** Each group member adds two mixed or decimal numbers. Answers will vary.

4. Each group member adds one mixed number and one decimal number. Answers will vary.

5. Share the methods you used to find the sums.

Unit 5, Lesson 21   Copyright © Houghton Mifflin Company

Activity Note You many want to give students two examples, such as 3.45 and $3\frac{4}{5}$.

 Math Writing Prompt

Explain Your Reasoning Add the greatest and least numbers. Explain how you compared the numbers and found the sum.

 Software Support

Course III: Module 4: Unit 2: Adding Decimals

③ Homework and Spiral Review

5-21
Homework **Goal:** Additional Practice

✓ Include students' completed Homework page as part of their portfolios.

5-21
Remembering **Goal:** Spiral Review

This Remembering page would be appropriate anytime after today's lesson.

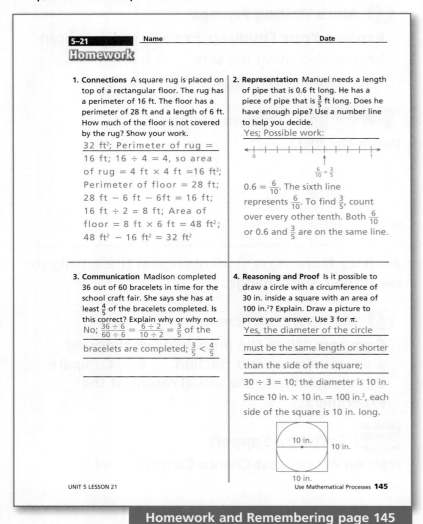

5-21 Name _____ Date _____
Homework

1. **Connections** A square rug is placed on top of a rectangular floor. The rug has a perimeter of 16 ft. The floor has a perimeter of 28 ft and a length of 6 ft. How much of the floor is not covered by the rug? Show your work.
32 ft²; Perimeter of rug = 16 ft; 16 ÷ 4 = 4, so area of rug = 4 ft × 4 ft =16 ft²; Perimeter of floor = 28 ft; 28 ft − 6 ft − 6 ft = 16 ft; 16 ft ÷ 2 = 8 ft; Area of floor = 8 ft × 6 ft = 48 ft²; 48 ft² − 16 ft² = 32 ft²

2. **Representation** Manuel needs a length of pipe that is 0.6 ft long. He has a piece of pipe that is $\frac{3}{5}$ ft long. Does he have enough pipe? Use a number line to help you decide.
Yes; Possible work:
$0.6 = \frac{6}{10}$. The sixth line represents $\frac{6}{10}$. To find $\frac{3}{5}$, count over every other tenth. Both $\frac{6}{10}$ or 0.6 and $\frac{3}{5}$ are on the same line.

3. **Communication** Madison completed 36 out of 60 bracelets in time for the school craft fair. She says she has at least $\frac{4}{5}$ of the bracelets completed. Is this correct? Explain why or why not.
No; $\frac{36 \div 6}{60 \div 6} = \frac{6 \div 2}{10 \div 2} = \frac{3}{5}$ of the bracelets are completed; $\frac{3}{5} < \frac{4}{5}$

4. **Reasoning and Proof** Is it possible to draw a circle with a circumference of 30 in. inside a square with an area of 100 in.²? Explain. Draw a picture to prove your answer. Use 3 for π.
Yes, the diameter of the circle must be the same length or shorter than the side of the square; 30 ÷ 3 = 10; the diameter is 10 in. Since 10 in. × 10 in. = 100 in.², each side of the square is 10 in. long.

UNIT 5 LESSON 21 · Use Mathematical Processes **145**

Homework and Remembering page 145

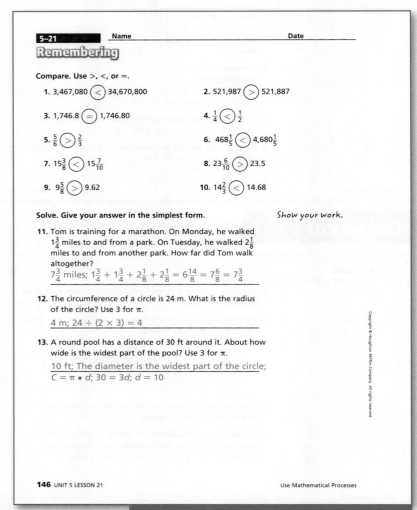

5-21 Name _____ Date _____
Remembering

Compare. Use >, <, or =.

1. 3,467,080 (<) 34,670,800
2. 521,987 (>) 521,887
3. 1,746.8 (=) 1,746.80
4. $\frac{1}{4}$ (<) $\frac{1}{2}$
5. $\frac{5}{6}$ (>) $\frac{2}{3}$
6. $468\frac{1}{5}$ (<) $4,680\frac{1}{5}$
7. $15\frac{3}{8}$ (<) $15\frac{7}{10}$
8. $23\frac{6}{10}$ (>) 23.5
9. $9\frac{5}{8}$ (>) 9.62
10. $14\frac{2}{3}$ (<) 14.68

Solve. Give your answer in the simplest form. *Show your work.*

11. Tom is training for a marathon. On Monday, he walked $1\frac{3}{4}$ miles to and from a park. On Tuesday, he walked $2\frac{1}{8}$ miles to and from another park. How far did Tom walk altogether?
$7\frac{3}{4}$ miles; $1\frac{3}{4} + 1\frac{3}{4} + 2\frac{1}{8} + 2\frac{1}{8} = 6\frac{14}{8} = 7\frac{6}{8} = 7\frac{3}{4}$

12. The circumference of a circle is 24 m. What is the radius of the circle? Use 3 for π.
4 m; 24 ÷ (2 × 3) = 4

13. A round pool has a distance of 30 ft around it. About how wide is the widest part of the pool? Use 3 for π.
10 ft; The diameter is the widest part of the circle; $C = π \cdot d$; 30 = 3d; d = 10

146 UNIT 5 LESSON 21 · Use Mathematical Processes

Homework and Remembering page 146

Home or School Activity

 Real-World Connection

Sale Advertisements Have students find sale advertisements in the newspaper or on the Internet.

Then have students look for fractions used in the advertisements, such as $\frac{1}{3}$ off the original price. Have students find the fraction of the original price that is paid. For example, you pay $\frac{2}{3}$ of the original price if it is on sale for $\frac{1}{3}$ off.

Allow students to share with the class. Have students determine the best sale for related items.

Unit Review and Test

UNIT 5

Lesson Objectives

● **Assess student progress on unit objectives.**

The Day at a Glance

Today's Goals	Materials
1 Assessing the Unit ▶ Assess student progress on unit objectives. ▶ Use activities from unit lessons to reteach content. **2 Extending the Assessment** ▶ Use remediation for common errors. There is no homework assignment on a test day.	Unit 5 Test, Student Activity Book pp. 229–230 or Hardcover Book pp. 229–230 Unit 5 Test, Form A or B, Assessment Guide (optional) Unit 5 Performance Assessment, Assessment Guide (optional)

Keeping Skills Sharp

Quick Practice 5 MINUTES	
Goal: Review any skills you choose to meet the needs of your class. If you are doing a unit review day, use any of the Quick Practice activities that provide support for your class. If this is a test day, omit Quick Practice.	**Review and Test Day** You may want to choose a quiet game or other activity (reading a book or working on homework for another subject) for students who finish early.

1 Assessing the Unit

Assess Unit Objectives

🕐 **45 MINUTES** (more if schedule permits)

Goal: Assess student progress on unit objectives.

Materials: Student Activity Book or Hardcover Book pp. 229–230, Assessment Guide (optional)

▶ Review and Assessment

If your students are ready for assessment on the unit objectives, you may use either the test on the Student Book pages or one of the forms of the Unit 5 Test in the Assessment Guide to assess student progress.

If you feel that students need some review first, you may use the test on the Student Book pages as a review of unit content, and then use one of the forms of the Unit 5 Test in the Assessment Guide to assess student progress.

To assign a numerical score for all of these test forms, use 10 points for each question.

You may also choose to use the Unit 5 Performance Assessment. Scoring for that assessment can be found in its rubric in the Assessment Guide.

▶ Reteaching Resources

The chart lists the test items, the unit objectives they cover, and the lesson activities in which the objective is covered in this unit. You may revisit these activities with students who do not show mastery of the objectives.

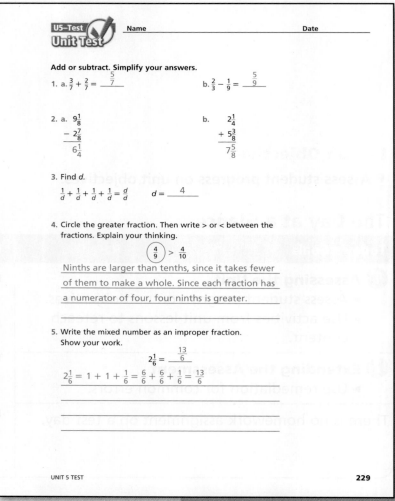

Student Activity Book page 229

Unit Test Items	Unit Objectives Tested	Activities to Use for Reteaching
1–2	**5.1** Add and subtract fractions and mixed numbers with like and unlike denominators.	Lesson 1, Activity 1 Lesson 3, Activities 1–2 Lesson 7, Activities 1–2 Lesson 8, Activities 1–2 Lesson 14, Activity 1 Lesson 15, Activity 1 Lesson 16, Activity 1
4, 6, 7	**5.2** Compare and order fractions, decimals, and mixed numbers.	Lesson 2, Activities 1–2 Lesson 9, Activity 1 Lesson 18, Activities 1–2 Lesson 19, Activities 1–2
3	**5.3** Relate fractions and wholes.	Lessons 4–6, Activity 1

U5–Test
Unit Test

Name _____ Date _____

6. Write these fractions in order from **least to greatest**.

$\frac{3}{8}$, $7\frac{1}{2}$, $\frac{4}{4}$, $\frac{8}{16}$, $\frac{5}{2}$ $\frac{3}{8}$, $\frac{8}{16}$, $\frac{4}{4}$, $\frac{5}{2}$, $7\frac{1}{2}$

7. Write these numbers in order from **greatest to least**.

$\frac{3}{5}$, 5.202, $\frac{100}{100}$, 0.7, $\frac{8}{5}$ 5.202, $\frac{8}{5}$, $\frac{100}{100}$, 0.7, $\frac{3}{5}$

8. Write the fraction that is equivalent to $\frac{9}{10}$. Show your work.

$\frac{32}{40}$ $\frac{81}{100}$ $\boxed{\frac{36}{40}}$

$\frac{32 \div 4}{40 \div 4} = \frac{8}{10}$ $\frac{36 \div 4}{40 \div 4} = \frac{9}{10}$

_____

Solve. Simplify your answer.   *Show your work.*

9. Kendra has 6 red marbles and 2 blue marbles in a bag. She reaches in and chooses one without looking. What is the probability that it is a blue marble?

$\frac{1}{4}$

10. **Extended Response** Terry worked in the garden for $\frac{3}{4}$ hour. Peter worked in the garden for $\frac{1}{6}$ hour more than Terry. How many hours did they work in the garden altogether?

First, calculate how long Peter has worked.

Add both fractions together. $\frac{3}{4} + \frac{1}{6} = \frac{11}{12}$

Peter has worked $\frac{11}{12}$ hour. Now add

these two together to calculate the total

number of hours they worked in the garden

altogether. $\frac{3}{4} + \frac{11}{12} = \frac{20}{12} = 1\frac{2}{3}$

Together, they have worked $1\frac{2}{3}$ hours in the

garden.

* Item 10 also assesses the Process Skills of Problem Solving and Communication.

230 UNIT 5 TEST

Student Activity Book page 230

Unit Test Items	Unit Objectives Tested	Activities to Use for Reteaching
5, 8	**5.4** Find equivalent fractions.	Lesson 6, Activity 2 Lesson 11, Activities 1–2 Lesson 12, Activities 1–2 Lesson 13, Activities 1–2 Lesson 18, Activities 1–2 Lesson 19, Activities 1–2
9	**5.5** Express the probability of an event as a fraction.	Lesson 17, Activities 1–2 Lesson 21, Activity 2
10	**5.6** Solve problems involving fractions.	Lesson 9, Activities 2–3 Lesson 10, Activity 1 Lesson 14, Activity 2 Lesson 20, Activities 1–2

▶ Assessment Resources

Free Response Tests
Unit 5 Test Student Activity Book or Hardcover Book pp. 229–230
Unit 5 Test, Form A, Assessment Guide

Extended Response Item
The last item in the Student Book test and in the Form A test will require an extended response as an answer.

Multiple Choice Test
Unit 5 Test, Form B, Assessment Guide

Performance Assessment
Unit 5 Performance Assessment, Assessment Guide
Unit 5 Performance Assessment Rubric, Assessment Guide

▶ Portfolio Assessment

Teacher-selected Items for Student Portfolios:

- Homework, Lessons 3, 6, 9, 11, 13, 14, 15, 16, 17, and 21

- Class Activity work, Lessons 3, 8, 10, 15, 17, and 21

Student-selected Items for Student Portfolios:

- Favorite Home or School Activity

- Best Writing Prompt

② Extending the Assessment

Unit Objective 5.1

Add and subtract fractions and mixed numbers with like and unlike denominators.

Common Error: Ungroups Incorrectly

When ungrouping is necessary for a subtraction, students may forget to add the fractional part of the mixed number to the ungrouped whole.

Remediation Encourage students who are experiencing difficulty to write out all of the steps. For example, when ungrouping $2\frac{1}{4}$, write $2\frac{1}{4} = 1 + \frac{4}{4} + \frac{1}{4} = 1 + \frac{5}{4}$. They can also think of ungrouping in terms of money. Two one-dollar bills and one quarter is the same amount of money as 1 one-dollar bill and 5 quarters.

Unit Objective 5.2

Compare and order fractions, decimals, and mixed numbers.

Common Error: Misidentifies the Greater Fraction

Some students may think the greater denominator indicates the greater fraction.

Remediation Remind students that the <u>d</u>enominator tells the number of <u>d</u>ivisions of the whole. If the same whole is divided into more parts, each part must be smaller. Talk about sharing a pizza. Ask students which piece will be bigger—the one they will get if the pizza is shared equally by 4 friends, or the one they will get if the pizza is shared equally by three friends.

Unit Objective 5.3

Relate fractions and wholes.

Common Error: Writes an Incorrect Denominator

Students may have trouble deciding into how many parts the whole has been divided.

Remediation Draw a square divided into four smaller squares on the board and shade one of the smaller squares. Write $\frac{part}{whole}$ beside the picture. Ask students how many parts are shaded and how many parts are not. Then ask how many parts make up the whole. Ask why it doesn't make sense to say that the picture represents $\frac{1}{3}$.

Unit Objective 5.4

Find equivalent fractions.

Common Error: Has Difficulty Determining Equivalence

Some students find it difficult to compare fractions for equivalence.

Remediation Encourage students to look for the relationship between the numerators and compare it to the relationship between the denominators. Write $\frac{2}{3} \longrightarrow \frac{4}{12}$ on the board. Ask students what the 2 on the left has been multiplied by to get 4 and what the 3 on the left has been multiplied by to get 12. Since the answers are different, the fractions are not equivalent.

Unit Objective 5.5

Express the probability of an event as a fraction.

Common Error: Records Probability Incorrectly

Students may be confused about what each part of the fraction represents when it describes a probability.

Remediation Discuss with the class the meaning of the numerator as the number of favorable outcomes and the denominator as total number of outcomes. To reinforce the ideas, roll a number cube, and ask students to name the possible outcomes. Write 6 for the denominator in a probability fraction. Then ask about the number of favorable outcomes for an event, such as rolling a 1 or rolling an even number. Record the appropriate number in the numerator.

Unit Objective 5.6

Solve problems involving fractions.

Common Error: Forgets to Simplify the Answer

Some students may not remember to write their answers in simplest form.

Remediation Remind students that answers are often easier to understand when presented in simplest form. This may involve regrouping or finding the simplest equivalent fraction, or both. For example, the answer $\frac{20}{12}$ hours can be regrouped to $1\frac{8}{12}$ hours, then further simplified to $1\frac{2}{3}$ hours.

Unit 6 Overview

Volume, Capacity, and Weight

IN THIS UNIT, students examine and apply important relationships in measurement. They begin by using what they know about length and area to develop a formula for volume. Then students change the length or the area of a figure and predict how the volume will change. Later in the unit, students compare volume and capacity, and mass and weight. Activities in this unit provide students with opportunities to build familiarity with both metric and customary units of measure.

Skills Trace	
Grade 4	**Grade 5**
• Convert among customary or metric units of length, capacity, and weight or mass. • Apply units of length to calculate area and volume. • Choose the appropriate unit of measure and tool. • Solve problems involving customary or metric units of measure. • Solve problems involving elapsed time.	• Convert among customary or metric units of length, capacity, and weight or mass. • Apply units of length to calculate area and volume. • Choose the appropriate unit of measure and tool. • Solve problems involving customary or metric units of measure. • Relate length, area, and volume. • Identify the use of negative numbers in real-world situations. • Solve problems involving elapsed time.

Unit 6 Contents

Unit 6   Assessment

✓ Unit Objectives Tested	Unit Test Items	Lessons
6.1 Find the volume of a rectangular prism.	1–3, 5, 9	1, 2
6.2 Solve problems involving capacity, mass, and weight.	6–8, 10	3, 4
6.3 Solve problems involving elapsed time.	4	7

Assessment and Review Resources

Formal Assessment	Informal Assessment	Review Opportunities

Formal Assessment

Student Activity Book
- Unit Review and Test (pp. 255–256)

Assessment Guide
- Quick Quiz 1 (p. A60)
- Quick Quiz 2 (p. A61)
- Quick Quiz 3 (p. A62)
- Test A—Open Response (pp. A63–A64)
- Test B—Multiple Choice (pp. A65–A66)
- Performance Assessment (pp. A67–A69)

Test Generator CD-ROM
- Open Response Test
- Multiple Choice Test
- Test Bank Items

Informal Assessment

Teacher Edition
- Ongoing Assessment (in every lesson)
- Math Talk (in every lesson)
- Portfolio Suggestions (p. 637)

(123) Math Talk
- ▸ The Learning Classroom (p. 614)
- ▸ Math Talk in Action (pp. 583, 588, 597, 608, 628)
- ▸ In Activities (pp. 618, 622, 624, 630)
- ▸ Solve and Discuss (pp. 584, 592, 597, 598, 603, 604, 610, 612, 621, 622, 623, 629)
- ▸ Student Pairs (pp. 589, 592, 619, 620, 631, 632)
  Helping Partners (pp. 612, 628)
- ▸ Small Groups (pp. 598, 602, 609, 610, 622, 623, 631)

Review Opportunities

Homework and Remembering
- Review of recently taught topics
- Spiral Review

Teacher Edition
- Unit Review and Test (pp. 635–638)

Test Generator CD-ROM
- Custom review sheets

Planning Unit 6

Lesson NCTM Focal Points NCTM Standards	Resources	Materials for Lesson Activities	Materials for Going Further
6-1 **Cubic Units and Volume** NCTM Focal Points: 3.2, 3.3, 3.4, 3.5, 3.6, 3.8, 5.1 NCTM Standards: 3, 4, 8	TE pp. 581–586 SAB pp. 231–234 H&R pp. 147–148 AC 6-1	Centimeter or inch cubes	Centimeter or inch cubes Meter sticks Math Journals
6-2 **Relate Length, Area, and Volume** NCTM Focal Points: 3.2, 3.3, 3.4, 3.5, 3.6, 3.8 NCTM Standards: 2, 3, 4, 6, 7, 9	TE pp. 587–594 SAB pp. 235–238 H&R pp. 149–150 AC 6-2 MCC 25 AG Quick Quiz 1	Centimeter-Grid Paper (TRB M18)	Centimeter or inch cubes Centimeter-Grid Paper (TRB M18) Math Journals
6-3 **Measures of Capacity** NCTM Focal Points: 5.1, 5.2 NCTM Standards: 1, 3, 4, 8	TE pp. 595–600 SAB pp. 239–240 H&R pp. 151–152 AC 6-3 MCC 26	Containers and boxes	Customary and metric measuring cups and spoons Eyedropper Variety of containers Math Journals
6-4 **Measures of Mass and Weight** NCTM Focal Points: 5.1, 5.2 NCTM Standards: 1, 4, 8	TE pp. 601–606 SAB pp. 241–242 H&R pp. 153–154 AC 6-4 MCC 27, 28	Balance scale and classroom objects (optional)	Math Journals
6-5 **Working With Measurement Units (Optional)** NCTM Focal Point: 5.2 NCTM Standards: 1, 4, 9	TE pp. 607–616 SAB pp. 243–244 H&R pp. 155–156 AC 6-5 AG Quick Quiz 2	Several plastic containers Several objects	Centimeter ruler Scissors Box-shaped objects Math Journals

Resources/Materials Key: TE: Teacher Edition SAB: Student Activity Book H&R: Homework and Remembering
AC: Activity Cards MCC: Math Center Challenge AG: Assessment Guide ✓: Grade 5 kits TRB: Teacher's Resource Book

NCTM Standards and Expectations Key: 1. Number and Operations 2. Algebra 3. Geometry
4. Measurement 5. Data Analysis and Probability 6. Problem Solving 7. Reasoning and Proof
8. Communication 9. Connections 10. Representation

Lesson NCTM Focal Points NCTM Standards	Resources	Materials for Lesson Activities	Materials for Going Further
6-6 **Temperature (Optional)** NCTM Focal Point: 7.3 NCTM Standards: 1, 4, 5, 6, 7, 9, 10	TE pp. 617–626 SAB pp. 245–250 H&R pp. 157–158 AC 6-6	None	Calculator Math Journals
6-7 **The Passing of Time** NCTM Standards: 1, 4, 6	TE pp. 627–634 SAB pp. 251–254 H&R pp. 159–160 AC 6-7 AG Quick Quiz 3	Calculator	Clock face (optional) Index cards Rulers Scissors Math Journals
Unit Review and Test	TE pp. 635–638 SAB pp. 255–256 AG Unit 6 Tests		

Hardcover Student Book

- Together, the Hardcover Student Book and its companion Activity Workbook contain all of the pages in the consumable Student Activity Book.

Manipulatives and Materials

- Essential materials for teaching *Math Expressions* are available in the Grade 5 kits. These materials are indicated by a ✓ in these lists. At the front of this Teacher Edition is more information about kit contents, alternatives for the materials, and use of the materials.

Independent Learning Activities

Ready-Made Math Challenge Centers

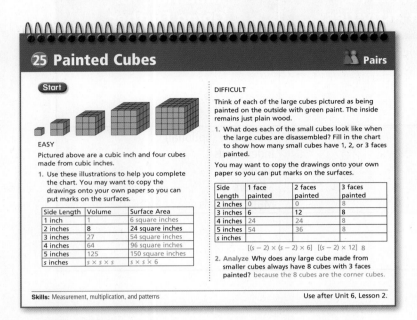

25 Painted Cubes — Pairs

Start

EASY

Pictured above are a cubic inch and four cubes made from cubic inches.

1. Use these illustrations to help you complete the chart. You may want to copy the drawings onto your own paper so you can put marks on the surfaces.

Side Length	Volume	Surface Area
1 inch	1	6 square inches
2 inches	8	24 square inches
3 inches	27	54 square inches
4 inches	64	96 square inches
5 inches	125	150 square inches
s inches	$s \times s \times s$	$s \times s \times 6$

DIFFICULT

Think of each of the large cubes pictured as being painted on the outside with green paint. The inside remains just plain wood.

1. What does each of the small cubes look like when the large cubes are disassembled? Fill in the chart to show how many small cubes have 1, 2, or 3 faces painted.

You may want to copy the drawings onto your own paper so you can put marks on the surfaces.

Side Length	1 face painted	2 faces painted	3 faces painted
2 inches	0	0	8
3 inches	6	12	8
4 inches	24	24	8
5 inches	54	36	8
s inches	$[(s-2) \times (s-2) \times 6]$	$[(s-2) \times 12]$	8

2. Analyze Why does any large cube made from smaller cubes always have 8 cubes with 3 faces painted? because the 8 cubes are the corner cubes.

Skills: Measurement, multiplication, and patterns   Use after Unit 6, Lesson 2.

Grouping Pairs

Materials Cubes (optional)

Objective Students find patterns for volume, surface area, and painted faces of cubes.

Connections Computation and Algebra

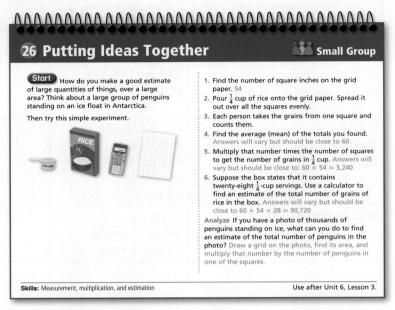

26 Putting Ideas Together — Small Group

Start How do you make a good estimate of large quantities of things, over a large area? Think about a large group of penguins standing on an ice float in Antarctica.

Then try this simple experiment.

1. Find the number of square inches on the grid paper. 54
2. Pour $\frac{1}{4}$ cup of rice onto the grid paper. Spread it out over all the squares evenly.
3. Each person takes the grains from one square and counts them.
4. Find the average (mean) of the totals you found. Answers will vary but should be close to 60.
5. Multiply that number times the number of squares to get the number of grains in $\frac{1}{4}$ cup. Answers will vary but should be close to: $60 \times 54 = 3,240$
6. Suppose the box states that it contains twenty-eight $\frac{1}{4}$-cup servings. Use a calculator to find an estimate of the total number of grains of rice in the box. Answers will vary but should be close to $60 \times 54 \times 28 = 90,720$

Analyze If you have a photo of thousands of penguins standing on ice, what can you do to find an estimate of the total number of penguins in the photo? Draw a grid on the photo, find its area, and multiply that number by the number of penguins in one of the squares.

Skills: Measurement, multiplication, and estimation   Use after Unit 6, Lesson 3.

Grouping Small Group

Materials $\frac{1}{4}$ cup rice, Inch-Grid Paper (TRB M1), calculator

Objective Students use area to estimate the number of grains of rice in a box.

Connections Real World and Estimation

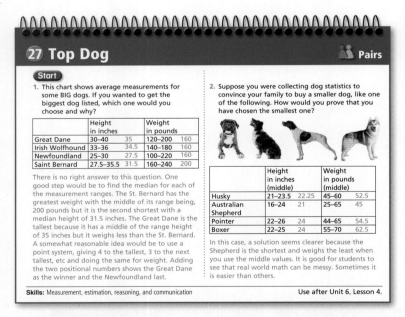

27 Top Dog — Pairs

Start

1. This chart shows average measurements for some BIG dogs. If you wanted to get the biggest dog listed, which one would you choose and why?

	Height in inches		Weight in pounds	
Great Dane	30–40	35	120–200	160
Irish Wolfhound	33–36	34.5	140–180	160
Newfoundland	25–30	27.5	100–220	160
Saint Bernard	27.5–35.5	31.5	160–240	200

There is no right answer to this question. One good step would be to find the median for each of the measurement ranges. The St. Bernard has the greatest weight with the middle of its range being, 200 pounds but it is the second shortest with a median height of 31.5 inches. The Great Dane is the tallest because it has a middle of the range height of 35 inches but it weighs less than the St. Bernard. A somewhat reasonable idea would be to use a point system, giving 4 to the tallest, 3 to the next tallest, etc and doing the same for weight. Adding the two positional numbers shows the Great Dane as the winner and the Newfoundland last.

2. Suppose you were collecting dog statistics to convince your family to buy a smaller dog, like one of the following. How would you prove that you have chosen the smallest one?

	Height in inches (middle)		Weight in pounds (middle)	
Husky	21–23.5	22.25	45–60	52.5
Australian Shepherd	16–24	21	25–65	45
Pointer	22–26	24	44–65	54.5
Boxer	22–25	24	55–70	62.5

In this case, a solution seems clearer because the Shepherd is the shortest and weighs the least when you use the middle values. It is good for students to see that real world math can be messy. Sometimes it is easier than others.

Skills: Measurement, estimation, reasoning, and communication   Use after Unit 6, Lesson 4.

Grouping Pairs

Materials None

Objective Students compare the size of dogs, using a table of measurements.

Connections Measurement and Real World

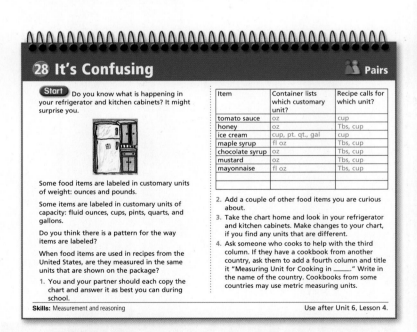

28 It's Confusing — Pairs

Start Do you know what is happening in your refrigerator and kitchen cabinets? It might surprise you.

Some food items are labeled in customary units of weight: ounces and pounds.

Some items are labeled in customary units of capacity: fluid ounces, cups, pints, quarts, and gallons.

Do you think there is a pattern for the way items are labeled?

When food items are used in recipes from the United States, are they measured in the same units that are shown on the package?

1. You and your partner should each copy the chart and answer it as best you can during school.

Item	Container lists which customary unit?	Recipe calls for which unit?
tomato sauce	oz	cup
honey	oz	Tbs, cup
ice cream	cup, pt. qt., gal	cup
maple syrup	fl oz	Tbs, cup
chocolate syrup	oz	Tbs, cup
mustard	oz	Tbs, cup
mayonnaise	fl oz	Tbs, cup

2. Add a couple of other food items you are curious about.
3. Take the chart home and look in your refrigerator and kitchen cabinets. Make changes to your chart, if you find any units that are different.
4. Ask someone who cooks to help with the third column. If they have a cookbook from another country, ask them to add a fourth column and title it "Measuring Unit for Cooking in _____." Write in the name of the country. Cookbooks from some countries may use metric measuring units.

Skills: Measurement and reasoning   Use after Unit 6, Lesson 4.

Grouping Pairs

Materials Food items at home, recipe book

Objective Students list units of measurement for food items.

Connections Measurement and Real World

Ready-Made Math Resources

Technology — Tutorials, Practice, and Intervention

Use online, individualized intervention and support to bring students to proficiency.

Help students practice skills and apply concepts through exciting math adventures.

Extend and enrich students' understanding of skills and concepts through engaging, interactive lessons and activities.

Visit **Education Place**
www.eduplace.com

Visit www.eduplace.com/mx2t/ and find family, teacher, and student materials, activities, games, and more.

Literature Link

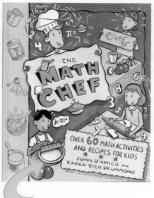

The Math Chef

The Math Chef
Children will learn about metric and customary measurement in this book of recipes written by Joan D'Amico and Karen Eich Drummond. The recipes include everything from cherry-baked apples to tortilla 'n' cheese fiesta salad! Students also will find math facts and math activities interspersed among the recipes.

Unit 6   Teaching Resources

Differentiated Instruction

Individualizing Instruction

Activities	Level	Frequency
	• Intervention • On Level • Challenge	All 3 in every lesson

Math Writing Prompts	Level	Frequency
	• Intervention • On Level • Challenge	All 3 in every lesson

Math Center Challenges	For advanced students
	4 in every unit

Reaching All Learners

English Language Learners	Lessons	Pages
	1, 2, 3, 4, 5, 6, 7	581, 587, 591, 595, 601, 607, 617, 627
Extra Help	Lessons	Pages
	2, 5, 6, 7	590, 610, 619, 620, 622, 631
Special Needs	Lesson	Pages
	6	618, 623
Advanced Learners	Lessons	Pages
	2, 4	589, 604

Strategies for English Language Learners

Present this problem to all students. Offer the different levels of support to meet students' levels of language proficiency.

Objective Review three-dimensional shapes and volume.

Problem Draw a square, rectangle, cube, and rectangular prism on the board. Write *two-dimensional*, *three-dimensional*, and *volume*.

Newcomer

• Point to the square and then the cube. Say: **A square is two-dimensional. A cube is three-dimensional.** Have students repeat. Continue with other shapes.

Beginning

• Model a cube. Say: **A cube takes up space. It has volume.** Have students repeat. Point to the square. Ask: **Does a square have volume?** no

• Say: **A square is two-dimensional.** Ask: **Is a cube two-dimensional?** no **three-dimensional?** yes Continue with other shapes.

Intermediate

• Have students identify the shapes. Model a cube. Ask: **Which has volume, a cube or a square?** cube

• Say: **Three-dimensional shapes have volume. A cube is __.** three-dimensional Continue with the rectangular prism.

Advanced

• Have students identify each shape. Say: **We measure length × width × height to find __.** volume Say: **Cubes and rectangular prisms have __.** volume

• Say: **Shapes with volume are three-dimensional.** Have students identify the three-dimensional shapes.

Connections

Language Arts Connection
Lesson 2, page 594

Multicultural Connection
Lesson 3, page 600

Real-World Connections
Lesson 5, page 616
Lesson 7, page 634

Science Connection
Lesson 4, page 606

Social Studies Connection
Lesson 6, page 626

Math Background

Putting Research into Practice for Unit 6

From Current Research: Volume Measure

The measure of volume presents some additional complexities for reasoning about the structure of space, primarily because units of measure must be defined and coordinated in three dimensions. The research conducted often blends classroom study with description of individual change, so this section and the one that follows on angle measure reflect this synthesis.

An emerging body of work addresses the strategies that students employ to structure a volume, given a unit. For example, Battista and Clements (1998) noted a range of strategies employed by students in the third and fifth grades to mentally structure a three-dimensional array of cubes. Many students, especially the younger ones, could count only the faces of the cubes, resulting in frequent instances of multiple counts of a single cubic unit and a failure to count any cubic units in the interior of the cube. The majority of fifth-grade students, but only about 20% of third-grade students, structured the array as a series of layers. Layering enabled students to count the number of units in one layer and then multiply or skip-count to obtain the total number of cubic units in the cube. These findings suggest that, as with area and length, students' models of spatial structure influence their conceptions of its measure.

Classroom studies again suggest that forms of representation heavily influence how students conceive of structuring volume. For example, third-grade students with a wide range of experiences and representations of volume measure structured space as three-dimensional arrays. Unlike the younger students described in the Battista and Clements (1998) study, all could structure cubes as three-dimensional arrays. Most even came to conceive of volume as a product of area and height (Lehrer, Strom, & Confrey, 2002).

Battista (1999) followed the activity of three pairs of fifth-grade students as they predicted the number of cubes that fit in graphically depicted boxes. He found that student learning was affected both by individual activity and by socially constituted practices like collective reflection. Thus, traditional notions about trajectories of development may need to be revised in light of more careful attention to classroom talk and related means of representing volume.

Lehrer, Richard. "Developing Understanding of Measurement." *A Research Companion to Principles and Standards for School Mathematics.* Eds. Jeremy Kilpatrick et al. Reston: NCTM, 2003. pp. 190–191.

Other Useful References: Volume, Capacity, and Weight

Battista, M. T. (1999). Fifth graders' enumeration of cubes in 3D arrays: Conceptual progress in an inquiry classroom. *Journal for Research in Mathematics Education, 30,* pp. 417–448.

Battista, M. T., & Clements, D. H. (1998). Students' understanding of three-dimensional cube arrays: Findings from a research and curriculum development project. In R. Lehrer & D. Chazan (Eds.), *Designing learning environments for developing understanding of geometry and space* (pp. 227–248). Mahwah, NJ: Erlbaum.

Learning Math: Geometry. Annenberg/CPB Learner.org. 1997–2004. <www.learner.org/resources/series167.html>.

Learning Math: Measurement. Annenberg/CPB Learner.org. 1997–2004. <www.learner.org/resources/series184.html>.

Lehrer, R., Strom, D., & Confrey, J. (2002). Grounding metaphors and inscriptional resonance: Children's emerging understanding of mathematical similarity. *Cognition and Instruction 20,* pp. 359–398.

National Council of Teachers of Mathematics. *Learning and Teaching Measurement* (NCTM 2003 Yearbook). Ed. Douglas H. Clements. Reston: NCTM, 2003.

National Council of Teachers of Mathematics. *Principles and Standards for School Mathematics.* Reston: NCTM, 2000.

Getting Ready to Teach Unit 6

Measurement

Volume and Capacity
Lessons 1, 2, and 3

Students begin this unit by examining cubes and arranging them in layers to create rectangular prisms. By doing this, students internalize a clear concept of volume that they can draw on when they are asked to develop a formula for volume. $V = l \times w \times h$ becomes a meaningful statement for them because they see volume as one layer $l \times w$ multiplied by h (= number of layers).

While volume is a measure of the amount of space an object takes up, capacity is a measure of how much a container can hold. Volume is measured in cubic units: cubic centimeters, cubic meters, cubic inches, and so on. Capacity is usually measured in "liquid" units, such as liters, gallons, and ounces.

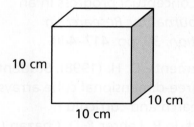

The volume of this prism is 1,000 cu cm.
It is 1 dm × 1 dm × 1 dm.

The capacity of this container is 1 L.
The mass of this container filled with water is 1 kg.

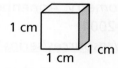

Volume: 1 cu cm

Capacity: 1 mL
Mass: 1 g if filled with water

Weight and Mass
Lesson 4

Because we most often talk about the weight or mass of objects on the surface of Earth, we often use the two terms interchangeably. In fact, they refer to different properties.

Mass is a measure of the amount of "stuff," or matter, in an object. The mass of an object is the same on the moon as it is on Earth, because the amount of "stuff" in the object does not change.

Weight is a measure of the pressure an object exerts downward because of gravity. Your weight is less on the moon than it is on Earth, because there is less gravity on the moon's surface than there is on Earth's surface. Weight can be measured on a scale with a spring, such as a common bathroom scale.

Both metric and customary measures are used in this unit. Working with metric units builds facility with decimals and powers of 10; working with customary units can involve a deeper understanding of multiplicative comparisons and unit fractions. Both types of measures are used in this unit.

Basic Multiplication and Division Fluency

Students should continually work toward fluency for basic multiplication and division facts. Use checkups to assist students in monitoring their own learning. In the Teacher's Resource Book (TRB) you will find several pages for diagnosing and practicing basic multiplication and division.

TRB M58 Diagnostic Quiz for Basic Multiplication	TRB M66 Scrambled Multiplication Tables
TRB M59 Diagnostic Quiz for Basic Division	TRB M67 Blank Multiplication Tables
TRB M60 Basic Multiplication Practice	TRB M68 Multiplication for 10s, 11s, 12s
TRB M61 Basic Division Practice	TRB M69 Division for 10s, 11s, 12s
TRB M62 Multiplication for 3s, 4s, 6s, 7s, 8s, 9s	TRB M83 Factor Puzzles for 3s, 4s, 6s, 7s, 8s, 9s
TRB M63 Division for 3s, 4s, 6s, 7s, 8s, 9s	TRB M84 Factor Puzzles for 6s, 7s, 8s
TRB M64 Multiplication for 6s, 7s, 8s	TRB M85 Blank Factor Puzzles
TRB M65 Division for 6s, 7s, 8s	

See the Basic Facts Fluency Plan for information about practice materials.

Cubic Units and Volume

REAL WORLD Problem Solving

Vocabulary

face
edge
vertex
volume
cubic unit
rectangular prism

Lesson Objectives

● Visualize the cubic units contained in a cube or solid rectangular figure.

● Use a formula to calculate the volume of a rectangular prism.

The Day at a Glance

Today's Goals	Materials	
1 **Teaching the Lesson** **A1:** Identify the parts of a cube. **A2:** Explore the concept of volume as cubic units. **A3:** Develop a formula for calculating volume, and use it to solve problems. **2** **Going Further** ▶ Differentiated Instruction **3** **Homework and Spiral Review**	**Lesson Activities** Student Activity Book pp. 231–234 or Student Hardcover Book pp. 231–234 and Activity Workbook pp. 96–98 (includes Family Letter) Homework and Remembering pp. 147–148 Centimeter or inch cubes	**Going Further** Activity Cards 6-1 Centimeter or inch cubes Meter sticks Math Journals

123 Use Math Talk today!

Keeping Skills Sharp

Daily Routines	English Language Learners
Nonroutine Problem Is it possible to draw a quadrilateral with at least 3 obtuse angles? Draw an example and a counterexample with angle measures. Yes; Example: 3 obtuse angles: 105°, 91°, and 115°. The fourth angle: 360° − 311° = 49°. Counterexample: 3 obtuse angles: 175°, 150°, and 130°. These angles total 455° > 360°. A quadrilateral cannot have these 3 obtuse angles.	Model a cube and draw one on the board. Identify the *face* and *edge* on the actual cube. Have students repeat. • **Beginning** Point to the board. Ask: **Is this an edge or a face?** Label each. • **Intermediate** Point to the board. Say: **This is a/an __.** face, edge Ask: **Are there 4 or 6 faces?** 6 **How many edges are there?** 12 • **Advanced** Have students identify the edge and face on the drawing. Have them tell about each.

Teaching the Lesson

Attributes of a Cube

 15 MINUTES

Goal: Identify the parts of a cube.

Materials: centimeter or inch cubes (1 per student), Student Activity Book p. 231 or Hardcover Book p. 231 and Activity Workbook p. 96

✔ **NCTM Standards:**
Geometry
Measurement
Communication

▶ **Describe a Cube** | WHOLE CLASS |

Distribute the centimeter or inch cubes or display a demonstration cube.

● Name some objects you use that are cubes. Possible answers: number cubes for board games, ice cubes (not always cube-shaped), sugar cubes, stock cubes for soup, caramels

Explain that the sides of a cube are called *faces*.

● What is the shape of each face of a cube? square

● Are all the faces congruent? yes

● How do you know? They are all square and they all have the same side length.

Discuss exercises 1 and 2 on Student Book page 231 as a class. If students have difficulty recognizing the number of faces a cube has, have them recall any number cubes they may have used while playing board games and describe the faces of those cubes.

● What numbers are on the faces of a number cube for a board game? 1 to 6

● So how many faces does a cube have? 6

Ask students to complete exercises 3–4.

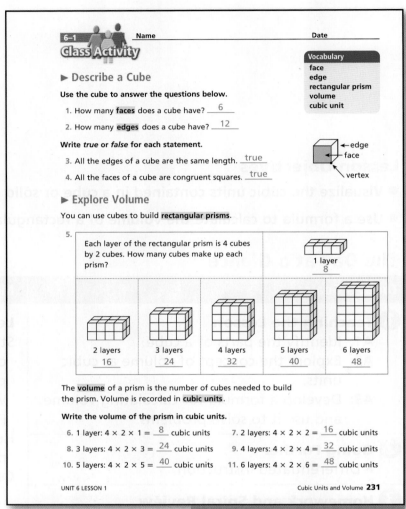

Student Activity Book page 231

The Learning Classroom

Building Concepts To support building coherence, have students take turns briefly summarizing the previous day's lesson at the beginning of each math class. Alternatively, you may have a student summarize at the end of each lesson. Either way, if you do this regularly, students will get used to making mental summaries of math concepts and making conceptual connections.

Visualize Volume

 20 MINUTES

Goal: Explore the concept of volume as cubic units.

Materials: Student Activity Book p. 231 or Hardcover Book p. 231 and Activity Workbook p. 96, centimeter or inch cubes

 NCTM Standards:
Geometry
Measurement

▶ Explore Volume WHOLE CLASS

Hold up a unit cube. Explain that the cube measures 1 unit on each edge and is the standard used for finding the volume of a solid figure. The volume of a solid figure will be the number of same-size cubes that fit into it, filling the space so that there are no gaps.

Ask the students to describe how they can figure out the amount of space inside a box. Encourage them to carry the discussion as far as they can and, if possible, include a description of how to calculate the amount of space. If necessary, lead the students to understand that the idea of measuring the amount of space inside a box is the same as finding the volume of that box. See a sample of classroom dialogue in the Math Talk in Action below. Volume is stated in cubic units because volume measures the number of unit cubes that will fit in the box.

 Math Talk in Action

How can you find the number of unit cubes that will fit in a box?

Lilah: You can fill the box and count them.

What if you don't have enough unit cubes to fill the box?

Lilah: You can make a layer of cubes to cover the bottom of the box. Then you need to find the number of layers.

Percy: You can stack some cubes to find how many layers you need.

Lilah: Right. Then you multiply the cubes in a layer by the number of layers.

Cubic Units Have students look at exercise 5 on Student Book page 231. Ask the class to look at each prism and determine its volume by counting individual cubes. Remind students to include the label *cubic units* when they tell the volume of each prism.

1 layer: $4 \times 2 \times 1 = 8$ cu units
2 layers: $4 \times 2 \times 2 = 16$ cu units
3 layers: $4 \times 2 \times 3 = 24$ cu units
4 layers: $4 \times 2 \times 4 = 32$ cu units
5 layers: $4 \times 2 \times 5 = 40$ cu units
6 layers: $4 \times 2 \times 6 = 48$ cu units

Invite students to imagine adding one layer to the six-layer prism and to name the volume of that prism (56 cubic units). Have students complete exercises 6–11. Remind students to include the word *cubic* or the symbol *cu* as part of their answer.

 Alternate Approach

Use Cubes to Find Volume If students need a more concrete approach to finding volume, have them use cubes to build a prism layer by layer. Students build the bottom layer and count the number of cubes in it. Then they build up the remaining layers. Finally, students count the total number of layers and multiply it by the number of cubes counted for the bottom layer. To confirm that this number is the volume of the prism, students can take the prism apart and count the number of cubes in it. The number should match their calculated answer. Students can use cubes to find the volume of the prisms in Exercise 5 on Student Book page 231.

 Ongoing Assessment

Ask students to calculate the total number of cubes. How many cubes are in:

▶ 6 layers of 2 by 4 rectangles?

▶ 10 layers of 3 by 3 rectangles?

▶ 9 layers of 10 by 10 rectangles?

① Teaching the Lesson (continued)

Activity 3

Solve Volume Problems

 25 MINUTES

Goal: Develop a formula for calculating volume, and use it to solve problems.

Materials: Student Activity Book or Hardcover Book p. 232

✓ **NCTM Standards:**
Geometry
Measurement

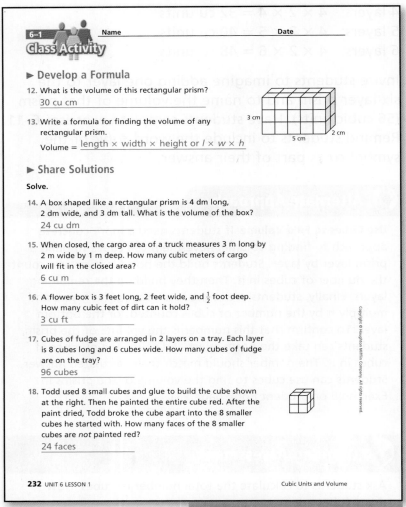

Student Activity Book page 232

► Develop a Formula INDIVIDUALS

Talk about volume as finding the area of the base ($l \times w$ or B) and then counting how many layers there are (h). Show the formula for volume with parentheses that highlight the area of the base.

$(l \times w) \times h = V$ or $V = Bh$

After students complete exercise 12 on page 232, ask:

● How do you find the area of a rectangle? multiply length by width

● How do you find the volume of a rectangular prism? multiply length by width and then by height

● How is finding volume different from finding area? Possible answer: To calculate volume you must include height.

For exercise 13, have students write a formula for finding the volume of a rectangular prism and then share their completed formulas by writing them on the board. Accept any formula that multiplies the length and the width and the height. If the traditional formula does not appear on the board, you may want to introduce it now: $V = l \times w \times h$, or $V = lwh$.

► Share Solutions WHOLE CLASS

Math Talk Use **Solve and Discuss** for exercises 14–18, emphasizing the idea that volume is always given in cubic units. Invite a few students to work at the board while others work at their desks. Students give their solutions and explain their thinking. Encourage other students to listen carefully and ask questions. Classroom discussions may include:

● For exercise 14: $4 \times 2 \times 3 = 24$ cu dm. The bottom layer is 4×2, or 8 cu dm. There are 3 layers, so $8 \times 3 = 24$ cu dm.

● For exercise 15: $3 \times 2 \times 1 = 6$ cu m. The cargo area has only one layer.

● For exercise 16: $3 \times 2 \times \frac{1}{2} = 3$ cu ft of dirt. Measurements need not be whole numbers, and answers may not be whole numbers.

● For exercise 17: $8 \times 6 \times 2 = 96$ cubes. The bottom layer is 8×6, or 48 cubes. There are 2 layers.

● For exercise 18: 24 faces are not painted red. The 8 individual cubes each have 6 faces, so there are 48 faces altogether. After the larger cube was assembled and painted, paint covered 24 of those faces, so 48 faces − 24 painted faces = 24 unpainted faces.

② Going Further

● Intervention   Activity Card 6-1

Different Dimensions   Activity Card 6-1 ●

Work: In Pairs

Use:

• 36 Centimeter or inch cubes

1. **Work Together** Build a rectangular prism with centimeter cubes. Then record the dimensions of the prism in a table like the one below.

Dimensions of Rectangular Prisms			
	Length	Width	Height	Volume
Prism A				
Prism B				

2. Build a second rectangular prism, using a different number of cubes. Record the dimensions in your table.

3. **Math Talk** How did you find the volume of each prism? How can you check your results? Possible answer: The volume is the product of length × width × height; you can check the volume by counting the cubes in the prism.

Unit 6, Lesson 1   Copyright © Houghton Mifflin Company

Activity Note Review the meaning of volume before students begin. If necessary, show the students a model that is 3 by 2 by 2 and then count the 12 cubes that compose it.

 Math Writing Prompt

Explain Your Thinking If you turn an object upside down or onto its side, does its volume change? Explain your answer.

 **Software Support**

Warm-Up 46.23

▲ On Level   Activity Card 6-1

Different Dimensions—Same Volume   Activity Card 6-1 ▲

Work: In Pairs

Use:

• 36 Centimeter or inch cubes

1. **Work Together** The rectangular prism below has a volume of 36 cubic units.

6 by 3 by 2

2. **Predict** Can you build three other rectangular prisms with a volume of 36 cubic units? Test your prediction. List the dimensions of each rectangular prism you build.

2. Yes; accept all prisms whose dimensions include three factors whose product is 36.

3. **Math Talk** How did you choose the dimensions of the prisms you built? Possible answer: We chose 3 numbers whose product equals 36.

Unit 6, Lesson 1   Copyright © Houghton Mifflin Company

Activity Note Have all of the students who built prisms compile a list of possible dimensions for the given volume.

 Math Writing Prompt

Summarize In your own words, describe how centimeters, decimeters, and meters are related, and how cubic centimeters, cubic decimeters, and cubic meters are related.

 Software Support

Ice Station Exploration: Frozen Solids, Level J

■ Challenge   Activity Card 6-1

Estimate Volume   Activity Card 6-1 ■

Work: In Small Groups

Use:

• Meter sticks

1. Estimate the dimensions of your classroom in meters, and record your estimate.

2. Use your estimate to calculate the volume.

3. **Work Together** Measure the dimensions of the classroom to the nearest meter.

We think the classroom is about 5 meters by 10 meters by 2 meters high. The volume is 5 × 10 × 2 = 100 cu m

4. Compare the actual volume with the estimate.

5. **Math Talk** Discuss the strategies you used to make your estimates.

Unit 6, Lesson 1   Copyright © Houghton Mifflin Company

Activity Note Discuss possible benchmarks, such as the height of a door, the length of a floor tile, or the width of a desk, to use in estimating the dimensions of the classroom.

 Math Writing Prompt

Solve a Problem A box measures 10 cm on each side. How many square centimeters of paper are needed to cover all the faces of the box?

 DESTINATION Math· **Software Support**

Course III: Module 5: Unit 1: Rectangles and Squares

③ Homework and Spiral Review

For Homework, students calculate volume to solve word problems.

This Remembering activity is appropriate anytime after today's lesson.

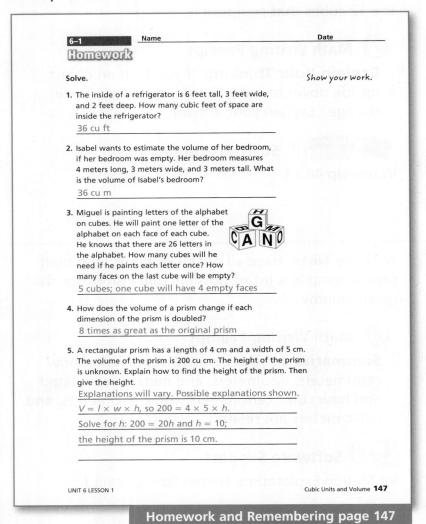

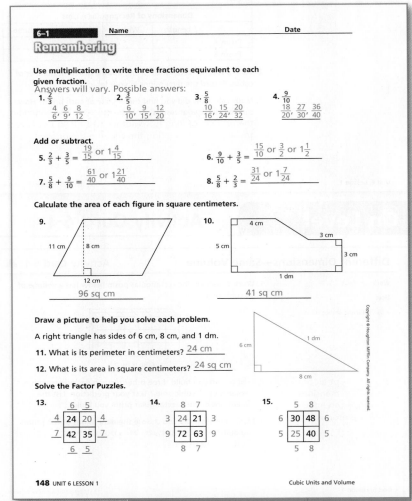

Home and School Connection

Family Letter Have students take home the Family Letter on Student Activity Book page 233 or Activity Workbook page 97. This letter explains how the concepts of volume, capacity, and weight are developed in *Math Expressions*. It gives parents and guardians a better understanding of the learning that goes on in math class and creates a bridge between school and home. A Spanish translation of this letter is on Student Activity Book page 234 and Activity Workbook page 98.

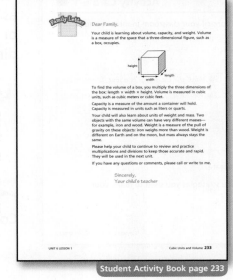

Student Activity Book page 233

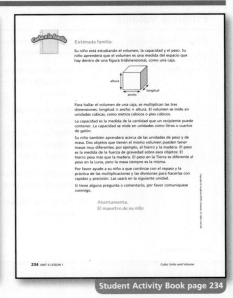

Student Activity Book page 234

Relate Length, Area, and Volume

REAL WORLD Problem Solving

Lesson Objectives

- Identify whether a situation involves measuring length, area, or volume.
- Examine and apply relationships among figures measured in one dimension, two dimensions, and three dimensions.

Vocabulary

one-dimensional
two-dimensional
three-dimensional

The Day at a Glance

Today's Goals	Materials
1 Teaching the Lesson **A1:** Identify whether a situation involves measuring length, area, or volume. **A2:** Calculate the length of a missing edge of a figure, given the volume and other dimensions. **A3:** Discover how area and volume increase when dimensions increase. **2 Going Further** ▶ Problem Solving Strategy: Estimate to Solve Problems ▶ Differentiated Instruction **3 Homework and Spiral Review**	**Lesson Activities** Student Activity Book pp. 235–237 or Student Hardcover Book pp. 235–237 Homework and Remembering pp. 149–150 Centimeter-Grid Paper (TRB M18) Quick Quiz 1 (Assessment Guide) **Going Further** Student Activity Book p. 238 or Student Hardcover Book p. 238 Activity Cards 6-2 Centimeter or inch cubes Centimeter-Grid Paper (TRB M18) Math Journals 123 Use Math Talk today!

Keeping Skills Sharp

Daily Routines	English Language Learners
Homework Review Let students work together to check their work. **Strategy problem** Fabric is on sale for these prices: Orange, $3 per yard; blue, $4 per yard; yellow, $2.50 per yard; and white $1.50 per yard. Irma needs to buy 3 different colors of fabric with a total length of 2 yards. She has a budget of $6. What fabrics could she buy? Possible answer: 0.5 yd blue for $2, 0.5 yd orange for $1.50, 1 yd yellow for $2.50; $2 + $1.50 + $2.50 = $6	Write *dimensions*, *length*, *width*, and *height* on the board. Say: **Length, width, and height are dimensions.** Draw a line. • **Beginning** Say: **We can only measure the length of a line.** Ask: **Is a line one-dimensional?** yes Continue with a square and a cube. • **Intermediate** Ask: **What can we measure?** length Say: **A line has 1 __.** dimension Continue with other shapes. • **Advanced** Have students identify the dimensions of a line, square, and cube.

Teaching the Lesson

Applications of Length, Area, and Volume

20 MINUTES

Goal: Identify whether a situation involves measuring length, area, or volume.

Materials: Student Activity Book or Hardcover Book p. 235

✓ **NCTM Standards:**
Geometry
Measurement
Connections

▶ **Compare Length, Area, and Volume**

WHOLE CLASS

Ask the students to define the terms *one-dimensional*, *two-dimensional*, and *three-dimensional*, using words and pictures. Together, read the definitions at the top of Student Book page 235, and discuss how the terms relate to length, area, and volume.

To prepare students to do exercises 1–8, you might ask:

● How many length measurements do you need to find the area of a rectangle? 2; length and width

● How many length measurements do you need to find the volume of a box or rectangular prism? 3; length, width, and height

Invite students to suggest an appropriate unit of measure (either in customary or metric measurements) for each situation. Encourage students to discuss how they got their answers. See a sample of a classroom dialogue in the Math Talk in Action below.

 Math Talk in Action

What kind of figure has one dimension?

Eartha: a line or line segment

How do you describe the size of something that has one dimension?

Daniel: You can tell how long it is.

What kind of figure has two dimensions?

Eartha: Any kind of quadrilateral.

Daniel: Triangles, too. Anything that's flat.

6–2 **Class Activity**   Name _____ Date _____

Vocabulary
Length one-dimensional
Area   two-dimensional
Volume three-dimensional

▶ **Compare Length, Area, and Volume**

Length tells how wide, tall, or long something is. Finding length requires one measurement. Length is **one-dimensional** and is measured in length units.

Length [1 cm]

Area tells how much surface a figure covers. Finding area requires two length measurements. Area is **two-dimensional** and is measured in square units.

Area [1 cm × 1 cm]

Volume tells how much space an object occupies. Finding volume requires three length measurements. Volume is **three-dimensional** and is measured in cubic units.

Volume [1 cm × 1 cm × 1 cm]

Tell if you need to measure for length, area, or volume. Then write the number of measurements you need to make.

1. How much water is in a swimming pool? ___volume; 3___

2. How tall are you? ___length; 1___

3. How much carpet is needed for a floor? ___area; 2___

4. How far is it from a doorknob to the floor? ___length; 1___

5. How much sand is in a sandbox? ___volume; 3___

6. How much wallpaper is needed for one wall? ___area; 2___

7. How long is a string? ___length; 1___

8. How much space is there inside a refrigerator? ___volume; 3___

UNIT 6 LESSON 2   Relate Length, Area, and Volume **235**

Student Activity Book page 235

How do you describe the size of something that has two dimensions?

Daniel: Tell how much surface it covers.

Eartha: That's the area. You tell the size in square units.

Daniel: To measure it, you have to measure both dimensions.

What kind of figure has three dimensions?

Eartha: A box or a ball.

Daniel: Any real object, actually.

How do you describe the size of something that has three dimensions?

Daniel: Tell how much space it takes up.

Eartha: That's the volume.

Daniel: You tell the size in cubic units and measure three dimensions.

Find an Unknown Edge

 20 MINUTES

Goal: Calculate the length of a missing edge of a figure, given the volume and other dimensions.

Materials: Student Activity Book or Hardcover Book p. 236

 NCTM Standards:
Geometry
Measurement
Algebra

▶ Cubic Relationships WHOLE CLASS

Have students complete exercises 9–14. Invite them to explain how they calculated each answer and, if necessary, remind them to include the appropriate unit labels in their answers. As students share their explanations, write the appropriate equation on the board to help them become familiar with simple algebraic expressions.

Ask students to complete exercises 15–18.

▶ Compare Relative Sizes WHOLE CLASS

Cubic Meters and Cubic Centimeters Remind students that a centimeter cube has a volume of 1 cubic centimeter. Ask students how they think this volume compares to the volume of 1 cubic meter. Discuss the relationship between the lengths of the sides of a 1-cm and a 1-m cube. (Since 1 m = 100 cm, the side of a meter cube is 100 times longer than the side of a cm cube.)

Have **Student Pairs** decide how they could express the volume of 1 cubic meter in centimeters. (*A* of the base = 100 cm × 100 cm, or 10,000 cm. There are 100 layers, so *V* = 10,000 × 100 = 1,000,000.) Lead students to see that the volume of 1 cu m is 1 million times the volume of 1 cu cm.)

Ask students the same question about cubic inches and cubic feet. Lead them to see that since 1 foot = 12 inches, a cubic foot is equal to 12 × 12 × 12 = 1,728 cubic inches.

6-2
Class Activity

Name _____ Date _____

▶ Cubic Relationships

Solve.

The sides of a cube are 3 centimeters long.

9. What is the area of each face? _9 sq cm_

10. What is the volume of the cube? _27 cu cm_

Sides = 3 cm

A cube has a volume of 8 cubic meters.

11. What is the length of each edge? _2 m_

12. What is the area of each of its faces? _4 sq m_

Volume = 8 cu m

One face of a cube has an area of 16 square inches.

13. What is the length of each edge? _4 in._

14. What is the volume of the cube? _64 cu in._

Face Area = 16 sq in.

Describe a real-world situation for each.
Answers will vary.

15. measuring length

_____

16. measuring area

_____

17. measuring volume

_____

18. **Challenge** A box has a volume of 24 cubic inches. Two of the faces of the box are squares. Its length is 3 times its width. What are the dimensions of the box?
_2 in. by 2 in. by 6 in._

236 UNIT 6 LESSON 2   Relate Length, Area, and Volume

Student Activity Book page 236

Differentiated Instruction

Advanced Learners The factors of 24 include 1, 2, 3, 4, 6, 8, 12, and 24. Since two opposite faces of the prism are squares, one of the factors represents the length of the sides of the squares. Students will most likely use guess and check to discover that the dimensions are 2 in. by 2 in. by 6 in.

✓ Ongoing Assessment

Ask:

▶ How do you know whether to solve a problem for length? area? volume?

▶ Why should you always include the units in your answers to these problems?

Activity 3

Change Dimensions

  20 MINUTES

Goal: Discover how area and volume increase when dimensions increase.

Materials: Centimeter-Grid Paper (TRB M18), Student Activity Book or Hardcover Book p. 237

 NCTM Standards:
Geometry
Measurement
Algebra

▶ Double One Dimension of a Figure

INDIVIDUALS

Have students draw a 1-by-3 rectangle on grid paper. Ask them to keep doubling the length of the 1-cm side and have them record what happens to the area.

	Area
1-by-3	3 sq cm
2-by-3	6 sq cm
4-by-3	12 sq cm
8-by-3	24 sq cm

● What happens to the area when you double one dimension? You double the area.

▶ Double Two Dimensions of a Figure

INDIVIDUALS

Ask students to complete exercise 19 on Student Book page 237 independently and to explain their conclusions. Doubling the length of each side makes the area four times as large. Students can see this relationship easily if they draw a picture like the one shown.

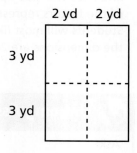

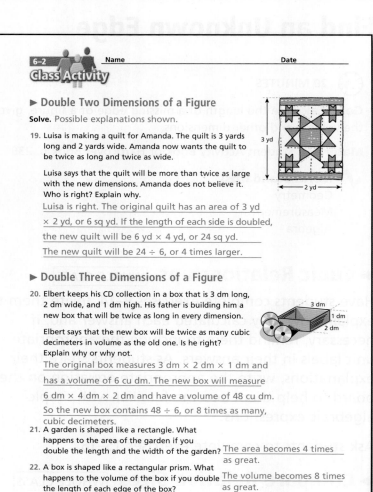

Student Activity Book page 237

Differentiated Instruction

Extra Help If students have difficulty visualizing how doubling affects area, ask them to use grid paper to explore the concept. Have students

• Draw the original rectangle.

• Double the width, and draw the new rectangle. How does the area change? The area is two times the size.

• Double the original length, and draw the new rectangle. How does the area change? The area is two times the size.

• Double both the width and the length of the original, and draw the new rectangle. How does the area change? The area is four times the size.

▶ Double Three Dimensions of a Figure

WHOLE CLASS

Have the class read exercise 20 on Student Book page 237 and solve it together. Doubling the length of the sides will result in the volume being eight times greater, or 48 cubic decimeters instead of 6 cubic decimeters.

Encourage the class to try to visualize the situation: the bottom layer of the new box will be four times as large (just as the quilt in the previous problem became four times as large), and the new box will have two layers because it will be twice as tall. So, four times as large and two times as tall is the same as $4 \times 2 = 8$.

Sketch a 1-by-1-by-1 box on the board. Ask questions as you complete a table to show what happens as you double the length of one side.

Side	Side	Side	Volume
1	1	1	1 cu cm
2	1	1	2 cu cm
4	1	1	4 cu cm
8	1	1	8 cu cm

● What happens to the volume when you double the length of one side? It doubles.

Repeat the activity by doubling the length of two of the sides.

Side	Side	Side	Volume
1	1	1	1 cu cm
2	2	1	4 cu cm
4	4	1	16 cu cm
8	8	1	64 cu cm

● What happens to the volume when you double two dimensions? It becomes four times as large.

Invite students to complete exercises 21 and 22 on Student Book page 237.

Formulate a Generalization Ask the class to state a generalization related to the doubling they just discovered. Help them relate the generalization to the number of dimensions in a figure. For example:

● Length is one-dimensional. If we double it, it becomes two times as long.

● Area is two-dimensional. If we double each length, we have $2 \times 2 = 4$. It becomes four times as large.

● Volume is three-dimensional. If we double each length, we have $2 \times 2 \times 2 = 8$. It becomes eight times as large.

● The factor 2 (the double) occurs once, twice, or three times, depending on whether the shape has one dimension, two dimensions, or three dimensions.

Teaching Note

Math Background Some students may be familiar with exponents. Exponents tell the number of factors in a product of equal numbers. So 4^2 is another way to write 4×4, and 4^3 is another way to write $4 \times 4 \times 4$.

The standard way to write the symbols for area and volume units is to use exponents. So 10 sq cm is written as 10 cm^2 and 10 cu cm is written as 10 cm^3. The exponent is equal to the number of dimensions of the figure being measured.

For **English Language Learners,** the use of color is often helpful when discussing exponents. Have students come to the board and write the base number in white and the exponent in another color. Have them write the base and exponent for $2 \times 2 = 4$ (4^2) and $2 \times 2 \times 2 = 8 = (2^3)$ and explain in their own words what an exponent represents.

 **Quick Quiz**

See Assessment Guide for Unit 6 Quick Quiz 1.

Going Further

Problem Solving Strategy: Estimate to Solve Problems

Goal: Use estimates to solve problems. Recognize when underestimates and overestimates are appropriate.

Materials: Student Activity Book or Hardcover Book p. 238

✓ **NCTM Standards:**
Geometry
Measurement
Problem Solving
Reasoning and Proof

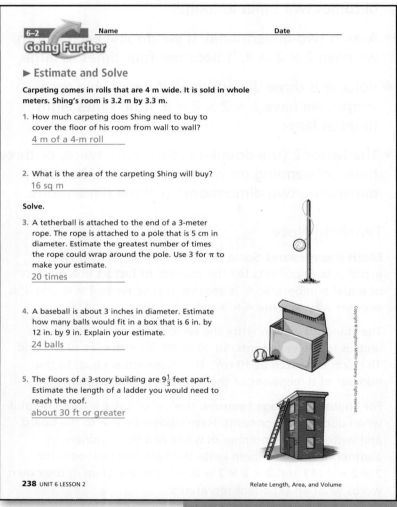

Student Activity Book page 238

▶ Estimate and Solve WHOLE CLASS

Discuss when an overestimate or underestimate is reasonable to solve a problem. For example:

- If 13 students travel in cars with 4 students in each car, how many cars do they need? The closest estimate is 3 cars, but then 1 student would be left behind. So they would need 4 cars.

- If the ceiling of a room is $9\frac{1}{2}$ feet high, how many 2-foot-high boxes can you stack in the room? We might estimate $10 \div 2 = 5$ boxes, but that won't work because only 4 boxes will fit.

Use **Solve and Discuss** to complete exercises 1–5. Have the students read exercise 1.

- Estimate the area of Shing's room.
  about $3 \times 3 = 9$ sq m

- Is the actual area greater or less than 9 sq m? Why?
  greater; each side is greater than 3.

- Is this a good estimate for buying the carpet? Why?
  No; the carpet has to be wider and longer than 3 m.

Have students solve the word problems.

For exercise 3, you might ask, "If the real value of π is greater than 3, will your estimate be greater than or less than the actual answer?" Less than

In exercise 4, students should see that they need to use the diameter to figure out how many balls fit along each dimension of the box.

In exercise 5, discuss why an exact answer of 28 feet is not a good estimate. The ladder has to lean against the wall and needs to be longer than 28 feet.

▶ Irregular Shapes STUDENT PAIRS

Estimate Volume Have **Student Pairs** work together to estimate the volume of irregular shapes, such as a stapler, in the classroom. Students should generalize that they can compare the object to a rectangular prism and then estimate the volume.

Differentiated Instruction

Build Boxes

Activity Card 6-2 ●

Work: In Pairs

Use:
- 36 Centimeter or inch cubes

1. Make a rectangular box using one layer of cubes that is different from the one shown. Record the volume of the box.

2. Add three more layers, one at a time. Record the number of layers and the volume of each new box, as shown below.

1 layer	2 × 6 = 12 cubes
2 layers	2 × 12 = 24 cubes
3 layers	3 × 12 = 36 cubes
4 layers	

3. **Predict** What patterns do you see in what you recorded about each layer in your box? Suppose you added one more layer. Predict the volume of the box. Possible answer: Each new layer increases the volume by an amount equal to the original volume.

Unit 6, Lesson 2   Copyright © Houghton Mifflin Company

Activity Note Another way of writing the volume of the first layer of the box shown is 1 × 12 = 12, which is the height times the area of the base.

 Math Writing Prompt

Explain Your Thinking How can you measure and find the volume of a rectangular box?

 **Software Support**

Warm-Up 46.25

Square Areas That Grow

Activity Card 6-2 ▲

Work: In Pairs

Use:
- Centimeter-Grid Paper (TRB M18)

1. **Work Together** Make a design using squares. Begin with a 1-by-1 unit square in the upper left corner of your grid.

2. Draw new squares, increasing the length and width by 1 unit each time. Make a table to record the growth in area.

3. **Look Back** What pattern do you see in the number of square units that you added each time you made a new square?
Possible answer: The increase in area is the sequence of odd numbers beginning with 3, 5, 7, and so on.

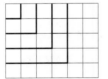

Square	Area	Increase in area
1-by-1	1	
2-by-2	4	3
3-by-3	9	5
4-by-4	16	7
5-by-5	25	9

Unit 6, Lesson 2   Copyright © Houghton Mifflin Company

Activity Note Be sure that students understand that they must count all the square units within each new square to find the area.

 Math Writing Prompt

Make a Drawing Sketch a picture of a box with a volume of 100 cm³. Label the dimensions. How do you know that the volume is 100 cm³?

 Software Support

Ice Station Exploration: Polar Planes, Level S

Use 12 Cubes

Activity Card 6-2 ■

Work: In Pairs

Use:
- Centimeter or inch cubes

2. Possible prisms are:

1 × 1 × 12

2 × 1 × 6

2 × 2 × 3

3 × 1 × 4

Students lists may include variations of the same dimensions, such as 1 × 12 × 1.

1. **Work Together** Build as many rectangular prisms as you can that have a volume of 12 cm³.

2. Make a list of all the possible dimensions that you found for the rectangular prism.

length	width	height

3. **Math Talk** Discuss the strategies you used to find the dimensions of the prisms. How can you be sure that you have included all possible dimensions? Possible answer: Make an organized list of 3 numbers whose product is 12.

Unit 6, Lesson 2   Copyright © Houghton Mifflin Company

Activity Note Suggest that students begin by listing the factors of 12 and then making an organized list of combinations of 3 factors whose product is 12.

 Math Writing Prompt

Use Reasoning The base of a triangular prism has half the area of the base of a rectangular prism. Both prisms have the same height. How are their volumes related?

 DESTINATION Math® **Software Support**

Course III: Module 5: Unit 1: Rectangles and Squares

③ Homework and Spiral Review

6–2
Homework **Goal:** Additional Practice

✓ Include students' Homework page 149 as part of their portfolios.

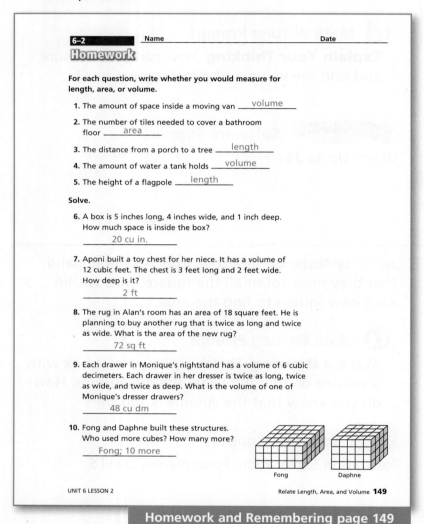

6–2
Homework

Name _____ Date _____

For each question, write whether you would measure for length, area, or volume.

1. The amount of space inside a moving van ___volume___

2. The number of tiles needed to cover a bathroom floor ___area___

3. The distance from a porch to a tree ___length___

4. The amount of water a tank holds ___volume___

5. The height of a flagpole ___length___

Solve.

6. A box is 5 inches long, 4 inches wide, and 1 inch deep. How much space is inside the box?
___20 cu in.___

7. Aponi built a toy chest for her niece. It has a volume of 12 cubic feet. The chest is 3 feet long and 2 feet wide. How deep is it?
___2 ft___

8. The rug in Alan's room has an area of 18 square feet. He is planning to buy another rug that is twice as long and twice as wide. What is the area of the new rug?
___72 sq ft___

9. Each drawer in Monique's nightstand has a volume of 6 cubic decimeters. Each drawer in her dresser is twice as long, twice as wide, and twice as deep. What is the volume of one of Monique's dresser drawers?
___48 cu dm___

10. Fong and Daphne built these structures. Who used more cubes? How many more?
___Fong; 10 more___

Fong   Daphne

UNIT 6 LESSON 2   Relate Length, Area, and Volume **149**

Homework and Remembering page 149

6–2
Remembering **Goal:** Spiral Review

This Remembering activity is appropriate anytime after today's lesson.

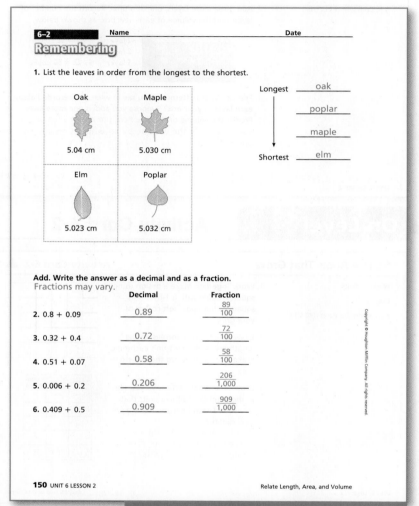

6–2
Remembering

Name _____ Date _____

1. List the leaves in order from the longest to the shortest.

Oak	Maple
5.04 cm	5.030 cm
Elm	Poplar
5.023 cm	5.032 cm

Longest ___oak___
___poplar___
___maple___
Shortest ___elm___

Add. Write the answer as a decimal and as a fraction.
Fractions may vary.

	Decimal	Fraction
2. 0.8 + 0.09	0.89	$\frac{89}{100}$
3. 0.32 + 0.4	0.72	$\frac{72}{100}$
4. 0.51 + 0.07	0.58	$\frac{58}{100}$
5. 0.006 + 0.2	0.206	$\frac{206}{1,000}$
6. 0.409 + 0.5	0.909	$\frac{909}{1,000}$

150 UNIT 6 LESSON 2   Relate Length, Area, and Volume

Homework and Remembering page 150

Home or School Activity

Language Arts Connection

Different Definitions Have students think of as many different definitions as they can for the word *volume* and have them write a sentence for each definition.

594 UNIT 6 LESSON 2

Measures of Capacity

REAL WORLD **Problem Solving**

MINI UNIT 6 LESSON 3

Lesson Objectives

- Explore the relationship among metric and among customary units of capacity.
- Solve problems involving metric and customary measures of capacity.

Vocabulary

capacity
liter
kiloliter
milliliter
cup
pint
quart
gallon

The Day at a Glance

Today's Goals	Materials

1 Teaching the Lesson
  A1: Compare volume and capacity.
  A2: Convert among metric units of capacity.
  A3: Convert among customary units of capacity.
 	
2 Going Further
  ▶ Differentiated Instruction
 	
3 Homework and Spiral Review
	Lesson Activities
	Student Activity Book pp. 239–240
	  or Student Hardcover Book
	  pp. 239–240
	Homework and Remembering
	  pp. 151–152
	Containers and boxes
	
	Going Further
	Activity Cards 6-3
	Customary and metric
	  measuring cups and
	  spoons
	Eyedropper
	Variety of containers
	Math Journals
	
	123 *Use* **Math Talk** *today!*

Keeping Skills Sharp

Daily Routines	English Language Learners
Homework Review Set aside time to work with students needing extra help. **Mental Math** When you count pennies by skip counting, what place value are you actually starting with but never say? hundredths If you count pennies by twos, 2 pennies, 4 pennies, and so on, what are you skip counting by? 0.02, or 2 hundredths How will this change if you count dimes by twos? 0.2, or 2 tenths	Write *capacity, L, pt,* and *qt* on the board. Say: **Capacity is how much liquid a container can hold.** Model containers. • **Beginning** Say: **This container can hold 1 L of water. Its capacity is 1 L.** Have students repeat. • **Intermediate** Say: **This holds 1 L of water.** *Liter* **is a unit of __.** capacity **Its capacity is 1 __.** liter Continue with other containers. • **Advanced** Have students identify the units of measurement and tell about liquids that come in similar containers.

① Teaching the Lesson

Activity 1

Volume and Capacity

 10 MINUTES

Goal: Compare volume and capacity.

Materials: containers and boxes

✓ **NCTM Standards:**
Measurement
Communication

▶ Compare and Contrast Volume and Capacity WHOLE CLASS

In the two previous lessons, students explored volume and learned that it was a measure of the amount of space occupied by a geometric solid. To contrast volume

with capacity, display a container that is usually associated with liquids, such as a cup or a milk jug, and a box. Write the terms volume and capacity on the board and explain that although both terms in a general way can refer to the amount of space inside an object, volume is a "dry" measure and capacity is a "wet," or liquid, measure.

● Name containers that are commonly used for liquid capacity. Possible answers: milk jug, juice box, water bottle

● Name items you might measure with volume units. Possible answers: a packing box, storage space, a refrigerator, trunk space in a car, cargo space in a truck

Activity 2

Metric Measures of Capacity

 20 MINUTES

Goal: Convert among metric units of capacity.

Materials: Student Activity Book or Hardcover Book p. 239

 NCTM Standards:
Geometry   Measurement

▶ Decimals and Capacity WHOLE CLASS

Write the number 1,000 on the board.

● What is 1,000 ÷ 10? 100

Write 100 underneath 1,000, and continue to divide by 10.

● What is 100 ÷ 10? 10

● What is 10 ÷ 10? 1

● What is 1 ÷ 10? 0.1

● What is 0.1 ÷ 10? 0.01

● What is 0.01 ÷ 10? 0.001

Remind students that these decimal relationships are the basis for the relationships among all metric units of measurement. Together, discuss what students recall about metric prefixes from their work with length.

Read aloud the introductory material on Student Book page 239, or read it together. To work with metric units of capacity, students need to understand the relationships shared by the units, especially liters, kiloliters, and milliliters. Have students study the table.

● Is a kiloliter to the left of a liter, or to the right of a liter? to the left

● Which is greater, a kiloliter or a liter? kiloliter

● A kiloliter is 1,000 times as great as a liter. Explain how the table shows this. To change liters to kiloliters, you must multiply by 10, by 10, and then by 10 again; $10 \times 10 \times 10 = 1,000$.

● Is a milliliter to the left of a liter, or to the right of a liter? to the right

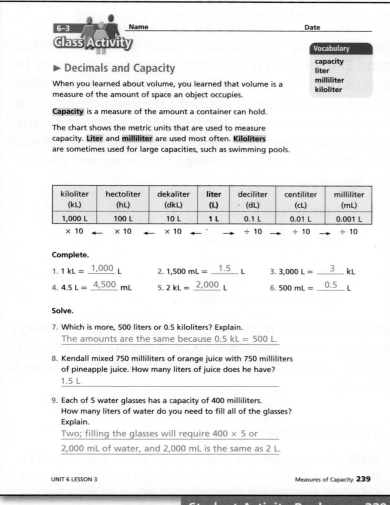

Student Activity Book page 239

6–3

Class Activity

Name _____ Date _____

▶ **Decimals and Capacity**

When you learned about volume, you learned that volume is a measure of the amount of space an object occupies.

Capacity is a measure of the amount a container can hold.

The chart shows the metric units that are used to measure capacity. **Liter** and **milliliter** are used most often. **Kiloliters** are sometimes used for large capacities, such as swimming pools.

Vocabulary
capacity
liter
milliliter
kiloliter

kiloliter (kL)	hectoliter (hL)	dekaliter (dkL)	liter (L)	deciliter (dL)	centiliter (cL)	milliliter (mL)
1,000 L	100 L	10 L	1 L	0.1 L	0.01 L	0.001 L

× 10 ← × 10 ← × 10 ← → ÷ 10 → ÷ 10 → ÷ 10

Complete.

1. 1 kL = __1,000__ L   2. 1,500 mL = __1.5__ L   3. 3,000 L = __3__ kL

4. 4.5 L = __4,500__ mL   5. 2 kL = __2,000__ L   6. 500 mL = __0.5__ L

Solve.

7. Which is more, 500 liters or 0.5 kiloliters? Explain.
   The amounts are the same because 0.5 kL = 500 L.

8. Kendall mixed 750 milliliters of orange juice with 750 milliliters of pineapple juice. How many liters of juice does he have?
   1.5 L

9. Each of 5 water glasses has a capacity of 400 milliliters. How many liters of water do you need to fill all of the glasses? Explain.
   Two; filling the glasses will require 400 × 5 or
   2,000 mL of water, and 2,000 mL is the same as 2 L.

UNIT 6 LESSON 3   Measures of Capacity **239**

- **Which is smaller, a milliliter or a liter?** milliliter

- **A milliliter is 1,000 times as small as a liter. Explain how the table shows this.** To change liters to milliliters, you must divide by 10, by another 10, and then by 10 again; dividing by 10 three times is the same as dividing by 10 × 10 × 10, or by 1,000.

- **Describe the mathematical relationship shared by all of the units in the table.** Any unit is 10 times as great as the unit immediately to its right, and 10 times as small as the unit immediately to its left.

Have the class work cooperatively to discuss and complete exercises 1–6. Challenge students to decide the answers using only mental math. Then use **Solve and Discuss** for exercises 7–9.

 Math Talk in Action

What metric prefixes are related to each number in the chart?

Enrique: The number 1,000 is kilo-, as in kilometers.

Lauren: And 0.01 and 0.001 are *centi-* and *milli-*, as in centimeters and millimeters.

What metric prefixes are related to ten and one tenth? Think about the word *decimal*.

Lauren: A decimeter is a length, but is it 10 m or 0.1 m?

Tao: Deci- ends in *i* like *centi-* and *milli-*, so I think it's less than 1. So a decimeter is 0.1 m.

Enrique: Then 10 m is a dekameter.

Does anyone remember what 100 meters is? There's an area measure called a hectare.

Lauren: A hectameter?

Enrique: I think it's hect-OH-meter, like kil-OH-meter.

Teaching Note

Math Background The metric system has simple and elegant relationships between length, volume, capacity, and even mass. A cubic decimeter of water is exactly equivalent to one liter and has a mass of one kilogram. A cubic centimeter of water is equivalent to one milliliter and has a mass of one gram.

 Ongoing Assessment

Ask students what metric unit might best be used for different liquid amounts.

▶ What unit would you use to measure gasoline for a car? drops of liquid medicine? water falling over Niagara Falls?

① Teaching the Lesson (continued)

Activity 3

Customary Measures of Capacity

 20 MINUTES

Goal: Convert among customary units of capacity.

Materials: Student Book Activity or Hardcover Book p. 240

✓ **NCTM Standards:**
Measurement
Number and Operations

▶ Fractions and Capacity SMALL GROUPS

Students may find it more difficult to convert within the customary system than within the metric system. For example, to change one metric unit to another, a student needs only to multiply or divide by multiples of 10, often using mental math. Changing customary units is more involved. For example, a typical way to

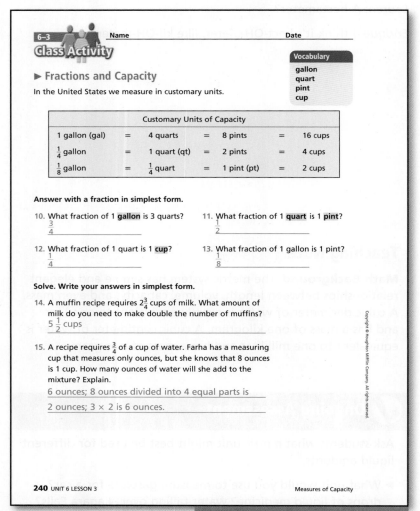

Student Activity Book page 240

determine the number of pints in 1 gallon is to think that since 2 pints = 1 quart and 4 quarts = 1 gallon, the number of pints in 1 gallon is 2 × 4, or 8.

Read aloud the introductory material on Student Book page 240, or read it together. Encourage students to discuss the different relationships shown in the table. To help them practice applying the relationships, you might choose to write the following exercises on the board, and others like them. Then have students work collectively or in **Small Groups** to discuss and decide the answers.

4 pints = ___8___ cups

6 pints = ___3___ quarts

8 quarts = ___2___ gallons

1 gallon = ___16___ cups

Use **Solve and Discuss** for exercises 10–15. Encourage students to use the table to help decide the answers and to commit the relationships shown in the table to memory.

Teaching Note

Math Background The metric system (SI) was developed in the 17th and 18th centuries to establish a simple, easily used system of weights and measures that would be universally acceptable to the countries of the world. The metric system is built on a foundation of seven basic units, and all other units are derived from them.

SI BASE UNITS		
Name	**Symbol**	**Quality**
kilogram	kg	Mass
second	s	Time
meter	m	Length
ampere	A	Electrical current
kelvin	K	Temperature
mole	mol	Amount of substance
candela	cd	Luminous intensity

The United States is the only industrialized country in the world that does not use the metric system as its predominant system of measurement.

② Going Further

Differentiated Instruction

● Intervention — Activity Card 6-3

Estimate Liquids — Activity Card 6-3 ●

Work: In Pairs

Use:
- Customary and metric measuring cups and spoons, eyedropper, variety of containers

1. **Work Together** Estimate the number of milliliters in one cup. Then check your estimate. Estimates will vary; about 240 mL.

2. Estimate the number of milliliters in a teaspoon and in a tablespoon. Check both estimates. Estimates will vary; 1 teaspoon is about 5 mL and 1 tablespoon is about 15 mL.
3. **Look Back** How can you use what you have observed about metric measures of capacity to estimate the capacity of other containers? Test your strategies with different small containers.

Unit 6, Lesson 3　　　　　Copyright © Houghton Mifflin Company

Activity Note Before students begin the activity, give them a visual benchmark for milliliters by reminding them that some medicines are dispensed with an eyedropper, which holds about 1 mL.

✎ Math Writing Prompt

Show What You Know List some items that you can measure by volume and others that you can measure by capacity.

Soar to Success Math Software Support

Warm-Up 43.23

▲ On Level — Activity Card 6-3

Leaky Faucets — Activity Card 6-3 ▲

Work: In Pairs

1. A faucet that leaks 30 drops in a minute can waste 10 liters of water in a day. Make a table to show the total amount of water wasted at the end of each day for a week.
2. Write an equation to show the amount of water wasted, W, in days (d).
$W = 10 \times d$
3. Use the equation to calculate how long it will take for a kiloliter of water to leak from the faucet.
100 days:
$1 \text{ kL} = 1,000 \text{ L}$
$W = 10 \times d$
$1,000 = 10 \times d$
$100 = d$

Day	Leakage
1	10L
2	20L
3	30L
4	40L
5	50L
6	60L
7	70L

Unit 6, Lesson 3　　　　　Copyright © Houghton Mifflin Company

Activity Note Before students begin, remind them that 1 kiloliter equals 1,000 liters. To write the equation, students must express the amount wasted in terms of the number of days passed.

✎ Math Writing Prompt

Change Units Use two examples to explain how to change a capacity in milliliters to liters and how to change a capacity in kiloliters to liters.

MegaMath Grades K-6 Software Support

Ice Station Exploration: Arctic Algebra, Level K

■ Challenge — Activity Card 6-3

Gasoline Consumption — Activity Card 6-3 ■

Work: In Small Groups

2. 4 hr, 240 mi, 8 gal;
5 hr, 300 mi, 10 gal

1. Read the problem below.

A car traveling at 60 miles per hour uses 2 gallons of gasoline in one hour. How far can the car travel on one gallon of gasoline?

2. Make a table to show distance and gallons used for each hour of a five-hour trip.

3. Solve the problem, and then write an equation relating gallons, g, to distance, d. 60 mi ÷ 2 = 30 mi; $d = 30 \times g$

Hour	Distance	Gallons used
1	60 mi	2 gal
2	120 mi	4 gal
3	180 mi	6 gal

Unit 6, Lesson 3　　　　　Copyright © Houghton Mifflin Company

Activity Note Some students may think that the equation $30d = g$ expresses 30 miles per gallon. Have them use substitution to check if the equation they wrote is correct.

✎ Math Writing Prompt

Solve a Problem How can you pour exactly 4 L of water into a large bucket if you have only a 5-liter container and a 3-liter container?

✖ DESTINATION Math Software Support

Course III: Module 6: Unit 1: Displaying and Analyzing Data

Measures of Capacity　**599**

3 Homework and Spiral Review

6–3 **Homework** **Goal:** Additional Practice

For Homework, students convert among metric and among customary units of capacity to solve word problems.

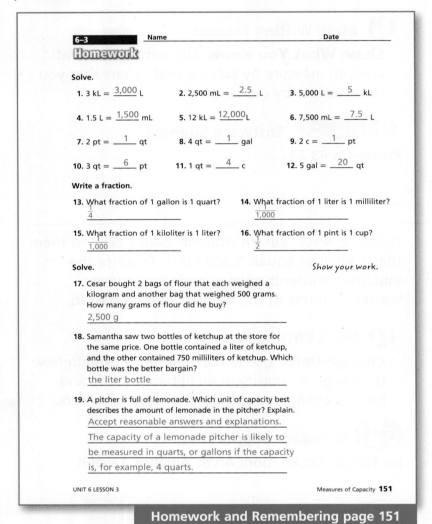

6–3 **Homework** Name ______ Date ______

Solve.

1. 3 kL = 3,000 L
2. 2,500 mL = 2.5 L
3. 5,000 L = 5 kL
4. 1.5 L = 1,500 mL
5. 12 kL = 12,000 L
6. 7,500 mL = 7.5 L
7. 2 pt = 1 qt
8. 4 qt = 1 gal
9. 2 c = 1 pt
10. 3 qt = 6 pt
11. 1 qt = 4 c
12. 5 gal = 20 qt

Write a fraction.

13. What fraction of 1 gallon is 1 quart? $\frac{1}{4}$
14. What fraction of 1 liter is 1 milliliter? $\frac{1}{1,000}$
15. What fraction of 1 kiloliter is 1 liter? $\frac{1}{1,000}$
16. What fraction of 1 pint is 1 cup? $\frac{1}{2}$

Solve. *Show your work.*

17. Cesar bought 2 bags of flour that each weighed a kilogram and another bag that weighed 500 grams. How many grams of flour did he buy?
2,500 g
18. Samantha saw two bottles of ketchup at the store for the same price. One bottle contained a liter of ketchup, and the other contained 750 milliliters of ketchup. Which bottle was the better bargain?
the liter bottle
19. A pitcher is full of lemonade. Which unit of capacity best describes the amount of lemonade in the pitcher? Explain.
Accept reasonable answers and explanations.
The capacity of a lemonade pitcher is likely to be measured in quarts, or gallons if the capacity is, for example, 4 quarts.

Homework and Remembering page 151

6–3 **Remembering** **Goal:** Spiral Review

This Remembering activity is appropriate anytime after today's lesson.

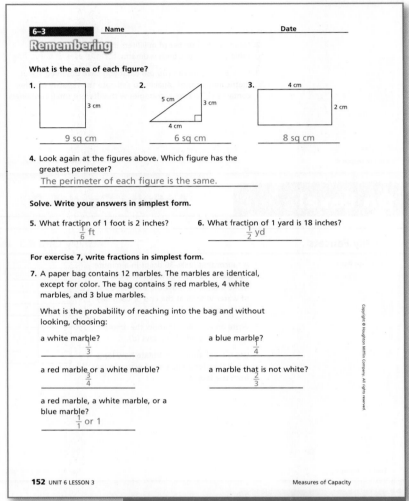

6–3 **Remembering** Name ______ Date ______

What is the area of each figure?

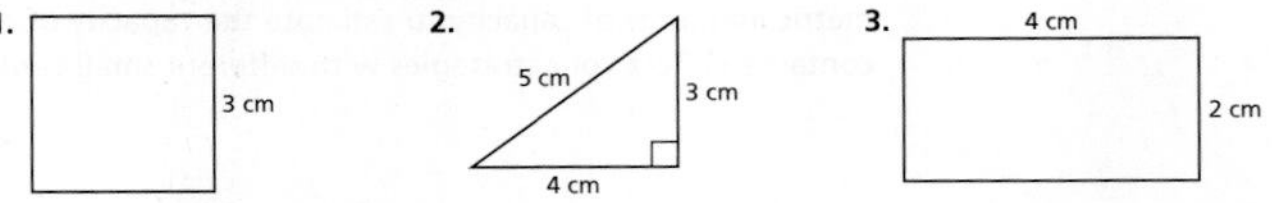
3 cm
5 cm
3 cm
4 cm
4 cm
2 cm

1. 9 sq cm
2. 6 sq cm
3. 8 sq cm

4. Look again at the figures above. Which figure has the greatest perimeter?
The perimeter of each figure is the same.

Solve. Write your answers in simplest form.

5. What fraction of 1 foot is 2 inches? $\frac{1}{6}$ ft
6. What fraction of 1 yard is 18 inches? $\frac{1}{2}$ yd

For exercise 7, write fractions in simplest form.

7. A paper bag contains 12 marbles. The marbles are identical, except for color. The bag contains 5 red marbles, 4 white marbles, and 3 blue marbles.
What is the probability of reaching into the bag and without looking, choosing:
a white marble? $\frac{1}{3}$
a blue marble? $\frac{1}{4}$
a red marble or a white marble? $\frac{3}{4}$
a marble that is not white? $\frac{2}{3}$
a red marble, a white marble, or a blue marble? $\frac{1}{1}$ or 1

Homework and Remembering page 152

Home or School Activity

Multicultural Connection

Recipe Research Find a recipe for a dish that comes from a culture different from your own. List all the capacity units and amounts that are used in the recipe.

Measures of Mass and Weight

Vocabulary

mass
kilogram
gram
milligram
ounce
pound
ton

Lesson Objectives

● Explore the relationships among metric units of mass and among customary units of weight.

● Solve problems involving metric measures of mass and customary measures of weight.

The Day at a Glance

Today's Goals	Materials	
1 Teaching the Lesson 　**A1:** Discuss the similarities and differences between mass and weight. 　**A2:** Convert among metric units of mass. 　**A3:** Convert among customary units of weight. **2 Going Further** 　▶ Differentiated Instruction **3 Homework and Spiral Review**	**Lesson Activities** Student Activity Book pp. 241–242 or Student Hardcover Book pp. 241–242 Homework and Remembering pp. 153–154 Balance scale and classroom objects (optional)	**Going Further** Activity Cards 6-4 Math Journals *Use* **Math Talk** *today!*

Keeping Skills Sharp

Daily Routines	English Language Learners
Homework Review See if any problem caused difficulty for many students. **Mental Math** Find the number that is 0.01 greater and the number that is 0.01 less than each of the given numbers. **1.** 3,950　　　**2.** 16,008.79 **3.** 57.114　　　**4.** 913.2 1. 3,950.01, 3,949.99; 2. 16,008.80, 16,008.78; 3. 57.124; 57.104; 4. 913.21, 913.19	Write *mass* on the board. Draw a balance with equal sized cubes *A* and *B*. Cube *B* has a greater mass. Ask: **Are these the same size?** yes ● **Beginning** Say: **Cube *B* has a greater mass.** Have students repeat. ● **Intermediate** Ask: **Do they have the same mass?** no **Which has a greater mass?** *B* ● **Advanced** Have students compare the mass of the two cubes.

1 Teaching the Lesson

Measures of Mass and Weight

 20 MINUTES

Goal: Discuss the similarities and differences between mass and weight.

Materials: balance scale and classroom objects (optional)

✔ **NCTM Standards:**
Measurement
Communication

▶ Compare and Contrast Measures of Mass and Weight WHOLE CLASS

Although the terms mass and weight are sometimes used interchangeably, the terms do not have the same meaning. Use the following example to help students understand the difference.

● Suppose your weight on Earth is 60 pounds. Because the force of gravity on the Moon is only $\frac{1}{6}$ as much as the force of gravity on Earth, your weight on the Moon would be $\frac{1}{6}$ of your weight on Earth. If you could go to the Moon and stand on a scale, how much would you weigh? $\frac{1}{6}$ of 60 pounds, or 10 pounds

You might ask students for the weight of a 60-pound person on other space objects with these approximate forces of gravity compared with Earth.

Mercury or Mars	$\frac{1}{3}$	20 pounds
Jupiter	$2\frac{1}{2}$	150 pounds
Pluto	$\frac{1}{25}$	$2\frac{2}{5}$ pounds

Then ask whether the mass would change on each planet. No, the mass stays the same.

 Math Talk Have students work in **Small Groups** and discuss why mass does not change regardless of location. Then have groups share with the class and compare answers.

Students should explain that the mass stays the same, because the amount of matter doesn't change by traveling to the Moon or another space object. Your body is made up of an amount of material. This amount is your mass; it is the same whether you are on Earth or on the Moon. In other words, you are the same mass in each place. But your weight is different.

✋ Alternate Approach

Balance Scale Have students compare some classroom objects for weight (or mass). They can use a box of pencils, a tape dispenser, a stapler, scissors, and so on. Ask them to order the objects from lightest to heaviest. Then have them check their predictions by using a balance scale. Have them continue checking and comparing until they get all the objects in the correct order.

Teaching Note

Math Background Mass is a difficult concept to define for students. Sir Isaac Newton (1642–1727) defined mass as the quantity of matter. Students may then ask, "What is matter?" This would involve a discussion of the concept of density. Two objects of exactly the same volume may have different masses because the matter or "stuff" in one object is more densely packed than in the other—like packing more stuff in a suitcase of the same size.

Weight depends on the pull of gravity, the concept for which Newton is most famous. In the customary system, pounds are used to measure weight and slugs are used to measure mass. The metric unit of weight is the newton (N), named after the famous Sir Isaac, of course, and the metric unit of mass is the kilogram.

The Learning Classroom

Helping Community It will be important to take some class time to discuss what *good helping* is all about. Students may come up with a list that can be posted in the classroom. It is important that they understand that good helping does not mean telling answers, but it means taking other students through steps so that they come up with the answer themselves.

Metric Measures of Mass

 20 MINUTES

Goal: Convert among metric units of mass.

Materials: Student Activity Book or Hardcover Book p. 241

✔ **NCTM Standard:**
Measurement

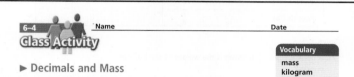

6–4	Name					Date

Class Activity

Vocabulary
mass
kilogram
gram
milligram

▶ **Decimals and Mass**

Mass is the amount of matter in an object. Heavier objects have more mass. This table shows the metric units that we use to measure mass. We use **kilogram**, **gram**, and **milligram** most often.

kilogram (kg)	hectogram (hg)	dekagram (dkg)	gram (g)	decigram (dg)	centigram (cg)	milligram (mg)
1,000 g	100 g	10 g	1	0.1 g	0.01 g	0.001 g

× 10 ← × 10 ← × 10 ← → ÷ 10 → ÷ 10 → ÷ 10

Complete.

1. 1 kg = __1,000__ g   2. 500 mg = __0.5__ g   3. 2,000 g = __2__ kg

4. 2.5 g = __2,500__ mg   5. 4 kg = __4,000__ g   6. 5,000 mg = __5__ g

Solve.

7. Hiro has 5 kg of potatoes and 2 kg of onions. He plans to use 3 kg of potatoes and 0.5 kg of onions for a recipe. How many kilograms of each will not be used?
   2 kg of potatoes and 1.5 kg of onions

8. Javier estimates there are 2.5 kg of books in his book bag. Mavis estimates there are 1,500 g of books in her book bag. If the estimates are reasonable, who is carrying the heavier bag? Explain.
   Javier; 1,500 g is the same as 1.5 kg; 2.5 is greater than 1.5

9. A United States nickel has a mass of 5 g. A cloth bag contains 1 kg of nickels. About how many nickels are in the bag? Explain.
   about 200; 1 kg = 1,000 g and 1,000 ÷ 5 = 200

UNIT 6 LESSON 4   Measures of Mass and Weight **241**

Student Activity Book page 241

▶ **Decimals and Mass** WHOLE CLASS

Read aloud the introductory material on Student Book page 241, or read it together. Invite students to discuss the table.

● How do the prefixes of the units compare with the prefixes of the units of capacity in the previous lesson? They are the same prefixes.

Review how to use the table to help to change units of mass. For example, to change from a larger unit (such as kilograms) to a smaller unit (such as grams), you need to multiply the number of kilograms by 10, by 10, and by 10 again. It is helpful for students to recall that multiplying a number by 10, by 10, and by 10 again is the same as multiplying that number by 10 × 10 × 10, or 1,000. Multiplying a number by 1,000 is the same as moving the decimal point 3 places to the right.

● Describe how to change milligrams to grams. Divide the number of milligrams by 1,000, or move the decimal point 3 places to the left.

Have the students work together to discuss and complete exercises 1–6. Challenge students to use only mental math. Then use **Solve and Discuss** for exercises 7–9.

Teaching Note

Math Background A *tonne*, sometimes called a metric ton, is 1,000 kg. It is equivalent to about 2,200 pounds. A lowercase "t" is the symbol for tonne. 1,000 L, or 1 kL, of water has a mass of one tonne.

Ongoing Assessment

Ask students what metric unit is best used to measure different objects.

▶ What would you use to measure the mass of a strawberry? a pumpkin? a drop of water?

1 Teaching the Lesson (continued)

Activity 3

Customary Measures of Weight

 20 MINUTES

Goal: Convert among customary units of weight.

Materials: Student Activity Book or Hardcover Book p. 242

 NCTM Standards:
Measurement
Number and Operations

▶ Fractions and Weight WHOLE CLASS

Write the words *ounces*, *pounds*, and *tons* in a horizontal row on the board. Remind students that these units are the customary, or common, units we use to measure weight. Then invite volunteers to write, in the appropriate column, an object whose weight is likely to be measured with that unit. For example, you might measure a coin in ounces, a textbook in pounds, and an automobile in tons.

During this activity, students will work with fractions and must write fractions and mixed numbers in simplest form. Prior to completing the activity, you might choose to review how to simplify fractions.

● What operation do we use to change a fraction to simplest form? division

● How do we use division to change a fraction to simplest form? Divide the numerator and the denominator of a fraction by the same number.

● Whenever possible, what number should you divide by to change a fraction to simplest form? greatest common factor (or greatest common divisor) of the numerator and of the denominator

Teaching Note

Language and Vocabulary The term *ounce* has two meanings, one for capacity (how much a container can hold) and one for weight. Explain that sometimes the capacity unit is referred to as a *fluid ounce*. The weight measure was once called an *ounce avoirdupois*, the system of weights in which 16 ounces equals 1 pound. An older system used the *ounce troy*, which had 12 ounces in a pound. This system is still in use today by goldsmiths and jewelers.

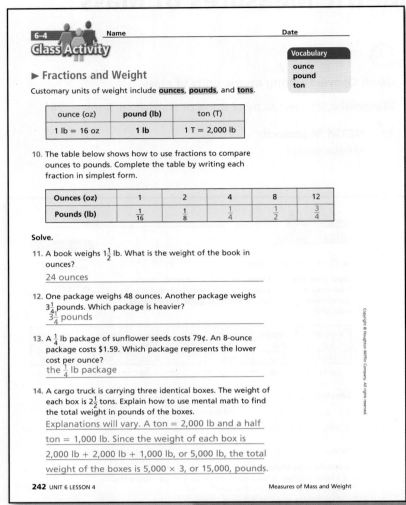

Student Activity Book page 242

Use **Solve and Discuss** for exercises 10–14. As students work, encourage them to memorize the equivalent units that are presented in the lesson.

$$1 \text{ pound} = 16 \text{ ounces}$$

$$1 \text{ ton} = 2,000 \text{ pounds}$$

Differentiated Instruction

Advanced Learners Point out that in the customary measurement system, a standard ton is equal to 2,000 pounds and is also called a short ton. Students may enjoy the challenge of discovering what a long ton is, and sharing their findings with their classmates. (A long ton = 2,240 pounds and is occasionally used to measure the displacement of ships.)

② Going Further

Intervention — Activity Card 6-4

Equivalent Measures — Activity Card 6-4

Work: In Pairs

1. Copy the diagram below showing two weights balanced on a scale.

2. Measures will vary. Some possible measures include:
2,000 mg and 2 g
5 g and 0.005 kg
1,000 lb and $\frac{1}{2}$ T
4 oz and $\frac{1}{4}$ lb

2. Take turns. One partner writes a weight below one side of the scale. The other partner writes a weight below the other side to balance it, but uses a different unit in the same system. For example, 1,000 mg and 1 g.

3. **Math Talk** Which measurement system do you prefer to use? Explain why. Possible answer: The metric system, because it is easier to find equivalent measures.

Unit 6, Lesson 4   Copyright © Houghton Mifflin Company

Activity Note If students are ready for it, encourage them to include some examples that include fractions or decimals. For example: 500 mg = 0.5 g.

✎ Math Writing Prompt

Investigate Mathematics Explain how to calculate how many ounces are in 1 ton.

 **Software Support**

Warm-Up 39.10

On Level — Activity Card 6-4

Changing Units — Activity Card 6-4 ▲

Work: In Pairs

1. Copy and complete the table to show how to convert kilograms to pounds. Remember: 1 kg is equal to about 2 lb.

Kilograms	Pounds
1	2.2
2	4.4
3	6.6
4	8.8

2. Use the data in the table to write a general equation relating weight in pounds (p) to kilograms (k). $p \approx 2.2 \times k$

3. **Work Together** Find other conversions between measurement systems to share with your class. For example, about how many kilometers equal 1 mile?
Possible answer: about 1.6 km

Unit 6, Lesson 4   Copyright © Houghton Mifflin Company

Activity Note Some students may think that the equation $k \approx 2.2 \times p$ relates kilograms and pounds. Have them use substitution and the values in their table to check if their equation is correct.

✎ Math Writing Prompt

Explain Your Thinking Why do we say that astronauts in space are "weightless" even though their mass remains the same as it is on Earth?

 Software Support

Ice Station Exploration: Arctic Algebra, Level K

Challenge — Activity Card 6-4

Write an Equation — Activity Card 6-4 ■

Work: In Pairs

1. Read the following situation.

- It costs $15 an hour to rent a bicycle for 1 hour.
- Each additional hour costs $10.
- Any time over 1 hour is rounded up to the next whole hour.

2. Together, write an equation for the cost (c) of renting a bike for any number of hours (h).
Possible answer: $c = (h - 1) \times \$10 + \$15$

3. **Write About It** Explain why your equation will work for any number of hours.

Unit 6, Lesson 4   Copyright © Houghton Mifflin Company

Activity Note If students have difficulty writing the equation, have them write an equation for a 2-hour rental. Then go back and substitute c into the equation for cost and h into the equation for hours.

✎ Math Writing Prompt

Use Appropriate Units Write about some animals you might weigh in ounces, pounds, or tons. Include an estimate of each animal's weight.

 Software Support

Course III: Module 2: Unit 3: Two-digit Multipliers

③ Homework and Spiral Review

6-4 Homework Goal: Additional Practice

For Homework, students convert among metric and among customary units of mass and weight to solve word problems.

6-4 Remembering Goal: Spiral Review

This Remembering activity is appropriate anytime after today's lesson.

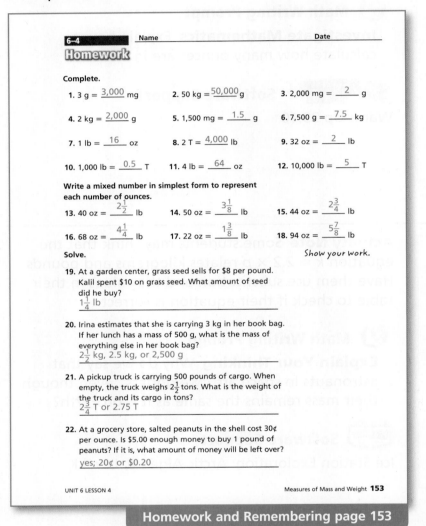

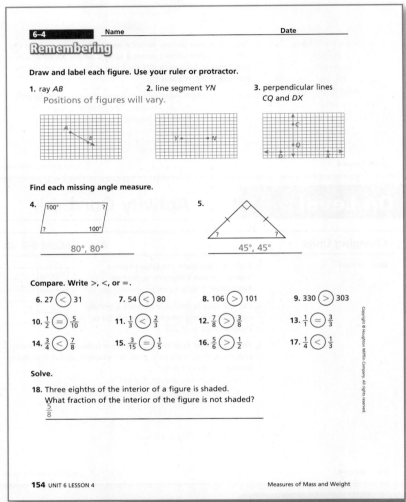

Home or School Activity

Science Connection

Birth Weights The average human baby weighs 7 pounds 5 ounces at birth. Use science books, encyclopedias, or the Internet to research the average birth weights of various animals. Show your information in a table organized from least to greatest weight.

Working with Measurement Units (Optional)

REAL WORLD Problem Solving

Lesson Objectives

- Convert, add, and subtract metric and customary units.
- Estimate metric and customary measurements.
- Compare metric and customary units.

The Day at a Glance

Today's Goals	Materials

1 Teaching the Lesson
  A1: Convert metric and customary units of capacity, mass or weight, area, and volume.
  A2: Add and subtract compound measurement units.
  A3: Compare metric and customary measures.
  A4: Use benchmarks to estimate metric and customary measures.
 	
2 Going Further
  ▶ Differentiated Instruction
 	
3 Homework and Spiral Review
	Lesson Activities
	Student Activity Book pp. 243–244 or Student Hardcover Book pp. 243–244
	Homework and Remembering pp. 155–156
	Several plastic containers
	Several objects
	Quick Quiz 2 (Assessment Guide)
	
	Going Further
	Activity Cards 6-5
	Centimeter ruler
	Scissors
	Box-shaped objects
	Math Journals
	
	123 Use Math Talk today!

Keeping Skills Sharp

Daily Routines	English Language Learners
Homework Review Have students explain how they found the answers. Look for the errors. **Strategy Problem** Uli spent $32 to buy a total of 10 tickets for both adults and children. An adult ticket costs $4, which is twice the price of a children's ticket. How many of each ticket did she buy? Uli's cost $4 ÷ 2 = $2. Try 5 adult and 5 children's: 5 × $4 = $20; 5 × $2 = $10; $20 + $10 = $30, too little. Try 6 adult = $24; 4 children's = $8; $24 + $8 = $32	Write *pound, kilogram, metric,* and *customary* on the board. • **Beginning** Point and say: **A kilogram is a metric measurement.** Ask: **Is a pound a metric measurement?** no **Is a pound a customary measurement?** yes • **Intermediate** Ask: **Which is metric, a kilogram or a pound?** kilogram Say: **A pound is a __ measurement.** customary • **Advanced** Have students identify the units and say which type of measurements they are.

① Teaching the Lesson

Convert Metric and Customary Measurements

 30 MINUTES

Goal: Convert metric and customary units of capacity, mass or weight, area, and volume.

Materials: Student Activity Book or Hardcover Book p. 243

✔ **NCTM Standards:**
Number and Operations
Measurement

▶ Metric Measurements WHOLE CLASS

Ask for Ideas Invite volunteers to share what they know about the metric system of measurement. If necessary, point out that the metric system is formally known as the *International System of Units* (*SI*), and it is widely used around the world in a variety of disciplines. (The United States is the only industrialized country in the world that does not use the metric system as its predominant system of measurement.)

Make sure students understand that the metric system of measurement is a base 10 system, which means that multiples of 10 are used to derive larger and smaller units, with 1,000 being the most common multiple used.

Capacity Invite volunteers to define the term *capacity*. Capacity is a measure of the amount a container can hold. Point out that the *liter* is a common metric unit of capacity, and write the capacity relations shown below on the board or overhead.

$$1 \text{ liter (L)} = 1,000 \text{ milliliters (mL)}$$
$$1,000 \text{ liters (L)} = 1 \text{ kiloliter (kL)}$$

Special Relationship You may want to share with students that there is a special relationship among metric measurements for water only. When measuring water, 1,000 cubic centimeters of water are equivalent to 1 liter of water, which weighs 1 kilogram. You will find further information on page 581I of this Teacher Edition.

 Math Talk in Action Discuss the relations.

• **Explain how we can change any number of liters to milliliters.**

Mario: The prefix *milli-* means one-thousandth.

Shania: A liter is more than a milliliter, so multiply the number of liters by 1,000.

• **How can we change any number of liters to kiloliters?**

Rhondell: The prefix *kilo-* means 1,000.

Kyle: A liter is less than a kiloliter, so divide the number of liters by 1,000.

Write the following statements on the board and ask students to explain how to find the missing numbers.

2,000 L = ___ kL 2; divide by 1,000
3 L = ___ mL 3,000; multiply by 1,000
5,000 mL = ___ L 5; divide by 1,000
8 kL = ___ L 8,000; multiply by 1,000

Generalize Ask students to state the operation that is used to change a smaller unit (such as liters) to a larger unit (such as kiloliters), and state the operation that is used to change a larger unit (such as liters) to a smaller unit (such as milliliters). Use division to change a smaller unit to a larger unit; use multiplication to change a larger unit to a smaller unit.

Teaching Note

Math Background In today's activity (and in other upcoming activities) students will not explore every metric unit. Instead, they will only work with those units that are widely used.

Class Management

One part of making everyone responsible for listening to one another is to make sure that the explainers are talking loudly enough and that they are talking to the whole class, not just you.

Have students use a pretend microphone initially to remind them to talk loudly. The pretend situation frees them to talk more loudly than they usually can and to look directly at their "audience." In some cultural backgrounds children are not supposed to talk loudly, especially to the teacher, or gaze directly at the teacher.

▶ Compound Metric Units SMALL GROUPS

Point out that some conversions involve compound (e.g., more than one) units.

Capacity Have **Small Groups** discuss possible ways to complete the conversions shown below and share their methods with the class.

1 L 500 mL = ___ mL 1,500
7 L 250 mL = ___ mL 7,250
2.6 L = ___ L ___ mL 2; 600
4.005 L = ___ L ___ mL 4; 5

Mass Although the terms weight and mass are often used interchangeably, mass is, strictly speaking, a measure of how much matter is in an object, whereas weight is a measure of the gravitational pull on an object. Point out that common units of mass include gram (g), kilogram (kg), and milligram (mg), with gram being the standard or benchmark unit.

Write the prefixes shown below on the board to remind students of their meanings.

$$\text{kilo} = 1,000 \quad \text{milli} = \frac{1}{1,000}$$

Have different **Small Groups** discuss possible ways to complete the conversions shown below and share their methods with the class.

4 kg = ___ g 4,000
8,000 g = ___ kg 8
2 kg 375 g = ___ g 2,375

Encourage students to offer and complete other mass conversions.

Area and Volume Invite volunteers to explain the concept of area (a measure of the amount of surface covered or enclosed by a figure) and volume (a measure of the amount of space an object occupies).

Draw the figures and write the formulas shown below on the board. As a class, discuss how to find the area of the rectangle and the volume of the cylinder, and then name those measures. $A = 1.8 \text{ m}^2$ and $V \approx 240.21 \text{m}^3$ (using 3.14 for π)

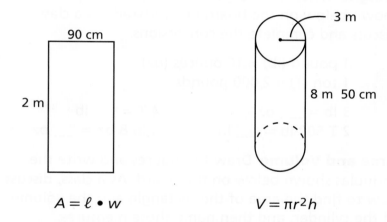

$$A = \ell \cdot w \qquad\qquad V = \pi r^2 h$$

Make sure students recognize that the dimensions of each figure must be changed to a common unit before the formulas can be used. For example, the 90-centimeter base of the rectangle must be changed to meters, or the 2-meter height must be changed to centimeters. (90 cm = 0.9 m or 2 m = 200 cm). Although either conversion will produce a correct answer, converting to meters gives us an answer that is more easily understood or visualized (1.8 m²) than converting to centimeters (18,000 cm²).

Summarize Culminate the activity by having students note that compound units must sometimes be converted to one common unit before multiplication (or division) can be performed.

Teaching Note

Math Background You may wish to share these relationships with the students. For water, 1 mL = 1 cubic cm and has a mass of 1 g. 1,000 cubic cm = 1 Liter and has a mass of 1 kg.

Activity continued ▶

① Teaching the Lesson (continued)

Activity 1

▶ Compound Customary Units

WHOLE CLASS

Capacity Write the capacity relations and the exercises shown below on the board or overhead. As a class, discuss and complete the conversions.

> 1 pint (pt) = 2 cups (c)
> 1 quart (qt) = 2 pints
> 1 gallon (gal) = 4 quarts
>
> 6 c = ___ pt 3   3 gal = ___ qt 12
> 2 qt 3 c = ___ c 11   1 gal 1 pt = ___ pt 9

Weight Write the weight relations and the exercises shown below on the board or overhead. As a class, discuss and complete the conversions.

> 1 pound (lb) = 16 ounces (oz)
> 1 ton (T) = 2,000 pounds
>
> 3 lb = ___ oz 48   4 T = ___ lb 8,000
> 2 T 500 lb = ___ lb 4,500   5 lb 8 oz = ___ oz 88

Area and Volume Draw the figures and write the formulas shown below on the board. As a class, discuss how to find the area of the rectangle and the volume of the cylinder, and then name those measures.
$A = 112$ in.^{2} and using 3.14 for π, $V \approx 42.39$ ft^3

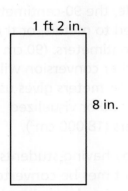

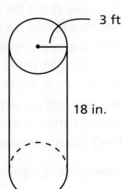

1 ft 2 in.

8 in.

3 ft

18 in.

$A = \ell \cdot w$ $V = \pi r^2 h$

Remind students that the dimensions of each figure must be changed to a common unit before the formulas can be used.

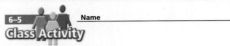

6–5
Class Activity

Name _____ Date _____

▶ Convert Measurements

Write *multiply by 1,000* or *divide by 1,000* to complete each sentence.

1. To change grams to kilograms, _divide by 1,000_.
2. To change grams to milligrams, _multiply by 1,000_.
3. To change kiloliters to liters, _multiply by 1,000_.
4. To change milliliters to liters, _divide by 1,000_.

Use the information in the table below to complete exercises 5–16.

Metric	Customary
kilo = 1,000	1 pint (pt) = 2 cups (c)
milli = $\frac{1}{1,000}$	1 quart (qt) = 2 pints
	1 gallon (gal) = 4 quarts
1 gram (g) = 1,000 milligrams (mg)	1 pound (lb) = 16 ounces (oz)
1 kiloliter (kL) = 1,000 liters (L)	1 ton (T) = 2,000 pounds

5. 3,040 mL = _3_ L _40_ mL
6. 1 gal = _8_ pt
7. 72 oz = _4_ lb _8_ oz
8. 4 c = _1_ qt
9. 4,300 g = _4_ kg _300_ g
10. 5 T = _10,000_ lb
11. 1 g 1,000 mg = _2_ g
12. 3 kL 1,000 L = _4_ kL
13. 2 L 500 mL = _2,500_ mL
14. 7 kg = _7,000_ g
15. 2 qt 2 c = _5_ pt
16. 1 gal = _16_ c

17. Write an example to show that the statement below is true. *Examples will vary.*

Multiplication is used to change a larger unit to a smaller unit.
To change grams to milligrams, multiply the number of grams by 1,000; 5 grams = 5,000 milligrams.

18. Write an example to show that the statement below is true. *Examples will vary.*

Division is used to change a smaller unit to a larger unit.
To change milliliters to liters, divide the number of milliliters by 1,000; 3,000 milliliters = 3 liters.

UNIT 6 LESSON 5   Working with Measurement Units **243**

Student Activity Book page 243

▶ Convert Measurements WHOLE CLASS

Discuss and complete exercises 1–4 as a class.

Have students work in **Small Groups** and use **Solve and Discuss** for exercises 5–18. Invite a volunteer from each group to share the group's answers to exercises 17 and 18 with the class.

Differentiated Instruction

Extra Help For students who have difficulty with customary measures of capacity, suggest that they make Study Sheets. They might include these measures.

1 cup = $\frac{1}{2}$ pint   1 quart = 2 pints

2 cups = 1 pint   1 gallon = 8 pints

4 cups = 1 quart   1 gallon = 4 quarts

16 cups = 1 gallon

---

610 UNIT 6 LESSON 5

Add and Subtract Measurements

 30 MINUTES

Goal: Add and subtract compound measurement units.

Materials: Student Activity Book or Hardcover Book p. 244

✓ **NCTM Standards:**
Number and Operations
Measurement

▶ Add and Subtract Metric Measurements ⬚WHOLE CLASS⬚

Have students recall that whenever they subtract two whole numbers, they must ungroup whenever the number being subtracted is greater than the number they are subtracting from, and they must regroup whenever they add two whole numbers if the sum in any place is more than 9. Point out that in a related way, ungroupings and regroupings must often be performed when subtracting or adding two measures.

Capacity Write the exercises shown below on the board and have students work cooperatively to discuss the computations and find the answers.

$$
\begin{array}{r}
3\ \text{L } 750\ \text{mL} \\
-\ 1\ \text{L } 200\ \text{mL} \\
\hline
2\ \text{L } 550\ \text{mL}
\end{array}
\qquad
\begin{array}{r}
4\ \text{L } 300\ \text{mL} \\
-\ 1\ \text{L } 900\ \text{mL} \\
\hline
2\ \text{L } 400\ \text{mL}
\end{array}
$$

$$
\begin{array}{r}
5\ \text{L } 600\ \text{mL} \\
+\ 2\ \text{L } 150\ \text{mL} \\
\hline
7\ \text{L } 750\ \text{mL}
\end{array}
\qquad
\begin{array}{r}
2\ \text{L } 700\ \text{mL} \\
+\ 6\ \text{L } 500\ \text{mL} \\
\hline
9\ \text{L } 200\ \text{mL}
\end{array}
$$

Make sure students understand the ungrouping of 4 L 300 mL (as 3 L 1,300 mL) to complete the subtraction, and understand the regrouping of 8 L 1,200 mL (as 9 L 200 mL) to simplify the sum.

Mass Write the exercises shown below on the board and have students work cooperatively to discuss the computations and find the answers.

$$
\begin{array}{r}
4\ \text{g } 400\ \text{mg} \\
-\ 1\ \text{g } 300\ \text{mg} \\
\hline
3\ \text{g } 100\ \text{mg}
\end{array}
\qquad
\begin{array}{r}
6\ \text{g } 200\ \text{mg} \\
-\ 3\ \text{g } 700\ \text{mg} \\
\hline
2\ \text{g } 500\ \text{mg}
\end{array}
$$

$$
\begin{array}{r}
3\ \text{g } 500\ \text{mg} \\
+\ 5\ \text{g } 350\ \text{mg} \\
\hline
8\ \text{g } 850\ \text{mg}
\end{array}
\qquad
\begin{array}{r}
1\ \text{g } 650\ \text{mg} \\
+\ 2\ \text{g } 900\ \text{mg} \\
\hline
4\ \text{g } 550\ \text{mg}
\end{array}
$$

Make sure students understand the ungrouping of 6 g 200 mg (as 5 g 1,200 mg) to complete the subtraction, and understand the regrouping of 3 g 1,550 mg (as 4 g 550 mg) to simplify the sum.

▶ Add and Subtract Customary Measurements ⬚WHOLE CLASS⬚

Capacity Write the exercises shown below on the board and have students work cooperatively to discuss the computations and find the answers.

$$
\begin{array}{r}
2\ \text{gal } 3\ \text{qt} \\
-\ 1\ \text{gal } 1\ \text{qt} \\
\hline
1\ \text{gal } 2\ \text{qt}
\end{array}
\qquad
\begin{array}{r}
6\ \text{gal } 1\ \text{qt} \\
-\ 2\ \text{gal } 2\ \text{qt} \\
\hline
3\ \text{gal } 3\ \text{qt}
\end{array}
$$

$$
\begin{array}{r}
5\ \text{gal } 1\ \text{qt} \\
+\ 3\ \text{gal } 2\ \text{qt} \\
\hline
8\ \text{gal } 3\ \text{qt}
\end{array}
\qquad
\begin{array}{r}
4\ \text{gal } 3\ \text{qt} \\
+\ 1\ \text{gal } 3\ \text{qt} \\
\hline
6\ \text{gal } 2\ \text{qt}
\end{array}
$$

Make sure students understand the ungrouping of 6 gal 1 qt (as 5 gal 5 qt) to complete the subtraction, and understand the regrouping of 5 gal 6 qt (as 6 gal 2 qt) to simplify the sum.

Activity continued ▶

Activity 2

Weight Write the exercises shown below on the board and have students work cooperatively to discuss the computations and find the answers.

$$\begin{array}{r} 2\text{ lb } 8\text{ oz} \\ -\ 1\text{ lb } 6\text{ oz} \\ \hline 1\text{ lb } 2\text{ oz} \end{array} \qquad \begin{array}{r} 5\text{ lb } 4\text{ oz} \\ -\ 2\text{ lb } 9\text{ oz} \\ \hline 2\text{ lb } 11\text{ oz} \end{array}$$

$$\begin{array}{r} 3\text{ lb } 1\text{ oz} \\ +\ 3\text{ lb } 9\text{ oz} \\ \hline 6\text{ lb } 10\text{ oz} \end{array} \qquad \begin{array}{r} 1\text{ lb } 12\text{ oz} \\ +\ 4\text{ lb } 10\text{ oz} \\ \hline 6\text{ lb } 6\text{ oz} \end{array}$$

Make sure students understand the ungrouping of 5 lb 4 oz (as 4 lb 20 oz) to complete the subtraction, and understand the regrouping of 5 lb 22 oz (as 6 lb 6 oz) to simplify the sum.

Generalize As a class, compare and contrast adding and subtracting whole numbers with adding and subtracting metric or customary measures. Make sure students emphasize the differences when units in each system are ungrouped and regrouped.

Ongoing Assessment

▶ Explain how regrouping and ungrouping tons, pounds, and ounces are different from regrouping and ungrouping kilograms, grams, and milligrams.

▶ Explain how regrouping and ungrouping gallons, quarts, pints, and cups are different from regrouping and ungrouping kiloliters, liters, and milliliters.

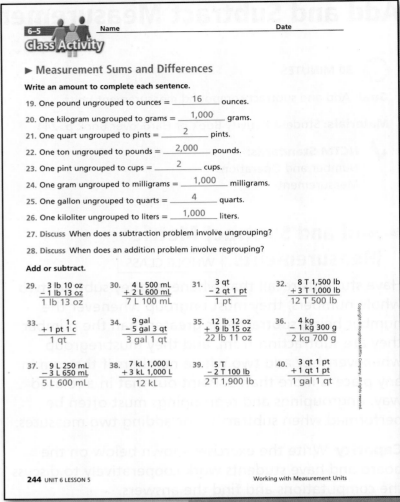

6-5
Class Activity
Name _____ Date _____

▶ **Measurement Sums and Differences**

Write an amount to complete each sentence.

19. One pound ungrouped to ounces = ___16___ ounces.

20. One kilogram ungrouped to grams = ___1,000___ grams.

21. One quart ungrouped to pints = ___2___ pints.

22. One ton ungrouped to pounds = ___2,000___ pounds.

23. One pint ungrouped to cups = ___2___ cups.

24. One gram ungrouped to milligrams = ___1,000___ milligrams.

25. One gallon ungrouped to quarts = ___4___ quarts.

26. One kiloliter ungrouped to liters = ___1,000___ liters.

27. Discuss When does a subtraction problem involve ungrouping?

28. Discuss When does an addition problem involve regrouping?

Add or subtract.

29.
$$\begin{array}{r} 3\text{ lb } 10\text{ oz} \\ -\ 1\text{ lb } 13\text{ oz} \\ \hline 1\text{ lb } 13\text{ oz} \end{array}$$
30.
$$\begin{array}{r} 4\text{ L } 500\text{ mL} \\ +\ 2\text{ L } 600\text{ mL} \\ \hline 7\text{ L } 100\text{ mL} \end{array}$$
31.
$$\begin{array}{r} 3\text{ qt} \\ -\ 2\text{ qt } 1\text{ pt} \\ \hline 1\text{ pt} \end{array}$$
32.
$$\begin{array}{r} 8\text{ T } 1,500\text{ lb} \\ +\ 3\text{ T } 1,000\text{ lb} \\ \hline 12\text{ T } 500\text{ lb} \end{array}$$

33.
$$\begin{array}{r} 1\text{ c} \\ +\ 1\text{ pt } 1\text{ c} \\ \hline 1\text{ qt} \end{array}$$
34.
$$\begin{array}{r} 9\text{ gal} \\ -\ 5\text{ gal } 3\text{ qt} \\ \hline 3\text{ gal } 1\text{ qt} \end{array}$$
35.
$$\begin{array}{r} 12\text{ lb } 12\text{ oz} \\ +\ 9\text{ lb } 15\text{ oz} \\ \hline 22\text{ lb } 11\text{ oz} \end{array}$$
36.
$$\begin{array}{r} 4\text{ kg} \\ -\ 1\text{ kg } 300\text{ g} \\ \hline 2\text{ kg } 700\text{ g} \end{array}$$

37.
$$\begin{array}{r} 9\text{ L } 250\text{ mL} \\ -\ 3\text{ L } 650\text{ mL} \\ \hline 5\text{ L } 600\text{ mL} \end{array}$$
38.
$$\begin{array}{r} 7\text{ kL } 1,000\text{ L} \\ +\ 3\text{ kL } 1,000\text{ L} \\ \hline 12\text{ kL} \end{array}$$
39.
$$\begin{array}{r} 5\text{ T} \\ -\ 2\text{ T } 100\text{ lb} \\ \hline 2\text{ T } 1,900\text{ lb} \end{array}$$
40.
$$\begin{array}{r} 3\text{ qt } 1\text{ pt} \\ +\ 1\text{ qt } 1\text{ pt} \\ \hline 1\text{ gal } 1\text{ qt} \end{array}$$

244 UNIT 6 LESSON 5   Working with Measurement Units

Student Activity Book page 244

▶ Measurement Sums and Differences

WHOLE CLASS

Direct the class to use **Solve and Discuss** to complete exercises 19–28 on Student Book page 244.

Ask students to work **Individually** or paired with a **Helping Partner** to discuss and complete exercises 29–40.

Metric and Customary Measures

 20 MINUTES

Goal: Compare metric and customary measures.

 NCTM Standards:
Number and Operations
Measurement
Connections

► Compare Metric and Customary Capacity WHOLE CLASS

Ask for Ideas Having a general sense of how metric and customary units compare is a useful skill. Ask students to suggest reasons why it may be helpful to understand how liters compare to quarts or gallons or how milliliters compare to cups and pints.

Write the general relationships shown below on the board or overhead. (Make sure students understand that the relationships are only approximations, and not exact.)

> 1 quart is about 1 liter.
> 1 cup is about 250 milliliters.

As a class, discuss possible answers to the following questions.

● Which is more, 1 cup or 1 milliliter? 1 cup

● Four cups is about the same as how many liters? 1 liter

● One liter is about the same as how many pints? 2 pints

● If you drink 2 cups of juice, will you drink more or less than 1 liter of juice? less

● About what fraction of a liter is a cup? $\frac{1}{4}$

Challenge students to pose and answer additional questions.

► Compare Metric Mass and Customary Weight WHOLE CLASS

Write the general relationships shown below on the board or overhead, and emphasize that the relationships are only approximations.

> 1 kilogram is about $2\frac{1}{4}$ pounds.
> 1 ounce is about 30 grams.

Discuss possible answers to the following questions as a class, and then challenge students to pose and answer additional questions.

● Which is more, 1 pound or 1 kilogram? 1 kilogram

● Which is more, 1 ounce or 1 gram? 1 ounce

● Four kilograms is about the same as how many pounds? 9 pounds

● About how many grams is 1 pound? about 480 grams

► Compare Metric and Customary Length WHOLE CLASS

Ask for Ideas Give students an opportunity to recall any metric and customary length relationships they learned about in Unit 2 Lesson 6. 1 in. ≈ 2.5 or $2\frac{1}{2}$ cm; 1 dm ≈ 4 in.; 1 yd ≈ 90 cm; 1 yd ≈ 0.9 or $\frac{9}{10}$ m; 1 mi ≈ 1,600 m; 1 mi ≈ 1.6 km; 1 km ≈ 0.6 or $\frac{5}{8}$ mi

Activity 4

Estimate Measurements

 25 MINUTES

Goal: Use benchmarks to estimate metric and customary measures.

Materials: several plastic containers, several objects

 NCTM Standard:
Measurement

▶ Estimate Metric and Customary Capacity WHOLE CLASS

Bring a variety of empty, plastic containers from home and display them in the classroom. Provide students with metric and customary capacity benchmarks (such as "This container has a capacity of 1 liter, and this container has a capacity of 1 gallon.") and ask them to use the benchmarks to estimate the capacities of the other containers.

If water is available, students could pour water to check the reasonableness of their estimates.

 Quick Quiz

See Assessment Guide for Unit 6 Quick Quiz 2.

▶ Estimate Weight or Mass WHOLE CLASS

Estimate Mass Display a variety of small objects. If the objects have a weight label, use a piece of easily-removable tape to hide the label.

Provide students with metric mass and customary weight benchmarks (such as "This object has a mass of 500 grams, and this object has a weight of 1 ounce."). Then ask students to use the benchmarks to estimate the mass or weight of the other objects. One way for students to make an estimate is to hold the benchmark object in one hand and the object to be estimated in the other hand.

If a scale is available, students could use metric and customary weights to check the reasonableness their estimates.

The Learning Classroom

Math Talk Aspire to make your classroom a place where all students listen to and understand one another. Explain to students that this is different from just being quiet when someone else is talking. This involves thinking about what a person is saying so that you could explain it yourself. Also, students need to listen so that they can ask a question or help the explainer. Remind students that listening can also help you learn that concept better.

②Going Further

Differentiated Instruction

Intervention — Activity Card 6-5

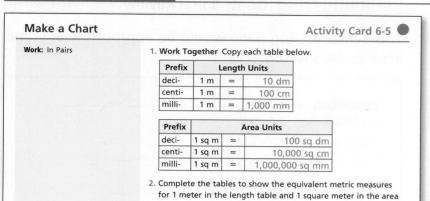

Make a Chart — Activity Card 6-5 ●

Work: In Pairs

1. **Work Together** Copy each table below.

Prefix	Length Units		
deci-	1 m	=	10 dm
centi-	1 m	=	100 cm
milli-	1 m	=	1,000 mm

Prefix	Area Units		
deci-	1 sq m	=	100 sq dm
centi-	1 sq m	=	10,000 sq cm
milli-	1 sq m	=	1,000,000 sq mm

2. Complete the tables to show the equivalent metric measures for 1 meter in the length table and 1 square meter in the area table.

Unit 6, Lesson 5   Copyright © Houghton Mifflin Company

Activity Note Students may wish to use the metric length equivalencies to sketch the subdivisions of a square meter before completing the area units. Ask students to identify any patterns they see.

 Math Writing Prompt

Explain Your Thinking Explain why an area of 1,000 sq cm is the same as an area of 10 sq dm.

 **Software Support**

Warm-Up 38.16

On Level — Activity Card 6-5

Match Game — Activity Card 6-5 ▲

Work: In Pairs

Use:
• Centimeter ruler
• Scissors
• Several box-shaped objects

1. Together with your partner, choose two objects with about the same volume.

2. On your own, measure the dimensions of your object and calculate the volume. Compare results with your partner and check each other's work.

3. You earn one point if the difference in volumes is greater than 10 cu cm. Your partner earns one point if the difference in volumes is less than 10 cu cm.

4. Repeat the activity. The first player to earn 5 points wins.

Unit 6, Lesson 5   Copyright © Houghton Mifflin Company

Activity Note Before beginning the activity, remind students of metric benchmarks that can help them estimate. Have students discuss any particular strategies they use to select the second object.

 Math Writing Prompt

Explain Your Thinking About how many 2-liter bottles of water are equivalent to one gallon? Explain how you know.

 Software Support

Ice Station Exploration: Frozen Solids, Level J

Challenge — Activity Card 6-5

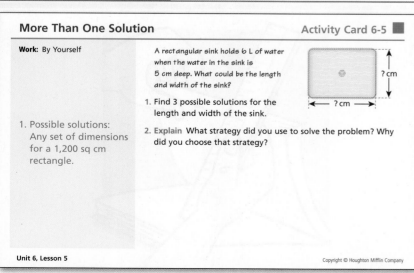

More Than One Solution — Activity Card 6-5 ■

Work: By Yourself

A rectangular sink holds 6 L of water when the water in the sink is 5 cm deep. What could be the length and width of the sink?

1. Find 3 possible solutions for the length and width of the sink.

2. **Explain** What strategy did you use to solve the problem? Why did you choose that strategy?

1. Possible solutions: Any set of dimensions for a 1,200 sq cm rectangle.

Unit 6, Lesson 5   Copyright © Houghton Mifflin Company

Activity Note Suggest that students look for a hidden question in the problem. They need to know the volume equivalent in cubic centimeters for 6 liters; 6 L = 6,000 mL = 6,000 cu cm.

 Math Writing Prompt

Summarize Information Describe how the metric system works by describing how the prefixes are related.

 **Software Support**

Course III: Module 5: Unit 1: Rectangles and Squares

③ Homework and Spiral Review

6–5
Homework **Goal:** Additional Practice

✓ Include students' Homework page 155 as part of their portfolios.

6–5
Remembering **Goal:** Spiral Review

This Remembering page would be appropriate anytime after today's lesson.

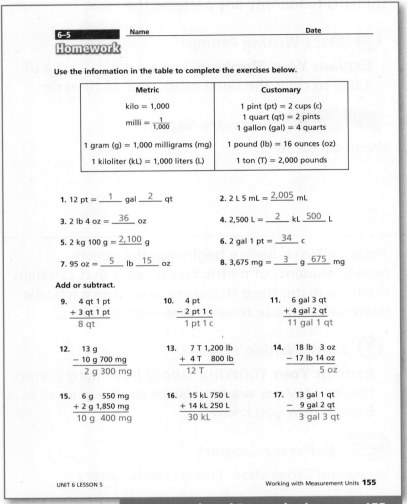

6–5 Name _____ Date _____
Homework

Use the information in the table to complete the exercises below.

Metric	Customary
kilo = 1,000	1 pint (pt) = 2 cups (c)
milli = $\frac{1}{1,000}$	1 quart (qt) = 2 pints
	1 gallon (gal) = 4 quarts
1 gram (g) = 1,000 milligrams (mg)	1 pound (lb) = 16 ounces (oz)
1 kiloliter (kL) = 1,000 liters (L)	1 ton (T) = 2,000 pounds

1. 12 pt = __1__ gal __2__ qt
2. 2 L 5 mL = __2,005__ mL
3. 2 lb 4 oz = __36__ oz
4. 2,500 L = __2__ kL __500__ L
5. 2 kg 100 g = __2,100__ g
6. 2 gal 1 pt = __34__ c
7. 95 oz = __5__ lb __15__ oz
8. 3,675 mg = __3__ g __675__ mg

Add or subtract.

9.   4 qt 1 pt
    + 3 qt 1 pt
    ――――――――
       8 qt

10.   4 pt
     − 2 pt 1 c
    ――――――――
      1 pt 1 c

11.   6 gal 3 qt
    + 4 gal 2 qt
    ――――――――――
      11 gal 1 qt

12.   13 g
    − 10 g 700 mg
    ――――――――――
      2 g 300 mg

13.   7 T 1,200 lb
     + 4 T   800 lb
    ――――――――――――
       12 T

14.   18 lb 3 oz
     − 17 lb 14 oz
    ――――――――――――
         5 oz

15.   6 g   550 mg
    + 2 g 1,850 mg
    ―――――――――――――
      10 g 400 mg

16.   15 kL 750 L
    + 14 kL 250 L
    ――――――――――――
      30 kL

17.   13 gal 1 qt
     − 9 gal 2 qt
    ――――――――――――
      3 gal 3 qt

UNIT 6 LESSON 5   Working with Measurement Units **155**

Homework and Remembering page 155

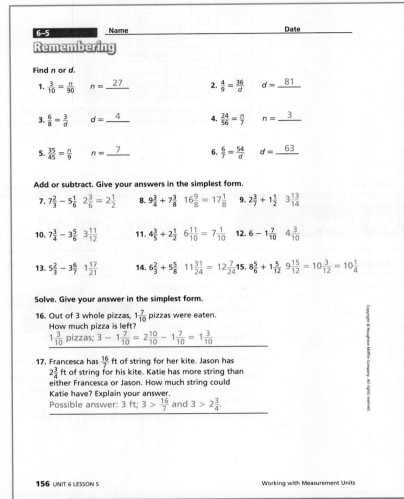

6–5 Name _____ Date _____
Remembering

Find n or d.

1. $\frac{3}{10} = \frac{n}{90}$ $n = $ __27__
2. $\frac{4}{9} = \frac{36}{d}$ $d = $ __81__

3. $\frac{6}{8} = \frac{3}{d}$ $d = $ __4__
4. $\frac{24}{56} = \frac{n}{7}$ $n = $ __3__

5. $\frac{35}{45} = \frac{n}{9}$ $n = $ __7__
6. $\frac{6}{7} = \frac{54}{d}$ $d = $ __63__

Add or subtract. Give your answers in the simplest form.

7. $7\frac{2}{3} - 5\frac{1}{6}$ $2\frac{3}{6} = 2\frac{1}{2}$
8. $9\frac{3}{4} + 7\frac{3}{8}$ $16\frac{9}{8} = 17\frac{1}{8}$
9. $2\frac{3}{7} + 1\frac{1}{2}$ $3\frac{13}{14}$

10. $7\frac{3}{4} - 3\frac{5}{6}$ $3\frac{11}{12}$
11. $4\frac{3}{5} + 2\frac{1}{2}$ $6\frac{11}{10} = 7\frac{1}{10}$
12. $6 - 1\frac{7}{10}$ $4\frac{3}{10}$

13. $5\frac{2}{3} - 3\frac{6}{7}$ $1\frac{17}{21}$
14. $6\frac{2}{3} + 5\frac{5}{8}$ $11\frac{31}{24} = 12\frac{7}{24}$
15. $8\frac{5}{6} + 1\frac{5}{12}$ $9\frac{15}{12} = 10\frac{3}{12} = 10\frac{1}{4}$

Solve. Give your answer in the simplest form.

16. Out of 3 whole pizzas, $1\frac{7}{10}$ pizzas were eaten. How much pizza is left?
    $1\frac{3}{10}$ pizzas; $3 - 1\frac{7}{10} = 2\frac{10}{10} - 1\frac{7}{10} = 1\frac{3}{10}$

17. Francesca has $\frac{16}{7}$ ft of string for her kite. Jason has $2\frac{3}{4}$ ft of string for his kite. Katie has more string than either Francesca or Jason. How much string could Katie have? Explain your answer.
    Possible answer: 3 ft; $3 > \frac{16}{7}$ and $3 > 2\frac{3}{4}$.

156 UNIT 6 LESSON 5   Working with Measurement Units

Homework and Remembering page 156

Home or School Activity

 Real-World Connection

What's the Width? Ask students to estimate the widths of several different-sized books in customary and in metric units. Then have students use customary and metric rulers to find the exact widths. Students can display their estimates and exact widths in a table.

Temperature (Optional)

Lesson Objectives

● Solve problems involving Fahrenheit and Celsius temperatures.

● Identify appropriate measurement tools and units.

● Interpret and make a stem-and-leaf plot.

Vocabulary

degree Fahrenheit (°F)
degree Celsius (°C)
stem-and-leaf plot

The Day at a Glance

Today's Goals	Materials
1 Teaching the Lesson **A1:** Identify benchmark Fahrenheit temperatures; solve Fahrenheit temperature problems. **A2:** Identify benchmark Celsius temperatures; solve Celsius temperature problems. **A3:** Compare Fahrenheit and Celsius temperatures. **A4:** Choose an appropriate measurement tool or unit. **A5:** Apply understanding of place value to develop and interpret a stem-and-leaf plot. **2 Going Further** ▶ Math Connection: Integers on the Number Line ▶ Differentiated Instruction **3 Homework and Spiral Review**	**Lesson Activities** Student Activity Book pp. 245–249 or Student Hardcover Book pp. 245–249 Homework and Remembering pp. 157–158 **Going Further** Student Activity Book p. 250 or Student Hardcover Book p. 250 and Activity Workbook p. 99 Activity Cards 6-6 Calculator Math Journals

123 *Use* **Math Talk** *today!*

Keeping Skills Sharp

Daily Routines	English Language Learners
Homework Review Have students discuss and resolve issues from their homework. **What Went Wrong?** Dani had $3\frac{1}{2}$ lb of flour. She used $1\frac{5}{7}$ lb. According to her calculation, she should have $2\frac{3}{14}$ lb left. She actually has $1\frac{11}{14}$ lb left. What went wrong with her calculations? She switched the fractions and subtracted: $3\frac{5}{7} - 1\frac{1}{2} = 3\frac{10}{14} - 1\frac{7}{14} = 2\frac{3}{14}$.	Draw a thermometer on the board. Label *degrees Fahrenheit (°F)* and *Celsius (°C)*. Write *thermometer* and *temperature*. ● **Beginning** Ask: **Do we use a *thermometer* to measure *temperature*?** yes **Can we measure in °F or °C?** yes ● **Intermediate** Say: **We use a thermometer to measure__.** temperature **We can measure in degrees __or degrees__.** Fahrenheit or Celsius ● **Advanced** Have students identify the thermometer, its use, and both scales.

Teaching the Lesson

Fahrenheit Temperature

 25 MINUTES

Goal: Identify benchmark Fahrenheit temperatures; solve Fahrenheit temperature problems.

Materials: Student Activity Book or Hardcover Book p. 245

✔ **NCTM Standards:**
Measurement
Reasoning and Proof
Number and Operations
Problem Solving

▶ Discuss Fahrenheit Temperature

WHOLE CLASS   Math Talk

Ask for Ideas Ask students to share what they know about degrees Fahrenheit and Fahrenheit thermometers. Make sure that the following ideas are part of the discussion.

● Thermometers are tools that are used to measure temperature.

● Fahrenheit is a temperature scale.

● The abbreviation used to represent Fahrenheit temperature is °F.

● The benchmark Fahrenheit temperatures are 212°F (water boils) and 32°F (water freezes).

Differentiated Instruction

Special Needs Some students may need to use an index card, held horizontally, to read temperatures on the thermometer. For students who have a hard time finding the numbers of degrees between two temperature readings, suggest that they "bracket" the numbers by placing sticky notes at the upper and lower temperatures and counting the degrees in between.

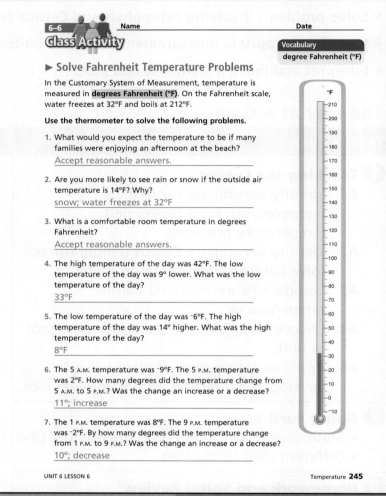

Student Activity Book page 245

Have students look at the Fahrenheit thermometer shown on Student Book page 245, and ask them to explain how to decide what number of Fahrenheit degrees each tick mark represents. 1°; each interval of 10° is divided into ten equal parts (10° ÷ 10 = 1°)

Point out that, although we must write a − sign for a negative temperature, no sign is written when we write positive temperatures. Stated a different way, any number without a sign is assumed to be a positive number.

Temperatures Across Zero Read aloud (or write on the board) the situations shown below. For each situation, have students find the missing temperature by counting tick marks on the thermometer that is pictured on Student book page 245. Also for each situation, encourage students to explain how arithmetic may be used (instead of counting tick marks) to find the missing temperature. For example, if the starting temperature is 3° and the decrease is 5°, a student may think: "Moving 3° to 0° is 3°, and by moving 2° more (for a total of 5°), I find that the answer is ⁻2°."

Start:	⁻6°	**Start:**	10°
Change:	8° increase	**Change:**	15° decrease
End:	2°	**End:**	⁻5°
Start:	3°	**Start:**	⁻2°
Change:	6° decrease	**Change:**	3° increase
End:	⁻3°	**End:**	1°
Start:	2°	**Start:**	⁻5°
Change:	6° decrease	**Change:**	8° increase
End:	⁻4°	**End:**	3°

Differentiated Instruction

Extra Help Display a plastic container of lukewarm water, a plastic container of cool water, and a thermometer. Have students take turns moving the thermometer from one container to the other to observe the changes in temperature.

The Learning Classroom

Helping Community Students may fear doing their math work in public because they are afraid to be incorrect. Emphasize that errors help us learn. A safe culture develops in this type of classroom because students do not fear criticism when they make mistakes. You can model this for students as you make your own errors. Fixing your errors models a healthy approach for students.

▶ Solve Fahrenheit Temperature Problems PAIRS

Have **Student Pairs** discuss and complete exercises 1–7 on Student Book page 245.

After the activity has been completed, invite a volunteer from each pair to share their answers for exercises 1–3 with the class.

Teaching Note

Math Background Make sure students understand that all measurements are approximations. In other words, no measurements are exact.

Although temperature is typically measured to the nearest whole degree, it is very unlikely that a temperature is an exact whole number of degrees. For example, a room temperature of 68 °F may be 68.3 °F if measured to the nearest tenth of a degree. If measured to the nearest hundredth of a degree, the temperature may be 68.32 °F. And so on. Therefore, a given temperature (such as 68 °F) is only an approximation.

The same concept is true for other types of measurements, including length and weight; each is an approximation.

Activity 2

Celsius Temperature

 20 MINUTES

Goal: Identify benchmark Celsius temperatures; solve Celsius temperature problems.

Materials: Student Activity Book or Hardcover Book p. 246

 NCTM Standards:
Measurement
Reasoning and Proof
Number and Operations
Problem Solving

▶ Discuss Celsius Temperature

WHOLE CLASS

Ask for Ideas Ask students to share what they know about degrees Celsius and Celsius thermometers. Make sure that the following ideas are part of the discussion.

- Celsius is a temperature scale.

- The abbreviation used to represent Celsius temperature is °C.

- The benchmark Celsius temperatures are 100 °C (water boils) and 0 °C (water freezes).

Temperatures Across Zero Review how to find an unknown:

- starting temperature, given an ending temperature and an increase or decrease.

- ending temperature, given a starting temperature and an increase or decrease.

- change in temperature, given a starting and an ending temperature.

(See the previous page for examples of each type of problem.)

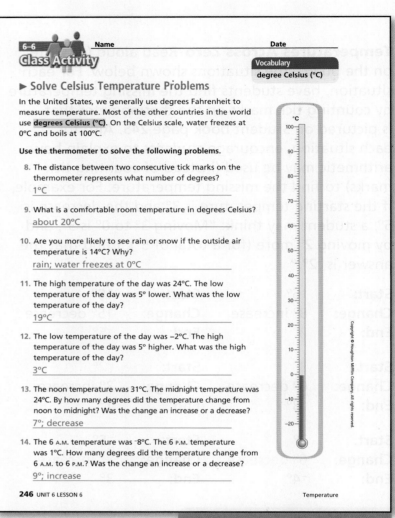

Student Activity Book page 246

▶ Solve Celsius Temperature Problems

PAIRS

Have **Student Pairs** work together to discuss and complete exercises 8–14 on Student Book page 246.

Differentiated Instruction

Extra Help Cut out pictures of measurable objects from newspapers and magazines. Distribute the pictures and give students an opportunity to describe all of the different ways the objects could be measured. For a picture of a book, for example, students may suggest that the length, width, and thickness of the book could be measured with a ruler, and the weight of the book could be measured with a scale.

Compare Fahrenheit and Celsius Temperatures

 25 MINUTES

Goal: Compare Fahrenheit and Celsius temperatures.

Materials: Student Activity Book or Hardcover Book p. 247

 NCTM Standards:
Measurement
Number and Operations
Problem Solving

▶ Estimate Temperatures   `WHOLE CLASS`

As a class, use **Solve and Discuss** to complete exercises 15–20 on Student Book page 247.

Exercise 20: The goal of the discussion is not for students to derive the exact formulas ($°F = °C \times \frac{9}{5} + 32$ and $°C = (°F - 32) \times \frac{5}{9}$) that are used to convert the temperatures. Instead, the goal is to derive a *general* formula that can be used, preferably with mental math, to *estimate* or *approximate* the temperatures.

Give students an opportunity to compare the corresponding temperatures and discuss possible ways to estimate. Possible methods include doubling the °C and then adding 25 or 30 to estimate the equivalent °F temperature, and halving the °F and then subtracting 15 to estimate the equivalent °C temperature.

Again, the goal of the discussion is for students to develop a method that gives them a *general sense* of the equivalent temperature.

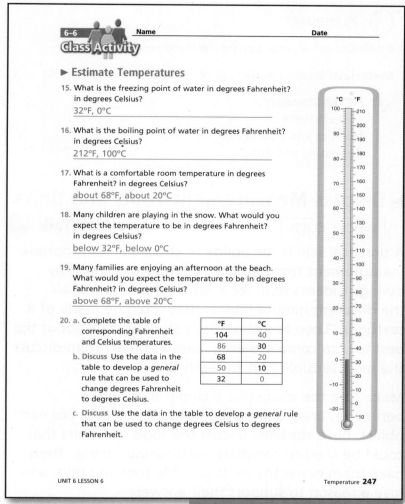

Student Activity Book page 247

The Learning Classroom

Student Leaders When students explain their work, they need to stand beside their work and point to parts of it as they explain. Using a pointer that does not obscure any work enables all students to see the part of the drawing or math symbol that is being explained.

Teaching the Lesson (continued)

Choose Appropriate Tools and Units

 20 MINUTES

Goal: Choose an appropriate measurement tool or unit.

Materials: Student Activity Book or Hardcover Book p. 248

 NCTM Standards:
Measurement
Number and Operations
Reasoning and Proof

▶ Discuss Measurement Tools and Units

| WHOLE CLASS | Math Talk |

A practical skill is the ability to choose an appropriate measurement tool and unit. Introduce this skill by asking students to make a list on the board of all the different measurements that could be made of a textbook. Then as a class, have students talk about the best tool to complete each measurement. Then discuss the most sensible unit for each tool.

Make sure the discussion includes finding the perimeter, area, and volume of some objects. For each object, have students discuss the tools and units that could be used to complete each measurement. Then have them name the most sensible tool and unit, and give a reason to support their answer.

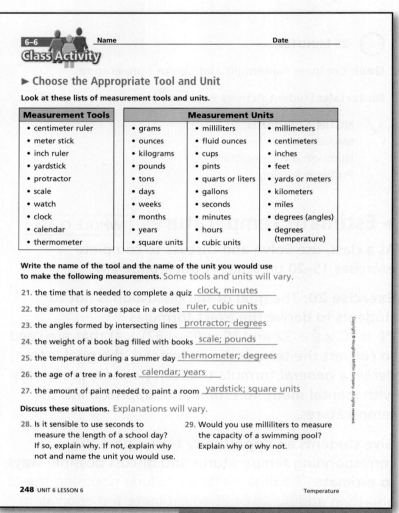

Student Activity Book page 248

▶ Choose the Appropriate Tool and Unit   SMALL GROUPS

Arrange students to work in **Small Groups** to discuss and complete exercises 21–27 on Student Book page 248. Have students work cooperatively as a class and use **Solve and Discuss** to complete exercises 28–29.

Differentiated Instruction

Extra Help Display pictures (cut from newspapers, magazines, and other sources) of a variety of objects and measuring tools. Give students an opportunity to discuss the objects and tools, and match each object with an appropriate measuring tool.

Activity 5

Display Temperatures

 25 MINUTES

Goal: Apply understanding of place value to develop and interpret a stem-and-leaf plot.

Materials: Student Activity Book or Hardcover Book p. 249

✓ **NCTM Standards:**
Data Analysis and Probability
Representation
Number and Operations

▶ Discuss Stem-and-Leaf Plots

WHOLE CLASS

Ask for Ideas Have students share what they know about stem-and-leaf plots.

On the board, write the following data table and the incomplete stem-and-leaf plot as students work in pairs to copy the information on a sheet of paper.

Quiz Scores (number correct)					
19	20	18	18	20	19

Quiz Scores (number correct)	
Stem	Leaf

Legend:

Emphasize Place Value Use questioning to help students understand that data in a stem-and-leaf plot are displayed by place value.

Have **Student Pairs** write the quiz scores in order from least to greatest and then complete the plot by writing a stem and a leaf for each score. Discuss a possible legend or key that will help a reader make sense of the display.

Quiz Scores (number correct)	
Stem	Leaf
1	8 8 9 9
2	0 0

Legend: 1 | 8 = 18

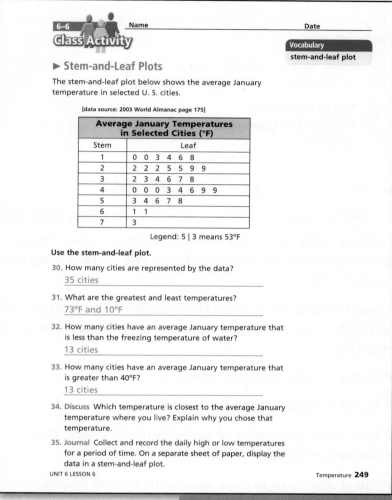

Student Activity Book page 249

▶ Stem-and-Leaf Plots SMALL GROUPS

Direct students to work in **Small Groups** to complete exercises 30–33 on Student Book page 249. Then have students compare answers.

Use **Solve and Discuss** to complete exercise 34.

You might choose to have students complete exercise 35 as a class project.

Differentiated Instruction

Special Needs Some students may need to use index cards, held vertically, to read individual numbers on a stem-and-leaf plot.

Going Further

Math Connection: Integers on the Number Line

▶ Integers in the Real World

WHOLE CLASS

Math Talk

In this activity, students will connect what they know about numbers on a thermometer with integers on the number line.

Have students recall from their study of Fahrenheit and Celsius temperatures that integers can be positive or negative.

● Name several positive integers. 1, 2, 3, and so on

● Name several negative integers. ⁻1, ⁻2, ⁻3, and so on

● Give some examples of real-world situations that involve positive and negative numbers.

Invite students to list the situations on the board. If the context of money and checking accounts is not listed, point out that checking accounts involve positive numbers when balances are greater than zero, and negative numbers when balances are less than zero.

Also give students an opportunity to suggest real-world situations that generally involve only positive numbers (such as tropical temperatures, for example), and only negative numbers (such as depth below sea level, for example).

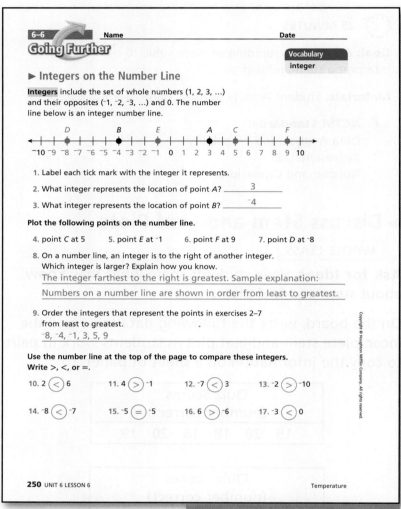

Student Activity Book page 250

▶ Integers on the Number Line

WHOLE CLASS

Complete exercises 1–17 on Student Book page 250 as a whole-class activity.

 Ongoing Assessment

▶ Give an example of a measurement that involves negative numbers.

Differentiated Instruction

Intervention — Activity Card 6-6

Temperature Pairs
Activity Card 6-6

Work: In Pairs

1. −20°C
   0°C
   34°F
   50°F
   20°C
   86°F
   37°C
   212°F
   110°C

1. **Work Together** Organize the list of temperatures from lowest to highest.

| 34°F | 0°C | −20°C | 50°F | 86°F |
| 20°C | 110°C | 37°C | 212°F | |

2. **Write About It** Describe your strategies for organizing the list of temperatures.

3. On your own, choose a temperature in degrees Fahrenheit and a temperature in degrees Celsius from the list above. Write a sentence describing a situation that relates to each temperature.

Unit 6, Lesson 6   Copyright © Houghton Mifflin Company

Activity Note Suggest that students order the Celsius temperatures separately from the Fahrenheit temperatures and then use benchmark temperatures for both systems to organize the final list.

✏ Math Writing Prompt

Use Reasoning Describe the difference in the clothing you might wear for temperatures of 30°F and 30°C.

Soar to Success Math ★ Software Support
Warm-Up 49.04

On Level — Activity Card 6-6

Show What You Know
Activity Card 6-6

Work: In Pairs

1. On your own, write a brief description of a situation that is weather or temperature related. Do not give any temperatures. An example is shown.

   > When Janice left to go to school she wore a jacket but still felt cold. On her way home she was too warm so she put her jacket in her backpack.

2. **Decide** Exchange papers. Write a reasonable temperature range in °C to match the situation.

3. Exchange papers again. Confirm that the temperature range given is appropriate.

4. Repeat the activity for a new situation.

Unit 6, Lesson 6   Copyright © Houghton Mifflin Company

Activity Note Suggest that students use benchmarks to help them determine a sensible range for each situation.

✏ Math Writing Prompt

Estimate Explain how the Celsius scale makes it easy to remember the freezing point and boiling point of water. How does this help you estimate temperatures on the Celsius scale?

MEGA MATH Grades K-6 Software Support
The Number Games: Tiny's Think Tank, Level P

Challenge — Activity Card 6-6

Predict and Verify
Activity Card 6-6

Work: By Yourself

Use:
• Calculator

1. Select 10 temperatures in degrees Fahrenheit.

2. Estimate each temperature in degrees Celsius.

$$°C = (°F - 32) \div 1.8$$
$$°F = (°C \times 1.8) + 32$$

3. Use a calculator and the formulas above to check your predictions.

4. **Write About It** What strategies did you use to make your predictions?

Unit 6, Lesson 6   Copyright © Houghton Mifflin Company

Activity Note Remind students to be careful about inputting numbers and operations in the correct order. Some calculators do not use Order of Operations.

✏ Math Writing Prompt

Explain Your Thinking Will a temperature recorded in degrees Celsius always be less than the same temperature in degrees Fahrenheit? Explain.

✦ DESTINATION Math· Software Support
Course III: Module 4: Unit 3: Multiplying Decimals

3 Homework and Spiral Review

Homework **Goal:** Additional Practice

✓ Include students' Homework page 157 as part of their portfolios.

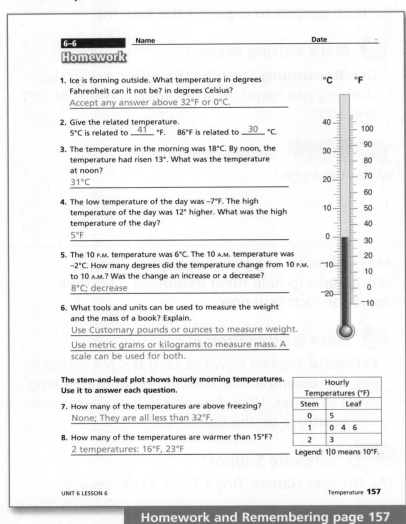

Remembering **Goal:** Spiral Review

This Remembering page would be appropriate anytime after today's lesson.

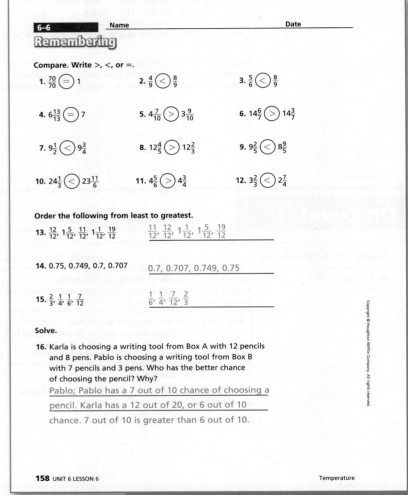

Home or School Activity

Social Studies Connection

World Temperatures Have students choose a city they would like to visit. Students should do research to find the city's average monthly high and low temperatures in °F and in °C. Student will display the temperatures in a table or bar graph. Display students' work in the classroom.

Sydney, Australia—Average Annual Daily High and Low Temperatures

	High	Low	High	Low
Jan.	79°F	66°F	26°C	19°C
Feb.	79°F	66°F	26°C	19°C
Mar.	77°F	64°F	25°C	18°C
Apr.	72°F	59°F	22°C	15°C
May	66°F	54°F	19°C	12°C

The Passing of Time

Lesson Objectives

- Solve problems involving elapsed time.
- Convert clock time, calendar time, and compound units of time.

Vocabulary
analog clock
digital clock

The Day at a Glance

Today's Goals	Materials
① Teaching the Lesson **A1:** Find elapsed time to the hour, half-hour, and quarter-hour; convert clock time. **A2:** Add and subtract time. **A3:** Convert calendar time and compound units of time. **② Going Further** ▶ Differentiated Instruction **③ Homework and Spiral Review**	**Lesson Activities** Student Activity Book pp. 251–254 or Student Hardcover Book pp. 251–254 Homework and Remembering pages pp. 159–160 Calculator Quick Quiz 3 (Assessment Guide)	**Going Further** Activity Cards 6-7 Clock face (optional) Index cards Rulers Scissors Math Journals

123 *Use Math Talk today!*

Keeping Skills Sharp

Daily Routines	English Language Learners
Homework Review Have students work together to check their work. **Reasoning** Sylvia has a spinner with colored sections. The probability of landing on red is $\frac{2}{5}$, and the probability of landing on blue is $\frac{1}{10}$. Are there other sections on the spinner? Explain how you know. If so, decide on color(s) for the other sections, and give the probability for landing on each color. Yes; $\frac{2}{5} = \frac{4}{10} + \frac{1}{10} = \frac{5}{10} < 1$, so there are more sections. Possible answer: Green: $\frac{3}{10}$; yellow: $\frac{2}{10}$ or $\frac{1}{5}$.	Draw a picture showing the sun at noon on the board. Write 12 *noon*, *A.M.*, and *P.M.* Draw a sun to the left and the right. Write 9 *A.M.* on the left and 9 *P.M.* on the right. - **Beginning** Ask: **Is 12 noon the middle of the day?** yes **Does *A.M.* mean before noon?** yes. **Does *P.M.* mean after 12 noon?** yes - **Intermediate** Ask: **Which means before 12 noon. *A.M.* or *P.M.*?** *A.M.* Say: *P.M.* means after 12 __. noon - **Advanced** Have students tell about *A.M.* and *P.M.* in relation to *noon*.

Teaching the Lesson

Elapsed Time

 20 MINUTES

Goal: Find elapsed time to the hour, half-hour, and quarter-hour; convert clock time.

Materials: Student Activity Book or Hardcover Book pp. 251–252

 NCTM Standards:
Measurement
Number and Operations

▶ Compare Different Clocks   WHOLE CLASS

Invite a volunteer to read aloud the three paragraphs at the top of Student Book page 251. Encourage students to share any additional information they may know about analog and digital clocks.

Math Talk in Action

Give students an opportunity to discuss what they know about telling time using an analog clock.

Discuss the numbers.

Jason: The numbers represent hours.

Zara: There are 12 numbers, so an analog clock can show 12 hours.

Alex: After 12 hours, the time repeats.

Discuss the marks that are on the edge of the clock face.

Gillian: The marks represent minutes.

Maurie: There are 60 marks altogether.

Patrice: So there are 60 minutes in an hour.

How can we decide if it's A.M. or P.M. by looking at an analog clock?

Kris: We can't tell.

Jodie: If it was midnight the last time the hour hand was at 12, the clock shows A.M.

Rendell: If it was noon the last time the hour hand was at 12, the clock shows P.M.

Discuss exercises 1–7 as a class.

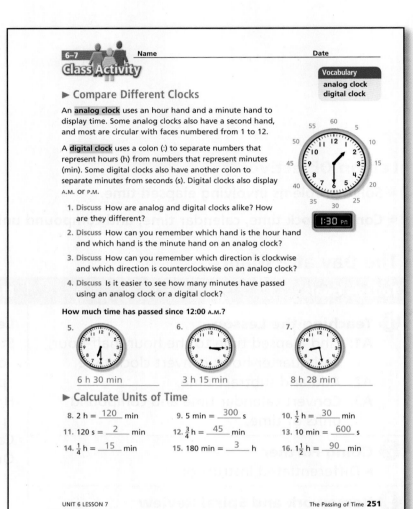

Student Activity Book Page 251

▶ Calculate Units of Time   INDIVIDUALS

Spend a few minutes reviewing all of the time relationships students can think of (such as 1 min = 60 s and 1 h = 60 min). Then have them work individually or paired with a **Helping Partner** to complete exercises 8–16.

Teaching Note

Common Error It is a mistake for students to assume that all time relationships are precise. Make sure they understand that although some relationships are precise (such as 1 hour is *exactly* 60 minutes), others are approximations (such as 1 year is *about* 365 days).

► Solve Elapsed-Time Problems

WHOLE CLASS

Introduce the activity by having students work cooperatively to discuss and solve the three situations shown below.

Write the situations on the board. (Note that none of the situations involve ungrouping, regrouping, or times across 12:00.) For each situation, have students discuss how to decide if addition or subtraction is used to solve the problem.

Starting Time: 4:15 P.M.
Elapsed Time: ?
Ending Time: 7:45 P.M.

7:45 P.M. − 4:15 P.M. 3:30	3 hours 30 minutes

Starting Time: 2:09 A.M.
Elapsed Time: 9 h 32 min
Ending Time: ?

2:09 A.M. + 9:32 11:41 A.M.	

Starting Time: ?
Elapsed Time: 5 h 30 min
Ending Time: 8:30 P.M.

8:30 P.M. − 5:30 3:00 P.M.	

Generalize Lead students to generalize that addition is used if we are looking for a time in the future (such as finding an end time when a start time is given), and subtraction is used when we are looking for a time in the past (such as finding a start time when an end time is given.)

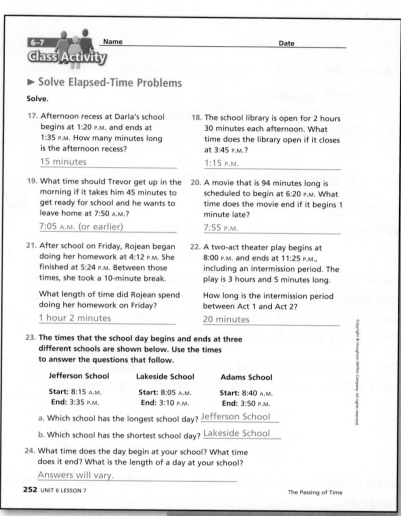

Student Activity Book Page 252

Exercises 17–24 On Student Book page 252, have students work cooperatively, using **Solve and Discuss** to complete these exercises.

Teaching the Lesson (continued)

Activity 2

Add and Subtract Units of Time

 40 MINUTES

Goal: Add and subtract time.

Materials: Student Activity Book or Hardcover Book p. 253

✓ **NCTM Standards:**
Measurement   Number and Operations
Problem Solving

▶ Discuss Elapsed Time

WHOLE CLASS   **Math Talk**

Write on the board: 10:48 A.M.
                          − 2:15 A.M.

Have students suggest a word problem that matches the times. For example, Ms. Loren began her shift at work last night at 2:15 A.M. Her shift ended at 10:48 A.M. How long was Ms. Loren's shift?

Ask students to discuss the problem, explain why subtraction is used, and then find the answer.

        10:48 A.M.
       − 2:15 A.M.
         8:33   = 8 hours 33 minutes

Give students an opportunity to decide if the answer is sensible.

▶ Ungroup Hours WHOLE CLASS

Write on the board: 5:25 P.M.
                          − 2:50 P.M.

Have students suggest a word problem that matches the times. Then invite a volunteer to show the solution on the board and to justify each step.

- Subtract the earlier time from the   4:85
  later time.   5̶:2̶5̶ ̶P̶.M̶.̶
- Need more minutes.   − 2:50 P.M.
                                             2 h 35 min
- Ungroup 1 h as 60 min.

- Add 60 min to 25 min.

- Subtract minutes from minutes,
  then subtract hours from hours.

▶ Regroup Minutes WHOLE CLASS

Read the following problem aloud:

For exercise, Katarina walks 45 minutes each day. How many hours and minutes does she walk in one week?

Discuss how to solve the problem, and invite volunteers to write different ways on the board. Add 45 minutes seven times or multiply 45 minutes by 7.

Discuss how to regroup the number of minutes (315) to hours and minutes. Divide 315 by 60 or repeatedly subtract 60 from 315 until fewer than 60 minutes remain.

Have students verify that the answer (5 h 15 min) is sensible.

▶ Calculate Total Time WHOLE CLASS

Read the following problem aloud.

In the morning, Jimmie needs 1 hour 10 minutes to get ready for school. His bus arrives 7:08 A.M. What is the latest Jimmie should wake up on a school morning?

Discuss how to solve the problem, and invite a volunteer to perform the computation on the board.

        6:68
       7̶:0̶8̶ A.M.
      − 1:10
       5:58 A.M.

Make sure students recognize that it is not possible to subtract 10 minutes from 8 minutes, which results in a need to ungroup 1 hour as 60 minutes.

▶ 24-Hour Time WHOLE CLASS

Explain to students that a day begins at 12:00 A.M. To find 24-hour time, find the number of hours and minutes that have passed since 12:00 A.M. Write on the board:

        2:00 A.M. is 02:00 or 0200
        2:00 P.M. is 14:00 or 1400

Note that 24-hour times can be expressed with or without a colon. We say "two o'clock" or "oh two hundred" for 02:00 or 0200. We say "fourteen o'clock" or "fourteen hundred" for 14:00 or 1400.

Discuss why 12:15 A.M. is the same as 00:15. 0 hours and 15 minutes have passed since 12:00 A.M.

Discuss how to convert 8:30 P.M. to 24-hour time. There are 12 hours between 12:00 A.M. and 12:00 P.M. There are 8 hours and 30 minutes between 12:00 P.M. and 8:30 P.M. Add 12 hours plus 8 hours and 30 minutes to get 20:30.

▶ Elapsed Time Across Noon or Midnight WHOLE CLASS

Write on the board:

    4:10 P.M.
  − 9:35 A.M.

Have students suggest a word problem that matches the times. Then ask them to explain what needs to be done to solve the problem and to justify their answer. For example:

- Need more minutes to subtract, so ungroup 1 hour as 60 minutes.

    15:70
    3:70

- Need more hours to subtract, so change 3 hours 70 minutes to its equivalent time on a 24-hour clock. Then subtract.

    4:10 P.M.
  − 9:35 A.M.
    6 h 35 min

Give students additional practice changing 12-hour customary times to 24-hour times.

Differentiated Instruction

Extra Help If students consistently make mistakes in finding elapsed time across noon or midnight, suggest that they make a list hour by hour and then determine the leftover minutes. For example, for time from 10:45 to 3:15,

- 10:45 to 11:45 = 1 hour.
- 11:45 to 12:45 = 1 hour.
- 12:45 to 1:45 = 1 hour.
- 1:45 to 2:45 = 1 hour.
- 2:45 to 3:15 = 30 minutes.
- Add 1 + 1 + 1 + 1 = 4 hours.

  Add 4 hours + 30 minutes = 4 hours 30 minutes.

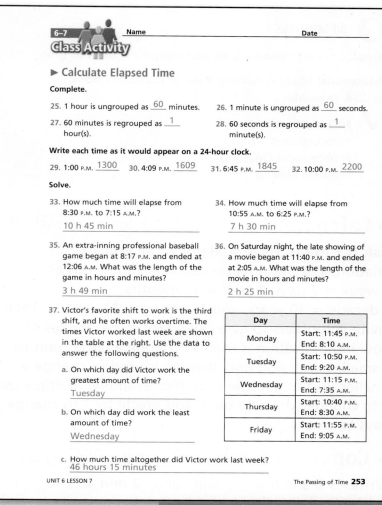

Student Activity Book Page 253

▶ Calculate Elapsed Time WHOLE CLASS

Complete exercises 25–28 on Student Book page 253 as a class activity.

Have students work as **Student Pairs** or in **Small Groups** to complete exercises 29–32.

For exercise 37, students can distribute the workload by having one student calculate the elapsed time for Monday, another student calculate the elapsed time for Tuesday, and so on.

Activity 3

Convert Units of Time

 30 MINUTES

Goal: Convert calendar time and compound units of time.

Materials: Student Activity Book or Hardcover Book p. 254, calculator

✓ **NCTM Standards:**
Measurement
Number and Operations
Problem Solving

▶ Calendar Units of Time   WHOLE CLASS

Ask for Ideas Have students recall precise relationships that involve calendar time (such as 1 week = 7 days, 1 year = 12 months, 1 decade = 10 years, and 1 century = 100 years). Then invite volunteers to give calendar-time examples of how multiplication is used to change a larger unit to a smaller unit, and how division is used to change a smaller unit to a larger unit. (For example, multiply by 7 to change weeks to days, and divide by 7 to change days to weeks.)

▶ Compound Units of Time   WHOLE CLASS

Write "3 h 5 min = ___ min" and "2 min 45 s = ___ s" on the board. Invite volunteers to demonstrate on the board two or more ways to make each conversion.

60 min + 60 min + 60 min + 5 min = 185 min
(3 × 60 min) + 5 min = 180 min + 5 min = 185 min

60 s + 60 s + 45 s = 165 s
(2 × 60 s) + 45 s = 120 s + 45 s + 165 s

▶ Estimate Time   WHOLE CLASS

Invite three volunteers to each write a number of hours and minutes on the board. Give students an opportunity to discuss how the sum of the times could be estimated. For example, one way to estimate is to round each number of minutes to the nearest hour and then add. Challenge students to suggest a variety of strategies.

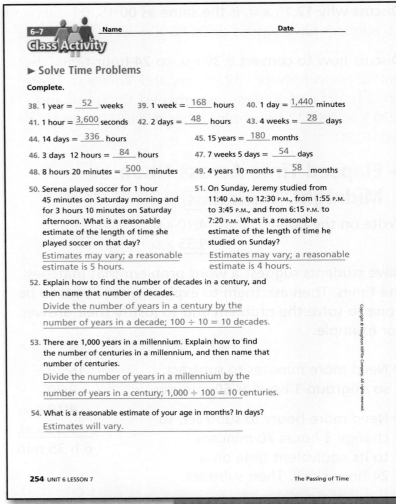

6–7
Class Activity
Name _____ Date _____

▶ **Solve Time Problems**

Complete.

38. 1 year = __52__ weeks   39. 1 week = __168__ hours   40. 1 day = __1,440__ minutes

41. 1 hour = __3,600__ seconds   42. 2 days = __48__ hours   43. 4 weeks = __28__ days

44. 14 days = __336__ hours   45. 15 years = __180__ months

46. 3 days 12 hours = __84__ hours   47. 7 weeks 5 days = __54__ days

48. 8 hours 20 minutes = __500__ minutes   49. 4 years 10 months = __58__ months

50. Serena played soccer for 1 hour 45 minutes on Saturday morning and for 3 hours 10 minutes on Saturday afternoon. What is a reasonable estimate of the length of time she played soccer on that day?
Estimates may vary; a reasonable estimate is 5 hours.

51. On Sunday, Jeremy studied from 11:40 A.M. to 12:30 P.M., from 1:55 P.M. to 3:45 P.M., and from 6:15 P.M. to 7:20 P.M. What is a reasonable estimate of the length of time he studied on Sunday?
Estimates may vary; a reasonable estimate is 4 hours.

52. Explain how to find the number of decades in a century, and then name that number of decades.
Divide the number of years in a century by the number of years in a decade; 100 ÷ 10 = 10 decades.

53. There are 1,000 years in a millennium. Explain how to find the number of centuries in a millennium, and then name that number of centuries.
Divide the number of years in a millennium by the number of years in a century; 1,000 ÷ 100 = 10 centuries.

54. What is a reasonable estimate of your age in months? In days?
Estimates will vary.

254 UNIT 6 LESSON 7   The Passing of Time

Student Activity Book Page 254

▶ Solve Time Problems   PAIRS

Encourage **Student Pairs** to complete the exercises on Student Book page 254.

 Ongoing Assessment

Ask questions such as these that involve an unknown elapsed time, an unknown starting time, and an unknown ending time.

▶ How much time elapses from 3:45 P.M. to 5:10 P.M.?

▶ What time is 4 hours 36 minutes before 9:20 A.M.?

▶ What time is 15 hours 50 minutes later than 1:30 P.M.?

 Quick Quiz

See Assessment Guide for Unit 6 Quick Quiz 3.

Intervention   Activity Card 6-7

How Much Time?   Activity Card 6-7 ●

Work: In Pairs
• Clock face (optional)

1. Write a time on a piece of paper using A.M. or P.M. Do not tell the time to your partner.

2. Decide which partner will show his or her time first. Then look at the first time.

3. Next, look at the second time. Finally, find the elapsed time between the first and second times. Partners switch roles and repeat the activity.

4. **Explain Your Thinking** Explain how you calculated the elapsed time when the time crossed midnight or noon.

Unit 6, Lesson 7   Copyright © Houghton Mifflin Company

Activity Note If students struggle finding elapsed times, you may want to limit the times to whole hours or half-hours only.

✓ Math Writing Prompt

Make Connections Give three examples of situations when you might need to know how much time has passed.

 **Software Support**

Warm-Up 48.15

On Level   Activity Card 6-7

Find the Time   Activity Card 6-7 ▲

Work: In Pairs
Use:
• 6 Index cards, 3 per partner
• Rulers
• Scissors

1. Divide each index card vertically into two halves. Cut each index card in half.

2. On each half write a time and indicate A.M. or P.M.

3. Mix up the cards and turn them face down.

4. Each partner turns one card face up.

5. **Work Together** Calculate the elapsed time from the time on the first card to the time on the second card.

6. Continue until all of the cards have been used.

Unit 6, Lesson 7   Copyright © Houghton Mifflin Company

Activity Note If students finish early, have them order the times from earliest in the A.M. to closest to midnight.

✓ Math Writing Prompt

Explain the Difference Explain what a digital clock can show that an analog clock does not show.

 Software Support

The Number Games: Tiny's Think Tank, Level D

Challenge   Activity Card 6-7

Can She Finish?   Activity Card 6-7 ■

Work: By Yourself

3. Yes; Possible explanation:

• It will take her 120 rows × 5 min per row or 600 minutes to complete the scarf.

• 600 min ÷ 60 min per h = 10 h to complete the scarf.

• 7 days × 2 h per day = 14 h.

• Since 10 h < 14 h, she will complete the scarf.

1. Read the following word problem.

It takes 5 minutes for Remi to crochet a row in a scarf. She had 120 rows left to crochet. This week she can devote 2 hours each evening to working on the scarf. Will she complete the scarf in this time?

2. What hidden question do you need to answer before you can answer the question asked. Possible answer: How many minutes will it take her to complete the scarf?

3. Solve the problem. Write a step-by-step explanation of how you found the answer. See left column.

4. Write your own multistep word problem that involves time. Exchange problems with another student and solve each other's problem.

Unit 6, Lesson 7   Copyright © Houghton Mifflin Company

Activity Note The problem can be solved in many ways. Have students compare and discuss the different solution methods they used. Have them list a hidden question for each method.

✓ Math Writing Prompt

Write a Problem Express 132 minutes in hours and minutes. Write a word problem involving time that has an answer of 132 minutes.

 DESTINATION **Software Support**
Math

Course III: Module 2: Unit 3: Two-digit Divisors

③ Homework and Spiral Review

Homework **Goal:** Additional Practice

✓ Include students' Homework page 159 as a part of their portfolios.

Remembering **Goal:** Spiral Review

This Remembering page would be appropriate anytime after today's lesson.

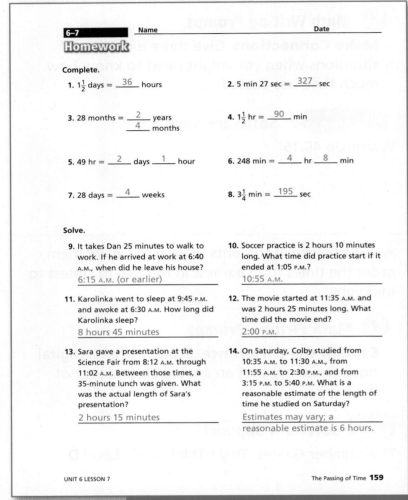

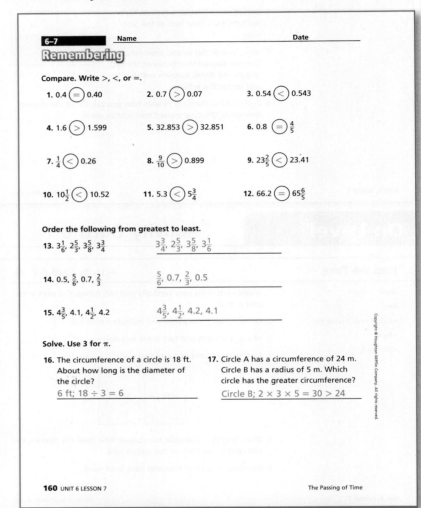

6-7 Homework — Name — Date

Complete.

1. $1\frac{1}{2}$ days = __36__ hours

2. 5 min 27 sec = __327__ sec

3. 28 months = __2__ years __4__ months

4. $1\frac{1}{2}$ hr = __90__ min

5. 49 hr = __2__ days __1__ hour

6. 248 min = __4__ hr __8__ min

7. 28 days = __4__ weeks

8. $3\frac{1}{4}$ min = __195__ sec

Solve.

9. It takes Dan 25 minutes to walk to work. If he arrived at work at 6:40 A.M., when did he leave his house?
6:15 A.M. (or earlier)

10. Soccer practice is 2 hours 10 minutes long. What time did practice start if it ended at 1:05 P.M.?
10:55 A.M.

11. Karolinka went to sleep at 9:45 P.M. and awoke at 6:30 A.M. How long did Karolinka sleep?
8 hours 45 minutes

12. The movie started at 11:35 A.M. and was 2 hours 25 minutes long. What time did the movie end?
2:00 P.M.

13. Sara gave a presentation at the Science Fair from 8:12 A.M. through 11:02 A.M. Between those times, a 35-minute lunch was given. What was the actual length of Sara's presentation?
2 hours 15 minutes

14. On Saturday, Colby studied from 10:35 A.M. to 11:30 A.M., from 11:55 A.M. to 2:30 P.M., and from 3:15 P.M. to 5:40 P.M. What is a reasonable estimate of the length of time he studied on Saturday?
Estimates may vary; a reasonable estimate is 6 hours.

UNIT 6 LESSON 7 — The Passing of Time **159**

6-7 Remembering — Name — Date

Compare. Write >, <, or =.

1. 0.4 $=$ 0.40

2. 0.7 $>$ 0.07

3. 0.54 $<$ 0.543

4. 1.6 $>$ 1.599

5. 32.853 $>$ 32.851

6. 0.8 $=$ $\frac{4}{5}$

7. $\frac{1}{4}$ $<$ 0.26

8. $\frac{9}{10}$ $>$ 0.899

9. $23\frac{2}{5}$ $<$ 23.41

10. $10\frac{1}{2}$ $<$ 10.52

11. 5.3 $<$ $5\frac{3}{4}$

12. 66.2 $=$ $65\frac{6}{5}$

Order the following from greatest to least.

13. $3\frac{1}{6}, 2\frac{5}{3}, 3\frac{5}{8}, 3\frac{3}{4}$ — $3\frac{3}{4}, 2\frac{5}{3}, 3\frac{5}{8}, 3\frac{1}{6}$

14. $0.5, \frac{5}{6}, 0.7, \frac{2}{3}$ — $\frac{5}{6}, 0.7, \frac{2}{3}, 0.5$

15. $4\frac{3}{5}, 4.1, 4\frac{1}{2}, 4.2$ — $4\frac{3}{5}, 4\frac{1}{2}, 4.2, 4.1$

Solve. Use 3 for π.

16. The circumference of a circle is 18 ft. About how long is the diameter of the circle?
6 ft; 18 ÷ 3 = 6

17. Circle A has a circumference of 24 m. Circle B has a radius of 5 m. Which circle has the greater circumference?
Circle B; 2 × 3 × 5 = 30 > 24

160 UNIT 6 LESSON 7 — The Passing of Time

Homework and Remembering page 159

Homework and Remembering page 160

Home or School Activity

 Real-World Connection

Estimate the Time Have students write down the time they start an activity, such as playing a game of ball or going shopping with a family member. When the activity is over, ask them to estimate how long it took. Then students check the time and calculate the exact time.

> *Grocery Shopping*
> *Start: 11:15 A.M.*
> *Estimated time: almost two hours*
> *Finish: 1:20 P.M.*
> *Exact time: 2 h 5 min*

Unit Review and Test

Lesson Objective
● Assess student progress on unit objectives.

The Day at a Glance

Today's Goals	Materials
1 **Assessing the Unit** ► Assess student progress on unit objectives. ► Use activities from unit lessons to reteach content. **2** **Extending the Assessment** ► Use remediation for common errors. There is no homework assignment on a test day	Unit 6 Test, Student Activity Book or Student Hardcover Book pp. 255–256 Unit 6 Test, Form A or B, Assessment Guide (optional) Unit 6 Performance Assessment, Assessment Guide (optional)

Keeping Skills Sharp

Daily Routines 5 MINUTES	
If you are doing a unit review day, go over the homework. If this is a test day, omit the homework review.	**Review and Test Day** You may want to choose a quiet game or other activity (reading a book or working on homework for another subject) for students who finish early.

Assessing the Unit

Assess Unit Objectives

45 MINUTES (more if schedule permits)

Goal: Assess student progress on unit objectives.

Materials: Student Activity Book or Hardcover Book pages 255–256; Assessment Guide (optional)

▶ Review and Assessment

If your students are ready for assessment on the unit objectives, you may use either the test on the Student Book pages or one of the forms of the Unit 6 Test in the Assessment Guide to assess student progress.

If you feel that students need some review first, you may use the test on the Student Book pages as a review of unit content, and then use one of the forms of the Unit 6 Test in the Assessment Guide to assess student progress.

To assign a numerical score for all of these test forms, use 10 points for each question.

You may also choose to use the Unit 6 Performance Assessment. Scoring for that assessment can be found in its rubric in the Assessment Guide.

▶ Reteaching Resources

The chart lists the test items, the unit objectives they cover, and the lesson activities in which the objective is covered in this unit. You may revisit these activities with students who do not show mastery of the objectives.

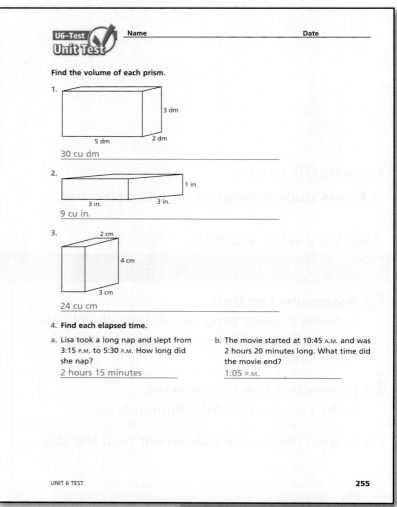

Student Activity Book page 255

Unit Test Items	Unit Objectives Tested	Activities to Use for Reteaching
1–3, 5, 9	**6.1** Find the volume of a rectangular prism.	Lesson 1, Activity 2 Lesson 2, Activity 2
6–8, 10	**6.2** Solve problems involving capacity, mass, and weight.	Lesson 3, Activity 1 Lesson 3, Activity 2 Lesson 4, Activity 1 Lesson 4, Activity 2
4	**6.3** Solve problems involving elapsed time.	Lesson 7, Activity 1 Lesson 7, Activity 2

636 UNIT 6

▶ Assessment Resources

Free Response Tests
Unit 6 Test, Student Activity Book or Hardcover Book pages 255–256
Unit 6 Test, Form A, Assessment Guide

Extended Response Item
The last item in the Student Book test and in the Form A test will require an extended response as an answer.

Multiple Choice Test
Unit 6 Test, Form B, Assessment Guide

Performance Assessment
Unit 6 Performance Assessment, Assessment Guide
Unit 6 Performance Assessment Rubric, Assessment Guide

▶ Portfolio Assessment

Teacher-selected Items for Student Portfolios:

- Homework, Lessons 2, 5, 6, and 7
- Class Activity work, Lessons 3 and 4

Student-selected Items for Student Portfolios:

- Favorite Home or School Activity
- Best Writing Prompt

② Extending the Assessment

Unit Objective 6.1
Find the volume of a rectangular prism.

Common Error: Doesn't Label the Answer

In writing answers to problems, students may not include a unit of measure with their numerical answers.

Remediation Point out that a measurement problem usually requires a unit of measure with the answer. Emphasize that it is important to look back at the problem to see what unit of measure is needed for the label. Remind students that answers must show the units used. For example an answer of 3 might mean 3 cm or 3 cu cm. This is especially important if dimensions are given in different units.

Common Error: Has Difficulty Visualizing Three-Dimensional Objects

Some students may have difficulty looking at a two-dimensional picture of a rectangular prism and visualizing the three-dimensional object that the picture represents.

Remediation Provide students with actual rectangular prisms, such as books or small boxes, and encourage them to look for pictures of these prisms. Point out that the objects are often drawn from slightly above, rather than from straight on, so the top and sides are visible. Also, give students practice using cubes to build a variety of solid figures.

Common Error: Confuses Area and Volume

Some students may confuse area and volume when choosing a unit.

Remediation Demonstrate that determining the area of a plane figure requires two factors— length and width.

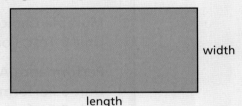

Demonstrate that determining the volume of a solid figure requires three factors—length, width, and height.

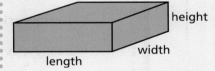

Common Error: Uses an Incorrect Formula

Some students may fail to apply the correct formula when solving a word problem. For example, a student may assume an area problem to be a volume problem, and vice versa.

Remediation Encourage students to draw a picture to represent the problem, and then use their drawing to determine if they need to find the area or volume.

Unit Objective 6.2
Solve problems involving capacity, mass, and weight.

Common Error: Doesn't Use the Correct Units

Some students do not remember to check for units used in their calculations and answers.

Remediation Remind students that answers must show the correct units. They should ensure the same units are used before adding or multiplying. For example, to calculate volume when given dimensions in centimeters and decimeters, students must convert some measures so all of them are in the same units.

The answer should also be stated using the correct units. For example, students might write an answer of 12 cm when the unit should be cubic centimeters. Encourage students to state the given units, and the units that they will use for answers.

Unit Objective 6.3
Solve problems involving elapsed time.

Common Error: Doesn't Calculate Time Correctly Across Noon

Some students make errors in determining elapsed time when it crosses noon.

Remediation Suggest that students write elapsed time hour by hour and then add the leftover time. For example,

- 10:45 to 11:45 equals 1 hour
- 11:45 to 12:45 equals 1 hour, for a total of 2 hours
- 12:45 plus 20 minutes equals 12:65, or 1:05.

Student Glossary

Glossary

A

acre A measure of land area. An acre is equal to 4,840 square yards.

acute angle An angle whose measure is less than 90°.

acute triangle A triangle with three acute angles.

addend One of two or more numbers added together to find a sum.

Example:

$$7 + 8 = 15$$

addend   addend   sum

Add On Method for Subtraction Find the difference between two numbers by adding to the lesser number to get the greater number.

adjusted estimate A new estimate that is made using the Digit-by-Digit method of dividing when an overestimate or underestimate has been initially made.

analog clock A clock that uses an hour hand and a minute hand to display time. Most are circular and have a face numbered from 1 to 12. Some analog clocks also have a second hand.

angle A figure formed by two rays or line segments with a common endpoint.

apex The vertex of a cone.

area The amount of surface covered by a figure measured in square units.

array An arrangement of objects, symbols, or numbers in equal rows and equal columns.

Associative Property of Addition Changing the grouping of addends does not change the sum.

Example:
$$3 + (5 + 7) = (3 + 5) + 7$$

Associative Property of Multiplication Changing the grouping of factors does not change the product.

Example:
$$3 \times (5 \times 7) = (3 \times 5) \times 7$$

average (See mean)

axis A line, usually horizontal or vertical, that is labeled with numbers or words to show the meaning of a graph.

axis of rotation A line about which a figure is rotated.

Glossary **S1**

Glossary (Continued)

B

bar graph A graph that uses bars to show data.

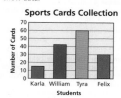

Sports Cards Collection

base of a figure For a triangle or parallelogram, a base is any side. For a trapezoid, a base is either of the parallel sides. For a prism, a base is one of the congruent parallel faces. For a pyramid, the base is the face that does not touch the vertex of the pyramid.

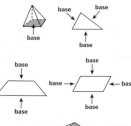

base of a power The number that is used as a factor when evaluating powers.

Example: In 10^3, the 10 is the base.

basic ratio A ratio in simplest form.

Example: The ratio 12 to 8 simplifies to 3 to 2.

billion One thousand million.
1,000,000,000

billionth One thousandth of a millionth.
0.000000001

C

capacity A measure of how much a container can hold.

categorical data Data expressed as words that represent categories.

Example: Color (red, blue, yellow, and so on)

Celsius The metric temperature scale. Water freezes at 0°C and boils at 100°C.

centimeter A unit of measure in the metric system that equals one hundredth of a meter. 1 cm = 0.01 m

1 cm

change minus A change situation that can be represented by subtraction. In a change minus situation, the starting number, the change, or the result will be unknown.

Example:

Unknown Start	Unknown Change	Unknown Result
$n - 2 = 3$	$5 - n = 3$	$5 - 2 = n$

change plus A change situation that can be represented by addition. In a change plus situation, the starting number, the change, or the result will be unknown.

S2 Glossary

Example:

Unknown Start	Unknown Change	Unknown Result
$n + 2 = 5$	$3 + n = 5$	$3 + 2 = n$

circle A plane figure that forms a closed path so that all the points on the path are the same distance from a point called the center.

circle graph A graph that uses parts of a circle to show data.

Zak's Book Collection

circumference The distance around a circle.

clockwise The direction in which the hands of a clock move.

collection situations Situations that involve putting together (joining) or taking apart (separating) groups.

column A part of a table or array that contains items arranged vertically.

combination situation A combination situation is one in which pairs or sets are counted. Tables can be used to show combinations.

Types of Sandwiches

	Cheese	Peanut Butter	Tuna
White	W + C	W + PB	W + T
Wheat	Wh + C	Wh + PB	Wh + T

common denominator A common multiple of two or more denominators.

Example: 6 could be used as a common denominator for $\frac{1}{2}$ and $\frac{1}{3}$:
$$\frac{1}{2} = \frac{3}{6} \quad \frac{1}{3} = \frac{2}{6}$$
$$\text{so } \frac{1}{2} + \frac{1}{3} = \frac{3}{6} + \frac{2}{6} = \frac{5}{6}$$

Commutative Property of Addition Changing the order of addends does not change the sum.

Example: $3 + 8 = 8 + 3$

Commutative Property of Multiplication Changing the order of factors does not change the product.

Example: $3 \times 8 = 8 \times 3$

comparison situation A situation in which two amounts are compared by addition or by multiplication. An additive comparison situation compares by asking or telling how much more (how much less) one amount is than another. A multiplicative comparison situation compares by asking or telling how many times as many one amount is as another. The multiplicative comparison may also be made using fraction language. For example, you can say, "Sally has one fourth as much as Tom has," instead of saying "Tom has 4 times as much as Sally has."

complementary angles Angles having a sum of 90°.

complex figure A figure made by combining simple geometric figures like rectangles and triangles.

composite number A number greater than 1 that has more than one factor pair. Examples of composite numbers are 4, 15, and 45. The factor pairs of 15 are: 1 and 15, 3 and 5.

cone A solid figure with a curved base and a single vertex.

congruent Exactly the same size and shape.

Example: Triangles ABC and PQR are congruent.

continuous data Data that represent an accumulation without interruption. Each data point is related to the data point before and after it.

Example: Temperature reading over a 24-hour period: 45°, 47°, 52° and so on.

coordinate A number that determines the position of a point in one direction on a grid.

coordinate plane A system of coordinates formed by the perpendicular intersection of horizontal and vertical number lines.

counterclockwise The direction opposite to the direction the hands of a clock move.

Glossary **S3**

S4 Glossary

Student Glossary (Continued)

---

counterexample An example that proves that a general statement is false.

cube A rectangular prism that has 6 faces that are congruent squares.

cubic centimeter A metric unit for measuring volume. It is the volume of a cube with one-centimeter edges.

cubic meter A metric unit for measuring volume. It is the volume of a cube with one-meter edges.

cubic unit A cubic unit of volume made by a cube with all edges one unit long.

Example: Cubic centimeters and cubic inches are cubic units.

cup A U.S. customary unit of capacity equal to half a pint.

cylinder A solid (three-dimensional) figure with two curved, congruent bases.

D

data Pieces of information.

decimal number A representation of a number using the numerals 0 to 9, in which each digit has a value 10 times the digit to its right. A dot or decimal

point separates the whole-number part of the number on the left from the fractional part on the right.

decimeter A unit of measure in the metric system that equals one tenth of a meter. 1 dm = 0.1 m

degree A unit for measuring angles. Also a unit for measuring temperature. (See Celsius and Fahrenheit.)

denominator The number below the bar in a fraction. It tells the number of unit fractions into which the 1 whole is divided.

Example: 4 is the denominator.

$\frac{3}{4}$ ← denominator

diagonal A line segment connecting two vertices that are not next to each other.

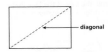

diameter A line segment from one side of a circle to the other through the center. Also the length of that segment.

difference The result of a subtraction.

Example: 54 − 37 = 17
difference

digit Any of the symbols 0, 1, 2, 3, 4, 5, 6, 7, 8, or 9.

Glossary (Continued)

digital clock A clock that has a colon (:) separating digits representing hours from digits representing minutes. Some digital clocks also have another colon to separate minutes from seconds. Digital clocks also display A.M. or P.M.

Digit-by-Digit A method used to solve a division problem.

Example:

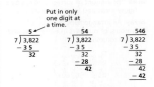

dimension The height, length, or width.

Examples:
A line segment has only length, so it has *one* dimension.
A rectangle has length and width, so it has *two* dimensions.
A cube has length, width, and height, so it has *three* dimensions.

discrete data Data that involve counting. In a set of discrete data, each number is exact and the numbers are not related to each other.

Example: The heights of five trees: 18 ft, 35 ft, 20 ft, 40 ft, 28 ft.

Distributive Property You can multiply a sum by a number, or multiply each addend by the number and add the products; the result is the same.

Example:
$$3 \times (2 + 4) = (3 \times 2) + (3 \times 4)$$
$$3 \times 6 = 6 + 12$$
$$18 = 18$$

divisible A number is divisible by another number if the quotient is a whole number with no remainder.

Example: 15 is divisible by 5 because 15 ÷ 5 = 3

dot array An arrangement of dots in rows and columns.

double bar graph Data is compared by using pairs of bars drawn next to each other.

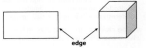

E

edge A line segment that forms as a side of a two-dimensional figure or the part of a three-dimensional figure where two faces meet.

edge

---

elapsed time The amount of time that passes between two times.

equal groups Groups that have the same number of objects.

equation A statement that two expressions are equal. An equation always has an equals sign.

Example: 32 + 35 = 67
50 = 75 − 25
1 + 10 + 40 = 53 − 2

equilateral Having all equal sides.

Example: An equilateral triangle

equivalent Representing the same number or amount.

equivalent fractions Two or more fractions that represent the same fractional part of 1 whole.

estimate Find *about* how many or *about* how much. A reasonable guess about a measurement or answer.

evaluate To substitute a value for a letter and then calculate to simplify the expression.

even number A whole number that is a multiple of 2. An even number ends with a 0, 2, 4, 6, or 8.

Example: 68 is an even number because it is a multiple of 2; 2 × 34 = 68.

example A specific instance that demonstrates a general statement.

expanded form A way of writing a number that shows the value of each of its digits.

Example: Expanded form of 835:
800 + 30 + 5
8 hundreds + 3 tens + 5 ones

Expanded Notation A strategy used to solve multiplication and division problems.

67 × 43

43 = 40 + 3
× 67 = 60 + 7
60 × 40 = 2,400
60 × 3 = 180
7 × 40 = 280
7 × 3 = 21
2,881

43
× 67
2,400
180
280
21
2,881

3,822 ÷ 7

expression A combination of one or more numbers, variables, or numbers and variables with one or more operations.

Examples: 4
6n
6n − 5
7 + 4
2(3 + 4)

exponent The number in a power that tells how many times the base is used as a factor.

Example: In 10^3, the 3 is the exponent.

F

face A flat surface of a three-dimensional figure.

Glossary (Continued)

factor One of two or more numbers multiplied together to make a product.

Example:

$$4 \times 5 = 20$$

factor factor product

Factor Puzzle A two-by-two table that is made from the cells in two rows and two columns of the Multiplication Table. It can be used to solve proportions. The unknown number in the ○ will be 5 × 3 = 15.

Fahrenheit The temperature scale used in the United States. Water freezes at 32°F and boils at 212°F.

floor plan A scale drawing of a room as seen from above.

foot A U.S. customary unit of length equal to 12 inches and $\frac{1}{3}$ yard.

fraction A number that is the sum of unit fractions, each an equal part of a set or part of a whole.

Examples: $\frac{3}{4} = \frac{1}{4} + \frac{1}{4} + \frac{1}{4}$
$\frac{5}{4} = \frac{1}{4} + \frac{1}{4} + \frac{1}{4} + \frac{1}{4} + \frac{1}{4}$

front-end estimation A method of estimating that uses the left-most digit in each number and replaces all of the other digits with zeros.

Example:
4,588 → 4,000
−2,616 → −2,000
2,000 estimated difference

function A consistent relationship between two sets of numbers. Each

number in one of the sets is paired with exactly one number in the other set. A function can be shown in a chart, or as a set of ordered pairs.

Example: The relationship between the number of yards and the number of feet.

$$f = 3y$$

Yards	1	2	3	4	5	6	7
Feet	3	6	9	12	15	18	21

G

gallon A U.S. customary unit of capacity equal to 4 quarts, 8 pints, and 16 cups.

gram The basic unit of mass in the metric system.

greater than (>) A symbol used when comparing two numbers. The greater number is given first.

Example: 33 > 17
33 is greater than 17.

greatest Largest.

growing pattern A number or geometric pattern that increases.

Examples: 2, 4, 6, 8, 10…
1, 2, 5, 10, 17…

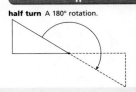

H

half turn A 180° rotation.

---

height The perpendicular distance from a base of a figure to the highest point.

hexagon A six-sided polygon.

histogram A graph in which bars are used to display how frequently data occurs between intervals.

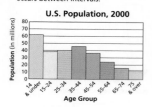

U.S. Population, 2000

hypothesis A statement used as the basis of an investigation.

I

Identity Property of Multiplication The product of 1 and any number equals that number.

Example: $10 \times 1 = 10$

image The new figure that results from the translation, reflection, or rotation of a figure.

improper fraction A fraction whose numerator is greater than or equal to the denominator.

Example: $\frac{3}{2}$

inch A U.S. customary unit of length. There are 12 inches in 1 foot.

1 inch

inequality A statement that two expressions are not equal.

Examples: $2 < 5$
$4 + 5 > 12 - 8$

integer The set of integers includes the set of positive whole numbers (1, 2, 3, …) and their opposites (–1, –2, –3, …) and 0.

inverse operations Opposite or reverse operations that undo each other. Addition and subtraction are inverse operations. Multiplication and division are inverse operations.

Examples: $4 + 6 = 10$, so $10 - 6 = 4$
$3 \times 9 = 27$, so $27 \div 9 = 3$

isosceles trapezoid A trapezoid with one pair of opposite congruent sides.

isosceles triangle A triangle with at least two congruent sides.

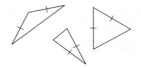

Glossary **S9**

Glossary (Continued)

K

key A part of a map, graph, or chart that explains what symbols mean.

kilogram A unit of mass in the metric system that equals one thousand grams. 1 kg = 1,000 g

kiloliter A unit of capacity in the metric system that equals one thousand liters. 1 kL = 1,000 L

kilometer A unit of length in the metric system that equals one thousand meters. 1 km = 1,000 m

L

least Smallest.

least common denominator The least common multiple of two denominators. Example: 6 is the least common denominator of $\frac{1}{2}$ and $\frac{1}{3}$.

length The measure of a line segment, or of one side or edge of a figure.

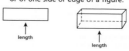

less than (<) A symbol used when comparing two numbers. The smaller number is given first.
Example: $54 < 78$
54 is less than 78.

line A straight path that goes on forever in opposite directions.
Example: line AB

line graph A graph that uses a broken line to show changes in data.

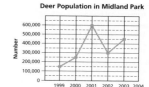

Deer Population in Midland Park

line plot A diagram that shows the frequency of data on a number line.

line of symmetry A line such that if a figure is folded on that line, the two parts will match exactly.

line of symmetry

line segment Part of a line that has two endpoints.

line symmetry A figure has line symmetry if it can be folded along a line to create two halves that match exactly.

Linked Multiplication Column Table A Multiplication Column Table that also has a column showing the unit that links the terms in each ratio.

S10 Glossary

Example: This table shows the ratios of two rates, $3 per day and $5 per day, and the linking unit, days.

Days	Noreen ③	Tim ⑤
0	0	0
1	3	5
2	6	10
3	9	15
4	12	20

liter The basic unit of capacity in the metric system.

M

mass The measure of the amount of matter in an object.

mean (average) The size of each of n equal groups made from n data values. The mean can be found by adding the values in a set of data and dividing by the number of such values.

Example: 75, 84, 89, 91, 101
$75 + 84 + 89 + 91 + 101 = 440$,
then $440 \div 5 = 88$. The mean is 88.

measure of central tendency The mean, median, or mode of a set of numbers.

median The middle number in a set of ordered numbers. For an even number of numbers, the median is the number halfway between the two middle numbers.

Examples: 13 26 **34** 47 52
The median for this set is 34.
8 8 **12 14** 20 21
The median for this set is 13.

meter The basic unit of length in the metric system.

milligram A unit of mass in the metric system that equals one thousandth of a gram. 1 mg = 0.001 g

milliliter A unit of capacity in the metric system that equals one thousandth of a liter. 1 mL = 0.001 L

millimeter A unit of length in the metric system that equals one thousandth of a meter. 1 mm = 0.001 m

misleading A comparing sentence containing language that may trick you into doing the wrong operation.

Example: John's age is 3 *more* than Jessica's. If John is 12, how old is Jessica?

mixed number A number represented by a whole number and a fraction.

Example: $4\frac{2}{3}$

mode The number that appears most frequently in a set of numbers.

Example: 2, 4, 4, 4, 5, 7, 7
4 is the mode in this set of numbers.

Multiplication Column Table A table made of two columns from a multiplication table.

Days	Dollars
0	0
1	3
2	6
3	9
4	12
5	15
6	18
7	21
8	24
9	27

multiplication table A table that shows the product of each pair of numbers in the left column and top row.

multiplier The factor used to multiply the numerator and denominator to create an equivalent fraction.

Example: A multiplier of 5 changes $\frac{2}{3}$ to
$\frac{5 \times 2}{5 \times 3} = \frac{10}{15}$.

Glossary **S11**

Glossary (Continued)

N

negative number A number less than zero.

Examples: –1, –23, and –3.5 are negative numbers.

net A flat pattern that can be folded to make a solid figure.

net for a cube

non-unit fraction A fraction with a numerator greater than 1.

Examples: $\frac{3}{4}$ or $\frac{4}{8}$ or $\frac{10}{8}$.

number sentence Describes how numbers or expressions are related to each other using one of the symbols =, <, or >. The types of number sentences are equations and inequalities.

Examples: $25 + 25 = 50$
$13 > 8 + 2$

numerical data Data that consist of numbers.

numerator The number above the bar in a fraction.

Example: The numerator is 2.

$\frac{2}{3}$ ← numerator

It tells how many unit fractions there are: 2 of the $\frac{1}{3}$.

O

oblique lines Lines that are not parallel or perpendicular.

obtuse angle An angle greater than a right angle and less than a straight angle.

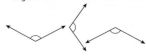

obtuse triangle A triangle with one obtuse angle.

odd number A whole number that is not a multiple of 2. An odd number ends with 1, 3, 5, 7, or 9.

Example: 73 is an odd number because it is not a multiple of 2.

one-dimensional Having only length as a measure. A line segment is one-dimensional.

operation A mathematical process. Addition, subtraction, multiplication, division, and raising a number to a power are operations.

Order of Operations A set of rules that states the order in which operations should be done.
1. Compute inside parentheses first.
2. Simplify any exponents.
3. Multiply and divide from left to right.
4. Add and subtract from left to right.

ordered pair A pair of numbers that shows the position of a point on a coordinate grid.

Example: The ordered pair (3, 4) represents a point 3 units to the right of the y-axis and 4 units above the x-axis.

S12 Glossary

Student Glossary (Continued)

origin The point (0, 0) on a two-dimensional coordinate grid.

ounce A unit of weight or capacity in the U.S. customary system equal to one sixteenth of a pound or one eighth of a cup.

overestimate An estimate that is greater than the actual amount.

Example: A shirt costs $26.47 and a pair of jeans cost $37.50. You can make an overestimate by rounding $26.47 to $30 and $37.50 to $40 to be sure you have enough money to pay for the clothes.

P

parallel The same distance apart at every point.

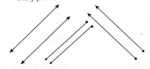

parallelogram A quadrilateral with both pairs of opposite sides parallel.

parentheses Symbols used to group numbers together.

$$7 + (3 \times 4) = 19$$

parentheses

partial products Products of the smaller problems in the Rectangle Sections method of multiplying.

Example: The partial products are highlighted.

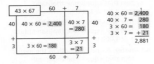

pentagon A polygon with five sides.

percent Percent means out of a hundred or per hundred. The numerator of a fraction that has 100 as the denominator is followed by the % sign: 50% is $\frac{50}{100}$ or a value equivalent to $\frac{50}{100}$.

perimeter The distance around a figure.

perpendicular Lines, line segments, or rays are perpendicular if they form right angles.

Example: These two lines are perpendicular.

pi A number equal to the circumference of a circle divided by its diameter, or about 3.14. Pi is often represented by the symbol π.

Glossary **S13**

Glossary (Continued)

pint A U.S. customary unit of capacity equal to half a quart.

place value The value assigned to the place that a digit occupies in a number.

Example: 235

The 2 is in the hundreds place, so its value is 200.

plane A flat surface that extends without end.

polygon A closed plane figure with sides made of straight line segments.

pound A unit of weight in the U.S. customary system.

pre-image A figure before its transformation.

prime factorization A whole number written as the product of prime factors.

Example: Prime factorization of 30:
$2 \times 3 \times 5$

prime number A number greater than 1 that has 1 and itself as the only factor pair. Examples of prime numbers are 2, 7, and 13. The only factor pair of 7 is 1 and 7.

prism A solid figure with two congruent parallel bases.

pentagonal prism

probability A number between 0 and 1 that represents the chance of an event happening.

product The result of a multiplication.

Example: $9 \times 7 = 63$

product

proof A demonstration of the truth of a general statement.

proportion An equation that shows two equivalent ratios.

Example: 6 : 10 = 9 : 15

pyramid A solid with a polygon for a base whose vertices are all joined to a single point.

Q

quadrilateral A two-dimensional figure with four sides.

quart A U.S. customary unit of capacity equal to $\frac{1}{4}$ gallon or 2 pints.

quarter turn A 90° rotation.

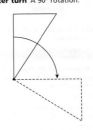

S14 Glossary

R

radius A line segment that connects the center of a circle to any point on that circle. Also the length of that line segment.

range The difference between the greatest and the least number in a set.

ratio A comparison of two or more quantities in the same units.

Ratio Table A table that shows equivalent ratios.

Example: This table show ratios equivalent to the basic ratio, 3 : 5.

③	⑤
0	0
3	5
6	10
9	15
12	20
15	25
18	30
21	35
24	40

ray A part of a line that has one endpoint and extends without end in one direction.

rectangle A parallelogram with four right angles.

Rectangle Rows A method used to solve multiplication problems.

Example:

Rectangle Sections A method used to solve multiplication and division problems.

Example:

$3{,}822 \div 7$ Build a new section with each leftover amount.

Glossary **S15**

Glossary (Continued)

rectangular prism A solid that has congruent rectangular bases.

reflection A transformation that flips a figure onto a congruent image. Sometimes called a *flip*.

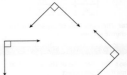

reflex angle An angle greater than 180°.

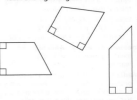

remainder The number left over after dividing a number by a number that does not divide it evenly.

Example: 43 ÷ 5 = 8 R3
The remainder is 3.

Repeated Groups Groups with the same number of objects are Repeated Groups.

Example: 2 + 2 + 2 = 6
There are 3 repeated groups of 2.

repeating pattern A pattern consisting of a group of numbers, letters, or figures that repeat.

Example: 1, 2, 1, 2, ...
A, B, C, A, B, C, ...

○ □ ○ ▲ ○ □ ○ ▲

rhombus A parallelogram with congruent sides.

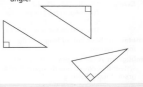

right angle An angle that measures 90°.

right trapezoid A trapezoid with at least one right angle.

right triangle A triangle with one right angle.

S16 Glossary

T4 Student Glossary

rotation A turn. A transformation that turns a figure so that each point stays an equal distance from a single point, the center of rotation.

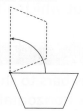

rotational symmetry The property of a figure that allows it to fit exactly on itself in less than one full rotation.

round To find the nearest ten, hundred, thousand, or some other place value.
Example: 463 rounded to the nearest ten is 460.
463 rounded to the nearest hundred is 500.

row A part of a table or array that contains items arranged horizontally.

• • • • •

S

scale Numbers or marks arranged at regular intervals that are used for measurement or to establish position. In a scale drawing, the scale tells how the measurements in the drawing relate to the actual measurements.

scale drawing A drawing that is made in proportion to the size of a real object.

scalene triangle A triangle with no equal sides is a scalene triangle.

Short Cut Method A method used to solve multiplication problems.
Example: 43 × 67

	Step 1	Step 2	Step 3	Step 4	Step 5

short word form A way of writing a number that uses digits and words.
Example: Short word form of 12,835: 12 thousand, 835

shrinking pattern A number or geometric pattern that decreases.
Example: 15, 12, 9, 6, 3,…
25, 20, 16, 13, 11,…

similar Having the same shape but not necessarily the same size. The lengths of the corresponding sides are in proportion.

similar figures

---

simplest form A fraction is in simplest form if there is no whole number (other than 1) that divides evenly into the numerator and denominator.
Example: $\frac{3}{4}$ This fraction is in simplest form because no number divides evenly into 3 and 4.

simplify To find a result. To rewrite a fraction as an equivalent fraction with a smaller numerator and denominator.
Example: $\frac{3}{6} = \frac{1}{2}$

situation equation An equation that shows the action or the relationship in a problem.
Example: 35 + n = 40

slant height The height of a triangular face of a pyramid.

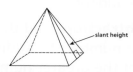

solution equation An equation that shows the operation to perform in order to solve the problem.
Example: n = 40 − 35

square A rectangle with four congruent sides.

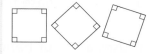

square number The product of a whole number and itself.
Example: 3 × 3 = 9
9 is a square number.

square root The square root of a number n is a number that when multiplied by itself equals the number n.
Examples: 4 is the square root of the number 16.

square unit A unit of area equal to the area of a square with one-unit sides.
Examples: square meters and square inches

square yard A unit of area equal to the area of a square with one-yard sides.

standard form The form of a number written using digits.
Example: 2,145

stem-and-leaf plot A display that uses place value to organize a set of data.

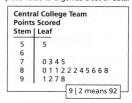

Central College Team Points Scored

Stem	Leaf
5	5
6	
7	0 3 4 5
8	0 1 1 2 2 2 4 5 6 6 8
9	1 2 7 8

9 | 2 means 92

straight angle An angle of 180°.

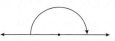

sum The result of an addition.
Example:

53 + 26 = 79

addend   addend   sum

---

supplementary angles Angles having a sum of 180°.

surface area The total area of the two-dimensional surfaces around the outside of a three-dimensional figure.

T

table Data arranged in rows and columns.

term in a pattern A number, letter, or figure in a pattern.
Example: The second term in this number pattern is 10.
5, 10, 15, 20, 25,…

three-dimensional Having length measurements in three directions, perpendicular to each other.

ton A unit of weight or mass that equals 2,000 pounds.

tonne A metric unit of mass that equals 1,000 kilograms.

transformation Reflections, rotations, and translations are examples of transformations.

translation A transformation that moves a figure along a straight line without turning or flipping. Sometimes called a *slide*.

trapezoid A quadrilateral with exactly one pair of parallel sides.

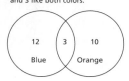

triangle A polygon with three sides.

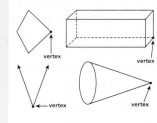

U

under estimate An estimate that is less than the actual amount.
Example: A shirt costs $26.47 and a pair of jeans cost $37.50. If you brought $60 to pay for the clothes because you rounded $26.47 to $25 and $37.50 to $35, you made an under-estimate and did not have enough money.

ungroup Rewrite a mixed number with a different whole number and fraction part or rewrite a whole number with different numbers in the places.
Example: $4\frac{2}{3} = 3\frac{5}{3}$ or 100 + 20 + 3 = 90 + 30 + 3

unit Something used repeatedly to measure quantity.
Examples: Centimeters, pounds, inches, and so on.

unit fraction A fraction with a numerator of 1.
Examples: $\frac{1}{2}$ and $\frac{1}{10}$

---

unsimplify Rewrite a fraction as an equivalent fraction with a greater numerator and denominator.
Examples: $\frac{1}{2} = \frac{3}{6}$

V

variable A letter or symbol that represents a number.

Venn Diagram A diagram that uses overlapping circles to show the relationship between two (or more) sets of objects.
Example: This Venn diagram shows that of 25 students surveyed, 12 like the color blue, 10 like the color orange, and 3 like both colors.

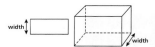

12   3   10
Blue   Orange

vertex A point that is shared by two arms of an angle, two sides of a polygon, or edges of a solid figure. The point of a cone.

vertex   vertex
vertex   vertex

view A two-dimensional representation of what a three-dimensional figure looks like from the front, side, or top.

volume The measure of the amount of space occupied by an object.

W

width The measure of one side or edge of a figure.

width

width

word form The form of a number written using words instead of digits.
Example: Six hundred thirty-nine

X

x-axis The horizontal axis of a two-dimensional coordinate grid.

x-coordinate A number that represents a point's horizontal distance from the y-axis of a two-dimensional coordinate grid.

Y

y-axis The vertical axis of a two-dimensional coordinate grid.

yard A U.S. customary unit of length equal to 3 feet or 36 inches.

y-coordinate A number that represents a point's vertical distance from the x-axis of a two-dimensional coordinate grid.

Teacher Glossary

A

acre A measure of land area. An acre is equal to 4,840 square yards.

acute angle An angle that measures less than 90°.

acute triangle A triangle in which each of the three angles is acute.

addend A number to be added in an addition equation. In the equation $7 + 4 + 8 = \square$, the numbers 7, 4, and 8 are addends.

Add On Method for Subtraction Find the difference between two numbers by adding to the lesser number to get the greater number.

adjusted estimate A new estimate that is made using the Digit-by-Digit method of dividing when an overestimate or underestimate has been made initially.

analog clock A clock that uses an hour hand and a minute hand to display time. Most are circular and have a face numbered from 1 to 12. Some analog clocks also have a second hand.

angle A figure formed by two rays or line segments that meet at an endpoint.

apex The vertex of a cone.

area The amount of surface covered or enclosed by a figure measured in square units.

array An arrangement of objects, pictures, or numbers in equal columns and equal rows.

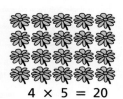

5 × 4 = 20   4 × 5 = 20

5 × 4 = 4 × 5

Associative Property of Addition The property that states that changing the grouping of addends does not change their sum. For all numbers *a*, *b*, and *c*, $a + (b + c) = (a + b) + c$.

Associative Property of Multiplication The property that states that changing the grouping of factors does not change their product. For all numbers *a*, *b*, and *c*, $a \times (b \times c) = (a \times b) \times c$.

axis A line, usually horizontal or vertical, that is labeled with numbers or words to show the meaning of a graph.

axis of rotation A line about which a figure is rotated.

B

bar graph A graph that uses bars to show data. The bars may be vertical or horizontal.

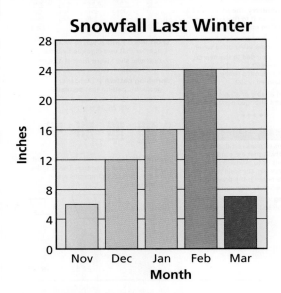

base of a figure For a triangle or parallelogram, a base is any side. For a trapezoid, a base is either of the parallel sides. For a prism, a base is one of the congruent parallel faces. For a pyramid, the base is the face that does not touch the vertex of the pyramid.

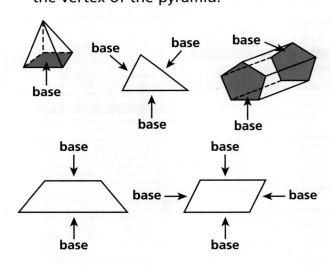

base of a power The number that is used as a factor when evaluating powers.
Example:
In 10^3, the 10 is the base.

basic ratio A ratio in simplest form.

billion One thousand million or 1,000,000,000.

billionth One thousandth of a millionth or 0.000000001.

break-apart drawing A drawing that students create to show the relationship between addition and subtraction.

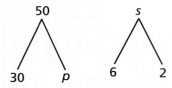

C

capacity A measure of how much a container can hold, also used to describe the volume of fluids such as water or sand.

categorical data Data expressed as words that represent categories.

Celsius The metric temperature scale.

centimeter (cm) A metric unit of length equal to 0.01 $(\frac{1}{100})$ meter.

change minus A change situation that can be represented by subtraction. In a change minus situation, the starting number, the change, or the result will be unknown.

change plus A change situation that can be represented by addition. In a change plus situation, the starting number, the change, or the result will be unknown.

circle A plane figure with all points the same distance from a fixed point called the center.

circle graph A graph used to display data that make up a whole. (Also called a pie graph or a pie chart.)

circumference The distance around a circle.

Class Multiplication Table Poster A poster in table form that displays the multiplication facts.

Multiplication Table

X	0	1	2	3	4	5	6	7	8	9
0	0	0	0	0	0	0	0	0	0	0
1	0	1	2	3	4	5	6	7	8	9
2	0	2	4	6	8	10	12	14	16	18
3	0	3	6	9	12	15	18	21	24	27
4	0	4	8	12	16	20	24	28	32	36
5	0	5	10	15	20	25	30	35	40	45
6	0	6	12	18	24	30	36	42	48	54
7	0	7	14	21	28	35	42	49	56	63
8	0	8	16	24	32	40	48	56	64	72
9	0	9	18	27	36	45	54	63	72	81
10	0	10	20	30	40	50	60	70	80	90
11	0	11	22	33	44	55	66	77	88	99
12	0	12	24	36	48	60	72	84	96	108

clockwise The direction in which the hands of a clock move.

collection situations Situations that involve putting together (joining) or taking apart (separating) groups.

column In a data table, a vertical group of cells. In an array, a group of items arranged vertically.

combination A selection of members of a set when the order is not important. Combinations = choices for 1st item × choices for 2nd item.

common denominator The same denominator that is needed in order to add or subtract fractions; any common multiple of the denominators of two or more fractions.

Commutative Property of Addition The property that states that changing the order in which numbers are added does not change the sum. For all numbers a and b, $a + b = b + a$.

Commutative Property of Multiplication The property that states that changing the order in which numbers are multiplied does not change the product. For all numbers a and b, $a \times b = b \times a$.

Teacher Glossary (Continued)

comparison A method of showing whether one quantity is greater than, less than, or equal to another quantity. Multiplicatively, there are two ways in which students may make comparisons. If students are comparing 2 circles and 6 squares, the comparison could be expressed as:

1) There are 3 times as many squares as circles.

or

2) There are $\frac{1}{3}$ as many circles as squares.

complementary angles Two angles for which the sum of their measures is 90°.

complex figure A figure made by combining simple geometric figures like rectangles and triangles.

composite number A number greater than 1 that has more than two factors. Examples of composite numbers are 10 and 18. The factor pairs of 10 are 1 and 10 and 2 and 5. The factor pairs of 18 are 1 and 18, 2 and 9, and 3 and 6.

cone A solid figure with a circular base and a single vertex.

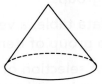

congruent Exactly the same size and shape.

continuous data Data that represent an accumulation without interruption. Each data point is related to the data point before and after it.
Example: Temperature reading over a 24-hour period: 45°, 47°, 52°, and so on.

coordinate A number that determines the position of a point in one direction.

coordinate plane A system of coordinates formed by the perpendicular intersection of horizontal and vertical number lines.

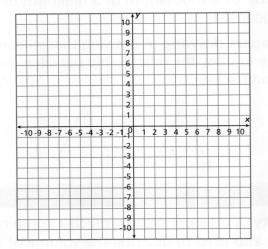

count-bys Products that are found by counting-by a particular number; 5 count-bys would be 5, 10, 15, 20, 25, and so on; 3 count-bys would be 3, 6, 9, 12, and so on.

counterclockwise The direction opposite to the direction the hands of a clock move.

counterexample An example that proves that a general statement is false.

cube A rectangular prism with six congruent square faces.

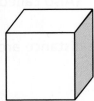

cubic unit A unit for measuring volume such as a cubic inch or cubic centimeter. It is the volume of a cube with 1-unit edges.

cup A customary unit for measuring capacity. There are 2 cups in 1 pint.

cylinder A solid with two curved, congruent bases.

D

data Pieces of information.

decimeter A metric unit of length equal to 0.1 ($\frac{1}{10}$) meter.

degree (°) A unit for measuring angles. Also a unit for measuring temperature. (See **Celsius** and **Fahrenheit**.)

denominator The number below the bar in a fraction. It tells the number of equal parts into which the one whole is divided.

diameter A line segment from one side of a circle to the other through the center. Also the length of that segment.

difference The result of a subtraction.

digit Any of the symbols 0, 1, 2, 3, 4, 5, 6, 7, 8, or 9.

digital clock A clock that has a colon (:) separating digits representing hours from digits representing minutes. Some digital clocks also have another colon to separate minutes from seconds. Digital clocks also display A.M. or P.M.

Digit-by-Digit A method of dividing in which students estimate and determine each digit of the quotient.

dimension A way to describe how a figure can be measured. The height, length, or width.

discrete data Data that involve counting. In a set of discrete data, each number is exact and the numbers are not related to each other.

Distributive Property The property that states that when two addends are multiplied by a factor, the product is the same as when each addend is multiplied by the factor and those products are added. For all numbers a, b, and c, $(a + b) \times c = (a \times c) + (b \times c)$.

divisible A number is divisible by another number if the quotient is a whole number with no remainder. The number 6 is divisible by 3 but not by 4.

Division Cards Cards that display a division exercise on one side along with a corresponding multiplication fact. The missing quotient is shown as an unknown factor in the multiplication fact. The reverse side shows the missing quotient and unknown factor.

double bar graph A graph in which two data sets are compared by using pairs of bars drawn next to each other.

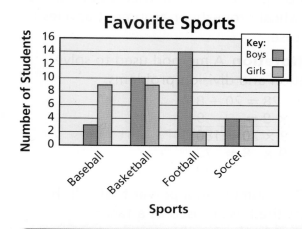

E

edge The line segment where two faces of a three-dimensional figure meet.

elapsed time The amount of time that passes from the start of an event to its end.

equal groups Groups that have the same number of objects. Concept used in multiplication and division situations.
$5 \times 6 = 30$. There are 5 equal groups of 6 items.

equation A statement that two expressions are equal.

$12 - 5 = 7 \qquad 3 + 1 = 4 \qquad 5 = 2 + 3$
$6 = 8 - 2 \qquad 6 + 2 = 4 + 4$

equilateral triangle A triangle that has three congruent sides and three congruent angles.

equivalent Representing the same number.

equivalent fractions Fractions that represent the same number. $\frac{1}{2}$ and $\frac{2}{4}$ are equivalent fractions.

estimate (noun) A number close to an exact amount. An estimate tells *about* how much or *about* how many.

Teacher Glossary (Continued)

estimate (verb) To make a thoughtful guess or to tell *about* how much or *about* how many.

evaluate To substitute a value for a letter and then calculate to simplify the expression.

even number A number that is a multiple of 2. The ones digit of an even number is 0, 2, 4, 6, or 8. Even numbers are those that can be divided into two equal groups.

example A proposed problem, used to prove that a mathematical property or argument applies to a specific case.

Expanded Notation A method used to solve multiplication and division problems.

Example:

$$
\begin{array}{r}
28 = 20 + 8 \\
\times\, 9 = \qquad 9 \\
\hline
9 \times 20 = 180 \\
9 \times\ \ 8 = \ \ 72 \\
\hline
252
\end{array}
$$

exponent The number in a power that tells how many times the base is used as a factor.
Example: In 10^3, the 3 is the exponent.

expression One or more numbers, variables, or numbers and variables with one or more operation signs.

F

face A flat surface of a three-dimensional figure.

factor One of two or more numbers multiplied to find a product.

Factor Puzzle A two-by-two table that is a part of a multiplication table, with one missing number.

Fahrenheit The temperature scale used in the United States.

floor plan A scale drawing of a room as seen from above.

foot A customary unit of length equal to 12 inches.

front-end estimation A method of estimating that uses the left-most digit in each number and replaces all of the other digits with zeros.
Example:

$$
\begin{array}{r}
4{,}588 \longrightarrow \ \ 4{,}000 \\
-2{,}616 \longrightarrow -2{,}000 \\
\hline
2{,}000 \ \text{estimated difference}
\end{array}
$$

function A relationship between two sets of numbers. Each number in one of the sets is paired with exactly one number in the other set, for example, the relationship between yds and ft.

G

gallon A U.S. customary unit for measuring capacity. One gallon is equal to 4 quarts.

Geometry and Measurement Poster

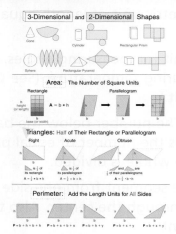

gram The basic unit of mass in the metric system. A nickel weighs about 5 grams.

growing pattern A number or geometric pattern that increases.
Examples: 2, 4, 6, 8, 10…
1, 2, 5, 10, 17…

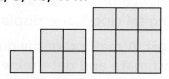

H

half turn A 180° rotation.

height The perpendicular distance from a base of a figure to the highest point.

hexagon A six-sided polygon.

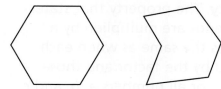

histogram A graph in which bars are used to display how frequently data occurs between intervals. The labels for the bars are numerical intervals.

hypothesis A statement used as the basis of an investigation.

I

Identity Property of Multiplication The product of 1 and any number equals that number.

image The new figure that results from the translation, reflection, or rotation of a figure.

improper fraction A fraction with a numerator that is greater than or equal to the denominator.

inch A customary unit of length equal to $\frac{1}{12}$ foot.

inequality A statement that two expressions are not equal.

integer The set of integers includes the set of positive whole numbers (1, 2, 3, …) and their opposites ($^-1$, $^-2$, $^-3$, …) and 0.

inverse operations Opposite or reverse operations that undo each other. Addition and subtraction are inverse operations. Multiplication and division are inverse operations.

isosceles trapezoid A trapezoid with a pair of opposite congruent sides.

isosceles triangle A triangle with at least two congruent sides.

K

key A part of a map, graph, or chart that explains what symbols mean.

kilogram A metric unit of mass equal to 1,000 grams.

kiloliter A metric unit of capacity equal to 1,000 liters.

L

leading language Language in a comparing sentence that suggests which operation to use to solve the problem.

least common denominator The least common multiple of two or more denominators.

length The measure of a line segment, or one side or edge of a figure.

line An infinite set of points forming a straight path extending in opposite directions.

line graph A graph that uses line segments to show changes in data. A line graph is often used to display data that changes over time.

line of symmetry A line that divides a figure into two opposite congruent parts.

line segment Part of a line that has two endpoints.

line symmetry A figure has line symmetry if it can be folded along a line to create two halves that match exactly. Also called reflection symmetry.

Linked Multiplication Column Table A Multiplication Column Table that also has a column showing the unit that links the two terms in each ratio.

liter The basic unit of capacity in the metric system.

M

mass The amount of matter in an object. Mass is constant; weight varies because it is subject to the effect of gravity on matter.

mean (average) The size of each of n equal groups made from n data values. The mean can be found by adding the values in a set of data and dividing by the number of such values.

measure of central tendency The mean, median, or mode of a set of numbers.

median The middle number when a set of numbers is arranged in order from least to greatest. For an even number of numbers, the median is the average of the two middle numbers.

meter The basic unit of length in the metric system. A meter is a little longer than a yard.

milligram A metric unit of mass equal to 0.001 ($\frac{1}{1,000}$) gram.

milliliter A metric unit of capacity equal to 0.001 ($\frac{1}{1,000}$) liter.

millimeter A metric unit of length equal to 0.001 ($\frac{1}{1,000}$) meter.

Teacher Glossary (Continued)

misleading language Language in a comparing sentence that may cause you to do the wrong thing.

Example: John's age is 3 more than Jessica's. If John is 12, how old is Jessica?

mixed number A number represented by a whole number and a fraction. For example, $3\frac{1}{5}$ is a mixed number.

mode The number or numbers that occur the most often in a set of data.

Multiplication Column Table A table made of two columns from a multiplication table.

multiplication table An array of numbers with rows and columns labeled from 1 through 12. The product of the labels is found in the cell where the row and column intersect.

multiplier One of the factors in a multiplication equation. The factor used to multiply the numerator and denominator to create an equivalent fraction.

N

negative number A number less than zero.

net A two-dimensional flat pattern that can be folded into a three-dimensional figure.

non-standard unit A unit of measure not commonly recognized, such as a paper clip. An inch and a centimeter are standard units of measure.

non-unit fraction A fraction that is built from unit fractions. $\frac{2}{3}$ is a non-unit fraction because it is built from the unit fractions $\frac{1}{3} + \frac{1}{3}$.

number sentence A mathematical statement to show how numbers or expressions are related. Number sentences can be equations or inequalities.

numerator The number above the bar in a fraction. The numerator tells the number of unit fractions being described.

numerical data Data that consist of numbers.

O

oblique lines Lines in the same plane that intersect to form non-right (acute or obtuse) angles.

obtuse angle An angle that measures more than 90° and less than 180°.

obtuse triangle A triangle with one angle that measures more than 90°.

odd number A number that is not a multiple of 2. The ones digit of an odd number is 1, 3, 5, 7, or 9. Odd numbers cannot be divided into two equal groups.

one-dimensional Having only length as a measure. A line segment is one-dimensional.

operation A mathematical process. Addition, subtraction, multiplication, division, and raising a number to a power are operations.

ordered pair A pair of numbers that shows the position of a point on a graph.

Order of Operations A set of rules that state the order in which operations should be done.

origin The point (0, 0) on a two-dimensional coordinate grid.

ounce A unit of weight or capacity in the U.S. customary system equal to one sixteenth of a pound or one eighth of a cup.

overestimate An estimate that is greater than the actual amount. A quotient that is too large when the Digit-by-Digit estimating method of division is used.

P

parallel Lines in the same plane that never intersect are parallel. Line segments and rays that are part of parallel lines are also parallel.

parallelogram A quadrilateral in which both pairs of opposite sides are parallel and opposite angles are congruent.

parentheses ( ) Symbols used to group numbers or variables in an equation or expression; parentheses can also tell which operation to perform first.

partial products Products of the smaller problems in the Rectangle Sections method of multiplying.

43 × 67	60	+	7
40	40 × 60 = 2,400		40 × 7 = 280
+ 3	3 × 60 = 180		3 × 7 = 21

$$40 \times 60 = 2{,}400$$
$$40 \times 7 = 280$$
$$3 \times 60 = 180$$
$$3 \times 7 = +\ 21$$
$$2{,}881$$

pentagon A polygon with five sides.

percent Percent means out of a hundred or per hundred. The numerator of a fraction that has 100 as the denominator is followed by the % sign: 50% is $\frac{50}{100}$ or a value equivalent to $\frac{50}{100}$.

perimeter The distance around a figure.

perpendicular Lines, line segments, or rays are perpendicular if they form right angles.

pi (π) A number equal to the circumference of a circle divided by its diameter. Two common approximations used for pi are $\frac{22}{7}$ and 3.14.

pint A U.S. customary unit for measuring capacity. One pint is equal to two cups or half a quart.

place value The value assigned to the place that a digit occupies in a number.

Place Value Parade Poster The place values from thousands to thousandths presented so students can see the ten-for-one trades between places and the symmetry around the ones place.

Place Value Parade

Thousands	Hundreds	Tens	Ones	Tenths	Hundredths	Thousandths
1,000.	100.	10.	1.	0.1	0.01	0.001
$\frac{1{,}000}{1}$	$\frac{100}{1}$	$\frac{10}{1}$	$\frac{1}{1}$	$\frac{1}{10}$	$\frac{1}{100}$	$\frac{1}{1{,}000}$
$1,000.00	$100.00	$10.00	$1.00	$0.10	$0.01	$0.001
kilometer km	hectometer hm	dekameter dkm	meter m	decimeter dm	centimeter cm	millimeter mm

plane A flat surface that extends without end.

point symmetry The property of a figure that can be turned less than a full turn (360°) and still look the same as it did before the turn. Also called rotational symmetry.

polygon A closed plane figure made up of three or more straight line segments for its sides.

pound A U.S. customary unit for measuring mass. One pound is equal to sixteen ounces.

pre-image A figure before its transformation.

prime factorization A whole number written as the product of prime factors.
 Example: Prime factorization of 30:
 2 × 3 × 5

prime number A number greater than 1 that has 1 and itself as the only factors.

prism A 3-dimensional figure that has two parallel congruent bases and parallelograms for faces. Prisms are named by the shape of their bases.

probability The mathematical science of measuring and estimating predictability. A number between 0 and 1 that represents the chance of an event happening.

product The answer to a multiplication. In the problem 3 × 4 = 12, 12 is the product.

proof A method to establish that a mathematical property or argument is true.

proportion An equation that shows two equivalent ratios.

pyramid A solid whose base can be any polygon and whose other faces are all triangles that meet at a point called the vertex.

Q

quart A U.S. customary unit for measuring capacity. One quart is equal to 32 ounces.

quarter turn A 90° rotation.

R

radius A line segment that connects the center of a circle to any point on the circle, or the length of that line segment.

Teacher Glossary (Continued)

range The difference between the greatest number and the least number in a set of data.

ratio A comparison of two or more quantities in the same units.

Ratio Table A table that shows equivalent ratios.

ray Part of a line that starts at an endpoint and goes on without end in one direction.

rectangle A parallelogram with four right angles.

Rectangle Rows Method A method used to solve multiplication problems.

Example:

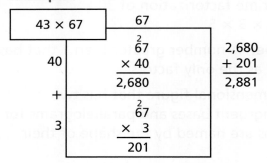

Rectangle Sections A method used to solve multiplication and division problems.

Example:

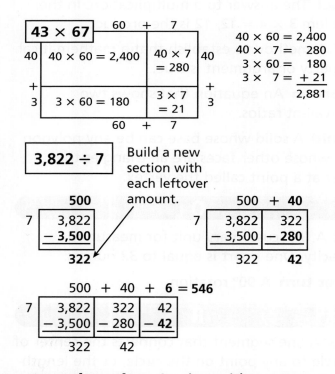

rectangular prism A prism with congruent rectangular bases.

reflection A flip. A transformation that moves a figure about a line to form a congruent image.

reflection symmetry See **line symmetry**.

reflex angle An angle with a measure that is greater than 180° and less than 360°.

remainder In division, the number left over after dividing two numbers that are not evenly divisible. In the division example 32 divided by 6, the quotient is 5 with a remainder of 2. There are 5 groups of 6 and one more group that has only 2 items (the remainder).

repeating pattern A pattern consisting of a group of numbers, letters, or figures that repeat.

Example: 1, 2, 1, 2, …
A, B, C, A, B, C, …

⚪ ⬜ ⚪ 🔺 ⚪ ⬜ ⚪ 🔺

right angle An angle that measures 90°.

right trapezoid A trapezoid that has at least one right angle.

right triangle A triangle with one right angle.

rotation A turn. A transformation that turns a figure so that each point stays an equal distance from a single point, the center of rotation.

rotational symmetry See **point symmetry**.

round To find the nearest ten, hundred, thousand, or some other place value. The usual rounding rule is to round up if the next right digit is 5 or greater and round down if the next right digit is less than 5.

row A part of a table or array that contains items arranged horizontally.

scale Numbers or marks arranged at regular intervals that are used for measurement or to establish position. In a scale drawing, the scale tells us how the measurements in the drawing relate to the actual measurements.

scale drawing A drawing that is made in proportion to the size of a real object.

scalene triangle A triangle with no equal sides.

T14   Teacher Glossary

Secret Code Cards (decimal and whole number) Cut-out cards used to teach place value from thousandths to thousands. Students assemble the cards to show various numbers.

Short Cut Method of Multiplication A strategy for multiplying. It is the current common method in the United States.

Step 1	Step 2
$\overset{7}{2}8$	$\overset{7}{2}8$
$\times\ 9$	$\times\ 9$
$\overline{2}$	$\overline{252}$

short word form A way of writing a number that uses digits and words.
   Example: Short word form of 12,835:
           12 thousand, 835

shrinking pattern A number or geometric pattern that decreases.
   Examples: 15, 12, 9, 6, 3,…
           25, 20, 16, 13, 11,…

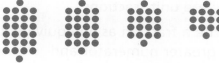

similar Having the same shape but not necessarily the same size. The lengths of the corresponding sides are in proportion.

simplify a fraction To divide the numerator and denominator of a fraction by the same number to make an equivalent fraction made from fewer but larger unit fractions.

   Example:

$$\frac{5}{10} = \frac{5 \div 5}{10 \div 5} = \frac{1}{2}$$

situation equation An equation students write to represent a story problem. It represents a literal translation of the problem. It may or may not have the unknown isolated on one side of the equals sign.

slant height The height of a triangular face of a pyramid.

solution equation A situation equation that has been rewritten so that the unknown is on the right side of the equals sign. It is related to the operation needed to solve the problem rather than to a literal translation of the story problem.

square A rectangle with four congruent sides.

square centimeter A metric unit for measuring area that is one centimeter on each side.

square foot A customary unit for measuring area that is one foot on each side.

square inch A customary unit for measuring area that is one inch on each side.

square number The product of a whole number and itself.

square root The square root of a number n is a number that when multiplied by itself equals the number n.
   Example: 4 is the square root of the number 16.

square unit A unit of area equal to the area of a square with one-unit sides. A square unit can refer to a standard or non-standard unit.

square yard A customary unit for measuring area that is one yard on each side.

standard unit A recognized unit of measure, such as an inch or a centimeter. A non-standard unit of measure might be a paper clip.

stem-and-leaf plot A display that uses place value to organize a set of data.

Central College Team Points Scored	
Stem	Leaf
5	5
6	
7	0 3 4 5
8	0 1 1 2 2 2 4 5 6 6 8
9	1 2 7 8

9 | 2 means 92

straight angle An angle that measures 180°.

subtract To take away from.

Teacher Glossary (Continued)

sum The answer when adding two or more addends. In the addition equation, 3 + 2 = 5, 5 is the sum.

supplementary angles Two angles having a sum of 180°.

surface area The total area of the two-dimensional surfaces of a three-dimensional figure.

symmetry See **line symmetry** and **point symmetry**.

T

Target A transparent square used to find a product in the Multiplication Table. A product is found in a cell at the intersection of a row and a column.

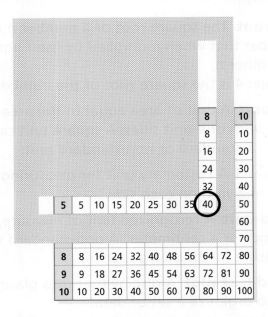

term in a pattern A number, letter, or figure in a pattern.
Example: The second term in this number pattern is 10.
5, 10, 15, 20, 25, …

three-dimensional (3-D) Having length measurements in three directions, perpendicular to one another.

ton A customary unit for measuring mass. One ton is equal to 2,000 pounds.

tonne A metric unit of mass that equals 1,000 kilograms.

transformation Reflections, rotations, and translations are examples of transformations.

translation A slide. A transformation that moves a figure along a straight line without turning or flipping it.

triangle A closed figure with three sides.

turn A figure that is rotated around a point or axis; also referred to as a rotation. The size and shape of the figure remain the same. (See **rotation**.)

two-dimensional (2-D) Having length measurements in two directions, perpendicular to each other.

U

underestimate An estimate that is less than the actual amount. A quotient that is too small when the Digit-by-Digit estimating method of division is used.

ungroup To break into smaller groups in order to subtract. For example, 1 hundred can be ungrouped into 10 tens and 1 ten can be ungrouped into 10 ones.

unit fraction A fraction that is one equal part of a whole. $\frac{1}{3}$ and $\frac{1}{4}$ are unit fractions.

unsimplify Rewrite a fraction as an equivalent fraction with a greater numerator and denominator.

V

variable A letter or a symbol that represents a number in an algebraic expression.

Venn Diagram A diagram that uses overlapping circles to show the relationship between two (or more) sets of objects.
Example: This Venn diagram shows that of 25 students surveyed, 12 like the color blue, 10 like the color orange, and 3 like both colors.

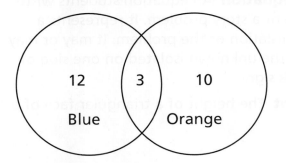

vertex A point common to two sides of an angle or polygon, or two edges of a solid figure. Also, the point of a cone.

view A two-dimensional drawing that shows what a solid looks like from the front, side, or top.

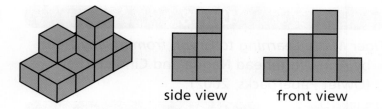

side view   front view

volume The measure of the amount of space occupied by an object.

W

width One dimension of a 2- or 3-dimensional figure.

X

x-axis The horizontal axis of a two-dimensional coordinate grid.

x-coordinate A number that represents a point's horizontal distance from the *y*-axis of a two-dimensional coordinate grid.

Y

yard Customary unit for measuring length. One yard is equal to three feet; one yard is equal to thirty-six inches.

y-axis The vertical axis of a two-dimensional coordinate grid.

y-coordinate A number that represents a point's vertical distance from the *x*-axis of a two-dimensional coordinate grid.

Recommended Books

Basic Facts Fluency Plan

Anno's Mysterious Multiplying Jar, by Masaichiro and Mitsumasa Anno (Putnam Juvenile, 1999)

Math Strategies That Multiply: The Best of Times, by Greg Tang, illustrated by Harry Briggs (Scholastic Press, 2002)

One Grain of Rice: A Mathematical Folktale, by Demi (Scholastic Press, 1997)

Unit 1

O, Say Can You See?, by Sheila Keenan and Ann Boyajian (Scholastic Nonfiction, 2007)

Math-terpieces: The Art of Problem-Solving, by Greg Tang, illustrated by Greg Paprocki (Scholastic Press, 2003)

The Sundae Scoop, by Stuart J. Murphy, illustrated by Cynthia Jabar (Harper Collins, 2003)

Unit 2

Building with Shapes, by Rebecca Weber (Compass Point Books, 2004)

Unit 3

Polar Bear Math: Learning About Fractions from Klondike and Snow, by Ann Whitehead Nagda and Cindy Bickel (Square Fish, 2007)

Unit 4

Sir Cumference and the Great Knight of Angleland: A Math Adventure, by Cindy Neuschwander, illustrated by Wayne Geehan (Charlesbridge Publishing, 2002)

Sir Cumference and the Dragon of Pi, by Cindy Neuschwander, illustrated by Wayne Geehan (Charlesbridge Publishing, 1999)

Unit 5

Fraction Action, by Loreen Leedy (Holiday House, 1996)

Unit 6

The Math Chef: Over 60 Math Activities and Recipes for Kids, by Joan D'Amico and Karen Eich Drummond (Jossey-Bass, 1996)

Unit 7

The Amazing Impossible Erie Canal, by Cheryl Harness (Aladdin, 1999)

7 × 9 = Trouble!, by Claudia Mills (Farrar, Straus, and Giroux, 2004)

Unit 8

Tiger Math: Learning to Graph from a Baby Tiger, by Ann Whitehead Nagda and Cindy Bickel (Owlet Paperbacks, 2002)

Unit 9

Go, Fractions!, by Judith Stamper, illustrated by Chris Demarest (Grosset & Dunlap, 2003)

Unit 10

Find the Constellations, by H. A. Rey (Houghton Mifflin, 1976)

Unit 11

Piece = Part = Portion: Fractions = Decimals = Percents, by Scott Gifford (Tricycle Press, 2003)

Jumanji, by Chris Van Allsburg (Houghton Mifflin, 1981)

Unit 12

Sir Cumference and the Sword in the Cone, by Cindy Neuschwander, illustrated by Wayne Geehan (Charlesbridge Publishing, 2003)

Mummy Math: An Adventure in Geometry, by Cindy Neuschwander, illustrated by Bryan Langdo (Henry Holt and Company, 2005)

Index

Index (Continued)

Index (Continued)

E

Index (Continued)

Index (Continued)

Index (Continued)

Index (Continued)

Index (Continued)

Index (Continued)

Index (Continued)

Index (Continued)

Index (Continued)

Index (Continued)